Women's Evangelical

Commentary
NEW TESTAMENT

Women's Evangelical Commentary
NEW TESTAMENT

edited by

Dorothy Kelley Patterson &
Rhonda Harrington Kelley

HOLMAN
REFERENCE

NASHVILLE, TENNESSEE

Women's Evangelical Commentary
New Testament

ISBN: 978-0-8054-9567-6

Dewey Decimal Classification: 225.7
Subject Heading: BIBLE. N.T. COMMENTARIES\WOMEN

Printed in the United States of America

1 2 3 4 5 6 7 • 14 13 12 11

TABLE OF CONTENTS

Introduction vii
How to Study the Bible xiii
Cutting It Straight xxi
Contributors xxxi
Abbreviations of Bible Books .xxxv
Transliteration Key to Greek and Hebrew. xxxvii

Introduction to the Gospels 1
Matthew. 11
Mark 77
Luke 129
John 191
Acts 251
Romans 355
1 Corinthians. 413
2 Corinthians. 463
Galatians 509
Ephesians. 533
Philippians. 573
Colossians 595
1 Thessalonians. 623
2 Thessalonians 641
1 Timothy. 653
2 Timothy 691
Titus 721
Philemon 741
Hebrews. 749
James. 791
1 Peter 809
2 Peter 841
1 John 857
2 John 875
3 John 881
Jude 887
Revelation 895

Index of Features. 989
Maps

INTRODUCTION

The *Women's Evangelical Commentary: New Testament* is the initial volume in a library of helpful resources and is the first of a two-volume commentary set. The Old Testament volume is scheduled to be released in the summer of 2011. These unique tools make a special effort to address adequately the biblical texts about which women are asking questions. God's Word will be opened through systematic exposition by women for women on subjects important to women.

A commentary by definition is an expository treatise or a series of comments or annotations on a Scripture text. This New Testament volume is much more than exposition. The introductory sections include discussions on author, date of writing, recipients, setting, themes, and the genre of literature, as well as an outline to guide the reader through each book in a systematic way. The heart of the volume, however, is an exposition of the text of each book with special attention to challenging verses, idiomatic phrases, difficult words, and passages of interest to women. Selected word studies and discussion of literary and stylistic matters are included.

Women mentioned in the text are examined in profile with summarized information about their lives so that the reader can see their life challenges and how they trusted God to solve them. There is no attempt to idealize their lives; rather, they are presented in the midst of good and bad choices, faithfulness and disobedience, piety and self-centeredness. You can reach out and touch these women, who become your examples of what to do or not do, your models for inspiration, your mentors for spiritual growth. The summary profiles are tools for highlighting information on women, not because women on the pages of Scripture are more prominent than men and not because women are superior in their devotion to spiritual things, but merely because one of the goals of this volume is to introduce contemporary women to women of the Bible.

Articles on how to study the Bible and other topics related to the interpretive process offer thought-provoking scholarship, devotional meditations, and the practical outworking of faith from the pens of women. Charts are used to consolidate and summarize helpful information in an analytical and memorable way. A pronunciation guide for key names of people and places and appropriate maps are provided with each book. Devotional sections called "Heart to Heart" include illustrations as well as practical insights and helpful applications of the text. User-friendly indexing and a suggested bibliography for further study are included. Occasionally an excursus, a more in-depth discussion, has been inserted by the editor to pursue special topics of interest whenever further explanation is needed.

The ultimate goal is to provide a tool to walk a woman through the Bible in woman-to-woman exposition of God's Word. Opening God's Word to women through a comprehensive study of Scripture prepared by women for women on subjects important to women is not really a modern phenomenon. In the Apostle

Paul's discussion on church order, he instructed spiritually mature women to teach women who were fresh and new to the faith (Ti 2:3-5).

Are the women who have contributed to these volumes really qualified to write commentaries? The team of women assembled includes both seasoned expositors and a number of young women who have recently completed their training in biblical studies and who come to the task of biblical exposition with excellent academic preparation as well as enthusiasm for a new and fresh opportunity to put these tools to work in the marketplace of ideas. These women—the experienced and the newly equipped expositors—do not come to this task to interpret Scripture from their own perspectives or from the view of a supposed superior feminine scholarship or from any suggestion that the Bible must be reinterpreted by women to escape the alleged "oppression" of the patriarchal society described in Scripture. They come with stellar academic preparation to do serious exposition with a special passion for opening the Word of God to other women.

No interpreter approaches the sacred Book without presuppositions. The question of personal biblical interpretation comes out of what you bring to the table in beginning your process of examining the text. For this commentary project the editors have settled on these presuppositions:

- The Bible is God's Word; it is true, without error, the only standard of truth, and God's objective revelation.

- Through the Bible God reveals

  - Himself as Father, Son, and Holy Spirit—the Holy Triunity,
  - the nature and condition of human beings—male and female,
  - God's way of reconciling His creation to Himself,
  - God's standards for how women and men relate to Him and to one another, and
  - God's power and wisdom for walking in His ways.

- The Bible can be understood by ordinary women and men.

- The Bible must be interpreted in its plain and natural sense.

Since Scripture provides all you need for "life and godliness," the way you approach Scripture will affect the power Scripture has in your life. You should come to Scripture with the same mindset as you would come to an audience with God. If you approached God, you would come with your mind focused and your heart ready to respond to what God might tell you. Your attentiveness to God and your readiness to obey Him will enhance or limit your understanding of His Word.

God is consistent, and so is His Word. Those whose hearts are not set on obedience to God delight to find apparent contradictions in Scripture. This skepticism serves as an excuse for them to persist in a life of disobedience, of doing their own thing, of picking and choosing what they will believe and obey. When your heart is right, you may not understand a portion of Scripture or the relationship between various portions of Scripture, but you proceed in your study knowing that God does not contradict Himself and that through the disciplined application of time-honored interpretive principles and through His Holy Spirit, He will make plain to you what He is saying.

The godly woman seeks to conform her beliefs and behavior to Scripture, not the other way around. She welcomes the help of fellow believers in this task, including those who write commentaries. Each of you is like the Ethiopian official whom Philip asked if he understood what he was reading as he traveled from Jerusalem back to Ethiopia. His response is as yours, "How can I . . . unless someone guides me?" (Ac 8:31).

Every woman needs this guidance. The task of the commentator is to make clear the meaning of Scripture and challenge the reader to fashion her life accordingly. Modern mentality defines freedom as the ability to set your own standards and chart your own course. However, freedom in the Bible is defined primarily in relationship to God's law. Natural notions of freedom are based on a radical misreading of the human condition. Freedom in this natural or popular sense is a path of disaster because it will lead you away from the One who created you and desires to restore you to a right relationship with Himself and with one another.

Freedom in the Bible is defined primarily in relationship to God's law. God's natural law and His moral law define the conditions of life—abundant, overflowing life. The words "law" and "command" carry a negative connotation, not because "law" is negative but because human hearts and minds have been gravely distorted by sin. In order for a woman to say with integrity to God, "I delight in Your law; I love to do Your will," some radical reorientation has to take place in her heart.

Scripture describes this radical change in many ways. One of the most familiar is the new birth. Different women come to this change in different ways. One of the common threads is the recognition of God's law, the awareness that you have violated that law and that you don't have within yourself the ability to measure up to God's high standards. These realizations are coupled with the good news that past violations are completely forgiven through Christ's death and that power to measure up to God's expectations is available for the asking day by day.

Genuine freedom is born in this way. Genuine freedom produces the ability and the desire to live the kind of life that not only fulfills the commands of the law but also develops an even more complete and demanding love, enabling you to submit to God and to do His will. Nowhere in Scripture is there an admonition to embrace life in terms of your own rights. As God's creation, in relation to Him, the Creator, you have no intrinsic and inalienable rights. You must be totally sold out to Him and under the authority of His Word (Pr 3:5-6).

Why a commentary for women? The psalmist has a timely word describing a great company of women as they brought the good news (Ps 68:11). What a worthy task for women to be numbered among those who love His Word and take "the good news." Although the commentators are all women and in a sense write from that perspective, the Word of God is not to be interpreted through the "gender lens." God's Word is for women and men, but this particular resource, without apology, is prepared primarily for women to use.

The commentators have a passion for woman-to-woman exposition, and the passages selected for comment within the limits of a one-volume commentary on the New Testament were selected with the volume's audience in mind. However, in interpreting those passages, the contributors have been committed to evangelical hermeneutical principles that have been tried and proven throughout the generations.

Women have shown themselves to be uniquely sensitive to spiritual matters. Survey any Christian book store and you will find that far more Bibles and spiritual resources are purchased by women. More women than men are involved in Bible study whether in homes, churches, or community gatherings. Many women sense that their innermost personal needs can be met by a word from God. Even injustices and tragedies can be endured through the comforting presence of the Holy Spirit, and Scripture is the most vital link to the comforts offered by the heavenly Father.

There have already been some ventures into this arena. Egalitarians[1] and feminists have produced several one-volume commentaries and a host of other biblical resources. Elizabeth Cady Stanton published *The Woman's Bible* in 1895. She stated her purpose as achieving for women freedom from what she alleged to be the "oppression" of Scripture. Although Stanton did comment on passages she believed to be of interest to women, she also removed verses she thought were tainted with a male bias. Using an experiential method of interpreting Scripture, she placed herself over Scripture, molding her interpretation of the text to fit her own life and agenda. Her position has continued to be the ideological foundation for feminist theology in which individual choices and personal experience become the ultimate basis for interpreting Scripture.

In 1995 Dorothy Patterson and Rhonda Kelley led the editorial team producing *The Woman's Study Bible.*[2] The team of women accepted the absolute veracity and uniqueness of the Bible. They did not need revisionism or accommodation or relativism. Those women were committed to study Scripture and pull out its meaning to present to women the Creator's purpose for their lives. That project proved that women from many different denominations, ethnic backgrounds, and occupations could accept a word from God as not only true but also binding for all. Their training and giftedness were willingly harnessed to open the Scriptures with a determination to find a word from God for women who are hurting from injustices and who are burdened with the problems of life. The guidelines for biblical exposition formulated by the editors years ago are still appropriate. It is clear that women working within carefully defined hermeneutical boundaries can make some unique contributions to the task of woman-to-woman biblical interpretation:

- *A distinctive exegesis* demands pulling out the meaning of the text rather than reading into the text your own personal whims.

- *Intuitive scholarship* links discerning intuition with the discipline of scholarship, providing an innovative dimension to evangelical interpretation.

- *Nurturing sensitivity* inspires new and exciting ways to encourage and motivate.

- *Mentoring friendships* undergird spiritual bonding by offering common ground instead of polarity in the quest to understand and interpret Scripture.

- *Creative service* connects the mind and heart to present inspiration and guidance that are not only fresh and relevant but also firmly anchored in biblical boundaries.

Without doubt these guidelines push to the forefront both strengths and weaknesses found in the Creator's design of the feminine mystique.

Intuition is a gift associated almost exclusively with women. A woman can become so attuned to the assets of this powerful and useful gift that she forgets the boundaries of disciplined study formulated throughout the generations. A woman must be careful not to "throw out the baby with the bath water." She should use her God-given intuitions to prompt interest and draw attention to areas where more disciplined study is needed, but she must conscientiously work with hermeneutical principles faithfully used through the generations.

Maternity is also a God-given gift, but it is not reserved for bearing and rearing children. The nurturing instinct at the heart of maternity brings unique instincts for encouragement and inspiration. In studying Scripture, nurturing can be a valuable force in motivating the student of Scripture to take what she has learned in exposition and apply those truths to living the Christian life.

The woman-to-woman mentoring described by Paul in the book of Titus grows out of the fertile ground of God-created femininity. Friendships are not limited to women by any means, and yet there seems to be a unique relational spark among women, who then form life-changing, long-lasting, and far-reaching friendships among themselves. Yet both the nurturing and mentoring cannot reign unchecked when it comes to Bible study groups and inductive Bible study; they must be anchored to didactic instruction, which sometimes includes pulling from Scripture a "hard word" that is not comforting or appealing when compared to what you personally want to believe or do. Scripture must also convict and correct, often a painful process but ultimately deeply rewarding.

The ways women serve in the church and kingdom also fall into an area that demands guidance as well as inspiration. No woman (or man) has complete freedom to do whatever she feels gifted or called to do. The unique creativity of women exemplified in the Bible must line up with God's clear boundaries revealed in Scripture regarding the channels in which that creativity is expressed. God's guidelines don't vary with cultural norms and values.

Defiance of the boundaries turns service into doing your own thing, which may indeed provide something good for some and even offer what may appear to be satisfying spiritual results. However, to resist God-given boundaries becomes a means of moving obedience to God from absolute mandate for you to selective choice by you.

Any woman who uses the commentary must remember that the first and most important step to studying Scripture is always a personal reading of the text of Scripture, letting its words speak to your heart. God promises that these words "will not return to Me empty" (Is 55:11). Nevertheless, a woman who believes that she needs no help in study of the vast depths of Scripture exercises overconfidence or naïveté. Unlocking God's Word is often expedited through the help of capable and committed commentators who share the results of their years of disciplined study. These commentators offer to any woman who comes reverently to Scripture with an open heart and ready mind an effective and helpful catalyst for personal study of the Holy Book.

Bible study booklets are not and were never meant to be commentaries. In fact, you cannot prepare a Bible study on any level effectively unless you have gathered for yourself commentaries by those who have prepared themselves in a formal way to explain the Scripture. A capable Bible teacher will study carefully biblical exposition done by trained scholars and teachers in order to understand clearly the meaning of the text before she begins to write Bible lessons or teach Scripture to others.

There are also a number of devotional volumes bearing the designation of "commentary" but without any systematic exposition of the Scripture. While these do offer encouragement and help for the Christian life, which is important, this project in biblical exposition is definitely different and uniquely distinct in comparison to other products prepared specifically for women. For a woman to profit from this volume, she must first have a desire to know what God says and then at least be open to doing what He demands. This volume has as its goals:

- to challenge women to make a systematic journey through the Scriptures in search of God's truth and message;

- to give women an opportunity to receive clear biblical exposition prepared by women with formal training in theological and biblical studies, including the biblical languages, with special emphasis upon those passages of Scripture, especially the difficult-to-interpret verses, that speak to women; and

- to learn how to find biblical solutions to life's problems and answer questions about life choices and decisions through personal study and the interpretation of God's Word.

Charles Haddon Spurgeon, one of history's finest biblical expositors, raised an interesting discussion in his volume *Commenting and Commentaries.* He described how the commentators would relate to the students of Scripture as "a glorious army . . . whose acquaintance will be your delight and profit." He also offered a warning: "It seems odd that certain men [and this certainly could be women] who talk so much of what the Holy Spirit reveals to them, should think so little of what he has revealed to others."[3]

Never has there been a time when women were any more diligent in pursuing the study of God's Word. May God grant to the women who use this commentary renewed commitment of personal time and resources that will unlock the riches of God's Word to all women who pursue the high and holy task of serious study of God's Word. We pray that the *Women's Evangelical Commentary: New Testament* will be a resource for that study.

Notes

[1] The dictionary defines an egalitarian as one who believes in the equality of all people. However, in contemporary society many insist that no distinction in roles can exist in "equality." The Bible presents equality and role distinction as different, but compatible, aspects of human existence. There is a difference between who a person is and what a person does.

[2] Published by Thomas Nelson Publishers, Nashville, Tenn., 1995. Dorothy Kelley Patterson, General Editor; Rhonda Harrington Kelley, Managing Editor. Because Dr. Kelley and I poured into the volume much of our own personally developed material, especially in its charts, maps, portraits, and topical notes, you will find some adaptations of these personal resources in this series of volumes.

[3] Charles H. Spurgeon, *Commentating and Commentaries,* revised edition (Grand Rapids: Kregel Publications, 1988), 9.

HOW TO STUDY
THE BIBLE

God communicates with us primarily through His written Word (Ps 19:7-11). For any woman who desires to be a serious student of God's word there are certain obvious qualifications:

- a personal relationship with Jesus Christ, which brings the indwelling Holy Spirit (Jn 16:13);

- a deep reverence for God's Word (Pr 1:7);

- a passion to know God's Word (2 Tm 1:12; 3:14-17); and

- an utter dependence on the Holy Spirit to guide and direct and teach (Jn 14:26).

Scripture can become within your life an illuminating and powerful reminder that God speaks, acts, awaits, and loves you (2 Pt 1:19-21). If you focus on the events of history alone, you will see God in the light of human questioning and personal needs; but if you add an understanding of the Word of God you will see women and men in light of God's judgment as well as His mercy and love. Only through immersing yourself in the study of His written Word can you understand with confidence God's ultimate justice and victory.

The uniqueness of the Bible truly sets this volume apart; there is none like it in all of history. The Bible is **inspired** (Gk. *theopneustos*, lit. "God-breathed or inspired of God," 2 Tm 3:16); it is **inerrant** (without error); it is **infallible** (trust-worthy in the sense that it cannot and will not lead you astray); it is **immutable** (without the constraints of time and unchanging).

The first and foremost step in understanding Scripture is a commitment to read its words, not haphazardly but with purpose, not just a passage here and there but the whole counsel of God. Before embarking on serious study of a focal passage, you should read the Bible in its entirety. Only then can you understand its flawless unity—what the great pastor/theologian W. A. Criswell called "the scarlet thread of redemption," a reference to the great central theme of the Lord's atonement and redemption. This compilation of 66 books—all inspired by the Holy Spirit—have a common purpose of reconciling man to God. The Bible not only makes you wise unto salvation (2 Tm 3:15), but its words also nurture and edify spiritually (2 Tm 3:16-17).

> ## *Question*
> ## *How can I read the entire Bible?*
>
> ### *Answer*
>
> You can begin in Genesis and read through to Revelation, and everyone should do so at least once. Reading three chapters each weekday and five on Sunday is one option.
>
> You can select various books at random or according to personal preference.
>
> The bottom line is that you must start and keep on reading—not for preparation to teach but simply to become familiar with Scripture—the broadest survey of the Bible as a whole in the shortest period of time.
>
> Reading does not take the place of day-in and day-out disciplined study, which alone provides a working knowledge of the Bible in all its parts. Anyone who dares to teach must never cease to learn.

As you read the Bible for personal study, keep a notebook. Let your notes be unstructured and for you alone. Don't worry about form or style. Just record any insights you glean from simply reading the words of Scripture without researching what others have said. Here is a note from my personal journal on Micah 2:9.

> 2:9 How appropriate to be in this book during the Thanksgiving season. Our one truly American holiday shows the Judeo-Christian foundation of our country better than anything else with its emphasis upon gratitude to God (3:6). The message of this book is like a dagger to my soul because of my lack of compassion and mercy.

Someone once said, "Good theology begins and ends in prayer." Without prayer, your Bible study can degenerate into a dull and monotonous chore of trying to remember facts and people and places for head knowledge. On the other hand, if your personal devotional time consists of prayer alone, you can move unconsciously toward believing that God's imprimatur is on whatever you want. However, when you bring together the knowledge you gain about God's creation order, His plan of redemption, His demands for holiness in life and work within the hallowed communication of prayer and seeking His face, you have established a helpful dialogue with God. The more carefully you hear His written word, the less likelihood of self-deception (Jms 1:22-25). Again, from my journal on Micah 6:8,

> 6:8 This challenge pricks my heart. God does not demand justice toward others but justice in our own personal actions of life. We are to be just and righteous personally. For others, He demands mercy, which is more than justice. For God, He demands still more — humility, the stripping away of any pride of our self-righteousness and mercy to others!

Question
How do I begin personal Bible Study?
Answer

What many call spiritual formation or personal quiet time begins with setting apart a definite time for personal Bible study—not preparation time for research or teaching or writing but purely a communication time exclusively with God. Then you must be persistent in guarding that time and using it wisely.

Once the time is set and you are serious about personal study, you are ready to move into a careful study of the biblical text, whether for further personal enrichment or in preparation to teach a passage. Your first reading should extend to the book as a whole, and you would do well to read it several times in close proximity, hopefully reading through the book in one sitting. I emphasize a different aspect of study with each reading. For example, my first reading is to get a broad acquaintance with the book, without making notes but only underlining or highlighting key ideas without trying to interrupt reading by looking at commentaries or other helps but looking carefully at the words while listening for the Spirit's direction and application. My second reading is to determine how the book is divided or outlined and note in my journal recurring themes, terms of interest, topics addressed. Here an entry from Micah 4:10,

> The promise of this verse is especially dear to my mother's heart, for I have felt the pain and labor of birth, and affliction surely the trials of recent years from our enemies can be compared to that awesome pain just as the Lord's redemption from the enemy's hand opportunity and may be compared to the joy of new life.

At this point you are ready to read the book by sections and summarize as you read. These summaries should eventually document the flow of the book's message. These readings should be done prayerfully and reverently, in the fear of the Lord.

Using this method you read the text independently without consulting other sources until you have begun to come, under the tutelage of the Holy Spirit, to your own understanding of the meaning of text. You have not been sidetracked with minute interpretation but have been able to master the overall message of the words themselves.

The most careful study of Scripture is exegesis or verse-by-verse study in which you move slowly and deliberately through the text without trying to sidestep difficult verses, considering the interdisciplinary nature of Scripture. These steps can be helpful in such study:

- Consider parallel passages in which the same thought is expressed in two independent passages (e.g., "fear of the Lord" as found in Pr 31:31 and also in 1 Pt 3:2).

Question
What should I look for in this personal reading of the text itself?

Answer

Look for these elements:

- The principal or most important subject addressed
- Any outstanding lessons
- Verses for focus and memorizing
- Prominent people and places mentioned—are there any role models?
- References to the central message of Scripture—Christ and His atonement
- Practical applications to life and work
- Devotional thoughts for meditation

- See how one passage casting light on another (e.g., an understanding of the creation order in Gn 2 in explaining the relationship between men and women in the home, Eph 5:21-31, and in the church, 1 Tm 2:9-15).

- Use the meaning of one passage to further define another (e.g., love as defined in 1 Co 13 and then further elucidated in 1 Jn 3:16).

- Further develop original principles to be modified and explained in relation to some new set of circumstances (e.g., the relationship between women and men clearly established through generations but then in question because of cultural changes and now defined through an understanding of egalitarianism vs. complementarianism).

Resources play heavily into personal study—whether for your own edification or to help you in teaching others. Grammatical tools can also be helpful, such as diagramming sentences.

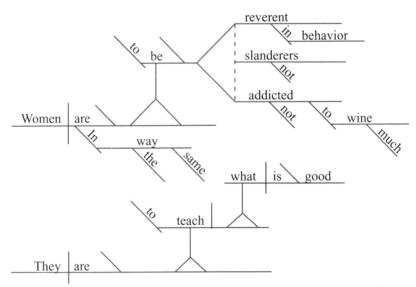

Also include literary evaluation (e.g., what genre—history, parable, prophecy, poetry, epistle or letter), consideration of figurative language (e.g., whether straightforward sharing of information or some veiled figurative device), the meaning of key words (e.g., how they function as to part of speech and role in the sentence, significance of the word in the passage, other occurrences of the word in Scripture, which can be seen by consulting a concordance), looking at the historical context (identifying author, determining date and place from which book was written, identity and circumstances of recipients, and especially determining authorial intent, i.e., what the author meant by what he wrote).

Question
What kind of sources should I use?

Answer

There are some primary general references and resources you should always consult:
- Find verses quickly and examine how the words are used throughout Scripture by using a **concordance** of the Bible (not an abridged one as found in the back of your Bible but an unabridged desk copy).
- Detailed information about words, people, places, and events can be found in a **Bible dictionary**.
- An overview of individual books of the Bible and general information on the books can be found in a **Bible handbook**.
- Pinpointing geographical locations, often together with a description of the history and significance of the place, is best done in a **Bible atlas**.
- **Translations and paraphrases** of the Bible are helpful to express the best understanding of a passage.
- A **Harmony of the Gospels** is essential for any study of the four Gospels.
- **Charts** and graphics are helpful organizational and clarifying tools.
- **Bible commentaries** are absolutely essential for genuine exegetical study—and you need more than one (see suggestions in bibliographies found at the end of each book's commentary in the *Women's Evangelical Commentary on the NT*).

Once you have worked your way systematically and carefully through the text you are ready to study the theological content of your text. With the big picture of the entire passage before you, you can better understand the flow of the author's message. The most accurate interpretation is always found in comparing Scripture with Scripture. Here are some safeguards as you work your way through that process:

- Obscure passages must be interpreted in light of passages that are crystal clear.

- Beware of trying to build a major doctrine on one verse or even several isolated verses.

- Gain understanding of doctrines by reviewing many verses and sections of Scripture.

- If, in your human evaluation, two doctrines appear to contradict each other, accept both, realizing that you will never understand the mind of God.

- Study brief passages in light of lengthier passages.

- Consider that the New Testament helps to interpret the Old Testament and vice versa.

- Timeless principles are found in timely manifestations of those principles.

- Systematic passages should take priority over incidental passages.

- Teaching or didactic passages will make more clear symbolic or practical passages.
- Every part of Scripture must be viewed in light of its overall emphasis.

Application is the finale to your study of Scripture, but all practical lessons must be governed by disciplined and tested principles of hermeneutics. The Bible is a book of principles and not merely a catalog of solutions for every situation. Principles are indeed clearly stated, but you must also be sensitive to the spirit of God's word since Scripture will not directly address every subject. The emphasis of Scripture is on inner commitment to holiness of life and obedience to God rather than a pseudo-spiritual cloak of outward acquiescence to whatever seems relevant in your own thinking. You must make a distinction between what the Bible records (e.g., slavery) and what it approves (e.g., male headship in the home and church). Express commands to individuals in Scripture are not necessarily the will of God for you, nor is it necessary for you to have a literal reproduction of a biblical situation in order to determine God's will for you.

General Principles of Hermeneutics	
Rule of Regeneration (1 Co 2:14)	You must have a personal relationship with Jesus Christ in order to understand His Word.
Rule of Authority (2 Tm 3:16-17)	You must accept the Bible as the authoritative word of God.
Rule of Preparation (Ps 119:33-40)	You should not attempt to study the Bible until you are ready to pray for and accept the Holy Spirit's instruction in understanding the truths contained therein.
Rule of Organization (2 Tm 2:15)	Read the Bible through from beginning to end. Organize the section you want to study and summarize what you learn.
Rule of Natural Interpretation (2 Tm 2:7)	Read the Bible in a natural way as you would any other book, believing that God says what He means and means exactly what He says. Interpret the Bible literally unless the structure of the context clearly indicates that the passage is symbolic or figurative.
Rule of Christocentric Interpretation (Lk 24:25-27)	Keep Christ at the center of the biblical message.
Rule of Contextual Consideration (Ps 119:105-112)	You can prove anything by isolating verses, but you maintain the integrity of the text when you consider its meaning in context.
Rule of Common Sense (Mt 11:28-30)	The Bible was written to be understood by you and me and anyone who comes earnestly to learn from its message. Someone has said that the Bible is deep enough for theologians to swim and shallow enough for a child to understand.
Rule of Pneumatic Guidance (Jn 16:13)	Only the Holy Spirit can ultimately give understanding to Scripture.

Personal study is definitely the first step in preparing to teach the Bible. You must discover what the passage really says and discover what it means by following good hermeneutical principles and by harmonizing the text with its context and with the whole of

Scripture. You are then ready to make an outline and to prepare an introduction to draw your pupils into the study as well as a conclusion to persuade them to move to action. In the heart of your teaching, challenge them to think and make practical applications to life.

In an entry to her personal journal in August, 1554, Elizabeth I of England penned these words about what Scripture meant to her:

> *I walk many times into the pleasant fields of the Holy Scriptures,*
> *where I pluck of the goodsome herbs of sentences by pruning,*
> *eat them by reading, chew them by musing, and lay them up at*
> *at length in the high seat memorie, by gathering them together,*
> *that so having tasted their sweetness I may the less perceive the*
> *bitterness of this miserable life.*

We would do well to follow her lead in letting the word of God permeate and mold our lives.

Dorothy Kelley Patterson

CUTTING IT STRAIGHT:
THE NEED FOR A SOUND
HERMENEUTIC

Mary A. Kassian

"When you interpret Scripture, cut it straight!" is the advice Paul gave Timothy. He said, "Be diligent to present yourself approved to God, a worker who doesn't need to be ashamed, correctly teaching the word of truth" (2 Tm 2:15). "Correctly teaching" (Gk. *orthotomounta*, "cutting straight, holding a straight course, doing right, rightly dividing") suggests the imagery of a farmer cutting a straight furrow, a builder cutting a stone, or a tentmaker cutting the cloth. Precise, faultless workmanship is indicated.

Imagine that you wanted to build a fine piece of furniture. Would you succeed if you began to haphazardly cut without a pattern or guide? Of course not. Your chair would end up crooked. There is a right way and a wrong way to build. Enthusiasm and hard work aren't enough; a craftsman needs a good plan, good methods, and good tools. It is the same with interpreting Scripture. According to Paul, there is a right way and a wrong way to handle it. Correctly handling requires diligence, care, precision, and skill—the right attitude *and* the right method—the right heart and the right hermeneutic.

Hermeneutics (Gk. *hermēneuō*, "interpret") is the process of interpretation. Its name comes from the Greek myth of Hermes, the winged messenger of Mount Olympus, who was assigned to interpret the sayings of the Oracle at Delphi. Biblical hermeneutics is concerned with finding the true meaning of a particular passage in the Bible. Over the course of history, scholars have proffered several views regarding what constitutes an appropriate hermeneutic for Scriptural interpretation.

- Some scholars employ a *mystical* methodology. They argue that due to the supernatural nature of revelation, the interpreter's task is to uncover multiple and/or hidden meanings in the text.

- Others support the opposite—an *anthropocentric* methodology. This approach emphasizes that the Bible was written by human authors. Hence, supernatural elements must be minimized and the text must be understood in light of human opinion, culture, and reason.

- Still others utilize a *thematic* methodology. These scholars maintain that interpretation must conform to a predetermined interpretive key, or system of doctrine, which is regarded to be the "theme" of a particular passage or book or the overall theme of Scripture.

Obviously, these approaches would come up with very different meanings for the same text. In the story of Jonah and the great fish, for example, a mystical interpreter might conclude that solitude and seclusion in a small, dark place is the appropriate punishment or penance for being disobedient. An anthropocentric interpreter, on the other hand, would argue that the account is merely figurative—Jonah wasn't actually swallowed by a great fish—rather, the author used this illustration to convey the darkness Jonah felt in his spirit after disobeying God. Finally, a thematic interpreter, who had chosen "liberation" as her interpretive key, might argue that the point of the passage is to reveal God's attitude toward those who do not actively pursue the liberation of oppressed people.

While each of these approaches is based on true observations and assumptions about the Bible as supernatural, written by men, and containing coherent themes, none constitutes a sound hermeneutic. Evangelical Christians believe that a sound hermeneutic cannot be based on an *interpreter's* assumption about Scripture. Instead, since the Bible is one's final authority, the basis for a sound hermeneutic must be gleaned from Scripture itself. A sound hermeneutic is internally rather than externally based. The Bible itself is the best resource for establishing the principles and processes of biblical interpretation.

Using Scripture, evangelicals have established certain hermeneutic presuppositions regarding the inspiration, inerrancy, authority, necessity, sufficiency, clarity, and unity of the word, as well as practical guidelines for biblical interpretation. This *biblicistic* approach is commonly called the "literal-grammatical-historical" method. It seeks to establish the "main and plain" meaning of the text. Interpreters who stray from this method commonly stray from historic, biblical orthodoxy. An inauthentic hermeneutic leads to an inauthentic interpretation. Therefore, to know and adhere to the established hermeneutic presuppositions and guidelines is imperative.

Presuppositions for Hermeneutics

The first presupposition of a sound hermeneutic is that Scripture is inspired by God. There are frequent claims in the Bible that all the words of Scripture are God's words. In the Old Testament, the introductory phrase "This is what the LORD says" appears hundreds of times. In the New Testament, Paul maintains, "All Scripture is inspired by God" (2 Tm 3:16). Peter concurs that "no prophecy ever came by the will of man; instead, moved by the Holy Spirit, men spoke from God" (2 Pt 1:21).

Scripture is the word of God. It is inspired by Him. Moreover, because the Bible says that God cannot lie or speak falsely (Ti 1:2; Heb 6:18), a sound hermeneutic upholds Scripture as inerrant. The Bible is right, true, and without error. Psalm 12:6 says, "The words of the Lord are pure words, like silver refined in an earthen furnace, purified seven times." When Jesus prayed to the Father, He affirmed, "Your word is truth" (Jn 17:17). A *biblicistic* belief in the inspiration and inerrancy of Scripture has practical hermeneutical implications. You cannot regard the teachings of a biblical author as mere personal opinion, nor can you dismiss them as mistaken or erroneous. The words of the Bible are the words of God. To disbelieve or disobey any word of the Bible is to disbelieve or disobey God.

Scripture teaches that its own words are divinely inspired and inerrant. God's Word presents itself as authoritative, necessary, and sufficient for godliness. Every child of God is obliged to obey its mandates. The Lord commands believers to obey and keep His Word (Dt 12:32, Jn 14:23; 1 Jn 5:2). He says, "I will look favorably on this kind of person: one who is humble, submissive in spirit, and who trembles at My word" (Is 66:2). The Word is essential for sustaining your relationship with the Lord. Jesus says, "Man must not live on bread alone but on every word that comes from the mouth of God" (Mt 4:4). Neglecting the Word affects the spirit like neglecting food affects the body. The Word is absolutely necessary for spiritual life and health. The Word is also sufficient for spiritual life. No other book is required. God's children do not need to rely on other texts to "fill-in-the-blanks." "All Scripture is inspired by God and is profitable for teaching, for rebuking, for correcting, for training in righteousness, so that the man of God may be complete, equipped for every good work" (2 Tm 3:16-17). Peter affirms that God has given you "everything" you need for life and godliness (2 Pt 1:3-4). Scripture is your standard—your authority. It is *what* you need. And it is *all* you need.

The authority, necessity, and sufficiency of Scripture have important hermeneutical implications. The authority of Scripture means that the text has a greater authority than the person interpreting it. Whenever an interpreter claims to have more insight into a text or biblical principle than a biblical author, she is guilty of putting self above Scripture— a grave error in hermeneutics. The necessity of Scripture indicates that interpreters cannot simply disregard passages that are unpopular or uncomfortable, nor can they shrug them off as unimportant or unnecessary. The sufficiency of Scripture means that interpreters ought not to rely on external sources to interpret the Bible or enhance its meaning, nor can they cite other texts as being equal in importance or authority.

A hermeneutic based on Scripture upholds the inspiration, inerrancy, authority, necessity, and sufficiency of the word of God. Two final presuppositions are the clarity and unity of Scripture. A sound hermeneutic maintains that God's commands and directions are clear—not hidden. The Bible teaches that the character of Scripture is such that even the "simple" can correctly understand its words and be made wise by its truths. "The testimony of the Lord is trustworthy, making the inexperienced wise" (Ps 19:7). Understanding Scripture is not a privilege reserved for the theological elite. Scripture's truth is "evaluated spiritually" (1 Co 2:14). Understanding it aright is as much a moral/spiritual exercise as an intellectual one. With the help of the Holy Spirit, every believer is able to read and understand the Bible with confidence that she has done so with a reasonable amount of acuity.

The clarity of Scripture has important hermeneutical implications. Interpreters cannot claim that a passage's meaning is so obscure and unclear that it cannot be understood and applied. Certainly, some passages are more difficult to interpret than others, but this shortcoming is on the interpreter's part rather than on the part of the Word of God. God chose to communicate with humans using human language. Therefore, interpreters are responsible to approach the Bible as they would any other human communication—to determine as accurately as possible what the authors intended their audience to understand, believe, and obey. Interpretations that rely on obscure or uncommon meanings of words, interpretations that go against the plain, obvious meaning of the text, and/or interpretations claiming that only the theological elite are privy to biblical knowledge do not uphold the hermeneutical presupposition affirming the clarity of the Word of God.

The final presupposition of a sound hermeneutic addresses the unity of Scripture, which is closely related to presuppositions regarding the inspiration and inerrancy of the Word of God. "Every word of God is pure"—not just some of the words, but *every word* (Pr 30:5). If the whole Bible is inspired, then all the words of Scripture are the products of a single divine mind and will naturally constitute a cohesive message. Moreover, if all of God's words are true, then His message will not contradict itself. Hence, every passage of Scripture must be regarded as part of a unified whole. This fact, too, has important hermeneutical implications. An interpreter cannot determine the meaning of one passage or verse independent of the rest of Scripture. "Scripture interprets Scripture." Furthermore, she cannot pit Scripture against Scripture—arguing that one passage is accurate, while another is mistaken. The task of harmonizing Scripture and understanding the individual parts in light of other parts and the whole can be a challenge. But the basic presupposition regarding the unity of Scripture maintains that this is not only possible but necessary. A sound hermeneutic begins with the premise that the harmony is already there and that the interpreter's task is to search it out. Interpreters are required to treat the Bible organically and ought always to look for its internal links, which are there in profusion for those who have eyes to see them.

Hermeneutical presuppositions have implications for the manner in which a woman handles a text and consequently for her conclusions and applications: The position of the wheel dictates the direction and destination of the vehicle. That's why it's so important to approach Scripture with presuppositions that are firmly grounded in the Word of God. Biblical beliefs about the inspiration, inerrancy, authority, necessity, sufficiency, clarity, and unity of the Word are the only authentic basis from which to begin.

Guidelines in Hermeneutics

A sound hermeneutical system builds upon biblically based presuppositions with literal-grammatical-historical hermeneutical guidelines, a method that uses the ordinary rules of human language to interpret an author's meaning. "Literal" means that interpreters take the words for what they mean in their normal or plain sense without implying that all forms of communication are woodenly treated in the same way. This approach acknowledges that doctrinal truth can be conveyed symbolically or figuratively, as well as through parables, poems, or typology. For example, a literal approach does not interpret Jesus' statement, "I am the door" (Jn 10:7), to mean that He has hinges and a handle. No. A literal approach takes various types of communication into account. Symbolic language is interpreted symbolically; figurative language, figuratively; and poetic language, poetically. "Literal" simply means that the interpreter looks for the plain, obvious, and ordinary meaning of any given type of communication.

"Grammatical" indicates that interpreters follow standard rules of grammar. They recognize linguistic tools such as similes, analogies, and metaphors, and interpret meaning in light of their normal grammatical use. "Historical" means that interpreters seek with diligence to determine the historical background and context before rendering an interpretation. To neglect the history of the time period in which the text was written is like stripping a conversation from its context. The literal-grammatical-historical method maintains that the meaning of a text is the author's intended meaning and that the author's intention can be derived most accurately by observing the facts of history and the common rules of language and communication. The literal-grammatical-historical method includes common-sense hermeneutical guidelines such as "context determines meaning," "obscure yields to plain," and "incidental yields to didactic."

A basic hermeneutical guideline is that the context of a passage helps determine the meaning of that passage. The Bible is rooted in history and must therefore be interpreted in light of its historical context. To ascertain the geographic and cultural contexts of a passage when seeking to determine meaning is also helpful. However, by far the most important consideration is the textual context of the passage under consideration. Interpreters must be careful to examine the immediate context of surrounding verses as well as the overall purpose and plan of the book.

Another hermeneutical guideline, "obscure yields to plain," dictates that difficult teachings in Scripture be interpreted in light of those that are obvious and plain. The guideline, "incidental yields to didactic" indicates that verses mentioning a topic in passing (incidentally) be interpreted in light of those that specifically (didactically) address and offer explicit instruction on a given issue.

The literal-grammatical-historical method includes guidelines for determining the cultural applicability of a text. Certain biblical texts were meant to be applied only in a specific time and culture, whereas others were intended to transcend time and culture. In order to discern which teachings are transcultural in contrast to those that are culture-bound, you must first determine the reasons given for the principles. If the author's reasons are based on culture, then the principle itself may be culture-bound. But if the reasons are based on unchanging principles, then the facts themselves should be honored. Because you as an interpreter live in a different time and culture than when the principle was transmitted and recorded, determining the correct application of biblical principles can sometimes be a challenge. Nevertheless, following standard hermeneutical guidelines, you can determine which biblical principles are applicable today.

Interpretative Challenges for Women

The need for a sound hermeneutic is particularly important for the 21st-century Christian woman. The philosophy of feminism permeates the media and mainstream societal institutions. The current milieu is such that the Bible's teaching on gender radically counters popular thought. Thus, there is a tremendous pressure on theologians to update and revise historic interpretations of what the Bible has to say about the role relationship between men and women. Proponents argue that the church must change its doctrinal stance on the role of women in order to remain relevant. Alarmingly, many feminist theologians have violated basic hermeneutic presuppositions and rules in order to justify doing so. Evangelical theologians—egalitarians in particular—are not exempt from this error.

Feminist and egalitarian interpreters often violate basic hermeneutic presuppositions when interpreting passages that deal with gender issues. To begin, many approach the Bible with a predefined interpretive key. They assume that "liberation" or "equality" is the crux of the Bible's message. All passages are interpreted accordingly. Passages that teach distinct roles for male and female are dismissed, minimized, or rationalized in light of this crux. For example, in Ephesians 5 women are commanded to be submissive to their husbands. Feminists/egalitarians often argue against this by citing a *crux interpretum* based on Galatians 3:28, "There is no . . . male or female; for you are all one in Christ Jesus." They argue that the Bible's theme of equality dictates the meaning of Ephesians 5. However, a thematic methodology does not constitute an authentic hermeneutic. Its starting point is skewed, and its conclusions are therefore suspect.

A sound hermeneutic maintains that all Scripture is inspired by God, or literally, God-breathed (2 Tm 3:16). Scripture comes directly from God. Feminist/egalitarian theologians often do not honor this presupposition. They argue that some portions of Scripture are so male-biased, so influenced by the writers' own prejudices, that these are rendered inapplicable. For instance, they mention that since Paul received his training under Gamaliel, one of the most famous rabbis, and since Paul was socialized in a chauvinistic society, for him to believe in the inferiority of women was natural. This belief influenced his writings about the role of women. Accordingly, the passages in which Paul addresses the role of women were not inspired by God but by the apostle's own prejudices. The difficulty with this approach is that any disagreeable passage may be similarly dismissed. One could just as easily say that Paul was expressing his own viewpoints when he spoke of sexual morality or doctrine. All Scripture would thus be subject to dismissal as uninspired and inapplicable purely on the basis of the interpreter's judgment.

The inerrancy of Scripture is another hermeneutical presupposition that is violated in order to bring the Bible in line with feminist philosophy. When feminist/egalitarian interpreters encounter passages with which they disagree, they often label them as inauthentic and/or incorrect. However, if you cannot rely on what the Bible says about the role of women as absolute truth without any mixture of error, then how can you rely on what it says about the nature of humanity, salvation, interpersonal and family relationships, sexual lifestyles, the will and emotions, and a host of other issues? An errant Scripture would merely be a reflection of ancient philosophy and psychology with little else to offer. Also, as church history has repeatedly shown, groups who begin questioning the validity of small details of Scripture eventually question larger doctrines as well.

When feminist/egalitarian interpreters disregard hermeneutical presuppositions of inspiration and inerrancy, they also violate the basic presupposition of the authority of the Word of God. When an interpreter determines which parts of Scripture are inspired and which parts reflect the author's human bias—or which parts are correct and which are errant, that interpreter has assumed authority over the Bible. Instead of submitting to the Bible's instruction, the interpreter forces the Bible to submit to her own preconceived notions about what constitutes truth.

The hermeneutical presuppositions regarding the necessity and sufficiency of Scripture are also violated by some feminist/egalitarian interpreters. These interpreters regard biblical directives about gender roles as antiquated and irrelevant to contemporary women. In doing so, they imply that women and men can rely on their own personal sense for what feels natural, right, and fair in male-female relationships. In essence, they maintain that turning to the Bible for help in this regard is unnecessary. Furthermore, in order to justify a feminist interpretation, many of these interpreters employ a self-determined system of hermeneutics. In other words, they regard the Bible as open to their own alterations. They argue that its ideas about the role of women were meant to "evolve" and "transform" over time. Paul's vision for an equal "neither male nor female" paradigm was meant to gradually come to fruition. Having achieved "equality" to a greater extent than Paul and his contemporaries, today's women must interpret Scripture in light of contemporary understanding. In essence, these interpreters are saying that Paul's words in the Bible cannot stand alone. They must be augmented with a more enlightened view—the contemporary feminist one. This approach violates the hermeneutical presupposition about the sufficiency of Scripture. Scripture is sufficient. You do not need the added "benefit" of a contemporary mindset in order to interpret it correctly.

The clarity of Scripture is another hermeneutical presupposition that many feminist/egalitarian interpreters violate. For example, they argue that biblical authors did not use certain Greek words, such as "head" (Gk. *kephalē*), in the plain, ordinary sense of the word. They argue that Paul's intended meaning is an obscure one that is not evident to the ordinary reader. They maintain that when Paul used the word *kephalē*, he meant "source" and not "authority." Therefore, the verses in which he states that the husband is the "head" in the husband-wife relationship do not really mean what they appear to mean. The meaning is only evident to the theological elite who have access to obscure documents that contain rare, unusual word definitions. Notwithstanding that the word *kephalē* means "headship" in thousands upon thousands of biblical and extrabiblical instances, these feminist/egalitarian scholars propose that Paul intended a meaning so uncommon and rare that only now, after two thousand years of biblical interpretative history, can his true meaning be understood. But the introduction of new word meanings that radically change the historic interpretation of a text ought to be regarded with a great deal of suspicion—as should the claim that only those educated in the minute nuances of Greek and Hebrew can understand and interpret the Bible. Some interpreters would like you to believe that the Bible's teaching on the role of women is very complex and difficult, if not impossible, for the ordinary person to understand. But the supposition that average, ordinary believers cannot understand the main and plain meaning of Scripture violates the principle of the clarity of the Word of God.

The final hermeneutical presupposition frequently violated by feminist/egalitarian interpreters is the unity of Scripture. Instead of regarding the Bible as unified, they propose that certain passages and authors contradict each other. These interpreters often quote Scripture "against" Scripture. For instance, they cite Galatians 3:28 to discount the teaching in the Epistles regarding male/female role distinctions. But the unity of Scripture means that the Bible's message regarding the role of women in the home and church is harmonious throughout. Scripture does not contradict Scripture.

Feminist/egalitarian interpreters do not always honor standard hermeneutical presuppositions, nor do they abide by hermeneutical guidelines. Traditional historic interpretation maintains that the text says what it means and means what it says. The interpreter is to ascertain exactly what the biblical author said and derive its intended meaning from that alone. However, in order to support an egalitarian interpretation, interpreters often stray from the accepted hermeneutical rules of "context determines meaning," "obscure yields to plain," and "incidental yields to didactic."

The most glaring example of taking a verse out of context is the manner in which feminist/egalitarian scholars interpret Galatians 3:28. In the context of Galatians 3–5, the question is addressed: "Who may become a child of God and on what basis?" (see Gl 3:28). The central issue in Galatians 3 and 4 is the role of the law in relation to faith. A strong secondary theme is that both Jew and Gentile come to God on the basis of faith. The Galatians were trying to reestablish external requirements, in particular the observance of Old Testament laws, as the basis for joining the Christian church (Gl 3:3-5). The Galatians were advocating circumcision, the Old Testament mark of the covenant between the individual and God, as an entrance requirement for the Christian community. Uncircumcised Gentile men would be required to be circumcised, and women would be excluded from this spiritual privilege. In this context Paul stated, "There is no Jew or Greek, slave or free, male or female, for you are all one in Christ Jesus." Therefore, in context, Galatians 3:28 teaches that Gentiles, females, and those in the lower classes of society can enter into a spiritual relationship with God on the same basis as Jewish men. Circumcision is not a prerequisite. Paul wasn't even discussing male-female relationships in this verse. He was discussing who could become a Christian and on what basis. To use this verse out of context in order to argue that the Bible supports the obliteration of male-female roles is a hermeneutical error.

Another basic hermeneutical rule is that obscure passages are to be interpreted in light of those whose meaning is plain. In other words, clear passages are used to determine the meaning of unclear passages and not vice versa. Unfortunately feminist/egalitarian inter-preters often give obscure passages more prominence. For example, Romans 16:7 says, "Greet Andronicus and Junia, my fellow countrymen and fellow prisoners. They are out-standing among the apostles, and they were also in Christ before me." The Greek phrase "outstanding *among* the apostles" can also be translated "well known *to* the apostles." Feminist/egalitarian interpreters often cite this verse as a New Testament example of a female apostle and as support for bolstering their case for ordaining women as pastors/elders. They argue that the translation is more accurate and that "outstanding among the apostles" indicates that Junia *was*, in fact, an apostle. The difficulty with this reasoning is that Romans 16:7 is unclear about Junia's relationship to the apostles. "Among" the apostles could mean that she was merely a friend or acquaintance of the apostles, or it could mean that she was actually a member of that group. No case can be made on the basis of this verse alone. But there are many other Bible verses (e.g., 1 Co 11; 1 Tm 2:11-12; 3:1-16; Ti 1) that clearly address the appointment of apostles and the prerequi-sites for eldership. None of these indicate that such a role was or is considered appropri-ate for women. If you interpret Romans 16:7 in light of the clear passages, you must conclude that Junia was not an apostle. To give any verse veiled in obscurity more weight in interpretation than all passages in which the meaning is plain constitutes a breach of sound hermeneutics.

When interpreting the Bible, verses with obscure meanings must yield to those verses that are clear and plain. Furthermore, passages in which topics are mentioned in passing (incidentally) must be subordinate to passages that directly (didactically) address the issue at hand. Feminist/egalitarian interpreters often violate this principle. Again, their use of Galatians 3:28 is a prime example. Galatians 3:28 is a theological statement about the fundamental equality of all people in their standing before God and mentions gender only incidentally. The practical implications for male-female social relationships are not addressed. Therefore, biblical role relationships cannot be decided solely on this basis but must be determined from the interpreter's broader understanding of Scripture—an understanding formed by studying passages that directly address the role relationship between men and women. Didactic passages on the role of men and women advocate a structured relationship in both the home and church wherein the male assumes a position of leadership and authority. To use Galatians 3:28, an incidental passage, as the basis for understanding role relationships, violates sound hermeneutics.

Finally, feminist/egalitarian interpreters often go against sound hermeneutics when they inappropriately relativize Scripture in order to squeeze it into the modern cultural setting. This move limits the application of a biblical text to a specific culture or time in history when the text itself actually demands a wider application. These interpreters rela-tivize biblical texts that they feel are inappropriate in the contemporary social context—such as those that teach the submission of women in marriage and affirm male pastors/elders in the church. But Paul's rationale for role relationships is based on eternal truths such as the created order and the relationship of Christ to the church. Since the reasons are not culture-bound, to dismiss the principle as only pertaining to Paul's time is improper. Unfortunately, many wrongly dismiss eternal Christian doctrine by labeling it culturally relative. They say that certain parts of Scripture are *inapplicable* simply because they are not currently *popular.*

The trend, in many contemporary evangelical churches, is to accommodate the Word of God to bring it more in line with contemporary thought on the roles of men and women. In order to handle the Bible correctly, it is imperative that scholars consistently employ a sound hermeneutic and take care not to violate the principles and processes of biblical interpretation.

𝒜 𝒲orkman 𝒜pproved to 𝒢od

In the ancient world there was no paper money, only coins. Metal was heated until liquid, poured into molds and allowed to cool. The coins were relatively soft, so some people cheated and shaved them down. At one point, more than eighty laws were passed in Athens to stop this widespread practice. But some money changers refused to deal with altered coins. They put only genuine full-weighted money into circulation. Such men were identified as "approved" (Gk. *dokimon*, "genuine, tried and true, respected"). Paul used this same word when he admonished his friends: "Be diligent to present yourself *approved* to God, a worker who doesn't need to be ashamed, correctly teaching the word of truth" (2 Tm 2:15). God desires that you approach His Word with integrity—like the money changers who refused to accept and circulate shaved-down coins. He approves of those who diligently work at "rightly dividing" His Word. In order to "cut it straight," interpreters must approach this task with sound hermeneutics.

𝐵ibliography

*Black, David Alan, and David S. Dockery. *Interpreting the New Testament*. Nashville: Broadman & Holman, 2001.

Carson, D. A. *Exegetical Fallacies*. Grand Rapids: Baker Book House, 1984.

*Conzelmann, H., and A. Lindemann. *Interpreting the New Testament: An Introduction to the Principles and Methods of N.T. Exegesis*. Peabody, MS: Hendrickson Publishers, 1988.

Kassian, Mary A. *Women, Creation and the Fall*. Westchester, IL: Crossway Books, 1990.

*Kaiser, Walter C., Jr., and Moises Silva. *An Introduction to Biblical Hermeneutics*. Grand Rapids: Zondervan, 1993.

*Klein, W. W. *Introduction to Biblical Interpretation*. Nashville: Thomas Nelson, 2004.

*Long, V. Phillips. *Foundations of Contemporary Interpretation*. Grand Rapids: Zondervan, 1996.

Mayhue, Richard. *How to Interpret the Bible for Yourself*. Winona Lake, IN: BMH Books, 1997.

McQuilkin, J. Robertson. *Understanding and Applying the Bible: An Introduction to Hermeneutics*. Chicago: Moody Press, 1992.

Thomas, Robert. *Evangelical Hermeneutics*. Grand Rapids: Kregel Publications, 2002.

*Virkler, Henry A. *Hermeneutics: Principles and Processes of Biblical Interpretation*. Grand Rapids: Baker Book House, 1995.

Zuck, Roy B. *Basic Bible Interpretation: A Practical Guide to Discovering Biblical Truth*. Wheaton: Victor Books, 1991.

Zuck, Roy. *Rightly Divided: Readings in Biblical Hermeneutics*. Grand Rapids: Kregel Publications, 1996.

*For advanced study

WEC
CONTRIBUTORS

Ann Bowman teaches New Testament Language and Literature at the International School of Theology in San Francisco, California, and has been affiliated with the Campus Crusade for Christ since 1970. She previously taught in West Africa. A frequent speaker and prolific writer as well as recipient of numerous awards, she lives in Buena Park, California.

Betsy Durand received her Master of Divinity in Women's Studies from Southeastern Baptist Theological Seminary in December 2003. She lives in Wake Forest, North Carolina, where she stays busy as a full-time homemaker and mother of two boys. She also leads the Women's Ministry at North Roxboro Baptist Church, where her husband serves as pastor. She grew up as a missionary kid in Israel, learning Modern Hebrew and gaining a special appreciation and love for the Jewish people.

Candi Finch received her Master of Divinity in Theology with Women's Studies from Southwestern Baptist Theological Seminary in May 2005 and is currently pursuing her Doctor of Philosophy degree in Systematic Theology from Southwestern. She lives in Fort Worth, Texas. Because she has a heart to see teenage girls become mature disciples of Christ, she is actively involved as a Sunday School teacher and small group mentor in the student ministry at Glenview Baptist Church.

Christa Friel is pianist and Coordinator for Vocal and Instrumental Ensembles at First United Methodist Church Graham. A published hymn writer, she is a speaker and worship leader for women's conferences and retreats. She has a Master of Divinity with Biblical Languages and plans to complete her Doctor of Philosophy degree in Theology in May 2007 from Southwestern Baptist Theological Seminary. She lives in Fort Worth, Texas, where she is a member of Wedgewood Baptist Church.

Sharon Gritz is a freelance writer living in Fort Worth, Texas, with her husband Paul and teenage daughter Lydia. Dr. Gritz has served as Adjunct Professor of New Testament at Southwestern Baptist Theological Seminary. She enjoys writing adult Bible study curriculum. She teaches younger children in an inner-city mission as well as adults and children at University Baptist Church.

Trish Hawley is Instructor in Women's Ministry and Women's Ministry Coordinator at the New Orleans Baptist Theological Seminary. She has a Master of Divinity in Women's Studies from Southeastern Baptist Theological Seminary and plans to complete her Doctor of Philosophy degree in May 2006 from the Southern Baptist Theological Seminary. She lives in New Orleans, Louisiana, and is actively involved in the Women's Ministry at First Baptist Church.

Tamra Hernandez has a Master of Divinity with Biblical Languages and is a doctoral student in theology at Southwestern Baptist Theological Seminary. She and her husband have one teenage son, a cancer survivor, and live in Fort Worth, Texas, where they are members of Wedgewood Baptist Church.

Donna Hicks has a Bachelor of Science degree from the University of South Carolina and a Master of Divinity degree in Biblical Studies from the New Orleans Baptist Theological Seminary, where she has also completed further post-graduate studies. She is a member of Morningside Baptist Church in Spartanburg, South Carolina.

Jennie Huffines received a Master of Divinity in Women's Studies from Southeastern Baptist Theological Seminary and serves as Women's Ministry Director at Osborne Baptist Church. She enjoys teaching and speaking to women as well as mentoring college-age girls. She is a homemaker who lives in Brown Summit, North Carolina, with her husband and daughter.

Mary Kassian is an award-winning author, international speaker, and distinguished professor of Women's Studies at Southern Baptist Seminary in Louisville, Kentucky. She has published several books, including *The Feminist Mistake,* and has written numerous Bible studies for women, including *In My Father's House, Conversation Peace,* and *Vertically Inclined.* She was also a section editor and contributor to *The Woman's Study Bible.*

Rhonda Harrington Kelley (B.A., M.S., Ph.D.) is the president's wife and Professor of Women's Ministry at the New Orleans Baptist Theological Seminary. She is also a Christian author and speaker. Formerly the director of speech pathology at Ochsner Medical Center, Dr. Kelley completed advanced degrees at Baylor University, and University of New Orleans. She lives in New Orleans, Louisiana, with her husband Chuck and is Director of Women's Ministry at First Baptist Church.

Emily Hunter McGowin plans to complete her Master of Divinity in Theology from the George W. Truett Theological Seminary in the fall of 2007. She has authored and co-authored several articles and book reviews, some of which have appeared in *Faith and Mission, The Journal of the Evangelical Theological Society*, and *The Truett Journal of Church and Mission*. She lives in Fairfield, Texas, with her husband Ron, who is the Pastor of Youth at First Baptist Church.

Kathy McReynolds is a professor in the English Bible and Apologetics programs at Biola University. Dr. Reynolds has written several books and articles on theology, ethics, and discipleship as they pertain especially to women. She lives in La Mirada, California, with her husband and three children. She and her family are long-time members of Whittier Area Community Church.

Dorothy Kelley Patterson (B.A., Th.M., D.Min., D.Theol.) is a homemaker who helps her husband Paige Patterson, president of Southwestern Baptist Theological Seminary, by serving as Professor of Theology in Women's Studies. With graduate and post-graduate degrees in theology, Dr. Patterson teaches, speaks, and writes for women. She is a member of the Evangelical Theological Society, serves on the Advisory Board for the Council for Biblical Manhood and Womanhood, and attends Birchman Baptist Church. The Pattersons reside in Fort Worth, Texas, but travel extensively throughout the world. Their children are married: Armour and Rachel Patterson live in Arizona; Carmen and Mark Howell, with their daughters Abigail and Rebekah, live in Houston, Texas.

Ashley Smith is an adjunct professor of Women's Ministry at the Criswell Bible College in Dallas, Texas. She has a Master of Divinity in Women's Studies from Southeastern Baptist Theological Seminary and speaks regularly for women's events. She and her husband, Dr. Steven Smith, live in Mansfield, Texas, with their daughter Jewell.

Donna Thoennes is Assistant Professor in the Torrey Honors Institute at Biola University and involved in ministry to women, engaged couples, and college students at Grace Evangelical Free Church in La Mirada, California. Dr. Thoennes particularly enjoys ministering alongside her husband Erik in their home, at Biola, on missions trips, and at the church where he serves in pastoral ministry.

Joy White received her Master of Divinity degree in Women's Studies from Southeastern Baptist Theological Seminary, Wake Forest, North Carolina. She is currently working on a Doctor of Philosophy in Systematic Theology from Southeastern. She resides in Fort Worth, Texas, with her husband Thomas, who is a professor and administrator at Southwestern; their daughter Rachel; and their two dogs.

HCSB BIBLE BOOK ABBREVIATIONS

Old Testament		*New Testament*	
Gn	Genesis	Mt	Matthew
Ex	Exodus	Mk	Mark
Lv	Leviticus	Lk	Luke
Nm	Numbers	Jn	John
Dt	Deuteronomy	Ac	Acts
Jos	Joshua	Rm	Romans
Jdg	Judges	1 Co	1 Corinthians
Ru	Ruth	2 Co	2 Corinthians
1 Sm	1 Samuel	Gl	Galatians
2 Sm	2 Samuel	Eph	Ephesians
1 Kg	1 Kings	Php	Philippians
2 Kg	2 Kings	Col	Colossians
1 Ch	1 Chronicles	1 Th	1 Thessalonians
2 Ch	2 Chronicles	2 Th	2 Thessalonians
Ezr	Ezra	1 Tm	1 Timothy
Neh	Nehemiah	2 Tm	2 Timothy
Est	Esther	Ti	Titus
Jb	Job	Phm	Philemon
Ps	Psalms	Heb	Hebrews
Pr	Proverbs	Jms	James
Ec	Ecclesiastes	1 Pt	1 Peter
Sg	Song of Songs	2 Pt	2 Peter
Is	Isaiah	1 Jn	1 John
Jr	Jeremiah	2 Jn	2 John
Lm	Lamentations	3 Jn	3 John
Ezk	Ezekiel	Jd	Jude
Dn	Daniel	Rv	Revelation
Hs	Hosea		
Jl	Joel		
Am	Amos		
Ob	Obadiah		
Jnh	Jonah		
Mc	Micah		
Nah	Nahum		
Hab	Habakkuk		
Zph	Zephaniah		
Hg	Haggai		
Zch	Zechariah		
Mal	Malachi		

TRANSLITERATION CHARTS

Greek Transliteration Chart

Greek	English	Greek	English	Greek	English
α	a	ι	i	ρ	r
β	b	κ	k	σ	s
γ	g	λ	l	τ	t
δ	d	μ	m	υ	u
ε	e	ν	n	φ	ph
ζ	z	ξ	x	χ	ch
η	ē	ο	o	ψ	ps
θ	th	π	p	ω	ō

Hebrew Transliteration Chart

Hebrew	English	Hebrew	English
א	'	ל	l
ב ב	b v	מ	m
ג	g	נ	n
ד	d	ס	s
ה	h	ע	'
ו	w	פ פ	p ph
ז	z	צ	ts
ח	ch	ק	q
ט	t	ר	r
י	y	שׁ שׂ	s sh
כ	k	ת	t
Vowels			
ְ	e, vocal shewa	ֵ	ē
ַ	a	ִ	i
ָ	a	ֹ	o
ָ	o	ֻ	u
ֶ	e	וּ	u

INTRODUCTION
TO THE GOSPELS

Everyday Life in the New Testament World

The Jewish population in Israel at the time of Jesus has been estimated to be about five or six hundred thousand. The population of Jerusalem was probably close to twenty-five or thirty thousand. Some scholars have suggested that Galilee had as many, if not more, Gentiles than Jews ("Galilee of the Gentiles," Mt 4:15). Many people lived in the two main cities—Sepphoris and Tiberias; however, the vast majority of the population lived in over two hundred small villages in and around Galilee. Each of these small villages had no more than about one thousand in population. At the time of Christ about four million Jews lived in the Roman Empire.[1]

The entire Roman Empire was estimated to have had about fifty million inhabitants. The major cities throughout the empire were extremely crowded, with people living in very close quarters. Rome probably had about one million residents. Alexandria had approximately seven hundred fifty thousand people and Antioch five hundred thousand.[2]

The Roman Empire had a sophisticated road system for the ancient world. Major highways linked most of the main cities. Although the country had mainly dirt roads, travel was relatively easy. Quite possibly a soldier on horseback could travel between twenty to fifty miles a day; a wagon could journey seven or eight miles a day; and, on foot, a man could walk twenty miles in a day. However, travel could be quite dangerous; so people did not often travel too far from home. The roads were lined with inns and hideaways in which many thieves and pirates lodged. For the most part, roads traveled often were considered relatively safe, but desolate roads were very risky (see Lk 10:29-37). This constant threat of danger was precisely why hospitality was so important to the early Christian travelers.

In the time of Jesus, wealthy families usually lived in large multistory brick villas complete with an inner atrium where large groups of people could gather. Ordinary people often lived in one-room, two-level houses in which the living quarters were separated from the animal stalls. They were built with plain exteriors and were modestly decorated. Many people did not own furniture, except perhaps a mat for sleeping and an outdoor oven for cooking. Living conditions in general were unsanitary, as runoff gutters for sewage and trash ran down the middle of the street.[3]

Fathers arranged marriages. In the first century, rabbis set the age for the betrothal of girls at 12 and of boys at 13. After a marriage proposal, the fathers began to negotiate the bride price. The father of the prospective bride was to be compensated for the loss of a worker. A girl was not considered property. The bride price was based on the reputation of the bride's father. If the girl was ever in need, she could receive that bride price back for her own use.

After agreeing upon the bride price, a couple was engaged, which meant much more in New Testament times than it does in the modern era. If the engagement was broken, the person responsible was liable to be fined. During the engagement period, no sexual relations were permitted (see Mt 1:18-25). Jewish men were expected to marry by 18 years of age, Roman men by 25, and Greek men by age 30. Jewish, Roman, and Greek girls were usually married by their mid-teens.[4]

The family was of central importance in Israel in New Testament times. Women were praised in many references in the Torah, and a woman's role has been identified as essential to the spiritual well-being and continuation of each generation of Judaism. Rabbis would often say, "He who has no wife dwells without good, without help, without joy, without blessing, and without atonement" (*Bereshit Rabbah* 17:2). Children were considered a blessing from God, but they had no voice or advocate in the larger social world. Godly living meant knowing one's role and functioning well in it. Fathers worked to provide for their families; mothers took care of domestic matters; children were expected to obey their parents with honor and respect.

Romans usually ate four meals daily with both meat and dairy products in the menu. Poorer Jews ate only two meals a day. Bread was coupled with fruit, nuts, or vegetables. Fish was available in abundance in Galilee. Wine was the drink of choice since it was considered safer and healthier than milk or water. But wine in the first century, unlike modern alcoholic beverages, contained no additives and was heavily diluted with water. After the day was done, people usually spent hours in conversation with good friends. There was little else to do in the evening, so good fellowship was valued highly.

Jewish men normally wore a tunic, sandals or shoes, and some kind of head covering. For prayer, traditionally the Jewish man wore a prayer shawl and phylacteries, leather bands containing important Scriptures, bound around his head and on his left arm. A Jewish man usually had a beard. Jewish women wore colorful garments, a shawl, or some covering over their heads, and, when they could afford it, jewelry and other cosmetics. Women usually had long hair.

In about the second century BC, rabbis began to teach Jewish boys who had reached the age of six. At synagogues across the Mediterranean world, the boys received primarily religious instruction based on the Torah—the five books of Moses. Young girls were not usually formally educated, but they were taught by their mothers how to care for the home. This development of an educational system for young Jewish boys was probably spurred on by the influence of the Greeks. The Greeks placed high importance on education; however, Greek education was available to both boys and girls.

The manufacturing of clothes, pottery, and metal was at the heart of the industries operating in New Testament times. Carpentry and basket weaving were also important occupations in Israel. Bankers and money changers could also make a good living. Around the Sea of Galilee, fishing provided a good income. However, farming was the mainstay in most of Palestine.

Three main languages were spoken in and around Palestine in the first century: Hebrew, Aramaic, and Greek. Evidence for diversity of languages can be found, such as on the inscription written in Hebrew (or Aramaic), Greek, and Latin and placed above Jesus' cross. Jesus probably spoke all three languages.

Only one or two percent of the population of the Roman Empire was considered wealthy. This included the emperor's court and many military commanders. The bureaucracy necessary to serve the wealthy probably was responsible for making another three or four percent of the population rich. A small "middle class" could take care of their own daily needs and set aside some savings as well. However, most of the population

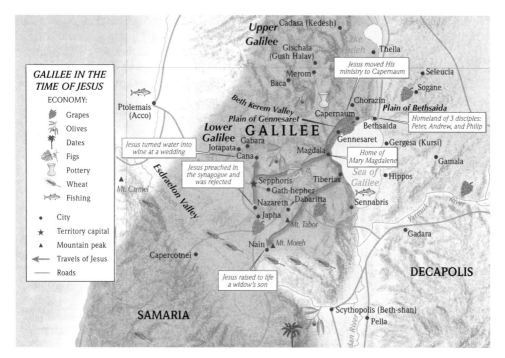

GALILEE IN THE
TIME OF JESUS
ECONOMY:
- Grapes
- Olives
- Dates
- Figs
- Pottery
- Wheat
- Fishing
- • City
- ★ Territory capital
- ▲ Mountain peak
- ← Travels of Jesus
- ---- Roads

Upper Galilee

Cadasa (Kedesh)
Gischala (Gush Halav)
Thella
Jesus moved His ministry to Capernaum
Seleucia
Merom
Baca
Sogane
Beth Kerem Valley
Chorazin
Plain of Bethsaida
Plain of Gennesaret
Capernaum
Bethsaida
Homeland of 3 disciples: Peter, Andrew, and Philip
Lower GALILEE
Galilee Gabara
Gennesaret
Gergesa (Kursi)
Jesus turned water into wine at a wedding
Jotapata
Magdala
Home of Mary Magdalene
Gamala
Cana
Jesus preached in the synagogue and was rejected
Sepphoris
Tiberias
Sea of Galilee
Hippos
Ptolemais (Acco)
Gath-hepher
Mt. Carmel
Nazareth
Dabaritta
Sennabris
Esdraelon Valley
Japha
Mt. Tabor
Gadara
Yarmuk River
Nain
Mt. Moreh
Capercotnei
DECAPOLIS
Jesus raised to life a widow's son
SAMARIA
Scythopolis (Beth-shan)
Pella
Jordan River

were poor farmers or laborers who barely made enough to meet their daily needs. Most of Jesus' disciples probably came primarily from this latter category.

For the Jewish people religious holidays and appointed festivals provided a time of entertainment and relaxation. They were both festive and reflective. Hellenized Jews also enjoyed sporting events, which included Olympic Games, chariot races, and gladiator contests. Greeks and Romans participated in numerous annual holidays, temple rituals, and patriotic celebrations for entertainment.

The mind-set of first-century Jews, Romans, and Greeks has provided insight into a number of cultural values quite distinct from the modern Western cultures.[5]

- *Honor/shame.* One cannot overestimate the importance of honor and shame in ancient society. Money and prestige paled in importance compared to the responsibility of honor and the devastation of shame. What mattered most was for one to conduct himself honorably in all things. Jesus' honor, though constantly challenged by the religious leaders of His day, was never tainted.

- *Individual versus group personality.* The first-century Mediterranean culture was much more group-centered than modern Western culture. Allegiance to family, extended family, friends, religious association, and society in general was of utmost importance. Jesus was quite countercultural in this respect. Jesus did not belittle His own family or devalue the importance of the biological family unit. God created the family and provided structure and guidelines for its well-being (see Gn 2:18-24; Ps 78:1-7). Jesus, however, did present family relationships among believers as not only temporal but also eternal! He clearly affirmed relationships within the extended kingdom family (Mk 3:31-35).

- *Perception of limited goods.* In a world not dominated by capitalist methods, people naturally assumed there was a limited supply of goods. Therefore, the farmer who had a year of good crops was expected to share with the poor. And, when friends did share their wealth, the one who was assisted was honor-bound to repay them. Instead of saying "thank you" in the ancient world, people simply returned the favor by a genuine give-and-take attitude. In this sense Jesus was also countercultural when He insisted on sharing with the poor, expecting nothing in return. Those who gave sacrificially would look for a reward in the life to come.

- *Character plus performance.* Good deeds were important in the first century, but good character was a prerequisite for good deeds. What mattered most was a person's character. Truly good deeds flowed from within.

- *Purity/cleanness and impurity/uncleanness.* Since no equivalent in the modern world really exists for these concepts, grasping their importance in the first-century Jewish context may be difficult. Old Testament teachings on purity, or what was considered clean, versus what was unclean pricked the consciences of ancient Jews. They were diligent to keep themselves pure, knowing that if they allowed themselves to become unclean, they would forfeit the opportunity to worship with the people of God. To be unclean was to be put out of the community. In a society that valued relationships extending beyond the family to the household of faith, any isolation from the community was a devastating experience. An extensive set of rules (see Lv 11–18) dictated when and how a person became unclean and then included the steps needed to be declared clean again.

- *Present, past, and future.* Many in the modern generation tend to live in the future. They rarely live in the moment, and they most certainly devalue the past. In the ancient world, the present was of utmost importance, then the past, and finally the future. Most people were poor; therefore, the future was uncertain at best. An individual's identity and self-understanding were closely related to the past. But the present was all he had, and he lived primarily in the moment. Jesus certainly affirmed the value of living in the present (see Mt 6:11,34).

What Are the Gospels?

By both ancient and modern standards, the Gospels are unique. Unlike ancient writings they are not merely a collection of hero stories. They are not narratives written by Jesus about Himself. They are not like modern biographies in that they omit much background information and historical data on the main character. Even though the Gospels are unlike ancient writings in some respects, they are certainly more like ancient Middle Eastern writings than they are like modern Western literature. They are not bound by linear thinking. Clearly in many contexts the authors of the Gospels organized their materials based on a particular topic or theme and not chronologically. The authors' main concern was showing that Jesus is the Son of God. The order of events seemed secondary. Therefore, one ought not to assume a chronological sequence unless the author's presentation requires it.

The Gospels are really *theological biographies*. Each proclaims Jesus to be the author of salvation; each was written from a specific theological perspective. All four Gospels claim a trustworthy and true message. Moreover, the overall intent of the authors was to elicit a response from their readers (or hearers). Once people received the good news about Jesus, they could not remain neutral.

The Synoptic Gospels: Matthew, Mark, and Luke

In the late 1800s the German biblical scholar J. J. Griesbach named Matthew, Mark, and Luke the *Synoptic* Gospels because many of the details, though arranged differently in each of the three Gospels, were very similar. The term *synoptic* means "seeing together."

Until the seventeenth century, the most common approach to the four Gospels was to try to harmonize them. The first such attempt, called the *Diatessaron* (Gk. lit. "through four"), was in the second century. Throughout the history of the church many of the great church fathers (e.g., Augustine) and others (e.g., Calvin) have followed suit. Scholars generally accepted that Matthew, Mark, and Luke were written in that order and that since John knew about these works, he chose to focus on other aspects of Christ's ministry.

Beginning in the seventeenth century, many Enlightenment thinkers, primarily in Germany, began to call into question this traditional approach to understanding the Gospels. D. F. Strauss (1808–1874), for example, rejected the traditional interpretation of the Gospels and argued that most of Jesus' claims and actions were myths, which were then fashioned into stories created by Jesus' followers, thereby turning Jesus of Nazareth into Jesus the Christ. No one with a high view of Scripture could accept this interpretation.

Studying the Life of Jesus

The primary sources for studying the life of Jesus are the four Gospels. Even though these sources have been vehemently attacked by some scholars, the Gospels have withstood repeated attacks and are still considered by all evangelical New Testament scholars to be thoroughly reliable. The existing manuscripts of the Gospels are in very good condition. The oldest known Gospel fragment is the John Ryland's papyrus, containing John 18:31-33 and dating to approximately AD 130. The five oldest and most complete copies of the New Testament date from about the fourth and fifth centuries, and they do contain all the Gospels.

The fact that more than five thousand ancient manuscripts, from fragments to entire books, are available attests the Gospels' reliability. More manuscript evidence exists for the New Testament than for any other document from antiquity. External evidence for the reliability of the Gospels that goes well beyond manuscript evidence is also available. Testimony comes from archaeology, from non-Christian writers, and from the rest of the New Testament. Consequently, when it comes to the historical reliability of the Gospels, believers can be assured that God's Word has been preserved uncorrupted down through the centuries.

Outside of the Gospels, references to Jesus are scanty. The first-century Jewish historian Josephus called Jesus a wise man who "wrought surprising feats," and he said that after His crucifixion "on the third day he appeared to them restored to life."[6] Second-century writers such as Tacitus and Suetonius referred to the death of Jesus and to the existence of some of His followers.[7] In a letter to Trajan, Pliny the Younger stated that the Christians from his area in Asia Minor "sang in alternate verse a hymn to Christ, as to a god."[8] Lucian, also from the second century, referred to Christ as the "first law giver" of Christians and a "crucified sophist."[9]

Those outside the Christian community did refer to Jesus, and they essentially did not contradict the Christian testimony about Him. But in reality these references do not provide any additional insight into the study of the life of Christ beyond what was recorded in the Gospels.

Jesus spent most of His life in Palestine, which is roughly the size of Vermont. In New Testament times, Palestine was divided into three major sections: Galilee in the north, Samaria in the central section, and Judea in the south. As mentioned earlier, Galilee had a large Gentile population. Samaria originally was identified with the northern kingdom of Israel (2 Kg 17:29). After the kingdom fell to the Assyrians, most Israelites were sent into exile, and exiles from other nations were forced into Samaria by the Assyrians. Many of those remaining as a remnant in the land intermarried with Gentiles and were even drawn into worshiping pagan gods. When the rebuilding of the temple began, Ezra and Nehemiah refused to include the Samaritans (Ezr 4:1-3; Neh 4:7), which intensified the animosity that had long existed between the north and the south. Even in the time of Jesus, friction remained between the Jews and Samaritans to the extent that the Jews refused to pass through Samaria when they traveled from Galilee to Judea (Lk 9:52-54; 10:25-37; 17:11-19; Jn 8:48). Judea had the heaviest concentration of Jews. Most of Jesus' ministry took place in Galilee and between Galilee and Jerusalem.

Jesus and Women

There are over forty references to women in the Gospels, either in narratives or in the teachings of Jesus. Women—Jesus' mother Mary, Elizabeth and Anna, Mary and Martha, and many others—were directly associated with Jesus.

Women traveled with Him and ministered to His needs: Mary Magdalene, from whom seven demons had been cast; Joanna, the wife of Chuza, the manager of Herod's household; Susanna; and possibly many others. MANY OTHERS (Gk. *heterai pollai*, Lk 8:3), a plural feminine noun and adjective, seemingly referencing other women who were not named, and indicating more than a few. These women supported Jesus by their own means. Quite possibly many put themselves in harm's way. Doubtless many made extraordinary personal sacrifices. Women numbered among this courageous group were a far cry from the typical image of the sheltered and sequestered Palestinian woman of the first century.

The fact that women traveled with Jesus, supporting Him and learning from Him, is of extraordinary significance. For one thing, in Judaism, women were not allowed to learn the Torah. They might learn informally, but a woman would not associate herself with a traveling rabbi in order to become his disciple; neither would she engage in formal religious studies. This traveling group of women affirmed that Jesus' ministry went beyond the normative limitations set upon women. It testified not only to the dignity Jesus bestowed on women but also to His confidence in their desire to learn spiritual things and in their ability to do so and then to use what they had learned in kingdom service.

Jesus ministered to many women: the widow of Nain, the woman who was crippled by a demon, the widow with her two tiny coins, the woman at the well, Peter's mother-in-law, the woman taken in adultery, Jairus's daughter, the woman with chronic bleeding, and the Syrophoenician woman. All of these incidents showed Jesus to be either gentle or firm, as needed. But none of them ever portrayed Jesus as having anything other than a high view of women. His actions were in stark contrast to those with the relatively low view of women pervasive throughout Palestine in the first century.

One way to understand Jesus' high view of women is to examine some of His parables, such as the parable of the lost coin, in which He used women and an item associated with women to make His point. In the parable of the persistent widow, the widow was definitely portrayed in a favorable light against the unfair rulings of the unjust judge (Lk 18:1-8). Although she was one of the helpless in society, she demonstrated incredible strength and faith as she dealt with the unjust judge.

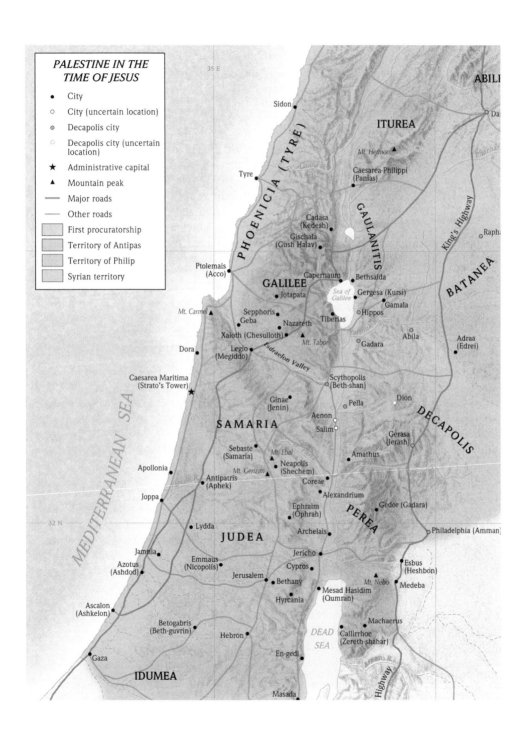

PALESTINE IN THE
TIME OF JESUS

- ●   City
- ○   City (uncertain location)
- ◉   Decapolis city
- ◌   Decapolis city (uncertain location)
- ★   Administrative capital
- ▲   Mountain peak
- ──   Major roads
- ──   Other roads
- ▢   First procuratorship
- ▢   Territory of Antipas
- ▢   Territory of Philip
- ▢   Syrian territory

ABIL

35 E

Sidon

ITUREA

Da

PHOENICIA (TYRE)

Mt. Hermon ▲

Caesarea-Philippi
(Panias)

Tyre

GAULANITIS

King's Highway

Pharpar

Cadasa
(Kedesh)

Gischala
(Gush Halav)

Rapha

Ptolemais
(Acco)

Capernaum   Bethsaida

BATANEA

GALILEE

Sea of
Galilee

Gergesa (Kursi)

Jotapata

Gamala

Mt. Carmel ▲

Sepphoris
Geba

Nazareth

Tiberias

Hippos

Xaloth (Chesulloth)

Mt. Tabor ▲

Gadara

Abila

Dora

Legio
(Megiddo)

Esdraelon Valley

Adraa
(Edrei)

Caesarea Maritima
(Strato's Tower) ★

Scythopolis
(Beth-shan)

Dion

MEDITERRANEAN SEA

Ginae
(Jenin)

Pella

DECAPOLIS

Aenon

SAMARIA

Salim

Gerasa
(Jerash)

Sebaste
(Samaria)

Mt. Ebal ▲

Amathus

Apollonia

Mt. Gerizim ▲

Neapolis
(Shechem)

Antipatris
(Aphek)

Coreae

Joppa

Alexandrium

Ephraim
(Ophrah)

Gedor (Gadara)

PEREA

Philadelphia (Amman)

32 N

Lydda

Archelais

JUDEA

Jericho

Jamnia

Emmaus
(Nicopolis)

Cypros

Esbus
(Heshbon)

Azotus
(Ashdod)

Jerusalem

Bethany

Mt. Nebo ▲   Medeba

Ascalon
(Ashkelon)

Hyrcania

Mesad Hasidim
(Qumran)

Betogabris
(Beth-guvrin)

Hebron

DEAD
SEA

Machaerus

Callirrhoe
(Zereth-shahar)

Gaza

En-gedi

IDUMEA

Masada

Arnon R.

Highway

With respect to social change in general, Jesus showed little interest in merely changing social conditions for women. He gave His attention to matters of the heart, knowing that when hearts are right, actions will be right. Jesus did portray some women in need, but in no way did His words demean them. Women described in the Gospels clearly had dignity. The women who were first at the tomb were among the first in a long line of women who have borne witness to the Savior through the generations.

A woman was first at the cradle, lovingly nurturing the Christ child, and last at the cross, refusing to leave her Son and Savior in His darkest hour. Other women served the Savior during His incarnation and have continued to do so throughout the subsequent generations. Jesus was more than a mere man, and one could never compare Him or His actions with even the greatest prophet or teacher. He did reach out to every woman, as to every man. He drew each to Himself in loving care; He taught without condescension; He answered questions and made arguments graciously; He corrected without malice; He praised with sincerity; and He always affirmed any act of obedience. His humor was pure and without sarcasm. He indeed instructed women and mapped out His plans for their lives. He honored the creation order and never pushed or expected a woman to act as a man, but delighted in women who, as women, served Him and the kingdom. As a man in His earthly tabernacle, He treated women with dignity and honor.

Notes

1 See, for example, Joachim Jeremias, *Jerusalem in the Times of Jesus* (Philadelphia: Fortress, 1969), 205; and Robert H. Gundy, *Survey of the New Testament*, rev. ed. (Grand Rapids: Zondervan, 1981), 21.
2 See Craig Blomberg, *Jesus and the Gospels* (Nashville: Broadman and Holman, 1997), 55.
3 Ibid., 58–59.
4 Much of what is in this entire section is based on the discussions of Craig Blomberg and of Thomas Lea and David Alan Black, *The New Testament: Its Background and Message* (Nashville: Broadman and Holman, 2003).
5 This list is taken from Blomberg's *Jesus and the Gospels.*
6 Josephus, *Antiquities* 18.63–64, Loeb Classical Library, English translation by Louis H. Feldman (Cambridge: Harvard University Press, 1981).
7 Tacitus, *Annals* 15.44; Suetonius, *The Lives of the Caesars* 6.16.
8 Pliny, *Letters* 10.96.
9 Lucian, *The Passing of Peregrinus* 13.

Women in the Life of Jesus

Women in Jesus' Geneology

- Tamar (Mt 1:3)
- Rahab (Mt 1:5)
- Ruth (Mt 1:5)
- Uriah's wife (Bathsheba, Mt 1:6)

Women in parables

- Woman baking with leaven (Mt 13:33)
- Woman with lost coin (Lk 15:8-10)
- Persistent widow (Lk 18:1-8)
- Pregnant women and nursing mothers (Mk 13:17)
- Ten virgins (Mt 25:1-13)

Women in the life of Jesus

- Mary, mother of Jesus (Mt 1:16-25; 2:11; 13:55; Mk 6:3; Lk 1:26-56; 2:1-52; Jn 2:1-12; 19:25-27; Ac 1:14)
- Elizabeth (Lk 1:5-25)
- Mary and Martha (Mt 26:6-13; Mk 14:3-9; Lk 10:38-42; Jn 11:1-5; 12:1-8)
- Mary Magdalene (Lk 8:2-3)
- Joanna, wife of Chuza (Lk 8:2-3)
- Susanna (Lk 8:2-3)
- Mother of Zebedee's sons (Mt 20:20-21)

Women who had one-time encounters with Jesus

- Anna the prophetess (Lk 2:36-38)
- Samaritan woman (Jn 4:1-42)
- Sinful woman who washed Jesus' feet (Lk 7:36-50)
- Woman caught in adultery (Jn 8:1-11)
- Woman in the crowd (Lk 11:27-28)

Women Jesus mentioned in conversation

- Mother vs. daughter (Mt 10:35)
- Poor widow with two tiny coins (Mk 12:41-44)

Women at the cross

- Mary Magdalene (Mt 27:55-56; Mk 15:40-41; Jn 19:25-27)
- Mary, mother of Jesus (Jn 19:25-27) (possibly referred to as Mary, the mother of James in Mt 27:55-56; Mk 15:40-41)
- Salome (Mk 15:40-41), also called the mother of Zebedee's sons (Mt 27:55-56)
- Mary, wife of Clopas (Jn 19:25-27)

Women at the tomb

- Mary Magdalene (Mt 27:61; 28:1; Mk 16:1-8; Lk 24:10; Jn 20:1-2)
- "The other Mary" (Mt 27:61; 28:1; possibly the mother of James in Mk 16:1-8; Lk 24:10)
- Salome (Mk 16:1-8)
- Joanna (Lk 24:10)

Women who had miraculous encounters with Jesus

- Peter's mother-in-law (Mt 8:14-17; Mk 1:30-31)
- Syrophoencian woman and her daughter (Mt 15:21-28; Mk 7:24-30)
- Jairus's daughter (Mk. 5:21-23,35-43; Lk 8:40-42a,49-56)
- Woman with bleeding (Mk. 5:25-34; Lk 8:42b-48)
- Widow of Nain and her son (Lk 7:11-15)
- Woman crippled 18 years (Lk 13:10-13)

MATTHEW

Introduction

Title

The Gospel of Matthew presents Jesus as the Jewish Messiah, the Anointed One, the One who came to fulfill the Old Testament Law and the Prophets. The Gospel contains five major discourses given by Jesus during His three-and-one-half-year ministry. Matthew strategically placed the sermons in his Gospel in order to demonstrate to his audience that Jesus is the divine Son of God.

Matthew linked each sermon or discourse with a narrative section in order to emphasize a common theme. The first sermon (chaps. 5–7) was linked with the healing narrative of chapters 8–9 in order to highlight Jesus' divine authority. Matthew 9:35 closely mirrored the language in 4:23, which could suggest that these chapters represented a unit.

In the second sermon (chap. 10), Jesus commissioned the 12 disciples and warned them of certain opposition. The narrative section of chapters 11–12 demonstrated that the warning in chapter 10 had become fact. Chapter 13 represented a turning point in Matthew's Gospel as it became increasingly clear that Jesus was moving His followers to choose whether they were with Him or against Him. As the Jews became increasingly hostile to Jesus and His message, the door to ministry among the Gentiles opened (13:53–14:36).

With this change in the focus of Christ's ministry, Matthew reversed the sermon-narrative sequence. In Matthew 16:21–17:27, Jesus' repeated discussions on the cost of discipleship were followed by a sermon in chapter 18, which was given exclusively to believers and involved issues concerning the church. In Matthew 19:1–25:46, Jesus warned of the coming judgment on unbelievers, especially within the nation of Israel. The last three chapters of Matthew recorded the events of Christ's arrest, trial, death, and resurrection. The last verses in Matthew (28:16-20) provided the final proof of Jesus' divine authority: the apostles were commissioned by Him to go and make disciples of all nations.

Setting

Matthew did not state specifically what precipitated his work, but many commentators acknowledge that he wrote his Gospel while in Antioch of Syria. Antioch was a Greek-speaking community with a large Jewish population. Internal evidence shows that Matthew made several references to Gentiles and one reference to Syria (Mt 4:24). External evidence also supports some city along the coast of Phoenicia or Syria as the place of composition (Ac 11:19,26-27; 15:23). Ignatius, the bishop of Antioch, was one of the first church fathers to reference Matthew's Gospel.

Author

Although evidence available to determine authorship is not conclusive, ample support exists to identify Matthew, the tax collector and an apostle of Jesus, as the author of the Gospel that bears his name. An inscription placed at the beginning of some of the early manuscripts of the Gospel states that "Matthew, also called Levi, a converted tax collector and one of Jesus' twelve apostles" wrote it. One of the most important pieces of evidence supporting Matthew's authorship comes from Papias. His words have been translated and interpreted in many ways, but he basically asserted that "Matthew composed [compiled] his Gospel [sayings] in the Hebrew [Aramaic] language [dialect, style], and everyone translated [interpreted] as they were able."[1]

Some scholars have debated the veracity of this quote. However, although Jewish by birth, Matthew's job as a customs officer for the Roman government would have called for skills in Aramaic (the spoken language of the Jews) as well as in the widely used official Greek language. Matthew could have written in Hebrew or Aramaic some of Jesus' sayings that later formed the foundation of his Gospel.

Another objection raised against Matthean authorship is that an apostle would not rely on someone who was not an apostle (i.e., Mark) to develop his work and that the supposedly overall anti-Jewish flavor of the Gospel militates against Matthew, a Jew, as the author. With regard to the first objection, the possibility of Mark's heavy reliance on Peter's testimony to write his Gospel has been fairly well established. Peter was part of the inner circle of disciples who were closest to Jesus and, thus, would have proved a reliable source for Mark. In light of this, Matthew would not have had any qualms with relying on Mark to authenticate and augment his material if he chose to do so. However, the strong case for Matthean priority makes this issue moot.

In light of all that has been said, one can safely assume that Matthew, the tax collector who became a member of Jesus' inner circle of apostles, wrote the Gospel that has borne his name throughout the generations. Concerning the priority of Matthew's Gospel, the burden of proof lies on those arguing for Markan priority. A host of evangelical scholars spanning the generations, as well as testimony of the early church fathers, have not only affirmed the Apostle Matthew (also known as Levi) as its author but also have argued vigorously for the priority of Matthew's Gospel.

Date

Dating Matthew is also a matter of controversy. Some modern scholars insist that Matthew must be dated between AD 85 and 100. They support this conclusion in several ways. Clearly Matthew's audience was comprised of primarily Jewish Christians who were struggling to break with Judaism. Before AD 70 when the Romans destroyed the temple, Jewish thought and practice were quite diverse. After the destruction of the temple, only two Jewish groups continued to exist: Rabbinic Judaism (a continuation of the Pharisaic tradition) and Jewish Christianity (Jews who accepted Jesus as the Messiah and openly identified themselves with Him).

Matthew's concern to show Jesus as the fulfillment of Old Testament prophecies and the One to carry out God's redemptive plan was more plausible in a situation where only *two* groups were competing to show which one was the true heir of Jewish heritage. However, very little in Matthew's Gospel supports a date after AD 70. Matthew clearly acknowledged the existence of more than one Jewish sect in his Gospel. Those who support a later date point to the fact that Jesus "predicted" the destruction of the temple. Therefore, they assume that the composition of the Gospel must be after its destruction in AD 70.

There is a counterpoint to that argument: If Jesus is indeed the Son of God, as Matthew portrayed Him to be, certainly He could predict the future. Only those who assume that Matthew was misguided about Jesus' identity would argue that Jesus could not have announced future events with accuracy. Matthew also discussed the temple tax, offerings, and rituals, as well as the importance of keeping the Sabbath. Based on the context of the discussions, the inclusion of these elements in Matthew's Gospel makes more sense if one accepts that the temple was still standing.

In light of these issues, the internal evidence supports an earlier date for Matthew. However, the external evidence gives the greatest amount of support for an earlier date. Irenaeus stated that Matthew wrote his Gospel "while Peter and Paul were preaching the gospel and founding the church in Rome,"[2] which is consistent with a date in the 60s. This statement was also endorsed by Eusebius, who indicated that Papias, bishop of Hierapolis in Phrygia about AD 130, first associated Matthew with the Gospel.[3] Therefore, one is wise to conclude that Matthew was written sometime in the 60s and before the fall of the temple in AD 70.

Recipients

The recipients of Matthew's Gospel were primarily Jewish. The text shows that Matthew's audience was engaged in a struggle, either having just broken with Judaism or being in the process of trying to break from it. Matthew was concerned about the plight of the Jewish Christians, but clearly throughout his Gospel Matthew also included the Gentiles in God's plan of redemption. Therefore, Gentiles were also among the recipients. Some have argued that Matthew's Jewish emphasis was intended to show Gentile Christians how to appropriate their new Jewish heritage. Matthew's Gospel was surely intended to be circulated, but the primary destination is generally understood to be Antioch in Syria.

Major Themes

Conflicts with Jewish religious leaders. While Matthew is certainly the most Jewish of the Gospels, it also details most precisely the clashes between Jesus and the Jewish authorities. Those who followed Jesus had to embody a righteousness that exceeded that of the scribes and Pharisees (5:20). Matthew 23 recorded one of Christ's most scathing rebukes of the religious leaders. Based on His words the scribes and Pharisees clearly failed on all accounts to practice true righteousness (Mt 23:1-36).

Particularism and universalism in the Gospel. In some passages of Matthew, Christ seemed to limit His mission to the Jews (10:5-6,23; 15:24). Matthew's use of "the kingdom of heaven," the phrase used by the Jews to describe God's reign, also seemed to point to a Jewish mission. At the same time, however, Matthew is the only Gospel that described the visit of the Gentile magi who came to worship the newborn King (2:1-2). Matthew included three parables that predicted the ruin of the Jewish leaders as well as the warning that the kingdom of God would be taken away from them and given to a nation producing fruit (21:18–22:14). Only Matthew recorded Christ's teaching concerning the sheep and the goats, depicting universal judgment (chap. 25), and the Great Commission, inviting all people to become disciples (chap. 28).

Matthew represented Jesus' ministry in two stages. Before His death and resurrection, Jesus made an appeal first to the Jews. As opposition mounted and the Jewish leaders finally rejected His offer, the disciples were to go out after Christ's death and resurrection and continue to proclaim His message to all people. From the very beginning of Matthew's Gospel, the Gentile mission was foreshadowed. The priority was to go first to the Jews because they were God's chosen people and the recipients of His covenant with Abraham. Nevertheless, the extension of that covenant to the Gentiles was embraced by the Apostle Paul. Jesus died for all, and the invitation to salvation has always been available to all.

Discipleship within the church. In Matthew the disciples were represented in a much more favorable light than they were in Mark (Mt 8:26; 13:51; 14:33). Disciples in general were addressed with very endearing terms such as "little ones." Matthew is the only Gospel to refer specifically to the church and to give instructions concerning discipline and forgiveness within the church community (16:18; 18:15-35).

Views of Jesus. In Matthew, Jesus was often called the Son of David, a witness to Christ's royal heritage as the seed of King David. This title occurred nine times in Matthew's Gospel and was consistent with his portrayal of Jesus as the Jewish Messiah. "Lord" is another

---

Pronunciation Guide

Abijah	_uh BIGH juh_	Jotham	_JOH thuhm_
Abiud	_uh BIGH uhd_	Judea	_joo DEE uh_
Achim	_AY kim_	Manasseh	_muh NASS uh_
Ahaz	_AY haz_	Matthan	_MAT than (th as in thin)_
Amminadab	_uh MIN uh dab_	Nahshon	_NAH shahn_
Amon	_AM uhn_	Naphtali	_NAF tuh ligh_
Aram	_A (a) ruhm, AHR uhm_	Nazareth	_NAZ uh reth_
Asa	_AY suh_	Obed	_OH bed_
Azor	_AY zawr_	Perez	_PEE rez_
Bethlehem	_BETH lih hem_	Pharisees	_FEHR uh seez_
Boaz	_BOH az_	Rahab	_RAY hab_
Capernaum	_kuh PUHR nay uhm_	Ramah	_RAY muh_
Decapolis	_dih KAP oh liss_	Rehoboam	_ree huh BOH uhm_
Eleazar	_el ih AY zuhr_	Sadducees	_SAD joo seez_
Eliakim	_ih LIGH uh kim_	Salmon	_SAL mahn_
Eliud	_ih LIGH uhd_	Shealtiel	_shih AL tih el_
Galilee	_GAL ih lee_	Syria	_SIHR ih uh_
Hezekiah	_HEZ ih kigh uh_	Uriah	_yoo RIGH uh_
Hezron	_HEZ rahn_	Uzziah	_uh ZIGH uh_
Jechoniah	_jek oh NIGH uh_	Zadok	_ZAY dahk_
Jehoshaphat	_jih HAHSH uh fat_	Zebedee	_ZEB uh dee_
Jerusalem	_jih ROO suh lem_	Zebulum	_ZEB yoo luhn_
Joram	_JOH ruhm_	Zerah	_ZEE ruh_
Josiah	_joh SIGH uh_	Zerubbabel	_zuh RUHB uh buhl_

title used by Matthew in a slightly different way than in the other Gospels. Jesus was described as "Lord" in many different contexts in which the title simply meant "master," a word often used for those in authority. But in certain contexts in Matthew, the title could have suggested His divinity, as in passages describing His ability to heal (8:2,6,25; 9:28).

However, one must realize that the modern-day usage of "Lord" as a unique title of divinity was not necessarily so limited in the New Testament era (see 1 Pt 3:6 where Sarah was cited as using the title for her husband). Many did believe Jesus came from God, while refusing to acknowledge that He was (and is) God. In this light, "Lord" (Gk. *kurios*) was both a common term indicating one in authority and on some occasions a more exclusive connotation of divinity.

Christ was referred to as Immanuel ("God is with us"; 1:23) only in Matthew. This name foreshadowed His promise in Matthew 28:20, "I am with you always, to the end of the age." By far the most distinctive title for Jesus in Matthew is Teacher (19:16). He is the Teacher of a higher order of righteousness.

Outline[4]

I. THE IDENTIFICATION OF JESUS: WHO HE IS (1:1–4:11)
- A. The Genealogy and Birth of Jesus (1:1–2:23)
- B. The Preparation for Jesus' Ministry (3:1–4:11)
  1. His forerunner (3:1-12)
  2. His baptism (3:13-17)
  3. His testing (4:1-11)

II. THE DEVELOPMENT OF JESUS' MINISTRY: WHAT HE DID (4:12–16:20)
- A. The Beginning of Ministry (4:12-25)
  1. Preparing for ministry (4:12-16)
  2. Calling out disciples (4:17-25)
- B. Preaching: The Sermon on the Mount (5:1–7:29)
- C. Healing the People (8:1–9:38)
- D. The Opposition to Jesus' Mission (10:1–12:50)
  1. Identifying and sending out the apostles (10:1-15)
  2. Predicting opposition (10:16-42)
  3. Experiencing opposition (11:1–12:50)
- E. Predicting Progressive Opposition toward Jesus (13:1–16:20)
  1. Explaining opposition: kingdom parables (13:1-52)
  2. Enacting opposition: from Jew to Gentile (13:53–16:20)

III. THE CLIMAX OF JESUS' MINISTRY (16:21–28:20)
- A. A Focus on Coming Death and Resurrection (16:21–18:35)
  1. The implications for disciples (16:21–17:27)
  2. The implications for the church (18:1-35)
- B. The Road to Jerusalem: The Coming Judgment (19:1–25:46)
  1. True discipleship vs. condemnation for the Jewish leaders (19:1–22:46)
  2. Judgment on the temple and the nations (23:1–25:46)
- C. An Account of Jesus' Ultimate Destiny (26:1–28:20)
  1. Passion and crucifixion (26:1–27:66)
  2. Resurrection and proclamation of the good news (28:1-20)

Exposition of the Text

THE IDENTIFICATION OF JESUS: WHO HE IS (1:1–4:16)

The Genealogy and Birth of Jesus (1:1–2:23)

1:1 From the very beginning, Matthew intended to show the connection between Jesus and the Old Testament. He presented Him first as the Christ (Gk. *Christou*, "anointed one"), the Jewish equivalent for Messiah. In Jesus' day the Jewish people were filled with messianic expectations, and many would-be messiahs appeared. To further his claim that Jesus was the true Messiah, Matthew also referred to Jesus as **the Son of David** and **the Son of Abraham**.

The Jews understood that the Messiah would descend from the royal line of David. God made a covenant with David and swore that David's kingdom would be established forever (2 Sm 7:12-16). Isaiah foretold that God's gracious promise would be fulfilled through King David's greater Son:

> For a child will be born for us, a son will be given to us, and the government will be on His shoulders. He will be named Wonderful Counselor, Mighty God, Eternal Father, Prince of Peace. The dominion will be vast, and its prosperity will never end. He will reign on the *throne of David* and over his kingdom, to establish and sustain it with justice and righteousness from now on and forever. The zeal of the LORD of Hosts will accomplish this (Is 9:6-7, emphasis added).

Obviously Jesus was the "Son of Abraham" if He was the "Son of David." But Matthew mentioned Abraham specifically for at least one important reason. God promised Abraham that through his offspring, "all the peoples on earth will be blessed through you" (Gn 12:3; see also 17:7; 22:18). With these two titles, the Son of David and the Son of Abraham, Matthew was highlighting the two stages of Christ's ministry: to the Jew first, then to the Gentile. In so doing, he was planting the seed for the idea of the "Great Commission" in chapter 28. As D. A. Carson said, "Jesus the Messiah came in fulfillment of the kingdom promises to David and of the Gentile-blessings promises to Abraham."[5]

1:2-17 Matthew's genealogy differs from Luke's genealogy (Lk 3:23-38), and the traditional understanding is that Matthew presented Jesus' lineage through Joseph's line,[6] while Luke followed Mary's genealogy. Matthew's primary aim was to show that Jesus was the greater Son of David, the one who would bring the divine blessings first to Israel and ultimately to all nations. Hence, he focused on King David, and he included a number of Gentile women. Matthew wanted to show the full spectrum of people, from royalty to "peasantry," who would be invited to partake in the kingdom blessings. Luke, on the other hand, intended to show from the beginning the universal nature of the Gospel. (See Lk 3:23-28 for more discussion on his purpose.)

Only Matthew included five women in his genealogy: **Tamar, Rahab, Ruth, Uriah's wife** (Bathsheba), and **Mary**. All of these women had Gentile roots except Mary. What they all had in common, however, was their somewhat questionable reputation.

Tamar was a daughter-in-law of Judah and wife to his sons, first Er and then Onan (see Gn 38). When Er and Onan died as a result of their sins, Judah was afraid to give his third son as a husband to Tamar. So Judah sent Tamar back to live in her father's house with a promise that he would give her his third son in marriage when the time was right. Tamar learned that her father-in-law had deceived her concerning marriage to his youngest son; Jewish law dictated that a relative provide heirs for the widow's deceased husband. The laws of levirate marriage (Dt 25:5-6) assured a man's lineage by allowing the deceased man's widow to become the wife of his brother in order to produce children to perpetuate the man's name and secure his property. Tamar devised a plan; she disguised herself as a prostitute so that Judah did not recognize her and lured Judah into sleeping with her. Tamar asked for a young goat in payment, and Judah gave her his cord and staff with a promise that he would return with the goat. When he sent his servant with the goat, the "prostitute" Tamar was nowhere to be found. Later Judah found out that his daughter-in-law was pregnant. He swore he would have her burned at the stake, but then she produced his cord and staff. At that time Judah announced that she was more "righteous" than he. She had done, according to Jewish law, what he refused to do.

Rahab was a prostitute who lived in Jericho at the time of Joshua (see Jos 2). She took in the two spies Joshua sent into the city to survey the land before Israel attacked. When the king of Jericho heard about the spies, thus endangering their lives, Rahab hid them and then sent them out of Jericho in a different direction so they would not be captured. Rahab committed herself to the God of Israel, and her life was spared when the Israelites attacked Jericho. She became the mother of kings.

Ruth, a Moabite woman, married a Jew who had immigrated with his family to her homeland of Moab (see Ru 1–4). Her husband died, and as a widow she moved back to Judah with her mother-in-law Naomi. Boaz, a distant relative of Ruth's first husband, owned land in Judah, and Ruth went to glean leftover grain from his fields. The two met, and Boaz showed an interest in the young Moabite widow. Ruth visited Boaz late one night as he slept on his threshing floor. Ruth did not do anything inappropriate with Boaz, even though her actions might have been questioned because she visited the threshing floor at such a late hour. Boaz later became Ruth's kinsman-redeemer and husband. Because of the constant hostilities between Moab and Israel in Ruth's time, the Israelites despised the Moabites. Nevertheless, Ruth so distinguished herself in the land of Judah that she became known as "a woman of noble character" (Ru 3:11), and she even found herself in the line of the Messiah.

Bathsheba was the wife of Uriah, a soldier in King David's army (see 2 Sm 11–12). While King David's armies were away at war, David saw Bathsheba bathing on her porch. He summoned her and slept with her, and she became pregnant. David tried to cover his adultery by bringing Uriah home from battle and enticing the valiant soldier to spend a time of intimacy with his wife. When the honorable Uriah refused to sleep with his wife while his fellow soldiers were on the battlefield, David sent him back to the battlefield and ordered Joab to put Uriah on the front line, where his death would be certain. David was severely disciplined by the Lord for his sin. After mourning the death of her husband, Bathsheba became David's wife. The baby of David and Bathsheba died as a consequence of their sin, but Bathsheba conceived again and gave birth to Solomon, who became one of the greatest kings of Israel.

Mary, who became the mother of Jesus, was betrothed to Joseph, but she was found to be with child before the marriage was consummated (see Lk 1:1–2:20). Joseph could well have divorced her on grounds of unfaithfulness. But, as a righteous man, Joseph believed the Lord, who told him that Mary's conception had occurred by the power of the Holy Spirit.

> *No one is too "disreputable" for Jesus.*

For Matthew to include women in his genealogy was surprising, but to mention women with questionable or scandalous reputations was shocking. Perhaps Matthew's point was that if the Messiah had such people in His lineage, He could most certainly save all people. No one is too "disreputable" for Jesus.

1:18-25 One of the first questions in a modern reader's mind when considering the virgin birth of Christ is the historicity of its claim.

- That the early Christians would make up such an event is highly unlikely. Unlike the Greco-Roman myths of virgin births, the narratives in both Matthew and Luke are simple, straightforward, and unassuming. If the virgin birth of Christ was purely fictional, embellishment, not simplicity, would have characterized the account.

- If the virgin birth was simply invented, one would expect to find much more correlation between what Matthew and Luke recorded about the event and its fulfillment of Old Testament prophecy. In some cases the writers did record straightforward, literal fulfillment. That the Messiah would be born in Bethlehem, for instance, is a literal fulfillment. But primarily, the Gospel writers relied on the use of typology. According to R. T. France, typology is

"the recognition of a correspondence between New and Old Testament events, based on a conviction of the unchanging character of the principles of God's working, and a consequent understanding and description of the New Testament event in terms of the Old Testament model."[7] Matthew used typology many times throughout his Gospel. One example is found in 2:15 where he referred to Jesus' flight out of Egypt.

In light of these and many other examples that could be given in support of the historicity of the virgin birth of Christ, there is no good reason to doubt the authenticity of this event.[8]

In keeping with his focus on Joseph in the genealogy, Matthew highlighted that Joseph was **a righteous man** who did not want **to disgrace** (Gk. *deigmatisai*, "expose, make an example of, humiliate publicly") Mary after learning of her pregnancy. Joseph could have divorced Mary on the charge of infidelity privately in the presence of witnesses or publicly before a court of rabbis. As with many Old Testament writers, righteousness was a very important concept for Matthew (see 3:15; 5:20). The engagement or betrothal in Jewish culture was taken very seriously and was considered a binding contract between a man and woman, even though no physical intimacy would have taken place. This formal commitment could only be dissolved by divorce. Joseph knew that Mary's child was not his, but he believed what the Lord revealed to him about the conception in a dream: **What has been conceived in her is by the Holy Spirit**. In accordance with the command of the Lord, Joseph named the child **Jesus**, a Greek equivalent of Joshua, which means "*Yahweh saves*" (v. 21).

Matthew pointed out that Christ's birth fulfilled the prophecy found in Isaiah

7:14, **See, the virgin will become pregnant, and give birth to a son, and they will name Him Immanuel**. The Hebrew word for VIRGIN (*'almah*) suggested a young woman of marriageable age. There is no example in Scripture in which *'almah* refers to a young woman who is not a virgin (Gn 24:43; Sg 1:3; 6:8). But the Septuagint, the Greek translation of the Old Testament, used *parthenos*, which specifically meant "a woman who had never had sex." In using this same term, Matthew confirmed that Isaiah's prophecy was now complete in Jesus and precisely identified Mary as a virgin. In accordance with God's command, Joseph named the child Jesus. The names Jesus and Immanuel combine to provide a picture of Christ's deity.

The Journeys of Mary		
Location	**Purpose**	**Reference**
Bethlehem	Mary traveled with Joseph to be registered in his ancestral village. There Christ was born.	Lk 2:1-7
Jerusalem	Jesus was presented at the temple, and the prophetess Anna bore witness to Him.	Lk 2:22-38
Bethlehem	The magi visited Jesus.	Mt 2:1-11
Egypt	Joseph and Mary, with Jesus, fled Bethlehem for safety.	Mt 2:13-15
Nazareth	The family returned home.	Mt 2:19-23

2:1-11 Jesus' birth **in Bethlehem** was a direct fulfillment of Micah 5:2. Bethlehem (Hb. "house of bread") was located about five miles south of Jerusalem. Also known as Ephrath (Gn 35:19), it was the city of David's ancestors and the site of Rachel's tomb (2:18). While Jewish leaders did not recognize the significance of this event, the magi, astrologers from the East who studied the stars as a way to understand present and future events, recognized its importance. The WISE MEN (Gk. *magoi*) were probably an educated group of philosophers, scientists, or astrologers—possibly from a priestly class, coming from Persia or Babylon. The word describing the wise men was also used of Babylonian priests or men who were especially gifted in the interpretation of dreams and stars and was used in the Septuagint in Daniel 2:2 to describe the "diviner-priests" to whom King Nebuchadnezzar gave orders to interpret his dream. The English word "magician" comes from this Greek word.

Although the text does not record the number of wise men, the fact that three gifts were presented has led to the tradition of "three" wise men. Imagine the uproar in the court of King Herod the Great as the magi came to him, looking for the one who had been born **King of the Jews**! King Herod and all of Jerusalem were troubled (Gk. *etarachthē*, "stirred, unsettled and thrown into confusion, frightened"). Herod was one of the cruelest rulers of all time, and he did not hesitate even to murder members of his own family if they appeared to be a threat to his throne. In fact, Caesar Augustus, the Roman emperor, used a play on the Greek words to say that it was safer to be Herod's pig (Gk. *hus*) than Herod's son (Gk. *huios*). When the magi came to Herod looking for the King of the Jews, he undoubtedly began plotting how he could eliminate this new threat to his throne. Herod called in the **chief priests** and scribes, who were supposed to be watching for the coming of the promised Messiah, to inquire where Christ was to be born. He then instructed the wise men to report to him when they found the Christ child.

There was a common tradition that suggested the announcement of special births through some phenomenon in the heavens, especially with the stars. The historians Josephus, Tacitus, and Suetonius, as well as the poet Virgil, all affirmed a universal expectation of the coming of an extraordinary king. The magi may have also been aware of the Jewish hope for a Messiah coming out of a remaining influence from the Jewish captivity in Persia (539–332 BC). Because historians had already suggested the appearance of a new world ruler, these men were immediately captivated by what they saw in their study of the stars. They made their way to Jerusalem not solely on the basis of the stars, but because of their findings from other studies. The star was seen again by the wise men over the house where Joseph, Mary, and Jesus lived. The term **house** (Gk. *oikian*) pro-

vided a clue that Mary and Joseph were no longer in a stable with animals but had moved to a permanent dwelling somewhere in Bethlehem. Additionally, Jesus was referred to as a **child** (Gk. *paidon*) instead of as a baby (Gk. *brephos*, see Lk 2:16), which suggested that Jesus could have been as old as two years when the magi visited Him. When the wise men saw Jesus, **they worshiped Him**. The words for FALLING DOWN and WORSHIP (Gk. *pesontes prosekunēsan*) were used to describe the act of falling down before someone to kiss his feet. These wise men were pagan astrologers; and when confronted with the King of Kings in the form of a young child, they could do nothing but fall down in awe of His majesty and splendor. They presented Christ with three gifts: **gold, frankincense, and myrrh**. Gold was prized for its beauty and worth and was associated with royalty; frankincense, a fragrant spice, was taken from the bark of trees and used in incense; and myrrh was a costly perfume often used in embalming the dead.

The Wives of Herod the Great, King of Judea
Matthew 2:1-19; Luke 1:5

Wife	Description	Children	Descendants
Mariamne II	Daughter of the high priest Simon	Herod Philip	Salome (daughter of Herod Philip and Herodias, Mt 14:1-12; Mk 6:17)
Mariamne I	Hasmonean princess; Herod's favorite wife	Salampsio; Alexander; Cypros; Aristobulus	Herod Agrippa I (King of Judea, Ac 12:1-24); Bernice (Ac 25:13; 26:30); Drusilla (Ac 24:24); Herod Agrippa II (King of Judea, Ac 25:13–26:32); Mariamne
Malthace	A Samaritan	Herod Antipas (Tetrarch of Galilee); Archelaus (King of Judea, Mt 2:22)	
Cleopatra		Herod Philip (tetrarch of Iturea; Lk 3:1)	
Doris		Antipater	
Other wives	Five unnamed	Other children	

Heart to Heart:
What Is Your Reaction to Jesus?

In Matthew 2:1-11 people were confronted with the reality of Christ: Herod the Great, the chief priests and scribes, and the wise men. When Herod heard about this new King of the Jews, he reacted in anger and condemnation because he felt Jesus posed a threat to his throne and his way of life. Unfortunately, many people in contemporary society react the same way when they come face-to-face with the truth of Jesus the Savior—they reject Him because they feel He threatens their way of life. The chief priests and scribes had been looking for the coming Messiah for hundreds of years, but because Jesus did not fit their mold, they rejected Him. Only the wise men accepted Christ as the promised King and worshiped Him in reverence.

Have you rejected Jesus because you have some preconceived notions about who God is or how He should act? God desires that you have a relationship with Him, and that is precisely why Jesus Christ came to the earth. By living a perfect life and offering Himself as a sacrifice for sin on the cross at Calvary, Jesus overcame the barrier that sin had created between God and His creation. You have a choice: Will you reject Christ like Herod and the chief priests and scribes, or will you accept Him like the wise men, who in their worship of Christ displayed how truly wise they were?

2:12-15 Having been warned in a dream about Herod's intent to kill Jesus, Joseph took Mary and Jesus **to Egypt**. Matthew saw this as a fulfillment of Hosea 11:1, **Out of Egypt I called My son**. Matthew drew the correlation between what happened to Israel when they went down to Egypt and what was happening to Jesus. Joseph and his family stayed in Egypt **until Herod's death**, which occurred in 4 BC.

2:16-18 Herod had slaughtered two of his own sons, Aristobulus and Alexander, and their mother, Mariamne I, even though she was considered his favorite wife (Herod had ten wives). Herod's acute paranoia claimed victim after victim, and in verse 16 Herod FLEW INTO A RAGE (Gk. *ethumōthē lian*—the adverb *lian* coupled with the verb *ethumōthē* stressed the intensity of Herod's anger and rage; he became *violently angry*) when he learned he had been OUTWITTED (Gk. *enepaichthē*, "deceived, tricked") by the wise men, who had been warned in a dream not to report to Herod when they learned of the Christ child's location. Slaughtering all the male children under two years of age in Bethlehem and its surrounding region was not a surprising move for a ruler so ruthless and paranoid and prone to violence. The fact that Herod chose to kill all the children under two years of age supports the theory that Jesus was at least a toddler at the time the wise men visited Him.

Verse 18 presents another example of Matthew's use of typology. In Jeremiah 31:15, women at the time of the exile were mourning the loss of their children. **Rachel** was a wife of Jacob and the mother of Joseph and Benjamin (see Gn

29–31). She lost both of her children to Egypt and was a "type" of all Israelite women who mourned the loss of their children. Matthew applied this theme at the time of Herod's slaughter to the mothers of Bethlehem who lost their children two years and under. Rachel herself died in childbirth on the way to Bethlehem (Gn 35:16-20). The site of her traditional tomb in Bethlehem is still revered by Jews.

Also striking are the words of Jeremiah 31:16, "Keep your voice from weeping and your eyes from tears, for the reward for your work will come—this is the Lord's declaration—and your children will return from the enemy's land." Possibly with this verse in mind, Matthew declared that Jesus and His family returned from Egypt after the massacre.

2:19-23 After the death of Herod the Great, his kingdom was divided among three of his sons: Herod Archelaus, Philip, and Herod Antipas. Archelaus, one of Herod's sons by his wife Malthace, took after his father in many ways. He was known for his great building projects as well as his cruel and inhumane rule. The Jews sent a delegation to Caesar Augustus in Rome to protest Archelaus's tyranny, and in AD 6, Rome removed Archelaus from power for his incompetence. Matthew noted that Joseph and Mary would not settle in Judea because they **heard that Archelaus was ruling over Judea**; instead, they settled in Galilee, where Herod Antipas ruled as the tetrarch of Galilee and Perea.

The statement, **He will be called a Nazarene,** in this precise wording (v. 23), is nowhere to be found in the Old Testament. But Matthew introduced the quote as representing the teachings not of one prophet, but of the **prophets** in general. He evidently had no specific Old Testament reference in mind but was possibly summarizing several prophecies made concerning the obscurity of the place of Christ's birth and childhood. Several explanations have been suggested:

- Some believe Matthew was implying that Jesus was a Nazirite and encouraged others to take a similar vow (see Nm 6), but nowhere in Scripture is Jesus identified as a Nazirite.

- The religious leaders of the first century used "Nazarene" as a term of contempt—a way of expressing their scorn toward Jesus (see Jn 1:46).

- In Isaiah 11:1 there is a reference to a "branch" (Hb. *netser*) growing out of the roots of Jesse (see Jr 23:5; Zch 3:8; 6:12), which would indicate that Matthew could have considered this prediction as spoken through the prophets.

- Some critics simply describe the phrase as a scribal note or oversight.

- The more natural explanation seems to result from the many references to Jesus as a resident of Nazareth, which again could have, and probably would have, been attributed to the prophets.

Blomberg points out that Matthew's infancy narratives stressed three key themes: Jesus was the hope of Israel; blessings would be extended to Gentiles; and Jesus was the legitimate King.[9]

The Preparation for Jesus' Ministry (3:1–4:16)

His forerunner (3:1-12)

3:1-12 Although Matthew did not record the date when John the Baptist began his ministry in the wilderness, Luke did record the year (in the fifteenth year of the reign of Tiberius Caesar, Lk 3:1). John, the son of the priest Zechariah and of Elizabeth, who was a relative of Jesus' mother Mary, was 30 years old when he began preaching in the **Wilderness of Judea.** This rocky region was located in the lower Jordan Valley and was not densely populated. However, as John began preaching, people came from far and near to hear his radical message.

John's message had two themes: the call to repentance and the nearness of the kingdom of heaven. REPENT (Gk. *met-anoeite*, "have a change of heart, change one's ways") linked the idea of sorrow for one's actions with turning around and embracing new actions. The emphasis was not on sorrow but on a change of actions. Biblical repentance did not end at being sorry for your actions; repentance meant turning from one way to an entirely different course. The imminence of the **kingdom of heaven** referred to a specific Jewish understanding of God's reign but was also virtually the same idea as what was called the "kingdom of God" in the Gospels of Mark and Luke. The Jewish people were awaiting the kingdom of heaven, so John the Baptist's words would not have been foreign to them. His ministry was foretold by Isaiah (Is 40:3), and the people were coming to him, confessing their sins in hopeful expectation of the coming kingdom.

John the Baptist singled out the **Pharisees and Sadducees**, calling them a **brood of vipers** and warning them to flee from the coming wrath (3:7). The Pharisees (meaning "the separated ones") were a sect of Jewish leaders who controlled the synagogues and were seen as the religious authorities by the Jews. The Sadducees (meaning "the righteous ones"), a rival party of the Pharisees, were made up of wealthy men who exercised considerable political influence over the Jews because many of them were members of the Sanhedrin. By singling out these two groups, John foreshadowed Christ's ministry in which He often confronted the religious and political leaders about their hypocrisy.

John pointed out to the Jewish leaders that they could not appeal to their ancestry as children of Abraham to save them. Only a person who had repented of his wicked ways and trusted Christ for salvation could enter the kingdom of heaven (v. 2). John demanded proof of genuine repentance before he would baptize anyone: **Produce fruit consistent with repentance** (v. 8). Do not misunderstand John's statement. John was not saying that a person was saved by works; however, he was saying that a person's lifestyle would demonstrate whether or not he had experienced true salvation and repentance.

John used two metaphors to describe the reality of judgment for anyone who did not repent: the **ax** and **fire** (v. 10) and the **winnowing shovel** (v. 12). When a tree no longer produced fruit, it would be cut down with an ax and burned with fire. Fire often represented judgment in the Old and New Testaments. John did not shy away from proclaiming the truth of God's message—judgment awaited any person who did not repent and accept Christ's free gift of salvation.

The second metaphor John used was that of the winnowing shovel. John proclaimed that when Christ came, He would divide the **wheat** and the **chaff** (v. 12) with his winnowing shovel. When harvest time arrived, farmers would gather up the wheat with the chaff and bring it to the threshing floor. In order to separate the grain from the chaff (the empty shells that covered the grain), the farmer would take the forklike winnowing shovel and throw his harvested grain into the air. The grain would fall to the ground as the worthless chaff blew away in the wind.

His baptism (3:13-17)

3:13-17 Jesus came from Galilee to be baptized by John the Baptist, but John tried to stop Jesus, knowing that he, rather than Jesus, was the one in need of baptism. BAPTIZE (an anglicization of Gk. *baptizō*, "baptize") originally meant "to

Jewish Sects in the New Testament

Pharisees

Name	Dates of Existence	Origin	Segments of Society
Pharisees = "the Separated Ones" with three possible meanings: • separating themselves from people • separating themselves to the study of the law ("dividing" or "separating" the truth) • separating themselves from pagan practices	Existed under Jonathan (160–143 BC) Declined in power under John Hyrcanus (134–104 BC) Began resurgence under Salome Alexandra (76 BC)	Probably spiritual descendants of the Hasidim (religious freedom fighters of the time of Judas Maccabeus)	Most numerous among the Jewish parties (or sects) Probably descendants of the Hasidim—scribes and lawyers Members of the middle class—mostly businessmen (merchants and tradesmen)

Beliefs	Selected Biblical References	Activities
Monotheistic Viewed entirety of the Old Testament (Torah, Prophets, and Writings) as authoritative Believed that the study of the law was true worship Accepted both the written and oral law More liberal in interpreting the law than were the Sadducees Quite concerned with the proper keeping of the Sabbath, tithing, and purification rituals Believed in life after death and the resurrection of the body (with divine retribution and reward) Believed in the reality of demons and angels Revered humanity and human equality Missionary minded regarding converting the Gentiles Believed that individuals were responsible for how they lived	Mt 3:7-10; 5:20; 9:14; 16:1,6-12; 22:15-22,34-46; 23:2-36 Mk 3:6, 7:3-5, 8:15; 12:13-17 Lk 6:7; 7:36-39; 11:37-44; 18:9-14 Jn 3:1; 9:13-16; 11:46-47; 12:19 Ac 23:6-10 Php 3:4b-6	Developed oral tradition Taught obedience to the law as the way to God Changed Judaism from a religion of sacrifice to a religion of law Progressive thinkers regarding the adaptation of the law to new situations Opposed Jesus because He would not accept the teachings of the oral law as binding Established and controlled synagogues Exercised great control over general population Served as religious authorities for most Jews Took several ceremonies from the temple to the home Emphasized ethical as opposed to theological action Legalistic and socially exclusive (shunned non-Pharisees as unclean) Tended to have a self-sufficient and haughty attitude

Sadducees

Name	Dates of Existence	Origin	Segments of Society
Sadducees = Three possible translations: • "the Righteous Ones"—based on the Hebrew consonants for the word "righteous" • "ones who sympathize with Zadok," or "Zadokites"—based on their possible link to Zadok the high priest • "syndics," "judges," or "fiscal controllers"—based on the Greek word *syndikoi*	Probably began about 200 BC Demise occurred in AD 70 (with the destruction of the Temple)	Unknown origin Claimed to be descendants of Zadok—high priest under David (see 2 Sm 8:17; 15:24) and Solomon (see 1 Kg 1:34–35; 1 Chr 12:28) Had a possible link to Aaron Were probably formed into the high priest's party about 200 BC	Aristocracy—the rich descendants of the high-priestly line (however, not all priests were Sadducees) Possibly descendants of the Hasmonean priesthood Probably not as refined as their economic position in life would suggest

Beliefs	Selected Biblical References	Activities
Accepted only the Torah (Genesis through Deuteronomy—the written law of Moses) as authoritative Practiced literal interpretation of the law Rigidly conservative toward the law Stressed strict observance of the law Observed past beliefs and tradition Opposed oral law as obligatory or binding Believed in the absolute freedom of human will—that people could do as they wished without attention from God Denied divine providence Denied the concept of life after death and the resurrection of the body Denied the concept of reward and punishment after death Denied the existence of angels and demons Materialistic	2 Sm 8:17; 15:24 1 Kg 1:34 1 Chr 12:26-28 Ezk 40:45-46; 43:19; 44:15-16 Mt 3:7-10; 16:1,6-12; 22:23-34 Mk 12:18-27 Lk 20:27-40 Jn 11:47 Ac 4:1-2; 5:17-18; 23:6-10	In charge of the temple and its services Politically active Exercised great political control through the Sanhedrin, of which many were members Supported the ruling power and the status quo Leaned toward Hellenism (the spreading of Greek influence)—and were thus despised by the Jewish populace Opposed both the Pharisees and Jesus because these lived by a larger canon (The Pharisees and Jesus both considered more than only Genesis through Deuteronomy as authoritative.) Opposed Jesus specifically for fear their wealth/position would be threatened if they supported him

Jewish Sects in the New Testament

Zealots

Name	Dates of Existence	Origin	Segments of Society
Refers to their religious zeal Josephus used the term in referring to those involved in the Jewish revolt against Rome in AD 6—led by Judas of Galilee.	Three possibilities for their beginning: • during the reign of Herod the Great (about 37 BC) • during the revolt against Rome (AD 6) • traced back to the Hassidim or the Maccabees (about 168 BC) Their certain demise occurred around AD 70–73 with Rome's conquering of Jerusalem.	According to Josephus, the Zealots began with Judas (the Galilean), son of Ezekias, who led a revolt in AD 6 because of a census done for tax purposes.	The extreme wing of the Pharisees

Beliefs	Selected Biblical References	Activities
Similar to the Pharisees, except for strong belief that only God had the right to rule the Jew; patriotism and religion became inseparable Believed that total obedience (supported by drastic physical measures) must be apparent before God would bring in the Messianic Age Were fanatical in their Jewish faith and in their devotion to the law—to the point of martyrdom	Mt 10:4 Mk 3:18 Lk 6:15 Ac 1:13	Extremely opposed to Roman rule over Palestine Extremely opposed to peace with Rome Refused to pay taxes Demonstrated against the use of the Greek language in Palestine Engaged in terrorism against Rome and others with whom they disagreed politically [Sicarii (or Assassins) were an extremist Zealot group who carried out acts of terrorism against Rome.]

Herodians

Name	Dates of Existence	Origin	Segments of Society
Based on their support of the Herodian rulers (Herod the Great or his dynasty)	Existed during the time of the Herodian dynasty (which began with Herod the Great in 37 BC) Uncertain demise	Exact origin uncertain	Wealthy, politically influential Jews who supported Herod Antipas (or any descendant of Herod the Great) as ruler over Palestine (Judea and Samaria were under Roman governors at this time)

Beliefs	Selected Biblical References	Activities
Not a religious group—but a political one. Membership was probably comprised of representatives of varied theological perspectives	Mt 22:5-22; Mk 3:6; 8:15; 12:13-17	Supported Herod and the Herodian dynasty. Accepted Hellenization. Accepted foreign rule

Essenes

Name	Dates of Existence	Origin	Segments of Society
Unknown origin	Probably began during Maccabean times (about 168 BC)—around the same time as the Pharisees and the Sadducees began to form. Uncertain demise—probably in AD 68–70 with the collapse of Jerusalem	Possibly developed as a reaction to the corrupt Sadducean priesthood. Have been identified with various groups: Hasidim, Zealots, Greek influence, or Iranian influence	Scattered throughout the villages of Judea (possibly including the community of Qumran). According to Philo and Josephus, about 4,000 in Palestinian Syria

Beliefs	Selected Biblical References	Activities
Very strict ascetics. Monastic: most took vow of celibacy (adopting male children in order to perpetuate the group), but some did marry (for the purpose of procreation). Rigidly adherent to the law (including a strict rendering of the ethical teachings). Considered other literature as authoritative (in addition to the Hebrew Scripture). Believed and lived as pacifists. Rejected temple worship and temple offerings as corrupted. Believed in the immortality of the soul with no bodily resurrection. Apocalyptically oriented	None	Devoted to the copying and studying of the manuscript of the law. Lived in a community sense with communal property. Required a long probationary period and ritual baptisms of those wishing to join. Were highly virtuous and righteous. Were extremely self-disciplined. Were diligent manual laborers. Gave great importance to daily worship. Upheld rigid Sabbath laws. Maintained a non-Levitical priesthood. Rejected worldly pleasures as evil. Rejected matrimony—but did not forbid others to marry

dip under," with the idea of totally enveloping one substance in another. Baptism was a well-known ceremony performed as a sign of repentance in the time of Jesus. For a Christian, baptism is a public testimony symbolizing putting off the old life and identifying with the new life in Christ. It has a threefold significance.

- A public confession that Jesus died and rose again, picturing His death, burial, and resurrection.

- A public testimony of the experience of regeneration, showing death to an old life and resurrection to walk in the newness of life in Christ. Only the believer who has experienced the new birth is a candidate for baptism.

- A declaration of the believer's confidence that he will be raised from his own death and burial when Christ returns.

Only Matthew recorded Jesus' response to John's protest concerning Jesus' request for baptism, **Allow it for now, because this is the way for us to fulfill all righteousness** (v. 15). What was Jesus' purpose for being baptized? He certainly did not need to confess any sins to John. By being baptized, Jesus publicly endorsed John's ministry and message, and He personally displayed obedience to the will of God the Father. In fact, in verses 16-17 God the Father verbally expressed His approval of Jesus' baptism. Each person of the triunity was represented as Jesus formally entered into His Messianic ministry: God the Son in His incarnation, God the Father as **a voice from heaven**, and God the Holy Spirit **like a dove** descending from heaven.

His testing 4:1-11

4:1-11 The Synoptic Gospels all place the temptation of Jesus after His baptism.

The writers did not necessarily intend to write a chronological account of Jesus' life, but the sequence here is significant. God the Father acknowledged Jesus to be His Son; then, as recorded in both Matthew and Luke, **the Devil** referred to Him as **the Son of God**. This acknowledgement served as a double endorsement of Christ's divinity.

But Jesus still was to undergo temptation. The word **TEMPTED** (Gk. *peirasthēnai*) means "solicit to sin." The Bible is clear that God never tempts anyone to sin, but He allows men and women to be tempted. As the final Lawgiver and final Prophet, Jesus **fasted 40 days and 40 nights** (v. 2) in the wilderness—in the same general region where John had been preaching. He was tempted in three significant ways: to turn **stones** into **bread**, (Mt 4:7; Dt 6:16) to be rescued supernaturally from death, and to receive **all the kingdoms of the world** (Mt 4:10; Dt 6:13). Jesus accomplished what Adam, in his Edenic paradise, could not do when faced with temptation. Jesus resisted the Devil and thus became the "Greater Adam." In every instance, He used Scripture to defend Himself against the enemy's attacks.

In each temptation Jesus was enticed to use His heavenly Sonship in a way inconsistent with His divine mission. Jesus knew that obedience to God's word was more necessary than eating bread. He did not test God by protecting Himself, but He relied on His confidence in God's promise of constant protection. Jesus did not in any way swerve from His undivided allegiance to God the Father. The Son was to be King, but He was also to live in complete submission to the Father's authority.

THE DEVELOPMENT OF JESUS' MINISTRY: WHAT HE DOES (4:12–16:20)

The Beginning of Ministry (4:12–4:25)

Preparing for ministry (4:12-16)

4:12-16 For Jesus to begin His earthly ministry in **Galilee of the Gentiles** (v. 15) is significant. Matthew was not interested in Galilee merely for its own sake, but because Christ's ministry there was a fulfillment of prophecy. In Isaiah 9:1-2 the Messiah was promised "to Galilee of the nations," highlighting again His preordained mission to all nations. Christ's light dawned first in the darkest of places.

As far as the Jews were concerned, Galilee was a despicable place far from the religious influence of Jerusalem. Matthew recorded that Christ said He came to call not the righteous but the sinner to repentance (see 9:13). His light and grace penetrated every dark place.

Capernaum, a city **in the region of Zebulun and Naphtali** (v. 13), was larger than Nazareth and situated on the northwest shore of the Sea of Galilee. It was a hub of political and commercial life in Galilee and attracted many Gentiles because of the fishing mart. It proved to be an ideal place for Jesus' ministry, and He made His home in Capernaum.

Jesus' Ministry as Fulfillment of Scripture in Matthew

Aspects of His Ministry	Fulfillment Passage in Matthew	OT Prophecy
His virgin birth and role as God with us	Mt 1:18,22-23	Is 7:14
His birth in Bethlehem and role as Shepherd	Mt 2:4-6	Mc 5:2
His exile years in Egypt and messianic role as God's Son	Mt 2:14-15	Hs 11:1
His upbringing in Nazareth and role as Messiah (Hb. *nezer*, "branch")	Mt 2:23	Is 11:1
His preaching ministry in Galilee and role as light to the Gentiles	Mt 4:12-16	Is 9:1-2
His healing ministry and role as God's Servant	Mt 8:16-17	Is 53:4
His reluctance to attract attention and His role as God's chosen and loved Servant	Mt 12:16-21	Is 42:1-4
His teaching in parables and His role in proclaiming God's sovereign rule	Mt 13:34-35	Ps 78:2
His humble entry into Jerusalem and role as King	Mt 21:1-5	Zch 9:9
His betrayal, arrest, and death and His role as Suffering Servant	Mt 26:50,56	The prophetic writings as a whole

Calling out disciples (4:17-25)

4:17-22 This section provided the setting for Matthew's first sermon-narrative sequence. Jesus' message was the same as had been presented by His forerunner John the Baptist: **Repent, because the kingdom of heaven has come near!** (v. 17). Two sets of brothers, **Simon** and **Andrew**, together with **James** and **John**, were among the first to be called to follow Jesus

(4:18-22). Simon and Andrew were **fishermen** by trade, and probably knew Jesus before this encounter by the **Sea of Galilee** (Jn 1:40-42). When Jesus called them to **fish for people** (see Mk 1:14-20, excursus from the editor), they **immediately** (Gk. *eutheōs*, "at once, soon") left their business and accepted His call. The other set of brothers, James and John, were in their boat with their father **mending their nets**, and they **immediately** left their **boat and their father** to follow Christ.

4:23-25 Verse 23 displays the threefold ministry of Christ while He was on the earth: teaching, preaching, healing. He taught **in their synagogues** (Gk. *sunagōgais*, assemblies). During the exile the Jewish nation was cut off from worshiping in the temple, so synagogues became the centers of worship, community, discipline, and religious instruction. Even after the temple was restored, synagogues remained an important part of the religious life of the Jews, and Jesus went to the synagogues with His teaching ministry.

Christ's preaching and healing ministry was well underway before He delivered the Sermon on the Mount. News about Him had spread as far as the region of Syria with its heavy Gentile population. The "darkness," which plagued the people of Galilee and beyond, was demonstrated by the various kinds of sufferings and ailments Christ healed.

Preaching: The Sermon on the Mount (5:1–7:29)

The Sermon on the Mount is one of the most well-known biblical texts, quoted often by both believers and unbelievers. Thousands of pages have been written about its contents and meaning. Though believers have never been able to meet perfectly the demands of Jesus' words, they have been challenged to strive toward the standard He set, through the

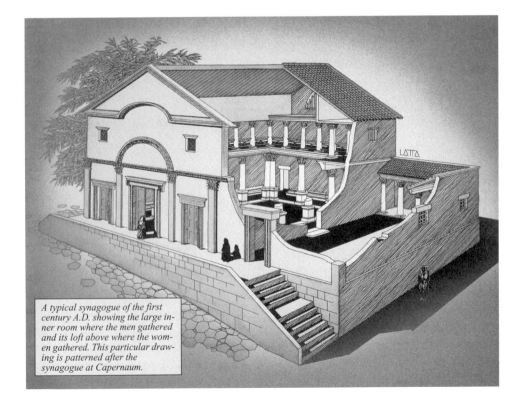

A typical synagogue of the first century A.D. showing the large inner room where the men gathered and its loft above where the women gathered. This particular drawing is patterned after the synagogue at Capernaum.

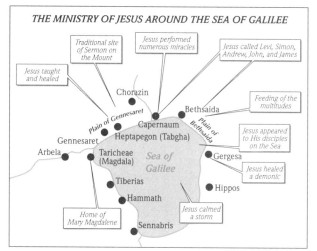

THE MINISTRY OF JESUS AROUND THE SEA OF GALILEE

- Jesus taught and healed
- Traditional site of Sermon on the Mount
- Jesus performed numerous miracles
- Jesus called Levi, Simon, Andrew, John, and James
- Feeding of the multitudes
- Jesus appeared to His disciples on the Sea
- Jesus healed a demonic
- Jesus calmed a storm
- Home of Mary Magdalene

Chorazin
Plain of Gennesaret
Bethsaida
Capernaum
Plain of Bethsaida
Gennesaret
Heptapegon (Tabgha)
Arbela
Taricheae (Magdala)
Sea of Galilee
Gergesa
Tiberias
Hammath
Hippos
Sennabris

power of the Holy Spirit, demonstrating in every way full submission to Jesus. The Sermon on the Mount, then, is not about righteousness by works but about living a life consistent with genuine repentance, which then bears fruit.

The Sermon was meticulously structured to communicate Jesus' demand for a greater righteousness (5:17-20). The teachings are essentially grouped into units of three. The Beatitudes and the "salt and light" passages formed the introduction (5:3-16). Six illustrations of the greater righteousness followed, contrasting the Old Testament Law with Christ's ethic (5:21-48), then three examples of true piety (6:1-18), followed by three teachings about money and anxiety (6:19-34) and then by three sections on how to treat others (7:1-12). Jesus concluded His sermon with three examples, focusing on the only two responses possible for those who heard Him—acceptance or rejection (7:13-27).[10]

The greater righteousness, then, involved a total and complete change of heart. Righteousness goes beyond mere works by producing good fruit consistent with this heart change (5:20). It involves seeking God's kingdom and His righteousness first (6:33) and treating others as you would want to be treated (7:12). Righteousness holds God's will to be

supreme (7:21), and unswerving allegiance to Jesus Christ produces security in Him (7:24-25).

In every way the Sermon on the Mount was designed to demonstrate Jesus' authority as the final Lawgiver. Reminiscent of Moses' trek up Mount Sinai to receive the law from the God of Israel, Jesus **went up on the mountain** (5:1), sat down, and delivered His message. But unlike Moses, He did not receive His message from a higher authority. Christ *is* the higher authority! The crowd was amazed after He finished speaking because He spoke as "one who had authority" (7:29). This message was exactly what Matthew wished to communicate to the people, and especially to the religious leaders. Jesus—the Son of David, the Son of Abraham—is greater than Moses. When Moses came down from the mountain, the people of Israel responded negatively to him, and judgment fell upon them. When Jesus "came down from the mountain" (8:1), the people followed Him, and He demonstrated His authority (and His greater righteousness) by various healings and miracles. Clearly, then, Matthew intended to show that, based on who Christ is, all believers must strive to embrace the greater righteousness about which He taught.

5:1-12 In the Sermon on the Mount Jesus presented an upside-down kingdom. The very things valued by the Greco-Roman world—wealth and fame— were devalued in Christ's kingdom. BLESSED (Gk. *makarioi*, "blessed, fortunate") is usually understood to mean "happy," but this concept does not capture its real meaning. More precisely the word suggests the idea of "being congratulated" because God's favor is granted to the individual.

The blessedness described in the Beatitudes is not a quality characteristic of human beings but a trait of God Himself. Only God imparts this blessedness ... [It] cannot be demanded from God but rather is the result of fulfilling the prescribed conditions set before you by the Lord Himself. Blessedness is a characteristic exclusively bestowed by God upon the believer, and it is attainable by you only because God dwells in your heart.[11]

Since this blessedness comes from within, it is neither caused nor affected by outside circumstances. Its source and point of reference is God. Social and spiritual aspects of life are woven through each Beatitude. Believers are characterized by their humility and confidence in God. Through the Beatitudes Christ explained His personhood and His ministry, which were marked by humility and sacrifice.

Beatitudes for Women[12]			
Blessed Are . . .	**Character Quality**	**Description**	**References**
Those who are poor in spirit (Mt 5:3)	Humility	Stripped of pride and sensitive to God's ministry in their behalf	Is 61:1; Lk 4:16-21; 7:22
Those who mourn (Mt 5:4)	Sensitivity	Responsive to personal sinfulness and tenderhearted toward one another	Is 61:2; Ec 3:1-8; Lk 19:41; Jn 11:33,35
Those who are gentle (Mt 5:5)	Meekness	Demonstration of self-control and submission	Mt 6:33; 1 Pt 3:1-7
Those who hunger and thirst for righteousness (Mt 5:6)	Obedience	Desire to hear and do the will of God	Lk 1:53
Those who are merciful (Mt 5:7)	Compassion	Outworking of faith to meet the needs of others	Lk 1:58
Those who are pure in heart (Mt 5:8)	Holiness	Lifestyle of set-apartness, including thoughts and actions	Ps 24:4-6
Those who are peacemakers (Mt 5:9)	Reconciliation	Forbearance instead of retaliation; forgiveness of wrongs; restoration of fellowship	Rm 3:25; 12:18; Eph 4:32; Php 1:3-5; Ti 3:2; 1 Jn 1:7

Beatitudes for Women [12]			
Blessed Are . . .	**Character Quality**	**Description**	**References**
Those who are persecuted for righteousness (Mt 5:10)	Commitment	Steadfast loyalty that cannot be broken	Lk 13:34-35; 2 Th 2:15-17; 2 Tm 2:3
Those who are insulted and persecuted (Mt 5:11)	Patience	Willingness to endure suffering	1 Pt 2:19-21; 3:14; Rv 12:11

The world despised anyone who was considered weak, but Jesus taught that anyone who recognizes his own spiritual poverty and helplessness is ready for spiritual growth. The POOR (Gk. *ptōchoi*, from root meaning "crouch," suggesting a beggar who kneels in hope that his need will be supplied by another) IN SPIRIT (v. 3) could refer to those who are both spiritually impoverished and socially and economically oppressed.

Nowhere in Scripture is poverty or absence of possessions declared to be the path to spiritual blessing. The poor of whom Jesus spoke were those marked by godly humility. The emphasis was upon emptying yourself to make room for God. One who is poor cannot satisfy her own needs; she is driven by her poverty to dependence upon God. When self-sufficiency and pride are stripped away, you are ready to be responsive to God, His word, and the gracious ministries He sends to meet your need. As with most godly character traits, the pattern is found in the life of Jesus. He came into the world in a humble setting—a stable manger in an insignificant village. There is no way into the kingdom of God other than with the poverty of spirit that comes from emptying yourself of pride, self-reliance, and self-sufficiency and in contrast filling yourself with God, His strength, and God-sufficiency. You then forget about building up your self-image because you have chosen to live out the God-image in your life. The emphasis is on God's power instead of your resourcefulness.

The New Testament uses the phrase **kingdom of heaven** (v. 3) in three ways. In the Sermon on the Mount, as is often the case, all can be included in the meaning:

> *You forget about building up your self-image because you have chosen to live out the God-image in your life. The emphasis is on God's power instead of your resourcefulness.*

- the kingdom of God within the heart of a believer (Mt 6:33);

- the body that includes all believers on earth (Lk 11:2); and

- the kingdom prepared for believers after death (Mt 16:19; Lk 9:62).

In each case God ushers in the kingdom, and Jesus reigns over it. Only the poor in spirit, claiming no personal merit, can enter because grace, and not works, opens the door.

Those who mourn (v. 4) echoed Isaiah 61:1 and may have referred to those who, having confessed spiritual poverty or personal sinfulness, grieved over spiritual impoverishment. However, the meaning cannot be confined to sorrow over sin. Again the reader finds a paradox since most people do not recognize sorrow as a blessing. Followers of Christian Science even deny the existence of physical illness and suffering. However, sorrow and death will always be present. Still this Beatitude does not suggest that physical suffering or loss of a loved one or any other tragedy of life would bring blessing merely as a payment for grief. Spiritual mourning indicates a sensitive consciousness of sin and an accompanying sorrow because of that sin (Jms 4:9). Those who mourn recognize who they are; they see purpose in sorrow and suffering; they allow that sorrow to give glory to God. Tragedies become stepping stones to the heart of God and His comfort (Pss 63:6-8; 77:2-6). Grief prompted by the sin itself, rather than only by the consequences of the sin that might have affected you adversely, produced sanctified sorrow.

They will be COMFORTED (Gk. *paraklēthēsontai*, "encourage, console, cheer up," from the same root as *paraklētos*, "the one called alongside" and the name identifying the Holy Spirit). The Holy Spirit enables you to cry out for help because He not only brings conviction but also awakens within you sorrow over sin (Jn 16:7-11). As the believer mourns over her sin, the Holy Spirit who abides within does His work to give comfort and joy and enables her to persevere, even in the midst of sorrow and suffering. The Greek verb is in the passive voice and the future tense, implying not only assurance for the present but also security for the future. The cycle of comfort will be continuous because the Holy Spirit dwells now and forever in the believer's heart. The blessedness should not be construed as coming from the path of sorrow itself but from the comfort accompanying the believer in the journey (2 Co 1:3-4).

The **gentle** (Gk. *praeis*, "humble, meek," v. 5) were not the weak or cowardly. They were those who, under the pressures of life, had learned to bend their wills and to set aside their own notions as they stood before the greatness and grace of God. They were characterized by humble trust rather than arrogant independence as they exercised self-control of life and actions, submitting to the authority of Christ. Your focus must move from dependence on your own gifts and abilities to genuine dependence upon God. In humble recognition of her sinfulness, the believer has emptied her life and now

Heart to Heart: A New Beginning

For years, in the land of Israel, Jewish women have made regular pilgrimages to what they and all the world once called the Wailing Wall, located on the Temple Mount in the heart of the Old City of Jerusalem. There, especially on the Sabbath, which begins on Friday evening and extends until sundown on Saturday, they would approach the wall with their tears of genuine grief for the tragedies suffered by their people, especially because of their exile from the holy city of Jerusalem. Many still go to this site, but it has a new name. It is now called the Western Wall because the tears are now tears of joy and thanksgiving that the Jewish nation once again presides over Jerusalem and that the Jews can worship in freedom at this holy place. Tears do not have to mean despair and hopelessness. Mourning can be the door to a new beginning.[13]

stands before the Lord, seeking to please and serve Him by cheerfully obeying His commands and graciously submitting to the authorities God has placed in her life.

Again the paradox is clear: The world associates gentleness with weakness, but in God's eyes strength characterizes the one who harnesses her life in order to maintain God-control. Gentle self-control prepares the way for God-control. Just as inheritance of the land was an expression of God's intervention and deliverance for Israel (Dt 4:1; 16:20), to **inherit the earth** was a temporal manifestation of the heavenly kingdom to come and another way to express God's sovereign rule. Enjoying that inheritance is possible because of a God-given spirit of contentment (Ps 37:16; Pr 15:16).

The first four Beatitudes describe the character of one who has been awakened and filled with the Spirit of God:

- Being poor in spirit, you realize your own inadequacy and need and are humble before the Lord.

- You are conscious of your own sinfulness and thus mourn.

- You are gentle before the Lord and allow God to control your life.

- You are not self-righteous, but realize only God Himself can offer what is needed. The key is spiritual sensitivity—a complete change of perspective.

Each Beatitude builds upon the previous one and prepares for those that follow.

Those who **hunger and thirst for righteousness** (v. 6) have a craving for righteousness, comparable to such physical hunger and thirst as was known only in lands where people died for want of food or water. Health and growth were marked by a good appetite but an appetite that was rarely satisfied. Even so God has placed in His creation an insatiable hunger for

Himself—a God-shaped vacuum only He can fill. RIGHTEOUSNESS (Gk. *dikaiosunē,* "what God requires, what is right, what is just") equaled the will of God. Matthew used this word seven times in his Gospel, and five times the word was used in the Sermon on the Mount (3:15; 5:6,10,20; 6:1,33; 21:32). In the Greek text the noun was prefaced by the article (lit. "the righteousness"), demanding a character from which right actions flowed. God's standard for righteousness is the life of the Lord Jesus. The text does not say that the person full of righteousness would be blessed; rather the one blessed would "hunger and thirst" or yearn after righteousness, realizing the journey of spiritual nurture never ends. The desire for spiritual sustenance must be renewed daily even as in your physical appetite. The word for FILLED (Gk. *chortasthēsontai,* "feed, be satisfied, eat one's fill") is in the passive voice, indicating the filling was to be done by an outside agent. The Lord did the filling. The verb is in the future tense, affirming that the filling was not a one-time event. God means for the filling to continue to supply nourishment and satisfaction.

The emphasis turns from character to how character is shown in relationship to others. The **merciful** (Gk. *eleēmones,* "sympathetic") are moved to pity and compassion—sympathetic to the suffering of another. However, this mercy is not merely pity or a natural emotional response to need. To extend mercy God's way is an act of the will, and once extended, mercifulness draws more mercy. The religious leaders of Jesus' day prided themselves in doing deeds of service, but their hearts were often indifferent to the sufferings of others (Mk 3:1-6). Mercy ruled out merit and overshadowed other attributes of God. God's justice was

Excursus from the Editor: Gentleness in the Gender Lens

A woman, in her position as a wife, is able to reflect the position of the believer in relationship to Christ in a unique way. She acknowledges her position as one of respect for her husband, not because of the demands of human law but because God Himself assigned the wife to be a helper to her husband. Some have found tension in the possibility of a difference between virtues as assigned in a general way to all Christians and virtues appropriated by gender (i.e., because you are a man or woman).

A careful look at Scripture seems to suggest that rather than different virtues for men and women, there is a difference in how these virtues held in common are applied individually—whether in timing or degree. In both Ephesians 5 and 1 Peter 3, the instruction given for submission is addressed specifically to wives, not to husbands, and the application of the teaching occurs within the domestic setting. A husband esteems his wife as does a wife her husband, but the directive given to wives consistently throughout Scripture frames a wife's appropriate response to her husband in such a way that her submission to her husband becomes a benchmark in their unique relationship with each other (Eph 5:22; Col 3:18; Ti 2:5; 1 Pt 3:1). This submission is mutual only in the sense that no one has absolute personal autonomy. A husband is not licensed for self-determination. He, too, has been assigned by God to perform certain duties to his wife—loving her as Christ loved the church and leading her with a servant's heart.

A husband does not submit to his wife in the same way that she submits to him any more than Christ is to submit to the church in the same way the church submits to Him. Rather, a husband submits to his wife by a willingness to provide, protect, and lead her even at the cost of his life, just as Christ loves and leads the church, even to laying down His life.

Accordingly, the gentleness and quietness that are to characterize the spirit of a woman are uniquely illustrated within marriage in a wife's obedience to the divine directive that she submit to her own husband. Nevertheless, gentleness is a "fruit of the Spirit" and thus a reflection of the character of God in the believer's life (Gl 5:22-23). Consequently, those who are gentle or meek will be true heirs to the inheritance of God (Mt 5:5). Strength submitted to God and sanctified by Him works itself out as service to others. Men, too, are encouraged to model this fruit of the spirit, gentleness (Gl 5:22), especially in the way a husband would treat his wife (1 Pt 3:7).

For whatever reasons, however, God issues His directive with purpose and foresight, as well as a unique orderliness (1 Co 14:40), even though those whom He created may not understand what He is doing and the why or wherefore of what He demands (Is 55:8). A man and woman may receive the same spiritual chal-

lenge and yet appropriate it in different ways, according to the respective role assignment each has been given by God.

The character qualities any woman is called upon to emulate would commonly be understood as de facto Christian virtues and thus ideals for all believers. By the same token, however, women are sometimes specifically addressed in Scripture, and in those cases the message must have a special application to them.

Nevertheless, for whatever reasons, Peter specifically challenged women to seek a "gentle and quiet spirit," and he described this attitude as "very valuable in God's eyes" (1 Pt 3:3-4). The virtue of gentleness was described by some as especially prized in women, perhaps because in 1 Peter a lofty challenge was offered to women, one which echoed the message of the Apostle Paul in his writings (Eph 5:22-24; Col 3:18; Ti 2:4-5).

The imperishable beauty of a "gentle and quiet spirit" enables a wife to submit to her husband's authority, even if he is an unbeliever, because she knows that God Himself has challenged her to this course of action, and her obedience is to Him (1 Pt 3:1-2). Sarah's husband Abraham was not an unbeliever, but even in uncertain, unpleasant, and dangerous situations she chose to submit to her husband and trust God (Gn 12:1-8,10-20; 20:1-18).

There is no basis to suggest that Moses or Peter taught that wives should obey their husbands blindly in whatever a husband instructs his wife to do. Though a wife's model for her submission to her husband is her submission to Christ, submitting to a husband is never portrayed as being the same or equal to submitting to Christ. Wives must obey God first and foremost (Ac 5:29), but a wife's submission to her husband is a command from the Lord.

Peter did not imply that this gentle and quiet attitude would prohibit suffering; rather he acknowledged that suffering would come (1 Pt 2:18-20; Mt 5:44-45). Yet the clear message is that spiritual strength, coming from self-control prompted by God-control within the heart, can and will overcome discouragement and even physical weakness (1 Pt 3:6). You dare not run from adversities, for they become God's universities. You cannot escape trials, for they are the fabric into which the threads of your life will be woven. You cannot avoid suffering, for it will bring the fragrance of Christ to your testimony. Whatever else is involved, certainly submission is the yielding of yourself to the authority and direction of another—an attitude that would be impossible without a "gentle and quiet" spirit (1 Pt 3:4).

A gentle and quiet spirit exhibits a dependence upon the Lord and the courage to obey His directives even in the midst of the uncertainties of living with an unbeliever. Such human gentleness does not preclude godly boldness. Rather, the gentleness is founded upon unwavering confidence in the Lord as the One who enables you to stand for right, even in the midst of overwhelming difficulties (Est 5:2-8).

Boldness, as presented in Scripture, is not a reference to obnoxious or aggressive behavior; nor is it the result of personal self-determination. Boldness is the result of God's work within the human heart. As such, this gift can bring God's Word to the forefront to address those with whom you seek to share a word of divine wisdom—a gift to be sought by every believing woman (Ac 4:29-31). Rahab the prostitute acted boldly to provide an escape for the Israelite spies and thus deliverance for God's people. Because she did so, God included her and her family in His deliverance (Jos 6:17,22-25). He even gave Rahab a place of honor in the lineage of Messiah (Mt 1:5).

Abigail, whose husband was a godless fool, made a bold personal appeal to David and in so doing saved the lives of her household and eventually became a queen (1 Sm 25:23-35,39-42). Gentleness and boldness are not antithetical. Boldness prompted by your confidence in God and kept within the boundaries the Lord has set is a beautiful and effective accompaniment to gentleness. A woman marked by boldness that has been tempered with gentleness can accomplish great things for God and receive His blessing in so doing. [14]

---

satisfied by the sacrifice of His Son, and that was mercy. It moved beyond feelings to prompt helpful action as a response to need.

The **pure** (Gk. *katharoi*, "clean, guiltless") **in heart** (v. 8) are people who are morally upright and holy and not just ritually cleansed. They have a lifestyle not only different and set apart in what they do but also marked by a difference in thought and motivation. To be "pure in heart"[15] is to be obsessed by God and controlled by Him. This purity is an inner fountain that feeds all you do and say. The pure in heart do not harbor ill intentions toward anyone and are obsessed with pursuing genuine godliness. Those whose debt has been paid by Christ on the cross will indeed see God. Having been redeemed, they enter into His holy presence, and they see things as God sees them. Many of the religious leaders in Jesus' day observed the laws concerning ritual cleanliness of the body; however, their hearts were far from God. Only a person who turns to Christ to cleanse him of his sins will ever **see God** (Heb 12:14).

The **peacemakers** (v. 9) strive for harmony in all areas of life as a reflection on the inner peace that God brings to His children. Jesus taught that peace will only come when people have peace with God. This Beatitude raises the bar to the highest intimacy with the heavenly Father (Mt 5:45). The word moves beyond the idea of political and economic stability to include total well-being in the spiritual realm as well. Peacemakers (Gk. *eirēnopoioi*) want more than an end of conflict. They want healing among the people, ultimately dependent on reconciliation with God.

This derivation of the Greek word for *peacemakers* is used only here in the New Testament. It refers to individuals who make peace and seek reconciliation rather than to one who is passive and seeking peace at any cost. A peacemaker works at establishing peace. As a peacemaker you must separate yourself from your own interests and whims and what is best for you. You must become others-oriented with a deep concern for others and for how the kingdom would be impacted by your actions. You are willing to suffer injustice in order for peace to reign and Christ to be magnified.

To be **called sons of God** (v. 9) was not a gender assignment but an honorable title that went beyond personal identification to acknowledge publicly your relationship to the Lord and your place in His family. All children of God would not become peacemakers; this task required spiritual discipline and maturity.

Those **persecuted for righteousness** (v. 10) will have the **kingdom of heaven**. The last Beatitude has come full circle to offer the same reward as the first. Perhaps no other Beatitude displayed the paradoxical nature of Christ's kingdom better than this last one. Persecution was considered a blessing in Christ's kingdom because it allowed a person to empathize with the sufferings of Christ. Jesus did not promise that the one who endured false accusations and persecutions would be vindicated; nevertheless, a reward in heaven awaited the person who had persevered.

When you mold your character and life after Christ, you experience the same opposition Christ experienced. Persecution begins when you commit yourself to Christ, and it intensifies as you become more and more like the Savior. A clash between two worldviews that cannot be reconciled hastens persecution. The world expects compromise and the path of least resistance, but Christ demands a gentle spirit and purity of heart and life. Believers should not expect to escape persecution, but they can count on God's faithfulness. Three categories of suffering were described (v. 11):

- **Insult** (Gk. *oneidisōsin*, "reproach, revile, heap insults upon") referred to verbal abuse and taunting words.

- **Persecute** (Gk. *diōxōsin*, "seek after, strive for," and in its root meaning "pursue") carries the sense that the

world was running after believers to cause them suffering.

- **Falsely say every kind of evil against you** (Gk. *pseudomenoi*, "lying") referred to defamation of character or deception by falsehood.

The tense of each of these verbs describing these categories of suffering suggests the event happened at a particular time in the past instead of being an ongoing and continual action. Persecution happens, but it is not necessarily a continuous experience. There is a window of hope for earthly relief and the assurance of ultimate heavenly deliverance. In verse 12 Jesus used a strong word to express rejoicing (Gk. *chairete* from the root meaning "grace"), and it was amplified with another verb, suggesting increasing intensity of joy (Gk. *agalliasthe*, "rejoice greatly, jump for joy"). The persecution in itself did not bring joy but often affirmed that you belonged to Christ, giving you a unique opportunity to glorify Christ and bear your testimony for Him.

5:13-16 In the Beatitudes, Jesus encouraged His followers to display characteristics that would set them apart from what the prevailing culture valued. To make sure that none of His listeners thought being countercultural meant separating yourself from the people immersed in that culture, Jesus called them to be **salt** and **light**. Salt was primarily a food preservative in Jesus' day; when salt became mixed with other impure substances, it lost its effectiveness as a preservative. In Syria or Palestine it would not have been uncommon to see salt scattered on the ground when it lost its usefulness. In order for Christ's disciples to be effective in the world, they have to live in the world. Salt must touch what it purifies and preserves. When salt touches, it can sting and burn. Character and witness would be paramount in bringing about

Excursus from the Editor: Gender-Inclusive Language

The question has been asked as to why the text reads "sons [instead of "children"] of God." In 1 John 5 and elsewhere believers were identified with the title "children." Though any answer is subjective at best, perhaps one possibility would be to understand the meaning of "children" as suggesting youth, even immaturity. On the other hand, the designation of "son" suggests strength and authority and especially the idea of inheritance. Jesus, the preacher who delivered this sermon, called Himself the "Son of God" so that the designation "sons of God" identifies "peacemakers" with Him who is the ultimate Peacemaker in a unique way (see Eph 2:15-17; Col 1:20-21).

Sonship packs meaning beyond the cursory understanding. In no way is the term "son" used in this context meant to suggest the omission of women from Jesus' kingdom. One of the best verifications of sonship is likeness to the Father. God the Father was called "the God of peace" (Heb 13:20). He sent out ambassadors to pursue reconciliation and peace (2 Co 5:20). Jesus, the Son, is the Prince of Peace (Is 9:6), and He is to be a Mediator of peace (1 Tm 2:5). Jesus entered the world with an angelic chorus proclaiming "Peace on earth" (Lk 2:14), and He left the world with "Peace I leave with you" (Jn 14:27). The Holy Spirit is the divine Comforter who seals believers with His peace (2 Co 1:22).

Sonship expressed an intimate relationship. As a son, the peacemaker portrayed the work of the Father in His task of reconciliation. The most important aspect of this peacemaking was the commitment to bring about God's redemptive work in the midst of a hurting world. The task was not reserved for men but open to any believer who would accept the challenge and fulfill the requirements. The work of peace is sweet and blessed. In addition to the Beatitudes, peace is linked to pureness of heart in Hebrews 12:14 and James 3:17.

The promise was not that such a peacemaker would be made *a child of God, which would be a reference to being made in His image and likeness; rather the commitment was that the peacemakers would be* called *"sons of God," suggesting that they were already regarded as sons. In fact, the verb is in the passive voice to affirm that the sonship had already been established through a divine act in the past, and they were different from the rest of the world because they were the children of God. In other words, to be called "sons of God" indicated having godly characteristics.*

vital change in the world, but this effort to influence the world would prove costly.

Light often symbolized purity and therefore became an excellent metaphor for God's revelation of Himself. Jesus Himself is the true light (Jn 1:9) and the light of the world (Jn 8:12), and His followers are to be the light **of the world** (v. 14). Apart from Christ, people are lost in darkness. His followers' lives are to act as beacons pointing people to Christ.

5:17-20 Christ came not only to fulfill the Law but to show that He is the true interpreter of the Law. Jesus honored the Law, every syllable of it and even small strokes. In Jesus' words, **not the smallest letter** (Gk. *iota*) **or one stroke of a letter** (Gk. *kepaia*, the "title" or "form" referring to a small stroke that distinguishes among several similar Hebrew letters) would be removed. Of course, the coming of Christ brought some of the law to completion, while other requirements await His coming again, **until all things are accomplished** (v. 18).

Verses 21-48 contain six illustrations of the kind of righteousness Jesus required of His followers. Not only did Jesus condemn murder, adultery, divorce, oath-taking, and retaliation as did the law, but He also denounced hatred, lust, and pride, attitudes that stood behind such behaviors. Further, Jesus commanded love of enemies, which was the way mandated for His disciples as they sought to be perfect as their Heavenly Father. The Greek word, translated PERFECT, is *teleios*, meaning "complete" or "mature," or even having the idea of "being initiated." Hence, one evidence of Christian maturity is love of your enemies—a goal reached only with great effort and endurance. Becoming "perfect" for the believer is a journey, not to a sinless life, but with the intent to complete the journey in a God-glorifying way.

5:21-26 The first illustration concerned the commandment about **murder**. Jesus must have shocked His audience when He put murder on the same level as anger and careless words. The use of the word **fool** in verse 22 is noteworthy and showed the severity with which Jesus condemned wrong thoughts and attitudes. Jesus used the Aramaic word *raca*, which literally had the sense of being EMPTY-HEADED, an oriental term of abuse and insult. The fact that Jesus does not use the Greek word *moros* (having the same meaning) sheds light on the audience of the book of Matthew. Matthew must have

Heart to Heart:

Influence

Influence is a gift from God and in some ways especially so for women, whose God-given maternal, nurturing nature makes the path of influence even more effective. Women must not be content simply to slow the destructive forces in modern society. It is not enough to protect just your own hearth. Rather, you must commit yourself to become a preserver of biblical values and virtues and a beacon of God's light with a beam that extends far beyond your own inner circle. For the sake of your children and grandchildren, you must set out to change your neighborhood, your city, your state, your nation, and the world!

been written for readers who, though they spoke Greek, could also understand the Aramaic term without additional explanation.

5:27-30 The second illustration addressed the subject of **adultery**. Jesus taught that it was not enough simply to refrain from the act of adultery. **Lust**, too, was sinful and was the beginning point for actually committing adultery. **Everyone** included men and women, married or single. Jesus condemned fornication as well as ADULTERY (Gk. *emoicheusen*, "commit adultery") or the choice to engage in extramarital sexual intimacies. Jesus' command to **gouge ... out** the eye and **cut ... off** the hand was not meant to be taken literally yet provided a vivid picture of the seriousness of sin.

5:31-32 The Old Testament allowed a man to give his wife **a written notice of divorce** if some uncleanness was to be found in her (Dt 24:1). This allowance was often abused, and men divorced their wives for many different reasons. Jesus rejected this practice on the grounds of the sanctity of marriage (see Mt 19); He continued to call His followers to a higher standard than what the Jewish law demanded. Unfortunately, in contemporary society, Christians are no different from non-Christians in this area, with half of all Christian marriages ending in divorce. **Sexual immorality** (Gk. *porneias*, "unlawful sexual intercourse, unchastity, fornication") has been exhibited in various ways in the New Testament:

- voluntary sexual intercourse between a man and woman who are not married (1 Co 7:2; 1 Th 4:3);

- all forms of unchasteness (Jn 8:41; Ac 15:20,29; 1 Co 5:1; 6:13,18; Eph 5:3); and

- prostitution (Rv 2:14,20-21).

5:33-37 Jesus taught that all stated commitments are uttered in the presence of God and thus considered binding. He also condemned the hypocritical use of **oaths** by the religious leaders who taught that oaths omitting God's name were not binding and could be broken. Some, fearing they would not be able to keep a promise, might **swear** by something less than God's name, such as **heaven** or **earth** or **Jerusalem**. Jesus totally rejected this practice because a person of integrity has no need for oaths since his word is trustworthy.

5:38-48 Jesus quoted from Leviticus 24:20 and taught that His followers were not to **resist** evil with evil. He did not deny the common *lex talionis* (law of retaliation) as a principle of legal justice. The law insisted upon adequate punishment. However, Jesus did have a kingdom focus and thus a higher standard. He decried a slap across the **cheek** intended to insult one who was supposed to be inferior. In contrast to the behavior of the Pharisees, disciples of Christ were to accept insults and were to go the extra mile when asked to do so by the Romans. The ultimate principle was love of one's enemies, and that standard is still applicable, and even mandatory for every believer. The rabbis had corrupted the statement of summary of the law by adding to Scripture their own words, **and hate your enemy** (5:43; see Lv 19:18). By tampering with God's Word, they were able to define their neighbors, eliminating the hated **Gentiles** and Samaritans. On the other hand, Jesus called for unconditional love toward all just as God's love extends to all (v. 45).

6:1-4 The greater righteousness demanded that acts of religious devotion not be merely external but truly motivated from a heart that was right before the Lord. Religious acts that issue from a pure heart were done **in secret**; the Father—and not the response of people—was the focus. Public prayer and fasting and even good deeds were not forbidden, but Jesus was cautioning against wrong motivation. Giving **to the poor** (v. 2) was not required by Jewish law, yet it was considered especially praiseworthy. Some people would **sound a trumpet** (a figurative way of calling attention to your deeds) when they gave to the poor so they would be commended for their acts. Jesus called these people HYPOCRITES (Gk. *hupokritai,* "pretenders, actors, interpreters," and "anyone who impersonated another"). The Greek root meant "wearing a mask" or "pretending." Jesus used this strong word to denounce people who pretended to be pious.

6:5-15 The model prayer (vv. 9-13) illustrated *how* to pray rather than prescribing necessary words to use. Jesus contrasted the insincere prayers of **hypocrites** with the proper way to pray. This prayer, summarizing the teachings of Jesus about God's kingdom, is also known as the "Disciple's Prayer" or the "Lord's Prayer." Jesus addressed God as FATHER (Gk. *Pater,* Aramaic *abba*), which was an intimate term carrying the sense of "Daddy." Presenting God as an accessible, caring parent was unheard of in the first century.

God's forgiveness cannot be earned. It is a gift. But God's forgiveness can be blocked by your unwillingness to forgive those who have sinned against you.

6:16-18 As the disciples were told to perform their good deeds in *public* so that others might praise the Father (5:16), so they were now told to do their religious deeds in *private* in order that the deeds would not be motivated by human praise. The point was the same. In both cases, to bring praise to the Father is paramount. If good deeds in general are not performed in public, the Father is not praised. If religious deeds are performed merely in public, the Father is not praised. Hypocrisy must be avoided in both cases.

Teachings from the Lord's Prayer

Phrase	Meaning	References
Our Father in heaven (Mt 6:9)	Recognize who God is.	Rm 8:15
Your name be honored as holy (Mt 6:9)	Worship Him because of who He is.	Pss 18:3; 96:8
Your kingdom come/Your will be done (Mt 6:10)	Seek the will of God and do it. His Word is the path to finding His will.	1 Jn 5:14
Give us today our daily bread (Mt 6:11)	Ask God to meet even your most mundane needs to accomplish your spiritual duties.	Php 4:9
And forgive us our debts (Mt 6:12)	Ask God to forgive your debts and your failures to obey Him.	Ps 66:18; Hs 14:2
And do not bring us into temptation; deliver us from the evil one (Mt 6:13)	Seek a way of escape from the evil of temptation—protection, not removal from any trials but from judgment that comes when you are overcome by trials.	1 Co 10:13; Jms 1:2-3
For Yours is the kingdom (Mt 6:13)	This benediction acts as a doxology.	

Fasting (Gk. *nesteuontes,* "abstaining from food") is a spiritual discipline exclusively between a believer and God, serving to draw a believer closer to God. Jesus assumed that His disciples would fast. He fasted for 40 days to prepare for ministry and strengthen His soul for the confrontation with Satan (Mt 4:1-2). Jesus stressed that God is not moved by fasting itself but rather by the turning of the hearts of His people to Him. Fasting must come from a right motive, or it loses its significance.

6:19-24 In this section the same point was made concerning God's place in a disciple's life. God, not possessions, must be at the center of the disciple's life. If not, no amount of "good" behavior would account for anything. What a disciple values reveals where his **treasure is**. You cannot serve both **God** and **money**. And you cannot hide where your true loyalty lies. The **eye**, which is the mirror of the soul, will reveal the truth. It will show whether you serve **light** or **darkness**, God or money.

6:25-34 The one who has God as her treasure need not fear the lack of material needs, for God will provide. The true disciple must seek **God and His righteousness** before all else and trust God to provide for her needs. Jesus modeled this principle throughout His entire ministry; as disciples you should follow His example. The **cubit** is a measurement defined as the length of a woman's forearm from the inside of the elbow to the end of her longest finger.

7:1-12 Christ's disciples were to treat others as they wanted to be treated (7:12). The religious leaders failed to do this. However, only by treating others well would the greater righteousness be served and **the Law and the Prophets** fulfilled. Those committed to God and His righteousness must not be like the hypocrites and judge others without first judging themselves. A disciple must use discernment.

In this context, the disciple's priority is continually to seek God. If you seek God to meet your daily needs and if you treat others as you want to be treated, then the two greatest commands—to love God supremely and to love your neighbor as yourself—will be fulfilled in your life as a disciple. The "Golden Rule" and the principle of reciprocity embodied in it summarize the moral and ethical requirements for those who choose to follow Christ. Its standard of conduct goes beyond what is normally expected.

7:13-29 With three illustrations, Christ showed that there are only two ways to respond to His message—either to accept Him or to reject Him. There is no middle road. The road leading to life is narrow, so Jesus' followers must strive to stay on the straight and narrow path. There are many who will endeavor to lead a disciple astray. But Christ assured His followers that a false prophet would be recognized by his fruit. Jesus used these parables to illustrate His teaching on personal righteousness: the two gates (vv. 13-14); the two trees (vv. 15-23); and the two foundations (vv. 24-28).

In verses 21-23 Jesus gave His would-be followers a most stern warning. He would recognize His true disciples by *their* obedience. Only those who do the will of the Father would enter the kingdom of heaven, and the Father's will was for His followers to believe in the One He sent. Thus, to do the will of His Father even imperfectly is to model yourself and conform your life to what Jesus taught and how He lived (vv. 24-27).

> *Thus, to do the will of His Father even imperfectly is to model yourself and conform your life to what Jesus taught and how He lived (vv. 24-27).*

Jesus' command, "Repent because the kingdom of heaven has come near" (4:17), must be met with seriousness and with genuine, fruit-bearing repentance. Jesus' words call for a decision. The popular opinion was that virtually all would be saved, but Jesus suggested the opposite. Only a few will be saved.

Healing the People (8:1–9:38)

In this narrative sequence, Matthew has introduced two very important matters:

- As the sovereign interpreter of the Law, Jesus demonstrated His authority by performing various miracles. He also demonstrated His greater righteousness by living under the Law (8:4) and by even extending its boundaries in His interpretation (9:30; see 6:1).

- The greater righteousness is attained by *faith*. Faith was explicitly mentioned five times in this narrative sequence (8:10,26; 9:2,22,29). Jesus praised and rewarded all who exercised faith in Him, but He rebuked those who exercised little faith (8:26).

8:1-4 Jesus' first demonstration of His power was healing a leper. Lepers were considered unclean, and all were forbidden to touch them because anyone who touched a leper would become unclean from the encounter. Not only did Jesus heal the leper, but **He touched him** as well. The leper exercised faith by his words, **You can make me clean**. By touching and healing the leper, Jesus demonstrated His authority over sickness and disease. Jesus was not bound by earthly laws and rituals.

8:5-13 In the next instance, Jesus interacted with someone else, a Gentile **centurion**, who was considered unclean. The centurion believed in Christ's authority and power to heal his **servant**. Matthew recorded that Jesus not only healed the servant but also commended the centurion, claiming that He had not seen such faith in anyone in Israel. Jesus then confirmed that the Gentiles would have a place **at the table with Abraham, Isaac, and Jacob in the kingdom of heaven**,

while the **sons of the kingdom** (the Jews) would **be thrown** out. This incident is a hint of the coming conflict between Christ and the Jewish leaders.

The little girl was brought back to life because of the faith of her father. The woman with the bleeding displayed her own extraordinary faith. She believed that if she just touched Jesus, she would be made well. Her disease was obviously not life threatening; but it made her unclean and, therefore, an outcast in society. When Jesus acknowledged her, He referred to her as **daughter** (9:22). He acknowledged her faith in Him, and at that moment she was accepted by Him.

The mother-in-law, the little girl, and the woman all had in common that, as female in gender, they were not highly valued in Jewish or Greco-Roman society. By interacting with them, Jesus was doing something new in Israel. He was openly placing value upon girls and women, something that had not been done to the extent of His standard. Jesus did not show partiality; the benefits of His kingdom were for everyone who would come to Him in faith.

8:14-22 When Jesus entered **Peter's house** and saw Peter's **mother-in-law lying in bed with a fever**, He healed her, and she **began to serve Him**. This focus on Jesus was consistent with Matthew's overall intent to highlight His authority. This woman served Him, recognizing with gratitude what He had done for her. Of all the healing that occurred that night, she was singled out, possibly because she played such a vital role in the overall success of the evening.

According to Matthew, Christ's healing ministry is a fulfillment of Isaiah 53:4, "He Himself bore our sicknesses and He carried our pains." In 8:20, Jesus referred to Himself as **the Son of Man**, a phrase occurring in the Greek text 81 times in the Gospels, 69 of which are found in the

Women Healed by Jesus

Woman	Faith	Jesus' Response	Her Response	Reference
Peter's mother-in-law	The faith of her family was demonstrated.	He healed her fever.	After being healed, she arose and served those present.	Mt 8:14-15; Mk 1:30-31; Lk 4:38-39
All who were sick	In faith, people came to Jesus for healing.	He healed all who were sick and cast out spirits as well.	None given.	Mt 8:16-17; Mk1:32-34
The hemorrhaging woman	Jesus was impressed with her faith.	After feeling her touch him, He saw her and healed her.	She received the healing she sought and must have rejoiced.	Mt 9:20-22; Mk 5:25-34; Lk 8:43-48
The Canaanite woman's daughter	The mother was persistent and worshiped Jesus.	Her request was heard and answered when He healed her daughter.	None given.	Mt 15:21-28; Mk 7:24-30
The infirm woman	Not stated.	Upon seeing her, He called to her and healed her.	She was healed by being made straight and began glorifying God.	Lk 13:11-13

Synoptics. In every instance Jesus referred to Himself. The title spoke of His self-humiliation, stressed His humanity, and possibly foreshadowed His suffering.

- When others inquired about following Jesus, He did not hide the reality of His life and ministry. He caused those asking questions to look into their hearts.

- For example, Jesus challenged the scribe of verse 19 with His statement in verse 20. Jesus instructed him to make sacrifices to be one of His followers. A similar exchange between Jesus and another disciple is recorded in verses 21-22.

8:23–9:38 Jesus demonstrated His power over nature and the demonic realm. He manifested His authority to forgive sins, to raise the dead, to heal the chronically ill, to open the eyes of the blind, and to loose the tongues of those unable to speak. There were a variety of responses to His deeds, manifesting strong faith, faltering faith, or open rejection of faith.

The calming of the wind and the waves prompted His disciples to ask, **What kind of man is this?** (8:27). But the demons knew exactly who He was and what He could do. The scribes accused Jesus of blasphemy because He claimed the power to forgive sins. But the healing of the paralytic provided ample proof of His authority in this arena. To solidify this proof, Matthew included an account of his own calling to follow Jesus in this section. He quoted Jesus as saying, **I didn't come to call the righteous, but sinners** (9:13). Following this quote, Matthew inserted a question about fasting, which, on the surface, may seem out of place in this miracle narrative. However, the parable in 9:15-17 clearly suggested that Christ was doing a new thing in Israel, where both the old and the new would be preserved and restored in Him and in the covenant He would inaugurate.

As Jesus was speaking this parable, one of the Jewish **leaders** (the only one in this encounter to approach Jesus with true faith) interrupted with news that his **daughter** was dying (9:18). The Jewish leader believed that Jesus could restore life. On the way to the man's house, **a woman who had suffered from bleeding for 12 years** was healed because of her faith that Jesus could heal her. Just as Jesus restored the woman to health and the young girl to life, He was also the One who fulfilled Old Testament law and introduced the new covenant. The key for each person is to trust in Christ.

The next two miracles Matthew recorded show Jesus responding to true faith, opening the eyes of the blind and driving out a demon who robbed a man of speech. The response of the people linked these healings with the previous question about fasting and the subsequent healings of the woman and the girl: **Nothing like this has ever been seen in Israel!** (9:33).

The Pharisees accused Jesus of possessing a demon, foreshadowing the ensuing opposition to His ministry. But Jesus' preaching and healing in chapters 5–9 attested not to the power of the Devil but to the presence of the kingdom of heaven.

Similar to the verses that signaled the first sermon-narrative sequence (4:23–5:1), 9:35-38 indicate the beginning of the second. Jesus **saw the crowds** and **He felt compassion for them** because they were like lost sheep. He gave His disciples an object lesson that compared the crowd to a ripe field ready for harvest.

The Opposition to Jesus' Mission (10:1–12:50)

Identifying and sending out the apostles (10:1-15)

10:1-4 Matthew first mentioned Jesus' **12 disciples** (Gk. *mathētas*, "learners") at this point, but one may safely assume that these men had been with Jesus before He

Heart to Heart: Your Ministry in Your Home

According to Jewish custom, a woman's duty and honor were to serve those who entered her home. This passage demonstrated that Jesus not only physically healed Peter's mother-in-law, but He also restored her dignity by enabling her to perform again her womanly role in the home.

Serving was one way a woman maintained her status of usefulness in her home. The home was the woman's domain, and she brought honor to her husband by maintaining it and overseeing its functions. Her tasks included serving guests.

In the same way today, women strive to maintain their homes with grace and hospitality to all who are their guests. When a woman suffers sickness, emotional pain, or the trials of a bad day, Jesus can heal her and restore her so that she can be the woman of grace in any situation, whether in the home or in another setting. In so doing she brings honor to Jesus, to herself, and to those around her.

delivered the Sermon on the Mount. Matthew called these men **apostles** (10:2). By using the term APOSTLE (Gk. *apostolōn*, "one sent out"), Matthew indicated that Jesus sent the disciples out with His personal authority and as His representatives. He sent workers out fully equipped by His power to minister as He had done. These men were given **authority** to drive out **unclean spirits** and **to heal every disease and sickness** (v. 1).

Jesus' Disciples

Name	Description	References
Simon (Hb. *hearing*) Peter or Cephas (Gk., *rock*)	He was a strong leader and among the first called by Jesus as a disciple. He was the brother of Andrew and worked in his father's fishing business. He wrote 1 and 2 Peter.	Mt 10:2; 16:16; Mk 3:16; 13:3; Lk 5:8; 6:14; Jn 1:42; Ac 1:13
James (Hb. *he who grasps the heel*), son of Zebedee	He was a fisherman who worked with his father and his brother John. Jesus nicknamed James and John the "Sons of Thunder." James was later executed by Herod Agrippa I.	Mt 4:21; 10:2; Mk 1:19; 3:17; 13:3; Lk 6:14; Ac 1:13
John (Hb. *the Lord is gracious*), son of Zebedee	He was the brother of James and was part of the inner circle. The Fourth Gospel, several epistles or letters, and the book of Revelation have been attributed to him. John was called the Beloved Disciple, and Jesus singled him out from the cross to take care of His mother Mary.	Mt 4:21; 10:2; Mk 1:19; 3:17; 13:3; Lk 6:14; Ac 1:13
Andrew (Gk. *manliness*)	Originally a fisherman, he was also a disciple of John the Baptist but later followed Christ. He brought his brother, Simon Peter, to Christ.	Mt 4:18; 10:2; Mk 3:18; 13:3; Lk 6:14; Jn 1:40-44; Ac 1:13
Philip (Gk. *horse lover*)	He was a disciple who came to Jesus early. He was from Bethsaida in Galilee, as were Peter and Andrew.	Mt 10:3; Mk 3:18; Lk 6:14; Jn 1:43-48; Ac 1:13
Bartholomew (Aram. *son of Tolmai*), also known as Nathanael	He was Philip's companion on several missionary journeys. It is possible that Bartholomew is the Nathanael whom Philip brings to Christ.	Mt 10:3; Mk 3:18; Lk 6:14; Jn. 1:44-51; Ac 1:13
Matthew (Aram. *gift of God*), also known as Levi	A former tax collector; the Gospel of Matthew has been attributed to him.	Mt 9:9-13; 10:3; Mk 3:18; Lk 6:15; Ac 1:13
Thomas (Hb. *twin*)	He was most famous for doubting the resurrection of Jesus.	Mt 10:3; Mk 3:18; Lk 6:15; Jn 14:5; 20:24-29; Ac 1:13
James (Hb. *he who grasps the heel*), son of Alphaeus	Little is known about him other than that he was called James "the younger" or "the less" in order to distinguish him from the son of Zebedee.	Mt 10:3; Mk 3:18; Lk 6:15; Ac 1:13
Thaddaeus (Hb. *breast or heart*)	Also known as Judas, son of James, possibly he went by his nickname, Thaddaeus, because of the disgrace that was attached to the name *Judas*.	Mt 10:3; Mk 3:18; Lk 6:16; Ac 1:13

Jesus' Disciples		
Name	Description	References
Simon (Hb. *hearing*) the Zealot (Gk. *zealous one*)	He was one of the lesser known apostles. His nickname, "the Zealot," could have been used to distinguish him from Simon Peter or could refer to his personality or his political allegiance.	Mt 10:4; Mk 3:18; Lk 6:15; Ac 1:13
Judas Iscariot (Hb. *man of Kerioth*)	Some take his name as that of cities in Judea and Moab, but others take it to mean *assassin* or *false one*. He is infamous for betraying Jesus and then hanging himself out of guilt and regret.	Mt 10:4; Mk 3:19; Lk 6:16; 22:3; Jn 13:26-30

Matthew provided a list of the names of the 12 apostles (vv. 3-4). In each list found in the Gospels (see also Mk 3:16-19 and Lk 6:14-16), Peter was listed first and Judas Iscariot was listed last. These men came from varied backgrounds and experiences; yet before they met Christ, none lived a life of which the world would have taken note. However, Christ saw something unique in each one of these men, prompting Him to choose them to be His representatives to the world. Christ poured His life into them, even though He knew they would desert Him for a time or even betray Him, as in the case of Judas Iscariot.

10:5-15 Jesus' next sermon was divided into two sections, giving instructions specifically for ministry during Jesus' lifetime and words of wisdom for future generations of disciples who would come after Jesus' death and resurrection (vv. 16-42). The Twelve were to go only to the **lost sheep** of Israel (a reference to Jesus' concern for the "sheep without a shepherd," 9:36). There was a sense of urgency with regard to getting the message out. It would be better for the sinful cities of **Sodom and Gomorrah** than for any of the lost sheep of Israel who refused to welcome these sent by the Lord (vv. 5-15), an allusion that emphasized the certainty and magnitude of God's judgment.

Predicting opposition (10:16-42)

10:16-26 Several things come into focus concerning the later generations of disciples (vv. 16-42). First, there would be hostility toward them simply because they were associated with Jesus' name. This hostility would be widespread, ranging from the synagogue to the streets to the homes. If the Son of Man had been persecuted, His followers were sure to be, too.

Verse 23 is especially difficult to interpret in this context. In the previous section concerning the specific ministry of the Twelve, it would not have been difficult to understand. Nevertheless, the verse implied that the Jewish people would play an important role in the ongoing ministry of the church, an observation that seems consistent with Matthew's overall purpose.

Second, the only proper response to such persecution was to fear God. Looking back to Jesus' teachings concerning reliance on God in the Sermon on the Mount (6:25-34), Jesus reassured the disciples that God was in control (10:26). Therefore, they must fear Him alone. He reminded them that death was not final for the believer (v. 28), and He continued to express His loving care for all of His creation (vv. 29-31).

Third, reminiscent again of the Sermon on the Mount, Jesus declared that there are only two responses: acceptance or rejection (7:13-27). There is no middle road. The depiction of family strife must be understood in this context. Those who professed to follow Him must have unswerving allegiance to Him, even if following Christ brought alienation from family or if it cost your own life. His call was to single-minded devotion, even in the midst of division. Ultimately, all will be judged by their obedience to Christ (7:21-23).

Christ never disregarded or devalued family relationships. God created the family and gave clear instructions throughout the Scriptures concerning His will for families. However, concerning Christ and devotion to Him, all else must take second place (v. 37). The first command is always to love God with all one's being.

Experiencing opposition (11:1–12:50)

11:1-30 The sermon portion of this second sermon-narrative sequence predicted future opposition to the disciples' mission. This narrative section emphasized the rising opposition to Christ's mission.

Chapter 11 begins with a segment that tied the importance of John the Baptist to his role in Jesus' ministry. While sitting in prison, John had begun to have questions about Jesus' identity, so **he sent** some of **his disciples** to ask Jesus about his concerns. Though he was the forerunner of Christ's ministry, understandably doubts had arisen in his mind. Christ answered John's question indirectly by pointing to the miracles He was performing. His words must have encouraged John to stand firm in his faith (vv. 4-6).

Jesus praised John as far greater than the Old Testament prophets and as the one who fulfilled the prophecies concerning Elijah. However, John's understanding was not complete. The disciples would witness Jesus' crucifixion, resurrection, and His ascension; and they would have an even more complete witness to share. Jesus praised John, but He rebuked the

Jewish people for refusing to respond to both Jesus' and John's message. Foreshadowing the openness of the Gentiles to His message, Jesus condemned the heavily populated Jewish towns where He ministered for their lack of repentance (vv. 20-24).

By contrast, Jesus praised the Father (11:25-30) for His way of revealing Himself to people. Here is a paradox. God's revelation was **hidden . . . from the wise and learned** (v. 25). These would seem to be the most likely to understand, but pride and self-sufficiency kept them from getting it. On the other hand, **infants** are dependent by nature and tend to have a desire to learn (v. 25). The good news of the gospel was available to all who wanted to listen and learn. Yet underlying this discussion was Jesus' clear affirmation of the Father's will (v. 26). Jesus had an exclusive relationship with the Father and delighted to do the will of the Father (v. 27).

Here is a beautiful interweaving of God's sovereignty and human free will. God's elective purposes could not be thwarted by sinful man, and the choices mirrored in human responsibility would not be cast aside because of divine whim. Yet God did reveal or conceal according to His pleasure.

Jesus taught another lesson in discipleship, using the common **yoke** as a metaphor (vv. 28-30). The yoke was Jesus life' and teachings—not the law. Followers of Christ were indeed free from the law, but they were not free to do as they pleased. They were to be harnessed to Christ. The yoke was a harness in which two animals pulled together. One harness often was larger, designed for the stronger and more experienced animal, so that the younger animal could be trained and guided by its mentor. Jesus invited **all** who were **weary and burdened** to come to Him for **rest**. In the context, **all** seemed to refer to both

Jew and Gentile, stressing Christ's mission to both groups. And this could be the ultimate point Matthew intended to make.

12:1-45 In this section, the opposition to Jesus' mission was more apparent. The rising clamor began with Jesus' claims about Himself as being **greater than the temple** (v. 6), **Jonah** the prophet (v. 41), and King **Solomon** (v. 42). His miracles provided ample evidence for His claims (v. 13). The healing that He performed on the Sabbath caused the Pharisees to want to destroy Him (v. 14). When Jesus learned of their plot, He **withdrew**. Crowds **followed Him, and He healed them all**, advising them to tell no one of His deeds.

With these events, Matthew claimed that Isaiah's prophecy was **fulfilled** (see Is 42:1-4). In this context, Christ's character was contrasted with that of the Pharisees. Unlike the religious leaders, the true servant of the Lord was gentle and merciful (see also 11:29; 12:7). The Gentile nations would put their hope in this humble Servant of the Lord, corroborating the testimony Jesus gave of Himself (11:28-30).

In light of Jesus' healing of a **demon-possessed man** who was **unable to speak** (12:22), the Pharisees accused Him of being empowered by the devil. Jesus clearly showed them that their accusation could not be true because a **kingdom divided against itself** would not stand. Jesus again showed that there were only two ways to respond to Him: acceptance or rejection (v. 30). Those who rejected Him could **be forgiven** if they repented and accepted Him. But blasphemy **against the Holy Spirit**, or attributing to Satan the work of the Holy Spirit—which the Pharisees were indeed doing—would **not be forgiven** (vv. 31-32).

This rebuke was by far the strongest yet from the religious leaders. They were clearly an example of the bad trees mentioned in the Sermon on the Mount (7:15-20). Jesus bluntly called them **evil**, for their evil words revealed their evil hearts. While the warning about words in this context was meant for the Pharisees, it stands as a warning to all who use their words without thought of eternal and/or temporal consequences (12:33-37).

When the Pharisees asked for **a sign,** Jesus compared Himself to **the prophet Jonah** (v. 39), alluding to His own death and resurrection. These words were the first specific mention of His future suffering. Jesus rebuked the Pharisees by citing historical examples of the willingness of the Gentiles to listen to Jonah and Solomon (vv. 39-42). These were mere men and people recognized the importance of their messages; yet here stood Jesus, the awaited Messiah, and the religious leaders who studied the Scriptures could not recognize the One before them.

The hardness of this generation of Jews was more sharply defined as Jesus described the **unclean spirit** that left and then returned to a man who had been cleansed (v. 43). This reference was to the "cleansing" power of His ministry. When the demon returned, the condition of that man would be **worse than at first**—an indication of just how hardened this generation would become (v. 45).

12:46-50 In this scene Jesus poignantly described the characteristics of a person who was for Him and not against Him. The one who was for Him would be doing **the will** of His **Father in heaven**. In this way Jesus elevated spiritual relationships above natural/biological relationships. Jesus was not denigrating His mother and brothers; He was simply giving priority over all human relationships to the will of His Father. D. A. Carson illuminated Jesus' understanding of family in the context of other relationships:

For, had He not entered into earthly kinship solely for the sake of the higher spiritual relationship which He was about to found? Thus, it was not that Christ set lightly by His mother, but that He confounded not the means with the end. . . . We do not make ourselves Jesus' close relatives by doing the will of his heavenly Father. Rather, doing the Father's will *identifies* us as his mother and sisters and brothers (cf. 7:21). The doing of that will turns on obedience to Jesus and his teaching, according to Matthew, for it was Jesus who preeminently revealed the will of the Father (cf. 11:27).[16]

Predicting Progressive Opposition toward Jesus (13:1–16:20)

Explaining opposition: kingdom parables (13:1-52)

13:1-9 This third sermon-narrative sequence represented a crucial turning point in Christ's ministry. Only those who would do the Father's will were true followers of Christ (12:46-50). From this point the polarization between those who would follow Christ and those who would not came into sharp contrast. In verses 1-52, the polarization was explained through parables. A PARABLE (Gk. *parabolais*, "proverb, figure, symbol") is basically a metaphorical narrative. Two Greek words are linked—*para*, meaning "near, beside, along," and *ballō*, meaning "throw, put, place, bring," and thus with the sense of literally "bringing alongside." Throughout much of church history, the parables of Jesus were understood to be allegories with each detailed part having its own particular meaning. This method fell out of favor in the nineteenth century when

Adolf Julicher pointed out the problems associated with allegorical interpretations of the parables. Julicher argued very persuasively that each parable had a main point and that the details must not be allegorized.

An ALLEGORY (Gk. *alla*, meaning other, and *agoreuō*, meaning "proclaim") is a literary device in which a narrative is used to teach truth. The content of the allegory is not meant to be literal. It is similar to but more extended than a metaphor. Although allegory can be used as an effective teaching tool, to misuse this literary device by drawing attention away from or even by distorting didactic or teaching passages is to cause the interpreter to misread and thus misinterpret the passage. Jesus used allegory in the parables of the soils and of the tares (13:24-30,36-43).

Although some allegorical interpretation is appropriate as the biblical context allows, the more natural method of interpretation remains dominant.

- The parables of Jesus were written in a particular context so that the main point could be discovered if that same point was translated into a contemporary context.

- The parables of Jesus were vehicles for proclaiming the kingdom. Therefore, it was vitally important to understand the meaning of the kingdom in the ministry of Jesus.

The kingdom lay at the heart of Jesus' message, and its meaning was expressed most poignantly in His parables. Joachim Jeremias summed up the importance of the parables in this way:

> The hour of fulfillment has come; that is the keynote of them all. The strong man is disarmed, the powers of evil have to yield, the

physician has come to the sick, the lepers are cleansed, the heavy burden of guilt is removed, the lost sheep is brought home, the door of the Father's house is opened, the poor and the beggars are summoned to the banquet, a master whose kindness is undeserved pays wages in full, a great joy fills all hearts. God's acceptable year has come. For there has appeared the one whose veiled majesty shines through every word and every parable—the Savior.[17]

The overall function of a parable was to call forth a response from the hearer. The kind of response evoked really depended on the heart of the listener. In this section Jesus began to separate His listeners into outsiders (those who did not have responsive hearts) and insiders (those who responded favorably). Only in Matthew were the parables divided evenly: those addressed to the public (vv. 1-35) and those given specifically to the disciples (vv. 36-52).

Jesus' main focus in all His teachings was the kingdom of heaven or the kingdom of God. The kingdom of God could refer to different ideas:

- a covenant into which one enters,

- a future entity yet to be fully established,

- an unexpected coming event separating the righteous from the wicked,

- the establishment of a recognizable social order,

- a present experience of Jesus' words and deeds, or

- an entity over which God reigned as King.[18]

The kingdom of God, according to Jesus, most certainly had present and future dimensions. By the power of the Holy Spirit, a believer simply could not underestimate what she could do now. However, she had to be realistic about the kinds of things she could truly accomplish. Believers in this world were still in enemy territory. Jesus never made the church identical to the kingdom of God.

13:10-17 Parables have been described as "an earthly story with a heavenly meaning." Indeed Jesus did often use examples drawn from daily life (13:24-30,45-46) or from nature (13:1-7,31-32) to teach spiritual truths. The details used to tell the story are not necessarily significant, though often they play a part in the lesson to be taught. What Jesus taught and what His hearers understood were not always the same, but the application to life is just as relevant today as it was when the parable was delivered.

13:18-23 The **parable of the sower** provided a key to understanding not only Jesus' other parables but also His teachings in general. This parable indicated the kind of hearers who had been around Jesus since the beginning of His ministry; but in this late hour, the weeding out process had to begin. This particular parable has been interpreted in many ways, but clearly the only harvest in which a farmer would be truly interested would be the one that produced good, mature fruit (13:8), which was the main point of the story.

> The Word of God is proclaimed and causes a division among those who hear; God's people receive the Word, understand it, and obediently fulfill it; others fail to listen because of a hardened heart, a basic superficiality, or a vested interest in riches and possessions.[19]

Heart to Heart:
The Kingdom of Heaven

For Jesus, the ethics of the kingdom of God involved every arena of life. Godly character must precede conduct. Love of God and love of neighbor are the foundations of His ethic. He commanded that those who would follow Him must love and serve others, even if they endured suffering and death in the process. Jesus was deeply concerned about justice and mercy. He said that He came to seek and to save the lost. This included first and foremost the outcast and lowly of society. He was "pro-life" in the truest and most genuine way. Jesus taught much about the use of material possessions. He was quite aware of who He was and what He came to do.

Before Jesus explained the meaning of this parable, His disciples asked Him why He was speaking in such terms (13:10). Here the division between insiders and outsiders was made plain. Parables were for insiders. Clearly, too, according to other passages, outsiders also understood His stories; but the difference between the insiders and outsiders lay in the fact that the latter did not respond appropriately. True spiritual understanding was characterized by a willing heart. Once the meaning of the story had been made clear, an unwilling heart would only become more hostile. The Isaiah quote made clear that, with regard to the outsiders, Jesus was speaking to a people who were already hostile to His message (Is 6:9-10; Mt 13:14-15).

13:24-43 The **wheat**, the **weeds**, and the "large net" (v. 47) described events surrounding the Judgment Day. Although at times evil might appear to be winning out and seemingly there was little difference between God's people and those who followed the evil one, God's purposes ultimately would not be thwarted.

The **mustard seed** and **yeast** revealed that God's kingdom would be much larger than expected, especially considering the way in which it began. The reference to **the birds** was most likely a reference to the Gentile believers (see Ezk 17:23).

13:44-52 The treasure and the pearl could be interpreted in two ways. The **treasure** and the **pearl** spoke of the priceless value of the kingdom, or they indicated the need to sacrifice all to attain it. Either way, the main point was that one must do whatever it takes to submit to the rules of God's kingdom.

Once the crowd was dismissed (13:36), Jesus fully explained to His disciples the meaning of these parables. The discerning (Jewish) disciple, who had been instructed in the kingdom, could now understand the ways in which Jesus' teachings were similar or dissimilar to Jewish law.

Enacting polarization: from Jew to Gentile (13:53–16:20)

13:53-58 As the narrative section of this third sequence began, the hardness of the Jewish leaders and people was more pronounced, and Jesus now focused on the Gentiles. The highs and lows of the disciples' faith have also been highlighted in this section. In fact, faith, unbelief, rebellion, and acceptance all have been placed side by side in this entire section. Jesus was first rejected by the people in **His hometown** of Nazareth. He **did not** perform **many miracles there because of their unbelief** (v. 58).

Questions	Answers
	Herodias *Matthew 14:3-12*
Who?	Member of the Herodian dynasty; daughter of Aristobulus, son of Herod the Great; wife of Philip I (her uncle) then Herod Antipas; mother of Salome
What?	Cunning woman, controlling wife, and manipulative mother who demanded the head of John the Baptist on a platter
When?	During the first-century ministries of John the Baptist and Jesus
Where?	Lived in Tiberias, the capital of Galilee and a city built by her husband
Why?	Sought power and corrupted her daughter; became the New Testament counterpart of Jezebel in the Old Testament

See also Mk 6:14-24; Lk 3:19-20.

14:1-12 Herod the tetrarch (Herod Antipas) was ultimately responsible for the cruel and inhumane murder of **John the Baptist**, the forerunner of Jesus. "Herod," a title, described a number of rulers. He, as other members of his family, was a ruthless and paranoid tyrant. His father Herod the Great had been responsible for the slaughter of innocent babies in Bethlehem following the visit of the magi (2:16). His murder of John was prompted by John's condemnation of Herod's adulterous and incestuous relationship with

Herodias (see her portrait chart), the **wife** of his **brother** Philip (14:3-4). Herod may have been intrigued by John, but Herodias hated him. She forced Herod's hand and achieved her goal of getting rid of John (14:6-11).

14:13-36 The rebellion and unbelief of the Roman officials was apparent in the account of the beheading of John the Baptist (14:1-12). Several miracles were sandwiched in between this account of Roman hostility and the rebellion by Jewish leaders against God's Word in favor of their tradition (15:1-9). In contrast to this wicked behavior, Jesus fed the **5,000** and **healed** many who were **sick** (14:13-21,34-36). He was overwhelmed by **compassion** for these people. The One who performed these miracles and walked **on the sea** was none other than the Son of God. The proclamation came from the lips of the disciples themselves, and they **worshiped Him** (14:33). The Messiah's power, compassion, and authority stood in stark contrast to the evil behavior of the secular and religious authorities. Peter's **little faith** was also contrasted with the disciple's proclamation to highlight further the disequilibrium caused by Jesus' ministry.

15:1-20 After Jesus rebuked the religious leaders for their blatant disregard of God's Word, He denounced them. The confused disciples were concerned that Jesus had offended the Pharisees (15:12), but Jesus rebuked the disciples for their lack of understanding (15:16-20).

15:21-28 Matthew contrasted the disciples' lack of understanding with the Gentile woman's understanding of Jesus. This **Canaanite woman** lived in the Gentile region **of Tyre and Sidon**. She referred to Jesus as the **Son of David**, a sure recognition of His identity as the Messiah, and then begged Him to heal her **daughter**. As the disciples wanted to send the people away to the villages to get food (showing their lack of faith, 14:15), they also urged Jesus to

send her away (15:23). The disciples still did not understand fully the nature of Christ's ministry. But He would not be deterred; neither would the Gentile woman.

This Canaanite woman clearly had not only tremendous **faith** but also an understanding of religious matters (v. 28). She must have learned about the Jewish expectations of a Messiah and must have believed that He would one day come.

The Canaanite Woman: *A Desperate Mother* *Encounters Jesus* *Matthew 15:21-28*	
Her Requests	**His Responses**
"Have mercy on me, Lord. . . . My daughter is cruelly tormented by a demon" (v. 21).	He did not say a word to her (v. 23).
"Lord, help me!" (v. 25).	"It isn't right to take the children's bread and throw it to their dogs" (v. 26).
"Yes, Lord. Even the dogs eat the crumbs that fall from their masters' table!" (v. 27).	"Woman, your faith is great. Let it be done for you as you want" (v. 28).
See also Mk 7:24-30.	

The Lord tested the Canaanite woman's faith by claiming He had come only for

the lost sheep . . . of Israel (v. 24). Her response revealed a still greater faith. Although she understood that as a Gentile she was despised by the Jews, she was not deterred; she admitted her unworthy status before Christ. Rather than turning her away, Jesus rewarded her faith and healed her daughter. So, with a Gentile woman's perseverance and faith, Christ began His ministry to the Gentiles.

15:29-31 Jesus moved from Tyre and Sidon to **Galilee** of the Gentiles, climbed up a **mountain**, and **sat** down. **Crowds came to Him** and **He healed them** all, and the people gave **glory to the God of Israel**, indicating that the people were probably primarily Gentile. There was a clear connection between this scene and the one just before the Sermon on the Mount, when Jesus' ministry was strictly to the Jews (4:23-25).

15:32-39 Driven by **compassion** again, Jesus fed the **4,000**. This time the people were primarily Gentiles, testifying again to the change in the focus of His ministry. But one thing had not yet changed: the disciples' fledgling faith. They were concerned about the apparent lack of **bread**.

16:1-12 After the feeding Jesus left for Magadan (15:39, or Magdala), a site near the Sea of Galilee. Shortly thereafter, He was **approached** by the **Pharisees and Sadducees**, who **asked Him** for another **sign**. But this time **no sign** would **be given**. Jesus then warned His disciples about the

Heart to Heart: *Who He Is*

Every woman longs for heaven where God is, but you are invited to be in heaven with Him right now—to be happy with Him at this very moment. Being happy with Him now means trusting Him as Savior, loving as He loves, helping as He helps, giving as He gives, serving as He serves, rescuing as He rescues, and having Him with you 24 hours a day.

yeast of the Pharisees and Sadducees (vv. 6,12). But they did not yet understand, and Jesus rebuked them (vv. 8-11). After Jesus recounted His miracles with the bread, they finally got Jesus' point.

This narrative section was clearly characterized by contrasts. The starkest of them all is the one that juxtaposed the Gentile woman's faith with the consistent lack of understanding on the part of the disciples, who had witnessed so much of the ministry of Christ and yet continued to exhibit a lack of faith. But Matthew intended to show their growth, too.

16:13-20 In the very next scene, for the moment at least, their faith began to take on a much firmer character. In **the region of Caesarea Philippi**, a region well known for its pagan worship, Simon Peter made his great confession concerning Jesus' identity, **You are the Messiah, the Son of the living God!** (v. 16). Jesus affirmed Peter's confession and acknowledged that God the Father was responsible for revealing this truth. Jesus also changed Simon's name to **Peter** (Gk. *Petros*, "a specific rock") and claimed that **on this rock** (Gk. *petra*, "a rocky crag" or "massive rock") He would **build** His **church**, and **the forces of Hades** would **not overpower it**. Several interpretations are possible:

- Jesus may have been speaking in Aramaic, as is found in some early manuscripts like the *Peshitta* (written in a cognate language to Aramaic, i.e., Syriac). *Cephas* (Aram.) could be used interchangeably for both the proper name and for the word "rock," which then could be a reference to Simon Peter himself as the rock.

- Some say Matthew could have been more precise in identifying Peter as the stone and Jesus as the large rock by using the Greek word *lithos* (stone of any size) for the latter. However, that would have erased an effective

literary device or wordplay. There would have been no pun.

- Clearly, Peter was addressed, and this rock could be the Christological confession—Peter's words containing the truth of the Christian faith, i.e., who Christ is, not only the Messiah or anointed one but also the Son of God (v. 16).

In the context, either of the last two interpretations is possible. Peter identified Jesus; then Jesus identified Peter. Yet the most important event in the chapter was Peter's inspired confession of faith.

THE CLIMAX OF JESUS' MINISTRY (16:21–28:20)

A Focus on Coming Death and Resurrection (16:21–18:35)

The implications for disciples (16:21–17:27)

16:21-23 Jesus called Peter **an offense**. And, though Peter became an instrument of Satan for a brief moment (v. 23), Jesus Himself had already announced that even death could not destroy or "overpower" (Gk. *katischusousin*, "prevail, be victorious over") the church (v. 18). This interpretation in no way necessitated the idea of a pope or apostolic succession. The reference to Peter as a "rock" might simply be a recognition of his leadership role among the apostles or, as previously suggested, could be a reference to his confession. CHURCH (Gk *ekklēsian*, "assembly") refers to those who have been called out, and in the New Testament the word became the designation for Christians who joined together in a common purpose. HADES was the transliteration of the Greek word used to reference the "underworld" or "place of the dead."

The "keys of the kingdom" (v. 19) was obviously a metaphor for the gospel. Peter used these keys at Pentecost (Ac 2:14), at Samaria (Ac 8:14), and as a witness to Cornelius (Ac 10). In Greek the verb tense is most accurately expressed as "will have already been bound" (in the sense of *forbid*) and "will have been already loosed" (in the sense of *permit*). Peter certainly was not given authority to forgive sins, but his pronouncement was that the forgiveness of sins was dependent upon what heaven had already willed.

16:24-28 At this point the sermon-narrative sequence was reversed. In this section, Jesus sought to teach His disciples the true nature of discipleship. Those who would **follow** Him must, like Him, **take up** their own crosses. His entire message emphasized the radical commitment needed to follow in His steps. There can be no neutral ground. Those who would follow Him must be willing to **lose** everything in this life for His sake. The bottom line was that anyone who followed Christ must be willing to suffer. But Jesus assured them that they would be rewarded when He returned in the glory of **His kingdom**.

17:1-13 In the transfiguration, **Peter, James,** and **John** were given the opportunity to see Christ in His glory. They were singled out for this opportunity because they were the closest to Christ; they formed His "inner circle" of companions. During this amazing experience they saw **Moses and Elijah**, the giver of the law and the greatest prophet, **talking with** Jesus (v. 3). Though Peter objected, Moses and Elijah were taken away, and **Jesus** was left there **alone**. The disciples learned of the true supremacy of Christ— worthy of wholehearted discipleship. In language similar to what was uttered at the baptism of Jesus, God the Father acknowledged Jesus as His **beloved Son** in whom He took **delight** (v. 5). But this time He told Peter, James, and John to **listen to** Jesus alone. True discipleship entails unswerving devotion to the Son of

God. **The disciples** now **understood** that **John the Baptist**, the forerunner of Christ, was the Elijah who was to come.

17:14-23 When the disciples came down from the mountain, they were met by **a man** whose **son** had **seizures and** suffered **severely**. The disciples **couldn't heal him**. **Jesus rebuked** not only the **demon** (v. 18) but also the unbelief of an entire **generation** (v. 17). Their unbelief, however, did not stop Jesus from healing **the boy**. The disciples, who were given authority over demons earlier, were curious as to **why** they could not **drive it out** (v. 19).

Matthew communicated the point that true discipleship requires faith, even faith as small as **a mustard seed**, the smallest seed known in that region (v. 20). Their faith was important now, more than ever, because the time was near when Jesus would no longer be with them physically. They would have to learn to depend solely on His unseen presence. Jesus reminded them again that He was **about to be betrayed**, killed, and **on the third day**, He would **be raised up** (vv. 22-23). The fact that the disciples were **deeply distressed** showed that the mustard seed of faith had yet to take root.

17:24-27 Matthew alone reported this event. It has been interpreted in numerous ways. Verse 24 seems to establish the fact that the Jewish temple tax for the upkeep of the sanctuary—not a Roman tax—was being considered (Ex 30:12-14; 38:26; 2 Chr 24:6). The amount required was the didrachma or **double drachma**, the equivalent of wages for about two days' work. Verse 25, then, resembles a parable and involves a question concerning civil taxes. The main point of the question is that, just as royal **sons** are exempt from the **taxes** imposed by their fathers, so Jesus was exempt from the tax imposed by His Father. Jesus, in other words, acknowledged the temple tax to be an obligation to God; but as God's Son, He was exempt. But so as not to **offend**, Jesus would pay the tax. He directed Peter to **catch** a **fish**, which contained the **coin** for making payment of the taxes owed. Jesus paid Peter's tax, too (v. 27). But, to what extent was Peter like Jesus? Jesus extended sonship to all who followed Him; therefore, the sons were exempt from the temple tax, too.

But Jesus set an example in humility for His disciples (18:1-5). He veiled His identity as God's Son as He moved toward the cross. Yet in moving toward the cross, He was inaugurating the time when the significance of the temple would fade. But until that time, the temple tax was expected to be paid, and so He paid the tax. As with so many things, the disciples did not fully understand the significance of Jesus' example until much later.

The implications for the church (18:1-35)

After unveiling in the narrative section His future suffering and having corrected certain misunderstandings concerning the true nature of discipleship, Jesus, in this fourth sermon, dealt with what His death and resurrection would mean for the church: humility and forgiveness, characteristics most perfectly emulated by Christ.

18:1-9 Having been asked by His disciples about who would be the **greatest in the kingdom**, Jesus **called a child** to come out of the crowd. The greatest in His kingdom would be one who modeled childlike dependence on God. The idea is not "childishness," implying a perpetual state of immaturity, but childlike, implying that the mature or "perfect" believer is one who is completely dependent on God to meet all of his needs (6:25-34). Matthew 18:6-9 makes clear that believers ought to do all they can to avoid causing even a child, one of the least of Christ's

followers, to stumble. God has His eye on all of His flock, no matter how insignificant they might appear to others.

18:10-14 The parable of the lost **sheep** (vv. 10-14) fell within the context of Jesus' teachings for His disciples. Jesus continually emphasized that the gospel was to be given to all. Jesus was the Shepherd who could not be content, even knowing that all but one sheep were safe. He had to **search for the stray**. Only when all the sheep had been drawn to Him could He rejoice.

18:15-20 Jesus taught His disciples how to resolve disputes among believers (vv. 15-17). Forgiveness is essential for the church. When one believer **sins against** another, the one offended is to **go** to that believer and point out the wrong. If the offending believer is unrepentant, church discipline must be invoked. If there is still no repentance, excluding the unrepentant one from fellowship is appropriate. With the ease of filing lawsuits today, this procedure is most difficult to pursue; and, unfortunately, it is rarely practiced.

As Paul pointed out in 1 Corinthians 6:1-11, lawsuits among believers are due mainly to spiritual immaturity. So lawsuits among believers were a symptom of a deeper spiritual problem. The remedy, then, to problems in the church is not to be found in the courtroom, but in the heart. Humility and forgiveness must be central in the ministry of the church. God wants His children to live in harmony and join together in serving Him. The Bible does provide a plan for resolving conflicts:

- The believer must face the conflict, acknowledge that the conflict exists, and accept whatever fallout comes as a result (v. 15).

- Only if one-on-one efforts fail should the believer reach out to others for help in solving the conflict (v. 16).

- Finally, if the conflict cannot be resolved by the individuals or their peers, then the matter must come before the church to be settled (v. 17).

The emphasis is never punitive. God is in the business of redemption. Believers, too, must respond lovingly. The believer who has been wronged must ultimately forgive and move forward in harmony (see Php 4:2-7).

18:21-35 The parable of the unforgiving slave was given in response to Peter's question concerning how many times a believer could **sin against** another and be forgiven. Jesus' response is that true repentance must always be met with forgiveness, more than **70 times** over! The rabbis taught that a sin, when there was repentance, should be forgiven a few times, but then there was to be no forgiveness. Peter's suggestion that you should forgive **seven times** would have been considered generous, but Jesus came with another unbelievable challenge—unlimited forgiveness.

There was no comparison between what was owed the **king** and what was owed the **slave**. This parable does not contradict the previous teaching on church discipline. The key here is *true* repentance. The one who truly changes his behavior ought to be forgiven one hundredfold. But where true repentance was not manifested, judgment would be unrelenting. God has forgiven believers an overwhelming debt; how could those same believers refuse to forgive the small offenses of others? Some have argued that verses 34-35 provide evidence that God's grace could be taken away. But Ridderbos points out,

> Whoever tries to separate man's forgiveness from God's will no longer be able to count on God's mercy. In so doing he does not merely forfeit it, like the servant

in the parable. Rather he shows that he never had a part in it. God's mercy is not something cut and dried that is received only once. It is a persistent power that pervades all of life. If it does not become manifest as such a power, then it was never received at all.[20]

The Road to Jerusalem: The Coming Judgment (19:1–25:46)

True discipleship versus condemnation for the Jewish leaders (19:1–22:46)

19:1-12 This fifth narrative section opened with Jesus responding to various questions, sparking the occasion to warn of the coming judgment. As the cross loomed closer, teachings on the meaning of true discipleship and the condemnation of the Jewish leaders who had rejected Him took on new urgency.

Jesus left Galilee for **the region of Judea across the Jordan** (v. 1). By heading toward Judea, Jesus deliberately put Himself even closer to Jerusalem, where He had already predicted He would be killed (16:21). He was met by **large crowds** and **healed** many in the region of Judea.

Some **Pharisees** among the crowd **approached** Jesus **to test Him** (19:3). The word for **TEST** (Gk. *peirazontes*, "try, test") is the same word used in Matthew 4:1 where Jesus was led into the wilderness to be tempted by the Devil. This word can take on an evil sense as in Matthew 4:7 and mean to solicit or tempt to sin. Clearly from the text in Matthew 19:3 the Pharisees had evil intentions when they questioned Jesus about divorce. **They asked, "Is it lawful for a man to divorce his wife on any grounds?"** During this time, there was a debate going on between the Pharisaic schools of Shammai and Hillel. Moses allowed a man to divorce his wife in such cases where he found "something improper" about her (Dt 24:1). The controversy was over whether this injunction was limited to sexual unfaithfulness or whether it could be applied in a wider context. The Shammai school took the strict view that divorce was allowed only in cases of sexual immorality. The Hillel school held that the statute could be applied to practically any action that displeased a husband. In the modern era, such a position would have provided grounds for putting away or seeking divorce even if a wife burned her husband's breakfast toast.

Matthew and Mark recorded this incident. The accounts have differences and similarities, but there are no contradictions. Both Matthew and Mark are straightforward in noting Jesus' return to the creation order (vv. 4-6) to support His rejection of divorce rather than citing the teachings of one of the popular rabbis. Then Matthew chose to focus on the **divorce papers** and Jesus' reference to uncleanness, which He defined more narrowly than many as **sexual immorality** (Gk. *porneia*, referring to a broad range of forbidden sexual practices, v. 9). Mark, on the other hand, assumed the sexual immorality and simply noted Jesus' word that breaking the vows of commitment in marriage would be tantamount to **adultery** or having sexual intimacy with someone other than your wife or husband.

Because marriage was a metaphor used by the Lord to illustrate His own relationship to believers and to the church, He had a stern word for any who broke the vows of marriage. Ultimately, then, God's answer to this problematic issue was not found in laws or legal codes or traditions or even human choices. God returned to His creative design for the man and the woman, their holy and committed union, and His plan to use that sacred union as a tool for revealing Himself and His faith-fulness. God cannot and will not compromise His principles; neither does He lower His standards. However, God redeems and restores all who seek Him and His forgiveness. Jesus came not to reduce the law's demands but to enable those who rely on Him to live according to God's high standards.

In His reply, Jesus appealed to neither view. He certainly did not recommend or require divorce (Gk *apostasion* from *apoluō*, "sending away" and thus "breaking fellowship") under any circumstances. He never suggested that the innocent must divorce the one guilty of unfaithfulness (see Hs 3:1-3). Rather, He acknowledged the permission Moses granted for a divorce certificate (Dt 24:1-4), noting that such would be used only because of hardened hearts (Mt. 19:8). Mark's audience was primarily Gentile, and both Jew and Gentile societies recognized adultery as grounds for divorce, so there was little reason for Mark to elaborate on the clause concerning adultery. Matthew's audience, on the other hand, was primarily Jewish, giving him a reason to show Jesus as immersed in Jewish debate. In any event, the Pharisees had taken the permission of the law granted by Moses and made it a command, and in the process they had allowed human choices and circumstances to circumvent God's plan and purpose.

Matthew and Mark agreed that faithfulness to marriage vows, in accordance with the creation commandment, must be a top priority. God's plan was permanent monogamy (Gn 2:24; see also Mk 10:7-8). The modern application of Jesus' teaching on divorce must heed several considerations:

- God's primary intention for marriage is lifelong commitment; therefore, maintaining the marital union is absolutely essential (Mt 19:6).

- Jesus put the rights of husband and wife on equal footing (Mk 10:11-12).

- Some Christians may never marry, which does not mean they are settling for second best; Paul the apostle was single (1 Co 7:7-9).

- Divorce may be permitted (though not mandated) if a believing spouse is deserted by an unbelieving spouse (1 Co 7:10-16).

- Physical, sexual, or emotional abuse in a marriage situation must be dealt with in a compassionate and firm manner within the context of church discipline.[21]

Reasons God Rejects Divorce
• Marriage is a divine institution the Lord used to teach His children about their relationships to Him (Gn 1:27; Mt 19:4-5).
• Marriage is God's design, operates under His authority, and carries His imprimatur (Mt 19:4-5).
• Marriage brings two people together as one flesh, testifying to the permanence God planned for this most intimate union (Mt 19:6).
• Jesus pointed to the example of the first couple (Mt 19:8).
• Remarriage following unjustified divorce compounds sin (Mt 19:9).

19:13-15 Children were then **brought to** Jesus in order to receive His blessing, but **the disciples rebuked them**. The **kingdom of heaven** belongs to those who are childlike, and Jesus Himself loved the children (v. 14).

19:16-30 The issues moved from marriage and family to the proper use of earthly possessions. The rich young ruler was concerned about his eternal destiny and questioned Jesus about the good things he must **do to have eternal life**. Jesus' initial response seemed strange.

Was Jesus implying that He Himself was not good (v. 17)? Or was He reminding the young man that He was God? Matthew suggested that Jesus was trying to point the ruler to the ultimate standard of goodness. Jesus quoted from the Ten Commandments, and the young ruler confessed that he had **kept all these**, but he **still** admitted a **lack**. When Jesus told him to **go** and **sell** all his possessions so that he might have true **treasure in heaven** and then to **follow** Him, the rich young ruler walked away. Jesus' commands here must be taken together: Altruism or any humanitarianism without commitment to Christ counts for nothing toward eternity.

Jesus did not command His followers to sell all their possessions and follow Him while living a life of utter poverty. Indeed, many have understood these verses to teach just that. Jesus' point was that if one's **possessions** would keep him from full allegiance to Christ, he must immediately divest himself of these things. Jesus' emphasis was always on the heart within rather than the possessions or position without.

> *Jesus' emphasis was always on the heart within rather than the possessions or position without.*

Using hyperbole, Jesus showed how difficult it is for the **rich ... to enter the kingdom of heaven** (v. 23). He did not condemn people because they had wealth. Entrance into the kingdom of heaven can only happen through God's grace, and many Jews had come to equate wealth and prosperity with a ticket to heaven. For those who have left everything to follow Him, blessings in this life (primarily through the fellowship of God's people) and in the life to come, will follow. Jesus realized that wealth would bring dangers and challenges in the spiritual realm (v. 23). Matthew added that in the life to come the Twelve would **sit on 12 thrones, judging the 12 tribes of Israel** (v. 28). Paul, as the apostle to the Gentiles, also spoke to the matter, indicating that all believers would take part in judging the world (1 Co 6:2-3).

20:1-16 The parable of the vineyard workers, peculiar to Matthew's Gospel, seemed to support the statement of Jesus that "many who are first will be last, and the last first" (19:30). The parable stressed the equality of all believers, regardless of when they came to work for Christ. Jesus assigned rank or position as well as rewards and opportunities. He determined what was to be required. God was interested in more than how much work would be done; He required faithfulness to the task assigned.

20:17-34 As Christ's impending time of suffering drew ever closer, His servanthood was emphasized. For the third time since Peter's confession, Jesus told His disciples that He was **going** to suffer in **Jerusalem**, be killed, and **on the third day** be raised to life. This time there was no immediate reaction from the disciples. But in the very next scene **the mother of** James and John **approached** Jesus to request that her **two sons** sit beside Jesus **on** His **right** and **left** in His **kingdom** (v. 21). Mark's account of this incident did not mention the mother, but Matthew included this historical fact. The passage revealed that despite Jesus' repeated warnings about His upcoming suffering and His teachings on humility, James and John, and seemingly their mother as well, were still concerned about prestige and power (v. 21). Whether this unholy ambition originated with these brothers or with their mother, the misplaced priority was unfortunate and served as an occasion for Jesus to remind the Twelve once again of the cost of discipleship (Lk 9:23).

Zebedee's Wife	
Matthew 20:20-28	
An ambitious request drew varied reactions and a loving response.	
Request of an ambitious mother: "Promise, that these two sons of mine may sit, one on Your right and the other on Your left, in Your kingdom" (v. 21).	**Jesus answered:** "You don't know what you're asking. Are you able to drink the cup that I am about to drink?" (v. 22).
Reaction of eager brothers: "We are able" (v. 22).	**Jesus told them:** "You will indeed drink My cup. But to sit at My right and left is not Mine to give" (v. 23).
Reaction of jealous colleagues: When the 10 disciples heard this, they became indignant with the two brothers (v. 24).	**Jesus called them over and said:** "You know that the rulers of the Gentiles dominate them. . . . It must not be like that among you" (vv. 25-26). "Whoever wants to be first among you must be your slave" (v. 27). "The Son of Man did not come to be served, but to serve" (v. 28).

A lesson learned from this New Testament woman: Selfish ambitions may lead others to react poorly, but Jesus' loving response is patient and kind. See also Mk 10:35-45.

Jesus wanted His disciples to come to Him with their questions and requests, but He must have grieved over this inappro-priate request that showed James and John had an inflated view of themselves and a complete misunderstanding of what it meant to follow Christ. With great sensitivity, Jesus did not abruptly reject this devoted mother's request. Rather, He used the question as a springboard for correcting her misunderstanding and teaching valuable lessons, such as humility and servanthood (Mt 20:26-28). True discipleship involved submission and service. Jesus' disciples were to follow in the footsteps of their Master who **did not come to be served, but to serve, and to give His life—a ransom for many** (20:28). Salome (see Mk 15:40) came to get something, but she left the Savior's presence having made the supreme sacrifice for any mother giving her two sons to Christ, James (a leader in the early church, Ac 12:17; 15:13) and John (the disciple whom Jesus loved, and the one used by the Holy Spirit to pen a Gospel and three epistles bearing his name as well as the book of Revelation, Jn 13:23).

The healing of the **two blind men** was an example of Christ's servanthood and a testimony of faith and true discipleship. As the healing of two demon-possessed men in the Gadarenes was recorded at the beginning of Christ's ministry, coming after Jesus' rebuke of the little faith displayed by the disciples, so Matthew mentioned at the end of Christ's earthly ministry the healing of two blind men immediately after a demonstration of the disciples' still faltering faith.

The demons identified Christ clearly, though they were certainly not His disciples! However, Mark mentioned that one of the demon-possessed men wanted to go with Jesus (Mk 5:18). These blind men recognized Jesus as the **Son of David**. After their healing, **they followed Him**.

21:1-22 The triumphal entry marked the beginning of the end of Christ's earthly ministry. His entrance into Jerusalem was a fulfillment of Isaiah 62:11 and Zechariah 9:9. As He rode on the **donkey**, large crowds lined the road to Jerusalem shouting, **Hosanna to the Son of David!** clearly recognizing His kingly status (v. 9). As **He entered Jerusalem**, however, the crowds referred to Him as **the prophet Jesus from Nazareth in Galilee** (v. 11). This reference most likely was a foreshadowing of the coming challenge to His authority. Jesus immediately challenged the practices in **the temple complex** by driving the money changers from His Father's house. But **the blind and the lame came to Him** there, **and He healed them** (v. 14). The children cheered, calling Him **the Son of David**, while the scribes and the Pharisees were indignant at the use of such a title. But the Old Testament Scripture quoted by Jesus confirmed the wisdom of the children. The curse of the barren **fig tree** served two purposes in this context:

- Israel is often likened to a fig tree (Jr 8:13; 24:1-8), and the reference was symbolic of the coming judgment upon Israel.

- This lesson on faith was the last lesson given to the disciples before the Lord's suffering came.

21:23-27 In this section, the harsher condemnation of the Jewish leaders was highlighted with a series of their questions, in which Jesus' authority was challenged and then answered with a series of His parables. Jesus also baffled His enemies with some of His own questions.

The chief priests and the elders of the people questioned Jesus' **authority** (v. 23). He fired back with a question concerning the nature of **John's baptism**. The question forced the religious leaders to take an agnostic stance. Then Jesus shared three parables in which He made perfectly clear that the kingdom of heaven was being taken away from the Jews and given to a people who would listen—most notably the very people that the religious leaders despised: "tax collectors and prostitutes" (v. 31).

21:28-32 The parable of the two sons, peculiar to Matthew, disclosed that the religious leaders rejected the way of righteousness, but the tax collectors and prostitutes accepted it; therefore, the kingdom of heaven would be theirs.

21:33-45 The parable of the vineyard owner showed that the religious leaders' disobedience would result in the kingdom's being **given to a nation** that would be committed to **producing . . . fruit**. The symbolism is clear: God was the **landowner**; the **vineyard** was Israel; the **tenant farmers** were the religious leaders; the **slaves** were the prophets, including John the Baptist; and the **son** was Jesus. Three main points emerge from this story:

- God is patient.

- The rebellious will be destroyed.

- The church will replace Israel as the center of Christ's work of salvation.

22:1-14 The parable of the **wedding banquet** also demonstrated how the religious leaders **paid no attention** to the call of God. The invitation for **everyone** to join the banquet was a reference to the Gentiles and to all whom the religious leaders would certainly deem unworthy for such an occasion. The invitation was broad, but all did not respond positively to the message. There were requirements to the divine invitation. The **chosen** were the ones who committed to do the will of the Father (v. 14; see 7:21).

22:15-22 A series of confrontations with the **Pharisees**, the **Herodians**, and the Sadducees were recounted. The Pharisees, or "separated ones," largest of the Jewish sects, developed the oral tradition and became the interpreters of the law. They were legalistic and self-righteous. The Herodians, who were supporters of Herod and his dynasty, were a political group with members from various religious perspectives, including many who were wealthy and influential and, needless to say, pro-Roman in their commitment. These groups came together to ask Jesus about paying **taxes to Caesar**. Rather than their testing Him, Jesus' answer tested them. **They were** so **amazed** that all they could do was to withdraw from Him.

22:23-33 That **same day** the **Sadducees**, who acknowledged only the five books of Moses to be authoritative and who said, as a result, that there was **no resurrection**—an event not mentioned in the Pentateuch—approached Jesus with a question concerning a childless widow who had been married to a succession of the brothers of her deceased husband. They were appealing to the tradition of levirate marriage (Dt 25:5-6) in which a brother married the childless widow of his deceased brother in order to secure the property for and ensure the lineage of his deceased brother.

Jesus quickly pointed out their ignorance of Scripture and showed them that the Torah, which they held as the Word of God, affirmed the resurrection. Though marriage according to human understanding would not exist **in heaven**, happiness would not be absent because of a lack of sexual intimacy. Heavenly relationships will, in fact, surpass even the most intimate relationships on earth. This time Matthew pointed out that the crowds were **astonished at His teaching**.

22:34-40 When asked about the two greatest commandments, Jesus pointed out that they were to love God wholeheartedly and to **love your neighbor as yourself**. For the Jewish people, to love God was fundamental to all life, and the command from Deuteronomy 6:5 was well known. Hillel taught that Leviticus 19:18, which commanded love of one's neighbor, was also a fundamental mandate. But Jesus put both of these commandments together in such a way that for one to do otherwise would be nonsense. For Jesus said, **all the Law and the Prophets depend on these two commandments** (v. 40). A right relationship to God was prerequisite to producing a right relationship to others.

22:41-46 Finally, Jesus asked a question: How could the Pharisees view the Messiah as merely a human descendant of David? Jesus quoted Psalm 110, widely understood to be written by David. Two "lords" are mentioned in that psalm. The first clearly referred to *Yahweh* (the personal name of God). The second could be an earthly master; but since there had been no human being in Israel higher than **David**, the reference must have been to **the Messiah**. Therefore, the Messiah must be higher than David. The title "Son of David" had often been used to show the descent of Messiah, but few people realized that the Messiah would also be God's Son. Jesus illustrated that in these verses. Unable to refute such logic, the Pharisees walked away speechless.

In every confrontation, Jesus responded with supreme logic and Scripture. With such weapons, the religious leaders were humiliated and defeated, which fueled their rage against Him.

Judgment on the temple and the nations (23:1–25:46)

23:1-39 This fifth and final sermon began with a scathing diatribe against the Jewish leaders. Mark gave only a brief account of this sermon, whereas Matthew went into great detail. Its inclusion in the Gospel of Matthew is consistent with Matthew's overall purpose to present Jesus as **the Messiah**—the sole, authoritative interpreter of the Law and the Prophets. Looking back to many of the teachings in the Sermon on the Mount, Jesus showed how the Pharisees failed to practice the greater righteousness (compare especially the content of chapters 5–6 with 23:2-22). They did not practice what they preached. Everything they did was for the eyes of men. They **neglected** the deeper **matters of the law—justice, mercy, and faith** (v. 23). Inside they were **full of hypocrisy and lawlessness** (v. 28).

Some have described this chapter as the most anti-Jewish in all the New Testament. However, Jesus, too, was a Jew. He was not condemning every Jewish religious leader (see Jn 3). He was denouncing bitter hypocrisy. **The chair of Moses** (v. 2) was probably a reference to the stone chair located at the front of the synagogue. The teacher occupied this chair of honor and influence, and to be **seated** there would suggest becoming the honored teacher's successor. Only Jesus was qualified to sit in the chair of Moses. Jesus' diatribe was very similar to those of many of the Old Testament prophets, who on many occasions decried the deeds of wayward Israel and Judah. Jesus did not attack the task of teaching in the synagogues. His words of criticism were for the self-righteous teachers. Jesus also lamented over Jerusalem, calling for nothing more than His people's willingness to accept Him. The return of Christ came into focus here as well.

24:1-14 In the previous section, Jesus condemned the religious leaders for their preoccupation with external things and their neglect of inward things. Phylacteries, leather boxes containing Scripture written on small scrolls, were worn on the left arm and on the forehead by Jewish men—a practice continued among orthodox Jewish men even in the modern era (Ex 13:9,16; Dt 6:8; 11:18). Some of these religious leaders had turned what was to be a personal reminder of God's words into a public spectacle to draw attention to their supposed spiritual devotion. Now, the disciples **called His attention to the temple buildings** (external things). Surely they must have understood at this point that one greater than the temple was with them. But rather than rebuke them, Jesus used the occasion to draw their attention to the future—the last days.

After telling the disciples of the future destruction of the temple, Jesus was asked: What will be **the sign of Your coming and of the end of the age?** (v. 3).The judgment on the temple and on the nations came to the forefront. Many false messiahs would appear and **deceive many**; then there would be wars, famines, and earthquakes. These things have happened throughout human history. But Jesus likened the events to **birth pains**, meaning they would increase in frequency and intensity (v. 8).

Widespread **persecution** of the disciples would come, and **the love of many** would **grow cold** (v. 12). But the kingdom message would continue to spread. The emphasis must be upon the necessity of faith and obedience and not upon a projected timetable of events. Suffering and sorrow would be widespread (v. 21).

24:15-31 The **abomination that causes desolation** (v. 15) is found in Daniel 9:27; 11:31; 12:11. This phrase was a prophecy with more than one fulfillment. It did refer to the desecration of the temple, especially the altar of sacrifice, where in 168 BC Antiochus Epiphanes erected a statue of Zeus and sacrificed a swine. References to this phrase in many places in the New Testament identified the antichrist, especially in the book of Revelation. When antichrist appeared, there would be an increased sense of urgency to get out of Judea. **False prophets** would **arise** at this time as well.

But there would be no mistaking the return of Christ. He came the first time in humility and obscurity, seeking to save the lost. But when He returns, He will light up the sky, announcing the coming judgment.

24:32-35 The **parable** of **the fig tree** was especially important in this context. This GENERATION (Gk. *genea*, "nation, race, offspring") may refer to the nation of Israel, reaffirming her continued existence until the last days, or the expression may simply suggest "age" or "time period" in general. The word may also suggest a particular time frame, as a 30- or 40-year period, in which case these signs described in the text would have begun to be fulfilled before that generation passed away (see also Mt 11:16; 12:39, 41-42,45; 16:4; 17:17; and 23:36).

24:36-51 In this section of the sermon, Jesus stressed three very important points:

- **No one** except the Father **knows** the day or hour of Christ's return (v. 36).

- Disciples should be watchful and ready for His return in all circumstances.

- While waiting for the King to return, the disciples' watchfulness must be manifested in service.

Foolish and Sensible Virgins
Matthew 25:1-13

Foolish Virgins	Sensible Virgins
Took lamps but no oil	Took lamps with oil
Asked for some oil	Answered "no" because they wanted to be prepared for the bridegroom
Went to buy oil	Went to meet bridegroom
Not ready for the Son of Man to return	Ready for the Son of Man to return
Lesson of the Parable: Be ready for the coming of the Son of Man (Christians must prepare for Jesus' return).	

Matthew gave a more extended treatment of the "waiting period" than any of the other Gospels. A key theme in Matthew is true discipleship. Jesus probed His listeners, warning them to be watchful and ready: A genuine disciple is consistently practicing watchfulness and service (24:51; 25:12,30,46).

Women and the Parables of Jesus

Parable	Audience	Application	Reference
The lamp under a basket	The disciples	All of your words and actions should give testimony to God's redemptive and transforming grace.	Mt 5:14-16; Mk 4:21-22; Lk 8:16-17
The marriage	The Pharisees and the disciples of John the Baptist	In Christ's companionship, joy will be found.	Mt 9:15; Mk 2:19-20; Lk 5:34-35
The patched garment	The Pharisees and the disciples of John the Baptist	Jesus came to make all things new.	Mt 9:16; Mk 2:21; Lk 5:36
The children in the marketplace	The multitudes concerning John the Baptist	Those who rejected Jesus and John could not be satisfied. Beware of focusing on personal whims.	Mt 11:16-17; Lk 7:31-32
The leaven	The multitude on the seashore	Beware of sin, for it makes its way into life, corrupting and drawing away from the good and true.	Mt 13:33; Lk 13:20-21
The pearl of great price	The disciples	The relative value of the gospel exceeds all else.	Mt 13:45-46
The wedding garment	The chief priests and the Pharisees	Your life must be kept pure and holy.	Mt 22:10-14
The sensible and foolish virgins	The disciples on the Mount of Olives	Be prepared and watchful for Jesus' return.	Mt 25:1-13
The wedding feast	The chief priests and the Pharisees	Do not reject God's invitation to salvation.	Mt 22:2-9; Lk 14:16-23
The lost coin	The Pharisees and scribes	Christ's love is for sinners, and He is determined to draw them to Himself.	Lk 15:8-10
The persistent widow	The disciples	Pray fervently and persistently.	Lk 18:1-8

Each of the five parables in 24:42–25:46 focused on some aspect of watchfulness. The days of the Son of Man would be like **the days of Noah** (v. 37). The flood came unexpectedly on the people as they went about their business. So the warning was to expect the unexpected. If the Son did not know the time of His return, "How cheerfully should we his followers rest in ignorance that cannot be removed, trusting in all things to our Heavenly Father's wisdom and goodness, striving to obey his clearly revealed will, and leaning on his goodness for support."[22]

The faithful slave was prepared at all times, faithful even when his master's delay was long (v. 46). In the end, he would be greatly **rewarded**. The **wicked slave**, on the other hand, was lax in his responsibilities and would be **cut** into **pieces** and assigned **a place with the hypocrites** (vv. 50-51).

25:1-30 The parable of the **10 virgins** has been interpreted in many ways. The point of the story, however, was straightforwardly the delay of the bridegroom. The **foolish** virgins had some oil in their lamps, but the delay of the bridegroom revealed their lack of preparation; **they didn't take oil with them**. The oil was an important object lesson in the story, showing that the foolish virgins were unprepared for the delay of the bridegroom and so they were shut out in the end. The response of the virgins to the bridegroom's delay distinguished the **SENSIBLE** (Gk. *phronimoi*, "thoughtful, wise") from the **FOOLISH** (Gk. *morai*, "stupid," transliterated into English as "moron"). The major theme is preparation for the Son of Man's return.

Women with Jesus in His Last Days			
The Woman	**The Event**	**Her Ministry to Jesus**	**Reference**
Mary, unnamed in Matthew but identified in John	Jesus' anointing at Bethany	She anointed Jesus' head with expensive and fragrant oil.	Mt 26:6-13; Jn 11:1-44
Unnamed female servants	Peter's testing	They questioned Peter about his association with Jesus.	Mt 26:69-72
Pilate's wife	Jesus' trial	She pleaded with her husband to release Jesus, whom she believed was righteous.	Mt 27:17-19
Unnamed women	The journey to the crucifixion site	They mourned for Jesus.	Lk 23:26-29
Mary Magdalene; Mary (Jesus' mother, possibly referred to as the mother of James and Joseph in Mt 27:55-56); Salome (the wife of Zebedee, and the mother of disciples James and John); Mary (the wife of Clopas and the sister of Mary and thus the aunt of Jesus)	Jesus' crucifixion and burial	They remained with Jesus through His time of suffering and prepared His body for burial.	Mt 27:55-56; Jn 19:25-27
Mary Magdalene; Mary (the mother of James); Joanna	Jesus' resurrection	They announced His resurrection to the disciples.	Mt 28:1-10; Lk 24:1-12

25:31-46 The separation of **the sheep** and **the goats** was not a parable per se, even though it had some parabolic elements: sheep, goats, and the **shepherd**. The story illustrated a truth: God knows who belongs to Him. The story had overtones similar to Matthew 10:40-42. Though this story has been subject to varied interpretations, given the specific context, it is probably best to understand **the least of these brothers of Mine** to be Christ's disciples (25:40). The fate of the nations was determined by how they treated Christ's followers, who endured severe suffering for the gospel's sake. Jesus identified with His followers to the extent that He saw their treatment as His (Ac 9:5). Those who treated His followers with kindness would be rewarded; those who neglected or ignored them would themselves be ignored and rejected in the end. To respond to Jesus' love was to obey His commands. To obey His commands was to reach out to others in love. Christ's divine authority over all nations, which came into sharp focus in chapter 28, was briefly highlighted here.

An Account of Jesus' Ultimate Destiny (26:1–28:20)

Passion and crucifixion (26:1–27:66)

26:1-56 Thursday evening. The plot against Jesus was twofold. First, the Jewish leaders **conspired** to **kill Jesus**. Second, Judas, spurred on by what he considered a "waste" of oil for Jesus' anointing (Jn 12:3-6), plotted with the Jewish leaders to **hand** Jesus **over** to them. Sandwiched between these two acts of treachery was the one act of faith in this entire section: Jesus' anointing in Bethany. And this act was performed by a woman. In a sequence similar to the one in Matthew 15:21-28, where the Gentile woman's faith is juxtaposed with the rebellion of the Jewish leaders and the

unbelief of the disciples, so the faithfulness of a woman is spotlighted here.

The **Passover** was the setting for many hurtful events for Jesus. At this last Passover, Jesus predicted Judas's betrayal, Peter's denial, and the disciples' abandonment of Him. The Passover, celebrated every year, was a very important feast commemorating the delivery of Israel out of Egypt. The elements of the ceremony observed by the Jews included the following:

- A blessing and the first cup of wine: "I will deliver you . . ." (Ex 6:6).

- The meal of unleavened bread, bitter herbs, greens, and roasted lamb, each symbolizing details associated with the first Passover.

- Second cup of wine: "I will free you from slavery to them . . ." (Ex 6:6).

- The singing of a song of praise (Pss 113–114).

- The breaking of bread and the eating of the meal.

- Third cup of wine and the end of meal: "I will redeem you . . ." (Ex 6:6).

- The singing of another song of praise (Pss 115–118).

- Fourth cup of wine: "I will take you as My people, and I will be your God" (Ex 6:7).[23]

While reciting this liturgy, Jesus proclaimed that a new Passover was about to be inaugurated by the shedding of His blood. Jesus then instituted the Lord's Supper by using two symbols—the **unleavened bread** (a reminder of the hasty departure of God's people from Egypt, Ex 12, and a symbol of His **body**, which would be broken at His death, v. 26) and the **fruit of the vine** (symbolic of His **blood**, which would be shed on the cross, v. 28). This celebratory event looked back to Jesus' death on the cross and forward to His return. The betrayal by Judas signaled the beginning process leading to the new covenant. Matthew added that Judas asked if Jesus had spoken of him, and Jesus replied that it was indeed he (i.e., Judas). Peter and the other disciples protested that they would **never deny** Christ, even if refusal to deny Him meant death.

But then they went to **Gethsemane** (lit. "oil press," the garden located across the Kidron Valley at the foot of the Mount of Olives), which became the place where loyalty was to be tested. The Father confirmed that His Son's suffering was indeed His will; and Jesus, in prayer and anguish, submitted to His Father's will. The disciples closest to Jesus (Peter, James, and John, who were with Him on the Mount of Transfiguration), on the other hand, were not even able to remain faithful to pray with Him. When Judas came with his companions and greeted Jesus with the traditional kiss of friendship (which in this case became the "kiss of death"), Jesus' disciples abandoned Him, thus failing the test of loyalty. The **30 pieces of silver** paid to Judas would have been the value of a male or female slave gored to death by an ox (26:15; see Ex 21:32).

To highlight further Jesus' loyalty to the Father's will, Matthew added the words of Jesus concerning the **legions of angels** whom His Father would send upon His request for deliverance. But the Scriptures detailing the will of His Father had to be fulfilled. If Jesus had requested deliverance from His assignment, the Father's will would not have been fulfilled. So Matthew once again emphasized the supremacy of God's will in everything.

26:57–27:66 Friday. Jesus was condemned by the Sanhedrin, denied by Peter, handed over to Pilate, and eventually crucified on what has long been called "Good" Friday. Matthew highlighted the fact that Jesus went to the Jews first, where He was placed **under oath** and asked if He were **the Messiah, the Son of God** (v. 26:23). Jesus answered affirmatively and announced His return, when He would come in power and glory.

Servant Girl Matthew 26:69-75	
Reference	**Biographical Information**
Mt 26:69-70	An unnamed servant girl used by God to confront Peter, who denied Christ
Mk 14:66	One of the high priest's servants
Jn 18:17	The slave girl who was the doorkeeper
See also Mk 14:66-68; Lk 22:56-57; and Jn 18:17.	

Then Jesus was sent to a Gentile, the Roman leader **Pilate**, where He was again asked if He were **the King of the Jews**. Jesus acknowledged that fact. During both inquisitions, to the amazement of His opponents, Jesus' demeanor was one of quiet acceptance and gentle response, in keeping with the prophecies spoken about Him (Is 42:1-4). Before both the Jews and the Gentiles, Jesus had made His confession to being the Messiah, the Son of God, the King of Israel.

Between Christ's two confessions concerning Himself are the confessions of two others—Peter and Judas. Their confessions revealed much about these men. Matthew, who alone added the account of Judas's hanging, intended the reader to understand that Peter's confession led to repentance, but Judas's words of regret merely signaled his remorse and thus ultimately his doom. Instead of returning to Jesus as Peter did, Judas went to Christ's enemies, who could offer no help at all. These events fulfilled Scripture. Divine foreknowledge and sovereignty, together with human responsibility, came into play here as part of the divine economy.

God knew what Judas would do. Yet Judas made his own choices; he had every opportunity to repent, but he chose to go his own way (vv. 14,25,48-50). Judas later regretted what he did; he was full of remorse (Gk. *metameletheis*, "regret, be sorry, change of mind"), and he even returned the money he received for betraying Jesus (27:3-5). However, he did not repent. **Blood money** could **not** be placed **in the temple treasury** (27:6-7); so the legalistic religious leaders, wanting to observe the letter of the law, used the money to buy a **field** in which **foreigners** would be buried.

Jesus. The people chose a hardened criminal over Jesus (27:20-21). Pilate then declared himself innocent of Jesus' blood. The crowd answered Pilate by saying, **His blood be on us and on our children!** These words have often been used to promote the view that the Jewish people and their descendents were solely responsible for the death of Jesus. This belief has fueled anti-Semitic causes and crimes for 2,000 years. This view is a grave distortion of Scripture. According to Scripture, all people through every generation until today had a role in the death of Jesus. Isaiah 53, identified as the heart of God's message of redemption in Scripture, spoke to the role of God and of mankind in Jesus' suffering and death.

Pilate's Wife
Matthew 27:11-25
Pilate's Interrogation
"Don't You [Jesus] hear how much they are testifying against You?" (v. 13). "Who is it you want me to release for you— Barabbas, or Jesus who is called Messiah?" (v. 17). "What should I do then with Jesus, who is called Messiah?" (v. 22). "I am innocent of this man's blood" (v. 24).
His Wife's Intuition
"Have nothing to do with that righteous man, for today I've suffered terribly in a dream because of Him!" (v. 19).

Mary, Mother of Jesus	
Matthew 27:55-61	
Her Story	**His Story**
Followed Jesus to Jerusalem	Mt 27:55; Mk 15:40; Lk 23:49
Sacrificed her son to ministry	Mt 10:3; Lk 24:18
Ministered to Jesus	Mt 27:55; Mk 15:41; Lk 8:2-3
Supported His work	Lk 8:2-3
Witnessed His death on the cross	Mt 27:56; Mk 15:40; Lk 23:49
Anointed His dead body	Lk 23:56
Observed His burial in Joseph of Arimathea's tomb	Mt 27:61; Mk 15:47
Visited the empty tomb	Mt 28:1; Mk 16:1-4; Lk 24:2
Heard from an angel of His resurrection	Mt 28:5; Mk 16:5-8; Lk 24:6
Met the risen Savior	Mt 28:9-10
Told others of His resurrection	Mt 28:11; Lk 24:9-10

The inclusion of the words from Pilate's wife concerning the innocence of Christ (27:19) and the crowd's statement claiming responsibility for Jesus' death were also peculiar to Matthew's passion account (27:25). Pilate himself evidently believed Jesus was innocent, since he tried to release him by offering his accusers a deal he thought they could not resist. He offered to release one of two prisoners: Barabbas, a violent insurrectionist, or

Yet He Himself bore our sicknesses, and He carried our pains; but we in turn regarded Him stricken, struck down by God, and afflicted. But He was pierced because of our transgressions, crushed because of our iniquities; punishment for our peace was on Him, and we are healed by His wounds. . . . Yet the LORD was pleased to crush Him, and He made Him sick (Is 53:4-5,10).

In addition to the perspective expressed by the Prophet Isaiah, Jesus spoke of His own death as a choice He actively embraced: "No one takes it [My life] from Me, but I lay it down on My own. I have the right to lay it down, and I have the right to take it up again" (Jn 10:18).

So while Matthew's Gospel showed the prominence of the Jewish leadership in the death of Jesus, their role has to be interpreted in a much wider context. God's grace is offered regardless of the part any individual played in the death of His Son. In the 30 years following Jesus' resurrection the most ardent disciple of Jesus, Saul of Tarsus, was a man of the same mind-set as those crying, **Crucify Him!** He had given his full energies to persecuting followers of Christ until he himself met Christ and sought His forgiveness.

Matthew gave careful details of Jesus' crucifixion, of His burial, and of the measures taken to ensure that no one stole Jesus' body from the tomb given by Joseph of Arimathea. He also gave attention to some of the cosmic events surrounding the death of Jesus (27:39-44, 51-53).

Resurrection (28:1-20)

28:1-20 Sunday. Only Matthew recorded the visit of the chief priests and the Pharisees to Pilate. They asked for a guard to secure Christ's tomb. Christ's teaching concerning His resurrection was well-known, even among His enemies. Matthew recorded that the women conquered their fears and ran back to report to the 11 disciples the good news of Christ's resurrection. On their way the risen Christ **met them**, and they **worshiped Him** (v. 9).

Uniquely in Matthew, the scheme of the Jewish leaders to explain away Christ's resurrection was recorded (vv. 11-15). Matthew undoubtedly recorded this event to counter **this story**. Known as the "Great Commission," verses 16-20 summarized Matthew's main themes found throughout his Gospel: the importance of discipleship, the universal mission of the church, Christ's commandments as a reflection of God's will for all believers, and the perpetual teaching ministry of Christ as the final and sovereign Interpreter of the Law.

The risen Savior's strategy, simple yet profound, was explained clearly. Jesus first called His disciples to Himself. He took time to teach them; He let them learn about Him by spending time with Him. Then He sent them out. The structure of the passage indicates that the heart of disciple-making is simple to understand:

- Going in evangelism in order to **make disciples** (v. 19a).

- **Baptizing** the converts—those who have accepted Christ (v. 19b).

- **Teaching** the baptized disciples to grow through obedience to the Lord's standards (v. 20a).

Sharing the gospel was vitally important, but Jesus also challenged His disciples to lead those who embraced the gospel into obedience to Christ through believer's baptism and through learning the disciplines of the Christian life.

Other observations can be made from the account of Jesus' final days as recorded in Matthew's Gospel:

Heart to Heart:
Women and the Great Commission

The best way to appreciate the presence of women disciples in the New Testament is to study the Great Commission in context. The female disciples were not only there at the most difficult and dangerous point in Jesus' ministry, but they also became indispensable as models of how Christ's followers were to pursue His marching orders for the church, even until the end of the age. Yet, although you may understand the vital parts of the Great Commission, you may still easily miss the important role of the women disciples. Certainly, the presence of women in the various passages that led to the challenging commissioning appeal is obvious. But just how closely these events tie the women to those statements is frequently overlooked.

When Jesus gave His apostles the command to witness and make disciples, He used contextual examples of women disciples to illustrate what it means to be a disciple and to share a witness. Therefore, you must consider the presence and roles of the women seen in the broad context surrounding the words of the Great Commission. Striking artistic portraits of women disciples have been blended together to make a wonderful composite of devotion to Christ and a commitment to share the gospel. As a woman in the modern era, you have an open door and the divine anointing to direct your energies and creativity into using every opportunity to share the gospel with those who cross your path.

- When Jesus was arrested in the garden of Gethsemane, initially Peter responded with the sword and was rebuked by Jesus. The disciples all "deserted Him and ran away" (26:56), perhaps seriously questioning their own personal commitment to Christ and opening themselves to public scrutiny of the level of commitment in their discipleship.

- The women were also mentioned as they followed Christ from afar to the cross and to the tomb (27:55-56), along with Joseph of Arimathea, who had become a disciple (27:57).

- The women at the empty tomb were the first to witness the resurrection and were instructed by Christ to tell the apostles of His resurrection (28:5-10).

Women were present at both the crucifixion (27:55-56) and burial (27:61) of Jesus, and they were the first ones to see Him after His resurrection (28:9-10). They were, in effect, commissioned by the risen Lord to announce His resurrection to His disciples (28:8-10), which added to their ministries to the Lord. The devoted women who remained with Jesus at the cross and followed Him to the tomb were in the right place at the right time to deliver the glorious news of His resurrection. The Lord honored their faithfulness by entrusting them with these wonderful words of hope and victory to be delivered to the disciples.

Bibliography

*Albright, W. F., and C. S. Mann. *Matthew.* Garden City: Doubleday, 1971.

*Alexander, J. A. *The Gospel According to Matthew.* New York: Scribner, 1860.

*Allison, D., and W. D. Davies. *A Critical and Exegetical Commentary on the Gospel According to St. Matthew.* ICC, 3 vols. Edinburgh: T & T Clark, 1988–97.

Balch, David L., ed. *Social History of the Matthean Community.* Minneapolis: Fortress, 1991.

Blomberg, Craig L. *Matthew.* New American Commentary, vol. 22. Nashville: Broadman and Holman, 1992.

Broadus, John. *Commentary on the Gospel of Matthew.* Valley Forge: American Baptist Publication Society, 1886. Reprint, Grand Rapids: Kregel Publications, 1990. Citation is to the Kregel edition.

*Carson, D. A. *Matthew.* Expositor's Bible Commentary, vol. 8, ed. Frank E. Gaebelein. Grand Rapids: Zondervan, 1984.

*France, R. T. *The Gospel According to Matthew* [rev. TNTC]. Leicester: IVP; Grand Rapids: Eerdmans, 1985.

*France, R. T. *Matthew: Evangelist and Teacher.* Exeter: Patermoster; Grand Rapids: Zondervan, 1989.

Green, Michael. *Matthew for Today.* London: Hodder & Stoughton, 1988; Dallas: Word, 1989.

Keener, Craig. *A Commentary on the Gospel of Matthew.* Grand Rapids: Eerdmans, 1999.

Mounce, Robert H. *Matthew* [NIBC]. Peabody: Hendrickson, 1991.

Patterson, Dorothy Kelley. *BeAttitudes for Women.* Nashville: Broadman and Holman Publishers, 2000.

*Ridderbos, H. N. *Matthew* [BSC]. Grand Rapids: Zondervan, 1987.

* For Advanced Study

Notes

[1] Papias is quoted in Eusebius' *Ecclesiastical History* 3.39.16.
[2] Irenaeus, *Against Heresies* 3.1.1.
[3] See Eusebius, *Ecclesiastical History* 5.8.2.
[4] The layout of my outline was adapted from Craig L. Blomberg, *Matthew*, New American Commentary, vol. 22 (Nashville: Broadman and Holman, 1992), 128–29.
[5] D. A. Carson, *Matthew,* Expositor's Bible Commentary, vol. 8 (Grand Rapids: Zondervan, 1984), 62.
[6] The word "whom" in verse 16 is feminine, making it clear that only Mary is Jesus' biological parent.
[7] R. T. France, *The Gospel According to Matthew,* (Grand Rapids: Eerdmans, 1985), 40.
[8] See J. Gresham Machen, *The Virgin Birth of Christ* (New York: Harper & Row, 1930), for one of the most solid defenses of the virgin birth narratives.
[9] Blomberg, 202.
[10] Dale C. Allenson Jr., *The Structure of the Sermon on the Mount,* JBL 106 (1987): 423–25.
[11] Dorothy Kelley Patterson, *BeAttitudes for Women* (Nashville: Broadman and Holman, 2000), 10.
[12] Ibid., 48.
[13] Ibid., 68.
[14] Ibid., 86–89.
[15] Ibid., 200.
[16] Carson, 299–300.

[17] Joachim Jeremias, *Rediscovering the Parables* (New York: Scribner, 1966), 181.

[18] E. P. Sanders, *Jesus and Judaism* (London: SCM; Philadelphia: Fortress, 1985), 141–50.

[19] Simon Kistemaker, *The Parables of Jesus* (Grand Rapids: Baker, 1980), 29.

[20] Ridderbos, *Matthew* (Grand Rapids: Zondervan, 1987), 346.

[21] For a more in-depth study on divorce and remarriage, see Craig Blomberg, "Marriage, Divorce, Remarriage and Celibacy: An Exegesis of Matthew 19:3-12," *Trinity Journal* n.s. 11 (1990): 161–96.

[22] John Broadus, *Commentary on the Gospel of Matthew* (Grand Rapids: Kregel Publications, 1990), 493.

[23] Graham N. Stanton, *The Gospels and Jesus* (Oxford: OUP, 1989), 257.

M ARK

Introduction

Mark's Gospel is straightforward yet vivid, succinct yet unrelentingly passionate, simplistic yet deeply profound. The simplicity of its message is a no-non-
sense account of the life, death, and resurrection of Jesus Christ. There are no
genealogies, no details on the birth of the Christ child, no description of His
childhood. Mark began with Jesus as an adult entering His ministry.

Mark's facts are accurate; he did indeed record events of history. However, he
presented his material as a preacher would his sermon. Even historical facts are presented in a fresh, vigorous, and passionate way. The book's simplicity has led many
to conclude that this brief Gospel is basically a superficial account of Jesus' life.

Mark often used a few verses to present what other Gospels would describe in
several chapters. For example, compare the description of Jesus' temptation in Matthew 4:1-11 with Mark's account (1:12-13). But closer examination of the shortest
account of the life of Jesus reveals a straightforward unfolding of the gospel with a
keen analysis and spiritual depth appealing even to the most serious student of the
life of Christ. Yet every mother will be delighted to know that Mark presents the
good news of Jesus Christ so simply that even a child can understand it.

Mark's Gospel can be divided into two main sections. The first eight chapters
are filled with action-packed narratives recounting Jesus' miracles and the crowd's
unceasing amazement, focusing on the power of His ministry. The fast-moving
pace of these accounts was emphasized by the use of the adverb IMMEDI-
ATELY (Gk. *euthus*, "straight, right, upright"). The word occurred first in
the quote from Isaiah 40:3 as "straight" (1:3), an obvious reference to preparation for the coming of the Messiah. The word continued to be used
throughout the book in the Greek text as an introduction to section divisions
(1:12). In English, the word is translated in various ways but with the same
idea of denoting urgent or straightforward action. Mark used this word more
than forty times. By comparison, the word was used seven times by Matthew,
once by Luke, and only three times by John. In the Greek text, Mark frequently
used the "historical present," a grammatical device in which present-tense verbs
are vehicles for past-tense action, giving a more vivid and moving picture, especially when introducing transitions in Jesus' ministry (e.g., 1:12,21,40).

The last eight chapters turn to Christ's passion. The fast-paced tempo of the
book slows down immensely as the suffering and death of Christ become the
all-consuming focus. Some have argued that Mark, as no other Gospel, reflects
the centrality of the cross in early Christian thought.

Title

Although the title of the Gospel of Mark bears Mark's name, the book is anonymous, without mention of anyone as the specific author throughout its text.

Mark's assumption could have been that his penning of the volume was common knowledge and not necessary to mention, or he may have wished to defer any attention to his recording of the Gospel in order to emphasize the fact that ultimately the words came from the Holy Spirit who guided his work. Perhaps even the exact wording of the title, which has been associated with the book from the end of the first century, suggests the latter explanation. At the very least, the association of Mark with this Gospel in its title indicated his early connection to the recording of its message. The Gospel "According to Mark" (Gk. *kata Markon*) clearly suggested that the Gospel itself was not Mark's but rather was Mark's account of the Gospel. The content of the Gospel came from God alone.

Setting

Tradition, as well as much of the external evidence, has associated Mark's Gospel with Rome. Three sources—the anti-Marcionite Prologue to Mark, Irenaeus, and Clement of Alexandria—supported a Roman origin. Chrysostom (AD 400), on the other hand, attributed origin of Mark's writing to an Egyptian setting (around AD 200). However, the internal evidence fits better with Rome. The Roman historian Tacitus described in detail the tragic and devastating fire that destroyed more than half the city of Rome in AD 64. Strong rumors placed the blame for setting this fire on the emperor Nero, who, in turn, tried to hold the Christians responsible. The emperor's malicious attack opened the door for unprecedented persecution of the fledgling followers of Christ.

> But neither human help, nor imperial munificence, nor all the modes of placating Heaven, could stifle scandal or dispel the belief that the fire had taken place by order. Therefore, to scotch the rumor, Nero substituted as culprits, and punished with the utmost refinements of cruelty, a class of men, loathed for their vices, whom the crowd styled Christians. Christus, the founder of the name, had undergone the death penalty in the reign of Tiberius, by sentence of the procurator Pontius Pilatus, and the pernicious superstition was checked for a moment, only to break out once more, not merely in Judaea, the home of the disease, but in the capital itself, where all things horrible or shameful in the world collect and find a vogue. First, then, the confessed members of the sect were arrested; next, on their disclosures, vast numbers were convicted, not so much on the count of arson as for hatred of the human race. And derision accompanied their end; they were covered with wild beasts' skins and torn to death by dogs; or they were fastened on crosses, and when daylight failed were burned to serve as lamps by night. Nero had offered his Gardens for the spectacle, and gave an exhibition in his Circus, mixing with the crowd in the habit of a charioteer . . . in spite of a guilt which had earned the most exemplary punishment, there rose a sentiment of pity, due to the impression that they were being sacrificed not for the welfare of the state but to the ferocity of a single man.[1]

In view of this severe persecution and for many even martyrdom, Mark wrote to comfort believers; but in an intensely personal and practical way, he also prepared them for possible suffering by presenting them with the Suffering Servant. The way of Christ is the way of the cross, and Mark prepared his readers for their suffering by giving them a vivid account of the suffering of Jesus. About one third of the Gospel of Mark was devoted to the death of Jesus. His suffering was made explicit not only in the passion account but also all through Mark's narratives about the life of Christ:

- In the temptation experience, Jesus was with wild animals (1:13).

- Jesus suffered from misunderstandings on the part of His family (3:21) and people in general (3:22,30).

- He described in detail the cost of discipleship (8:34-38).

- He made references to persecutions (10:30,33-34,45; 13:8-9,11-13). Mark's ultimate message was noted in this way: "Faithfulness and obedience as a follower of Jesus Christ will inevitably lead to suffering and perhaps even death."[2]

Genre

The movement of the events recorded in this Gospel was more rapid than the pace of the other Gospels. One might call it a journalistic style in which the emphasis was on presenting the facts without augmentation and adornment. All three Synoptic Gospels (Matthew, Mark, and Luke) covered much of the same material. Although Matthew and Luke recorded more events, Mark often tended to give more details on the events he recorded. His words were colorful and full of action as he emphasized what Jesus was doing rather than what He was teaching. Yet Mark presented Jesus as the Master Teacher, while showing His humanity in having vividly presented a full range of emotions—from heartfelt compassion (1:41) to righteous indignation (3:5).

Author

Although the Gospel of Mark is anonymous in the sense that its author did not specifically identify himself in the text, the early church fathers, including Irenaeus, Tertullian, Clement of Alexandria, Origen, Jerome, and the Muratorian canon (the oldest known list of books of the New Testament, AD 180–200), all seemed to point unanimously to John Mark, the young companion of Peter and Paul, as the author of the Gospel that even now bears his name (see Ac 12:12,25; 13:5,13; 15:37; Col 4:10; 2 Tm 4:11; Phm 24; 1 Pt 5:13). In some of the references to John Mark, he is simply called John. The context identifies him with certainty, however. John Mark accompanied Paul and Barnabas when they returned to Antioch from Jerusalem (Ac 12:25), and he also accompanied these men on their first missionary journey (Ac 13:5). Obviously, he was an extraordinary young man who was called out for unique service and ministry.

Unfortunately, Mark was perhaps remembered most for his dispute with Paul, which began with his impromptu desertion of the missionary team at Perga in Pamphylia (Ac 13:13). Paul reacted in a very negative way and refused to accept Mark's return for the second missionary journey. A fight over this impetuous young man caused Barnabas, a cousin of John Mark, to leave his partnership with Paul (Ac 15:36-39). Barnabas and Mark then sailed for Cyprus, at which time mention of them faded out of Acts. Yet Mark must have found a way back into Paul's favor since he appeared in the Pauline epistles (Col 4:10; Phm 24). At the end of his life, the Apostle Paul gave evidence of Mark's full restoration to his fellowship and ministry (2 Tm 4:11). Mark was probably a Jewish Christian from the Judean province. His mother provided a meeting place for the early church in Jerusalem (Ac 12:12).

Some modern scholars reject Markan authorship for these reasons:

- The author could not have been Jewish because the Gospel lacks a Jewish flavor.

- The author could not have been a companion of Paul because this Gospel lacks Pauline theological emphases.

- The author could not have learned the material from Peter because of the negative ways in which the disciples, especially Peter, are portrayed.

- The material for the Gospel could not have come from one primary source because critical studies have shown a complex history for the Gospel tradition.

In response to these critical suppositions, many conservative scholars have made observations:

- The more Gentile flavoring of the Gospel merely points out that the audience to whom Mark was addressing his message was primarily Gentile. The Gentile flavor of the content of this Gospel does not prove that the author was non-Jewish.

- The emphasis on the cross in the latter part of the Gospel is indeed consistent with Pauline thought, and in such a brief Gospel, and one influenced primarily by Peter, one would not expect an extensive discussion of Pauline theology.

- Actually one would expect the more negative view of the disciples, especially Peter, as more likely coming from Peter himself, who was likely Mark's primary source.

- Mark's dependence on Peter for much of his material does not necessarily rule out the use of other sources.

- In light of the fact that Mark was an obscure character with mixed success in ministry endeavors, anyone who wanted this work to be taken seriously would not likely have selected John Mark as the author if he were not indeed the author. Whomever one selects as the author, the interpretation of the Gospel depends little on the human author since the primary focus for all Scripture is its divine origin.

The most important piece of evidence supporting John Mark as the author came from the early church historian, Eusebius. In *Ecclesiastical History* Eusebius recorded the words of Papias, who cited an elder named John (probably the Apostle John) as teaching that John Mark was the interpreter of Peter:

> Mark became Peter's interpreter and wrote accurately all that he remembered, not indeed, in order, of the things said or done by the Lord. For he had not heard the Lord, nor had he followed him, but later on, as I said, followed Peter, who used to give teaching as necessity demanded but not making, as it were, an arrangement of the Lord's oracles, so that Mark did nothing wrong in writing down single points as he remembered them. For to one thing he gave attention, to leave out nothing of what he had heard and to make no false statements in them.[3]

The early history of the church thus had a strong tradition identifying Mark as the author of this Gospel primarily because of Mark's close association with Peter as his primary source and an eyewitness to the words of Christ and the events of His life and ministry. The modern objections do not outweigh the overwhelming testimony of the early church that John Mark penned this Gospel.[4]

Date

With regard to dating the Gospel, the external evidence is divided; consequently, the Gospel cannot be dated with precision. Eusebius quoted Clement as saying:

> When Peter had preached the word publicly in Rome and announced the gospel by the Spirit, those present, of whom there were many, besought Mark, since for a long time he had followed him and remembered what had been said, to record his words. Mark did this, and communicated the gospel to those who made request of him. When Peter knew of it, he neither actively prevented nor encouraged the undertaking.[5]

Irenaeus, on the other hand, has been understood to suggest that Mark wrote his Gospel after Peter died. According to Irenaeus, Mark wrote after the "exodus" of Peter and Paul. He stated specifically that "Mark the disciple and interpreter of Peter also transmitted to us what he had written about what Peter had preached."[6] EXODUS (Gk. *exodus*, "departure, death") in this context may simply mean that Peter "exited" from Rome to minister somewhere else. Even if this were not the case, Irenaeus stated only that the transmission of the Gospel, not its composition, occurred after Peter's death.

Internal evidence does not seem to demand a date after AD 70. Objections that have been raised against a date earlier than AD 70 are generally motivated by antisupernaturalism. The argument is that Jesus' "prediction" of the destruction of the temple demanded a post-70 date for composition of the Gospel. This argument against an earlier date loses credibility *unless* one believes that Jesus was unable to predict the future. If the Gospel were dated after AD 70, one would have expected Mark to mention a catastrophe of the magnitude of the destruction of the temple and even Jerusalem.

The general consensus is that if Mark wrote during Peter's lifetime, and external evidence generally seems to support such a conclusion; and if Peter was martyred during Nero's persecution before AD 68, then Mark must have penned his Gospel sometime between AD 64 and 68.

Recipients

As is true with Matthew and John, Mark did not specifically identify his recipients, but many internal indicators point to Roman believers.

- Fewer references from the Old Testament are made than are found in other Gospels.

- Mark tended to explain Jewish traditions and his translation of Aramaic words or phrases (e.g., 3:17; 5:41), perhaps indicating a Gentile audience who would have needed such explanations (e.g., 7:2-4).

- Mark dealt quite a bit with persecution and martyrdom (8:34-38; 13:9-13), which would be of special interest to Roman Christians who had suffered greatly under Nero and other emperors.

Major Themes

The Message about Jesus as good news. Some scholars have pointed out that Mark may have been among the first to refer to the story of Jesus Himself (and not merely His teachings) as the gospel, *the good news.* In several places throughout his work, Mark wove the term *gospel* into his story (8:35; 10:29). The Greek word (*euangelion*, also translated *good news*) occurs seven times in Mark, four times in Matthew, and never in Luke or John. In any case, Mark was faithful to gather and systematize the activities as well as the teachings of Jesus. Although especially committed to presenting the suffering and death of Jesus, Mark also was careful to present a full Christology in describing Jesus as fully human and fully divine. Although he opened the door for the Gospel to the Gentiles, he was faithful to identify Christ as the Son of David and the Jewish Messiah.

Imminent eschatology. Mark was faithful to declare that Christ would return and that no one knew when He would return. Mark knew well the tendency for people to attempt to tie Christ's return with a particular historical event. He then refused to be preoccupied with the end of the age in the future but rather put his emphasis on calling the faithful to devote themselves to being faithful disciples in the present.

Disciples and discipleship. With regard to the Twelve, Mark frequently recorded their failures and misunderstandings. Their hearts were hard, they displayed a continual lack of faith, and they often did not grasp the significance of Christ's miracles (4:40; 6:51-52; 8:4,14-21). They lacked the faith to carry out Christ's commands (9:14-29). Their "blindness" was contrasted with Christ's miracles of opening the eyes of the blind (8:22-26; 10:46-52). Ultimately, as is well-known, Peter denied Christ, Judas betrayed Him, and the disciples fled when Christ was arrested. However, Mark also showed that the Twelve did respond to Christ's initial call (1:16-20; 2:13-14; 3:13-19), and they did receive the secrets of the kingdom while outsiders were kept in the dark (4:14-20; 7:17-23).

For Mark, following Christ brought not only the expected joy of ministry and commitment but also the sorrow of rejection and suffering. He saw the disciples of Jesus as unexpected but genuine believers, ordinary people with the same successes and failures as any new convert. Perhaps that is one reason for Mark's very practical approach to discipleship.

Mark's Portrait of Jesus

Son of God. Since Mark opened his Gospel with this title for Jesus (1:1), clearly its use guided his narrative in a significant way. Mark's argument that Jesus was the Son of God was coupled with a demonstration of His divine power. Jesus' interactions with the crowds, His many healings and exorcisms, and His stilling of the storm all demonstrated His power. When Jesus died, even the Roman centurion described Christ as God's Son. In light of these examples, clearly Mark intended to present Jesus as more than merely human.

Son of Man. In Matthew's Gospel, the title "Son of Man" was a favorite phrase Jesus used of Himself (Mt 8:20). In the Gospel of Mark, this title was used in the same way and was usually connected to Jesus' humanity and His suffering (8:31).

Redeemer. Jesus declared that He came to give His life as a ransom for many (10:45). While this phrase did not recur in Mark's Gospel, the great emphasis on the passion narrative showed the significance of redemption for Mark. Indeed, Mark seems to have devoted more space than any other Gospel writer to the passion narrative. This emphasis on the cross is consistent with early Christianity. Without question Mark presented Christ as One who had come to suffer.

Healer. Mark's devotion of so much attention to Christ's healing ministry is significant for an understanding of his portrait of the Savior. One can find in Mark's Christology an attempt to keep two essential truths about Christ in balance: His ultimate glory and the centrality of the cross. Perhaps Mark's Gospel is the best at balancing an emphasis on both Jesus' divinity and His humanity.

Christ. Jesus' title, the "Christ" (Gk. *christos*, the "Anointed One," equivalent to the Hebrew title Messiah), occurs in the opening statement (1:1) but is not used again until the account of Peter's confession (8:29). The title occurs eight times in the Greek text of Mark's Gospel. Although appearing only once in the first half of the Gospel, it is significant nonetheless. Chapters 1–8 seem to build toward the riveting confession of the Apostle Peter.

Appearances of Women in Mark's Gospel

The prominence of women among Jesus' devoted and loyal contemporaries is notable. They were drawn to Him by their own needs and by His powerful presence and message. They came for healing, for forgiveness, for the power to find a new and fulfilling life, and for His benediction of blessing on their children. The examples in the Gospels are many:

- The timid woman who touched the tassel on His robe; when found out, she "came with fear and trembling, fell down before Him" to thank him (Mk 5:33).

- The aggressive Canaanite woman, who would not be put off by the fact that she was not Jewish (Mk 7:25-30).

- The women who provided for Him out of their own resources (Lk 8:3).

- The mothers whose children He took "in His arms, He laid His hands on them and blessed them" (Mk 10:15-16). The plural verb has an understood subject. From this historical era, mothers would have likely been the ones presenting their children. "People" can be understood as the subject, but the word *laos*, meaning people, is not found in the Greek text.

When women were deep in sin, Jesus forgave them (Jn 4:1-42; 8:1-8). When they were humiliated, He stood up for them (Jn 8:1-8). When they suffered social wrongs, He defended them (Lk 7:36-50). When they had abilities to offer, He used these (Lk 8:2-3); and even when they expressed effusive devotion to Him, He lovingly reminded them of the main thing: "A woman from the crowd raised her voice and said to Him, 'The womb that bore You and the one who nursed You are blessed!' He said, 'Even more, those who hear the word of God and keep it are blessed!'" (Lk 11:27-28). The word translated EVEN MORE (Gk. *menoun*, "rather, on the contrary, indeed, much more") is used correctively, not to chastise words of devotion but to note that words in themselves are not enough. Mary was blessed more because she shared in the blessings of all who would hear the word of God and keep it.

Pronunciation Guide

Alphaeus	al FEE uhs	Herodias	hih ROH dih uhs
Bartholomew	bahr THAHL uh myoo	Idumea	id yoo MEE uh
Bartimaeus	bahr tih MEE uhs	Iscariot	iss KAR ih aht
Beelzebul	bee EL zee buhl	Jairus	JIGH ruhs, JAY uh ruhs
Bethphage	BETH fuh jee, BETH fayj	Judean	joo DEE uhn
Bethsaida	beth-SAY ih duh	Nazareth	NAZ uh reth
Boanerges	boh uh NUHR jeez	Pharisees	FEHR uh sees
Capernaum	kuh PUHR nay uhm	Sadducees	SAD joo sees
Galilee	GAL ih lee	Sidon	SIGH duhn
Gennesaret	gih NESS uh ret	Syrophoenican	sigh roh-fih NEE shuhn
Gerasenes	GEHR uh seens	Thaddaeus	THAD ih uhs
Gethsemane	geth SEM uh nih	Tyre	TIGHR
Golgatha	GAHL guh thuh, gahl GAHTH uh	Zebedee	ZEB uh dee

Outline[7]

I. PROLOGUE TO THE GOSPEL (1:1-13)
- A. Preparing the Way by John the Baptist (1:1-8)
- B. Going Through the Waters of Baptism (1:9-11)
- C. Experiencing Temptation in the Wilderness (1:12-13)

II. THE MINISTRY OF CHRIST IN GALILEE (1:14–8:30)
- A. The Authority of Jesus and the Blindness of the Pharisees (1:14–3:6)
  1. The selection and enlistment of disciples (1:14-20)
  2. Jesus' miracles of healing (1:21–2:5)
  3. Jesus' conflict with religious leaders (2:6–3:6)
- B. The Parables and Signs of Jesus and the Blindness of the People (3:7–6:6a)
  1. Ministering to the multitude (3:7-12)
  2. Setting apart the 12 apostles (3:13-19)
  3. Encountering opposition (3:20-35)
  4. Teaching through parables (4:1-34)
  5. Demonstrating power with miracles (4:35–6:6a)
- C. Jesus' Ministry to the Gentiles and the Blindness of His Disciples (6:6b–8:30)
  1. Defining the mission and experiencing opposition (6:6b-29)
  2. Continuing the miracles and teaching (6:30–8:26)
  3. Hearing Peter's confession of faith (8:27-30)

III. THE PASSION OF CHRIST (8:31–16:20)
- A. Predictions of Death and Defining of Discipleship (8:31–10:52)
  1. The cross and resurrection foreshadowed (8:31-33)

2. The requirements for discipleship (8:34-38)
3. The transformation (9:1-13)
4. Healing a boy (9:14-29)
5. Announcement of betrayal (9:30-32)
6. True servanthood (9:33-50)
7. Teaching on divorce (10:1-12)
8. Blessing of the children (10:13-16)
9. Jesus and a seeker (10:17-31)
10. Discussion with His disciples (10:32-52)

B. Jesus' Teachings at the Temple (11:1–13:37)
 1. Triumphal entry and judgment (11:1-26)
 2. Teaching and debate (11:27–12:44)
 3. Prediction of destruction and announcement of Christ's return (13:1-37)
C. The Climax of Jesus' Life (14:1–16:20)
 1. Preparation for suffering (14:1-72)
 2. Crucifixion and burial (15:1-47)
 3. Resurrection (16:1-20)

Exposition of the Text

A PROLOGUE TO THE GOSPEL (1:1-13)

Preparing the Way by John the Baptist (1:1-8)

1:1 The lengthy opening phrase provided a title for the Gospel—**The beginning of the gospel of Jesus Christ, the Son of God**. The GOSPEL (Gk. *euangelion*, "good news") of JESUS (a transliteration or anglicized form of the Greek rendition of the Hebrew *Joshua*, meaning "Yahweh saves") CHRIST (Gk. *Christos*, "anointed one," equivalent to Hebrew *Mashiach*, a title so closely associated with Jesus that it became part of His name) was further defined with the phrase describing Jesus Christ as "the Son of God" (Jesus addressed God as "Father" and the Father referred to Jesus as "My Son"). Interestingly, this phrase was used sparingly; yet it appeared at the beginning (1:1) and close to the ending (13:32) of the Gospel, serving as bookends to support and emphasize this foundational truth of Jesus' unique relationship to the one

and only true God. Who He is (one commissioned by God for a specific task) and what He came to do (the Father's bidding) are essentially unfolded in His name and in that phrase, and His character and mission permeate this Gospel from start to finish. By definition the gospel message presented hope and deliverance.

1:2-3 Mark planted a firm foundation with the phrase **As it is written**, for thereby his readers are taken back to the Old Testament and the One described by the prophets. The true Messiah must fulfill Old Testament prophecy. The verb in the perfect tense affirms that although the reference is to something in the past, the results continue in the future, underscoring the authority of what has been recorded in the Gospel as inextricably connected to what has gone before. The authority of Scripture is unchanging. Mark quoted infrequently from the Old Testament, but here he pointed to **Isaiah the prophet**, a reference in some manuscripts as simply "the prophets." In any case, the reference to the Old Testament was paraphrased from Isaiah 40:3,

Malachi 3:1, and Exodus 23:20. The multiple references only strengthen its bonding to the Old Testament. The quotations were adopted by Mark to use in connection with John the Baptist.

1:4-6 Mark moved his readers into the life of Christ rather abruptly as he introduced the Messiah's forerunner, **John**. John the Baptist may have had some contact with the Essene community at Qumran simply because they were all inhabitants of this desert area. However, there is absolutely no evidence of his involvement with this ascetic group, and his many differences with them certainly leave no reason to assume that he was one of the Essenes. They practiced baptism as a self-administered ritual cleansing, but John's baptism of repentance was very different. On the other hand, there are some carefully recorded facts about John:

- His father was the priest Zechariah (Lk 1:5).

- His mother Elizabeth was a relative of Mary, the mother of Jesus (Lk 1:36).

- His conception came to a barren and infertile womb (Lk 1:7).

- His designation as the forerunner of Messiah was announced before his birth (Lk 1:13-17).

- His primitive dress (Mk 1:6).

- His simple diet (Mk 1:6).

- His ascetic lifestyle was without self-indulgence and marked by simplicity (Mk 1:6).

- In the Greek text he is identified as John without the traditional description, "the Baptist."

The wilderness was a desert, the barren and uninhabitable Jordan River area located at least twenty miles from Jerusalem. The most distinct aspect of John's ministry was his baptizing. Jewish proselytes practiced self-immersion, and the Essenes at Qumran went through repeated self-administered ceremonial washings. John advocated a BAPTISM (Gk. *baptisma*, "ritual washing, dipping under," transliterated into English as baptism of REPENTANCE (Gk. *metanoias*, "change of mind, change of heart, turning from one's sins, changing one's ways"), carrying the idea not only of a change of mind but also of a change of action. **Baptism of repentance** can be interpreted two ways: baptism produced by repentance or baptism characterized by repentance. John's straightforward call to repentance cannot be construed as suggesting that baptism itself produced forgiveness. The phrase translated **the forgiveness of sins** has been troubling to many, and its meaning hinges on the Greek preposition *eis* with a range of meanings (*into, to; in, at, on, upon, by, near; among; concerning*). The word can refer to purpose with the understanding of "leading to" or "causing" (because of) or "attaining a goal" (with the end result). Logically, the sense seems to be that forgiveness of sins is the end result of repentance. Baptism is an outer, symbolic manifestation offering a clear, public testimony that the inner work of repentance has already taken place.

John's baptism was unique because he called for repentance of sins before he would administer baptism, and thus those whom he baptized signaled a deliberate turning from the old path to a new. Obviously baptism was symbolic of a life cleansed from sin, of dying to sin and arising to walk in a new life, and of what Jesus did (His death, burial, and resurrection). Josephus, a first-century Jewish historian, supported this assumption in the following words:

But to some of the Jews the destruction of Herod's army seemed to be divine vengeance, and certainly a just vengeance, for his treatment of John, surnamed the Baptist. For Herod had put him to death, though he was a good man and had exhorted the Jews to lead righteous lives, to practice justice towards their fellows and piety towards God, and so doing to join in baptism. In his view this was a necessary preliminary if baptism was to be acceptable to God. They must not employ it to gain pardon for whatever sins they committed, but as a consecration of the body implying that the soul was already thoroughly cleansed by right behavior.[8]

John's message was radical. His baptism indicated that repentance had already occurred. He called to repentance those who believed that their ancestry could save them.

1:7-8 Mark's focus continued steadfastly to be on Jesus as he noted the testimony of John the Baptist on the superiority of Christ. John **baptized . . . with water** and noted that the water baptism he administered was only preparatory to the baptism **with the Holy Spirit** to be administered by the coming Messiah. Just as John's baptism submerged the repentant individual under the water, the Messiah's baptism would immerse him "with the Holy Spirit," from which would come the transforming power of God. Initially this baptism announced by John came at Pentecost (see Ac 1:5; 2:1-4), then in Samaria (Ac 8:14-17), and even upon Cornelius and other Gentiles (Ac 10:34-48; 11:16-18). Paul also testified that the Holy Spirit "baptized" or immersed the believer into the body of Christ (1 Co 12:13).

Going through the Waters of Baptism (1:9-11)

1:9-11 Most evangelical scholars set the beginning of Jesus' public ministry when He was about 30 years of age (c. AD 27). He spent His childhood in Nazareth in Galilee. Two events pinpoint the beginning of His public ministry: His baptism (vv. 9-11) and His temptation (vv. 12-13). Jesus did not need John's baptism of repentance because Jesus was sinless (Heb 4:15). However, He did seek out John, and He insisted on baptism at John's hands. Ultimately the reasons for this surprising event are in the divine economy, but there are these considerations:

- Jesus wanted to connect Himself to the forerunner who prepared the way for Him.

- Jesus used this public event to set the course for His ministry.

- Jesus humbled Himself to identify with those He came to save.

Here the three persons of the triunity are present:

- Jesus the Son in His fleshly tabernacle.

- **The** Holy **Spirit** coming down **like a dove** at the baptism (v. 10) and then driving the Son into the wilderness (v. 12).

- The Father (**voice . . . from heaven**) declaring His delight in the Son on the occasion of Jesus' baptism (v. 11).

The Father clearly expressed the Son's essential identity, **My beloved Son**, and also affirmed His approval of the Son's role, **I take delight in You**. Jesus did not become God's Son at His baptism. The verb tenses in these two affirmations are richly revealing. The words **YOU ARE** emphasized the eternal and essential relationship between the Father and Son. "I take delight in" described the Father's pleasure and indicated the implied performance of a particular function in history. William Lane paraphrased this twofold affirmation, "Because you are my unique Son, I have chosen you for the task upon which you are about to enter."[9] The Father's commendation of the Son happened at this event, but it was based on an eternal relationship.

Experiencing Temptation in the Wilderness (1:12-13)

1:12-13 The brevity of this account is no less vivid or revealing, and Mark alone mentioned **wild animals**—perhaps because of the nature of the persecution of Christians in Rome. "The Spirit DROVE (Gk. *ekballei*, "force or drive out, send away, cast or throw out") Him" was not suggesting that Jesus was forced to go because of His reluctance but rather underscored that this time of testing was a necessary event in the divine plan. Jesus was TEMPTED (Gk. *peirazomenos*, put to the test, try) "by SATAN" (Gk. transliteration of Hebrew word meaning "adversary"). Mark did not record victory but seemed to present Jesus' entire ministry as a continuing conflict with the Devil. Surely the trials of Christ serve as an example and encouragement to His followers.

THE MINISTRY OF CHRIST IN GALILEE (1:14–8:30)

The Authority of Jesus and the Blindness of the Pharisees (1:14-3:6)

The selection and enlistment of disciples (1:14-20)

1:14-20 Mark noted that Jesus began His ministry in Galilee after the imprisonment of John. Although the details as to when Christ's ministry began were seem-

ingly not important to Mark, showing that the forerunner had completed his mission moved the entire focus to Jesus. Mark did not want anything to detract from **the good news**, and Jesus was the One with "the good news." The idea that "the TIME is fulfilled" (Gk. *kairos*, "a favorable, opportune, significant time") was not a reference to chronological time (Gk. *chronos*, "extension or period of time") but pointed to the time appointed and foretold through the prophets for God's activity on earth. The prophecies would be fulfilled in Jesus. In Jesus, the **kingdom of God** is **near**. In the Old Testament the kingdom of God was not specifically mentioned, but the idea was present throughout. The kingdom of God (or the kingdom of heaven in Matthew) was central to Jesus' teachings, with both a present and future aspect. In Jesus, God's rule was present on earth. But the kingdom also had a future dimension (Mt 8:11). Soon after the announcement of the kingdom, Jesus found **Simon** (Peter) and **Andrew**, along with **James** and **John**, on the shore of the Sea of Galilee and commissioned them to follow Him. He called them to **fish for people**. In keeping with Christ's mission, the people must have an opportunity to be rescued from impending judgment. These chosen men would carry out His mission. The situation was urgent, so the men **immediately** left everything **and followed** Christ.

Jesus' miracles of healing (1:21–2:5)

1:21-28 Miracles were an important testimony of the power of the gospel. Mark recorded 17 miracles for individuals and alluded to others. Jesus' work was made more difficult as the people became more interested in miracles to solve their physical problems than in the heart solution needed for their spiritual needs. However, never was faith dependent upon a miracu-

Inclusive Language

Inclusive language has begun an exclusivity that changes the grammar and syntax of classic language. The phrase "fish for people" (1:17) is an example I have chosen to alert you to what may become a dangerous trend of accommodating even the work of translation to modern agendas. The words translated "people" (Gk. anthrōpōn, "man, mankind") can be translated as "people" or "human beings," but for centuries the generic usage of "mankind" had been used in translation in this passage as throughout the text of Scripture, perhaps because this particular word fits in tandem with the Genesis account introducing God's creation in His image in the creation order as "man" (Hb., adam, "man or mankind"), in which the use of "man" as a reference to mankind in Genesis 1:26 is then defined as "male and female" (Gn 1:27). The generic use is continued in verses like Psalm 1:1, "O How happy is the man . . . ," which certainly is not restricted to males but includes females as well because it is the well-established generic usage. Note also the translation philosophy on gender language for the Holman Christian Standard Bible in the introduction found in copies of the HCSB. I appreciate the faithfulness of this group of translators; but in the translation of this particular word, I differ with the choice they made. Each interpreter must consider these choices carefully.—DKP, editor

lous deed, nor was a supernatural phenomenon necessary to prove the deity of Christ. The miracle would only support and enhance faith and provide a sign and a testimony of divine power.

Mark grouped together three healing miracles to portray Christ's divine power. The language Mark used is vivid, urgent, and full of emotion. The events Mark recorded seemed to have taken place on one particular **Sabbath** day. **Capernaum**, Peter's hometown, became a base for Jesus' Galilean ministry. As Jesus entered the SYNAGOGUE (transliterated from Gk., a word referring to the Jewish meeting place for prayer and for study of the Scripture), He was met by "a man with an unclean spirit." Jesus ultimately came to destroy the Devil's work, and He encountered an evil spirit early in His ministry. The spirit knew Jesus and what He came to do. Jesus cast out the **unclean spirit** with a simple command (v. 25). He needed no

magic formula. Because Jesus **was teaching** as one with power and **authority**, the crowds were **amazed**. The word AMAZED (Gk. ethambēthēsan, a verb in the pluperfect passive indicative form) carries the sense that as long as Jesus taught, the crowds would keep on being amazed.

1:29-34 The details Mark used to describe the healing of Peter's mother-in-law suggest an eyewitness account. **He went to her, took her by the hand, and raised her up** (v. 31). The phrases **as soon as** and **at once** (vv. 29-30) connoted the urgency of the matter. Once she was well, she served **them**, all who were present. Matthew says that she served Jesus, choosing to identify specifically the most important one she served, while Mark's reference was more general (cp. Mt 8:14-17; Lk 4:38-41).

1:35-39 Jesus drew His strength and power for ministry from His Father. After a busy night of healings and exorcisms,

Simon's Mother-in-Law		
Identified	Mother-in-law of the Apostle Simon Peter	v. 30
Incapacitated	Lying in bed with a fever	v. 30
Invaluable	They told Him about her	v. 31
Inspiring	He went to her, raised her up, and she began to serve	v. 31

Jesus arose **early in the morning** to seek His Father. Jesus prayed when facing a crisis (6:46; 14:32-41). The crisis here is the somewhat superficial response of those who heard His good news. **Simon and his companions** came looking for Jesus with the message that everyone was **searching for Him**. Mark used the term "companions" (v. 36) instead of disciples. The people seemed interested only in being healed. Mark emphasized that although healings are important, they were not the primary purpose for Jesus' coming; He came primarily to **preach** the good news (v. 38). Jesus always has been much more than a miracle worker; He is the Son of God.

1:40-45 A man with a serious skin disease is the phrase translating the Greek *lepros*, which is transliterated into English as "leper." Because of an infectious skin disease, a leper experienced social as well as physical suffering. By law he was required to wear torn clothes, let his hair be unkempt, and then cry out "unclean" (see Lev 13:45-46), and he had to live alone outside the camp. This leper approached Jesus directly, believing Jesus could heal him. Mark was the only Gospel writer to add the phrase **moved with compassion**. Jesus **touched** the leper and cleansed him. He told him to **say nothing** but gave him instructions to **go . . . to the priest** to **offer what Moses prescribed for cleansing**. Instead the leper **spread the news** about his healing. Because of Jesus' fame, the people came **from everywhere** to see Him, and Jesus was forced to leave the towns and go to **deserted places** because of the crowds. The people still followed Him there, but they seemed to have a shallow response to Jesus, responding not to who He was but to what He could do. The miracles actually seemed to blind people to the truth.

Jesus' conflict with religious leaders (2:6–3:6)

Five incidents were described in which Jesus was involved in controversy by challenging important Jewish traditions, which brought Him into conflict with the self-righteous Jewish leaders in Galilee. These leaders felt threatened because Jesus seemed to know their thoughts before they spoke, and He exposed their true character. He was very popular with the people, for they had never known a man like Him. Near the end of his Gospel, Mark also recorded a similar series of five additional controversies, which took place when Jesus was in Jerusalem (11:27–12:37). These incidents claim no chronological sequence but are grouped topically to record conflicts between Jesus and His opponents. Believers in every age must defend their faith under attacks from unbelieving detractors. Perhaps this series of encounters between Jesus and those who opposed Him was part of Mark's preparation for his narrative on Jesus' passion. In any case, Jesus brought a new and fresh understanding of the kingdom of God, with an emphasis on the newness of life found in regeneration.

2:6-12 In the first controversy, which occurred at the healing of a paralytic, Jesus showed that He was able to forgive sins. The Pharisees found this idea blasphemous because they failed to accept Jesus as who He truly was—God in flesh. In Jewish teaching, even the Messiah could not forgive sin. BLASPHEMING is simply a word anglicized from the Greek language. It describes profane and irreverent speech about God, and the Old Testament penalty for blasphemy was death (Lv 24:16). Nevertheless, Jesus proved His authority by doing the work only God could do. This act of healing actually had three miraculous elements:

- Jesus even knew the scribes' thoughts before they spoke (Mk 2:8).

- Jesus performed a physical healing for the paralytic (v. 11).

- Jesus forgave the paralytic's sins (v. 5).

Jesus evidently had returned to the house of Simon Peter: "It was reported that He was at home" (2:1; see 1:29). In any case, the dwelling would probably have consisted of a few rooms and a courtyard with an outside stairway leading to a flat roof, often fashioned from branches and mud. Creating an opening in such a roof would not be difficult. All were **astounded and gave glory to God**, and in so doing acknowledged Jesus as God (v. 12). Physical healing was important to Jesus but always secondary; spiritual healing was primary and most essential.

The use of **Son of Man** more than 14 times (2:10,28; 8:31,38; 9:9,12,31; 10:33–35; 13:26; 14:21 [twice], 41, 62) made this title the most frequent Christological designation in Mark's Gospel. Jesus always used this phrase as a self-descriptor in the Gospels. Nothing in Scripture states why Jesus chose this title for Himself. Perhaps the phrase combined His deity and humanity with a measure of

ambiguity, which would then force an individual to make his own choice about Jesus. Was He merely a man? Was He the Son of God—the promised Messiah? Mark understood that Jesus was human, as the title suggested, but Mark knew that Jesus was more than a man.

2:13-17 The **sinners** whom Jesus came to forgive included **tax collectors** like **Levi the son of Alphaeus** and others who realized their need for a spiritual healing. There is a strong, almost universal tradition that Levi and Matthew are one and the same (see parallel account in Mt 9:9). Some have suggested that Levi was his given name and Matthew (Aram., "gift of God") was the name he was given when he became an apostle. Name changes often accompanied dramatic changes in life.

Levi was a tax collector for Herod Antipas, the tetrarch of Galilee, and was despised by the Jews. There was a major route from Damascus to the Mediterranean coast for which Capernaum would have been a strategic site for a tollbooth on entering Galilee. When Levi was called out by Jesus, he most certainly knew there would be no turning back to his old profession with its financial security.

The **Pharisees** or "separated ones" were developers of what came to be known as the oral tradition (the *Talmud* and *Mishnah*). They were the official interpreters of the law. They were very legalistic and obsessed with observing the Sabbath in certain ways and performing rituals. Anyone who did not follow their interpretation of the law was a sinner and thus unclean, not fit for their fellowship or interest. Jesus likened His ministry to that of a physician. The sinners, or spiritually **sick**, realized their need; the **righteous** did not. The righteous to whom Jesus referred were probably these Jewish leaders, such as the Pharisees, who were depending on their works to make them right with God. Matthew added the Old Testament text, "For I desire loyalty and not sacrifice" (Hs 6:6; see Mt 9:13), giving a better indication that Jesus was addressing these leaders, for they knew the words of the prophets well. Mark may have omitted the quote because his audience was mainly Gentile. In any case, Mark made his point. Jesus was not looking for deeds of righteousness but, rather, for a heart of repentance. Interesting for women in verse 15 is the phrase "RECLINING (Gk. *katakeimai*, "lie down, dine") at the table." Although seemingly Jews did sit for everyday meals, a festive or formal meal prompted reclining on a mat at a low table and leaning on the left elbow while eating. Sinners (Gk. *hamarōloi*) here seems to be more a reference to those who, because of their poverty or circumstances, could not keep all the law, especially the tedious additions in the oral law added by the religious leaders. They were outcasts and despised by these leaders.

2:18-22 Jesus clarified the purpose of **fasting**. Familiar key elements were involved in the metaphors Jesus used in response to the question about fasting: a groom, cloth, wine, and wineskins. Jesus rejected fasting because the **groom** (a metaphor for God in the Old Testament) was there. But when the groom had gone away, then fasting would begin (Jesus' death was not specifically mentioned here because the timing was not yet right for such a revelation). The metaphors of the **cloth** as well as of the **wine** and **wineskins** reflected that a new age had come, one in which the old Mosaic law would not suffice. The old system of Jewish law and oral tradition was incompatible with the new cloth and new wine. No one had ever been able to keep the law to perfection. Jesus was ushering in a new king-

dom. He fulfilled the law and became the way of salvation for all.

2:23-28 Jesus challenged the Pharisees' understanding of the purpose of **the Sabbath**. In the first scene Jesus' disciples clearly broke the Jewish oral tradition by **picking some heads of grain** on the Sabbath. (An entire treatise of the *Mishna*, i.e., *Shabbath*, was dedicated to the subject of the Sabbath. See especially *Shabbat* 7:2; *Yoma* 8:6.) Jesus claimed to be the **Lord even of the Sabbath**, the only one who had the authority to interpret the true meaning of the Sabbath. The Pharisees had turned the Sabbath into something God never intended through their additions of human rituals and traditions to the law. The refreshing God intended by Sabbath rest had become restrictive and oppressive. The Old Testament did forbid work on the Sabbath (Ex 20:8-11), but the scribes then enumerated their own lists, including reaping, which the Pharisees then interpreted as "picking some heads of grain." Jesus here confronted the religious leaders and restored an understanding of the Sabbath according to divine plan and purpose. Human need was to take precedence over ceremonial law. Jesus then cited 1 Samuel 21:1-6, where David and his men **ate the sacred bread.** The "bread of presentation" or 12 loaves, representing the 12 tribes of Israel, was placed on the table in the Holy Place of the tabernacle or temple (see Ex 25:30; 29:32; Lv 24:5-9) to establish that people—not ritual—should take precedence on the Sabbath (Mk 2:25-26). Note that even though David's action did violate the law, he was not condemned for it. Jesus, of course, did not declare the law itself invalid but simply interpreted it properly to include exceptions under certain conditions. Sabbath rest and the ceasing of normal pursuits were to give opportunity for refreshing renewal and for special worship and service to God. Mark's reference to **Abiathar** (v. 26) is not in conflict with the Old Testament account in which Ahimelech is identified as the priest (1 Sm 21:1-6). As the son of Ahimelech (1 Sm 23:6), Abiathar was evidently involved in the incident as well since both were priests at the time. David's close association with Abiathar would prompt Jesus to mention him with David.

3:1-6 Later, at **the synagogue**, Jesus also established that it was lawful **to do good** on the Sabbath by healing a man with **a paralyzed hand**. When Jesus asked the religious leaders a question concerning good and evil with regard to the Sabbath, **they were silent**. Jesus looked at them "with anger and sorrow at the "HARDNESS (Gk. *pōrōsei*, "dullness, insensibility") of their hearts." A vivid description of Christ's feeling utterly distressed was expressed uniquely in

Mark's Gospel. The emotion of ANGER (Gk. *orgēs*, "wrath, retribution") in Jesus was not an impulsive outburst or uncontrolled explosion with the intent of seeking revenge. Rather, divine anger is always a righteous response to sin—what one might call righteous indignation or what a righteous man feels in the presence of full-blown evil. Anger itself is never a sin, for a believer's senses and emotions should prompt action when there is injustice or evil. The key is for anger, as with all emotions, to be under God's control. Jesus had a settled disposition against evil and hypocrisy, but His response was always governed by His own character. Jesus healed the man. The extent of the **hardness** of the religious leaders became clear when they conspired on how to **destroy Him** (v. 6).

Controversial Encounters Found in Mark [10]	
Controversy	**Reference in Mark**
Over Jesus' right to forgive sins	2:1-12
Over Jesus' fellowship with tax collectors and "sinners"	2:13-17
Over the disciples' freedom from fasting	2:18-22
Over the disciples' picking grain on the Sabbath	2:23-27
Over Jesus' right to do good on the Sabbath	3:1-6
Over the nature of Jesus' family	3:20-21,31-35
Over the source of Jesus' power to exorcise evil spirits	3:22-30
Over the disciples eating with unwashed hands	7:1-5,14-23
Over setting aside the commands of God on the part of the Pharisees and teachers of the law of God in order to observe their own tradition	7:6-13
Over the legality of divorce and God's intention for marriage	10:1-12
Over Jesus' authority to cleanse the temple and John's authority to baptize	11:27-33
Over paying taxes to Caesar and giving God His due	12:13-17
Over marriage in the resurrection, the power of God, and the witness of Scripture	12:18-27
Over the most important commandment	12:28-34
Over the nature of the Messiah—the son of David or David's Lord	12:35-37

The Parables and Signs of Jesus and the Blindness of the People (3:7–6:6a)

Ministering to the multitude (3:7-12)

3:7-12 Having demonstrated the authority of Jesus by describing the blindness and hostility of the Jewish religious leaders, Mark next illustrated the blindness of the people. Mark did not say specifically why Jesus withdrew, but Matthew noted that Jesus withdrew, knowing there was a plot to kill him (Mt 12:14-15), which indicated significant opposition to His ministry. Jesus' fame had spread as far as the southern part of Judea. By including the information about readying **a small boat** for escape, Mark clearly indicated that huge crowds were swarming Jesus. As demons left people, they shouted Christ's identity; but He silenced them because Jesus wanted to keep the focus on His ultimate destiny, the cross. With Jesus' widespread fame, making His identity known prematurely might have disrupted His ultimate mission.

Setting apart the 12 apostles (3:13-19)

3:13-19 Jesus **went up the mountain and summoned those He wanted**, whom He designated as **apostles**, so that these 12 men could share in His ministry. Also, He was preparing these men for their future ministry, which would take place after His death and resurrection. James and John, the sons of Zebedee, were assigned the nickname **BOANERGES** (an English transliteration of the Greek word) or "Sons of Thunder" (Gk. *huioi*, "sons" *Brontēs*, literally "thunder"), perhaps because of their impetuous personalities (see 9:38; 10:35-45; Lk 9:54) or maybe even because of their thunderous preaching. The men Jesus chose were an unusual group including four fishermen, a tax collector, and a member of a radical political party. None of the disciples were trained religious leaders.

Encountering opposition (3:20-35)

3:20-35 Mark contrasted Jesus' disciples with His opponents through two rather hostile encounters. He did so by dividing up the narrative concerning Jesus' encounters with **His family** (3:20-21,31-35) so that His encounter with the scribes came in between, a way of presenting these two events unique to Mark's Gospel. This literary device was used to draw attention or to interpret the events by using one to offset the other. He linked the two encounters to allow for a more dramatic effect (see vv. 20-21), which is characteristic of Mark's fast-moving treatise, and to fix the reader's attention on the centrality of God's will in Jesus' message.

With the reactions of Jesus' family presented as bookends surrounding the hostility of the scribes, the skepticism of Jesus' own biological family was seen more clearly. Members of His own family said, **He's out of His mind**, revealing how little His family understood Him and no doubt adding to His hurt and discouragement, but certainly their rejection was not equal to the harsh accusation of the Pharisees. So who are the relatives of Jesus? Only those, whether biologically related or not, who determined to do **the will of God** (vv. 33-35). In a culture that valued family relations above all else, Jesus' claims were radical indeed. Nevertheless, there is no hint that Jesus was undermining the family and its relationships, for the family was commissioned by the Creator God, and Jesus was the agent of creation (Gn 2:8-25; Jn 1:1). Jesus simply used the visit of His family to teach a spiritual truth.

The scribes admitted that Jesus performed miracles, but they charged that Jesus must be empowered by the Devil or be demon-possessed in order to cast out the Devil. Their charge was both self-contradictory and self-condemning. The Devil would not thwart his own work; other Jewish exorcists were casting out demons by the power of God. The point Jesus ultimately made was that attributing God's work to demons is blasphemous and could not be forgiven. You cannot commit the "unpardonable sin" (a sin for which there is no forgiveness) unless you know what you are doing. Before this tragic step from which there is no turning back, you become so hardened in unbelief that despite knowledge and understanding, you make a conscious choice to adopt a pattern of willful defiance toward God. The Pharisees reached this point when they attributed the work of the **Holy Spirit** to Satan. In light of this opposition, Jesus began to "weed out" those who were against Him from those who were with Him.

Teaching through parables (4:1-34)

4:1-20 This section is one of the few that Mark devoted strictly to the teachings of Jesus. Its importance lies in revealing what the kingdom of God is like, how it grows, and who can actually enter the kingdom. Jesus used PARABLES (a transliteration of Gk. *parabolais*, "proverb, figure, symbol" from *para*, meaning "beside," and *ballō*, "throw," literally "to throw beside") as His primary tool for teaching truths. In essence, this method used comparison, placing a concrete situation readily known by the pupil next to a biblical truth or spiritual lesson.

Some **parables** were easily understood and readily revealed truth (12:12); others required an explanation for understanding (4:13-20). Jesus did sometimes veil the truth from those who heard Him, such as those who persisted in unbelief and those seeking to end His ministry or destroy His

message. Parables were used so that believers would understand immediately or with an explanation, while unbelievers would not grasp the meaning. The hearing without understanding was the result, not the purpose, of the message (see Is 6:9-10). The fact that the parable contained an admonition to listen at the beginning (v. 3) and end (v. 9) would seem to affirm that the parable's meaning is not always readily clear.

In the parable of **the sower**, the only harvest about which the farmer cared was the one that produced mature fruit. The sower was the same in each planting, but the soils were different. The emphasis was on the different kinds of **soil** and the ways the gospel was received in each. Accordingly, only true disciples yield fruit. Jesus used parables to reveal secrets (v. 11) not previously understood. For those who were already on the **outside** (i.e., out of touch with God, persistent unbelievers), the message of the kingdom would further alienate them. But for those who were open to Jesus' message, greater maturity and discipleship would result.

4:21-34 The next three parables concerned spiritual perception of the message of the kingdom and the specific growth of **the kingdom**. The parable of the **lamp** and measures was used in different contexts in Matthew and Luke, but here in Mark it was a stern exhortation to be spiritually perceptive. Jesus did not come for His kingdom to be **hidden** but to be revealed fully to all. The more you appropriate spiritual truth now, the more you will receive in the future. If you do not make spiritual perceptiveness a high priority now, even the little spiritual perception you think you have **will be taken** from you. In other words, you had better wonder if you have truly made a commitment to Christ and are counted as His disciple if pursuing spiritual understanding is not a priority. Those who don't have an interest in spiritual things will soon find themselves falling further **away** from the kingdom (v. 25).

The parable of the secretly growing **seed**, which is unique to Mark, had to do with the mysterious way the kingdom of God **grows**. All a farmer could do was plant the seed. He would not understand how the seed grows because that is a MYSTERY (Gk. *mustērion*, "secret, mystery," referring in this context to something that cannot be known apart from God's revelation). Thus, the point of the parable was this:

> The fruit is the result of the seed; the end is implicit in the beginning. The infinitely great is already active in the infinitely small. In the present, and indeed in secret, the event is already in motion. . . . Those to whom it has been given to understand the mystery of the Kingdom (4:11) see already in its hidden and insignificant beginnings the coming kingdom of God.[11]

The kingdom of God was **like** the **mustard seed** because the kingdom, too, appeared weak and insignificant in the beginning. But in the end it would be great, powerful, and all-consuming. "The example of the mustard seed should prevent us from judging the significance of results by the size of the beginnings."[12]

The summary statement on the parables emphasized again that Jesus' disciples, the ones on the "inside," were privy to the secrets of the kingdom in a way that no others were. Moreover, true insiders are characterized by a spiritual hunger for the things that have to do with the kingdom of God. If this hunger is not present, you must question whether you are truly on the inside.

Demonstrating power with miracles (4:35–6:6a)

In a dramatic display of miraculous powers, Mark showed Jesus' triumph over hostile forces in nature (4:35-41), in the demonic realm (5:1-20), and in death and chronic illness (5:21-43). Jesus' tremendous display of divine power made the blindness and hostility of the world look ludicrous. Though Jesus' message and ministry were powerful, He was still ultimately rejected. Mark was preparing his readers for the cross.

4:35-41 Jesus often demonstrated His power over nature itself by harnessing its elements. With the calming of the storm, the disciples were desperately fearful, and they were compelled to ask, **Who then is this?** Their faith still left much to be desired. **The wind and the sea** knew the voice of their Master, but the disciples had yet to learn to recognize it.

5:1-20 Healing of demon possession showed the victory of the supernatural over unusually powerful forces of evil. **The demons** (wicked, unclean spirit-beings) also knew His voice. They did not need to ask who He was. But they had to ask Him for **permission** to go where they wanted to go.

Jesus did not engage in lengthy conversations with demons and frequently forbade them to speak (1:34). Mark paid extraordinary attention to the details surrounding the healing of the man possessed by the legion of demons. Some would question Jesus' assigning these animals to destruction. Of course, the demons, not Jesus, actually destroyed the swine (5:13).

Nevertheless, Jesus always showed that He cared more for mankind, created in His own image and redeemed by His own blood, than for animals. The demons, of course, were determined to destroy. When they could not destroy the man, they settled for **the pigs**. The account is riveting precisely because Mark walked the reader

Demons	
Information	**Reference**
Could act as personal and intelligent beings	Ac 16:16-18
Sought to express themselves through another living creature	Mt 12:43-45
Could achieve supernatural strength	Lk 8:29; Ac 19:13-16
Were aware of the destiny God planned for them	Mt 8:29; 2 Pt 2:4
Were apparently fallen angels who took part in Satan's rebellion	Is 14:12-15; Ezk 28:14-15; Jd 6
Can attack through temptation, direct opposition to God's work, and by influence, oppression, and possession	Mt 4:1-11; Mk 5:1-5; Lk 13:10-17; Ac 16:16-18
Can cause physical illness	Mt 12:22; 17:14-18; Mk 9:17-25
Can generate emotional turmoil	1 Sm 16:14; Mk 5:1-5
Can deceive, causing people to believe lies	Ac 5:3
Can draw people to embrace worldly wisdom	Jm 3:13-16
Can entice people to accept doctrinal error in the place of truth	1 Tm 4:1-5

through the agony characterizing the daily life of this man (vv. 2-5).

Believers need not look for demons, but they must be aware of their existence and influence and be prepared to stand against them (Eph 6:10-12; 1 Pt 5:8-9). The only permanent protection from demon possession is to be born again, which includes the permanent indwelling of the Holy Spirit from that day forward (1 Co 6:19). The believer is to put aside sinful practices and remove any demonic influences. Incorporating the disciplines of prayer and Bible study prepares a believer for battle against Satan and his demons.

The command, **Go back home to your own people, and report to them how much the Lord has done for you** (5:19), was in stark contrast to Jesus' command to the leper in 1:44, "See that you say nothing to anyone." Jesus had a reason for commanding silence. The **Decapolis** was a league of ten Greek cities largely populated by Gentiles (thus the presence of a herd of pigs would not be surprising) and located to the east of the Sea of Galilee and the Jordan River. In 6:6b–8:30, Jesus

launched His ministry to the Gentiles, and the man possessed with demons was in Gentile territory.

New Testament scholars have debated the location of this miraculous exorcism. Matthew identified the place as "the region of the Gadarenes" (Mt 8:28), located only six miles from the lake; Mark (5:1) and Luke (Lk 8:26) record Gerasa, which was about 30 miles from the lake. Here the reading is inconsequential to the meaning of the passage. Variants do occur in the extant manuscripts, as would be inevitable with hand-copying and centuries of transmission. The miscopying of a scribe, however, is a far cry from any error in the inspired, Spirit-breathed autographs. This encounter was the beginning of Jesus' future miracles. Mark may have regarded this incident "as the inauguration of the mission to the Gentiles." Outsiders from beyond Jordan had been coming to Jesus (3:8), but now Jesus was coming to them.

5:21-43 Jairus and the **woman** with an issue of blood also knew the voice of the Master. Again with riveting, heart-pounding narrative, Mark recounted the details of the circumstances drawing these two desperate people to Christ. Jesus refused to neglect the needs of the humble woman who interrupted His encounter with an influential synagogue leader (5:22-26). The stories read like eyewitness accounts. These incidents probably did not occur in chronological order but were brought together because of their common theme and purpose. The stories of the "man with an unclean spirit," Jairus's daughter, and the "woman suffering from bleeding" all have to do with ritual uncleanness. Mark did not explain the location of the woman's bleeding, but it was probably in her uterus. In any case, it was not only a physical burden for her but one with serious spiritual and social consequences since it made her unclean and thus condemned to live as an outcast (Lv 15:25-30). Jesus rejected ritual uncleanness, and He related to everyone whatever the social status or gender or ethnic background. Jewish law mandated that contact with graves, blood, or death made one ceremonially unclean. In both encounters human efforts had failed; yet Jesus succeeded because of His power and because of the faith of these two—one a religious leader and the other a humble woman. Each came to Jesus because of personal faith.

The Woman with an Issue of Blood		
Her Need	**Her Approach**	**Jesus' Response**
12 years of bleeding physically (Lk 8:43)	Came from behind as a humble seeker of healing (Mt 9:20)	Marked by sensitivity—He knew that his garment had been touched in love (Mk 5:30)
Loss of financial resources (Lk 8:43)	Touched the tassel on His robe (Mt 9:20)	Bearing hope—go in peace (Mk 5:34)
Rejection by others because of her uncleanness (see Lv 15:25-33)	Believed Jesus could heal her (Mt 9:21)	Delivering healing—He knew He could heal her. Knowing a personal encounter was essential, He called for her to step forward (Mk 5:30)

Jairus, whose name was omitted in the Matthean account (Mt 9:18), was a prominent Jewish leader (Mk 5:22). As **one of the synagogue leaders**, he undoubtedly was responsible for leading worship and giving instructions to the people. Since the text did not suggest any earlier contact with Jesus, one can assume that Jairus knew Jesus only by reputation. Yet he believed Jesus could heal his young **daughter**. His request for Jesus to touch his daughter, **lay Your hands on her so she can get well** (Gk. sōthē, "save") **and live** (v. 23) was a commonly understood prelude to healing among the Jews (6:5; 7:32; 8:23,25). The use of the Greek verb meaning "save" was appropriate since in all Jesus' miracles recorded in Mark 5, physical healing served as a metaphor for spiritual deliverance from sin and was understood in a theological sense as ultimate healing or salvation. Jairus' request to Jesus for the laying on of hands could also have been his way of urging Jesus' personal presence and attention to the needs of his dying daughter.

On the way the pressing crowd, especially the woman who stopped Jesus seeking her own healing, resulted in a costly delay. Yet when the message **your**

daughter is dead (v. 35) came, whether Jesus believed that the child was dead or that the report was false, there was no finality in death for Jesus. Whether the child had fallen into a deep coma or slipped into eternity, Jesus had the power to renew or restore life. The verb **asleep** (Gk. *katheudei*) was often used as a metaphor for death (see 1 Th 4:13-15). Most evangelical commentators accept that meaning here. The **people weeping and wailing loudly** (v. 38) were probably professional mourners who would have been summoned even without a direct word from Jairus because of his prominence in the community. Even the death of a poor man would merit some public display of mourning, a custom still in vogue in much of the world in the modern era. Jesus dismissed the mourners and even grieving friends, not because of personal annoyance or even secrecy, but in order to contrast their lack of faith and unbelief with the faith of the believing father Jairus (v. 36). Jesus knew that the story of this young girl's resurrection would be told. When He gave the family **strict orders that no one should know about this** (v. 43), Jesus was simply seeking enough privacy to leave the home and continue His ministry. He knew that there was still much before Him in His journey to the cross.

The Daughter of Jairus		
Her Need	**Her Approach**	**Jesus' Response**
Healing and life (Mk 5:23,35)	Having personal helplessness—intervention was made by her father (Mk 5:23)	Listening with sensitivity (Mk 5:23-24)
	Exercising faith in Jesus' power (Mk 5:36)	Going in compassion (Mk 5:24,36)
	Waiting for Jesus' timing	Doing what no one else could do (Mk 5:41-42)

There was little doubt that the demonstration of Christ's amazing powers in this section proved a great comfort to Mark's original audience. These accounts offered assurance that the Son of God, who triumphed over such hostile forces, could protect them. For example, the woman who was bleeding would have made anyone she touched unclean; when she touched Jesus, she became clean. Jesus not only healed her physically and removed the cause of social rejection, but He also met her spiritual needs: **Daughter, . . . your faith has made you well** (Gk. *sesōken,* save). This miracle became more extraordinary because it happened without conscious effort on Jesus' part but, of course, with His full knowledge. And even if the worst happened, the persecuted church in Rome would know that Jesus would be with them through every trial.

6:1-6a The wind and the waves, demons, sickness, and death all responded to Christ. They recognized His authority and had to respond. But the people from Nazareth could not see what was so special about the man from their **hometown**. To them Jesus was merely a carpenter, **the son of Mary**. Though He was invited to **teach in the synagogue** (He was well known as a teacher) and though His preaching was just as powerful there as anywhere else, the people of Nazareth **were offended by** Him (6:1,3). Jesus **was amazed at their unbelief**.

Although Jesus' family lived in Nazareth, He went there as a rabbi with His disciples. His mission was to preach the good news. How unfortunate that the people of Nazareth allowed their everyday knowledge about Jesus (who came from the home of an ordinary craftsman) to block the spiritual understanding He offered to them. The rejection He experienced there was a sign of what was to come. Even His family joined in this rejection (6:4; see also 3:20-21,31-35).

One should not be shaken by Mark's statement, **He was not able to do any miracles there** (6:5). Of course the entire Gospel, and the New Testament as a whole, point clearly to the omnipotence of God. God and His Son (also fully God) could do anything, but Mark acknowledged that Jesus chose to limit Himself based on the response of the people. One is again reminded that Jesus was not setting out to impress people as a miracle worker. His miracles were kingdom centered. In an atmosphere of unbelief, Jesus chose not to exercise His power through miracles. Throughout His ministry, His miracles were in response to faith.

Jesus' Ministry to the Gentiles and the Blindness of His Disciples (6:6b–8:30)

Defining the mission and experiencing opposition (6:6b-29)

6:6b Mark showed, through a demonstration of Jesus' teachings and the riveting accounts of His miracles, the true nature of discipleship and the blindness of the people. Those who were true disciples responded to His teachings on the kingdom of God. But the world in general rejected these truths. Thus, they were on the outside. The second literary scheme began with Mark's description of significant opposition to Jesus, bringing the section to a close, opening the following

section with Jesus' withdrawal and the commissioning of the disciples in a new region. This time Jesus withdrew from His own people, as He was on the verge of beginning His ministry among the Gentiles.

6:7-13 As a result of the success of His village ministry, Jesus commissioned **the Twelve** to assist in His endeavors. The disciples had been prepared for this ministry. They were originally called to "fish for people" (1:17); Jesus gave them special attention on several occasions (3:7,13; 4:10). They had seen His amazing miracles and heard His powerful teaching. What they needed to do now was to have complete trust in God to meet all their needs on their journey. The mission assignment to the Twelve was patterned after Jesus' ministry: preaching **that people should repent** (v. 12), **driving out . . . demons** (v. 13), **and healing** the sick (v. 13).

6:14-29 King Herod heard of all that Jesus was doing and feared that **John the Baptist** had **been raised from the dead** to haunt him. Herod's concern about John being raised from the dead was not as motivated by Jesus' ministry per se as by a guilty conscience over his murder of John. Traditionally, according to the Jewish historian Josephus, John was imprisoned and executed at Machaerus, a fortress located in modern-day Jordan (ancient southern Perea). Indeed, John's death did foreshadow the death of Jesus. John the Baptist had refused to overlook the blatant adultery of Herod Antipas and **Herodias**. The daughter of Aristobulus, a son of Herod the Great and Mariamne, Herodias had married her uncle Philip, also a son of Herod the Great. Herodias's husband Philip was the half brother of Herod Antipas, who was ruling during the days of John; but she was living out of wedlock with Herod Antipas. Although Herod was embarrassed when John denounced his adulterous relationship, he himself seemed intrigued by John and **was protecting him** for a time. Herodias, however, was furious and immediately sought to destroy the prophet. Her daughter Salome not only showed no surprise with her mother's request to her to ask for **John the Baptist's head** but added two enhancements

of her own: she wanted the head **on a platter—right now!** (v. 25).

Mark's Gospel has two passion (suffering) narratives: the passion of John and the passion of Jesus. A passion narrative presents the story of someone's death. There are interesting parallels between these two passion narratives:

The Queens of the New Testament [13]		
Name	**General Information**	**Reference**
Bernice	• Older daughter of Herod Agrippa I • Wife of her uncle, the king of Chalcis • Consort to her brother Herod Agrippa II • Guest of Festus, with her husband Agrippa, to whom Paul delivered his defense • Mistress to Roman emperors Vespasian and Titus	Ac 25:13,23; 26:30
Candace	• Title used by the queens of Ethiopia • Possibly a recipient of the gospel through her imperial staff member who accepted Christ as Savior and was baptized by the evangelist Philip • According to tradition, she also became a Christian	Ac 8:27-28
Drusilla	• Herod Agrippa I's younger daughter • Wife of Aziz of Emesa • Wife of Procurator Felix of Judea • Guest of Felix before whom Paul appeared	Ac 24:24
Herodias	• Daughter of Aristobulus and Bernice (sister to Herod Agrippa II) • Granddaughter of Herod the Great • Wife of her uncle, Herod Philip • Mother of Salome, according to the Jewish Historian Josephus • Consort to Herod Antipas (her brother-in-law) • One responsible for the death of John the Baptist	Mt 14:1-2; Mk 6:17
Queen of the South	• Nikauli, according to the Jewish historian Josephus • Visitor to Solomon's court • Queen whose historic visit to Solomon was noted by Jesus	1 Kg 10:1-13; Mt 12:42; Lk 11:31
Unnamed queen in the book of Revelation	Personification of the city of Babylon—known for its wickedness and destruction	Rv 18:7-10

- The respect for John the Baptist and Jesus by Roman rulers—Herod and Pilate, respectively (v. 20; 15:5,14).

- The hatred experienced by John and by Jesus from their enemies—

Herodias and the Jewish religious leaders respectively (v. 24; 11:18).

- The yielding to pressure to kill John and Jesus by Herod and Pilate, respectively (v. 26; 15:15).

- The mention of disciples coming for the body and burial in a tomb (v. 29; 15:43-46).[14]

Numerous historical questions have been raised concerning Mark's account of John the Baptist. Most of them have to do with Josephus' account of the incident. The most probable solution is that Josephus emphasized the political motives behind Herod's actions, while Mark zeroed in on the moral aspects. Calvin observed:

> We behold in John an illustrious example of that moral courage, which all pious teachers ought to possess, not to hesitate to incur the wrath of the great and powerful, as often as it may be found necessary: for he, with whom there is acceptance of persons, does not honestly serve God.[15]

Continuing the miracles and teaching (6:30–8:26)

6:30-44 Apart from Jesus' resurrection, the feeding of the 5,000 was the only miracle recorded in all four Gospels (6:30-44; Mt 14:13-21; Lk 9:12-17; Jn 6:5-13). Again the miracle pointed to the kingdom. Jesus not only provided for the multitude's need for food, but He was also revealing Himself as Messiah to **His disciples** and training His disciples to **give them something to eat** (v. 37) rather than sending **them away**. The disciples participated in this miracle. They learned valuable lessons. They did not themselves have what was needed, but the little they gave to Jesus would be multiplied. They could share the resulting abundance and even have leftovers to be gathered. Jesus showed Himself to be a man of great **compassion**, a supplier of needs when resources were unavailable, and the One whose authority extended to the elements of the natural world. The Greek word here translated COMPASSION (*esplagchnisthē*, "have pity, feel sympathy, be moved") is used only by or about Jesus in the New Testament (6:34; Mt 18:27; Lk 10:33). The word goes beyond pity and encompasses the idea of supplying help. The numbering of the crowd was based on counting the **men**. Adding women and children would have greatly increased the number.

6:45-52 Jesus **made His disciples get into the boat and go on ahead of Him** to **Bethsaida**, which was on the northeast shore of the Sea of Galilee. Mark mentioned for the second time Jesus' prayer session (1:35; 6:46). The next time he mentioned a time of prayer was in the garden of Gethsemane (14:32-36). Jesus prayed when a crisis came or when He experienced a temptation not to carry out God's plan. Prayer marked His life and prompted the disciples to ask Him to teach them to pray (Lk 11:1).

6:53-56 These verses contain a summary of Jesus' ministry in Galilee before departing into other territories, similar to summaries in 1:32-34 and 3:7-12. Jesus' fame had spread far and wide. And when the people **touched** Him, not the **tassel of His robe** but their faith in the One who wore it, the Healer Himself, **made them well**.

7:1-8 Apparently this section is a unit linked by a common theme concerning uncleanness. The major emphasis is that Jesus rejected the oral interpretation of and addition to the written law. The early church evidently struggled with how to respond to Mosaic law and especially to dietary laws. Jesus rejected the religious leaders' interpretation of the ritual uncleanness. Jewish ritual and tradition had to be put into perspective in order to move forward in reaching Gentiles with the gospel. Ritual washings required of priests in the Old Testament had been expanded by the scribes and Pharisees as a requirement affecting all Jews.

Contemporary believers must be cautious in embracing the letter of divine mandate while ignoring the spirit of Scripture. This section, similar to the accounts of conflict found in 2:1–3:6 and ultimately showing why Jesus was now turning to the Gentiles, served as an introduction to Jesus' ministry among the Gentiles. Mark explained the **tradition of the elders** (a large mass of oral tradition about the law, v. 3) to his audience. He even gave an example, which reflected in many ways the low view of the Gentiles held by Jewish religious leaders. After being in the **marketplace** and coming in contact with the **unclean** (Gentiles), the Pharisees would **wash** themselves as a way of purification. Ceremonial washing was one of many traditions and rituals added to the law that they observed.

Jesus contrasted **the command of God** with **the tradition of men**, pointing out that in many ways their traditions were out of step with the heart of God's commands. Jesus had no mercy on religious leaders who were supposed to be examples for the people. HYPOCRITES (a transliteration of Gk. *hupokritōn*, "those who pretend to be other than what they are") originated as a Greek theatrical term describing someone who acted the part of another. The Greek root *krinō*, meaning "judge," is linked to the Greek preposition *hupo*, meaning "under" and thus having the sense of judging under. The actors of the ancient world wore a series of masks as they assumed the identities of the characters they were playing. In other words, the Pharisees were masking their internal beliefs behind their external rituals. Their insincerity and radical inconsistency, although covered by pretense, was uncovered by Jesus.

7:9-13 The example Jesus gave the Pharisees affirmed the fifth commandment: **Honor your father and your mother**. Anyone who cursed his mother or father would receive the **death** penalty (Ex 20:12). Jesus then demonstrated how tradition added by the religious leaders easily subverted this command.

According to the tradition, a son only had to declare what he intended to give **his father or mother** as **Corban**, and that **gift** would be designated as belonging to God. **No longer** could the son be required to use the designated gift to assist his parents. In the practice of *Corban,* the Pharisees effectively nullified for children the commandment to honor their parents. If the son later regretted his gift of *Corban*, the Pharisees would then demand that his earlier vow be kept (see Nm 30:2). Evidently this gift, when **committed to the temple**, did not have to be surrendered immediately. The child could continue to use the property until his own death when the remainder would then go to the temple. The son denied his parents, enriched himself, and then gave God what was left. God's intent in giving the command had been negated by the tradition of man (v. 13). The Pharisees in effect used the letter of one commandment to **invalidate** the intent of another commandment. By such a declaration, a son legally excluded his parents from benefiting from the gift. In other words, he dedicated something to God but then disobeyed God's mandate in using it. Again, stressing the letter of the law and adhering to the Pharisees' interpretation and additions to the law subverted the true intent of the law.

This interchange revealed the seriousness of God's commandments and the wickedness of anyone who was seeking to get around them. A stern warning was addressed to anyone who wanted to shirk his responsibilities.

7:14-23 Specific food regulations had been expanded to the point that some religious leaders wanted to determine whether a person was righteous or unrighteous by the food he ate. Jesus condemned them because real uncleanness is decided by the heart, not food (7:18-23). True defilement is internal (in the heart) and not external (determined by what you do or do not do). God is not impressed with a list of rules; neither is a person harnessed by rules (Col 2:20-23).

Jesus returned to the issue of defilement. True defilement was not associated with dirty hands but **the things that** came **out of a person**. Uncleanness was determined by moral principles, not by routine ritual. Food and drink did not make one unclean, even if imbibed with unclean hands or declared unclean by food laws. Rather, evil thoughts and wicked behavior from the heart made one unclean. Jesus was fulfilling the law in the Old Testament. If **all foods** were **clean**, ritual washings were not necessary, and the barriers between Jews and Gentiles were abolished.

The disciples did not understand this idea. In verse 19b, Mark explained Jesus' teaching to his readers. Mark wanted to emphasize the freedom of Gentiles by plainly stating Jesus' rejection of Jewish ceremonial law as the path to righteousness.

7:24-30 Typically, the Jews had no relationships with Gentiles because of ritual uncleanness. But Jesus distanced Himself from the Jewish oral traditions; and, in contrast to these traditions, He revealed the true nature of uncleanness.

Jesus associated Himself with a Gentile woman, perhaps as an outward protest against these laws. He showed by example the futility of these laws. This encounter highlighted Jesus' mission to the Gentiles. Jesus' rejection of the ceremonial law would have encouraged the Gentiles to believe that the gospel was for them as much as it was for the **Syrophoenician** woman. Mark gave more details about the woman's circumstances than did Matthew; but unlike Matthew, he left out

phrases such as "Son of David" and "lost sheep of Israel." He also did not mention the fact that the disciples wanted to send the woman away (Mt 15:23). These omissions may have been made purposely because of his Gentile audience.

The women with whom Jesus had His longest conversations were not Jewish women, as one might expect because of the stigma Jews attached to non-Jews. Rather the women were Gentiles: the Syrophoenician woman (Mk 7:24-30) and the Samaritan woman (Jn 4:1-42). In the accounts of Matthew and Mark, this Syrophoenician woman's encounter with Jesus was recorded in the section between the feeding of the 5,000 and the feeding of the 4,000. This arrangement highlighted the contrast between the feeding of thousands of people and the woman's request for a few **crumbs**. The overall effect of this sequence portrayed this woman as having an extraordinary faith.

The woman came to Jesus with an urgent request. Her daughter was suffering terribly from **an unclean spirit**. Jesus' first response to her at a glance seemed uncharacteristically harsh. However, Jesus was neither indifferent nor insensitive; rather, He wanted to test the faith of this Gentile woman and use her faith as a testimony to the disciples. He told her, **It isn't right to take the children's bread and throw it to the dogs** (7:27). The Jews often referred to the Gentiles as "dogs," but here the reference is a diminutive form, meaning small dogs kept as household pets rather than scavengers of the streets.

But more amazing than Jesus' initial response to the woman was her response to Him. Clearly she understood Jesus' messianic mission. Matthew noted in his parallel passage (Mt 15:21-28) that she referred to Jesus as the "Son of David" and indicated that Jesus viewed His ministry as being first to the Jews and then to the Gentiles (Mt 15:24; Ac 13:46; Rm 1:16). But the woman also understood that the Jewish Messiah's mission went beyond Israel's borders. Based on this understanding, she appealed to Jesus. The woman showed herself to be not only intelligent and perceptive but also a woman of deep and unshakable faith. The woman must have impressed the disciples for both Matthew and Mark to give such attention to her encounter with Christ early in His ministry to the Gentiles.

7:31-37 Only Mark included the healing of the **deaf** and mute **man** (vv. 31-37). Perhaps he included it because the healing occurred in Gentile territory. The word translated **SPEECH DIFFICULTY** (Gk. *mogilalon*, "having difficulty in speaking, mute, dumb") is a *hapax*, used only here in the Greek New Testament (vv. 32,35), but it is also found once in the Septuagint (the Greek translation of the Old Testament) in Isaiah 35:6, a passage describing mute people shouting for joy when Messiah comes. This passage is one of only three in which Jesus used saliva in order to heal someone (see also Mk 8:23; Jn 9:6). Although Jesus still wanted to keep His presence and identity unknown (Mk 7:24,36), at this point in His ministry it was impossible.

Heart to Heart:
Keeping the Main Thing the Main Thing

Jesus' desire for privacy was not based on personal comforts, nor were His withdrawals efforts to veil His message in secrecy. He wanted to keep the focus on the gospel—the good news of salvation—rather than letting His message be twisted into merely the personal attention of sensationalism associated with miracles and healing. In the modern era, there is still a struggle to keep the main thing first. Yes, you must respond to human need. And God does indeed heal physical bodies. Nevertheless, the most important task for believers today remains the sharing of the good news of Christ's atonement for the sins of all. The primary mission of miracles is calling women and men to Christ and discipling them in the Christian life.

8:1-10 As happened earlier in Jesus' ministry, large crowds followed Him. **They had nothing to eat**, and out of compassion He wanted to feed them (vv. 1-9). He did feed them and, as always, what He provided was sufficient—and the people were satisfied (v. 8). Jesus was still in Gentile territory, so He was merely performing the same miracle for the Gentiles He had done for the Jews (6:31-44).

The theme uniting these parallel events was spiritual understanding or the lack of it.

Jesus sounds a call to spiritual understanding in 7:14-18, but the disciples fail to understand after each feeding miracle (6:52; 8:14-21). The miracles of healing—the opening of the ears of the deaf man (7:31-36) and the eyes of the blind man (8:22-26)—are symbolic of and prepare the way for the opening of the spiritual understanding of the disciples.[16]

Parallel Events in Mark		
6:31-44	Feeding the multitude	8:1-9
6:45-56	Crossing the sea	8:10
7:1-23	Conflict with Pharisees	8:11-13
7:24-30	Discussion about bread	8:14-21
7:31-36	Healing	8:22-26
7:37	Confession of faith	8:27-30

8:11-21 To further this theme of spiritual understanding and lack of it, **the Pharisees** asked for **a sign from heaven**. Even this request was insincere. Again Jesus was being TESTED (Gk. *peirazontes*, "put to the test, tempted, tried"). The same word was used to describe Satan's tempting of Jesus (1:13). They did not look at His miracles as signs that would help them believe; rather, they saw Jesus' miracles as an opportunity to entrap Him. Jesus responded that **no sign** would **be given**. Interestingly, in the Gospels, Jesus' miracles were often described as *dunamis* (Gk.), or "mighty acts." However, the Pharisees asked for a SIGN (Gk. *sēmeion*, "something known or distinguished") or evidence from Jesus. Mark omitted the phrase "except the sign of Jonah" (Mt 16:4) but mentioned Jesus' deep sigh (Mk 8:12). The phrase SIGHING DEEPLY (Gk. *anastenaxas*, "giving a great groan") is found only here in the New Testament. Jesus' expression showed His disappointment with the unbelief of those who certainly should have known better. Moreover, the disciples' lack of faith at this point was exasperating to Jesus. But the disciples' failure spurred Jesus to warn them concerning the YEAST (Gk. *zumēs*, "a substance used to make bread rise"), which in the New Testament often symbolized evil. Yet here it might have been a metaphor for the teaching of the Pharisees and for the evil disposition of Herod, or perhaps for both it symbolized their common unbelief (vv. 11-21). The disciples failed to realize that the **bread** they actually had was the spiritual provision of Christ Himself.

8:22-26 A question has often been raised as to why Jesus led this man **out of the village** before healing him. Most of the recorded miracles were done in public settings and at the point of initial encounter. This occasion and two others (Jairus's daughter, 5:35-43, and the deaf mute, 7:31-37) were healings done elsewhere. The motive for the other two must have been a way for Jesus to help the men with their faith. As to why Jesus did not follow His usual pattern and heal instantly,

> He did so most probably for the purpose of proving, in the case of this man, that he had full liberty as to his method of proceeding, and was not restricted to a fixed rule. . . . And so the grace of Christ, which had formerly been poured out suddenly on others, flowed by drops, as it were, on this man.[17]

This miracle, recorded only by Mark, was the second that pointed to the Old Testament expectations of the Messiah (see 7:24-37). Both miracles revealed the "opening of the eyes" of the disciples, who were finally recognizing Jesus as the Messiah. The disciples, as well as the people in general, wanted a ruler who would solve their problems and make their lives easier. On the other hand, Jesus' mission was to make their eternity sure. Jesus refused to allow earthly desires for healing, yearnings for provisions of need, and ambitions for political positions to overshadow or divert His focus from the ultimate work of salvation. He even warned His disciples about talking (v. 30).

Hearing Peter's confession of faith (8:27-30)

8:27-30 There was remarkable parallelism between the healing of the blind man and the growing understanding of the disciples:

Healing and Revelation		
Blind Man	**Parallelism in this Passage**	**Disciples**
8:22	Circumstances	8:27
8:23-24	Partial sight—partial understanding	8:28
8:25	Sight—understanding	8:29
8:26	Injunction to silence	8:30

The disciples' understanding was not complete at the time (8:32), but the parallelism still was valid.

Caesarea Philippi was built on the site of ancient Paneas (also called Banias) by Philip the tetrarch. Its ruins remain a popular archaeological site and are beautifully located at the foot of Mount Hermon with gushing springs that are identified as one of the sources of the Jordan River. Jesus **asked** a question first of **His disciples**. Contrary to what some modern scholars have said, the fact that Jesus hesitated to reveal Himself as **Messiah** early in His ministry does not mean He did not believe Himself to be the Messiah. He clearly accepted the title (8:29).

> And this is hardly surprising; for the title, in spite of all the false and narrow hopes which had become attached to it, was peculiarly fitted to express his true relation both to the OT and to the people of God . . . the title, applied to Jesus, designates him as the true meaning and fulfillment of the long succession of Israel's anointed kings and priests, the King and Priest . . . the

Prophet anointed with the Spirit of God, who fulfills the long line of Israel's prophets; and the One in whom the life of the whole nation of Israel finds its fulfillment and meaning, in whom and for whose sake the people of Israel were, and the new Israel now is, the anointed people of God.[18]

THE PASSION OF CHRIST (8:31–16:20)

Predictions of Death and Defining of Discipleship (8:31–10:52)

The cross and resurrection foreshadowed (8:31-33)

The third and final section in the Gospel of Mark was built around Jesus' three predictions concerning His suffering and death (8:31; 9:31; 10:33-34). The "secret" was now out in the open. The Son of Man must go to Jerusalem, suffer, die, and on the third day be raised to life.

8:31-33 Jesus had alluded to His coming suffering and death, but the disciples still did not understand (v. 32). Here Jesus became more direct to be sure they understood what He had been saying. Peter rebuked Jesus because he did not understand the true mission of the Messiah. Jesus saw Peter's effort to divert Him on His path to the cross as the same temptation Satan offered in the wilderness when Jesus began His ministry. In His stinging rebuke of Peter, Jesus still refused to act on His own apart from the Father's will. Jesus did not demand martyrdom to secure salvation. However, He was clear that one who comes to Christ must remove all claims so that Christ is in complete control.

The requirements for discipleship (8:34-38)

8:34-38 Mark also emphasized what Christ's suffering meant for those who

> # Heart to Heart:
> ## The Cost of Discipleship
>
> *The cost of following Christ is to put one's entire life on the line, holding nothing back. It is the way of the cross. Mark alone recorded Jesus' words "and the gospel" in verse 35, highlighting the preaching of the message for which His followers must give their lives, emphasizing also the gospel's call to service. Sometimes you may find it easier to die for Christ, knowing you will be immediately ushered into His presence to experience the glories of heaven, than to live for Him, which may demand daily sacrifices and difficulties along the way.*

would follow Him. In many places throughout this section, Mark stressed the true nature of discipleship: denying yourself, taking up your cross, and following Him. Denying yourself is not to deny a particular thing. Nor is it asceticism and the denial of many things, and certainly it is not self-hatred. Rather, the idea is to **deny** self-focus, refusing to make yourself the center of life. God becomes the center of all life. To bear the **cross** was to make the same journey Christ made—a way of suffering and death to self, giving up even what is most dear for Christ. You move from self-control to God-control.

This section also was intended to show Jesus' move to Jerusalem from Galilee, where He spent most of His ministry time. Much of this section is a travel narrative. The last healing in Jericho moved the narrative right to the entrance of the Holy City.

Unlike Matthew, Mark did not record Jesus' words of praise concerning Peter's insight into the Lord's true identity. Peter's confession was significant and accurate as far as it went. However, Mark's account stopped with a declaration that Jesus is the promised Messiah (v. 29). Although some manuscripts of Mark include "Son of God," the earliest and best do not, meaning that unlike Matthew

(Mt 16:16-19), Mark's account probably did not include these very important words identifying Jesus as not only the Messiah but as God (v. 29).

Jesus' mandating their silence about His identity was much more difficult to understand than His forbidding their reporting on His healings (v. 30). Perhaps most important in this regard would be Jesus' effort to circumvent or correct the popular, but incomplete, view of His messiahship because of its insufficiency in not clearly stating His deity. In fact, Jesus followed these words of warning with His own explanation of His coming death and resurrection (v. 31). Perhaps Peter had in mind a traditional Jewish, popular messiahship of a leader who would free the people from Roman tyranny, one that did not involve suffering. At this time no Jew would envision a Messiah who faced suffering and death. Jesus wanted to dispel this traditional view right away.

The transformation (9:1-13)

9:1-13 Jesus had a way of strengthening His statement by using what was here translated **I ASSURE YOU** (Gk. *amēn*, "truly, indeed"). The word moved from Hebrew via transliteration just as it has moved by anglicization into English. Jesus' puzzling statement did not necessarily imply that **some standing** before Him would not die. Rather, He was saying that some standing there, but not all, would witness the transfiguration. More than anything these words offered encouragement and anticipation for the coming kingdom (9:1).

Although Mount Tabor has been considered the traditional site of the transfiguration, many scholars believer the choice unlikely because of the ancient fortress located there. A better location seems to be Mount Hermon, located about 12 miles north of Caesarea Philippi. Peter's suggestion of erecting tabernacles would not only indicate that **Elijah** and **Moses** were of the same importance as Jesus but also would have diverted Jesus from the cross in the process (v. 5). The TRANSFIGURATION (Gk. *metemorphōthē*, "changed in form") was an actual event that showed Christ's glory. Truths were illuminated through this extraordinary event:

- Jesus was the fulfillment of the Law (represented by Moses) and of the prophets (represented by Elijah).

- Jesus prefigured the glory that would be His at the time of His return.

- All believers were represented (Moses represented those who had died and been buried, Dt 34:5-6; Elijah was translated without dying and represented those who remain alive at the time of Christ's return, 2 Kg 2:11).

- This event demonstrated beyond doubt that Jesus was more than He appeared to be, i.e., God in human flesh.

- The transfiguration was also meant for the spiritual training of those who were with Him. Jesus' words, **Elijah really has come** (v. 13), referred to John the Baptist who "will go before Him in the spirit and power of Elijah" (Lk 1:17), thus fulfilling the prophecy

of the forerunner who was to prepare the way for Messiah (see Is 40:3; Mal 3:1-2; 4:5).

Healing a boy (9:14-29)

9:14-29 Mark told the story of the demon-possessed boy with urgency, dramatic detail, and intense emotion. Only Mark recorded Jesus' question to the father (v. 21). And only Mark recorded the father's desperate plea: **I do believe! Help my unbelief** (v. 24). This plea for help demonstrated what the disciples needed to do in order to cast out the demon in the first place: they needed to seek God in prayer and ask for help as a true disciple would do. Perhaps the disciples had begun to believe that the power to cast out demons was their own, or perhaps they assumed that they controlled the power and thus determined when it would be used. The disciples had had success in casting out demons (6:13). Jesus gave an instructive reply, reminding the disciples of the real source of power, which is available to all believers through **prayer**. FASTING (Gk. *nēsteia*, "going without food"), although not included in all early manuscripts, is a natural response when one's entire focus of body and mind is turned to God. Prayer and **fasting** often go hand in hand because in praying with your heart and mind fixed upon God, the mundane needs of the body are overshadowed with the urgency of the spiritual battle before you. Fasting for the Jews was observed for different reasons:

- as part of observing the Day of Atonement (Lv 23:27-32);

- as a sign of mourning (1 Sm 31:13; Est 4:1-3);

- as personal or corporate repentance (1Sm 7:6; Dn 9:3-19);

- as a way of calling out to God during suffering or sickness (2 Sm 12:16-23);

- as part of important decision-making (2 Ch 20:1-18; Est 4:16).

Fasting was never meant to be a perfunctory ritual to attract the attention of others but rather a very private and personal means of drawing a believer closer to God.

Announcement of betrayal (9:30-32)

9:30-32 Three times Jesus predicted His own suffering and death (8:31-33; 9:30-32; 10:32-34). In each case, He used the opportunity to teach His disciples, following the prediction with a section on what it means to be a disciple of Christ (8:34-39; 9:33-37; 10:35-45). Jesus made it clear that to follow Him would be contrary to current Jewish understanding and expectation. His true mission as Messiah was to suffer and die for the sins of all people. Genuine discipleship demanded complete commitment to Him, coupled with selfless service for others whom they would encounter.

True servanthood (9:33-50)

9:33-37 In another lesson on discipleship, Jesus discussed the meaning of true greatness, which was never the advancing of oneself but rather the pouring out of one's life in service to others. Jesus set the highest example of self-denial and sacrificial service even to giving His life (10:45). The disciples still did not understand. Jesus then illustrated His point with a young **child**. The most humble, helpless, vulnerable, and seemingly insignificant one in the kingdom was called out to illustrate the demeanor demanded in discipleship and to provide an opportunity for Jesus to affirm His love and recognition of the value of the children (v. 37). Jesus made clear again that greatness in His kingdom was not determined by position or possessions but by having a servant's heart and humble spirit.

9:38-41 Jesus by no means erased the exclusivity of the gospel. There is only one way for salvation (Rm 10:9,13). However, within the body of believers should be an inclusive spirit of love—not to violate one's conscience by supporting what you believe to be contrary to Scripture (Ac 5:29) but by being loving and kind in the way you interact with those whose approach is different than your own. Two cannot walk together unless they have agreed on the nonnegotiables, the great doctrines of faith, but there is a place for diversity of methodology (vv. 39-40). He may have been warning the Twelve that they were not His only disciples. Others had committed themselves to follow Christ and to do His work.

9:42-48 Jesus was stressing that the destructive nature of evil demanded a radical offensive action. He was certainly not calling for mutilation of the body; rather, He was emphasizing the necessity of avoiding eternal punishment or jeopardizing one's right standing with God whatever the cost. HELL (Gk. *geennan*) is derived from the Valley of Hinnom (Hb. *ge'hinnom*), which is a valley southwest of what is known as the Old City of Jerusalem. During the monarchy, occult practices—even cremation of babies as sacrifices to pagan gods like Baal and Molech (2 Kg 23:10; Jr 7:31-32; 32:35)—were followed here by apostasizing Jews. In later years the place became a trash dump and was known as the place of destruction by fire, Gehenna (Jr 31:40). The place continued as a dumping ground for garbage and sewage during the intertestamental time. This metaphor was Jesus' most effective description to warn His hearers that the torments of **hell** are real and eternal and thus should be avoided at all costs.

9:49-50 Verse 49 must be connected to verse 43. Therefore, Jesus was affirming the eternal fire awaiting unbelievers in the day of punishment. Since the disciples had already been told that they were the "salt of the earth" (Mt 5:13) to preserve against decay and to season the world with Christlike character, being useful to the Lord, the mention of **salt** here was meant to illustrate a vivid contrast. The tragedy of the lack of salt would become readily apparent. Here it represented purification. Jesus admonished His followers to prevent decay and to preserve life.

Teaching on divorce (10:1-12)

10:1-12 In their interchange with Jesus, the Pharisees were not interested in answers to difficult questions; they wanted only to entrap Jesus (v. 2, **to test Him**). Perhaps they remembered that Herod Antipas had murdered John the Baptist because of John's condemnation of Herod's marriage to Herodias and thought Herod would get rid of Jesus for the same reason. **Divorce** remains a challenging issue to consider. The Jews generally were one-minded in allowing divorce, but they differed on the acceptable grounds for divorce. The religious leaders themselves were divided into two camps and could not agree:

- Shammai and his followers interpreted "something improper" (Dt 24:1) more strictly as being immorality, such as adultery.

- Hillel and his followers believed that anything the husband found distasteful in his wife fell in this category.

Jesus' response was a classic rebuke in which He cut to the heart of the issue by answering their question with one of His own. Again the Pharisees were willing to disregard the intent of the law (see 2:23–3:6; 7:1-23). God established the first union between one man and one woman as a permanent covenant commitment. Jesus knew the religious leaders would appeal to Moses, and He did not question or throw out the law in His answer. However, He noted that Moses' permission to divorce (v. 4) was accommodating human weakness (v. 5). Jesus not only returned to the creation account and God's first unveiling of His plan for marriage, but He also noted that divorce was a concession to human stubbornness—HARDNESS (Gk. *sklērokardian*, "stubbornness of people hard to teach") "of your hearts." There is forever a tension in the Creator God's perfect will and the actions of His sinful creation.

Jesus also leveled the ground between husband and wife in the arena of marital commitment (vv. 10-12). Jesus again went beyond the Jewish religious leaders because He acknowledged that for a man to commit infidelity against his wife made him an adulterer as well. The moral obligation within the marriage covenant in the teachings of Jesus was the same for husband and wife. Jesus even recognized the right of a wife to divorce her husband, which had not been allowed in Judaism.

Jesus not only went to the heart of the problem—human rebellion was shifting the focus from divine plans—but He also lifted the discussion beyond Mosaic law to God's original plan at **creation**. God intended for one man and one woman to become inseparably **one** being, mirroring the unity within the godhead (Gn 1:27). Indeed, Jesus condemned all divorce, whether by husband or wife, as being contrary to His plan. Christians, as did the Jews before them, have fallen short on the divine mandate. However, God forgives divorce as any other sin.

Blessing of the children (10:13-16)

10:13-16 Jesus emphasized the importance of childlike faith, in which dependence upon the Lord was mandated over self-reliant trust in one's personal strength and ability. Jesus also clearly embraced the **children** with loving affection. He underlined the sanctity of each life as precious and valuable.

Jesus and a seeker (10:17-31)

10:17-31 Jesus loved the wealthy young man and revealed to him the weaknesses in his spiritual understanding. Jesus looked into the heart of this confident young man; He knew the self-reliant young man was putting his possessions in first place in his life. To put Christ first in his life, the man must first get rid of the things that commanded his greatest devotion and upon which he depended for security. Jesus illustrated the truth through irony and hyperbole (v. 25). The warning was serious, but it was presented in a humorous way.

The disciples were truly puzzled since the Jews placed great emphasis on wealth as a divine blessing. On the other hand, Jesus saw wealth as a diversion of trust from God to self. The final word affirms again that salvation is totally the work of God, and no one can achieve entrance to the kingdom with his own efforts. Jesus never tried to whitewash the Christian life, but He promised believers:

- They would **receive . . . more** than they gave up (vv. 29-30).
- They would experience difficulties and **persecutions** (v. 30).
- They would have **eternal life** (v. 30).
- They would see some surprising reversals (v. 31).

Discussion with His disciples (10:32-52)

10:32-34 Jesus then gave His third prediction of His own passion, offering more details of what He would experience as He and His disciples walked **to Jerusalem**: betrayal (v. 33), sentence of **death** (v. 33), delivery to **Gentiles** (v. 33), being mocked (v. 34), being **spit on** (v. 34),

being flogged (v. 34), execution (v. 34), and resurrection (v. 34).

10:35-45 Jesus presented a second lesson on greatness (see 9:33-37), which was also a third lesson on discipleship. Rather than focusing on position and prominence for yourself, Jesus defined another paradox, reversing human reasoning and defining greatness as serving others. He clearly said that one who would be great in His kingdom would be a SERVANT (Gk. *diakonos*, "helper," v. 43) and a SLAVE (Gk. *doulos*, v. 44)—not just to Jesus Himself but to all. Jesus culminated His instruction with an example of His own service, even to laying down His life (v. 45) as a RANSOM (Gk. *lutron*, "price paid for release, means for redeeming") or what is paid to free someone from bondage. The death of Christ is the redemption of one who trusts in Christ and seeks forgiveness from sin (see Rm 6:20-23; Heb 2:14-18; 1 Pt 1:18-19). Also significant is the allusion to the substitutionary nature of His atonement in the phrase FOR MANY (Gk. *antipollōn*, more literally "in the place of, instead of many").

Mark also uniquely paralleled the request of James and John (vv. 35-45) with their discussion on who would be the greatest (9:30-37). Both discussions defined true greatness, and both followed a prediction of Jesus' passion. Both accounts revealed just how spiritually blind the disciples were at times.

10:46-52 The accounts of Matthew and Mark were often parallel on this part of Jesus' Judean ministry. In Matthew there were two blind men in Jericho begging for healing (Mt 20:29-34). There was no contradiction when Mark focused his discussion on one of the blind men evidently for reasons specific to his purpose. Matthew recorded that Jesus and the disciples met these blind men "as they were leaving Jericho" (Mt 20:29); Mark noted that they met the men as **they came to Jericho** (v. 46). In Jesus' day there was a Jericho dating back to the Old Testament era and another Jericho dating to the New Testament period. The old Jericho was largely abandoned, but the new one was larger and much more populated. One can visit both of these archaeological sites, which are close together in distance but distinct in location, even now. The healings may have taken place somewhere between these two cities.

Mark alone named one of the blind men—**Bartimaeus**; and Mark described all the graphic details surrounding this event (vv. 49-50). Bartimaeus referred to Jesus as the **Son of David**, a messianic title. In Mark's Gospel, this title only appeared twice (v. 47; 12:35); in the latter reference, Jesus used it to describe Himself. Jesus did not silence Bartimaeus, indicating that He accepted the title.

When Jesus was near Jerusalem and the fulfillment of His mission, keeping His identity secret was no longer necessary. The opening of the blind man's eyes is juxtaposed with the blindness of the religious leaders with whom Jesus was about to engage in Jerusalem.

Jesus' Teachings at the Temple (11:1–13:37)

Triumphal entry and judgment (11:1-26)

Jesus' ministry within Jerusalem included the triumphal entry and the cleansing of the temple (11:1-19), His instructions to the disciples (11:20-26; 12:35-44; 13:1-37), and His conflicts with the religious leaders (11:27-33; 12:1-34). The hostility of the religious leaders who were instrumental in bringing about Jesus' death was vividly described.

11:1-11 With regard to the importance of the triumphal entry, the unique way in which Jesus entered the city combined hints of His messiahship as the Son of David with an explicit statement of the spiritual dimension. He was the fulfillment of prophecy, and He brought deliverance, although not in the political ways the people envisioned. This entry was humble and lowly as prophesied (Zch 9:9) and stands in contrast to His victorious return to usher in His kingdom (Rv 19:11). HOSANNA (Hb, meaning "save now") was first used to call for God's power to save, but by this time the word had become a joyous shout of praise or call for victory (v. 9).

11:12-14 The nation of Israel and her hypocritical religious leaders were represented by the barren **fig tree**, which looked good on the outside but bore no fruit (v. 13). Jesus cursed the tree, and it withered (v. 21), prefiguring God's judgment on Israel. Some question Jesus' response because of Mark's interjection concerning **the season** for harvest fruit. One does well to remember that such a statement could merely serve as a device to alert the reader to consider the lesson in the event. **Bethphage** (lit. "house of figs") must have been close to Jerusalem, but its location is not noted on maps. **Bethany** was only two miles east of Jerusalem and seemed a popular stop for Jesus as He often stayed in the home of His friends Lazarus, Mary, and Martha (v. 1; Mt. 21:17; Jn 12:1).

11:15-22 Following the account of the fig tree was the cleansing of **the temple** and then a return to the fig tree. Mark might have had a purpose for arranging his material in this way. The judgment symbolized by the cursing of the fig tree might have been a precursor of what was to come in the temple, emphasizing the barren state of Judaism, just as the cleansing judgment of the temple could be prophetic of the coming destruction of Jerusalem (chap. 13). Not only were the people not fed spiritually, but also the temple had been taken over by the charlatan money-makers who found their profit in dishonest practices—and all in the name of religion (vv. 15-17). They charged inflated prices for sacrificial animals, excluding the participation of poor people in offering sacrifices.

Even the priest had allowed politics to enter the spiritual realm. The chief priests had been descendants of Zadok (see 1 Ch 24) from the days of Solomon until the time of Antiochus IV. From that time onward each conquering ruler selected the high priest. Officers of the temple then came from the wealthy and influential families of Jewish society.

11:23-26 Considering the context, Mark could have been directing the attention of his readers away from the sorrow prompted by the cursing of the fig tree (a metaphor for Israel) and to the faithfulness of God. Only by trusting Him, not by their acts of worship, could they find salvation and have their needs met. There are often figures of speech used in Scripture, such as Jesus' hyperbole concerning throwing a **mountain** into **the sea** to make the point that God is able to do anything. However, God's omnipotence did not presuppose the Creator's willingness to acquiesce to any whim or request from His creation. Nevertheless, God's character remains a reminder of His loving care for His children and His determination to be involved in their lives in a providential way. Faith is a key in the phenomenon of answered prayer. Yet faith includes an element of submission to the Father and to His will. To pray believing includes submitting yourself to accept whatever God wills when you pray.

As far as your posture when praying, the text does not mandate standing since in Scripture both standing and kneeling are mentioned as acceptable positions for praying. More important is the relationship between prayer and forgiveness. Nothing negates prayer as much as an unforgiving heart (see Mt 6:13-14; 7:7; 17:20; 18:19; Lk 11:9; 17:6). This forgiveness is certainly not to be interpreted as questioning the security of the salvation of one who has been redeemed, which offers absolute assurance of your position in Christ for all eternity. On the other hand, your fellowship with other believers and with the Father is dependent upon your having a pure heart before Him. If you harbor an unforgiving spirit toward your brother or sister in the Lord, you have broken your fellowship with the Father as well. Your position in Christ is secure, but your separation from the delights of fellowship with Him is not to be taken lightly.

Teaching and debate (11:27–12:44)

With respect to these teachings and debates, Matthew and Mark contain similar accounts of this section (see Mt 21:23–22:46 on Christ's interchange with the religious leaders), except that Matthew recorded the parable of the wedding banquet not found in Mark's Gospel (22:1-14). However, Matthew omitted the story about the widow's coins found here (12:41-44).

12:1-12 Jesus used this parable to expose the plot on His life and the coming divine judgment on all who rejected Him. The **man** represented God; the **tenant farmers** represented Israel; the **slave**[s] represented the prophets; the **beloved son** represented Jesus. Clearly this parable seemed to be directed against the religious leaders who opposed Jesus' ministry from its inception. The messianic implications were there. Jesus was understood to be the son in the parable. He applied the quotation from Psalm 118:22-23 to Himself (vv. 10-11). He presented His coming rejection by the people themselves and His death at their hands.

12:13-17 Again Jesus was in conflict with the religious leaders. The Herodians (identified as men who supported Herod) and the Pharisees were not usually united, but here they joined forces in an attempt to **TRAP** (Gk. *agreusōsin*, "catch off guard"), a word implying deceit, often used to describe catching an animal in a trap. Using flattery, they addressed an issue that did seem to present an impossible issue for Jesus. If He instructed the people to **pay taxes** they thought unfair, they would undoubtedly turn on Him; if He suggested anarchy against Roman government, He would be arrested. The Herodians paid taxes willingly to gain favor with government leaders, but the Pharisees did so only grudgingly. Jesus acknowledged the responsibility of the people and their spiritual leaders to their government, but He did not fail to affirm that any obligation due the state was less important than their foremost responsibility to God (v. 17).

12:18-27 The **Sadducees**, mentioned only here in Mark's Gospel, did not believe in the **resurrection** (v. 18). Some historians have claimed that they accepted only the Pentateuch as Scripture, but all are agreed that they did not accept the oral tradition of the scribes and Pharisees. The Sadducees tried to entrap Jesus with a question about the resurrection. Jesus responded with a counter question showing their lack of understanding of **the Scriptures** and ignorance concerning **the power of God**. The question alluded to the Jewish law of levirate marriage in which **a wife** whose husband died without a male heir would marry her husband's brother in order to produce an heir and preserve her deceased husband's name and property. Jesus corrected the Sadducees on their misunderstanding of the resurrection, affirming that there would be no marriage in heaven, which made their question moot.

12:28-34 When **one of the scribes** asked Jesus, **"Which commandment is the most important of all?"** Jesus **answered** him directly, quoting from Deuteronomy 6:4-5 (vv. 29-30) and Leviticus 19:18 (v. 31). He used *shema* (Hb.), so named because the initial word begins with "listen" (v. 29). This Jewish confession of faith was recited then and now by devout Jews evening and morning. The reference to FIRST (Gk. *prōtē*, "leading, foremost, most important") might have been more a reference to significance than to sequence. Jesus not only answered His critics, but He confounded them. Their response changed from one encounter to the next:

- "They left Him and went away" (v. 12).

- "They were amazed at Him" (v. 17).

- **No one dared question Him any longer** (v. 34).

12:35-37 Jesus fulfilled all Scripture. In reversing the question-and-answer session, Jesus posed His own question. He understood that the question here was not concerning the validity of Scripture itself but rather an attempt to determine how Scripture should be interpreted. Even in the modern era, within the kingdom this challenge remains at the forefront. Since **David** was speaking of his descendant as his **Lord**, not a characteristic way for fathers to refer to their sons, he must have had in mind someone who was more than a son or descendant. Jesus did not deny His Davidic descent, but He was correcting the misunderstanding, among His followers and the people, that the Messiah was to be a liberating ruler. Jesus showed that He was more than **the Son of David**. As the Son of Man, Jesus represented not only the Jews but also humanity.

12:38-40 Often there is misunderstanding of the difference between clergy and laity. Here the religious leaders showed their pride and arrogance by wearing garments associated with their ecclesiastical office and by demanding and receiving a special deference from the people (v. 38). They also had special seating **in the synagogues** and experienced prestigious expressions of honor and protocol at festive events (v. 39). They forgot that they themselves were servants of God who should be seeking to honor Him and serve others in behalf of Him. They were to be supported by the people, but they had again abused this practice for unlawful gain and at the expense of those among the people who were most vulnerable (v. 40).

Heart to Heart: Loving Your Neighbor

Who is a neighbor (Gk. poleōs, "the inhabitants of a city")? The word is rather inclusive—those who live in your home, in your community (including those who serve you), in your church, in your workplace and those with whom you do business, and even those whom you meet casually in your recreational pursuits.

Jesus, in the context of His life and ministry, seemed to have expanded the circle of those who are considered a neighbor. According to Jesus, the neighborhood is the world. All are to fall under the shadow of loving concern. He had a formula for expressing love that cannot be misunderstood: you are to love and thus value others as you would yourself. What is called the "golden rule" is the path to peace and harmony for all. Furthermore, Jesus added stature and importance to the mandate when He denominated it a commandment and second only to the command to love God Himself. In other words this command to love your neighbor is one of two parts that make the whole of the Christian life.

12:41-44 After Jesus' encounters with the religious leaders, He sat down in the temple court. Interestingly, He was in the court of women, a place in which both men and women could gather and also where the **treasury** was located. **A poor widow** caught His attention. She put in the box two tiny **COINS** (Gk. *lepta*, the smallest coin in Palestine, each valued at about one-eighth of a cent), the smallest currency in circulation among the Jews at that time. Yet her gift was genuinely sacrificial. Jesus paid attention even to the smallest details. This scene is sharply contrasted with the disciples, who, upon visiting the same temple, noticed the "impressive buildings" (13:1). Character, not concrete, impressed Jesus. The amount of a gift was not as important as the attitude of the heart (2 Co 9:6-7).

Prediction of destruction and announcement of Christ's return (13:1-37)

The discourse on the last days of Jesus, known as the Olivet Discourse and delivered on the Mount of Olives (v. 3), was by

Women Ministering to Jesus

Woman	Her Ministry	Practical Application	Reference
Mary	Nurturing Jesus as He grew into manhood	Mothers are to rear their children by nurturing them in the Lord (Eph 6:4).	Lk 21:51-52
Susanna	Supporting Jesus' ministry with her energies and resources	Women have opportunity to invest time, energy, and resources (1 Tm 6:17-19).	Lk 8:1-3
Mary of Bethany	Listening to Jesus as He taught spiritual truth	Women must take time to study God's Word and to listen for His voice (2 Tm 2:15; Heb 4:12).	Lk 10:39
Samaritan woman	Hearing Jesus share the gospel, accepting His grace, sharing her testimony with others	Women, too, have the responsibility to share the good news of the gospel (1 Pt 3:15).	Jn 4:28-30
The mother-in-law of Simon Peter	Extending hospitality to Jesus and His disciples	In a sense, all hospitality is offered ultimately to Jesus (Col 3:17,23-24).	Mk 1:29-31
The widow with two tiny coins	Generously supporting the kingdom	The Lord never expects you to give more than you have—only to be generous with what has been entrusted to you (Heb 6:10).	Mk 12:41-44
Mary of Bethany	Preparing Jesus' body for burial	Even mundane tasks are important (Mk 14:8).	Mt 26:6-13
Mary Magdalene	Staying with Jesus even when He was rejected, giving the first proclamation to His resurrection	Women must stand firm in the faith even in times of discouragement and persecution (Rm 8:35-39; 2 Co 3:23). They must be ready to share the good news of the resurrection (1 Pt 3:15).	Mt 27:55; Jn 19:25; 20:1-18

far the longest teaching segment in Mark's Gospel. The discourse was part of the APOCALYPTIC (from Gk. root *apoka-luptō*, "reveal, disclose," and thus claiming to reveal the future) genre and was also identified as "The Little Apocalypse," typically symbolic in many ways, and commonly used in Jesus' day. Some scholars question whether or not Jesus said the words attributed to Him, preferring to assign the words to editors or other sources, but the words clearly represented Jesus' teachings and contained appropriate instruction to prepare the disciples for His death.

13:1-13 In addition to the discussion of what is to come, Mark's Gospel was a testimony, including the words of Jesus Himself, encouraging and exhorting His followers to prepare for His imminent return and to warn them against the deceivers who would come to pull them away, leaving for the generations to come a legacy of instruction for living the Christian life.

Jesus warned His disciples about the danger of being deceived in very graphic terms:

• **Many will come in My name,** false messiahs (v. 6).

- **Wars and rumors of wars** (vv. 7-8), with the most immediate example being the coming war with Rome, which resulted in the destruction of Jerusalem in AD 70, followed by a host of conflicts, until the present era.

- **Earthquakes . . . and famines** (v. 8), natural disasters that would continue to escalate.

- Persecutions (vv. 9-13), which not only attacked Jesus and His disciples but which have continued throughout the generations of those who honor Christ. The phrase HAND YOU OVER (Gk. *paradōsousi*) runs as a thread through verses 9-12, appearing three times in the Greek text. In verse 12 the word is translated "betray," and the same word is used repeatedly in chapters 14 and 15 in reference to the betrayal of Jesus and His being handed over to His enemies.

The signs announcing the end of the age are confined to a remote future, but these signs did begin in the generation contemporaneous with Jesus. Yet the signs continue into the future and notably are not exhausted or ended in the present era, underscoring the absolute reliability of Jesus' words not only for the time in which He lived but until now and into the future.

Jesus spoke of the near future, which would be the destruction of Jerusalem and the temple in AD 70, and of the distant future or the great tribulation. Mark's record of the teaching of Jesus' last days was also full of exhortations and imperatives concerning practical, ethical living. The discourse was not delivered merely to satisfy curiosity about the future. Rather, Jesus combined information on what was coming in the future with an exhortation to live and bear witness in a hostile world.

The emphasis was on being vigilant and spiritually alert since no one knows the time of Jesus' return (vv. 32-33).

13:14-23 Jesus referred to the **abomination that causes desolation** (13:14; see Dn 9:27; 11:31; 12:11; Mt 24:15) or the great tribulation and the appearance of antichrist. ABOMINATION (Gk. *bdelugma*, "something detestable, sacrilegious object") was a reference to anything that is repulsive to God or the idolatrous practices and immorality (Dt 29:16-17; 1 Kg 11:6-7; Ezk 8:9-18). The reference to OF DESOLATION (Gk. *erēmōseōs*, "lonely, uninhabited place") addressed the result produced by the "abomination." In other words, the events coming would be so detestable that God's people would even abandon the temple. The first fulfillment came in 168–167 BC when Antiochus Epiphanes, a Syrian ruler, erected an altar to Zeus and sacrificed a pig on it, defiling the temple altar of burnt offering. Then a second fulfillment came with the destruction of the temple in AD 70, and final fulfillment will come when antichrist desecrates the temple and breaks his covenant with Israel in the middle of the great tribulation (see Dn 9:24-27; 2 Th 2:3-4; Rv 13:14-15).

13:24-37 No one but the Father **knows** the day or the hour of Christ's return. Jesus clearly told His disciples that they would not know the date and time set by **the Father** (v. 32; Ac 1:7), for a determined focus on the future could hinder their main mission, which was to preach the good news. The coming of Christ described in verses 24-27 is not the rapture or translation of the church (1 Th 4:13-18; 1 Co 15:51-58), but the return of **the Son of Man** (v. 26) following the great tribulation (vv. 14-23) and inauguration of the "millennial" kingdom (Rv 19:11-21).

The Climax of Jesus' Life
(14:1–16:20)

Preparation for Suffering (14:1-72)

The passion of Christ was central for Mark as for all four Gospels. Of the 661 verses in the book of Mark, 128 of them were devoted to the Lord's passion, and a total of 242 recounted the last week of His life. The suffering of Christ was all-consuming for Mark. And, as has been mentioned many times, there was a good reason for Mark's emphasis. The church to whom he was writing was undergoing heavy persecution. For their own encouragement they needed to hear about the trials of the One whom they served.

A series of events delivered Jesus to death:

- the betrayal by Judas, one of His inner circle (vv.10-11)

- the desertion of most of those closest to Jesus (vv. 27-31,50)

- the religious and civil trials (vv. 53-65; 15:1-5)

- His crucifixion (15:16-41).

14:1-2 None of these events took Jesus by surprise. He knew from eternity past His mission (10:45) and the ultimate victory that would be His (16:6,19-20). THE PASSOVER (Gk. *pascha*) and "the Festival of UNLEAVENED Bread" (Gk. *ta azuma*, without yeast, with the article *ta* or "the" used to describe the Feast), which was celebrated subsequent to Passover, were important to the Jews. **The Passover** reminded the Jews of that last night their forefathers spent in Egypt where the angel of death killed all the firstborn in Egypt but "passed over" the homes of all who displayed the blood of the slain lamb over the doorpost. All the Jewish households who were obedient and trusted God's Word were spared. The subsequent **festival** lasted seven days and

commemorated the exodus from Egypt (see Ex 12:1-51).

14:3-9 Jesus' sufferings were highlighted in this section by betrayal and denial. Like Matthew, Luke, and John, Mark highlighted Mary's devotion to Christ as she **anointed** Jesus in preparation for His **burial**. She was identified as Mary of **Bethany**. In the midst of this dark hour in Jesus' life, she stood out as a model of committed devotion. Mary gave her attention to Jesus and ministered to Him; He in turn expressed gratitude to her and recorded her testimony for generations to come (v. 9).

14:10-26 Perhaps because **Judas** went immediately to **betray** Jesus, he was identified as one of those who questioned Mary's use of extravagant oil to anoint Jesus (vv. 4-5; Jn 12:4-6). BETRAY (Gk. *paradoi*, "hand over") was not only a deceitful act, but the one who would "hand over" a friend was without honor. Especially would this dishonor fall upon one who would eat (an important act of friendship) with the man he intended to betray (v. 20). A comparison of the accounts of this final meal Jesus had with **His disciples** suggests that Judas evidently did leave the meal before the institution of the memorial supper by the Lord (vv. 20-21). Judas had not questioned Mary's extravagance because of his concern for the poor but because of his own greed (Jn 12:4-6).

Jesus used two familiar symbols when He instituted the Lord's Supper with His disciples: **bread** (v. 22) and the **cup** or **fruit of the vine** (vv. 23-25). The reference to drinking of the cup **in the kingdom of God** must point to a time beyond Jesus' crucifixion and resurrection and to the Lord's return to establish His glorious kingdom (v. 25).

14:27-31 Jesus again quoted the Old Testament (Zch 13:7) in order to present a poignant picture of the desertion of the

---

Heart to Heart:
She Did What She Could

When a woman offers to Christ her committed devotion in service to Him personally, as did Mary in her anointing of Jesus, or to someone else in His name, she will always be rewarded. Perhaps the one she serves or to whom she gives sacrificially will express loving gratitude, but far more important to her is the commendation of the Savior, who does indeed note every deed of loving-kindness done in His name (see Heb 6:10).

Have you ever been hurt because your sacrifice went unnoticed by husband or child, by parent or sibling, by friend or foe? Don't dwell on what is not said or gratitude not given, but instead offer your kind word or deed for another to Christ. He will receive it as a gift to Himself, and your testimony will be etched in the stones of eternity honoring Him and opening the door for Him to honor you. Do what you can do with what you have, while you can, where you are.

---

disciples during His hour of suffering and death. He used the metaphor of **the shepherd** to describe Himself in relation to the disciples (His **sheep**). The difficulty lies in understanding **run away**, which in some versions is translated "fall away" (Gk. *skandalisthesesthē*, "cause to sin, be led into sin, desert, have doubts"). The verb has a wide range of meanings, but the context, especially the quote from Zechariah, does help in interpreting the meaning here. Nothing interprets Scripture as effectively as another passage of Scripture. The disciples would not lose their salvation (a premise clear throughout the whole of Scripture, Jn 10:28-29); rather, they would falter in their faith and thus abandon Jesus for a time. Few people realize their weaknesses, and **Peter** certainly fit this model. Despite the bold disciple's interruption and rebuttal, Jesus announced that Peter would not only fulfill the prophecy but would do it soon and repeatedly (v. 30). Jesus even used one of His favorite words for emphasis (Gk.

amen, "truly, indeed"), translated here **I assure you**.

14:32-42 Gethsemane, an anglicization of the Greek word meaning "oil press," was a garden located on the Mount of Olives. Jesus often went there to **pray**. This prayer was not uttered by one who was weak or fearful. No matter how much Jesus suffered from knowing the temporary alienation from the Father was coming, He chose the path of obedience with determination, knowing the divine necessity for His death to make atonement for all who would turn to Him in faith.

14:43-52 Evidently those who were sent to **arrest** Jesus did not know Him. His popularity at that time may have made it difficult for the religious leaders to find people who knew Jesus and were willing to betray Him in this way. Rabbis were often greeted by their disciples with the common sign of affection and esteem—the **kiss**. Judas probably feared for his own life and thus chose this deceptive

Jewish Feasts and Festivals			
Name	**Reference**	**Date of Celebration**	**Significance**
Passover	Ex 12:2-20; Lv 23:5	Nisan (Mar./Apr.)	Commemorated God's deliverance of Israel out of Egypt.
Festival of Unleavened Bread	Lv 23:6-8	Nisan (Mar./Apr.)	Commemorated God's deliverance of Israel out of Egypt. Included a day of firstfruits for the barley harvest.
Festival of Weeks, or Harvest (Pentecost)	Ex 23:16; 34:22; Lv 23:15-21	Sivan (May/June; seven weeks after Passover)	Commemorated the giving of the law on Mount Sinai. Included a day of firstfruits for the wheat harvest.
Festival of Trumpets (Rosh Hashanah)	Lv 23:23-25; Nm 29:1-6	Tishri (Sept./Oct.)	Signaled the day with a blowing of the trumpets to begin the new civil year.
Day of Atonement (Yom Kippur)	Lv 23:26-33; Ex 30:10	Tishri (Sept./Oct.)	On this day of fasting the high priest made atonement for the nation's sin.
Festival of Booths or Tabernacles (Sukkot)	Lv 23:33-43; Nm 29:12-39; Dt 16:13	Tishri (Sept./Oct.)	Commemorated the forty years of wilderness wandering.
Festival of Dedication or Festival of Lights (Hanukkah)	Jn 10:22	Kislev (Nov./Dec.) and Tebeth (Dec./Jan.)	Commemorated the purification of the temple by Judas Maccabaeus in 164 BC.
Festival of Purim or Esther	Est 9	Adar (Feb./Mar.)	Commemorated the deliverance of the Jewish people in the days of Esther.

means of identifying Jesus for those who sought to do Him harm. This action in itself showed how little Judas knew about the Savior. Judas expected resistance.

One of those is a reference to Simon Peter (v. 47; Jn 18:10). Many believe the **certain young man** who left **naked** was an autobiographical reference to Mark since such trivia would be an unusual inclusion unless it was imbedded in the mind of the author himself (v. 51), and its inclusion served to add to the authenticity of the entire book.

14:53-64 Jesus had two trials—religious and civil. The religious trial involved a progression:

- Before Annas, the father-in-law of the high priest Caiphas and a former high priest himself (Jn 18:19-24)

- Then Caiphas, **the high priest**, who had assembled **all the chief priests, the elders, and the scribes** (vv. 53-65)

- Formal condemnation by the Sanhedrin (Lk 22:66-71).

In the religious trials Jesus was charged with **blasphemy** because He affirmed that He was indeed the Son of God (14:61-64). Jesus also appeared before Pilate in a civil trial, without which He would not have been crucified (15:1-15). Although the Jews, especially their religious leaders, had much freedom to pursue their own ends, only the Roman government could condemn for capital crimes. Here Jesus was accused of treason and of causing a public insurrection against the Roman government, and Jesus did indeed affirm that He was "King of the Jews" (15:2).

14:65-72 Peter did show his deep affection for and commitment to Jesus by following Him into an area where he also would be at risk. However, as with many believers, he allowed his human fears to overcome his spiritual resources, which were available to give him strength for the difficult times.

Crucifixion and burial (15:1-47)

Because of Mark's emphasis on the suffering of Christ's disciples all through his Gospel, his consideration in a more in-depth fashion of the sufferings of Christ Himself seemed appropriate. Modern Christians living in the affluent West generally do not like to focus on the horrors of the crucifixion because they are too negative for a people who put a premium on comfort. Women especially would much rather focus on the "relational" aspects of the gospel. But without

the cross, there would be no meaningful relationships. One cannot study the Gospels with an understanding heart without coming to the conclusion that the tragic journey along the Via Dolorosa (Lat. "the Way of Sorrow") is good news. It is the only way to heaven. Mark made it abundantly clear: The Via Dolorosa is not for Jesus only but for all who would follow Him. The crucifixion is essential to faith.

15:1-20 The Roman government had a **custom** of releasing a prisoner for the Jews during the Festival of Unleavened Bread because of its commemoration of the release of the Hebrews from Egyptian bondage as a gesture of goodwill. **Pilate** believed they would choose Jesus for release over the criminal **Barabbas**. However, once the Jews made their choice of Barabbas, Pilate proceeded not only to condemn Jesus to death by crucifixion but also to call for flogging and scourging, which was a barbaric, senseless, cruel punishment in which the victim was **stripped** to the waist with his hands bound to a stationary pole while he was mercilessly whipped. The whip itself was a torturous instrument consisting of a handle with attached leather thongs weighted with jagged pieces of bone and rock. The victim was most assuredly disfigured and often died from this ordeal (v. 15).

15:21-47 Even the Romans recognized crucifixion as the most hideous death. GOLGOTHA (Gk. *Golgothan,* transliterated into Greek and English from the Aramaic name of a hill near the site of Jerusalem in Jesus' day) was the place of execution, located outside the city walls. The meaning is found in the text, the SKULL PLACE (Gk. *kraniou,* "skull," 15:22; Mt 27:33; Lk 23:33; Jn 19:17). As He was being crucified, Jesus refused the sedating drink traditionally offered by the women of Jerusalem to make the excruciating pain more bearable for the victim (v. 23). Unknowingly the Roman soldiers themselves fulfilled the ancient prophecy (see Ps 22:18), which they would never have done purposefully (v. 24).

Look, He's calling for Elijah (v. 35) may have been the crowd's misunderstanding of **Eloi** (Aram. *elōi,* my God), which the people thought sounded like the name of Elijah. However, perhaps more likely is the interpretation that the crowd was taunting Jesus since Elijah (Hb. "my God is *Yahweh"*) was regarded as one who would prepare the way for the Messiah (9:11-13; see also Mt 17:3) and since Elijah was reported to have been in intimate conversation with Jesus at the time of His transfiguration (9:4; see also Lk 9:30-31).

The following order of events culminating in Jesus' death was assembled from a summary of the accounts found in all four of the Gospels:

- The Passover meal was eaten with the disciples (14:12-21; Lk 22:14-16, 24-30)
- Jesus' washing of the disciples' feet (Jn 13:1-20)
- Judas' departure from the meal (Jn 13:21-30)
- Jesus' institution of the memorial supper (14:22-26; Lk 22:17-20)
- Jesus' prayer in Gethsemane (14:26, 32-42)
- Judas's betrayal of Jesus (14:43-46; Jn 18:2-12)
- Jesus' appearance before Annas the former high priest (Jn 18:13-14, 19-24)
- Jesus' condemnation by the high priest Caiphas and the Sanhedrin (14:53,55-65)
- Peter's denial of the Lord (14:66-72; Jn 18:15-18, 25-27)

- Jesus' formal sentencing before the Sanhedrin (Lk 22:66-71)
- Jesus in the court of Pilate (15:1-15; Jn 18:28-38)
- Jesus before Herod Antipas (Lk 23:6-12)
- Jesus' sentence delivered by Pilate (15:6-15; Lk 23:13-25)
- Jesus' flogging (15:15-20; Jn 19:1-14)
- Jesus' crucifixion (15:23-32)
- Jesus' death (15:37)
- The tearing of the curtain of the sanctuary (15:37-38; Mt 27:50-54)
- The piercing of Jesus' side (Jn 19:31-37).

The tearing of **the curtain of the sanctuary . . . from top to bottom** made clear that God was in control, and it was a reminder that through Christ's death all would have direct access to God (v. 38; see Heb 10:19-22). Even **the centurion**, the Roman soldier in charge of the band of soldiers assigned to keep order among the people and execute the ordered crucifixion, recognized that Jesus is the Son of God (v. 39), a fact that would have special significance in Mark's Gospel, since it was primarily directed to a Gentile audience. This seasoned military officer was strangely moved and drawn to Jesus. Whether or not the military official realized the full meaning of his words, he clearly identified Jesus as **God's Son**.

Resurrection (16:1-20)

Mark's Gospel has theological distinctives. Christ's passion was the apex of His ministry as the Suffering Servant. He came to give His life as a ransom for many (10:45). The disciples' failure was also noted in reference to betrayal, denial, and even desertion. All happened as Jesus predicted. The crucifixion and resurrection confirmed that Jesus is the Son of God, and those who would follow Him must be willing to walk the path of suffering with Him.

A plausible explanation for the brevity of Mark's account of the resurrection could be that his original audience was already quite familiar with the details of this world-shaking event. Furthermore, he might not have retold the story in order to highlight the balance needed and the tension associated with living the Christian life before Christ's return.

There are more similarities than differences between the contents of the Gospels penned by Mark and Matthew. However, some of the differences may be important in understanding the role of the women who were disciples of Jesus Christ. Those differences included one significant addition to Matthew's account, two seemingly purposeful deletions, and another long-debated possible deletion or change.

The addition has to do with Mark's description of the women disciples viewing the crucifixion. After naming the same three women (15:40) as in Matthew (Mt 27:56, if, as many believe, Salome was the mother of James and John, the sons of Zebedee), the passage referred to "many other women" who had "come up with Him to Jerusalem" (15:41). Though not specifically numbered or named, other women, beyond those specifically named in the Gospel passages, followed Jesus.

The first deletion has to do with any mention of the Jewish leaders or Roman guards, both of whom played prominent roles in Matthew's account (27:62-66; 28:2-4,11-15). In their absence, the narrative starting at Mark 15:40 described only those who were disciples of Jesus. The attention paid to the women disciples, including identifying them by name (15:40-41; 15:47–16:10), was remarkable during a time when women were not at the forefront in public gatherings.

Women, without the labor-saving devices or convenient help of the modern era, were needed in their homes to care for their households and children; they were busily engaged in the mundane tasks essential for a family's life and health. There is no hint in Scripture that any women serving Christ in special ways neglected their homes or families in so doing.

16:1-8 The second deletion, which was more subtle, had to do with the mention of fear (v. 8) without the allusion to "great joy" recorded in Matthew's account (Mt 28:8). Fear on the part of the women fit the unusual encounter they experienced. Interestingly, in verse 8 the word translated FEAR (Gk. *ephobounto*, "fear, be afraid") is also used to mean "worship" or "reverence." Certainly, there must have been increased heartbeat and uncertainty—elements of physical fear. However, in verse 6 the word translated DON'T BE ALARMED (Gk. *ekthambeisthe*, "greatly surprised or distressed") has a different connotation. The women experienced awe and reverence for the risen Christ. Especially in the latter case, the women were not in any sense portrayed in a bad light but with a very positive report of their reverence for Christ. In fact, the women also fled from the tomb just as the male disciples had run away from Christ and had failed to stand by Him at the time of His arrest, trial, and crucifixion. Even more tragic is the fact that the women said nothing to anyone (16:8). The tragedy is that women and men have failed Christ in His life and in the subsequent generations. How comforting and glorious is the grace that overlooks human weakness and gives another opportunity for service.

There is no need, as some feminists attempt to read in victim mentality, to compare these women with the men who were disciples. First, Paul himself warned believers not to compare themselves with others (2 Co 10:12). More important, for women and men the goal is always to glorify Christ. Each woman must bear her own faithful testimony to Him. These women ultimately did just that (16:10). Jesus, remembering the loving acts of devotion from women who faithfully served Him, entrusted to the women disciples the message of His resurrection (16:7-8), not based on their merit or performance but as a gracious gift and opportunity.

16:9-20 These last verses of Mark's Gospel have had unusual scrutiny and thus engendered considerable debate. A number of textual critics have questioned whether or not these concluding verses were penned by the Gospel's author or added by an editor at a later time. The two earliest manuscripts, and generally the ones most respected as reliable, as well as others, had nothing after verse 8. These critics primarily appealed to internal evidence (e.g., a difference between verses 9-20 and the remainder of the Gospel). Others note that to end with verse 8 would be an abrupt and inappropriate ending. Yet as has been wisely noted by some, the abrupt ending follows an abrupt beginning of the Gospel. Mark hardly noted anything in Jesus' life before moving into the events of His ministry. Throughout the Gospel he was not concerned with smooth transitions. Also, Mark may have wanted an "open" ending as evidence that the story of Christ was not complete. By ending with announcing that the women "said nothing to anyone" (v. 8), perhaps Mark was admonishing his readers to pick up the gauntlet and proclaim the good news themselves.

Many who maintain verse 8 as the ending of the Gospel in surviving early manuscripts further argue that final verses penned by Mark must then have been lost.

The majority of the extant manuscripts of the Gospel do contain the full 20 verses, but most of these manuscripts are late in dating. What is most important for anyone seeking to interpret these verses is that whatever the precise ending of Mark may be, the verses in the canon of Scripture entrusted to believers in subsequent generations, when properly interpreted, will not cause confusion or generate erroneous doctrine. No doctrine is built upon one isolated passage; thus you must continue to search the whole counsel of God in interpreting Scripture. These verses essentially summarize the postresurrection appearances of Christ, including the Great Commission. Other Gospels record the same events.

Perhaps some of the most difficult verses to understand occur in this section (vv. 17-18). The apostles had recorded instances describing their power to exorcise demons (Ac 16:16-18). There was also a phenomenon at Pentecost in which the apostles communicated with people in languages they had never studied or those hearing the gospel understood languages with which they were not familiar. Whether a gift of speaking or hearing or both, a linguistic miracle happened at Pentecost (Ac 2:1-12). Trampling on snakes was associated with the powers accorded the Seventy who were sent out by the Lord (Lk 10:1-20), and the Apostle Paul shook off a poisonous viper on Malta (Ac 28:3-6). These happenings recorded in Acts were Pentecost and post-Pentecost events, but the point is that such occasional phenomena are noted; but they were not the norm, even if extended beyond the apostolic circle to include other believers. Neither were such miracles the focus. Jesus and the good news of the gospel occupied center stage in Mark and throughout the New Testament.

In the providences of God, the Lord promised to watch over and care for His people in their missionary endeavors. This protective care included God's occasional intervention on behalf of His servants. The fact that Peter and Paul evidently died as martyrs indicates that the Lord did not intervene in every crisis, but incidents recorded from their lives and the lives of others showed that sometimes God did intervene in miraculous ways.

There is evidence of the existence of 16:9-20 as early as Irenaeus (second century), who regarded the verses as genuine. Whatever the final verdict will be concerning the ending verses of Mark, one can have full confidence that the presence or absence of these verses does not affect the overall integrity of the book or compromise any major doctrine associated with the historic Christian faith. Amazingly God's Word has been so carefully preserved that even in debate and uncertainties among scholars, its authenticity in authority and lack of contradiction reigns supreme.

Bibliography

Brooks, James. *Mark.* The New American Commentary, vol. 23. Nashville: Broadman Press, 1991.

*Calvin, John. *Commentary on a Harmony of the Evangelists*. 3 vols. Grand Rapids: Baker, 1979.

Cole, Alan. *The Gospel According to Mark.* Leicester: IVP; Grand Rapids: Eerdmans, 1989.

*Cranfield, C. E. B. *The Gospel According to Saint Mark.* Cambridge: Cambridge University Press (CUP), rev. 1977.

*Gundry, Robert. *Mark: A Commentary on His Apology for the Cross*. Grand Rapids: Eerdmans, 1993.

Martin, R. P. *Mark: Evangelist and Theologian*. Grand Rapids: Zondervan, 1972.

*Moule, C. F. D. *The Gospel According to Mark*. Cambridge: CUP, 1965.

*Taylor, Vincent. *The Gospel According to Saint Mark*. London: Macmillan, 1952.

* For advanced study

Notes

1. Tacitus, *Annals* 15.44.

2. See Walter W. Wessel, "Mark," in Expositor's Bible Commentary, vol. 8, ed. by Frank E. Gaebelein (Grand Rapids: Zondervan, 1984), 610.

3. Eusebius, *Ecclesiastial History* 3:39.15

4. See Blomberg, *Jesus and the Gospels* (Nashville: Broadman & Holman, 1997), 123–124.

5. Eusebius, 6.14.6–7.

6. Irenaeus, *Against Heresies* 3.1.38–41.

7. The idea for this outline was adapted from Blomberg's outline.

8. Josephus, *Antiquities* 18:5.2.

9. William Lane, *The Gospel According to Mark* (Grand Rapids: Zondervan, 1974), 58.

10. Adapted from *Holman Book of Biblical Charts, Maps, and Reconstructions* (Nashville: Broadman & Holman, 1993), 71.

11. J. Jeremias, *The Parables of Jesus* (London: SCM: 1963), 153–53.

12. D. E. Nineham, *St. Mark* (Baltimore: Penguin, 1963), 144.

13. Adapted from *The Woman's Study Bible* (Nashville: Thomas Nelson Publishers, 1995), 1656.

14. Lane, 215.

[15] John Calvin, *Commentary on a Harmony of the Evangelists,* 3 vols. (Grand Rapids: Baker, 1979), 2:222.

[16] Wessel, 686.

[17] Calvin, 2:285.

[18] Ibid., 270–271.

L UKE

Introduction

The universal appeal of the Gospel of Luke has captivated a wide audience down through the ages. This Gospel has portrayed Jesus in the deepest, most intimate sense as a friend to outcasts and sinners. The Gospel of Luke has many features in common with both Matthew and Mark but has numerous unique characteristics as well. For instance, like Matthew, Luke opened his Gospel with the birth of Jesus; but, unlike Matthew, Luke's work did not record many of the lengthy sermons of Jesus. Like Matthew and Mark, Luke recorded many of Jesus' miracles, but each evangelist brought a unique perspective to the same event.

What is wholly unique to the third Gospel is what is commonly known as "Luke's Central Section" (9:51–18:14), which contains Jesus' teachings from His itinerant ministry. Some of the parables in this section are recorded in Matthew and Mark, but for the most part, the material in this section is almost exclusively Lukan.

Some commentators have found it difficult to discern the overall thematic structure. However, what needs to be kept in mind is that this Gospel is the first part of a two-volume set. The book of Acts is the second part. A fuller understanding of the purpose of Luke's Gospel will only be satisfied with consideration of the volumes as one unit.

There are several good reasons to believe that the same person wrote both Luke and Acts:

- Both works are addressed to Theophilus (Lk 1:3; Ac 1:1).

- The author of Acts acknowledged a previous work, presumably the Gospel of Luke.

- The two volumes have a number of themes in common.

- The overall structure of both works is very similar.

This last point is one of the strongest pieces of evidence supporting a single author for both Luke and Acts. The Gospel begins with Jesus being born under Roman rule, then traces Jesus' travels from Galilee, through Samaria and Judea, and finally to Jerusalem, ending with Jesus' rejection by the Jews in Jerusalem and culminating with His death and resurrection. Then the book of Acts opens with Jesus' commission to the disciples to take the good news of His death and resurrection from Jerusalem to Judea, to Samaria, and to all the Gentiles. Acts then ends accordingly with the Apostle Paul preaching the gospel in Rome, under Roman rule.

Title

In the Greek text the Gospel bears the simple banner "According to Luke" (Gk. *kata Lukan*), a nondescript title but one that keeps the emphasis where it needs to be. The words indeed came through or by way of Luke, but the message of the book came from God.

Setting

Scholars have noted Antioch, Corinth, Greece, and Rome as places where Luke could have penned Luke and Acts. However, any effort to pinpoint the exact place where this Gospel originated is speculative and cannot be known with certainty. Such information would add little to an understanding of the message of Luke. Luke may have begun his research for these books during Paul's imprisonment in Caesarea (Ac 24:23). However, the writing process probably began during Paul's imprisonment in Rome.

Luke did give his readers a "purpose statement" (Lk 1:1-4). First, the Gospel was dedicated to Theophilus. It was written to build up and to confirm his faith. But one is probably safe to assume that the work was intended for a wider audience than Theophilus. It was written to win new converts and to build up those who were already converted.

Luke was concerned with advancing the Christian movement as a whole. His goal was to provide a trustworthy account of the Christian faith, and he relied on the reports of eyewitnesses (since he noted that he himself was not an eyewitness, 1:1-4), his own careful investigation of other written accounts (1:1), and perhaps even his consideration of oral tradition circulating through the church in order to establish his claims (v. 2).

Luke desired to give his readers a basis for their knowledge (v. 4). His thoroughness and his painstaking attention to detail were meant to assure believers that the events described happened just the way he recorded them. One would do well not to labor over the priority of a particular Gospel or even the traditions concerning how the respective Gospels were compiled but rather to give attention to the gospel message as it has been passed down, carefully preserved and lovingly delivered even to the present generation.

Genre

Luke's writings have almost always been denominated as near perfection in grammar and stylistic structure. He wove together colorful words as well as specialized vocabulary of both medical and theological terms in a unique and classical way. He used Hebrew and Aramaic expressions correctly but also showed literary skill in Greek. However, of greater importance to the reader is the distinctive and accurate detail Luke brought to recording historical events while conveying a theological message.

Author

Though the writer does not give his name in the book, Luke has traditionally been recognized as the author. Lukan authorship was never questioned until the last half of the nineteenth century. Luke was a Gentile doctor[1] who traveled with Paul and died at the age of 84 in Boetia, Greece. Internal and external evidence can be cited to support Lukan authorship, and one of the most convincing proofs is that the early church fathers consistently attributed the third Gospel to Luke, the companion of the Apostle Paul. The Muratorian Canon (AD 180), for instance, says, "The third book of the Gospel, according to Luke, Luke that physician, who after the ascension of Christ, when Paul had taken him with him as companion of his journey, composed in his own name on the basis of report." Even before this, the heretic Marcion (AD 135) acknowledged Luke as the author of the third Gospel.

Irenaeus not only named Luke as the author of the third Gospel, but he also claimed that Luke was Paul's closest companion. The author of the book of Acts closely associated himself with Paul (Ac 16:10-17; 20:5-15; 21:1-18; 27:1–28:16); these sections are known as the "we" passages because the author of the book of Acts identified himself as Paul's traveling companion through the use of the first-person plural pronoun. Whereas the use of the first-person plural by the author of Acts would not be considered hard evidence for Lukan authorship, it does add support to that conclusion. Paul also mentioned Luke in Colossians 4:14; Philemon 24; and 2 Timothy 4:11. The author of the Gospel of Luke indicated that he was a second-generation Christian who was in a position to investigate the person and works of Jesus.

All told, the internal and external evidence seem overwhelmingly to support the idea that Luke, the faithful companion of Paul, was the author of both Luke and Acts. However, as is true with any "anonymous" book not bearing the name of its human author, the attention is turned even more to the ultimate author—the Holy Spirit who inspired the words. The book's content comes from God, and its veracity is not determined by the identity of its human author.

Date

Luke and the book of Acts were probably written sometime between AD 59 and 63. With respect to dating Luke, two main points need to be kept in mind:

- the dating of the book of Acts and the fact that Luke did not record what ultimately happened to the Apostle Paul, namely, his martyrdom, but merely brought his readers up-to-date; and

- the destruction of Jerusalem in AD 70, prophetically recorded in Luke 21:20-24 as coming in the future.

First, based on the structure and content of both Luke and Acts, apparently Luke was written before Acts. Luke neither mentioned the Neronian persecution nor Paul's death, both of which occurred in AD 64 or 65. Had Luke written Acts after these two events, he would probably have mentioned them. Second, one does not have to date Luke after the fall of Jerusalem in AD 70 based on Jesus' prediction of its destruction in Luke 21, unless she is predisposed to discount the supernatural.

Recipients

The diverse and universal nature of Luke's Gospel makes it difficult to nail down one specific community. Nevertheless, some internal clues seem to suggest a predominantly Gentile-Christian community. The prologue (1:1-4) holds the key. First, the addressing of Theophilus and the mention of several secular rulers at the beginning of the Gospel suggests a Gentile audience. Some scholars have suggested that Theophilus was not a real person, assuming that his name (Gk. "lover of God" or "friend of God") acted as a code name to refer to a Gentile official in the Roman army or perhaps as a discreet pseudonym designed to protect a believer who was highly placed in government.

Some speculation identified Theophilus with Titus Flavius Clemens, Domitian's cousin, whose wife Domitilla was a Christian. Titus fell out of favor with the emperor on the charge of "atheism" (a term used by the Romans to describe Christians because they refused to worship all the Roman "gods"), and he was executed.

The use of "most excellent" to describe Theophilus may support that he was not only an actual person but also a person of rank. Both Luke and Acts give prominence to God-fearers who were a part of the secular society but still monotheistic in their own personal persuasions—perhaps because they had heard or read the Jewish Scriptures (7:1-10; Ac 10:1–11:18; 18:26-39).

On a broader scale, Luke may have been writing to Gentiles in general to give them a clear account of Jesus. The compassion of Jesus for social outcasts throughout the Gospel and the movement of Jesus' ministry progressively from a Jewish to a specifically Gentile context suggested a more extensive Gentile audience. Additionally, Luke did not seem to show interest in the fulfillment of messianic prophecy as was seen in Matthew. But Luke did portray Jesus as a "light to the Gentiles," which further suggested a predominantly non-Jewish audience. Unlike Matthew, Luke traced Jesus' genealogy back to Adam, showing Jesus' relationship to both Jews and Gentiles.

Luke's book would have brought considerable hope to these first-century, non-Jewish readers. At a time when they had given up hope on the pagan gods and been disillusioned by the teachings concerning luck and fate, here was a Savior for all people. Jesus cared about people; He lived and died and rose again for them. Luke told this story with a conviction that would have brought hope even to those who were most downtrodden and that has continued to be true until now.

Major Themes

Without question, Luke's central and overriding theme is that Jesus is the Son of God and Savior of all who turn to Him in faith for salvation, regardless of ethnicity, gender, or socioeconomic status (1:1-4). There are secondary themes that have been developed as well.

Salvation for all people. Two of the key passages in the Gospel of Luke are 2:10-11, which says, "Don't be afraid, for look, I proclaim to you good news of great joy that will be for all the people: today a Savior, who is Messiah the Lord, was born for you in the city of David" and 19:10, which says, "The Son of Man has come to seek and to save the lost." The entire Gospel of Luke portrayed Jesus as the compassionate Savior who extended forgiveness to outcasts and sinners. This compassion was illustrated in the story of the sinful woman who washed Jesus' feet with her tears and anointed His head with oil (7:36-50) and in the parables of the lost sheep, coin, and son in Luke 15. The high priority of evangelism and sharing the good news was woven throughout the book.

The Holy Spirit. Luke mentioned the Holy Spirit more than any other Gospel writer. One of his characteristic phrases is "filled with the Spirit" (Lk 1:15, 41; also Ac 2:4; 4:31). The Spirit overshadowed Mary in the conception of Jesus (Lk 1:35) and filled John the Baptist (1:15) and his mother Elizabeth (1:41). The Spirit was on Simeon and inspired him to prophesy about the future of the Messiah (2:25-35). Jesus was full of the Holy Spirit and was led by the Spirit into the temptation (4:1). Jesus, quoting from Isaiah, testified that the "Spirit of the Lord" was upon Him (4:18). Jesus promised the Holy Spirit as an answer to prayer (11:13). The work of the Holy Spirit was also a dominant theme throughout the book of Acts, in which the Spirit is mentioned about 70 times (Ac 1:4-5,8; 2:4,17-18,38; 10:19,38,44).

Prayer. Prayer was a special concern to Luke. In many instances throughout Luke, Jesus was engaged in prayer (5:15; 9:18; 11:1). Only Luke mentioned the fact that Jesus was praying when the Spirit descended on Him in baptism (3:21), when He chose the Twelve (6:1), and when He was on the mountain at the time of the transfiguration (9:29). Luke also recorded Jesus' special teachings and parables on prayer (11:1-13; 18:1-8).

Recording Christian history. That Luke had in mind to write a "salvation" history was clear from his prologue, in which he stated that he intended to give an orderly account of all that had happened since Jesus' birth and from what has commonly been accepted as his addition of a sequel, namely, the book of Acts, in which Luke continued to trace the work of the apostles in building the early church. Luke-Acts taken together displayed the sovereign work of God in bringing salvation to the ends of the earth. There is little doubt that Luke wanted to communicate that God is ultimately in charge of human history.

Jerusalem. Luke is commonly known as the most "Gentile" of all the Gospels. But this understanding of Luke could be misleading. Jerusalem, the center of Jewish culture, was of central importance in Luke. In this third Gospel, Jesus "resolutely" sets out for Jerusalem in order to fulfill His destiny. In fact, Luke's central section recorded Jesus' teachings while He was "making his way to Jerusalem" (Lk 13:22). The Gospel of Luke ended at the temple in Jerusalem, and the book of Acts began at the temple in Jerusalem. Luke seemed to go out of his way to acknowledge that the Jews were God's holy people and that Jerusalem was His holy place. But it was also just as clear throughout Luke-Acts that God was moving beyond Jerusalem and beyond a merely Jewish religion. He was doing a new thing in Israel by inaugurating the fulfillment of Judaism. Christ *is* the fulfillment of Judaism; He did not come merely to preserve Judaism or to reform it.

Stewardship of material possessions. Luke emphasized throughout his Gospel that Jesus' followers were not to store up riches on earth exclusively for themselves. In his beatitude section only Luke juxtaposed warnings to the rich with the blessings to the poor (6:24-26). The parables of the rich fool (12:13-21) and of the rich man and Lazarus (16:19-31) were stern warnings against those who spent all their wealth solely on themselves and their own interests. The unjust steward was commended by Jesus because he handled his worldly wealth wisely; believers were expected to do the same (16:1-13). Zacchaeus voluntarily gave up to half of all he had (19:1-10), and the faithful steward put his master's concerns above his own (19:11-27). Luke's message concerning the use and abuse of material possessions could be a difficult one for the affluent West of the modern era to hear, but these words must be taken to heart nonetheless. While clearly in Luke to be both Christian and rich is not impossible, rich Christians are admonished not to be tightfisted toward the needy (12:33; 14:33; Ac 2:44-47).

Women and their role in Jesus' ministry. Luke gave far more attention to women than did the other Gospels. Mary and Elizabeth were given special attention in the events surrounding Jesus' birth (chaps. 1–2). Anna, a poor widow serving in the temple, prophesied about Christ (2:36-38). A sinful woman was singled out and forgiven by Christ (7:36-50). Luke acknowledged the women who supported Christ during His earthly ministry (8:1-3). A crippled woman was healed on the Sabbath (13:10-17). The women at the cross and those who announced the resurrection were also given special attention in Luke (23:27-31; 23:55–24:11).

Portrait of Jesus in Luke

Friend of outcasts. No other Gospel portrayed Jesus' relationship to outcasts quite to the extent that Luke did. Four groups are highlighted:

• Samaritans and Gentiles

• women

• the poor

• tax collectors and sinners

Samaritans and Gentiles were hated among the Jews. Yet they were the ones singled out by Jesus on more than one occasion throughout the Gospel of Luke:

• the parable of the good Samaritan (10:25-37)

• the story of the 10 lepers in which only the Samaritan returned to give thanks to Jesus for his healing (17:11-19)

Also, Jesus' Gentile mission was foreshadowed in the parable of the great supper (14:23) and fully unveiled in the book of Acts.

Luke, more than any other Gospel writer, focused on Jesus' ministries to women (and their ministry to Him). The poor and the downtrodden received special attention in Luke. While at the synagogue in Nazareth, Jesus quoted from Isaiah the passage that characterized His ministry. He was God's anointed, commissioned "to preach good news to the poor" (4:18).

The profound paradox of God's relationship to sin and sinners comes through with beautiful clarity in Luke's Gospel. Jesus takes sin seriously, and Jesus loves sinners. These two truths cohere in Jesus' atoning death for sinners.

In some contexts "sinner" refers to those who had broken Jewish oral tradition and cultural norms. In other contexts, sinners were those who had violated God's law. Among the worst of sinners in Jesus' day were tax collectors. Yet Luke recorded two accounts of God's transforming grace in the lives of these men who were despised by their fellow Jews:

• the parable of the Pharisee and the tax collector (18:9-14) and

• the account of Zacchaeus' encounter with Jesus (19:1-10).

Those who had a profound sense of their having violated God's standards were drawn to Jesus. They were not disappointed. Like Zacchaeus, they were forgiven and experienced the desire to do all that God requires.

Jesus' encounter with Zacchaeus took place as He was on His way to Jerusalem to pay the price for the sins of the world by laying down His life. Zacchaeus could not have known the price of the peace, forgiveness, and new life that Jesus imparted to him that day in Jericho. By displaying Jesus' compassion toward the lost, Luke wanted his readers to understand that no sinner was so far gone that God's salvation could not reach him. This powerful theme has drawn sinners through the ages to Luke's Gospel.

Prophet. Only Luke told the story of the widow from Nain whose son was raised from the dead by Jesus. In response to this amazing miracle, the people of the town glorified God and said, "A great prophet has risen among us" (7:16). Only Luke cited Jesus' reference to Himself as a prophet (13:33). These two uniquely Lukan passages have led some scholars to speculate that Luke's entire purpose for his "central section" (9:51–18:34) was to portray Jesus as the "prophet" spoken about by Moses in Deuteronomy 18:15. In this section many themes parallel the theology found in Deuteronomy: Jesus was sent as God's messenger to warn a rebellious generation of its coming destruction only to be rejected. Luke's use of the Old Testament is best understood as a prophetic use, showing that all of Scripture points to Jesus and must be fulfilled by Him.

Themes in Luke	
Theme	**Examples from Luke**
Theology	Word of God (5:1; 6:47; 8:11,13-15,21; 11:28) Jesus as Savior (1:69; 2:11; 19:9) The present kingdom of God (11:20; 19:9) The Holy Spirit (1:35,41,67; 2:25-27; 3:22; 4:1,14; 11:13; 24:49)
Concern for women	Elizabeth (1:5-25,39-45,57-66) Mary (1:26-56; 2:1-20,41-52) Anna (2:36-38) The widow of Nain (7:11-12) The "sinner" who anoints Jesus' feet (7:36-50) Women disciples (8:1-3) The woman searching for her lost coin (15:8-10) The persistent widow petitioning the unjust judge (18:1-8) The sorrowful women along the way to the cross (23:27)
Concern for the poor/warnings to the rich	Blessings on the poor (6:20-23) Woes on the rich (6:24-26) The rich fool (12:16-20) The rich man and the beggar Lazarus (16:19-31)
Concern for social outcasts	Shepherds (2:8-20) Samaritans (10:25-37; 17:11-19) Tax agents and "sinners" (15:1) Gentiles/all people (2:32; 24:47)
The Christian life	Gratitude and joy (1:46-55,68-79; 2:14; 15:7,10,24,32; 17:16,18; 24:53) Prayer (3:21; 6:12; 9:18; 11:1-13; 18:1-14) Proper use of material possessions (6:32-36; 10:27-37; 12:32-34; 16:1-13) Changed lives in imitation of Christ (9:3-5,16; 10:2-16,38-42; 12:41-48; 22:24-27) Repentance/faith (3:7-14; 5:32; 10:13; 11:32; 13:3-5; 15:7-10; 24:47)

Pronunciation Guide

Abijah	*uh BIGH juh*	Melshi	*Mel shee*
Addi	*AD igh (eye)*	Menan	*MEE nan*
Amminadab	*uh MIN uh dab*	Methuselah	*mih THOOZ uh luh*
Arphaxad	*ahr FAX ad*	Naggai	*NAG igh (eye)*
Caiaphas	*KIGH uh fuhs*	Nahor	*NAY hawr*
Cainan	*KAY nuhn*	Nahshon	*NAH shahn*
Cosam	*KOH sam*	Neri	*NEE righ*
Eber	*EE buhr*	Obed	*OH bed*
Eliakim	*ih LIGH uh kim*	Peleg	*PEE leg*
Eliezer	*el ih EE zuhr*	Quirinius	*kwih RIN ih uhs*
Elmodam	*el MOH dam*	Reu	*REE yoo*
Esku	*Ehsk yoo*	Rhesa	*REE suh*
Gennesaret	*gih NESS uh ret*	Salmon	*SAL mahn*
Heli	*HEE ligh*	Semei	*SEM ih igh (eye)*
Hezron	*HEZ rahn*	Serug	*SEE ruhg*
Iturea	*it yoo REE uh*	Shealtiel	*shih AL tih el*
Joannas	*joh AN uhs*	Shelah	*SHEE luh*
Jonan	*JOH nan*	Terah	*TEE ruh, TEHR uh*
Jorim	*JOH rim*	Theophilus	*thee AHF ih luhs (th as in thin)*
Jose	*JOH sih*		
Lysanias	*ligh SAY nih uhs*	Tiberius	*tigh BIHR ih uhs*
Mahalalel	*muh HAL uh lihl*	Trachonitis	*trak uh NIGH tiss*
Matthat	*MAT that (th as in thin)*	Zachariah	*zak uh RIGH uh*
Mattathiah	*mat uh THIGH uh*	Zerubbabel	*zuh RUHB uh buhl*
Melchi	*MEL kigh*		
Melea	*MEE lee uh*		

Outline

I. INTRODUCTION TO JESUS' MINISTRY (1:1–4:13)
  A. Preface to the Gospel (1:1-4)
  B. The Birth and the Infancy of Jesus (1:5–2:52)
    1. The annunciation of the birth of the forerunner John (1:5-25)
    2. The annunciation of the birth of Jesus (1:26-38)
    3. Mary's visit to Elizabeth (1:39-56)
    4. The birth of John the Baptist (1:57-80)
    5. The birth of Jesus (2:1-20)
    6. The presentation of Jesus in the temple (2:21-40)
    7. The childhood of Jesus (2:41-52)
  C. Preparation for Jesus' Ministry (3:1–4:13)
    1. The work of John (3:1-20)
    2. The baptism of Jesus (3:21-22)

3. The genealogy of Jesus (3:23-38)

4. The temptation of Jesus (4:1-13)

II. MINISTRY IN AND AROUND GALILEE (4:14–9:50)

A. Preaching in Nazareth (4:14-30)

B. Beginning a Healing Ministry (4:31-44)

C. Calling the First Disciples (5:1-11)

D. Participating in Controversies with the Jewish Leaders (5:12–6:11)

E. Formalizing the Call to Discipleship (6:12-49)

F. Focusing on the Question of Jesus' Identity (7:1–8:3)

G. Hearing the Word of God Correctly (8:4-21)

H. Illustrating Jesus' Authoritative Word (8:22-56)

I. Coming to the Christological Climax (9:1-50)

III. JESUS' TEACHING "EN ROUTE" TO JERUSALEM (9:51–18:34)

A. Discipleship in the Shadow of the Cross (9:51-62)

B. The Mission of the Seventy (10:1-24)

C. The Mandate for Double Love (10:25-42)

D. The Teaching about Prayer (11:1-13)

E. The Controversy with a Pharisee (11:14-54)

F. The Preparation for Judgment (12:1–13:9)

G. Kingdom Reversals (13:10–14:24)

H. The Cost of Discipleship (14:25-35)

I. The Seeking and Saving of the Lost (15:1-32)

J. The Use and Abuse of Riches (16:1-31)

K. The Teachings on Faith (17:1-19)

L. The Coming of the Kingdom (17:20–18:8)

M. The Requirements for Entering the Kingdom (18:9-30)

N. Conclusion and Transition (18:31-34)

IV. JESUS IN JUDEA: MINISTRY NEAR AND IN JERUSALEM (18:35–21:38)

A. From Jericho to Jerusalem (18:35–19:27)

B. Entry into Jerusalem (19:28-48)

C. Jesus' Teaching during the Final Week (20:1–21:38)

V. THE CLIMAX OF JESUS' LIFE (22:1–24:53)

A. Passover (22:1-71)

B. Crucifixion (23:1-56)

C. Resurrection (24:1-53)

Exposition of the Text

INTRODUCTION TO JESUS' MINISTRY (1:1–4:13)

Preface to the Gospel (1:1-4)

1:1-4 Following the format for prefaces found in many other documents of his day, Luke used a highly stylized form of literary Greek. Routinely all Greek historians justified their research and reliabil-ity, and Luke seems to have done the same. Luke's purpose was to give an "orderly account" of the person and works of Jesus. But this was not confined to a chronological account. In fact, his purpose had more to do with thematic order. He intended to detail salvific or theological history and to give his readers a firm basis for the knowledge they had received. **Most honorable Theophilus** (transliteration from Gk., lit. "lover of God") was probably a person of distinction, possibly a statesman or Roman official or perhaps even a religious leader. His exact identity is unknown. The name may also have served as a literary device for addressing all believers, who would be "lovers of God" by virtue of their commitment to Christ. Theophilus may not have been a believer, but he was a God-fearing man who had obviously received some instruction in the faith. In any case, Luke was careful to assure Theophilus of the veracity of the Gospel.

The Birth and the Infancy of Jesus (1:5–2:52)

The annunciation of the birth of the forerunner John (1:5-25)

Beginning in verse 5, Luke changed his style of Greek from the highly formal style to the standard *koine* or populist language. This abrupt change led many scholars to speculate about the sources Luke used to develop this section. Some have suggested that he might have been translating from sources written in either Hebrew or Aramaic. Others have suggested that Luke might have personally interviewed either Mary or Elizabeth, since these women were part of the focus in his birth narrative.

Only Matthew and Luke record the events surrounding Christ's birth, each author with his own emphases according to his overall purpose. Matthew developed his narrative around the Old Testament prophecies fulfilled by Jesus' birth, while Luke was concerned with showing God's plan of salvation for all people. Luke is unique among the four Gospels in showing the familial relationship between John and Jesus. While clearly Luke wanted to point out the similarities between John and Jesus, he also wanted to

show the significant differences between them. With respect to similarities, John's birth was foretold (v. 13) as was the birth of Jesus (vv. 26-33). Then the relationship between Elizabeth and Mary was clarified (vv. 39-56), followed by a narration of the birth and growth of both John (vv. 57-80) and Jesus (2:1-52). Throughout this section, then, the similarities between John and Jesus are highlighted. Both came from godly Jewish parents who were visited by angels; both mothers experienced the power of the Holy Spirit and were told of the salvific significance of their children, whose ministries would offer spiritual consolation and even social changes to both Jews and Gentiles (vv. 11-17,26-35). Both sets of parents experienced some disbelief but were eventually filled with joy and praise at the working of God in their lives (vv. 39-56). Luke also detailed the circumcision, naming, and maturation of both John and Jesus (vv. 57-80; 2:21-52).

As for differences, Luke pointed out at least two ways in which Jesus is greater than John:

- The virgin birth clearly sets Jesus above John.
- John was the forerunner to Jesus, who is the only Savior, the Christ, and the Lord of all.

1:5-25 There were approximately 18,000 priests in Israel at the time Zechariah was called to minister in the temple; so this was definitely a once-in-a-lifetime opportunity for him. Zechariah's disbelief concerning the angel's announcement of the birth of John was met with judgment, probably because as a priest he should have been familiar with the Old Testament accounts of God's power to open the womb of barren women (Gn 21:1-7; 25-21; 30:22; 1 Sm 1:1-19).

The description of this couple as **righteous in God's sight** precluded their infertility as being the result of their sin. Although imperfect because of their humanity, they were truly devoted to God and faithfully served Him (vv. 5-6).

Other Old Testament women had suffered from childlessness (Sarah, Gn 17:16-17; Hannah, 1 Sm 1:5-11), but none was any more publicly rewarded than Elizabeth, who was blessed with a child even in her old age. The unexpected reversal of her infertility served as another way of pointing to God's miraculous intervention in what would be impossible— humanly speaking.

The appearance of **an angel of the Lord** was a supernatural event specifically noted and thus affirming its historicity (v. 11). **Your prayer has been heard** would be a welcome response to any petition (v. 13). Although Zechariah may have been praying for the long-awaited messianic redemption, more probably the reference was to the heartfelt prayer of a godly couple for a child to continue the generations. The answered prayer was further enhanced with the angel's prophetic announcements of the child's name **John** (Gk. *jōannēs,* linking the Hebrew name of God with *hānan,* meaning "showing favor" or "being gracious").

No woman dare miss the atmosphere surrounding the birth of a child (even to elderly parents for whom conception would seem neither wise nor convenient). Yet **joy** (Gk. *chara,* "gladness") **and delight** (Gk. *agalliasis,* "exultation, extreme joy") are followed by an allusion to **many will rejoice** (Gk. *charēsontai,* "show favor, bestow"). What superlatives these are, describing the joy accompanying even the birth of Jesus' forerunner. The good news was amplified by the exciting announcement of the coming birth, which would fulfill the eschatological hope of Israel. There is also a contrast between the **fear** that overcame Zechariah (1:12) and the joy promised to those who

would celebrate the birth of Messiah (v. 14).

Since some of the requirements for a Nazirite are not mentioned, the more logical explanation seems to be that John was called to live a set-apart life, including a commitment to serve God in a unique way (Lv 10:9). The Nazirite vow as recorded in the Old Testament was more extensive (Nm 6:2-15):

- to abstain from alcoholic beverages (6:2)

- to refrain from cutting hair (6:5)

- to avoid contact with dead bodies (6:7-9).

More important than what was forbidden for John was what was promised by God. In the Old Testament the Holy Spirit came upon a prophet later in life, but John the Baptist would **be filled with the Holy Spirit while still in his mother's womb** (v. 15), showing again God's supernatural intervention as well as giving subtle affirmation to life in the womb as worthy of divine protection and as receiving an endowment for service.

One cannot help but be encouraged with the promise **to turn the hearts of fathers to their children** (v. 17). Even as part of a synonymous parallelism alongside what follows, you cannot dismiss the straightforward admonishment to families to restore godly leadership in the home. But taken as a whole, the assurance was given that John the Baptist would call fathers to turn to their children with love and compassion, persuading their offspring to look to God. On the other hand, **the disobedient** (were called to accept with commitment and sacrifice) **to the understanding** (Gk. *phronēsis,* "way of thinking," "insight") **of the righteous** (v. 17).

For Elizabeth to keep **herself in seclusion for five months** would hide her pregnancy from public view (v. 24). Whether this action was her choice because of innuendos from curious neighbors was not apparent. Even Mary was unaware of the pregnancy of her relative Elizabeth (v. 36). On the other hand, this seclusion may have been God's plan to follow His timing on these glorious events. In any case, when Elizabeth did appear, she was quick to acknowledge with humble gratitude what God had done in removing the stigma of her barren womb and giving her new usefulness in His divine purpose (v. 25).

The annunciation of the birth of Jesus (1:26-38)

1:26-38 Mary, too, was approached by an angel, and she questioned how this birth could come about, since she had never "known" a man. Zechariah had expressed his doubt (v. 20) with a seemingly innocent question. But on Mary's part this question was not so much an indication of unbelief as it was a sincere inquiry concerning how conception could possibly come about any other way (v. 34). God's power over reproduction was at work respectively in the wombs of both Mary and Elizabeth and was completely consistent with His supernatural powers revealed elsewhere (vv. 35-36). In Elizabeth's case there were clearly Old Testament examples of barren women becoming pregnant (Sarah, Gn 21:1-7; Hannah, 1 Sm 1:1-19); but with Mary, what she was being promised by the angel was unprecedented! VIRGIN (Gk. *parthenos*), although sometimes translated with a broader meaning as "maid," is clear here in its more restrictive sense.

Mary, the Mother of Jesus Luke 1–2	
Mary's Life	**Luke's Account**
Her Significance	Virgin of Nazareth engaged to Joseph (1:26-27)
Her Selection	Favored by the Lord, blessed among women (1:28)
Her Sanctity	Found favor with God (1:30)
Her Submission	"May it be done to me according to Your word" (1:38)
Her Service	• Gave birth to Jesus (2:6-7) • Loved God (2:19) • Raised Jesus in the faith (2:27) • Accepted His destiny (2:34) • Followed His teachings (2:51)
Her Sorrow	• Saw Jesus crucified on the cross (23:49) • Saw Him buried (23:55-56)
Her Salvation	• Found His empty tomb (24:1-5) • Experienced His resurrection (24:6-10) • Spoke of His resurrection (24:11-12) • Joined the disciples in the upper room (Acts 1:14)
See also Mt 1:16-25; Mk 3:21; Jn 2:1-5; 19:25-27.	

Luke referred to the Holy Spirit repeatedly in the first four chapters (1:41,67,80; 2:25-27). In the description of conception, the Holy Spirit would OVERSHADOW (Gk. episkiasei, "cast a shadow, cover") Mary, suggesting the powerful presence of God (v. 35). The same word is used in the accounts of the transfiguration (9:34; Mt 17:5; Mk 9:7) to describe the overshadowing of the cloud from which God spoke, identifying Jesus as His Son.

A woman cannot help but be touched by Mary's servant heart. She submitted to the inevitable shame and suffering that would accompany a premarital pregnancy. Her submission was to God (v. 48) and served as the crowning touch to her humble confidence in the Lord (v. 38).

As a side note, it has been argued by many that the people of the first century did not understand the laws of nature and thus were gullible to believe in the supernatural, especially in the idea of a miraculous "virgin birth." However, precisely because Mary understood the laws of nature, she questioned the angel. The fact is that an understanding of the supernatural is enhanced by an understanding of the natural. Mary clearly knew that what Gabriel had promised her could not come about naturally (v. 34).

Mary's visit to Elizabeth (1:39-56)

1:39-56 Throughout this narrative Luke has interwoven the lives of the two women—different in age and in season of life but the same in their spirit of commitment, which prompted each to offer herself to the Savior. Both mothers were told of the place their sons would hold in the divine economy, and each accepted her own role and that of her son with humble obedience. As soon as the sound of Mary's voice was heard, John leaped inside the womb of his mother and Elizabeth was **filled with the Holy Spirit** (v. 41). Nowhere is Mary called the "Mother of God," but she is clearly identified as the mother of Jesus, the Messiah (v. 43).

Mary responded to Elizabeth with a hymn of praise, one similar in context to the words spoken by Hannah in 1 Samuel 2:1-10. Mary's hymn, known as the *Magnificat*, spoke of the deliverance of Israel, both spiritual and physical; but it also told of the illumination that would come to the Gentiles. The hymn was marked by these distinctions:

- many Old Testament phrases and references (v. 54; see Ps 98:3),

- evidence of the deep piety of Mary with character traits appropriate for the mother of the Lord (vv. 47-48),

- affirmation of her personal knowledge about the Old Testament (vv. 50-53),

- call to action in meeting physical needs (vv. 51-53), and

- consciousness of her own role in the divine economy (vv. 46-49).

Some suggest that Luke composed this hymn, implying that the literary masterpiece could not have come from a young peasant girl. Such conjecture dismisses the matter of divine inspiration, which by definition surpasses human ability and giftedness to place a heavenly message in an earthly vessel. Although one would assume that Mary, as most young women in her peer group, was uneducated, the text does not say so. She, as the chosen vessel to nurture the Messiah, may have had some unique opportunities for learning; she may have had extraordinary giftedness with the ability to recall the Old Testament Scripture, which she probably had heard repeatedly in her home and in the synagogue. Whether the song came to her in a moment of inspiration or over time in private meditation, Mary was noted by Luke as the human composer of these meaningful and beautifully fashioned words that have been recorded for the generations. The mother of the Lord Jesus was indeed an extraordinary woman.

Mary actually described herself as the **slave** (Gk. *doulēs,* "female servant") of the Lord. There is no hint of an oppressive bondage imposed by another but rather a self-determined submission to God's will (vv. 38,48).

Mary's Song Luke 1:46-55	
Mary's Praise	**God's Blessings**
Proclaims God's greatness (v. 46)	Looked with favor on His slave (v. 48)
	Has done great things for me (v. 49)
	Extended mercy from generation to generation (v. 50)
Rejoices in God (v. 47)	Has done mighty deeds (v. 51)
	Scattered the proud (v. 51)
	Toppled the mighty (v. 52)
	Exalted the lowly (v. 52)
	Satisfied the hungry (v. 53)
	Sent rich away empty (v. 53)
	Helped Israel (v. 54)
	Spoke forever (v. 55)
See also 1 Sm 2:1-10, Hannah's Song.	

gave praise to God. His hymn is commonly called the *Benedictus* (Latin for "blessed"). Like Mary's hymn, it speaks

Elizabeth Luke 1:5-25,57-66		
Name Meaning	→	"God is my oath"
Father	→	Aaron, a priest
Husband	→	Zacharias, a priest
Hometown	→	Jerusalem
Cousin	→	Mary, mother of Jesus
Son	→	John the Baptist, forerunner of Jesus
Legacy	→	She was righteous before God, followed His commandments, and was blameless (1:6)

The birth of John the Baptist (1:57-80)

1:57-80 After John was born, Elizabeth's relatives **were going to name him** after his father **Zechariah**. But Elizabeth protested, claiming that his name was to be **John**. When her relatives asked her husband Zechariah about it, he quickly agreed with his wife. At that moment, Zechariah's tongue was loosed and he

of rescue from Israel's physical enemies, of spiritual restoration, and of blessings to the Gentiles (vv. 68-79). The covenant God made with Abraham was being fulfilled, and this covenant included blessings to all nations. John's childhood and adult years were briefly mentioned, speci-

Heart to Heart: Forever Friends

ℬecause God created women to be relational, they need friends. Women are encouraged by other women who have faced similar life experiences. Elizabeth and Mary, who were cousins, also became forever friends. The expectant mothers shared joy as they awaited the births of their God-given sons. Elizabeth's gift of hospitality and wise counsel endeared her to young Mary. Their special friendship must have continued as they raised their sons, nurtured their families, and followed their Lord. Their mentoring relationship is a model for Christian women today. The affirmation and advice of the older woman strengthened the younger woman, who had been chosen by God to give birth to Jesus Christ, the Savior of the world. God often uses women to teach and train other women (Ti 2:3-5). Seek to develop some forever friendships with Christian women.

fying that he resided **in the wilderness**. This description of the forerunner cleared the way for the entrance of the Messiah.

The birth of Jesus (2:1-20)

2:1-7 The census called for every Jew to register in his home city. All women were included in the mandate as well. Augustus reigned during this time (27 BC to AD 14). His scheduling of the census set the stage for fulfillment of prophecy— the birth of Messiah in Bethlehem (Mc 5:2). Publius Sulpicius **Quirinius was governing Syria** (v. 2). As a prominent Roman who seems to have been governor twice, he directed the census. His first reign (6 to 4 BC) fits Luke's account. Although no specific birthdate is recorded, Luke's emphasis on the census would add to its historical importance in determining the timing of Jesus' birth. Since Herod the Great was alive at the time of Jesus' birth and for some months thereafter, His birth would have been before 4 BC, which is the recorded date for Herod's death. The Jewish historian Josephus also recorded the census under Quirinius as taking place between AD 6 and 7. In any case, the general historical setting is clear, and Luke's integrity remains strong as a careful historian.

The engagement or betrothal (Hb. *kiddushin*) between Mary and Jospeh (v. 5) differed greatly from the modern concept of engagement. Its contractual nature was serious and as officially binding as marriage, but betrothal did not open the door for consummating the marriage. The circumstances surrounding Jesus' birth emphasize that He was born into a humble earthly family.

About six months after John was born, Jesus was born in Bethlehem in Judea. He came into the world and was laid in a manger or **a feeding trough** for the animals. The word translated **inn** (Gk. *kataluma*, "guest room") suggested that

Joseph and Mary had made plans to stay with a family in Bethlehem, a common practice among travelers since the inns themselves were often dirty and dangerous; but, because of the census, which involved the coming of *all* people from the area, many others would have made the same plans. There was simply not enough room in the few small homes to meet the needs of everyone required to come. So Joseph and Mary were given shelter in the area with the animals of the household. In small Palestinian homes, this area would have meant the ground level of the home, which was often separated from the raised portion of the house by a feeding trough.[2]

2:8-20 The timing of Jesus' birth almost certainly was not during December since the **shepherds were staying out in the fields** (v. 8). The months spent out in the fields began as early as March but must have ended by November because of the weather. Luke emphasized the humble beginnings of the Savior even further by recording the announcement made to the shepherds. Shepherds were despised in the first century for their lifestyles; some had the reputation of being thieves. Nevertheless, to such lowly people, the angels announced the birth of God's Son, **a Savior, who is Messiah the Lord** (vv. 10-11). "Savior" is the most distinctive title for Jesus in Luke, while "Lord" is more prevalent in Acts. The **heavenly host** presented a doxology with heavenly and earthly components: **Glory** (Gk. *doxa*, "splendor, brightness") belongs to God, but His favor (Gk. *eudoxia*, "good will, good pleasure") rests upon His creation (v. 14). These very humble and ordinary men—shepherds—became the first evangelists to proclaim the Savior's birth. They delivered **the message they were told about this child** (v. 17).

The presentation of Jesus in the temple (2:21-40)

2:21-24 During childbirth a woman became unclean because the flow of blood and the bodily discharge associated with the birth were considered impure. **Eight days** was the set period for preparing for the **circumcision** of a male child, at which time medical science has since affirmed that the coagulants reach their maximum effectiveness, making that day the safest time for the minor surgical procedure. Both Jesus and His forerunner John were circumcised according to Jewish law (v. 21; 1:59), embracing the covenant mark God had given to Abraham (Gn 17:12-14; 21:4; Lv 12:3). After seven days circumcision would occur on the eighth day. For a male child the mother was considered unclean for an additional 33 days (see Lv 12:1-5) or a total of 40 days. Then the mother had to offer a sacrifice and present her first son to the Lord (Nm 18:15). Luke was careful to note that Mary and Joseph fulfilled the law:

- **He was named Jesus** (v. 21; see 1:31).

- He was circumcised on the eighth day (v. 21).

- Mary completed her days of **purification** (v. 22).

- Mary and Joseph presented Jesus, the firstborn male, to the Lord in Jerusalem (vv. 22-23).

- They offered a sacrifice of **a pair of turtledoves or two young pigeons** (v. 24), as expected from a humble, poor family (Lv 2:6-8).

2:25-35 Mary's first visit to the temple after Jesus' birth took place on the eighth day, the appointed time to circumcise Him. Joseph and Mary "brought Him" to the "temple to present Him to the Lord" (v. 22) and offer the prescribed sacrifices. Soon after they arrived, they were approached by a devout and aged man named **Simeon** (vv. 25-27). Simeon was seeking the fulfillment of the messianic prophecy when Israel would be restored, and God promised him that he **would not** die **before** seeing Christ. Filled with the Holy Spirit, he prophesied over the baby Jesus and spoke of His future. His parents were amazed at what he said about their child (v. 33). Then Simeon turned and spoke directly to Mary: **Indeed, this child is destined to cause the fall and rise of many in Israel and to be a sign that will be opposed**—*and a sword will pierce your own soul*—**that the thoughts of many hearts will be revealed** (italics added).

Simeon, unknown except for these prophetic words, proclaimed in eloquent words now known as *Nunc Dimittis* from the initial words of the Latin translation of his song of praise ("now you let depart"; see the Old Testament influence in Is 40–55). Simeon was part of the remnant of Judaism looking for the Messiah's coming. Simeon linked **the Lord's Messiah** (v. 26) with **Your salvation** (v. 30), making clear that Jesus as Messiah came to be God's salvation.

Anna		
Luke 2:36-38		
This brief account gives much information about Anna.		
v. 36	→	a prophetess
v. 36	→	a daughter of Phanuel
v. 36	→	of the tribe of Asher
v. 36	→	well along in years
v. 36	→	widowed after 7 years of marriage
v. 37	→	widow for 84 years
v. 37	→	did not leave the temple
v. 37	→	fasted and prayed
v. 38	→	saw the Savior
v. 38	→	thanked God
v. 38	→	spoke of Him to all people

Mary was told by the **righteous and devout** Simeon that her Son's ministry would bring both grief and joy to Israel and that she herself would be wounded by the events in His life (vv. 34-35). As His mother, Mary would have naturally been disturbed by this prophetic word concerning her Son's destiny. As His disciple, the word would have been equally disturbing. The most intimate thoughts of her heart would be revealed and laid bare before her Son. She learned that His life and mission would fill her future with intense pain and suffering, both as a mother and as a disciple. This was Mary's double-edged **sword** (v. 35).

2:36-40 Anna the elderly **prophetess** also thanked God for Jesus and spoke about Him in her own words of testimony **to all who were looking** for **the redemption of Jerusalem** (vv. 36-40). The words of Simeon and Anna set Jesus apart from John by showing that the ministry of Jesus was destined to surpass the ministry of John. Simeon saw the Christ child and was ready to die (v. 29); Anna saw Him and began to bear witness to those who would listen (v. 38).

Excursus on the Women Associated with Jesus' Birth

Interestingly, John followed the example of his mother's prebirth Spirit-filled status. Elizabeth's unborn son leaped for joy inside her womb as Elizabeth herself cried out in joy on the occasion of Mary's greeting. The perfectly timed movement of the baby is almost surely an indication of the filling of the Spirit "while yet in his mother's womb" (1:15). The other evidence is that the baby leaped for joy—an emotion that is beyond the capability of an unborn baby. Some might say that Elizabeth was engaging in overstatement or that she was trusting a gut-level impression when she claimed that the baby leaped for joy at Mary's greeting. Remember, though, her words were in the power of the Holy Spirit, and joy is certainly a prominent fruit of the Holy Spirit in a person's life. Elizabeth's Spirit-filled words have, unfortunately, usually faded into unimportance in light of Mary's longer response in her hymn, the Magnificat. Yet clearly Elizabeth's blessing is what prompted and prepared the way for Mary's response. Some even suggest that Elizabeth helped Mary compose the words of the hymn, since Mary stayed with Elizabeth for about three months. In any case, Elizabeth's words were also significant and Spirit-inspired.

Elizabeth did not usurp the role of her husband Zechariah. Rather she faithfully affirmed what God had revealed to her. When she told her friends that her son was to be named "John," they protested and looked to Zechariah, who immediately wrote, "His name is John" (1:63). Even without his speech, Zechariah remained the head of his home. Often in marriage, the weakness of one is an opportunity for the encouragement of the other. Oneness in marriage does express itself even in service to Christ. Zechariah's faith left him without the ability to speak; Elizabeth's faithfulness to the Lord and her commitment as a helper to her husband prompted her to bear testimony even when Zechariah could not speak (1:42-45). John was filled with the Spirit from before his birth, and both of his parents were also faithful to be used by the Spirit (1:42-45; 67-79).

Elizabeth lived up to her godly reputation (1:5-6). Though Zechariah had doubted what the angel had told him about Elizabeth's miraculous pregnancy (1:18-20), he quickly regained his perspective and finished with strong praise to the Lord (1:62-79).

The traditional Catholic view of Mary identifies her as the "Mother of God," accompanied by concepts like her immaculate conception and bodily ascension, which are efforts to exalt her to a status above other human beings. In the popular piety of Catholicism, she is even viewed as the "mediatrix," and universally Catholicism holds her up as one to whom you can pray with the assurance that she has special access to her Son. The other position, commonly held among Protestants, has often expressed a reaction against these innovations by saying virtually nothing about Mary other than to affirm the virgin conception. Such overreaction fails to recognize the remarkable and exemplary character of this amazing woman.

Mary was indeed "the mother of our Lord" (1:43) and at the same time a woman whose gentle behavior was highly esteemed in her day. But there is much more in the New Testament portrayal of Mary, which is complete with colorful glimpses into her unique role and God-honoring spirit.

Mary moved from being the young mother from whose womb came the Son of God to becoming a faithful disciple of Jesus, the Son of God. The journey was rough at times, and her life was intriguing. From receiving the angel's greeting in Luke 1:28 to the prayer meeting she attended in the upper room in Acts 1:13-14, Mary has had much to teach women who have followed Christ as disciples throughout history.

The genealogies in Matthew 1 and Luke 3 have provided necessary information about Mary's family background. The Old Testament announced that the Messiah was to come from the tribe of Judah, specifically, from the lineage of King David. Matthew traced the Messiah's genealogy through Abraham while Luke went back even further to Adam.

Because of the Old Testament prophecies, Jesus' ancestry was important. Joseph, the husband of Jesus' birth mother Mary, had to be of the right lineage. Therefore, the genealogical records in Matthew and Luke are very significant. Most agree that Matthew contains Joseph's genealogy, showing Christ's royal and legal right to the throne of David; and Luke traces Mary's ancestry, emphasizing Christ's connection to the entire human race since the record goes back to Adam. Both genealogies support the fact that Joseph and Mary were qualified, legally and relationally, to be the parents of the Messiah. As a descendant of David, Mary had a rich heritage. She had royal blood flowing through her veins!

Even though she was well aware that someday the Messiah Himself, the Savior of Israel, would come through a member of her own family line, she did not know just how intimately involved she would be in the Messiah's coming. Her ancestry put her in the lineage of Messiah, but her godly character ultimately prepared her to be the mother of the Son of God.

Even though Gabriel's words "troubled" Mary, there was no mistake. She was the right young woman, one who was **HIGHLY FAVORED** *(Gk. kecharitōmenē, "bestow favor upon, bless") by the Lord (1:28). The Greek root charitō links the word to "grace" (Gk. charis). Mary was herself a recipient of God's grace. Mary had found grace with God, and that favor would be poured out on all people through the divine offspring she would bear (1:30-31). Her Son would reign on David's throne forever and receive a kingdom that would never end (1:32-33).*

Mary's inspired song, the Magnificat (1:46-55), is a remarkable testimony to Mary's knowledge of many Old Testament themes, especially salvation. Its words revealed her insight into God's plan and purposes for His people. The Old Testament phraseology and concepts she used are reminiscent of Hannah's song (1 Sm 2:1-10). Some scholars believe that Hannah's song served as a model for Mary. Mary's godly character and attitude of servanthood certainly linked her to Hannah. Mary would have known about Hannah, who put herself at the Lord's disposal and gave up her son Samuel (1 Sm 1:28), when she submitted herself to God to carry His Son (Lk 1:38).

The biblical truth woven throughout Mary's song teaches much about the character of God and His purposes in salvation history (1:50-51). But the song also revealed that she was a "learner" of God before she became a disciple of Christ. She was a "follower" of God in the way of the old covenant. She was confident that God would come through. Like other faithful Jews, she had anticipated the day when Messiah would come. Mary could not have imagined that she would be chosen to play such a significant role in the blessed event.

Being Jesus' mother must have added a unique and sometimes complicated dimension to the discipleship process. For instance, her motherly instinct would not give her an advantage in the discipleship process or make the transition into discipleship any easier. Discipleship is not a natural and easy process for anyone. But that was especially true for Mary, who knew Jesus first as her child. The things she would naturally do as His mother she would have to learn to do in a different way as His disciple. As His mother she would naturally love Him, but as His disciple she would have to learn to love Him as her Savior and Lord. As His mother, she would have naturally provided for Him, but as His disciple she would have to learn to trust in His providence. As His mother, she would naturally have sacrificed for Him, but as His disciple she would have to accept His sacrifice for her sins and learn from Him the deeper meaning of a sacrificial life.

Anna's encounter was a new beginning: She continued to speak of Jesus to all those who were looking for the redemption of Jerusalem. There was an interesting resemblance between the description of Anna in Luke 2:36-38 and the passage in which Paul described the widow in the early church (1 Tm 5:3-16). A widow was one who was truly alone, with no one to care for her, trusting God exclusively for her welfare. Her trust and hope were expressed in prayers day and night, a practice for which Anna was well-known (Lk 2:37; see 1 Tm 5:5). Thus, though absolutely nothing is known about Anna's family or means of support, the brief description of her temple life is remarkably close to Paul's description of widows as:

- *above reproach (1 Tm 5:7)*

- *over sixty years old (1 Tm 5:9)*

- *the wife of only one man (1 Tm 5:9)*

- *having a reputation for good works (1 Tm 5:10).*

Nothing is said about children or a home and hospitality. Prayer may well have been a primary part of the job description for these widows (1 Tm 5:5). Anna would have been a classic model for daily supplications. Her example also clearly showed that an older widow can still be an active, effective disciple fully committed to the Lord. If Anna had married in her later teens, as was common in that society, married only 7 years, and widowed for 84 years before she had the opportunity to see the baby Jesus in the temple (Lk 2:38), she had likely been a fixture in the temple precincts for nearly a century.

Not just her length of service was impressive about Anna the disciple, but her joyful enthusiasm must have been contagious. Rather than being cynical or full of questions about the newly designated Messiah, Anna began to thank God immediately and continued to overflow in testimony about the newborn Redeemer, probably for the rest of her life. Although the Holy Spirit was not mentioned in the cameo appearance of Anna, the Spirit was clearly in control.—DKP, editor

---

The childhood of Jesus (2:41-52)

The incident between the young boy Jesus and the erudite Jewish leaders in the temple, recorded only by Luke, sheds light on an event in the life of Jesus before He officially began His ministry. He astounded the religious leaders by asking penetrating questions (v. 46). Many scholars bemoan the fact that Luke did not say more about Jesus' childhood. Luke did not attempt to give a detailed account of Jesus' early years, but he did provide this brief vignette showing Jesus' *humanity.*

The boy Jesus submitted to His parents by going home with them. And under their nurture He grew and matured, honoring Mary and Joseph as other children were expected to honor their parents.

2:41-52 Joseph, Mary, and Jesus, along with many other relatives, **went up** to Jerusalem to celebrate the **Passover**. When the time of feasting was over, the family left for Nazareth thinking that Jesus was with them. They began to look for Him in their company; but when they could not find Him, **they returned to**

Jerusalem. After three days, Joseph and Mary finally **found** Jesus **in the temple**. Joseph and Mary were clearly anxious and upset over the situation. Jesus' response was **Didn't you know that I had to be in My Father's house?** (v. 49). Luke's notation that Mary and Joseph did not understand what Jesus was saying to them reflected His parents' continuing misunderstanding at this point concerning who He was (v. 50).

Luke again said that Mary **kept all these things in her heart** (v. 51b). In other words, she considered everything that took place and was willing to learn and grow from the experience. From Mary, women who follow Christ can learn the value of a willing spirit, of asking questions, and of **searching** (v. 48) for answers. Even as Jesus' mother Mary did not fully understand Him, every believer faces this challenge and has a constant need to grow in the knowledge of Him.

Mary, as a fellow sufferer and faithful disciple, manifested her "growing pains" in both her words and actions, as she struggled through the transition from mother to disciple. Only a few glimpses of her are given during Christ's ministry, but they are revealing. Mary was confused over Jesus' actions and concerned for His reputation. The discipleship (and suffering) of Mary was most clearly presented in John's Gospel. John mentioned her only two times, and in both places he respectfully referred to Mary as "the mother of Jesus" (Jn 2:1; 19:26-27). This reference is significant because in both passages she was seen with Jesus' other disciples. John did not separate her from the disciples into a separate category but actually portrayed her as one who, like the others, was following Jesus. In both situations, Jesus was conversing with Mary, and His authority was clear. She, like the other disciples, was there at the beginning of Jesus' earthly ministry (Jn 2:1-11). She

was also there at His death and resurrection (Lk 24:10-11; Jn 19:26-27). Therefore, Mary, like the other disciples, was a reliable witness to these extraordinary events, and Jesus did not fail to give loving deference to her as His mother, a gesture giving her no special preference in the kingdom, yet maintaining an expression of gratitude for her sacrificial investment in His life.

Preparation for Jesus' Ministry (3:1–4:13)

The work of John (3:1-20) and the baptism of Jesus (3:21-22)

3:1-22 Luke's introduction of John the Baptist not only reflects historical precision and accuracy, but it also bears much similarity with some of the introductions of the Old Testament prophets (Is 1:1; Jr 1:1-3; Hs 1:1; Am 1:1). God's Word is not abstract and impractical; specific historical situations are included.

Luke's opening chapters present many of the same themes as Matthew but appealing to a broader Gentile audience. For example, in quoting Isaiah 40, Matthew only quoted verse 3, while Luke included verses 4 and 5 and the words **everyone will see the salvation of God**. Matthew singled out the Pharisees and Sadducees as those who came to hear John and who were addressed by him. But Luke recorded John's address to the crowd. Luke gave the fuller account in which John the Baptist raised the question concerning what they should do to bear fruit in keeping with repentance. The people, the **tax collectors**, and the **soldiers** were all instructed by John the Baptist concerning how they should live their daily lives. They were to **share with** those who were in need. They were not to be greedy but were to live as a people of integrity. Luke emphasized the practical and concrete. He was concerned about the social aspects of the life of faith. Even in Jesus' baptism (3:21-22), Luke was the only one to mention that **the Holy Spirit descended on Him** [Jesus] **in a physical appearance like a dove** (3:22). The work of God through the Holy Spirit is seen not only in the life of the Savior but also in the everyday lives of believers.

The genealogy of Jesus (3:23-38)

3:23-38 The genealogy presented here in Luke appealed to a broader audience than the one in Matthew. Luke emphasized Christ's humanity and His universal appeal. Luke did not start Jesus' genealogy with Abraham as did Matthew, but he traced Jesus' lineage with an emphasis on the humanity, showing that Jesus was the Son of Adam as well as the divine Son of God. Some scholars have suggested that Luke presented Christ's natural and royal ancestry through Mary while Matthew presented Christ's legal and royal ancestry through Joseph. Yet Luke still substantiated His messianic claim by noting Jesus' descent from David. Only the ancestors from Heli (v. 23) to Zerubbabel (v. 27) are found in other accounts. Luke seemed primarily concerned with presenting Jesus as the Savior of all people, not just the Jews. With the exception of verses 23-27, you can find the genealogy in the Old Testament (see Gn 5:3-32; 11:10-26; Ru 4:18-22; 1 Ch 1:1-4,24-28; 2:1-15).

Some have commented extensively on the difference between the genealogies in Matthew (1:1-17) and here in Luke (3:23-38). In summary, consider these options for explaining the differences:

- One gives legal descent and the other physical descent, which occurred especially when the law of levirate marriage was involved (see Dt 25:5).

- Both Mary and Joseph descended from David but by different branches of the family.

The latter seems more likely as noted in earlier discussion

The temptation of Jesus (4:1-13)

4:1-13 The **40 days** (v. 2) probably served as a reminder of the wilderness experience of Israel after the exodus (Nm 14:33; 32:13; Dt 2:7), or it could be a flashback to the 40 days Moses spent on the mountain (Dt 9:9). With Israel, God was testing His people; with Jesus, Satan was allowed to tempt the Son of God. Every believer *will* be tempted. The certainty of that is clear; the pattern is unveiled; the way out is available (see 1 Co 10:13).

> *Every believer will be tempted. The certainty of that is clear; the pattern is unveiled; the way out is available (see 1 Co 10:13).*

You should note that God never *tempts* His people (Jms 1:13) in the sense of trying to get them to sin or to do evil. That would be contrary to His divine nature. He *allows* Satan to tempt His children since nothing happens unless God lifts His hand and allows it. In this sense, God tests His people by letting them make choices.

Here the one who opposes God is called the **Devil** (Gk. *diabolou*, a compound of *dia* or "through" and *ballō* or "throw," "cast"), "the one who casts through" (v. 2). Clearly his power is always limited. This temptation account is also discussed in Matthew 4:1-11.

Luke's account of the temptation parallels Matthew's except that he reversed the order of the last two scenes. The reason for this difference may have to do with Luke's interest in Jerusalem (v. 9), which Matthew did not specifically mention by name. On the other hand, Matthew may have wanted to end his account with a kingdom emphasis. Since he was writing primarily to a Jewish audience, he may not have felt the name of "the holy city"

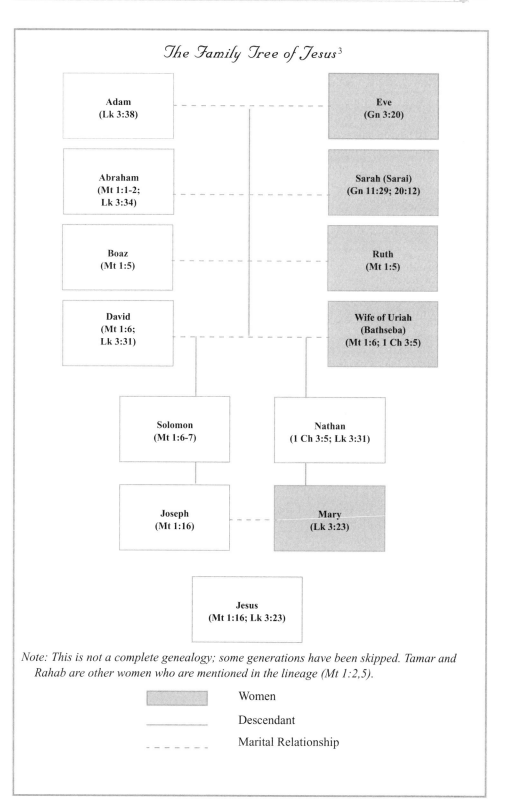

The Family Tree of Jesus³

Adam
(Lk 3:38)

Eve
(Gn 3:20)

Abraham
(Mt 1:1-2;
Lk 3:34)

Sarah (Sarai)
(Gn 11:29; 20:12)

Boaz
(Mt 1:5)

Ruth
(Mt 1:5)

David
(Mt 1:6;
Lk 3:31)

Wife of Uriah
(Bathseba)
(Mt 1:6; 1 Ch 3:5)

Solomon
(Mt 1:6-7)

Nathan
(1 Ch 3:5; Lk 3:31)

Joseph
(Mt 1:16)

Mary
(Lk 3:23)

Jesus
(Mt 1:16; Lk 3:23)

Note: This is not a complete genealogy; some generations have been skipped. Tamar and Rahab are other women who are mentioned in the lineage (Mt 1:2,5).

Women

Descendant

Marital Relationship

necessary (Mt 4:5). Also, in Matthew the Devil left Jesus and angels came to attend to Him (Mt 4:11). Luke recorded that the Devil left Him only **for a time** (Lk 4:13). There is no mention of angels (Mt 4:11) or wild animals (Mk 1:13). It is not uncommon for various accounts penned or described by different individuals to present or emphasize the details noted as important to the respective author. There is no contradiction here, simply helpful differences that reaffirm the importance of all working together to give the whole. Luke was very interested in the work (and the ultimate demise) of the Devil throughout his Gospel.

MINISTRY IN AND AROUND GALILEE (4:14–9:50)

Preaching in Nazareth (4:14-30)

4:14-30 Luke is the only writer to emphasize that Jesus began His ministry in Galilee **in the power of the Spirit** (v. 14). This scene concerning Jesus' visit and ultimate rejection at His hometown in Nazareth is described with more detail than Matthew and is perfectly fitted for Luke's overall purpose. The event took place during Jesus' Galilean ministry. The sequence in which it is recorded does not affect its meaning. The Synoptics are not tied to a strict chronological sequence. Their flexibility in placing the events in Jesus' ministry probably had more to do with the interest and emphasis of each author. Luke may have placed the account here because he felt it was most important and would thus make a meaningful introduction to ministry in Galilee. Jesus' rejection in Nazareth laid out the overall themes of His mission and highlighted the conflicts that were to come (4:16-30). Matthew and Mark placed it later in their respective sequences of events (Mt 13:53-58; Mk 6:1-6).

When Jesus **entered the synagogue** He **was given** the **scroll** of Isaiah, and He found the passage that described His overall mission (Is 61:1-2; see also 58:6). Both the physical and spiritual aspects of the Messiah's ministry were seen in these few verses. The people **were amazed** at His words, but their questions concerning His identity as **Joseph's son** (v. 22) hint at their unbelief. Jesus' response was harsh, a **proverb** (v. 23) that was undoubtedly well-known by the common people. Jesus used it to make a crucial point (v. 24). Those who are recognized as great in other places are not recognized as such at home.

Jesus' statements concerning the prophets Elijah and Elisha (vv. 25-27) pointed out the deeper meaning behind His use of the proverb. As the prophets of the Old Testament were rejected by the people of Israel, so would Jesus be rejected by the people. But the Gentiles would benefit from such a rejection. The people of Nazareth were so infuriated that they sought to kill Jesus. But He escaped unharmed (vv. 28-30).

Beginning a Healing Ministry (4:31-44)

4:31-44 Following on the heels of Jesus' proclamation of the purpose of His mission in Nazareth came a demonstration of its truth. Jesus entered a synagogue in **Capernaum**, His new hometown. His **authority** was revealed when a demon-possessed man addressed Him **with a loud voice**, begging to be left alone. Jesus silenced the demon and cast it out (v. 35). As at Nazareth, the people were amazed at His teaching and authority (v. 32). But there was a difference in their response. His identity was not questioned. In fact, the demons verified that He is the Son of God. Unbelief was not immediately evident in this context; therefore, Jesus' healing ministry advanced and culminated with the healings at Simon Peter's house.

Peter's **mother-in-law** was the first to draw Jesus' attention (v. 38). After He **rebuked** her **fever**, she served the group (see also Mk 1:29-31). Soon her house was filled with those who needed the Master's touch.

At daybreak, Jesus moved to **a deserted place**. Mark emphasized that He went there to pray (Mk 1:35). Luke pointed out that the crowds **tried to keep Him from leaving**, but Jesus noted that He must go and **proclaim the good news about the kingdom of God to the other towns** (Lk 4:43). Jesus' statement about the good news at the synagogue in Nazareth was tied to His proclamation concerning the nature of His mission, which may be why Luke arranged these events in this order. Only Luke recorded these events before his account of the call of the disciples. The connection between the Messiah's proclamation of His mission and the demonstration of His works could not be missed. The connection between words and works was an important emphasis for Luke.

Calling the First Disciples (5:1-11)

5:1-11 The calling of the first disciples is paralleled in Matthew (Mt 4:18-22) and Mark (Mk 1:16-20), but Luke gave a fuller and more interesting account of the event. Because **the crowd was pressing in on Jesus**, He got into Simon's boat and taught the people from a position away from the shore. Luke made clear that those first disciples had a good chance to hear Jesus teach just before He called them. They had heard Him before this time (see Jn 1:40-42), but perhaps this insight from Luke indicated that their decision to follow Jesus was not one made impulsively but after hearing His teachings. Further, Jesus actually helped these poor fishermen by guiding them to the

catch of their lives. They had **worked hard all night** but with nothing to show for it. At Jesus' command, however, they **let down** their **nets** and brought in such a large load that their boats **began to sink** (vv. 6-7).

Simon Peter's confession concerning his own true nature was highly significant. Peter showed here an understanding not only of his own inadequacy but also of his own sinfulness (v. 8). Luke often focused on an individual in order to draw attention to Jesus. Here Jesus' holiness and power were contrasted with Peter's weakness and sinfulness.

The radical nature of discipleship is also emphasized here. Luke alone mentioned that the disciples **left everything** to follow Jesus (v. 11). Later, Luke demonstrated further the cost of true discipleship (Lk 14:33). The obedience of the disciples was also a striking aspect of this account. At Jesus' word, Simon let down his net, and at Jesus' word the disciples left everything **and followed Him**.

The placement of the calling of the first disciples in the overall context of Luke seems to have been carefully considered. Luke first established the nature of Jesus' ministry (4:14-44). Then he was ready to demonstrate the sovereignty of the Messiah first by Jesus' interaction with Peter (a sinful but obedient man) and then with other outcasts and sinners in future encounters. Note the excursus in Mark 1:14-20 for a discussion of the translation issue concerning **people** (Gk. *anthropous*) in 5:10.

Participating in Controversies with the Jewish Leaders (5:12-6:11)

In this section Luke paralleled Mark quite closely, but the placement of these events following Luke's account of the calling of the first disciples, especially Peter, gives the Lukan account a slightly different sense. As with Matthew and

Mark, Luke was concerned to show the reasons why Christianity went beyond ancient Judaism. Luke showed Jesus' conflicts with the religious leaders in order to demonstrate the Lord's authority to heal and to forgive sins and to reveal His superiority over the old traditions of Judaism.

5:12-16 First, Jesus healed the leper, which demonstrated not only His authority over disease but also His compassion for the sick. **Serious skin disease** seemed to be synonymous with leprosy. The disease is not necessarily equivalent to modern-day Hansen's disease, but its victims were repulsive to society, and there was no known cure. The most astounding thing Jesus did in the eyes of the people was to touch the man (5:13) since lepers were considered unclean by the people and the religious leaders. Obviously this simple gesture communicated concern in a way nothing else would. The man's humble statement, "**Lord, if You are willing, You can make me clean**," affirmed his confidence in Jesus' ability to heal and thus Jesus' divinity, His authority, and His power (v. 12). Jesus not only responded with "**I am willing**" (v. 13), but He gave instructions to the man seeking help with the message **be made clean** (Gk. *katharisthēti,* "purify, declare ritually acceptable"), and the leper was healed **immediately** (Gk. *eutheōs*), the word used so frequently in Mark's fast-moving Gospel.

News about Jesus **spread** quickly despite His admonition to **tell no one** (v. 14), and the crowds following Him were overwhelming. Jesus never called for silence to forbid the spread of the gospel but rather to allow Him to do the work the Father had given Him before His time for the cross came. He felt a constant urgency to do His work. The news of healings increased His popularity but hindered His work. Jesus, in order to escape the crowds, went to lonely places to pray.

Second, Jesus manifested His authority to forgive sins, which drew heavy criticism from the Jewish leaders. Not only did Jesus heal, but the healing validated His claim that He could forgive sins.

15:17-26 Evidently the **Pharisees and teachers of the law** had heard enough about the popularity of Jesus as a teacher that they felt it necessary to hear and judge what He was teaching the people (v. 17). Here Jesus' power to heal is coupled with His power to forgive sins. Luke showed his own keen theological understanding when he included **alone** (Gk. *monos,* "only") to indicate the uniqueness of Jesus' authority to **forgive sins**, which was reserved for God alone (v. 21). Luke used this opportunity to make clear that Jesus is indeed God.

Blasphemies were capital crimes and called for stoning of the perpetrators (Lv 24:14-16). This act described not merely speaking against God but insulting or slandering the character of God. The religious leaders believed Jesus had committed blasphemy because they did not accept Him as God (Mk 2:7).

Jesus again turned a question into a counter question in order to create a hypothetical situation the religious leaders could not answer (15:22-23). Even while continuing His controversial encounters with the religious leaders, Jesus never lost sight of the paralytic man who had turned to Him in faith (v. 24). The man could not fulfill Jesus' command except with God's healing power. His obedience was thus based on faith (v. 25), and by being obedient he awakened glory to God in his own heart and in the hearts of the people who were looking on. The people described what they had seen as **incredible things** (Gk. *paradoxa,* "strange, wonderful, remarkable, unusual, marvelous," v. 26).

5:27-32 Jesus bestowed favor on those who seemed least worthy and helped them. First a demoniac received Christ's touch (4:31-37), then a paralytic (5:17-26), and finally **a tax collector** (vv. 29-32). When Jesus called, Levi (Matthew) left **everything behind** and followed Him. Only Luke emphasized this total obedience on the part of Levi. In all three Synoptic Gospels, Levi's dinner and guests led to questions about religious practices (vv. 29-32). The outcome was that Jesus' mission involved a radical break with traditional religious practices. He did not come merely to add to what was already practiced. His ministry involved something that was radically new. This profound difference was seen in the company He kept (v. 32).

5:33-39 The bridal metaphor is used here and elsewhere throughout Scripture. In the Old Testament Israel was the unfaithful bride (see Hs 3:1), and in the New Testament the church was compared to a bride in her relationship to Christ, the Bridegroom (Jn 3:29). Jesus' answer was radical as He contrasted the joy of the wedding with the sorrow of the absence of the bridegroom. He anticipated His coming death (v. 35). Jesus used both garments (a new, unwashed, and thus unshrunk, cloth that was sewn into an old and seasoned garment) and **wineskins**, which, because when sewn together they were watertight, were often used to hold liquids. The new skins had good elasticity and could adjust to the volume of the liquid during the aging process. However, the old skins were rigid and could easily burst under pressure. The gospel Jesus brought could not be absorbed into Judaism because it was radically new.

6:1-11 The Gospels mentioned three Sabbath controversies. Two occurred in the Synoptics and one in John 5. In each instance Jesus made several points:

- The Sabbath is for man's benefit (Mk 2:27).
- **The Son of Man is Lord of the Sabbath** (v. 5).
- The Sabbath is for good deeds (v. 9).
- God the Father and the Son both work on the Sabbath (Jn 5).

The origin of the Sabbath was not only rooted in the creation account and in the Ten Commandments of the Old Testament; it was also deeply grounded in Jewish rabbinic tradition. The Sabbath came weekly, and its observance became a matter of public knowledge. Therefore, observance of the Sabbath (the seventh day of every week reserved for worship and rest) provided fertile ground for debate. If the religious leaders were going to trap Jesus, how He viewed the Sabbath provided a perfect issue. Both incidents recorded as happening on the Sabbath juxtaposed human need with Jewish ceremonial law.

Apparently Jesus took the initiative, not waiting for the man's request. The man's illness was not life threatening, or rabbinical law would have allowed him medical help. However, Jesus' point is that when healing can be provided, it should not be delayed.

Jesus observed the Sabbath but not according to their oral traditions and ceremonial additions to the law. For Him it remained a day of rest and worship. Plucking the grain was work, but it was prompted by the need for food. Jesus maintained that ceremonial law ought only to be the means to an end and so should become a servant to any higher moral law (vv. 3-5).

Jesus healed the man with the paralyzed hand on the Sabbath and infuriated the religious leaders so that they began discussing what they might do to him. Luke's language is not as specific as that of Matthew and Mark in this context (see

Mt 12:14; Mk 3:6); he nevertheless accurately portrayed the hostility the religious leaders had toward Jesus. Jesus had clearly established that He, not the Pharisees and other religious leaders, through His role as **Lord of the Sabbath,** would rule and properly interpret how the Sabbath should be observed.

Formalizing the Call to Discipleship (6:12-49)

6:12-19 Jesus now gained momentum in His ministry with the appointment of the Twelve as apostles (see Mt 4:18-21 for further discussion on the calling out of the Twelve). Jesus spent the entire **night in prayer**, an indication of His feeling great need in the challenges before Him. As Jesus' ministry advanced, the controversy with the religious leaders heated up. Jesus needed the wisdom and guidance of the Father. Even Jesus probably was not in the habit of praying all night (v. 12). But on this occasion, nothing less than a lengthy and extended night of prayer could suffice for the Son of God. What a scene when Jesus and His disciples came down from the mountain! Multitudes gathered to Him to hear Him and to be healed by Him (v. 17). Unlike Matthew, Luke stressed that **the whole crowd was trying to touch** Jesus **because power was coming out from Him**. The night of prayer had energized Him with the power of God, and that power resonated and overflowed through the crowd.

6:20-49 Although the setting for this sermon and the Sermon on the Mount in Matthew (see Mt 5-7) is considered the same by many, others believe the difference in content suggests two different settings of the sermon. Of course, there are very logical choices:

• The same location and sermon were in view, but they are described by two men from their different perspectives.

• The same location but two different, yet similar, messages were delivered to different audiences.

• Two similar sermons were delivered by Jesus in different locations with the heart of the message, namely, the nature of the Christian life, being the same but with varying content—a situation common among modern-day itinerant preachers each of whom tends to have a keynote message for which he is known.

The context of this passage and of Matthew 5-7 is undoubtedly the same. But there are some stark differences between the two in terms of content. There is no reason to question the trustworthiness of Luke's account since to do so is to question Scripture itself. Such questioning is not warranted when you keep in mind that Luke's purpose in presenting the material was seemingly quite different from Matthew's, and his audience was different as well.

The first thing noted in terms of differences between the sermon as recorded in Matthew 5-7 (see extensive discussion in commentary on Matthew) and in Luke 6 is that Luke added several woes in his listing of the Beatitudes. Luke included what are called "kingdom reversal" passages, which became more prevalent in the central section of his book, where he nailed down the rigorous demands of discipleship. However, this short introduction to such reversals described what the call to discipleship entailed.

Luke emphasized not only the spiritual but also the physical and practical aspects of discipleship, as in his mention of the **poor** and **hungry** in the negative section on woes. Also Luke's use of **laugh** (Gk. *gelasete*, v. 21) was a different nuance than Matthew's "be comforted" (Mt 5:4). The promise of great **reward** in heaven (v. 23) did not suggest a works salvation

---

Heart 🐾 Heart:
The Blessing of Sorrow

*P*erhaps you are asking: how can sorrow be a blessing? While not all sorrow seems like a blessing, Christians can be assured of joy that will come when they remain faithful even while mourning (v. 21). A faithful woman who is blessed can see the purpose in sorrow for the glory of God. In her book, BeAttitudes for Women, *Dorothy Patterson concluded: "Sorrow leads us to Christ, and that sorrow when carried triumphantly, draws others to Christ most effectively. Sorrow seems to be an integral part of service and obedience." When you face sorrow, have confidence in God. Draw near to Christ, the Light of the world, in your darkest hours. Know that He will turn your tears into laughter. Whether or not you feel joy, you can be assured that "Jesus makes joy the final stanza of every midnight song."*[4]

---

but rather blessing from the Lord and personal vindication for faithfulness under fire. The **rich** were not singled out to receive **woe** because of their wealth but rather because they had chosen to seek fulfillment of their desires on earth instead of future kingdom blessings (v. 24). They did not see value in spiritual disciplines.

The second significant difference was that, unlike Matthew, Luke did not mention anything concerning the law and the Pharisees. The entire section of the Sermon on the Mount concerning Christ and His relationship to the law, as well as His discussion on prayer and fasting (Mt 5:17-42; 6:1-18), was omitted by Luke. Some conclude that this omission was made because Luke was writing primarily to a Gentile audience. Gentiles would not have been as concerned about the law and Christ's response to it. Luke did record the sections in the Sermon on the Mount concerning prayer as well as Jesus' discussion on God and possessions but not until his central section (Lk 11:1-13; 12:22-34), where the meanings of these

passages take on a slightly different character than they have in Matthew.

With regard to formalizing the call to discipleship, Luke found these four elements of utmost importance:

• blessings and woes (6:20-26)

• love for enemies (6:27-36)

• judging others (6:37-42)

• a test to prove the genuineness of professing to be a disciple given in two illustrations: a tree and its fruit (6:43-45) and then the wise and foolish builders (6:46-49).

Focusing on the Question of Jesus' Identity (7:1–8:3)

7:1-10 Both Matthew (8:5-13) and Luke record the healing of the centurion's servant but with slightly different details. Matthew noted that the man himself came to ask for the healing, while Luke recorded that the man sent **Jewish elders** to make the request on his behalf. Some modern scholars have claimed that this difference poses a significant problem concerning the accuracy of the account.

Upon closer look, however, apparently Luke, as often was the case, gave a more complete narrative than Matthew. It was an ancient custom to allow a person to speak through his agents. Matthew did not mention the Jewish elders' involvement. Luke, on the other hand, recorded their intervention (vv. 3-5). Luke's account of the healing of the centurion more clearly foreshadowed Christ's ministry to the Gentiles and had a striking resemblance to the conversion account of the Gentile centurion Cornelius in Acts 10. Nevertheless, both Matthew and Luke agreed that this event demonstrated Jesus' authority ever more clearly.

7:11-17 With Jesus' authority in focus, Luke dealt with the question concerning Jesus' identity. Rather than appealing to Christ's divinity, especially in light of His previous demonstration of divine authority (7:1-10), Luke revealed Him as a "prophet," even though Jesus had just raised the widow's son from the dead. Much has been said about Christ's **compassion** for this woman, considering that the young man was her **only son** and that **she was a widow**, an important point. The raising of the widow's son was similar to Elisha's raising of the Shunammite's son (2 Kg 4:8-37). Luke seemed to recognize this similarity as evidenced by his comment that the crowd responded to this miracle by saying, **A great prophet has arisen among us** (v. 16). Also, only in Luke did Jesus refer to Himself as a prophet (13:33). Many scholars have seen Luke's entire central section as paralleling Deuteronomy, where mention was made of the "prophet" who is to come and to whom everyone should listen (Dt 18:15). There is much to commend this view. Indeed, Luke's entire use of the Old Testament should be understood to teach that all Scripture points to Jesus and is all about Him.

Questions	Answers
Where?	In the city of Nain (v. 11).
Who?	A widow whose only son had died (v. 12).
When?	Jesus saw her and had compassion (v. 13).
How?	Jesus brought her son back to life (v. 14).
What?	The dead son sat up and spoke to his mother (v. 15).
Why?	They glorified God and told about Him all around (vv. 16-17).

Widow of Nain — *Luke 7:11-17*

7:18-35 Jesus' ministry raised questions in the mind of another "prophet"—John the Baptist. John sent messengers to ask questions of Jesus. Jesus sent them back to John with the assurance that He (Jesus) is **the One** who was **to come** (vv. 22-23). Then Jesus praised John the Baptist to the crowd. While John indeed came in the spirit and power of Elijah, Luke wanted his readers to know that Jesus was the great Prophet unparalleled by any other (vv. 21-23).

7:36-50 Unlike Matthew, Luke recorded the kind of people who responded to John's message: tax collectors and sinners. They were the ones who acknowledged God's way of righteousness. Then Luke provided an extended example of the kind of person who responded to Jesus, namely, the sinful woman.

Jesus was at the house of a Pharisee, one who "rejected the plan of God" for himself (7:30). When the sinful woman entered the Pharisee's home, she did not go to the Pharisee, but she immediately directed her attention and service to Jesus (vv. 37-38). The Pharisee retorted **to himself** that **if** Jesus truly **were a prophet**, He **would know ... what kind of woman** she was. Luke was showing the challenge made to Jesus' identity.

Jesus responded to Simon's complaint with a parable about **two debtors**, one who had been forgiven a small debt and the other a much larger one. Jesus intended to compare the woman with the debtor who was forgiven more and then to show that her sins were forgiven. The woman **loved much**. Because of this devotion, Jesus proclaimed that her sins were forgiven. She had demonstrated that Jesus' forgiveness awakened in her heart the desire to serve Him more sacrificially (vv. 47-48).

Interestingly, the woman's focus was on Jesus' feet. In 14 short verses, Jesus' feet were mentioned seven times. Prophesying about the salvation that would come to Israel through the Messiah, Isaiah said, "How beautiful on the mountains are the *feet* of the herald, who proclaims peace, who brings news of good things, who proclaims salvation, who says to Zion, 'Your God reigns!'" (Is 52:7, italics added). Jesus' ministry to the sinful woman is a beautiful demonstration of the fulfillment of Isaiah's prophecy. A Pharisee who was quite learned in the Word of God did not recognize this truth. But a sinful woman, an outcast, acknowledged the prophecy and demonstrated her understanding of it by focusing on the *feet* of the greatest *Prophet,* the One destined to bring her peace and salvation (v. 50). Luke in this passage was demonstrating a kingdom reversal at its finest.

8:1-3 Unique to Luke was this account of the women who supported Christ's work, yet another example of the unlikely people who responded to Christ and His message. These women were healed of various diseases and illnesses by Jesus. Seven demons had come out of **Mary . . . Magdalene**. Luke did not specify how **Joanna, the wife of Chuza**, and **Susanna** were healed; but they were among the

Sinner at Simon's House
Luke 7:36-50
Steps to Forgiveness
Confession ➔ "I am a sinner" (vv. 36-39).
• She washed His feet with her tears.
• She wiped His feet with her hair.
• She kissed His feet.
• She anointed His feet with fragrant oil.
Cleansing ➔ "Your sins are forgiven" (vv. 40-49).
• She was forgiven of many sins.
• She loved much.
Commission ➔ "Your faith has saved you. Go in peace" (v. 50).

many **supporting** Jesus **from their** own **possessions**. Luke emphasized the sacrifice and commitment made by these women. For women to be a part of the party traveling with itinerant preachers in the first century was uncommon.

Jesus had large crowds following Him in groups—probably for protection and possibly even for fellowship. When the young boy Jesus was thought to be part of the group traveling from the temple, the entourage was large enough that Mary and Joseph did not initially realize Jesus was not in the group (Lk 2:41-52).

Women never traveled alone and did not travel as much as men because of the difficulties and dangers as well as their responsibilities in the home. In this case, for women to be included in the large entourage would not have been as unusual as the fact that they were obviously considered among the inner circle of disciples and were specifically named as part of the group. There is no indication in the text as to the length of travel or distance covered or how far they went from their homes. From the high value Jesus placed on children and the home, you can be sure that He was not encouraging women to neglect their home responsibilities. (Note the frequency with which He used the family metaphor in His teaching.) Jesus recognized women as full-fledged disciples, something completely unheard of in His day. These women not only gave sacrificially of their resources, but they also exhibited extraordinary devotion and selfless service to Jesus, giving of their time and energy to be a part of His traveling ministry. There were many generous women who contributed to the ministry of Christ.

Joanna and Susanna *Women Who Supported Jesus* *Luke 8:1-3*	
Joanna	**Susanna**
• Wife of Chuza, Herod's servant • Wealthy believer • Healed by Jesus • Supported Jesus' ministry • Sacrificed for the gospel • Visited the tomb of Jesus (23:55) • Witnessed His resurrection (24:10)	• Follower of Jesus • Healed by Jesus • Leader among Christian women • Financial supporter of Jesus • Loved by Jesus
See also Mk 15:40-41.	

Hearing the Word of God Correctly (8:4-21)

8:4-21 Those who are true disciples will not only hear the Word but also put its truths into practice. The practical side of Christian living is extremely important for Luke. The first-century Romans were intensely practical as well. So this message would have resonated with them.

Parables were a popular tool used by Jesus (5:36-39; 6:39,44-45,47-49; 7:41-42), and the account of the parable of the sower is found in all three Synoptic Gospels (Mt 13:1-23; Mk 4:1-20; Lk 8:4-15), but in some ways it is more detailed and extended in Luke, although Luke seemed to abbreviate the account with some notable omissions. In each case the author interjected a brief section on the purpose for parables between the presentation of the parable and the explanation of its meaning.

Parables had a dual function: to reveal truth to the disciples (called by some the insiders) or genuine seekers and to conceal the message from enemies (also called outsiders) or those who sought to harm Jesus (v. 10). The central theme in Jesus' parables was **the kingdom of God**. Jesus used metaphors that would be understood by those who wanted to find meaning in His message.

Luke's focus seemed to be on enduring in the faith and bearing fruit, ideas that find their fullness in Luke 14:25-34, where the cost of discipleship is fully disclosed. Luke intended to leave his readers with no doubts concerning the nature of discipleship. If true disciples are not enduring and bearing fruit, they must be ready to lose even what they think they might have. They must take an internal inventory in order to verify to whom they really belong (vv. 16-18).

Jesus in no way dishonored His family (vv. 19-20), but here He is affirming those who obey God (v. 21). The way to be close to Jesus—as close as His own family—is to hear His Word and do it. The Word of God is the final authority in the life of every believer. In other words, those who belong to Christ hear Him and obey Him (vv. 19-21).

Illustrating Jesus' Authoritative Word (8:22-56)

8:22-56 Jesus, the Savior of outcasts and sinners, demonstrated His divine authority by exercising power over nature (vv. 22-25), over demons (vv. 26-39), and over sickness and death (vv. 40-53), and He commanded complete obedience from His followers. In these passages, Luke provided illustrations of Jesus' authoritative word.

An Excursus on Mary Magdalene

Mary Magdalene, demon-possessed and literally "enslaved" to evil, was intimately acquainted with the evil powers of the prince of darkness himself. When she was set free from her darkness, she became a servant to the Light (Lk 8:1-3). Mary Magdalene's witness goes far beyond her verbal proclamation. She was a remarkable example of a faithful and loyal disciple.

Many women have had hurtful experiences. You learn from Mary Magdalene that your past, no matter how "dark" it was, need not hinder you on the path to discipleship. You may never be able to "forget" your past; but you can, like Mary, overcome it and serve Christ.

Mary was from a little village called Magdala[5] (Jn 19:25), located on the northwest shore of the Sea of Galilee. Thus, "Magdalene" was probably not Mary's family name but represented the town from which she came. Magdala was predominately Gentile and not respected among the Jews. In fact, the rabbis attributed its fall to immorality. How Mary Magdalene became demon possessed is not known.

The fact that seven demons were cast out of her (Mk 16:9; Lk 8:2) indicates that she must have been actively involved with "the powers of darkness" to some degree. What characteristics of demon possession Mary manifested are unknown, but those around her sensed that something was desperately wrong. The most vivid description of multiple demon possession in the Gospels was a man from the region of the Gerasenes who met Jesus on the shores of the Sea of Galilee (Mk 5:3-5).

This man was in unspeakable agony and was greatly feared by his community. Mary Magdalene could have experienced some of these same horrors. There is little doubt that her release from bondage was dramatic and life changing, and she immediately manifested her gratitude by her actions (Lk 8:3).

> Being a faithful witness involves more than verbal proclamation; it is living your life as characterized by service to the Master.

The significance of Mary Magdalene's witness of the risen Christ was brought to light in John's portrayal of her (Jn 19:25; 20:1,18). Matthew gave the most focused attention to her courage. She was boldly present at the cross and tomb, despite the possible consequences (Mt 27:56,61; 28:1). Mark shed further light on the steadfastness of Mary Magdalene and the other women disciples at the cross and tomb (Mk 15:40-47; 16:9).

Nowhere was Mary Magdalene's role as a faithful witness to the risen Christ more clearly seen than in John's Gospel. He focused on Mary as the first to bear witness of Christ's resurrection (Jn 20:10-18). The Apostle John gave a more intimate look at the conversation between Jesus and Mary (Jn 20:15-17). As Jesus released Mary from bondage, so will He release you from your past in order to serve Him. Being a faithful witness involves more than verbal proclamation; it is living your life as characterized by service to the Master.

Jesus raised some interesting questions during each miracle. After calming the winds and the waves, Jesus asked His disciples, **Where is your faith?** (v. 25). **Fearful and amazed**, they responded with their own question, **Who can this be?** (v. 25), which showed that the disciples continued to be slow in understanding Jesus' true identity.

Before casting legions of demons from the possessed man, Jesus asked the demons, **What is your name?** (v. 30). Luke gave a vivid account of the destructive nature of demon possession. The man, when he was set free, begged to go with Jesus; but, instead, Jesus **sent him away** to his hometown so that he could bear witness about what had happened to him. (See further discussion in Mark 5:1-20.)

When the woman who had an issue of blood touched Him, Jesus asked, **Who touched Me?** (v. 45). The woman came to Him trembling with fear and confessed what had happened. He sent her away with the assurance that her faith made her well (8:48; see further discussion in the parallel passage on the healing of the bleeding woman as well as on the resurrection to life of Jairus's daughter in Mk 5:21-43). The significance was not in what Christ's questions revealed about Himself, but what His questions revealed about His hearers. They trembled at His words and deeds. And this awesome power was precisely what Luke wanted to communicate about Christ and His authority.

Coming to the Christological Climax (9:1-50)

9:1-9 In this section, Luke basically followed the accounts of Matthew and Mark of events leading up to Peter's confession of Christ, but there are some significant differences to be mentioned. Unlike Matthew, Luke gave a truncated version of the commissioning of the Twelve (vv. 1-6), perhaps because of his intended Gentile audience and overall purpose. The lengthier version was especially appropriate for Matthew, who was writing to a Jewish audience. The section concerning "only the lost sheep of Israel" (Mt 10:6) would not have fit Luke's overall purpose. The instructions recorded would certainly heighten the importance and urgency of the task assigned (vv. 3-5).

The passage concerning Herod's desire to see Jesus is unique to Luke (vv. 7-9). For John the Baptist to be on Herod's mind and conscience was not surprising. Herod did not see Jesus at this time but did come face-to-face with Him when Pilate sent Jesus to him (23:8-11). Since Luke sought to reveal Jesus as the greatest prophet, these verses might have been important for Luke's overall purpose because of the references to **Elijah** and **the ancient prophets** (v. 8).

9:10-36 The feeding of the 5,000 was recorded in all the Gospels (see Mk 6:30-44). Jesus had intended to go away with His apostles for some rest; but, instead, the crowds discovered His whereabouts and came to Him. Jesus had compassion on them, healed their sick, and fed all of them with **five loaves and two fish** (vv. 16-17). Luke in his account specified that Jesus **spoke to them about the kingdom of God** (v. 11), an important concept for Luke. He recorded this event just before Peter's confession (vv. 18-20), Jesus' prediction of His death (vv. 21-22), Jesus' teaching on discipleship (vv. 23-27), and the demonstration of the kingdom's power in the transfiguration (vv. 28-36).

After Peter made his confession (vv. 18-20; see further discussion on Mt 16:13-19), Jesus told His followers what it would cost them to follow Him (vv. 23-27). When Jesus posed the question concerning His identity to His disciples,

He most assuredly expected more from them than the rumors floating among the people or the innuendos coming from the religious leaders (v. 20). Peter's succinct answer came: **God's Messiah** (Gk. *ton Christon tou Theou*, literally "the Christ of the God" or "the anointed one of God"). The HCSB translators chose to use the Hebrew title "Messiah," which also means "anointed one." Luke did not include the more explicit words "the Son of the Living God" (Mt 16:16), but he does emphasize the divine nature of Messiah in the phrase "God's Messiah" (v. 20).

Luke added that the cross was to be taken up **daily** (v. 23). This addition unique to Luke fit his emphasis on the practical side of Christian living, which was to be lived out daily and in every way.

The transfiguration of Christ (vv. 28-36) was the most significant event between His birth and His passion. All of the Synoptic Gospels recorded this phenomenal event. Luke emphasized the suffering that lay ahead for Jesus. He did so through the conversation Jesus had with Moses and Elijah (v. 31). Luke's account contained several important themes:

- The eight days (v. 28). Matthew and Mark recorded "after six days," with the idea being that it was roughly a week. Luke was more precise in that he wanted to draw the parallel between Moses' wait for the revelation of God on Mount Sinai (Ex 24:15-16) and Jesus' wait on this mountain.

- The mountain, Moses and Elijah (v. 30).

- Jesus' death (v. 31).

- The tabernacles (v. 33).

- The cloud (v. 34).

Two events are important in understanding these themes: the exodus (Ex 24)

and the return of Christ (1 Th 4:16-17; Rv 1:7). These two frames of references—one past and one future—shed light on the overall purpose of the transfiguration event.

Only Luke mentioned Jerusalem in the context of the transfiguration. Jerusalem, as the dwelling of God and the center of salvific activities, was highly significant to Luke. This event prefigured Jesus' determination to set out for Jerusalem (9:51).

9:37-50 The healing of the demon-possessed boy further demonstrated the power and greatness of God. As a physician, Luke noticed the physical responses similar to those caused by epilepsy; yet he was more concerned with the demonic source of the boy's suffering. Luke left out the section concerning the disciples' lack of faith precisely because he wanted the focus to be on **the greatness of God** (v. 43). However, he did record a shortened account of the argument among the disciples concerning **who would be the greatest** (v. 46). As with the healing of the boy, Luke's account did not include Jesus' lecture to the disciples concerning true greatness.

The point of Jesus' reference to the **little child** (v. 48) is not to illustrate simple faith as in Matthew 18:2-4; neither is it to illustrate a disciple who comes in the name of Jesus as in Matthew 10:40-42. In almost every society, position, prominence, prestige, and power are the symbols associated with success and accomplishment. Jesus could see the seeds of such shallow thinking germinating in the minds and even issuing forth in the talk of His disciples. Taking advantage of the presence of a "little child," Jesus positioned him before them. No one present would have been impressed with the greatness or prestige of that child. Yet surprisingly Jesus suggested that humility, obedience, faith, and dependence upon

God are qualities that set one apart for greatness in a heavenly assessment.

This man had actually been seen **driving out demons in Your** (Jesus') **name**. He was **not against** Jesus even though he apparently had not yet officially joined the followers of Christ (vv. 49-50). Perhaps Luke was remembering the unwillingness of some in the Jerusalem church to accept Paul (Ac 23:1-22). In any case, while contending for the faith and maintaining its tenets faithfully is important, believers dare not close themselves to any servant of Christ just because he is outside of their immediate circle. Furthermore, the man who used the name of Jesus should not be rejected, even though he did not yet belong to the group of believers. He was possibly on the way to receiving Christ. Therefore, they were not **to stop him** (v. 50).

JESUS' TEACHING "EN ROUTE" TO JERUSALEM (9:51–18:34)

Discipleship in the Shadow of the Cross (9:51-62)

9:51-62 Luke's central section extends from 9:51 through 18:34. While some of the material used by Luke in this section has also been recorded in Matthew and Mark, the arrangement of the material in Luke is uniquely his. Some of the most beloved and well-known passages of Scripture, such as the parables of the good Samaritan (10:30-37) and the prodigal son (15:11-31), are found in this section.

With His passion set before Him, Jesus was **determined to journey to Jerusalem** (v. 51), a modern idiom for the Semitic expression to "set his face towards." This idea is drawn from a prophecy where the Messiah, the obedient Servant, was contrasted with Israel, the rebellious servant: "The Lord GOD will help Me; therefore I have not been humiliated; therefore I have set My face like flint, and I know I will not be put to shame" (Is 50:7).

Jesus **sent messengers ahead**, and they entered a Samaritan village, but they were quickly turned away, much to the displeasure of James and John. When the disciples wanted **to call down fire** on the village, Jesus **rebuked them** and then moved on to **another village**. Jesus was entering Samaritan territory, an indication of the beginning of His Gentile ministry. (See discussion on Samaria in the Introduction to the Gospels.) Throughout this section Jesus ministered in Samaria and Judea. While there was relatively little said about Jesus' traveling from one place to another, there were some indications that He was on His way "to Jerusalem" (9:51,53; 10:38; 13:22,32-33; 17:11). An indication of the cost of following Jesus was laid out early in this lengthy section. Letting someone else bury your father or saying good-bye to your family was akin to saying that Jesus has priority over familial and even customary religious duties. Jesus' pointed response, though short, ought not to be taken lightly (v. 62). To follow Jesus meant a radical transfer of your loyalty. "Following him is not a task which is added to others like working a second job.... It is everything. It is a solemn commitment which forces the disciple-to-be to reorder all their other duties."[6]

The Mission of the Seventy (10:1-24)

10:1-24 In an event unique to Luke, Jesus sent out messengers to go into **every town and place** where Jesus was planning to go to prepare the way for Him. The word **others** seemed to indicate that the 70 were in addition to the Twelve, who may have remained with Jesus. There is some textual variance concerning whether Jesus sent out 70 or 72. In the various extant manuscripts "70" is found more frequently. Some have conjectured that a scribe would have been more likely to change "72" to "70" since the latter number appeared frequently and prominently in Scripture (70 elders in Ex 24:1; Nm 11:16,24; 70 offspring of Jacob in Ex 1:5; Dt 10:22; 70 nations in Gn 10:2-31 or 72 nations in the Septuagint reference; 70 members of the Sanhedrin). In any case, the meaning is not affected, and either number probably suggested a representative for each nation of the world corresponding to the 70 names in Genesis 10.

There was an urgency to this missionary task. They were to put aside the usual extra items with which one would travel.

Even time-consuming greetings along the road were to be bypassed, not as a discourteous response to those encountered but as a means of moving forward with an urgent task. On the other hand, a prescribed greeting was given for those who received them (v. 5). That greeting centered on PEACE (Gk. *eirēnē*, "harmony, order"), the traditional Hebrew greeting. The word is also a synonym for the blessing of salvation.

Son of peace (v. 6) was denoting a believer. Of course, if the household did not have believers, the blessing would not be effective.

Excursus on the Teachings of Luke's Central Section

The material found in Luke's central section (9:51–18:34) is not systematically paralleled in Matthew and Mark. While some of the sections are found in Matthew and Mark (cp. Lk 10:13-16 with Mt 11:21-24 and Lk 18:18-23 with Mk 10:17-22), Luke's arrangement of the material is unique. This section contains almost exclusively Jesus' teachings. While it may appear on the surface that Luke was tracing Jesus' steps from Galilee to Jerusalem in chronological and geographical order, there is little evidence that he was in fact doing this. The material in this section was arranged topically, not chronologically. Given the way in which the material was arranged, Luke may well have intended to relate Jesus' teachings in such a way as to reveal what things were most important to Jesus while He was living under the shadow of the cross.

Some of the most compelling outlines of Luke's central section have little to do with chronology. Several scholars have persuasively argued that many of the passages in this section closely parallel some of the themes found in Deuteronomy. If this is indeed the case, Luke may well have been portraying Jesus as the Prophet who was to come (Dt 18:15). Some of the themes significant to Luke— the coming judgment on Israel, the acceptance of the kingdom by the outcasts of society, and the foreshadowing of the Gentile mission—can also be found in many sections in Deuteronomy (see for example Dt 28–33). While Luke in his narrative had certainly been careful to this point to portray the religious leaders in a somewhat favorable light, this section contains many of the sharp rebukes against the religious leaders found in Matthew and Mark.

God's judgment on **Sodom**, one of the cities destroyed with burning sulfur (Gn 19:24), was well-known. Jesus indicated that God's judgment on these cities mentioned would be far greater than what happened to Sodom (vv. 12-15).

Jesus' visit to **Chorazin**, whose location is uncertain, is mentioned only here (v. 13). **Tyre** and **Sidon** were pagan cities. They would not escape condemnation for their unbelief, but the cities of Galilee had greater responsibility because they had the advantage of the ministry of Jesus Himself (vv. 14-15).

Bethsaida was near the site for the feeding of the five thousand (v. 13; 9:10-17). **Capernaum**, located on the western side of the Sea of Galilee, had also been the site of ministries by Jesus. For these cities of Galilee to reject Jesus after His ministries and teaching among them would mean greater judgment than what God had poured out on the pagan cities.

The commissioning of the 70 closely parallels the commissioning of the Twelve in Matthew 10:5-15. If Jesus was in Perea at this time, His presence could have indicated that this mission was especially to Gentiles. The fact that the 70 were representative of the Gentile nations listed in Genesis 10 seems to support this conclusion. Sending the men **in pairs** (10:1) enabled them to help and support one another, but there was another reason. Jewish law required two witnesses for the condemnation described (vv. 10-11; see Dt 19:15).

The demise of the Devil through the message and work of Christ was also a very important theme to Luke, as he mentioned the Devil's presence and work several times throughout the narrative. With the coming of the kingdom of God, the Devil's end was assured (vv. 18-19).

The Mandate for Double Love (10:25-42)

10:25-42 This section contains what are considered two of the best-known stories in Scripture: the parable of the good Samaritan and the story of Mary and Martha. Luke seemed to link these two stories to the question from the **expert in the law**. Jesus told the parable of the good Samaritan in response to the legal expert's question: Who is your **neighbor**? The basic lesson was that you must show compassion to all who are in need, even to your worst enemy. Clearly the priest and the Levite did not understand this concept. The shocking point of this story is that even your enemy is to be treated as your neighbor.

How does the predicament of Mary and Martha fit into this context? The key to understanding Mary and Martha can be found in the first of the greatest commandments: love for God. As was shown in the parable of the good Samaritan, loving your neighbor is vitally important; but such sacrifice can draw attention away from appropriate love for God. Therefore, Luke shared the story of Mary and Martha in order to show that love and devotion to God ought never to be compromised, not even for good deeds. Defying all social norms of His day, Jesus proclaimed that Mary had chosen to sit and learn from Him, and her **right choice** would **not be taken away from** her (v. 42). Even for Gentile believers, the two greatest commandments, which originated in the Jewish Old Testament, were vitally important, and their importance has been vividly illustrated.

The Teaching About Prayer (11:1-13)

11:1-13 The well-known prayer Jesus taught His disciples can also be found in Matthew 6:9-13. The prayer was a pattern for believers since the prayer began with **Father**, a noun of address for God reserved exclusively for Jesus and His followers. Jesus, of course, had a unique relationship with the Father reserved only for Himself. However, the term was also a special one for believers because the endearing name with the intimacy and respect engendered was a beautiful way to affirm the link Jesus established between the Father and His children, who came to the Father through their relationship with Jesus, the Son of God. Anyone who accepts Jesus' atoning death on the cross is reconciled to God by becoming His spiritual child.

The first petitions relate to God: the honoring of His name through your worship and adoration and the acknowledging of His rule in your life (v. 2). The second group of petitions relates to the individual: provision of sufficient food for sustenance (v. 3), forgiveness of your sins and your forgiveness of others to make possible your personal fellowship with God (v. 4a), faithfulness in God's protection during times of testing (v. 4b). God does not seek to lure His children into doing evil (Jms 1:1-15), but He allows testing to strengthen character and nurture commitment.

The parable involved a reluctant host and persistent visitor. The visitor was asking for bread because he had been on a long journey, but at first the host refused to give the petitioner anything. However, because of the petitioner's persistence, not his friendship, the host acquiesced to the request. PERSISTENCE (Gk. *anaideia,* "shamelessness," impudence") essentially connoted the idea of annoying persistence. Jesus promised that God will give good gifts (in this case, the Holy Spirit) to those who shamelessly and boldly ask of Him. In this context, Luke intended that his readers focus not so much on God's response as on the response of the believer. Believers are to love God and their neighbors, and they are to be bold in prayer. Perhaps the ultimate picture presented in this vivid parable is the contrast between the way God answers the prayers of His children in contradistinction to the way believers respond to the petitions of one another.

Heart to Heart:
Women of Worship and Work

Jesus taught His followers the importance of worship and work through the lives of two sisters from Bethany. While Mary was sitting at the feet of Jesus (10:39), Martha was busy in the kitchen (10:40). Frustrated by her sister's lack of assistance, Martha sought the support of their house guest, Jesus. He lovingly but firmly replied, "Martha, Martha, you are worried and upset about many things, but only one thing is necessary. Mary has made the right choice, and it will not be taken away from her" (10:41-42). While work, including mundane household tasks, is essential, women often become so distracted by daily demands that they lose focus on nurturing their relationships with the Lord. Christian women must worship and work—knowing Him and serving Him.

The Controversy with a Pharisee (11:14-54)

11:14-54 These passages concerning the conflicts between Jesus and the Pharisee have parallels in both Matthew and Mark (see Mt 12:1-45 for a more in-depth treatment). Luke undoubtedly chose to record these controversies at this particular point in his narrative. For the Pharisees to attribute Christ's miracles to the work of Satan called into question not only Christ's authority but also the authority of the word of God itself. Perhaps for that reason, Luke added within this context a passage concerning the woman who blessed the womb that bore Jesus (vv. 27-28). Jesus responded by saying that true blessedness is found in hearing the word of God and keeping it (vv. 27-28).

Jonah's message had brought immediate and far-reaching repentance (vv. 29-30; Jn 3:5-10). The **queen of the south**, namely, the queen of Sheba, had traveled a great distance just to hear the wisdom of **Solomon** (v. 31; see 1 Kg 10:1-13). Jesus was far **greater than** Jonah or Solomon, and His message was far more powerful. The people of Nineveh and the queen of the South might also have been understood as representing Gentile participation in the Old Testament faith.

This metaphor is challenging in that the **eye** was not primarily to give light, as you might assume a **lamp** to do. Rather the eye is to receive light. You cannot generate your own light (v. 35). The light must come from the outside (v. 36), and that light is God's Word, which functions as a lamp (v. 36). There is also the possible application in your life: To receive this light will cause you to illuminate the gospel through the rays of your life.

Jesus elevated the word of God in the midst of His conflicts with the Jewish leaders, who were clearly denigrating that word by attributing Jesus' work to the Devil. Not only is God's word supreme, but also Jesus Himself is greater than the kings and the prophets of the Old Testament (vv. 29-32). However, unlike the Gentiles, the religious leaders did not recognize Him. That they were **full of darkness** is clear from the scathing rebuke Jesus leveled against the Pharisee at dinner (vv. 39-44). When the Pharisee saw that Jesus did not wash His hands in the traditional manner, **he was amazed**. Jesus took this opportunity to expose the religious hypocrisy of the Jewish leaders (vv. 38-39). The Pharisees had become obsessed with ceremonial cleanness and with fulfilling rituals such as tithing, while ignoring the heartfelt repentance and commitment demanded by the gospel.

Rue was a shrub with stringent odor growing on hills in the Holy Land (v. 42). Jesus affirmed their commitment to tithing even their garden herbs and vegetables, but He also warned that stewardship went beyond this ritualistic practice to include attitude of heart and discipline of life. This inconsistency seemed to be the overall point of this entire section. Jesus' controversies with the Pharisees exposed their religious hypocrisy, which would soon be judged.

The Preparation for Judgment (12:1–13:9)

12:1-12 The previously mentioned judgment is seen in full light here. The disciples and the crowds are warned against religious **hypocrisy** (vv. 1-3). Jesus used **yeast**, an old fermented dough used as a rising agent in new dough, to continue His discussion of the Pharisees' hypocrisy, which was spreading through their teachings as yeast did in dough.

Jesus exhorted His listeners to fear God alone and to acknowledge Christ (vv. 4-12). Jesus was emphasizing the value of all of His creation by pointing to one of the most insignificant—the sparrow, which was used for food by the poor. These words served as a reminder of God's providential care, which extended even to the smallest details of life (vv. 6-7). **One who blasphemes against the Holy Spirit** has a hardened heart toward God and opposes God's work with a full understanding of what he is doing (v. 10). Jesus' disciples were warned about greed and exhorted instead to do good works, knowing that if they did not, they would be punished based upon the level of their knowledge of their master's will (vv. 13-48). (See discussion on Matthew 12:31 concerning blasphemy against the Holy Spirit.)

12:13-21 Greed is a self-centered desire for wealth or possessions (v. 15). Greed generally escalates as a person acquires more possessions. The man's greedy character becomes apparent in his own actions (vv. 17-19). Religious leaders were frequently called upon to mediate disputes concerning inheritances; but Jesus refused to be drawn into dividing up possessions, not because He did not have the right or authority to decide the dispute or because He was insensitive to the problem. Jesus directed His remarks to matters of the heart.

12:22-34 Just as with greed, **worry** can affect anyone, whatever his position in life. An attitude of anxiety is destructive to the physical life and hurtful to spiritual testimony (vv. 22-26). HEIGHT (Gk. *ēlikian*, "stature, years, maturity") in this context seems to suggest the span of life. Again Jesus clearly noted the value of every life and the loving care He poured out on all of His creation (v. 24). To use your energies in worry over things you cannot control—whether great or small— is futile and inappropriate. God does not overlook the necessities of His children according to His plan for their lives. When He allows suffering or even deprivation, such is never wasted in the divine

economy. Drinking of the cup of His sufferings is never to be taken lightly. The privilege must be embraced for the opportunity of testimony and means of glorifying the Father.

Alongside right attitudes is the mandate for God-given priorities (v. 31). Not only does God provide what is needed, whether in abundant outpouring or measured inner strength, but He also has given a clear pattern for right priorities. Clearly God demands your first and foremost allegiance (v. 31), and you must spend time with Him in personal intimacy and fellowship. For those who choose to marry, these are clear directives concerning loyalty and loving devotion to your husband or wife (Gn 2:24; Eph 5:22,25; 1 Pt 3:1-7) and nurturing care for your children (Ps 127:3; Eph 6:4). Once God and home are honored, then come the opportunities for ministry and service in the kingdom of Christ beyond home.

Jesus' concluding admonition to **sell your possessions and give to the poor** (v. 33) has been interpreted by some as a suggestion that the disciples get rid of possessions that might deter their service to Christ and by others as a call to help those less fortunate than they by their own personal sacrifice. First, there is no suggestion to give up *all* possessions. Rather the emphasis seems to be that material possessions are not on a par with a life set apart unto God. The issue is not how much you have but how what you have affects your commitment to Christ (v. 34).

12:35-48 Jesus noted again the importance of readiness for His **return**, using the metaphor of a **master** and his **slaves**, who were responsible for protecting and caring for their master's household and being ready or **alert** for his return (v. 37).

The severity of punishment for unfaithfulness is clear. Whether the phrase **cut him to pieces** is a means of portraying severe punishment or, more likely, a metaphor for emphasizing the separation from God and His people is not as important as the understanding that the penalty for unfaithfulness is great indeed (v. 46). The idea of degrees of punishment is presented here (v. 48). One who sins in ignorance does not have the same responsibility as one with full knowledge and understanding. God is absolutely just in administering His wrath. However, the main tragedy is separation from God; and that is the penalty for all who reject Him.

12:49–13:9 Fire is used to symbolize divine judgment or refining purification or the coming of the Holy Spirit (12:49). The context seems to point to judgment. The reference to **baptism** (12:50) as in Mark 10:38 seems to be used as a reference to His coming death, at which time He would be immersed in His suffering on the cross. When Jesus spoke of **division** in contrast to **peace**, He was alluding to the separation of believers from unbelievers (12:51). Elsewhere Jesus does talk about bringing peace (1:78-79; 2:14; 7:50). Indeed Jesus' coming brought the opposite of peace—division even among families and friends (12:52-53)—because some not only would reject Christ themselves but would be angry with any who received Him.

People are forced to make a choice: either they are for Christ or against Him. There is no middle ground. Those who do not understand this choice and its consequences have a lack of discernment concerning the times in which they live. Therefore, Jesus' followers must do everything they can to be reconciled with God, who is here described as their **adversary** (12:57-59) because anyone who does not take personal responsibility and repent will perish (13:1-5).

Repentance and fruit-bearing are both necessary, or judgment will come (13:6-8). Some very stern warnings against hypocrisy and indifference—warnings that, unfortunately, the modern Western church has ceased to heed—are recorded in this section. Jesus must be feared, loved, and obeyed.

Kingdom Reversals (13:1–14:24)

Who actually understood Jesus' message and repented? Those whom you would least expect. In this section Luke indulged in one of his favorite themes: kingdom reversals. This section can be divided into two closely associated parts (13:10-35; 14:1-24). Each part begins with a healing on the Sabbath, followed by two parables, and finally concludes with a longer narrative concerning who will and who will not enter the kingdom of God. The predominant theme of this section has to do with the reversal of the expectation concerning who will enter the kingdom. In keeping with this theme, to put God in one's debt was rebuked by Christ, while eternal reward was promised to those who followed Him with no "expectation" for repayment (14:14b, 15-24).

13:1-9 The unrest and upheaval undoubtedly produced revolution among the people and tyranny from those governing. The Jewish historian Josephus corroborates such revolts, and this incident seems to be a reference to people killed by Pilate as they were making sacrifices (v. 1), which would suggest the event took place in the Jerusalem temple. Jesus did not assign blame solely to Pilate or to **these Galileans** who suffered, but He used this opportunity to remind His listeners of the sinfulness of all and thus the need for all to **repent** (v. 3).

Jesus then used the familiar **fig tree** to represent Israel. Despite its lack of fruit, the tree received an additional year of grace (v. 8). However, Israel remained in danger of God's judgment if the nation continued to reject her Messiah.

13:10-17 In the first mention of the Sabbath, Luke recorded that a woman **who had been disabled by a spirit for over 18 years** had been set free. Evidently she had a spinal problem, which had crippled her body (v. 11). Demonic activity seemed to be responsible for her chronic and lengthy illness (vv. 11,16), although Luke does not say that the woman was demon possessed. Ultimately all evil and sickness would be attributed to Satan. Here Jesus initiated the healing without a request from the woman (v. 12), showing His compassion. She was healed immediately, and all knew the healing was of God (v. 13). **The leader of the synagogue** was indignant; he rebuked Jesus, though not directly addressing Him, for healing on the Sabbath (v. 14). Jesus likewise answered him with a general statement to all who would elevate ritualistic observances over extending healing and mercy. He used their willingness to extend mercy to an animal instead of to one of God's people as an example of their hypocrisy (v. 15). After Jesus' questions concerning what was most important to do on the Sabbath, the Jewish leader, and not Jesus, was humiliated. The phrase **daughter of Abraham** indicated her Jewish heritage (v. 16).

13:18-30 This scene was followed by two parables about **the kingdom**: one that pointed out its unlikely beginnings and one that exhorted believers to make every effort to stay on the narrow path leading to the kingdom. The idea is not so much emphasizing the growing process as noting how what seems very insignificant can be the beginning of something great and wonderful. A tiny **seed** becomes a mighty tree (vv. 18-19); a small amount of **yeast** can change a measuring of **flour** by spreading itself through the **mixture** and increasing its volume (vv. 20-21). Jesus clearly presented the responsibility and accountability of the individual (v. 24).

The Disabled Woman
Luke 13:10-17
Her Life
• Daughter of Abraham, a faithful Jew
• Lived in the region of Perea
• Attended synagogue on the Sabbath
Her Illness
• Disabled by a spirit for over 18 years
• Bent over and could not straighten up
Her Healing
• Jesus laid hands on her
• Her health was restored
• She glorified God
Her Challenge
• Religious leaders criticized Jesus for healing on the Sabbath
• She was bound by Satan for 18 years
Her Redeemer
• Humiliated the hypocritical religious leaders
• Restored her health

Many will try to enter and won't be able has nothing to do with personal merit or diligence. Jesus had already made clear that the key was personal repentance (13:3,5). Even to be at the table with Jesus (**we ate and drank in your presence**, v. 26) was not enough. The closing proverb in this section probably for Luke's audience would have been understood as the inclusion of the Gentiles and a recognition of the unbelief in Israel. However, the article used in the Greek text is omitted in the English version, indicating that the designation was not meant to suggest all Gentiles would now be first and all Jews last, for some Jews did believe, and many Gentiles did not believe (v. 30).

13:31-35 Sandwiched between these two Sabbath healings is a brief allusion to Jesus' death. After Jesus received the Pharisees' warning that **Herod** was trying **to kill** Him, He referred to Himself as a **prophet** and claimed that a true prophet could not die **outside of Jerusalem** (v. 33). He then lamented over Jerusalem—the city of His future passion

(v. 34). Nevertheless, Jesus was still "on His way" to Jerusalem. Nothing would deter Him, not even Herod (Is 50:7).

14:1-6 On the second mention of the Sabbath, Luke described the healing of a man **whose body was swollen with fluid** (v. 2). This condition is described in the Greek text as *hudrōpikos*, "dropsy or edema." The text does not indicate whether this man was an invited guest, an intruding man seeking help, or someone planted by the Pharisees to entrap Jesus. The matter of healing on the Sabbath was further complicated with the obvious elevation of rituals and traditions above concern for the well-being of people. Again Jesus' wisdom left the religious leaders speechless.

14:7-24 This scene was followed by Jesus' teachings on humility, followed by the parable of **the large banquet**. **Those who were invited** (the Jews) made **excuses** for not coming. Therefore, those who gathered at this great table were the most unlikely: **the poor, maimed, blind, and lame**. As is characteristic of Luke, the outcasts of society were so favored that it seemed that the favored of society became the outcasts. **Humiliation** is often the result of a lack of humility (v. 9). Throughout these verses the emphasis was upon humility and how that is essential in coming into God's kingdom. There is no coercion in the strong invitation **make them come in** (v. 23); rather there is strong persuasion for those who might feel hesitant to come to the great banquet because of their own personal unworthiness.

The Cost of Discipleship (14:25-35)

14:25-35 Although Luke recorded that the least likely were invited into the kingdom of God, he never implied that entrance into the kingdom would be easy. To the contrary, **the cost** of discipleship is high; those who desire to enter the kingdom ought to reflect deeply on the sacrifice that is necessary in order to do so (v. 27).

Again, parables unique to Luke form the heart of this section. Jesus gave stern warnings to any who would use family responsibilities as an excuse to abandon a radical commitment to Him. Jesus did not suggest dishonoring parents or neglecting family responsibilities. Love for Jesus should be so great that love of family would seem like hatred by comparison. All other loyalties are subordinate to your devotion to Christ. Sometimes to follow Christ means giving up even the most precious earthly relationships. Ultimately you must be willing to lay down your life for Christ since to **bear** your **own cross** was often an expression indicating death (v. 27). Only those who have committed themselves to Christ and who have persevered over the long term are truly saved. Here the text does call for giving up all. For a genuine believer, all she has belongs to God. She has given up control of her life and possessions. She becomes God's steward to manage all that belongs to her. Christ must be set above everyone and everything in a person's life. Nothing less will do. While the cost of following Christ is high (vv. 28-30), the cost of not following Him is higher still (vv. 31-32).

Seeking and Saving the Lost (15:1-32)

This part of Luke's central section contains some of the most beloved parables in the Gospels. They describe the deep love God has for wayward sinners. They also affirm the joy of the heavenly Father when the lost are recovered. First and foremost, God forgives and restores. Movement in the trilogy of parables shows an increase in value: a sheep, a coin, and a son. The tragedy of lostness is vividly portrayed but always overshadowed by the joy of finding the precious object that has been lost.

15:1-7 The religious leaders complained about the **tax collectors** because they considered them thieves and thus linked them with all who were immoral or **sinners**. To eat at the same table with them would have been unthinkable (vv. 1-2). Jesus was not suggesting that anyone did not need repentance. Rather He was describing the Pharisees and scribes as so self-righteous that they had not realized their need for **repentance** (v. 7). There are some interesting analogies in this parable. The shepherd sought his lost sheep, and Jesus actively seeks anyone who is lost (19:10). Also even as the shepherd called for a celebration when he found the lost sheep, Jesus rejoices over receiving a sinner who comes home in repentance (v. 7).

15:8-10 Women who married in the ancient world often wore headpieces that were adorned with valuable coins. Perhaps the coins were part of her dowry, the savings she had put aside, ornaments to accessorize her head covering, or some combination of these. In any case, **10 silver coins** (Gk. *deka*, "ten"; *drachmas*, "silver coins") would have been a treasured possession. Since these coins are mentioned only here in the New Testament, their exact value is uncertain, but some have suggested the number of coins probably meant they were all she had. One coin would have been typically one day's wages. To lose something this valuable would have been considered a shameful and irresponsible act.

Undoubtedly the scene was an humble home, with probably few if any windows, explaining the diligence of her search (v. 8). When she found the lost treasure, her joy had to be shared with all. The lesson in this parable comes at several points. First, the seeking **woman** is a model of every woman's search for the treasure of

Lost and Found *Luke 15:8-10*	
What was lost?	• One of one hundred sheep (15:1-7) • One of ten coins (15:8-10) • One of two sons (15:11-32)
What was found?	• The lost sheep • The lost coin • The lost son
What was learned?	• God seeks to save even one lost sheep. • God rejoices when one sinner repents. • God celebrates when one lost child returns.

the gospel, the inheritance awaiting those who will repent and believe and trust Jesus for salvation. Second, the joy engendered by the woman's happy celebration over finding her lost coin is compared to the **joy in the presence of God's angels over one sinner who repents** (vv. 9-10). Nowhere is there any indication that the woman in this parable is to represent God. Jesus clearly unveiled the lesson as being found in the joy over finding the precious coin as parallel to the joy in heaven over a sinner who repents.

15:11-32 According to Deuteronomy 21:17 in a family of two brothers, the older son would receive a **double portion** or two-thirds of his father's estate. Although not unusual then or now for a father to divide his estate before his death (v. 12), to liquidate any portion of the estate before the father's death was probably not the norm; and certainly for **the younger son** it proved to be foolish and irresponsible (vv. 13-14). The **distant country** was probably beyond the Jewish borders since the son's job was **to feed pigs** (v. 15), unclean animals for the Jews and a sign of utter degradation for any Jew.

The heart of this parable is to showcase God's unconditional love in receiving sinners who have repented and His joyous celebration on their return (vv. 20-24). First, Jews focused on the son, who initiated the process of reconciliation when he (the younger son) CAME TO HIS SENSES (Gk. *eis eauton de elthōn*, lit. "came to himself," a phrase expressing a Semitic idiom for repentance). When he realized his wrongdoing (v. 18), even noting that ultimately he had **sinned against heaven**, he took the first step in repentance. He then clearly noted his own unworthiness in asking his father to accept him as merely **one of your hired hands** (v. 19), which meant the son understood he did not deserve to be treated as a son but as a hireling who could be dismissed at any time. Then the attention turned to the father. Jesus portrayed the father's response in a unique way. Uncharacteristically the father **ran** to his repentant son, receiving him with joyous celebration (v. 20). The gifts of the father carried symbolism: **the best robe**, a sign of important position; **a ring**, a symbol denoting authority; and **sandals**, usually suggesting luxury since servants and common people did not usually have them (v. 22). Also **the fattened calf** was indicative of a special occasion since meat was not regularly included in the ordinary diet (v. 23).

The metaphor is rich in its symbolism between the son as **dead** or **lost** on one hand and then **alive again** or **found** on the other. Physically the son had been lost and was dead to his father through his abrupt departure from the family circle, but there was also the spiritual dimension in which he had been dead in sin, and now through his repentance he had returned alive and was found.

The lesson of the parable was not complete without a look at the older brother. For whatever reason, he was not present when the celebration began. When he did arrive, he was disrespectful of his father

(vv. 28-30). He used abrupt and commanding words, such as **Look** (Gk *idou*, "see, listen"); he described his work in the family business as **slaving** (Gk *douleuō*, "serving, obeying"), certainly not a term indicating joyful labor as you would expect from one working in a family business from which he profits (v. 29); he showed discontent with what he had received and even compared that with what had been given to his brother, a practice forbidden in Scripture (vv. 29-30, see 2 Co 10:12); he sharply criticized not only his brother but also his father. Nevertheless, the father remained constant and faithful. He did not condemn his older son, but he continued to emphasize the joy over receiving the younger son who had repented and returned home (vv. 31-32).

The Father through the Son seeks to save the lost. The parable about the lost son is the climax of this section. There are three vital lessons to be learned as you read the parable through the eyes of each character:

- Wayward individuals, no matter how far they have wandered off, can and must repent.

- God is always waiting to welcome the repentant sinner home.

- Those who consider themselves upright ought never to look down on those whom they consider "unworthy" of God's grace and forgiveness.

The Use and Abuse of Riches (16:1-31)

16:1-13 This section contains parables that are unique to Luke, and they are among the most difficult to interpret. The subject is possessions and wealth. The **manager** (Gk. *oikonomon*, "steward") was one entrusted with managing the property and **possessions** of another (v.

1). He was called to account and was dismissed for his mismanagement. He was not accused of dishonesty but rather carelessness and lack of productivity. He was in a panic because he was **not strong enough to dig**, that is, he was not prepared for physical labor (v. 3).

The manager then proceeded to try to recoup by ingratiating himself to the **debtors** of his master so that they would take care of him in the future (v. 4). Again the manager sought to help himself at the expense of his master.

Jesus did not identify the **master** (v. 8; Gk. *kurios*, "lord"). Was he the **rich man** (v. 1) or Jesus Himself? The context would seem to support identifying the rich man as the master. Rather than considering the words of commendation (v. 8) as endorsing dishonest action, you could consider the exact wording of the text, **because he had acted astutely**, as merely praising the manager for acting with prudence in collecting what he could.

> *You may have wealth and serve God, but you cannot enslave yourself to your possessions and keep God as your most important focus.*

The theme of stewardship was then summarized as Jesus warned against a divided heart, noting that you cannot be addicted to money and possessions and still give wholehearted devotion to God (v. 13). You may have wealth and serve God, but you cannot enslave yourself to your possessions and keep God as your most important focus.

16:14-18 The Pharisees, who loved **money**, scoffed at Jesus' teaching (vv. 14-15). The Pharisees failed to take seriously **the Law and the Prophets**, to which they gave lip service. They continued to miss its real message. Jesus upheld the authority of the Old Testament (v. 17). He used a strong hyperbole to affirm that. The validity of the Old Testament was never in question; Jesus upheld Scripture explicitly in His teaching and implicitly in His life.

Only a brief part of Jesus' teaching on divorce and remarriage was recorded by Luke. You cannot purport to accept the accuracy and authority of Scripture and suggest that there is internal contradiction. Luke and Matthew presented the same teaching with minor differences, which would be expected from reports by two different people. Luke omitted the phrase "except in a case of sexual immorality" (Mt 5:32); he recorded that **everyone who divorces his wife and marries another woman commits adultery** (v. 18) rather than Matthew's words "causes her to commit adultery" (a case in which Luke does not refute what Matthew says any more than Matthew is differing with Luke; both are true, but the emphasis of each writer varies from the other).

In each account, the man who "marries a divorced woman" (Mt 5:32) or who **marries a woman divorced from her husband** (Lk 16:18) commits adultery. Although neither Matthew nor Luke discussed a wife's divorcing her husband, which would have been very unusual in Israel, Mark did (Mk 10:12). There was no attempt to suggest a woman divorced by her husband was penalized. These words were addressed to serious followers of Christ who wanted their lives to be totally consistent with the standards of Christ. They were well aware that this standard was more demanding, and they knew that they could not always understand the ways of God (Is 55:8-9).

16:19-31 In the parable of the rich man and Lazarus, the **rich man** was a lover of money who was an unfaithful steward of his possessions (v. 19). He never repented during his lifetime. He knew well the Old Testament commands to care for the poor and needy, but he ignored such commands. On the other hand, **Lazarus**

(transliteration of Gk. *Lazaros*, from Hb. *Eleazar*, "he whom God has helped") was **a poor man** who had been blessed for his faithfulness. The phrase **Abraham's side** became an expression for "heaven."

The rich man was described as **being in torment** (v. 23), which indicated that death for an unbeliever does not mean annihilation; rather there is continual consciousness during the irreversible torment endured (vv. 24-26). Although these vivid words fall within a parable and thus are not an actual description of hell, they do coincide with other biblical information on the place of torment (Is 66:24; Mt 18:8-9; 25:41). There are some clear statements concerning the nature of hell:

- the awareness of what was forfeited (v. 23)

- the flame (v. 24)

- the memory of opportunities ignored (v. 25)

- the separation from God and the blessings accompanying His presence (v. 26)

- the permanence of this condition (v. 26).

The rich man did not suffer the penalties of separation from God because of his wealth but because of his attitude toward his wealth.

Jesus again returned to the supremacy of Scripture when He described the rich man's plea for the resurrection of Lazarus as a messenger to his family to warn them of the penalty of rejecting God. Abraham's response pointed to an attitude of unbelief. Rejecting the Scriptures would not be changed even by one who had risen from the grave (v. 31), as would be even more evident when Jesus Himself arose **from the dead**.

The Teachings on Faith (17:1-19)

Luke continued with more teachings on faith as he returned to the warnings concerning sin, repentance, and forgiveness that Jesus delivered to His disciples. The relationship between faith and duty was unveiled in the short parable of the unworthy servant, which was unique to Luke and which provided a perfect illustration of salvation by grace through faith alone.

17:1-10 The term **OFFENSES** (Gk. *skandala*, "trap, temptation, that which offends, stumbling block") was also used to describe traps used to catch animals, but in the New Testament it is most often a metaphor for whatever leads people into sin (v. 1). A **millstone** was a substantially heavy round stone used to grind grain. Women sometimes used the smaller ones, but often an animal's strength was required to accomplish the task. **These little ones** could be a reference to children, but the context would seem to identify them as new or perhaps weak believers (v. 2).

The number of times forgiveness is to be offered was not the issue but rather the importance of being willing to forgive others (v. 4). Perhaps **the apostles** felt they needed an extra portion of faith in order to be forgiving. The **mustard seed** provided an object lesson for how little faith would be required to accomplish even what seemed impossible.

Jesus returned to the theme of servanthood, emphasizing how diametrically opposed to the world His teachings are. Instead of trying to rule or lord it over others, Jesus called for humble service as the path to greatness in His kingdom. To be Christlike called for going beyond duty (v. 10).

17:11-19 As Jesus passed through **Samaria and Galilee** on His way **to Jerusalem**, He healed the 10 lepers. He told them to go show themselves **to the priests** according to the law (Lv 14:2).

Only one returned to say thank you, and **he was a Samaritan**. Jesus acknowledged the man's faith. The healing of the 10 lepers, and especially of the Samaritan leper, provided a powerful demonstration of "salvation" through grace or faith alone. Nothing anyone can do will repay Christ for His grace; the only response for those who have received His grace is to offer gratitude, and the Samaritan did precisely that.

The Coming of the Kingdom (17:20–18:8)

17:20-37 In response to a question raised by a Pharisee concerning the timing for the coming of **the kingdom of God**, Jesus answered the **when** question with an interesting and enigmatic phrase—not **with something observable** (Gk. *meta paratērēseos),* which may include any or all of these ideas:

- not to be introduced with visible signs;

- not to come through the process of human observation;

- not to be ushered in by certain rituals or traditions.

Certainly the context is clear that the kingdom of God as understood here will come suddenly and without warning or time to make preparations once the process has begun (vv. 20-21).

Jesus answered that the kingdom would not come visibly, but would be **among you** (v. 21). The discussion is parallel to what is found in Matthew and Mark about the appearance of the kingdom of God (Mt 24; Mk 13). Luke balanced the present and future aspects of the kingdom by stressing that the kingdom was indeed present in the ministry of Jesus (Lk 17:21). This emphasis does not preclude the kingdom as seen in a different way in the consummation at the end of time, but rather there is also a sense in which the

kingdom comes in the lives of those who accept God's rule in their lives. His appearance at the end of the age will be quite clear to all (v. 23). Many scholars have accused Luke of de-emphasizing and suggesting a delay in the return of Christ in his narrative, which is a misunderstanding of Luke's purpose for this passage.

In this central section Luke stressed kingdom reversals, the acceptance of outcasts and sinners into the kingdom, and the elevation of the poor as being as important as the rich (14:7-24). Luke was attempting to show that, on the one hand the kingdom of God was already at work in the earthly ministry of Jesus, while, on the other hand, it was yet to come in fullness and power (vv. 22-37). The suddenness of His return is further affirmed in Jesus' examples of Noah (vv. 26-27) and Lot's wife (v. 28). Lot's wife was a reminder of what happens to one who is obsessed with material possessions. She lost everything (Gn 19:26).

18:1-8 Jesus then returned to the theme of prayer in a parable about the persistent widow. Of course, the message is not that you should bombard the Lord again and again with every request or desire you have. Rather, you see God's working through His masterful timing, teaching His children, and building character and virtue in the process of struggle. Every believer is reminded of God's desire that your petitions come to Him and that He is moved by your sufferings and the misunderstandings you suffer.

The **judge . . . who didn't fear God or respect man** would be typical of the pagan secularist in the judicial world. As a local judge, he was easily accessible to the people. The phrase WEAR ME OUT (Gk. *hupōpiazē,* "treat roughly," lit. "seize or arrest under") has the sense of "holding down" or "gaining control." Idiomatically the phrase can be understood as "damaging the reputation of someone."

The contrast between a corrupt judge and a helpless woman cannot be overlooked. Of course, God cannot be compared to a crooked and corrupt judge, but the difference in power between God and His creation is far greater than between a judge and his subject. Yet God patiently listens to His children in their hours of trial, and He is moved by their pleas. If an unjust judge is moved by a lowly widow, how much more a loving heavenly Father by His children. If even unjust judges could be persuaded to give justice through persistent intercession, then certainly God would be faithful to mete out justice. In other words, the kingdom of God will not be shut to those who persistently seek entry according to God's terms (vv. 7-8).

Persistent Widow
Luke 18:1-8

A lesson in perseverance:
- Pray to Him always.
- Do not become discouraged.
- Keep offering your petition to Him.
- Be persistent in coming to Him.
- Cry to Him day and night.
- He will respond.

The Requirements for Entering the Kingdom (18:9-30)

18:9-30 As Luke brought his central section to a close, he again drew attention to those who would enter the kingdom of God. The parable of the Pharisee and the tax collector is a powerful and poignant example of one who received the mercy and favor of God—not the one who, as the Pharisee, boasted in his own righteousness, but the one who, as the tax collector, acknowledged that he was a sinner and in need of mercy. He who was seeking mercy gained entrance into the kingdom of God.

The one who was humble as a child belonged in the kingdom of God (vv. 15-17). Jesus never suggested that children would become part of the kingdom just because they were children. However, childlike humility and faith were attitudes necessary for receiving God's grace.

The ruler may have been a member of the prestigious Sanhedrin or perhaps the leader of a synagogue (v. 18) since he began his conversation with Jesus by trying to flatter Him. The one who would come to God on divine terms and then willingly follow Jesus (vv. 18-30) would be a true member of the kingdom of God. Indeed, for the rich to enter the kingdom of God was hard. The wealth in and of itself was not evil; rather, what that wealth could potentially do to the human heart was the issue. Luke was not claiming that everyone must be materially poor to enter the kingdom; but certainly all must put Christ first, above all people and possessions, in order to enter the kingdom. Riches must remain in their proper place, that is, subservient to Christ and His authority.

This young man tried to justify himself by his deeds, testifying that he had kept the law from his youth (vv. 20-21). Yet no one can keep these laws. Even this young man fell easily before the commandment against covetousness (Ex 20:17) because he could not part with his material possessions (Lk 18:22-23). Ultimately he depended more on what his wealth provided than what God offered. Some commentators have suggested that **the eye of a needle** was an especially narrow gate into Jerusalem, but there is no archaeological evidence for such. More likely the expression is simply a figure of speech emphasizing how difficult it would be for a man enchained in material possessions to enter the kingdom (vv. 24-25).

What an extraordinary way to end this remarkable section. Luke's central section contained many things that were difficult for the affluent West to hear. Nevertheless, as Luke so painstakingly pointed out, those who truly belong to Christ would heed His message and obey it.

Conclusion and Transition (18:31-34)

18:31-34 Jesus predicted His death for the third time (v. 33). He reiterated that He would be **handed over to the Gentiles, mocked, spit on**, flogged, and finally killed (v. 32). Then He would **rise on the third day** (v. 33). But His disciples did not grasp what He said. Still Jesus expressed a strong sense of destiny as He quickly approached Jerusalem.

JESUS IN JUDEA: MINISTRY NEAR AND IN JERUSALEM (18:35–21:38)

From Jericho to Jerusalem (18:35–19:27)

18:35-43 Luke and Mark recorded these events in similar ways, but Luke made some significant additions. The healing of the **blind man near Jericho** demonstrated that Jesus was the **Son of David** and the Messiah. Luke also showed Jesus' concern for the needy. In Luke's account alone this incident was described as moving the newly healed man and the people to give glory to God through the work of Jesus (v. 43). The blind man knew Jesus even when he could not see Him (vv. 38-39). He not only was healed physically, but he also received spiritual sight. He came to know Jesus (vv. 41-43).

19:1-10 The account of **Zacchaeus**, unique to Luke, contained what many believe is the key verse in all of Luke: **For the Son of Man has come to seek and to save the lost** (v. 10). The story also showcased several primary Lukan themes:

- the universal nature of the gospel (vv. 2-4);
- the problem of wealth (v. 2);
- Christ's ministry to tax collectors and sinners (v. 7);
- the joy of giving to the poor (v. 8);
- salvation (vv. 9-10) .

Jericho was an important toll site in ancient Palestine. Zacchaeus was trying to see who Jesus was, not merely out of curiosity or even to see the performance of miracles (v. 3). His heart was ready as noted by his initial response to Jesus (v. 8). Tax collectors were known for their fraud. They could officially collect whatever amount they chose and keep anything above what was required by the government. The law, in cases of fraud, required only the return of the amount defrauded plus one fifth (Lv 6:5; Nm 5:6). However, theft had a stiffer penalty—restoration of at least four times the amount stolen (Ex 22:1). Zacchaeus was under such conviction that he immediately recognized what he had done as theft and committed to **pay back four times as much** (v. 8). Also, when he spoke of giving **half of** his **possessions to the poor**, he was not talking about his income but rather all that he had (v. 8). The change in his life had been dramatic and inclusive of every area of lifestyle. Salvation was granted to Zacchaeus, not because of his promised good deeds, but because he was **a son of Abraham**, probably a reference to his sharing the faith of Abraham. Perhaps more likely Jesus was referring to the fact that Zacchaeus, even though a tax collector, was among those to whom the Messiah had come to minister (vv. 9-10).

19:11-27 The **parable** of the **10 minas** is linked to the story of Zacchaeus by the words, **As they were there listening to this** (v. 11). Luke was again dealing with Jesus' teaching about the future and God's purpose in history. The *mina* was a Greek monetary unit. Each slave received about three months' wages. They understood that this money was to be used to **engage in business** (v. 13). Jesus commented on three of the slaves, two of whom did well (vv. 16,18). The third slave was ruled by his fear of the nobleman and did nothing (vv. 20-21). Then he defended his irresponsibility by attacking the character of the nobleman (v. 21), who simply turned the tables and reacted as the slave said he would (vv. 22-24).

The parable of the 10 minas fulfills four important functions:

- It clarifies the time of the appearance of the kingdom of God.

- It realistically portrays the coming rejection and future return of Jesus.

- It delineates the role of a disciple in the time between Jesus' ascension and His return.

- While similar to Matthew 25:14-30, it makes a unique contribution at this point in Luke's Gospel.

Entry into Jerusalem (19:28-48)

19:28-44 The uniquely Lukan contribution in these passages was the account of Jesus' reaction as He saw the city of Jerusalem. Luke did not record Jesus' actual "entry" into Jerusalem. Instead, he emphasized Jesus' approach to Jerusalem (v. 11).

Bethany is on the eastern slope of the Mount of Olives about two to three miles from Jerusalem. It is still so identified today. **Bethphage** was near Bethany, but its exact location remains unknown (v. 28). The **Mount of Olives,** still well-known in Jerusalem, is strategically important as an eastern route coming down the mountain (2,660 feet above sea level) into the Kidron Valley and then

through the Eastern or Golden Gate on to the temple mount (v. 37).

In verse 41, Jesus was still approaching Jerusalem. Luke's account was not a contradiction to the accounts of Matthew and Mark, both of which clearly emphasized Jesus' entry to Jerusalem. Rather, Luke was making a theological point. While Luke agreed that Jesus was the "king" who deserved a triumphal entry, he belabored the point that Jesus was moving toward the place of rejection, which would be the city of Jerusalem.

Jesus stated that **the stones would cry out** if His disciples did not recognize the importance of this day and were silent (v. 40; see Hab 2:11). Then Jesus Himself **wept** over the city that would reject Him. Luke zeroed in on Jesus' concern for the city of Jerusalem and also recorded His prediction of its future destruction (vv. 43-44). **The time of your visitation** referred to the time when salvation and blessing would come.

19:45-48 Jesus had spent much time teaching in the temple, an emphasis in Luke's Gospel. Now in His role as Messiah He came to cleanse the temple. Here Luke noted the first clear reference to the efforts of Jesus' enemies to kill Him (v. 47). At this point the people did not share the feelings of their religious leaders (v. 48).

Those who were selling referred to the merchants who sold animals and other things to be used for sacrifices and offerings (v. 45). Commercial activity in **the temple complex** was awkward at best; but without competition or controls, there were unequal exchange rates and exorbitant prices.

Jesus' Teaching During the Final Week (20:1-21:38)

20:1-19 Luke added some unique descriptions in his account of Jesus' last week before His crucifixion. The religious leaders still challenged Jesus' authority (vv. 1-2). Again and again Jesus has proven through His teachings, healings, and other miracles that He is "the Son of the Most High" (1:31-33), "the Messiah and the Savior" (2:11), "the Holy One of God" (4:34), and "the Son of David" (18:38-39). Jesus used His counter question to respond (see also discussion in Mt 21:23-27). The religious leaders did have a dilemma because **the people** believed that **John was a true prophet** (v. 6). Their claim to ignorance (v. 7) simply made them look incompetent to fulfill the functions assigned.

In the parable of the vineyard owner, in the accounts by Matthew and Mark, one of the servants is killed. In Luke, only the killing of the son is mentioned. The allegorical nature of the parable is readily noted. Luke may be fashioning his account in relation to his overall purpose. The **vineyard** represented Israel (v. 9; see Is 5:1-7); the **owner** represented God (v. 13); the **slave(s)**, the Old Testament prophets (vv. 10-12); the **son**, Jesus (vv. 13-15); the **tenant farmers**, the religious leaders (vv. 9-12); and the others, the Gentiles (v. 16). Luke demonstrated more poignantly the coming judgment of Israel.

The response of Jesus' listeners may suggest that they understood the allegory's forecast of the destruction of Jerusalem (v. 16). Jesus then used Psalm 118:22 to add a prediction of His death and again to refute the popular notions concerning His messiahship (v. 17). Jesus knew that He was to be the stone over which Israel would stumble and then **be broken** (v. 18). The **cornerstone** was unique, bearing the weight and stress where two walls are joined and without which the entire structure would collapse (v. 17).

20:20-26 The **denarius** was a small silver Roman coin bearing the image of the ruling emperor on its face and was equiv-

alent to a day's wages in value. Jews ages 14 to 65 were required to pay a tax **to Caesar** (Tiberius) and to the government of Rome. Of course, the Jews resented greatly having to pay these taxes, which collectively often amounted to over one-third of a person's income.

Luke spoke frankly of **spies** (Gk *egkathetous*, "ones hired to lie in wait") seeking to entrap Jesus (v. 20). However, again Jesus went to the heart of the matter, not pandering to those who espoused political compromise or encouraging others who tried to incite revolt. Instead He just presented the classic principle of good citizenship: Pay for the benefits you enjoy from the government whatever is required by the government (v. 25). But Jesus added another dimension with His mandate to **give** back **to God** what belonged to Him, which first and foremost would be obedience.

20:27-40 There will be no death in heaven, which makes the Sadducees' issue moot since there will be no need for births to continue the generations (vv. 34-36; see the commentary on Mk 12:18-27 and Mt 22:23-33).

20:41-44 David, the second king of Israel, was identified as the one through whose lineage the Messiah would come. In His humanity, Jesus was a descendant of David (Lk 3:31) when He came in His incarnation as a baby in Bethlehem. He was also clearly David's **Lord** in that as the eternal Son of God, He had existed before David. The section of Psalm 110 quoted here was undoubtedly coming from what Luke considered a messianic psalm. The psalm does in fact affirm that the Messiah is indeed greater than and possesses more authority than David, who was considered Israel's greatest king.

20:45-47 Jesus made universal application with His warnings concerning the religious leaders. They had attacked Him again and again as a group and thus

Religious Leaders in the New Testament
Luke 20:27-40

Name	Description	References
Pharisees	• Monotheistic • Believed study of law was true worship • Controlled synagogues • Religious authorities for Jews • Opposed Jesus	Mt 3:7-10; 5:20; 9:14; 16:1,6-12; 22:15-22,34-46; 23:2-3 Mk 3:6; 7:3-5; 8:15; 12:13-17 Lk 6:7; 7:36-39; 11:37-44; 18:9-14 Jn 3:1; 9:13-16; 11:46-47; 12:19 Ac 23:6-10 Php 3:4-6
Sadduccees	• Directed temple services • Politically active • Materialistic strict adherence to the law • Opposed Pharisees and Jesus	Mt 3:7-10; 16:1,6-12; 22:23-34 Mk 12:18-27 Lk 20:27-40 Jn 11:47 Ac 4:1-2; 5:7-18; 23:10
Zealots	• Similar to Pharisees • Believed God alone was ruler • Fanatical in Jewish faith • Opposed Roman rule • Believed in the total obedience to the law	Mt 10:4 Mk 3:18 Lk 6:15 Ac 1:13
Herodians	• Not a religious group • Political group • Diverse theological perspectives • Supported Herod • Accepted foreign rule	Mt 22:5-22 Mk 3:6; 8:15; 12:13-17
Essenes	• Rigidly adhered to the law • Rejected temple worship • Devoted to copying the law • Lived together in community • Rejected worldly pleasure	None

Adapted from *Holman Book of Biblical Charts, Maps, and Reconstructions*, pp. 88-91.

identified themselves as His enemies. Undoubtedly, in a general way, they were ostentatious in their appearance not only with **long robes** but also with their very public rituals and traditions by which they attempted to display religious devotion (v. 46). Spurning the poor, they even neglected responsibilities to their own parents (see Mk 7:9-13) and lacked sensitivity to widows. Perhaps when serving as executors of the estates of these helpless women they would squander their humble estates through assessing fees and collecting expenses (v. 47).

21:1-4 The **temple treasury** had 12 trumpet-shaped treasure boxes according to the Talmud. Since they were located in the court of the women, the widow could have entered without being noticed. Yet Jesus saw her and immediately knew of her sacrificial gift of **two tiny coins**, worth only a fraction of a day's wages—but all she had (vv. 2-4).

21:5-38 Jesus gave a straightforward warning about the false teachers, some of whom would claim to be the Messiah and many of whom would make predictions about the end-times (v. 8). He also warned

Money in the Bible[7]		
Biblical Unit	**Reference**	**Equivalents**
talent	Ex 25:39; Mt 18:24; 25:15	3,000 shekels; 6,000 bekas
shekel	Gn 23:15; 1 Sm 12:21	4 days' wages; 2 bekas; 20 gerahs
bekah	Ex 38:26	½ shekel; 10 gerahs
gerah	Ex 30:13; Lv 27:25; Ezk 45:12	$\frac{1}{20}$ shekel
drachma	1 Ch 29:7; Lk 15:8; 19:13	1 day's wage
piece of silver	Zch 11:13; Lk 22:5	1 day's wage
mite or copper coin	Mk 12:42; Lk 21:2	1½ of a Roman kodrantes; $\frac{1}{16}$ of a denarius
denarius	Mt 22:19; Lk 15:8; 20:24	25 denarii; 1 day's wage
penny or quadrans	Mk 12:42	¼ of an assarius

about the coming persecution from the Gentiles and from the Jews. These warnings began to be fulfilled with a very intense time of persecution for believers between the death of Jesus and the destruction of Jerusalem in AD 70.

Luke included an extended explanation of the destruction of Jerusalem (vv. 20-24). His description was vivid and intense. Jesus described events that would take place in the immediate future (AD 70) and in the distant future (the time of His return).

The prophecy concerning the temple's destruction was fulfilled in AD 70 when the Roman general Titus captured Jerusalem and destroyed the temple (vv. 5-6). Jesus also noted the long siege of Jerusalem by the Romans before the fall of the city (v. 20). Evidently, according to Eusebius, the Christians fled Jerusalem and took refuge at Pella, a town near the Sea of Galilee and east of the Jordan River (v. 21).

Pregnant women and nursing mothers would certainly be among the most vulnerable in war. Being uprooted from their homes or surviving a siege would be difficult enough by oneself. Having children and being concerned about their many needs would be a source of almost unbearable pressure (v. 23). A condition

that usually brought joy and life would mean sorrow and death.

The phrase **the times of the Gentiles** (v. 24) indicated that the Gentiles would have control over Jerusalem until God determined the end of that rule. This domination of Jerusalem and Palestine would continue up to and including the last three and a half years of the great tribulation (see Rv 11:1-2). Antichrist would annul the covenant made with Israel at the beginning of the great tribulation. He would then pour out his wrath against the Jews until Christ intervenes upon His return to establish His earthly kingdom.

All things (v. 32) must be in reference to the destruction of Jerusalem and thus **this generation** would have the most natural understanding, a reference to those who were listening to Jesus speak. Jesus did seem to move in His discussion from **that day** as a reference to the destruction of Jerusalem as a type of judgment to come (v. 34) and the final judgment, which would come at the consummation of all things.

Jesus did not promise escape from death for His disciples or any of His followers (v. 18). In fact, He affirmed that some would die (v. 16). Rather He was emphasizing that they would be lovingly carried through these sufferings by the Lord and ultimately have life eternal with Him (v. 19). Jesus' words concerning false Christs were left out in this context but recorded in 17:23. Also missing from Luke's description of the end-times was an account of the gathering of the elect (Mt 24:31; Mk 13:27). Instead, Luke recorded Jesus' teaching concerning future **redemption** (v. 28).

The account ended with Jesus' exhortation for the need of watchfulness (v. 36). Only Luke recorded the details of this watchfulness. Believers were to be on guard, **so that your minds are not dulled from carousing, drunkenness, and worries of life, or that day will come on you unexpectedly like a trap** (vv. 34-36). This detailed emphasis was in keeping with Luke's concern with practical daily living. His message is sorely needed in today's church, as people seem to be even more distracted now than at other times in the history of the church.

THE CLIMAX OF JESUS' LIFE (22:1–24:53)

Passover (22:1-71)

22:1-6 Luke presented the most vivid and moving Passover account among the three Synoptic Gospels. **The Festival of Unleavened Bread** followed immediately after the Passover (observed Nisan 14–15, which came in early spring) and lasted seven days (vv. 1,7). The Jews ate unleavened bread to commemorate their deliverance from the slavery of Egypt since their ancestors had done this on the night of their hasty departure from Egypt (see Ex 12). Luke began his account with a description of Judas's plot **to betray Jesus** (vv. 3-6). Only Luke mentioned that this betrayal was ultimately the work of Satan. Luke was careful to show that Jesus' mission meant the ultimate demise of the Devil. Throughout his narrative, Luke had

referred to Satan's activity and to his ultimate downfall (10:18-20). But in this context Satan was still at work, causing dissension and seeking to interfere with Jesus' mission (22:23). **Satan entered Judas** in order to move him to betray Jesus (v. 3). Judas then became the instrument of Satan to accomplish his purpose of trying to destroy Jesus' life and ministry.

22:7-30 In preparing for Passover, Jesus noted that the disciples were to follow **a man carrying a water jug** (v. 10). Since carrying water was done by women, a man doing this task would be easily spotted. The meal would have been eaten **when the hour came**, which would have been immediately after sundown on the fifteenth of Nisan (v. 14). Both at the table and in the garden, Luke captured Jesus' intense feelings concerning all that was happening to Him. As He reclined at the table, Jesus said, **I have fervently desired to eat this Passover with you before I suffer** (v. 15). In Greek these words are intense, more literally, "with desire I have desired."

During the Passover meal, four cups were shared, of which Luke mentioned two—one before and one after the bread:

- a cup of thanksgiving before sharing the bread (v. 17)

- a cup of **the new covenant** after supper (v. 20; Mt 26:27-29; Mk 14:23-25; 1 Cor 11:25-26).

Paul focused attention on one cup:

- a "cup of blessing" (1 Co 10:16), which ties the Passover and the Lord's Supper together.

Despite some textual questions raised by critics, the authenticity of verses 19-20 has not been questioned by evangelical scholars. Recall from Luke's prologue (1:1-3) that he collected his data from different sources. With that in view, one can reasonably assume that Luke combined his descriptions of Jesus' Passover in the company of His disciples with the Lord's institution of the Lord's Supper. This explains the reference to two cups.

The Lord's Supper brought new significance to the ancient Passover meal. The disciples clearly understood the metaphor Jesus used, speaking of the **bread**, which was broken as His **body** would be, and of **the fruit of the vine** as the **blood** He would shed in His vicarious atonement (see 1 Co 11:23-26).

The "new covenant" was one of grace and forgiveness based upon the sacrificial death of Christ on behalf of sinners (see Jr 31:31-34). Although Judas was present at the time of the Supper (22:21), apparently he did not actually partake of the elements (see Jn 13:26-30). Luke had received an account of the information Jesus shared with the apostles at the time of the Passover celebration; but even if he knew the exact order of events, he was not bound to follow that order. Thus some slight differences in the accounts do occur. However, there are no contradictions within the accounts.

22:31-34 Satan asked Jesus **to sift** Peter as **wheat** (v. 31). **You**, however, is plural, a reference to all the disciples (v. 31). But Jesus prayed specifically for Peter (**you** is singular in v. 32). Peter's leadership among the other disciples was evident as Jesus instructed him to **strengthen** his **brothers** after he **turned back** to the Lord (v. 32).

22:35-38 Jesus gave instructions to the disciples, including an update on their itinerant ministries. Although some have suggested that Jesus was now calling for an armed revolt, the context, as well as Jesus' overall teaching, does not support this interpretation. Jesus could have been using irony in suggesting that some disciples who had considered His way adequate and the best now wanted to abandon

it because of difficulties encountered. However, more likely Jesus knew that far greater persecution than any they had known was coming, and He wanted to admonish them to prepare for it (vv. 36-38). He ended the discussion abruptly because of the lack of understanding on the part of His disciples (v. 38). Rather than a reversal of any earlier instructions, Jesus was more likely addressing an exception or plan for a time of crisis (v. 38) as symbolic of the upheaval to come.

22:39-46 In the garden, Luke recorded that Jesus' **sweat became like drops of blood falling to the ground**, indicating the immense stress and agony He was experiencing (vv. 43-44). **This cup** was a figurative way of describing that which was allotted to a person (v. 42). The expression was a reminder of the Passover supper already past and of the crucifixion death still to come.

22:47-71 With a grand entrance and **with a kiss** (a customary greeting between friends in the Middle East), Judas betrayed his master while Jesus was literally in mid-sentence in the garden of Gethsemane, located at the Mount of Olives (v. 47). A student might also kiss his teacher or rabbi as a sign of respect and honor. For Judas to betray Jesus with a kiss made his act even more unconscionable. The "holy kiss" was also a greeting in the early church, offering blessing and expressing unity within the body (Rm 16:16; 2 Co 13:12; 1 Th 5:26). Jesus reminded Judas, **this is your hour**, an acknowledgment of more than the **darkness** of night at the time of Jesus' arrest (v. 53). Satan was at work. Although Satan seemed to have victory in this hour, Jesus would have the ultimate hour of victory. The **temple police** whisked Jesus away and **brought Him** to the **house** of the high priest. In the passage concerning Peter's denial, Luke recorded that Jesus **turned and looked at Peter** (v. 61). With this description Luke was again capturing the intensity of the moment in which a friend denied a friend.

Not long after this, Jesus was mocked and beaten. He was then brought **before** the **Sanhedrin** where He was questioned about His identity. Here Jesus made His great confession that He is **the Messiah**, the **Son of Man**, the One who will be **seated at the right hand** of God.

Crucifixion (23:1-56)

23:1-56 The **whole assembly** referred to the Sanhedrin (v. 1). Luke made a few unique contributions to the crucifixion narrative. First, he mentioned that when **Pilate** (Pontius Pilate, Roman governor, AD 26–36) found out that Jesus **was a Galilean**, he **sent Him to Herod**, who was **in Jerusalem** at the time (vv. 6-12). Herod interrogated Jesus, **mocked Him**, and then **sent Him back to Pilate**. That day, Luke noted, **Herod and Pilate** had become **friends** (v. 12). Luke may have included this incident because he had more interest in local politics than did Matthew or Mark, or perhaps because his audience was primarily Gentiles who were themselves interested in politics in general.

Second, Luke recorded Jesus' words to the **Daughters of Jerusalem**, a tender and affectionate designation (vv. 28-31). Jesus told them not to **weep** for Him but for their great city, which would be destroyed. Barren women who had no children would be fortunate in the sense that they would not have to see their children suffer and die in the awful destruction coming (v. 29). An indication of this was seen in what they were doing to Him. Luke's concern for the future Jerusalem was clearly evident here.

Third, Luke was the only one to mention that **one of the criminals** crucified with Christ repented and actually acknowledged Jesus as God. He knew

that Jesus was innocent, and he also had heard about the kingdom Jesus was about to enter (vv. 41-43). **Paradise** was a Persian loan word meaning "garden" or "park" (v. 43). In the New Testament it was used as a synonym for heaven, and in the Septuagint (Greek translation of the Old Testament), it was used to describe the garden of Eden. The splitting of the curtain in two was symbolic of the fact that Jesus' death made the sacrificial system unnecessary because now the people could have direct access to God through Christ and His supreme sacrifice on the cross (v. 45; see Rm 5:2).

Jesus' innocence and His coming kingdom were two important themes to Luke throughout his narrative. Here he reminded his readers of the reality of these concepts at a point in his narrative when there could be every reason to doubt them.

Luke mentioned **the women** merely as part of the larger crowd **watching** Jesus suffer on the cross (v. 49). Even noting that they **followed** (Gk. *sunakolouthēsasai*) likely speaks of discipleship but does not capture the full significance of the role of these women in this context. Out of **all who knew Him**, the women were specifically mentioned. These women disciples did not turn away or distance themselves after Jesus died. They courageously followed **Joseph of Arimathea** to the tomb (v. 55).

Like a good historian, Luke also assured his readers of the credentials of the one who offered to bury Jesus. Joseph of Arimathea (ancient Ramah, Jr 31:15, which belonged to Samaria in Old Testament times and Judea in the New Testament period) **was a good and righteous man**, one who could confirm that Jesus was indeed a just man, and in this way, could by inference validate the trustworthiness of Christianity (vv. 50-51). He was a wealthy **member of the Sanhedrin** and evidently a secret follower of Christ. Jewish law would not allow a body to remain on the cross after sunset on the Sabbath. Crucified criminals were usually dumped in common burial grounds, but Joseph gave up the newly carved stone **tomb** he had prepared for his own use. Preparation of the body would have included **wrapping it** in strips of **linen** that had been interwoven with **spices** (v. 53).

Resurrection (24:1-53)

24:1-53 As soon as restrictions associated with reverence for the Sabbath permitted, several women disciples returned to the tomb (23:56–24:1). The women were visiting the tomb, not to confirm Jesus' resurrection as He had announced, but to be sure that His body had been prepared properly for burial (v. 1) They did not expect to find an empty tomb (vv. 2-3)! Two angels appeared, telling them of the resurrection and reminding them that Jesus had predicted this event (vv. 4-7). The women, according to Luke's account, were the only disciples present at the first appearance of the resurrected Jesus. They then were privileged to go immediately and inform the apostles about what had happened (vv. 8-9).

Each of the three Synoptic Gospels speaks to a truly surprising degree on the presence of women disciples at the crucifixion and resurrection of Jesus. They were present at Jesus' lowest point at the cross, and they were honored to be the first witnesses to His resurrection. These women provided a wonderful testimony of faithful service and witness.

Women at the Cross
Luke 24:1-12

The Woman	The Event	The Reference
Mary, the mother of Jesus Mary, the wife of Clopas and aunt of Jesus Mary Magdalene	The crucifixion of Jesus	Jn 19:25-27
Women from Galilee Mary Magdalene Mary, mother of James and Joseph[8] Salome, wife of Zebedee	The crucifixion and burial of Jesus	Mt 27:55-56
Mary Magdalene Mary, the mother of Jesus Joanna	The resurrection	Mt 28:1-10; Lk 24:1-12

Luke's extended account of the resurrection of Jesus provided an astounding conclusion to the major theme developed throughout the Gospel—*the saving mission of Christ.* He also set the stage for the development of the early church in the book of Acts. No one account captures the essence of Jesus' saving mission better than the Emmaus story (vv. 13-35). The **first day of the week** (v. 1) is Sunday. The Sabbath ended the week for Jews. Sunday became the day of worship for believers (Ac 20:7), showing the importance of the resurrection to the Christians of the first century. Unique to Luke, this moving account sent a clear message concerning the nature and fulfillment of Jesus' mission. Emmaus (modern-day Kubeibeh) was located about seven miles northwest of Jerusalem.

Six major themes emerge from this **final** section:

- Jesus is the fulfillment of Scripture (24:26-27,44-48).

- Jesus was made known during fellowship at the table, possibly a reminder of the Last Supper (vv. 30-35).

- The reality of Christ's humanity and of His bodily resurrection was emphasized (vv. 36-43).

- Luke's overall interest in the power of the Holy Spirit was manifested in the prediction of the Spirit's role at Pentecost (vv. 48-49).

- All of the resurrection appearances in Luke happened in Jerusalem, and at the time the disciples returned to the temple. Jerusalem had an important role in God's redemptive plan (vv. 52-53; Ac 1:8).

- Only Luke mentioned the ascension of Jesus (vv. 50-51).

The disciples were overwhelmed with the reality of Jesus' resurrection (v. 37). Jesus proved Himself to be alive by showing them **His** pierced **hands and feet** and asking them to touch Him (v. 39). Then He asked for food and ate (vv. 41-43), not because He needed nourishment but to affirm the reality of His physical presence among them.

Luke's concluding verses (vv. 46-53) provided transition to his second volume, the book of Acts. Luke then continued his historical record, taking up in the book of Acts where the Gospel of Luke ended.

Bibliography

Bock, Darrell L. *Luke*. NIV Application Commentary. Grand Rapids: Zondervan, 1996.

Evans, Craig A. *Luke (*NIBC). Peabody: Hendrickson, 1990.

Liefeld, Walter L. *Luke*. Expositor's Bible Commentary, vol. 8. Grand Rapids: Zondervan Publishing House, 1984.

Lockyer, Herbert. *All the Women in the Bible*. Grand Rapids: Zondervan, 1988.

*Maddox, Robert. *The Purpose of Luke-Acts*. Edinburgh: T & T Clark, 1982.

*Marshall, I. Howard. *Luke: Historian and Theologian*. Exeter: Paternoster; Grand Rapids: Zondervan, rev. 1988.

Marshall, I. Howard. *The Gospel of Luke* (NIGTC). Exeter: Paternoster; Grand Rapids: Eerdmans, 1978.

Morris, Leon. *The Gospel According to Luke* (TNTC). Grand Rapids: Eerdmans, 1974.

Stein, Robert H. *Luke*. The New American Commentary, vol. 24. Nashville: Broadman Press, 1992.

* Advanced Study

Notes

[1] Whether Luke was Jew or Gentile cannot be settled with certainty, but most evangelical scholars identify him as a Gentile. He did avoid using Semitic words (6:14; 8:54; 22:42; 23:45), and he omitted, perhaps purposefully, the Jewish traditions associated with controversies among the Jews recorded by Matthew. Some even conclude that in his references to Jews, he does not seem to include himself as part of the group (4:44; 23:51; Ac 10:39; 13:5; 14:1; 17:1; 21:11).

[2] Kenneth E. Bailey, "The Manger and the Inn: The Cultural Background of Luke 2:7," *Near East School of Theology Theological Review* 2 (1979), 33–44.

[3] Adapted from *The Woman's Study Bible,* Dorothy Patterson and Rhonda Kelley, eds. (Nashville: Thomas Nelson Publishers, 1995), 1694.

[4] Dorothy Patterson, *BeAttitudes for Women* (Nashville: Broadman and Holman Publishers, 2000), 59–60.

5 The village is also referred to as "Magadan" (Mt 15:39) and "Dalmanutha" (Mk 8:10).
6 Robert J. Karris, *Invitation to Luke* (Garden City: Doubleday, 1977), 130.
7 Adapted from *The Woman's Study Bible*, 2135.
8 The name Joseph is also found as Joses in some translations.

JOHN

Introduction

One need not be a biblical scholar to realize the vast differences between the Synoptic Gospels and the Gospel of John. Jesus' birth and baptism, the calling of the Twelve, the parables, and the transfiguration are all absent in the book of John. Instead, John offers a series of lengthy discourses, which are primarily related to the "signs" or miracles done by Jesus. Some of these signs include turning water into wine and raising Lazarus from the dead. Not only are there notable theological differences between the book of John and the Synoptics, but also the language used by Christ in John is quite distinctive. These distinctives have led many modern scholars to question the historical reliability of John. Therefore, to spend a little time dealing with the question of the historical reliability of John is important.

The early church identified John's Gospel as the most valuable of all the Gospels. The early church fathers revered its depth of spiritual and theological insight. Unfortunately, the early heretics valued it, too. Many of them wrote their own works, which closely paralleled Johannine thought. One of the most influential heretics to embrace John was Valentinus, a second-century Gnostic. Irenaeus, however, saw that John's incarnational theology could be turned and used against the Gnostic heretics, as was done when the Arians taught that Jesus was merely a created being. Athanasius and the Council of Nicea used John's Gospel to affirm Christ's divinity.

Numerous commentaries and devotionals on John were produced from the age of the church fathers to Thomas Aquinas (1225–1274). This interest came to an end, however, beginning in the seventeenth century, with the dawn of the Enlightenment. Enlightenment thinkers for the most part rejected supernatural religion and started to question any and every account of the supernatural in Scripture. Many of them claimed that the Gospels were filled with fanciful stories meant to fool the uneducated masses. They denied many of the doctrines of orthodox Christianity, including, but not limited to, the divinity of Christ and His bodily resurrection.

The Apostle John, writing later than the Synoptic authors, was interested in presenting a theological Gospel, which would have appeal both to the philosopher and to the historian, as well as in developing for the early church a theological understanding of who Jesus really was. The Synoptic Gospels were written as the process of evangelization began with the incarnation of Christ and the unfolding of His life and ministry. The Gospel of John, written later, revealed the impact of Jesus' life and ministry on His followers as they grew in understanding and commitment.

However, with regard to the *Jewishness* of John, Israel Abrahams, an orthodox Jew and rabbinic scholar at Cambridge in the 1920s, said, "To us Jews, the

Fourth Gospel is the most Jewish of the four!" John used numerous Old Testament references and seemingly assumed that his readers were familiar with these references, which lacked the clarifying statements evident in Mark and Luke. Furthermore, the discourses of Jesus presuppose knowledge of the symbolism behind the Jewish festivals (2:13,23; 4:45; 6:4; 7:2,8,10-11,14,37; 10:22; 11:55-56; 12:1,12,20). John also understood the customs, culture, and land of first-century Palestine (2:1-10; 5:9-10; 9:14-16; 11:44; 19:31). All of these observations taken together in the Gospel of John seem to point to a decidedly Jewish background, one which moves away from second-century Greek religion and philosophy and maintains deep roots in first-century Judaism.

Most scholars are relatively certain that Matthew, Mark, and Luke were in some way dependent on one another. When John deviated from the Synoptics, critics raised questions. Nevertheless, one may also assume that John was familiar with the writings of Matthew, Mark, and Luke since he wrote his Gospel last.

In 1963, C. H. Dodd composed a thorough and revolutionary study of the Gospel of John. He concluded, "Behind the Fourth Gospel lies an ancient tradition independent of the other gospels, and meriting serious consideration as a contribution to our knowledge of the historical facts concerning Jesus Christ."[1] The Gospel of John then can be understood to be an independent and authoritative witness to the person and works of Jesus. John has a strong claim to historicity, even though it does not parallel Matthew, Mark, or Luke.

As for its structure, John can be divided into two sections (chaps. 1–11 and 12–21), one that focuses on Jesus' deeds (the signs) and another that reveals His passion (glory). The prologue of John (chap. 1) stresses Jesus' preexistence and His incarnation. It also presents the testimony of John the Baptist. Chapters 2–11 consist of seven miracles performed by Jesus, accompanied by seven lengthy discourses. These function as "signs" of Jesus' authority given so that people may believe.

Chapters 12–21 contain two major sections. After a brief introduction in chapter 12 describing the events that will lead to Jesus' death, chapters 13–17 recount Jesus' farewell discourse to His disciples. Chapters 18–21 then narrate the Lord's crucifixion and resurrection, and the reinstatement of the disciples.

Title

The simple title in the Greek text, "According to John" (Gk. *kata Ioannēn*), reflects the strength of evidence for the authorship of this Gospel. Parallel in form to the titles of the other three Gospels ("According to Matthew," "According to Mark," and "According to Luke"), the title of this Fourth Gospel identifies by name the apostle who, writing under the inspiration of the Holy Spirit, bears witness to Jesus the Christ on its pages.

Setting

Although the place of origin is not specifically identified, tradition, especially the writings of ancient historians Irenaeus and Eusebius, notes that John wrote from his home in Ephesus. Irenaeus had personal interaction with Polycarp, the revered pastor and martyr who knew John personally. As one of the large and prominent cities of the ancient world, Ephesus had a church founded by the Apostle Paul (Ac 19:1-20) during the time he was evangelizing Asia.

Other places suggested for consideration include Alexandria, Antioch, and Palestine. However, in each case the argument is based on circumstantial evidence—e.g., a discovery of fragments of the Gospel, allusions to John in other literature associated with the region, or the association of its content with a certain region.

Unless the acceptance of Ephesus, based on the testimony of trustworthy witnesses, can be shown to be false, one does well to accept their account. After all, they are far closer to the events in question than those interpreters, many of whose presuppositions are at variance with both historic Christian faith and with evidence that in any other context would meet criteria of historical reliability. Several commentators even mention the unique caveat concerning a railway station located in a small Turkish village near ancient Ephesus. The station bears the name "Ayasoluk," which scholars identify as a corruption of the Greek *haios theologos*, literally "holy theologian," a popular designation for the Apostle John among the followers of Eastern Christianity.[2]

Genre

The word "gospel" (Gk. *euangelion*, lit. "good messenger," evolving into "good news") in the New Testament seems to imply oral teaching or instruction or preaching. The Gospels are a unique literary form that has both biographical and historical characteristics. The Gospels employ various literary conventions and subgenres to accomplish their purpose of bearing witness to Jesus Christ. Some have described the genre of Gospel as growing out of the preaching of the early church. Nevertheless, the Gospel of John is set apart from the other Gospels with its own unique arrangement of content and written style and way of focusing on the life, death, and resurrection of Jesus.

Author

There are currently four views concerning who wrote the Gospel of John:

- The Gospel was compiled either by John the son of Zebedee or by one of his close followers.

- The Gospel was a devotional treatise written by a pious believer in the second century.

- The Gospel was the production of a community of Christians who may have possessed the Synoptics and some of Paul's letters.

- The tradition was utterly reformed to reflect the community's own history.

The internal evidence, however, points decidedly to a person described as "the beloved disciple" (13:23; 19:26; 20:2; 21:7,20) as the best candidate for penning the Gospel. In these Scripture passages, John the son of Zebedee has been identified as the "beloved disciple." The most striking evidence for this identification is the context of John 21, a fishing scene that introduced Peter, Thomas, Nathanael, and the two sons of Zebedee. Peter is not the beloved disciple, and there is no evidence that Thomas or Nathanael knew Jesus so intimately. Of the sons of Zebedee, James was martyred early (Ac 12:2), leaving John the son of Zebedee as the only possibility. The other internal evidence pointing to John as the author of the Fourth Gospel is as follows:

- John was one of the Twelve and a part of the "inner circle" of disciples, which included Peter and James.

- The Gospel referred to disciples by name as a matter of course, but John is not listed among them. This "silence" can be explained if the "beloved disciple" is a phrase concealing John's role or perhaps the unique way in which John discretely refers to himself.

In 1881, B. F. Westcott gathered together indirect internal evidence pointing to the son of Zebedee as the author:

- The author was a Jew of Palestine.
- The author was an eyewitness.
- The author was an apostle.

As for external evidence, the early church fathers overwhelmingly point to John the son of Zebedee as the author of the Gospel that bears his name. Fourth-century church historian Eusebius recorded Irenaeus' testimony concerning the matter. According to Irenaeus, John lived in Ephesus, where his church "became a true witness of the apostolic tradition." Irenaeus also discussed authorship of the Gospels. After writing about Matthew, Mark, and Luke, he says, "Lastly, John, the disciple of the Lord, who had leaned back on his breast, once more set forth the Gospel while residing in Ephesus." Irenaeus's source for this information was none other than the bishop of Smyrna, Polycarp, who was personally instructed by John. Irenaeus says the following about Polycarp:

> Polycarp was not only instructed by apostles and conversant with many who had seen the Lord, but was appointed by apostles to serve in Asia as Bishop of Smyrna. I myself saw him in my early years, for he lived a long time and was very old indeed when he laid down his life by a glorious and most splendid martyrdom. At all times he taught the things which he had learnt from the apostles, which the Church transmits, which alone are true.[3]

In the second century, Justin Martyr (c. 100–165), Tertullian of Carthage (160–215), and Clement of Alexandria (155–220) all testify that the author of the Fourth Gospel is the Apostle John.

Date

As with the issues concerning the authorship of the Gospel of John, the early church provided some vital testimony concerning the dating of the work. Early church tradition dated the Fourth Gospel to the end of the first century, probably during the reign of Domitian (81–96). John was an old man ministering in Ephesus at this time. The combination of the testimonies of Irenaeus (*Against Heresies* 3.1.1, 3.3.4), Polycrates, Papias, Polycarp, and Clement, all quoted by Eusebius (*Ecclesiastical History* 3.31.3, 3.39.4, 5.20.4-6, 6.14.7) point to this approximate dating for the book of John. Eusebius and Jerome also affirmed this time frame.

Recipients

There have been some interesting studies done concerning the first recipients of this Gospel. A popular view concerning the makeup of this community has described its development in two stages. The first stage involved Jewish Christians who lived in Palestine in the mid-first century. This community found itself increasingly at odds with the

Jewish authorities and was finally excommunicated from the synagogues (Jn 9:22; 12:42; 16:2). They needed encouragement and instruction in their faith. The second stage involved a predominantly Gentile audience who lived in Asia Minor during the first century. This pagan constituency needed to be drawn to faith in Christ and then nurtured in that faith. Both Jewish and Hellenistic emphases are found in John. There is no indication in the text concerning the precise geographical location of the intended audience. However, the fact that John carefully explained Jewish traditions, translated Jewish names, and located Palestinian sites might suggest that at least Gentiles located outside of Palestine were included among those for whom he wrote.

Major Themes

John's theme is clearly stated: "But these are written so that you may believe Jesus is the Messiah, the Son of God, and by believing you may have life in His name" (20:31). The chronological or logical sequence of events is not his focus. John must have been overwhelmed by the spiritual needs of a fledgling but growing church. He sensed the lack of understanding of the Old Testament, especially among the Gentile converts. John became the writing theologian, determined to bring to the church an understanding of Jesus and the gospel and of how to defend the faith in a hostile world. John also clearly included the necessity for a response from his readers. Faith in Christ was not simply intellectual assent to a belief system but had to be accompanied by genuine commitment to respond appropriately.

Eternal Life and Death. Unlike Matthew, Mark, and Luke, John described eternal life and death as beginning immediately. One's response to Jesus determined whether he was alive or dead (1:14; 3:18; 5:24). However, the idea of future hope was not absent in John (5:25-29; 6:39; 12:25,48; 14:3,28). Some scholars have considered John's "eternal life" passages as equivalent to the "kingdom" passages in the Synoptics. John's use of "eternal life" instead of kingdom, may have communicated more effectively with a largely Hellenistic audience.

The Election and Security of Believers. There are several passages in John that affirm the security of the believer: "This is the will of Him who sent Me: that I should lose none of those He has given Me but should raise them up on the last day" (6:39). "My Father, who has given them to Me, is greater than all. No one is able to snatch them out of the Father's hand" (10:29). In the upper-room discourse, Jesus attested that the disciples did not choose Him, but He chose them (15:16). However, in John 15, Jesus exhorted the believer to *abide* in Him. Anyone who does not abide in Him is in danger of being cut off and destroyed.

The Holy Spirit as Comforter. While the work of the Holy Spirit is quite prominent throughout the Gospel of Luke, here in John the work of the Spirit receives a different emphasis. In John 14–16, the Holy Spirit is described as fulfilling five roles to benefit the believer:

- Helper (14:15-18)
- Interpreter (14:25)
- Witness (15:26)
- Prosecutor (16:5-11)
- Revealer (16:12-15).

"The Jews." Like Matthew, John has been accused of being anti-Jewish. The term "the Jews" occurs 68 times in John, and some argue that the designation is consistently used in a derogatory sense. However, a close look at the context reveals that *Ioudaioi* merely distinguishes "Judeans" from Galileans. Therefore, the term is not necessarily used in a demeaning way. John did intend to show, however, that Jesus fulfilled all the Jewish traditions and rituals. With Jesus, the new covenant is inaugurated. Therefore, those who believed in Jesus became the chosen people of God.

Miracles as Signs. Whereas in the Synoptic Gospels, "signs" are often used in a negative sense, in the Gospel of John their function is to give reason to believe that Jesus is the Messiah, the Son of God (2:11; 4:53-54). However, even in John, signs were not always viewed in a positive light (4:48). In fact, at the end of John, Jesus said, "Blessed are they who did not see, and yet believed" (20:29 NASB). Three stages of faith are evident in John:

- an infant stage that is open to faith (a requirement before any signs are given),

- a growing faith based on signs, and

- a mature faith that needs no signs.

Dualisms. John is fond of using sharp contrasts such as light versus darkness, life versus death, love versus judgment, above versus below, spirit versus flesh, truth versus falsehood, believers versus unbelievers. John pointed to one Truth and one Lord. What ultimately mattered for eternity was what one would do with Jesus. Those who believed would have eternal life. Those who did not believe would die. John strongly exhorted a young church buffeted by hostile enemies inside and out to stay on the straight and narrow path of faith. For that reason, love and unity were vitally important throughout the book of John.

Portrait of Jesus in John. John introduced Jesus. He made clear His extraordinary nature as the incarnate Son of God (1:1,14).

Logos. This term, although not used by the Synoptic writers, has a long and complex history in both Hellenistic and Jewish settings. In non-Jewish settings, the term generally meant a life force or world soul that permeated the earth. In Jewish settings, it referred to the spoken word of God. Both these settings seem to refer to the way God or the gods reveal themselves to mankind. John was likely using this term precisely because of its uses in other contexts in order to reveal that Jesus is the full expression of the Logos, the only way, the truth, and the life. He is the One who ultimately reveals the truth of God.

Lamb of God. John also introduced and covered thoroughly the atonement of Christ (1:29; 3:14-15; 10:11). Only in John's writings was Jesus identified as the "Lamb of God" (27 times in the book of Revelation). In John 1, John the Baptist calls Jesus "the Lamb of God, who takes away the sin of the world" (v. 29). This reference is undoubtedly to Jesus' role as the ultimate sacrificial lamb of the Passover.

God. Much has been made of John's references to the deity of Christ. The seven "I am" statements of Christ all allude to His exalted nature:

- the bread of life (6:35),

- the light of the world (8:12),

- the door for the sheep (10:7),

- the good shepherd (10:11),
- the resurrection and the life (11:25),
- the way, the truth, and the life (14:6), and
- the true vine (15:1).

However, while John's Christological understanding is clear, Matthew, Mark, and Luke clearly attest to Christ's deity as well. The passages concerning His virgin birth, His authority to forgive sins, His power over the Devil and nature, and His death and resurrection manifest brilliantly Jesus' divinity.

Pronunciation Guide

Aenon	*EE nahn*
Arimathea	*ar ih muh THEE uh (TH as in thin)*
Barabbas	*buh RAB uhs*
Bethany	*BETH uh nih*
Bethesda	*buh THEZ duh*
Bethsaida	*beth-SAY ih duh*
Caiaphas	*KAY uh fuhs, KIGH uh fuhs*
Capernaum	*kuh PUHR nay uhm*
Cephas	*SEE fuhs*
Clopas	*KLOH puhs*
Gabbatha	*GAB uh thuh*
Golgotha	*GAHL guh thuh, gahl GAHTH uh*
Magdalene	*MAG duh leen, mag duh LEE nih*
Malchus	*MAL kuhs*
Nathanael	*nuh THAN ay uhl (TH as in thin)*
Nazarene	*NAZ uh reens*
Nicodemus	*nik uh DEE muhs*
Rabbouni	*ra BOO nigh*
Salim	*SAY lim*
Sychar	*SIGH kahr*
Tiberias	*tigh BIHR ih uhs*

Outline

I. INTRODUCTORY TESTIMONY
(1:1-51)
  A. The Prologue (1:1-18)
  B. The Testimony (1:19-51)

II. THE TESTIMONY OF SIGNS AND
DISCOURSES (2:1–11:57)
  A. Jesus and Jewish Institutions
  (2:1–4:54)
    1. Water into wine—a new joy
    (2:1-12)
    2. Temple cleansing—a new
    temple (2:13-25)
    3. Jesus, Nicodemus, and the
    Baptist—a new birth
    (3:1-36)
    4. Jesus, the Samaritan
    woman, and the official's
    son—a new diversity of
    followers (4:1-54)
  B. Jesus and Jewish Festivals
  (5:1–10:21)
    1. Healing the paralytic and
    imitating the Father
    (5:1-47)
    2. The true Passover: the bread
    of life (6:1-71)
    3. The true tabernacles: living
    water and the light of the
    world (7:1–9:41)

    4. The good shepherd and
    oneness with the Father
    (10:1-42)
  C. Jesus as the Resurrection and
  the Life (11:1-57)

III. THE TESTIMONY OF DEATH AND
RESURRECTION (12:1–20:31)
  A. Actions in Preparation for
  Death (12:1-50)
    1. Anointing at Bethany
    (12:1-11)
    2. Entry into Jerusalem
    (12:12-50)
  B. Teaching in Preparation for
  Death (13:1–17:26)
    1. Servant ministry versus
    betrayal (13:1-38)
    2. Farewell discourse
    (14:1–16:33)
    3. High priestly prayer
    (17:1-26)
  C. Events Surrounding Death
  Itself (18:1–20:31)
    1. Arrest, trials, and crucifixion
    (18:1–19:42)
    2. Resurrection (20:1-29)
    3. Purpose of the Gospel
    (20:30-31)

IV. CONCLUDING TESTIMONY (21:1-25)
  A. The Reinstatement of the
  Disciples (21:1-23)
  B. The Epilogue (21:24-25)

Exposition of the Text

INTRODUCTORY TESTIMONY (1:1-51)

The Prologue (1:1-18)

The Gospel of John begins with one of the greatest statements about Jesus Christ ever penned. There are other Christological passages, but none surpasses these verses (1:1-18). The words are a literary masterpiece, but even more important is the profound statement of theological understanding of the person and work of Jesus Christ found herein.

1:1-5 John began his prologue with the affirmation that the Word, Jesus Christ, preexisted with God (1:1-18). He already *was* when this beginning occurred. Even John's introductory phrase, **in the beginning**, paralleled the opening words of

Genesis. Genesis 1:1 addressed the "beginning" of creation; whereas John 1:1 described the incarnation of God in Christ. God—the Word, the Second Person of the triunity—assumed a human body and nature in order to accomplish redemption.

WORD (Gk. *logos*, "a thing uttered, speech, language") has the nuance of going beyond mere sound, expressing a full communication appealing to all the senses. The Hebrew understanding of the Old Testament Scripture designated Messiah as the divine unveiler for God's wisdom and as the conduit of His power. Although the idea of *logos* belonged to Greek philosophy, John used the word in a broader sense to include Hebrew ideas as well. The *logos* described by John predated any philosophical ideas (v. 1). The verb WAS (Gk. *ēn*) is in the imperfect tense, indicating continuing action in past time or continual timeless existence. On the other hand, in verse 3, the aorist verb WERE CREATED (Gk. *egeneto*, "become") has the sense of one creative event or coming into being in contrast to the continuous existence noted in verses 1 and 2. For Christ to create all things would then lead to the logical conclusion that He Himself was not created. Ultimately, "word" denotes the unique communication between the Creator God and His creation. This communication reached its zenith with Christ as God in human flesh (v. 14).

Creation occurred with a "word" (vv. 1-3; Ps 33:6), including in this expression creativity and energy. John packed meaning into "word" by identifying it as the source of everything visible and even including the invisible of precreation eternity. Without question John assigned universal significance to Jesus Christ and noted His preexistence as well as His ever-present and unending authority.

The phrase "the word was WITH (Gk. *pros*, "with or towards," used here with the accusative case and thus having the sense of "face-to-face with") God" was uniquely crafted to include His equality as deity Himself and His distinction of identity as "the Word" (v. 1). Eternal coexistence and absolute unity is clear. Verse 2 repeats and amplifies this coexistent unity of God.

Three truths undergird the understanding of the triunity of God:

- His preexistence is affirmed, **in the beginning was the Word** (v. 1). BEGINNING (Gk. *archē*, "starting point") refers to the time before creation, a qualitative rather than a temporal expression.

- The Word is distinct in His own role within the Godhead, **the Word was with God** (v. 1), yet having the idea of harmony and fellowship.

- His deity is clear, **the Word was God** (v. 1). God (Gk. *theos*) lacks the article, an anarthrous construction and thus the predicate noun, which emphasizes equality.

This passage is definitive in understanding the person and work of Christ. Christ would bring LIFE (Gk. *zōē*), suggesting "power to make alive and renew energy needed for all activity," and LIGHT (Gk. *phōs*), denoting "enabling force" for all to see and observe God working in the world. John expressed this latter phenomenon in a unique way using the verb OVERCOME (Gk. *katelaben*, suggesting the idea of "seizing, grasping, or overcoming") in expressing how the light would "catch or overtake" and conquer the darkness (v. 5). Christ's work on the cross would be the ultimate overpowering of darkness with light. Yet, heresies did develop around this crucial doctrine of the faith.

After battling these heresies, the church developed a definitive creed refuting these major heresies and proclaiming that Christ is truly God and truly man—one person with two distinct natures without confusion, change, or division. Jesus is undiminished and untarnished deity (vv. 1,14,18; see also Php 2:6-11; Col 2:9; Heb 1:1-13). He is the God-Man, possessing full humanity without in any way lessening His deity (4:6; 11:35; 12:27).

Heresies and the Doctrine of Christ	
Denying the reality of the two natures	*Docetism* developed first, denying the full humanity of Christ.
	Ebionism denied the full deity of Christ.
Denying the integrity of the two natures	*Sabellianism* recognized that Jesus, as God the Father, became the Son by incarnation, which denied the distinction of persons within the Godhead.
	Arianism declared that the Son was neither eternal nor immutable; the Son was subordinate in His being to the Father. The Arians translated John 1:1b as, "the Word was a god" because the definite article was absent in the Greek text. They considered Christ to be the first created being and not God Himself. This heresy was refuted by the Council of Nicea (AD 325).
	Apollinarianism asserted Christ's full deity but denied His full humanity. This heresy was rejected by the Council of Constantinople (AD 381).
Confusing the proper unity of the two natures	*Nestorianism* called for two separate natures and two separate persons without unity. This heresy was condemned by the Council of Ephesus (AD 431).
	Eutychianism suggested that the union of the divine and the human resulted in one theanthropic nature (part God and part man) of Christ.

Ultimately, John was clear that Jesus is indeed the eternal God who came in human flesh, asserting full deity and perfect humanity in one person. In conclusion, orthodox Christianity, based on John's clear teaching, demands:

• recognition of Jesus' two natures,

• integrity of the divine and human natures respectively, and

• the union of these two natures in one person.

Triunity has been never more clearly and carefully presented.

1:6-8 The followers of John the Baptist continued to be active as a group even after John's death (Ac 18:25; 19:1-3). Although there is no evidence of their elevating the martyred leader above Jesus, the Gospel writer wanted to be sure there was no misunderstanding on the distinction between the Baptist and Jesus. Throughout the book of John, the primary function of John the Baptist was to testify concerning Jesus. While this understanding was also true in the Synoptic Gospels, they included many other aspects of John's ministry that are missing here. The apostle primarily presented the work and ministry of John the Baptist (v. 7) rather than recording his birth and the details of **his** early ministry.

John is the human agent for presenting Jesus as the Word. The word SENT (Gk. *apestalmenos*, "commission") carries the sense of authority as with a personal representative, and the verb's perfect tense indicates the permanent and enduring nature of his assignment (v. 6). The word translated WITNESS (Gk. *martuērsē*, "testify or affirm") is a distinctive Johannine word and precisely established the importance of testimony to the claims of Jesus as the God/Man. "Witness" later evolved into the English word "martyr," a reference to one who suffers or dies for his beliefs. The Baptist did indeed seal his **witness** with death at the hands of Herodias (Mk 6:14-29). John spoke from the human perspective and sought to revive the people and awaken them to their spiritual needs. Yet the Baptist's role is always presented as subordinate to that of Jesus (v. 8; 3:22-30). He never tried to usurp the divine "Word," whose heavenly light far surpassed his own earthly light of witness (vv. 8-9). "The Word" was present "in the beginning" (v. 1); John came upon the scene at a divinely appointed time.

1:9-13 Christ is presented as **the true light**. The meaning of TRUE (Gk. *alēthinon*, "real, genuine, authentic") does not necessarily call for the contrasting idea to be "false." Rather the emphasis is on completeness and clarity, as if coming out of the shadows. Under the radiance and brightness of Christ, all else seems dim and inadequate (v. 9). Ultimately, revelation is only in and **through Him**. The phrase GIVES LIGHT (Gk. *phōtizei*, "shed light or instruct") emphasized His purpose to make Himself and His will clear to everyone. The present tense verb affirms that this revelation can only be found in Him. There is no assumption

that all would accept Christ but rather the clear understanding that the witness and revelation are intended for all (v. 12).

The Johannine meaning of RECOGNIZE or know (Gk. *egnō*) suggests more than intellectual knowledge—perhaps the understanding of "being in a right relationship" (v. 10). From the perspective of John and other New Testament writers, for the Jews to reject Jesus was incomprehensible. From their viewpoint, this rejection could not have been their lack of knowledge but must have been their conscious determination to reject what they knew (v. 11).

Interestingly the two appearances of HIS OWN are different in gender. The first (Gk. *idia*) is a neuter reference to one's personal belongings, i.e., the land of Israel; the other (Gk. *idioi*), a masculine form, referred to His people. Jesus **created** the world, and it belonged to Him; but the people He created rejected Him (v. 11).

There is a direct contrast to this rejection in verse 12, where BELIEVING (Gk. *pisteuousin*) indicates an active and continual commitment to Christ. It is not merely head knowledge. Belief is inextricably linked with RECEIVING (Gk. *parelabon*, "taking to one's side or welcoming"). To receive goes beyond belief to include confidence that what is being received is trustworthy (v. 12) for one to embrace. The word "children" (Gk. *tekna*) suggests endearment and connection. These were not linked biologically **of blood** or by human decision, that is, **the will of the flesh** (v. 13); they were not natural **children of God**. But by believing and receiving, they became His children; the relationship was spiritual.

1:14-18 Although Gnosticism did not appear until later, reaching its full strength in the second and third centuries, John battled what might be called "incipient

Gnosticism," which claimed that Jesus only *seemed* to be human since Christ could not have been both sinless and human. Gnostics regarded the spiritual as inherently good and the earthly, i.e., the created world, as evil. Gnostics refused to see any connection between the sins of the body and spiritual things. Therefore, in their thinking they could worship on a spiritual level while remaining free to do as they pleased in everyday living. John countered with unveiling Christ's humanity (4:6-7; 11:35; 12:27; 19:30). Jesus took His human nature at His incarnation, but He did not lose any of His deity. He was truly the God-Man.

In John 1:1, "the Word" was a reference to eternal deity; here **the Word became flesh**, involving a change in Him. In the incarnation Jesus did just that: He entered into the domain of humanity. Through His birth, He came into the human world and TOOK UP RESIDENCE (Gk. *eskēnōsen*, "live in a tent or take temporary residence") as the executor of His Father's will in human flesh (v. 14). His incarnation was temporary; His fleshly tent was God's residence, replacing the ancient tabernacle in the wilderness (Ex 40:34-38). The Greek word evolved from the same root as "tabernacle" and was used in the Septuagint. It contained the same consonants as the Hebrew word *shekinah*, a reference to God's glory. Hence, John was comparing the incarnation to the time when God's presence was among His people, "tabernacling" with them in the desert of Sinai. Yet, Jesus' glory has a unique dimension in that He is **the One and only Son** (v. 14).

Never was there a hint of philosophical musing; rather John said, **We observed His glory**, indicating a reality personally experienced. The incarnation was the most perfect and complete revelation of THE ONE AND ONLY SON (Gk.

monogenous, "unique"), literally a "one of a kind" Son. With no equal from all of humanity, He alone was able to reveal the Father fully (v. 14).

The contrast between **the law** and **grace** (Gk. *charis*) was addressed. There was no negative swipe at the divine standard of righteousness, which was represented in "the law," but God was the embodiment of "grace." The coming of Christ, God's ultimate gift, unveiled God's way for salvation (v. 17).

The words **No one has ever seen God** (v. 18), though sometimes puzzling, are absolutely true. In fact, the word order in the Greek text adds emphasis as the word "God" appears first, and the clause ends with the Greek *pōpote*, meaning "ever, at any time," with the Greek *oudeis*, meaning "no one," in between. The Son is said to be AT THE FATHER'S SIDE (Gk. *ōn kolpos*, lit. "being in the bosom"), a Hebrew idiom denoting the intimate relationship between a child and his parents (v. 18). BEING (Gk. *ōn*) is a present participle, implying not only preincarnate existence but also constant and continual association. No statement more clearly expresses intimate association and close following and thus God's compassion for the world.

The verb in the phrase HE HAS REVEALED HIM (Gk. *exēgēsato*, "explain or interpret") is transliterated into English as exegesis. The incarnation is the ultimate teaching or expounding of God's Word and was often used to proclaim divine secrets (v. 18). God cannot be understood by ordinary human senses, but the life and words of Jesus provide all one needs to know God and His purposes for life. God as a being is so beyond human comprehension that He cannot be seen. Only through spiritual eyes can one know Him. However, He chose to reveal Himself in physical form through Jesus.

Thus, John revealed in his prologue that Jesus is both divine and human. John's

focus on the Word becoming flesh emphasized Christ's humanity. He first established Christ's deity (a point with which
his opponents disagreed), and then he
established Christ's humanity (a point
with which they did agree).

The Testimony (1:19-51)

John the Baptist's primary function in
the Fourth Gospel was to testify of Jesus.
He clearly stated that he was not the Messiah. He was the one who was to testify
concerning the Messiah. There is no
explicit mention of Jesus' baptism by
John in this Gospel. The focus was exclusively on Jesus. The Apostle John may
have been attempting to combat a sect
worshiping John the Baptist in his community.

1:19-28 John, the apostle/evangelist,
gave little attention to John the Baptist in
the way he was presented in other Gospels
(Mt 3:1-6; Mk 1:2-6; Lk 1:1-24,57-80;
3:1-13). He immediately went to the heart
of the forerunner's purpose.

In this Gospel, the Baptist was identified as the one doing the baptizing (v. 25).
Although the baptizing done by John the
Baptist seemed similar to the Jewish proselyte's baptism—complete immersion,
which was required to remove all evil
from the one seeking membership in the
holy community of followers of *Yahweh*.
However, this Jewish baptism was
self-immersion. John added the agent for
baptism, and the baptism he proclaimed
was a picture of personal confession of
repentance and commitment to faith in
Christ.

John's suggested identification with **Elijah** might have reflected the Jewish
expectation of Elijah's return before Messiah would come (Mal 4:5-6), especially
since John the Baptist and Elijah were
similar in their unorthodox dress and
ascetic tendencies. The Baptist denied the
connection. Finally the people inquired

about his identity forthrightly. John used
the words of **Isaiah the prophet** (Is 40:3)
to describe his task of preparing for
Messiah:

- He was a **voice**, which, of course,
  would be useless without a message
  (v. 23).

- He was to prepare or **make straight
  the way of the Lord** (v. 23).

- He was to **baptize** (v. 26).

Yet in all his tasks, the Baptist understood
his role in contradistinction to that of
Jesus the Christ (v. 27). Untying sandals
was the menial task of a slave, and thus
the Baptist did not see himself even as
worthy of being a slave of Jesus, emphasizing again the exalted nature of Jesus.

Bethany across the Jordan (v. 28) is
not the same village (located near Jerusalem) in which Lazarus and Mary and
Martha lived. Since the site has not been
identified with any certainty, some suggest that it is Betharba (lit. "the place of
crossing"). However, the only sure information about the village is that it was not
a populated area, which may be why the
location is uncertain.

1:29-51 This next section recorded a
series of happenings that occurred on successive days:

- First, John was questioned by interro-
  gators from Jerusalem (vv. 19-28),
  which has already been discussed.

- Second, John offered a paean of
  praise as Jesus approached (vv.
  29-34).

- Third, John the Baptist introduced
  Jesus to John's own disciples (vv.
  35-42). He announced that Jesus **is
  the Lamb of God who takes away
  the sin of the world**; two disciples
  took notice (vv. 35-37). One was
  Andrew; the other was not named.
  They quickly turned from following

John the Baptist **and followed Jesus**. Andrew called Peter.

- Fourth, Jesus left for Galilee (vv. 43-51). **Jesus found Philip**, who then brought **Nathanael** to Jesus. This initial calling in Judea seems to have occurred before the formal calling of the disciples by the Sea of Galilee, which is recorded in the Synoptic Gospels (Mt 10:1-15; Mk 3:13-19; Lk 6:12-16).

Throughout John's witness, his focus is on Jesus. The phrase "the Lamb of God" prefigured the sacrificial nature of Christ's mission and atoning work (v. 29). The metaphor of the "lamb" taking away sin is found frequently in the Old Testament (Gn 22:2-8).

In verse 30, a significant change sets this verse apart from verse 15 with these words: **after me comes a man** (Gk. *anēr*, "man or husband," emphasizing maleness more than does the generic term *anthropos*). Some commentators see this distinction as alluding to the headship of Christ over His followers as paralleled in the husband's headship over the wife in marriage (see 1 Co 11:3; Eph 5:22-23), a principle clearly taught in the Pauline epistles.

John the Baptist did know Jesus; they were relatives (Lk 1:36). However, he had not known Him as Messiah; and here, for John, the Holy Spirit began to unveil Jesus as the Christ, the Messiah (v. 31).

This section summarized Johannine Christology:

- Jesus is the Passover **Lamb** (v. 36), which identified Him as the sacrifice meeting Old Testament requirements.

- Jesus was preexistent—fully God and fully man in His incarnation, which enabled Him to make atonement (v. 30).

- Jesus made atonement to provide salvation, and He linked Himself **with the Holy Spirit** as the one who intercedes for believers at the divine throne (v. 33).

- Jesus was "the only Son," who truly embodied God and through His incarnation clothed Himself with humanity (v. 14).

Many titles were used to describe Jesus. He was described as "the Lamb of God" (a picture of the Passover lamb that was slain when the children of Israel were delivered from Egypt, Ex 12:1-13), a **Rabbi** (lit. "master or teacher," a title of respect used by students in addressing a wise and honored teacher, v. 38), **Messiah** (lit. "anointed one," v. 41), **the Son of God** and **King of Israel** (v. 49). He was the one described **in the Law** and the Prophets (v. 45).

Cephas, a Greek transliteration of an Aramaic term meaning **Rock**, was not commonly used as a proper name in either language. The Greek equivalent was used in Matthew's Gospel (Mt 16:18). The term is used as a nickname and became so popular (perhaps because it seemed to suit him well) that his given name **Simon** became secondary in importance. Note also the common way of identification: referring to a boy or a man with the phrase **son of** (Hb. *ben* or Ar. *bar*) attached to the name of his father (v. 42).

Jesus took the initiative in calling out Philip (v. 43), who, as Andrew and Peter, was likely a fisherman. His hometown **Bethsaida** (v. 44, lit. "house of fishing") was in Galilee. Nathanael's reference to **Nazareth** (v. 44), a city not mentioned in the Old Testament, revealed the insignificance of Jesus' hometown at the time He began His ministry. Jesus' interaction with Nathanael is noteworthy (vv. 47-51). Jesus referred to Nathanael as **a true Israelite** in whom there was **no deceit**. Perhaps there is a play on words here between two names—Jacob and Israel.

Jacob means "deceiver," and yet here Jesus identified a man from Israel (i.e., the House of Jacob) as one without deceit. Nathanael, overwhelmed with wonder at the omniscience of Jesus, called Jesus "the Son of God" and "the King of Israel." Jesus then promised to Nathanael greater wonders. Jesus' description of **the angels of God ascending and descending on the Son of Man** may be a reference to Jacob's dream about the ladder to heaven (Gn 28:10-12). Nathanael could find an encouraging word in this flashback. Jacob received an overwhelming blessing from God despite his deceitful life. How much more did Nathanael, in whom there was no deceit, have to anticipate (vv. 47,51). There may also be a clear allusion to Christ's future death and resurrection. The writer John clearly exalted Christ throughout the first chapter by consistently referring to His glorious person and to His future works.

THE TESTIMONY OF SIGNS AND DISCOURSES (2:1–11:57)

Jesus and Jewish Institutions (2:1–4:54)

Water into wine—a new joy (2:1-12)

Chapters 2–4 are bracketed by the miracles performed in Cana. The changing of the water into wine and the healing of the official's son are the only two miracles in the book of John specifically designated "signs." The narratives in this section show the new and unique ministry of Jesus in contrast to the traditions and rituals of the Jews. This new age would bring a new joy (2:1-12), a new temple (2:13-25), a new birth (3:1-36), and a new diversity of those who were offered salvation (4:1-54). These events are generally understood to have taken place before Jesus' Galilean ministry. One must be cautious about trying to follow Jesus' movements with a precise plan. The Gospel was never meant to be a travelogue. To rearrange and try to harmonize with any agenda, including travel, might have destroyed or at least distorted the message of the text.

2:1-12 A perfect example of the aforementioned warning came with the words **on the third day** (v. 1) since in chapter 1 three "next" days are mentioned (1:29,35, 43). Instead of rehearsing the many efforts of explaining such unimportant temporal minutiae, let the reader note that to pinpoint time issues and geographical locations with precision is difficult, if not impossible. In attempting to do so one risks missing the message and failing to understand the rich theological truths found herein.

Perhaps the best explanation for this "third day" reference is to consider it more than a chronological time designation but rather a way of pointing forward to the third day coming. The "third day" expression has great theological significance because of the resurrection.

Sometime early in His ministry, Jesus, His disciples, and His mother Mary were all invited to **a wedding** in Cana, a town in Galilee not precisely identified as to location but designated by most as a village about nine miles north of Nazareth (the hometown of Nathanael, 21:2). While they were there, the host ran out of wine. Weddings in the ancient world could last even a week. To run out of wine would cause great social embarrassment to the host and was considered quite inhospitable. Mary, understanding the dilemma, asked her Son to get involved. Mary was only mentioned in this Gospel here and at the cross (19:25-27). Mary was well aware that her Son had the ability to remedy the situation, and she was not afraid to ask Him to intervene. Jesus' response to His mother was neither disrespectful nor inappropriate. A paraphrase of the Greek text would be, "What [is it] to me and to you, woman? **My hour has not yet come**" (v. 4). John often stressed that Jesus' time of exaltation had not yet come. The Son is always in submission to God's will and His timing.

The offensive term seems to be **woman** (v. 4, Gk. *gunai*), which is a polite form of address used by Jesus here and elsewhere to address other women (4:21; 20:13; Mt 15:28; Lk 13:12), instead of the more affectionate term "Mother." He had chosen to use this formal noun of address, which seemed to push the event into a more formalized and thus less intimate relationship. His public ministry had already begun. Family members often use more generic designations of one another in public settings. Jesus might also have been consciously trying to change Mary's thinking as a mother in order to spare her additional suffering when His hour would come. Jesus was still her Son during His last hours on the cross, but He was now her Lord as well.

Clearly Mary was not offended by her Son's words, and with confidence she still anticipated that He would intervene in some way, which indeed He did. But He chose to do so without calling attention to the miracle (v. 7).

Also of interest to women is John's identification of the household staff as **servants** (v. 5, Gk. *diakonois*, "helpers, deacons, deaconesses"). The latter two meanings noted in a lexical footnote remind readers that other uses of *diakonois*, whether masculine or feminine, singular or plural, do in fact have root meanings of service without suggestion of ecclesiastical hierarchy (cf. Rm 16:1).

John also noted that the water changed into wine came from **jars** used **for Jewish purification**. The Jews used water generously in their rites for cleansing and purification, and these stone (or clay) water pots would have stored the water to be used for washing rituals. Each of the six pots would have contained about 20 to 30 gallons of water. The symbolism was clear: *Jesus' new "wine" of the new covenant would replace the old "water" of the old tradition.* Jesus turned water into the wine of joy in contrast to Moses who turned wine into the blood of judgment (Ex 7:14-24). Wine (although heavily diluted, perhaps three parts water to one part wine) was a common beverage with meals. Jesus **displayed His glory, and His disciples believed in Him** (v. 11).

This first sign (Gk. *sēmeion*, "act or miracle") certainly contained the meaning that this act was designed to lead those who observed to belief in Jesus as the Messiah, the Son of God, as is noted in what follows in the text. He "displayed [Gk. *ephanerōsen*, "making visible or clear"] His glory." The abundance of wine (an Old Testament metaphor for joy) Jesus produced was one way of manifesting His Messianic glory, which resulted in belief (Gk. *episteusan*) among the disciples. The word implies more than intellectual assent, including the idea of having confidence in or a trusting commitment (v. 11).

Temple cleansing—a new temple (2:13-25)

2:13-25 Jesus, with His mother and brothers, moved from Cana in the hills of Galilee to Capernaum, a village in Galilee (v. 12). Here again interpreters are confused because the Synoptics place the cleansing of the temple at the end of Jesus' ministry (see Mt 21:10-17; Mk 11:15-19; Lk 19:45-46), while John included the event early in Jesus' ministry. Again, readers must be reminded that chronological arrangement is not the purpose of John's Gospel (cf. Jn 20:31). Some suggest that there were two temple cleansings despite the fact that only one is mentioned in each Gospel. The matter seems to be more logically resolved by

The Wedding at Cana
John 2:1-12

The Place	• A wedding • In Cana of Galilee
The People	• Mary, the mother of Jesus • Jesus Christ • Jesus' disciples
The Problem	• The host ran out of wine (there was a physical need). • Mary sought the help of her Son.
The Power	• The water was turned into wine. • It was good wine. • Jesus performed the miracle. • This was His first sign of power in public. • He was glorified. • His disciples believed.

beginning with the belief that Scripture is true and accurate in what is recorded. However, considerable differences may occur as each writer pursues his written record according to purposes given to him by the Holy Spirit.

John's narrative in general differed from the Synoptics. **Sheep and oxen** were not specifically mentioned in the Synoptics; the Synoptics did not record Jesus' words, **Destroy this sanctuary, and I will raise it up in three days** (2:19). However, Matthew and Mark did attest that Jesus' words were repeated by those who were present at the crucifixion (Mt 26:61; Mk 14:57-58). These words would have made an impression on the crowd so that they might well remember them. Jerusalem in general and the temple in particular were the center of Jewish life. As the central place for worship, the temple marked the dwelling place of God Himself. The infant Jesus had been brought to the temple by His parents for circumcision (Lk 2:21-24,27), and, at the age of 12, Jesus was found in that same temple in deep theological discussion with the religious leaders (Lk 2:46-47).

This cleansing symbolized that the temple, along with the ceremonies and rituals

that accompanied it, was about to be replaced. Jesus' body represented the new temple and the destruction was a reference to His death just as the rebuilding referred to His resurrection (v. 19). The disciples later understood the significance of this event and believed, seeing it as the fulfillment of Psalm 69:6. In fact, **many** were putting their trust in Him at that time because of **the signs He was doing**. Yet the message was being communicated that belief based solely on miracles was not necessarily true faith.

Jesus, Nicodemus, and the Baptist—a new birth (3:1-36)

3:1-21 Nicodemus, a pious and respected teacher who was a Pharisee and a member of the Sanhedrin, was presented as an example of a person who merely believed in signs without truly understanding Jesus' message (3:1-12). His coming to Jesus by **night** could have been for secrecy to protect his own reputation, to avoid delay of crowds, to ensure privacy in conversation, or simply because he could not wait (v. 2). The phrase **I assure you** (Gk. *amēn*, "truly" or "indeed") is commonly used for emphasis and personal affirmation (vv. 3,5,11).

Jesus' teaching on the new birth was confusing to Nicodemus (v. 4). BORN (Gk. *gennēthē*, "born or begotten") AGAIN (Gk. *anōthen*, "from above or from heaven, again or anew"). Both ideas are included. The renewal can come only from a heavenly source, emphasizing the origin of salvation (Gl 4:19). Nicodemus knew a rebirth physically was impossible, but Jesus pointed to the necessity of spiritual birth as a parallel to physical birth. He used the word SPIRIT (Gk. *pneuma*, "power, wind, breath") to carry a double entendre with the emphasis on the power brought with the Spirit as He enters a life (v. 5). The reference to **water** is not so easily explained. These options are to be considered:

- Water baptism is regenerative in itself, an idea antithetical to the New Testament teaching of salvation by grace. Verse 5 emphatically does not teach baptismal regeneration. One of the most basic principles for interpreting Scripture is that difficult passages must be interpreted in light of what is crystal clear (e.g., Jn 3:16 and Eph 2:8-9).

- Water is associated with the natural physical birth, which is accompanied by a flow of water.

- Water is a metaphor for God's Word, which does have cleansing quality (15:3; 1 Pt 1:23).

- Water is a metaphor for the washing of regeneration and renewing of the Holy Spirit (Ti 3:5), suggesting that one enters the kingdom of heaven through this process.

Both the second and last options fit within the whole of Scripture. For contrast and linking of two parts, Jesus' statement should perhaps be interpreted as reminding Nicodemus that just as he experienced physical birth coming into the earthly realm, he must also experience spiritual birth to enter the heavenly kingdom. However, linking water and spirit as a reference to life would have been an easily understood metaphor in the desert regions of the ancient land. Nicodemus must have responded to Jesus' appeal since he later participated in the public burial of Jesus by his contribution of aloes and spices to prepare the body for burial (19:39-41).

> *One thing is certainly clear: Legalism or doing certain things or outward conformity or not doing what was forbidden would not guarantee admission to heaven. Only a radical inner transformation can prepare a person for the kingdom of God.*

One thing is certainly clear: legalism or doing certain things or outward conformity or not doing what was forbidden would not guarantee admission to heaven. Only a radical inner transformation can prepare a person for the kingdom of God. The Old Testament references in verses 13 and 14 would have been familiar to Nicodemus (Gk. name meaning "innocent of blood"), who as a Pharisee (v. 1) had long studied Scripture—even committing much of it to memory. He was also a member of the prestigious Jewish ruling council, the Sanhedrin (v. 10). In answer to his question, Jesus stated, **No one has ascended into heaven, except the One who descended from heaven—the Son of Man** (v. 13). No one, including Elijah who was translated to his heavenly reward in a chariot of fire (2 Kg 2:11), descended as did Jesus in His incarnation, living, dying, and then arising to ascend in the glory of His resurrection to take His place at the right hand of the Father (Mk 16:19). Jesus then turned to history by way of illustrating the salvific message He was preparing to share (v. 14). Moses in the wilderness was used to prefigure the crucifixion through the lifting up of the bronze snake in the midst of people who were dying from the venomous bites of the snakes in their midst (Nm 21:4-9). The Old Testament event pointed to Jesus who would be lifted up on the cross as the sacrifice necessary for salvation (vv. 16-18; 8:28; 12:32-34).

Eternal life emphasized the quality of life and its enduring nature even through ages to come. This biblical concept is more than immortality; it includes not only the soul but also the body. God created mankind for life and not death. "Eternal life" is inextricably linked to regeneration. In this text LIFE (Gk. *zōēn*, "living thing" in contrast to Gk. *bios*, "manner of life" or "period of duration of life") is modified by ETERNAL (Gk. *aionion*, "unending, everlasting, for all time"), a word used only by John in conjunction with life (vv. 15,16,36; 4:14,36; 5:24,39; 6:27,40,47, 54,68; 10:28; 12:25,50; 17:2-3). Having "eternal life" goes beyond living forever. Those confined to eternal punishment will experience its suffering throughout eternity. The experience is one that can never be exhausted because it is imperishable. Clearly this concept of eternal life involves an eschatological or future dimension as well as the present reality (3:36; 5:24; 6:47; 1 Jn 5:13).

The discussion concerning whether these words of salvific importance (3:16-21) came directly from Jesus or from John is a moot issue since every word of Scripture is God-breathed. The message is clear: Salvation is a gift for all who believe and trust in the Lord. God is the initiator and executor in salvation. Yet each person has a choice on how he responds.

Some have tried to present this picture of lostness as divine gloom and doom. However, one cannot miss the positive emphasis of a loving God drawing His children to Himself through His unconditional love and unending mercies. The contrast between belief and unbelief is clear as is the result of each.

3:22-36 The ministries of John the Baptist and of Jesus went on simultaneously for a time. But as time passed, Jesus' ministry grew as the Baptist's role began to fade. In the words of John the Baptist: **He must increase, but I must decrease** (v. 30).

The location of **Aenon** (v. 23, meaning "springs") may have been south of Bethshan, which seems more likely, or close to Shechem. **Salim** may have been an earlier name for Bethshan. The dispute between the disciples following John and those following Jesus was natural (vv. 25-26). What should be noted, however, is that John the Baptist not only refused to participate in the pettiness, but he also continued to affirm his own subordination to Jesus (vv. 27-30).

The closing verses of this chapter seem to summarize in testimony the person and work of Christ:

- Jesus came **from above** and His authority **is above all** (v. 31).

- Jesus spoke from personal observation (v. 32).

- Jesus stated **God's words** (vv. 33-34).

- **The Father loves the Son and has given all things into His hands** (v. 35), entrusting the Son to accomplish His purposes.

- Relationship to the Son is absolutely essential to escape **the wrath of God** (v. 36). In this verse both Greek participles *pisteuōn*, BELIEVING, and *apeithōn*, BEING DISOBEDIENT, are in contrast. One is either continually believing or being persuaded, or she is willfully defying

the word of God and thus refusing
to be persuaded.

Jesus, the Samaritan woman, and the official's son—a new diversity of followers (4:1-54)

4:1-2 Jesus obviously honored, encouraged (v. 1), and participated in baptism, having been baptized Himself by John the Baptist (Mt 3:13-17). Yet by His own words, He **was not baptizing,** suggesting these conclusions:

- Baptism is important and significant.

- Baptism is not optional.

- Baptism, although important, is not necessary for salvation.

4:3-42 John purposefully provided a remarkable contrast of characters by juxtaposing the encounter of Jesus with Nicodemus (3:1-21) and with the Samaritan woman (4:1-26) with a transition between the two. Nicodemus was a Pharisee, a powerful male Jew, who was well educated with special training in all matters concerning Jewish religious life. The Samaritan woman, on the other hand, was likely poor, uneducated, and a social outcast. Yet both experienced the loving witness of Jesus; both struggled with understanding the simple message; both responded and bore witness in their own respective ways (Nicodemus, 19:39; the Samaritan woman, 4:28,39).

When John recorded that Jesus **had to travel through Samaria,** a phrase punctuated by the Greek *edei* ("must, necessarily, ought, should"), one is reminded that Jesus never traveled at His own pleasure or because of human pressure; He waited for and received direction from the Father (Ps 40:8).

The area called **Samaria,** located on the main road between Judea and Galilee, about 40 miles north of Jerusalem, was the capital of the territory occupied by the 10 northern tribes of Israel. So much hostility existed between Samaria and Judah that the northern kings were unwilling for their subjects to worship at the Jerusalem temple. They set up a sacrificial system in their own territory. The area has remained hated by the Jews and a trouble spot even in the modern era. The Jews preferred to avoid the route, and most seemed to take alternate routes despite the longer distance.

The Samaritans, a remnant of Jews who intermarried with Gentiles during the Assyrian captivity endured by the northern kingdom (2 Kg 17:5-6,24), were considered by the Jews to be half-breeds because of their intermarriage with the pagan people among whom they were forced to live. The monotheism of Israel did become dominant, but with some innovations, including a rival temple on Mount Gerizim, located about 40 miles north of Jerusalem (v. 20). A small Samaritan community continues to worship there. The Samaritans traditionally celebrate Passover outdoors under a full moon in order to reenact the first Passover as faithfully as possible. The Passover lamb is slain. At sunset the men who are heads of households take their lambs to the area for sacrifice. The lambs' throats are cut simultaneously; the blood is drained from the carcasses; the animals are skinned and roasted. The meal begins about midnight.

Since the disciples went to purchase food, some commercial interactions occurred (v. 8). Perhaps the phrase, **for Jews do not associate** (Gk. *sugchrōntai,* "having dealings with or associating on friendly terms") **with Samaritans,** had more to do with sharing vessels for food or, as here, for drink (v. 9).

Although **Jacob's well** is not mentioned in the Old Testament, the traditional site in ancient **Sychar** (vv. 5-6) is identified in the modern era as it has been for centuries. Gathering water was usually done in early morning or late afternoon and not at noon, the hottest part of the day. Some commentators identify **about six in the evening** as the sixth hour (Gk. *ektos*, v. 6), which if determined from 6 a.m. would mean noon; but according to the Roman plan, the time would be reclaimed either from midnight or noon, making the hour—whether early morning or late afternoon—more appropriate for hauling water. Whether the woman was fetching water at the usual time or deliberately going at midday to avoid other people matters not. The fact that the presence of others was not mentioned might make the latter a more reasonable explanation.

Jesus broke social and religious norms in three significant ways:

- He spoke to a woman (v. 7).

- He interacted with someone from a different ethnic and religious background (and one despised by the Jews, v. 9).

- He associated with someone who had obviously indulged in immoral behavior (v. 17).

John showed the absolute impartiality of the gospel message, which ignores social and religious boundaries and is extended to all.

Heart to Heart:
Women as Witnesses (Jn 4:1-30)

*O*n an ordinary day and in an extraordinary way, Jesus gave "living water" to a sinful woman who came to the well for water. Crossing all social barriers, Jesus offered the scorned woman redemption and eternal life. By faith she was saved. The forgiven woman, no longer ashamed, returned to her city to share the good news: "Come, see a man who told me all the things I have done; this is not the Christ, is it?" (Jn 4:29). The Samaritan woman testified of the Lord's work in her life, and many who had shunned her in the past responded to her witness. Jesus later challenged His disciples to witness in Jerusalem, Judea, Samaria, to the ends of the earth—in their own neighborhoods and around the world (Ac 1:8). Redeemed women today must be witnesses of His life-changing grace.

In verses 10-15, Jesus turned the conversation to spiritual matters. For Jewish purification rituals, flowing water was often preferred to well water, and the reference may mean "flowing water" in contradistinction to well water. In the Old Testament *Yahweh* is referred to as "the fountain of living water" (Jr 2:13; 17:13). Jesus described the Holy Spirit as providing "streams of living water" (Jn 7:38), resulting in the endless supply—a blessing of eternal life. The woman immedi-

ately acknowledged that she would like this **living water** (v. 15). Jesus then focused on her personal life (vv. 16-19). Not only did Jesus' omniscience come into play, but Jesus also demonstrated His compassion even for the outcasts of society. Yet He required them to repent since repentance is the necessary condition for all who come to him. The woman was impressed by Jesus' ability to penetrate her life and thoughts. She not only responded to the invitation to take the "living water," but she also went out and told everyone she saw that she had met **a man who told** her **everything** she **ever did** (vv. 28-29).

Despite the woman's attempt to change the subject, she was moved to take the conversation precisely where Jesus wanted it to go (vv. 20-24). As a result, Jesus accomplished His purpose to bring her to salvation. John's purpose was also served: He showed Jesus Himself as being the replacement for all holy places. Jesus revealed Himself as the Messiah (vv. 25-26). He came into the world as one from the lineage of David and from the tribe of Judah (v. 22). Jesus described God as Spirit. He had no limitations of time and space (omnipresent). No idols or images were needed since the divine presence resides within every believer.

The Jews of Samaria expected the Messiah (v. 25) because there were prophecies about Him in the Pentateuch. However, because they rejected the rest of the Old Testament, their understanding was flawed and incomplete. Jesus identified Himself as **the One** (v. 26). The woman acknowledged this but with little understanding of what that meant. Even the disciples called Jesus "Messiah" before they came to an adequate understanding of what that designation really meant. The title "Messiah" in the Old Testament, as the title "Christ" in the New Testament, was connected to the announcement of a coming "anointed one." Jesus continued to reveal Himself as the woman began to grow in her understanding of who He is. How affirming of John's stated purpose (Jn 20:31) for other Samaritans to come to believe through her testimony (4:42).

Later Jesus would challenge His disciples to witness in Samaria (Ac 1:8), and Philip began a mission there (Ac 8:5). But the first witness in Samaria came from the testimony of a sinful, immoral woman whose life was changed by an encounter with Christ. She received the "living water" and was forgiven, cleansed, and revived.

Jesus' disciples were shocked to find Him speaking **with a woman**. But Jesus exhorted His disciples to recognize **the fields** ready for spiritual harvests. He used the analogy of the grain harvest to emphasize the urgency of harvesting souls. There was more work to be done, regardless of the immediate results (vv. 37-38). **Many Samaritans** came to believe in Jesus as **the Savior of the world**.

The Samaritan Woman
John 4:1-26

Jesus met a sinful woman at the well in Samaria. Though tired from His journey, the Savior offered forgiveness and freedom to this woman in bondage.

Freedom from <u>Self</u>	• Personal limitations • Human weaknesses • Sinful lifestyle
Freedom from <u>Social Prejudice</u>	• Religious differences • Racial barriers • Limited understanding
Freedom from <u>Sin</u>	• Immoral behavior • Adulterous relationships • Rejection of God

Excursus: The Samaritan Woman

The woman of Samaria is known by her lifestyle and ethnic heritage more than her name. In fact, her name is not mentioned. During His earthly ministry, Jesus came in contact with this woman under ordinary circumstances in an extraordinary way. Because of her unethical lifestyle, she was "unacceptable" to those around her. People went out of their way to avoid her.

John referred to her as a "woman of Samaria" (Jn 4:7). By leaving her unnamed, perhaps the apostle was attempting to give his audience a deeper impression of her perceived unworthiness or to focus more on the woman's unacceptable lifestyle. John may not have known her name. Perhaps, on the other hand, the apostle wanted to emphasize how Jesus valued those considered unacceptable by the world. This woman did have a troublesome immoral background.

> No woman, whatever stigma she may bear, is excluded from Christ's call to discipleship.

Christ brought out the best in the Samaritan woman. In the process of unveiling her dark past (v. 17), He brought to light a woman. Many women, even if known by a good name, carry baggage from their past. They know what it is like to feel unknown, unworthy, and unacceptable. A message of hope and inspiration comes from the life of the Samaritan woman. Christ saw more than her sin and degradation. He saw a woman in need, a woman with the potential to be a fruitful disciple. And He gave her a chance to come to Him in faith. She, in turn, broke from the religious traditions of her own people and from her own personal sin and followed Him on the path of discipleship.

The fact that John even recorded Christ's encounter with this unnamed and "unacceptable" Samaritan woman communicates a powerful message. No woman, whatever stigma she may bear, is excluded from Christ's call to discipleship. Jesus' ministry was revolutionary in many ways, but it was especially so with regard to women.

Jesus did not avoid women or look down on them. On the contrary, with every encounter He gave them an opportunity to believe and to become His disciples, as is clearly seen in His encounter with the Samaritan woman. Christ decisively broke through the barriers created by her sinful lifestyle and brought out the best in her. And she responded to His call to discipleship. Because she responded to Christ's call cautiously but with determination, she stands as a noble example of a woman who became a committed and witnessing disciple of Christ.

The Samaritan woman was the first "witness" to the Samaritan people concerning the works of Jesus. Her role as a disciple is clearly seen. The most important role of discipleship in Johannine theology is the proclamation of Jesus' true identity. Though she was slow to believe at first, her testimony still bore fruit and her witness stood firm (vv. 36-38).

4:43-54 Both Matthew and Luke recorded the healing of the centurion's slave (Mt 8:5-13; Lk 7:1-10). John recorded Jesus' encounter with **the royal official,** who asked for the healing of his son (v. 46). Both men were prominent and powerful, and both were from Capernaum. John used this account to demonstrate that miraculous signs can produce faith. Since John identified this event as the **second sign** (v. 54), the two events in Cana (cf. 2:11) would seem to be related in some way. Whether a Jew or Gentile, the **royal official** surprisingly sought the help of Jesus, the son of a humble carpenter (vv. 46-47). The reference to **his whole household** (v. 53) in the ancient world would include his immediate and extended family as well as servants. The head of the household would obviously be very influential in determining the spiritual direction of those who found shelter under his roof. Certainly there was no way to enter the household of faith without believing, and the verb (Gk. *pisteusen,* "believe") would affirm that understanding.

Jesus and the Jewish Festivals (5:1–10:21)

Healing the paralytic and imitating the Father (5:1-47)

Chapters 5–10 represent another literary unit, describing the events that took place when Jesus was in Jerusalem for the religious festivals. This section supplements the Synoptic record of Jesus' Galilean ministry. John meticulously showed that Jesus was the fulfillment of the Jewish festivals: Passover, Tabernacles, and Hanukkah (Dedication). In John's Gospel the feeding of the 5,000 and Jesus' walking on water, which did not occur in Jerusalem, were recorded as taking place around the time of the Passover. In John, these miracles were followed by a lengthy discourse on the Bread of Life (chap. 6), in which the symbolism was closely related to the bread of the Passover meal.

5:1-15 The healing of the paralytic was significant because it sparked a controversy with the Jewish leaders, who began to plot how they might kill Jesus (vv. 17-18); and the discourse following this event revealed Jesus' relationship with the Father.

The healing took place on a Sabbath. Jesus was **by the Sheep Gate,** one of the entrances carved into Jerusalem's city wall. The group of pools were actually deep stone reservoirs collecting rainwater to be used for drinking and other necessities. Water has always been a precious resource in the Middle East. The **pool called Bethesda** was especially prominent as a gathering place for the sick and maimed because the people believed healing properties were in its waters (v. 3). The tradition concerning **the moving of the water** is not found in extant Greek manuscripts dated prior to AD 400. This brief section (parts of vv. 3-4) may have been based on popular tradition and thus have been added by a scribe as an effort to explain the bubbly flow of the water that occurred from time to time (v. 7). This insignificant textual problem does not undercut the miracle or clear meaning of the text in any way.

Near the modern Church of St. Anne is a group of pools many archaeologists have identified as this popular ancient site. At this pool Jesus singled out a man and asked if he wanted **to get well** (v. 6). Jesus perceived a relationship between the man's illness and past sin (v. 14). What that sin might have been is not indicated. John made no mention of the man's response to Jesus after their second encounter but reported that the Jews began to persecute Jesus as a result of His healing the man on **the Sabbath.** Although the Jewish festival is not identified (v. 1), evidently this Sabbath controversy is focused on the proper requirements for keeping the Sabbath. The Sabbath, the day God rested from His creative activity of fashioning the world and all in it (Gn 2:2-3), was the seventh day of the week. It became a holy day set apart for rest and worship for all Jews, and the concept has carried over into Christianity with setting aside the first day of the week (commemorating the resurrection) or Sunday.

Among the Jews, desecrating the Sabbath was punishable by death, and the criteria for dishonoring the Sabbath were greatly expanded in the numerous oral laws that had been added to the Law of Moses. The prohibition against carrying one's bed had been added to that oral tradition (v. 10).

The man's negative attitude was apparent and seemingly did not change. He was so indifferent and ungrateful that he did not even inquire about Jesus' identity (v. 13).

5:16-41 John seemed to focus not on the paralytic's response to Jesus but rather on the Jews' response to Jesus. Evidence for this conclusion can be seen in the discourse following this event in which Jesus defended His actions (vv. 19-47).

Jesus' disregard for Sabbath regulations was not the only thing upsetting the Jewish religious leaders. They actually sought His life because of His **calling God His own Father**, thus **making Himself equal with God** (v. 18). John, of course, stated his own purpose as showing that Jesus is indeed the Son of God (20:31).

The parallel between the Son and the Father was continually asserted by John. Never is the Father subordinate to the Son. Rather, the Son is sent by the Father, obedient to the Father, and committed to glorifying the Father (5:23,27,30; 6:44; 8:28-29). The Son was given power by the Father **to pass judgment** (5:27). Jesus described His relationship with the Father as being one in which He is *ontologically*

(of the same essence or being) equal with the Father yet *functionally* subordinate to Him. "The Father initiates, sends, commands, grants; the Son responds, obeys, performs his Father's will, receives authority."[4]

Human action is a manifestation of human commitment (v. 29; see also Eph 2:10; Jms 2:14-17). But there is no hint of a works' salvation. These verses are among the few eschatological references in John. The idea is that human works simply bear testimony to decisions in the hearts of individuals—whether to follow righteousness or wickedness.

Jesus presented four witnesses who affirmed His claims (vv. 31-47): John the Baptist (vv. 33-35); His own deeds (v. 36); the Father (vv. 37-38); and Scripture (vv. 39-47). The Jews were tied to the legacy of the great lawgiver Moses (v. 45). Jesus presented Himself as a living testimony to the Father, and He challenged their unbelief and rejection of Him (v. 43). Jesus did affirm that Moses wrote Scripture (v. 46), and these verses are critically important to affirming Jesus' view of Scripture. He believed that Moses wrote the Pentateuch. Either He was wrong or He accommodated Himself to the Jewish tradition or He was correct in affirming the Mosaic authorship of the Torah. The latter, of course, is the only option consistent with His deity.

The True Passover: The Bread of Life (6:1-71)

6:1-21 The **mountain** Jesus ascended was east of the **Sea of Galilee**, an area known as the Golan Heights (v. 3). The feeding of the 5,000 was the one miracle recorded by all the Gospel writers (Mt 14:15; Mk 6:35; Lk 9:12); only Luke failed to mention the "walking-on-water miracle" (Mt 14:22; Mk 6:47; Jn 6:15-21). In verse 7, Philip was astonished by Jesus' request to feed the large multitude. Even though **200 denarii** amounted to almost two-thirds of a yearly wage (Mt 20:2), still this sum could not feed the 5,000 men plus the women and children assembled. The crowd tried to **take Him by force** because they were convinced after seeing Jesus' miracles, especially His feeding the crowd of people with so few resources, that He was the conquering king they needed to lead them in overthrowing the Roman government and setting up a new kingdom through which they would benefit (vv. 14-15). The disciples continued to show spiritual immaturity as Jesus came to rescue them in the midst of a storm (v.19). As is characteristic, John used these fourth and fifth sign miracles to introduce another lengthy discourse from Jesus.

This "Bread of Life" discourse (6:22-40) was significant because it functioned in John's narrative much the way the parable of the sower did in the Synoptic Gospels. Jesus used this discourse as a "weeding out" tool to separate true believers from those who followed Him merely to benefit from His miracles. Also, the discourse clearly communicated that Jesus, as the Bread of Life, was the true fulfillment of the Passover. The Passover is mentioned elsewhere in John (2:13,23; 6:4; 11:55; 12:1; 13:1; 18:28,39; 19:14).

6:22-71 Jesus implored the crowd to seek that which would endure—**the food that lasts for eternal life** (v. 27). When asked by the crowd what these works might be, Jesus responded by saying that **the work of God** is to **believe in the One He has sent** (v. 29).

Faith based on the performing of miracles is not enough. A contrast is made between Jesus and Moses, under whose leadership God supplied *manna* to feed the Israelites as they left Egypt and made their journey through the wilderness for 40 years (v. 31). The *manna*, a small, round wafer that appeared with the morn-ing dew and thus designated **bread from heaven** (v. 31), was gathered by the people, made into cakes, and baked or boiled (Ex 16:13-36). The Old Testament *manna* was a prototype pointing to Jesus, **the real bread from heaven** who would provide unfailing sustenance and satisfaction (vv. 32-33).

I am the bread of life is the first of seven "I am" axioms, which are recorded only in John. The metaphors Jesus used include:

- bread of life (6:35,41,48,51),
- light of the world (8:12; 9:5),
- door of the sheep (10:7,9),
- good shepherd (10:11,14),
- resurrection and the life (11:25),
- way, truth, and life (14:6), and
- true vine (15:1,5).

> *Only those who are true believers are secure. Hence, one must make sure that her faith is based solely on Christ Himself and not merely on His miracles!*

John continued to build an understanding of the theological underpinnings of salvation. Jesus clearly attributed the initiation of salvation to God, who draws all unto Himself (v. 37; see also 1:12-13). God's grace is continual and inexhaustible and without bounds.

One must have faith in Jesus Himself (vv. 30-31). *True* followers of Christ have great assurance because Christ will not lose a single one the Father has given Him (vv. 37-40). These verses support the eternal security of the believer. However, one must not ignore the immediate context of these verses. Only those who are true believers are secure. Hence, one must make sure that her faith is based solely on Christ Himself and not merely on His miracles!

There has been much debate concerning the meaning of eating Christ's flesh and drinking His blood (vv. 51-58). Some have argued that these words are a reference to the Eucharist. However, nothing in the immediate context warrants this interpretation. Rather, eating Christ's flesh and drinking His blood are vivid metaphors describing the kind of relationship true believers must have with Christ. Just as food is necessary to sustain physical life, so partaking of Christ, the Bread of Life, is required for spiritual life (vv. 54-57). They must be willing to identify with Him and assimilate His life within their own lives so that they would be willing to suffer and die with Him. This assimilation is accomplished by taking in, being formed by, and obeying His Word. Clearly not many who were following Jesus at the time were willing so to identify themselves with Him. Many walked away because the teaching was too **hard** (vv. 60-66). After this, Jesus addressed **the Twelve** (v. 67). Verses 68-71 represent the kind of confession given by Peter in the Synoptic Gospels. Jesus is **the Holy One of God**, and He alone has the words of eternal life. Thus, John was presenting the Twelve as *true* followers of Christ because they were the ones who stuck with Him.

The true tabernacles: living water and the light of the world (7:1–9:41)

Chapters 7–9 are intended to show Jesus as the fulfillment of the Feast of Tabernacles. The Feast of Tabernacles or Feast of Ingathering or Feast of Booths was celebrated "on the fifteenth day of the seventh month" (Lv 23:34), beginning five days after the Day of Atonement (*Yom Kippur*) and lasting seven days (Lv 23:33-36; Dt 16:13-17). Each family gathered in Jerusalem and built temporary shelters or booths in which they would live during the entire festival. This temporary housing was symbolic of the years the Israelites spent wandering in the desert after leaving slavery in Egypt before entering Canaan, and these dwellings represented shelter and protection. The feast was a time of thanksgiving for the harvest, which marked their transition from nomadic living to more permanent housing in their own land. John's allusion to the feasts highlighted the way Jesus fulfilled the Old Testament celebration and added to them ongoing spiritual significance.

7:1-9 Some raise the question of fearfulness on the part of Jesus when **He did not want to travel in Judea because the Jews were trying to kill Him** (v. 1). Jesus had no fear in the sense of human anxiety, but He was committed in His subordination to the Father to the timing of His mission. He did make changes in His itinerary to avoid those who sought His life because His time had not yet come (v. 8; 2:4; 7:30; 8:20).

John began this section by juxtaposing the true belief of the disciples (6:68-71) with the unbelief of Jesus' own brothers (7:1-5). The perpetual virginity of Mary advocated by some is certainly challenged in the references to other sons of Mary and Joseph (v. 3; 2:12; Mk 3:21,31-35; 6:3). A similar scene was recorded in Mark 3:20-35, in which Jesus' family members came to silence Him because they believed He was out of His mind. Although His brothers did not understand Him, the disciples who believed in Him did. In John's narrative, this contrast between belief and unbelief, displayed respectively by the Twelve and by Jesus' brothers, was a foreshadowing of similar things to come as Jesus later went alone to the festival (v. 10).

7:10-36 Jesus responded to the question concerning the origin of His teachings (vv. 15-16). The Jewish leaders could not understand how Jesus could know the

Scripture so thoroughly, teach with clarity, and speak with authority without formal training in rabbinical schools. THE SCRIPTURES (Gk. *grammata*, "letters of the alphabet or education"), when used in plural form, referred to a document, epistle, or book. Here, as is common elsewhere, the reference is to rabbinical learning under a rabbi. TRAINED (Gk. *memathēkōs*, "learn or study") has the sense of one who has passed through the school of the masters. The Sanhedrin expressed the same shock over the bold teaching of Peter and John because they had not been trained (Gk. *agrammatoi*, "unlettered") by the rabbis (Ac 4:13). The teaching rabbis were not as concerned about explaining the Scriptures as much as training their pupils to recite the opinions of the teachers of the law. They saw the opinions of other rabbis, especially the oral tradition, as the chief component in learning. Jesus certainly did not fit their mold, and they challenged His right to teach. Jesus responded quickly and decisively that His teaching was vested in the authority of **the One who sent** Him (v. 16). Jesus also placed squarely upon His accusers the responsibility for determining the work of God (6:28-29), which if they had done would have revealed that indeed His teaching was **from God** (vv. 17-18). In so doing Jesus reached to the heart of their challenging His teaching by raising His own counter questions concerning their understanding of the law and their willingness to manipulate it. He used their desire **to kill** Him (v. 19), which was contrary to the prohibition of murder in the Decalogue (Ex 20:13), to show they were in violation of their own standard. Jesus also noted that the law forbade all but emergency medical attention; however, the religious leaders allowed **circumcision** but not healing **on the Sabbath** (vv. 19-20).

The Dispersion (v. 35) or Diaspora extended through several centuries of history, during which time the Jews were forced out of Palestine and scattered throughout the world. First the Assyrians invaded and captured the land or the northern kingdom in Israel (722 BC), and then the Babylonians captured the southern kingdom or Judah (586 BC). In both of these overwhelming defeats, the people were slaughtered and taken out of the land and into captivity. Among the remaining remnant, some who experienced famine or disasters simply immigrated to other countries for food or work. By the time of Christ there were as many Jews living outside the land as in the land. Jesus was aware of the crowd's hostility and predicted His coming death, albeit in a veiled manner so that the people were not certain of His meaning (vv. 33-36).

7:37-52 Rituals accompanying the feasts often included the pouring out of water to picture God's provision of water to the people during their wandering in the wilderness (Ex 17:6) and in times of drought in the land (1 Kg 18:45). This provision of water was temporary relief to their thirst. Therefore, considering their life in an arid, desert terrain, the people would understand the metaphor of Jesus' offer of thirst-quenching water as ultimate sustenance and satisfaction. The **living water** was imagery Jesus took from the Old Testament (see Is 32:15; 44:3; Ezk 39:29; Jl 2:28-32) to use as a metaphor for the gift of the Holy Spirit to be poured out on the disciples after Jesus' death and resurrection. Obviously the people were ignorant of the fact that Jesus was born in Bethlehem (Jn 7:1-42).

Nicodemus appeared again and attempted to protect Jesus from His accusers (vv. 50-52), which probably indicated that he had indeed been converted in his earlier encounter with Jesus (3:1-3). Nicodemus here intervened openly in behalf of Jesus even in the midst of the hostile religious establishment of which he had been a part.

7:53–8:11 The unfolding of the narrative concerning the **woman caught in adultery** is consistent with Jesus' character and His ministry. The story could have been handed down by word of mouth and then finally integrated into the Gospel of John. There is no good reason to doubt its authenticity.

The pericope is not found in the Alexandrian text or in most of the prominent ancient versions; but it is found in almost 1,000 manuscripts, and commentary on the passage is found in the fourth-century writings of Augustine and Jerome. Whether or not the details of this event were penned by John himself or added later is immaterial. No questionable doctrinal position is found, and the account is seen by many as appropriate to this sequence of events. The theme of judging has been introduced (v. 51), and the story flows naturally. Some commentators do not consider the passage Johannine in style and view it as not fitting the context; yet for most evangelicals, as well as Roman Catholic theologians, the pericope is regarded as being canonical.

Most important is the lesson found in the story. Jesus gave an incomparable example of how He dealt with His legalistic critics who were testing His commitment to the law and attempting to entrap Him, while reaching out to the sinful woman—considered untouchable—in her need. He never glossed over moral standards but graciously extended mercy. No one could bring together what seemed to be polar opposites as did Jesus.

Heart to Heart:
Forgiveness and Light

The scribes and Pharisees asked Jesus a trick question that skeptics ask today: How can you forgive one so sinful? The loving response of Jesus to His judgmental followers is a pattern for every generation: "Neither do I [Jesus] condemn you. Go, and from now on do not sin any more" (Jn 8:11). The sinful woman, though ungodly and immoral, was not condemned by Jesus. Christians are not to judge those who sin. Forgiveness is the Christlike response. God can reach out to the fallen with His saving grace and work through Christians if His followers will love and receive sinners. Forgiveness is not earned or deserved; it is freely given by those who love the Lord. If those who live in darkness are forgiven, they can walk in the light. Don't be like the scribes and Pharisees who thought the sins of the adulterous woman were beyond forgiveness. Know that God forgives and restores all who sin. Share this hope with women who feel the shame and guilt of their sins. Assure them as Jesus did: "I am the light of the world. Anyone who follows Me will never walk in the darkness but will have the light of life" (Jn 8:12).

Only the woman was presented (v. 4) in this account; whereas in the Torah both the man and the woman (if betrothed or engaged) were to be put to death by stoning (Dt 22:23-24) and by an unspecified method if the woman were married (Lv 20:10; Dt 22:22). Jesus' conclusion was not what they expected but continued to confound them (v. 7). Jesus in no way ignored sin and its consequences, but here He saw the hearts and motivation of these self-righteous accusers who were using a woman to accomplish their own purpose of seeking to entrap Him. In Jewish law the witness was to cast the first stone when capital punishment was involved (Dt 17:5-7). The accusing group slowly departed, beginning with the most revered members and **the older men** (Gk. *presbuterōn*). Surely this woman must have been shocked and overwhelmed to meet a man who, instead of exploiting and using her for his own lustful and selfish purposes, showed loving concern and extended forgiving grace. Jesus not only refused to condemn her, but He redeemed and restored her. Only Jesus as the sinless One could forgive her sin (1:29).

The Forgiven Adulteress John 8:1-12	
The Judge	Jesus Christ (v. 1)
The Courtroom	The temple complex (v. 2)
The Accusers	The scribes and Pharisees (v. 3)
The Accused	An unnamed woman (v. 3)
The Crime	Adultery (v. 3)
The Evidence	Caught in the act (v. 4)
The Penalty	Death by stoning (v. 5)
The Motive	To trap Jesus and accuse Him of breaking the law (v. 6)
The Defense	• Jesus wrote on the ground with His finger (v. 6). • He said, "The one without sin among you should be the first to throw a stone at her" (v. 7). • Again He wrote on the ground (v. 8).
The Response	They left one by one (v. 9).
The Verdict	• Jesus asked, "Has no one condemned you?" (v. 10). • Jesus responded, "Neither do I condemn you. Go, and from now on do not sin any more" (v. 11).

8:12-20 John did not indicate the exact timing of these words from Jesus, but they were delivered during His visit to Jerusalem and possibly some time after the Feast of Tabernacles. While in the temple complex, Jesus made a second proclamation: **I am the light of the world** (v. 12). During the Feast of Tabernacles the great Menorah or lampstand was lighted. The special lighting in the court of the women initiated the festival on the first night and probably continued except on the eve of the Sabbath. The lights, of course, were symbolic, reminding the people of the pillar of fire that led them through the wilderness (Ex 13:21; Nm 9:15-23). Undoubtedly the spiritual lessons were also helpful in calling the people to recommitment to *Yahweh,* who so faithfully had led and would continue to lead them. Jesus in His second "I Am" declaration utilized His Old Testament symbol and imagery to reveal Himself as being the Light to reveal divine truth in a nation overcome by moral and spiritual darkness (v. 12; see also 1:4,9). Its shadow would have been cast over the court of the women where Jesus was teaching. This declaration brought Jesus into sharp conflict with the Pharisees, who challenged

His claim and questioned the legitimacy of His testimony concerning Himself (v. 13). Jesus had already called forth witnesses to His words: the testimony of John the Baptist, His own works, the imprimatur of the Father, and the affirmation of Scripture (5:33-47). However, for these self-righteous religious leaders, nothing would satisfy.

The question from the Pharisees (v. 19) could have been a legitimate inquiry reflecting the confusion in their own minds just as easily as an insult to Jesus' paternity. One is always wise to move slowly when considering judging motivations in the hearts of others. Nevertheless, even when Jesus answered, they refused to acknowledge His connection to the Father; and they continued to ask the same questions (v. 25) and ignore His answers. Despite their hostility, Jesus was protected from them until His work was completed (v. 20).

Thirteen trumpet-shaped containers were placed in **the treasury** as a place for receiving offerings from the people (see Mk 12:41-44 and the account of the widow who gave her "two tiny coins"). The treasury is commonly noted as being in the court of women within reach of women whose sacrificial giving has been a matter of record through the generations.

8:21-29 Throughout the Gospel of John there is a path to the cross. **When you lift up the Son of Man** is another marker (v. 28). LIFT UP (Gk. *hupsōgēte*, "raise high, exalt") was used in reference to the cross (3:14) with which Jesus compared the "pole" on which the "bronze serpent" was mounted in the wilderness (Nm 21:9). The word often has the sense of setting something in a place of prominence or exalting. John later developed this theme more clearly in chapter 12 (12:32).

The Jews knew exactly what Jesus was claiming—He declared Himself to be the Old Testament "I AM that I AM"—God Himself. The words I AM (Gk. *egō eimi*) are significant, occurring three times in this discourse (vv. 24,28,58). Some commentators believe these words are alluding to the title of God, revealed to Moses when he was commissioned by Yahweh God to lead the enslaved Israelites out of Egypt (Ex 3:14). Jesus' claim cannot be missed: Jesus is *Yahweh* God of the Old Testament. Rich in meaning, the title affirms preexistence and eternality. But the lesson does not stop with this affirmation of unity with the Father. The following phrase **I do nothing on my own** (v. 28) affirms yet again the Son's subordination, as the Redeemer and bearer of the message of salvation, to the Father. Four times Jesus noted that He had been sent by the Father (vv. 16,18,26,29). The Son's devotion to the Father and His voluntary obedience to the will of the Father provide a perfect model for biblical submission. Equality in being but uniqueness in role is again affirmed. Here is a climatic declaration of the gospel and a beautiful unfolding of the theological foundations for the Godhead.

8:30-47 John appealed again to one of his favorite themes: Only those who have genuine faith are truly disciples, and they alone will experience true spiritual freedom (vv. 30-33). The people appealed to their relationship to Abraham to show that they had **never been enslaved to anyone** (v. 33). But Jesus quickly pointed out the true **descendants of Abraham** in contrast to those who are children of the Devil (vv. 34-47). He set forth clearly the requirements for discipleship.

Jesus made clear that disobedience to God would mean slavery in the sense that in so doing one not only increases alienation from God and prevents fellowship with God but also falls more and more into the grasp of the evil one, making escape more and more difficult (v. 34). The participle translated COMMITS (Gk. *poiōn*, "make, do, cause, bring about, produce") is in the present tense, implying a continual habit of sinning, not merely intermittent acts. Jesus used the analogy from the family to contrast a son whose status in the family had permanent bonds and the privileges rightfully his because of family bonds with the slave who as an outsider could not claim family ties or privileges (v. 35). His point was clear: Genuine freedom was not in their ancestry but in Christ (v. 36). True heirs of Abraham are not merely those who have descended from his loins physically but those who have accepted and exercised his faith. Sin controls and binds, and only Christ can offer freedom from that bondage, which then enables one to do what she ought in order to please God (v. 36).

Blind trust in religious tradition and rituals or depending upon one's ancestry or trying to obey the law and oral traditions would be futile. They were indeed **descendants of Abraham**, a holy nation elect and chosen by God; but their sinful rebellion had caused them to be repeatedly enslaved in Egypt, Babylonia, Persia, Syria, and at this time by the Romans. Far more important than political freedom was spiritual freedom, and that would be found only in Christ.

When Jesus asked the rhetorical question **Why don't you understand** (Gk. *ginōskete*, "know, find out, perceive"), He went clearly to the root of the problem. The people were INHERENTLY UNABLE (Gk. *ou dunasthe*) to LISTEN (Gk. *akouein*, "hear, give heed to, understand"). The latter word entailed more than hearing words but rather included the idea of paying attention to and incorporating into life what has been heard. It is hearing with intent to obey.

The people did not respond with obedience and commitment to Jesus because their allegiance was to another. They belonged to their **father the Devil**. Here Jesus gave a clear warning concerning the Devil and described his work in detail (v. 44):

- His name DEVIL (Gk. *diabolou*, "slanderer") describes his work. The Greek preposition *dia*, meaning "through," is combined with the Greek verb *ballō*, meaning "throw or cast" or even "assault, strike." The Devil then is the one who "casts through" or slanders.

- He is the father of those who oppose God.

- "He was a MURDERER (Gk. *anthrōpoktonos*, *anthroposan* or "man" linked with *kteinō*, meaning "slay or kill") from the beginning." He deceived Adam and in doing so, he robbed him, and all who came after, of life and immortality. This rare compound word is unique. *Anthropos*, referring to man, is a common word; but *kteinō* is not even found in the lexicon of words used in the Greek New Testament. In fact, seemingly only here is this compound word found in the New Testament. According to Liddell and Scott's classical Greek lexicon, the word is used frequently by the Greek poets with the sense of "kill or slay."[5] Not only was Jesus thoroughly skilled in usage of the Greek language, but He was very precise in expressing the truths He sought to teach. The seriousness of the evil one brought forth what seems to be a uniquely coined word to describe the Devil's evil intent.

- He **has not stood** in the **truth**. STOOD (Gk. *stēken*, "stand firm") suggests a steadfast stance, which might allow some wiggle room; but Jesus reinforced the Devil's assault against truth by adding "because there is no truth in him." Lying was a pattern for his life. **He speaks from his own nature**.

- **He is a liar and the father of liars**. The Devil uttered the first lie in the garden of Eden, and he continues to breed deceit into everyone with whom he has influence or control (Gn 3:4).

8:48-59 To accuse Jesus of being a demon-possessed **Samaritan** was an expression of heightened hostility and determined opposition as well as a double slur against His character. With the "Samaritan" designation, which in itself was a figure of speech expressing **dishonor**, the Jews probably were referencing Jesus' differences with their traditional interpretations of the law since they viewed any differences as heresy. In John's Gospel, Jesus was accused of demon possession three times (7:20; 8:52; 10:20), a label probably understood as meaning "deranged" or "crazy." Such disrespectful name-calling was typical of mob reaction. Jesus was straightforward in refuting their allegations concerning His character, and He was clear in connecting Himself with the Father and in revealing that His purpose was to glorify the Father and accomplish His will above all else (vv. 49-51).

The Jews had no understanding of eternal life and considered that concept ridiculous and nonsensical. Jesus distinguished between physical death and spiritual death and simply affirmed that one who believed in Him would not suffer spiritual death but would in fact inherit life everlasting (v. 52; see also Rv 2:11; 20:6).

Jesus was often subtle in the verbal affirmations of His deity. He chose to live His life and do His work so that His deity would not be questioned with any objective consideration. He never denied that He was God, but He did continually point to the Father and glorify Him, knowing that in so doing He would be vindicating Himself.

His reference to **My day** was looking forward to His redemptive work on the cross (v. 56). He did allude to His deity in a veiled way, **Before Abraham was, I am** (v. 58), implying continuing existence without beginning or end. "I am" in the Jewish mind was recognized as a title of deity (Ex 3:14). Obviously the crowd, perhaps inflamed by the religious leaders in their midst, understood exactly what Jesus was saying. They tried to stone Him, and He simply vanished from them, not because of fear or intimidation but because His time had not yet come (v. 59; see 7:30).

9:1-41 Jesus once again healed on the **Sabbath** (v. 14). The one He healed had been **blind** all his life. Jesus healed in an unusual way (v. 6). Using this method, Jesus could be accused not only of breaking the Old Testament law concerning the Sabbath but also of breaking the Pharisaic law forbidding the use of spittle on the Sabbath. The man whose sight was restored confessed faith in Jesus and even proceeded to worship Him. He clearly had seen the light. His "sight" (faith or belief) was juxtaposed with the Pharisees' "blindness" (unbelief).

Blindness was undoubtedly common in the ancient world. Jesus had healed others who were blind (Mt 9:27-31; 12:22; 15:30; 21:14; Mk 8:22-26; 10:46-52). In the view of the Jews, whether from a birth defect, infection, advanced age, or as a side effect from some other debilitating illness, blindness was the result of sin. Some Jews believed the man could have sinned while still in his mother's womb, or he could have sinned before his conception (an idea from the Greek philosopher Plato). On the other hand, perhaps the sin of his parents brought this affliction upon their son (see Ex 20:5; 34:7; Nm 14:18).

The Bible does trace suffering to moral causes. For example, death came ultimately to all because of Adam's sin (Rm 5:12-21). Children do sometimes suffer because of the sins of their parents (Ex 34:7). One of the greatest tragedies of sin comes in its far-reaching effect, hurting the innocent as well as the guilty. Personal sin can also cause suffering (Dt 28:15-68; Jr 31:30). However, biblical teachings have been distorted and misunderstood. Jesus replied clearly that in this case the man's blindness had been allowed so **that God's works might be displayed in him**. What a comforting blessing to know that in suffering one can exalt Christ (Rm 8:28; 1 Pt 2:21). In this healing, Jesus not only showed His power to restore physical sight, but He also revealed His power to give spiritual sight and light. He used another "I am" metaphor—**I am the light of the world** (v. 5).

The **pool of Siloam** (v. 7), located just inside the wall in the southeastern corner of the city of Jerusalem, was built in the first century to improve public access to the waters from the Gihon Spring. As early as the eighth century BC, King Hezekiah built a 583-yard tunnel bringing waters from the Gihon Spring into Jerusalem in the event of a siege by his enemies. This engineering masterpiece, called Hezekiah's tunnel, was built through solid rock. The Siloam pool, measuring 20 by 30 feet, is used as a source of water even today.

The fact of the man's healing could not be disputed. Too many family members and friends who knew of his lifelong affliction now saw that condition completely reversed (v. 8) so that even Jesus' enemies had to acknowledge what had

happened; yet their unbelief was set (v. 16). The skepticism of the stubborn and hard-hearted religious leaders did not deter the man who had been healed, who now with physical sight restored had also received spiritual sight and responded with gratitude and praise (vv. 25,38). The Pharisees could see physically, but they chose to remain blind spiritually (vv. 40-41). They refused to act on the revelation of truth they had received.

God listens to **anyone** who is **God-fearing and does His will** (v. 31). The Greek word *theosebēs* with the sense of "devout, religious, pious" is understood to have the sense of reverencing God, describing one who is a sincere worshiper of God. One who is "God-fearing" does God's will. The fear of the Lord is interwoven throughout Scripture as a mark of one who has set herself apart unto the Lord. It is more than reverential awe, including a loving devotion on the part of one toward another who is so loved and respected that you cannot bear to disappoint that Exalted One in your heart and mind.

The Good Shepherd and oneness with the Father (10:1-42)

10:1-21 John began with a phrase especially peculiar to his Gospel, **I assure you** (Gk. *amēn, amēn*, "firm, faithful, true"). This adverb or particle of affirmation and assent was used repeatedly to present Jesus' affirmation of His person or His mission (1:51; 5:19,24-25; 6:26,32,47,53; 8:34,51,58; 10:1,7; 12:24; 13:16,20,21,38; 14:12; 16:20,23) and for special emphasis elsewhere (3:3,5,11; 21:18). Here (10:1) Jesus used the device to introduce an allegory that explained His ministry.

When the flocks of several shepherds mingled together, the sheep still recognized the familiar voice of their own shepherd and followed him (v. 4). The shepherd also knew his sheep, not merely by a family brand but **by name** (v. 3). The shepherd fed his sheep, led them to water, and kept them from harm's way. In order to do this task, the shepherd often found himself in danger. Jesus introduced two more "I am" statements: **I am the door of the sheep** (v. 7) and **I am the good shepherd** (v. 11). These metaphors were clearly understood by the people to whom Jesus spoke, for the sheep were important to sustaining life, providing food and clothing. Again the metaphor is rich in Old Testament imagery (Pss 23:1; 79:13; 80:1; Ezk 34:15). Jesus' proclamation of Himself as the Good Shepherd was the fulfillment of Ezekiel 34. Jesus used the contrast between Himself as the Good Shepherd and the religious leaders who, as the false shepherds described by the prophet, failed to lead the people faithfully. A shepherd might sleep at the entrance to the sheepfold to give maximum protection to his flock. The sheep pen, built from mud-bricks or local rough-hewn stones or sometimes simply a cane, had only one opening in order to protect the sheep from predators and/or **A THIEF** (Gk. *kleptēs*, "deceiver or imposter") and a **ROBBER** (Gk. *lēstēs*, "plunderer, bandit, revolutionary"). The slight nuances of meaning suggest in the former, trickery and deceit, and in the latter, violent plunder. Together the dangers are vividly portrayed (v. 1). Jesus used the metaphor of "the door" to emphasize that only He could provide access to God and to reaffirm His willingness to lay down His life for His sheep (vv. 7-10).

The **other sheep that are not of this fold** is a reference to the Gentiles who were not of the "fold" of Judaism (v. 16). Gentiles as well as Jews would share in the salvation He brought and would be under one Shepherd. **A hired man** was not intent on bringing harm to the sheep, but he was more concerned about his own well-being (v. 13). The approach of a predator would send him fleeing (v. 12). Jesus used this analogy to show the difference between Him as the shepherd and the religious leaders, who indeed might do some good things for the sheep but would never sacrifice themselves for the sheep.

10:22-42 Jesus was in Jerusalem in December (Jewish month of *Kislev*) for the **Festival of Dedication**, which occurred a few months before the Passover, at which time He would give His life. **Solomon's Colonnade** was a magnificent structure with its roof supported by rows of 40-foot high pillars. Solomon built the oldest porches on the east side. Jesus was walking on the west porches built by Herod. These porches were used for people as a place to pray and meditate and by rabbis as a place for teaching (v. 23).

The Feast of Dedication (*Hanukkah* or the Feast of Lights) is not mentioned in the Old Testament. This festival was established to commemorate the dedication of the temple by Judas Maccabaeus December 25, 165 BC, after the temple had been desecrated by Antiochus Epiphanes, the king of Syria, in 167 BC. Antiochus tried to abolish the Jewish religion by attacking Jerusalem and profaning the temple complex with the sacrifice of swine on the altar. Judas Maccabaeus and his brothers retaliated and defeated Antiochus. They cleansed the temple and rebuilt the altar and restored worship. This feast is still celebrated by Jews every December and lasts eight days with the lighting of a candle each day. (Accordingly, the *Hanukkah* Menorah has 8 branches.)

Eternal security is one of the most wonderful blessings for those who belong to Christ (v. 28). The Greek text uses a double negative (*ou mē*, literally "not not"). *Ou* is used in questions where an affirmative response is expected, and *mē* is used in questions where a negative answer is expected. The two together carry the strongest assertion—a solemn and absolute assertion. God not only initiates salvation, but He also accomplishes that redemptive work; and believers are forever secure in the hands of both the Father and the Son.

The Jews challenged Jesus quite plainly about His identity. They still did not understand because they were **not** His **sheep** (v. 26). His sheep listened to His voice. No one could snatch His sheep from Him because the Father **is greater than all** (v. 29). The conclusion of His reply was considered by the Jews to be blasphemous because Jesus declared, **The Father and I are one** (v. 30). This carefully worded answer testified to the two individual persons in the godhead, while "one" (Gk. *hen*, a neuter pronoun) affirmed the unity of nature.

To refute this charge of blasphemy, Jesus quoted from Psalm 82:6, which refers to evil judges as "gods." The Jews allowed their own judges to be called gods because of the divine origin of the civil authority they wielded and the justice at the foundation of their system of jurisprudence (v. 34). Since the Jews had expressed no antagonism against the Hebrew psalmist, they were on shaky ground to use this means for an attack on Jesus. Surely they were continually amazed at Jesus' grasp of the Old Testament—even obscure passages and minute details. He knew the Scriptures, and He could explain them far and beyond any man (vv. 35-36). The point is that, if Scripture acknowledges evil judges to be authorities on earth in a limited sense, then why should Jesus not apply the term to Himself, one who is clearly God's unique Son.

Jesus as the Resurrection and the Life (11:1-57)

John ended the first half of his Gospel with the most dramatic of Jesus' miracles: the raising of Lazarus from the dead. Jesus had brought people back from death previously in His ministry, but this occasion was the most significant because Lazarus had been dead for four days. According to Jewish tradition (*Genesis Rabbah 100,* 164a), the soul stayed near the body for only three days. Hence, Lazarus was dead in every sense of the word. The Jews believed that after the passing of this much time his soul was gone.

Verses 1-16 provide the background leading up to the miracle; verses 17-44 detail what happened when Jesus arrived in Bethany; and verses 45-57 describe the response of the religious leaders who plotted to kill Jesus because of the miracle.

The narrations of John and Luke (Lk 10:38-42) spotlight similar characteristics in Mary and Martha. In John, as in Luke, Martha is busy; but Mary is waiting on the Lord. Martha, for example, ran to meet Jesus when He arrived in town, while Mary stayed at home to wait (v. 20). When Martha lamented to Jesus that if He had been present, her brother would not have died, she was confessing her faith in His power (vv. 21-22). Jesus responded to this confession by saying, "I am the resurrection and the life" (v. 25). Then Martha confessed further that she believed Jesus to be the Messiah, the anointed One sent from the Father (v. 27). Martha's confession about Christ bears some striking similarities to Peter's confession (Mt 16:16).

Whereas Peter had the privilege of seeing Jesus' transfiguration after his confession, Martha had an up-close and personal viewing of the resurrection power of Christ after her confession. Jesus testified to being the resurrection and the life by raising Lazarus from the dead.

The event was deeply moving for believers and unbelievers alike. Even Jesus displayed some powerful emotions at the scene (vv. 33,35). John noted that Jesus was filled with both grief and anger—grief over the death of His friend and anger, perhaps at the unbelief of some who were present. The unbelievers quickly reported the resurrection of Lazarus to the Pharisees. Feeling threatened by Jesus, they plotted to kill Him. However, the high priest Caiaphas prophesied about the death of Jesus (v. 50). John then elaborated on the meaning of this prophecy (vv. 51-52). Jesus' death was not merely planned by a handful of religious leaders; it was ultimately part of God's sovereign plan of redemption.

11:1-16 Lazarus (Hb. "one whom God helps," a derivation from the name Eleazer) was a personal friend of Jesus. Some even suggest, based on verse 3, that he was "the disciple whom Jesus loved." While most commentators do not take that view, all would affirm from Jesus' own testimony that He loved Lazarus (v. 5). The testimony of **Mary**, a Greek personal name equivalent to the Hebrew Miriam (probably meaning "bitter" from Hb. *Mara*; see Ru 1:20), affirms her devotion to Christ until now (v. 2). **Martha** (Hb. "lady—as of the house") arose to the challenge of her name with her efficiency in managing her household and extending hospitality (Lk 10:38,40; Jn 11:20; 12:2). **Bethany** (Hb. "house of figs or unripe figs" or "house of sorrow or misery or affliction") was located on the eastern slope of the Mount of Olives **about two miles away** from Jerusalem and probably within an hour's walk (v. 18). The mountain obscured Jerusalem and set the village apart in seclusion, perhaps making it a worthy retreat for quiet renewal and thus very useful to Jesus. Tradition associates the gathering of invalids and outcasts and thus the designation "house of suffering."

Jesus seemed determined to delay going to Bethany despite the message concerning Lazarus's serious illness (vv. 4-6). He demonstrated His omniscience in knowing the moment of Lazarus's death and His omnipotence in knowing He would restore Lazarus to life (v. 11). Again He demonstrated His humanity (loving concern for a friend, vv. 35-36) and deity (power to raise one from the dead, v. 44). Jesus described Lazarus's death as falling **asleep** (v. 11). Sleep was used as a euphemism for death (vv. 11,14) in the New Testament here and elsewhere (Mt 9:24; Ac 7:60; 1 Co 15:6; 1 Th 4:13).

Thomas is mentioned individually (Jn 16) as is the style in John's Gospel— the disciples are noted as individuals or in small groups or alluded to as the Twelve (6:67,70-71; 20:24) but never enumerated in a comprehensively complete listing as in the Synoptic Gospels. Thomas is mentioned four times by John (v. 16; 14:5; 20:24-28; 21:2). Here Thomas expected Jesus would be killed. He is most often remembered for his skepticism; here, on the other hand, his loving loyalty is apparent.

11:17-37 Burial usually took place the day of death because of the hot climate and lack of knowledge about preserving the body. The body would be prepared for burial by anointing with special and expensive spices and ointments and then by wrapping the body in strips of white cloth. Jesus did not begin His journey from across the Jordan (10:40) until a day or two after Lazarus died (11:6), which, together with a journey of several days to reach Judea, meant that He did not arrive until **four days** after Lazarus' burial (v. 17). Jewish tradition claimed that the soul hovered over the body three days, in hope of a reunion, until decomposition of the body began to be evident. However superstitious and untrue, the widespread acceptance of this idea may have played into

Jesus' timing of His arrival in Bethany. No Jew could doubt that the resurrection of Lazarus from the grave after four days was indeed a miracle (v. 45).

Martha showed her familiarity with the Old Testament teaching on **the resurrection** (v. 24), and she affirmed her faith in Jesus' power over death (vv. 21-22). Jesus added to her understanding by declaring Himself to be "the resurrection" (v. 25)— a very important revelation for Jesus to entrust to Martha.

Jesus significantly timed His fifth "I am" statement, **I am the resurrection and the life** (v. 25; 6:35; 8:12; 10:9,11), since His mission in Bethany was to demonstrate His power to raise the dead, a meaningful foreshadowing or guarantee that those who physically died in Him would nevertheless be raised to eternal life in the future (v. 26). Paul clearly affirmed this principle in noting that indeed all die in Adam, but he also added that all in Christ will be made alive (1 Co 15:22). Thus, the only ultimate escape from death does not interrupt the physical cycle of decay that entered the world with sin, but for those who commit themselves to Christ, eternal life and bodily resurrection to join Christ is assured.

John, more than the other Gospel writers, revealed the deep compassion of Jesus. Jesus knew that Lazarus would be restored to life, yet still He was greatly moved. He was ANGRY (Gk. *enebrimēsato*, "scold, censure, warn sternly") with the sense of speaking harshly. The mourners had just questioned His power and His motives. His sorrow, mingled with the tense situation, brought out His humanity and moved Him greatly. The same word is used again in verse 38. Certainly Jesus was not angry with Mary or Martha, whom He had come to encourage and comfort, but He may well have felt angry indignation against sin as the cause of all suffering and death. The hypocrisy and sinfulness of the religious

leaders and people who gathered to mourn might also have awakened His righteous anger.

Jesus was also DEEPLY MOVED (Gk. *etarazen*, "stir up, disturb, unsettle") in the sense of being troubled or agitated for the same reasons. As a man, Jesus experienced the same emotions as all of humanity (vv. 33,35). Tears came, as noted with the most brief and poignant verse (v. 35), "Jesus WEPT" (Gk. *edakrusen*, "shed tears"). For "tears" John used a hapax, a word not used elsewhere in the Greek New Testament. Of course, He shared the sorrow of the loss, though temporary, of a friend and the pain of seeing those whom He loved suffer, but even more than these typically human responses, He recognized the hopelessness of the people who still did not believe. Surely His mission and work of redemption weighed heavily upon His heart.

11:38-57 The conversation between Jesus and Martha concluded with Martha's confession of faith:

> *A verbal confession must become a valid lifestyle. The mark of Christ must be evident in your life.*

I believe You are the Messiah, the Son of God, who was to come into the world (v. 27). She had all the components for a great confession of faith:

- She recognized Jesus as the Messiah, the anointed one.
- She acknowledged Him as the Son of God.
- She included His incarnation, linking His humanity to His deity.

Nevertheless, as with Peter and his confession, the story did not end here. When Martha arrived at the tomb of Lazarus, her lack of understanding surfaced again (v. 39), and Jesus reminded her that she **would see the**

glory of God if she **believed** (v. 40). The lesson is clear: Using the right words does not necessarily mean you understand the message. What sets apart a committed follower of Christ is the determination to live so that you are "fleshing out" the words into a life of obedience to Christ, whatever the cost. A verbal confession must become a valid lifestyle. The mark of Christ must be evident in your life.

Jesus addressed the Father concerning His work, remembering His mission, **so they may believe You sent Me** (v. 42). The prayer showed His one-mindedness with the Father (vv. 41-42; see also 20:31). Jesus knew and did the will of the Father. This miracle had surpassed the others and prompted a gathering of the **Sanhedrin**, which included 70 priests of whom some were Sadducees, and which, as the Jewish Supreme Court, met in Jerusalem. The high priest was added to the group in order to break any tie that might occur (v. 47). They were greatly troubled by Jesus' popularity with the people, which made it difficult for them to get rid of Him.

Mary and Martha of Bethany *John 11:1-45*	
Mary, the sister who worshiped	**Martha, the sister who worked**
She relished His presence.	She extended His grace.
• Focused on Him • Prioritized time with Him • Was sustained by Him	• Welcomed Him • Opened her home • Exuded warmth and hospitality
She respected His Word.	She noticed His needs.
• Hungered for the truth • Understood His teachings • Sought His guidance	• Fed Him • Housed Him • Served Him tirelessly
She received His power.	She accomplished His work.
• Demonstrated her love • Sacrificed her all • Accepted His praise	• Served others joyfully • Encouraged fellowship • Ministered in practical ways
Martha welcomed Jesus; Mary sat at His feet (Lk 10:38-39). Martha served Him dinner; Mary anointed His feet (Jn 12:2-3) Both Mary and Martha *worshiped* and *worked*.	
There are times to sit and worship and times to serve and work. Christian women must worship the Lord and serve Him.	
See also Mt 26:6-13; Mk 14:3-9; Lk 10:38-42; and Jn 12:1-8.	

Caiaphas, who was high priest that year and the son-in-law of Annas who himself served as high priest and who was mentioned in connection with Jesus' trial, uttered a profound statement; and despite His own prejudices, he spoke the words of God (v. 51), not realizing that God was using him to deliver a prophecy concerning Jesus and His redemptive purpose (v. 50). He set forth clearly the substitutionary nature of the atonement (v. 50). The word FOR (Gk. *huper*) clearly means "in behalf of or in the place of." God uses even His enemies to deliver His message.

The response to Jesus' miracle was diverse. On the one hand, **many of the Jews . . . believed in Him** (v. 45), but **some of them went to the Pharisees** (v. 46) as spies to betray Jesus.

Excursus: The Discipleship of Mary and Martha

Mary and Martha were faithful and loyal friends of Jesus, supporting Him through the challenges of life. They were also genuine disciples. As faithful friends and loyal disciples of Jesus, they exemplified honesty, integrity, and service. With two very different personalities, the women expressed their discipleship in different ways. Martha was distracted by preparations to serve Jesus, and Mary sat at the feet of Jesus (Lk 10:38-42).

Choosing the "better" action, Mary was sitting at the feet of Jesus and learning from Him (Lk 10:42). Mary's discipleship may seem more evident, but Martha also was learning from Jesus. Mary appeared to know what Martha needed to learn. However, Martha's service was not the object of correction. Rather her venting displeasure and judging Jesus' motivation were the issues in view. Jesus affirmed the importance of learning from Him as prerequisite to all else.

Martha could choose to learn from Christ's gentle correction and consider Mary's example of sitting at Jesus' feet as first in importance, or she could continue to "serve" Jesus in her own way. Perhaps Mary could submit herself to Jesus and learn from Him with greater ease than could her sister Martha. Martha was exemplary of an eagerness to serve Jesus, and for that she is also worthy to be emulated.

Mary, Martha, and Lazarus were intimate friends and disciples of Jesus. Even so, Jesus did not come right away when He heard of Lazarus's illness. As far as Mary and Martha knew, Jesus was "too late." Their brother was dead, and they were without hope of saving him. Perhaps they felt their Lord had failed them. But they did not understand the whole picture. Their loss had been orchestrated for a divine purpose. Their tragedy would bring glory to the Son of God (v. 4).

In keeping with John's overall purpose (20:30-31), the seventh and greatest "sign" of the Fourth Gospel further manifested Christ's deity so that the world might believe in Him. The Son of God demonstrated His power over death. Lazarus's resurrection evoked faith in some people (11:45), but it also hardened many others. In their fury to suppress the truth, the Pharisees heightened their opposition against Christ. Consequently, this miraculous event was another step in the direction of His own death and resurrection—the ultimate witness to His divine mission. However, Mary and Martha could not initially comprehend this heavenly plan. They were not able to see past their tears. Blinded by the pain of their loss, they experienced only the "here and now." Their faith was severely tested.

The secure and predictable lives of Mary and Martha in Bethany were shattered by the mysterious absence of their Lord during their time of greatest need. They stayed close to their home, trying to make sense of their brother's untimely death. They waited, knowing He would come.

Lazarus and his sisters were close to Jesus (11:3,5). They readily opened their home to Jesus when His ministry brought Him to Jerusalem (Lk 10:38). He may well have spent His last week on Earth at their home (Mt 21:17). Mary, Martha, and Lazarus held a special place in the Lord's heart. He spent a significant amount of time in the little village of Bethany.[6]

Mary and Martha spoke the truth about how they felt, and Christ listened and met their innermost needs. His grace and truth brought them hope and healing. Jesus listened to them, felt their pain, and responded to their needs. He heard their words and felt their emotions. His own display of emotion indicated that both His ears and His heart were open to them. He felt their loss deeply and wept with them (11:33-35). Though Jesus knew exactly what the outcome was going to be, He was still moved to weep with His beloved friends over the death of their brother (11:35). He did not view their tears as a lack of faith.

Jesus was never guilty of "bad timing." He knew that the glory of God would be displayed in this tragedy. The resurrection of Lazarus would strengthen faith in the followers of Christ, while moving unbelievers toward Him. Their pain would not be in vain. As disciples, Mary and Martha held tenaciously to their faith, and in God's timing the truth was revealed to them. They saw the glory of God and even came to understand His ultimate purpose for their trial. They witnessed an incredible miracle that confirmed a universal truth: God has the power to raise the dead. He can transform a hopeless predicament into a glorious victory. Tragedy was an opportunity for God to manifest His sovereignty, power, and love.

Several crucial principles related to discipleship can be gleaned from John 11:

- *God is always in control. Jesus was aware of Lazarus's situation and knew exactly what He was going to do. He allowed Lazarus's death to take place because He had a greater plan (v. 4). As a result, Mary and Martha learned much about the sovereignty of God.*

- *Mary and Martha were secure enough in their relationship with Christ to be honest with Him. They did not attempt to "bury" their true feelings. They were not silent. They took a risk and learned that the Lord accepted both the good and the bad in them.*

- *Sometimes God allows genuine needs to go unmet temporarily, which could result in deep pain. However, He can then bring about a greater good through the experience of suffering for His glory and for the strengthening of faith. Mary and Martha needed Jesus to heal their sick brother. The need was not fulfilled, and Lazarus's death was the result. Although they were not aware of it, Jesus planned for a greater good to come out of this loss—the demonstration of His power over the grave and the consequent belief of many of those who witnessed His raising of Lazarus from the dead (11:45).*

As was clearly seen in the lives of Mary and Martha, faith is absolutely necessary in a growing discipleship. Faith did not prevent them from experiencing pain and loss, but it enabled them to reach out for Christ in their time of need (11:3). Jesus honored their faith. He interacted with them on the basis of their loving and trusting relationship. He drew near and embraced them with His grace and truth. This study of Mary and Martha has many valuable lessons for women who seek to be Christ's disciples. Maturity often comes through extreme adversity. The ordeal of their brother's death and the subsequent encounter with Jesus in John 12 caused Mary and Martha to grow as His disciples. Mary and Martha were in their home in Bethany. In the context of a dinner given for their honored guest Jesus, their maturity as disciples was beautifully displayed (Jn 12:1-3), although in different ways. Their actions clearly reflected their unique personalities.

For the first time, though, Mary is seen as the focus of a particular scene. Indeed, Mary's act of devotion, the anointing of Jesus for burial, was extremely significant and showed her understanding of His mission. And her insight is starkly contrasted with the failure of other disciples to understand.

What Mary learned at the feet of Jesus and what she witnessed of His power to raise her brother from the dead fueled her spiritual growth. Her theological insight and sacrificial service stand as a solid witness to her growth as a disciple. The evidence of Martha's maturity is actually best seen in what is not written.

> In Jn. 12 there are no complaints by Martha and no hint of a rebuke to Martha—she serves quietly. . . . In comparing the portraits of Martha in Lk.10 and Jn.12, we note that Martha appears in the same role in both cases . . . Lk.10 makes it clear that a woman must first orientate her priorities so that the good portion comes first, being the one thing necessary. Having her priorities straight (as in Jn.12) she can assume a role that servants usually performed. This role is given new significance as a means of serving the Master and manifesting discipleship to and love for Him.[7]

Both Mary and Martha stand out as shining examples of servanthood and discipleship. From beginning to end, their "actions have spoken louder than their words." In fact, the very last time Mary and Martha appear in John 12, their words are not even recorded—only their actions. Maybe there is a lesson for us in this as well.

THE TESTIMONY OF DEATH AND RESURRECTION (12:1–20:31)

Actions in Preparation for Death (12:1-50)

Anointing at Bethany (12:1-11)

12:1-11 Six days before the Passover, **Martha was serving** (v. 2), and from what follows one can assume Mary was again sitting at the feet of Jesus (v. 3). Martha served without complaining, perhaps offering her service and hospitality as a gift to the Lord. While Matthew and Mark both mentioned Mary's anointing of Jesus, only John noted when the anointing took place—on the Saturday before what is now known as Palm Sunday. Mary poured on Jesus' feet a jar of perfume that was worth more than a year's wages (v. 5).

Anointing was usually for the head. Mary showed her own deep humility as she chose to pour the costly, **fragrant oil** over Jesus' feet. Only the lowliest servant attended the feet of guests, which would be dirty and dusty. No act could have been any more symbolic of her personal devotion to Christ and of her desire to sit at His feet to learn and to worship. The use of her hair to dry His feet was not common in the ancient world. Perhaps this act was yet another way of humbling herself by letting down her hair, usually bound or braided as customary for women in public, to complete the act of service.

For the anointing Mary used "a pound of **FRAGRANT OIL**" (Gk. *murou*, "ointment, perfume, or myrrh"), an aromatic ingredient also used to embalm bodies (19:39), and **NARD** (Gk. *nardou*, "oil") or spikenard, which was a fragrant oil derived from the hair stem of a plant growing in northern India (v. 3; Mk 14:3; see also Sg 1:12; 4:13-14). The "nard" was described as **PURE** (Gk. *pistikos*, "fit to be trusted, genuine"), a fitting allusion to the holiness of God that resided in the nature of Jesus, and **EXPENSIVE** (Gk. *polutimos*, "of great worth, valuable"), which was a reminder of the precious life He would lay down in payment for the sins of the world. Judas placed on the oil a monetary value of **300 denarii**, the equivalent of about a year's wages for the common laborer (v. 5).

Mary's actions were symbolic of preparing a body for burial. Perhaps sensing that Jesus' death was imminent, she used her most precious possession (Nothing in the text suggests that she took the family resources to purchase an extravagant oil, but rather she was willing to give up something she already had that was valuable to her). Because the imported spices and ointments were quite costly and yet occupied little space, they were often stored as an investment or life savings.

Because Lazarus's resurrection from the dead had verified Jesus' power over death, the **chief priests** wanted to kill him as well as Jesus. They were Sadducees and thus did not even believe in the resurrection of the dead. A living Lazarus would cause them to lose influence and power over the people.

Judas protested Mary's gift. Jesus knew the heart of Judas (6:20) and was well aware of his coming betrayal. Other disciples had fallen away and deserted Him, but Judas remained, perhaps hoping for financial gain or powerful position—some way to enrich himself as he had already done through his position as treasurer (12:6). John made clear that Judas **cared** nothing for **the poor** (v. 6). Caring for the poor was a command of the Old Testament (Dt 15:11). However, what Mary did was quite appropriate under the circumstances.

Unusual expense at a funeral was not regarded as unseemly; why should anyone object if the ointment which would otherwise have been used to anoint his dead body in due course was poured over him while he was still alive and able to appreciate the love which prompted the action?[8]

Entry into Jerusalem (12:12-50)

12:12-50 All of the Gospel writers mentioned Jesus' final entry into **Jerusalem**, but John supplemented the Synoptic accounts by adding some unique details. The crowds were enthralled with the miracles of Jesus and mesmerized by His teachings (v. 9). The excitement of the Passover celebration undoubtedly added to their festive mood. Palm trees had long been symbolic of victory and success, and to carry **palm branches** was a mark of triumph and honor. Images of their beautiful symmetry and graceful silhouette often adorned the temple. They were especially used in constructing booths for the Feast of Tabernacles. They were a natural addition to the celebratory entry to Jerusalem, accompanied by the joyous shouts of **Hosanna** (transliterated from Hb., lit. "save now please"), which was used as an official word of welcome for dignitaries. The palm branches and spontaneous word of victory suggested that the people were thinking of liberation and deliverance as they used the words of the psalmist (Ps 118:25-26). Yet Jesus rejected the political aspirations of the people by choosing to enter the city on a lowly **donkey** rather than on the back of a powerful horse.

Upon seeing Jesus' entry into Jerusalem, the Pharisees exclaimed that **the world has gone after Him**! (v. 19), a unique note from John, which prepared the way for John's mention of the **Greeks** who came to Jesus. These "Greeks" may have been God-fearing men like Corne-

lius (Ac 10) or proselytes. The designation is one generally inclusive of Gentiles. The raising of Lazarus from the dead had far-reaching effects. Certainly these words offered a prophetic voice of what would come through Jesus' atonement for the sins of the world—Jews and Gentiles (v. 32).

Jesus' parable about the **grain of wheat**, which fell to the ground and died had an application through the paradox of the man who lost eternal life because of his fixation on physical life and temporal passions, while the man who had God as the first priority in his life would receive **eternal life** (vv. 20-29; Mt 6:33; Lk 12:15,22). **The ruler of this world** is one of the ways John identified Satan (v. 31; 14:30; 16:11; 2 Co 4:4; Eph 2:2; 6:12). In the garden, the man and woman fell prey to his wiles as a result of their disobedience and were driven out of their Edenic paradise by God. Seemingly Satan had won, especially in light of Jesus' coming death. However, the opposite was true since through Jesus' crucifixion Satan's power would be forever broken.

The expression **hates his life** was not meant to suggest contempt for oneself and certainly was not an allusion to a low value of life or suicidal tendencies. Again John used a colorful figure of speech—a hyperbole—to emphasize the importance of right priorities—commitment first and foremost to God, which would include a commitment to serve others.

The climax of the parable came when Jesus emphatically stated that, in His death, He would **draw all people** to Himself (v. 32). "All people" is not a suggestion of universalism in the sense that all will be saved. However, it does provide assurance that Christ died for all and draws all to Himself, without regard for ethnic or gender or economic status (v. 32).

John's use of the phrase **lifted up** (Gk. *huphōthō*, "raise high, exalt," used exclu-

Excursus from the Editor: Liberation Theology

Liberation theology is an approach to the interpretation of Scripture that identifies the Bible's central theme as "liberation" or setting men and women free from physical, social, political, and economic bondage. Their approach comes out of the exodus motif found in the Old Testament (Ex 12:31-51). Certainly liberation is important and is one of many themes in Scripture, but the heart of biblical liberation is being freed from the power and penalty of sin (Gl 4:4-7). Social and political liberation and the reapportioning of wealth or economic reordering of society are not the most important goals. Liberation theologians interpret Scripture to support all ideologies of political and economic freedom in an effort to free the poor and oppressed of the world. They think such a movement will usher in an age of peace in which they see all ethnic and economic distinctions overcome and erased, setting up an earthly utopia. Their quest for liberation by necessity establishes personal experience as the primary factor in interpreting and applying Scripture.

Feminist theologians often embrace the precepts of liberation theology. In fact, their ideology seems to unfold from the roots of liberation theology. They demand that the Bible be interpreted in light of the liberation of women, whom they consider as the largest group enduring oppression. Any passage in Scripture that does not support their view is considered "nonauthoritative."

Jesus never suggested, nor does one find anywhere in Scripture, that meeting the needs of the poor and oppressed is not important. Christians more than others have traditionally addressed social inequities and economic disparities in selfless ways. However, meeting these physical needs is not the heart of the gospel. Jesus defended women (Lk 7:44; 10:38-42; Jn 12:1-3). In fact, Jesus addressed the issue of the poor in relation to His own messianic task in a particular way when Mary of Bethany used a costly fragrance to anoint Him (Jn 12:1-8). He did not disparage acts of generosity toward the needy, but He recognized that her anointing was part of His path to the cross and to the redemption of the world. Also, in an earlier encounter with Mary, Jesus commended her giving her time to learning the Scripture even when she could have used her energies for meeting the mundane needs of the poor and oppressed (Lk 10:38-42). In Jesus' encounters with Mary, one can clearly see the balance missing from liberation theology. The emphasis moves from exalting Christ and recognizing His redemptive mission to lifting up humanity and spending all one's time and energy to improve physical conditions in society. —DKP, editor

---

sively by John to refer to Jesus' death, 3:14; 8:28; 12:32,34, but elsewhere with the sense of "exalting") has a double

meaning: The crucifixion of Christ would ultimately lead to His exaltation as well as to redemption (3:16). Once again, the people did not fully understand the meaning of His words (v. 34). The disciples seemed to understand that Jesus' death was imminent; yet they could not comprehend that the Messiah could be "lifted up" to die (Dn 7:13-14).

John referred to the prophecies of Isaiah concerning the hardness of the Jews (Is 53:1, the Suffering Servant passage, and 6:10, Isaiah's unique and magnificent vision of God). The message was again straightforward: The Messiah would be glorified through His suffering. Jesus then implored the people again to believe in Him (Jn 12:44-50).

Teaching in Preparation for Death (13:1–17:26)

Servant ministry versus betrayal (13:1-38)

13:1-30 This section contains some of the most moving moments in Jesus' life recorded in all the Gospels. The simplicity of Jesus' act of washing the feet of His disciples (v. 5) and His command to the disciples to love one another (13:34) combined to offer a challenge of great difficulty for emulating in daily life because of the profound irony suggested as God Himself assumed the posture of a humble servant.

Jesus knew who He was and where He was going. His hour had finally come (v. 1). The timing of the Last Supper has been hotly debated (vv. 1-2). Jesus did say that He was going to observe the Passover with His disciples (Mt 26:18; Mk 14:14; Lk 22:11), but no mention is made of the Passover lamb in any of the accounts. Moreover, the crucifixion occurred on Friday, and the official Passover began at sundown on Friday. The symbolism of Jesus' death as the Passover Lamb becomes more poignant in this light. However, this timing would mean that His Last Supper with the disciples must have

been Thursday evening, after which He went out to be betrayed and arrested. There are logical reasons explaining what seem to be discrepancies in timing, but the fact remains that what is important is the Lord's laying down His life and His preparation of the disciples for that overwhelming sorrow. One's attention then should rest on the events, not the calendar.

Jesus' strong sense of identity and mission moved Him to perform this extraordinary act of service. The washing of feet clad only with sandals and filthy from walking miles on dusty, dirty roads was a common practice for a host to offer to those who had been guests invited for a meal. However, the slaves or lowest-ranking servants of the house were responsible for this mundane task. None of the disciples volunteered to do what needed to be done. So, having waited until after the meal, Jesus dramatically assumed the posture of a servant, showing in vivid reality His own humility and setting the pattern for His disciples as they would minister to one another in His absence (v. 2). The detailed description must have come from one of the Twelve, who were present at this poignant time. And here Jesus, Son of the Most High God, performed a menial task. By washing the feet of the disciples, Jesus offered a powerful example of the type of service and love which His disciples were expected to emulate (v. 14).

When Jesus came to Peter, He was met first with an emphatic refusal from the impetuous disciple: **You will never wash my feet—ever** (Gk. *ou mē,* "absolutely never"), using in the grammatical construction a double negative for emphasis (v. 8). Jesus replied, just as empathically, that to be a partaker in the gospel, Peter must share this experience. Peter was reminded that there was always purpose in what Jesus did and that absolute obedience and surrender on Peter's part were necessary. As Peter again tried to carry the

Lord's plan beyond its intended boundaries, Jesus used Peter's words to distinguish between foot-washing, an act of loving devotion and an example of humble service, and the ordinances of baptism and the Lord's Supper, both of which Jesus commanded. The only other mention of footwashing in the New Testament involved devout widows who were to offer hospitality and loving service to the saints, especially the poor (1 Tm 5:10). Most evangelicals do not prescribe footwashing or *pedilavium* (Lat. "foot bath") since the act is nowhere prescribed or commanded as an ordinance in the New Testament. Common observance in the early church was an act of hospitality and a way of expressing love and offering service to one another. Those who had experienced regeneration needed only to have cleansing from daily sins since regeneration was once and forever.

John set Jesus' ultimate act of love and service in stark contrast with Jesus' prediction of Judas's betrayal and Peter's denial. These men had been His closest companions for three years. For Jesus to wash the feet of one whom He knew would harm Him in the future made His service all the more astounding (v. 21).

Jesus spoke of **the one who ... has raised his heel against Me** (v. 18) with an idiomatic expression used by the psalmist and now prophetically fulfilled, meaning one who is taking advantage of another (Ps 41:9). Judas's betrayal did not surprise Jesus (Jn 6:20), but it must have been an overwhelming sorrow to Him. The announcement must have surprised His disciples, however (vv. 21-22). The reference to **one of His disciples, the one Jesus loved** (v. 23) has aroused debate as to who might have had this position of honor. Some have suggested Lazarus, but the weight of evidence points to John. In speaking of himself, John's use of veiled language

would seem appropriate. Although **reclining close beside Jesus** (more literally "reclining on the bosom of Jesus") would be a natural description of the one next to Jesus since customarily all reclined around a low table during meals, but certainly a person next to Jesus would have a place of honor and would enjoy more intimate conversation with Him.

Judas, a common name, was probably from Kerioth (Hb. "cities"), once a fortified city of Moab (Jr 48:24,41; Am 2:2), which would explain the descriptor **Simon Iscariot's son** (13:2). John noted that, as a keeper of the group's money, Judas had stolen a portion for himself (12:5-6). Perhaps John used the transitional phrase **it was night** (v. 30) to underscore the spiritual darkness into which Judas was catapulting himself.

13:31-38 The **new commandment** was in contrast to the old (Lv 19:18; Lk 10:27) in the sense that Jesus introduced a new motive and dimension (Jn 13:34-35). "New" denoted a fresh and improved approach. Jesus used an affectionate vocative or familiar address, **children** (Gk. *teknia*), to express His loving concern as He delivered an important admonition to His disciples (v. 33). Peter had genuine affection for Jesus (v. 37), but he was impetuous and impatient. Jesus knew that Peter was not yet ready to stand in the line of fire (v. 38).

Roosters, usually crowing at midnight and then at three in the morning, were so reliable with their crowing that tradition says the Roman guards changed their shifts according to this reliable time indication. Jesus prophesied that Peter would deny Him **three times** before dawn.

Farewell discourse (14:1–16:33)

14:1-31 The Farewell Discourse, or the "Upper-Room Discourse" as more commonly noted, has been one of the most appreciated and revered sections by believers in every era. This intimate and moving account of Jesus' instructions to His disciples took place after Jesus' last Passover meal and was recorded in detail by John. Chapters 14–17 resemble the established genre of a farewell discourse in Jewish literature. When the death of a great leader was imminent, naturally he would be moved to prepare his followers for living and continuing his work after his departure.

Sandwiched between Jesus' discussion on His departure and return (14:1-31 and 16:5-33) are His words of admonition to "remain in Him" (15:1-17) and His warning concerning the hatred of the world to be incurred by His followers (15:18–16:4). The main teaching of this entire discourse contained Christ's encouraging revelation concerning the person and work of the coming **Holy Spirit**, who would ultimately bring them comfort and give them courage (v. 26). He would never leave them (vv. 16-17). The ultimate purpose of this discourse was to help the disciples understand Christ's death and resurrection. The Spirit would shed further light on the person and work of Christ (v. 26).

This section is built around four questions from four different disciples.

- Peter was the first to ask where Jesus was going (13:36). Jesus answered that He was returning to the Father **to prepare a place** for them (14:1-4).

- Jesus' claim that they knew the way to where He was going prompted **Thomas** to ask about **the way** (14:5). Jesus told them plainly that He is the way, the true and living way **to the Father** (14:6-7).

- Philip insisted that he would still like to see the Father (v. 8). In response, Jesus made four points:

1. The Father is in Him (vv. 9-10).

2. His miracles testify that the Father is in Him (v. 11).

3. Those who believe will do **greater works than** He (vv. 12-13).

4. If a believer asks for **anything** in accordance with His desires, He **will do it** (v. 14).

- This prompted Judas (not Iscariot) to ask the final question: Why would He only reveal Himself to believers? (v. 22). Jesus' answer was that people must choose to follow Him. Those who do will have the Triune God dwell with them forever.

In verses 15-21, Jesus promised that He would give **another Counselor**, the Holy Spirit, who would **be with** them **forever**. Once Jesus returned to the Father, the Holy Spirit would in a sense stand in the Lord's place. He would be their helper, interpreter, witness, and revealer. The Father, Son, and Holy Spirit in their fullness will be with the believer who obeys and loves Him (Jesus).

The **dwelling places** (Gk. *monai*, "staying place, room, abode") may be referring to places where the disciples can find peaceful living (vv. 2,23) but is probably more a reference to permanent dwelling places. Jesus knew the disciples were anticipating some heavenly prepared place. Although the text is not explicit with details on location, Jesus Himself is to be the escort (see 1 Th 4:13-18), and fellowship with Him is to extend throughout eternity (Jn 14:3). Jesus' future return is also promised (v. 3). His return was as certain as His departure. Life was as certain as death (v. 19). He would depart in order **to prepare** for their future coming to Him.

Thomas was skeptical and full of doubt, and he expressed those feelings honestly. He in no way rejected Jesus, for he had already expressed a willingness to die for Him (11:16).

Jesus' answer was startling and authoritative and without vacillation. He gave the disciples the sixth "I am" statement: **I am the way, the truth, and the life** (v. 6). The Old Testament imagery continued as with the Israelites who, through the exodus, experienced their way out of Egyptian bondage, as in the truth through the giving of the law on Sinai, and as in the life they had never experienced before in the promised land of Canaan. Jesus portrayed Himself as the way out of the bondage of sin, into the truth of revealing Himself to provide a means to live life set apart unto God, and as the life of satisfaction and rest found in following Christ. With these words Jesus settled once and for all that He is the only way of reaching the Father. Jesus noted that He had presented the Father as no one else could do. The disciples were promised that to **know** Jesus would also mean they would **know** the **Father** (v. 7). KNOW (Gk. *egnōkeite)* implies more than intellectual acceptance and includes the idea of experience or knowledge affirmed with personal understanding.

The COUNSELOR (Gk. *paraklēton*, "advocate, helper, intercessor, comforter") is a reference to the Holy Spirit. The word's etymology links the preposition *para* ("near or alongside") with the verb *kaleō* ("call or summon"), giving the idea of "one who appears in another's behalf." The Holy Spirit is called alongside believers to give help and advice:

- He is a person.

- He is God.

- He has unique functions within the divine triunity.

Fire, oil, water, and a dove are symbols used to represent the Holy Spirit's presence, as is wind or breath (Gk. *pneuma).*

The neuter gender of this word does not justify viewing the person of the Holy Spirit merely as an impersonal power or force. The references to the Spirit affirm His intellect, emotion, and will (v. 17; 15:26; 16:7,13), and personal pronouns are appropriate and necessary in reference to Him.

ANOTHER (Gk. *allon*, meaning specifically "another of the same kind") is a key word. The Holy Spirit is not new on the scene, for the Spirit was an active participant in creation (Gn 1:2), in calling out individuals to specific tasks (Jdg 3:10; 12:24-25; 14:6), as an agent in baptism (Mt 3:11; Mk 1:8; Lk 3:16; Jn 1:33), and as part of the new birth (Jn 3:5). What was new after Jesus' departure was the intimate and permanent indwelling of the Spirit in the heart of every believer (15:26; Ac 2:33; 5:31-32). That indwelling or baptism of the Spirit comes at the moment of conversion and never ceases. The work of the Holy Spirit is not as visible as that of the Father and Son, since His function is to glorify the Son, which would mean that He does not call attention to Himself. Still He has specific work to do: teaching or illuminating God's Word (v. 26; 16:13), reproving and convicting and judging (16:8-11), regenerating (3:5), praying and interceding for believers (Rm 8:26), comforting (Jn 14:16), renewing (Ti 3:5), guiding into truth (Jn 16:13), empowering (Mt 28:19-20; Ac 1:8), testifying (Jn 15:26), restraining evil (2 Th 2:6-7). The indwelling is instantaneous and permanent, but believers may pursue the "filling" of the Spirit, and from that filling comes the real power (Eph 5:18).

The Holy Spirit also inspired the writers of Scripture and the prophets (2 Tm 3:16; 1 Pt 1:21-22; Nm 11:29; Ezk 2:2). At conversion He acts as a seal or guarantee of salvation (Eph 1:13; 4:30), and in the Christian life the Spirit bestows the fruit of Christlike virtues (Gl 5:22-23) and distributes gifts equipping believers to do the work of the kingdom (Rm 12:3-13; 1 Co 12:1-11; Eph 4:7-16; 1 Pt 4:10-11). God acts through, reveals His will to, and empowers His children to do His work by way of the Holy Spirit.

Peace (Gk. *eirēnēn*, "tranquility, unity") was not the cessation of conflict and difficulty. Even Jesus spoke of being troubled and agitated about the existing circumstances of life (Jn 12:27), and He knew a violent and painful death awaited Him. However, in the midst of sorrow and suffering and injustice, Jesus had confidence in the Father so that He could move without fear along the journey before Him (Jn 14:27). **The ruler of the world** was a

reference to the Devil (v. 30), who was continually present to sow his discord and deceit.

15:1-17 In this section Jesus exhorted His followers to **remain in** Him and to love one another. In true Johannine style, verses 1-8 present only two alternatives— either one remains in the "vine" and bears fruit, or one does not. Those who remain are pruned so that they may become more fruitful; those who do not remain are burned. *Those who do not remain, were never really true believers.* In verses 9-17, Jesus defined further what counts as "Christlike love." It is sacrificial service. In fact, fruit (v. 2) is "expressed" in sacrificial service.

Heart to Heart:
Abide in Him

One of a Christian's greatest life challenges is to abide in the Lord, to remain close to Him, and to be faithful to Him. Spiritual discipline is necessary to "walk in Him" daily. But the rewards of disciplined living are great. There are blessings to those who abide in Him.

In this passage, Jesus taught His disciples the power of abiding faith. Seven times Jesus said "remain." Christians are to remain in the Lord and in His Word. While it is tempting to focus on self or follow others, Christians must be devoted to Him alone.

This section began with the seventh and final "I am" statement: I am the true vine (v. 1). Jesus used the analogy of a vine and branches to teach that dependence on Him produces fruit (v. 4). He identified Himself as the "true vine," God as the vineyard keeper, and Jesus' followers as the "branches" (vv. 2,5). A branch apart from the vine and without the care of the keeper cannot produce fruit. A Christian apart from Christ and without the provision of God cannot live a Christlike life and bring glory to God. Are you abiding in Him and His Word? Are you producing fruit? If not, recommit yourself to Him. If

so, rejoice in this promise: **If you remain in Me and My words remain in you, ask whatever you want and it will be done for you. My father is glorified by this: that you produce much fruit and prove to be My disciples** (vv. 7-8).

In the Old Testament the vine represented Israel (Ps 80:8; Is 5:1-7; Jr 2:21), and the prophet spoke of Israel as becoming a wild and useless vineyard. Jeremiah also compared Israel to a degenerate plant, and Hosea complained about Israel as being an empty vine. In contrast, Jesus became the true (Gk. *alēthinē*, "genuine") or authentic vine (v. 1). Using the literary device of allegory, Jesus promised to produce fruit (v. 5) in the lives of believers. The branches had no life within themselves but received and sustained life by being attached to the vine. God the Father, as the vine keeper, would be available to help a faltering vine (v. 16). Those without fruit were either counterfeit followers or unproductive disciples (v. 4), and probably the former. Those who were false followers and fruitless would be cast into the fire (v. 6). There is no undercutting the security of genuine believers but simply affirmation on the fate of those who were not genuine disciples. Discipleship is affirmed by fruit-bearing.

Prayer is a powerful tool for believers, and there is no difference between the presence of Christ and the impact of His words—both act as a governing force. Love has ever been the motivation for obedience, and obedience in turn is a demonstration of love (vv. 9-10).

The Holy Spirit comes from the Father, and He is commissioned by the Son (v. 26). The Spirit is fully God and not subordinated in His personhood in any way; rather this "procession" testifies to the operation or function within the Godhead.

The Spirit is especially needed in the believer's life in times of pressure and upheaval. The world opposed Christians because of ignorance (v. 21) and because unbelievers are rebuked by the life of Jesus and His holiness, which means those who follow Him and emulate His standards will also be hated (v. 22).

15:18–16:4 Jesus warned His disciples that they would be hated because He was hated. Those who would hate them were really without excuse. Those who had eyes to see could have witnessed Jesus' teachings and His deeds. The Spirit would give them boldness and inner strength in times of trial. Jesus was sternly warning them to be prepared for what was coming.

16:5-33 In this final section, Jesus returned to the subject of His departure. He began by further discussing the work of the Holy Spirit. Unless Jesus left, the Spirit would not come to them. The phrase **sorrow has filled your heart** (v. 6) suggested a lingering spirit of gloom and doom among the disciples, who still did not understand what would happen when Jesus departed and the Holy Spirit moved into their hearts (v. 7). The convicting power of the Holy Spirit operates in these ways:

- **He will convict the world about sin** (v. 8), namely, its ultimate manifestation, which is an individual's unbelief and the failure to place his trust in Christ.

- He will convict the world of **righteousness** because He is returning **to the Father**, having conquered sin and death through His resurrection (v. 10).

- He will convict the world **about judgment, because the ruler of this world has been judged** (v. 11), and indeed the Devil was judged in the cross and resurrection. The Holy Spirit convicts of sins committed, righteousness forfeited, and judgment coming.

The Spirit's assignment to **guide you into all the truth** certainly applied to the writing of the New Testament documents, but the Spirit's guidance does not stop at the canon of Scripture (v. 23). God has not inspired subsequent revelation to the degree of the God-breathed canon of Scripture; but He still illuminates what He has inspired for believers.

Also in this section Jesus reminded His disciples that their grief would **turn to joy** (v. 20). His departure would bring the coming of the Holy Spirit. His resurrection would turn their sorrow into joy (v. 22). The vivid analogy to a woman's experience in childbirth strikes a familiar cord and is not a new image for Scripture. Here the present application seems to be a reference to the resurrection of Christ, at which time their sorrow would be exchanged for joy. However, there is also eschatological hope for future joy even beyond what could be experienced on earth (v. 22). In the Old Testament, Israel's sorrow and difficulty in awaiting the coming of the Messiah and deliverance were compared to a mother's experience in birth pangs (Is 26:17-19; 66:7-9). Jeremiah 13:21, Micah 4:9-10, and Hosea 13:13 use the same imagery to present simultaneously Israel's present suffering from their disobedience with their future hope of deliverance. Even in Jesus' absence they can ask for anything they want in His name (according to His will). However, mentioning the name of Jesus was never meant to be a magic formula for receiving an affirmative answer to one's petition. Rather, using the name of Jesus should be a personal reminder that every request is subject to His standards and subservient to His will and purpose.

The Prayer of Jesus John 17:1-26	
Targets of His Prayer	**Topics of His Prayer**
Jesus Himself (vv. 1-5)	"Glorify Your Son so that . . . " • the Son may glorify the Father (v. 1) • the Son may give eternal life to all given to Him by the Father (v. 2)
His disciples (vv. 6-19)	• protect them from the evil one (vv. 11,15) • so that they may be one (v. 11) • that they may have the Son's joy completed in them (v. 13) • sanctify them (vv. 17,19)
All believers and the world (vv. 20-26)	• that believers may all be one (vv. 21,22,23) • that the world may believe that the Father sent the Son (vv. 21,23) • that the world may know that the Father has loved them (v. 23) • that those the Father has given to the Son may be with Him (v. 24) • that those the Father has given to the Son may see His glory (v. 24) • that the Father's love may be in them (v. 26) • that the Son may be in them (v. 26)

Figures of speech (Gk. *paroimiais*, "proverbs") are useful tools in communication, to share spiritual truths through earthly human ideas (v. 25). Jesus knew when plain and straightforward speech was necessary and when it would be understood by His hearers (v. 29). Meantime, figurative speech was a way of illustrating the truths He was imparting. One should not be surprised that living in the world, which is ruled by the Devil, brings **suffering** (Gk. *thlipsin*, "pressure, affliction, trouble," v. 33). Whether in reference to outward pressures and circumstances or a reference to inner anguish from the message Jesus had given, suffering was inevitable.

High priestly prayer (17:1-26)

17:1-26 This prayer truly is the "Lord's Prayer"—for Himself, His disciples, and for all those who would believe in Him. His personal petitions consisted mainly of requests to help Him finish His mission. He spoke plainly of His preexistence and of the glory He had before the creation of the world. He also clearly defined eternal life.

Jesus' main concern for His disciples was that they be protected from the enemy (v. 15). He prayed that they not be overpowered by the Devil but that they become sanctified, growing in the grace and knowledge of God (v. 17). Although some suggest disparagingly that Jesus was not praying for the world in this context, one must remember that this section was part of the Upper Room discourse, where Jesus was primarily concerned with preparing the Twelve for life after His departure. Therefore, these verses must be interpreted in this light. Jesus was concerned for the lost since other contexts demonstrate that clearly (see Lk 15:7, 10,23,32; 19:10). His main concern in these verses, however, is for the Twelve, that those who believe His message might dwell in unity. In some profoundly mysterious way, the church reflects (or ought to reflect) the divine triunity. Believers must, by the power of the Holy Spirit, dwell in unity.

Eternal life (Gk. *aiōnios zōē*) has several dimensions—purchased in the past through the Lord's atonement, keeping believers in the present from day to day, and securing the future when faith is consummated for eternity in the presence of the Lord (v. 3). Jesus affirmed the completion of His mission and work assigned to Him by the Father, knowing that through His obedience the Father had been glorified (v. 4). Because He had been obedient to the Father's will, Christ would be exalted in the glories of heaven (v. 5).

A precious promise contained in Jesus' prayer is the assurance that **not one of them is lost** (v. 12). Some suggest that Jesus failed in the case of Judas, **the son of destruction**, but Judas perished because he rejected Christ. Even then, God's plan was accomplished and the Scripture fulfilled. Judas made his own choice, but God in His omniscience knew what that choice would be in eternity past, and that choice had personal consequences for Judas and eternal significance in God's plan for redemption.

Christians are in the world. Jesus recognized that they could live in the world without being bound to its mind-set (v. 16). Jesus did pray for the protection of His children **from the evil one**, a reference to the Devil (v. 15). The disciples were needed in the world to share the good news of the gospel.

Sanctification is linked with truth, i.e., the Word of God, which provides a sure and unchanging standard for life. Jesus knew the importance of being sanctified (Gk. *hagiason*, "dedicated, purified") or set apart unto the Lord for His disciples, and the only way to that goal was through the working of God's Word in their lives (v. 17).

Jesus not only stressed the importance of the love of believers one for the other (13:34), but He also admonished them to achieve unity (Jn 17:21-22), not in the sense of seeking sameness but becoming like-minded in order to present the gospel to the world in the best possible way.

Events Surrounding Death Itself (18:1–20:31)

Arrest, trials, and crucifixion (18:1–19:42)

18:1-40 Judas knew to look for Jesus in Gethsemane since Jesus often sought the quiet of this garden for prayer and meditation. Located on the lower slope of the Mount of Olives, this site is still marked by a grove of ancient olive trees (v. 1).

Peter was obviously devoted to Jesus and courageous enough to risk his own life to defend Jesus against the arresting mob. He was armed and took action impulsively. Although Jesus told Peter, **"Sheathe your sword!"** there is no hint of pacifism here but rather Jesus' conscious determination to follow the Father's plan and timing (v. 11). The **company of soldiers** (Gk. *speiran*) may have been guards from the Jewish temple, but they were probably joined by a contingency of Roman soldiers (known as a "cohort," a tenth of the legion, about 300 to 600 men) so the arrest would be legal. The troops were accompanied by a throng of religious leaders. The party seemingly evolved into an armed mob (v. 3).

In the account of Jesus' passion, John to a large degree paralleled the Synoptic Gospels. However, John did include some material that was not recorded in Matthew, Mark, or Luke. For instance, John noted the fact that Jesus was brought before Annas, the father-in-law of Caiaphas who had preceded him in office (18:12-14,19-24), for an informal trial. Since Jewish law claimed that the role as high priest was one held for life, Annas still exercised authority and influence.

The identity of **another disciple** (v. 15) is not stated in Scripture. Some have speculated that it might have been Joseph of Arimathea, who later made his own personal tomb available for Jesus' burial, or Nicodemus, who is mentioned as helping Joseph prepare Jesus' body for burial. However, the person most often identified in this way in the book of John seems to be John himself. In any case, this individual had the distinction of being known by the high priest.

Although the Sanhedrin, the Jewish Supreme Court, had the authority to assess the death penalty, they could not carry out execution without the approval of the Roman government (v. 31). **The gover-**

nor's headquarters (Gk. *praitōrion*, transliterated as Praetorium, "imperial guard") was probably located close to the palace of Herod (v. 28). The Jewish religious leaders would not enter for fear they would be defiled and unable to eat the Passover meal.

John also recorded that Jesus' side was pierced while He was on the cross (19:31-37) and described the significance of this piercing—that Scripture would be fulfilled (19:36; see also Ps 34:20). John stated quite clearly that he witnessed these things and testified about them so that his readers might believe.

Perhaps there is no better witness to the significance of the crucifixion than Jesus' words, which were contained in seven statements—three from the book of John—as He hung on the cross:

- "Father, forgive them, because they do not know what they are doing" (Lk 23:34).

- "I assure you: Today you will be with Me in paradise" (Lk 23:43).

- First to Mary, "Woman, here is your son," and then to John, "Here is your mother" (Jn 19:26-27).

- "My God, My God, why have You forsaken Me?" (Mk 15:34).

- "I'm thirsty" (Jn 19:28).

- "It is finished" (Jn 19:30).

- "Father, into Your hands I entrust my spirit" (Lk 23:46).

The last words of Jesus on the cross, especially **It is finished** (v. 30), were not to announce the end of Jesus' life but rather to proclaim the completion of His mission from the Father. The verb is in the perfect tense, signifying something accomplished in the past with continuing results in the present and future. Most important—the crucifixion is not the cause of death but rather the fact that

Jesus did die a physical death as the substitute for all mankind (vv. 33-34). Joseph of Arimathea was mentioned in all the Gospels (v. 38; Mt 27:57-60; Mk 15:42-46; Lk 23:50-56). He was wealthy, a member of the Sanhedrin, a God-fearing man, and in the end a follower of Christ. His daring request became a public confession of his faith in Christ (v. 38). Joseph and Nicodemus (v. 39), as members of the Jewish Supreme Court, had much more to lose than most of the other followers of Jesus. With the Jews' hostility toward Jesus, even their lives, not to mention livelihoods and reputations, were on the line.

From Jesus' final words, clearly love of enemies and steadfast commitment to the will of God were supreme. In Christ's death was modeled commitment to the two greatest commandments: loving God and loving neighbor, and loving them to the uttermost.

19:1-16 Pilate had Jesus **flogged** (Gk. *emastigōse,* "whip, scourge, punish"), a cruel and inhumane punishment in which the victim was bound to a post with the skin of his back fully exposed and then whipped 39 times (13 blows to the victim's chest and 26 to his back) by a soldier or some man of strength. The leather whip had pieces of bone and lead interwoven. The flesh was torn, and the ordeal served to hasten death. (For a timeline of Jesus' final week, see the commentary on Mk 15:21-47.)

The Roman governor Pontius Pilate (AD 26–36) was procurator of Judea during Jesus' public ministry and at the time of His arrest, trial, and crucifixion (Mt 27:11-26; Lk 3:1; 23:1-25). He was directly accountable to the emperor Tiberius Caesar for all Roman governance in Judea. If the Jews filed a formal complaint against him, he could lose his position and perhaps his life (Jn 19:12). John recorded Pilate's verdict of "not guilty" (**I find no**

grounds for charging Him, v. 4), proving that Jesus was not found guilty of any crime against Rome. Jesus did make clear that Pilate's power was temporal and limited, while Jesus' power was eternal and without limit (v. 11). Jesus also made clear the degrees of culpability. Judas, one of His inner circle, had greater knowledge and thus would bear greater guilt. There are degrees to the offensiveness of sin, and the more one knows the truth, the greater is her accountability before God.

Pilate pronounced his official decision to turn Jesus over to the Jews **in a place called the Stone Pavement** (Gk. *lithostrōton,* "paved with stones"; Hb. *Gabbatha*) from a raised platform outside in front of the Praetorium (v. 13). The response of the Jewish **chief priests** was astounding. They expressed their allegiance to the pagan emperor they hated and under whose governance they had long chafed (v. 15). The depth of their spiritual degradation was nowhere any more clear than in the hypocrisy of this act of betrayal (see Jn 1:11).

19:17-42 Pilate's hatred or ridicule for the Jews was evident in the title he placed over Jesus on the cross. Ironically, that title was exactly right (v. 19). The fact that its message was **in Hebrew, Latin, and Greek** only enhanced the importance of Jesus' death as having universal influence (v. 20). Hebrew was the language of the Jews and the common tongue for the people of Judea. Latin was the official language of the Roman Empire, and Greek was the language of the marketplace as well as the eastern provinces of the empire.

Several women remained at the cross—Jesus' mother Mary, her sister Salome, Clopas' wife Mary, and Mary Magdalene. **The disciple He loved**, whom most evangelical commentators believe to be John, remained with them. Jesus' tender affection and sense of responsibility to

His mother is nowhere more apparent than here (vv. 25-27). Jesus took seriously the responsibility of the firstborn son to provide for His mother. He assigned John to be her provider and protector.

Roman law required that criminals being crucified remain on the cross until dead, however long that might be. The bodies were then left to the vultures. Breaking the legs often hastened death (v. 31). Jewish law complicated this crucifixion scene because it required that the body be removed the same day and buried before evening, especially when the Sabbath was approaching (v. 31). Since Jesus was already dead, His legs were not broken, fulfilling another prophecy (vv. 33,36; Ps 34:20).

Resurrection (20:1-29)

20:1-29 John devoted more space to the resurrection account than any of the other Gospel writers. In this chapter, Peter and John (the beloved disciple) are juxtaposed. Both of them ran to the tomb and found it empty, but only the beloved disciple **saw and believed** (vv. 3-10). The rest of the chapter spotlights the interaction between Mary and Jesus (vv. 11-18) and between the disciples and Jesus (vv. 19-29).

The first day of the week would have been the day after the Sabbath, beginning at sundown on Saturday and ending at sundown on Sunday. The visit from the women occurred early on Sunday morning. John mentioned only **Mary Magdalene**, but others are noted in the Synoptic Gospels (v. 1; Mt 28:1; Mk 16:1; Lk 24:10). **The other disciple** (v. 3) seems to be the Apostle John, who spoke of himself humbly in this way.

The Jewish custom of wrapping the dead body with long strips of cloth and then placing a napkin over the face would suggest that getting out of this mummy-like grave clothing would

require a struggle and leave a disheveled mess. However, not only were the grave clothes still there, indicating the body had not been stolen, but they were neatly **folded** (vv. 6-7).

Fear of the Jews indicated why Joseph of Arimathea had not come forward earlier to identify himself as a disciple (19:39) as well as why the apostles were gathering behind **locked doors** (20:19). On the other hand, Mary Magdalene went alone to the tomb of Jesus **while it was still dark** (20:1), while Simon Peter and the beloved disciple waited until it was becoming daylight to go (20:2-8). Mary Magdalene is a wonderful example of eagerness to minister to and to honor the Lord. The risen Lord Jesus chose to send her to His **brothers** (20:17) before the apostles received Christ's command, sending them out with the message of forgiveness in the power of the **Holy Spirit** (20:21-23). Mary had the honor of being the first messenger commissioned by the risen Christ.

In John, Mary Magdalene was the carrier of the news about the empty tomb and the resurrected Lord to the other disciples. Perhaps the bookend effect created by the repeated wording, "because of his fear of the Jews" in 19:38 and "because of their fear of the Jews" in 20:19, is a literary touch that spotlighted this woman disciple. That wording is found elsewhere in John only in 7:13, a reference to why many Jews would not openly seek Jesus. This observation affirms the courage of Mary Magdalene, who faithfully bore her testimony in a fearful situation (20:18).

Jesus' salutation, **Woman,** was the polite way of addressing a woman. Mary did not recognize His voice then, but immediately when He uttered her name, she knew it was the Lord. Mary used the affectionate and respectful address **Rabbouni** (Aram. "my master, my teacher"). When Jesus said to Mary, **Don't cling to**

me (v. 17), He was not concerned about being touched since He asked Thomas to touch Him (v. 27). Rather, He wanted Mary to realize that He was there only temporarily. His return to the Father was imminent. "Brothers" included more than His siblings. The disciples now were related to Him in a new way because of His representing them to the Father (Heb 2:11-12). Jesus used **My Father and your Father** because Mary's relationship to God was different from His own (v. 17).

The phrase **He breathed on them** (v. 22) again used Old Testament imagery (Gn 2:7; Ezk 37:9). Christ imparted spiritual life in the same way God gave physical life to Adam. This bestowal of the Holy Spirit on the disciples was a precur-sor of what would take place at Pentecost (Ac 2:1-4). God does not look to any man to decide whether or not to forgive (v. 23). However, those who represent Him in sharing the gospel are recognized by for-giving or not forgiving sins, depending on whether the one who hears the message of salvation accepts or rejects Christ as Sav-ior. Because the first two verbs are aorist tense, which implies a one-time action, and the other verbs are in perfect tense, which suggests a continuation and ongo-ing of the action of the former verbs, a more literal translation would be thus: "Those whose sins you forgive have already been forgiven; those whose sins you do not forgive have not been for-given" (see comments on Mt 16:19).

Mary Magdalene *John 20:1-18*	
Her life <u>before Christ</u>	• From Magdala on the Sea of Galilee • Suffered from demon possession • Family background unknown • Held high social position and wealth • Healed by Jesus Christ
Her life <u>with Christ</u>	• Disciple of Jesus Christ • Traveled with Jesus in ministry • Cared for the needs of Jesus • Supported His work financially • Spent Jesus' last day with Him • Witnessed the trial of Jesus • Saw Him nailed to the cross • Comforted Jesus as He died
Her life <u>after Christ</u>	• Witnessed the burial of Jesus Christ • First to witness His resurrection • Told the disciples of His resurrection • Received comfort from angels • Encountered the risen Savior • Announced His resurrection • Spread the gospel for the rest of her life
See also Mt 27:56,61; 28:1; Mk 15:40,47; 16:9; Lk 8:2; 24:10; Jn 19:25.	

Purpose of the Gospel (20:30-31)

20:30-31 Thomas's confession of faith in Christ is a great spontaneous testimony of genuine belief (v. 28). Thomas had moved from the lowest measure of faith—doubt and unbelief—to the highest confidence and faith. **My Lord** was Jesus' title used by His disciples, and **my God** was full acknowledgment of His deity.

John included Jesus' last beatitude (v. 29) in this Gospel. Jesus pronounced a blessing on those who, unlike Thomas, would never see Him in the flesh but yet would exercise faith and believe in Him and His resurrection. Immediately following is the purpose statement of the entire Gospel (v. 31). These verses describe in essence the overall strategy, subject, and purpose of the book of John. The *strategy* is to describe the works of Jesus as "signs" in order to illustrate Jesus' character, His power, and His appeal to human need. The main *subject* of the Gospel is Jesus Christ, **the Son of God**. He would fulfill God's purposes for the Jewish people and for the entire world. The *purpose* is that the readers might **believe** in Him. To believe in Jesus means to accept the revelation of God that comes through Jesus in its totality, to acknowledge His divine authority, and to accept the commission He gives to His disciples. The acceptance of the entire scope of this belief is beautifully illustrated in chapter 21.

CONCLUDING TESTIMONY (21:1-25)

The Reinstatement of the Disciples (21:1-23)

21:1-23 The miracle of the catch of fish in this passage was much like the account of the initial call of the disciples recorded in Luke 5:1-11; the action of Simon Peter is in character with other representations of him (Mt 16:21-23; 26:33-35; Jn 13:36-38; 18:10-11,15-18,25-27; 20:6); the reference to "sheep" closely followed the metaphor in 10:1-18; verse 19 used language concerning Peter that is applied to Jesus in 12:33. Another important point of this section has to do with John's desire to quell the rumor that he would not die before Christ's return.

John introduced a play on words in the exchange between Jesus and Peter. Jesus asked Peter, **Do you love Me?** three times (vv. 15,16,17). Three times Peter had denied Christ (18:16-17,25-27), and Jesus, in restoring Peter, gave him three opportunities to affirm his love for the Lord. In the first two questions, Jesus used the Greek verb *agapas* ("value, esteem, feel generous concern, be faithful towards, delight in") with a sense of fixing upon the idea of self-giving, a love committed without concern for "what is in it for me." Peter, in all three responses used the Greek verb *philō* ("manifest kindness or affection, like, have fondness for") in the sense of having high regard or affection for one because you see value in that one. The two words can be almost synonymous, but in this exchange the context seems to support a shade of difference. Perhaps Peter was cautious in his avowal because of his bitter disappointment over having denied Jesus earlier. However, Jesus seemed to be making His point concerning the nature of Peter's love, coupling the question of love with the responsibility of ministry for Christ—**feed** (Gk. *boske*, "tend," vv. 15,17) and **shepherd** (Gk. *poimaine*, "guide, protect," v. 16; "nurture," v. 16) **My lambs** (Gk. *arnia*) in verse 15 and **My sheep** (Gk. *probate*) in verses 16 and 17. Both "lambs" and "sheep" denote tenderness and suggest care and protection. Jesus also prophesied that Peter would die as a martyr because of his commitment to follow Christ (vv. 18-19). Many interpret **stretch out your hands** as a reference to crucifixion. According to tradition, Peter was crucified in Rome between AD 64 and 68, and he insisted on being crucified upside down because he did not feel worthy to die as his Savior did.

THE EPILOGUE (21:24-25)

21:24-25 The epilogue contains many descriptions that suggest the author was an actual participant in the events taking place. However, in a peculiar sense these words were also penned for a people who were far removed from these events (v. 24). When the Fourth Gospel was written, the New Testament literature (such as the Synoptic Gospels and perhaps some of Paul's letters) was probably already circulating and becoming well-known. John freely admitted that he recorded only a mere pittance of Jesus' words and deeds. Yet his testimony has enriched the church throughout the generations.

Bibliography

*Borchert, Gerald L. *John 1–11*. The New American Commentary, vol. 25A. Nashville: Broadman and Holman, 1996.

*_____. *John 12–21*. The New American Commentary, vol. 25B. Nashville: Broadman and Holman, 2002.

*Bruce, F. F. *The Gospel of John*. Grand Rapids: Eerdmans, 1983.

*Carson, D. A. *The Gospel of John*. The Pillar New Testament Commentary. Grand Rapids: Eerdmans, 1991.

Hendriksen, William. *New Testament Commentary: Exposition of the Gospel According to John*. Grand Rapids: Baker Book House, 1953.

*Hengstenberg, E. W. *Commentary on the Gospel of John*. Volumes 1–2. Minneapolis: Klock & Klock Christian Publishers, Inc., 1980 Reprint. Originally Edinburgh: T & T Clark, 1865.

Keller, Phillip. *A Shepherd Looks at the Good Shepherd and His Sheep*. Grand Rapids: Zondervan, 1978.

Morgan, G. Campbell. *The Gospel According to John*. London: Marshall, Morgan & Scott, Ltd., n.d.

*Morris, Leon. *The Gospel According to John*. Revised edition. Grand Rapids: Eerdmans, 1995.

Phillips, John. *Exploring the Gospels: John*. Neptune, NJ: Loizeaux Brothers, 1988.

Tenney, Merrill C. *John*. The Expositor's Bible Commentary, vol. 5. Grand Rapids: Zondervan, 1981.

Thomas, David. *The Gospel of John: Expository and Homiletical Commentary*. Grand Rapids: Kregel Publications, 1980.

*Westcott, Brooke Foss. *The Gospel According to St. John: The Greek Text with Introduction and Notes*. Thornapple Commentaries. Edited by A. Westcott. Grand Rapids: Baker Book House, 1980.

Witherington, Ben, III. *John's Wisdom: A Commentary on the Fourth Gospel*. Louisville: Westminster/John Knox, 1995.

*For advanced study.

Notes

1 C. H. Dodd, *Historical Tradition in the Fourth Gospel* (New York: CUP, 1963), 423.
2 Gerald L. Borchert, *John 1–11,* The New American Commentary, vol. 25A (Nashville: Broadman and Holman, 1996), 94.
3 Irenaeus, *Against Heresies* 3.3.4; Eusebius, *Ecclesiastical History* 4.14.3.
4 D. A. Carson, *The Gospel According to John* (Grand Rapids: Eerdmans, 1991), 251.
5 Henry George Liddell and Robert Scott, *A Greek-English Lexicon*, 9th ed. (Oxford: Clarendon Press, 1966), 1001.
6 Note the mention of Bethany in Mt 26:6; Lk 10:38; 24:50; Jn 12:1.

[7] Ben Witherington, *John's Wisdom; A Commentary on the Fourth Gospel* (Louisville: Westminster/John Knox Press, 1995), 112, 115–116.

[8] F .F. Bruce, *The Gospel of John* (Grand Rapids: Eerdmans, 1983), 257.

ACTS

$\mathcal{I}$ntro$\tilde{d}$uction

Acts, one of the most exciting books in the New Testament, is action packed, providing relevant details pertaining to the spread of the gospel and the beginning of the Christian church. Covering a span of 30 years, Acts recounts the expansion of the church from its Jewish roots in Jerusalem all the way to Rome, the center of the Roman Empire.

For several reasons, Acts is a significant book in the New Testament:

- Acts functions as a hinge between the Gospels and the Epistles or Letters. Acts is the only historical sequel to the Gospels in the Bible, providing the background and setting for many of the Pauline Letters. If the church did not have Acts, all that is known about the beginnings of Christianity would be the bits gathered from Paul's letters.

- A reading of Acts enables believers to understand God's purposes and plans for the church. The book furnishes principles for revival and missionary work; it gives guidance for church government; it teaches how to disciple believers and how to grow churches; and it presents a strategy for evangelizing the world.

- Acts presents essential doctrine, providing the foundation for the doctrine of the Holy Spirit. Over 50 times in its 28 chapters the Holy Spirit is mentioned. Acts provides the historical model for the doctrine of the church, showing how the church began and expanded. Acts also provides insight, through apostolic sermons found throughout the book, into many other doctrines, such as the person and work of Christ, and the doctrine of salvation.

$\mathcal{T}$itle

Acts was originally written as a sequel to the Gospel of Luke (see Lk 1:1-4; Ac 1:1-2). During the first century Acts and Luke likely circulated as a two-volume set. Early in the second century, the two works separated, and Luke became identified with the other three Gospels, thus forming and circulating as the Gospels. Acts apparently did not have a fixed title until around the third century.

Acts was referenced by a number of second-century writers. Irenaeus (c. AD 130–190), bishop of the church of Lyons in Gaul, described Acts as "Luke's witness to the apostles." Tertullian (c. AD 150–220) referred to it as "Luke's Commentary," and the Muratorian Canon (c. AD 170–200) deemed it "The Acts of All the Apostles." The earliest known reference to the modern rendering "The Acts of the Apostles" occurred around AD 160 in the anti-Marcionite prologue to Luke.

The controversy over the title in the second century has continued in the modern age. Some commentators suggest that "Acts of the Apostles" is not the most accurate title for the work. They argue that the book does not contain all the acts of all the apostles. Other than listing all the apostles in chapter 1 and a few other minor refer-ences, only the ministries of Peter and Paul are emphasized. A second criticism given is that the title fails to note the importance and centrality of the Holy Spirit throughout the book; thus some have proposed "The Acts of the Holy Spirit." Nevertheless, notwithstand-ing the emphasis in Acts on the outpouring of the Holy Spirit in Jerusalem (2:1-4), Samaria (8:17), Caesarea (10:44-46), and Ephesus (19:6), the content of the book is much broader than this title proposes, which could suggest a combination of the two titles—"The Acts of the Holy Spirit Through the Apostles." Others have argued vehemently that the work should be called "The Acts of the Apostles." Current scholars frequently shorten the title to "Acts" (Gk. *praxeis*, a word often used to describe the "acts" of great men). Since the book tells the story of how the Holy Spirit accomplished great acts through men and women of the early church, Acts is a fitting title.

Setting

The book of Acts extends Luke's carefully investigated narrative of the life and teachings of Jesus the Christ to include the early history of the church. The Gospel of Luke closed with the ascension of Jesus and His promise to send power "from on high" (Lk 24:49) to the disciples as they followed His instructions to "stay in the city" of Jerusalem. The first chapters of Acts describe the fulfillment of this promise to send the Holy Spirit; the rest of the book traces the spread of the gospel and the church from its birth in Jerusalem to the far reaches of the Roman Empire.

The historical convergence of three civilizations facilitated this movement of the gospel message and the transformation of Christianity from a Jewish sect into a world religion. The Roman Empire unified the Mediterranean world under a central government that pro-vided peace, stability, and freedom to travel among the various provinces under Roman rule. The predominant language across the empire was Greek, and Greek thought domi-nated the intellectual climate. Nevertheless, both the history and theology of Christianity were rooted in the Old Testament (known as the *Septuagint* in its Greek translation) and Jewish life. Jews of the Dispersion (or *Diaspora*) lived throughout the Roman Empire. Luke was an eyewitness to the missionary thrust of the early church and was especially familiar with Paul's journeys to the major cities dotting the coasts and major islands of the Mediterranean and Aegean Seas. Paul planted churches particularly in large population centers such as Ephesus, a city with approximately 250,000 people. In such metropolitan areas, Paul and his companions not only found Jewish synagogues but also encountered the marketplaces of ideas in the Greco-Roman world. Luke himself demonstrated in Acts a literary "ear" attuned to the various cultural and linguistic idioms of his time, employing the diction of Roman governors and Hellenistic Jews alike. Overall, in both his Gospel and Acts, Luke consciously sets the story of Jesus and His message into a global context of the world history and geography of his day.

Genre

Although the book of Acts reflects elements of the literary style and philosophical con-victions of other historians of antiquity, its unique character defies precise categorization. Certainly, the genre of Acts is that of historical narrative. In the tradition of Greek histori-ography, Luke summarized several formal speeches, provided detailed accounts of Paul's voyages, and generally recorded events in an episodic style. However, the book is also an extension of Luke's Gospel and therefore of the proclamation of the gospel. While Acts is certainly a historical record of the birth and missionary enterprise of the church, its focus is consistently on the transformation of ordinary people who give their lives to Christ and are thereby filled with the Holy Spirit. Luke wrote from the perspective of a believer, watching and participating in the gospel's powerful and widespread penetration of his world. Acts is an accurate historical witness to the truth of the gospel.

Author

Although Luke never named himself as the author, internal and external evidence both confirm his authorship. Internally, three primary lines of support exist. The first lies in the relationship between the Gospel of Luke and Acts. Luke and Acts have a common style, structure, and vocabulary, reaffirming that the same author produced both. This judgment has been universally accepted. In addition, both books are addressed to "Theophilus" (Lk 1:3; Ac 1:1). Acts 1:1 referenced the author's "first narrative . . . about all Jesus began to do and teach." When coupled with the fact that the last chapter of Luke provides a summary of the main themes of the first chapters of Acts, the latter book is readily accepted as a continuation of Luke.

A second internal indication for the Lukan authorship of Acts has to do with what are commonly called the "we" passages (16:10-17; 20:5-15; 21:1-18; 27:1–28:16). In the Acts narrative, the author transitioned from the third-person plural "they" to the first-person plural "we," indicating that the author traveled with Paul during portions of Paul's missionary journeys. From the "we" passages, one learns that whoever wrote Acts traveled with Paul to Rome. Since the prison letters were most likely written during the two years of Paul's imprisonment in Rome, one can determine who was with Paul at that time. From Colossians one learns that Tychicus (Col 4:7), Onesimus (Col 4:9), Mark (Col 4:10), Aristarchus (Col 4:10), Jesus called Justus (Col 4:11), Epaphras (Col 4:12), Demas (Col 4:14), and Luke (Col 4:14) were all with Paul in Rome. Additionally, from Philippians one learns that Timothy (Php 2:19) and Epaphroditus (Php 2:25) were with Paul. Of these, Aristarchus, Mark, Timothy, and Tychicus are mentioned in Acts through the use of the third person; thus none of them is the author. Since Demas later deserted Paul (2 Tm 4:10), he is not a viable option. Since Epaphroditus joined Paul after his arrival in Rome, he could not have described the voyage to Rome, nor could have Epaphras since he also arrived in Rome at a later date. That leaves Justus, Onesimus, and Luke as possible authors. Since no church tradition asserts that Justus or Onesimus wrote Acts, Luke is by far the most likely candidate.

A third internal indication for the Lukan authorship of Acts has to do with its excellent use of the Greek language. While some have attempted to argue that the author of Acts had to be a physician due to the use of technical medical terms within the book, these same terms were used by other first and second-century historians who were not physicians, such as Josephus. Nevertheless, the superb grammar and eloquence of Acts clearly reflects an educated writer. As a physician (Col 4:14), Luke would have been a well-educated man capable of this level of scholarship.

External evidence also supports the Lukan authorship of Acts. Tradition unanimously asserts that Luke wrote Acts. Irenaeus asserted that both the third Gospel and Acts were written by Luke, the physician and traveling companion of Paul. Likewise, the Muratorian Canon, Origen, Tertullian, and others all affirmed Luke's authorship. Since Luke was a somewhat obscure figure in the Bible—only mentioned three times—the church fathers would not likely have mistakenly attributed the work to Luke. If they had been wagering guesses concerning the author, they would have chosen a more prominent figure. Lukan authorship will be assumed for the remainder of this work.

Biblical knowledge about Luke as a person comes only from Paul's writings. In Colossians 4:14, Paul called him "the loved physician." In Philemon 24, Paul called him his "co-worker." Paul also indicated in 2 Timothy 4:11 that only Luke, possibly a Gentile Christian, was with him during his first imprisonment.

Early church tradition provides additional details about Luke's life. According to the anti-Marcionite prologue, Luke was a native of Antioch, Syria. He never married and died at age 84 in Boeotia. Luke's Antioch origin is logical, for 16 of the 18 times the place is mentioned in the Bible are in Acts. As one commentator noted, if Luke resided in Antioch, he would have met Barnabas, Paul, and Peter. He could have heard the gospel message, been converted, and become a disciple of the apostles. While it cannot be proven, Luke's association with Antioch is a likely possibility.

Date

Acts concludes with Paul's two-year imprisonment in Rome; therefore, the book must have been written during or after approximately AD 62. Logically, his writing would have been before the destruction of Jerusalem in AD 70 since Luke likely would not have ignored an event of such magnitude. Additionally, Luke would not have omitted Paul's death and martyrdom, which probably occurred between AD 66 and 68. Nor did Luke mention the Neronian persecutions, which began after the great fire of Rome in AD 64. Therefore, the Gospel of Luke was most likely completed shortly after Paul was released from his first imprisonment, with most of his writing prior to and during the imprisonment, putting the date of composition between AD 61 and 63.

Recipients

Like the Gospel of Luke, Acts is addressed to Theophilus (Gk., "lover of God," v. 1). The actual identity of Theophilus remains an enigma, as Luke and Acts provide the only known historical references to him. Theophilus could have been a new convert in need of full knowledge concerning the initiation and growth of Christianity or an interested Greek whom Luke hoped to convert to Christ. It has also been suggested that Theophilus was Paul's attorney for his defense in Rome. A more likely suggestion is that Theophilus was a high-ranking Roman official since Luke 1:3 refers to him as "most honorable Theophilus." One commentator pointed out that HONORABLE (Gk. kratistos), a title of respect describing Theophilus, was usually used for a person with social status and wealth, a conclusion supporting the idea that Theophilus was a high-ranking Roman official. This title was also used of Felix (Ac 24:3) and of Festus (Ac 26:25). Others believe that Luke was not addressing a specific individual named Theophilus but rather anyone who is a "lover of God." Although no conclusive answer can be discerned, Luke wrote the book to be read by many.

Theme

Many commentators consider Acts 1:8 the theme verse. In this verse, Jesus outlined the strategy for the apostles to fulfill the "Great Commission" (Mt 28:18-20; Lk 24:46-48). The verse also provided the basic geographical outline of the spread of the gospel as depicted in Acts. The good news of the gospel was first shared in Jerusalem (chaps. 1–5), then in Judea and Samaria (chaps. 6–8), and eventually all the way to Rome and "the ends of the earth" (chaps. 13–28). Although Rome is not literally "the ends of the earth," Luke effectively showed the potency of the gospel message and its spreading via the ministry of Christ's followers who had been empowered by the Holy Spirit.

The power and presence of the Holy Spirit is a second theme in Acts. In the book's 28 chapters, Luke mentioned the Spirit over 50 times. Although the Holy Spirit is not mentioned in 11 of the chapters, His activity pervades the entire book. The Holy Spirit is a gift to every believer (2:38); empowers believers to witness (1:8; 4:31); guides believers (8:29; 10:19; 16:6-7); and guides the church (13:2). The Holy Spirit was also essential in both the formation and fulfillment of the Scriptures (1:16; 4:25). From start to finish the work of the Holy Spirit is evident in Acts.

The ministries and lives of women in Acts are highlighted perhaps more than in any other New Testament book. The author of Acts demonstrated how women had an active and significant role in the formation of the early church. In Acts, Luke wrote about Lydia, who placed her faith in Christ and exercised her gift of hospitality by opening her home to Paul and his traveling companions (16:15). He also wrote about Sapphira, whose lie to the Holy Spirit resulted in the loss of her life (5:3-10). Godly women, such as Dorcas, who was miraculously raised from the dead by Peter (9:36-43), and Priscilla, who ministered alongside her husband, are included in the book. From beginning to end Luke noted important women who played key roles in the formation of the apostolic church. Discussions of these women will be included throughout the commentary.

Pronunciation Guide

Achaia	uh KAY yuh	Epicurean	ep ih kyoo REE uhn	Ptolemais	tahl uh MAY uhs
Adramyttium	ad ruh MIT ih uhm	Eunuch	YOO nuhk	Publius	PUHB lih uhs
Aeneas	ih NEE uhs	Gaius	GAY yuhs	Pyrrhus	PIHR uhs
Agabus	AG uh buhs	Gallio	GAL ih oh	Rhegium	REE jih uhm
Agrippa	uh GRIP uh	Gamaliel	guh MAY lih uhl	Sadducees	SAD joo sees
Amphipolis	am FIP uh lihs			Salamis	SAL uh miss
Ananias	an uh NIGH uhs	Hamor	HAY mawr	Salmone	sal MOH nih
Antioch	AN tih ahk	Iconium	igh (eye) KOH nih uhm	Samos	SAY mahs
Apollonia	ap uh LOH nih uh	Joppa	JAHP uh	Sanhedrin	san HEE drihn
		Lasea	luh SEE uh	Sapphira	suh FIGH ruh
Appius	AP ih uhs	Lucius	LYOO shuhs	Sceva	SEE vuh
Aquila	AK wih luh, uh KWIL uh	Lycaonian	lik ay OH nih uhn	Secundus	sih KUHN duhs
Aristarchus	ehr iss TAHR kuhs	Lydda	LID uh	Seleucia	sih LYOO shih uh
Artemis	AHR tih miss	Lystra	LISS truh	Sergius Paulus	suhr jih uhs-PAW luhs
Assos	ASS ahs	Macedonia	mass uh DOH nih uh		
Barsabbas	bahr SAB uhs	Manaen	MAN uh en	Shechem	SHEK uhm
Beroea	bih REE uh	Medes	MEEDS	Simeon, called Niger	SIM ih uhn / NIGH guhr
Bithynia	bih THIN ih uh	Mesopotamia	mess uh puh TAY mih uh	Sopater	SAHP uh tuhr, SOH puh tuhr
Caesarea	sess uh REE uh	Miletus	migh LEE tuhs	Stoic	STOH ihk
Caiaphas	KAY uh fuhs, KIGH uh fuhs	Mitylene	mit uh LEE nih	Syracuse	SIHR uh kyooz
Cappadocia	kap uh DOH shih uh	Mnason	NAY suhn	Syrtis	SUHR tiss
		Mysia	MISS ih uh	Tarsus of Cilicia	TAHR suhs / sih LISH ih uh
Cauda	KAW duh	Nicanor	nigh KAY nawr		
Cenchreae	SEN kree uh	Nicolaus	NIK oh luhs	Tertullus	tuhr TUHL uhs
Chios	KIGH ahs	Pamphylia	pam FIL ih uh	Theophilus	thee AHF ih luhs (th as in thin)
Claudius Lysias	KLAW dih uhs LISS ih uhs	Paphos	PAY fahs, PA fahss		
Cnidus	NIGH duhs	Parmenas	PAHR mih nuhs	Thessalonica	thess uh loh NIGH kuh
Cornelius	kawr NEE lih uhs	Parthians	PAHR thih uhns	Timon	TIGH mahn
Cos	KAHS	Patara	PAT uh ruh	Titius Justus	TIT ih uhs-JUHS tuhs, TIH shuhs (Roman)
Crispus	KRISS puhs	Pharisee	FEHR uh see		
Damacus	duh MASS kuhs	Philippi	FIH lih pigh		
Demetrius	dih MEE trih uhs	Phoenicia	fih NISH ih uh	Troas	TROH az
		Phrygia	FRIJ ih uh	Trophimus	TRAHF ih muhs
Derbe	DUHR bih	Pisidia	pih SID ih uh		
Drusilla	droo SIL uh	Porcius Festus	pawr shuss FESS tuhss	Tyrannus	tigh RAN uhs
Elamites	EE luhm ights			Tyre	TIGHR
Elymas	EL ih mass	Prochorus	PRAHK uh ruhs		
Ephesus	EF uh suhs				

Outline

I. INTRODUCTION (1:1-11)

   A. The Prologue (1:1-3)

   B. The Promise of the Holy Spirit (1:4-8)

   C. The Ascension (1:9-11)

II. PETER: MISSIONARY TO THE JEWS (1:12–12:25)

   A. The Spread of the Gospel to Jerusalem (1:12–5:16)

   B. Opposition to Christianity in Jerusalem (5:17-42)

   C. The Selection of the Seven Deacons (6:1–8:3)

   D. The Spread of the Gospel in Judea, Galilee, and Samaria (8:4–9:31)

   E. The Spread of the Gospel as Far as Phoenicia, Cyprus, and Antioch (9:32–12:25)

III. PAUL: MISSIONARY TO THE GENTILES (13:1–28:31)

   A. The Spread of the Gospel through the Region of Phrygia and Galatia (13:1–15:35)

    1. Paul's first missionary journey (13:1–14:28)

    2. Conflicts in the church (15:1-35)

   B. The Spread of the Gospel into Macedonia (15:36–21:14)

    1. The separation of Paul and Barnabas (15:36-41)

    2. Paul's second missionary journey (16:1–18:23)

    3. Paul's third missionary journey (18:24–21:14)

   C. The Spread of the Gospel to Rome (21:15–28:31)

    1. Paul's arrest (21:15–22:29)

    2. Paul's defense before the Sanhedrin (22:30–23:10)

    3. The plot against Paul (23:11-35)

    4. The accusation against Paul (24:1–26:32)

    5. Paul's journey to Rome (27:1–28:31)

Exposition of the Text

INTRODUCTION (1:1-11)

The Prologue (1:1-3)

1:1-3 The first few verses indicate that Luke and Acts shared a common author and were compiled as a two-part work. Verses 1-11 serve as a bridge between the account of Jesus' life and ministry in the Gospel of Luke and the historical account of the development of the apostolic church in Acts. The author Luke began Acts by briefly summarizing the conclusion of the Gospel of Luke, highlighting the **40 days** Jesus ministered on the earth after the resurrection (v. 3), the promised coming of the Holy Spirit (vv. 4-8), and the ascension (vv. 9-11).

Acts, like the Gospel of Luke, is addressed to **Theophilus**, whose Greek name means "lover of God" or "friend of God." Theophilus might have been a specific individual to whom Luke was writing, or the name could have symbolized all who love God (see extended discussion in "Recipients" within the introduction). The author also referred to his **first narrative**, the Gospel of Luke, which was **about all that Jesus began to do and teach** (v. 1). Luke did not mean by "all" that the Gospel of Luke included everything that Jesus did and taught; rather, he used the word to denote all that he recorded in the third Gospel. Acts continued the record of the ministry Jesus "began" while on the earth.

The brief mention of the ascension, **the day He was taken up** (v. 2), paralleled the Gospel of Luke's closing words: "He left them and was carried up into heaven" (Lk 24:51). The ascension occurred after the crucifixion of Christ (**after He had suffered**), after He had **presented Himself alive** to the apostles with **many convincing proofs**, and **after He had given orders through the Holy Spirit to the apostles**. The orders Jesus gave to His apostles were twofold: to wait on the promised Holy Spirit (Lk 24:49; Ac 1:4-5) and to be His witnesses beginning in Jerusalem (Lk 24:47-48; Ac 1:8).

Clearly from the reference to the apostles **whom He had chosen**, one can deduce that the apostles were not randomly chosen men (v. 4). Jesus came in God's perfect timing (Gl 4:4), and He chose apostles ordained by God.

The Promise of the Holy Spirit (1:4-8)

1:4-8 While Jesus was with the apostles during His last days on earth, **He commanded them not to leave Jerusalem, but to wait for the Father's promise** (v. 4). Jesus had previously instructed the disciples that upon His departure, the Father would send the Holy Spirit who would guide them in all truth (Jn 14:19-26; 16:7-13). The disciples must wait for the Holy Spirit who would empower them from on high (Lk 24:49). Jesus said that the time of the Holy Spirit's arrival was **not many days from now** (Ac 1:5). The awaited arrival would come on the "Day of Pentecost," approximately 50 days after the resurrection and only 10 days after the ascension (2:1-13).

The unprecedented boldness characterizing the witness documented throughout the book of Acts was inevitable for these reasons:

- the infallible testimony of many eyewitnesses who had seen the resurrected Christ;

- the unique phenomenon of One who died and was placed in the grave and then arose;

- the disciples' first-hand understanding that Jesus had conquered death.

The promise of the Holy Spirit was foreshadowed by the ministry of John the Baptist. John had **baptized with water,** but the time was coming when people would **be baptized with the Holy Spirit** (1:5). John's baptism with water differed from the ordinance given to the church. John's baptism symbolized repentance, while a believer's baptism has an even greater significance, identifying the believer with Christ in His death, burial, and resurrection. The baptism of the Holy Spirit occurs only once in a Christian's life at the point of salvation, when the Holy Spirit enters the believer to take up permanent residence (v. 5; see Rm 8:9). The baptism of the Holy Spirit is an entirely divine activity that comes, like salvation itself, through grace and not by human effort. It is the ascension gift to the church. It is not a "second blessing" or some exclusive experience subsequent to conversion. Believers may be filled with the Holy Spirit again and again after conversion, at which point the Spirit is received (see Eph 5:18). Renewal experiences have been common among believers through the generations. This baptism of the Spirit is different from the continuing and repeated actions of being "filled with the Spirit" (Eph 5:18) and living by the Spirit (Gl 5:25).

Anticipating the coming of the kingdom, the apostles asked Jesus if he was **restoring the kingdom to Israel** (Ac 1:6). This question was a logical response because they linked the outpouring of the Holy Spirit with the coming of the promised kingdom (see Ezk 36; Jl 2:28–3:1; Zch 12:8-10). The apostles had not yet forsaken their belief that Jesus' goal was to establish His kingdom in their day and during their generation. They fully believed the kingdom belonged solely to Israel. Jesus chose not to answer their question about timing, for it was not for them **to know times or periods that the Father has set by His own authority** (Ac 1:7). Jesus had already told them that no one knows the day or hour but the Father (Mt 24:36). Instead of answering their question, Jesus refocused them on His mission for the world. He shifted from their focus on Israel and a restoration of the Jewish state, deliverance from Rome, and even the establishment of the messianic kingdom to His mission by reiterating His plan for the evangelization of the world. The word TIMES (Gk. *chronous*, "moment or occasion"), meaning "an epoch or extended block of time," together with PERIODS (Gk. *kairous*, "season or age"), meaning "set or limited period of time marked by the right circumstances," indicates that God has an overall agenda for all the generations and also purposeful plans for every season or age.

Jesus' plan for the evangelization of the world as well as a rough outline for the book of Acts is summarized in verse 8. Empowered by the Holy Spirit, the apostles **will be** Christ's **witnesses in Jerusalem** (chaps. 1–7), **in all Judea and Samaria** (chaps. 8–12), **and to the ends of the earth** (chaps. 13–28). This mandate, expressed with future tense verbs ("will receive" and "will be"), can be understood as both a command and a prophetic promise. The heart of Jesus' commission is the challenge to be WITNESSES (Gk. *matures*). "Witness" is a key word in the book of Acts as it is used 29 times as either a verb (*martuerō*) or a noun (*martus*). By definition, to bear witness means "to testify

to the truth of what one has seen, heard, or known." To be a witness for Jesus has been costly for many men and women who faithfully shared the gospel and as a result suffered torture and even death. In Acts, this was the case with both Stephen (7:59-60) and James (12:1). Many Christians throughout history have lost their lives due to a faithful witness. Eventually the Greek word for witness (*martus*) was anglicized as "martyr." In Acts, Luke illustrated how the church obediently carried out this mandate (2:47; 4:31,33; 6:4,7; 8:4) and how God intervened at particular times to provide direction for taking the mission across new cultural thresholds and into additional geographical regions (8:16-17,26,29; 10:9-16, 19-20; 11:20-21; 13:2; 16:9-10; 18:9-10; 23:11).

The evangelization of the world would begin in Jerusalem, the very city where Jesus was crucified. This plan was strategic because Jewish pilgrims attended festivals in Jerusalem each year during Pentecost. Many of these would become seed planters for the early expansion of the church. The church would expand to Judea (the larger region in which Jerusalem was located) and Samaria (the region to the north of Judea). Eventually, the church would expand "to the ends of the earth." While some believe that this latter reference is to Rome, since Acts concluded in Rome, more likely Jesus was referring to a genuinely worldwide witness.

All believers received their commission concerning what to do until Jesus returns. The Holy Spirit was poured out in the church collectively, a sign of the Lord's assignment to this entity to spread the gospel throughout the world. Clearly the Holy Spirit was to be the Guide for implementing this holy commission, and there were indispensable ingredients necessary to accomplish this awesome task:

- the authority of Christ;

- the presence of Christ;

- the power of the Spirit; and

- the saints who were obedient and available.

The Ascension (1:9-11)

1:9-11 The ascension of Christ was mentioned three times in the Bible (1:9-11; Mk 16:19-20; Lk 24:50-51). These accounts noted that from the Mount of Olives, Jesus lifted up His hands, blessed His disciples, and was **taken up** by a **cloud** into **heaven** (Ac 1:9) where He sat down at the right hand of God (Mk 16:19). The unique contribution of Acts to the ascension narrative concerns the details of Christ's return (Ac 1:10-11). Other Scriptures confirm that one day Christ will return again to the Mount of Olives to set up His earthly kingdom in the same way He ascended into the clouds (Dn 7:13; Mt 24:30; 26:64; Lk 21:27; Rv 1:7; 14:14).

PETER: MISSIONARY TO THE JEWS (1:12–12:25)

The Spread of the Gospel to Jerusalem (1:12–5:16)

1:12-14 After witnessing the ascension of Christ, the apostles obeyed Jesus' command and **returned to Jerusalem from the mount called Olive Grove**, more commonly referred to as the Mount of Olives, which was **a Sabbath day's journey away** (v. 12). A Sabbath day's journey was equal to three fourths of a mile. They could have traveled this distance. No restrictions applied because they traveled on a Thursday, 40 days after the resurrection.

The women and Jesus' **brothers** joined the 11 apostles (v. 14). **Mary the mother of Jesus** was among the women, this encounter being the last mention of her in the New Testament. Mary Magdalene, Mary the wife of Clopas, Martha, Joanna, Susanna, and Salome, as well as others, were possibly present. These women had been a vital part of Jesus' ministry, accompanying Him when He traveled and supporting Him financially (Lk 8:1-3). Some of them followed Jesus from Galilee before His crucifixion (Lk 23:27), stood at a distance from the cross when He died (Jn 19:25), made the necessary preparations for His burial (Lk 23:55-56; 24:1), and reported the news of Jesus' resurrection to the 11 apostles (Lk 24:9-10). These faithful followers of Christ gathered in **the room upstairs** to pray with the apostles (Ac 1:13).

1:15-26 Over the course of the 10 days between the ascension and Pentecost, the believers in Jerusalem gathered together to pray and to discuss the vacancy among the apostles left by the departure of Judas Iscariot (vv. 16-20). The text indicates that **Peter stood up among the brothers**. Depending on the context, the Greek word used here for **BROTHERS** (Gk. *adelphōn*, "near kinsman or associate") can refer to men and women or to siblings. The term is not gender specific. This generic reference may well be to brothers and sisters in the family of God. Luke noted that the group numbered approximately **120** (v. 15). This number may have been significant because Jewish law required 120 men to establish a community with its own council. Luke might have been asserting that the group of believers was now large enough to form its own community.

In Peter's speech to the 120 Jerusalem believers, he recounted Judas's death, and he called for his replacement, referring to the Old Testament (v. 20). According to Acts, **this man**, meaning Judas, **acquired a field with his unrighteous wages** (v. 18). The Gospel of Matthew provided more specific details, noting that Judas returned the money he received for betraying Jesus to the chief priests and the elders. They then bought the **Field of Blood** (see Mt 27:3-9). Luke simply noted in Acts that Judas's money purchased the "Field of Blood" (Aram. *Hakeldamach*). Matthew demonstrated that the purchase of the field fulfilled Scripture, while Luke showed that Judas received what he deserved—a horrible death. Luke provided the more vivid account of Judas's death (Ac 1:18). Matthew only noted that Judas hanged himself (Mt 27:5). Even though Luke omitted this information, one can deduce Judas's **falling headfirst** resulted from his being suspended. The rope either broke due to the weight of his body, or someone cut the rope. While falling, Judas's body probably struck a sharp object, causing his body to **burst open**.

The Old Testament words, **Let his dwelling become desolate; let no one live in it** (Ac 1:20; Ps 69:25) predicted Judas's removal from office. The necessity of a replacement for Judas came from Psalm 109:8 (Ac 1:20). Significantly, the number of apostles paralleled the 12 tribes of Israel. The apostles would "sit on 12 thrones, judging the 12 tribes of Israel" (Mt 19:28). Peter noted that the new apostle would come **from among the men who** had **accompanied** the apostles **the whole time the Lord Jesus went in and out among** them, from Jesus' baptism to His ascension. The replacement also had to have witnessed Jesus' resurrection (Ac 1:21-22).

The apostle was to come "from among the men" (v. 21). A woman apostle was not an option, even though women had been a part of kingdom service throughout Jesus' ministry. The leadership role of an apostle belonged exclusively to men. Jesus had purposefully chosen 12 men to be His apostles and the replacement would be a man as well.

Two men meeting the requirements for apostleship were proposed: **Joseph, called Barsabbas, who was also known as Justus, and Matthias** (v. 23). To determine who the **Lord** had **chosen** as the replacement, they began by praying (v. 24). Unable to make a decision on their own, they decided to **cast lots**, and **the lot fell to Matthias** (v. 26). Casting lots was an Old Testament practice for discerning the will of God when a prophet was not available (Pr 16:33). After the outpouring of the Holy Spirit at Pentecost, this practice became unnecessary, as the Holy Spirit guides believers into all truth (Jn 16:13).

2:1-13 The day of Pentecost (Gk. *pentēkostēs*, "fifty") occurred approximately 50 days after the resurrection of Christ.[1] "Pentecost," the Feast of Weeks or Harvest in the Old Testament, was one of three annual feasts that brought all devout Jewish men to Jerusalem (see Ex 23:16; 34:22-23; Lv 23:15-21). When this eventful day arrived, **they were all together in one place** (Ac 2:1). Whether this group included only the 12 apostles or the 120 believers mentioned in 1:15 is unclear. The context seems to indicate the larger number (vv. 6-11). The **place**, which is referred to as a "house" in verse 2, was most likely the room upstairs in which the believers had been gathering for prayer (v. 1). The house was probably located close to the temple.

The word **suddenly** described the Spirit's arrival (v. 2), emphasizing the element of surprise, even though before His ascension Jesus said the Spirit would arrive not many days from now (1:5). Three signs accompanied the Spirit's arrival:

- **a sound like that of a violent rushing wind**

- **tongues, like flames of fire**

- the supernatural ability **to speak in different languages.**

For the first two signs, Luke, unable to explain verbally what happened, employed descriptive similes. He did make clear that this was a supernatural occurrence (2:2). The sound **filled the whole house** while the flames of fire **rested on each one** (v. 3), a change from the corporate resting of the Spirit on the nation of Israel to the indwelling of the Spirit in the hearts of individual believers. In Jewish tradition wind and fire both indicated God's holy presence. Fire was well-known to the Jews as an Old Testament symbol of the divine presence (Ex 3:2-5; 13:21; 24:17; 40:38). These "tongues" of fire were undoubtedly visible symbols that God was overshadowing their gathering. In both Hebrew and Greek, the word used for wind is synonymous with the word for Spirit. The wind represented the Spirit of God (Ezk 37:9,14). Luke wanted his readers to know that the Spirit's arrival meant God's presence.

When the promised Spirit arrived, **they were all filled with the Holy Spirit** (Ac 2:4). This initial filling of the Spirit was the baptism of the Spirit Jesus spoke about in Acts 1:5. While believers may be repeatedly filled with the Spirit, the baptism of the Spirit occurs only once, at the point of salvation. Significantly "all" were filled. The gift of the Spirit is not reserved for the most devout Christians but is a gift given to every believer. **The Spirit gave** those assembled at Pentecost the ability to speak in different languages (v. 4). This reference is not to ecstatic utterances as alluded to in 1 Corinthians 12–14. The words spoken at Pentecost were understood by those from various lands who were in Jerusalem for Pentecost, even though the languages were new to the speakers. DIFFERENT LAN-GUAGES (Gk. *heterais,* "another" in

the sense of a different kind; *glōssais,* "tongue or speech" in the sense of spoken language) in this context cannot be a reference to "unknown tongues." There was a language barrier because of visiting Jews who did not have an understanding of Hebrew or Aramaic. A linguistic miracle was the best option for communicating the gospel to the pilgrims coming from different regions outside Judea. Of course, Koine Greek as the *lingua franca* or common language could have been used, but God chose to reveal Himself in an extraordinary way that would not be missed by letting the people hear the message of salvation in their own respective languages (vv. 7-8).

There were Jews living in Jerusalem, devout men (v. 5). Although this group might include Jews visiting Jerusalem for Pentecost, they were primarily the Jews of the Diaspora who lived near the temple for the purpose of studying the law (v. 5). They represented the world at large. The **multitude** that **came together** was **confused** because **each one heard** the **Galileans speaking in** their **own language** (v. 6). Since all of the apostles were from Galilee, they alone could have been speaking, or the designation could have been to the believers in general since a majority of them would have been from Galilee. Luke then listed the nationalities represented at Pentecost, beginning in the east and moving towards the west (vv. 9-11). At least 15 languages were spoken and understood that day. In a sense, Pentecost was a reversal of the tower of Babel (Gn 11:1-9). At Babel, God confused the language so that people no longer understood each other, while at Pentecost God orchestrated a linguistic miracle allowing people from diverse lands to hear about **the magnificent acts of God** (Ac 2:11). The foundation was laid for an evangelistic effort among the Gentiles throughout the Roman Empire. While some embraced the truths spoken about Christ, others rejected the message, accusing the believers of being **full of new wine** (v. 13).

2:14-40 In response to the accusations of being drunk, **Peter stood up** with the support of the 11 other apostles and clarified that they were **not drunk** because it was **only nine in the morning** (vv. 14-15). Instead, they witnessed an act of God and a fulfillment of the prophecy **spoken through the prophet Joel** (vv. 16-21; Jl 2:28-32).

From beginning to end Peter's expository sermon came from Scripture. He quoted Joel 2:28-32, Psalm 16:8-11, and Psalm 110:1. He wanted his hearers to know that the coming of the Holy Spirit fulfilled Scripture as did the death, burial, and resurrection of Jesus Christ the Messiah. God poured out His **Spirit on all humanity** without discrimination: sons, daughters, young men, old men, male and female slaves (Ac 2:17). Through Jesus, salvation was made available to all (v. 21).

Some of Joel's prophecy was yet to be fulfilled (vv. 19-20). Even now believers enjoy messianic blessings, but more awaits those followers of Christ at His return when He establishes the millennial kingdom and ushers in eternal blessedness. MIRACLES (Gk. *dunamesi*, "works of power,"), WONDERS (Gk. *terasi*, "phenomena compelling attention or a second look"), and SIGNS (Gk. *sēmeiois*, "indication by which something is known") work together to describe the mighty works of Jesus and His disciples (v. 22). "Miracles" were a manifestation of power; "wonders" emphasized the physical way that power functioned and its result; "signs" summarized the spiritual significance of the wonder-causing miracles. God's sovereignty allowed Jesus to be nailed "to a cross" and killed, not accidentally,

but according to "God's determined plan and foreknowledge" (v. 23).

As prophesied by the **patriarch David**, Jesus **was not left in Hades and His flesh did not experience decay** (v. 31; Ps 16:10). HADES (Gk. *hadēs*, "underworld or death") is a word transliterated into English and interpreted by many as the place of the departed dead. Some make a distinction, considering "Hades" as a place for the unrighteous dead, while the righteous would go to "Abraham's bosom" (cp. Lk 16:19-31). However, in this context, the meaning seems to be that Jesus' body will not decay despite His suffering and death and thus "Hades," as *Sheol* (Hb.), would be understood as simply the place of the dead. Four proofs of Jesus' resurrection and ascension were provided by Peter:

- the prophecy of Psalm 16:8-11 and the presence of David's tomb (Ac 2:25-31)
- the witnesses of the resurrection (v. 32)
- the supernatural events of Pentecost (v. 33)
- the ascension of Christ, David's greater Son (Ps 110:1; Ac 2:34-35).

Because of these proofs Peter proclaimed that **the house of Israel** can **know with certainty** that Jesus is **both Lord and Messiah** (v. 36), titles legitimately belonging to Jesus because of His resurrection and ascension. The title Lord equates Jesus with *Yahweh*, the God of the Old Testament. The title Messiah (Gk. *Christon,* "anointed one") demonstrates that Jesus is the long awaited Jewish Messiah. Peter delivered this message to his Jewish audience. He blamed the Jews for the crucifixion of Jesus with the inclusion of the phrase **whom you crucified** (v. 36). Although the Romans physically nailed Jesus to the cross, the

Jewish religious leaders used their influence to insist on His death.

Peter's sermon **pierced** many of the Jewish listeners **to the heart**. They were convinced of the truths about Jesus and convicted of their sins. In desperation they asked the apostles, **what must we do?** (v. 37). Peter, still acting as the spokesman for the apostles, first commanded them to REPENT (Gk. meta-noēsate, a "change of direction or a change of purpose"), turning from sin to Christ, the essential beginning point for salvation (v. 38). This verb is second-person passive imperative, indicating a mandate for all to repent (i.e., you repent). However, "be baptized" is in third person imperative, which changes the emphasis to the individual's responsibility to act. Baptism is thus not a prerequisite for salvation but a personal choice for completing obedience to Christ with a public testimony of repentance and faith. Then Peter commanded them to BE BAPTIZED (Gk. baptisthētō, "immerse"), a public testimony of their repentance and trust in Christ. The English word "baptized" was transliterated rather than translated from the Greek language.

Some controversy surrounds the inclusion of a baptismal command with the phrase **for the forgiveness of your sins** (v. 38). There are two primary views. First, both repentance and baptism are necessary for salvation. This view is not viable because many other verses of Scripture clearly indicate that the forgiveness of sins results from faith alone (Jn 3:16; Rm 4:1-7; 11:6; Gl 3:8-9; Eph 2:8-9). Peter himself spoke of forgiveness of sins on the basis of faith alone (Ac 5:31; 10:43; 13:38-39). Additionally, the thief on the cross next to Jesus was never baptized; yet Jesus promised him a place in paradise (Lk 23:39-43). For these reasons, baptism is not essential for salvation.

A second and more plausible view translates Acts 2:38, "Be baptized . . . because of the remission of your sins." The Greek preposition eis, here translated BECAUSE OF, can also mean "on the basis of," which in this case would indicate that forgiveness of sins is the basis or reason for baptism. As with English prepositions, the word has a host of meanings. This translation is also appropriate in other verses (Mt 3:11; Mk 1:4). The process of translation is affected by other passages of Scripture, which in this case clearly teach that genuine faith in Christ is the only requisite for salvation. Forgiveness for sins does not come as a result of baptism but rather through what baptism symbolizes—the death, burial, and resurrection of Jesus.

Salvation and the accompanying **gift of the Holy Spirit** were promised to all who trust Christ for their salvation, **as many as the Lord our God will call** (Ac 2:39). This salvation came not only to the Jews of Peter's day but also comes to future generations and for **all who are far off,** which included the Gentiles.

2:41-47 Due to the supernatural movement of the Holy Spirit, **about 3,000 people** repented, believed, and were baptized, demonstrating their full identification with Christ. These new converts were immediately **added to them**—to the church in Jerusalem—on the basis of their faith and baptism (v. 41). Additionally, disciples were devoting **themselves to the apostles' teaching, to fellowship, to the breaking of bread, and to prayers**—four elements critical to discipleship (v. 42). The new believers received in-depth teaching about their faith, engaged in corporate fellowship with other believers in the church, participated in the Lord's Supper, and were active in prayer.

The FEAR (Gk. phobos, "amazement") or reverential awe that "came over everyone" was a result of the realization of the power and majesty of God. The **many wonders and signs** performed **through the apostles** authenticated their message about Christ (v. 43).

All the believers were together and had everything in common (v. 44). Unity marked the early church. They cared for one another, giving **as anyone had a need** (v. 45). This voluntary selling and sharing of goods was not compulsory but the result of their deep commitment to both God and each other. Some have erroneously interpreted this passage to support communism. Clearly Christian unity was distinct from this evil social ideology:

- Christian communal life began with a community of baptized believers, which meant instant rejection socially

and economically and often persecution from government.

- Wealthy believers like Barnabas (4:36-37) voluntarily gave generously to meet the needs of other less fortunate believers.

- Believers never sought to establish dependence upon the state or upon others; they worked hard within a hostile world. There is no evidence that communal life became a pattern.

They met daily both publicly **in the temple complex** and privately **from house to house** to enjoy life **with gladness and simplicity of heart** and to grow in their faith (v. 46).

Heart to Heart: Baptism and Salvation

Acts 2:38 states, "Repent and be baptized for the remission of sin." Acts 22:16 states, "Arise and be baptized and wash away your sins." By focusing on verses like these, some religious groups suggest that baptism is required for salvation. However, a study of the New Testament will reveal that this understanding cannot be confirmed by the whole counsel of God.

The New Testament teaches that salvation comes by grace through faith and not by baptism (Jn 3:16,36; Eph 2:8-9). Another refutation of baptismal regeneration is found in the story of the thief on the cross, whom Jesus promised would join Him in paradise on that day (Lk 23:43).

Baptism constitutes a very important step of obedience in following the commands of Jesus Christ. However, salvation does not require baptism. The elderly woman saved on her death bed does not have to be baptized in order to go to heaven, and the child who professes Christ but is not quite ready for baptism does not have to be baptized. Baptism constitutes the first step of obedience of a believer, not a requirement for salvation.

3:1-10 The healing of the lame man is one of the wonders and signs performed by the apostles (2:43). The miracle occurred **at three in the afternoon,** one of the three daily hours **of prayer** for Jews. Many people would have been on hand to witness this miracle at this time (3:1). The text indicates that the lame man begged **every day at the temple gate called Beautiful**, a large and ornate gate inside the temple mount on the eastern side, separating the court of Gentiles from the court of women. Peter, apparently with John looking on, performed the healing **in the name of Jesus Christ the Nazarene** (v. 6). To invoke the name of Jesus means to call upon His authority and power. The healing was **at once** and complete since the man **jumped up**. The man then entered the temple complex with Peter and John, **walking, leaping, and praising God** (v. 8). After 40 years of disability, the man **who used to sit and beg** was **walking and praising God** (v. 10).

3:11-26 Due to the miraculous healing and the man's exuberant response, a crowd of **amazed** people **ran towards** Peter, John, and the healed man, gathering at **Solomon's Colonnade** (5:12). The Colonnade, an impressive structure with a portico of columns running along the east side of the outer court of the temple and extending over 300 yards, was a place where believers often met together. Seizing the opportunity, Peter, who had denied Christ three times approximately two months earlier, in an amazing transformation began preaching his second major sermon in Acts.

Peter began by identifying the source of the healing—not his or John's **own power or godliness**, but rather the power of **Jesus** who was **glorified** by **the God of Abraham, Isaac, and Jacob** (vv. 12-15). By using this familiar Old Testament depiction of God employed throughout the Old Testament, Peter emphasized continuity with the Old Testament prophets. God's **Servant Jesus** was the Messiah and the Suffering Servant spoken about by the prophets (Is 42:1-4; 52:13–53:12).

As in his sermon at Pentecost, Peter laid blame for the crucifixion of Jesus on the Jews, providing more details by noting that the Jews **handed over** Jesus to be crucified even though **Pilate . . . had**

decided to release Him (Acts 3:13-15). The Roman governor Pontius Pilate recognized Jesus' innocence and attempted to release Him; however, the Jews requested that the **murderer** Barabbas be released instead (Mt 27:15-26; Mk 15:6-15; Lk 23:13-25).

This lame man walked **by faith in** Jesus' **name** (Acts 3:16). Is it the faith of Peter and John or the faith of the lame man previously healed? Perhaps both. For Peter and John to perform the miracle required their faith, and for the man to stand up and walk required faith on his part. Clearly the healing occurred as a result of faith in Jesus.

After confronting the Jews with the crucifixion of Christ, Peter acknowledged that they **did it in ignorance**, as Jesus previously stated while on the cross: "They do not know what they are doing" (Lk 23:34). The Jews alone should not be held responsible. This redemption via the cross had been **predicted through the mouth of all the prophets** (Acts 3:20-24). The death of Christ was no surprise but a fulfillment of prophecy to provide atonement for the sins of all.

Peter pleaded with his Jewish listeners to **repent and turn back** (v. 19), which in other translations (e.g., the King James Version) is rendered "repent . . . and be converted." Peter wanted them to be saved so that their sins would be WIPED OUT (Gk. *exaleiphō*, "remove, destroy"), implying a complete blotting out or erasing of sin. When one trusts Christ for the forgiveness of sins, Christ removes those sins as far as the east is from the west (Ps 103:12). Peter stressed that repentance and conversion bring the forgiveness of sins.

When Jesus returns, He will set up a millennial (or 1,000-year) kingdom on earth, and the living Jews of that day will experience the **seasons of refreshing** that **come from the presence of the Lord** (Acts

3:19; Rm 11:26). Until that day, which is **the times of the restoration of all things**, Jesus will remain in **heaven** (v. 21). The Jews had been awaiting the establishment of the earthly millennial kingdom spoken about **by the mouth of His holy prophets from the beginning** (v. 21).

As examples of those prophets, Peter quoted the words of **Moses** (vv. 22-23; Dt 18:15-19) and referenced Samuel, who, in the days of his youth, was given his prophetic role, and Abraham (Acts 3:24-25). The **Prophet** or Messiah, coming **from among your brothers**, would be of Jewish descent (v. 22). Additionally, He would come from the seed of Abraham since through Abraham's seed **all the families on the earth will be blessed** (v. 25; Gn 12:3; 18:18; 22:18; 26:4). God's **Servant** Jesus was the One sent first to the Jewish people, in an attempt to **bless** them; yet they rejected Him (Acts 3:26).

4:1-4 While Peter and John were **speaking to the people** who had observed the lame man's healing (3:1-10), they were **confronted** by three interacting groups of people: **the priests, the commander of the temple guard, and the Sadducees** (v. 1). The priests were primarily Sadducees. The commander of the temple guard, a powerful person next in rank to the high priest and a member of a leading priestly family, maintained order in the temple area. The Sadducees were a Jewish sect whose members came from the priestly line and controlled the temple. They had several defining characteristics:

- They did not believe in a bodily resurrection.

- They denied the existence of angels and spirits.

- They were loyal to the Roman government and sought to maintain the status quo.

- They were powerful and wealthy.

- They accepted only the Pentateuch, the first five books of the Old Testament.

Understandably, the Sadducees **were provoked** because Peter and John **were teaching the people and proclaiming** the resurrection (v. 2), a teaching in direct opposition to their beliefs. Additionally, Peter and John attracted a crowd, which caused the temple authorities to fear a riot. If a riot ensued, the priestly power and authority of the religious leaders could be taken away by the Romans. Therefore, **they seized** Peter and John, putting them in prison **until the next day** for **it was already evening** and too late for a trial (v. 3). Nevertheless, many Jews had already **heard the message** about Jesus and **believed**. In spite of the opposition, the number of believers continued to grow. Luke noted that "the number of MEN (Gk. *andrōn*, "male") came to about 5,000" (v. 4), the total of believing men at the time. Since "men" is not a gender neutral term, this number would not have included the women and children who had believed.

4:5-12 The next day Peter and John stood trial before the **rulers, elders, and scribes**, or the Sanhedrin, Israel's supreme court (Mk 15:1). **Annas the high priest** was actually the former high priest (AD 6–15) and the father-in-law of **Caiaphas**, the current high priest (AD 18–36). Annas, whose power had been removed by the Romans, was still regarded by the Jews as the high priest, thus possessing considerable power. **John** is a possible reference to Jonathan, one of Annas's sons, who later replaced Caiaphas as high priest in AD 36. Nothing is known about **Alexander,** though he may likely have been one of the **members of the high-priestly family** in attendance at the trial. Someone in this group, likely Annas or Caiaphas, questioned Peter and John about the healing (Acts 4:6-7).

The leaders of the Sanhedrin did not question the reality of the healing because a lame man known to everyone now walked. Instead, the Sanhedrin wanted to know **by what power or in what name** the healing had been performed (v. 7). Facing persecution, the power of **the Holy Spirit,** as Jesus had promised, enabled Peter to speak boldly yet succinctly in answering the questions from the Sanhedrin much as he had answered questions earlier from the crowd (3:11-26; Lk 12:11-12)). The healing was accomplished by the power and in **the name of Jesus Christ the Nazarene** (Acts 4:10). The Jews rejected Jesus and were responsible for His death. Peter noted that Jesus was **the stone despised by you builders** (v. 11; Ps 118:22). Peter identified the Jewish rulers as the "builders." Jesus' death was not final because **God raised** Jesus **from the dead,** and it was by His power that the once lame man was **standing** before the Sanhedrin **healthy** (Acts 4:10). With steadfast commitment to the Lord, Peter spoke the truth about Jesus to the Sanhedrin, concluding by stating that Jesus is the only way to heaven (v. 12). Thus, no other religion, even in this modern age of religious pluralism, can provide a way to heaven. The inerrant Word of God clearly states that there is only one Savior—Jesus Christ.

4:13-22 Although **Peter and John** were **uneducated and untrained men,** they spoke with a **boldness** that **amazed** their prosecutors (v. 13). These fishermen were without formal training in any rabbinical schools. Nevertheless, it was apparent that **they had been with Jesus**, providing unique credentials for their task. The unimpressiveness of these men was impressive. They learned much during the years they spent traveling and ministering alongside Him.

Ordering Peter and John to leave, they **conferred among themselves**. They could not **deny** that the man had been healed, yet they

> *The unimpressiveness of these men was impressive.*

could not afford to allow teaching and healing in Jesus' name to continue (vv. 15-16). Since Peter and John had not broken any laws, they could not find a **way to punish them**; so they merely threatened the apostles and **ordered them not to preach or teach at all in the name of Jesus** (v. 17), which did little to hinder Peter and John. They were **unable to stop speaking about what** they had **seen and heard** (v. 20). Both men had been radically changed by Jesus and chose to obey God rather than men. One of Jesus' last commands to them was to be His witnesses, and they were determined to keep that command (1:8; Mt 28:18-20). Even though the miracle angered the Sanhedrin, it had a positive impact on at least some people who **were all giving glory to God over what had been done** (Acts 4:21).

4:23-31 Upon their release, Peter and John returned literally **to their own** (Gk. *idious*), alluding to their friends or companions. Translators added the word **fellowship** for clarity. They returned to their own fellow believers, friends, and apostles (v. 23). When the group heard about what **the chief priests and elders had said** to John and Peter, they prayed, raising **their voices to God unanimously**. Once again Luke highlighted the unity of the apostolic church. Their prayer began with an acknowledgment that God is the Creator of **heaven, the earth, and the sea, and everything in them**. As the **Master** and Creator, God controls all things (v. 24). They prayed Scripture, recognizing the authority and truthfulness of the words of God that were written **through the Holy Spirit**. The believers equated **the Gentiles** with the Romans;

the peoples with the people of Israel; **the kings** with Herod Antipas; the tetrarch or ruler of Galilee and Perea (Lk 3:1); and **the rulers** with **Pontius Pilate**, the Roman governor of Judea (Mt 27:1-13). All of these **assembled together** fought against Jesus, not understanding that God's sovereign plan would **take place** (Acts 4:25-27; Ps 2:1-2). The gathered group of believers, praying about their current situation, could have easily been intimidated by the threats of the powerful Sanhedrin; however, they prayed for **boldness**, not protection, in speaking His word (v. 29). Perhaps they remembered Jesus' words from His Sermon on the Mount (Mt 5:10-12).

For whatever reason, the believers were totally committed to God, calling themselves His **slaves** (Acts 4:29). After they finished praying, God displayed His presence as **the place where they were assembled was shaken**. This physical manifestation of the presence of God was not unlike what happened at Pentecost. This divine sign was not a chance occurrence. God answered their prayers, and they all **began to speak God's message with boldness** (v. 31). This fresh in-filling was God's refueling these believers according to their needs in a new situation.

4:32-37 Luke concluded this section of Acts by discussing the state of the church. He described the group as a **multitude**, indicating its considerable growth. Even though they were large, they were in complete unity, being **of one heart and soul**. No one regarded their possessions as their own because they genuinely cared for each other and shared when there was **a needy person among them** (v. 34). When a need arose, **all those who owned lands or houses sold them** and **brought the proceeds** to the apostles who would then distribute them (vv. 34-35). Specifically, a man **the apostles named Barnabas**

(Aram. "son of encouragement") gave generously. Barnabas, a significant figure later in Acts, was named **Joseph**, but due to his righteous character and encouraging demeanor his name was changed to Barnabas (vv. 36-37). Barnabas was a Hellenistic Jew (i.e., his residence was located within the Roman Empire) and a kinsman of John Mark (Col 4:10).

5:1-11 A contrast is introduced by the transitional word **But** (v. 1). While Barnabas provided a good example of sharing (4:36-37), **Ananias** (Gk. form of *Hananiah*, "*Yahweh* has dealt graciously") and **Sapphira** (Gk., "beautiful or a blue gem") provided a negative one. Feigning piety, the married couple **sold a piece of property** and pretended to give all of the proceeds to the church but instead **kept back part of the proceeds** for themselves (vv. 1-2). Possibly the example of Barnabas' Spirit-led generosity prompted Ananias and Sapphira to desire that same approval. In any case, the actions of Ananias and Sapphira demonstrated an improper motive in giving.

No law required the early believers to sell their land and give it away. In fact, Peter said to Ananias, **Wasn't it yours while you possessed it? And after it was sold, wasn't it at your disposal?** (v. 4). Ananias and Sapphira could have done what they pleased with the land. Christians are to give what they have decided in their heart to give, not reluctantly or under compulsion, for God loves a cheerful giver (2 Co 9:7). Their failure to give would not have been sin; their sin was that they lied **to the Holy Spirit** (Acts 5:3), which was lying **to God** (v. 4).

In contrast to the Spirit-led giving of Barnabas, Ananias was led by Satan. Satan **FILLED** (Gk. *eplērōsen*, "possess fully") his "heart to lie to the Holy Spirit" (v. 3), connoting the idea of control or influence. This same Greek verb was used in the command "be filled

Heart to Heart:
Salvation in Christ Alone
(Acts 4:12; 8:26-40; 10:1-48)

The importance of Acts in determining the way of salvation cannot be under-estimated. Many people embrace "pluralism," believing that the world's major religions provide independent paths to a saving relationship with God. However, Acts indicates both implicitly and explicitly that salvation can only be obtained through Jesus Christ (4:12).

Does this mean that apparently devout people of other faiths will not go to heaven? Yes, it does. For further evidence of this conclusion take the story in Acts 8, where the Ethiopian official was instructed by Philip. First, the Ethiopian was a devout man. He traveled thousands of miles to worship in the outer areas of the Jewish synagogue. He read the prophet Isaiah as he traveled. Despite the Ethiopian's religious nature, the Holy Spirit instructed Philip to share the gospel with him. If this man were going to be saved through another religion, there would have been no reason for Philip to go to him in the first place.

Additionally, consider the man named Cornelius: "He was a devout man and feared God along with his whole household. He did many charitable deeds for the Jewish people and always prayed to God" (Ac 10:2). Why did he need to hear about Jesus Christ? Yet God in a vision told Peter to share the gospel with this man. Being religious is not enough. Salvation comes by grace through faith in Jesus Christ alone.

Knowing that Jesus Christ is the only way should encourage every woman to be bold in sharing her faith and to take an active role in missionary efforts to spread the gospel. Every person should take seriously the gospel message of Jesus Christ.

with the Spirit" (Eph 5:18). As a result of his sin, **Ananias dropped dead** (Acts 5:5). **Three hours** later, after repeating the same lie, Sapphira instantly **dropped dead** (vv. 9-10). The text does not indicate how they died, but the assumption is that they died as the judgment of God since **great fear came on the whole church and on all who heard** (v. 11). The same Spirit that brought God's blessing to believers also convicted believers of sin. This judgment helped purify the

church, creating an awareness in the new believers of the seriousness of sin. "God is not mocked. For whatever a man sows he will also reap" (Gl 6:7). Ananias and Sapphira sowed lies and deceit, and they reaped judgment and a premature death. They wanted to appear more generous than they were. Was this sin so dreadful as to merit death? Perhaps the severity of judgment underscored the importance of keeping the church pure in these early days of its existence and reinforced the difference made by the filling of the Spirit. A timely lesson is provided: The Spirit of God cannot be deceived.

5:12-14 Even after the persecution of Peter and John (4:13-22) and the purging of Ananais and Sapphira from the church (5:1-11), the church continued to prosper and grow. God answered the believers' prayers for **signs and wonders** (v. 12), which authenticated the apostles' message and enabled them to witness more effectively. The miracles were done **through the hands of the apostles** (v. 12). God used all the apostles, not just Peter, to perform miraculous works.

ALL (Gk. *hapantes*, "the whole people, everybody") was an ambiguous term describing those who met in Solomon's Colonnade. Some versions attempt to clarify by stating "all believers," but this interpretation is not required by the original manuscripts. In the face of persecution, the believers prayed for complete boldness (4:30). It is unlikely that they were then afraid to meet in public. The "none of the rest" (5:13) likely refers to unbelievers. In other texts the identical Greek word for REST (*loipōn*, "remaining") is used to refer to those "who have no hope" (1 Th 4:13; 5:6). The deaths of Ananias and Sapphira scared all but the genuine believers. Despite the hesitancy the unbelievers had in joining the group of believers, **both men and women** were being saved **in increasing numbers** (v. 14). This first specific mention in Acts of believing women did not mean that many had not already been saved earlier.

Many more people were healed by Peter and the apostles. Specifically, Peter's healing ministry had developed such a huge reputation that **the sick** were carried **into the streets** in case **Peter** passed by. People hoped they would be healed if **at least his shadow might fall on some of them** (v. 15). **Sick people** as well as **those**

who were tormented by unclean spirits were **all healed** (v. 16). Luke made a distinction between those with common sicknesses and those with unclean spirits. Only the Gospels and Acts mention people tormented by unclean or evil spirits. The rest of the New Testament is silent about this issue. Around the time of Jesus' ministry and shortly thereafter, a proliferation of people affected with demon possession appeared. The Bible never describes believers as being tormented by unclean spirits. This sickness is only applicable to the lost.

Opposition to Christianity in Jerusalem (5:17-42)

5:17-32 As a result of the spreading influence of believers, specifically the apostles, **the high priest took action** (v. 17). This high priest could be either Annas or Caiaphas. **All his colleagues** and **those who belonged to the party of the Sadducees** referred to those Luke mentioned previously in Acts (see notes on 4:5-12). **The apostles**, more than just Peter and John, were put **in the city jail** (v. 18). The high priest made good on his earlier threat. The apostles would be punished for continuing to teach, preach, and heal in Jesus' name.

God sent **an angel of the Lord** to free the apostles from jail (v. 19). This angel of the Lord should be distinguished from "the angel of the Lord" in the Old Testament, who was often identified as the preincarnate Christ (a Christophany). Upon freeing the apostles, the angel told them to **stand in the temple complex, and tell the people all about this life** (v. 20). These apostles returned to where they had been arrested and continued to do what they had been doing. This jail miracle was the first of three recorded in Acts (see 12:6-10; 16:26-27).

The next day **the high priest** and his colleagues **convened the Sanhedrin** (see notes on 4:5). In contrast to the previous trial of Peter and John, the entire Sanhedrin, **the full Senate of the sons of Israel**, was in attendance (v. 21). The Sanhedrin was composed of 70 people plus the high priest, who presided over the council. These 71 men formed the ruling body of the Jewish people. Despite all precautions taken, the prisoners still escaped without the knowledge of the prison guards, baffling **the captain of the temple police and the chief priests** (v. 24). Their amazement provided further proof that the apostles' escape was truly miraculous.

Someone, undesignated in the text, **reported** to the Sanhedrin that the apostles were **in the temple complex and teaching the people** (v. 25). The **captain** of the temple police, previously referred to as the commander of the temple guard (see notes on 4:1-4), personally went along with **the temple police** and escorted the apostles before the Sanhedrin. The guards **brought** the apostles **in without force** because **they were afraid the people might stone them**. The apostles did not fear stoning because they were regarded highly by the people (2:47; 5:13). Rather the captain and the temple police feared being stoned for their rearresting the apostles (vv. 26-27).

Acquiescing that they had disobeyed the orders not to teach in Jesus' name, **Peter and the apostles** gave reason for their noncompliance: **We must obey God rather than men** (v. 29). The apostles were not laying aside all laws and governmental authority. Instead they were arguing that when the laws of God come in conflict with the laws of man, they must first and foremost obey God.

By using the phrase **God of our fathers**, the apostles were identifying with Judaism (v. 30). The God of whom they were speaking was not another god, but the God of Israel, the triune God who **raised Jesus up** and who **exalted** Him as

ruler and Savior. The apostles referred once again to the resurrection and to Jesus' place in heaven at the **right hand** of God (v. 31). The apostles did not fail to present the good news of the gospel message, even in the face of their persecutors. They concluded their defense with a testimony that they were **witnesses of these things**, meaning they had personally witnessed the death, burial, and resurrection of Christ. More importantly, **the Holy Spirit** was a witness to these things as well (v. 32). Every believer receives the Spirit as soon as he determines to **obey** the gospel message and trust Christ for salvation.

5:33-42 The apostles' response **enraged** a majority of the Sanhedrin, to the extent that **they wanted to kill** the apostles. Although the Sanhedrin was primarily made up of Sadducees, Pharisees were members as well. The Pharisees represented the common Jews. The overall Jewish population sided with them, viewing them as the pious upholders of the law. They were in constant conflict with the Sadducees, who did not believe in angels and demons, the resurrection from the dead, and the reality of an afterlife. However, the Sadducees had to tolerate the Pharisees, who were supported by the majority of the public.

A Pharisee named Gamaliel offered a solution and became the first man to function as the friend of Christianity in court. Gamaliel was highly **respected by all the people** and recognized as the greatest **teacher** of his day (v. 34). He was the grandson of the great rabbi Hillel and the teacher of the Apostle Paul (22:3). Gamaliel wisely and in a timely manner suggested that they **be careful** and not act hastily with the apostles (v. 35). Citing Jewish history, he noted two uprisings that **came to nothing**. **Theudas**, who is not referenced in any other historical account, with **a group of about 400 men** rallied to no avail (v. 36). Likewise, **Judas the Galilean**, the founder of the Zealots, led a rebellion that failed (v. 37). For this reason, Gamaliel argued that the Sanhedrin should **stay away from** the apostles **and leave them alone** (vv. 38-39). Gamaliel insightfully noted that the Sanhedrin might **even be found fighting against God**. By the two men to whom Gamaliel compared Jesus, he likely thought the teachings of Jesus would also fade away. Some Pharisees followed Christ, but there is no record of the conversion of a Sadducee.

The Sanhedrin was **persuaded** by Gamaliel's advice. The apostles were **flogged**, ordered once again **not to speak in the name of Jesus and released** (v. 40). The flogging they received was probably a beating of 40 lashes, minus one to avoid breaking the legal limit (Dt 25:3). Instead of being discouraged by this severe persecution, the apostles rejoiced **that they were counted worthy to be dishonored on behalf of the name** (v. 41).

	Sapphira *Acts 5:1-11*	
The Deceivers	• Sapphira, meaning "beautiful" or "sapphire," a believer active in the early church in Jerusalem • Ananias, her husband, a man of wealth and promise	
The Deceit	• sold land • lied about the sale price • gave only some of the money to the apostles • kept some of the money for themselves • lied about how the money was allocated	
The Discipline	• failed God • asked by Peter, "Why did you agree to test the Spirit of the Lord?" (v. 9) • led to their destruction by greed • died with her husband Ananias as a result of their sin • always associated with deceit	

The Selection of the Seven Deacons (6:1–8:3)

6:1-7 Marked by the phrase **in those days**, an indefinite amount of time passed between the end of chapter 5 and the beginning of chapter 6. From later data in Acts, the time elapsing seems to be approximately five years after Pentecost.

Luke identified the believers as **disciples** for the first time in Acts. Luke's usage of the term "disciple" never referred to the Twelve, whom he referenced as "apostles" and one time in Acts as "the Twelve." The **number of the disciples** by this time had continued to grow—**multiplying** (v. 1) to 5,000 believing men (4:4) and, counting women and

children, perhaps to 20,000 believers in Jerusalem.

Because of the massive growth of the Jerusalem church, problems arose from inside (6:1-7) and outside the church (6:8–7:60). The church was then entirely Jewish in its composition. However, there were two groups of Jews. **The Hellenistic Jews** were complaining that **the Hebraic Jews** were overlooking **their widows** in the **daily distribution** (v. 1). The Greek-speaking **Hellenistic Jews,** part of the Diaspora, had not been born in Jerusalem but were living in Jerusalem. Their Greek influence caused a possible point of contention with the Hebraic Jews. In contrast, the **Hebraic Jews** spoke Aramaic and/or Hebrew and placed more value on preserving Jewish culture and customs.

In response to the complaint, **the Twelve** apostles gathered the believers together in search of a solution (v. 2). Due to the growth of the church and the many tasks to be completed, the apostles now needed to prioritize the tasks demanding their time. They would give up the ministry of waiting **on tables** and would devote themselves **to prayer and to the preaching ministry**. WAIT (Gk. *diakonein,* "serve") is the verb from which the Greek noun is transliterated into English as "deacon." TABLE (Gk. *trapezais*) may refer to tables used either for distributing food or as a point from which money is distributed. This task was important, especially related to the care of widows. However, **it would not be right** or pleasing to God for the apostles to forsake their primary task of preaching the word of God to serve tables (v. 2). Serving tables was not a lesser task; it simply was not the apostles' primary calling.

The **brothers**, used generically to mean believers in the church, selected **seven men** to assist the apostles by serving tables (v. 3). In essence, these men became the first deacons in the church. While it might have been easier for the apostles to select the men themselves, the apostles involved the church as a whole in making the decision, while they were guiding the process. The apostles cited several qualifications for these servants of the church (v. 3):

- They were to be **men**. Although women have a vital role in the church (Ti 2:3-5), men are commissioned by God to assume leadership roles over the congregation (Gn 1–3; 1 Tm 2:11-15).

- They were to be **of good reputation**, setting an example of godliness.

- They were to be **full of the Spirit**, completely yielded to God.

- They were to be marked with **wisdom**. They needed understanding and discernment for dealing with the daily affairs of the church.

The apostles' **proposal pleased the whole company** so the church began the selection process. The seven men selected all had Greek names, implying they were Hellenistic Jews (v. 5). **Nicolaus**, described as being **a proselyte**, must have been a Gentile convert to Judaism (v. 5). Perhaps the choice of men who were probably Hellenists (v. 5) would ameliorate the conflict concerning the alleged neglect of Hellenistic widows by the Palestinian Jews who were controlling the financial resources assigned to caring for the widows. A conflict that caused the first major division in the early church had to be addressed in a timely way. The newly selected servants of the church stood and the apostles **prayed and laid their hands on them**, commissioning them for their ministry, to finalize the selection process (v. 6).

Luke concluded this section with another progress report (1:15; 2:41; 4:4; 5:14; 6:7; 9:31; 12:24; 16:5; 19:20; and 28:31). These reports conclude sections and are helpful in subdividing the book as well as following the advancement of the gospel. As a result of the appointment of these men three things occurred:

- **the preaching about God flourished**

- **the number of the disciples in Jerusalem multiplied greatly**

- **a large group of priests became obedient to the faith.** The Christian message began to penetrate the temple walls, reaching even the priests.

6:8-15 Stephen (Gk. *Stephanos*, "crown"), **full of faith and the Holy Spirit** (v. 5) and **full of grace and power**

Heart to Heart:
Deacons (6:1-7)

Who chooses them? According to the pattern set forth in Acts 6, the congregation should choose from among themselves men who meet the qualifications given in 1 Timothy 3:8-13. Failure to meet these qualifications does not prohibit a man from ministry, but he is prohibited from holding the office of deacon.

What is ordination? Although not a magical rite of passage conferring a special power on someone, ordination is not to be taken lightly. Both pastors and deacons are set apart by the congregation in a meaningful way, which is commonly identified as ordination. After prayer and serious consideration, a spiritually qualified person is set aside for the work of the ministry. The church gives its approval to this person as did the congregation in Acts 6. If a church takes the responsibility seriously, ordination can be a meaningful experience by which those not worthy to serve are prohibited from ever possessing such roles.

What do they do? In some churches the deacons act as a board of trustees or a ruling body; however, Acts 6 indicates, as does the word "deacon" (Gk. diaconos), that this role calls for service. The deacons are to serve, not rule, the church. The final authority for the church lies in the congregation. For example, in the Lord's Supper, the pastor usually asks the ordained or set-apart men to come to the front. The pastor then hands the elements to the ordained servants who pass out the elements to the congregation. This service in a symbolic way represents the role of deacons in a church.

(v. 8), was obviously an extraordinary individual who, like the apostles, performed **great wonders and signs among the people** (v. 8). Until this point in Acts, only the apostles performed miracles. Some from the **Freedmen's Synagogue** began to argue **with Stephen** (v. 9). "Freedmen" were slaves who had been freed or their descendants. Divisions within the Jewish community were manifested in multiple synagogues—one for the **Cyrenians and Alexandrians**, one for those **from Cilicia and Asia**, and one for these "freedmen" from all the regions. Frustrated by their lack of ability to debate with Stephen, these synagogue antagonists persuaded people to falsely claim that Stephen had been **speaking blasphemous words against Moses and God** (vv. 10-11), a serious offense punishable by death (Lv 24:16). This claim caused such a ruckus that Stephen was brought before **the Sanhedrin**, much as the apostles had been (Acts 6:12; see 4:5-22; 5:21-32). Additionally, false claims were made that Stephen had spoken against **the law** and the temple, referred to as **this holy place** (Acts 6:13). These claims followed the same as the earlier claims since Moses was so closely identified with the law and the temple was revered as the dwelling place of God.

Specifically, they accused Stephen of saying **Jesus** would **destroy** the temple **and change the customs . . . handed down** by **Moses** (v. 14). Stephen's accusers undoubtedly distorted the words he had spoken. In the next chapter Stephen provided a response.

7:1-53 The **high priest** asked Stephen, **"Is this true?"**, a reference to the charge of blasphemy. Stephen's response to this simple question formed the longest sermon in Acts. Although some have accused Stephen of historical inaccuracies, a careful study reveals his effective use of events from Israel's history and the citing of at least 22 verses from the Old Testament. Stephen turned the charges back on his accusers, indicating that they, not he, were the real blasphemers of God. Structurally, the speech falls into six sections:

- the promises of Abraham (vv. 2-8)

- the deliverance through Joseph (vv. 9-16)

- the deliverance through Moses (vv. 17-34)

- the apostasy of Israel (vv. 35-43)

- the real tabernacle of God (vv. 44-50)

- the rejection of the Messiah (vv. 51-53).

Stephen began his speech by identifying and even showing respect for his listeners, as his **brothers and fathers** (v. 2).

Obedient to God's call, Abraham **came out of the land of the Chaldeans and settled in Haran** (vv. 3-4). The city of Ur in the land of the Chaldeans, located between the Tigris and Euphrates rivers in southeastern Mesopotamia or modern Iraq, was Abraham's original home. Haran, located approximately 500 miles northwest of Ur, was his home before he moved to Palestine. Although Genesis 12:1-4 recorded Abraham's call while he was living in Haran, the call might have

been received previously while he was living in Mesopotamia. Or God could have spoken to Abram in both Ur and Haran, with the latter as a reinforcement of the earlier call (v. 2; see Gn 11:27-32; 12:1-3; 15:7; Neh 9:7).

After his father, Terah, **died,** 75-year-old Abraham was led by God to **move to this land in which you now live**, southern Canaan or modern Israel (v. 4; Gn 12:4). Even though Abraham had traveled hundreds of miles, he was not given **an inheritance in it, not even a foot of ground**. To Abraham, God gave the promises of Israel, even though he had neither the land nor the heir to possess it (v. 5).

Abraham's **descendants would be aliens in a foreign country**. Enslaved and oppressed for **400 years**, they were freed from that oppression through the judgment of the oppressing **nation** and would ultimately come and worship God **in this place**, apparently meaning Canaan (vv. 6-7; Gn 15:13-14). Stephen rounded off the length of time the Israelites were in bondage to 400 years. Later in Acts it is rounded to 450 years (Ac 13:20). Both numbers are approximate since most evangelical scholars identify the length of time as 430 years (Ex 12:40).

God gave Abraham **circumcision** as the sign of the **covenant** God had made with him (Ac 7:8; Gn 17:1-14). Circumcision is the surgical procedure performed on infant boys in which the foreskin is removed from the penis for reasons of health and hygiene. For the Jews, this procedure was a religious ritual distinguishing the male Jew, the descendant of Abraham, from the Gentile. God had commanded that circumcision be performed as a sign of His covenant with Abraham. God, who always keeps His promises, blessed Abraham with a son, **Isaac**, who then fathered **Jacob**, who was the father of the **12 patriarchs**—the founders of the 12 tribes of Israel (v. 8; Gn 35:23-26).

As a continuation of the history of Israel, Stephen moved to Joseph, one of the 12 sons of Jacob. Stephen summarized the story of Joseph from Genesis 37–46 (Ac 7:9-16). By using the story of Joseph, Stephen demonstrated that throughout history God's appointed leaders had been rejected by Israel just as Jesus was. What the patriarchs intended for evil, God used for good, saving the people of Israel from the famine (Gn 50:20). Even though Jesus was rejected by Israel, He was God's appointed One. The crucifixion, which the Jews intended for evil, God used to provide a way to save people from their sins (Rm 5:9).

Stephen alluded to **75 people in all** (Ac 7:14). In Genesis 46:26, the number was recorded as 66 people, which did not include Jacob, Joseph, Manasseh, and Ephraim. All those in Jacob's household numbered 70 (Gn 46:15,18,22,25), a number symbolizing completeness or perfection and significant in representing God's complete work in preparing Israel. Stephen's figure of "75," however, most certainly comes from the Septuagint, which added to the count the five grandsons of Joseph (Ac 7:14).

Shechem, located on the slope of Mount Ebal in northcentral Palestine, was an important city before the Israelites settled there. It became the first capital of the northern kingdom (1 Kg 12:1). Jacob bought land and settled in Shechem (Gn 33:18-19). The remains of Jacob and Joseph were returned to Canaan, or Shechem, for burial.

Stephen linked two important historical events: Abraham's purchase of Machpelah in Hebron (Ac 7:16; Gn 23:17-18) with Jacob's purchase of a field in Shechem (Ac 7:16; Gn 33:19). Some would suggest that Jacob bought the land in Shechem in the name of Abraham to be a family burial

ground. However, more likely Stephen was conflating or telescoping several accounts into a summary statement, as is suggested by use of the plural in Acts 7:16. A literary device like this would have been clearly understood by the Jews.

After the time of Joseph, the descendents of Abraham **flourished and multiplied in Egypt until a different king ruled over Egypt who did not know Joseph**. The new king probably knew about Joseph but chose to forget his great contributions to Egypt, due to the perceived threat of the greatly multiplying Israelites (vv. 17-19).

Along came Moses, the next prominent character in Israel's history. Stephen's discourse on Moses composed the longest section of his speech, probably because he was defending himself against the claim he had blasphemed Moses (Ac 6:11). He discussed all three of the major segments of Moses' life, each covering a 40-year span.

Moses was born during the years of the Egyptian oppression of the Israelites, when they were forced to **leave their infants outside so they wouldn't survive** (Ac 7:19). Perhaps sensitive to the accusation that he had blasphemed Moses, Stephen described him as **beautiful before God** (v. 20). Stephen described Moses as a man **powerful in his speech** (v. 22) in contrast to Moses' self-evaluation as "I have never been eloquent . . . because I am . . . hesitant in speech" (Ex 4:10). This difference is explained primarily in the tendency of a humble man not to praise himself. Moses did become a powerful man in what he said and did. Stephen had the perspective of history. God used the circumstances of Moses' life to prepare him for his future.

When Moses was **approaching the age of 40, he decided to visit his brothers, the sons of Israel** (Ac 7:23). Moses chose to identify himself with his biological relatives, refusing to be called the son of

Pharaoh's daughter and choosing instead to suffer with the people of God (Heb 11:24-25). One day Moses came to the **rescue** of a fellow Israelite, **striking down** and killing an **Egyptian** (Acts 7:24; Ex 2:11-12). When he attempted **to reconcile** fighting Israelites the next day, they rebelled against Moses, questioning his authority (Acts 7:26-28; Ex 2:13-14). For Moses to side with the Israelites in no way suggested that he was not trying to achieve a peaceful solution (Acts 7:26). The Exodus account more than anything showed Moses' concern for one who seemed helpless before the attack of another (Ex 2:11-14). Stephen provided only a summary of the Old Testament incident.

Moses fled Egypt because of his fear of the wrath of the pharaoh and because of the rejection of his people (Acts 7:29; Ex 2:15), and he **became an exile in the land of Midian** (Ex 2:15). Difficult to locate with exactness due to its nomadic culture, Midian is placed by most scholars east of the Gulf of Aqabah, in modern northwestern Saudi Arabia. While in the land of Midian, Moses married Zipporah (Hb., "small bird or sparrow"), whose father was Jethro, the priest of Midian. The couple had **two sons**, Gershom (Hb., "alien or sojourner") and Eliezer (Hb., "God helps," Ex 2:22; 18:2-4).

Stephen reversed the chronological order of events: God revealed Himself to Moses *after* He told Moses to remove his sandals (Ex 3:5-6); Stephen noted God revealed Himself before He told Moses to take off his sandals (Ac 7:32-33). In keeping with Stephen's overall purpose, he was emphasizing in a theological way that God's revelation of Himself is most important. The God appearing to Moses was *Yahweh*, the God of Moses' ancestors Abraham, Isaac, and Jacob who indeed had revealed Himself long before the burning bush (Ex 3:5-6). The use of **then**

(Gk. *eipe de*, "and or but") does not require chronological sequence.

There are several references to the **angel** who spoke to Moses (Ac 7:35,38; see also v. 53; Gl 3:19; Hb 2:2). In Exodus 19 the one who spoke to Moses was identified as the "LORD" (Hb. *Yahweh*). There are two possibilities:

- Stephen was assuming that God was speaking to Moses via an angel, or

- the "angel" may well have been God Himself appearing in what has been called a Christophany—an appearance of the preincarnate Christ, the Son of God.

The hearers of Stephen's speech belonged to a nation that from the onset rejected the law and worship of the true God. Even while receiving the Ten Commandments, God's people rebelled against Him, turning to idolatry (Acts 7:38-39). By implication Israel's rejection of Jesus continued to Stephen's lifetime.

After addressing his supposed blasphemy against Moses, Stephen dealt with the accusation that he blasphemed the temple, recounting the history of it (vv. 44-50). While the children of Israel were **in the desert**, they carried around with them a portable place of worship, traditionally referred to as the tabernacle, which was made **according to the pattern** God set (v. 44). Stephen referred to it as the **tabernacle of the testimony** because it contained the ark of the covenant, which in turn contained the "testimony" or the two tablets on which the Ten Commandments were inscribed.

Some see Stephen's description of Israel's time in the wilderness as one of apostasy (vv. 42-43) to be a contradiction to Amos, whom they suggest was describing this time as an exemplary period (Am 5:25). However, the context of the book of Amos clearly notes that the prophet is denouncing Israel.

Also Stephen frequently chose to use the Septuagint, as in his allusion to the words of Amos (Am 5:25-27). The Septuagint paraphrased this difficult Hebrew text, which gave a different emphasis and application. **The tent of Moloch** (Ac 7:43) came from the Septuagint. Stephen's point is that the Israelites did indeed make sacrifice but not to *Yahweh* God.

Stephen further broadened the prophecy of Amos to include both exiles Israel brought upon itself—the northern kingdom by the Assyrians, whose capital was in Damascus (Am 5:27), and the southern kingdom by the Babylonians whose capital was Babylon (Ac 7:43). This purposeful change in Stephen's application of the text in Amos would have been understood by his audience. However, this point would have infuriated them all the more.

The tabernacle was with the Israelites when they entered the promised land under the leadership of Joshua, and it remained with them **until the days of David** (v. 45). David wanted to build the temple to provide **a dwelling place for the God of Jacob**, but David's son **Solomon** actually **built** it (vv. 46-47).

The tabernacle, and eventually the temple, represented the dwelling place of God. The children of Israel gave these structures, symbolizing in an earthly way the presence of the sovereign God of the universe, great importance during their history. Particularly this symbolization can be seen by the holy of holies, their ultimate expression in a visible way of the holiness of God. However, Stephen noted that these structures could not truly contain God in all His glory. Instead, God's dwelling place, represented by His **throne,** is in **heaven** (vv. 49-50; Is 66:1-2). This response surely heightened the anger of his listeners.

The Sanhedrin's anger level grew with Stephen's conclusion, which applied his message directly to them (Ac 7:51-53). Previously, Stephen had used the first person, including himself in his references to the Jews, frequently making reference to "our fathers" and "our forefathers" (vv. 11,12,15,19,38,39,44,45). At this juncture, he switched to the second person, using "you" and "your" (vv. 51,52,53), separating himself from his accusers. Stephen's use of **stiff-necked people** was God's own characterization of Israel when they rebelled against Moses and worshiped the golden calf (Ex 33:5). Additionally, he accused them of having **uncircumcised hearts and ears**, meaning that while they were circumcised in the literal sense, their unresponsiveness and resistance to God's revelation made them like the Gentiles, who were unclean and unforgiven. Finally, Stephen accused them of **resisting the Holy Spirit** just **as your forefathers did** (Ac 7:51). Just as their forefathers had rejected Joseph, Moses, and many of the other prophets, so did they reject the Messiah. Just as their forefathers **killed those who announced beforehand the coming of the Righteous One**, so they killed Jesus when He came, becoming **betrayers and murders** (v. 52). Although the Sanhedrin knew the law, they had **not kept it**, rejecting the One to whom the law pointed (v. 53).

7:54-60 Stephen might have had more to say, but he seemingly was interrupted by the intense anger of the Sanhedrin (v. 54). Although the Bible normally portrays Jesus as sitting **at the right hand of God** (Ps 110:1; Rm 8:34; Col 3:1; Heb 1:3,13; 8:1; 10:12; 12:2; 1 Pt 3:22), Stephen viewed Him as **standing**, perhaps signifying that Jesus was standing in Stephen's defense or that He was standing to welcome Stephen into heaven.

Heart to Heart:
The Blood of the Martyrs Is the Seed of the Church

The modern-day church owes a great debt to those who, as Stephen, have given their lives to extend the gospel throughout the world. From the New Testament, extrabiblical documents, and oral tradition, a roll of martyrs can be produced:

- *John the Baptist was beheaded (Mt 14:1; Mk 6:27) around AD 32.*

- *Stephen was stoned (Ac 7:54-60) around AD 34 for preaching the gospel message.*

- *James, the son of Zebedee, was killed with a sword (AD 45).*

- *James, the brother of Jesus, was cast down from the temple and beaten (AD 63).*

- *Barnabas, Paul's companion, was dragged out of the city and burned (AD 64).*

- *Mark, author of the second Gospel, was dragged to be burned and died on the way (AD 64).*

- *The Apostle Peter was crucified upside down (AD 69).*

- *The Apostle Paul was persecuted and beheaded (AD 69).*

- *The Apostle Andrew was crucified (AD 70).*

- *The Apostle Bartholomew was tortured, flayed alive, and beheaded (AD 70).*

- *The Apostle Thomas was cast into a furnace with his side pierced (AD 70).*

- *Matthew, author of the first Gospel, was nailed to the ground and beheaded (AD 70).*

- *The Apostle Matthias was tied on a cross upon a rock, stoned, and beheaded (AD 70).*

- *Luke, the author of the third Gospel, was hanged on a green olive tree (AD 93).*

- *The Apostle John was banished to the Isle of Patmos (AD 97).*

- *Timothy, Paul's companion, was stoned to death (AD 98).*

Heart to Heart:
(Continued)

These are only a few of the thousands of Christian martyrs who have been tortured and murdered during the years following the resurrection of Jesus Christ. All Christians should count it an honor to suffer for their Lord, even if that means following in the steps of these martyrs.

Countless numbers of women have also sacrificed their lives for the sake of the gospel. Priscilla, with her husband Aquila, gave her life during the persecution of Nero around AD 70. Watching as her husband was killed for his faith, Valeria returned home, continuing to make herself known as a Christian and refusing to eat food offered to idols, saying, "I am a Christian, and can, therefore, in no wise eat that which is offered to Sylvanus, your god."[2] Soon after this statement, men seized her and beat her to death with sticks.

Felicitas watched the murder of her husband and then saw her seven sons put to death. Even in her great pain this woman refused to recant her faith. Instead she urged her sons: "Remain steadfast in the faith, and in the confession of Christ; for Christ and His saints are waiting for you. Behold, heaven is open before you; therefore fight valiantly for your souls, and show, that you are faithful in the love of Christ, wherewith He loves you, and you Him."[3] After watching various fates befall her sons, Felicitas was beheaded with the sword (AD 164).

Ancient Roman excavations still carry the inscription of Perpetua and Felicitas, who were violently put to death about AD 201. Perpetua had recently given birth and was still nursing her baby, and Perpetua's slave Felicitas was advanced in pregnancy when they were arrested. Roman law required them to wait for the birth of the child. Many pleaded with them, including Perpetua's father, for the sake of their children to deny the Lord Jesus Christ and offer a sacrifice to the Roman gods. However, these women were not fainthearted and remained steadfast until the end. Shortly after the birth, both Perpetua and Felicitas were led into the amphitheater where wild beasts were unleashed upon them in front of Roman crowds. The beasts failed to kill Perpetua and Felicitias. Thus, the Roman soldier had to slay them with a sword.

Dedicated women of faith have watched their husbands and children die, and they have given their own lives for the sake of the gospel. The blood of martyrs like these planted the seeds of faith that continued to accelerate the growth of the early church. All Christians must be willing not only to live for Christ but also to die for Him.

Old Testament Quotes in Acts
Acts 7:1-50

Quote	Old Testament	Acts
Let his dwelling become desolate	Ps 69:25	1:20
I will pour out My Spirit	Jl 2:28-32	2:17-21
I saw the Lord ever before me	Ps 16:8-11	2:25-28
He was not left in Hades	Ps 16:10	2:31
Sit at My right hand	Ps 110:1	2:34-35
The Lord your God will raise up for you a Prophet	Dt 18:15-19	3:22-23
In your seed all the families of the earth will be blessed	Gn 12:3; 18:18; 22:18; 26:4	3:25
The stone despised by you builders	Ps 118:22	4:11
Why did the Gentiles rage	Ps 2:1-2	4:25-26
Get out of your country	Gn 12:1	7:3
His descendants would be strangers	Gn 15:13-14	7:6-7
Who appointed you a ruler	Ex 2:14	7:27-28,35
I am the God of your forefathers	Ex 3:6,15	7:32
Take the sandals off your feet	Ex 3:5,7-8,10	7:33-34
God will raise up for you a Prophet	Dt 18:15	7:37
Make us gods	Ex 32:1,23	7:40
Did you bring Me offerings	Am 5:25-27	7:42-43
Heaven is My throne	Is 66:1-2	7:49-50
He was led like a sheep	Is 53:7-8	8:32-33
I have found David	I Sm 13:44; Ps 89:20	13:22
You are My Son	Ps 2:7	13:33
I will grant you . . . blessings	Is 55:3	13:34
You will not allow Your Holy One to see decay	Ps 16:10	13:35
Look, you scoffers	Hab 1:5	13:41
I have appointed you as a light for the Gentiles	Is 49:6	13:47
Who made the heaven	Ex 20:11; Ps 146:6	14:15
After these things I will return	Am 9:11-12; Is 45:21	15:16-18
You must not speak evil	Ex 22:28	23:5
Go to this people and say	Is 6:9-10	28:26-27

In response, the Sanhedrin **screamed** to drown out what they deemed blasphemous words. The phrase **they . . . stopped their ears** indicated that they quit listening altogether. They **rushed together**, indicating the immediacy of the action taken. Luke's usage of the word RUSHED (Gk. *hormēsan*, "to put in motion or incite") vividly portrays the Sanhedrin's fury. The same word was used to describe the mad rush of the herd of demon-possessed swine into the sea of Galilee (Mt 8:32; Mk 5:13). With disregard for all dignity and propriety of office, the highest court in Israel was reduced to an out-of-control, bloodthirsty mob.

Violating the law, which required the authorization of the Roman government to prosecute an offense calling for capital punishment, the mob **threw** Stephen **out of the city** and stoned him (Ac 7:58; Jn 18:31). From the apparent immediate action of the Sanhedrin, no formal vote was taken to determine Stephen's guilt or innocence. Instead, in anger they responded to what they perceived to be outrageously blasphemous statements, which according to Jewish law were punishable by stoning (Lv 24:14-16), and yet they ignored the civil law under which they were living.

Some regulations related to stoning were followed as **witnesses** were involved (Ac 7:58; see Dt 17:7). In order to throw the first stones, the witnesses removed their robes and laid them **at the feet of a young man named Saul**, who would later, as Paul, become a prominent figure in the apostolic church (Ac 7:58).

In response to his stoning, Stephen reacted much as Jesus did on the cross. While Jesus called on the Father to receive His Spirit, Stephen called on the **Lord Jesus** (v. 59), demonstrating how the early church clearly equated Jesus with the Father. Additionally, Stephen asked for the forgiveness of his persecu-

tors just as Jesus did (v. 60). Even in the face of death Stephen led a life completely yielded to the Spirit of God.

8:1-3 During the stoning of Stephen, **Saul** stood by giving his approval and guarding the clothes of those casting stones (7:58; 22:20). Saul, whose Roman name was Paul, possessed Roman citizenship since he had been born in the Roman city of Tarsus. He studied under the famous rabbi Gamaliel, becoming a scholar in Jewish tradition and in the interpretation of Scripture. As a Pharisee, Saul zealously committed himself to the teaching and practicing of Old Testament laws and traditions. He ardently persecuted first-century Christians. Stephen's burial is mentioned (v. 2), providing a bridge to the rest of Acts since Stephen's death led to the scattering of the believers and subsequently to the spread of the gospel into **Judea and Samaria** (v. 1). Saul apparently led in the **severe persecution** against **the church in Jerusalem** (v. 3), imprisoning both **men and women**. Women were actively involved in the early church and as a result experienced persecution.

The Spread of the Gospel in Judea, Galilee, and Samaria (8:4–9:31)

8:4-8 Philip, the first missionary named in Scripture and one of the seven men chosen to serve tables (6:5), became the central figure for the rest of this chapter. He went to **Samaria and preached the Messiah** (8:5). Translators have difficulties choosing the correct reading for verse 4, whether reading "a city in Samaria" or "the city of Samaria." Either way, Samaria was a region north of Jerusalem that contained a number of cities. In Luke's day there was not a city named Samaria. However, Sebaste, the capital city of the region, bore the name Samaria in Old Testament times. After the ancient city was destroyed by John Hyrcanus and his sons (107 BC), it was rebuilt in the style of a Greek city by Herod the Great and renamed Sebaste (Gk. *Sebastos*, "venerable or august," equivalent of Lat. "Augustus") in honor of Caesar Augustus.

Interestingly, the first missionary effort went to **Samaria**. The Jews hated the Samaritans, regarding them as heretical Jews and thus to be avoided at all costs. The Samaritans stood on the fringes of Judaism. They were not considered fully Jewish; neither were they Gentiles. They were regarded as half-breeds because the Jews had intermarried with Gentiles and begun to worship foreign gods. By New Testament times the Samaritans had shed their idolatry and returned to a form of Judaism. They accepted the Pentateuch and were looking for the coming Messiah. Nevertheless, the Samaritans continued to worship on Mount Gerizim instead of Jerusalem, which created great tension between the Jews and Samaritans.

The Samaritans were ready to receive Philip's message of the Messiah. Many of them had possibly heard about Jesus from the Samaritan woman Jesus encountered at the well of Sychar (Jn 4). The unnamed Samaritan woman's witness, combined with the preparation of the Holy Spirit, resulted in an effective ministry to the Samaritan people. Such a large number of people accepted Philip's message about Jesus that Luke noted **there was great joy in that city** (Ac 8:8).

8:9-25 In Samaria there was **a man named Simon,** who **previously practiced sorcery** (Gk. *mageuōn,* "practice magic," v. 9). Simon's sorcery, also described in the Bible as magic and witchcraft, resulted from demonic powers or trickery. It gave him the ability to exercise control over nature and people. Sorcery was such a serious sin that the Jews were forbidden to be involved in any form of sorcery (Dt 18:10-14). Revelation 21:8 notes that sorcerers will be cast into the

lake of fire. Simon's sorcery **astounded the Samaritan people** to the point they called him **the Great Power of God** (Ac 8:10), which may have indicated they were calling Simon "god." Upon hearing Philip's message about **the good news** of **Jesus Christ,** many of the Samaritan people, and ultimately **even Simon himself,** apparently realizing the heretical nature of sorcery and turning in faith to Jesus Christ, **believed** and **were baptized** (vv. 12-13). Simon's faith may not have been genuine because he later attempted to buy the power of the Holy Spirit. He was impressed with **signs and great miracles** that Philip performed and likely feigned belief in Christ in an attempt to gain the same power, which was far greater than his own demonic power (vv. 18-19). Even now the coined word "simony" refers to the buying of ecclesiastical offices in an unworthy and deceitful way. Many see this encounter as Christianity's first confrontation with the occult. Moses had warned the Israelites of this danger before they entered Canaan (Dt 18:9-14; see also Lv 20:6,27; Dt 17:2-5). The sorcerer Elymas also tried unsuccessfully to stop Paul and Barnabas in their witness to Sergius Paulus (Ac 13:8,12).

When the persecution arose against the Christians in Jerusalem, the apostles stayed behind, perhaps ministering to those who had been imprisoned (Ac 8:1). When they heard the Samaritans had **welcomed God's message,** the apostles **sent Peter and John to them.** The two apostles **laid their hands on** the Samaritans and **prayed** that **they might receive the Holy Spirit.**

Some argue that apostolic authority is required for one to receive the gift of the Holy Spirit. Accordingly, the Samaritans were given the gift of the Spirit when Peter and John laid hands on them. Since no apostles exist in modern times, according to this view, the gift of the

Spirit now comes from specific church leaders who are viewed as the successors of the apostles. This view finds little support. Later in this very chapter Philip baptized the Ethiopian eunuch who did not receive apostolic confirmation (8:36-39), and Paul received the Spirit without the involvement of the apostles (9:17). Presumably the Holy Spirit did deal with these Samaritan believers as He does with anyone who repents, believes, and is born into the kingdom of God (Jn 3:8). The apostles "laid their hands on them, and they received the Holy Spirit" (Ac 8:7). This extension of the ascension gift of the Holy Spirit came to the Samaritans as it had to the Jews at Pentecost (2:1-13). The collective outpouring did not mean that the Holy Spirit had not dealt with these believers individually. Note that they did not "speak in tongues," affirming the context in which this manifestation of the Holy Spirit must be understood.

Others try to use this passage to teach that Christians receive the Spirit subsequent to salvation. They argue that the gift of the Spirit is a second blessing, after salvation. They use this as an example of saved people who had not received the Holy Spirit. This view is not legitimate because it contradicts the clear teaching of Romans 8:9, which says anyone who does not have the Spirit of Christ does not belong to Him.

There are three possible interpretations of this passage:

- The Samaritans were not really saved as a result of Philip's witness. While they heard and believed the truths about Jesus, they did not come to a full understanding until the apostles arrived. This is not a good interpretation because the text indicates they were baptized as a result of their belief from Philip's witness, with no indication that they were baptized again. The continuing pattern throughout Acts is that people are first saved, then baptized (2:41; 8:36-39; 9:18; 18:8). If the Samaritans had been saved from the apostles' witness, their baptism would have followed.

- The Samaritans were saved as a result of Philip's witness, and they received the Spirit at that point as well. The encounter with the apostles provided visible evidence of the Spirit's indwelling. The difficulty of this interpretation is that it does not follow the plain reading of the text. Luke wrote that the Spirit **had not yet come down on any of them** and that "they received the Spirit" when the apostles laid their hands on them (vv. 16-17).

- The most plausible interpretation is that unusual circumstances led to an unusual occurrence. The Samaritans were genuinely saved as a result of Philip's witness, but they did not receive the Spirit until the encounter with the apostles. This phenomenon may be due to the transitional nature of Acts. The initial outpouring of the Spirit occurred in Jerusalem at Pentecost (2:1-4) and was later repeated as the church added new groups: the Samaritans (8:11-17) and then the Gentiles (10:44-47). This encounter with the Samaritans is the only instance recorded in Scripture where the reception of the Holy Spirit is not clearly noted as accompanying salvation.

The Holy Spirit does indeed baptize, indwell, and seal at the moment of faith, but this seeming delay may serve several purposes:

- The apostle's participation with the Samaritan believers assured the

Jewish believers that the faith of the Samaritans was genuine.

- The Samaritans may have thereby experienced special encouragement that they had been genuinely accepted by the Jerusalem church and included in the church universal.

Both purposes served to maintain the overall unity of the church.

Peter realized that Simon did not understand God's grace or the free nature of salvation (v. 20). The implication is that Simon was not a Christian, even though he had expressed belief and had been baptized (v. 21). Salvation requires more than mere mental assent, for even the demons believe in God (Jms 2:19). Simon, having no personal relationship with the **Lord**, asked Peter to **pray** for him rather than asking the Lord's forgiveness himself. Simon is not mentioned in the remainder of the New Testament. After ministering alongside Philip to the Samaritans, Peter and John returned to **Jerusalem, evangelizing many** Samaritan **villages as they traveled** (Ac 8:25). Whether or not Philip accompanied the apostles is unclear because the antecedent for "they" is not stated.

8:26-40 From later clarification in the text, the **angel of the Lord** was **the Spirit of the Lord** (vv. 29,39). Philip's location at the time he received this call is unclear. He may have still been in a Samaritan city or in Jerusalem. Gaza, approximately 50 miles southwest of Jerusalem, was one of five chief cities of the Philistines. Destroyed in the first century BC and rebuilt near the Mediterranean coast, the city was positioned along a major coastal highway only three miles inland from the Mediterranean Sea and connecting Egypt with the rest of the ancient world. The designation of **desert Gaza** most likely referred to the old city of Gaza, which is slightly north of the new city (v. 26).

Ethiopia here does not refer to the modern nation by that name but to ancient Nubia, the region stretching from Aswan in southern Egypt to Khartoum in the Sudan. The man was a **eunuch**, indicating he was deprived of his sexual organs. Eunuchs were considered especially trustworthy and were often in charge of harems. In this case, the eunuch held a high position in Ethiopia as the one **in charge** of the queen's **entire treasury**. **Candace** was not the name of the queen but the title used by the queens of Meroe, the capital city of ancient Ethiopia.

The Ethiopian was heading home after worshiping **in Jerusalem**. As a eunuch he would have been denied access to the temple (Dt 23:1). Nevertheless, he must have embraced some form of Judaism since he had made a pilgrimage to Jerusalem and was **reading the prophet Isaiah** when Philip encountered him (Ac 8:30).

The Ethiopian's confusion regarding the passage was understandable, for even the Jewish religious experts disagreed about the meaning of Isaiah 53:7-8 (Ac 8:31-33). Some taught that the **sheep** led to **slaughter** represented Israel, others believed Isaiah was referring to himself, while still others rightly understood the passage to refer to the Messiah.

In Acts and throughout the rest of the New Testament, gospel presentations begin by explaining the Scriptures. Biblical exposition is the example provided by Peter, Stephen, Philip, and Paul because the "sacred Scriptures, which are able to instruct you for salvation through faith in Christ Jesus" (2 Tm 3:15) are at the heart of this method. Gospel presentations devoid of the truths from God's Word lack power to convict and convince.

Wadi el-Hesi, running northeast of Gaza, has been the traditional site designated for the baptism, although geography is certainly not the emphasis of the passage. There are some textual issues with

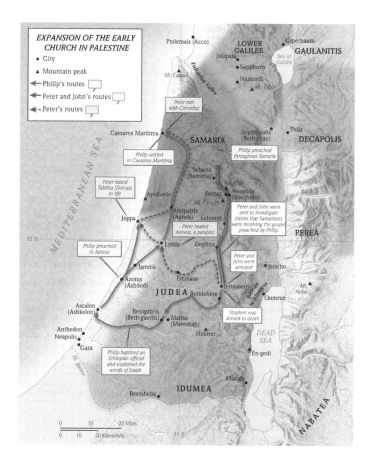

verse 37. However, the matter is hardly worth the time for investigation. The message is theologically sound. Even if added by a well-meaning scribe for clarification, the testimony is clearly stamped upon this encounter. Luke did not choose to record the details of the Ethiopian's conversion, but without a doubt this government official found the Lord (vv. 37-39). The Holman Christian Standard Bible includes the verse set apart in brackets with a brief footnote explaining the manuscript differences. Philip viewed the Ethiopian eunuch's faith in Christ as genuine, consenting to his request for baptism (v. 38).

Upon closer examination of this passage, clearly the Ethiopian was baptized by immersion:

• They had to come **to some water** (v. 36). If sprinkling were the mode of baptism, a large amount of water would not have been necessary.

• **Both Philip and the eunuch went down into the water,** and **they came up out of the water** (v. 38). If sprinkling or pouring were the mode, they would not have needed to wade into the water. The only logical reason for going into the water was to immerse.

• The Greek word transliterated into English as "baptism" literally means "to dip or to immerse."

Therefore, one can only assume that the eunuch's baptism by immersion was consistent with the New Testament pattern.

The connotation for Philip's departure, expressed as "carrying away," is similar to what happened to Elijah (v. 39; cp. 1 Kg 18:12; 2 Kg 2:16) and Ezekiel (Ezk 3:12,14; 8:3). Philip continued his ministry beginning with **Azotus**, the Old Testament city of Ashdod (1 Sm 5:1), another one of the five ancient Philistine cities, located about 18 miles north of Gaza and two and a half miles inland from the Mediterranean, an important center for producing purple wool in the first century. Philip evangelized **all the towns** along the Mediterranean coast **until he came to Caesarea**, which was approximately 60 miles north of Azotus. Philip had settled in Caesarea because about 20 years later Luke and Paul visited him and his four unmarried daughters there (Ac 8:40; 21:8-9).

Candace *Acts 8:26-40*		
The Kingdom	Meroe, the capital of Ethiopia, a region of Nubia just south of Egypt.	
The Queen	Candace, title for all the queens of Ethiopia.	
The Servant	A eunuch, trusted man of great authority, interested in the Old Testament.	
The Encounter	• Philip the Evangelist met the Ethiopian. • The eunuch engaged in a brief theological discussion. • The gospel was shared.	
The Response	• The eunuch believed: "I believe that Jesus Christ is the Son of God" (v. 37). • Philip baptized the eunuch. • The eunuch shared his faith. • Tradition has maintained that Candace was also saved.	

9:1-9 With the word **meanwhile**, Luke transitioned back to **Saul** who had been ravaging the church (8:1-3). Luke used the names Saul and Paul interchangeably. **Damascus,** an ancient city of importance existing as far back as the days of Abraham (9:2; Gn 14:15), was a commercial center where caravans converged from all directions, and it was the location for a large Jewish population. Saul realized that Christianity could spread throughout the world from Damascus because of its strategic location about 150 miles northeast of Jerusalem; therefore, he specifically sought to stop the spread of the movement to Damascus. The phrase **the Way** (Ac 9:2) was used to describe the Christian movement only in Acts (19:9,23; 22:4; 24:14,22), perhaps because Jesus referred to Himself as "the way" (Jn 14:6) or because the Christians were proclaiming "the way" of salvation (Ac 16:17).

Saul's conversion experience is highlighted several times in Acts as well as in his own writings (see 22:3-16; 26:4-18; 1 Co 15:8; Gl 1:12-16). The three accounts in Acts, while similar, have some minor differences. These differences can be explained by considering their purposes, settings, and audiences. In Acts 9:3-16, Luke reported the historical facts of Paul's conversion. In Acts 22:3-16, Luke recounted Paul's testimony in an address to an angry mob of Jews in Jerusalem using the first person. Acts 26:4-18, in which Paul sought to persuade Agrippa to become a Christian, also was recorded in the first person as Paul's personal revelation of the change in his life. All three of these accounts originated with Paul so that minor variations are unimportant.

While Saul heard a **VOICE** speaking to him, his companions only heard a

SOUND (Ac 9:4,7). Some translations indicate that Paul's companions also heard a voice because the Greek nouns (*phōnēn, phōnēs*) respectively used in each instance can both mean "sound" in the sense of a tone or voice and "articulated speech" in the sense of language. The HCSB accurately translates what Paul's companions heard as a sound, since other passages in Acts explicitly state that his companions did not hear a voice (22:9; 26:14). Although they heard the sound of a voice, they did not understand the words or message. Paul was the only human participant; those accompanying him were merely spectators.

By persecuting the church, which is the body of Christ (1 Co 12:27; Eph 1:22-23), Saul had been persecuting Christ Himself. Saul had considered himself a devout follower of God, yet he had been persecuting the very One who was God.

9:10-25 Ananias was undoubtedly one of the leaders in the Damascus church. Not much is known about him since Scripture refers to him only here. **The street called Straight** (v. 11), which still exists today, was one of the main routes through Damascus.

Several times in Acts God used visions to communicate with His people (see also 10:1-16; 16:9-10; 18:9-10). Interestingly, when Ananias entered the house, he greeted Paul as **Brother Saul** (9:17). No longer was Saul the feared persecutor of the church; he had become a brother in Christ, a member of the family of God. Although Ananias was the channel, Christ Himself commissioned Saul to be His ambassador, caused **scales** to fall **from his eyes**, and **filled** him **with the Holy Spirit** (vv. 17-18). Hence Paul later wrote that he had not received his apostolic commission from any mortal man but from the risen Christ (Gl 1:1,11-20). The expression **placing his hands on him** (Ac

9:12) was the bringing of an Old Testament custom into rabbinic Judaism as the means by which a student was commissioned as a rabbi (see Gn 48:14,20; Nm 27:15-17; Dt 34:9). In the New Testament sometimes hands were placed on one who was being healed (Mk 8:23-25; Ac 9:12,17) or blessed (Mt 19:13-15) or set apart for a particular ministry (Ac 6:6; 13:3) or given a visible sign of the outpouring of the Holy Spirit (Ac 8:17; 19:6). Paul must have been **baptized** by immersion. Otherwise, there was no reason for him to get up first (9:18b). Nevertheless, Luke omitted the details of the baptism, the place of baptism, and name of the person who baptized Paul. Some suggest that Paul was baptized in the River Abana because it flowed through Damascus close to Straight Street. Since no one else was mentioned, presumably Ananias baptized Paul. Additional details about Ananias' encounter with Paul were recorded in Acts 22:14-16 and 26:16-18.

Paul's first mission was to focus his evangelistic zeal on the Jewish population **in the synagogues** (the first journey—13:5,14; 14:1; the second journey—17:1-2,10,17; 18:4; the third journey—18:19; 19:8). Saul's arrival **in Damascus** had been expected, but his message was not. Instead of arresting the disciples of Jesus, Saul argued that their message about Jesus was true. The persecutor of the church joined the persecuted.

After many days had passed denotes the three years Saul spent in Arabia (Gl 1:17-18). By intermingling the current account from Luke with Paul's autobiographical account in Galatians, the following order of events can be constructed:

- Saul was converted and commissioned (Ac 9:1-19a).

- He preached in the synagogues in Damascus immediately after his conversion (19b-22).

- He went to Arabia where he resided for up to three years (Gl 1:17-18).

- He returned to Damascus (Gl 1:17).

- He fled from Damascus to Jerusalem.

Saul became quite an apologist, capably **proving** Jesus was **the Messiah** (Ac 9:22). As with Stephen, the Jews' inability to deal with Saul's arguments greatly angered them; therefore, they, along with the governor under King Aretas, **conspired to kill him** (v. 23). This time God had another plan. With the help of his new friends he was able to escape by being **lowered** in a **basket** through a window **in the wall** (v. 25). Wide walls were often built around cities for fortification and protection from enemies.

9:26-31 Narrowly escaping death, Saul went to **Jerusalem**. The disciples shunned him out of fear. **Barnabas** ("son of encouragement"), living up to his name, befriended Saul, introduced him **to the apostles and explained to them** Saul's conversion and total commitment to Christ (v. 27).

Gaining the acceptance of the apostles, namely Peter and James (Gl 1:18-19), Saul began to minister alongside them. **The Hellenistic Jews** were not from Jerusalem but from various parts of the Greek-speaking world. Angered by Saul's debating ability, the Jews **attempted to kill** him. **When the brothers**, likely a reference to the disciples in general, **found out** about the plan to assassinate Saul, they removed him from the city. They took him **to Caesarea,** a Mediterranean coastal city north of Jerusalem and a stopping point en route to his ultimate destination of **Tarsus** of Cilicia (Ac 9:30), located in the southeastern portion of Asia Minor in what is modern Turkey.

Throughout Acts, Luke provided the readers with summary statements about the progress of the spiritual and numerical growth of the church (see 2:47; 6:7;

12:24; 16:5; 19:20; 28:30-31). These statements, transitory in nature, concluded previous subjects and led into new subjects. With Saul's escape to Tarsus, the focus of Acts returned temporarily to Peter. With the removal of Saul from the area, the persecution of believers temporarily ceased and **the church** continued to increase **in numbers** (9:31). Jesus' command to be His witnesses in Jerusalem, in all Judea and Samaria, and to the ends of the earth had been partially fulfilled (1:8). The focus of the rest of Acts was the beginning of the spread of the gospel to the ends of the earth.

The Spread of the Gospel as Far as Phoenicia, Cyprus, and Antioch (9:32–12:25)

9:32-35 Peter no longer resided only in Jerusalem but traveled **from place to place**, ministering as he went (Ac 9:2). **Lydda**, which was known as Lod in the Old Testament (1 Ch 8:12), was located 25 miles northwest of Jerusalem and was situated at the important intersection of the road from Joppa to Jerusalem and at the heart of the trade route between Egypt and Damascus. Peter was in the city to visit the SAINTS (Gk. *hagious*, "holy or set apart," Acts 9:32). The term became synonymous with Christians in the early church, emphasizing that God declared believers in Christ to be holy and righteous in His eyes, set apart for His purposes.

The biblical text does not indicate whether or not **Aeneas** was a believer. Since Luke referred to him as **a man** instead of a disciple, some assume that he was not a follower of Christ. But since Peter's purpose apparently was to visit the saints, Aeneas was possibly a believer. **Paralyzed** and **bedridden for eight years** with no cure in sight, Aeneas was healed **immediately.** Although Peter spoke the healing words, he affirmed that

Aeneas was healed by **Jesus Christ**. Luke's designation of **all who lived** was likely a generalization, indicating that an enormous number of people placed their faith in Christ (v. 35). **Sharon**, a fertile plain about 10 miles wide and 50 miles long, extended from Joppa along the coast of the Mediterranean past Caesarea to Mount Carmel.

9:36-43 Joppa (modern Jaffa), just south of Tel Aviv, functioned as the major seaport of Judea. In the Old Testament, it was the place through which Solomon brought cedar beams from Lebanon to build the temple (2 Ch 2:16) and the place

from which Jonah sailed for Tarshish (Jnh 1:3). **A disciple named Tabitha** (Dorcas)**,** resided in Joppa (Ac 9:36). This instance is the only one in the New Testament in which a woman is referenced as a "disciple." Tabitha (Hb.) was more commonly known by her Greek name **Dorcas**. Both names mean "gazelle."

Dorcas **became sick and died** (v. 37). Some of Dorcas's Christian friends knew that Peter was only 10 miles away in Lydda, so they **begged** him to come. Luke did not explain what they wanted Peter to do; but since Tabitha's body was washed but not anointed for burial and her good

deeds were told to Peter when he arrived, they apparently believed he could restore her to life. As believers, they were familiar with the miracles Jesus had performed, and they had also heard of the miraculous deeds done by Peter in Lydda. According to Jewish custom a maximum of three days was allowed for burial. Dorcas was surrounded by **widows** to whom she had ministered while she was alive.

Peter had been present for all three resurrections of individuals from the dead, including the raising of Jairus's daughter (Mk 5:21-24,35-43; Lk 8:50-56), recorded in Scripture. Following the Lord's example, **Peter sent them all out of the room. He** then **knelt down, prayed,** and **said** "**Tabitha, get up**!" (Ac 9:40). In its Aramaic form, this verbal command, GET UP, differed from the words spoken by Jesus to Jairus's daughter by only one letter (Aram., *Talitha*, meaning "little girl" vs. *Tabitha* here).

As with the healing of Aeneas, the miracle **became known throughout** the region and **many believed in the Lord** (v. 42). Throughout Acts, Luke highlighted the many people who came to faith in Christ as a result of supernatural acts. Luke purposefully noted that Peter remained with **Simon** the **leather tanner** (v. 43). As a tanner, Simon worked with the skins of dead animals, having contact with the unclean, which was forbidden by Jewish law. Peter's acceptance of Simon prepares the way for his coming vision and mission to the Gentiles (ch. 10).

Dorcas *Acts 9:36-43*	
Her Name	• Dorcas (Gk.) or Tabitha (Hb.)
Her Home	• Joppa near Lydda
Her Character	• A disciple of Christ always serving others and doing acts of charity
Her Ministry	• Sewing garments for the widows
Her Illness	• Became sick, died suddenly, was prepared for burial
Her Testimony	• Peter and the disciples went to her. Widows mourned her death. Peter restored Dorcas to life. Many believed because of the miracle.

10:1-33 Chapter 10 signified a pivotal point for the church with the spread of the gospel to the Gentiles. One might have expected Paul, the apostle to the Gentiles, to be the bearer of the good news. Instead Peter was prepared for this task. Peter spoke at Pentecost, proclaiming the gospel to the Jews. He then went to Samaria to welcome the Samaritans into the church, and in Acts 10 he opened the way for the Gentiles to enter the church. Although other Gentiles such as the Ethiopian eunuch had been saved, this encounter uniquely demonstrated that the gospel was meant for the Gentiles as well as the Jews. Luke's length and repetitive structure placed emphasis on this account.

The spread of the gospel to the Gentiles overcame a seemingly impenetrable barrier that had existed between the Jews and the Gentiles. Devout Jews would not be guests in Gentile homes; neither would they eat food prepared by Gentile hands. Gentiles were considered unclean, and even to be in their presence was defiling. The gift of the Holy Spirit being poured out on the Gentiles, together with Peter's full acceptance of them, paved the way for the spread of the gospel beyond the Jews and to the whole world.

Built by Herod the Great and named after Caesar Augustus, **Caesarea** had great prominence, containing all the amenities of a great city: temples, a theater, a market, a hippodrome, an amphitheater, a racecourse, a palace, public buildings, an aqueduct, and a sophisticated man-made harbor. This Hellenistic-styled city located approximately 30 miles north of Joppa flourished, attracting primarily a Gentile population. Politically Caesarea functioned as the capital of the Roman province of Judea and possessed a significant military population.

Cornelius, a centurion, commanded a military unit of at least 100 soldiers (v. 1). His unit was a part of the **Italian Regiment** (about 600 men), which was part of the Roman legion (about 6,000 men). Law required centurions to be Roman citizens. The Gospels and Acts portray centurions in a favorable light (Mt 8:5-10; 27:54; Ac 22:25-26; 23:17-18; 27:6,43). Consistent with this, Luke described Cornelius as DEVOUT (Gk. *eusebēs*, a compound word linking *eu* or "good" with *sebomai* or "worship or reverence"), a man who "feared God, did many charitable deeds for the people, and always prayed to God" (10:2). When "devout" is linked with "fearing God," the reference is generally to a God-fearing proselyte. Luke used the term to refer to God-seeking Gentiles. As a God-fearer, Cornelius was a Gentile who had accepted many of the truths of the Jewish faith, but he had not become a full convert because he had not been circumcised (11:2-3). Cornelius even may have had a reserved seat in the synagogue because of his faithfulness, but he had not completed the transition to Judaism.

At about three in the afternoon, while he prayed in his house during one of the standard hours of prayer, Cornelius **distinctly saw in a vision an angel of God**, whom he later described as **a man in a dazzling robe** (v. 30). The male angel commended Cornelius for his **prayers** and his **acts of charity** (vv. 4,31), which were **a memorial offering before God** (v. 4). The term "memorial" is reminiscent of Old Testament sacrificial language. As a God-fearer and not a Jewish convert, Cornelius would have been barred from presenting offerings to God in the Jewish temple. Nevertheless, his acts of piety were not unnoticed, a point that Luke reiterated throughout the passage (vv. 2,4,22). Although Cornelius was a pious man devoted to the one true God, he needed the knowledge of Jesus Christ to be saved (4:12). God blessed Cornelius by providing him with that knowledge through Peter.

Peter went up to pray on the roof, which provided a solitary place (10:9). Noon was not one of the appointed times of prayer, but many of the more pious Jews prayed at that time (Ps 55:17).

The image Peter saw coming out of heaven indicated that it was a message sent from God (Ac 10:11). Some suggest that the **four corners** represented the ends of the earth, pointing ultimately to the worldwide mission (Rv 7:1). Both clean and unclean animals were represented (Ac 10:12). Leviticus 11 gave specific regulations about what Jewish people could and could not eat. In refusing to kill and eat, Peter attempted to be true to his Jewish faith. He had never eaten anything declared **unclean**, and he did not desire to do so now, despite his hungry appetite (Ac 10:14). But Peter overlooked what Jesus once said. Things like food cannot defile a person, but what comes from within—evil thoughts, greed, pride, and sexual immoralities—causes defilement

(Mk 7:17-23). The vision was repeated **three times** (Ac 10:16), emphasizing its importance.

Luke did not specify how the Spirit spoke to Peter, but Peter clearly understood and obeyed, having **no doubts at all** (vv. 20,23). LODGING (Gk. *exenise*, "to entertain as a guest," v. 23) described Peter's unexpected and utterly surprising hospitality. Peter must have begun understanding the meaning of his vision for him to be willing to entertain people he previously regarded as unclean.

The journey from Joppa to Caesarea was approximately 30 miles so they did not arrive until **the following day**. Cornelius understood the importance of this meeting, and he wanted **his relatives and close friends** to hear this sacred message as well (v. 24). Cornelius **worshiped** Peter (v. 25). The term used does not necessarily imply that Cornelius believed he was worshiping a deity. Instead Cornelius bowed in an attempt to pay the respect he believed to be fitting for a messenger of God. Not willing to be the object of any kind of worship, **Peter helped him up** to make clear to Cornelius the equality of all believers before God (v. 26).

The real meaning of Peter's message became crystal clear. Although his vision was of clean and unclean animals, by application God showed him that he **must not call any person common or unclean** (v. 28). Although Jewish law forbade a Jewish man to associate or visit a foreigner, Peter was willing to come to the home of a Gentile **without any objection** (v. 29). God had divinely prepared Peter for this moment, which would forever change the church.

Although Peter understood why God had called him to the house of Cornelius, Peter wanted to know the specifics of how it came to be (v. 33). Since Peter already knew the gist of Cornelius's story from the two servants and the soldier, perhaps he asked the questions so that all of the listeners would realize that this was an encounter ordained by God, as evidenced by the corresponding visions of him and Cornelius.

10:34-48 For each major segment of the Lord's commission (1:8), an outpouring on the body of believers collectively occurred as a symbol of heaven's approval of what was happening in kingdom ministry: the spreading of the gospel abroad to the Jew (2:1-4), to the Samaritan (8:4-17), and to the Gentile (10:34-44).

This statement in verse 35 is frequently misunderstood as advocating a works-based salvation. However, if that were true, there would have been no need for Peter to come and share the gospel with Cornelius, who was already regarded as an upright and God-fearing man. Instead Peter's statement needs to be understood within the larger context of his sermon, which clearly indicated that only those who believe in the name of Jesus will receive forgiveness of sins (v. 43). To work or to do righteousness certainly includes doing good deeds, but even though Jewish tradition accepts good deeds and works as sufficient for salvation, the author knows that such deeds or works never save or make one right with God.

The good news of peace through Jesus Christ was first sent to **the sons of Israel**. PEACE (Gk. *eirēnēn*, "blessing or tranquility") is the peace that comes through a right relationship with Jesus Christ (Rm 5:1-11). Although the gospel message was first for the Jewish people (Rm 1:16), Jesus **is Lord of all**. He came to earth and died for both Jews and Gentiles alike (Ac 10:36).

By utilizing the phrase **you know**, Peter assumed his audience possessed a familiarity with **the events** surrounding Jesus' life, beginning with **the baptism that**

John preached (v. 37). As in the Gospel of Mark, Peter's presentation of the life of Christ began with John the Baptist and concluded with the resurrection. For this reason as well as others, many have regarded Mark's Gospel as a reflection of Peter's theology. Peter then summarized the life, death, and resurrection of Jesus, this time not placing the blame for His crucifixion specifically on any group since the pronoun **they** is without a clear antecedent (v. 39). In Peter's previous sermons in Acts, he blamed the Jewish leaders (3:15; 4:10; 5:30). Peter placed emphasis in this sermon on the resurrection and post-resurrection appearances of Jesus (10:40-41). From the immediate context, one can assume that **us** referred to Peter and his Jewish companions. After the resurrection, Jesus appeared primarily to His closest followers, although He did appear to a group of 500 believers at one time (1 Co 15:6). Peter authenticated the genuineness of Christ's resurrection by testifying that he even **ate and drank with Him after He rose from the dead**. Acceptance or rejection of Jesus has eternal consequences—not a new message, but one of which **all the prophets** spoke (Ac 10:43; Is 53:11; Jr 31:34; Ezk 36:25-26). With this key point Peter prematurely concluded his sermon due to the coming of the Holy Spirit (Ac 10:44).

Apparently, once Cornelius and those gathered heard that forgiveness exists for all who believe in Jesus, they believed. As a result of their faith, the Holy Spirit came down and indwelt all who believed Peter's message. The visible manifestation of the Spirit was similar to that of Pentecost: They were **speaking in other languages and declaring the greatness of God** (v. 46). God in His providence knew that it would be hard to convince Peter's companions, **the circumcised believers**, that **the gift of the Holy Spirit** could be **poured out on the Gentiles also**

(v. 45). Therefore, He provided a convincing visible manifestation of the Spirit's arrival, one they had already experienced at Pentecost. Due to the similarity of this event with Pentecost, some refer to this as the "Gentile Pentecost."

As a result of their saving faith and subsequent gift of the Holy Spirit, Peter argued that the Gentiles should **be baptized**. Baptism came as a result of their faith. Luke failed to mention who performed the baptisms, perhaps because this information was not important.

11:1-18 Those who stressed circumcision (v. 2) can be more literally translated "those who were circumcised." These circumcised Jewish Christians could not understand why Peter, one of the key leaders in the church, **visited uncircumcised men and ate with them** (v. 3). Peter's actions blatantly violated Jewish custom. Peter, prepared for their objections, explained the circumstances beginning with his vision in Joppa.

In His sovereignty, God knew beforehand that Cornelius and his household would respond favorably to Peter's message about Jesus Christ (vv. 13-14). Peter saw no need to tell the circumcised believers the content of his message because they had heard him preach before and they knew the gospel message. For this reason, Peter jumped to the pouring out of the Holy Spirit on the Gentiles **just as on us at the beginning**, which equated the Gentiles' experience with the event of Pentecost (v. 15; Ac 1:5). As the words of Christ were fulfilled for the apostles at Pentecost, so they were fulfilled for the Gentiles at Cornelius' house. Peter used this event to justify the baptism of the Gentiles (Ac 11:17).

Peter's argument proved convincing, for his former critics **became silent**. They began to understand that God had a plan for the Gentiles as well as for the circumcised. The irate crowd of circumcised

Heart to Heart:
Household Baptisms in Acts
(10:48; 16:11-15,31-34; 18:8)

The book of Acts contains references to "household baptisms," a phrase sometimes used to support the practice of infant baptism. However, a careful analysis of these passages will reveal that no support arises from these passages for this practice. To the contrary, belief in Christ as a prerequisite to Christian baptism is consistently stated in Acts.

During Peter's visit Cornelius and his household received the Spirit and were baptized (10:48). However, Cornelius was described as "a devout man" and one who "feared God" (10:2). A young child does not have an understanding of fearing God.

Lydia and her household were baptized (16:15). Some have assumed that Lydia must have had children in the house and that these children would have been baptized. However, the evidence infers that Lydia had no husband or children. She was a seller of purple from the city of Thyatira, about 300 miles from Philippi. Had she been married, customarily she would have worked with her husband in the business or more likely presided over the home and cared for her children. Additionally, in verse 15 she referred to "my house," again implying that she had no husband and the house was hers alone. In verse 40, the house is referred to by Luke as "Lydia's house." The most logical explanation is that Lydia had no husband or children. She, together with those who worked for her in her house, accepted the gospel of Jesus Christ. Thus, all were believers who understood their commitment as individuals and were thus proper candidates for baptism.

Acts 16:31-34 discussed the salvation and baptism of the Philippian jailer and his household. However, before the baptism, Paul told them, "Believe on the Lord Jesus, and you will be saved—you and your household" (v. 31). Certainly Paul did not mean that the jailer could believe and everyone would be saved but that everyone in the house could believe and each, according to the exercising of his faith, would be saved. Belief in Christ was and is a prerequisite to Christian baptism. Additionally, he "rejoiced because he had believed God with his entire household" (v. 34). In infancy, one does not have the intellectual development to believe and, thus, should not be baptized.

Crispus "believed the Lord, along with his whole household" (Ac 18:8). This introductory phrase indicated that all in the household were capable of belief. Apparently no infants were present, and those who believed were baptized. Throughout Acts and the entire New Testament a consistent pattern of belief in Christ emerges first and Christian baptism follows. Thus, only a believer in Christ is a candidate for baptism.

believers became a group who **glorified God** for granting to the Gentiles **repentance resulting in life**, a phrase signifying salvation and highlighting the centrality of repentance in salvation (v. 18). The issue of inclusion of the Gentiles in the church would reemerge at the Jerusalem Council in Acts 15 since some men continued to teach that circumcision was necessary for salvation.

11:19-26 Luke returned to the martyrdom of **Stephen** (8:1-2), showing how his death resulted in the scattering of the church and the spread of the gospel **as far as Phoenicia, Cyprus, and Antioch** (11:19). The most prominent cities of Phoenicia, an area along the northeastern Mediterranean coast between Judea and Syria, were Tyre and Sidon. Most of this area lies within the boundaries of modern Lebanon. Cyprus, the home of Barnabas, is the third largest island in the Mediterranean and is located approximately 60 miles west of the Syrian coast. Antioch, the third largest metropolis in the Roman Empire, was located within the province of Syria. It became a key place for the spread of the gospel into the Gentile world.

Hellenists were Greek-speaking non-Jews. This movement was led by Hellenistic Jews from Cyprus and Cyrene **who came to Antioch** to share the gospel. Although Cyprus was close to Antioch, Cyrene was located in northern Africa. **Cyrenian** Jews were converted at Pentecost (2:10). In the Old Testament, "the hand of the Lord" could mean two things: God's power expressed in judgment (Dt 2:15; Jos 4:24; 1 Sm 5:7; 7:13) or God's power expressed in blessing (Ezr 7:9; 8:18; Neh 2:18). This instance refers to blessing because **a large number who believed turned to the Lord** (Ac 11:21). People not only believed the truths about Christ, but they turned from their sins and to the Lord. Mental belief in Christ is not

enough, for even the demons believe and shudder (Jms 2:19). Saving belief is always linked to repentance.

News of response to the gospel in Antioch soon **reached the ears of the church in Jerusalem**, who **sent out Barnabas** (Ac 11:22), a highly regarded man in the early church described by Luke as **a good man, full of the Holy Spirit and of faith** (v. 24; see also Ac 4:36). The apostles also trusted Barnabas just as, according to his word at an earlier time, they had accepted the persecutor Saul into the circle of believers (9:27). As a Greek-speaking Jewish Christian and a native of Cyprus, Barnabas was the best person to investigate the radical church growth movement and to assist in building up the church at Antioch.

Barnabas ("son of encouragement") genuinely cared about the welfare of these new believers. He desired that they live out their faith and share Christ with others daily. Initially in Acts, Luke was able to provide specific numbers, but by this point so many people had come to the Lord that they were beyond counting.

Mary Crowley said, "Being a Christian is not doing certain things but doing everything a certain way."

After spending a short time with the believers in Antioch, Barnabas realized he would need help discipling the new believers. So **he went to Tarsus** to enlist the help of **Saul** (Ac 11:25). Barnabas and Saul provided some guidance for **the church**, meeting with them and teaching **large numbers** (v. 26). They realized the greatest need of the church was for believers to be grounded doctrinally in the Word of God. As a result the church in Antioch flourished, eventually becoming the center from which missionaries embarked to share the gospel. Luke added that Antioch was the place where

the disciples were first called Christians (v. 26). The term "Christian" literally means "belonging to the party of Christ." What began as a nickname, and from some an insulting label, became a means of identifying those who lived and behaved like Christ. Mary Crowley said, "Being a Christian is not doing certain things but doing everything a certain way." Over a period of time the church separated from its roots of Judaism, becoming recognized as a distinct group. The Greek term *Christiamos* is only used three times in the New Testament (v. 26; 26:28; 1 Pt 4:16). Out of this predominately Gentile congregation were sent the first international missionaries (Ac 13:1-3).

11:27-30 Although Antioch is north of Jerusalem, the prophets went "**down**" because Jerusalem is at a much higher elevation than Antioch. **Prophets** in the New Testament differ slightly from the prophets in the Old Testament. In the Old Testament, the primary function of prophets was foretelling the birth and coming of Christ. Since this was no longer necessary, the New Testament prophets interpreted and preached God's word, encouraged the people, and predicted events. Prophets were highly regarded in the New Testament, ranking second only to the apostles (Eph 4:11).

Among the prophets who came from Jerusalem was **Agabus**, mentioned here for the first time in the New Testament (Ac 11:28). He reemerged later in Acts when he came to the assistance of Paul (21:10-11). PROPHETS (Gk. *prophētai*, "proclaimer or interpreter or one who speaks forth") had an important role in the early church. Under inspiration of the Holy Spirit, they not only announced future events but also revealed the will of God. These men were held in high esteem. Agabus's prediction of **severe famine** occurred around AD 39 (11:28). Luke, who wrote about this prediction after

it was fulfilled, noted that the famine came **during the time of Claudius**, the Roman emperor AD 41–54. Because of the prediction, **the disciples** in Antioch decided to begin a famine **relief** program for their sister congregation in Jerusalem. The support was not compulsory, but voluntary, each **according to his ability** (v. 29). Since Antioch fell within the bounds of the Roman Empire and would have therefore been affected by the famine as well, their sending support demonstrated a mature faith and generous hearts. **Barnabas and Saul** delivered the support **to the elders** (Gk. *presbuterous*) of the Jerusalem church. These elders functioned as pastors of the churches, and their primary responsibilities were preaching and teaching (1 Tm 5:17). Paul noted qualifications for elders in 1 Timothy 3:1-7, where the term "overseer" is used interchangeably with "elders."

12:1-19 Luke only provided a vague time reference for the martyrdom of James, the son of Zebedee and brother of John (vv. 1-2). One can surmise that his death occurred sometime after Barnabas and Saul delivered the relief offering to Jerusalem based on its location within Luke's report. **King Herod** is Agrippa I, the grandson of Herod the Great. Agrippa I ruled Judea AD 41–44. Therefore, this narrative occurred within that time span.

When Claudius, who had been one of Agrippa's childhood friends, became emperor in AD 41, he extended his kingdom to include Judea and Samaria. Throughout Agrippa's reign he continually sought the approval of the Jews. Although he was popular with the Pharisees because of his mixed Jewish descent and because he diligently kept Jewish customs, he sought additional ways to win their approval. For this reason, **Herod cruelly attacked some who belonged to the church**, specifically the leaders. Since the focus of this account is not the persecution but the triumph of the church, Luke did not provide many details. If **James** was executed in the Roman fashion, the phrase **with the sword** would mean he was beheaded (v. 2). If Herod used the Jewish mode of execution, the sword was thrust through James's body.

Herod intended to kill Peter, but since it was **during the days of Unleavened Bread,** he chose to wait (vv. 3-4). Executing Peter during the religious holiday might have offended the Jews, causing the reverse effect. Jews celebrated the Passover the evening of Nisan 14. It was followed by seven days of eating unleavened bread, ending on Nisan 21.[4] In this passage, Luke referred to the entire holiday period as "Passover" because Passover came before the Feast of Unleavened Bread. Herod intended to keep Peter in prison until **after the Passover**. In an effort to ensure that Peter remained in prison, Herod **assigned four squads of four soldiers each to guard him** (v. 4). Herod took every precaution because he had heard rumors of the apostles' previous escapes from jail (5:17-21). Four soldiers were guarding Peter at all times. Two were chained to him and two stood guard outside the prison (12:6,10).

Although his execution was scheduled for the next day, Peter did not fret about it. He had complete faith and trust in God. Since the light did not arouse Peter, the angel STRUCK (Gk. *pataxas*, "hit or slay") him. The angel had to do more than nudge Peter to wake him (v. 7). The word used suggests a strong blow. Throughout the narrative the angel was telling the groggy Peter what to do. Apparently Peter had been sleeping so soundly that he needed specific guidance from the angel (v. 9).

Luke did not provide details about the state of the guards, whether they were sleeping or in a God-ordered trance and unable to do anything. The escape was easy since even the gate leading into the city **opened to them by itself** (v. 10), underscoring God's active role throughout the escape. Luke provided specific details about this escape, authenticating its genuineness. Skeptics may claim that this escape was contrived by human means such as bribery, but Luke painted a clear picture.

Peter **went to the house of Mary, the mother of John Mark** (v. 12). Mary, a woman of means, with servants and a house big enough for the large group of believers to gather, was mentioned only here. Since Luke did not mention her husband, she might have been a widow. She was a brave woman of faith with the gift of hospitality, and she willingly opened her home to the church even in the face of persecution. She was the aunt of Barnabas (Col 4:10) and mother of John Mark, who later became a prominent figure in the early church and the author of the Gospel of Mark. Mary's house likely served as a regular place of worship for the Jerusalem church since Peter went straight there. Peter realized that the believers would be **assembled** and **praying** for him (v. 12).

A **servant** girl **named Rhoda** answered the door (v. 13). The fact that Luke mentioned the servant by name as well as the fact that Rhoda **recognized Peter's voice** indicate that Peter knew the members of Mary's household personally. Rhoda (Gk., "rose") had the duty of gate keeping. The praying Christians did not believe her announcement, calling her **crazy** (v. 15). Throughout Acts, Luke highlighted the great faith of the early Christians, but in this instance their lack of faith kept them from believing that Peter could have escaped from prison, perhaps because the memory of James' execution still lingered in their minds. They finally conceded that Rhoda might have seen **his angel** (v. 15). This response reflected the common Jewish belief that each person had a guardian angel resembling himself. Some believed that a person's angel often appeared immediately after his death.

Even Mary's large house would not hold all of the Jerusalem Christians. Therefore Peter asked the believers at Mary's house to **report** what had happened to him **to James and the brothers** (v. 17). This James, obviously not the James martyred earlier in the chapter, was the half-brother of Jesus, who was a leader in the Jerusalem church (Gl 1:19). Scholars disagree widely about the place Peter went, since staying in Jerusalem would not have been safe. Some say Antioch, others Caesarea, while still others suggest Rome. Luke omitted this detail from the text.

According to Justinian's code in Roman law, a guard who allowed his prisoner to escape was subject to the same penalty the escaped prisoner would have suffered. As a result, he ordered that the soldiers be led away to "their execution" (Ac 12:19). Although the Greek text does not use the explicit word for EXECUTION, translators do have good reason to interpret *apachthēnai* (Gk., "lead away") as implicitly, within this context, meaning exactly that the men would be led away to execution. For information on **Caesarea**, see notes on Acts 10:1.

12:20-25 With this account, Luke took a hiatus from the history of the church to provide some details from secular history. The death of Herod Agrippa I was relevant to the church because it opened the door for God's message to flourish and for the church to multiply (v. 24). Chronologically, this account occurred in AD 44, which was anywhere from several months to a year after Peter's escape from prison.

During Herod's reign, he became **very angry with the Tyrians and Sidonians** (v. 20). Tyre and Sidon were coastal cities located respectively 50 and 70 miles north of Caesarea. Since the days of Solomon, they had relied upon Judea for supplying food (1 Kg 5:9-12; Ezk 27:17). Due to the famine affecting Judea, the need in Tyre and Sidon was particularly severe. The text does not specify the nature of the conflict, but representatives from Tyre and Sidon presented themselves before Herod. They procured this opportunity by winning **over Blastus**, the king's personal servant **in charge of the king's bedroom**.

The historian Josephus described Herod's public address to them in detail, specifying that the festival was in honor of the Roman emperor Claudius. According to Josephus, Herod wore "a garment made wholly of sliver, and of a truly wonderful contexture" (*Jewish Antiquities* 19.343–350). When Herod took the stage, the people began to shout, **"It's the voice of god and not of a man!"** (Ac 12:22). According to Josephus, "The king did not rebuke them nor did he reject their flattery as impious." **Because he did not give the glory to God** but accepted the praise of the people, **an angel of the Lord** immediately **struck him**. Herod **became infected with worms and died** (v. 23). According to Josephus, Herod suffered five days of excruciating pain before his death. No longer did the disciples in Jerusalem have to worry about this infamous persecutor of the church. After Herod's death, first Felix and then Festus ruled in his place.[5]

Luke returned to where he left off in Acts 11:30 with **Barnabas and Saul**. After they had **completed their relief mission**, on which they had taken **John Mark**, they **returned to Jerusalem** (Ac 12:25). Formerly they had been in Antioch gathering relief for the famine-stricken Jerusalem church. Luke noted that they returned to Jerusalem, probably the trip during which they delivered the relief supplies. After making the delivery to the Jerusalem church, Barna-

Rhoda Acts 12:5-19	
Her Life	• Rhoda means "rose." • She lived in the first century during the reign of Herod the Great. • She was a servant of Mary, John Mark's mother. • She gathered with Christians to pray.
Her Lesson	• She prayed with other Christians for Peter's release from prison. • She heard a knock at the door during a prayer meeting. • She answered the door and recognized Peter's voice. • She ran to tell others and forgot to unlock the door for Peter. • She told others that Peter had been released.
Her Legacy	• She believed that God answers prayer. • She had a passion to share her faith. • She had joy in menial tasks.

bas and Saul apparently returned to Antioch. Verse 25 essentially functions as an introduction to the next chapter.

PAUL: MISSIONARY TO THE GENTILES 13:1–28:31

The Spread of the Gospel through the Region of Phrygia and Galatia (13:1–15:35)

Paul's first missionary journey (13:1–14:28)

13:1-3 The local church at Antioch was a prosperous and growing church composed largely of Gentiles. They actively sought to minister to others, demonstrated by their outreach to Gentiles in their city (11:19-36) as well as by their sending relief to the Jerusalem church (11:27-30). Now they determined to be the first church to send out missionaries (13:3).

Luke used the terms **prophets and teachers** to describe the five men he lists as leaders of the church. One can argue grammatically that in the Greek text the first three listed were prophets and the last two teachers (v. 1). The Greek particle *te*, which is not translatable but is simply used to connect pairs of words or coordinate clauses or similar sentences, serves to distinguish one set of coordinates from another. In this verse the first *te* introduces three names—Barnabas, Simeon, and Lucius—and the second *te* links two other names—Manaen and Saul. Since the word "prophets" (Gk. *prophētai*) occurs first, one would presume the first group fit that category and that "teachers" (Gk. *didaskaloi*) identified a second grouping. However, this fine point of grammar makes little difference in understanding the text, the important point being that all bases were covered. The church would receive what God's prophet would proclaim or "speak forth," and the people would be taught the whole counsel of God, including lessons from the Old Testament and from the life and instruction of Jesus Himself.

Since Barnabas and Saul were already described as teaching the congregation, one is wise to view all five men as prophetic teachers. These men spoke truth related to God's word as led by the Spirit.

Luke listed only men as the leaders of the church. Although women, such as Dorcas (9:36-43) and Mary the mother of John Mark (12:12), performed crucial ministries, their roles and assignments differed from those given to the men. Women did not function as teachers of men in the church.

Some suggest that the five men are listed in order of importance, beginning with **Barnabas** and concluding with **Saul.** Each man had something unusual in his background. The five men listed demonstrated the racial, cultural, and social diversity existing within the church at Antioch.

- Initially Barnabas's name is always listed before Saul's, but the order changed later in Acts. Barnabus, who was from Cyprus, was a peacemaker and often settled disputes between Jewish and Gentile Christians. He was also responsible for bringing Paul to Antioch.

- Since there were numerous Simeons, this **Simeon** was called **Niger** (Lat. "black"), probably reflecting that he had a darker complexion than the others and confirming that the early churches did not discriminate because of skin color.

- **Lucius the Cyrenian** was a native of North Africa, and possibly the person with Paul in Romans 16:1.

- **Manaen** is identified as **a close friend of Herod the tetrarch**. Another possible rendering is that "he was brought up with Herod the tetrarch" or "he was a foster brother of Herod the tetrarch." Herod Antipas, the son of Herod the Great, was tetrarch of Galilee and Perea during the life of Jesus. Therefore Manaen came from a royal social class.

- Saul, as already stated, was from Tarsus and was a trained rabbi and a Pharisee. He became one of the greatest Christian missionaries and was martyred for his faith.

They could refer to the five leaders alone or to the entire congregation at Antioch (Acts 13:2). One may argue that "they" identified the church since the entire congregation would have been involved in commissioning Barnabas and Saul. When these men returned, the missionaries reported to the church all that God had done (14:27). Additionally, later in Acts Luke indicated that the entire church, and not just the leaders, sent out Paul and Barnabas (15:2-3). Judging from the passages in Acts related to church governance (6:2-6; 15:4-30), apparently the entire congregation, rather than the leaders alone, had a role in decision-making and in the sending of missionaries.

The phrase "**MINISTERING** (Gk. *leitourgountōn*, "serve") to the Lord" indicates they were worshiping (Ac 13:2). In classical Greek this word was used to describe voluntary service to the state, but the word evolved to refer to the performance of service required by the state. In the New Testament era the word is used especially for the service rendered in a temple by a priest or servant. Performing service was truly a conduit for worship. Worship was accompanied by **FASTING** (Gk. *nēsteuontōn*, "going without food"), as they actively sought God's guidance. "Fasting" could be a private spiritual discipline or a public community effort to put aside food and/or drink for a set period of time. The early church used fasting in tandem with prayer in order to determine how best to move forward the spread of the gospel and how to respond to the challenges of persecution and difficulties they faced in a world hostile to the message of Christ and to those who embraced that message. God called **Barnabas and**

Saul (v. 2) to go and share the truth about Jesus with the Gentiles, beginning the task of spreading the gospel to the ends of the earth (1:8). From the time of his salvation, Saul had known his calling as the apostle to the Gentiles (9:15). Now Barnabas received this commission as well. How the Holy Spirit made His calling on the lives of Barnabas and Saul clear was not noted—perhaps because God's calling is one of those mysteries that remain to unfold according to divine timing and in a way unique to each situation. Certainly there is evidence that a compassion for the lost and a passion to share the gospel with those who had never heard were factors and must have helped the men to crystallize in their own hearts the divine call to pursue a God-assigned task.

To prepare Barnabas and Saul for their missionary service, the church **fasted, prayed, and laid hands on them** (13:3). Undoubtedly it encouraged Barnabas and Saul to know they had the prayers and support of the church behind them as they left.

13:4-12 Sent not only by the church but even more importantly **by the Holy Spirit**, Barnabas and Saul embarked from Antioch on what has been denominated as Paul's first missionary journey. Their path can be traced on the map entitled "The First Missionary Journey of Paul." From Antioch, they traveled 16 miles to **Seleucia**, a Syrian city that functioned as Antioch's eastern port on the Mediterranean coast. From Seleucia, they sailed approximately 70 miles to the city of **Salamis**, the chief port for the island of **Cyprus** (an island 138 miles long and 60 miles wide located in the eastern Mediterranean Sea). Barnabas understood the culture and customs of his homeland. By beginning their ministry in the **synagogues**, the missionaries were going first to the Jew, with the intent to go then to the Gentiles (v. 5). As a side note, Luke added that they **had John**, the cousin of Barnabas who previ-

ously had been identified as John Mark, with them **as their assistant**.

Upon leaving Seleucia, they traveled approximately 90 miles across the island until they came to **Paphos,** located on the southwestern coast and the capital of Cyprus. This immoral city was famous for its worship of Aphrodite. Although the group probably ministered as they traveled from Seleucia to Paphos, Luke chose not to give details on the journey. Instead he focused on two highlights of the ministry in Cyprus: the conversion of the **proconsul** (v. 12) and the defeat of a **false prophet** (13:4-12).

In Paphos the group encountered **a sorcerer** (v. 8), **a Jewish false prophet named Bar-Jesus** (v. 6), who became the first opposition to the gospel on their missionary journey. SORCERER (Gk. *magoi*, "magician or wise man") can be used to describe a counselor or honorable gentlemen (as with the "wise men" in Mt 2:1), or the word can refer to a fraudulent magician as here. This sorcerer was with the proconsul of the island, **an intelligent man** named **Sergius Paulus** (Ac 13:7). Proconsuls were appointed by the Roman senate, and they usually ruled for one to two years. Luke described him as an INTELLIGENT MAN (Gk. *andoi sunetō*, "sagacious, wise, understanding man"). His discernment became apparent as he sifted through the diverse options before him. As the proconsul, Paulus possessed great power, having absolute military and judicial authority on the island. Many men of position and power had personal sorcerers or magicians because of the widespread superstition. Of course, Barnabas and Saul were a threat to the false prophet's position with the proconsul and to his key source of income. Apparently the proconsul was searching for spiritual answers. He had listened to what the Jewish sorcerer had to say, but now he wanted to hear from the two missionaries. Luke added the sorcerer's name, **Elymas**, which was **translated** as "sorcerer" (v. 8). "Bar-Jesus," the name previously given, means "son of Jesus." The name Elymas was related more to his function, with a meaning similar to the word "sorcerer."

At this point, **Saul** emerged in the forefront (v. 9). While Barnabas's name had always been listed first, possibly indicating that he had been the leader of the group, from this point Saul's name is listed before Barnabas (except when they were in Jerusalem and in 14:14). From now on Luke chose to call Saul by his Roman name, **Paul** (13:9). Many people assume that Paul experienced a name change like Abram, whose name was changed to Abraham, or his wife Sarai, whose name was changed to Sarah (Gn 17:5,15). But this case was different. Luke indicated that "Saul" was "also called Paul" (Ac 13:9). Saul, the first Jewish king, was his Hebrew name. Paul was his Roman name (Lat. "diminutive or small"). Perhaps this switch came because he was short of stature or because of the focus of his ministry. Paul's mission throughout the rest of Acts focused on the Gentiles.

Paul, under the leadership of **the Holy Spirit**, confronted "the sorcerer," calling him the **son of the Devil**, in direct opposition to the sorcerer's name "son of Jesus" (v. 10). Paul revealed the false prophet's true character and pronounced a curse of temporary blindness that immediately took effect on him (v.11).

As a result of the miracle performed by Paul through the power of the Holy Spirit, the most influential person on the island of Cyprus placed his faith in Jesus Christ (v. 12). Seeing the power of God and receiving teaching about the Lord, the two missionaries helped the proconsul along the path of faith before they embarked on the next portion of their journey.

13:13-41 Although not on the Mediterranean coast, the city of **Perga** could be reached by sailing seven miles up the Cestrus River. Pamphylia was a small province on the southern coast of Asia Minor surrounded by mountains and foothills. For unknown reasons, perhaps because of the rough terrain, the change in leadership, or the focus on converting Gentiles, **John . . . went back to Jerusalem** (v. 13). Because of this desertion, Paul refused to take John Mark on a later journey, causing a disagreement between Paul and Barnabus, which resulted in their parting ways (15:36-39).

Antioch in Pisidia, located in modern Turkey, is to be distinguished from Antioch in Syria, the place from which they began their journey (13:14). The account of Paul's first sermon is the longest and best preserved. It easily divides into three sections, each beginning with the apostle's addressing his audience directly.

- Paul provided a brief summary from Israel's history, pointing to the promise of the Messiah (vv. 16-25).

- He showed how Jesus was the Messiah, touching on His rejection by the people, His crucifixion, and His resurrection (vv. 26-37).

- Paul provided an appeal for his listeners to believe in Jesus or face judgment (vv. 38-41).

Beginning his sermon, Paul addressed two distinct audiences, the **Men of Israel** and those **who fear God**, indicating that he had a mixed audience of Jews and God-fearing Gentiles (v. 16). He provided a brief summary of Israel's history, demonstrating how the people of Israel were God's chosen people. He highlighted the **forefathers** Abraham, Isaac, and Jacob; the **stay in the land of Egypt**; the exodus from Egypt; the **40 years** of wandering **in the desert**; and the conquest and possession **of Canaan** (vv. 17-18). The **seven nations** are listed in Deuteronomy 7:1. Paul came to 450 years by adding the 400 approximate years of captivity in Egypt (Gn 15:13), the 40 years they wandered in the desert (Nm 14:33-34), and allowing 10 years for Joshua to lead the Israelites in the conquest of the land (Jos 14:1-5; no number mentioned).

In his sermon Paul then moved to the time of the **judges** (six major judges—Othniel, Ehud, Deborah, Gideon, Jephtha, and Samson; and six minor judges—Shamgar, Tola, Jair, Ibzan, Elon, and Abdon) in Israel (Ac 13:20). **Samuel** bridged the gap between the judges and the kings. God gave them **Saul** for **40 years**. Because of Saul's disobedience to the word of the Lord (v. 21; 1 Sm 15:23), God removed him from office and **raised up David as their king**. Here the verses describing David demonstrate how Paul viewed the words of the Old Testament. Even though the psalmist said **I have found David** and Samuel called him **a man after God's own heart** (Ac 13:22), Paul attributed the words to God (Ps 89:20; 1 Sm 13:14), demonstrating that Paul believed the Scriptures accurately convey the words of God.

From David, Paul moved to Jesus, because **according to the promise** of Scripture, the Messiah would come from David's **descendants** (Ac 13:23; 2 Sm 7:12-16; Ps 132:11; Jr 23:5). All of God's work in and through His chosen people pointed to this epic event in history. To conclude this section, Paul preached about **John** the Baptist, who prepared the way for Jesus' **public** ministry. John's statement denying he was the Messiah and saying he was not even worthy to **untie the sandals on His feet** is found in all four Gospels (Mt 3:11; Mk 1:7, Lk 3:16; Jn 1:27). Paul used this example to point to the greatness of Jesus (Ac 13:24-25).

Again directly addressing both the Jewish and Gentile listeners, Paul began the second section of the sermon. Although the Jews were God's chosen people, the message of the gospel is for everyone. Like Peter (3:15; 10:39) and Stephen (7:52) before him, Paul laid the blame for Jesus' death on the Jews (13:27-28). Although the Romans carried out the killing of Jesus, the Jews **asked Pilate** for His execution.

Throughout the sermon, Peter stressed that everything about Jesus was a fulfillment of prophecy, from His birth to His death. By the phrase, **When they had fulfilled all that had been written about Him** (v. 29), Paul let his listeners know that nothing went unfulfilled in preparing for Jesus and in His mission of redemption. The following chart includes some of the prophecies fulfilled at the cross. Undoubtedly Paul recalled many of these fulfilled prophecies as he preached his sermon.

In 1 Corinthians 15, Paul noted that there were more than 500 "witnesses," including himself. Luke mentioned for the fifth time in Acts that witnesses to the resurrection existed (2:32; 3:15; 5:32; 10:39-41; 13:30-31). The testimony of the apostles—including Paul, the apostle to the Gentiles—was unanimous: Jesus was the risen Lord.

Paul then concluded his discussion on the resurrection as well as this second section of his sermon, demonstrating how the resurrection fulfilled **the good news of the promise that was made to our forefathers** (v. 32) and quoting several passages from the Old Testament (e.g., Ps 2:7). Since Jesus is the Son of God throughout all eternity and was recognized as God the Son throughout His earthly life (Lk 1:35; 3:22; 9:35), why does the passage say **today I have become Your Father**? At Jesus' resurrection He was exalted to the right hand of

Prophecies Fulfilled at the Cross

	Old Testament Prophecy	New Testament Fulfillment
The Messiah would be a reproach, and the people shook their heads at Him.	Ps 109:25	Mt 27:39
The crowds at the crucifixion site would stare at Him.	Ps 69:21	Lk 23:35
His executioners would divide His clothing among themselves by casting lots.	Ps 22:17	Lk 23:34
He would be given wine and gall for His thirst.	Ps 69:21	Mt 27:34
Jesus would cry from the cross, "My God, My God, why have You forsaken Me?"	Ps 22:1	Mt 27:46
Jesus would say, "Father, into Your hands I entrust My spirit."	Ps 31:5	Lk 23:46
Jesus' executioners did not break any of His bones.	Ps 34:20	Jn 19:34-36

God the Father. He was affirmed as the Son of God by believers (Rm 1:4).

Paul also quoted Isaiah 55:3 (Ac 13:34). God had promised David that through his descendant an eternal throne would be established and a kingdom would last forever (2 Sm 7:13,16). Jesus' resurrection confirmed this promise.

Paul's use of Psalm 16:10 related to the resurrection (Ac 13:35). Since David **fell asleep** (meaning he died), was **buried** and **decayed** (v. 36), the verse from Psalms was obviously not about him. Instead the reference is to Jesus. Paul used the Old Testament effectively to convince his listeners that Jesus is the risen Messiah.

In the third and final section of his sermon, Paul made an appeal to his listeners to believe in Jesus or face judgment. At this point Paul simply addressed his audience as **brothers**, identifying himself with the Jewish as well as the Gentile listeners (v. 38). The purpose of Paul's entire sermon led to this clear proclamation of the plan of salvation (vv. 38-39). Through belief in Jesus, all of their sins could be forgiven. In contrast, they **could not be justified through** obedience to **the law of Moses** (v. 39). Obedience to the law of

Moses could not free anyone from his sins. But the perfect life and atoning death of Jesus Christ satisfied the demands of the law, making the forgiveness of sins available to all who believe in Him (Gl 2:16).

As a warning for unbelief, Paul concluded his sermon with a verse pertaining in its original context to God's judgment of Judah (Hab 1:5). Paul used the words to warn any potential **scoffers** that there would be serious consequences for rejecting his message about Jesus the Messiah (Ac 13:41).

Many of the Jews and devout proselytes (Gentile converts to Judaism who had been circumcised) could not wait until the next week, so they **followed Paul and Barnabas** (v. 43). Taking advantage of the additional ministry opportunity, the two missionaries sought to ground the new believers in their faith. Those who truly embrace saving faith will never lose their faith, but continue in the grace of God (Jn 10:28).

Some variant texts indicate they gathered **to hear the** "word of God" (Ac 13:44). Whether "word" or **message**, they wanted to hear more teaching about the Lord Jesus through the Scriptures.

Paul and Barnabas boldly responded, indicating it was **necessary that God's message be spoken** to the Jews first (v. 46), which demonstrated why Paul always began his ministry in new locations at the synagogues. God's plan was that salvation should first be offered to the Jews, then the Greeks or Gentiles (1:8; Rm 1:16). This change of focus was in obedience to what the Lord commanded (Is 49:6).

Two necessary components of salvation are highlighted: divine election and the proper human response (Ac 13:48). APPOINTED (Gk. *tetagmenoi*, "order, determine") has the sense of "enrolled or inscribed." One cannot separate divine foreknowledge from election or God's appointment. God knew who would believe, and He ordered or predetermined that those who believed would be saved and thus "appointed" to eternal life (v. 48). There is always a delicate balance between human will or volition and divine providence. Yes, these Gentiles had to choose to believe, whatever the cost; but God's Spirit in their hearts prompted them by convicting and wooing them to Jesus. And upon their decision to believe, He **appointed** them for life to be partners of grace. **The religious women of high standing and the leading men of the city** joined together and **stirred up persecution against** the two missionaries **and expelled them from their district** (v. 50). Historians Josephus and Strabo both noted that many of the Gentile women were attracted to Judaism during the Diaspora. They not only attended the synagogues, but some of them became proselytes. Obviously religious women as well as men rejected the gospel and took part in direct opposition to the missionary efforts of the early church. Unlike Cyprus, where the most powerful person was converted, here the people of influence persecuted and

kicked Paul and Barnabas out of the area. Their **shaking the dust off their feet** probably resulted from Jesus' command to the apostles to shake the dust off of their feet when they left a town in which their words were not welcomed (v. 51; Mt 10:14-15). Since some in Antioch of Pisidia had rejected the truth about Jesus, the two followed the Lord's command in this symbolic act.

Nevertheless, not everyone in Antioch of Pisidia rejected the message about Jesus. They left behind a group of **disciples** who **were filled with joy and the Holy Spirit** (Ac 13:52). Although they experienced persecution, the fact that more people had accepted Jesus as Savior made the difficulties fade in importance.

14:1-7 After expulsion from Antioch of Pisida, Paul and Barnabas traveled approximately 90 miles southeast to the city of **Iconium**, located in the Galatian province and more specifically in the district of Lycaonia. Since **the same thing happened in Iconium**, as had happened in Antioch of Pisida, Luke provided a briefer account.

Paul and Barnabas began their ministry speaking in **the Jewish synagogue**, which resulted in the salvation of **a great number of both Jews and Gentiles** (v. 1). Although in Antioch the two had stated that their mission was now to the Gentiles, in each new city Paul and Barnabas started their ministry afresh, beginning with the Jewish population. Upon rejection of the gospel by the Jews, they would turn to the Gentiles.

Luke called Paul and Barnabas APOSTLES (Gk. *apostolois*, "ones sent as messengers"). Only here and in 14:14 did Luke call anyone an apostle other than the Twelve whom Jesus selected. Since the two were sent from the church in Antioch of Syria, they both can be called apostles or messengers in a general sense. However, only

THE FIRST MISSIONARY
JOURNEY OF PAUL
• City
← Paul's routes
— Via Sebaste

Paul encountered intense Jewish
opposition to the gospel

Paul and Barnabas fled Iconium
after a plot to kill them

Paul and Barnabas
mistaken for gods

Paul continued journey
after being stoned in Lystra

The church at Antioch sent Paul
and Barnabas on missionary work

Proconsul
Sergius Paulus
converted

MEDITERRANEAN SEA

Paul and the 12 disciples were officially apostles of Jesus Christ, because they are the only ones who received their commission directly from the risen Lord. Some question whether or not Paul was an apostle in this more specific sense. From the testimony of Scripture, clearly Paul regarded himself as an apostle and frequently began his letters with that designation (Rm 1:1; 1 Co 1:1; 9:1; 2 Co 1:1; Gl 1:1; Eph 1:1; Col 1:1; 1 Tm 1:1; 2:7; 2 Tm 1:1,11; Ti 1:1).

This effort **to assault and stone them** (Ac 14:5) was not an official sanction of the synagogue since a number of Gentiles were involved. However, perhaps the Jews instigated the assault since the official punishment for blasphemy was death through stoning. Paul and Barnabas were probably informed of the plan by one of the new believers. So they **fled** to continue their mission of **evangelizing** (vv. 6-7).

14:8-20 Lystra, a town surrounded by mountains, was approximately 20 miles south of Iconium. Luke failed to mention a synagogue in Lystra, perhaps because the city was too small for one. However, at least some Jews, including Timothy's Jewish mother, lived there (16:1). Faith was emphasized as a condition for receiving both physical and spiritual healing, as was commonly noted in the Gospels as well as in Acts. Believers should have faith that God has the power to heal, even if He chooses not to heal. The **lame** man demonstrated his faith by obeying Paul's command. He immediately **jumped up and started to walk around** (14:10). Although Luke did not mention the role of the Holy Spirit, the name of Jesus, or the power of God in this healing miracle, all these are clearly understood from the examples already provided (3:16; 4:10, 30; 9:34). This account closely paralleled Peter's healing of the lame man by the gate called Beautiful. In both miracles the men were "lame from birth" (3:2; 14:8); both Peter and Paul looked at the one to be healed (3:4; 14:9); and both men who were healed responded by jumping up and walking (3:8; 14:10).

Believing the two men were gods, the people **started to call Barnabas, Zeus, and Paul, Hermes**. From Greek mythology, Zeus was the king of the gods and Hermes was the god of speech. Because Paul **was the main speaker**, the crowd confused him with Hermes (vv. 11-12). According to Lystran legend, Zeus and Hermes in disguise had once visited the town seeking food and lodging. After being rejected by everyone but an elderly couple named Philemon and Baucis, the two gods sent a flood, drowning everybody but the hospitable couple. Not wanting to repeat their ancestors' supposed mistake, the people of Lystra sought **to offer sacrifice** to the two missionaries (v. 13).

Paul and Barnabas's method for sharing the gospel with the people of Lystra differed from their previous encounters in which their listeners at least understood the concept of God. Here they had to begin with something even more basic: the creation of the world. Paul and Barnabas told about how God created and sustained the Universe. Furthermore, God provided the **rain from heaven and fruitful seasons** and could satisfy their **hearts with food and happiness** (vv. 15-17).

Those arriving from **Antioch** of Pisidia exhibited determination, having traveled over 100 miles of rough terrain to try to kill the two missionaries. Perhaps insulted by Paul and Barnabas's refusal to accept their sacrifice, the Lystran people who once attempted to worship them were now

won over by the visiting Jews and tried to kill them (v. 19). Paul undoubtedly was knocked unconscious as a result of the stoning, explaining why his attackers assumed he was dead and testifying to the brutality of the attack. Amazingly Paul, having been stoned almost to death the previous day, walked 60 miles southeast to **Derbe** (v. 20). Paul later mentioned the stoning, along with many other persecutions (2 Co 11:23-27).

14:21-28 Luke provided few details about the work in Derbe, which was followed by backtracking **to Lystra, to Iconium, and to Antioch** (v. 21). Although they could have returned to Antioch of Syria by traveling through the mountains to Paul's hometown of Tarsus, they chose the longer and equally difficult path back through the towns they had already visited so that they could encourage the new Christians and help them establish leadership in their churches (vv. 22-23).

In addition to discipling the new believers, Paul and Barnabas helped the churches appoint leaders. The term APPOINTED (Gk. *cheirotonēsantes*, "choose or elect by raising hands") is used here and in 2 Corinthians 8:19. Although the text seems to indicate that Paul and Barnabas appointed the "elders," the use of this particular word makes it unlikely that they did so without the input of the congregation. Congregational appointment of leadership appears to be the common practice of the early church (v. 23; see 6:1-6). Nevertheless, clearly Paul and Barnabas had a role in the selection. The young churches, in which many of its members had been recently converted from paganism, undoubtedly needed the wisdom of the two apostles.

Elders (Gk. *presbuterous*, v. 23) is used interchangeably with the word for bishops/overseers (Gk. *episkopous*). The primary duty of the elder was preaching and teaching (1 Tm 5:17). Paul provided the church with a list of qualifications for elders (1 Tm 3:1-7).

After elders had been **appointed in every church** (Ac 14:23), Paul and Barnabas continued on their journey, still backtracking, passing **through Pisidia** into **Pamphylia,** now southern Turkey. After sharing the **message** of the gospel **in Perga**, they continued on to **Attalia**, located on the Mediterranean coast and serving as a harbor for Perga, the capital of the Roman province of Pamphylia (v. 24). Although not mentioned by Luke, when they arrived in Asia Minor, Attalia was probably their point of entry, since Perga was seven miles upstream from Attalia. For more information on Perga, see notes on Acts 13:13.

From Attalia, Barnabas and Paul **sailed** to **Antioch** in Syria, the starting place for their mission. Now that they had completed **the work** God had **entrusted** to them, **they reported** to **the church** all that **God had done** during the two years they were gone, especially the fact that God **had opened the door of faith to the Gentiles** (v. 27). They would remain there until the church sent them to Jerusalem to help clarify issues regarding the inclusion of Gentiles in the church.

Conflicts in the church (15:1-35)

15:1-35 Unnamed **men** from **Judea** came to Antioch and **began to teach** the Christians. These Judaizers, who apparently believed in Christ, taught that faith in Christ alone was not enough but must be coupled with keeping the law of Moses and circumcision (v. 1). This initial serious threat to the unity of the fledgling church resulted in the convening of the Jerusalem Council, a meeting of utmost importance for the church because the very nature of salvation was at stake (v. 2). The issue was not whether or not Gentiles could receive salvation but rather the matter of how they were saved. Specifically, must Gentiles become circumcised proselytes, embracing all the tenets of Judaism before they received salvation? Or did trust and faith in Jesus alone secure salvation?

The discussions and conclusions from this conference would be crucial for the future of Christianity. James, the half-brother of Jesus, presided over the meeting; and testimonies came from the foremost leaders of the church—Peter, Paul, Barnabas, and James (whose input was critical because he was a Palestinian Jew with no Hellenistic influence). Yet he, based on the Old Testament, agreed with Peter and Paul, whose personal experiences in evangelism had drawn them to an understanding of the universal appeal of the gospel. The Council did take action and reaffirmed the gospel (v. 7) as proclaiming salvation by faith alone (v. 9) through the grace of God (v. 11). That action was then ratified unanimously by the whole church (v. 22).

A key source of debate concerning the Jerusalem Council is related to Paul's letter to the churches in Galatia. Was this letter written before the Jerusalem Council or after? More specifically, does Paul's trip to Jerusalem mentioned in Galatians 2:1 coincide with the famine relief visit (11:27-30; 12:25) or with the Jerusalem Council? Both positions have important implications, and they both possess many convincing arguments. This commentator supports the traditional view that Galatians was written after the Jerusalem Council and subsequently provided Paul's viewpoint of the Council (Gl 2).[6]

Some others likely included Titus (v. 2; Gl 2:1). On the 250-mile journey to Jerusalem, the entourage **passed through both Phoenicia and Samaria, explaining in detail the conversion of the Gentiles** (Ac 15:3). For information about Phoenicia and Samaria, see notes on Acts 11:19 and Acts 8:4-8 respectively.

Some of the believers who were previously **Pharisees** objected to their successful mission to the Gentiles. They argued that the Gentiles needed to be circumcised and commanded **to keep the law of Moses** (15:5). In their opinion, since Paul and Barnabas had not done either of these, their ministry to the Gentiles was essentially invalid.

The issue had been raised and now must be resolved. So **the apostles and the elders assembled to consider** whether Gentiles needed to be circumcised and keep the law of Moses in order to be saved (v. 6). The church apparently was in attendance as well (vv. 12,22). After **much debate**, the specifics of which are unmentioned, **Peter stood up** and addressed the assembly (v. 7). From what follows, one can assume that the believers from the party of the Pharisees had already voiced their opinion.

Peter began by referring to his divinely orchestrated encounter with Cornelius (v. 7; 10:1–11:18). He referred to the Mosaic law as **a yoke**, which the Jews and their **forefathers** were not **able to bear** (15:10). The "yoke," a wooden piece placed on the necks or backs of farm animals, enabled two animals to pull a plow working together and thereby doubling what strength each would have had alone. As sinners, the Jews were unable to fulfill the law; thus their continued attempts to keep the law always resulted in failure. Although the law was good in and of itself, it was unable to save, for no one is justified by being obedient to the law but by faith. Jews and Gentiles alike were saved in the **same** manner, not by the law, but **through the grace of the Lord Jesus** (v. 11). The yoke as an instrument of bondage and hardship would improperly link Jews and Gentiles together. Gentiles should not be forced to undergo circumci-

sion or to keep the Mosaic law. From this point, Peter faded from the picture and the focus moved to Paul.

The ceasing of debate and silence of the assembly after Peter's speech implied that they had arrived at a consensus. The speech provided the perfect setting for the testimonies of Barnabas and Paul, who described **all the signs and wonders God had done through them among the Gentiles** (v. 12). They had already reported to the apostles and elders (v. 4), and now they shared their stories with the entire assembly. They likely described the conversion of Sergius Paulus, the proconsul of Cyprus (13:7-12), or the healing of the lame man in Lystra (14:8-10).

James, the pastor of the church in Jerusalem, issued a concluding statement. Jesus' half brother, who also authored the book bearing his name, would later be martyred for his faith. He quoted Amos as representative of the prophets, who were in agreement that God would save Gentiles. Because the text quoted (Am 9:11) differed from the Masoretic Text of the Hebrew Old Testament, some have raised questions. Perhaps James was quoting from the Septuagint (the Greek translation of the Old Testament); yet his quotation is not verbatim from that source. However, any supposed discrepancy is quickly resolved by recognizing that James was as inspired in his words as was Amos in his earlier statement. The Holy Spirit may choose to say virtually the same thing in two different ways, or He may choose to weave together different passages. He follows His own divine prerogative (Am 9:11-12; Is 45:21). The passage as quoted by James is absolutely trustworthy because the words are God-breathed.

David's tent is the Jerusalem temple, which, although still standing during the days of the Jerusalem Council, was destroyed approximately 20 years later in AD 70. The Gentiles will be included along with the Jews in His kingdom (vv. 16-18). James emphasized to the Jerusalem Council that Scripture did not indicate that the Gentiles had to become Jewish proselytes to enter the kingdom in the millennium; therefore, the requirement should not be imposed upon them now.

Circumcision and adherence to the law of Moses were **difficulties** Gentiles did not have to endure in order to be saved (v. 19). Nevertheless, the practical concern of table fellowship between Jews and Gentiles still needed to be addressed. A majority of the Jewish Christians still adhered to the dietary laws, not in an effort to gain acceptance before God but as a matter of custom and tradition. If Jews and Gentiles were to experience table fellowship together, the Gentiles would have to honor some of these basic laws, including abstinence **from things polluted by idols, from eating anything that has been strangled, and from blood** (v. 20). These requirements were not theological but sociological with the purpose of respecting the convictions of the Jewish believers in order to maintain unity in the church. The fact that Jewish communities were found in almost every city, with daily contact among Gentiles and Jews, made this consideration important. In later years, these rules would become inconsequential.

One additional rule did not directly relate to table fellowship. The Gentiles must **abstain . . . from sexual immorality** (v. 20). The Council assumed moral law, such as the Ten Commandments, which made this requirement seem repetitious since the commandment not to commit adultery was found in this common document. From Paul's letters one can deduce that this area was particularly difficult for the Gentile Christians. Paul frequently addressed the issue (1 Co 6:9,18; 2 Co 12:21; Gl 5:19). Someone had

rightly noted that Gentiles seemed more lax in the area of sexual standards than were the Jews, and the Jews saw themselves as radically different from the Gentiles in their standards. For example, the Jews would have nothing to do with someone whom they perceived as sexually immoral. Perhaps the Council included this rule not only for the sake of unity but also for an additional reminder to all of the importance of sexual purity.

Where at least 10 Jewish men were living in any area, they were required to establish a synagogue. The law of Moses was **read aloud** every **Sabbath** in the synagogue. Essentially, since there were Jews in every city who cherished the law of Moses, Gentile Christians should be sensitive and not be a stumbling block to their brothers in Christ (Ac 15:21; 2 Co 8:9).

As demonstrated throughout Acts, men fulfilled the leadership roles in the church. All that is known about **Judas** is that he was a prophet, as was **Silas**, who would later accompany Paul on his second missionary journey (15:32). Judas and Silas would bear the responsibility for delivering the **letter** to the church in **Antioch** (Ac 15:22-23).

Antioch, the capital of the two provinces of **Syria** and **Cilicia**, functioned as a single Roman district. Understood as a single address, the church in Antioch where the dispute had originally risen would be the recipient of the letter. Antioch would then disseminate the contents of the letter to the rest of the churches as needed.

The letter began with an explanation. Some from the Jerusalem church, who had **no authorization**, went out and said some troubling things (15:1-2). The apostles and elders wanted to clarify that these men spoke on their own behalf, not that of the church (v. 24). To rectify the situation, the Jerusalem church **unanimously decided** to send **Judas and Silas** to deliver the letter and **personally report the same things by word of mouth** (vv. 25-27). While the letter alone would have sufficed, the church did not want any confusion on the issue. The leaders wanted the believers of Antioch to know that this decision was made under the guidance of the Holy Spirit and should not be taken lightly. They desired **to put no greater burden on** the Gentile believers than **necessary** (v. 28). The letter then repeated what James had previously said (vv. 19-20) and refuted what the unauthorized people had said. Circumcision would not be a prerequisite to salvation. The congregation **rejoiced** over the contents because they deemed the requirements within it reasonable and not burdensome (v. 31).

The Spread of the Gospel into Macedonia (15:36–21:14)

The separation of Paul and Barnabas (15:36-41)

15:36-41 After an indeterminable amount of **time had passed**, **Paul** suggested to **Barnabas** that they **go back and visit** the Christians in the towns where they had **preached** on their first missionary journey, which is described in chapters 13 and 14, to **see how** the churches were **doing** and provide additional instruction as needed (v. 36). **Barnabas wanted to take along John Mark, who had deserted them** on their first missionary journey **in Pamphylia** (13:13), but **Paul did not think it** was **appropriate** since Mark had proven unreliable in the past (15:37-38). In addition to this **sharp disagreement**, Paul confronted Barnabas about some hypocrisy in his life (Gl 2:13). **Barnabas took Mark** and **sailed off to Cyprus** (Ac 15:39). His itinerary beyond Cyprus is uncertain because he faded from the book of Acts. He possibly visited the believers in Perga since other than Cyprus, this city was the only

place from the first journey not visited by Paul on his second missionary journey. Likely, the rift between Paul and Barnabas healed because Paul later briefly referred to him in a positive light (1 Co 9:6). In addition, Paul also changed his opinion about Mark, describing him as "useful to me for ministry" and as a "co-worker for the kingdom of God" (2 Tm 4:11; Col 4:10-11).

Paul and Silas traveled by ground north through **Syria** and into the province of **Cilicia**, which is modern Turkey, **strengthening the churches** as they went (Ac 15:40-41). Tarsus, Paul's hometown, was located in Cilica. They probably stopped there before crossing the Taurus mountains into southern Galatia, where Derbe and Lystra were located.

Second, the congregation must discipline members. Matthew 18 outlined the steps for church discipline. The final step is to bring the matter before the church. Jesus Himself stated that the church, not a board of elders or any other ruling body, held the final authority in church discipline (see 1 Co 5:4-5). Paul indicated the setting for this action was the assembly. The church is responsible for disciplining its members.

Third, the congregation should embrace its members. Paul did not command but urged the "majority" of the congregation to confirm their love by accepting a disciplined member back into the body (2 Co 2:6-8). From this passage and the fact that the church as a whole had a responsibility for its own purity, one can see that the congregation must have a role in accepting members.

What the congregation should *not* do. The congregation should not fight and bicker about matters of no importance. The color of the carpet or the type of chair in a Sunday School classroom will have little impact on the eternal destiny of lost souls. When the church turns its focus inward instead of outward, disputes occur that make congregational polity difficult. Additionally, when church discipline is not properly practiced, unregenerate members can create trouble. Church rolls overloaded with members who never attend should be purged or those members disciplined. The New Testament model is a regenerate church membership focused on fulfilling the commission of Jesus Christ to spread the gospel to the entire world.

Paul's second missionary journey (16:1–18:23)

16:1-5 Derbe and Lystra were cities Paul visited on his first missionary journey. Both were located in southern Galatia, the area now a part of modern Turkey. On his previous trip to Lystra Paul had healed a man lame from birth and was subsequently mistaken as Hermes, a god from Greek mythology. A little later he was stoned and left for dead by some Jews who had come from Antioch and Iconium looking for him (14:8-20).

In Lystra, there was **a disciple named Timothy**, who was **highly** regarded by the disciples at **Lystra and Iconium** (vv. 1-2). Timothy was likely converted on Paul's first missionary journey since Paul spoke of him as his "true child in the faith" (1 Tm 1:2). The two maintained a close relationship for the rest of Paul's life. Timothy's mother Eunice was **a believing Jewish woman, but his father was a Greek.** According to Jewish law, a child takes the religion of his mother, but in Greek law the father dominates in the home. As a result, Timothy was not circumcised according to Jewish tradition; however, he was taught the Scriptures from a young age (2 Tm 3:15). Paul wanted Timothy to accompany him and Silas on their journey, but the fact that Timothy was not circumcised created a problem. Although the Jerusalem Council established that circumcision was not a requirement for salvation (Ac 15:6-21), its absence was still a stumbling block for some Jews. Since many people in **those places** to which they would travel knew Timothy's **father was a Greek**, Paul **circumcised him** lest he become a hindrance to the gospel (16:3). Circumcision involved removing the foreskin from the male genitals. Jews performed this ritual on the eighth day after birth (Lv 12:3). Since Timothy had not undergone circumcision as a baby, he endured this painful procedure as a young adult for the sake of the gospel.

The **decisions reached** at the **Jerusalem** Council included the confirmation that circumcision was not a requirement for salvation, the practical necessity for Gentile Christians to obey some basic dietary laws for the purpose of table fellowship with Jews, and the command to abstain from sexual immorality (Ac 16:4; 15:20). News from the Jerusalem Council likely facilitated the outreach to the Gentiles.

16:6-10 The missionary group continued on **through the region of Phrygia and Galatia**, possibly indicating the region of Phrygian Galatia. When the political province of Galatia was created by the Romans in 25 BC, they incorporated a portion of the ethnic territory of Phrygia, while the remainder of Phrygia was incorporated into the province of Asia. Paul and company traveled this portion of Galatia, which included the cities of Antioch of Pisidia and Iconium, where Paul and Barnabas had visited previously. Next Paul intended to share **the message** of Jesus **in the province of Asia**, which was adjacent to Galatia (v. 6). Luke recorded that they **were prevented**—perhaps it was simply not God's timing. This area would have the opportunity to respond to the gospel at a later date, toward the end of this journey. The group passed through the province of Asia, taking a northern route until **they came to Mysia**, in the northwest section of Asia Minor. From there, the group attempted to go into **Bithynia**, to the north of Mysia, **but the Spirit of Jesus** once again prevented them. Paul never went into Bithynia, but the area was reached with

the gospel through Peter (1 Pt 1:1). **So, bypassing Mysia**, they traveled south **to Troas**, which was an important port city on the Aegean Sea 10 miles from the ancient site of Troy (Ac 16:7-8).

The area of **Macedonia** roughly corresponds to modern northern Greece. Paul considered his vision of the person calling him to Macedonia to be a mandate from God to preach the gospel in this province north of Achaia. This use of the pronoun **we** marked the addition of Luke, the author of Acts, to Paul's traveling group. When Luke joined the group, he was probably already a believer. (For more information about him, see the section entitled "Author" in the introduction to Acts.) Having traveled over 700 miles from their original destination of Antioch of Syria, Paul and Silas were ready to break new ground for the gospel.

16:11-15 Samothrace, an island in the Aegean Sea, was about halfway between Asia Minor and the Greek mainland. **The next day** they sailed **to Neapolis**, which was an important port city for Macedonia (v. 11). The famous Roman highway called the *Via Egnatia* ran through Neapolis. Beginning in Byzantium, this highway continued west to Philippi, on through Amphipolis and Thessalonica, and all the way to the Adriatic Sea. Upon hitting landfall in Neapolis, the group of missionaries followed this highway approximately 10 miles to get to the city of **Philippi** (v. 12).

Historically, Philippi, named for Philip II of Macedon, the father of Alexander the Great, was a city of importance. Additionally, in 42 BC, the forces of the first emperor, Octavian (later called Augustus Caesar), and Antony defeated the army of Brutus and Cassius, the assassins of Julius Caesar. In honor of the victory it became **a Roman colony.** For these reasons it was regarded as **a leading city** in that particular **district of Macedonia**.

The Timeline of Paul (AD)						
	1	**20**	**30**	**40**	**50**	**60**
Birth (Ac 22:3)	1–5 (?)					
Conversion (Ac 9:1-19)		34–35				
Ministry						
1st Trip to Jerusalem (Ac 9:26-29)			37–38			
2nd Trip to Jerusalem (Ac 11:27-30)				48		
1st Missionary Journey (Ac 13–14)				48–50		
Galatia						
Cyprus						
2nd Missionary Journey (Ac 15:39–18:22)					51–53	
Macedonia						
Achaia						
Greece						
3rd Missionary Journey (Ac 18:23–21:17)					54–57	
Asia						
Greece						
4th Missionary Journey (Ac 27–28)					59–60	
Caesarea						
Crete						
Malta						
Rome						
Writings						
1 Thessalonians					50–52	
2 Thessalonians					50–52	
Galatians					55–57	
1 Corinthians					56–57	
2 Corinthians					56–57	
Romans					55–59	
Ephesians						60–63
Philippians						60–63
Colossians						60–63
Philemon						60–63
1 Timothy						62–67
Titus						62–64
2 Timothy						66–67
Imprisonments						
Philippian Imprisonment (Ac 16:16-40)					58–60	
Caesarean Imprisonment (Ac 23:23–26:32)					58–60	
Roman Imprisonment (Ac 27–28)						60–63
Death						
Probably in Rome						67–68

Although Philippi was a city of considerable size, it contained minimal Jewish population because there was no synagogue, which required only 10 Jewish males. Therefore, **on the Sabbath**, the group **went outside the city gate by the river**, where they **thought there was a place of prayer** (v. 13). Although the exact location is unknown, they probably gathered at the River Gangites or at a stream that flows a short distance away from the city's west gate. A group of **women** had **gathered** to worship. Although Luke did not discuss the message, it was probably similar to what Paul had preached about Jesus in the synagogues earlier in his ministry (13:16-41).

Lydia was **from the city of Thyatira**, located in the Roman province of Lydda in Asia Minor and noted for its production of purple dye and dyed goods. Lydia herself was **a dealer in purple cloth** (v. 14). The purple dye was made from a shellfish called a murex and from the root of a madder plant. Therefore, it was extremely expensive and worn only by royalty and the wealthy. Lydia's business plus her ability to house the group of missionaries demonstrated that she possessed great wealth. In addition, Lydia, like Cornelius (10:1-8), **worshiped God**; yet she had not completely converted to Judaism. Luke noted that **the Lord opened her heart to pay attention to what was spoken by Paul** (16:14). Lydia obviously responded positively to Paul's message, genuinely believing that Jesus was the Messiah spoken about in the Old Testament Scriptures. Lydia became Paul's first convert on the European continent. As an outward expression of her new faith in Christ, she was **baptized** (v. 15) probably in the river near where they worshiped. The text also indicated that her household, including her servants as well as any family members old enough to fully comprehend and respond to the grace available through

Jesus Christ, was baptized. (For more information about household baptisms, see Heart to Heart: "Household Baptisms.") Hospitality is an important ministry for all Christians, especially women (1 Tm 5:9-10). In the ancient world, inns were often unavailable, too expensive, or too dangerous. By opening her home to the four missionaries, Lydia contributed considerably to their ministry. At her request, Paul and his companions accepted her invitation and most likely stayed with her for the rest of their time in Philippi.

16:16-24 In Philippi, there was **a slave girl** possessed by **a spirit of prediction** (Gk. *pneuma puthōna*, "spirit of divination," v. 16). According to the Greek legend, Python, the famous serpent at Delphi was destroyed by Apollo, who adopted the name of Pythia. The connection was readily apparent since Apollo was the mythical god of prophecy. Plutarch maintained that this term *puthōnes* applied to ventriloquists, and in the Septuagint this word is used for "familiar spirits" (Lv 19:31; 20:6, 27; 1 Sm 28:7).

The slave girl often **followed Paul** and his companions. The demon-possessed girl spoke truth, even using biblical terminology (Ac 16:17). The phrase **Most High God** was an Old Testament description of the God of Israel used by Abraham, the psalmist, and Daniel (Gn 14:22; Ps 78:35; Dn 5:18). The element of truth made her more dangerous. Since the girl agreed with the missionaries, some could have believed she was a part of their group and been deceived, bringing harm to the cause of Christ.

The **chief magistrates** were the officials of the Roman colony of Philippi responsible for trying civil cases and maintaining law and order (Ac 16:20). In front of these officials the accusers of Paul and Silas had two complaints, neither of which related to the current situation. First, they complained that Paul and Silas were **seriously disturbing** the **city.** Second, as **Jews** they promoted **customs** and practices that were **not legal** for **Romans to adopt or practice**. By highlighting their Jewish nationality, the accusers played upon the fears associated with recent political events (v. 21). About that time Emperor Claudius had expelled Jews from Rome for supposedly creating a religious disturbance (18:2). In an effort to avoid a similar situation and influenced by **the mob**, the magistrates **ordered them to be beaten with rods** without even giving them a chance to provide a defense (16:22).

Paul and Silas knew how to make the best of every situation. After receiving an unjust beating and being thrown in prison, they continued to trust God (v. 25). **Singing hymns** (Gk. *hunoun*, "sing hymn of praise," transliterated into English as "hymns") affirms the tremendous testimony that can come from this medium of worship and praise. Earthquakes occurred often in this region, but the timing and results of this quake demonstrated God's hand in the situation (v. 26). **The jailer** knew the law. If a Roman soldier allowed a prisoner to escape, no matter the cause, he paid with his own life (12:9; 27:42). Instead of facing a humiliating prosecution and an agonizing death, the jailer intended to commit suicide (16:27).

Paul stopped the jailer by letting him know that **all** the prisoners remained incarcerated. Luke did not indicate why the other prisoners did not flee. Perhaps they were still stunned by the **earthquake** or feared the consequences of being caught. Or perhaps they stayed as a result of what Paul and Silas said, which seems more likely since the jailer **rushed in, and fell down trembling before** the two missionaries (v. 29). Salvation has never been attained by being a good person, by going to church, or by being baptized.

Salvation comes only through belief in the Lord Jesus Christ. The jailer and **all his family** responded positively to the gospel message and **were baptized** immediately. The jailer was a changed man, marked by the newfound compassion he had for Paul and Silas. He took them **into his house** and **washed their wounds** and **set a meal before them** (vv. 33-34). He rejoiced not because his life had been physically saved by the securing of the prisoners but because he, along with his **entire household**, had received eternal life (v. 34). The mention of the jailer's household does not minimize the personal nature of the divine encounter with each individual:

- Paul used the singular verb in his exhortation to the jailer.

- Paul continually emphasized the personal nature of faith.

- Judaism had a rich heritage in the leadership of the husband and father in the home, and this model definitely extended to the spiritual arena; for the head of the family to lead and then be followed by others in the household who were moved by his example was a natural thing.

- Plain language in the text suggests that Paul's teaching and preaching extended beyond the jailer to include the entire household.

Luke did not indicate why the **chief magistrates** changed their opinion (v. 35). Perhaps the newly saved jailer pleaded for their release. When the jailer let them know that they could **go in peace**, Paul refused. For the first time in Acts, Paul revealed his status, and that of Silas, as **Roman citizens** (v. 37). According to the law, Roman citizens were protected from public beatings, imprisonment, and death without a trial. By denying these men their rights, **the magistrates** had broken the law. Paul demanded a public apology for the sake of the church. Without a public apology because of their public beating, the people of the city would always believe that Paul and Silas had been guilty of a crime, which could have caused unnecessary persecution of the new believers who had been associated with them. A public release from prison would help rectify the situation; therefore, Paul would only be appeased if the chief magistrates **themselves** came and escorted them **out** (v. 37).

Paul and Silas **departed** with Timothy and headed towards Thessalonica (v. 40). They apparently left Luke behind in Philippi because the "first person" or "we" sections temporarily ceased until Paul returned to the city on his third missionary journey (20:5). Luke likely remained behind so that he could continue the ministry and disciple the new believers.

Lydia
Acts 16:11-15,40

- A dealer of purple cloth (v. 14)
- From the city of Thyatira (v. 14)
- Lived in the city of Philippi (v. 14)
- Worshiped God (v. 14)
- Listened to the gospel (v. 14)
- Opened her heart (v. 14)
- Was baptized with her household (v. 15)
- Persuaded others to follow Christ (v. 15)

Paul and other followers of Christ entered the house of Lydia and encouraged one another before they departed from the city of Philippi.

17:1-9 Shortly after Paul and Silas were released from prison, they, along with Timothy, continued their journey heading west on the Egnatian Way towards Thessalonica. They passed **through Amphipolis and Apollonia**, cities providing good overnight stopping points for the travelers, breaking up the 100-mile trip from Philippi **to Thessalonica** (v. 1). Thessal-

A Fortune-Telling Slave Girl
Acts 16:16-24

Fortune-telling was widely practiced during the time of the early church. The Bible strongly condemns such practices (see Lv 19:26 and Jr 27:9). When Paul and Silas arrived in Philippi to preach the gospel, they met a young slave girl who was a fortune-teller—"a slave who had a spirit of prediction" (Ac 16:16). Her masters abused her by using her extraordinary abilities to predict the future for their personal profit. The girl taunted Paul and Silas as they preached. Paul was annoyed by the disruption and was convinced she was demon possessed. He exorcised the demonic spirit from her body in the name of Jesus Christ. Her masters retaliated against Paul and Silas, dragging them into the marketplace to be beaten and imprisoned. Though the fortune-telling slave girl was a hindrance, God empowered the ministry of Paul and Silas even in the prison where the Philippian jailer was saved.

onica was founded in 315 BC by Cassander, a general of Alexander the Great. He named the city after his wife, the daughter of Philip II and the half sister of Alexander. The city became the seat for the Roman governor and the capital for the entire province of Macedonia. It also possessed a great harbor, making it the chief seaport for Macedonia. Now this city is known as Salonica, the second largest city in Greece. Thessalonica possessed enough practicing Jews to demand a **synagogue**. As was Paul's custom, he spent his "Sabbath days" at the synagogue. Luke noted that Paul was there **on three Sabbath days**, indicating he ministered out of the synagogue for approximately three weeks (v. 2), after which he might have based his ministry out of the house of Jason (vv. 5-9). The group of missionaries remained in Thessalonica long enough to receive an offering from the Philippians (Php 4:16) and to establish work (1 Th 2:9).

Paul continually used Old Testament passages to show them how **the Messiah had to suffer and rise from the dead**. After grounding his argument in Scripture, he would proclaim **Jesus** as the **Messiah** (Ac 17:3). This method possessed similarities to his presentation in Antioch of Pisidia (13:13-41). He effectively persuaded some of the Jews, the **God-fearing Greeks** and **a number of the leading women** (17:4). The phrase "leading women" may denote women who held positions of authority in the city or women who were wives of prominent men since the phrase can also be translated "wives of the leading men." The latter translation is made explicit in some early textual interpretations. Luke did on occasion single out influential women who were converts in the congregation of Macedonia (16:14; 17:4,12), and without doubt in social and civic arenas Macedonian women did have influence as confirmed in extrabiblical sources. Again, however, whether these women had prominence of position or wealth in their own right or because they shared that influence with their husbands, the fact remains that women of influence did respond to the gospel, and, as with Lydia, they did devote their resources and energies to kingdom service. The main thrust of this passage seems to be that only **some of** the Jews were converted, while a great number of Gentile men and women were converted. Much of Paul's success came in his ministry to the Gentile population. Those who believed the truths about Jesus **joined Paul and Silas**, possibly indicating they formed a separate group that met independently from the synagogue in the house of Jason (v. 7).

Scripture says nothing about **Jason**. He was probably Jewish. Some even hypothesize that he was related to Paul (Rm 6:21). The accusers claimed Paul and Silas acted **contrary to Caesar's decrees** because they asserted **another king** (Ac 17:7). The motto "Caesar is Lord" prevailed throughout the Roman Empire. But Paul and Silas taught that only Jesus is Lord. Some perceived their commitment to Christ to be a direct assault against Rome and against Caesar himself. Although **the Jews stirred up the crowd**, the city officials took no action other than **taking a security bond from Jason and the others** (v. 9). The bond was a sum of money that would be forfeited should there be another disturbance.

17:10-15 To avoid further disruptions, Paul, Silas, and Timothy slipped away in the **night** for **Beroea**, which was 45 miles west of Thessalonica. This city in northern Greece is now called Verria. **A number of the prominent Greek women as well as men** were mentioned (v. 12; see note on 17:1-9). One could wish for the Beroean approach to examining the claims of Christ:

- They had open minds and hearts.
- They heard the word with eagerness and anticipation.
- They examined the Scriptures for themselves.
- They were willing to test the words of Paul in a discerning way.

So many people responded to the gospel message that the news got back to **the Jews from Thessalonica**. Still enraged at Paul, they traveled to Beroea where they once again effectively stirred **the crowds**. A similar situation occurred while Paul was on his first missionary journey. While ministering in Lystra, Jews from Iconium and Antioch of Pisidia came and rallied the crowds against Paul. As a result Paul was stoned and left for dead (14:19-20). In an attempt to avoid this same scenario, **the brothers immediately sent Paul away** while **Silas and Timothy** remained in Beroea. Some new converts probably

escorted Paul all the way to Athens. Once in Athens, Paul realized that evangelizing the province of Achaia would be an enormous task. Therefore he instructed his Beroean escorts to send **Silas and Timothy** to him **as quickly as possible** (v. 15).

17:16-34 Athens, an ancient city settled before 3000 BC, was named for Athena, the goddess of wisdom. It was located approximately 200 miles south of Thessalonica in the province of Achaia, five miles from the Aegean Sea. Regarded in Paul's day as the intellectual capital of the world, the city was known for its art, literature, and especially its philosophy. History's three most famous philosophers— Socrates, Plato, and Aristotle—called Athens home. Two other significant philosophers also resided in Athens at some point: Epicurus, founder of Epicureanism, and Zeno, founder of Stoicism. These philosophies were dominant in Paul's day.

In the marketplace Paul primarily encountered **Epicurean and Stoic philosophers**. The Epicureans (led by Epicurus, a contemporary of Zeno) taught that seeking pleasure and avoiding pain were man's greatest purposes. They were practical atheists and did not believe in an afterlife, nor did they believe that the gods concerned themselves with the affairs of men and women. In contrast, the Stoics (led by Zeno 360–260 BC, who taught from the *stoa* or porch), possessed a somewhat pantheistic belief system. Since god is all, all that exists is god. They believed that "logos" or reason created the universe and bound the entire cosmic order together so god is very impersonal. They taught that people should live in unison with nature, attain self-mastery, and suppress their desires. They were usually very self-centered and thus unloving towards others. However, when they failed, suicide often became their solution. Both philosophies stressed reason

over faith. Neither offered any hope for life in eternity.

The philosophers demeaningly dubbed Paul a **PSEUDO-INTELLEC-TUAL** (Gk. *spermologos*, "scavenger," figuratively "one who picks up scraps of knowledge or seed-picker"). The image of a "seed-picker" suggests a bird picking seeds indiscriminately in the barnyard. First used of birds and then of men collecting odds and ends in the market, essentially, they denigrated Paul as someone who grabbed scraps of ideas here and there and then attempted to pass them off as some great knowledge but with no depth of understanding and worth no more than the trash he peddled. They could not understand Paul's talk about a bodily resurrection because the Epicureans did not believe in existence after death, and the Stoics believed only the soul survived death. Others suggested Paul was **a preacher of foreign deities** because he told them **the good news about Jesus and the resurrection** (v. 18). They correctly understood that Paul preached Jesus as God, and they perhaps thought he used the term "resurrection" (Gk. *anastasin*, lit. "a raising or raising up") as the proper name of a goddess. They assumed that Paul was polytheistic as they were.

Nevertheless, Paul's teaching, although sounding **strange** to them, attracted some listeners. They wanted **to know** more about these new **ideas**. Their interest may not have been a genuine interest in the gospel but only an interest in **something new** (vv. 19-21).

Paul spoke to the **religious** Athenians from the **Areopagus** (v. 22), a hill about 370 feet high west of the Acropolis and behind the marketplace. The text indicates that Paul spoke in the middle of the Areopagus. Whether he spoke in the middle of that geographical location or in the midst of the Council of the Areopagus, which was so denominated because of its meeting place, is unclear. The Council was the supreme Athenian body for judicial and legislative matters, specifically pertaining to religion and education. Paul might have spoken formally to that group.

This sermon demonstrated how Paul effectively adapted the gospel message to his audience. He did not change the truth of the gospel, simply the manner in which he presented it. When addressing the Jews or worshipers of God, Paul presented the gospel using the proofs of Scripture (13:16-41). Since this audience had no concept of God or the Old Testament, Paul told them about Jesus from a different perspective, although he still grounded his statements in Scripture. This sermon is Paul's best preserved message to a pagan audience.

Paul began his speech to the "men of Athens" by noting that they were **EXTREMELY RELIGIOUS** (Gk. *deisidaimonesterous*, v. 22). This compound word links *deido*, "fear or revere" with *daimon*, "deities, evil spirits," and *stereos*, "firm, hard." The idea is that they were firm in reverencing their deities. Paul did not openly accuse his Athenian audience of anything wrong, such as superstition. The Athenians likely interpreted this remark as a compliment, but Paul subtly implied that their deities were evil spirits rather than gods. Paul attempted to find a commonality with his audience. As he had been exploring Athens, among the many idols and **objects of . . . worship** he discovered **an altar on which was inscribed: TO AN UNKNOWN GOD** (v. 23), an inscription Paul used as his basis to tell them about this God whom they did not know.

In contrast to the gods and idols of the Athenians, God **does not live in shrines made by hands** (v. 24; 1 Kg 8:27); neither does He need **anything** from the people He created (Ac 17:25; 1 Ch 29:14; Ps 50:7-15). In contrast to the Epicurean belief that the gods did not care about the affairs of men, this unknown God demonstrated concern over His creation, since **He Himself** gave **everyone life and breath and all things** (Ac 17:25; Gn 2:7; Is 42:5). **From one man**, God made **every nation of men to live all over the earth** (Ac 17:26; Gn 1:28). Paul was speaking of Adam, but he remained unnamed before Paul's pagan audience. This one God possessed sovereignty, decreeing both history (the **times**) and **boundaries** of the nations (Ac 17:26; Dt 32:8; Ps 74:17). Paul quoted two ancient poets who would have been familiar to his audience to provide support for what he said. First he quoted Epimenides (600 BC), who said, **"in Him we live and move and** have our being [**exist**]" (Ac 17:28). Then he quoted Aratus of Soli, Cilicia (300 BC) who said **For we are also His offspring** (17:28). Although both poets originally applied these quotes to Zeus, the king of the gods from Greek mythology, Paul used them in reference to *Yahweh,* the one true God. Using the truths of Scripture but presenting them in a way that would relate to his audience, Paul taught the Athenian people about the true character and nature of God, emphasizing both His power (transcendence) and His intimate involvement with His creation (immanence). In doing so, Paul portrayed a God mightier and more compassionate than any of the gods the Athenians had imagined. Paul demonstrated his broad range of interest and knowledge.

Having spoken about the character and nature of the one true God, Paul began to critique the Athenian culture and religious practices. In Athens, everywhere Paul looked, he saw idols made in the images of their false gods. He vehemently argued against this practice. Since God is the all-powerful Creator of the universe, the

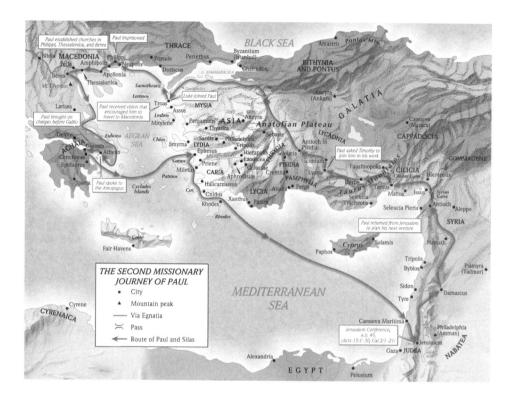

The following text boxes appear on the map:

- Paul established churches in Philippi, Thessalonica, and Berea
- Paul imprisoned
- Paul received vision that encouraged him to travel to Macedonia
- Paul brought on charges before Gallio
- Luke joined Paul
- Paul asked Timothy to join him in his work
- Paul spoke to the Areopagus
- Paul returned from Jerusalem to plan his next venture
- Jerusalem Conference, A.D. 49, (Acts 15:1-30; Gal 2:1-21)

THE SECOND MISSIONARY JOURNEY OF PAUL
- ● City
- ▲ Mountain peak
- — Via Egnatia
- ≍ Pass
- ← Route of Paul and Silas

Athenians should abandon this practice since the **divine nature** cannot be replicated by **gold or silver** (v. 29; Dt 5:8; Ps 115:1-2; Is 37:19; 44:9-10). Nevertheless, forgiveness could be found for this sinful practice. God could overlook their **ignorance** if they followed His command to **repent** (Ac 17:30). Paul emphasized the necessity of repentance because there would be **a day on which** God would **judge the world in righteousness by the Man He has appointed** (v. 31; Pss 9:8; 96:13; Is 66:16; Jr 25:31). Proof of the coming judgment was found in the fact that God sent Jesus and raised **Him from the dead**.

Paul's speech and particularly his mention of the **resurrection** prompted three responses. The first group **began to ridicule him**. It was inconceivable to them with their pagan frame of mind that a man could be raised from the dead (Ac 17:32). Paul's speech piqued the interest of the

second group, and they wanted to hear more. The third group **believed**, including **Dionysius the Areopagite**, who was one of the members of the upper echelons of the Athens Council (all of whom were at least 60 years of age and had held some high government office), and **a woman named Damaris** (v. 34). There is a strong tradition, noted in Eusebius, that Dionysius was the first bishop of Athens and that he died a martyr's death. Damaris does not seem to be his wife, and little is known about her.

While Paul did not labor in vain, only a few people accepted Christ, and no lasting church was established. His next stop in nearby Corinth proved more fruitful.

18:1-17 From Athens, Paul traveled approximately 50 miles west **to Corinth**, the capital of the province of Achaia. While Athens was known for its culture and learning, Corinth was known for its prosperity and immorality.

Damaris Acts 17:34	
Her Life	• An Athenian woman of distinction and prominence • Possibly one of the *hetairai* (intellectual women who associated with philosophers and politicians) • An idol worshiper
Her Legacy	• Heard Paul's sermon at Mars' Hill (17:22-34) • Became a believer (17:34) ignored the belittling of the unbelievers (17:32) • Courageously followed Christ (17:34) • Helped the early church spread the gospel (17:34)

Corinth prospered because of its strategic location at the point of convergence for land and sea-trade routes. Due to its location, trade moving north and south went through Corinth as did sea trade going east and west. Along with Corinth's prosperity was immorality of every kind. Immorality so characterized the city that the verb "to Corinthianize" meant to be sexually immoral.

In Corinth, Paul encountered a **Jewish** couple named **Aquila** and **Priscilla** (v. 2). Originally from **Pontus**, Aquila had moved to Rome. Inscriptions in the catacombs in Rome hint that Priscilla was from a distinguished family of high standing in Rome where the couple likely met.

The New Testament mentions Priscilla and Aquila six times (18:2,18,26; Rm 16:3; 1 Co 16:19; 2 Tm 4:19). Two times Aquila's name appeared before Priscilla's, and four times Priscilla is listed before Aquila. This styling of their names may be an indication of Priscilla's higher social status or that she had a more active role in the ministry or simply a gentlemanly courtesy or deference to a gracious woman. The text does not indicate one way or the other, so any conclusion is conjecture at best. In Acts, Luke always referred to Priscilla by her common name "Priscilla," while Paul preferred her more formal name, "Prisca."

As a result of an edict by **Claudius** the Roman emperor expelling all **Jews** from

Rome, Aquila and Priscilla had recently relocated to Corinth. Historical sources indicate that this edict occurred in the ninth year of Claudius's reign, which puts it around AD 49. Since Aquila and Priscilla arrived in Rome before Paul, he did not likely arrive in Corinth before the middle of AD 49.

Paul had a lot in common with the Jewish couple. First, they had a common faith. Since the Bible never mentioned Aquila and Priscilla's conversion or Paul's witness to the couple, it is assumed they were already believers when Paul met them in Corinth. Most likely the couple had heard about Jesus while living in Rome. Second, they had **the same occupation**. Aquila and Priscilla **were tentmakers by trade** as was Paul. As was common, they had a trade by which to earn a living (v. 3). For these two reasons Paul **stayed with them and worked** alongside them for the year and a half he was in Corinth. Since Paul was alone, whether a bachelor or widower, he must have found comfort and fellowship in this special friendship.

Paul began his ministry of proclaiming the gospel in a **synagogue** both to **Jews** and God-fearing **Greeks** (Ac 18:4). Earlier passages delineated how Paul shared the gospel in this situation, so there was no reason for Luke to recount it again (see 13:16-41).

Silas and Timothy joined Paul in Corinth, bringing a monetary gift from the Macedonian churches to support Paul's ministry (2 Co 11:9) and good news about the church in Thessalonica (1 Th 3:6-10). From Corinth, Paul wrote his first letter to the Thessalonians.

As a result of the gift from the Macedonian churches, Paul devoted more time to his ministry. Eventually the Jews resisted Paul's message, ultimately blaspheming Christ. From this point on in Paul's Corinthian ministry, he focused on **the Gentiles**. The phrase **he shook out his clothes** symbolized Paul's break in fellowship with the Jews due to their rejection of Jesus (18:6; see 13:51). Paul also told them, **"Your blood is on your own heads!"** (Ac 18:6). He had communicated the truth of the gospel to them and warned them of impending judgment, absolving himself from the situation. They would receive the due consequences for rejecting Jesus (Ezk 33:1-6).

Paul discontinued his ministry in the synagogue and began ministering **next door** out of **the house of a man named Titius Justus, a worshiper of God** (Ac 18:7). Evidently he was an uncircumcised Gentile who had come to know the Lord. Some scholars identify him as Gaius Titius Justus and thus the man mentioned in Romans 16:23 (written while Paul was in Corinth) and 1 Corinthians 1:14 (written from Corinth). As a Roman citizen, to have three names would have been common. He should not be confused with the Titus who accompanied Paul to Jerusalem for the Jerusalem Council (Ac 15:2; Gl 2:1).

Unlike Athens where few responded to the gospel, great things happened in Corinth. **Crispus,** along with Gaius, was baptized by Paul (1 Co 1:14). The example of this Jewish leader's faith in Christ probably drew many more people to Jesus. This missionary experience was different for Paul. In the past, he had been chased out of cities and stoned by the Jewish leaders. In Corinth, God granted him the opportunity to guide one of the leaders to belief in Christ. In addition to Crispus, his **household** and **many of the Corinthians . . . believed and were baptized** (Ac 18:8). This example is one of many throughout Acts where belief in Christ preceded baptism. The Holy Spirit was supernaturally moving among the Corinthians, and many people received salvation as a result.

The Lord encouraged Paul to continue his ministry in Corinth through **a night vision** (v. 9). In obedience to this vision, Paul remained for **a year and six months, teaching the word of God** among the people (v. 11). This residence in Corinth was Paul's first extensive stay while on a missionary journey.

Although Crispus, the leader of the synagogue had been saved, opposition still existed among the Jews in Corinth. The unbelieving **Jews made a united attack against Paul and brought him** before **Gallio**, the **proconsul of Achaia** (v. 12). The Roman Senate appointed the proconsul, who usually ruled, having complete judicial authority over their region for one or two years. Judging from historical documents and inscriptions, Gallio served as proconsul around AD 52. The Jews charged that Paul's teachings persuaded **people to worship God contrary to the law** (v. 13). Not believing that Roman law had been breached, Gallio essentially dismissed the case, leaving it up to the Jews to decide.

Somehow as a result of this ruling, **Sosthenes, the leader of the synagogue**, received a beating (v. 17). The text is unclear as to who attacked the Jewish leader. Some propose that the Gentiles attacked him due to a general atmosphere of anti-Semitism. This reading is supported by an early textual variant that reads "all the Greeks." Others propose that the Jews attacked him for sympathizing with the Christians. A man named Sosthenes is mentioned with Paul in the opening verse of 1 Corinthians. Perhaps he converted to Christianity. A third proposal is that the guards around **the judge's bench** beat Sosthenes for refusing to leave. The text is not clear so any possibility is conjecture at best.

As a result of Gallio's ruling, Christians continued to enjoy religious freedom. The church in Corinth continued to grow and eventually expanded throughout Achaia (2 Co 1:1; 11:10; 1 Th 1:7-8). Although only pertaining to Achaia, Gallio's ruling set a precedent for accepting Christianity under the umbrella of Judaism for the neighboring provinces.

18:18-23 Having been in Corinth for a year and half, Paul **said good-bye** to his fellow Christians and sailed to **Syria** (v. 18). Antioch in Syria was Paul's final destination. Before arriving there, he had brief stopovers in Cenchreae, Ephesus, Caesarea, and Jerusalem. **Priscilla and Aquila** accompanied him. Luke did not mention Silas and Timothy so they may have remained in Corinth to continue the ministry. Priscilla and Aquila did not go with Paul all the way to Syria but remained in Ephesus where a church met in their house (1 Co 16:19).

In **Cenchreae**, a port city five miles east of Corinth, Paul **shaved his head** because **he had taken a vow** (Ac 18:18). This vow may have been similar to the Nazirite vow (Nm 6:1-21). This type of vow involved abstaining from all fruit of the vine (wine, grape juice, grapes, raisins, etc), avoiding impurities such as contact with dead bodies, and not cutting one's hair. When time of the vow concluded, the person would shave his head and make a sacrifice at the temple in Jerusalem, throwing his hair into the fire. Usually someone made this vow for a specified amount of time,

although Samson (Jdg 13:5), Samuel (1 Sm 1:11), and John the Baptist (Lk 1:15) were Nazirites for life. Luke did not explain why Paul took this vow. Perhaps he was expressing thanks to God for the fruitful ministry and protection while he was in Corinth, as he had been promised in his vision.

From the port in Cenchreae, Paul, Aquila, and Priscilla sailed almost 300 miles across the Aegean Sea to the port city **Ephesus** on the coast of Asia Minor. Ephesus functioned as the capital of the province of Asia, where Paul had previously been prevented from ministry by the Holy Spirit (Ac 16:6). Paul's stop in Ephesus was brief, but later he ministered for three years in this strategic city (20:31).

Paul believed that God ordered his steps (v. 21). Leaving Aquila and Priscilla behind to continue the ministry in **Ephesus**, he sailed approximately 500 miles to **Caesarea** Maritima on the Palestinian coast (v. 22). He traveled inland and **went up** to Jerusalem. Traditionally pilgrims spoke of going "up" to the holy city, which sat high on Mount Zion. Paul likely traveled to Jerusalem to finish the fulfillment of his Nazirite vow. Upon leaving Jerusalem he conversely **went down** to **Antioch**, even though it lay several hundred miles north (v. 22). Paul concluded his second missionary journey at the place where he had started.

Not staying in Antioch long, Paul continued **traveling** from place to place **in the Galatian territory and Phrygia, strengthening all the disciples**, beginning his third missionary journey (v. 23). Before discussing this third journey in depth, Luke returned to Ephesus and the ministry of Aquila and Priscilla to Apollos. Early church tradition suggested a fourth journey westward toward Spain, which would have occurred after Luke completed the writing of Acts.

Paul's third missionary journey (18:24–21:14)

18:24-28 After Paul left Ephesus, **a Jew named Apollos** arrived in the city (v. 24). Apollos was from **Alexandria**, a city in northern Egypt known as a center for education and philosophy. Accordingly, Apollos was an educated man, **eloquent** and **powerful in the Scriptures**. The "Scriptures," as always throughout the New Testament, denoted the Old Testament. Apollos was the only person designated as powerful in the Bible. His unique gifts enabled him to be an avid witness for Christ. Apollos **had been instructed in the way of the Lord**, but one great gap appeared in his knowledge. INSTRUCT-ED (Gk. *katēchēmenos*, "make myself understood, inform, teach"), transliter-ated from Greek into English as "cate-chized," coming from "again" (Gk. *kata*) and "echo" (Gk. *echeō*). A student is taught by repetition, a tried and proven method of oral instruction that was especially popular among the He-brews through the generations. **He knew only John's baptism** (v. 25). What he knew **about Jesus** he taught **accurate-ly** and **boldly**, but he did not know the whole story (vv. 25-26).

When **Priscilla and Aquila heard** Apollos speak, they quickly recognized his fervent spirit and boldness as well as his areas of weakness. Apparently, all he knew came from the disciples of John the Baptist. Perhaps he knew that Jesus was the Messiah and something of His earthly ministry but nothing of the resurrection. Recognizing the great potential in Apol-los, the Christian couple **took him home and explained the way of God to him more accurately** (v. 26).

Some cite this example of Priscilla's teaching Apollos to support nullifying the teaching of 1 Timothy 2:12, which states that a woman should not "teach" or "have authority over a man." This account can-

not contradict 1 Timothy 2:12 for several reasons:

- *Priscilla taught alongside her hus-band.* She was not teaching Apollos by herself but assisting her husband. The text does not indicate who actu-ally did the teaching. Priscilla may have merely supported her husband as he taught Apollos.

- *The content of the teaching was evan-gelistic.* Aquila and Priscilla taught Apollos critical truths about the Christian faith. He did not have a full understanding of Christ. They explained the way to God more accu-rately to him.

- *The teaching occurred in a private place and not in a public service or class.* Aquila and Priscilla invited Apollos into the privacy of their home so they could help him more accu-rately understand the very nature of the Christian faith.

For these reasons, this account cannot be viewed as contradicting the clear teaching of other passages of Scripture.

As a result of Priscilla and Aquila's instruction, Apollos was adequately equipped for mission work. With the sup-port of **the brothers** in Ephesus, Apollos traveled to the city of Corinth in the prov-ince of **Achaia** (v. 27). There he had an effective ministry **vigorously** debating **the Jews in public, demonstrating through the Scriptures that Jesus is the Messiah** (v. 28). From Paul's frequent mention of Apollos's name in his first let-ter to the Corinthians, one can deduce that Apollos had an effective ministry there (1 Co 3:4-6,22; 4:6; 16:12).

19:1-7 Luke returned to Paul and the account of the apostle's third missionary journey. After concluding his second mis-sionary journey in Antioch, Paul ventured out again, traveling from place to place in

Priscilla, Aquila, and Apollos *Acts 18:1-18*	
Priscilla	• Often called by her more formal name, Prisca, by Paul (2 Tm 4:19) • A Jewess from Rome • A valued coworker in the early church (Rm 16:3) • One taught and trained personally by the Apostle Paul • Host, with her husband, for a house church (1 Co 16:19) • Ministered to Apollos with her husband Aquila
Aquila	• The husband of Priscilla • A Jewish man born in Pontus • A tent maker who offered lodging and work to Paul, who was also a tent maker • With his wife Priscilla, accompanied Paul on a missionary journey as far as Ephesus • A leader in the Ephesian church • Taught Apollos sound Christian doctrine
Apollos	• An educated Alexandrian Jew • Taught Christian doctrine by Priscilla and Aquila • Became an influential minister and powerful preacher

Galatia and Phrygia strengthening all the disciples (18:22-23). For information about this region, see notes on Acts 16:6-8. From Phrygian Galatia, **Paul** evidently continued his travel by land **through the interior regions** into the province of Asia until he **came to Ephesus** (19:1). On his way to Ephesus, Paul likely traveled through his hometown Tarsus, as well as through Derbe, Lystra, Iconium, and Antioch in Pisidia, visiting churches he had established on his first two missionary journeys.

When Paul arrived in Ephesus, **he found some disciples** (Gk. *mathētas*, "learners or pupils") of John the Baptist (v. 1). A disciple may be at varying stages in his learning process. Paul obviously sensed something about these men that made him question their understanding of salvation. Therefore, he asked them whether or not they had received **the Holy Spirit** when they **believed**. They responded that they had not **even heard that there is a Holy Spirit** (v. 2). Since John the Baptist had prophesied of the baptism of the Holy Spirit (Lk 3:16), these disciples were probably indicating that they had not heard about the Spirit's arrival.

They might not have heard about the death, burial, and resurrection of Jesus. While Apollos's knowledge about Jesus possessed some gaps, these men knew very little about Jesus.

Rebaptism in the Holy Spirit is not possible. Believer's baptism is a one-time occurrence just as the Spirit comes to dwell simultaneously within one who believes. This ordinance is significant because to follow Christ in baptism completes the new believer's obedience in salvation. When one is baptized for the wrong reason (i.e., when his knowledge of Christ is defective or even erroneous), the baptism is meaningless. Thus reimmersion for the right reasons is essential for obedience. The men at Ephesus had known only "John's baptism"; they were reimmersed immediately after accepting the gospel of the death, burial, and resurrection of Christ (Ac 19:5).

Once Paul realized they had received only **John's baptism** of **repentance**, he knew that their knowledge of Jesus, **the One** for whom John had prepared the way, was incomplete (v. 3). Upon hearing the truths about Jesus, they believed and **were baptized in the name of the Lord**

Jesus. At this point Paul **laid his hands on them**, and **the Holy Spirit came on them** (vv. 5-6). As a result, **they began to speak with other languages and to prophesy** (v. 6). Since they previously had not even heard of the Spirit, the Spirit's coming upon them served as tangible evidence of His power and as a symbol of heaven's approval of the work being accomplished—the spreading of the gospel abroad.

19:8-10 The Jews here must have been receptive since they allowed Paul to minister for **three months**. In Thessalonica, Paul only preached for three weeks before the Jews became jealous and ran him off (17:1-5). Paul's pattern of proclaiming the gospel first to the Jews, established on his first missionary journey, still stood. (For information on the phrase "the Way," see notes on Acts 9:2.)

Tyrannus, obviously a man of authority, was either the owner of **the lecture hall** or a philosopher who frequently taught there. Archaeologists have uncovered a site believed to be the location of this hall in the ruins of ancient Ephesus. According to tradition, Paul conducted discussions there **every day** (19:9) from 11:00 a.m. until 4:00 p.m. during the afternoon break when it would otherwise be unoccupied. The lecture hall offered a public setting where both Jews and Greeks could hear the gospel. Paul's ministry in Ephesus patterned his ministry in Corinth. First evangelizing the major metropolitan city of the region resulted in the natural spread of the gospel to the surrounding cities via Paul's converts. Consequently, the gospel became known not just in Ephesus but throughout the entire region of Asia Minor (modern Turkey).

19:11-20 In addition to the proclaiming of the word of the Lord, "extraordinary miracles" occurred in Ephesus (v. 11). Miracles often accompanied the outpouring of the Spirit (2:43; 5:12; 8:6,13). After Pente-cost, God performed miracles through the apostles. Before the Spirit came upon the Samaritans, God performed extraordinary miracles through the hands of Philip. In Ephesus, after the outpouring of the Spirit upon the disciples of John the Baptist, **God was performing extraordinary miracles by Paul's hands**. People would take cloths Paul had **touched** and bring them **to the sick** for healing. As a result, **diseases** and **evil spirits** would leave the sick (19:12). This unusual means of healing does not seem characteristic of apostolic healings elsewhere, even in the book of Acts. FACECLOTHS (Gk. *soudaria*, "handkerchiefs") were sweat rags or cloths worn around the head and used to wipe off sweat much as the "dew rag" in modern pop culture. "Work APRONS" (Gk. *simikinthion*, "aprons") were worn by the men. These obscure words likely denote cloths used for wiping off perspiration in the midst of hard labor. These cloths had no magical power in and of themselves but were a tangible representation of God's power working through the Apostle Paul. These miracles resembled the healings from Jesus' garment (Mk 5:27-34; 6:56) and from Peter's shadow (Ac 5:15).

Luke contrasted God's healing work through Paul with the false ministry of the **Jewish exorcists** who were immersed in the world of the demonic (19:13). Having observed Paul perform miraculous healings in the name of Jesus, the exorcists attempted to emulate his work, failing miserably. The spirits only knew **Jesus** as the One **whom Paul preaches** (vv. 13,15); they did not have a personal relationship with Him. The men who attempted this exorcism claimed to be the **seven sons of Sceva**, **a Jewish chief priest** (v. 14). Since there are no historical references to a high priest named Sceva, the exorcists possibly fabricated this position for their father in an attempt to procure a better reputation. These exorcists were **itinerant** (Gk. *perierchomenōn*, "go around, wander, make a circuit"), moving from place to place (v. 13).

When confronted, the evil spirit answered them by saying, **"Jesus I know, and Paul I recognize—but who are you?"** (v. 15). Unlike Jesus and Paul, they possessed no power and no authority from above. The evil spirit recognized this lack of power. Both Jews and Greeks came to recognize the genuine healing power in the name of Jesus through the hands of Paul and the inability for this to be replicated by sorcery (v. 17). The general disfavor toward witchcraft, sorcery, and necromancy caused a radical response (v. 19).

19:21-41 Paul realized that his time in Ephesus and the eastern part of the Roman Empire was coming to an end because the provinces of Syria, Galatia, and Asia had a substantial population of believers who were equipped to carry on the ministry (v. 21; Rm 15:23). The phrase **resolved in the Spirit** has two possible interpretations. Perhaps Paul decided in his human spirit to **go to Jerusalem** and then Rome, or he might have felt specifically led by the Holy Spirit to go. Since Paul felt as if he **must see Rome**, likely divine leading is involved. Although **Macedonia** and **Achaia** were not on the way to Jerusalem, Paul desired to go this way in order to encourage the believers and collect an offering for the poverty-stricken Jerusalem church (Ac 19:21; Rm 15:25-26). Before leaving Ephesus, Paul wrote a letter addressing some problems in the Corinthian church and asking them to begin collecting the offering. He had already collected an offering from the Galatian churches (1 Co 16:1-3). He also sent **Timothy and Erastus** ahead **to Macedonia** and then to Achaia to assist

with the problems in Corinth (Ac 19:22; 1 Co 16:10). Luke last mentioned Timothy in Acts 18:5 when he was ministering alongside Paul in Corinth. Every mention of Erastus in Scripture related to Corinth (Ac 19:22; Rm 16:23; 2 Tm 4:20).

During Paul's last months in Ephesus, **a major disturbance** arose concerning **the Way**, one of the designations for Christians (Ac 19:23; see notes on 9:2). So many people came to Christ, that "the Way" threatened the financial prosperity of some who made their living off of the worship of Artemis (Lat. *Diana*). Artemis of Ephesus should not be confused with the chaste huntress of Greek mythology. Instead, she was the goddess of fertility and the mother goddess of Asia Minor, who was most often depicted as a grotesque, multibreasted woman. The Roman Empire possessed at least 33 shrines devoted to Artemis, who was one of the most widely worshiped deities. Each year pilgrims would flock to Ephesus, the focal city for her worship, to the temple of Artemis, which was documented as one of seven wonders of the ancient world.

Demetrius, a silversmith, made his living constructing miniature **silver shrines of Artemis** (19:24). He showed that his greatest allegiance was to Artemis and the financial gain her worship afforded him (v. 27). In an effort to run Paul out of town and save his business, Demetrius effectively incited a riot.

The huge **amphitheater** of Ephesus held 24,000 people. **Gaius and Aristarchus,** two Christians from Macedonia, **were Paul's traveling companions** (v. 29). When Paul heard of the riot and the holding of his friends captive, he wanted to go and defend his faith, but some **disciples** and **provincial officials** prevented him (v. 30).

Alexander possibly wanted to make it clear that the Jews had nothing to do with the Christians; but when the crowd realized Alexander was a monotheistic Jew, they turned on him as well (vv. 33-34). The Ephesians took great pride in their heritage, and Artemis was closely tied to their culture and livelihood.

The city clerk functioned as the chief administrative officer of the city and as the liaison between the city and Roman provincial administration. He sought to maintain peace because he realized that the mob at the theater could be viewed as an unscheduled and illegal gathering, which could create problems with the Roman officials (v. 35). The word translated TEMPLE ROBBERS (Gk. *hierosulous*, "ones who commit sacrilege") combines the noun "temple" with the verb "rob" and was so commonly used to connote "temple plunderers" that Ephesian inscriptions with the word are still being uncovered. Because the heathen temples were storehouses for great wealth, there were instances of this crime (Rm 2:22) but obviously not in this case (Ac 19:37).

Heart to Heart: Goddess Worship

Goddess worship has again come to the forefront in modern culture. Some women trying to relate to a God they perceive to be male have turned to goddess worship, a popular wave of religious expression that encourages women to look for the goddess within and thereby to find strength based on their self-worth and inherent value. Goddess worship encourages women to worship false female deities as equal with God. This ideology is totally against the teaching of Scripture that all people become enemies of God because of their sinfulness (Rm 5:6-11). The Bible teaches that one can find remission of sin only through Jesus Christ. Naming self as a god is a total defiance of the truth that the Christian's body, upon salvation, becomes God's temple. This belief is a dangerous distortion of truth, and women should beware. Worship of oneself or of any goddess or god other than the one true *Yahweh* God causes great ruin, incurs the wrath of God, and indicates that one is not genuinely a child of the King. Paul reminded believers of their distinct honor and privilege in being God's sanctuary (v. 16). Having this perspective of life, behavior, and value, therefore, should lead Christians to live in an honorable way.

20:1-6 Luke omitted almost all the details about the final days of Paul's third missionary journey. Nevertheless, much of it can be pieced together through Paul's personal references to the journey in his letters, 2 Corinthians and Romans, which the apostle was writing during this time.

From Ephesus, Paul headed north to Troas on his way **to Macedonia** (v. 1; 2 Co 2:12-13). In Troas, he hoped to meet Titus, who had previously traveled to Corinth with a letter from Paul—a letter that is now lost (2 Co 7:6-8). In this letter to the Corinthians, Paul had confronted serious sin issues in the Corinthian church. Paul wanted to meet Titus so that he could get an update on the church. Not finding Titus in Troas, Paul continued his journey to Macedonia.

When Paul first came into Macedonia, he had a difficult time. He and his companions, including Timothy (2 Co 1:1), had no rest, and they were afflicted in every way (2 Co 7:5). But they were

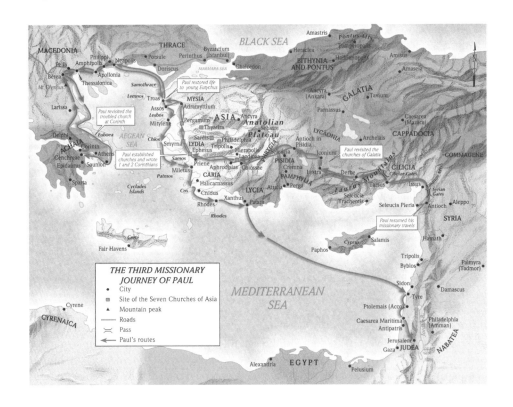

THE THIRD MISSIONARY
JOURNEY OF PAUL
• City
▣ Site of the Seven Churches of Asia
▲ Mountain peak
— Roads
✕ Pass
← Paul's routes

eventually comforted by the arrival of Titus and his good news about the repentance of the Corinthian church (2 Co 7:6-16). While in Macedonia, Paul **exhorted** the believers **at length** (v. 2), probably at least a year, and composed what would have been his fourth letter to the church in Corinth—2 Corinthians.[7]

From Macedonia, Paul continued to **Greece**, specifically to the city of Corinth in the province of Achaia. (For information on the city of Corinth, see notes on Acts 18:1.) During his **three**-month stay during the winter (vv. 2-3), Paul wrote the epistle to the Romans. From Corinth, Paul intended to head directly to Syria. After discovering a plot **devised against him by the Jews**, he decided to return **through Macedonia** (v. 3). Paul wanted to get to the Jerusalem church as quickly and safely as possible because he would be delivering the money he had collected

for Gentile churches. Paul focused on this offering throughout his third missionary journey. He demonstrated its importance by mentioning it in all of his epistles written during this time (Gl 2:10; 1 Co 16:1-4; 2 Co 8-9; Rm 15:25-32).

Representatives from many of the churches accompanied Paul back to Jerusalem to help deliver the offering: **Sopater . . . from Beroea, Aristarchus and Secundus from Thessalonica, Gaius from Derbe** (most likely a different Gaius than the man mentioned in 19:29), **Timothy, and Tychicus and Trophimus from Asia**, and apparently Luke from Phillipi, according to a logical conclusion based upon a reinstatement of the "we" passages beginning in Acts 20:5-6.

Some of the delegation traveled straight to **Troas** (see notes on 16:8), most likely to procure a ship for their trip to the Jerusalem coast, while the remain-

Greco-Roman Goddesses[8]	
Name	**Description**
Aphrodite (see also Venus)	The Greek goddess of sexual love and beauty, whose temple in Corinth supposedly employed 1,000 cultic prostitutes, contributing to the city's notorious immorality.
Artemis (see also Diana)	The Greek goddess of fertility, mother goddess of Asia Minor and helper to women in childbirth. Her temple was one of the seven wonders of the world (see Ac 19:21-40).
Athena (see also Minerva)	The Greek goddess of wisdom, fertility, and war. She was considered the guardian of Athens.
Ceres (see also Demeter)	The Roman goddess of agriculture. She was also known as the queen of the Dead.
Cybele	The Roman goddess known as "Mother-earth," whom many called "the Great Mother."
Demeter (see also Ceres)	The Greek goddess of grain and changing seasons. She was also known as the guardian of marriage.
Diana (see also Artemis)	The Roman goddess of fertility, hunting, and virginity (see Ac 19:21-40). She was also associated with the moon and with wild animals.
Hera (see also Juno)	The Greek goddess of women, marriage, and motherhood—she was the wife of Zeus.
Hestia (see also Vesta)	The Greek goddess of the hearth.
Juno(see also Hera)	The Roman goddess of women and of the rainbow. She was the wife of Jupiter and the queen of the gods.
Minerva (see also Athena)	The Roman goddess of wisdom, fertility, and war.
Venus (see also Aphrodite)	The Roman goddess of love and beauty. She was the mother of Cupid.
Vesta (see also Hestia)	The Roman goddess of the hearth.

der stopped in **Philippi** (see notes on 16:12) until after the Feast of **Unleavened Bread** (see notes on 12:3). From Philippi, it took them **five days** to reunite with the group in Troas. The reverse trip noted in Acts 16:11 only took two days, perhaps because of the direction of the winds. Once in Troas the entire group stayed for **seven days**, probably awaiting the departure of their ship (20:6).

20:7-12 The phrase **break bread** indicated Paul's traveling companions and some believers in Troas were celebrating the Lord's Supper (1 Co 10:16-17; 11:17-34), which was accompanied by Paul's extensive sermon. This worship service is one of the earliest references to their celebration of the Sabbath on Sunday instead of Saturday, according to Jewish tradition.

A young man named Eutychus, who was probably between the ages of 8 and 14, **sank into a deep sleep** while **sitting on a window sill** and **fell** out of the window **from the third story** and died (Ac 20:9). But Paul performed a resurrection miracle and restored the young man to **life** (vv. 10-12). This miracle paralleled ones in the Old Testament by Elijah (1 Kg 17:17-24) and Elisha (2 Kg 4:33-36). Around Paul, the miraculous must have become commonplace since after the miracle they resumed what they had been doing.

20:13-16 From Troas, Luke **sailed for Assos**, while Paul took the route via **land** (v. 13). Luke did not mention how the rest of their traveling companions made the journey, but some probably went with Luke and others with Paul. Assos was a port city only 20 miles south of Troas. On this short trip, Paul had additional time to instruct the believers from that region. Once in Assos, Paul boarded the ship and the group continued to **Mitylene**, a harbor on the southeast shore of the island of Lesbos approximately 30 miles south of Assos (v. 14). **The next day**, they **arrived** in **Chios**, an island south of Lesbos off the coast of Asia Minor. **The following day** they came **to Samos**, an island near Ephesus, **and the day after** that **to Miletus**, a city in Asia Minor 30 miles south of Ephesus (v. 15). Normally in Acts, Luke only highlighted Paul's major stops. Since he accompanied Paul on this portion of his journey, he provided specific details about the mode of travel.

Although Paul spent more time in Ephesus than in any other city on his missionary journeys, or perhaps because of that, he decided to bypass the city. He knew that if he stopped there, greeting all of the friends he had made during his three-year stay would take a considerable amount of time. He was in a hurry to make it to **Jerusalem** before **Pentecost** (v. 16).

20:17-38 Since Paul had not had the time to say good-bye to all of his friends in Ephesus, he compromised. He would speak to the leadership, who would convey his greetings to the rest of the church. Therefore, while he stayed in nearby **Miletus, he sent** for **the elders of the church** in Ephesus (v. 17).

Paul's farewell address to the Ephesian elders is the only sermon recorded from his third missionary journey and his only recorded sermon for a Christian audience.

As such, the message closely resembled Paul's epistles, which were addressed to Christian audiences. The sermon can be divided into three parts:

- a review of Paul's past ministry in Ephesus (vv. 18-21),

- a description of the present situation (vv. 22-27), and

- future responsibilities for the Ephesian elders (vv. 28-35).

Paul began his farewell address by reviewing his past ministry in Ephesus. Paul highlighted his **humility** even though to do so was often thought to be a sign of weakness in the Greco-Roman world. He wanted the Ephesian leaders to know the importance of humility in being Christlike (v. 19; Php 2:1-11). He also recalled his **tears**—due to **trials** and misunderstandings from fellow believers (Ac 20:19,31). Specifically he mentioned trials related to **the plots of the Jews**, even though the only trial Luke recorded about Paul in Ephesus was instigated by Gentiles (v. 19). Apparently Paul endured more trials than those recorded in Acts.

Paul then talked about his current situation. While in Ephesus, he had been compelled by the Spirit to go to Jerusalem (v. 22; 19:21) even though **the Holy Spirit** had warned him through many people, as later at Tyre and Caesarea (21:4,11), that **chains and afflictions** were awaiting him (20:23). Paul knew he had to be obedient to the Spirit, even if it meant imprisonment or death. Paul would later have the opportunity to do **the ministry** God had planned for him (v. 24) before priests (22:30–23:10), governors (24:1-21), and kings (26:1-23).

Paul prepared the fledgling group of believers for his departure (20:25). Aware that he faced severe persecution in Jerusalem, he realized he might never return to Asia Minor. Although some believe Paul returned there after his first Roman imprisonment, at this time he did not foresee the possibility.

In the third part of Paul's address to the Ephesian elders, he delineated to them their future responsibilities **as overseers to shepherd the church of God** (v. 20). Luke used the term OVERSEERS interchangeably with "elders" (vv. 17,28). (For more information about this office in the church, see notes on 14:23.) Paul used three terms to denote pastoral leadership: "elders" (Gk. *presbuterous*, 20:17), "overseers" (Gk. *episkopous*, "guardians, bishops," v. 28), and "to shepherd" (Gk. *poimainein*, "guide, protect, nurture," v. 28). The latter is a verb instead of a noun as in the case of the other terms. These terms are not suggesting levels of authority but rather diversity in function. They are used interchangeably and refer to differing responsibilities of the same man or of men who are pastors for the congregation. By using the terms "shepherd" and **flock**, Paul also brought out the Old Testament imagery (Jr 23:1-4; Ez 34:1-31). The primary duty of the elders was to care for the Christians in their churches as a shepherd cares for his flock by protecting it from **savage wolves** (Ac 20:29). Paul warned that attacks would come from both the outside—**come in among you**—and the inside— **from among yourselves** (vv. 29-30). From later New Testament writings, these warnings proved true (1 Tm 1:3-7,19-20; 2 Tm 1:15; 2:17-18; 3:1-9; Rv 2:1-7). Men, such as Hymenaeus and Alexander (1 Tm 1:19-20), Phygelus and Hermogenes (2 Tm 1:15), and Philetus (2 Tm 2:17-18) all caused problems for the Ephesian church. Paul especially wanted the elders to be on guard against **deviant doctrines** (Ac 20:30). Elders bore responsibility for the doctrinal integrity of the church. For **three years**, the length of

Paul's entire Ephesian ministry, Paul had provided them with an example of sound leadership. He set an example by continually yet lovingly **warning** them of the danger of doctrinal error, even doing so **with tears** (v. 31). Paul also set an example by not coveting **silver or gold or clothing** and through his work ethic (v. 33).

21:1-14 From Miletus, Paul and his group skirted the shoreline, stopping first 40 miles south at the small island of **Cos**, best known for being the location of the medical school founded by Hippocrates in the fifth century BC. **The next day** they sailed another 60 miles to the island of **Rhodes** and then to the city of **Patara** on the Lycian coast (v. 1). Each stop represented one day of travel. Once in Patara, the group **boarded** a larger ship that would take them all the way **to Phoenicia** (v. 2; see notes on 11:19). On their 400-mile journey across the Mediterranean Sea, the ship passed by **Cyprus**; continuing on their journey, approximately five days after leaving Patara, the group arrived in **Syria** (21:3). Although Luke stated that their destination was Phoenicia (v. 2), they arrived in Syria (v. 3). The two terms were somewhat interchangeable, Phoenicia being the more specific location and Syria the larger area, which encompassed Phoenicia. The ship harbored for approximately **seven days** to unload its cargo in the city of **Tyre**, a Phoenician coastal city located between the mountains of Lebanon and the Mediterranean Sea and known as a center for sea trade.

While in Tyre, Paul and his traveling companions **found** (Gk. *aneurontes*, "discover") **some disciples** (v. 4), which suggests that they were not acquainted with these believers and literally had to seek them out. Anywhere there were Christians, Paul knew he had a place to stay. Some view the Spirit-led admonition for Paul not to go to Jerusalem as a problem since he had previously been led by the Spirit to go there (19:21; 20:22). Most likely the current admonition was viewed as a warning of impending danger. The disciples cared for his welfare; therefore, having been warned by the Spirit that Paul faced danger, they advised him not to go, since they had no understanding that Paul's imprisonment was a part of God's greater plan for the spread of the gospel.

During their seven-day stay in Tyre, Paul and his traveling companions developed a close relationship with their newfound brothers and sisters in the Lord. To portray this close relationship, Luke noted that they **all**, even **their wives and children, escorted** them **out of the city**. In one week, Paul's group made a considerable impact on the Christians in Tyre.

From Tyre, they sailed 25 miles south to **Ptolemais**, known in both ancient and modern times as Acco (21:7; Jdg 1:31). Upon their arrival, they were **greeted** by some fellow believers they apparently already knew. In **Caesarea** Maritima, they stayed with **Philip the evangelist** for **many days** (Ac 21:8). Apparently the journey took less time than Paul expected, and he had plenty of time to make it to Jerusalem for Pentecost.

Luke noted that Philip **was one of the Seven** chosen to serve tables (Ac 6:1-7). Philip also ministered in Samaria and to the Ethiopian eunuch (8:4-40). Luke identified Philip's four **daughters** as "virgins," perhaps indicating their ability to devote themselves wholeheartedly to the ministry (1 Co 7:25-34). That they **prophesied** was fulfillment of the prophecy quoted by Peter at Pentecost (Ac 2:17; Jl 2:28). The text provided no details about the outworking of the ministry of the four prophetesses, but other passages of Scripture provide some parameters (1 Co 11:5; 14:3; 1 Tm 2:12). These women may have provided information to Luke for his writing of the Gospel of Luke and the book of

Acts, and the early church historian Eusebius noted that Papias received information from them.

Agabus, the prophet who predicted the famine in Acts 11:28, came **from Judea** while Paul and his companions were staying with Philip. He took **Paul's belt** that wrapped around his waist several times and **tied his own feet and hands**, symbolizing what would happen to Paul. He predicted that Paul would be imprisoned by **the Jews in Jerusalem** and delivered **into Gentile hands** (Ac 21:10-11). Paul had received this same message "town after town" (20:23). God used these warnings to prepare Paul for what was coming. God had called him to Jerusalem; therefore, he was going to go no matter what. Paul felt prepared for whatever came his way, even if it entailed imprisonment or death (21:13). Paul loved God more than he loved his own life.

The Spread of the Gospel to Rome (21:15–28:31)

Paul's arrest (21:15–22:29)

21:15-25 After spending several days with Philip in Caesarea, Paul and the representatives from the churches (20:4-5) journeyed the last 65 miles into **Jerusalem**. Luke identified himself as a member of the group, as suggested by his use of the pronoun **we** (21:15). **Mnason** was designated as **an early disciple,** perhaps indicating that he had received salvation at Pentecost (v. 16). His Greek name may indicate that he was a Hellenistic Jew, which would fit well with his willingness to house Gentile Christians. He obviously possessed considerable wealth since he had space to house Paul and his traveling companions. The Christians in Jerusalem **welcomed** the group **gladly** (v. 17).

After one night in Jerusalem, Paul and the representatives from the churches went to meet **James**, the half brother of

Jesus and leader of the church in Jerusalem, and the other **elders** (v. 18). The leaders rejoiced and **glorified God** at Paul's news, yet they feared the Jews' reaction (vv. 20-22). In Jerusalem a time of intense Jewish nationalism and political unrest had arisen; thus Paul's mission to the Gentiles with the gospel would not be well received by the Jewish population. Some people had accused Paul of teaching Jews to **abandon** both the law of **Moses** and the practice of circumcision (v. 21). But this was not the case. While Paul did not believe circumcision necessary for salvation, he obviously did not discourage Jews from the practice since he had already had Timothy circumcised (16:3). In an effort to appease the Jews and deal with the false rumors, the elders suggested that Paul perform a public act of Jewish piety. This action would help stifle the rumors because **everyone** would **know** that he was **careful about observing the law** (21:24). (For additional information about the requirements for the Gentiles, see notes on Acts 15:19-20.)

21:26-36 The **offering** from the four men likely included two pigeons and one lamb for each person, for a total of eight pigeons and four lambs (v. 26). **Jews from the province of Asia** who were in Jerusalem for Pentecost recognized Trophimus, who was a resident of Ephesus (v. 29). Seeing Paul, they stirred up the crowd by making three false accusations against him (v. 28):

• They claimed that he taught **everyone everywhere against our people.** Oddly, they accused Paul of being anti-Semitic, while he was participating in a Jewish custom.

• They accused him of teaching against the law, which was a serious accusation considering the setting. The Jews were particularly zealous for the law at Pentecost because it had become a

celebration of the giving of the law to Moses on Mount Sinai. A charge of this sort at this time would quickly infuriate the crowds who had traveled to Jerusalem for the sole purpose of celebrating the law.

• They accused Paul of teaching against **the temple** and provided an example, claiming that Paul **brought Greeks into the temple** (v. 29). While Greeks (uncircumcised Gentiles) could enter the outer parts of the temple complex, they were not allowed past the Court of the Gentiles. Allowing an uncircumcised male beyond that point would have **profaned** the **holy** temple. Since they had **previously seen** the Gentile **Trophimus** with Paul, they mistakenly assumed **that Paul had brought him** into the inner courts of the **temple complex**.

These serious claims, resembling the ones brought against Stephen, had resulted in Stephen's death (6:11-14).

The **chaos** attracted the attention of **the commander of the regiment**, who was on guard at the Fortress of Antonia, adjacent to the temple (21:31). From the towers there, he had a view of the entire temple complex. Troops were kept in readiness during festivals for outbreaks such as this. He, along with some of his **soldiers and centurions**, responded to the commotion **immediately** (v. 32). The commander, Claudius Lysias (23:26), was in charge of 1,000 Roman soldiers. At least 200 of them responded to this commotion, indicated by the use of the plural word **centurions** since a centurion commanded 100 men. With the arrival of the soldiers, the enraged Jews **stopped beating Paul**. Taking control of the situation, the commander took Paul **into custody**, which actually served to protect Paul (21:33). Had the Jews been left to their own devices, Paul would have been beaten to death. Unable **to get reliable information** in the chaotic situation, the commander **ordered** the soldiers to take Paul **into the barracks** (v. 34).

21:37-40 Right before they took him into the barracks, Paul shocked the commander by speaking to him in the Greek language (v. 37). Greek was the language of cultured and educated men and was not used by the common criminal he wrongly assumed Paul to be. Since Paul spoke Greek, the commander then assumed that Paul was **the Egyptian who had raised a rebellion** against Jerusalem some years earlier (v. 38). The historian Josephus recounted this event, noting that an Egyptian false prophet led men to the Mount of Olives in an effort to destroy the city walls and overthrow the Romans. Although hundreds of his followers died, the leader of the rebellion had escaped unscathed. Paul responded that he was not the Egyptian insurgent but a **Jewish man from Tarsus of Cilicia** (v. 39; see notes on 9:30).

The Daughters of Philip
Acts 21:7-14

"Philip the evangelist . . . had four virgin daughters who prophesied" (Ac 21:8-9).

- Philip was one of the seven disciples set apart for special service in the early church (Ac 6:1-7).
- He had four godly daughters.
- Each daughter had the spiritual gift of prophecy.
- They were probably unmarried and especially devoted to God.
- They shared the gospel and discipled women.
- They must have been well versed in Scripture.
- They worked among the leaders of the early church.

22:1-29 Paul began his defense as Stephen did in Acts 7, by addressing the crowd as "**brothers and fathers.**" This introduction identified him with his listeners and demonstrated respect. Although there had previously been "a great hush" (21:40), the crowd grew **even quieter** when they heard him speaking **in the Hebrew language** (22:2). Paul possessed their full attention. (For **Gamaliel**, see notes on 5:34.) Under Gamaliel, Paul received the best education available to a Jew. He emphasized his close ties to Judaism, stressing that he had been **zealous for God**, just as his listeners were (23:3). Paul had once **persecuted** those who belonged to **this Way**. Although Acts repeatedly refers to "the Way," Paul used "this Way," identifying himself with the movement he once persecuted. Here Paul acknowledged his role in **the death** and imprisonment of Christians (v. 4). Perhaps Stephen's stoning came to mind (7:54–8:3).

Acts provides three detailed accounts of Paul's conversion. The first account was told from Luke's perspective (9:1-19), while the other two accounts were told from Paul's (22:6-21; 26:4-23). He was addressing a Jewish audience, while in 26:4-23 he was talking to a predominantly Gentile audience. The diverse perspectives and different audiences account for the minor differences among the three accounts. (For the most detailed account of Paul's conversion experience, see the notes on 9:1-19.) Acts 22:6-9 paralleled Acts 9:3-8, although it does have three unique features. While 9:3-8 does not provide a time frame for the occurrence, Paul noted in this account that it occurred **about noon** (22:6). Acts 26:13 also affirmed that it was midday. Additionally, only this account described **Jesus** as **the Nazarene**, which was fitting for Paul's Jewish audience (22:8). The third unique feature of this account is Paul's notation that his traveling companions **did not hear the voice of the One who was speaking to** him. From all of the accounts one can deduce that Paul's companions heard a sound but did not "hear" (Gk. *ēkousan*, "listen to, heed, obey") the voice (v. 9). The choice of word suggests a possible nuance of meaning, which could suggest that Paul not only heard the sound of words but embraced the words with intent to obey.

Before his Jewish audience Paul openly confessed that he addressed Jesus as **Lord** immediately after Jesus revealed who He was (vv. 10-11). The other two accounts omit this detail. Paul's later account to the Gentile audience did not mention his encounter with Ananias because that portion of his testimony was not relevant for that audience (26:12-23). To his Jewish audience, Paul provided specific details about what Ananias said to him, specifically that he should preach Jesus **to all people** (22:15). Salvation comes as a result of **calling on His name**. Here, baptism is simply a metaphor for the washing **away** of **sins** (v. 16; see discussion on 2:14-40). Salvation is closely aligned with baptism in the New Testament but not in the sense of baptismal regeneration. Paul was already a Christian, and he was calling on new believers to give testimony of their salvation by submitting themselves to the ordinance of baptism (22:16). To speak of baptism as a "sacrament" is misleading since many have used that term with the connotation of "conveying grace." To suggest that grace comes from any rite or ritual is to violate the teachings of the New Testament.

After Paul told them about his baptism, he jumped ahead three years to his first trip to Jerusalem (cf. 9:26-29; Gl 2:18-19). Perhaps Paul referred to this divine vision he had while **praying in the temple** because it related to the mob's claim that he had defiled the temple. In the vision, God told him to **get out of Jerusalem quickly** (Ac 22:18). He needed to leave quickly because he faced persecution from disbelieving Hellenistic Jews (9:29). Again Paul reiterated his participation in the persecution of Christians, mentioning Stephen by name. Perhaps Paul used this emphasis to demonstrate the complete change in his own heart. The one who had been a persecutor of "the Way" now labored to share it. Even though Paul's primary calling was to share the gospel with the Gentiles, he practiced a "to the Jew first" strategy (9:15; 13:46; 14:27; 15:3,12; 21:19). Once Paul mentioned God's command for him to go **to the Gentiles**, the Jews quit listening to him, and their mob mentality returned (22:21-22).

Everything Paul said had been tolerable to them until he brought up his ministry to the Gentiles. That God would send someone to minister to the Gentiles was a blasphemous notion to the Jews. As Paul shook the dust off his feet at Antioch of Pisidia (13:51) and out of his clothes at Corinth (18:6), the Jews did so to demonstrate their opposition to Paul (22:22-23).

The phrase **examined with the scourge** indicated an interrogation accompanied by a brutal flogging in an attempt to **discover the reason** for the Jew's hostility towards him (v. 24). Right before the beating commenced, Paul brought up his **Roman** citizenship, as he had at Philippi (v. 25; 16:37). Although Roman citizenship could not technically be purchased, the commander indicated he had **bought** his **citizenship**, likely via a bribe, **for a large amount of money** (22:28). Possession of Roman citizenship afforded people certain rights and high status. Paul's citizenship provided protection, giving him the right to a Roman trial, exemption from the scourging, protection from execution, and eventually the right of appeal.

Paul's defense before the Sanhedrin (22:30–23:10)

22:30–23:10 For information on the chief priests and Sanhedrin, see notes on Acts 4:5 and 5:21. The commander did not gain much knowledge from this meeting, which resulted in a heated debate between the Pharisees and the Sadducees. Paul's ministry to the Gentiles on all of his missionary journeys had been in obedience to God. Paul's statement enraged **the high priest Ananias** (23:2). Ananias, not to be confused with Annas (4:6), served as high priest from AD 47 to 59. Noted for his cruelty, violence, and corruptness, his own people would later kill him. In his rage, Ananias "ordered" men standing by Paul "TO STRIKE (Gk. *tuptein*, "beat, wound") him on the mouth," indicating more than a mere slap on the face. The same verb was used to describe the mob's beating of Paul (21:32) and the Roman soldier's beating of Jesus (Mt 27:30).

The one appointed to judge Paul according to law violated the law by ordering Paul to be struck. The phrase **God is going to strike you** was not a curse but an acknowledgment that God would deal with Ananias justly (Ac 23:3). The phrase **whitewashed wall** is reminiscent of a tottering wall whose unstable condition had been disguised by a fresh coat of white paint (v. 3; Ezk 36:10-16). When some questioned Paul about his angry response towards the high priest, Paul acknowledged that he **did not know** that **it was the high priest** (Ac 23:5). There are several reasons why Paul did not know the high priest:

- Paul had been away from Jerusalem for over 20 years. Ananias took office during that time; hence, Paul did not know him.

- This was not the normal convening of the Sanhedrin; therefore, Ananias

may have not occupied his usual place or worn his robes of office.

- Some propose that Paul did not recognize him because of a personal eye condition that obscured his vision.

With these reasons in mind, Paul understandably did not realize that he was addressing the high priest. Since he quoted Scripture indicating you should **not speak evil of a ruler of your people** (v. 5; Ex 22:27), Paul obviously would not have spoken as rashly had he realized that Ananias was the high priest.

When Paul realized he stood in front of the **Sanhedrin**, which consisted of both **Sadducees** and **Pharisees**, he directed his appeal to the Pharisees, pointing out that he was not only **a Pharisee**, but **a son of Pharisees**, indicating that both his father and grandfather had been Pharisees. His declaration that he was a Pharisee demonstrated that he sought to uphold the law and that he believed in **the resurrection of the dead** (Ac 23:6). Doctrinally, the Pharisees and Sadducees disagreed. The **Sadducees** denied the **resurrection** as well as the existence of angels and demons. In contrast, **the Pharisees** affirmed **them all** (v. 8). (For more information about what the Sadducees and Pharisees believed, see notes on Acts 4:1 and 5:34 respectively.) Paul's statement that he was on trial for his belief in **the hope of the resurrection** caused the Pharisees to come quickly to his defense (23:9). Doing so, the Pharisees were not defending the resurrection of Jesus, but the concept of the resurrection and life after death. Fearing for Paul's safety and realizing he would not get any answers from the rioting Sanhedrin, **the commander** ordered some **troops to go down** and **rescue** Paul, bringing him back **into the barracks** in Fort Antonia (v. 10).

The plot against Paul (23:11-35)

23:11-22 The following night, the Lord appeared to Paul in his prison cell. Having the Lord by his side undoubtedly comforted Paul in his difficult circumstances. The Lord provided him with encouragement—commendation of Paul's past ministry in Jerusalem and a future prediction that Paul would survive the trials in Jerusalem so he could **testify** about Him **in Rome** (v.11).

The next day **the Jews** developed an assassination plan. To be BOUND UNDER A CURSE (Gk. *anethematisan*), from which the English word "anathema" comes, is a strong verb of commitment suggesting a person's binding himself in such a way that he calls upon himself a curse if he does not fulfill his oath. Paul's would-be assassins were willing to be **under a curse** from God if they did not take his life.

The son of Paul's sister heard about **their ambush**. This explicit reference to Paul's family members is the only one in Scripture. Fearing for his uncle's safety, Paul's unnamed nephew **came and entered the barracks and reported it to Paul** (v. 16). Since he could enter the barracks, Paul was not in solitary confinement and was afforded personal visits. Realizing the impending threat to his life, Paul got **one of the centurions** to take his nephew to Claudius Lysias, **the commander** (v. 17), who used privacy to protect the identity of the informant (v. 19).

23:23-35 Most excellent (Gk. *kratistos,* "most noble") was also used by Luke to describe Theophilus, the recipient of both Luke and Acts (1:1; Lk 1:3). Antonius Felix served as governor of Judea from AD 52 to 59. Felix and his brother Pallas were once slaves of Antonia, mother of the Emperor Claudius. Pallas, who was a favorite of Emperor Claudius, procured the current appointment for his brother.

This letter conveyed the basic content of the original letter (Ac 23:25), i.e., the commander's explanation of the situation. He asserted that he **rescued** Paul **because** of his Roman citizenship (v. 27). In truth, he had already arrested Paul and made preparations to scourge him when he discovered his citizenship. Claudius Lysias described Paul's appearance before the **Sanhedrin** as being **about disputed matters** in the Jewish **law**, which essentially asserted Paul's innocence of any crime against the Roman law, especially not a crime **that merited deaths or chains** (vv. 28-29). Because the **plot against** Paul forfeited his ability to carry out a safe trial in Jerusalem, the commander believed it best to move the trial to Caesarea (v. 30).

Antipatris was a military post about 40 miles from Jerusalem on the way to Caesarea. After reading the letter, Felix asked Paul **what province he was from** to determine if he had jurisdiction in the case (v. 31). Since the Roman province of **Cilicia** fell under the authority of the Roman legate of Syria—to whom Felix reported—therefore, he possessed jurisdiction for the case (v. 34).

The accusation against Paul (24:1–26:32)

24:1-9 After five days Ananias came to Caesarea along with **some elders and a lawyer named Tertullus**, who was most likely a Hellenistic Jew. He was enlisted to be the prosecutor. Whether a Jew or Roman, he was an excellent judicial orator. Tertullus diplomatically began by complimenting, no doubt insincere flattery, the judge Felix. He attributed the peace in the region to the rulership of Felix, a most desirable compliment because the primary task of rulers in that day was to maintain peace in their regions (v. 2). After precursory comments, Tertullus began his prosecution against Paul with three primary accusations:

- He depicted Paul as **an agitator among all the Jews throughout the Roman world** (v. 5). This serious claim would not be taken lightly by the Romans because they immediately attempted to squelch any threat to Roman peace (*pax Romana*). The Romans considered dissension in the Roman Empire as an act of treason against Caesar.

- Tertullus labeled Paul **a ringleader . . . of the Nazarenes**, because to be a leader of a religious sect without the approval of Rome was against the law. The term "Nazarenes" was derived from the hometown of Jesus, apparently another name for the Christians (v. 5).

- He claimed that Paul **tried to desecrate the temple**. On the basis of this charge, Tertullus claimed, the Jews **apprehended him** in order **to judge him according to our law** (v. 6). In actuality, the Jews never arrested Paul, nor did they plan on bringing him to trial. They simply tried to kill him (21:30-32).

24:10-21 After Tertullus concluded with the accusations, **the governor** provided **Paul** with the opportunity to defend himself against the claims. Instead of speaking in generalities as the prosecution had done, Paul addressed the specific incident that led to his incarceration. He argued that to claim he had been an agitator among the Jews was unsubstantiated and unprovable (vv. 12-13). Regarding the second claim, Paul acknowledged that he was a leader of the Christian movement called **the Way**. However, he did not view it as an additional **sect** because he worshiped the same **God** as the Jews, and he believed **all the things that are written in the Law and in the Prophets** as did the Jews (v. 14). Regarding the third claim, that he desecrated the temple, Paul again pleaded his innocence. While bringing **charitable gifts and offerings to** his **nation** at the temple, he was confronted by **some Jews from the province of Asia**. At the time, he was doing nothing wrong because he had been **ritually purified** (vv. 17-18). When Paul **stood before the Sanhedrin**, he argued that his accusers should only testify about what they had personally witnessed (v. 20). The real issue centered upon Paul's belief in **the resurrection of the dead**—a belief that sharply divided Jews. As such, the issue was theological, not civil or criminal. It did not belong in the Roman court of law; therefore, the charges should be dismissed.

24:22-27 Felix **adjourned the hearing** without making a decision under the pretext that he wanted to hear from Claudius **Lysias**, merely an excuse since he had already heard from Lysias in the form of a letter (v. 22). In the letter, Lysias had indicated that the real issue was a matter of Jewish law and that Paul was not guilty of any crime warranting death or imprisonment (23:29). In reality, Felix wanted to avoid making a decision because the right and just decision would have infuriated the Jews, possibly causing additional riots. Instead, Felix chose to placate the Jews by keeping Paul in prison. Since Paul was a Roman citizen who had not been found guilty of a crime, he was allowed **some freedom** in the form of frequent visits from **his friends** (v. 23).

Over the course of Paul's two-year imprisonment in Caesarea, he experienced frequent visits with Felix. On one occasion, Paul discussed **faith in Christ Jesus** with Felix and his third **wife**. The youngest daughter of Herod Agrippa I, **Drusilla** professed to be **Jewish** (v. 24; see notes on 12:1). Once married to the king of Emesa (in the province of Syria), she had been lured away by Felix, who had been struck by her beauty. At the age of 16, she married Felix and bore him a son. When Drusilla heard the good news of the gospel from Paul, she was not yet 20 years old. Approximately 20 years later, Drusilla and her son died in Pompeii during the eruption of Mount Vesuvius (AD 79).

Since Drusilla was Jewish, Paul probably reasoned with her from the Scriptures, showing how Jesus fulfilled Old Testament prophecy. **Righteousness, self-control, and the judgment to come** are sometimes called the "three tenses of salvation," beginning with how to be justi-

fied or made righteous by God, then learning to overcome temptation through self-mastery, and finally escaping the final judgment of God (24:25). Married to a woman whom he had lured away from her husband, Felix lacked both righteousness and self-control; thus, the realization that he faced judgment made him **afraid**. Although Felix was convicted of his sins, he put off making a decision for Christ. The fact that he later sought **money** in the form of a bribe from Paul, indicated that he never seriously pursued giving his life to Christ (v. 26).

Drusilla Acts 24:10-27	
Her Name	• Drusilla means "watered by dew" • A notable name among Romans
Her Family	• Granddaughter of Herod the Great • Youngest daughter of Herod Agrippa I, a persecutor of the church • Sister of Bernice • Wife first of King Aziz of Emesa • Later the wife of Felix, the Roman governor • The mother of Agrippa
Her Life	• She was a beautiful woman. • As a Jewess, she married a pagan. • She witnessed Paul's defense of the gospel before Felix. • She heard the good news of Jesus Christ. • She was convicted by the truth of Paul's message. • With Felix, she sent Paul back to prison.

When Paul had been in prison for **two years**, Felix was removed from office. His removal resulted from Jewish complaints to Rome about his brutality. He would have faced severe punishment from Emperor Nero if his influential brother had not interceded in his behalf. Not much is known about Felix's **successor, Porcius Festus,** because he died two years after assuming office in AD 62 (v. 27).

25:1-12 The chief priests and the leaders of the Jews, the Sanhedrin, **presented their case against Paul** to Festus and asked that Paul be sent **to Jerusalem**,

under the pretext that his trial would be heard there. They planned **an ambush** to **kill him** while in transport (vv. 2-3). Two years earlier, 40 Jews planned a similar ploy, enlisting the Sanhedrin as collaborators (23:15). This time the leaders themselves planned the ambush. Unaware of their plan, **Festus** denied their request, choosing for the time to keep Paul in **Caesarea** (25:4). Nevertheless, he invited the leaders back to Caesarea where they could air their accusations in formal court.

After spending a little over a week assessing the situation in Jerusalem, Festus returned to Caesarea along with Paul's accusers. Not wanting to delay Paul's case any longer, **the next day** Festus convened the court. The reference to **the judge's bench** meant an official Roman trial (v. 6). Although Luke did not delineate their charges, Paul's defense indicated that the charges were similar to those brought against Paul two years earlier when the case was tried before Felix (24:5-6). Paul again vehemently denied their charges (25:8), stating he had not **sinned at all** against **the Jewish law** (by being a leader of the Nazarenes)**, nor against the temple** (he did not desecrate it)**, nor against Caesar** (he had not incited riots).

After hearing both sides, Festus realized Paul had not broken Roman law. As such, Paul should have been acquitted of all charges. But like Felix before him, Festus realized this action would infuriate the Jews—causing unrest throughout Judea. Finally bowing to pressure from the Jews, he asked Paul to go **to Jerusalem** to **be tried** again on the same **charges** (v. 9). Although Festus intended to try the case, indicated by the phrase **before me,** Paul realized he would never receive a fair trial in Jerusalem—if he ever made it to trial. Paul argued that as a Roman citizen, he had the right to be judged right where he was, at **Caesar's tribunal** (vv. 10-11). Realizing that Festus had already been unduly influenced by the Jews and was thus unable to make a fair decision, Paul, as a Roman citizen, possessed the right to have his case heard in Rome by the emperor. After conferring **with his council**, Festus granted Paul's appeal (v. 12). This decision abdicated Festus of responsibility, allowing him to maintain amicable relations with the Jews without incriminating an innocent man. Paul at last had the opportunity to go to Rome and share the gospel with the most powerful person in the Roman Empire.

25:13-22 While Paul waited to begin his journey to Rome, **King Agrippa and Bernice** came to **Caesarea** to get acquainted with the new governor **Festus** (v. 13). King Agrippa (also known as Herod Agrippa II and Marcus Julius Agrippa II) and Bernice were two of the four children of Herod Agrippa I and the grandchildren of Herod the Great (Mt 2:1). Although Agrippa II never ruled over the main Jewish territory of Judea, Samaria, and Galilee as had his father, some regarded him the "king of the Jews" because he possessed the authority to appoint and remove the high priests. Twice a widow, Bernice, along with her two sons Berniceanus and Hyrancus, lived with her brother whom she never married. Rumors continually circulated about an incestuous relationship between the two siblings. Years later Bernice became the mistress of Titus, the son of Emperor Vespasian. Titus wanted to marry her, but for him to marry a Jewess would have been socially unacceptable. When he himself became emperor in AD 79, he abandoned his relationship with her.

Festus realized that King Agrippa, as king of the Jews, would have great insight into Paul's case. Since Festus was sending Paul to Rome, he had to write a letter to the emperor, similar to the one Claudius Lysias wrote to Felix (23:25-30). Because the matters related to the case dealt primarily with Jewish law, Festus sought Agrippa's opinion on the matter.

Festus presented his version of the events (25:15-21) paralleling Paul's account in 25:1-12. Festus provided a fairly accurate summary—the **Jews** wanted Paul convicted of a crime. Festus insisted upon a trial, which revealed the religious nature of the issue. Festus suggested taking the trial **to Jerusalem**, and **Paul appealed** to Caesar (25:21). The new piece of information concerned the nature of the disagreement—not merely over the belief in resurrection but over the resurrection of Jesus—between Paul and the Jews. Festus revealed his bias on the issue, stating Jesus was **a dead man whom Paul claimed to be alive** (v. 19). He, as the Jews, did not believe in the resurrected Jesus.

After hearing about the case, Agrippa expressed his desire: **"I would like** (Gk. *eboulomēn*, "to be willing or disposed") **to hear the man myself."** The verb is in the imperfect tense, suggesting that Agrippa had been wanting to hear Paul for a long time. From his working relationship with the Jews, he was undoubtedly familiar with the claims of Christianity and with the notorious ministry of Paul. He looked forward to meeting this leader of "the Way" in person. Festus agreed to Agrippa's request and promised him he would hear from Paul the next day (v. 22).

25:23-27 Paul's meeting before Agrippa was characterized by **great pomp** since all the important people in Caesarea were invited to the event, including the five high-ranking **commanders** of the Roman military and the **prominent men of the city** (v. 23). In essence, Festus used this opportunity to honor King Agrippa.

Festus emphasized that the Jews—in Jerusalem as well as Caesarea—wanted

Paul dead. Paul had **appealed to the Emperor**; therefore, Festus needed to explain the charges against Paul in a letter; but since Paul was innocent, he had **nothing definite to write**. "Emperor" (Gk. *kuriō*, "lord or master") was a title especially desired by Nero; therefore, Festus obliged with this identification (v. 26). For Christians, only Jesus is Lord, which became one of the earliest Christian confessions, in diametric opposition to the slogan "Caesar is Lord" (1 Co 12:3). In his address before Agrippa, Paul unashamedly called Jesus "Lord" (26:15).

26:1-11 Paul **stretched out his hand,** the common gesture of a first-century orator (v. 1). Paul cherished every opportunity to share the gospel. Jesus predicted that the disciples would be brought before governors and kings to bear witness to the nations. He also told them not to worry about what they should speak because they would not be speaking—the Holy Spirit would speak through them (Mt 10:18-20). Paul had this assurance as he testified before Governor Festus and King Agrippa.

Bernice *Acts 25:13,23; 26:30*	
Her Birth	• Eldest daughter of Herod Agrippa I • Older sister of Drusilla
Her Family	• She first married Marcus who died. • She married her uncle, Herod of Chalcis, who also died. • She had two sons—Berniceanus and Hyrancus. • She married Ptolemy, king of Cicilia.
Her Shame	• Consort to her own brother, Agrippa II • Mistress to two Roman emperors, Vespasian and his son Titus • Corrupt, immoral woman

The hope of the promise made by God to the **fathers** is the resurrection, specifically the resurrection of Jesus (v. 6). The reference to the **12 tribes** is a way

of delineating all of Israel or the Jewish people. After questioning the faith of his listeners, Paul readily admitted that at one point he himself lacked faith in the resurrection of Jesus. He **locked up many of the saints in prison,** and he had **cast** his **vote** that they be killed (v.10). The indication that Paul cast his vote did not necessarily mean he had been a part of the Sanhedrin. He was probably too young for service at the time; however, he may have filled the role of prosecutor for the Sanhedrin, therefore voting for the execution of imprisoned Christians. In sharing about his life before he became a Christian, Paul portrayed himself as zealous for the Jewish faith, even to the point of persecuting Christians, whom he believed distorted the faith (v. 11). His perspective totally changed with his conversion to Christ.

26:12-23 This third account of Paul's conversion and commission in Acts (see also 9:1-19; 22:6-21) provides the least information, omitting the details of his temporary blindness and of his encounter with Ananias. The emphasis in this account is on his commissioning from Christ, which in the other two accounts was tied to Ananias' visit. Paul received his commission from the Lord while on the Damascus road and again humanly speaking from Ananias.

By persecuting Christians, Paul persecuted the Lord Himself. Only this account stated that Jesus spoke **in the Hebrew language** and included the phrase. **"It is hard for you to kick against the goads"** (26:14). A goad is a long stick with a sharp pointed end, which was used by farmers to prod animals, particularly oxen, and point them in the right direction. The animals did not like being prodded; therefore, they would kick at the goad. Eventually the animals learned the futility of kicking and submitted to the farmer's direction. This Hebrew idiom expressed the futility of struggling against one's direction in life. In persecuting Christians, Paul had been struggling

against his destiny to become one of the greatest proponents for the Christian faith.

Before Paul's primarily Gentile audience, he especially emphasized his mission to the Gentiles and the truth of the gospel (vv. 16-18). While Paul wanted to explain his calling and commission, he also wanted his listeners to know how to receive the forgiveness of sins.

Jesus' appearance to Paul on the Damascus road was purposeful, not an arbitrary interruption in Paul's journey. Unbelievers are blinded to spiritual truth by Satan and are in spiritual darkness (2 Co 4:4). This contrast between **darkness** and **light** occuring throughout Paul's writings can be traced to his first personal encounter with Jesus (Rm 2:19; 13:12; 1 Co 4:5; 2 Co 4:6; 6:14; Eph 5:8; 1 Th 5:5). The contrast between darkness and light metaphorically pictured two differing ways of life. Jesus commissioned Paul to help **the Gentiles** turn from their dark sinfulness to the light of Jesus Christ. Forgiveness of sins is found only through Christ. Although salvation is only by grace through faith (Eph 2:8-9), sanctification naturally follows salvation. To be sanctified means to be set apart for Christ, to live one's life for the glory and honor of God.

Paul did not need to mention his missionary journeys because those areas fell beyond the jurisdiction of both Agrippa and Festus. Paul explained to his audience that the ultimate goal of his ministry was for Gentiles to "repent and turn to God, and do works worthy of RE-PENTANCE" (Gk. *metanoein*, "undergo a change in frame of mind and feeling or change in principle and practice"). The idea is reform or a change of behavior (v. 20). Paul's use of TURN (Gk. *epistrephein*, "to turn around, bring back, return") reinforces the meaning. Paul indicated that those who genuinely **repent and turn to God** will live life accordingly.

26:24-29 Festus proved to be an example of someone blinded by Satan. He could not understand the resurrection of Jesus. In his mind, no sane person would believe that a dead man came back to life. Therefore, Festus concluded that Paul must be **mad** (v. 24). Paul was not insane but spoke words consistent with the Old Testament prophets (v. 25). Paul realized that he would have a better chance convincing Agrippa than Festus. The phrase **this was not done in a corner** indicated that what Paul spoke about was common knowledge throughout Palestine (v. 26). Being a Jew himself and as the king of the Jews, Agrippa would have been well acquainted with Paul's teaching. Paul personalized the matter, addressing King Agrippa directly. He knew that if Agrippa embraced the message of the prophets he could demonstrate how the life, death, and resurrection of Jesus were a fulfillment of the prophets (v. 27). As a Jew, Agrippa could not deny his belief in the prophets, but he was not ready to affirm the truth of the Christian faith. Paul readily admitted his desire that Agrippa as well as everyone else believe in Christ. He wanted all to become as he was, minus the **chains**, meaning he wanted everyone to know the love of God found in Christ (v. 29).

Since they deemed Paul innocent, he could have been released. Although it would not have been illegal for Festus to free Paul, he would have risked offending the emperor. For this reason Paul's appeal would still have to be heard in Rome.

Paul's journey to Rome (27:1–28:31)

27:1-12 The remainder of Acts focuses exclusively on Paul's journey to Rome and his ministry in Rome. Paul had long desired to share the gospel in Rome (19:21). He knew the day would come because the Lord had promised him (23:11). Paul finally had the opportunity to go to Rome, but as a prisoner, not as he envisioned.

Luke, who reemerged in this chapter, was probably one of Paul's most frequent visitors. He accompanied Paul on the journey to Rome, providing vivid details of the voyage across the Mediterranean to **Italy** (27:1). **Julius**, a Roman **centurion** of the **Imperial Regiment**, allowed Paul a considerable amount of freedom and even prevented others from taking Paul's life (vv. 3,43). Luke noted that the ship came from **Adramyttium**, a city on the northwest coast of Asia Minor. **Aristarchus**, one of the representatives from the churches, had traveled to Jerusalem with Paul and accompanied him on this journey (v. 2; 20:4). Although this text does not state that he accompanied Paul as a prisoner, in Colossians Paul described him as a fellow prisoner (Col 4:10). The first day's journey brought them approximately 70 miles north of Caesarea to **Sidon.** While there, Julius **allowed** Paul to spend time with **his friends**, likely fellow believers from Sidon (Ac 27:3).

From Sidon, they sailed northwest, skirting **the northern coast of Cyprus**. They chose their route of travel **because the winds were against** them (v. 4). Sailing this way provided additional protection from the harsh winds. **After sailing through the open sea off** the coast of **Cilicia and Pamphylia**, they **reached Myra in Lycia** (v. 5). To reach Myra, they had sailed approximately 15 days and 500 miles. Myra was located about 40 miles east of the Lycian city Parta, a docking point for Paul on his third missionary journey (21:1). In Myra, **the centurion** procured another ship for him and his prisoners to finish their journey to Rome (27:6). It was an **Alexandrian ship** that made frequent trips to deliver grain from Egypt to Rome. Before the journey ended, the group would have sailed on three different ships—one from Caesarea to Myra, another from Myra to Melita, and still another from Melita to Rome.

From Myra, they **slowly** sailed west **for many days**. With **difficulty**, they finally came **as far as Cnidus** but were unable to dock there due to the severe **wind** (v. 7). A westward voyage on the Mediterranean usually took much longer than would the same voyage east, due to the adverse winds. One commentator suggested that an eastward voyage taking 10 days could extend to 50 to 70 days when going westward.[9] The group traveled during the winter, which was the most difficult and dangerous time for sailing.

Since they could not dock in Cnidus, they continued sailing, eventually reaching the city of **Salmone** on the easternmost portion of the island **of Crete**. The captain of the ship chose to sail on the southern side of the island to protect them from the winds. Salmone, a name of Phoenician origin, described a refuge from exposure to the wind.

The Fast was probably a reference to the Day of Atonement (also known as *Yom Kippur*), occurring between late September and early October. Sailing after that time of year would have been particularly dangerous due to the unsettling weather patterns on the Mediterranean Sea (v. 9). Understanding the extreme risk of traveling at that time of year, **Paul gave his advice** to those in charge (v. 10). The captain dismissed Paul's suggestion due to the unsuitability of **the harbor**. Going with the vote of **the majority**, they continued sailing west, hoping **to reach Phoenix**, a port only 40 miles from **Fair Havens** (v. 12).

27:13-38 They remained in Fair Havens until the conditions seemed favorable. **They weighed anchor**, meaning they raised the anchor of the ship and set sail along the island **of Crete**, heading for the city of Phoenix (v. 13). **The northeaster** or "Euraquilo" was **fierce** (Gk. *tuphōnikos*, "like a whirlwind"). Literally a typhonic wind—a whirling, cyclonic wind of hurricane force, came and hit the ship.

The wind swiftly blew the ship south **of a little island called Cauda** (the modern-day Greek island of Gaudos), located approximately 23 miles southwest of Crete (v. 16). In an effort to protect the ship, the crew did several things (v. 17):

- The crew, and possibly the passengers (since Luke uses **we**), hoisted **the skiff**, a lifeboat normally towed behind the main vessel, out of the water. During bad weather it was customary to remove it from the water.

- They **used ropes and tackle and girded the ship.** This process, known as frapping, involved wrapping cables around the ship's hull and cinching them tight, which provided additional support for the ship and enabled a better withstanding of the pounding from both the waves and the wind.

- They lowered **the drift-anchor**. Unable to know how far the winds had pushed them, they feared they would **run aground on the Syrtis**, a series of sandbars off the North African coast notorious for causing shipwrecks. They were located approximately 400 miles south of Cauda. The captain realized the northeastern wind could drive the ship that far off course; therefore, they lowered the drift-anchor to impede their movement.

The fact that the **sun** and the **stars** did not appear made navigation impossible (v. 20). **An angel of the God** indicated to Paul that he must **stand before Caesar** and so his life would be spared, together with the lives of **all those** with him (vv. 23-24).

Luke's designation of **the Adriatic Sea** (or Sea of Adria) should not be confused with the modern-day Adriatic Sea between the coasts of Yugoslavia and western Italy. The ancient writers called the north-central portion of the Mediterranean Sea between Greece and Italy the "Sea of Adria." During the storm, the ship drifted approximately 475 miles from Crete to the small island Malta, south of Sicily (v. 27). **A sounding** was made by throwing a weighted, marked line into the water. When the lead hit the bottom, the sailors could tell the depth of the water from the water marks on the rope. Not wanting to risk running **aground** in a **rocky place**, they **dropped four anchors from the stern** (the rear of the ship) to secure their location, and they **prayed for daylight to come** so that they could see land (vv. 28-29).

Paul realized that the sailors needed to stay on board for the sake of the passengers since they were the ones who knew how to maneuver the ship. Paul brought this fact to the attention of **the centurion and the soldiers**, who prevented the sailors' escape by cutting **the ropes holding the skiff** (vv. 31-32). Without a lifeboat, they depended all the more on the Lord's deliverance.

For the second time Luke mentioned that they had been **going without food** (vv. 21,33), perhaps because of seasickness, the difficulty of preparing food in the storm, or as a means of rationing the food so that it would not run out. At this point it was necessary for them to eat so that they would have strength to survive what ensued. Using a familiar Jewish proverb, **"not a hair will be lost from the head of any of you,"** Paul reminded everyone of God's promise to deliver them (v. 34; 1 Sm 14:45; 2 Sm 14:11; 1 Kg 1:52; Lk 21:18). Breaking bread did

not refer to an observance of the Lord's Supper because a majority of those on board were not Christians. Instead, Paul demonstrated his faith to all present by giving **thanks to God** for His provision and protection (Ac 27:35).

27:39-44 The time had come to abandon the ship. Fearing the repercussions if the prisoners escaped, the soldiers intended **to kill** them (v. 42). But **the centurion** came to the rescue **because he wanted to save Paul** (v. 43). Evidently Paul had garnered his respect over the course of the journey. Perhaps the centurion had even come to believe in Jesus.

28:1-6 Malta is a small Mediterranean island (only 16 miles long and 9 miles wide), lying approximately 60 miles south of Sicily and 180 miles north of Libya (v. 1). Settled by the Phoenicians, the island came under Roman rule in 21 BC. Although the island had a large degree of autonomy, Rome ruled through a governor. The shipwreck occurred only three miles from the entrance of what is interestingly known today as St. Paul's Bay. **The local people** were of Phoenician descent. The **viper** (Gk. *echidna*, "snake") was obviously a poisonous reptile (v. 3). Since today Malta has no known poisonous snakes, some claim this detail to be Luke's embellishment. However, even the recorded reaction of the natives indicated the snake was poisonous. Additionally, just because no poisonous snakes exist there in this era does not mean that none existed 19 centuries ago. By **Justice** (Gk. *dikē*, "penalty, punishment") the locals were referring to the Greek goddess *Dike* (translated here as "Justice"), the daughter of Zeus, whom they believed watched over all human affairs and reported to Zeus all wrongdoings so the guilty could pay for their crimes. By being bitten by the snake, Paul had received his due in their thinking (v. 4). When Paul **suffered no harm**, they **changed their minds**,

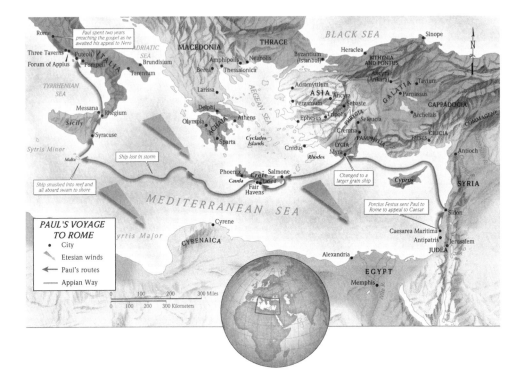

PAUL'S VOYAGE TO ROME
- City
- Etesian winds
- ← Paul's routes
- — Appian Way

deciding that **he was a god** instead of a murderer (v. 6). Paul had also been mistakenly called a god in Lystra (14:13).

28:7-10 Publius, a generous man, **welcomed** and **entertained** them **hospitably for three days** even though his father was **in bed suffering from fever and dysentery** (vv. 7-8). The text is not clear as to whether he welcomed the entire group of 276 (which would have been difficult) or just Paul and his personal companions. The healing of Publius's father was the only occasion in Acts when both **prayer** and the **laying** on of **hands** accompanied healing. Although Luke did not mention the spiritual reaction of the people, many probably came to believe in Jesus, since miracles in Acts often preceded faith (3:1-10; 5:14-16; 8:6-8). As a result of Paul's healing ministry on the island, **they heaped many honors** on them and provided them with **what** they **needed** for the remainder of their journey (28:10).

28:11-16 After spending **three months** on the island waiting for the bad sailing weather of winter to pass, they left on another **Alexandrian ship** headed for Rome. This ship bore the images of **the Twin Brothers as its figurehead** (v. 11). Ships often carried the insignia of Castor and Pollux, the twin gods who were the sons of Leda and Zeus in Greek mythology. People worshiped these two idols, represented by the constellation Gemini, throughout Egypt. Sailors believed them to be the protectors of the sea. From Malta, the ship sailed 90 miles north to **Syracuse**, an important harbor town on the east coast of Sicily (v. 12). After a brief stay of **three days**, they sailed north along the coast of Sicily 75 miles until they reached **Rhegium** (modern Reggio), a harbor town at the toe of Italy (v. 13). From there they sailed approximately 200 miles up the west coast of Italy to **Puteoli** (modern Pozzuoli), Italy's primary shipping port. Due to the favorable **south**

wind, the final leg of their sea journey took only two days. In Puteoli, they **found believers** with whom they stayed **for seven days** (vv. 13-14). Since the end of chapter 27, Julius and the Roman soldiers have completely disappeared from Luke's narrative of the journey, perhaps because Paul had earned their trust so much that they allowed him great freedom.

From Puteoli, they traveled the last 130 miles over land to **Rome** (v. 14), a city with over a million inhabitants and the dominating power of the world for two millennia (from the second century BC to the eighteenth century AD) as well as the capital of the Roman Empire with its population of 120,000,000 and land mass extending 3,000 miles east and west and 2,000 miles north and south.

Hearing about Paul's arrival, some of the believers from Rome came **as far as Forum of Appius** (approximately 40 miles from Rome) **and Three Taverns** (approximately 30 miles from Rome) to meet them (v. 15). They had long anticipated Paul's arrival because years ago Paul had written a letter to the church in Rome, indicating his desire to visit them (Rm 1:11,15; 15:23). While in Rome, the authorities **permitted** Paul **to stay by himself** in a rented house with a **soldier who guarded him** (Ac 28:16). Apparently, Paul was not deemed a flight risk; so with limited freedom he could minister fruitfully while under house arrest.

28:17-22 As on his previous missionary journeys, Paul sought to share the gospel with the Jews first even though they continually rejected it (v. 17; 9:20; 13:5, 14-41; 14:1; 17:1-4,17; 18:4; 19:8). Once the Jewish **leaders . . . gathered**, Paul explained his situation to them, making several key points:

- He had d**one nothing against** the Jewish **people** or **customs** (28:17).

- **The Romans** (namely Felix and Festus) decided he **had not committed a capital offense** (v. 18; 23:29; 25:25; 26:31-32). His **appeal to Caesar** was not because he had anything **against** his **nation** (28:19). Paul's Jewish listeners understood the hope of Israel to be the Messiah (v. 20). Paul did not immediately prove Jesus to be the prophesied Messiah—**the hope of Israel.** He saved this argument for a later time (v. 23).

The Jewish leaders had not heard about the charges against Paul previously. They had not **received any letters about** him **from Judea**, nor had any of the Jews **come** from Jerusalem and **reported or spoken anything evil** against him (v. 21). For this reason, they received Paul warmly and still desired **to hear** more about what he had to say. Nevertheless, they were **aware** of Christian teachings, and they realized those teachings had been rejected by Jews virtually **everywhere** (v. 22).

28:23-29 The phrase **kingdom of God** included not only the death and resurrection of Christ but also the eschatological significance of Christ's reign on earth. The phrase was used several times in Acts (1:3-6; 8:12; 14:22; 19:8; 20:25). Paul attempted to persuade them that Jesus was the Messiah, using the Old Testament Scriptures—**the Law of Moses and the Prophets** (v. 23). The leaders were divided over what Paul shared (v. 24). PERSUADED (Gk. *epeithonto*, "endeavor to convince") is in the imperfect tense, with the sense of "being persuaded," indicating that they were not yet fully convinced (v. 24).

The Jewish leaders finally agreed on something when Paul applied the words of Isaiah (Is 6:9-10) to his contemporaries. Like Israel in Isaiah's day, the Jews had deafened ears, spiritually blinded eyes, and calloused hearts (Ac 28:26-27). The news that the hope of Israel was also for **the Gentiles** angered the Roman Jews, just as it had angered the Jews in Judea. At this point **the Jews departed** because they were done listening to Paul, but they continued to **debate** the issue **among themselves** (vv. 28-29).

28:30-31 Luke concluded Acts with Paul's first Roman imprisonment. For **two whole years** Paul stayed **in his own rented house** with one soldier to guard him (vv. 16,30). While under house arrest, Paul remained active in the ministry (v. 31). During those two years he also wrote what are frequently called the Prison Epistles: Ephesians, Colossians, Philemon, and Philippians. Paul's imprisonment did not hinder the all-powerful truth of the gospel. Even in chains, Paul's prayer was that he would be bold in sharing the gospel (Eph 6:20).

Addendum: Paul's Life after Acts

According to church tradition, Paul was released from this imprisonment and carried on a ministry in the west—possibly in Spain. Later, Paul returned to Rome for a second, more harsh Roman imprisonment, during which he wrote the Pastoral Epistles—1 and 2 Timothy and Titus. This imprisonment concluded with his martyrdom as a result of Nero's persecution of Christians. Supposedly he was taken about a mile outside the city walls and beheaded around AD 65.

The apostles received power from on high as Christ promised (1:1-8). With the presence of the Holy Spirit, the apostles preached the gospel—the power of God for the salvation of all who believe (Rm 1:16). These few men, faithful to their witness, firm in their conviction, and persuasive in their presentation turned the world upside down for Christ. However, the book of Acts presents more than a historical account of great men and women. It presents the message of Jesus— the only name under heaven by which mankind must be saved (Ac 4:12) then and now. Thus, the commission given to the apostles remains the commission given to the church, and yet another generation filled with the Holy Spirit must proclaim the gospel to the entire world. Like Paul, all must be willing to suffer—even die for Jesus' name, willing to proclaim the gospel as Paul did—while in chains "with full boldness and without hindrance" (28:31).

Bibliography

Arnold, Clinton E., ed. *Zondervan Illustrated Bible Backgrounds Commentary,* vol. 2. Grand Rapids: Zondervan, 2002.

Brisco, Thomas V. *Holman Bible Atlas.* Nashville: Broadman and Holman, 1998.

*Bruce, F. F. *The New International Commentary on the New Testament: The Book of Acts.* Grand Rapids: Eerdmans, 1988.

Dockery, David S., ed. *Holman Concise Bible Commentary.* Nashville: Broadman and Holman, 1998).

_____. *Holman Bible Handbook.* Nashville: Holman Bible Publishers, 1992.

Halley, Henry H. *Halley's Bible Handbook.* Grand Rapids: Zondervan, 1965.

Holman Concise Bible Dictionary. Nashville: Broadman and Holman, 2001.

*Kaiser, Walter C., Jr., Peter H. Davids, F. F. Bruce, and Manfred T. Brauch. *Hard Sayings of the Bible*. Downers Grove, IL: InterVarsity Press, 1996.

*Kistemaker, Simon J. *New Testament Commentary: Exposition of the Acts of the Apostles*. Grand Rapids: Baker, 1990.

Larkin, William J., Jr. *The IVP New Testament Commentary Series: Acts*. Downers Grove, IL: InterVarsity Press, 1995.

Lea, Thomas D. *The New Testament: Its Background and Message*. Nashville: Broadman and Holman, 1996.

MacArthur, John. *The MacArthur New Testament Commentary: Acts 1-12*. Chicago: Moody Press, 1994.

_____. *The MacArthur New Testament Commentary: Acts 13-28*. Chicago: Moody Press, 1996.

*Marshall, I. Howard. *The Tyndale New Testament Commentaries: Acts*. Grand Rapids: Eerdmans, 2002.

*Nicoll, W. Robertson, ed. *The Expositor's Greek Testament,* vol. 2. Peabody, Mass.: Hendrickson, 2002.

Polhill, John B. *The New American Commentary: Acts*. Nashville: Broadman and Holman, 2001.

Stott, John R. *The Message of Acts: The Spirit, the Church and the World*. Downers Grove, IL: InterVarsity Press, 1900.

Van Braght, Thieleman J. *Martyrs Mirror: The Story of Seventeen Centuries of Christian Martyrdom from the Time of Christ to AD 1660*. Scottdale, PA: Herald Press, 2002.

Walvoord, John F., and Roy B. Zuck. *The Bible Knowledge Commentary: New Testament Edition*. USA: Victor, 1983.

*For advanced study

Notes

1 There appears to be some ambiguity as to when Pentecost truly occurred. Some commentators state that Pentecost occurred 50 days after the Passover, which would mean it was 50 days after the crucifixion. Others state that Pentecost occurred 50 days after the resurrection. Leviticus 23:4-16 delineates the Hebrew dating related to the sacred days surrounding Passover and Pentecost. According to Leviticus 23:5, the Passover occurred the fourteenth day of the first month (Nisan). Since the Jews followed a lunar calendar, this date varies according to modern calendars, falling between March and April of each year. The day after Passover, Nissan 15, marked the beginning of the week-long Festival of Unleavened Bread (Lv 23:6). The date of the Feast of Weeks or Pentecost was determined by counting from this time period "50 days until the day after the seventh Sabbath." Thus, the day of Pentecost was the fiftieth day from the first Sunday after Passover (see F. F. Bruce, *The Book of Acts,* The New International Commentary on the New Testament [Grand Rapids: Eerdmans, 1988], 49). Since Jesus was crucified on Passover and the day after was the Sabbath, Passover occurred that year on Friday, putting the Festival of Unleavened Bread on Saturday, which was the Jewish Sabbath. Counting 50 days from there would put the Pentecost in Acts 2 on a Sunday, 51 days after the crucifixion and 49 days after the resurrection.

2 Thieleman J. Van Braght, *Martyrs Mirror: The Story of Seventeen Centuries of Christian Martyrdom from the Time of Christ to AD 1660* (Scottdale, PA: Herald Press, 2002), 99.

3 Ibid., 110.

4 For additional information about the dating of Passover, see footnote 1.

5 Josephus, *The War of the Jews: On the History of the Destruction of Jerusalem*, Book I, Chapter XXXIII.

[6] For more information about this debate, see Simon J. Kistemaker, *New Testament Commentary: Exposition of the Acts of the Apostles* (Grand Rapids: Baker Book House, 1990), 533–536; Bruce, 282–285; and I. Howard Marshall, *Acts,* The Tyndale New Testament Commentaries (Grand Rapids: Eerdmans, 2002), 242–247.

[7] The first letter (1 Co 5:9) and third letter (2 Co 2:3-4) are lost. The second letter is 1 Corinthians and the fourth letter is 2 Corinthians. In addition to the letters, Paul made three visits to Corinth. The first visit he stayed for a year and a half on his second missionary journey. The second visit, which is not mentioned in Acts, was a brief one most likely during his three-year stay in Ephesus. He stayed for three months during the third visit to Corinth at the conclusion of his third missionary journey.

[8] Adapted from the *Woman's Study Bible*, ed. by Dorothy Kelley Patterson and Rhonda Harrington Kelley (Nashville: Thomas Nelson, 1995), 1845.

[9] Clinton E. Arnold, ed. *Zondervan Illustrated Bible Backgrounds Commentary,* vol. 2 (Grand Rapids: Zondervan, 2002), 471.

ROMANS

Introduction

Romans stands as one of the clearest statements of the gospel of Jesus Christ. As the longest and most formal of Paul's New Testament letters, Romans represents his systematic presentation of the theology of God's grace. This epistle answers the question, How can a person have a right relationship with God? Paul analyzed the spiritual condition of humanity and concluded that all have sinned and stand guilty before God. Against this indictment, he presented the good news of God's deliverance through Jesus Christ. All individuals may be saved through faith in Him and brought into a right relationship with God. In their union with Christ, believers enjoy victory over sin, the law as the way of righteousness, and divine forgiveness for their sins. Paul discussed the problem of reconciling God's promises to Israel with her rejection of the gospel, and he offered hope for his own nation. Finally, the apostle provided clear, practical guidelines on how believers should conduct their new lives in Christ and called them to make such a commitment.

The teachings in Romans have powerfully impacted people across the ages. They have prompted the conversion of humble women and men, as well as giants in the history of Christianity, such as Augustine, Martin Luther, and John Wesley.

Title

In its shortest form, the Greek title of this epistle is *pros Romaious*, "to the Romans." The title simply reflects the designated audience of this letter from Paul "To all who are in Rome, loved by God, called as saints" (1:7).

Setting

With the close of his third missionary journey, Paul had completed his mission to the East. He turned his eyes to the West and to Spain in particular. His westward focus would necessitate changing his missionary base from Antioch to Rome itself. Consequently, Paul wrote Romans not only to introduce himself and prepare the church for his visit but also to secure the prayers and support of the Roman believers for his Spanish mission. To enlist this backing the apostle systematically presented his message and theological position. He explained his doctrine to the church and applied it to practical issues in the daily lives of Christians. Unlike Paul's other letters, Romans does not refer to a local situation of the church but gives attention to timeless teachings.

Genre

The book of Romans primarily fits the genre of the personal letter. Paul's letter to the Romans follows the basic pattern of ancient Greco-Roman correspondence:

(1) an opening that identifies the writer and the recipients and then extends a greeting; (2) the body of the letter; and (3) the conclusion. The introduction and conclusion contain the more stylized and formulaic elements common to other ancient letters, but in each of his letters Paul modified the standard forms to suit his purpose of proclaiming the gospel. In Romans, Paul included a more extensive description of himself and of his addressees than would be typical for the opening of a letter (1:1-7). He also adapted the traditional Hellenistic greeting (Gk. *Charein*; see Ac 15:23 and Jms 1:1) to "Grace" (Gk. *Charis*), and added the traditional Jewish greeting of "peace" (Hb. *Shalom*, 1:3). The "Thanksgiving" element (1:4-7) was another distinctive feature of Paul's letters. The conclusion of a letter typically included a final wish or words of encouragement (15:14-32), a wish for peace or health (15:33), greetings (16:3-16), and sometimes a postscript. The pattern varied in Paul's letters, but the blessing or grace-benediction was always the final formal element of the closing (16:20), though not necessarily the final words of the entire document.

Despite the parallels between secular letter forms and the style of Paul's epistles, the letter to the Romans, like the other Pauline letters, reflects the particular situation of his audience. For example, the unusual length of Paul's introduction of himself reflects the need to emphasize his apostleship and common commitment to the gospel for believers, of both Jewish and Gentile origin, who had never met him. Also, although Romans is a personal letter, its central content or body is that of a systematic theological exposition of the gospel. Paul intertwined exposition and admonishment to argue for the power of the gospel to bring both spiritual salvation and ethical transformation.

Author

The first verse of Romans identifies Paul as the author. With almost no exception the church from postapostolic times until the present has accepted Pauline authorship. The style and content of the letter are so unmistakably Pauline that none have seriously challenged his authorship.

Date

Paul probably wrote Romans in early AD 57 on his third missionary journey during his three-month stay in Greece. He had already completed an extended ministry in Ephesus and then planned to travel to Jerusalem. His commendation of Phoebe of Cenchreae, the seaport of Corinth, and the mention of Gaius as his host suggest the apostle wrote from Corinth.

Recipients

Paul wrote to the church at Rome. These believers probably came to faith in Christ through the witness of merchants and other travelers who came to the capital of the Roman Empire and its largest city. Perhaps some of those who became Christians on the day of Pentecost returned home to Rome and shared the gospel of Jesus Christ. Although the church probably started from Jewish converts and still had a strong Jewish minority, the church was predominantly Gentile when it received Paul's letter.

Major Themes

Salvation—The main theme of Romans is salvation. Paul presented salvation in terms of the righteousness of God—the right standing God gives to believers—and faith. All people are sinners. They have no righteousness of their own to enable them to stand before a righteous God. As sinners, they need forgiveness. Though people are undeserving, God in His kindness reached out in love to provide the way of salvation through the cross of His Son. Jesus Christ's death paid the penalty for sin and enabled sinners to be forgiven and reconciled to God. Believers are declared righteous (or justified) by means of their faith in Jesus Christ. For Paul salvation represents the complete work of God alone. People can do nothing to gain right standing with Him. The theme of salvation has an interrelationship with the next two themes.

Righteousness of God—Paul used the phrase "righteousness of God" eight times and the term "righteousness" 33 times in Romans, showing the importance he attached to these concepts. The "righteousness of God" could mean an attribute of God, as in the righteousness that He displays (Rm 3:5,25), or it could signify the righteousness that comes from God, namely, the right standing that God gives sinners (Rm 3:21-22; 10:3). The death of Christ shows most clearly the righteousness of God. His death gives righteousness to those who believe. When God saves, He does so in a right way, by allowing His Son to pay the penalty of sin for sinners. The term "righteous" represents a legal term. Those whom God declares righteous have been pronounced "innocent." God has acquitted them through the saving work of Jesus on the cross. The righteousness of God means that God will always do what is right.

Justification—"Justification," a legal term meaning "to acquit or to declare not guilty," is God's action in which He declares that a sinner is righteous. Being righteous means having a right relationship with God. Justification is God's gracious gift. The death of Jesus forms the basis for the justification of believers. The means of this act of acquittal is the individual's faith in Jesus Christ. Good works do not achieve justification. God actually credits Christ's righteousness to sinners who believe and receive His gift. Justification by the work of Jesus on the cross means that God deals with sin and its penalty. God justifies in a way that is right, for God is righteous.

Law—Although Paul used "law" in a variety of ways in Romans, he primarily used the word in reference to the Mosaic law. He saw the law as very important and described it as one of Israel's great privileges. The law is meant for life (7:10). It is holy (7:12), spiritual (7:14), good (7:16), a source of instruction (2:18) and truth (2:20). God's law (7:22) is the standard by which He will judge people. Obedience to the law, though important, does not produce salvation. The law does not save, but it does give knowledge of sin and shows sinners that they need saving. Jesus Christ and His death show that the law is not the way of salvation. Justification is apart from the law. Believers are not under law but grace. They have died to the law through Jesus Christ. The Holy Spirit frees believers from the law's demands and fear of judgment.

Sin—Paul presented sin as serious and universal. All people are sinners. Their basic problem is sin. They refuse to do God's will and fail to do all that God wants. Sin enslaves people. As a power, it works for harm and evil. It kills people. Sin originated in Adam's fall. For Paul, the most significant aspect of sin is that Christ has overcome sin and its consequences. He died for sin. Consequently, sin no longer reigns. The cross reveals sin in all its evil and power because the death of God's Son was required to defeat sin. Believers are dead to sin because they are in Christ. They still face temptations, however, and have to defeat sin daily. The Holy Spirit helps believers to overcome sin and its temptations. Christ assures them of the final victory.

God's Sovereignty—God has complete power and authority over all creation as the potter has over the clay. He exercises His will absolutely without any help from humanity. God's sovereignty undergirds His work of salvation. In His sovereignty He designed a plan to achieve His saving purposes in the world. Men and women may not be able to comprehend how and why God acts because God has the freedom to do as He chooses to carry out His purposes. He always acts out of His love, mercy, and righteousness. He deals with all people fairly and desires all to be saved. He can save anyone He wills. In His sovereign will God elected Israel to be His special, chosen people. He does not, however, limit His election exclusively to the Jews. His sovereign purposes also include Gentiles. Divine sovereignty does not exclude human responsibility.

Holy Spirit—Christians have new life in Christ. This life is produced in them by the Holy Spirit. The process of being made holy and becoming more conformed to Christ is called "sanctification." God uses the enabling power and presence of the Holy Spirit in the lives of Christians to carry out this process. The ministry of the Spirit brings freedom from condemnation for believers. The Holy Spirit delivers them from sin and death. The Spirit establishes believers as children of God and provides the hope of glorification. The Spirit also intercedes for believers in their struggles to pray

Pronunciation Guide

Abba	*AB buh, AH buh*	Lucius	*LYOO shuhs*
Achaia	*uh KAY yuh*	Macedonia	*mass uh DOH nih uh*
Adriatic	*ay drih A (a) tik*	Narcissus	*nahr SISS uhs*
Ampliatus	*am plih AY tuhs*	Nereus	*NEE roos*
Andronicus	*an DRAHN ih kuhs*	Patrobas	*PAT roh buhs*
Antioch	*AN tih ahk*	Persis	*PUHR sis*
Apelles	*uh PEL eez*	Philologus	*fih LAHL oh guhs*
Aristobulus	*uh riss toh BYOO luhs*	Phlegon	*FLEE gahn*
Asyncritus	*uh SIN krih tuhs*	Phoebe	*FEE bih*
Cenchreae	*SEN kree uh, kihn KREE uh*	Propitiation	*pro pih shih AY shun*
		Sabaoth	*SAB ay ahth*
Epaenetus	*ih PEE neh tuhs*	Sosipater	*soh SIP uh tuhr*
Ephesus	*EF uh suhs*	Stachys	*STAY kiss*
Hermas	*HUHR muhs*	Tertius	*TUHR shih uhs, TUHR shuhss*
Hermes	*HUHR meez*		
Herodion	*hih ROH dih uhn*	Tryphaena	*trigh FEE nuh*
Illyricum	*ih LIHR ih kuhm*	Tryphosa	*trigh FOH suh*
Junia	*JOO nih uh*	Urbanus	*uhr BAY nuhs*

Outline

I. INTRODUCTION: PAUL INTRODUCED HIMSELF, HIS GOSPEL, AND HIS INTEREST IN THE ROMAN CHURCH (1:1-15).
   A. Paul Addressed the Church at Rome (1:1-7).
   B. Paul Explained His Interest in the Church at Rome (1:8-15).

II. PAUL PRESENTED THE THEME OF THE EPISTLE: SALVATION IS BY FAITH IN THE GOSPEL OF JESUS CHRIST (1:16-17).

III. ALL PEOPLE NEED SALVATION FROM GOD'S WRATH AGAINST SIN (1:18–3:20).
   A. God's Wrath Condemns the Pagan Gentiles (1:18-32).
   B. God's Wrath Condemns the Jews (2:1–3:9).
   C. God's Wrath Condemns All People (3:9-20).

IV. GOD'S RIGHTEOUSNESS PROVIDES JUSTIFICATION (3:21–5:21).
   A. God Provides Justification through the Work of Christ (3:21-31).
   B. Abraham's Example Confirms Justification by Faith (4:1-25).
   C. Justification Results in Benefits for Believers (5:1-11).
   D. Justification Delivers from Death and Gives Life (5:12-21).

V. JUSTIFICATION PRODUCES VICTORIOUS NEW LIFE FOR BELIEVERS (6:1–8:39).
   A. Believers Have Victory over Sin (6:1-23).
   B. Believers Have Victory over the Law as the Way of Righteousness (7:1-25).
   C. Believers Have Victory over Condemnation (8:1-39).

VI. THE PROBLEM OF ISRAEL'S UNBELIEF VINDICATES GOD'S RIGHTEOUSNESS (9:1–11:36).
   A. Paul Grieved over Israel's Rejection of Christ (9:1-5).
   B. God Displays His Sovereignty in Dealing with Israel (9:6-29).
   C. Israel Has Responsibility for Her Rejection of Christ (9:30–10:21).
   D. God Will Fulfill His Purposes for Israel (11:1-36).

VII. PAUL OFFERED PRACTICAL INSTRUCTIONS FOR CHRISTIAN LIVING (12:1–15:13).
   A. Believers Should Dedicate Themselves to God (12:1-2).
   B. Believers Should Exercise Their Spiritual Gifts in Humility (12:3-8).
   C. Believers Should Cultivate Christian Virtues (12:9-21).
   D. Believers Should Submit to Civil Authority (13:1-7).
   E. Believers Should Remember the Supremacy of Love (13:8-10).
   F. Believers Should Recognize the Urgency of Christian Living (13:11-14).
   G. Believers Should Seek to Build Up One Another (14:1–15:13).

VIII. PAUL CONCLUDED HIS LETTER TO THE ROMANS (15:14–16:27).
   A. Paul Gave His Reasons for Writing (15:14-33).
   B. Paul Commended Phoebe (16:1-2).
   C. Paul Greeted Friends in Rome (16:3-16).
   D. Paul Warned against False Teachers (16:17-20).
   E. Paul's Associates Greeted the Romans (16:21-24).
   F. Paul Offered Glory to God (16:25-27).

Exposition of the Text

INTRODUCTION: PAUL INTRODUCED HIMSELF, HIS GOSPEL, AND HIS INTEREST IN THE ROMAN CHURCH (1:1-15)

Paul Addressed the Church at Rome (1:1-7)

1:1 Paul presented his qualifications. He followed the usual letter writing form of his day by identifying himself and his readers and then greeting them. Romans contains the longest, most formal of his letter introductions because he was writing to a church he had not yet visited and desired to make clear the content of his teaching.

Paul described himself as **a slave of Christ Jesus**, affirming his complete loyalty to the Lord and his willingness to serve Him in obedient submission. God had **called** him to be **an apostle**, one commissioned and sent with authority. Paul did not choose this task. God chose him. God also set him apart with His gospel, to preach and live the **good news**. This good news has its source in God Himself.

1:2-6 Paul described the gospel. He did not present the gospel as if it were a new teaching. Rather, the gospel represented the fulfillment of God's unchanging plan and purpose as recorded **in the Holy Scriptures** through the promises given to the **prophets** years ago. The gospel focuses on God's **Son**, the Lord **Jesus Christ**. As to His human nature, Jesus **was a descendant of** King **David**. He was the promised Messiah. As to His divine nature, His **resurrection from the dead** declared Him to be **the powerful Son of God** and showed the power of the Holy **Spirit**. Paul described the gospel as God's plan of redemption for all **the nations** (or Gentiles). Christ Himself had given him the

gift (grace) of service as an apostle to tell Gentiles everywhere the good news so that they would believe in Jesus Christ and follow Him in **obedience**. Paul included the Roman Christians among the Gentiles called by God to belong to Christ Jesus.

1:7 Paul greeted the Romans. Since Paul greeted 28 people individually (most of whom he called by name) as well as others in selected households generally (16:1-16), the congregation in Rome must have been numerically strong. He described all the Roman Christians as **loved by God** and **called as saints**. God had set them apart for Himself to be His dedicated people. Paul greeted these believers with the spiritual blessings of unmerited favor and **peace from God** the **Father and the Lord Jesus Christ**.

Paul Explained His Interest in the Church at Rome (1:8-15)

1:8 Paul offered gratitude for the Romans. The Roman church had existed for some time in the political power center of the empire and evidently was already becoming well known. Paul thanked God through Jesus Christ for the Roman believers and the fact that their **faith** in Christ was **being reported** throughout the Greco-Roman **world**.

1:9-15 Paul shared his desire to visit the Romans doubtless not only because of the city's legendary reputation as the seat of government but also because of the reports coming about the faithful congregation of believers found there. By calling God as his witness Paul affirmed the sincerity of his claim that he prayed repeatedly for the Roman Christians. Perhaps because he had not personally visited Rome, the apostle felt the need to make this kind of solemn oath. He also noted that he served God with all his heart in living out and pro-claiming the gospel of His Son.

Paul desired to come to Rome and made that request of God. Yet, he wanted to come at the time and in the way of God's choosing, not according to his own plan. The apostle longed to visit the Romans, not for selfish reasons, but to **impart** a **spiritual** blessing to them so that they might be strengthened in the faith. He did not want the Romans to think he was boasting, so Paul added that they would mutually encourage one another by each other's faith.

The apostle wanted the Romans to know that he had tried to visit them many times, but circumstances beyond his control had prevented him. He wanted to reap a harvest of new converts to the Christian faith in Rome as he had among **Gentiles** in other areas. Since God had appointed Paul as apostle to the Gentiles, he felt an obligation to preach the gospel to all Gentiles, including those at Rome. Paul referred to **Greeks and barbarians** (v. 14). The Greeks, who spoke the Greek language, were the culturally elite in the Hellenistic world; the barbarians were those not yet tutored in the Hellenistic culture. Together they represented all Gentiles, and Paul's burden was to share the gospel with all. He felt this debt both to the cultured and the uncultured, **the wise and the foolish**. For his part he was ready **to preach the good news** in the capital of the empire.

PAUL PRESENTED THE THEME OF THE EPISTLE: SALVATION IS BY FAITH IN THE GOSPEL OF JESUS CHRIST (1:16-17)

1:16-17 Paul now presented the theme of the epistle: Salvation is by faith in **the gospel** of Jesus Christ. The GOSPEL (Gk. *euangelion* links *eu*, meaning "good" with *angelia*, meaning "mes-sage") is a "good message" and is the heart of salvation.

The apostle was ready to preach in Rome because he was **not ashamed of the gospel** of Christ. Many would have contempt for a crucified carpenter and the foolishness of the cross. Paul, however, gloried in the gospel even though his commitment to it had brought him suffer-ing and grief. He had no shame because the gospel is God's mighty, saving **power** to lift people up and change their lives. The redeeming power of the gospel results in deliverance from sin and the wrath of God toward it. It restores whole-ness to all that sin has destroyed.

Salvation has a universal scope. It is for **everyone, to the Jew first** and then **to the Greek** or Gentile, the totality of human-ity. At the same time, however, this salva-tion has a restriction. It belongs to those who believe, to those who trust in Jesus Christ and commit their lives to Him. The power of the gospel makes it possible for people to believe.

The gospel reveals the **righteousness** of God. People cannot know this by their own reasoning. God has to make it known to them. The terms "righteousness" and "righteousness of God" are central con-cepts in Romans. Righteousness is an attribute of God. It is also an activity of God. God acts decisively for the salvation of people and does so in a right way. He declares people righteous, giving them right standing before Him. Righteousness is also a quality of life God expects from believers, those who enjoy the status of righteousness.

Paul emphasized the centrality of faith. Righteousness begins with faith and ends with faith. People must recognize their complete insufficiency and rely on the sufficiency of God. The apostle supported his argument with a quote from Habakkuk 2:4. The one who is made **righteous by faith** shall **live**.

ALL PEOPLE NEED SALVATION FROM GOD'S WRATH AGAINST SIN (1:18–3:20)

God's Wrath Condemns the Pagan Gentiles (1:18-32)

Before explaining the gospel, Paul showed why God needs to put people right with Himself: All people are sinners. They have no righteousness of their own to enable them to stand before a righteous God.

1:18-25 The Gentiles rejected the knowledge of God and practiced idolatry. Just as righteousness is being revealed, so also is **God's wrath** continually being **revealed**. God's wrath is His personal, inflexible opposition to all sin, every evil. It is not emotional, irrational, or uncontrolled. It opposes idolatry, sinful rebellion against God, immorality, and sinful actions toward others. Unrighteous men and women by their wicked lives hinder and stifle the general **truth** about God, which is available to everyone.

God's wrath upon the Gentiles is justified because they failed to live up to the knowledge of God they possessed. God's WRATH (Gk. *orgē*), unlike most human anger, is not an uncontrolled explosive eruption but a consistent and holy response to that which is contrary to His will and nature. His wrath is directed toward offenses against Himself and others. Paul described God as giving sinful man over to the evil desires of his human heart (vv. 24,26,28). God's judgment is certain. However, God's pronouncement of judgment is accompanied by a note of sorrow. He is always consistent and just. Wrath is as much a part of God's character as is love. God's wrath is directed against evil and includes not only displeasure with present evil but also the ultimate defeat of evil (Mt 8:12). Men and women experience God's wrath only when they become part of evil and immorality. If God did not exercise wrath against evil, He would be unjust and even immoral. God takes the initiative and reveals enough of Himself so that those who sin and reject Him are guilty. The Gentiles sinned against the light they had, not against the light they had never received. They had received enough to know what is right. The created universe itself offers a natural revelation of the God who created it. What He has made and what people see lead them to understand **His invisible attributes—His eternal power and divine nature**. God has given people this revelation in nature, but many have chosen to ignore or reject it. They are **without excuse** (v. 20). The Gentiles **knew God**, but they deliberately rejected Him. They did not give Him the worship and gratitude He deserves.

The Gentile rejection of God led to their degradation. **Their thinking became** senseless, and their whole inner being became **darkened**. Those who rejected God claimed **to be wise**. In reality, they became fools. Instead of worshiping the One who is worthy of worship, they gave up **the glory of** the incorruptible **God**. They chose idolatry, worshiping the image of corruptible creatures—humans and animals—**instead of the Creator**.

Paul stated the consequences of the pagan world's refusal to worship God. Three times he affirmed that God gave them over. God allowed them to do what they wanted to do. He **delivered them over** (v. 24) to the consequences of their sin. Immersion in their own sin became their punishment. Their sinful desires led to sexual impurity. (Paul was probably referring to the practice of ritual prostitution.) This sexual impurity led in turn to the degrading of their bodies.

God abandoned these pagan Gentiles because of their idolatry. They exchanged the truth known about God for the lie of idolatry. In choosing the lie, Gentiles worshiped and served created things instead of the Creator. Although sin distorts, it does not remove the possibility of learning about Him in His creation (1:20). The mention of God the Creator led Paul to praise Him. Even though unacknowledged by many of His creatures, God's glory remains forever.

1:26-32 The Gentiles rebelled against God and practiced immorality. Paul gave in disgusting detail a long list of pagan vices, focusing on homosexuality in particular. The punishment for idolatry was being delivered over to shameful lusts, to impurity rising from unnatural passions or sexual perversion. Both **males** and **females exchanged natural sexual** relations for unnatural ones. These sinners **received** the due **penalty for their perversion** in themselves. They had darkened hearts; they understood God's truth but insisted on going their own way (1:24-25; Pr 3:7; 12:15; 14:12; 16:25).

Homosexuality is identified as the ultimate distortion of the creation order. This perverse human behavior is antithetical to the Creator's design biologically (for continuing the generations) as well as emotionally and psychologically (for the unique intimacy God planned between the man and woman). Paul evaluated homosexuality and sodomy by these criteria:

- sexual impurity (v. 24)
- degraded (vv. 24,26)
- lie (v. 25)
- unnatural (v. 26)
- lust (v. 27)
- shameless (v. 27)
- perversion (v. 27)

Other passages in Scripture address homosexuality (Lv 18:22; 20:13; 1 Co 6:9).

The sinners Paul was describing deliberately refused to have **God in their knowledge**. They preferred to know other things instead. Therefore, God gave them over to the consequences of their actions, to a depraved mind. They became incapable of making correct moral judgments. They continually did what is morally wrong and unacceptable. God, because of His respect for human freedom, does not force His way on anyone; but when people choose not to honor Him, He then gives them over to the results of their choices. In that sense, those who rejected God gave themselves over to all kinds of evil.

These unrighteous people knew enough of what God has revealed to know what is right and what is wrong. They knew that women and men who act as they did deserve death. Yet, they still practiced these evil acts and even applauded others who practiced such sins, encouraging vice in them. Paul's description of those who rejected God and rebelled against Him in the first century also characterizes people today who follow that same pattern.

God's Wrath Condemns the Jews (2:1–3:9)

Paul established the guilt of the Gentiles and their need of the gospel's righteousness. Now he turned to the Jews who had also failed to achieve a righteousness acceptable to God.

2:1-4 The Jews judged others hypocritically. Paul addressed an imaginary opponent who might have thought he was justified in condemning Gentile wickedness. Although his words are general enough to apply to Gentiles or Jews, the apostle apparently addressed his arguments toward the Jews. With their high moral standards, they would have thought themselves superior to the Gentiles and would have criticized them. Yet, those who pass judgment on others condemn themselves, for they are also guilty of sin.

Paul challenged Jewish complacency. God judges justly and fairly. No one will have special privileges. God judges on the basis of deeds done, not on status or nationality. Unbelieving Jews evidently felt exempt from divine judgment because of their descent from Abraham. The apostle insisted that they would not **escape God's judgment**. They were as guilty as the ones they judged. Those who think they will escape His judgment despise **God's kindness**. God does not punish sinners immediately. He directs His goodness and kindness toward bringing people to repentance, a change of mind demonstrated in turning away from sin and to a new life in Jesus Christ.

> $\mathcal{G}$od uses the law as the means or instrument of condemnation. It is not the guarantee of salvation, as many Jews believed.

2:5-11 Instead of repenting, the Jews behaved stubbornly and had **unrepentant hearts**. They refused to forsake sin and follow God's way. Therefore, they, too, would come under God's judgment. Like the Gentiles, they were **storing up** for themselves the **wrath** of God! On the day of judgment God's definite opposition to evil will reach its consummation. Also on that day, His **righteous judgment** (v. 5) will be revealed. Paul quoted Psalm 62:12 to summarize what judgment means. God will pay what is due personally to all individuals according to what they have done. Judgment is universal. Although salvation is by grace, judgment will be on the basis of works. Outward deeds express what one believes in the heart, giving evidence of faith or unbelief.

Judgment will result in one of two different rewards for each person: **eternal life** (v. 7) or **wrath and indignation** (v. 8). Those who put their trust in God,

not their own achievements, will receive that special quality of life lived in the presence of God. They set their minds on heavenly priorities—**glory, honor, and immortality** (v. 7), qualities that come from a close walk with God. In contrast, those motivated by self-centeredness reject the truth and obey unrighteousness. Their reward will be wrath and anger. Severe trouble comes to every human being who does evil. This punishment is universal, **first to the Jew, and also to the Greek**. Everyone who does good receives the blessings of glory, honor, and peace. God judges impartially. He shows **no favoritism** (v. 11) to any individual or nation.

2:12-16 God will judge all people. Paul made his first mention of the law in Romans 2:12. It does not matter whether or not everyone has received the law. All stand under God's condemnation. The Gentiles will perish not because they do not have the law but because they sin. All are judged according to the light they have. All suffer the consequences of sin whether or not they know the law. Since the Jews have the law and know what God expects of them, they will be judged by the law. God uses the law as the means or instrument of condemnation. It is not the guarantee of salvation, as many Jews believed.

The Jews could not plead their privileged position of having the law and hearing the law, which would not make them righteous. God justifies or declares **righteous** those who are **doers of the law** (v. 13). "Righteous" is a legal term equal to acquittal. The word is used when the accused is declared "not guilty." Theologically, it means the state of being right with God, of being acquitted when tried by Him. Paul was not saying people could be saved by obeying the law (v. 13).

Paul contended that the Gentiles have three witnesses to guide them.

- What the law required is written on Gentile *hearts*. They have a deep conviction of the rightness of some things. Their good deeds show that something within them points to what is right.

- Their *consciences* bear witness to them of their past actions, evaluating and passing judgment on deeds already committed.

- Their conflicting *thoughts* sometimes accuse them and other times defend them.

Gentiles have what they need to guide them on the right path. They know enough to understand what they ought to do. They have no excuse when they do wrong.

God will judge the secrets of people on the day of judgment. Judgment will be thorough and penetrating. Inward motives as well as overt acts will be judged. The gospel, however, includes the prospect of judgment mitigated through the mediation of Jesus Christ.

2:17-24 The Jews confused privilege and responsibility by failing to keep the law. To make his argument more vivid, Paul again addressed an imaginary opponent, a Jew. He noted by outlining the elements of Jewish pride how the Jew had failed to keep the law. The **Jew rest**[ed] **in the law** as the basis of all his hopes. He **boast**[ed] **in God**. He was proud of the fact that he knew God. He thought nobody else knew Him. By having the law, the Jew believed that he knew God's will and could **approve the things** that are excellent. The Jew was so certain of his superiority that he saw himself as **a guide to the blind** and **a light to those in darkness**.

God gave the Jews His revelation to share with others. The Jews should have received this gift with humility and thanksgiving, then shared it with others without a proud attitude. Since they had

the law, the very embodiment of knowledge and truth, they could have served as teachers to the Gentiles (whom they viewed as **ignorant** and **immature** with regard to spiritual matters).

With a series of rhetorical questions Paul accused the Jews of not practicing what they preach. They taught others the will of God but did not teach themselves. They admonished others **not** to **steal**, then they were dishonest themselves. They told others **not** to **commit adultery**, then they committed adultery. They denounced idolatry but robbed temples, which could mean that the Jews made profits by selling idols to Gentiles, thus achieving financial gain through the idolatry of others. Or, this accusation, as well as others, could show that Paul interpreted the law the way Jesus did in the Sermon on the Mount. Wrong motives and evil thoughts are as sinful as the acts themselves. Unfaithfulness to God could be seen as stealing from Him and as spiritual adultery. Robbing temples could mean irreverent disregard of God and holy things.

Paul pointed out the inconsistency between Jewish belief and practice in a summary, general indictment. The Jews boasted in God (v. 17) and also in the law, God's gift of revelation. Yet, because they disobeyed the law, the apostle insisted that they in fact dishonored the very God they, more than any other people, claimed to know and honor. Their failure at observing the law was so great that even Gentiles blasphemed the name of God (Is 52:5). Ironically, the Jews are supposed to promote the praise of God's name among the nations.

2:25-29 The Jews confused privilege and responsibility by depending on **circumcision**. Jewish self-confidence derived especially from circumcision. Circumcision, which refers to the surgical removal of the foreskin from the male sexual organ, had several purposes:

- It distinguished the seed of Abraham from the Gentiles (Gn 17:1-11).

- It reminded Israel of the covenant between Abraham and God, which extended to all of his descendants (Gn 17:9-14).

- It represented putting away evil and being set apart (Jr 4:4).

Though this outward sign was merely a testimony that the Jew was included in the covenant relationship God made with Abraham and Moses, many Jews made circumcision an end in itself. They failed to realize that the inward heart condition matters more than an outward physical sign.

Paul insisted that disobeying the law is as if one were to become **uncircumcised**. Covenant people should live as covenant people by obeying God's commands. Otherwise, circumcision, the sign of the covenant relationship, had no meaning at all. The reverse argument is also true. When those who are uncircumcised obey the law, their uncircumcision in effect becomes circumcision. Though the Jews considered the Gentiles as their inferiors, the uncircumcised Gentiles kept the spirit of the law and through their obedience became judges of the Jews. The Jews possessed the letter of the law and circumcision, the externals, but they were lawbreakers and guilty before God. The Gentiles, because of their obedience to the law, appeared in a more favorable light than the Jews. Being a real Jew and being marked by **true circumcision** (Rm 2:28) are inward and spiritual, not external and physical. Inward circumcision is done by the Spirit, not by conformity to the requirements of the law. This circumcision of the heart has precedents in the Old Testament (Dt 30:6; Jr 4:4; 9:26).

The true Jew received **praise from God**, who alone can see the inward state of one's heart. Paul used a play on words. The designation "Jew" derives from

"Judah," which means "praise." The right kind of praise does not come from people who see only the outward and observe only outward ritual.

3:1-8 The Jews raised objections to Paul's gospel. The apostle anticipated that the Jews would raise objections to the claims he had made in 2:17-29. He affirmed that possession of the law does not exempt the Jews from judgment and that physical circumcision is worthless apart from the inward condition of the heart. The Jews might have thought he had reduced them to a position of equality with the Gentiles. The apostle's argument was not intended to prove the equality of Jews and Gentiles in matters of privilege but in matters of sin and guilt before God.

Paul answered the first objection with a rhetorical question. His teaching had denied that **Jews have** any **advantage** over Gentiles and that their circumcision is of no benefit. However, the apostle insisted that the Jews do have an advantage (v. 2). God "entrusted" them with **HIS SPOKEN WORDS** (Gk. *ta logia tou theou*, lit. "the words of God"), a reference to the entire written revelation known as the Old Testament. ENTRUSTED (Gk. *episteuthēsan*, "believe in, have confidence in, someone or something entrusted to another") implies both the privilege of receiving "the words of God" and the responsibility to share those oracles with others.

A second objection the Jews might put forth was that Paul's teaching on condemnation contradicts the promises of God. They wondered whether God had failed in His purpose because some Jews did not believe or respond to God's goodness in giving them His oracles. (Paul would answer this question in detail in chaps. 9–11.) The apostle emphatically denied that God is unfaithful, insisting on God's absolute truthfulness and reliability. People, in contrast, will always fall short and ultimately are found to be liars. He supported his argument with a quote from Psalm 51:4. David, a man after God's own heart, was guilty of sin. David acknowledged his sin and believed that the righteous God was justified in judging him. Though God punished David for his sin, the Lord remained faithful to David.

Paul answered the final Jewish objection: His teaching makes God seem unrighteous. "If human failure demonstrates God's righteousness, then isn't God wrong, in fact, unrighteous, to punish people for their sin?" In this way of reasoning, the Jews believed that their sin should obligate God to exempt them from punishment since their sins did indeed reveal God's righteousness. It disturbed Paul so much even to use the word "unrighteous" in relation to the righteous God that he admitted apologetically that he was speaking only in human terms. Again he emphatically denied this claim with the strong assertion, **Absolutely not!** (v. 4) If this idea were true, who could judge the world? Since God will judge the world, the unrighteous must be punished. Unless this happens, what will take place is not judgment.

The apostle's objector acts as though the end justifies the means. If his lie magnifies God's truth to His glory, why should he be judged as a sinner? This argument is used by sinners trying to justify themselves. Some of Paul's contemporaries accused him, with his emphasis on salvation by grace, of actually encouraging sin in order to increase God's goodness and grace. The apostle identified such claims as slander. Those who reason and act in such a way **deserve** their **condemnation**.

God's Wrath Condemns All People (3:9-20)

Although Paul still continued to emphasize the Jews, he widened the scope of his argument in his summary (1:18–3:8). The whole world lies under God's condemnation because all people sin. The law gives knowledge of that sin. The apostle used a series of Scripture quotations to support his argument.

3:9-18 All people sin. Since all are sinners, no one has any advantage or defense. The words **both Jews and Gentiles** point to the universal nature of sinfulness. All people are under sin. Sin controls and condemns all who are under its power. Sin is a tyrant from whom individuals cannot free themselves. The apostle proved the universality of sin with the testimony of Scripture, primarily from the Psalms. The first quotation (3:10-12), from Psalm 14:1-3, summarized those to follow. Based on the standard of God's righteousness, all fall short, both Jews and Gentiles. There is no exception. Evidence shows that **no one** is **righteous**. **No one** even **understands** his lack of righteousness because he still chooses sin. All people fail to seek God and have no desire to worship Him. Sinners have other interests than God. They **have turned away** from His path. They have become **useless** and serve no good purpose. Their character has deteriorated. **No one . . . does good, . . . not even one**.

Sin affects the sinner's entire being, every part of the body: **throat**, tongue, lips, mouth, feet, eyes. With vivid word pictures Paul's quotes show the degradation of speech. Citing Psalms 5:9, 140:3, and 10:7, the apostle noted how a wicked mouth permanently speaks what is unclean, evil, and poisonous. What comes from such a mouth offends like the stench of an **open grave**. Such sinners keep using their **tongues** for treachery and deceit. The pattern of their lives is that of **cursing and bitterness** of speech.

Paul used Isaiah 59:7-8 to show the degradation of conduct. In their relationships with others, sinners' characteristic murderous and violent behavior leaves a path of destruction and misery. They know nothing of peace. They focus on bloodshed and destruction. Their sin separates them not only from God but also from others. What causes all these expressions of sin? Sinners have **no fear of God before their eyes** (see Ps 36:1).

3:19-20 The law gives knowledge of sin. Jews might object that the quotes Paul used refer only to Gentiles. The apostle corrected this misunderstanding. Everything in the Old Testament is addressed first to Jews. It convicts them of sin. God's righteous judgment will silence everyone. No human achievement, when measured against God's standards, will allow pride and boasting. Those who have the law have nothing to say before God. The whole world—Jew and Gentile alike—will become accountable to God and **subject to His judgment**. There will be no exceptions.

Paul provided the reason for every mouth's being stopped and every person's being made accountable to God: No one can be put right with God by works of the law. People are weak and unable to meet God's requirements. In fact, the law works by showing one his sin. The law reveals his failure and his need for the gospel. Good works do not earn salvation, but salvation inspires one to good works.

GOD'S RIGHTEOUSNESS PROVIDES JUSTIFICATION (3:21–5:21)

God Provides Justification through the Work of Christ (3:21-31)

Paul depicted universal sinfulness and the need for a right relationship to God. Now he explained how people overcome sinfulness and how God restores a right relationship by presenting the revelation of the righteousness of God, which is called the doctrine of justification. This

passage is central to understanding the entire Roman epistle.

3:21-26 Christ's death makes justification possible. The apostle contrasted justification by "works of the law" (v. 20) with justification by **grace** (v. 24) through **faith** (v. 22). **God's righteousness** refers to His way of giving women and men a right relationship with Him. This status before God is His free gift. This righteousness has now been brought to light in history through the person of Jesus Christ. This right standing from God does not depend on the law or keeping its demands. The gospel of grace has always been God's purpose, although its revelation had only recently been made. The entire Old Testament—**the Law and the Prophets**—bears witness to this truth.

This right standing with God or justification comes through faith in Jesus Christ. God justifies all who believe in Him. Faith does not earn salvation. Faith is the means through which God gives the gift of righteousness. The method of salvation remains the same for all sinners, Jews and Gentiles alike. The reason everyone must come to God through faith in Jesus Christ is that all people are sinners. They continually **fall short** of God's glory (v. 23), cut off from fellowship with Him and His presence. They fail to reflect His glory in not conforming to His holy image. Consequently, all need God's salvation.

Those who believe are justified. This legal term means they are acquitted of the guilt and charges brought by sin. God declares these believers righteous. He justifies them freely as a gift of His grace, His undeserved favor and generous goodness. There is no righteousness in a sinner himself. He can do nothing in himself for God to declare him righteous. Justification is God's gift. He justifies persons **by His grace through the redemption that is in Christ Jesus** (v. 24). "Redemption" refers to the release of prisoners of war or slaves by payment of a price. The death of Jesus on the cross paid a great price to purchase the freedom of sinners from their slavery to sin and to deliver them from the sentence of death.

Christ was a PROPITIATION (Gk. *hilastērion*, also translated "atonement, mercy seat"), a reconciling sacrifice. The word is used in the Septuagint to describe the golden cover of the ark of the covenant. This metaphor is a reminder of the Day of Atonement when the blood of the sacrificial animal was sprinkled on the mercy seat in the "most holy place" as atonement for the sins of the people (Lv 16:14-16). Propitiation suggests the idea of appeasing or satisfying. Christ's death satisfied divine justice and averted the wrath of God toward sinners. The means of Christ's propitiatory act was the shedding of His blood, that is, His death on the cross. By the shedding of His blood on the cross Christ became the **propitiation** (Rm 3:25) for the sins of humanity. God's holy nature required a sacrifice, and He Himself provided it through His Son. Christ serves as a propitiation only for those who believe, for faith is the means of appropriating the benefits of His death. Liberal theologians uncomfortable with the wrath of God and judgment of unrepentant sinners to hell have protested the translation "propitiation," suggesting rather "expiation," which, as forgiveness or cancellation of sins, is included in the meaning, yet inadequate to provide complete understanding of what Christ did on the cross. God's holiness demands punishment for sin. Propitiation satisfies the requirements of God's justice and cancels the guilt of man. It is a perfect and complete description of what Christ did on the cross for the atonement of His creation. God's love for His creation had to be reconciled with His perfect justice, and Jesus Christ through

His death on the cross satisfied the just demands of God and cancelled the sinner's guilt in perfect reconciliation.

The sacrifice of His Son shows God to be righteous because through Christ's death God satisfied the penalty for the sins of all who choose to accept His righteousness. This coverage included those sins previously committed by individuals who lived before Christ's death, those **sins** He had **passed over**. Justice demands that the guilty be punished. God's temporary suspension of wrath toward sins deserving punishment had seemed to call into question His perfect righteousness. The cross vindicated that righteousness. God's saving act showed that He is indeed just. The sacrifice of Jesus on the cross dealt decisively, and for all time, with sin. Unless Christ had died for sins, God could not be just in forgiving them. Previously God's righteousness had been obscured; now it is clearly revealed. The propitiatory death of Jesus makes possible the justification of sinners without compromising the moral character of God. The cross satisfies the claims of justice as well as the claims of mercy and grace.

3:27-28 Faith makes justification effective and excludes all **boasting**. Salvation by grace through faith excludes all boasting by any person, not just the Jews. Any works-oriented religion that claims human effort and merit as a means of acceptance with God could lead to pride and boasting. The **law of faith** (v. 27) cancels all teachings of salvation based on **works**. "Law of faith" is a reminder of God's decision to justify by faith alone. Christ's saving death removes any possibility of boasting. Grace allows no place for satisfaction in one's own achievement, for salvation is all from God, not by human effort.

Paul concluded that all people are **justified by faith apart from works of the** law. His insistence on faith emphasized justification as God's free gift.

3:29-30 Faith treats Jews and Gentiles the same way. Paul approached his argument from the viewpoint of monotheism. If there is only one God, as the Jews consistently have maintained, how can He be the God exclusively of any one people? Since no other God exists, the God whom the **Jews** worshiped must be the God of the **Gentiles** also. Since God is one and He alone is God, He has only one method of bringing justification to **circumcised** and **uncircumcised** alike. **Faith** is the only way for both Jews and Gentiles.

Heart to Heart: Good News!

You may think of yourself as a pretty good person. After all, you may not have committed any "major" sins. Yet, you have probably committed lots of "little" sins. Have you ever gossiped? criticized a fellow believer? hurt someone's feelings? Do you hold bitterness toward someone who has wronged you? All sins make you a sinner and separate you from God, who is holy. The gospel is good news indeed for you! God Himself declares you "not guilty" and makes you righteous. He restores you to a right relationship with Him because Christ died in your place and paid the penalty for your sins. His sacrifice gives you forgiveness and deliverance from sin and death. You do not have to do anything but trust in what God has done for you in Jesus Christ. By faith you can receive His free gift of salvation. Rejoice in God's work on your behalf through Jesus. Give thanks to Him for His righteousness bestowed on you.

3:31 Faith establishes the true purpose of the law. The Jews believed that God gave them the law. It showed them, His chosen people, the way of salvation. Now Paul seemed to be saying the law had no place. However, the apostle emphatically corrected that misunderstanding. Justification by faith does not **cancel the law**. If the law is properly understood, the law becomes the standard for measuring one's right standing with God. The gospel establishes the law in that it vindicates the law. The law brings an awareness of sin. Man's disobedience to the law made Christ's redemptive work on the cross necessary. If the cross was necessary, no person can become acceptable to God by fulfilling the demands of the law. God's plan of salvation did not set aside the law's demands. Rather, it gives the means of satisfying those demands. Thus, it **upholds the law**.

Abraham's Example Confirms Justification by Faith (4:1-25)

Paul wanted to establish that faith-righteousness is not an innovation. The true understanding of the Old Testament itself points to this. He used Abraham as the proof of his argument. The Jews looked to Abraham as the father of their nation and as one of the most righteous men who ever lived. They believed he was justified by his works, especially his circumcision. The apostle asserted, however, that Abraham was justified by his faith.

4:1-5 Abraham was justified by faith, not works. Paul imagined an opponent asking, "**What then** are we to **say** about our physical **forefather**? How did he achieve right standing with God?" Jewish teachers widely believed that Abraham was **justified by his works**. Paul assumed for the moment that this was true. In that situation Abraham had **something to brag about**. The apostle immediately dismissed the possibility, for no person, including Abraham, can boast **before God**.

Paul quoted Genesis 15:6 to show why Abraham had no reason to boast before God. Abraham BELIEVED (Gk. *episteusen*) God. In Greek the noun *pistis* is translated faith. Since English does not have a verbal form for this noun, *pisteuō* is translated "believe." One can easily see the connection between these two words in Greek with the obvious connotation of trust, reliance, and dependence. Abraham put his trust in God. Then, God CREDITED his faith as righteousness. "Credited" (Gk. *logizomai*) is an accounting term. Abraham's faith was credited to his account as righteousness, and his spiritual books were balanced (4:3). "Righteousness" means right standing with God. Nothing is said of Abraham's works even though the Jews thought of believing itself as a meritorious work. "Credited" rules out any idea of merit on the part of Abraham. God did the crediting. Faith is not a good work; it is trust in God. Abraham's righteousness was completely God's gift. Faith was the means by which he received this free gift.

If a person does some work, his pay is a matter of debt or the obligation of the employer. It is something that belongs to him. It is not a gift of grace. Those who do not work to obtain God's favor, however, but believe in Him are those whom God justifies. They do not trust in their works, but they trust in God. Their **faith is credited** to them **for righteousness**.

Paul showed the measure of God's grace when he described God as the One who justifies the ungodly—those completely without merit, even those who oppose Him, those who do not deserve being acquitted. God's grace extends to the vilest of sinners who truly believes. God's way of salvation requires women and men to produce nothing. They must only receive in faith God's free gift.

4:6-8 David affirmed righteousness apart from works. David pronounced a **blessing** on those **to whom God credits righteousness apart from works** (v. 6; Ps 32:1-2). Those people are blessed when God forgives their **lawless** deeds and covers their **sins**, never taking them into account. God extends grace and forgiveness toward sinners, toward those who refuse to conform to His law. Paul considered that one whose sins are forgiven and not counted against him as one credited with righteousness. Sin in a believer's life does not cancel justification. God does forgive. His gift of salvation is irrevocable.

4:9-12 Abraham was justified by faith before circumcision. The apostle raised the question, "When was Abraham justified, before or after he was circumcised?" The answer reinforced the justification-by-faith principle, for God credited Abraham's faith as righteousness years before he was circumcised at the age of 99. His circumcision had nothing to do with his justification. Circumcision served as the sign of what had already become a reality for Abraham because of his inner trust in God. Circumcision did not confer righteousness but confirmed it. It was a testimony to justifying faith.

Abraham's example made him the **father of all who believe but are not circumcised**, meaning the Gentiles. The uncircumcised also may be justified and have a right relationship with God. Abraham was also the **father of the circumcised**, the Jews, specifically those Jews **who** would **believe** and follow Abraham's example of faith—the faith he had while he was **uncircumcised**. Abraham is the father of all believers, circumcised and uncircumcised.

4:13-15 Abraham was justified apart from the law. God's **promise to Abraham** was **not through the law but through the righteousness that comes by faith**. The apostle defined the promise here as being the inheritance of **the world** by Abraham and his descendants. None of the Genesis passages detailing God's promises to Abraham use these precise words (see 13:15-17; 15:5,18; 17:2-8; 18:18; 22:17-18). However, God clearly did promise Abraham the land, numerous descendants, and the assurance that the entire world would be blessed through him. Perhaps in the sense that Abraham would be the father of all the family of faith, he would inherit the world. Some would note that this promise belongs also to Abraham's seed, whom Paul identified as Christ (Gl 3:16). God promised worldwide dominion to Christ (Php 2:10-11) and in Him to the spiritual seed of Abraham.

Paul explained why the promise could not be dependent on keeping the law. If those who are characterized by lawkeeping are heirs, faith is made useless. An empty faith contradicts Scripture, which affirms faith. This impotent faith would also cancel the promise. The promise speaks of a gift freely given. The law with its inflexible demands speaks of conditions to be kept. What would be given as a reward for work accomplished or laws obeyed would not be promise.

The law also **produces wrath** (Rm 4:15). Those who fail to keep its commands come under the condemnation of God, which is the opposite of what God's promise based on grace intends. The law shows to individuals their failures and their need of a Savior. It does not save. The only way to keep from breaking the law is to have no laws to break! If there were no law, there would be **no transgression** (v. 15), no overstepping God's standard.

4:16-25 Abraham's faith represents the standard for all believers. Paul concluded that the promise must be by faith so that it can be purely a matter of God's grace. Promise, faith, and grace belong together. Law, works, and merit stand together in a completely different sphere. Grace guarantees God's promise to all Abraham's spiritual descendants, believing Jews (those who are of the law) and believing Gentiles (those who are of Abraham's faith). Abraham **is the father of . . . all** who believe. His example of faith demonstrates the only way to God.

Paul appealed to the Old Testament prediction that Abraham would be **the father of many nations** (vv. 17-18; Gn 17:5) to support his argument. Abraham's place as spiritual father would be in the presence of God, the God in whom he believed. The apostle described God as the One who gives life to the dead, which, in the immediate context, probably refers to the fact that God enabled Abraham and Sarah to produce offspring even though their bodies were infertile, as dead, because of their advanced age. In a wider interpretation, God gives life to all those who are born again because of their faith in Jesus Christ. God is a life-giving God. He has overcome both physical and spiritual death.

God also **calls things into existence that do not exist** (Rm 4:17). Again, this reference could be to Isaac, the child of promise. Even before he was conceived, Isaac was real in the thoughts and purposes of God. Or, the reference could be to the nations of future believers whom God would call into existence at the right time and place in history. Those declared righteous before God were as dead, as people who did not even exist. God's creative call brings them into newness of life.

From a human perspective Abraham **believed against hope** because there was nothing from the world's point of view to support his faith. How could his old body produce a child? Yet, Abraham believed in the God who promised him that his **descendants** would be like the number of the stars, a multitude, thus making him the father of many nations. Hope in God is a certainty, for God can do what people cannot do. To have God is to have hope. Abraham never became **weak in** his **faith**, even when he thought of his body as already dead (he was 100 years old) and when he considered **the deadness of Sarah's womb** (she was 90). Instead of focusing on his own physical limitations, he focused on God and His promise.

As the years passed between the giving of God's promise and its fulfillment in the birth of Isaac, Abraham did not **waver in unbelief**. By means of his faith God gave him strength to wait. Abraham gave glory to God, ascribing to Him all that is due Him. He recognized and relied on God's faithfulness and power. By obeying God's command to circumcise all the males of his household as the sign of the covenant God would establish first with Abraham and then with Isaac, Abraham gave God glory. Abraham had a settled conviction that God could and would do what He had promised. Abraham's constancy in faith in God was **credited to him for righteousness** (vv. 3,5,9,22; Gn 15:6).

Paul knew the words of Scripture were written not for Abraham alone but had application for all who believe. All who believe in the pattern of Abraham, who place their faith in God, will have righteousness credited to them. The apostle

described God as the One **who raised Jesus our Lord from the dead**. This same God gave life to Abraham's dead body to make becoming a parent possible. Jesus was **delivered up** to death because of the transgressions of sinners. He was **raised** up **for** their **justification**.

Justification Results in Benefits for Believers (5:1-11)

Paul concluded his basic argument on justification by faith. Now he moved to the blessings received by the justified.

5:1-5 Believers have PEACE (Gk. *eirēnēn*), harmony with God. As a result of Christ's work of justification, believers now have peace with God. They are no longer His enemies, estranged from Him because of their sin. They are no longer objects of His wrath. Their new relationship of peace comes through the Lord Jesus Christ. This peace is especially meaningful in the midst of afflictions and trials because it bears testimony to a sweet reliance upon the providences of God to carry one through difficulties and on to endurance, character, and hope (v. 1).

Believers have peace and hope. Christ also introduces believers into the presence of God where they have continuous access. **This grace** (v. 2) is another way of referring to justification, the state of acceptance by God. This abiding new favorable status causes rejoicing **in the hope of the glory of God** (v. 2). For Christians, hope is a certainty. Now that believers have been made right with God, they can anticipate with confidence sharing in His glory. Even now they are being transformed from glory to glory (2 Co 3:18), but God has yet to reveal the final consummation (Rm 8:18).

Christians also exult in their **afflictions**. They can exult because they know God has accepted them and has supplied them with His grace. They also anticipate future glory. The strong word **AFFLIC-TIONS** (Gk. *thlipsesin*, "tribulation") refers to being under pressure, especially the pressure that comes from being a believer in a hostile world. The meaning, however, could include any real troubles that burden believers. Such difficulties should cause rejoicing because they produce steadfast **ENDURANCE** (Gk. *hupomonēn*, "living under"), a bearing up under pressure in the life of believers. The idea is holding out, standing firm, bearing up under, putting up with. This discipline in turn produces proven, tested character. This strength of character, whose testing has proven God's faithfulness, produces **HOPE** (Gk. *elpida*, "confident assurance"). This hope does not put believers to shame because God's love has flooded their hearts in abundance through the Holy Spirit God gave them at the time of their conversion.

5:6-11 Believers have reconciliation. The death of Jesus Christ on the cross showed the greatness of God's love because Christ died on behalf of **helpless** (morally weak), **ungodly** (rebellious to God's authority) people. He died at the appropriate time in God's divine purposes. Paul declared the immensity of Christ's death for undeserving people when he noted that it would not be easy to find someone to die for a righteous person, although perhaps someone with courage would **dare to die for a good person**. Christ died on behalf of individuals while they were sinners—not good, righteous people. God's action through Christ for sinners is based on Who He is, not on who a sinner is or what he has done.

Paul argued from the greater (the more difficult justification in the past) to the lesser (the less difficult deliverance from coming wrath). Being declared righteous is a present, accomplished fact, accomplished by the death (the blood) of Christ.

That new state has future implications. Through Christ believers will be saved from God's eschatological wrath. Christ's saving death has effectiveness beyond this life.

The apostle offered another contrast: Before justification believers were God's **enemies** (v. 10). After justification they **were reconciled to God** (v. 10). "Reconciled" means bringing together two parties who have been separated, making peace after an argument. God brought Christians back into a restored relationship with Himself **through the death of His Son**. Again, Paul pointed to the future dimension of this new relationship. Believers will be **saved** eternally by Christ's **life**, His resurrected life, as they share in that life with Him. They are in Christ; He is in them. This new status of **reconciliation** gives cause for rejoicing in God **through our Lord Jesus Christ**.

Justification Delivers from Death and Gives Life (5:12-21)

5:12-14 Paul discussed in detail the solidarity of mankind with both Adam and Christ. By comparing and contrasting Adam and Christ, he put forth the implications and far-reaching effects of their actions for all humanity.

Through one man, Adam, **sin entered** the human race, **and death through sin**. In some way all people inherit this sinful tendency from Adam. So, **death spread to all** people. When Adam sinned, humanity sinned because of its solidarity with him. What he did, those who followed did because they were in him. The one man, Adam, committed the one act; but the consequences of that act spread to all generations. **All sinned** (v. 12) could also refer to the sins committed by individuals.

Sin was in the world before God gave the law to Moses. With no law, there was no breaking of the law, so sin could not be charged to anyone's account. Yet, people still died from the time of **Adam** until **Moses**, even **those who did not sin** by breaking a direct command of God like Adam did. Death reigned, supremely sovereign over everyone with no exceptions, because the consequence of Adam's act passed to all humanity. Adam was **a prototype of the Coming One**, the Christ. His one act brought death to all, but the one act of the Coming One would bring life to all.

5:15-17 Although Adam was a prototype of Christ, Paul highlighted the differences between them. Adam brought disaster and death, while Christ brought abundant blessings and life. His gift differs from Adam's transgression (his going astray). By Adam's **trespass** many—the whole human race—died. God's grace gift and Christ's deed of **grace** freely **overflowed** to and benefited the totality of the human race, giving to them much more than what they had lost in Adam.

God's gift stands in contrast to Adam's sin. From this sin came God's **judgment, resulting in condemnation**. The one sin stands in contrast to many trespasses, which in turn are contrasted with the free gift, resulting in justification. **Condemnation** is contrasted with **justification** or being acquitted (v. 16). A final contrast is between death and life. Adam's act and Christ's act had different consequences. Adam's one trespass led to the rule of death for all. Those who receive **the overflow** of God's **grace** and **the gift of righteousness** (right standing with God) **reign in life through Jesus Christ**. The justified will reign.

5:18-21 As Paul continued to contrast the one man Adam to **the one man, Jesus Christ**, he noted that the consequences of Adam's disobedience as well as the result of Christ's obedience affected everyone universally. Adam's one transgression, deliberately breaking God's command, resulted in **condemnation** for all people,

while Jesus' righteous act resulted in justification, leading to eternal life for all people in Christ. Adam's **disobedience** constituted everyone as a sinner. Christ's **obedience** enabled everyone who believes to be declared righteous. Paul was not teaching universalism. Only those who believe are made righteous. Christ's work on the cross canceled out Adam's destructive trespass for those who are willing to appropriate His sacrificial gift.

The apostle answered the question, "What is the purpose of the law?" The law shows women and men that they are sinners. It increases the trespass by revealing what sin is and how serious it is. The law exposes the guilt of even supposedly moral people to show them that they, too, need grace to have a right standing with God. Where sin multiplies, however, grace multiplies even more. Sin reigns in death. Superabundant grace reigns through righteousness, resulting in eternal life through the Lord Jesus Christ.

In this whole discussion Paul did not mention Eve, who was the first to sin. He named Adam as representative of the human race. When the words "one man" appear in this passage, the apostle used the inclusive word (Gk. *anthropos*, "man, human being, person") instead of the gender specific word (Gk. *anēr*). Women and men alike sin.

JUSTIFICATION PRODUCES VICTORIOUS NEW LIFE FOR BELIEVERS (6:1–8:39)

Believers Have Victory over Sin (6:1-23)

Salvation begins with justification, the process of being declared righteous. Justification begins a new life for believers. Their process of growth is called "sanctification," "living godly, holy lives" or "becoming righteous." Their new life in union with Christ gives Christians victory over sin, or deliverance from meeting the demands of the law as the way of righteousness and from divine condemnation.

6:1-2 Believers should not continue in sin. Paul anticipated some might think an emphasis on justification by faith could lead to sin. He proceeded to raise and answer the questions of such objectors. The first question was framed: **Should we continue in sin** as the pattern of life and remain under its power so that grace may increase even more? Paul emphatically rejected this thinking. Believers have **died to sin**. They no longer are bound by sin. New life in Christ releases them from sin's power in their lives. Sin and life in Christ cannot coexist. Believers may still sin, but sin no longer dominates their lives.

6:3-11 Baptism illustrates the believer's union with Christ: dead to sin, alive to God. Those who have united themselves to Christ picture this union by being plunged into the waters of baptism, showing that they have been **BAPTIZED** (Gk. *ebaptisthēmen,* "immersed") into His death. Baptism is the transliteration or anglicization of the Greek word. The idea of the Greek word is a total enveloping of one substance in another. The argument for immersion as the proper mode for baptism is clearly made with the meaning of the word, coupled with the examples of Jesus and John. Paul's use of the imagery of baptism also effectively testifies to its public testimony of what transpires in conversion.

- The death, burial, and resurrection of Christ are pictured in the believer's immersion in baptismal waters.

- A believer also pictures his own regeneration, dying to the old life of sin and arising to a new life with Christ.

- Eschatologically, the believer is declaring his confidence in his reunion with Christ at His return.

Believers participate in His sacrificial death. United with Christ in death means death to a whole way of life, death to sin. Believers have died, and their baptism declares that fact. Verse 3 seems to speak of the believer's immersion into the body of Christ at conversion. To emphasize further this death to sin, Paul declared that Christians were buried with Christ by baptism into death. Burial depicts the finality and reality of death. Believers are really **dead to sin**. The old way of life has passed away. This death has a purpose, and baptism symbolizes that, too. Believers are raised up out of the burial waters to show that they also participate with Christ in His resurrection. God gives them a new kind of life in which to walk. Those who share in the death of Christ will certainly share in His resurrection. The new spiritual life of a believer does not come from within. It comes from union with Christ. A believer is decisively and permanently joined with Christ in death and in resurrection.

Paul pictured the believer's old self as crucified with Christ and completely destroyed. The purpose of this crucifixion was to abolish sin's control over the body. The text literally reads **body of sin** (6:6, Gk. *sōma hamartias*), picturing the body as an instrument of sin. Crucifixion with Christ makes this sinning body powerless. Before being united with Christ, believers were slaves to sin. Now they are no longer dominated by sin. Believers may still sin, but sinning does not characterize their lives. Dying to self and uniting with Christ ends the old way of life and frees one from sin's claims and mastery.

Since believers have died with Christ, they will also live with Him. Although this points to the future, bodily resurrection, it has implications for their lives here and now. Believers live unto Christ every day. They can know this with confidence because Christ has defeated death once for all. After He was raised from the dead, He lives forever. **Death no longer rules over Him** (v. 9). Instead, Christ rules supreme.

Christ died in relation to sin **once for all** (v. 10). Christ Himself was sinless. He came and lived in the world of sin and died for the sins of others. He decisively defeated sin and its power. He lives now wholly devoted to God and His glory. His resurrection life is eternal. In the same way, since believers are united with Christ, they should recognize that they, too, are dead once for all to sin and its control but forever **alive** in service **to God in Christ Jesus**.

6:12-14 Believers should offer themselves to God as weapons of righteousness. Paul appealed to Christians to become in practice what they already are in status. They have already died to sin and are justified. Sin, however, still remains in their lives. Negatively, believers are to stop letting sin rule in their mortal bodies (subject to weakness and physical death) so that they obey sin's evil desires. Also, they are to stop presenting any part of their bodies (hands, feet, mouth, eyes, ears) to sin to be used as **weapons** or instruments **of unrighteousness**. Positively, believers should decisively surrender themselves and all parts of their bodies **to God as weapons of righteousness**. Believers must live godly lives. This mandate is not an option. They belong to God, so they should use their bodies for His righteous purposes.

Paul gave the promise of victory over sin to encourage Christians. **Sin will not rule over** believers, even if they struggle intensely. God is on their side and offers His mighty resources. He will not let believers fail because they are not under law, which would make them slaves of sin and its condemnation, but they are **under grace**, which assures them of having a right standing with God. Sin no longer has lordship over them.

6:15-23 Believers are slaves of righteousness, not of sin. Paul repeated a similar but different question: Shall we sin occasionally **because we are not under law but under grace?** Any act of sin would not matter since grace abounds—believers could sin with impunity. The apostle emphatically denounced this thinking. He illustrated his argument with slavery. People are slaves to whatever master they obey. No one can serve two owners. There can be no compromise. Unbelievers are slaves to sin, for they obey its demands. Believers are slaves to obedience to God. Obedience to sin leads to death. Obedience to the gospel leads to righteousness.

Paul thanked God for His work in the lives of the Roman Christians. They had been slaves of sin but obeyed voluntarily the accepted Christian teaching to which they had committed themselves. They had been liberated from slavery to sin and its condemning power and had become slaves of righteousness. A life in service to righteousness produces satisfaction, joy, purpose, and meaning.

Paul noted he was speaking in human terms to explain why he would use the metaphor of degrading slavery to describe Christian service. He felt it necessary to use such a strong image because of their human weakness in discerning spiritual truths. He desired these believers to give themselves as wholeheartedly to God and righteousness as they had given themselves to the sin of moral impurity and increasing lawlessness in the past. Now they were to commit themselves to righteousness leading to sanctification, i.e., to ever-increasing holiness. Their lives should reflect their total commitment to God.

The apostle reminded believers again that they could not serve two masters. Any bondage requires total allegiance to the master served. When they were in bondage to sin, they could not serve righteousness. Before their life-changing commitments to Christ, believers had no benefit from the things they were doing. In fact, as believers they were ashamed now of those things. The sin-controlled life knows no shame. The outcome of their past sins was death. But now, believers **have been liberated from sin** and **enslaved to God** (v. 22). This new wholehearted commitment yields fruit that does not bring shame but gives birth to sanctification. Their ultimate end is eternal life.

Paul concluded his discussion on a triumphant note. He used a new metaphor with the word **WAGES** (Gk. *opsōnia*, "a soldier's pay, support or compensation"), which denotes the payment a general gives his soldiers. The wages of sin is death. In contrast, the free **GIFT** (Gk. *charisma*, "gift or favor") of God is eternal life. **Eternal life** (v. 23) refers to both a present possession and a future consummation. Believers do nothing to earn or deserve this gift. It is completely free. This eternal life comes through the mediation of the Lord Jesus Christ and His work.

Believers Have Victory over the Law as the Way of Righteousness (7:1-25)

Paul had stated that believers are not under the rule of law (6:14). Here he developed that statement and focused on the place of the law.

7:1-6 A marriage analogy illustrates how Christ sets believers free from the law. **The law has authority** over people **as long as** they are living. When they die, the authority of the law ends. An example

from marriage illustrates the binding nature of the law. A wife is **bound to her husband** (v. 2) by law as long as he is living. When her **husband dies**, the woman's legal obligation to the marriage law ceases. She is no longer a wife and is free to marry another. However, if the woman joins herself to another man while her husband is still alive, she is considered an **adulteress** because she has broken the law of marriage (Gn 2:24).

The law no longer has any binding authority over believers as a way of salvation because they have died to the law by their union with the crucified Christ. The purpose of this release from the law is twofold: that they might be joined to the resurrected Christ and that they might have fruitful lives for God. In their old sinful nature, the law aroused sinful passions in every part of the believer's body. Believers **bore fruit for death**. Because of their union with Christ in death, believers have died to what held them captive. They have been released from the penalties of the law through Christ's sacrificial death on the cross. The result of this freedom is the ability to serve God in a fresh, superior way as they are enabled by the Spirit. The old letter of the written law not only had no power to impart life, but also it could not enable service acceptable to God.

7:7-13 The relationship of the law to sin illustrates the believer's freedom from the law. Paul anticipated, especially from the Jews, who exalted the law, an objection arising that he was teaching that the law is evil. He raised the question, **Is the law sin?** He emphatically denied this misinterpretation of his teaching. The law helps people know what sin is. Paul would not have known the principle of sin apart from the law. Many know they have done wrong but do not know that wrongdoing is sin—rebellion against God. The law gives this understanding. It brings knowledge of sin and exposes sin for its true character. Paul gave a specific example about coveting. The law showed him that such inner craving for that which is not yours is sin.

> *Paul knew the law could not serve as a means of salvation for people, but it could produce guilt and give an awareness of sin.*

The apostle pictured sin as performing a military operation (**seizing an opportunity**, v. 11) and using the commandment as its starting point. For instance, how many people upon seeing a posted sign, "Wet Paint—Do Not Touch," will give in to the urge to touch the wet surface? The commandment produced a desire to do the very thing forbidden. The sin principle is powerful and active. Paul knew the law could not serve as a means of salvation for people, but it could produce guilt and give an awareness of sin. Apart from the law, sin is dead, dormant and inactive. The commandment rouses sin to action and shows its power.

Paul said that he was once **alive apart from the law** (v. 9). As a Jewish boy growing up in a Pharisee's home, he was never apart from the law. Paul meant that he had no consciousness of the law's inner demands or his rebellion against God. If anything, he felt that he obeyed God's law perfectly and took pride in his accomplishments. Then the realization came of what the commandment really required. This understanding brought the **sin**, which had been dormant within him, **to life**. The law showed Paul his sin and his condemnation before God. Now he realized his spiritual deadness. The commandment should have shown him the good and right path. To follow this revelation in obedience would have brought God's blessing and life. Yet, for Paul the commandment resulted in death because

he failed to follow God's will completely. This principle holds true for all people.

The apostle again described sin as a person (using personification, a figure of speech in which the attributes of a human being are given to an animal, an object, or an idea). Sin used the commandment as if it were a military base of operations and thus deceived Paul. Sin used the command to kill him. The law did not kill, but sin used the law to bring about the apostle's spiritual death. Sin within Paul caused him to do the very thing the law prohibited. He became a lawbreaker and thus was condemned.

7:7 The law is not sin. SIN (Gk. *harmartian*) is illuminated by the law (v. 13), exposing its hideous nature. Both Old and New Testaments have extensive vocabulary to describe sin. At the root of sin is the idea of missing the mark or failing to meet God's requirements. There is no exhaustive list of sins; rather, any act that misses God's perfect will is sin, separating the sinner from God. Hebrew words include these:

- *hattah*, stressing failure or mistake (Gn 4:7)

- `*asham*, emphasizing guilt (Is 53:10)

- *pesha'*, suggesting trespass (Pr 10:19)

- `*avon*, indicating iniquity (Lv 16:21)

There are even more words in Greek:

- *hamartia*, with the nuance of going astray or being off the standard (Rm 7:13)

- *paraptōma*, with the idea of stumbling or blundering (Eph 2:5)

- *parabasis*, emphasizing crossing the boundary (Rm 5:14)

- *anomos*, meaning no law or lawlessness, an attitude of disregard for God's law (1 Tm 1:9)

- *asebēs*, stressing ungodliness or irreverence (Rm 5:6)

- *aselgeia*, picturing excess and used in reference to all kinds of sexual immorality (Eph 4:19)

- *asōtia*, indicating carelessness and unnecessary extravagance (Eph 5:18)

- *parakoē*, suggesting a refusal to hear (Rm 5:19)

Although this listing makes no claim of being exhaustive, it does demonstrate the overwhelming devastation that accompanies sin and its disobedience to God.

On the contrary **the law is holy**, reflecting the character of God Himself. The commandment also is holy. This reference could be to all the commandments or to the tenth commandment on coveting, which Paul has used as his example. The **commandment is** also **just and** intended to bring **good**, not harm. The apostle always rejected the law as a means of salvation, but he affirmed its positive functions. The culprit is sin. Sin turns to wicked purposes what God intends for good.

Paul asked if what is **good** (the commandment) **caused** his **death**. He emphatically rejected this idea. The fault rested with sin. Sin used what is good (the law) to produce death in Paul. The victimized commandment revealed sin's true nature as utter evil and rebellion against God's ways, and it showed the utter depravity and seriousness of sin (**sinful beyond measure**).

7:14-25 The struggle against sin illustrates the believer's freedom from the law. Bible scholars debate whether this passage describes a pre-Christian or post-Christian experience. Paul was describing the struggle against sin for believers. Such a conflict is a normal part of the Christian life, and even the best Christians give in to sin's temptations.

Although Paul was probably speaking autobiographically, his experience characterized that of all believers. He and his readers knew **that the law is spiritual**, i.e., from God. The apostle, however, described himself as fleshly or carnal, **sold into sin's power**. Paul understood his moral weakness as a human being as well as sin's strength. He did not always do what he should do even when he desired to do so. He did **not understand** or approve what he was **doing**. He did not practice what he wanted to do but practiced what he hated. This lack of self-control shows sin's control and authority as master. Paul, the slave, obeyed even when he did not want to, even if his obedience was mechanical and not voluntary. He could not always resist sin's power and control. Since he was doing what he did not want to do, he was not really opposing the law. He was agreeing that **the law is good**. Paul concluded that he did not set out to do wrong; but the sin, which had taken up illegitimate residence in him, was pulling him into disobedience. Sin does not belong in the life of a believer, even though a believer finds it difficult, and even impossible, to eliminate its powerful influence completely.

Initially Paul spoke of doing what he did not want to do. Then he spoke of not being able to do what he wanted to do. He desired to do good but was unable to do so because nothing good lived within his flesh, meaning his fallen human nature. In his weakness he did not do the good he wanted to do **but practiced the evil** he did **not want to do**. He stated again that the sin indwelling him caused him to do what he did not want to do. The apostle was not refusing to take responsibility for his own actions. However, he did not sin carelessly. The Holy Spirit resident within prompted his spiritual nature to oppose the evil actions his flesh was committing.

Paul discovered that when he wanted **to do good, evil** was close by him. He could not escape it. In his inmost being the apostle **joyfully agreed with God's law**. The conflict, however, was within himself. The law of sin waged war against the law of his mind and made him prisoner to the law of sin in the parts of his body. All this struggle made Paul exclaim that he was **a wretched man** (v. 24). He did not like what sin did to him. He longed for deliverance from his physical body, characterized by death, because sin used his body as its instrument for doing wrong. His longing for deliverance led him to **thank God through Jesus Christ our Lord**. Paul had confidence he would triumph in the struggle. Jesus was his Deliverer. Mentally he knew he was **a slave to the law of God**, but physically he was a slave to sin. He lived in the tension of wanting to follow God in obedience but not always doing so.

Heart to Heart: Victory over Sin and Temptation

Becoming a Christian does not remove you from all sin and temptation. You will still have to struggle with sin. Paul's words assure you that this is a normal part of the believer's life. Sin is a powerful force. You will not always be able to resist its pull. Though this struggle will follow you throughout life, you do have hope. God promises deliverance. Victory is certain. You cannot overcome sin and temptation by your own self-determination and strength. You must look to the Lord Jesus for help. He has conquered sin once for all. He will fight by your side. Thank God, when you are in Christ Jesus, He no longer condemns you. Let Christ's enabling power through the indwelling Holy Spirit lift you to victory over sin.

Becoming a Christian does not remove you from all sin and temptation. You will still have to struggle with sin. Paul's words assure you that this is a normal part of the believer's life. Sin is a powerful force. You will not always be able to resist its pull. Though this struggle will follow you throughout life, you do have hope. God promises deliverance. Victory is certain. You cannot overcome sin and temptation by your own self-determination and strength. You must look to the Lord Jesus for help. He has conquered sin once for all. He will fight by your side. Thank God, when you are in Christ Jesus, He no longer condemns you. Let Christ's enabling power through the indwelling Holy Spirit lift you to victory over sin.

Believers Have Victory over Condemnation (8:1-39)

Chapter 8 summarizes the previous seven and serves as a climax to Paul's argument for righteousness by faith. The apostle has already shown how the justified life in Christ is a life of blessings (chap. 5), a life of victory over sin and holiness in union with Christ (chap. 6), and a life of freedom from the law (chap. 7). Now the apostle depicted the Christian life as one indwelt by the Holy Spirit and described the role of the Holy Spirit in the new life of a believer. The ministry of the Spirit brings freedom from condemnation.

8:1-8 The Spirit delivers believers from sin. For those in Christ Jesus **no condemnation now exists**. Condemnation is the opposite of justification. God has acquitted believers from sin's penalty and guilt. The sentence against them no longer applies because the life-giving Holy **Spirit has set** them **free in Christ Jesus**, delivering them from the enslaving power **of sin and death**. The Holy Spirit within believers gives them a new power to defeat sin.

The law could not rescue people from the power of sin and death because it had to depend on the weak human nature to fulfill its demands. God had to act personally to break sin's power. He did so **by sending His own Son** in the likeness of sinful **flesh**. Jesus was not a sinner Himself. He took the form of a man to defeat sin. Through Jesus, God condemned sin. The purpose of this condemnation was to fulfill **the law's requirement** in believers, those who walk **according to the Spirit**, not **the flesh**. The Spirit's work in believers accomplishes the law's demands. His enabling power helps believers to walk according to a standard they could never reach by themselves.

To walk by the Spirit means to set one's mind or whole being on the Spirit and spiritual matters, not on the things of the flesh that have been corrupted and dominated by sin. **Those whose lives are according to the flesh** are preoccupied with the things of this world. **Those whose lives are according to the Spirit** center their focus on the Spirit. The flesh opposes God and His interests. The mind that completely concentrates on the flesh and the things that relate to this earthly life is on a path that leads to **death**. It cuts itself off from all that brings life—from God Himself. In contrast, the mind that focuses on the Spirit finds **life and peace**. This mind lets the things of God dominate and allows the Spirit to guide and direct.

Those whose minds focus on the flesh and the things of this earth are **hostile** toward God. They do **not submit** themselves to God's law and are not even able to do so. Those who are in the flesh are so totally involved in this life that they **are unable to please God**.

8:9-11 The Spirit delivers believers from death. Believers are not in the flesh. Their lower nature no longer controls or characterizes their lives. They are in the Spirit because God's Spirit dwells in them. He then is the controlling influence in their lives because He has taken residence in their lives. Those people who do **not have the Spirit of Christ** do **not belong to Him** (v. 9). Being a Christian means having the Holy Spirit. The believer's body will die physically **because of sin**. Yet, **the Spirit is life** and brings life to the believer **because of righteousness**. God has already declared him righteous. The same **Spirit** of God **who raised Jesus from the dead lives in** believers. God will also bring life to the **mortal body** of a believer through the Spirit. The resurrection of believers is predicated upon the resurrection of Jesus Christ.

8:12-17 The Spirit establishes believers as children of God. Believers are not under obligation **to the flesh**, i.e., to live according to the flesh. The sin nature remains, but believers have no obligation to live by its dictates. The flesh has no ultimate control in their lives. Instead, they are obligated to live according to the Spirit. Those who **live according to the flesh** will **die**. Those who continually, day by day put to death—get rid of—the deeds of the flesh, with the Spirit's enabling power, will live.

The Holy Spirit is a person, not merely an impersonal moving force. He maintains intimate fellowship with believers as He resides within the heart of every child of God. In the Greek language, gender is assigned—grammatical gender rather than natural gender. Therefore, neuter is correct in Greek but requires the masculine in the English translation, **the Spirit Himself** (v. 16). Not only does the Spirit empower, but He also guides, protects, and confirms membership in God's family. All those who are **led by** the Holy Spirit are **God's sons**, His children. Being led by God's Spirit is the distinguishing feature of all God's people. The Spirit does not lead believers into **slavery** so that they again **fall back into fear**. He delivers them from fear and leads them into **adoption** (v. 15). Adoption gives to a child the rights and privileges of a family to which he does not belong by birth. The Spirit makes believers children, not slaves, of the heavenly family. As members of God's family, Christians can address the Lord in prayer in the warm, intimate terms a child would use: **"*Abba*, Father!"** (v. 15). The Spirit gives believers the assurance of membership in God's family by bearing witness with their inmost being that they indeed are **children** of God through faith in Jesus Christ.

Paul presented a bold image: The children of God are **heirs of God and co-heirs with Christ** (v. 17). These titles emphasize the assured position or relationship of believers who have indeed been adopted into God's family. Adoption into the family and acceptance of the responsibilities of discipleship also include sharing in the sufferings of Christ. The path of suffering, however, leads also to being **glorified with Him**.

> *Believers must expect sufferings in life, but the greatness of the coming glory makes current difficulties seem light.*

8:18-25 The Spirit provides the hope of glorification. The Roman Christians, like many first-century believers, lived in difficult times. Paul wanted to encourage these believers in the midst of their trials. He was certain that the **sufferings of the present time are not worth comparing** to **the glory to be revealed** to believers. This understanding put present problems in their right perspective. Believers must expect sufferings in life, but the greatness of the coming glory makes current difficulties seem light.

Not only do Christians suffer and long for glorification, but the whole **creation** does also. Paul personified creation in his description of its response—it **eagerly waits with anticipation** (vv. 23-25). This picture suggests a person leaning forward with great interest and desire. Creation is eagerly awaiting the revelation of the sons of God. With the fall of mankind, the creation also experienced a fall from what God intended into futility or frustration, the consequences resulting from human sin. Creation does not participate in this subjection willingly, but it does have hope. Creation, too, will ultimately be redeemed and transformed, sharing in the freedom from slavery to decay and **corruption** into the **freedom** of the glory of **God's children**. The present corruption of the physical world is not permanent. Even so, the whole creation groans with its present frustrating struggles of decay, but these pains suffered are meaningful like those of childbirth—a prelude to something new that is coming.

Like creation, believers also **groan within** themselves as they experience only partially all that God has in store for them. Believers possess the Holy Spirit as the **firstfruits** of coming glory, the hope of glorification. The image is from the Old Testament as the Hebrews brought to God an offering of the firstfruits of their harvest. By offering the firstfruits, they expected God to bless the remainder of the harvest. The presence of the Holy Spirit within believers is the guarantee of the full inheritance to come. Also like creation, believers wait eagerly for the completion of their **adoption**. God has already adopted believers into His family. With perseverance they wait for all the benefits and privileges of this status to be theirs in full measure, including the **redemption of** their **bodies** at the final resurrection when they will receive new, spiritual bodies not subject to decay and mortality. Believers will have bodies like that of the glorified Lord and will be conformed to His image. This hope is certain.

8:26-27 The Spirit **intercedes** for believers. The Holy Spirit also HELPS (Gk. *sunantilambanetai*, "lend a hand together, at the same time; to come to the aid of someone") weak believers. "Help" paints a word picture of the Spirit standing over against believers and pulling with them as they bear their burdens. Believers often **do not know** how they should **pray**. They struggle to know what is right, what needs others have, or what God's will is in a particular situation. The Holy Spirit Himself helps them to pray as they should. While they groan, unable to put into words their thoughts or requests, the Spirit takes these wordless sighs and transforms them into effective intercession. WEAKNESS (Gk. *astheneia*, "sickness, disease, timidity") could refer broadly to any area of weakness, but the context seems to point to difficulty in prayer.

As God **searches the hearts** (v. 27) of believers, He understands the inexpressible **groanings** (v. 26) of the Spirit within

them because He knows what the mind of the Spirit is. Believers may struggle with their own praying and be dissatisfied with their prayers, but they have confidence before God because they have a powerful intercessor, the Holy Spirit, who intercedes for them according to God's will.

8:28-30 The purpose of God brings freedom from condemnation and victory in triumphal living (vv. 1-2). God purposes good for believers. Paul did not say that everything happening is good in itself. Rather he recognized that even problems and crises cannot derail a sovereign God. Because God is omnipotent and omniscient and omnipresent, He is faithful to bring ultimate good even from the most tragic happenings (v. 28). He works **all things together** for **good**—not for all people in general but for believers. Paul described believers as those who love God and who are called according to His purpose. God called believers to saving faith in Jesus Christ, and they responded.

The specific good to which God causes all things to work is conformity to the image of Jesus Christ. Five key words describe God's saving purpose for believers.

He FOREKNEW (Gk. *proegnō*, lit. "know before, know in advance," v. 29), that is, He set His heart on or chose them beforehand.

He PREDESTINED them (Gk. *proōrisen*, "decide beforehand," v. 29). God initiated everything. He marked believers beforehand to become conformed to His Son's image so that Jesus would be the firstborn, the preeminent One, among many brothers. God planned for many children in His family.

CALLED (Gk. *ekalese*, v. 30) refers to being brought in. It is an effectual call—those called have already responded.

JUSTIFIED (Gk. *edikaiōsen*, "put into a right relationship with God," v.

30) means declared and treated as righteous.

GLORIFIED (Gk. *edoxasen,* "praise, honor, glorify," v. 30) refers to perfect conformity to the image of Christ, the ultimate state of believers when they become like Christ. Paul used the past tense of "glorified" because he was so certain that God's plan included glorification that he could speak of it as an accomplished fact.

Salvation from start to finish is an amazing event. Some steps happen simultaneously, but each is important:

• Foreknowledge (v. 30)

• Predestination (v. 30)

• Calling (v. 30)

• Contrition (2 Co 7:10)

• Repentance (Lk 13:3)

• Faith (Heb 11:6)

• Regeneration (Ti 3:5)

• Justification (Rm 8:30)

• Adoption (v. 15)

• Glorification (v. 30)

8:31-39 God's love in Christ brings freedom from condemnation. Knowing God's purpose should give believers a deep sense of spiritual security. God has shown through His saving acts that He is **for** believers (v. 31). In fact, no foe can ever prevail against believers with God on their side. God showed how far He would go on behalf of believers. He delivered up His own Son to an awful death by crucifixion. He **offered Him up** for sinners, a supreme demonstration of love. If He was willing to make such a sacrifice, would He not also with Christ freely give believers all things? God graciously gives believers all they need for life and godliness. He has already done the greatest thing. He will continue to do the lesser things.

Heart to Heart: Becoming Like Christ

God wants to make you like Jesus Christ! That is one of His purposes for your life. The Lord will use every resource and means available to do that, including people, circumstances, problems, and crises. Becoming like Christ is a lifelong process. It involves putting forth all your will and energy just like a soldier preparing for battle or an athlete training for a race. Are you reading the Bible regularly to know God's truths and how He wants you to live? Are you studying the Gospels to learn from Jesus' teachings and example? Do you spend time with the Heavenly Father in prayer, letting Him change your thinking and attitudes toward yourself, your situation, and the people in your life? Are you having fellowship with other believers? Is worship a priority in your life? Are you finding ways to serve God through ministry efforts? Are you trusting God when anxieties and difficulties seem to overwhelm you? Remember, God chose you to become like His Son. How blessed you are!

With the language of a legal court Paul raised the rhetorical question, **Who can bring an accusation against God's elect?** (v. 33). There will always be those who will accuse believers. Satan himself acts in this role of adversary. Yet, no charge will stand against those whom God has chosen because God Himself justifies them. The only One who could justifiably bring an accusation (since all sin is ultimately against Him) is the One who declares believers righteous.

Christ Jesus died to remove condemnation from those who trust in Him. He was **raised** to life, and those who are in union with Him share in that resurrected life. He sits at **the right hand of God**, sovereign and powerful to act on behalf of believers. He **intercedes** for them at the throne of grace.

Paul listed seven things that some might think could separate them from Christ's love. He asserted that nothing could do that, not **affliction**, **anguish**, **persecution**, **famine**, **nakedness**, **danger**, **or sword**, meaning execution (v. 35). The godly have always suffered (Ps 44:22). Believers will face suffering and persecution. Believers overwhelmingly conquer through God who revealed His love in the cross of Jesus Christ. The ability to triumph comes not from Christians themselves but from God. The apostle asserted with confident certainty a series of things that cannot separate believers from the love of God in Christ Jesus:

- **Death** cannot separate.

- **Life** with its pleasures, temptations, and trials cannot separate.

- No human or superhuman entity can do it.

- The list ends with a sweeping generalization—**any other created thing** (Rm 8:39)—that embraces anything Paul might have omitted. These things have no power to separate believers from God's love.

Heart to Heart: God's Love for You

Do you ever feel left out and think nobody loves you or cares about you? Paul's words provide wonderful encouragement for you. God loves you! He is on your side. If He is for you, who can be against you? He loved you so much that He did not even spare His own Son but offered Jesus up to death so that you can enjoy a personal relationship with the Almighty God, your Heavenly Father. Jesus Himself intercedes for you at God's right hand. Consequently, no one—not even you yourself—can condemn you. Not a single person or a single thing can ever separate you from God's love. His arms are always around you. You should not feel left out, nor should you think nobody loves or cares about you because God has included you in His family. He loves you, and He cares about you!

The Truth of God's Loving Care		
Truth	**Reference**	**Application**
God is for you.	Rm 8:31	No one can fight successfully against God.
He will freely give you all things.	Rm 4:17; 15:5; Jms 1:5	No one can outgive God.
He has justified you.	Rm 4:5; 8:33	God is the eternal judge of the universe. He is supra-supreme. No one outranks Him.
He prays for you.	Rm 8:26	He is the one who is able to answer all prayers.
You cannot be separated from His love.	Rm 8:35-39	His unconditional love covers all your transgressions.

THE PROBLEM OF ISRAEL'S UNBELIEF VINDICATES GOD'S RIGHTEOUSNESS (9:1–11:36)

Why does Israel stand separated from the love of Christ? Have God's promises failed or His purposes changed? Will salvation provided by Christ also be superseded in the future? Paul agreed that God had chosen Israel. He had given the Jews the covenants and the law. The Hebrew Scriptures have divine authority. How, then, could Paul claim that the law has been set aside for something new? How can Israel reject Jesus if they are God's chosen people and if even their Scriptures teach justification by faith? Can God reject His own chosen nation? Paul probably struggled with these questions himself, and the Jews confronted him with these issues. The apostle discussed the faithfulness of God in light of the doctrine of election.

Paul Grieved over Israel's Rejection of Christ (9:1-5)

9:1-3 Paul felt intense grief over Israel's rejection of Jesus Christ as the promised Messiah. He noted two witnesses as to the sincerity of his **anguish**: his union with Christ in whose presence he could not lie and his **conscience** enlightened by the Holy Spirit. To emphasize his personal concern for his own people, Paul expressed a prayer-wish—that he himself were **cursed and cut off from** Christ for the sake of his **brothers**. He longed to take the place of his kinsmen **by physical descent** (v. 3) in death so that they might become Christians and claim life.

9:4-5 The apostle identified his countrymen as Israelites. This term speaks of their having been chosen by God. Then he listed the great privileges belonging to the **Israelites** that demonstrated God's favor upon them. They possessed **the adoption**. God chose them as members of His family; they were not part of His family by nature. They experienced God's **glory**, His very own presence with them, in a special way unknown to other peoples. They received **the covenants** God made with various individuals, such as Abraham, Noah, Joshua, and David. God gave them His **law**, still their prized possession. They rejoiced in **the temple service** and the many **promises** of God, including the promise of a Messiah. The Israelites had esteemed **forefathers**, including Abraham, Isaac, and Jacob, men to whom God made promises before the giving of the law. **The Messiah** Himself was a physical descendant of their race. Mention of the Messiah led Paul to offer a doxology.

God Displays His Sovereignty in Dealing with Israel (9:6-29)

9:6-13 God works by election. A Jewish objector might infer from what Paul has said that Israel's unbelief means that **the Word of God has failed**, voiding all His promises. The apostle refuted the claim that God cannot carry out His purposes. He insisted that all of physical or biological Israel did not receive God's promises. God's saving purpose never applied to the whole ethnic nation but to a smaller group within the nation.

Paul developed his argument by quoting Genesis 21:12 to show that not all of Abraham's offspring were his true children. God made His promises to Isaac, the son of Abraham and Sarah and thus to the child of promise. Mere **physical descent** (v. 8) from Abraham (as was Ishmael through the concubine Hagar) did not mean automatically inheriting the promises of God. God reckoned Isaac as the seed from the very beginning, before he was even born. Abraham's age and Sarah's sterility required God's own intervention for Isaac to be born. His power enabled Sarah to conceive from Abraham's seed and to have a son.

The Jews could have contended that Isaac was the logical choice of God because he was the son of Sarah, Abraham's wife, and not the son of the slave girl. As twins, however, Jacob and Esau had the same mother and father. Even before they were born and before they had done anything good or bad, God chose Jacob for the spiritual line. He told Rebekah that **the older** brother would **serve the younger**, deliberately going against the cultural expectations of that day. God's choice of Jacob revealed His free sovereignty and demonstrated that election is not based on works. He chose Jacob before his character had formed and before he had accomplished anything. Election is based on God and His pur-

poses, not on any human achievement. God worked out His purpose according to His own way, choosing Jacob over Esau.

In speaking of Jacob and Esau, Paul was referring to nations, not individuals. His quoting of Malachi 1:2-3 reinforced this. **"Jacob I have loved, but Esau I have hated"** (Rm 9:13) could mean God loved Jacob more and Esau less. However, HATE (Gk. *emisēsa*, "hate, despise, disregard, be indifferent to") is a relative term as it is used here. Jesus used the same verb in suggesting that a man must hate his father and mother when he comes to Christ (Lk 14:26). Of course, Jesus who came to fulfill the law (cf. Ex 20:12), was not using the word "hate" as commonly understood. Rather He was making a contrast: One's love for parents would be as hate in comparison to his love for Christ. Esau was favored and greatly blessed by God (Gn 27:38-40). However, again God's blessings on Esau paled in comparison to His blessings upon Jacob. Possibly the best understanding here would be that God chose Jacob to fulfill His elective purpose for Israel, while rejecting Esau (cf. Mal 1:2-3). In this case, "hated" could signify "rejected." God rejected Esau (the nation Edom). He elected Jacob (the nation Israel) for the role of service.

9:14-18 God determines the objects of His mercy. Paul answered an imaginary objector who might have claimed God acts unjustly. This charge of injustice assumes some individuals are worthy of God's favor. The apostle strongly affirmed there can be no injustice with God. To act unjustly would be out of God's character (Ex 33:19). Instead of punishing Israel for its rebellion in the incident with the golden calf, God showed mercy and compassion for them. No people have any merit or rights before God. Salvation depends on God who shows mercy, not on any human effort.

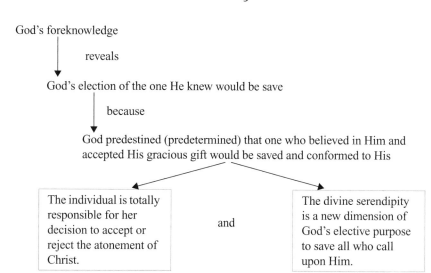

Understanding Election

God's foreknowledge

     reveals

God's election of the one He knew would be save

     because

God predestined (predetermined) that one who believed in Him and accepted His gracious gift would be saved and conformed to His

| The individual is totally responsible for her decision to accept or reject the atonement of Christ. | and | The divine serendipity is a new dimension of God's elective purpose to save all who call upon Him. |

God called out those whom He knew would accept His gift of salvation

God justified (made righteous) those who answered His call.

God glorified those called out and justified.

You must be careful not to try to reconcile the heavenly with the earthly. You accept what God has said about Himself—His faithfulness to call all to Himself and to embrace all who come. And you must not forget your personal responsibility to make your choice to accept or reject the Lord's atonement for you.

Paul used Pharaoh as another example. God raised this ruler up to his place in history for His own redemptive purposes. First, in the great events of the exodus God demonstrated His power in the face of Pharaoh's stubborn opposition. As a result of the liberation of His people from Egyptian slavery, God's name was proclaimed throughout the earth. The Egyptian ruler demonstrated the principle that God **shows mercy to whom He wills and He hardens whom He wills**. Paul was focusing on God's free merciful sovereignty, not on human responsibility. Pharaoh refused God's way and grace.

His unbelief and rebellion hardened his heart. God delivered him over to his own sin. God used Pharaoh's poor choices for His glory, but Pharaoh did what he wanted to do. God hardened Pharaoh in the wrong Pharaoh chose to do.

9:19-24 God has the right to create as He wills. Paul continued to dialogue with an imaginary opponent who raised another problem issue. If God is sovereign, how can people be held accountable for their actions, for who can resist God's will, His deliberate purpose? Why does God **still find fault?** The apostle could not imagine the creation talking back to the Creator God. Any such question asked is illegitimate. Those formed do not ask the One who formed them, **"Why did you make me like this?"** (v. 20). This is impertinent, inappropriate behavior. It implies that the sovereign God could give up His rightful power as Creator. It implies that the creature possesses more wisdom than God Himself. A person is in no position to ask such a question.

The apostle used the potter-clay image, employed also by the Old Testament prophets Isaiah (Is 29:15-16) and Jeremiah (Jr 18:1-6), to emphasize that God has the right and authority as the Potter to shape and use His creatures (the pots) as He desires. All people are created from the same material, but God assigns different roles to them, some for dishonorable or menial functions, such as Pharaoh, and others for honorable purposes, such as Moses and the Jews. The clay has no right to object to its shape or function. God alone understands His plan and the steps necessary to achieve it.

God **endured with much** longsuffering **objects of wrath ready for destruction** because He wanted to **display His wrath** and **make His power known**. He also desired to **make known the riches of His glory on objects of mercy that He prepared beforehand for glory**. God has patiently put up with the unbelieving Jews (objects of wrath) because He wanted to show mercy to both Jews and Gentiles. Those whom He "prepared beforehand for glory" (Rm 9:23, God's elect) include both Jews and Gentiles. He called out vessels of mercy from both groups.

9:25-26 God chose to extend His mercy to Gentiles. Paul listed a series of Old Testament quotes to support his belief that God had planned to show mercy to the Gentiles. Although Hosea 2:23 originally applied to the rebellious ten tribes of Israel, both Paul and Peter (1 Pt 2:10)

broadened the application to include the Gentiles as well. Those who were not God's people, He now calls His people. Those who were not His beloved, He calls beloved. Hosea 1:10 repeats this emphasis with the added thought that the Gentiles **will be called sons of the living God**. They will have all the rights and privileges of members of God's family.

9:27-29 God chooses to extend His mercy to a remnant in Israel. Paul had cited Hosea to show that God had included the Gentiles. Then he quoted Isaiah (Is 10:22-23; 28:22) to show God had excluded many Jews. Even though "Israel's sons" were very numerous, **only** a **remnant** would be **saved**. God had punished the nation, and without His intervening mercy Israel would have been totally destroyed, just **like Sodom** and **Gomorrah**. The Lord of the universe, however, **left a seed**, a remnant, a believing minority who inherited His promises and carried out His purposes. This remnant offers hope and shows that God has not rejected all of Israel. He has kept His promises.

Israel Has Responsibility for Her Rejection of Christ (9:30–10:21)

Paul had explained the rejection of Christ by the majority of the Jews based on God's sovereign choice. Next he emphasized the responsibility of the Jewish people themselves. Salvation involves both divine and human aspects, predestination (election) and freedom of choice. Divine sovereignty and human responsibility complement each other.

9:30-33 Israel tried to obtain **righteousness** through the works of the law. Historically, the Gentile nations had not pursued a right relationship with the one true God. **Pursue** reflects the idea of a race. Yet, they had obtained this righteousness, winning the race and gaining the prize, because they responded in **faith** to the proclamation of the gospel. In contrast, **Israel** historically had actively pursued obedience to the law, seeing the goal of their effort as a right standing with God. They, however, did not achieve righteousness because they pursued obedience to the law **not . . . by faith** but by their own **works**. They tried to gain acceptance by their own efforts instead of by accepting God's merciful grace. Paul used the words of the Prophet Isaiah (vv. 32-33; Is 8:14; 28:16) to show how the very One who should have been the object of their faith became instead **the stumbling stone** (Rm 9:32). The Jews could not accept the scandal of the cross, a crucified Messiah. This **stone in Zion** (v. 33) had two effects: the fall of some and the rise of others. The latter group embraced those who believed in Him, both Jews and Gentiles. These believers would not be ashamed when they finally stood before Him.

10:1-13 Israel rejected righteousness based on faith. Paul shared with his Christian brothers in Rome his deep, heartfelt concern for the Jews. He prayed **for their salvation**. The apostle knew from his own personal experience that the Jews had great enthusiasm for God. Yet, their very zeal often led to spiritual pride, especially because this zeal was not based on **knowledge**. Their misguided devotion did not know the nature of true righteousness. They were spiritually blind.

The Jews were also self-righteous. Since they did not know **God's righteousness** and tried to establish their own, they did not submit to His righteousness. They believed they could achieve right standing through their own efforts. Consequently, they stubbornly refused to submit to God's plan. They searched for righteousness the wrong way. The Jews did not understand that **Christ is the end of the law**. His atoning work decisively ended all attempts to achieve a righteousness based on obedience to the law. Christ is the end of any attempt to gain a right relationship with God by human effort **to everyone who believes** (v. 4), both Jews and Gentiles.

To support his theme that righteousness is by faith, Paul used another series of Old Testament quotes, beginning with Leviticus 18:5. If individuals did keep the whole law, they could obtain righteousness and life in that way. Such perfect obedience, however, is impossible for weak, imperfect humanity. Righteousness coming from faith in Christ is close and available (Dt 30:11-14). **The righteousness that comes from faith** (Rm 10:5) does not demand that people do the impossible. People do not need to **go up to heaven** to find Christ and bring Him down. Jesus has already come in the incarnation. Nor do people need to go to the place of the dead to bring Christ back to life. Jesus has already been resurrected. The message of faith that Paul and his associates were preaching declared that salvation by faith in Christ is within easy reach, **in your mouth and in your heart** (v. 8). Understanding the righteousness of God through Jesus Christ is not difficult. All people must do is believe.

Paul defined the message that calls for faith and results in salvation. People must CONFESS (Gk. *homologēsēs*, "say plainly, speak the same thing") with their mouths "Jesus is Lord" and believe in their hearts that God raised Him from the dead. The apostle placed confession before believing to parallel the words from the Deuteronomy quote, "mouth" and "heart." Of course, belief must precede confession. In fact, for confession to lead to salvation, one must agree with God in His judgments and in His remedy for redemption from sin. Verses 9 and 10 constitute one of the earliest confessions of faith. Belief (heart) refers to the inward aspect of faith, and confession (mouth) relates to the outward aspect. One can call Jesus "Lord" only with the help of the Holy Spirit (1 Co 12:3). Such a confession reflects a personal relationship with Christ. It publicly declares one's commitment to and faith in Jesus Christ. Belief in the resurrection of Jesus signifies belief in a living Savior. Confession of Christ as Lord is the earli-

est and most basic Christian confession. With verse 10, Paul restored the natural order: faith followed by confession. He made little distinction between **righteousness** and **salvation**. Both refer to the same experience. Believing with all of one's inner being, i.e., faith and trust, not works of the law, results in righteousness.

An Early Confession of Faith (Rom 10:9-10)

Truth Affirmed

- Confess the Lord Jesus.

- Believe.

- Formulate your confession of belief.

- Enjoy the security and benefit of salvation.

Application

- Speak with your mouth your acceptance of Jesus as Lord.

- Anchor your commitment to Christ in your heart.

- Believe God raised Jesus from the dead.

- You know that you are saved.

Send a preacher with a message (v. 15).
Proclaim the Word of God (v. 14).
Hear His word with an open heart (v. 14).
Call on Him for salvation (v. 14).

Paul affirmed the universal availability of salvation. Everyone who believes in Christ will not be disappointed. Believers will not **be put to shame** when they must give an account of themselves to God. The apostle also affirmed that salvation is the same for both Jews and Greeks (Gentiles). Despite their differences in race, culture, and religious background, no distinction exists at the foot of the cross. Both groups must come to God by grace through faith in Jesus Christ. There is only one way of salvation because there is only one Lord. Jesus stands ready to pour

out His boundless blessings to all who call on Him with no partiality.

Whoever **calls on the name of the Lord will be saved** (quoting Jl 2:32). The future tense implies the final consummation of salvation for believers. Calling on the name of the Lord expresses faith and parallels confessing Jesus as Lord (Rm 10:9). In the Old Testament "Lord" refers to *Yahweh*, the one true living God. Paul identified Jesus as Lord. This promise excludes no one. The Lord will save any person who sees his need and calls out for salvation.

10:14-21 Israel refused to respond to the preaching of the gospel. The apostle raised a series of rhetorical questions to show that calling upon the Lord for salvation does not take place apart from the proclamation of the gospel. He linked five key actions: calling, believing, hearing, preaching, and sending. In order to call on the Lord, people must first trust that the Lord can save them. In order to believe in Him, they must first hear Him (or **about Him**). This understanding reflects the first-century culture in which few people read or had access to "books." Instead, they received messages by word of mouth. So, to hear there must be those preaching. In order to preach, people must be sent. This shows their message is not their own and has an authority apart from themselves. Proclaiming the gospel message requires God's divine commissioning. Anyone who announces good news, especially the good news of the gospel, is welcome (Is 52:7). In a culture where most people traveled by foot, the feet of a good news messenger would indeed be beautiful or welcome.

However, not everyone who hears the good news obeys it. Paul was thinking of the Israelites in particular. He quoted Isaiah 53:1 to show that this had happened throughout history (Rm 10:16). Isaiah implied that not many believed the message. Paul gave a general truth: **Faith comes from what is heard**, the message; and **what is heard comes through the message about Christ**. Christ Himself is proclaimed through the message of the gospel. **What is heard** includes hearing with understanding and commitment. The gospel message creates faith in those who hear it (vv. 14-17).

Paul responded to someone who might object that the Jews have not heard the gospel. He affirmed that they had indeed heard the good news. He supported himself with the authority of Scripture (Ps

19:4). This verse speaks about the witness of God in creation. Paul saw a parallel to the widespread proclamation of the gospel. Jews in many areas, especially the Mediterranean world, had an opportunity to hear the gospel.

Others might have objected that the Jews did not understand the gospel. Paul answered that objection with quotes from the law (Dt 32:21) and the prophets (Is 65:1). He noted that the Gentiles who lacked spiritual **understanding** and who were not even looking for God had responded in faith to the gospel message. This should have provoked the Jews to **jealousy** and to a desire to have what the Gentiles had received. Yes, Israel had heard and had understood, yet they had responded with disobedience and defiance. They rejected the good news. The Jews had responsibility for their choices. God remained faithful by continually reaching out in love to faithless Israel.

God Will Fulfill His Purposes for Israel (11:1-36)

Paul had discussed God's sovereign election in choosing Israel and His mercy in including the Gentiles. He had recognized that disobedient Israel had human responsibility for her rejection of the gospel. Now the apostle affirmed that God had not abandoned His chosen nation. He would fulfill His purposes for the Jews and use the conversion of the Gentiles to do so.

11:1-10 God's purpose includes a remnant chosen by grace. God's rejection of Israel was not total. Paul gave himself as proof. He, too, was **an Israelite, a descendant of Abraham**, a member of **the tribe of Benjamin**, and a believer in Jesus Christ (v. 1).

The apostle asserted that God's rejection of Israel was an impossibility. **God has not rejected** the people **whom He foreknew** (v. 2). Paul gave an Old Testament example from the time of Elijah. The prophet felt isolated and alone as he witnessed the rejection of worship of the one true God. He felt he was the only one who remained faithful, and now others were seeking to kill him. God told Elijah, however, that **7,000** (a number representing perfection and completion) continued to worship Him faithfully. They had not submitted to **Baal** worship. God had preserved a faithful remnant. He would not desert those whom He had chosen. **In the same way** as in Elijah's day there remained **a remnant** of believing Jews, **chosen by** God's **grace** and not by the quality of their character or the works they had done. This minority obeyed God. They proved that God had not abandoned His people or His purposes.

Paul contrasted faith and works once more. One excludes the other. Only grace enables a person to be included in God's family and to have a right relationship with Him. If the remnant gains this relationship by grace, then the rest of the Jews must also see God's election as based on grace, not on any human effort.

The apostle summed up the consequences of Israel's choices. The Jews, though sincere, did not find the righteousness they were **looking for** because they sought for it in the wrong way, through works. **The elect** did obtain righteousness by grace. The disobedience of the rest led to the judicial result of hardening the heart. Paul gave the basis for this hardening through another series of Old Testament quotes (Is 29:10; Dt 29:4; Ps 69:22-23). God punished the Jews for their rebellion by giving them over to spiritual insensitivity. When people reject God's mercy through unbelief, hardening naturally and necessarily results. Those Jews who persist in unbelief will not escape disaster.

11:11-24 God's purpose includes the salvation of the Gentiles. Despite this bleak picture of the Jews, Paul saw hope for his people. They had indeed **stumbled**. He emphatically insisted, however, they did not stumble so as to fall or be beyond recovery. God used their transgression for His greater purpose, to bring salvation to the Gentiles. The Gentile reception of God's blessings would make the Jews **jealous** and desirous of that same salvation. The transgression of the Jews **brings** the **riches** of God's grace to the whole world. If their transgression and loss bring about this positive good, how much more abundance of blessings will their full conversion bring? The word translated FULL NUMBER (Gk. *plērōma*, "fullness, completeness"), in contrast to "remnant," could refer to the total number of unbelieving Jews who finally embrace salvation by grace. If the fall of Israel added richness to the Gentiles, how much greater would be the blessings when Israel repents and experiences God's fullness. Or, the reference could be to "fulfillment" in the sense of the fulfillment of God's purpose (vv. 11-12).

Paul addressed himself to the Gentile majority in the Roman church who might have wondered why the apostle to the Gentiles was discussing the Jews at such length. The apostle wanted to **magnify** his **ministry** to the Gentiles in order to move to jealousy his own people so that some of them might be saved. He would be the instrument God would use to bring about the conversion of the Jews. Paul did not see himself ushering in that time when **all Israel will be saved** (v. 26). He did see his Gentile mission as important in the purposes of God for the salvation of the Jews.

The rejection of the gospel by the Jews meant the **reconciliation** of the **world**. Many Gentiles had come to faith in Jesus Christ. If the Jews also accepted this good news and were accepted by God, it would mean coming to life from the dead. Literally, **life from the dead** (v. 15) speaks of the eschatological resurrection from the dead for all believers. Figuratively, "life from the dead" refers to a worldwide spiritual awakening brought about by the Jews being restored to a right relationship with God. Using the metaphors of **firstfruits** (v. 16; Nm 15:18-21) and **root** (Rm 11:16), Paul saw in the conversion of some of his contemporary Jews, the remnant, a guarantee of the future conversion of others, the nation. The few who were holy, set apart for God, sanctified the many.

Paul warned the Gentile Christians not to fall into the trap of spiritual pride. He used an allegory of olive trees. The cultivated olive tree represented the Jews; the wild olive tree represented the Gentiles. Branches of the cultivated olive tree—unbelieving Jews—were broken off. **Wild olive branches**—believing Gentiles—**were grafted in**. They shared in the "rich root" of the Jews, i.e., the foundation built on the patriarchs and God's covenant promises made to them. The apostle urged the Gentile Christians to stop boasting about their position before God and thinking themselves superior to the Jews who were now excluded. The Jewish root was supporting them.

The apostle imagined the Gentiles boasting that **branches were broken off so that** they could be **grafted in**. In their arrogance they assumed they were replacing Israel. Although he agreed with that statement, he cautioned them that **if God did not spare the natural branches** (v. 21), **He** would **not spare** them **either**. Faith does not allow boasting. Bragging means trusting in one's own efforts and not in God.

Paul contrasted two qualities of God, His **kindness and severity** (v. 22). The latter relates to His unyielding opposition to sin. His severity is directed **toward**

those who have fallen, i.e., unbelieving Jews. His **kindness** is toward those who believe and who continue to trust in God and not rely on themselves. The apostle was warning against proud complacency.

Paul offered hope to the Jews. God has the power to graft the Jews—if they believe—back into the cultivated tree. If the Gentiles, wild branches, were **grafted in against nature**, how much more will the natural branches be grafted back into their own **olive tree**. Since some Jews had already become believers, Paul thought it possible that many more would believe. God could do the impossible and graft them in again.

11:25-32 God's purpose includes the salvation of **all Israel**. Paul brought his discussion on the problem of Israel (chaps. 9–11) to a climactic conclusion. He referred to God's dealing with Israel as a MYSTERY (Gk. *mustērion*, "secret"), something unknown previously but now revealed by God. Without divine revelation, human intellect would not be able to discern His plan for the Jews. The Gentiles especially had no need to be conceited about this. They might have thought that Israel had no future and that they had replaced them. Paul corrected their misconception and pride. This mystery included a **partial hardening** (11:25) of Israel. A remnant that had believed had always existed. Only those who refused to believe had been hardened. This hardening is temporary—**until the full number of Gentiles** (v. 25) has received the gospel. The fulfillment of the Gentile mission would bring the lifting of hardness from Israel.

When the full number of Gentiles has come in, **all Israel will be saved**. Paul was not referring to each and every Israelite. He was speaking of the nation of Israel as a whole. There will be some Israelites whose lack of faith still excludes them. Instead of a remnant, however, the whole nation will turn to Christ. This will happen when the **Liberator**, Jesus Christ, comes **from Zion**, the heavenly city, at His return (v. 26). At that time the Lord will remove ungodliness from the Jews and **take away their sins**. Paul was pointing to a large-scale conversion of Israel at the time of His return. He confirmed this future prospect for Israel by quoting the authority of Scripture (Is 59:20-21). Israel will experience deliverance when God spiritually restores the new covenant. With their sins removed, the Jews will enjoy restored fellowship with God.

Paul identified the Jews from two perspectives or relationships. From the standpoint of **the gospel** they were **enemies** because of their rejection of Jesus. God was hostile toward them. The disobedience of the Jews led to the conversion of the Gentiles. God worked through the Jews' faithlessness to carry out His purpose. From the standpoint of God's **election** or choice, the Jews were **loved** for the sake of the promises God made to Abraham. God's purpose does not change. He does not take back what He has given. His **gifts** or special privileges to the Jews (Rm 9:4-5) and His **calling** of them **are irrevocable** (Rm 11:29).

God consistently worked out His purpose of justification and mercy to both Jews and Gentiles. He used one group to help the other. Paul reminded the Gentiles of their previous disobedience to God. God showed them **mercy** through the Jews' refusal to accept Jesus Christ. The Jews' disobedience resulted in mercy to the Gentiles, which brought the gospel to the Gentiles. God's mercy to the Gentiles resulted in mercy to the Jews. God **has imprisoned** (v. 32) together both Jews and Gentiles in their **disobedience**, but His ultimate plan is to show mercy to all. Jews and Gentiles alike are sinners. They have not escaped from their disobedience apart from God's mercy.

11:33-36 God deserves praise for His wisdom and ways. As Paul concluded his discussion on the difficult issue of Israel's unbelief, he burst into praise of God. All creation depends on God, including nations as well as individuals. Everything God does expresses His mercy, even if people do not understand His ways. God's purpose has an element of mystery and incomprehensibility. No one can fully understand the ways of God. No one can advise Him. He can never be **repaid** or outgiven. God is the Source, the Sustainer, and the Goal of all things. He deserves supreme **glory forever**.

PAUL OFFERED PRACTICAL INSTRUCTIONS FOR CHRISTIAN LIVING (12:1–15:13)

Paul often followed his doctrinal exposition with practical implications for the Christian life. He did the same in Romans with the transition word **Therefore** (12:1) pointing back to chapters 1–11. He had shown how God's mercy provides justification by faith for both Jews and Gentiles. Those whom God has declared righteous and put into a right relationship with Him must now live a righteous kind of life. Chapters 1–11 discuss right standing with God. Chapters 12–15 present right living.

Believers Should Dedicate Themselves to God (12:1-2)

12:1-2 These two verses represent the theme of Paul's practical application. Using the familiar generic address, **brothers**, he urged believers to respond with total commitment to God. The basis for this Christian living centers in **the mercies of God**. Because of all that God has done for believers in Jesus Christ, believers should willingly present themselves as a sacrifice to God. This **sacrifice** is **living** in contrast to the slain animals of the Jewish ritual and rises out of the new life in Christ, which is holy, dedicated to God and His will. This sacrifice is also pleasing to God because it reflects obedience to Him. Such a sacrifice constitutes believers' spiritual worship or REASONABLE (Gk. *logikēn*, "rational," transliterated into English as "logical") service. The "logical" service takes into account the season of life. What is appropriate for one time in life may not be consistent with priorities for another period. Negatively, believers should stop CONFORMING (Gk. *suschēmatizesthe*, "shaped by, living after the pattern of") to this age or world, which opposes God and lies under the control of Satan. The reference is to a temporary scheme of things dictated by the world or human circumstances. The new age should shape the lives of believers. On the other hand, believers should continually be TRANSFORMED (Gk. *metamorphousthe*, "changed in form") by the renewing of their minds. This change is radical, working from the inside out. Believers do not think like unbelievers. They are continually renewed in their thinking by the Holy Spirit. Their renewed minds will enable them to DISCERN (Gk. *dokimazein*, "examine, test, and approve") the will of God, that which is good, pleasing, and PERFECT (Gk. *teleion*, "completion, end, goal"). In the New Testament, perfection is not so much a reference to the absence of flaws as it is a way of expressing completion.

Believers Should Exercise Their Spiritual Gifts in Humility (12:3-8)

12:3-8 Paul applied the dedication believers should give to God in specific situations, first in relationships with other believers. When he referred to the **grace** (v. 3) given to him, Paul was thinking primarily of his apostleship. Paul was reminding the Romans of his authority to instruct. He wanted these believers to use their God-given gifts in humility, not thinking **more highly** of themselves than they ought. They were to think with sound judgment **as God has distributed a measure of faith** (v. 3) to each Christian. When believers recognize that their gifts come from God and can be used only in dependence upon Him, they cannot be arrogant but will have a proper opinion of themselves. Humility comes from faith— dependence on the saving grace of God in Christ.

Paul used the human body as an analogy of the Christian community. The **one body** has **many parts** with different functions. So also, the body of Christ has many parts with many functions, and each part is important. The apostle was describing the unity of the **one body in Christ** (v. 5), its diversity of members and gifts, and its mutuality or interdependence. All believers depend on the exercise of the gifts of others. Diversity is unified through mutual dependence. Christians cannot work independently of other believers. Recognizing unity, diversity, and interdependence will lessen the tendency to exalt one's gift over that of others. All gifts are important and should be exercised for the common good (1 Cor 12:7).

The apostle affirmed that believers have **different gifts** given to them by God's grace. These special endowments are to be used in His service. He did not provide an exhaustive list but named only seven gifts and how they were to be exercised.

- **Prophecy** (Rm 12:6) involves proclamation of God's direct word, delivered in faith, i.e., dependence on God.

- **Service** (v. 7) is a general term for ministry, probably to the material needs of believers.

- **Teaching** (v. 7) refers to helping believers know how to live, which was especially important in a time where there were few written documents.

- **Exhorting** (v. 8) refers to encouraging.

- **Giving** (v. 8) points to helping those in need, which should be done with generosity and free from mixed motives.

- Those who lead should do so **with diligence** (v. 8) and eagerness.

- Those who show **mercy** (v. 8) to people in distress, such as the sick and suffering, should do so **with cheerfulness**.

Believers Should Cultivate Christian Virtues (12:9-21)

12:9-12 Paul addressed every believer in this list of loosely connected exhortations. The primary command is to **love** sincerely. It comes first and in some sense summarizes all that follows. Love detests evil and clings to what is good. Christians should love each other as members of the same family—God's family. Love puts others first and never gets tired. It perseveres joyfully. **Persistence in prayer** (v. 12) should characterize the lives of believers. They should share enthusiastically and practice **hospitality**.

Believers should **bless** or call down God's good on **those who persecute** them. Love rejoices with those who are rejoicing and mourns with the mourners. Christians should have sympathy for others, feeling their joys and sorrows. Love seeks harmony and acts in humility. Christians should associate with the humble and not be conceited. Love never acts like the world, repaying **evil for evil**. It never takes revenge. Love acts in overcoming kindness to make enemies into friends. Believers should never give in to the temptation to retaliate, but rather they should overcome **evil with good**. Most of

these commands are easily understood. The difficulty lies in obeying them.

Believers Should Submit to Civil Authority (13:1-7)

13:1-7 Believers also have responsibilities beyond the church. Paul was writing to Christians in Rome, the capital of the empire. They needed to know what obligations believers have to the state. Also, the apostle had just written about not taking revenge and not repaying evil. What role does the government have in punishing evildoers?

Everyone, Christians and non-Christians alike, **must submit to the governing authorities** (v. 1). Paul gave the reason for this: All human **authority** comes ultimately **from God**. The authority that governments possess is a delegated authority. Submission does not mean obedience in all things. Believers must obey God rather than man (Ac 5:29) if the orders of authorities directly conflict with God's commands. They must also be willing to accept the consequences of their decisions. Those who resist the ruling authorities when they are ruling legitimately are rebelling against **God's command**. Those who oppose will suffer the consequences—the government's judgment or punishment. Believers must respect the state and its authority.

Those who obey the government have no reason to fear. In fact, the state will commend those who have **good conduct**. Believers should be law-abiding citizens. They do not have the freedom to choose whether or not to obey the government. Paul was speaking of the norm for governments. He was not dealing with persecuting authorities or those who reward evil and punish good.

Paul identified the government or its ruler as **God's servant** (v. 4). These rulers may have an exalted view of themselves or their positions of power and authority, but they are in reality God's servants, those responsible for the lowliest of tasks. They are ultimately responsible to God Himself. They serve His purposes. As God's servants, they enable their citizens to do good, to carry out God's will. Those who do wrong (probably referring to public acts of wrong) should continually fear because civil rulers have the authority to enforce punishment—they **carry the sword** (v. 4). They serve as instruments of God's wrath to punish wrongdoing and restrain evil.

In addition to the assignment to government as being God's servant, Paul gave two more reasons why believers should submit to its authority.

- The government punishes wrongdoing, so it is to their advantage not to bring God's wrath on themselves.

- They know it is the right thing to do, as indicated by the word **conscience** (v. 5).

The government cannot function without financial undergirding. Paul urged believers to **pay** their **taxes, since the authorities are God's public servants** (v. 6), continually attending to the tasks of government. Christians should pay all the taxes they owe: taxes and **tolls** (v. 7) or customs. They must also have the proper attitude toward these rulers, giving them **respect** and **honor** (v. 7). Although individual rulers may be unworthy, God has ordained the institution of government and placed these individuals in power. Christians should treat them with the dignity due them.

Believers Should Remember the Supremacy of Love (13:8-10)

13:8-10 Paul returned to the theme of believers loving others, including not only fellow Christians but people in general as well. The apostle had encouraged his readers to meet all their government obligations, such as taxes. Now he spoke of obligations in general. Christians should not continue in debt. They should pay financial indebtedness off as quickly as possible. One debt, however, can never be discharged—the debt to love others. Those who love all those who enter their lives have **fulfilled the law**. Believers can do this because the Holy Spirit produces this quality in their lives (Gl 5:22). He pours God's love into their lives (Rm 5:5).

The apostle gave four of the Ten Commandments dealing with relationships toward others as representative of the law from the second table of the Decalogue. **Any other commandment** (13:9) shows that these are not exclusive of other laws. Following Jesus' example, the apostle affirmed that all these are summed up by **"You shall love your neighbor as yourself"** (v. 9; Lv 19:18). "Neighbor" includes anyone who is near, anyone the believer encounters in daily life. Love does good for others. It does not wrong or harm them. Christians who love have performed all the law's requirements.

Believers Should Recognize the Urgency of Christian Living (13:11-14)

13:11-14 Paul presented an eschatological motivation for his exhortations on how Christians should conduct themselves, especially loving others—they know **the time**. Christ has come, bringing deliverance and new life. **It is already the hour** to **wake up** (v. 11) from spiritual lethargy because the consummation of their **salvation** (when Christ returns) is near. The apostle was calling his readers to urgent alertness.

Paul used **night** and **darkness** to symbolize evil and sin, while **daylight** and **light** symbolize what is good (vv. 12-13). The coming of Christ brought the beginning of a new day. The night of the old order is nearly over, and the daylight is near with Christ's return. Christians should discard any works related to darkness and their old way of life. They should put on **the armor of light** (v. 12) as soldiers preparing for battle with the powers of darkness. God provides this armor (Eph 6:13-18).

As people who belong to Christ and the daylight, believers are to live their lives with proper, decent behavior. The sins of darkness should not characterize them. The six sins Paul identified in verse 13 stem from focus on self and its desires. The first two deal with abuse of alcohol (**carousing and drunkenness**), the second two relate to sexual misconduct (**sexual impurity and promiscuity**), and the third pair deal with attitudes of self-will (**quarreling and jealousy**). These practices represent a failure to love.

Paul identified the armor Christians are to **put on with the Lord Jesus Christ** Himself (Rm 13:14). To put on the Lord Jesus Christ means to live in intimate union with Him, submitting to His lordship in every area of life. This means believers will make no plans to **satisfy the fleshly desires** (v. 14). They should give sin no opportunity in their lives. Christians have put on Christ at conversion (Gl 3:27). Throughout their lives, however, there is a continually taking off the old and putting on the new for renewal and growth.

Believers Should Seek to Build Up One Another (14:1–15:13)

Paul wrote to deal with the relationship between strong and weak Christians. The latter are not believers who are morally lax and easily susceptible to temptation. For the apostle, weak Christians are those with an immature faith who have overly scrupulous consciences that tend toward legalism. The weaker brothers at Rome possibly had a Jewish background. The strong possibly were those of Gentile backgrounds who did not observe the restrictions of their Jewish brothers and who celebrated their freedom in Christ. In reality, the identity of the weak and strong believers is not clear. The apostle wrote to warn and encourage both groups. He desired unity in the church above all. He wanted believers to live and minister with each other even though they may live out the Christian faith in different ways.

14:1-12 Believers should not judge one another. The church should **accept** and welcome with the warmth of friendship those who are **weak in faith**. Paul was not referring to saving faith. The weak are Christians. He was speaking of weakness in applying faith to the daily decisions of life or how believers should live. These weak believers should be accepted without judging their scruples or trying to change their minds or making them feel inferior. The strong should do nothing to discourage the weak.

Believers should not judge the dietary observances of others. For instance, some people in the Roman church believed they could **eat anything**. Others, the **weak** believers, following the dictates of their own consciences, ate **only vegetables** (v. 2). Perhaps the latter group wanted to avoid any possibility of eating meat offered to idols or desired to follow Jewish dietary laws. Paul did not give the reason for their being vegetarians. He insisted that each group respect the other. The strong should not despise the weak and feel superior to them. The weak should not pass judgment on the strong and think they are sinning because they do not observe their own scruples. **God has accepted** both strong and weak.

Paul used a household servant-master analogy. No one would think of criticizing someone else's slave. Such a servant stands accountable to his master only. It does not matter what others think, only what the

> ## Heart to Heart:
> ## A Critical Spirit
>
> *Unfortunately, a critical spirit and an attitude of spiritual superiority over others seem far too easy to cultivate. Let God's Word "straighten you out" in these areas. Do you criticize fellow believers or look down on them? Remember they, too, belong to Jesus as His servants. He alone is their Judge. Do you accept others despite their weaknesses and failures? Remember the Lord has accepted you in that very way. Do you go "full steam ahead" and do what you know the Lord has given you the freedom to do even if it offends a sister in Christ? Remember, God calls you to bear the weaknesses of those without strength and to avoid putting a stumbling block in their paths. You are not to please yourself but your neighbor for her good, to build her up. Remember that Jesus calls you to deny yourself. Decide now that you will walk in love and pursue what promotes peace and builds up others instead of tearing them down. Ask the Holy Spirit to remove your critical spirit and attitude of spiritual superiority.*

master thinks. In the same way both strong and weak believers are accountable to the Lord alone. The Lord accepts both and enables both to **stand** (v. 4).

Believers should not judge others who observe special days. First-century Christians differed on the observance of special days, possibly special feasts or fast days. The apostle stressed the importance of believers being convinced in their own minds whether such practices were right or not. They should not do what others do if they feel it is wrong. Both strong and weak act out of their convictions, trying to serve the Lord. They observe or do not observe special days as unto the Lord. They eat or do not eat as unto the Lord, and both give thanks for the food they do eat. Both are trying to do the will of God and act for His glory.

Christians **belong to the Lord** (v. 8), whether they are alive or dead, for even death cannot separate them from God and His love (Rm 8:38-39). Believers do not live to and for themselves but to and for

God. This obligation carries into the life to come. Alive or dead, believers belong to the Lord. The very purpose of Christ's dying and coming back to life was so that He might be the Lord of Christians, both the living and the dead. So, eating or not eating, observing a day or not, fall under His Lordship.

Paul asked why (weak) Christians should judge their fellow believers or why (strong) believers should regard their fellow believers with contempt. Both will have to stand before the judgment seat of God (2 Co 5:10). He alone is the true Judge and has the right to judge the actions of His children. His verdict is the one that counts. At that time everyone will do homage to God in worship. Bending the knee and confessing are not the behavior of judges. All believers will have to **give an account** of themselves **to God**. His judgment is personal and universal.

14:13-23 Believers should avoid making others stumble. Paul urged the Roman believers—both weak and strong—to stop passing judgment on one another. Instead of criticizing each other, they should determine **not to put a stumbling block or pitfall** in a brother's way (v. 13). A stumbling block impedes progress; a pitfall pictures a trap designed to capture a victim. Here the apostle was addressing the strong Christians. It did not matter to them whether or not they ate certain foods or observed certain days. They could change easily. If they encouraged their weaker fellow believers to do things against the dictates of their consciences, they were leading them into sin. The strong should set examples that do not lead to sin on the part of their weaker brothers and sisters. They should consider the effect their actions have on others.

Paul agreed with the convictions of the strong party. He affirmed that nothing is unclean in itself. Yet, he recognized that to those who considered something unclean, to them it was unclean. Until they changed their views on certain foods, they would violate their consciences to eat them. Believers should not do anything they think is wrong. The strong believers who go ahead and eat whatever they want deeply hurt their weaker fellow believers, not only because the latter see the former as sinning but also because their example may cause them to eat and thus violate their consciences, leading to spiritual ruin. Those who disregard the convictions of others are not **walking** in **love**. Christ died for these people, giving up His very life; yet the strong Christians are not willing to give up their favorite foods for them. Love is not selfish.

The apostle exhorted the strong not to let their freedom to eat **be slandered** (v. 16) because of their loveless misuse of this freedom. Then he moved the discussion to a higher level, to the spiritual and internal as opposed to the physical and external. **The kingdom of God** does not consist of eating and drinking but of **righ-teousness, peace, and joy in the Holy Spirit** (v. 17). These spiritual virtues produced by the Spirit, not diet, should have priority in the life of believers. Even the strong do not have unlimited freedom. They live under the authority of God's kingdom. Those who seek first the qualities of the kingdom are serving Christ, which makes them **acceptable to God and approved by** others.

Paul urged his readers **to pursue** earnestly harmony and edification in the church. Instead of criticizing or looking down on one another, believers should do those things that would promote **peace**. Instead of tearing each other down, Christians should build each other up. The apostle warned of the opposite action. Believers should never tear down God's work because of food. Even though all things are clean, they are evil if what believers eat causes fellow Christians to stumble or if weak believers eat with a guilty conscience. The better way would be for believers to abstain from meat and wine or abstain from doing anything that would make fellow Christians stumble. The goal should always be the building up of one another.

Paul exhorted the strong not to parade their faith (to do things without scruples the weaker believers cannot do) in front of the weak. Instead, they are to keep that to themselves before God. People are blessed who do not condemn themselves by doing something they know is right, i.e., their actions do not cause them doubts. The apostle also warned the weak not to eat if they had any doubts. Such action **is not from faith** (v. 23). It would condemn them and would be **sin** for those individuals. Paul wanted both the strong and the weak to act out of their own convictions and with a clear conscience. Faith—humble reliance on God—should motivate all that they do.

> *The strong have an obligation to bear weaknesses of those without strength.*

15:1-13 Believers should follow the example of Christ. Paul now spoke directly to the strong and included himself among them. The strong have an obligation to bear the weaknesses of those without strength. Though the scruples of the weak may cause problems and irritation for the strong, the latter can support and carry these weaker believers. They will not act selfishly to please themselves but will work for the unity of the Christian community even if that entails partially giving up their own freedom in Christ. The debt of love that can never be paid (Rm 13:8) may require self-denial and bearing the burden of the failings of others. The strong can take the initiative to solve conflict in the church. God has given them strength to help others.

Paul addressed all believers, exhorting them to please not only their fellow Christians, but also, expanding the application to their neighbors. This admonition does not mean doing anything others wish done or indulging them. The apostle put a limit on this pleasing. It must be done for the neighbor's good to **build him up**. The actions of believers must contribute to the spiritual growth of others. They must seek the good of others, not their own good.

Christ is the example to follow. He **did not please Himself** (v. 3). His commitment to do God's will and serve others brought Him suffering. As a consequence of His obedience, Jesus became the recipient of the insults of the people (Ps 69:9). The Lord did not seek His own interests but looked to meet the needs of others. Both strong and weak Christians should do the same.

Paul appealed to the Old Testament because he knew all the Scriptures written in previous years were written to teach Christians so that they might **have hope**.

Hope refers specifically to Christian hope, that of a saving relationship with God through Jesus Christ. The perseverance of believers in their Christian lives and the encouragement given by the Scripture promote this hope. God Himself is the source of the believers' steadfastness and encouragement. He gives these qualities to His children.

The apostle prayed that God would bring unity to the Roman church with its strong-weak conflicts. This unity would center in Jesus Christ, following His example. Its purpose would be worship. Paul desired these believers to **glorify God with a united mind and voice** (Rm 15:6). He exhorted believers—strong and weak—to **accept** each other (14:1) and based his exhortation on the fact that Christ has accepted them. Christ's acceptance of believers and their acceptance of one another bring praise to God and further His glory.

Christ became **a servant** of the circumcision, the Jews. Circumcision was the sign of God's covenant made first with Abraham and then continuing to his spiritual descendants. Jesus made known God's truth and confirmed God's faithfulness to the **promises** made **to the fathers**. God's promises find their fulfillment in Christ. The confirmation of the promises includes the call to the Gentiles. God's mercy in saving them and including them as part of His chosen people leads to their glorifying Him.

Paul again used a series of Old Testament quotations to support his argument that the Gentiles have always been a part of God's plan. These quotes show a progression in the role of the Gentiles. The first (Ps 18:49) speaks of the psalmist praising God **among the Gentiles** and singing praises to His name. God had given him victory over the Gentile nations. In the second (Dt 32:43), the Gentiles join with Israel in the praise of the Lord, for God gives salvation to both groups. In the last two quotes, the Gentiles join Israel in praising the Lord (Ps 117:1) and hoping in the Messiah, the root of Jesse (Is 11:10). If God can unite Jews and Gentiles, He can also unite the weak and the strong.

The apostle ended the doctrinal and practical sections of Romans with a prayer. He knew the believer's goal is not the right to eat and drink. Instead, his goal is joy, peace, and hope given by God through **the power of the Holy Spirit**. All this comes as a believer trusts in Him. The Holy Spirit desired that **the God of hope** (Rm 15:13), both the source and the object for the hope of Jews and Gentiles, fill them to overflowing with these spiritual blessings.

PAUL CONCLUDED HIS LETTER TO THE ROMANS (15:14–16:27)

Paul Gave His Reasons for Writing (15:14-33)

15:14-21 First, he shared his responsibility as apostle to the Gentiles. Paul had just finished giving some strong exhortations. The Roman Christians might have thought the apostle considered them immature. The apostle, however, had already spoken of their strong faith (Rm 1:8). Now with personal warmth (**my brothers**, 15:14) he shared his certain, continuing conviction that they were **full of goodness, filled with all knowledge, and able to instruct one another** (v. 14). "Goodness" refers to the Spirit's gift of moral excellence. "Knowledge" indicates that the Romans truly understood the Christian faith and knew the right things to do. They were able to admonish each other in mutual pastoral ministry.

Since the apostle had just noted the knowledge and ability of the Roman Christians in the faith, he explained why he had written. He confessed he had **writ-ten boldly on some points** for the purpose of reminding these believers of truths they perhaps already knew (or with which they were confronted for the first time). Paul wrote because of God's commissioning of him as the apostle to the Gentiles (the **grace given** to him). He took this calling seriously. This call included being **a minister of Christ Jesus to the Gentiles, serving as a priest of God's good news**. As a priest, he proclaimed the gospel. The purpose of Paul's priestly service was to present the Gentiles as an **offering** to God, **acceptable** and **sanctified by the Holy Spirit**. The Holy Spirit set the Gentiles apart to God as members of His chosen people. Paul preached so that the Gentiles might come to offer themselves to God as living sacrifices (Rm 12:1).

Paul's mission to the Gentiles had proved successful. Yet, he did not **boast** in his own accomplishment but **in Christ Jesus**, who enabled and strengthened him for this ministry. He was simply God's instrument. God had worked through him. The apostle boasted in the things pertaining to God. He **would not dare** to speak of **anything except what Christ** had **accomplished through** him—bringing the Gentiles to obedience. Christ achieved His purpose through what Paul said and did. The apostle's ministry had been confirmed by **miraculous signs and wonders** and enabled **by the power of** the Holy **Spirit**. He noted the extent of his proclamation in geographical terms, **from Jerusalem to Illyricum**, a Roman province northwest of Macedonia on the eastern shore of the Adriatic Sea (modern Yugoslavia and Albania). Paul had preached and established churches in the major centers of this area. His great ambition was to proclaim the gospel where Christ had not yet been named. He did not want to build on the **foundation** of another. Paul was not referring to competition in ministry. He usually worked with associates. He desired to see as many people as possible come to faith in Jesus Christ. Pioneer missionary labor meant going where no one else had yet gone to unreached people to plant new churches (Is 52:15).

15:22-29 Second, Paul shared his plans to visit Rome and Spain. He explained that he had been **prevented many times from coming** to Rome because of his pressing commitment to preach to those who had not heard the gospel in the east. He had followed the Spirit's leading. Now he felt he was ready to expand his focus. In fact, he believed he no longer had any church-planting work to do in the regions he had already visited. The apostle could follow the desire he had held for many years to visit the Roman Christians. He would not remain long in Rome, however, because his goal was to reach **Spain**, the western reach of the empire. He would enjoy fellowship with the believers for a while and hoped they would help him in his mission to Spain through their prayers, possible financial support, and even as coworkers. Perhaps Paul wanted to make Rome his missionary base for ministry to the west. His previous home church at Antioch would be too far away for this purpose.

Presently Paul was on his way **to Jerusalem** with the relief offering the Gentile churches in **Macedonia and Achaia** had collected to help the poverty-stricken Christians in the mother church at Jerusalem. The apostle had focused on this offering during his third missionary journey. He felt this trip to be so important that he delayed his longed-for trip to Rome. He saw the relief offering as an expression of love by the Gentile believers for Jewish Christians. He hoped this effort would bring unity and fellowship between the two groups who often dis-

puted with each other and thereby validate his Gentile mission.

Paul indicated to the Romans that the Gentiles participating in this offering were pleased to do so. They gave voluntarily with goodwill to this love offering. They had a spiritual debt to repay the Jewish Christians. This debt obligated them to share. The Jewish believers had shared their spiritual benefits, primarily the gospel of Jesus Christ, with the Gentiles. The least the Gentiles could do would be to minister to their **material needs**. Paul's immediate task at hand was the delivery of these funds to Jerusalem. When he had finished offering up this fruit, he would go to Spain by way of Rome. Paul expressed his quiet confidence that he would indeed come to Rome with the **fullness** of Christ's **blessing**.

15:30-33 Third, the apostle requested prayer from the Romans. He knew uncertain difficulties faced him in Jerusalem from hostile Jews and even legalistic Jewish Christians who had doubts about his work among the Gentiles. He urged them to **agonize together with** him in prayer to God on his behalf. AGONIZE (Gk. *sunagōnisasthai*, "help, assist, join with"), an athletic term, pictures the intense struggle of the athlete in competition. Paul based his appeal on the lordship of Jesus Christ and the love the Holy Sprit pours out on believers.

Intercessory prayer involves struggle. It puts believers in the fight against the forces of evil. Women in particular have felt the call to intercede for their families, their churches, their communities, and their country. Paul's words to the Romans remind them of the intense effort needed to pray and encourage them to persevere.

Paul had three specific requests for prayer. He desired prayer for his personal deliverance from the unbelieving Jews in Jerusalem. He had already had to leave

Heart to Heart: Intercessory Prayer

*H*ave you ever agonized in prayer on behalf of someone? Paul asked the Roman believers to agonize in prayer on his behalf. Are there people in your life who need your prayers? Intercessory prayer is a ministry that can occur in any place and at any time. It is a ministry in which the youngest child or the oldest adult can participate. Prayer is simply talking to God about other individuals and their needs. Paul's words remind us, however, that such prayer can involve intense struggle. It is urgent, serious business because it has eternal consequences. It releases God's power and all His spiritual resources on behalf of those for whom you pray. Will you accept the challenge of agonizing in prayer for another, especially for her spiritual growth? As a believer you can approach God's throne boldly to seek His mercy and help, not only on behalf of others, but also for yourself.

that city previously because of Jewish hostility. He also wanted the Romans to pray that the church in Jerusalem would accept the love offering from the Gentiles. These Jewish Christians were conservative, and all of them had not embraced the Gentiles as believers, especially since they did not observe the Mosaic law such as circumcision. If these two requests were answered, then Paul's third desire would become reality: He would come to Rome by God's will with joy and **be refreshed** by his fellowship with them. Paul added his own prayer benediction to this call for intercession that the God of peace be with all of the Roman Christians.

Paul Commended Phoebe (16:1-2)

Many people traveled in the first-century Roman empire. They often carried letters of recommendation from those who had friends in the city of their destination. For Christians, who practiced hospitality, these letters served to distinguish true believers from those who would take advantage of their generosity.

16:1 Paul's lengthy commendation of Phoebe likely indicates that she carried his letter to the Romans and delivered it to

the church in the capital city. She was from Cenchreae, serving as the port city of Corinth and located seven miles to her east. Phoebe's name meant "bright" or "radiant." Like many converts from pagan backgrounds, she kept her given name despite its connection to Greek mythology.

The apostle described this woman in three ways:

- She was a believing **sister**, a fellow Christian.

- She was a **servant of the church in Cenchreae**. The Greek word translated **SERVANT** (*diakonon*, "helper") definitely has the connotation of one who serves or ministers to another. It has been transliterated into English as deacon or deaconess. Countless women through the ages have given of themselves and their resources to the work of the kingdom. Their ministries in the local church have been myriad. In Acts 6:1-7, a group of men were called out to meet the physical and social needs of the congregation so that the apostles would not be distracted from their primary task of ministry of the Word (Acts 6:4). Were women also assigned official responsibilities in such service ministries? One cannot say with any certainty. In fact, this reference to Phoebe is the only one that could be understood in that way. If understood in the New Testament sense, a deacon or deaconess certainly needs no title to find ample opportunity for service. On the other hand, if being a deacon or deaconess is viewed as official spiritual leadership and if it is considered a position of authority over the congregation, as has evolved in many modern churches, other passages penned by the apostle Paul clearly provide additional guidelines (see 1 Tim 2:11-15; 3:8-13). The word certainly indicates that Phoebe had a servant's heart and that she used her energies to serve within her church family in some capacity.

- Phoebe was also for many a BENEFACTOR (Gk. *prostatis*, "helper," lit. "one standing before"). Lexicons define the term as "protectress, patroness, helper." The use of this word probably indicated that Phoebe was a woman of some wealth and position. She may have been a businesswoman. In any case, she was an important person. In fact, a woman would not be likely to be traveling alone in the first century. Phoebe may have been accompanied by her servants from her household. Paul stated that Phoebe had helped many people, including himself. He did not identify the nature of that help. Perhaps like Lydia of Philippi, Phoebe shared her material resources with those in need.

16:2 At any rate, Paul asked the Romans to **welcome** Phoebe **in a manner**

worthy of the saints. He also asked them to **assist her in whatever** ways **she** might **require**. Evidently Phoebe had some task to do in Rome, and the apostle wanted the Romans to help her, especially since she had helped Paul and the church in so many ways.

Phoebe *Romans 16:1-2*	
Phoebe's Life	• Name meaning "radiant or bright" • From the port city of Cenchrea • Woman of influence and status • Gentile Christian
Phoebe's Ministry	• <u>Sister</u> in the Lord • <u>Servant</u> of the church • <u>Saint</u> in the faith • <u>Helper</u> of many people
Paul's Role	• Commended her to the Christians in Rome • Asked them to welcome her in the Lord • Sought assistance for her ministry

Paul Greeted Friends in Rome (16:3-16)

Paul greeted 26 people by name and mentioned two more without using a name as well as noting several households. With the great amount of travel in the first century due to Roman peace and well-kept roads, Paul could well have known many people in a church he had not visited. Also, since he had not yet been to Rome, the apostle was anxious to establish the fact that they already had many relationships in common. The names are a mix of Greek, Latin, and Jewish. They indicate people from all strata of society, slaves and freedmen, singles and married, men and women, Jew and Gentile. They reflect the universal extension of the gospel. The repeated words "in Christ" or "in the Lord" throughout the list of names point to the commitment of all those named to the gospel of Jesus Christ.

Of the people mentioned, Paul identified nine women (ten including Phoebe). This was truly amazing in the male-dominated culture of that time. The acceptance and importance of women and their roles in the church is clear. They all gave valuable service to the Lord and kingdom causes.

16:3-16 Prisca and Aquila were a ministry team. They had worked with the apostle at Corinth and at Ephesus. Paul identified them as his **co-workers** and thanked them for risking their lives for him. He also sent greetings **to the church** that met **in their home**. House churches were common among the early Christians. Few other meeting places, apart from private homes, were available to those fledgling congregations.

Paul noted that several women had worked hard in the ministry for the Lord:

- **Mary** (v. 6);

- **Tryphaena and Tryphosa** (v. 12), who were probably sisters; and

- **Persis** (16:13), whom Paul called "beloved." She was very dear to him.

The apostle also greeted **Julia** (v. 15) and mentioned two unnamed women: the **mother of Rufus** (v. 13), who had mothered Paul at some time in his ministry, and the **sister of Nereus** (v. 15).

Andronicus and Junia (v. 7) could have been another husband-wife ministry team. However, there is considerable debate and no consensus among evangelical scholarship as to whether Junia is male or female (the masculine form differs only slightly from the feminine). In any case, they were among the earliest believers since they came to Christ before Paul was converted. As Paul's **fellow countrymen**, they were probably Jews.

Like Paul they, too, had suffered imprisonment for the sake of the gospel. Paul described them as **outstanding among the apostles**. Again the text lacks clarity on the nature of apostleship as used here. APOSTLES (Gk. *apostolois,* "messengers") in its most basic meaning is "ones sent." The term often refers to the twelve disciples who were called and sent by Jesus. The only other instances of the word's use in this way include Matthias, who succeeded Judas (Ac 1:26) and Paul himself (Ac 14:14). Here the word seems more logically used in its broader sense as designating those commissioned and sent out by the Lord to spread the gospel, as was Barnabas (Ac 14:14). In any case, these two were leaders in the Christian movement. Paul respected Junia, whether woman or man, and recognized this dedicated believer as having made a unique contribution to Christian ministry. There is no contradiction or confusion regardless of whether Junia is male or female. The meaning of the Greek word *apostolois,* translated in English as APOSTLES, is clear. How it is interpreted in this reference has ample evidence in the ways the word is used in the New Testament as a whole. Christ did send out men and women to share the gospel, but He did not abrogate the clear boundaries of Scripture in doing so.

Paul Warned Against False Teachers (16:17-20)

16:17-20 The apostle abruptly interrupted his greetings to give a strong warning about false teachers. The Romans were to **watch out** for these people (v. 17), implying they had not yet infiltrated the church, though the possibility existed that they might. Although Paul did not identify the nature of their error, these heretics did cause dissension and put up stumbling blocks contrary to the Christian

Women Mentioned by Paul in Romans

Name	Reference	Comments in the Text	Application
Phoebe (Gk. meaning "pure or "radiant")	Rm 16:1-2	• Gentile from Cenchrea, a port city • Described by Paul as a sister (Gk. *adelphēn*); a servant (Gk. *diakonov*, transliterated into English as *deacon*); one of the saints (Gk. *hagiōn*, "set apart, holy, morally pure," and often a reference to one who belongs to and is wholly devoted to God); a benefactor (Gk. *prostatis*,"helper, friend") • Probably a woman of wealth and influence and perhaps functioning in the world of commerce or government	Even wealth, position, and influence do not relieve a woman of the responsibility of humble service.
Prisca or Priscilla (Lat. "dutiful")	Rm 16:1-3; Ac 18:18,26; 1 Co 16:19; 2 Tm 4:19	• Described by Paul, together with her husband Aquila, as *fellow workers* (Gk. *sunergous*, lit. "work with") • Noted their dedication to risk their lives for the gospel • Highly esteemed by the churches • Hosted church in their own home	Work for Christ is woven into the warp and woof of life—in the tasks of home and marketplace.
Mary (Hb. "bitter")	Rm 16:6	Described by Paul as one who *has worked very hard*	Hard work, facing difficulties and obstacles, is part of the kingdom task.
Junia (Gk. feminine form). See comments in exposition concerning whether reference is to man or woman.	Rm 16:7	• Paul described as: "fellow countrymen" and "fellow prisoners" • "outstanding among the apostles" • followers of Christ before Paul's conversion	Whether male or female, God honors your work in His name.
Tryphena (Gk. "dainty") and Tryphosa (Gk. "delicate")	Rm. 16:12	Paul described them as women *who have worked hard in the Lord*	If their names indicated frailty or physical weakness of any kind, they still worked hard!

Women Mentioned by Paul in Romans (cont.)			
Persis	Rm 16:12	Paul described her as *my dear friend* and as one *who worked very hard in the Lord*	Working hard together builds and sustains friendships.
Unnamed mother of Rufus	Rm 16:13	Paul described her as like a mother to him	Maternity is a precious ministry to the saints.
Julia and unnamed sister of Nereus	Rm 16:15	Worthy of greetings from Paul	Gratitude for your service for Christ is not dependent on whether or not your name is remembered or mentioned.

Junia
Romans 16:7

- Jewish believer
- Mentioned with Andronicus
- Converted before Paul the Apostle
- Friend of Paul
- Imprisoned with Paul
- Diligent co-laborer in the faith

teaching the Roman believers had already learned. Those whose instruction differed from the sound doctrine they knew should be avoided. He urged them to keep away from such persons, not giving them any opportunity to deceive the Christians.

Romans were to avoid such people because they did **not serve our Lord Christ** but rather **their own appetites**. The phrase **such people** (v. 18) indicates that Paul did not have a definite group of false teachers in mind but anyone with this mindset. He had met many false teachers in his travels. He knew the type. These people used **smooth talk and flattering words** to deceive deliberately **the unsuspecting** or naïve (v. 18).

Paul had confidence in the Romans that they would not be so deceived. The report of their **obedience** was well known outside of Rome. Any misstep would also become well known. Their very faithful-

ness, which caused Paul to **rejoice**, made them a target. Consequently, the apostle urged them **to be wise** in **what is good** and **innocent** in **what is evil**. Despite any evil the believers would encounter, Paul confidently predicted that **the God of peace** (not dissension) would **crush Satan** (v. 20), the initiator of evil who would seek to sow discord among believers. God would do the crushing, but Satan would end up **under** the **feet** of the Christians. They would have the victory. **The grace of our Lord Jesus be with you** (v. 20) was Paul's customary closing benediction.

Paul's Associates Greeted the Romans (16:21-24)

16:21-24 The apostle's friends and associates who were with him in Corinth also sent their greetings to the Roman believers. This group included **Tertius**, Paul's amanuensis (secretary) who wrote the letter for him.

Paul Offered Glory to God (16:25-27)

16:25-27 The apostle ended his letter with a doxology of praise to God, which in essence summarized the teachings of the epistle. God is able **to strengthen** the Roman Christians and do for them whatever they need. This empowering is according to the gospel Paul had preached and had made his own and the proclamation he faithfully delivered about Jesus Christ. The gospel had been a mystery **for long ages**, but with the coming of Jesus Christ, God had revealed it. The gospel showed that Jesus explained and fulfilled the Old Testament Scriptures in every way according to God's eternal commandment. This revelation was for the purpose of leading **all nations** to believe and obey the gospel.

Bibliography

* Barrett, C. K. *The Epistle to the Romans.* Harper's New Testament Commentaries. New York: Harper & Row, Publishers, 1957.

* Bruce, F. F. *The Epistle of Paul to the Romans.* Tyndale New Testament Commentaries. Grand Rapids: William B. Eerdmans Publishing Company, 1963.

Corley, Bruce, and Curtis Vaughan. *Romans: A Study Guide Commentary.* Grand Rapids: Zondervan Publishing House, 1976.

* Cranfield, C. E. B. *A Critical and Exegetical Commentary on the Epistle to the Romans.* The International Critical Commentary. 2 vols. Edinburgh: T. & T. Clark Limited. Vol. 1, 1975; vol. 2, 1979.

* Dunn, James D. G. *Romans.* Word Biblical Commentary. 2 vols. Dallas: Word, Inc., 1988.

Harrison, Everett F. *Romans.* The Expositor's Bible Commentary, vol. 10. Grand Rapids: Zondervan Publishing House, 1976.

Moo, Douglas. *Romans 1–8.* Wycliffe Exegetical Commentary. Chicago: Moody Press, 1991.

Morris, Leon. *The Epistle to the Romans.* Grand Rapids: William B. Eerdmans Publishing Company, 1988.

Mounce, Robert H. *Romans.* New American Commentary, vol. 27. Nashville: Broadman and Holman, 1995.

* Murray, John. *The Epistle to the Romans.* The New International Commentary on the New Testament. Grand Rapids: William B. Eerdmans Publishing Company, 1959.

Phillips, John. *Exploring Romans.* Grand Rapids: Kregel, 2002.

* Advanced Study

1 CORINTHIANS

Introduction

On Paul's second missionary journey, he came to Corinth and built a strong friendship with fellow tentmakers, a Jewish couple named Aquila and Priscilla. Paul remained in Corinth about a year and a half, evangelizing and preaching in the Jewish synagogues. He encountered fierce opposition, but he also experienced great success. Even Crispus, the synagogue leader, trusted the Lord (Ac 18:8).

Paul spent much time with this influential church. While God worked in mighty ways, the church struggled for purity and maturity. Paul wrote the Corinthians several strong letters, diligently teaching doctrine and carefully explaining Christian behavior. Heated questions were addressed. Of particular interest are a number of passages specifically affecting women.

Title

Paul wrote at least three (some scholars posit four or more) letters "To God's church at Corinth" (1:2; 2 Co 1:1). The Greek title of the letter known in English as "Paul's First Letter to the Corinthians," or simply as "First Corinthians," is *pros Korinthiogō A*, "to the Corinthians A," derived from the letter's immediate recipients. Paul mentioned having written a previous letter (5:9), which is not extant. Rather than designating the epistle as the first one Paul had written to the church in Corinth, the title "First Corinthians" acknowledges this letter as the first of the two Corinthian letters accepted in the New Testament canon.

Setting

In 46 BC, Julius Caesar rebuilt Corinth as a Roman colony that prospered magnificently, growing to nearly 600,000 people. Its location on a narrow isthmus between northern and southern Greece gave it great importance and advantage in sea trade, drawing sailors and tradesmen from Asia and Europe.

As the political capital of Greece, Corinth was a seat of commerce and intellectual life with a reputation for luxury, sexual immorality, and even sacred prostitution. Its acropolis, the Acrocorinth, was used for defense and for pagan worship. On the Acrocorinth was located the temple to Aphrodite, which enticed many locals and foreigners (see chart on Aphrodite). The church faced hardships while protecting itself and reaching out to the world; however, its ministry effectively demonstrated the power of God.

Genre

First Corinthians is a letter from the Apostle Paul to the church in Corinth. The letter begins with the three-part salutation typical of ancient Greco-Roman written correspondence: name of the writer, identification of the recipients, and words of greeting. Unlike the letter to the Romans, 1 Corinthians is not a carefully crafted

---

Aphrodite

- Greek goddess of sexual love and beauty
- Roman counterpart: Venus
- Semitic (Phoenician) counterpart: Ishtar/Astarte
- Temple in Corinth reportedly employed 1,000 priestesses and cultic prostitutes

Aphrodite is not mentioned in 1 Corinthians, but the presence of her temple in the city figured prominently in the sexual immorality with which the church was dealing.

---

doctrinal treatise; rather, Paul responded personally and directly to a variety of troubling issues that had developed in the Corinthian church.

Author

Paul's authorship is almost universally accepted. The book not only is marked by his style but also bears his signature at beginning and end (1 Co 1:1; 16:21). Clement of Rome as early as AD 95 mentioned that 1 Corinthians had been written by Paul. This missionary and theologian was a bold and compassionate leader who preached the gospel of Jesus Christ to the Jew first and then to the Gentiles.

Date

The church at Corinth was established about AD 50 during Paul's 18-month residence there in the midst of his second missionary journey (Ac 18:1-17). Having received disturbing reports of sexual immorality within the Corinthian congregation while visiting Ephesus on his third missionary journey (Ac 19), the apostle penned a letter that obviously has been lost (1 Co 5:9-11). Subsequently he heard from "members of Chloe's household," who may have been members of the Corinthian church (1 Co 1:11), about divisions in the church and misunderstandings over the contents of the earlier letter. Soon thereafter he received another delegation with a letter containing questions (1 Co 7:1; 16:17) and promptly dispatched Timothy to Corinth (1 Co 4:17). Meantime he wrote a second letter, the extant 1 Corinthians, hoping it would reach Corinth before Timothy's arrival (1 Co 16:10). In light of these facts, Paul probably wrote 1 Corinthians near the end of his stay in Ephesus (1 Co 16:8; Ac 20:31) and before his departure for Macedonia (1 Co 16:5; Ac 20:1) about AD 56, and not later than AD 57. Although feeling it unwise to leave the work in Ephesus, he freely sent and received letters. This letter addressing conduct and answering timely questions was an effective means for him to mentor this congregation.

Recipients

At the time of the letter, Corinth was a thriving Roman colony with many of its inhabitants having immigrated from Italy and with a strong population of Greeks. Because of viable trade business, the city hosted a transient population and was home for many ethnic groups, mirroring diversity ethnically, culturally, and economically. Many Jews who lived in Corinth had been driven out of Rome by Claudius in AD 49.

Some of these Jews, including notable leaders, accepted Paul's message. Gentiles from varied backgrounds were also drawn to Paul's message. The church in Corinth was large and filled with members who were self-willed, rebellious against authority, and arrogant.

Into this unfavorable climate, confusion, and guilt, Paul introduced forgiveness, redemption, and joy.

Major Themes

With a compassionate firmness, Paul dealt with tough issues, including doctrinal errors and confusion about church order, sensualism and immorality, disunity and pride, and the abuse of Christian liberty and gifts. Love is a dominant theme (chap. 13). Love for God is mandated; love for others is explained. Self-love is presented as fatal and harmful, immature and destructive. Relationships are also a significant theme, including proper respect for one another and Christlike behavior toward others. Paul constantly emphasized focusing first on God and truth, then on others, introducing biblical foundations and a godly framework for ethical behavior.

Instruction on church order is carefully given to the young Corinthian congregation in an effort to help them understand the body of Christ. Christian solutions are presented for Corinthian dilemmas. Paul contrasted worldly and spiritual wisdom. He nurtured and cared for the Corinthians.

Issues Addressed in 1 Corinthians

- Gross sexual immorality (5:1; 6:15)
- Struggles for power and leadership (1:1-17)
- Denial of the resurrection of the body (15:12)
- Testimony in the workplace and community (8:10; 10:25)
- Taking fellow believers to court (6:1)
- The role of women in public worship (11:2-6; 14:34)
- Confusion about the Lord's Supper (11:21)
- Misunderstanding of spiritual gifts (12:1–14:40)
- Understanding love (13:1-13)
- Charitable offerings and gifts (16:1-4)

Pronunciation Guide

Achaia	*uh KAY yuh*	Gaius	*GAY yuhs*
Achaicus	*uh KAY ih kuhs*	Galatian	*guh LAY shuhn*
Apollos	*uh PAHL uhs*	Macedonia	*mass uh DOH nih uh*
Aquila	*uh KWIL uh*	Maranatha	*mahr uh-NATH uh*
Cephas	*SEE fuhs*	Priscilla	*prih SIL uh*
Chloe	*KLOH ee*	Sosthenes	*SAHS thuh neez*
Crispus	*KRISS puhs*	Stephanas	*STEF uh nuhs*
Ephesus	*EF uh suhs*		
Fortunatus	*fawr tyoo NAY tuhs*		

Outline

I. PAUL'S GREETING (1:1-9)

II. FACING THE ISSUE OF DISUNITY
(1:10–3:23)
   A. Maturity vs. Immaturity
      (1:10–3:4)
   B. A Foundation in Christ (3:5-23)

III. EXAMINING CHRISTIAN CONDUCT
(4:1–6:20)
   A. Managers of the Mysteries of
      God (4:1-5)
   B. Humility (4:6-13)
   C. Church Discipline (4:14–5:13)
   D. Lawsuits (6:1-11)
   E. Christian Liberty (6:12-20)

IV. ADDRESSING QUESTIONS OF THE
CHURCH (7:1–10:33)
   A. Perspectives on Singleness and
      Marriage (7:1-40)
   B. Considerations for Dealing
      with Food Offered to Idols
      (8:1-13)
   C. A Defense of Apostleship
      (9:1-27)

   D. Warnings from Israel's Past and
      Idolatry (10:1-22)
   E. The Abuse of Christian Liberty
      (10:23-33)

V. OUTLINING CONDUCT IN THE
CHURCH (11:1–14:40)
   A. Head Coverings and Women
      (11:1-16)
   B. Self-Control and the Lord's
      Supper (11:17-34)
   C. Spiritual Gifts and the Body of
      Christ (12:1-31)
   D. Loving Others and Spiritual
      Maturity (13:1–14:40)

VI. TEACHINGS ABOUT THE
RESURRECTION (15:1-58)

VII. CONCLUDING PERSONAL
REMINDERS (16:1-24)
   A. The Gift for the Church in
      Jerusalem (16:1-4)
   B. Plans for Paul's Travel
      (16:5-12)
   C. A Final Exhortation from Paul
      (16:13-24)

Exposition of the Text

PAUL'S GREETING (1:1-9)

1:1-9 Paul identified himself as the author, **an apostle** commissioned by God. Paul also mentioned **Sosthenes**, another leader who must have been familiar to the church since he joined Paul in writing the letter (v. 1). Paul then addressed the recipients of the letter and sent greetings in **the name of Jesus Christ our Lord** (v. 2). Since 1 Corinthians was written in an effort to resolve problems faced by the church, Paul's warm and loving touch was encouraging (v. 3). Knowing that he would later speak directly and forcefully, Paul reminded his spiritual children of his loving concern, expressing his appreciation

for them, **I always thank my God for you**, and reminding them of God's faithfulness (vv. 4-9). He was setting a context for the chastisement he would give concerning their un-Christlike behavior. Paul described "God's church," literally "the church of God," a New Testament phrase unique to Paul, as SAINTS (Gk. *hagiois*, "dedicated, hallowed, pure, righteous") or those set apart and holy unto the Lord (v. 2). Paul used a form of this word more than 60 times throughout his letters. The word served as a reminder to the Corinthians that they had been forgiven their sins and dedicated unto the Lord, a "sanctified" people who should live accordingly.

Chloe
1 Corinthians 1:11

Although little is known about Chloe, Paul knew her and called her by name. She obviously knew him well enough to send members of her household directly to him with a report. In contrast to secular society, in the church women were considered to be valuable and influential participants in the building up of the body of Christ.

Members of her household had spoken to Paul.	**Household** could refer to: • immediate members of her family • fellow worshipers of the church meeting in her house • servants belonging to her
They reported what was going on in the church.	• There were quarrels among the Corinthian believers over their leaders. • Paul did not say whether Chloe and/or the members of her household were involved in the dispute; they just reported the quarrels.

FACING THE ISSUE OF DISUNITY (1:10–3:23)

Maturity versus Immaturity (1:10–3:4)

1:10-13 Paul was concerned about **the divisions** the church was experiencing. QUARRELS (Gk. *erides,* "strife, discord, contention") were a serious threat to unity in the church. The word suggests a sharp challenge and contentious spirit (v. 11). Members were taking sides and trying to associate themselves with cliques and opposing groups. Apparently the church members were trying to identify themselves with particular church leaders according to who had **baptized** each (vv. 12-16). Paul was greatly distressed because the church members were wasting valuable time fighting one another about a meaningless issue. No competition should exist regarding the messenger but only gratefulness to God for His grace. The people were focusing on themselves and their temporal affairs rather than on God's plan. Paul was disturbed by the news he received from Corinth, and he passionately urged them, **in the name of our Lord Jesus Christ**, to find unity among themselves.

1:14-17 Paul had a clear understanding of his responsibility and his call to preach. Neither Paul nor any other man could bring salvation by preaching or baptizing. Paul understood his role as a preacher of the gospel; he was seeking only to glorify Christ and draw others to Him. The real changing power is in Christ Jesus, not in the character of the messenger or in the ability of the preacher to deliver the message. The messenger must point to Jesus, not himself. Paul emphasized that he himself did not preach **with clever words** (v. 17) because all the emphasis should be on the cross of Christ rather than on the talents of the orator.

Certainly Paul made one of the clearest distinctions between initial faith in Christ and water baptism, putting both into perspective. The foundation and heart of faith is the work of Christ on the cross. Baptism pictures that saving work (v. 17). In the name of wisdom, the Corinthians had introduced quarreling and divisiveness, aligning themselves with various leaders in the church and claiming for each leader superior wisdom over the others. Paul recognized that divine wisdom would appear "foolish" to the philosophers of the world (v. 20). The only true knowledge about

Divisions in the Corinthian Church
1 Corinthians 1:10

Reference	Source of Division	Solution
1:1–3:23	Envy and strife caused by immaturity	• Seek doctrinal understanding (1:10). • Build faith on God's power rather than man's wisdom (2:5). • Understand the role of servanthood (3:5-7).
5:1-13	Immorality in believers	Confront evil in the church (5:5; cp. Mt 18:15-20).
6:1-11	Lawsuits among believers	Choose an arbitrator with "standing in the church to judge" (6:4-5).
11:17-34	Improper observance of the Lord's Supper	• Evaluate your reasons for coming to the Lord's table (vv. 26-29). • Wait for one another (v. 33). • Eat at home to satisfy physical hunger (v. 34).
12:1–14:40	Misuse, abuse, and/or elevation of spiritual gifts	Understand that: • God is the source (12:5-7,11). • Diversity is the key (12:20). • Unity is the design (12:24-27). • Love is the discipline (12:31–13:13). • Maturity is the goal (14:1-25). • Order is the necessity.

God and all genuine wisdom comes through the Holy Spirit (Jn 14:26).

1:18-31 Paul emphasized the **power** of the cross to those who believe. Like the Corinthians, the people whom God addressed through the Prophet Isaiah were lacking in moral and ethical living (v. 19; Is 29:14). The first half of Isaiah was a message of judgment, while the remaining portion offered hope. The prophet chided God's people for living by their own **wisdom** and for failing to rely on God and serve Him with obedient hearts. In both Isaiah and 1 Corinthians, readers were reminded that even the wisest men fail in comparison to **God's wisdom** and perfection.

Your CALLING (Gk. *klēsin*, "invitation, position, vocation") amounts to an official summons from the Lord Himself to enter a personal and intimate fellowship with Him (v. 26). That call is not based on your intellectual acknowledgment or wisdom or on your position or status but strictly on the grace of God. The problem is never with God's ability to save but with people who have become accustomed to trusting in their own abilities or positions or resources instead of trusting the Lord. Your glory is in Christ alone (v. 31).

Paul, with great consistency, continued to drive home his point. None can know or understand God by reason or human wisdom alone. Man's mind is finite and cannot comprehend an infinite God; however, God was pleased to allow all—regardless of their intellectual prowess, education, or training—to be drawn into salvation by the Holy Spirit through a simple message that appeared foolish to those who considered themselves wise (v. 21). Paul admitted that the simplicity of the way God has chosen would cause some to have difficulty believing (v. 23). He explained that the salvation and mercy of God can never be fully understood but must be believed by faith, recognizing that the greatest human strength cannot exceed the perceived weakness of God (vv. 25,27).

Paul called readers to consider themselves honestly in the light of God's perfection and to realize that even the most honorable, desirable person is worthless and wicked compared to the majesty of God (v. 28). However, being **in Christ Jesus** gives inestimable value to believers by producing **righteousness, sanctification, and redemption** (vv. 30-31). Again, the emphasis was not on the individual but on Jesus.

2:1-5 This section includes critical life lessons for Christians. The power of God is not limited by human weakness. Paul understood this principle firsthand and felt it was critically important for the struggling Corinthian church to learn it as well. He reminded the Corinthians of their first encounter with the gospel message. Paul came in humility and human weakness, even calling attention to his lack of skill and ability. Paul recognized that he in himself had nothing to offer; but through the message of the crucified Christ, he had much to give. He placed all the emphasis and importance on Jesus and believed God's power made the difference.

The phrase **I was with you in weakness** (v. 3) should stand as a great encouragement to all. Although Paul was afraid, exhausted, and apprehensive, he did not let his weakness stop him from sharing the gospel. He did not rely on his ability, appearance, prosperity, experience, or confidence as the most important resources to fulfill his responsibility (v. 2). He came even in his inadequacy, which was so obvious that he was criticized. However, this fact was the persuasive ingredient in Paul's argument. Despite his own human weakness, God still used him to do mighty things (v. 5).

Some biblical characters with an unusual anointing from God appear superhuman and therefore seem beyond human standards. But this is not the full picture. Scripture offers examples of God using ordinary, even weak, people to accomplish His mighty work—as He empowers them. Paul's vulnerability should be comforting. Every Christian faces feelings of unworthiness. Paul explained early in the letter that "you were made rich in everything" (1:5), and "that you do not lack any spiritual gift" (1:7). Rather than expecting power from the wisdom of men, the Holy Spirit brings power beyond expectation (2:4).

2:6-9 In this chapter, Paul contrasted earthly wisdom and spiritual wisdom and emphasized that earthly wisdom is not eternal and will come to an end. WISDOM (Gk. *sophian*, "prudence, skill, knowledge") pertains more to the skillful use of intelligence and ability in living, having a sense of discernment for using what God has given—whether tangible or intangible (v. 6). In the Old Testament, wisdom does not refer to intellectual ability but to "one who looks to God for instruction in living." The wise Solomon noted that wisdom began with "the fear of the Lord" (Pr 1:7), which implies that even a very gifted individual who does not fear and reverence God is a fool (see Ps 14:1). In the New Testament, understanding wisdom begins with the light found in the Old Testament.

Paul saw worldly wisdom and God's wisdom as opposites. The Greeks depended on human mental prowess and insight to unravel the mysteries of life, but Paul relied on God's revelation in Christ (1 Co 1:30; Eph 1:8-9,17; 3:8-12). Accordingly God's wisdom in Christ is not **of this age** (2:6) and "the wisdom of this world is foolishness with God" (3:19). By contrast, God's wisdom is "taught by the Spirit" (2:13). Paul's testimony is clear:

- He humbled himself before the Lord without "brilliance of speech or wisdom" (v. 1);
- He exalted Jesus (v. 2);
- He admitted personal weakness (v. 3);
- He acknowledged supernatural power (v. 4);
- He affirmed the power of the gospel (v. 5).

God's wisdom was described as a MYSTERY (Gk. *mustēriō*, "secret"), which in the Bible has a different nuance of describing something hidden from human understanding until revealed and made clear through the Holy Spirit to believers (v. 7). Rulers, intellectuals, and authorities who only rely on earthly wisdom are unable to understand spiritual truths. However, this lack of understanding should not cause discouragement in believers but should urge them to pray for the enlightenment of the Spirit and to search out the truths of God.

Paul used the Old Testament to show the Jews in the congregation that Jesus was indeed the fulfillment of prophecy and to assure them of the promises passed down through God's chosen people affirming the consistency of the Old and New Testaments for modern readers. Isaiah recalled that many times since the beginning of the world God had moved mightily, beyond the comprehension of all men, to act on behalf of those who waited for Him (v. 9; Is 64:4).

2:10-16 Paul affirmed the Holy Spirit's work of drawing men to God and acting as a guide, teacher, and helper since Jesus was no longer present to minister (v. 11). Many believers were insecure without the physical presence of Jesus among them; they needed assurance that the Holy Spirit

would be their helper. He was the key to unlocking God's wisdom. Only God can know and reveal God. The Holy Spirit knows the wisdom of God because He is God.

The early Christians knew about *Yahweh* the God of Abraham. They were also familiar with God's Son Jesus because He walked among them in a tangible way. They were now beginning to understand the role of the Holy Spirit who was commissioned by the Father and the Son to remain with and indwell every believer. Paul assured the Corinthians that the Spirit of God knows the deepest things in the heart of God and will not lead believers astray but will serve to lead them to God in a way consistent with His Word already revealed. He also reminded them that they had not been given **the spirit of the world, but the Spirit who is from God**, **in order to know what has been freely given to us by God** (v. 12). Paul took time to teach the important doctrines of the faith. Women must also take time to study and teach these same doctrines with accuracy and excitement.

The **natural man** (or woman) cannot receive the things of God because they are **foolishness to him** (v. 14). FOOLISHNESS (Gk. *mōria*, anglicized as *moron*) suggests dullness and insipid and tasteless mediocrity—the response of people without spiritual sensitivities to the beauty and excellence of divine truth. Spiritual things and people cannot be rightly judged by those with a carnal mindset. NATURAL (Gk. *psuchikos*, "pertaining to life or soul") describes a man who does not have the Holy Spirit—he is worldly, unspiritual, fleshly, and "physical" (anglicizing the Greek word). The SPIRITUAL (Gk. *pneumatikois*, "pertaining to the Spirit") demands the regenerating work of the Spirit (v. 13).

Without the Spirit of God, no one can discern and accept the things of God. Paul emphasized that all would ultimately be judged by God; and, therefore, believers must examine themselves and evaluate whether or not their lives are surrendered to the purposes of God (vv. 13-16).

Note Paul's claim that his very words are inspired by God through the Holy Spirit—the principle of *verbal inspiration*, not in the sense of mechanical dictation that nullifies the author's unique personality but still affirming that the Spirit-inspired word of Paul is God's message to believers (v. 13).

The Two Types of Wisdom[1] *1 Corinthians*	
In the World—Worldly Wisdom	**Through the Spirit—Spiritual Wisdom**
Falling prey to envy, strife, and division (1:10; 3:3)	Pursuing unity (12:13)
The message of the cross is foolishness (1:18)	The message of the cross is the power of God (1:18)
God is not known (1:21)	The power of God is demonstrated (2:5)
Immature understanding (3:1; 14:20)	Developing maturity (2:6)
Will not last (3:15)	Will last (3:10-14)
Caught in personal craftiness (3:19)	Maintaining self-control and discipline (6:12; 9:27)
Boasting in men (3:21)	Boasting in the Lord (1:31)
Inflated with pride (4:6)	Marked by fear of the Lord and humility (2:3)
Pride in personal accomplishments (4:7)	Recognition of God as the source of everything (6:19-20)
Critical of leadership (4:8)	Submissive to spiritual leadership (14:37; 16:16)
Relying on the power of words (4:20)	Relying on the power of God (4:20)
Pride in human knowledge (8:2)	Having the mind of Christ (2:16)
Insisting on personal rights (8:9)	Becoming a servant of all (9:19)
Insensitivity to others (8:11)	Building up others (8:1)
Arrogantly wounding those who are weaker (8:12)	Seeking another's well-being (10:24)
Subject to falling into sin (10:12)	Escaping from temptation (10:13)
Scoffing at differences (12:21)	Respecting diversity (12:25)
Childish and infantile in thinking (14:20)	Walking in the way of love (13:1)

3:1-4 To challenge the people to mature in their faith, Paul reminded them what they were like before they came to know Christ. They had remained spiritual **babies** (v. 1). Paul loved the Corinthians enough to share that the **envy and strife among** them were evidences that they were still fleshly and **living like ordinary people** (v. 3). Persons who have not yet accepted Christ as Savior and Lord and received forgiveness of sin are fleshly, selfish, and enemies of God.

However, a person who has become a child of God with the Holy Spirit living within (2:12-16) is no longer an "ordinary" person. Based on the relationship with Jesus Christ, that person is honored, valued, and forever accepted in the family of God. Paul further pointed out that ordinary men seek position and separatism, but spiritual men should seek after humility and unity (v. 6). The Corinthians were preoccupied with attaining wisdom, and in the process they had respectively aligned themselves with their favorite leaders (v. 4). Their human pride asserted itself in an elitist attitude.

A Foundation in Christ (3:5-23)

3:5-17 Paul softened his language as he explained the role Christian mentors can play in a young believer's life. He was not discounting the importance of nurturing the lives of others and being grateful when others plant and water in your life (v. 6), but Paul defended the truth that **only God . . . gives the growth** (v. 7). God rewards those who work for His kingdom both by planting and watering, but God deserves credit for the growth.

Paul compared the Corinthian believers to a **field** and a **building** (v. 9), explaining that he **laid** the **foundation** for the building on which others would build (v. 10); one person cannot and should not do everything. Judgment will test and reveal **the quality of each one's work** (v. 13), and rewards for Christians will be determined accordingly (vv. 14-15). Believers are bond slaves to Christ, who has already extended undeserved mercy. He owes nothing, yet He chooses to bless and reward His workers with good things.

REWARD (Gk. *misthon*, "pay, wages, reward, or punishment") is to be understood as compensation for a task. The term may refer to monetary payment, but usually its connotation has to do with some aspect of divine evaluation of human activity. Jesus used the word several times in the Sermon on the Mount in reference to rewards that the ungodly receive in this life (Mt 5:46; 6:2,5,16; see also 2 Pt 2:13,15; Jd 11) in contrast to rewards that believers will receive in heaven (Mt 5:12; 6:1; see Mk 9:41; Lk 6:23,35; 2 Jn 8). Paul in 1 Corinthians used the term four times, all referring to the reward that comes from kingdom ministry. On the day of judgment the Lord will test by fire the purity of everyone's ministry. Some will receive a reward, while others will endure loss, though not the loss of salvation. This judgment is only for Christians and takes place immediately after the church has been raptured or translated into heaven (3:11-17). This judgment seat of Christ (Gk. *bēma*) is not the place for assigning eternal destiny to anyone but rather the time for determining and giving rewards to believers (Rm 14:10; 2 Co 5:10). Here are some things to note about this judgment:

- Only those who have the proper spiritual foundation in Christ will be able to appear at the *bēma* (v. 11).

- Throughout their lives believers build upon that **foundation**, a superstructure that may consist of the valuable and lasting—**gold, silver, costly stones**—or the unworthy and fleeting—**wood, hay, or straw** (v. 12).

- On the day of Christ's return, all works will be declared and **revealed by fire** (v. 13), an expression probably referring to the penetrating and discerning gaze of Jesus (cp. Rv 1:14; 2:18).

- Those Christian works with permanent value abide and become the basis for rewards (v. 14).

- Those works that are worthless or those that are improperly motivated will be **burned up** in the fire of Christ's gaze. Consequently, rewards may be limited, but the person **will be saved** (v. 15).

Paul also stressed the importance of accountability for believers. Even though growth is given by God, believers must not ignore their responsibility to serve in the role the Lord has given (v. 5). Paul explained that a believer who works lazily will still be saved but **like an escape through fire** (v. 15), identifying the seriousness of the matter. The Roman Catholic Church has appealed to this text to justify purgatory, but this "fire" is not to purge evil. It is to annihilate what is worthless. Furthermore, because of the Holy Spirit's indwelling, the believer's body is considered **God's sanctuary** (v. 16). Paul described the Corinthians as God's TEMPLE (Gk. *naos*, "temple, shrine," the same word used for a pagan temple, Ac 17:24). Most often this word denoted the Jewish temple in Jerusalem (Lk 1:21), but it also was used in reference to the heavenly sanctuary (Rv 14:15) or in a figurative sense to identify believers corporately (as here in 3:16) or individually (6:19). When used in contrast, *hieron* usually refers to the entire temple complex while *naos* indicates the innermost sanctuary or the holy of holies. The corporate application here addressed the believers at Corinth, or the local church, as the most holy place or the unique dwelling place of the Spirit of God. Division within the local church (3:4) would be a way of defiling the sanctuary of God and would call for His judgment. RUINS (Gk. *phtheirei*, "destroy, corrupt, spoil, seduce") is the verb used to describe the spoiler who attacks God's temple as well as the action God will take in response. When any individual ruins God's temple (i.e., the church or body of believers), God will ruin him.

3:18-23 Paul challenged believers not to be deceived by philosophies of the world. The Corinthians were God's only temple in Corinth (v. 17). Women in today's society are sometimes drawn to the importance and protection of personal rights in such popular ideologies as feminism and postmodernism. These are contrary to

God's wisdom and **futile** (v. 20). To receive the wisdom of God, you **must become foolish** (v. 18), recognizing your worthless and hopeless state without Christ. Paul cited two Old Testament passages to strengthen his argument (Jb 5:13; Ps 94:11).

Again addressing the divisive behavior, Paul stated that **no one should boast in men** (1 Co 3:21). Because Christians belong to Christ, they will ultimately win and reign. This eternal perspective shows the futility of placing importance on a temporal relationship instead of treasuring the eternal relationship of belonging to Christ. Believers are inseparably united with Jesus Christ, and He is one with God; therefore, believers are united with God the Father. Human nature may seek division, but living in unity with God is related to living in unity with others.

EXAMINING CHRISTIAN CONDUCT (4:1–6:20)

Managers of the Mysteries of God (4:1-5)

4:1-5 Paul reasserted his authority while reaffirming his role as a servant in teaching the Corinthians how to accept and respond to church leaders. Paul explained that leaders should be seen as **servants** (Gk. *hupēretas*, "helpers or assistants") **of Christ** (v. 1), doing the will of the Master. He also described them as **managers**, or stewards, **of God's mysteries** (v. 1). MANAGERS (Gk. *oikonomous*, "stewards, administrators, treasurers") are those in possession of and accountable for handling a valuable commodity. The compound word links "house" and "law," literally "the law of the house." MYSTERIES (Gk. *mustērion*) is a reference to the truths of God that cannot be discovered by an individual on her own. They must be, and they are intended to be, revealed by God Himself. Paul considered himself a custodian of God's revealed truth. His approval and accountability were only in Christ (v. 3). He was not trying to please men or even live up to his own expectations for his life. He affirmed that God is the only real judge, and He will bring to light all the intentions of the heart. Paul also explained that God will **praise** and reward His servants, affirming the fact that seeking approval and blessing from others will not bring the rewards that approval from God will bring.

Humility (4:6-13)

4:6-13 Paul was teaching these things so that believers would not give way to **pride** (v. 6). Paul noted that he had AP-PLIED (Gk. *meteschēmatisa*, "change, transform") these things to myself and Apollos." The sense of the Greek verb can suggest a transference in one's imagination (NKJV "figuratively transferred") and thus application. In other words, Paul's earlier statements were to be applied to himself and Apollos who would be "servants" and "managers" or stewards in order that the Corinthians would be taught not to think more highly of anyone than what is called for in Scripture. By this rule, no one in spiritual leadership would become inflated with self-importance. No person can **boast** or relish in any talent, ability, or skill because all are given by God (v. 7). To take credit for a characteristic that is not earned but given as a gift is ludicrous. Further, if all things are a gift, you cannot consider yourself superior to others. Paul used irony to express how the Corinthians had shown their false sense of pride and comfort in their spiritual position.

Paul used an interesting metaphor, describing the apostles as a SPECTA-CLE (Gk. *theatron*, "play" or anglicized as "theater") to illustrate the humiliation and suffering of indignities by the apostles. Yet in all God used these displays of weakness to demonstrate His power (v. 9). Paul contrasted the pride of the Corinthians with his own weakness and suffering for the cause of Christ (vv. 10-11). The apostle used a series of contrasts between the judgment of the world and His acceptance of that judgment. FOOLS (Gk. *mōroi*, "stupid," in the sense of being ridiculous) and WEAK (Gk. *astheneis*, "powerless, sick, feeble") were descriptors of the apostles in contrast to WISE (Gk. *phronimoi*, "sensible, thoughtful" with the nuance of being sagacious and smart) and STRONG (Gk. *ischuroi*, "mighty, powerful, weighty") in reference to the Corinthians. DISTINGUISHED (Gk. *endoxoi*, "honored, glorious, splendid" in which the word *doxa*, "glory," is linked with the preposition to mean "in the glory") is contrasted with DIS-HONORED (Gk. *atimoi*, "less honorable," in which the word *timē*, "precious," is prefaced by the alpha privative, which negates its significance and reverses its meaning to the opposite—in this case "despised"). Rather than affirming the inflated views they had of themselves, Paul led them to the reality that they were living for themselves instead of living for God. He and a few others were carrying the burden of persecution and furthering the gospel at a great cost, while the Corinthians were sitting back and enjoying the benefits of their position as children of God, a position that is not to be fully enjoyed until heaven (vv. 12-13). Yet here the apostle moved to a lesson on how to respond to mistreatment—timely for every generation. You BLESS (Gk. *eulogoumen*, "say good words," or deliver a eulogy, the anglicized word used to memorialize individuals) those who REVILE (Gk. *loidoroumenoi*, "insult") you. You ENDURE (Gk. *anechometha*, "put up with, accept, bear with," a compound word *ane* or "again" and *echō* or "have," meaning "you have again and again") when you are PERSECUTED (Gk. *diōkomenoi*, "to pursue with malignity"). The Corinthians were given a vivid admonition to return good for evil.

This message must have been incredibly difficult for the Corinthians to hear. Paul minced no words in casting blame. He held up their weakness and selfishness to the light of God's perspective and identified the real core issues of life. How could any congregation have listened to an indictment like this and not felt a great sting of pain? Although painful, these reminders are also extremely important to growth since, if accepted, they can prompt positive life change. Staying balanced may be one of life's greatest challenges. Paul acted as a catalyst, constantly calling people back from imbalance to a proper standing with Jesus.

Church Discipline (4:14–5:13)

4:14-21 Paul softened his words in verse 14, reminding the Corinthians of his great love for them. The Corinthians' behavior can be likened to a child going off to college who thinks she knows so much more than her "foolish" parents, only to find that her parents weren't so ignorant and unloving as she had thought. By calling himself their spiritual father (vv. 14-15), Paul was reminding the Corinthians that he had a family connection with them and desired their well-being—but not at the expense of their right behavior and understanding.

Paul urged the believers to quit living for themselves and follow his example (v. 16). **Imitators** (Gk. *mimētai*, from which comes the anglicized word "mimic") are those who copy or mimic another. Like a loving father, Paul intended to guide them and take care of them. He desperately wanted to be with them, but since his coming was impossible at that time,

he arranged to send **Timothy** in his place (v. 17).

Some were **inflated with pride**, thinking they had learned everything they needed. Yet Paul was sending Timothy to **remind** them **about my ways in Christ Jesus**. Paul explained that they had much correction to face. Moreover, Paul asked how they would like to receive correction when he came. Paul did not have in mind a physical **rod** but rather strong, corrective verbiage. Although the figure used suggested severity and warning, Paul clearly preferred to come **in love and a spirit of gentleness** (v. 21). Imagine a parent using similar language: "Do you want to make this hard or easy?" Paul's parenting skills came to the forefront as he trained these spiritual children to make their own wise choices. Paul knew that a life of obedience is a life of blessing, and he wanted the best for his spiritual children.

5:1-3 Paul found their participating in and allowing things that even non-Christians would find offensive to be shocking. SEXUAL IMMORALITY (Gk. *porneia*, "unlawful sexual intercourse, prostitution, unchastity, fornication") usually referred to sexual acts outside of marriage. Paul identified specifically one in the Corinthian congregation who was **living with his father's wife** (Gk. *gunaika*, probably a reference to the stepmother of the offender). The father might have been deceased, but in any case the liaison was forbidden, and they were living together without being married (Lv 18:7-8; 20:11). Even Roman law forbade such unions. Instead of being saddened by this behavior and dealing with it in a biblical way, the Corinthians were still **inflated with pride**, willing to overlook and tolerate this behavior. They were men-pleasers instead of God-pleasers, placing their own desires above obedience (1 Co 5:2).

5:4-5 Paul stated clearly that the guilty man ought to be **removed from among you** and allowed to come to the end of himself (v. 2), so that he might call out to God for mercy, **that his spirit** might be **saved in the Day of the Lord** (v. 5). He knew that if the church intimated in any way that this behavior was acceptable or that it was overlooked by God, the erring man would never experience repentance and forgiveness.

Paul's recommendation is clear and uncompromising. Realizing the seriousness of the situation and how quickly it could infect the rest of the church, Paul encouraged speedy and direct action. Although some might view discipline as harsh, Paul affirmed that his desire was for the ultimate salvation of the sinner and the protection of the church.

The timing seems to be a gathering for the Lord's Supper (v. 11, "do not even eat with such a person"). Some churches may have celebrated the memorial feast every time they gathered, and the intimacy of such a gathering for the congregation would provide the most appropriate setting for the action recommended. The authority to which Paul appealed, **in the name of our Lord Jesus** (v. 4), must be the method of discipline Jesus delineated in Matthew 18:15-18. Once proper steps had been taken, the whole matter must be taken to the church. Only then, if the sinful man rejected the discipline of the congregation, was he to be excluded. Church discipline (the last and most serious remedy to be used only if all else has failed) is always first and foremost about restoration, and it is the task of the congregation. Paul made no mention here of elders or bishops.

Turn that one over to Satan for the destruction of the flesh (v. 5) is a phrase about which commentators are divided, but there are some appropriate conclusions:

- Paul seemed to assume that the man involved in the incestuous relationship had never been saved. The primary purpose of whatever happened in the course of his discipline was to be certain "his spirit may be saved in the Day of the Lord" (v. 5).

- If the man had been saved, his restoration to the fellowship of the church was most important.

- The phrase DESTRUCTION (Gk. *olethron*, "slay, destroy, to be at point of death, render useless or worthless") "of the flesh" probably did not refer to physical death or disease but may have been a metaphor for rendering the fleshly nature of a man powerless. The word is used elsewhere in connection with God's judgment against sin.

- Churches in the modern era must give attention to the expulsion of unrepentant offenders through the process set forth in the New Testament, which, in a sense, is "turning that one over to Satan."

5:6-8 In every family the women who made bread would save some of the yeast for the next baking in order to ensure each week's bread would rise properly. Paul was saying that to tolerate even a little sin would affect the entire body. **Yeast** (Gk. *zumē*, "leaven") is part of a culinary metaphor used by Paul in which his readers were reminded that a very small amount of yeast permeates and spreads throughout all the dough mixture in a short time. The application is clear: To ignore this problem would open the door for fermentation or spoiling the whole church (v. 6). Jewish regulations concerning Passover emphasized this principle since all leaven must be removed from the house. The illustration was one with which women could readily identify. In that day, most women spent hours preparing meals, and bread was a main staple. Knowing the compassionate hearts of women, Paul wisely chose an illustration that would make clear to women the importance of supporting and encouraging church discipline and godly behavior. Paul understood the place of influence given to women and recognized that women who understood this important spiritual principle could positively influence the church.

Paul called the Corinthians to consider the past. During the time of Moses, the angel of death passed over only the homes that had been covered by the sacrificed blood of the innocent lamb. He likened that to the sacrifice of Jesus on the cross and pleaded with them to remember this sacrifice with **sincerity and truth** rather than **malice and evil**. Since Jesus died and thereby brought forgiveness of sin, believers are mandated to keep the Feast of Unleavened Bread ongoing in the sense of continually purging any sin that might corrupt the congregation. MALICE (Gk. *kakias*, "badness, wickedness, trouble"), a general word for evil, and EVIL (Gk. *ponērias*, "sinfulness"), a general word for the most despicable forms of sin, encompassed just about every manifestation of sinfulness (v. 8). In contrast, SINCERITY (Gk. *eilikrineias*, "purity of motive," from linking *krinō*, "judge," and *eile*, "sunshine") gives the sense of "judging in the sunshine or in penetrating light." Churches ought always to be pure in their commitment to the ways of the Lord and open to the scrutiny of God's truth.

5:9-13 Paul referenced a former **letter** in which he instructed the church **not to associate** with those practicing sexual immorality and clarified his instruction (see "Title" and "Date" sections in the introduction). Paul explained that he did not expect them to disassociate with non-believers who live in sin (v. 10), but he did encourage them to disassociate with anyone in the church (**who bears the name of brother**) who refused to live a life wholly consecrated to Christ (v. 11). God has called Christians to befriend and share the gospel with those who have not embraced the gospel message. To separate themselves totally from **the world** would be against God's plan for drawing people into His family through the sharing of personal testimony.

On the other hand, allowing men in the family to live as pagans is also against the plan of God. Paul explained that the believers should avoid those in the church who mask themselves with the name of a Christian brother. Such people should be judged, and believers should refuse **to associate** with an unrepentant brother. Paul noted the foolishness of judging those outside the church because God will do that; believers must **judge those who are inside** the church in order to keep the church pure and healthy (vv. 12-13).

Because the philosophies of tolerance and relativism are so prevalent in the modern era, many feel Paul's advice is harsh and wrong, but this instruction is inspired by God and given via the pen of the apostle to inspire righteous living and to provide protection of the church. Those who fail to uphold this standard are serving themselves alone, failing to obey God, and harming the entire church body.

Paul also issued a clear command to **put away the evil person** (v. 13; see 5:2; Dt 13:5; 17:7,12; 21:21; 22:21). Paul had a "no tolerance" policy. Discipline is best for everyone. Discipline allows unbelievers to see a clear distinction between the world and the church and gives the sinning brother the message that his behavior is unacceptable to God. Church members are accountable to the church body.

Discipline deters immoral behavior and keeps Satan from having a foothold in the church. The church remains pure and focused on the holy God. Discipline should not be mean-spirited, but it should be supported by all believers.

Lawsuits (6:1-11)

6:1-4 Paul addressed lawsuits among Christians, beginning with a logical explanation that when Christ returns, Christians **will** rule and **judge** the entire **world**. Based on this truth, for Christians to enter the law courts of the Gentiles and be judged by **unbelievers** is ridiculous. Paul was disheartened for two reasons:

- The church was not disciplined enough to control and train its members to observe ethical practices.

- The church, even after seeing this problem, did not deal with it wisely and promptly. Instead, they were letting unbelievers have an inside look at their problems and weaknesses. In a sense, Paul was saying, "Don't hang your dirty laundry out to dry. Clean up your own act and don't give unbelievers a reason to doubt the authenticity of Christianity. "

GO TO LAW (v. 1) and JUDGE (vv. 2-3) are translations of derivatives of the same Greek word (*krinō*, "make a distinction between, decide, resolve"). In verse 1, the present middle tense suggests the sense of "allow yourselves to be judged." Many words from this root are woven throughout the verses in this section. Judgment always involves the process of thinking through a situation and coming to a conclusion. The term could be used in a narrowly judicial sense, but judging in a more general sense may also be an option. In the New Testament, *krinō* most often refers to judging something or someone in general. In this instance the specific judicial setting is a human court (vv.

1,6). Paul's statement that the saints would "judge the world" and "the angels" (vv. 2-3) refers to the heavenly setting in which believers will rule in the future kingdom (cp. Rv 2:26-27).

If the saints looked to civil courts, several elements would be missing, including:

- the Spirit of God residing in the heart of the judge or arbiter, who would not have God's wisdom, and

- the judge's familiarity with anything beyond Roman law.

By going outside the congregation, their witness would be tarnished, if not destroyed, in the eyes of the pagan magistrates and people of the community. The Christians would be acting like pagans. Furthermore, if the world is to be judged by the saints, wouldn't they also be the best forum for judgment of even the SMALLEST (Gk. *elachistōn*, "least," a superlative of *mikros*, "small, insignificant," from which come English words with the prefix "micro") cases. The use of this word emphasizes Paul's estimate of the matters being disputed among the Corinthians as relatively unimportant and without consequence. In fact, perhaps he suspected that covetousness lay at the root of the problem (v. 8).

6:5-11 Much easier than cleaning up your own act and doing the hard work of following Christian principles or dealing with a brother according to Scripture, was letting someone else, namely, a civil judge, settle the matters the Corinthians didn't want to face. Greek culture, as modern society, was intrigued with litigation. Paul was not dismissing the need for justice; instead he was calling on believers to seek justice properly. Paul pointed out that they were not seeking the good of others but were ferociously fighting for their own rights and gain. He compared the Corinthians to a long list of evildoers

(vv. 9-10). Paul wanted them to understand the seriousness of their indiscretions.

Clearly this portion of the letter was not written solely to address eternal security; however, the subject matter falls right in line with passages teaching that a genuine believer cannot lose his salvation. First, those who live for themselves are obviously not surrendered to God and thus will not inherit heaven. Second, Paul acknowledged that some in the church were previously evildoers, but he also noted that they **were justified** by Jesus Christ. He is showing that God is willing to forgive and justify (v. 11). Paul was also showing that once a person was justified, his behavior would change, as evidence of his salvation. He was calling into question the authenticity of salvation for one who does not live for Christ because genuine salvation is evidenced by changed behavior.

Christian Liberty (6:12-20)

6:12-20 Apparently Paul was addressing some common Christian slogans, acknowledging first the new freedom from the law and a works-based salvation and still explaining that this new freedom should not be abused. Although there is liberty in Christ, this liberty should not free anyone to become enslaved by something else (v. 12). HELPFUL (Gk. *sumpherei*, "bring together" in the sense of being "good, better, useful") did not trump God's best; BEING UNDER THE CONTROL OF ANYTHING (Gk. *exousiasthēsomai*, "have the right over") was a reminder that nothing surpassed the authority of Christ (v. 12). God has given believers earthly blessings to enjoy but not to control them (v. 13).

Paul took the illustration further by explaining that **the body** was not to be used for personal fleshly desires but to serve **the Lord** (v. 13). Just as other

Scriptures affirm, the body is the temple of God, and thus the body is the Lord's (v. 19). Believers must realize that freedom from sin is enslavement to Christ (vv. 19-20).

Paul referenced Christ's resurrection from the dead as evidence that believers also will be **raised** by the **power** of God (v. 14). Scripture names Jesus as the head of the body (v. 15). At the moment of conversion, the believer becomes a member of the body of Christ (12:13) permanently, which, according to Paul's argument, makes any believer's part in fornication all the more reprehensible (6:15-16). Especially important is the connection Paul makes to God's plan for marriage (Gn 2:24), which refers to physical intimacy in marriage using the **one flesh** metaphor. What could be any more unthinkable than for a believer to be JOINED (Gk. *kollōmenos*, "unite, cling to") with the sense of being glued or welded together. Behaving immorally in the earthly body is like joining the holy, perfect Christ with a prostitute (1 Co 6:15). When sexual sin is committed, the two are joined in the flesh, so how then can one who is joined with the Lord also be joined with someone immoral—a vile misrepresentation of the mercy of Christ (v. 16). Paul urged believers not to wait or think about what they ought to do when faced with a questionable situation but to **flee from sexual immorality** (v. 18), which is especially damaging because this sin cannot be separated from the body, as evidenced by many consequences such as pregnancy out of wedlock and sexually transmitted diseases. The sole purpose of "sexual immorality" is the gratification of lust, which makes this sin quite heinous because of the obvious selfishness prompting the sin as well as the inevitable damage to personal spiritual sensitivities. Again, Paul appealed to the idea of the body as a SANCTUARY (Gk. *naos*, "dwelling place of God, the inner sanctuary itself"), probably an allusion to the temple in Jerusalem. The fact that the body was the residence for the Holy Spirit was no small matter (v. 19). Here Paul used the word most often associated with the holy of holies rather than *hieron*, which was most often used for the temple complex. He emphasized the value of the body and soul because of the high **price** paid by Jesus' perfect life, death, and resurrection (v. 20). This loving sacrifice of Jesus ought to be the motivation to live a holy and pure life.

ADDRESSING QUESTIONS OF THE CHURCH (7:1–10:33)

Perspectives on Singleness and Marriage (7:1–40)

7:1-7 Paul addressed questions about marriage raised by the Corinthians in previous correspondence (v. 1). He affirmed the single life, which he acknowledged as a profitable state in which to serve the Lord. He did explain, however, the preference for a person who is tempted morally to marry according to God's directives rather than remain single and live in sin (v. 2). Paul may have been responding here to some who were suggesting total abstinence, which in his view did not take into consideration the strength of natural, God-given desires. For the church to have had many practical questions regarding singleness and marriage was understandable. Ultimately Paul made clear that each individual has his own gift—whether celibacy or marriage—and both are a blessing when used according to divine guidelines (v. 7).

Paul clarified sexual conduct in marriage. Paul shared that the husband and wife did **not have authority over** their own bodies (vv. 3-4). Paul was encouraging healthy marriages and the right, proper, and fulfilling sexual life within God's design. Paul shared the same infor-

mation with both wives and husbands in a culture that generally deferred to the needs of the men. This evidence underscores Paul's attitude of concern toward both men and women to enjoy the blessings of God in their relationships with one another. The temptation to believe that Paul was chauvinistic in other instructions to women is thereby circumvented.

The mandate, **do not deprive one another** (Gk. *apostereite*, "steal, rob, defraud"), suggested that sexual abstinence within marriage was not acceptable and in fact was contrary to the purpose and commitment in this holy union. Paul explained the conditions to be met for a husband and wife to refuse to have sexual relations: agreement on the part of both, for a set **time**, and for the purpose of devoting themselves **to prayer** (v. 5). Then, Paul explained that normal marital activities should resume. Since Jewish men often took certain vows during which they withheld themselves from the marital bed to give special time to prayer and study of the Torah, Paul was demonstrating his equal concern for wives and husbands by insisting that the husband and wife must **agree** on this matter. **Lack of self-control** (Gk. *akrasian*, "self-indulgence") suggested that Paul was warning both parties of the dangers of prolonged abstinence. This consistent expression of love manifested in sexual intimacy should keep the marriage strong and healthy and protect it from temptation and destruction. Paul was clearly an advocate for marriage and offered great instruction to both men and women on how to fortify marriage.

There is no hint in verse 6 (nor in vv. 12,25,40) that Paul was departing from apostolic authority or Spirit-breathed transmission in order to insert his own opinions. His speaking is by **concession** or permission or under the direction of the Holy Spirit and is best understood by accepting the words within their immediate context in the ordinary sense of the words themselves. Paul had given a mandate prohibiting sexual abstinence in marriage (vv. 2-3), but then he gave a "concession" for the temporary abstinence, which was carefully defined but not mandated. Far from suggesting a lack of inspiration, Paul's use of these phrases reaffirmed the extent of inspiration, underscoring that Paul would not arbitrarily insert his own opinions but would speak only what God expressly gave to him through the Holy Spirit.

Paul expressed contentment in his single state and explained his happiness in the state in which God had placed him. However, Paul recognized that God has given different gifts to each, and all should be content with the gift that God has given. Marriage is a gift, and singleness is a gift. Both are gifts with purpose, and both should be celebrated with contentment. Mutuality in sexual intimacy and in marriage is clarified. Sex is not the privilege of the husband and duty of the wife, as popularly portrayed. Rather it is a privilege and duty for both, and first and foremost it should be an act of beauty glorifying the unity God designed.

7:8-9 Paul addressed people who were single by choice and by tragedy. One can be single and perfectly healthy and content. Some believe that Paul was previously married and widowed. If so, he would have known the joy of having a companion and the benefits of marriage. He was able to affirm both marriage and singleness.

As a single for all of his Christian life, Paul's "gift from God" (v. 7) was celibacy, the ability of an individual to live without conjugal relationships. God's plan for the man and his helper or counterpart to share life and responsibilities (Gn 2:18-24) was thwarted and distorted with the entry of sin. A need developed for men and women, who, as Paul, would

give themselves completely to "the things of the Lord" (1 Co 7:32-34). Celibacy did not become the norm but an exception with a gift bestowed by God to individuals for varying periods of time and a myriad of reasons. Paul certainly experienced feelings of loneliness and awkwardness common to many singles in a setting where most were married. His words specifically to singles ought to be viewed as an encouragement to many.

Life in Christ offers new purpose and direction for everyone. Paul was invigorated by his calling, and he made this passion the driving force of his life. He enjoyed putting all his energies into the ministry, which he considered an honorable and worthwhile existence.

Two explanations may be considered for understanding this challenging phrase **to burn with desire**:

- If the phrase is penal in nature, the idea is that lust will lead to divine judgment, an idea without biblical foundation since "lust" is simply intense desire.

- More likely here the idea is that if one does not have the gift of celibacy, he should marry instead of allowing unhealthy and ungodly desires to develop within (v. 9).

7:10-16 Paul turned his attention to **the married** (v. 10) with the reminder that his message was the directive of the Lord. The Bible's teaching on marriage rules out the idea of polygamy and same-sex unions. Neither of these options is scriptural or permissible. The sanctity of marriage is affirmed (v. 10). Paul has already explained that both marriage and singleness are important and acceptable. Here he addressed specifically concerns about marriage and divorce. Paul first addressed the wife, entreating her **not to leave her husband**. Many believe this mandate to women was caused by the new liberation women were experiencing because of their ability to choose personally whether or not to believe in Christ. This liberty, however, was being carried too far, and women were not only choosing to follow Christ but were also choosing to leave their unbelieving husbands in the process. Evidently Paul was describing a union established by non-believers, in which one was converted (v. 10). The question posed by the Corinthians who were newly converted, knowing it would be wrong for a believer to marry an unbeliever, pointed to whether or not union with an unbelieving partner makes the believer unacceptable to God. Paul reaffirmed that God honors the marriage for the sake of the believing partner. The picture suggested that the believer's "cleanness" or sanctification overpowers the unbeliever's "uncleanness." The unbeliever still must be converted (v. 16), but the sanctification extends to the marriage. Of course, an unbelieving spouse and children are **sanctified** or set apart—not with salvific reward, but with a salvific purpose to receive a unique and continual witness from the believing spouse. The marriage bond must remain intact, and both wives and husbands are expected to protect the sacred union.

Paul explained that a spouse who had been left alone should **remain unmarried**, leaving the possibility for reconciliation (v. 11). This strong directive is appropriate for a society with a 50-percent divorce rate even within the church. Paul made a few qualifications, explaining that a Christian married to an unbeliever must remain married and not seek divorce unless the unbeliever wanted to leave (v. 13). The hope was that the unbeliever would see the godly conduct and changed life of the believer and experience genuine repentance and salvation (v. 14). Paul also pleaded for the children to have an intact family with Christian influence.

On the other hand, Paul explained that if an unbeliever wanted to be released from the marriage, the believer could **let him** go and remarry (v. 15). Still, Paul called both the man and woman to live peaceably with one another and explained that the best solution was for the marriage to remain intact and for the individual family members to be reconciled to God.

7:17-24 Paul acknowledged the fact that many were and will be in uncomfortable or undesirable states when they are called out to become children of God. Paul instructed all people to be content, refusing to succumb to worldly or fleshly standards and instead relying on God. Paul gave examples of how one ought to remain, giving practical application to a hard truth. Because circumcision had become associated with Judaism, Gentles sometimes looked upon it with disdain (vv. 18-19). Paul explained that circumcision was no longer of great importance but that one's focus should be on obedience to the commands of Jesus. It was no longer for those who were uncircumcised to be circumcised or for those circumcised to seek to reverse the procedure (vv. 19-20). Paul next addressed slaves, explaining that if **a slave** could get out of a bad situation, then by all means he ought to get out; but if he could not easily do so, then he ought to **remain** and be content (v. 21). No one should force his way out of a situation because he is unhappy. When people are called to the Lord, they belong to the Lord; it is important to make the most of the state God has allowed and realize that He is in control of all circumstances, good and bad (v. 24).

Paul shared an especially important principle—all **were bought** with **a price** (v. 23). He did not express varying prices or values but implied that God has a genuine and equal love for all. This fact ought to give a person, in a good or bad situation, courage to go on and to find satisfaction in the truth of identity with Christ.

7:25-35 Paul offered an eternal perspective for unmarried men and women. With much talk of marriage and life circumstances, one can easily become consumed with details and overwhelming responsibilities. Human needs and desires change little with time. Paul was urging readers to live not as those temporally minded but as those spiritually minded.

Paul acknowledged that a single person with fewer attachments can serve the Lord in ways not possible for one who is married (v. 34). He affirmed this state of service for God's kingdom, **so that you may be devoted to the Lord without distraction** (v. 35). Paul explained that these instructions are not intended to hold a person back or keep her from God's will but to help a person keep a proper perspective.

7:36-40 Paul's reply is difficult to follow because the letter with the question he was answering has been lost. These verses are seemingly addressed to the father of a virgin daughter who is of **MARRIAGE-ABLE AGE** (Gk. *huperakmos*, "past the bloom of youth," v. 36). Apparently some in the Corinthian church were encouraging couples to endure lengthy engagements. **VIRGIN** (Gk. *parthenon*, "maiden or unmarried youth or chaste one") is apparently a reference to an unmarried daughter. In the ancient world, fathers had control over the marital plans of their daughters and could withhold a daughter from any marriage they considered unfitting or improper. Paul refuted this practice, expressing that it is fine to marry and better to marry than to disobey God's clear commands regarding sexual behavior.

Paul then spoke to widows. He released the women to marry upon the death of their husbands and again affirmed the importance of lifelong commitment. He left one requirement for remarriage. There is no exception. Christians must be committed to marrying **in the Lord** (v. 39), providing the best chance for a successful

home life and protecting the church. Knowing that widows had a vital ministry in the New Testament church, Paul expressed his opinion that a widow would be **happier** and more fulfilled in service if she remained single (v. 40).

This section of Scripture affirms the importance and value of marriage and offers very clear guidelines to the married, expressing the idea that getting marriage right is more important than simply being married. Paul also affirmed single living, giving significance to all in the body of Christ.

Considerations for Dealing with Food Offered to Idols (8:1-13)

8:1-3 This chapter addressed an issue that affected the church members, causing division and confusion as well as hurt and pain. The people lived in fear of pagan idols, which they believed controlled everything. The people were afraid of evil spirits and regularly made meat sacrifices to the idols so that they would not be overcome with evil spirits. The meats were later sold in the market.

Many new converts to Christianity had lived under this fear of evil spirits and idols before their conversions. All were faced with the acceptability of eating this meat because it was such an integral part of society. Wondering if it might be contaminated by evil spirits, many new converts were afraid that eating the meat would tempt them to return to idol worship (v. 7). Others easily recognized that idols were totally false gods and had no power over the crucified Christ. Because of their knowledge they had no fear or concern about eating this meat and rather enjoyed the freedom to do so (vv. 8-9).

Paul weighed in heavily on this group by taking a stab at what they perceived as superior knowledge and maturity. Immediately, he recognized that their knowledge had made them arrogant. Their

The Marriage Dilemma 1 Corinthians 7		
Current Situation	**Paul's Advice**	**Biblical Principle**
Unmarried	Marry (v. 2).	Avoid sexual immorality (vv. 2,9,36).
	Stay Single (vv. 8,26-27).	Remain devoted to the Lord without distraction (vv. 32-35).
Married	Do not deprive one another (v. 5).	• Authority over the body is given to respective spouse in marriage (vv. 3-4). • Deprivation is an invitation to temptation (v. 5).
Married, having left spouse	Remain unmarried or be reconciled to spouse (v. 10).	The Lord commands the wife not to leave her husband (v. 10).
Married to unbeliever who stays	Do not leave (vv. 12-13).	The Holy Spirit works in the lives of the spouse and of the children (v. 14).
Married to unbeliever who leaves	Let him/her go (v. 15).	You are not bound in such cases (vv. 15-16).

knowledge, which built them up **with pride**, was really taking them low in Christian maturity. Paul wanted them instead to grow in Christian maturity and to edify others rather than building themselves up by putting inordinate values in Christian liberty. Real love for God produces real love for God's children, brothers and sisters in Christ (v. 3).

8:4-6 Paul agreed that there was nothing wrong with eating the meat offered to idols. The knowledgeable group was right in recognizing that **no God but one** is to be loved, feared, and served. Paul promoted knowledge and doctrine and affirmed the truth of worshiping *Yahweh* God alone.

8:7-13 Paul's solid grasp of truth did not keep him from recognizing those with a tender **conscience** who felt it was improper to eat of this meat (v. 7). Paul pointed out that although some were right in believing that the idols were nothing, they were wrongly puffed up with pride because of their understanding. Paul noted that even though allowed, this practice was becoming **a stumbling block to**

the weak in the church with a tender conscience (v. 9).

CONSCIENCE (Gk. *suneidēsis*, "a seeing together") refers to your insight into yourself. The term usually has a moral aspect. The Greek word occurs only once in the Septuagint (Ec 10:20) and never in the Gospels. Your conscience recognizes an existing standard that you must follow (Ac 23:1; Rm 9:1; 2 Co 1:12; 1 Tm 1:5; 2 Tm 1:3; 1 Pt 2:19). Paul used *suneidesis* in an ethical rather than a moral sense (1 Co 8:7). The conscience may tell one believer something and another something else. These situations fall into the domain of Christian liberty. Some Christians in Corinth thought eating meat sacrificed to an idol was sinful, and Paul encouraged them to follow their consciences and not eat the meat. However, other Christians knew that this meat was not really defiled since the idols were "nothing" (v. 4), and Paul explained that they were at liberty to eat the meat with a clear conscience in certain situations (8:1-13; 10:25-30).

Instead of being prideful, the members ought to love one another enough to abstain from some permissible things in order to keep others whom they loved from stumbling. Again, Paul appealed to the Corinthians to put others before themselves. Paul provided general guidelines for ethical decisions:

- Will the action **cause my brother to stumble** (v. 13)?
- Will the action be edifying for me (10:23)?
- Will the action glorify God (10:31)?

These simple questions provide an ethical foundation, together with the leadership of the Holy Spirit, for godly decisions.

Paul affirmed the fact that God alone is worthy to be praised. He also affirmed the fact that idols are nothing and that it is permissible to eat from the meat offered to them. However, Paul later pled for those who were previously involved in idol worship, asking Christian brothers not to hurt one another. Paul insisted that wounding a brother is sinning against Jesus Christ, here emphasizing God's tender and sensitive love for all His children regardless of their background. Ministering to a Christian brother is much more important than personal satisfaction, freedom, or knowledge.

While food offered to idols is not an issue faced by modern churches, the principles are easily applied to the contemporary scene. Paul's clear commitment to the love and protection of Christian brothers and sisters is a valuable lesson.

Heart to Heart: The Obstacle Course of Faith

In this letter to the Corinthians, Paul mentioned two types of obstacles that may keep people from coming to faith in Christ or may lead them astray from their faith. The first is the trap or snare of CHRIST CRUCIFIED (Gk. skandalon, "that which offends, stumbling block"), which tripped up the wisdom-seeking Jews and the sign-seeking Greeks (1:23). Women who buy into the world's dream of success have difficulty getting over the foolishness of the cross. The very One meant to be the bridge to God becomes the stone over which the traveler stumbles (see Is 8:14-15).

Another snare is STUMBLING BLOCK (Gk. proskomma, "obstacle," 1 Co 8:9) coupled with NO OFFENCE (Gk. aproskopoi, "blameless," negated with an alpha privative, 10:32). The challenge to the Christian woman is to remove those obstacles of her own making along the pathway of faith. She must make choices that "seek . . . the good of the other person" (10:24) and make her above reproach. But she must never think that she can or should remove the obstacle of the cross. If someone is going to stumble on the pathway of faith, let it be over Christ crucified—not Christians vilified.

A Defense of Apostleship (9:1-27)

9:1-14 Some in the Corinthian church did not want to follow the leadership of Paul. They challenged his authority and apostleship. Paul used this controversy to answer questions about Christian liberty. He affirmed his right to receive payment for his work in the ministry but explained that he personally limited his compensation when it could be a stumbling block to others and keep them from coming into a relationship with Jesus Christ.

Just as they had asked him questions, now Paul asked them questions, making it clear in the process that his apostleship was real. He cited the fruit from his ministry among the Corinthians as evidence or a seal of that apostleship. Paul defended his Christian rights and the rights of other apostles. Perhaps Paul's apostleship was doubted because he chose to support himself by making tents unlike some other apostles. Paul explained in an extended paragraph that ministers of the gospel should receive compensation for their services in terms of material things, such as money or possessions. He supported his premise from the law (Dt 25:4) and illustrated it with the Levitical priesthood (1 Co 9:13; Lv 6:16,26; 7:6,31-32; Nm 5:9-10; 18:8-20,31; Dt 18:1). Paul ended his discussion by noting that he had chosen not to receive a stipend (1 Co 9:15). He further added emphasis to the necessity of divine compulsion for being able to preach the gospel (v. 16; Jr 20:9).

This support for the minister would, in fact, enable him to devote more time to the ministry of the gospel and benefit all. Rather than holding the minister back from accomplishing God's calling, churches should be supporting and encouraging those called by God.

9:15-18 Paul not only defended his right to accept payment but also his own right to refuse payment. He chose to preach the gospel without charge or expense to the people. He called this ability to preach without requiring pay a **REWARD** (Gk. *misthos*, "pay or wages," v. 18) and his **BOAST** (Gk. *kauchēma*, "pride or object of boasting," v. 15). This refusal gave him a sense of **obligation** to no one (v. 16), save the Lord from whom he drew his authority. He did not fully exercise his freedom and authority because he was more concerned about the gospel and others. It is certainly easier to demand your own way, especially when you are deserving. However, Paul had already surrendered his life first to Christ and then to others. He was very willing to sacrifice his comforts for the greater cause.

9:19-23 Paul explained that even though he had freedom in Christ, he had chosen to make himself a servant of others. Why would Paul do this? He explained it clearly. He conformed to the needs of others so that he might **win more people** to Christ (v. 19). Paul's complete focus and single-minded drive must be commended. Although total freedom in Christ was a reality in his life, he was willing to become **a slave** for the benefit to others, even at great cost to himself.

Although Paul's body was worn and abused, he worked incredibly long hours as a tentmaker for his livelihood and spent the rest of his time teaching and evangelizing. His schedule was exhausting, yet he did not want others to think he was financially motivated, nor did he want to burden other believers. His clarity and conviction must be admired.

Paul knew his audience. When he was witnessing to the Jews, he submitted himself to the Jewish law (v. 20). Paul lived much of his life tediously bound to the Jewish law. As a Christian, he was able to recognize that this law caused him to persecute, even kill, many Christians. Further, the overzealous commitment to Jewish law and tradition prompted the crucifixion of the Savior. Paul was still willing to revert to the Jewish law in order to reach Jews for Christ.

Paul next addressed his desire to reach Gentiles or those **outside the law** (v. 21). He went where they lived; he ate with them. Paul related to the Gentiles, not as a Jew who condemned them with the law, but as a fellow sinner, introducing them to the mercy and grace of God. Paul explained that he would never disobey **God's law** in order to become like someone else, but he did not hesitate to relate to them and make them feel comfortable even at his own discomfort.

Paul even addressed those who were weak physically, emotionally, financially, and in other ways (v. 22). He did not hesitate to share his personal weakness as testimony to God's unfailing strength and faithfulness. This example from the great apostle lends further credence to the power of personal testimonies shared with unbelievers. Paul used his personal testimony to lead many to Christ.

Women often have a natural willingness to sacrifice for others. They are happy to give up personal freedoms for the betterment of those suffering. Paul encouraged this behavior, not for personal satisfaction or recognition, but for the purpose of winning others to Christ, which was Paul's primary goal and the purpose for his life on earth. This passion should consume every believer. Paul closed this section by celebrating the benefits and blessings of rejoicing with someone who has been newly joined to God's kingdom. He considered this a great victory, and this occasion brought incredible joy. He wanted all to experience bringing others into the kingdom and being full partners in sharing the gospel message.

9:24 Although Paul did not rely on his communication ability, he was also not afraid to use his God-given oratorical skill. He unashamedly motivated readers to work like Olympians. He used the easily recognizable metaphor of a **race** to create urgency and competition and to add importance to his message. He challenged the Corinthians to "win." A good coach puts a difficult but attainable goal in front of his players. By encouraging the church to **run in such a way** as to **win**, he was telling them that they could win. This encouragement and vote of confidence must have been needed after the chiding the people had experienced under the apostle's disciplinary actions.

9:25-27 After convincing the people that they were able to win, Paul also motivated them with the prize to be won—not a perishable, temporal reward but an **imperishable one**—an honor that could never be forgotten, a record that could never be broken, a title that would be enjoyed eternally (v. 25). Unlike a beauty queen whose age will belie her crown or an athlete whose body will one day fail to achieve, the Christian's eternal enjoyment of heaven will be unending.

Because of this unbelievable reality, Paul urged the Corinthians to exercise **self-control**, run with purpose, and discipline the body (v. 25). He explained that the prize is so great, the hard work should easily be accepted in exchange for the honor. He also motivated them with his own commitment and conviction. He explained his regimen in hopes that others would follow, and he made himself vulnerable before them, sharing his genuine desire that they **not be disqualified** from the race for any reason (vv. 26-27).

Only one team wins, and most people are not on that team. Some have never won a significant award in their lives. For others, recognition may have occurred so long ago that it is difficult to remember. Here, Paul assured the greatest reward and allowed readers to understand that by identification with Christ, they are on the winning team!

Warnings from Israel's Past and Idolatry (10:1-22)

10:1-5 Paul struck the perfect balance between encouragement and reality. After challenging the Corinthians to run a mighty race, he warned them not to become prideful or self-centered. Even though their salvation had made them a part of God's family, Paul did not want the church presuming upon God's goodness. He used some familiar examples to bring home his point.

The Israelites were God's chosen people. They rejected Christ while the power of salvation through Jesus was made available to people of every race. Paul spoke of the Israelite forefathers and considered them the fathers of all who accept Christ, whether Jew or Gentile (vv. 1-2). With this example, Paul brought to mind the experience of the Israelites coming out of 400 years of slavery. The exodus was a well-known account with valuable lessons for the Corinthians.

Paul recalled how the Israelites were guided by **the cloud**, symbolizing God's presence and how they **passed through** the Red Sea in one of God's most dramatic miracles (v. 1). Moses represented the old covenant. The metaphor of baptism described their walking through the sea and being immersed and identified, along with Moses, **in the cloud and in the sea** (v. 2). They were required to have an individual faith, but this symbol was a reminder of future baptism in Christ Jesus as the representative of the new covenant.

Paul reminded the people of Israel's past, showing examples of how God powerfully moved in their lives to provide for their needs and to display His power. The **spiritual rock** (see Nm 20:11) was a reminder to the Jews that the rock from which the Israelites drank **followed them** thereafter to continue giving them water. Paul affirmed the real source of their sustenance—**Christ** (1 Co 10:4). But, he also reminded them that those who did not genuinely trust and serve God **were struck down**.

10:6-13 Paul did not merely mention their mistakes; he listed them. He told them not to worship other gods, not to seek selfish pleasure, and not to **commit sexual immorality** (vv. 7-8; see Ex 32:6). He mentioned the incident when the snakes killed those who were unfaithful (1 Co 10:9; see Nm 21:6). Complainers were not tolerated (1 Co 10:10). Paul softened these terrible consequences by explaining that God did not desire to harm His children but left these **as examples** of His willingness to exercise judgment if necessary (vv. 11-12).

Paul directly addressed the Corinthians' arrogance, urging them to be careful of an attitude of pride or a false sense of security. Like the Israelites of the past, they could easily **fall** (v. 12). Many a church leader has settled in his position of respect and power only to fall to the enemy and leave a congregation wandering in confusion. Both leaders and laity can fall and must be careful to avoid the snares of the evil one. Paul acknowledged that temptation **is common to humanity**, a reality that believers of every age must face. However, he reminded the church that **God is faithful** even in temptation, providing **a way of escape** as well as His power to resist the temptation (v. 13). Paul assured Christians that with the help of God, they could bear this burden.

10:14-15 The Corinthians were part of a society that suggested many ways to heaven and acknowledged many gods; those who had been exposed to this very common practice were tempted to slip back into **idolatry**. After worshiping many gods, to be committed to one God was very different. Since idol worship was such a commonly accepted cultural practice, few saw anything wrong with continuing to worship other gods along with *Yahweh* (v. 18).

The Israelites experienced this struggle; New Testament believers experienced it; and many today would say that Jesus is not *the* way to heaven but one of many ways. While there have been and will always be proponents of polytheism, Paul demanded that believers **flee from** and reject idolatry. He urged them to discern, **judge**, and realize that other gods cannot be worshiped along with Jesus.

10:16-18 Paul referred to **the cup of blessing** as **the blood of Christ** (v. 16), reminding all that Jesus is unlike any other religious figure, evidenced by the fact that He gave His own life to pay the sin debt of mankind. He explained that Christianity is wholly different from any religion; it cannot be placed in the same category with other belief systems. Paul skillfully lifted up Jesus above all others.

Paul described **the bread that we break** as **the body of Christ** (v. 16), naturally a picture of the **sharing** (Gk. *koinōnia*, "fellowship, close relationship, participation") "in the body of Christ": This communion refers to that which is held in common for believers; their fellowship centers on the cleansing "blood of Christ" (v. 16) and united body of believers (v. 17). Paul was drawing attention to the nature of salvation. He reminded the church that the sins of each person caused the death of Christ, and God was willing to forgive and reconcile mankind to a personal relationship to Himself. That reconciliation is priceless.

"Communion" for believers is a reminder of the sacrifice of Jesus and the life-saving covenant offered through His blood, prompting gratitude and thankfulness. It bears testimony to the exclusive nature of the gospel and to the impossibility of participating in communion with God while worshiping an idol.

10:19-22 Paul reminded the Corinthians that participating in or even condoning other religions, was like partnering with **demons** (v. 20). The Bible only offers two ways of understanding the world, good and evil—truth or lies. There is a true relationship with Jesus or empty hope in false religions. God can be worshiped or Satan can be worshiped.

Paul further emphasized that they could not be partners with God and also **be partners with demons**. God does not allow dual membership. Paul warned his readers not to provoke **the Lord to jealousy**. He understood that the death of Christ was an unimaginable sacrifice for God the Father, and failing to believe in Christ as the only way to heaven is essentially saying that the death of Christ was unnecessary and without purpose. Naturally this attitude would provoke God to jealousy in the defense of His Son. Paul reminded readers that God is much stronger than any other and not a force with which to contend (v. 22).

The Abuse of Christian Liberty (10:23-33)

10:23-26 Paul returned to his previous point that while there is now new freedom in Christ, this freedom should be restricted to those things that are helpful for building up others. Paul challenged readers to **seek** the **good of the other person** just as Jesus Christ did with His life, death, and resurrection. With this idea in mind, Paul further elaborated on the question of eating meat (v. 25). Using the Old Testament, Paul reminded his audience that everything in the earth belongs to the Lord; therefore, eating meat sold in the markets, even if it had been offered to an idol, was permissible. The MEAT MARKET (Gk. *makellon*, "food market") was an area where meat—sometimes from animals that had been sacrificed to idols—was sold.

10:27-30 Paul further expounded that believers should by all means build relationships with **unbelievers**. They should get to know them and spend time with them, and they should not rudely refuse what unbelievers offered to them (v. 27). The believers were to set an example but not make unbelievers feel uncomfortable or improper for eating something that God allows. Christians ought to be set apart and different because of their relationship to Christ, but they should not be offensive. Thinking of the other person rather than self is important, and doing what makes the other person comfortable, as long as the behavior does not call for disobedience before God, is preferred.

Paul explained that if a person had concerns about the food offered to idols, then Christians should not enjoy the food; they should put the concerns of the other person before their own desires (v. 28). This principle can be applied to many areas of life.

Helpful Hints for Exercising Your Christian Liberty 1 Corinthians 10:23-31 (cp. 5:12)	
Questions to ask about what is permissible:	• Will this bring me under its control? (5:12) • Will this be helpful to and/or build up others? (5:12; 10:23-24) • Will this offend others? (10:28-29,32) • Will this bring glory to God? (10:31)

Paul returned to defending his right to eat what he desired as long as he gave thanks to God (vv. 29-30). This issue was sensitive with the Corinthians, and Paul was reminding all that there must be a balance. Balance is challenging, but striving with a clean conscience toward God and others is worth the effort (vv. 31-33).

10:31-33 Paul beautifully closed the argument by bringing the focus to God, not to behavior, self, or others (v. 31). Pleasing God is the bottom line and should be the determining factor for behavior. Love and honor for God, not guilt or expectation, should be the motivation and guide. Likewise, evangelism should be motivated not by guilt or obligation but by love for Christ and others. Paul set the example—he conformed to the needs of others, not seeking his own gain or the approval of men but purposing to win others to Christ, which would bring glory to God. This idea gives Christians the proper balance.

OUTLINING CONDUCT IN THE CHURCH (11:1–14:40)

Head Coverings and Women (11:1-16)

11:1-3 This initial verse actually completes the preceding chapter. Boldly, Paul proclaimed that the Corinthians should imitate him (v. 1). He spoke as a father, not arrogantly, as he addressed difficulties in circumstances and character faced by these believers. The Corinthians, as many children after receiving discipline, needed assurance that they could obey. Paul seemed to be saying, "I am doing this; you can, too." He pointed those with doubts to Christ. All should be imitating Christ, and all must remember that God cooperates with and aids those who seek Him. Paul commended the believers for listening to him and learning from him. He then continued further in teaching on another controversial subject (v. 2).

Paul, no stranger to controversy, gratefully and wisely began his argument theologically. This strategy calmed emotions and removed personal threat. Paul explained **that Christ is the head of every man** (v. 3). HEAD (Gk. *kephalē*, "top, chief, one to whom others are subordinate") is used 11 times in verses 3-13. Although the word does not always carry the same meaning, the context clearly indicates whether the word is to be understood in the spiritual (vv. 3a,3b,4b,5b) or physical sense (vv. 4a,5a,5c,6,7,10,13). The word is best and most often understood to refer to "superior rank." Colossians and Ephesians also refer to Christ as the "head" (Eph 1:22; 4:15; 5:23; Col 1:18, 2:10).

In an attempt to avoid the natural implications of this clear passage, feminists Letha Scanzoni and Nancy Hardesty argue that "head" does not mean anything other than "source," an obscure meaning for *kephalē* at best. They say that Christ, as the agent of creation (Jn 1:3), is the source from which man came. They also note that the woman was taken from the side of the man, making man the "source" of woman (Gn 2:21).[2] This position runs into difficulty, beginning with the concluding phrase of 11:3, which according to their interpretive methodology implies that there was a time when Christ did not exist as there was a time when the man and woman did not exist. They then must conclude that Christ finds His origin in God the Father, which puts them in disharmony with Paul and the Christology he developed in Philippians 2 and Colossians.

There can be only one head on a body. Christ is the head of the man, **the man is the head of the woman, and God is the head of Christ** (v. 3). The conclusion of verse 3 does lay to rest supposed masculine superiority since Christ, as God, cannot possibly be inferior to God since they are one and the same. Likewise "the head

of the woman is man" does not imply inferiority of the woman or superiority of the man, while making clear the difference in the role assignment for each. God's order of creation is irrevocable and inviolable, and it supports clearly that God ordained subservience of men and women to Himself and that He models role distinctions and subordination in office with the incarnation of God in Christ. The relationship between God the Father and God the Son serves as a model for husbands and wives—equality in essence (Jn 14:9) and distinction in office (Jn 14:28). Both men and women were created in the image of God, and yet He gives to each a purposeful assignment.

This order comes from God. A person's complaints do not change the order or the need for the order. Order is not a reflection of personal worth or value but a prelude to purpose and effectiveness. Everyone wants to know his role and rank. Most jobs come with a description and chart explaining the pecking order. A lack of clarity causes more harm, confusion, and mistrust than an honest description of reality.

Paul was reminding all that order and authority are part of every area of life, including life in the Godhead. This truth should be a tremendous encouragement to all women. Christ does not shrink back from His role but clearly defines that role for the betterment of everyone. Ontologically, the three persons of the Trinity are equal in value and importance. Practically and functionally, however, their individual roles vary. If the persons of the triunity can find satisfaction and contentment in their assigned roles, then women ought to follow suit quickly. This understanding is also the basis for role differentiation among men and women in the home and in the church.

While not every text in Scripture provides reasons for following certain commands, this passage does offer thorough supportive reasoning. Women especially must be grateful for this explanation, recognizing that the creation does not inherently deserve explanation from their Creator, but they must appreciate and be all the more determined to obey when it is given.

Male headship in the home and church is necessary because of its reflection of the relationship between God the Father and Jesus the Son. While men and women are both created to reflect the image of God, they are given unique assignments on how to do so, a point clearly explained in these verses.

11:4-6 The ancient robes were rather androgynous. Men and women did not have the great diversity in clothing that is seen in the modern era. Since garments for both men and women were robes, the head covering became a clear distinction of gender. The verses addressing the cultural custom of head coverings explain their significance to society. This covering was a sign of a woman's submission to her husband and displayed a commitment of loyalty to him and his leadership. For a man to wear a head covering or for a woman to refuse to wear a head covering appeared to be a role reversal.

Paul previously linked the order of family and church relationships to the triunity of the Godhead (vv. 1-3); therefore a role reversal is not only contrary to God's design for mankind but also opposes God's nature and character. Essentially, this role reversal was a refusal to accept God's personal directives for men and women and a blatant disregard for His personhood.

The first role reversal occurred in the garden of Eden when Adam failed to fulfill his leadership responsibility by protecting his wife from the deception of Satan. Eve, likewise, refused to submit herself to her husband's leadership and instead asserted

herself, making her own willful and deadly choice. The fall inflated the natural tendency of women to disdain submission and of men to abuse authority (Gn 3:16). Husbands and wives will forever struggle for proper balance as a result of the first couple's poor choices.

Throughout the ages, many movements have occurred among women. The Greek and Roman cultures experienced backlash from women who were highly mistreated and degraded. Some women wanted to change their positions in society and have different opportunities. They wanted to discard traditional female roles and responsibilities, forsaking their families in order to be treated like men. These women were refusing to display the attributes of femininity and taking off the veils.

Paul made a distinction in how men and women would respectively adorn themselves when they would pray and prophesy in the church (vv. 4-5). With a wrong understanding of why Moses veiled himself (Ex 34:29-35), the Jewish men would cover their heads in prayer (1 Co 11:4). The modern practice by men in Judaism of wearing the *yarmulke* during the reading of the Torah and by the Hasidim (orthodox Jews) every time they go out in public is puzzling in light of Paul's admonition. The practice must go back as far as the *Mishna* of the first century and according to the *Talmud* had two purposes:

- to show reverence for God; and
- to indicate the shame of the sinner as he stood before God.

Was Paul doing battle with the Judaizers? Or was the fact that Corinth was primarily a Gentile congregation a reason for giving priority to Gentile social practices? Perhaps this impasse is encouragement for the interpreter to consider more seriously the theological platform of the apostle. Certainly men were not permitted to cover their heads when they prayed or prophesized in the Corinthian congregation, which was a distinct break with Judaism. The mandate was strengthened by Paul's use of DISHONOR (Gk. *kataischunei*, "put to shame, disappoint"), a strong word expressing the disgrace that would ensue if any man covered his head so that he would not reflect the glory of Christ. Paul explained that this covering was unnecessary for men because they were created to display God's image, glory, and rulership.

On the other hand, a woman who refused to cover her head was dishonoring her own head, or husband, by opposing the purpose God created her to fulfill. She was also taking value away from the importance of femininity by exclaiming that its importance was so little that it was much better simply to be like a man. The Creator took great efforts to carry out His intricate plan, using both men and women to display His image. For the creature to throw aside the Creator's design in favor of a lesser position is incredibly mind-boggling, shameful, and sad.

In addition, a woman who UNCOVERED (Gk. *akatakaluptō*, combining *kata* or "down" with *kaluptō* or "veil" and affixing the alpha privative to negate the word and thus lit. "not to veil down") her head was shaming her husband by suggesting that he was an unworthy leader (v. 5). Quite opposite to validating and supporting her husband's ministry, she was harming her husband's ability to rule his house well. The women were trying to be independent of men, and apparently the men were allowing, possibly even encouraging, this role reversal. Paul used a vivid image to depict the shame by suggesting that a woman might as well have SHAVED (Gk. *exuremenē*, lit. "shave with a razor"). He further noted that a woman's hair

had been given to her as a mark of glory (v. 15).

The striking importance of this letter for today's readers is jolting as many men of this generation have been so squashed by the modern feminist movement that they hardly know what it means to be men or leaders. There is a lack of understanding on the part of males and females to understand and fulfill their assigned and crucially important roles, and this deficiency has very obviously harmed society.

To summarize, Paul has given a rationale for insisting that women who pray or prophesy in the church cover their heads:

- The covered head was symbolic of a wife's submission to her own husband (v. 3).

- To refuse to acknowledge this headship publicly was a disgrace equal to having a shaven head (v. 5).

- The head covering demonstrated the submission of wives to their respective husbands as a visible sign of authority in the presence of ministering angels who were present in the congregation (v. 10).

- The foundation for these practical manifestations of obedience was God's order of creation, especially the prior creation of the man, who, in addition to being in the divine image with the woman, had been vested with the unique task of authority and was the one for whom the woman had been created (v. 8; see also Gn 2:18).

There is no hint of antagonism toward women. In fact, their ontological equality is beautifully affirmed in the divinely designed reciprocity of the relationship between husband and wife. The woman's subordination is the God-ordained manifestation of her divinely assigned role or function. Christ Himself is her example (v. 3).

The question in the modern era centers upon how these principles are to work themselves out for women. First, the natural sense of the passage establishes that there are boundaries and guidelines and that these are consistent and not contradictory with the whole of Scripture. Second, there is a clear distinction between theological foundations—headship and submission, on the one hand—and how these work themselves out in practical application—covering the head. Interpreters in every generation must build a sturdy bridge from the theological truth to relevant and practical application. Paul used the cultural setting of Corinth to dictate his application. Perhaps in the modern era, a woman shows her recognition of her husband's headship and authority more by wearing a wedding ring than a hat.

As today, secular attitudes were affecting people, particularly women in the church. Women who prayed and prophesied in church without this traditional head covering were making a statement that was clear to everyone. The desire to be viewed according to God's design as valuable is not wrong, but throwing aside the commands of God in order to accomplish earthly ends is wrong. Paul was getting to the heart of the matter. He was telling the congregation why this behavior was unacceptable and giving the women an opportunity to see the inevitable destruction from allowing personal choices to trump God and His plan.

Within Christianity the roles of both men and women changed. Men, who might have been physically able to strong-arm their wives and families, were now called to submit to God and model His loving servant leadership, viewing their wives as a significant and needed help for becoming all that God designed. Women were given an unmatched dignity and special honor. They were affirmed in intellect, position, and ministry. Women

were encouraged to study God's Word, share the gospel, and minister in the church. Women were also called to obey the commands of the Lord regarding their roles, honoring their husbands.

Although Paul affirmed the ministry and participation of women (v. 5), this involvement was qualified by certain guidelines. Paul exclaimed that women who disregarded these guidelines should carry their thoughts and behaviors to their logical conclusion by shaving their heads (v. 6). While this statement is somewhat difficult to understand today, it was clearly understood by the Corinthians. The only women whose heads were shaved or who wore short hair were prostitutes or adulteresses. Paul was saying get out in the open with your real beliefs. If you deny God's truth, then get out of the church and live what you really believe; but if you accept God's truth, embrace it fully and don't allow your behavior to invalidate your beliefs. A popular movement should not alter a person's ability or pride in standing tall for the gospel. Political pressure can often lead women to bow to secular role expectations, but Scripture encourages women to embrace fully God's design.

11:7-10 GLORY (Gk. *doxa*, "reputation, credit, honor") speaks of adornment, beauty, or a crown indicating high rank. Creating man from the dust of the earth was a display of God's majesty and glory. In this sense, the man pointed to and gave glory to God the Father. Woman, also created by God to display His image, was created not only from the man, but for the man as a helper (Gn 2:18). She has a different purpose, namely helping the man as a coregent of the earth. In this way, she is a beautiful adornment to him. Her character and graces should bring honor and glory to her husband, thereby increasing his value or high rank. The man and the woman have been interconnected from the beginning. The woman's creation was preceded by the man's (vv. 8-9); therefore, she should accept his authority and willingly bring him glory.

There is much confusion concerning the phrase **because of the angels** (v. 10). ANGELS (Gk. *angelous*, "one sent") may refer to "angels" in the sense of heavenly beings—special emissaries of God—or in the more general sense "messengers" as in Revelation 2 and 3 in reference to the pastors of the local congregations. Three interpretations are possible:

- The angels are a reference to the pastoral leadership of the Corinthian congregation, which would suggest the women submitted not only to the authority of their respective husbands but also to the spiritual authority of their pastors.

- These angels were fallen angels who might take advantage of the unveiled women who appeared to be immodest (see Gn 6:1-2). Fallen angels do exist (2 Pt 2:4; Jd 6), but it is highly unlikely that Paul would make reference to these angels as being in the worship services at Corinth. This view is considerably suspect since to build the interpretation of a difficult passage upon another obscure passage is questionable at best.

- Angels as heavenly beings created for the work of God would be the most natural understanding in the worship services. In this case, the presence of these exalted heavenly visitors ought to inspire these women to demonstrate their submission to their husbands and to God.

11:11-12 Knowing that this issue would be difficult for some to accept, Paul affirmed the value and importance of both men and women, who have equal opportunity to know God and experience His spiritual benefits. Both men and women are needed in the church, in life, and in marriage. Men and women need each other and cannot accomplish God's purpose alone (Gn 2:18). Even as the woman was created from the man, so every man who is born must also come from a woman. Paul was bringing a sense of essential equality through this point and closed with the reality that all things come from God. There is an exciting and satisfying element to the mystery in the relationship between men and women. God has created this beneficial and challenging dichotomy, and it must be recognized as from the Lord and as beautiful and without contention. Logically, no one should be prideful regarding his position or earthly assignment; neither should he be ashamed because each assignment, or in this case gender, comes directly from God, with intrinsic value and worth.

11:13-16 After laying down a lengthy and heavy theological treatise describing the Godhead and creation, Paul then said, **Judge for yourselves** (v. 13). He had given an exhaustive and clear argument. He was basically suggesting, "After all that I have explained, could anyone really think it is right for a woman to forsake her role and abandon her responsibility to reflect God and her husband rightly?" Nevertheless, Paul further buttressed his claim by natural argument. Didn't God create the woman's hair to grow in such a way that it is a natural covering for her? Doesn't even her hair point to the glory of her role and act as her covering?

ARGUE (Gk. *philoneikos*, "quarrelsome or contentious") has the sense of "strife-loving." Its etymology is interesting, linking "quarrel" (*neikos*) with "love" (*philos*), literally a person who loves a quarrel. Paul declared that **the churches of God** have **no other** (Gk.

toiautēn, "such, of this kind") **custom** (Gk. *sunētheian,* "habit"). In other words, Paul affirmed that there is no place for someone who loves to quarrel or argue in the church. He is not forbidding lively discussion of diverse opinions but rather combative confrontation, which brings hurt and division (v. 16).

The passage is clear, however, that while the symbol of authority can vary, the principle cannot. As expressed in these verses, the principle is based on Scripture and is universal and meaningful. This principle was well-understood by church leaders and churches that were committed to God's design.

Perhaps one of the best applications for today is the idea that men should look and behave as men and likewise women as women. None should shirk role or responsibility. Both should seek the respective position each was created to fill. Both should joyfully accept their appropriate created purpose and illustrate the teaching of the Creator accordingly.

In an androgynous culture this passage ought to influence men and women to display their obvious differences proudly for the purpose of bringing glory to God and His order. A role reversal, while in vogue with society, is a serious violation of Scripture with many harmful consequences.

The specifics of whether or not pants or short haircuts are permissible and whether hats are required are not nearly as important as the outcome of coming to church looking and behaving like a woman or, conversely, looking and behaving like a man. The importance of this principle has certainly been lost in society and the church, and its aftershock affects many other important ideas. Even the lack of etiquette and proper training among girls and boys is evidence of the blurring of the lines by the enemy and the flesh within the order established by God at creation.

The differences of the genders ought to be acted out and gladly embraced, offering importance and direction to all. A symbol is often protection for your weakness, a reminder of what you ought to do even when it is not something you desire to do. The head covering, or an appropriate symbol, serves to keep women in line with God's purposes and should be embraced with gratitude, not regarded with disdain.

Self-Control and the Lord's Supper (11:17-34)

11:17-22 In the previous instruction, Paul was addressing ecclesiology or church order. In this section, Paul was addressing the same subject but a different practice—the Lord's Supper.

Paul addressed the Corinthians' pride, selfishness, and desire for self-promotion. In New Testament times, the church would often have large feasts for fellowship together. These feasts were often followed by the Lord's Supper, which would be a celebration and remembrance of Christ's sacrifice and an encouragement for unity in the church as the body of Christ. However, rather than building one another up and supporting the whole body, the members were causing divisions and looking down on those who had little (v. 18). Some were puffing themselves up, drawing attention to those well-off and shaming the poor, refusing to share with them (v. 19). They were abandoning Christian behavior and thoughtfulness and instead celebrating drunkenness and lack of self-control (v. 21).

11:23-26 After hurting one another and behaving in a way that was not controlled by the Spirit of God, these presumptuous people would take communion together. This kind of behavior was totally contrary to the teachings of Christ, and, worse, their behavior drew attention to self rather than pointing to Christ.

Head Coverings for Women[3]

Full veiling does not seem to be part of the Old Testament culture. However, head coverings were important to women in biblical days. They not only offered protection from the elements but also served as symbols of modesty and, for a married woman, as a token of her commitment to her husband.

Type of Covering	Description
Headband (Hb. *shabis*)	A head ornament or front-band, probably of gold or silver (Is 3:18,20)
Headdress (Hb. *pe'er*)	Head coverings worn by women and men: • An ornamental head covering wound around the head by wealthy women (Is 3:20; Ezk 24:17) • The garland of the bridegroom or the turban worn by men as well as the cap worn by priests (Is 61:10; Ezk 24:17,23; 44:18)
Head covering (Gk. *peribolaios*, lit. "covering")	• Some kind of hair covering, perhaps even a shawl (1 Co 11:15) • The wearing of long, loose hair without a covering by an adulteress confirmed that such would be considered shameful (Nm 5:18). • The importance of the covering seems to be twofold: to show clear distinction between the sexes and to affirm publicly a wife's commitment to her husband's leadership (1 Co 11:2-16). • The custom may have been especially important to the Corinthians because of the pagan and immoral influence around them.
Veil • (Hb. *tsaciph*)	• Rebekah put on a veil when she approached Isaac before her marriage, perhaps as a sign of her betrothal. The veil was to be removed at the time of marriage (Gn 24:65). • Tamar used the veil to trick Judah (Gn 38:14,19).
• (Hb. *redid*)	• The veil-like, thin garment was probably for summer (Sg 5:7; Is 3:23).
• (Hb. *tsamah*)	• This face veil (lit. "locks") was probably ornamental, perhaps a long train of adornment for women of high social standing (Sg 4:1,3; 6:7; Is 3:23).
• (Hb. *mispachoth*	• This covering (probably a cap fitting close to the head) was associated with the activities of false prophetesses (Ezk 13:18,21).

The theological principle of God's creation order has remained unchanged even though its specific manifestations, such as a woman's covering her head in Corinth, have differed from place to place and culture to culture. This principle was evident in the chronological sequence of creation (1 Co 11:8-9). Furthermore, woman was man's "glory" (v. 7). This concept refers to the act of "manifesting or pointing to the role of another." The woman, who pointed to the man, was to be covered in the presence of God; while man, who pointed to God, was not. The practice was also followed "because of the angels" (v. 10). Paul reasoned that angels, the most submissive of all creatures, would be offended by noncompliance. Furthermore, God had provided a natural analogy that emphasized the appropriateness of the head covering: Women are naturally favored over men in the provision of hair on the head (vv. 13-15). Finally, Paul appealed to the universality of Christian practice (v. 16). The principle of headship was important, and its symbol was to be observed in all the churches.

The Lord's Supper was instituted by Jesus Christ. He commanded and asked that it be done as a **remembrance** and celebration of His sacrifice and love. The Corinthians were shaming this solemn and important event. Jesus ate the Last Supper with His disciples during Passover and just before He died (Mt 26:19-30). Jesus died at Passover as He became the new Passover Lamb (1 Co 5:7) and instituted this memorial supper to commemorate His death (11:24-25). The annual Passover celebration marked the deliverance of the Jews from Egypt (Ex 12:24-27).

The events in the Supper continue to speak eloquently to believers. The symbolism of the **bread** as His broken **body** and **the cup** as His shed **blood** reenact in the believer's heart the vicarious death of Jesus in his behalf. Therefore, no believer should come to the Lord's table with unconfessed sin (1 Co 11:28), and the Supper is for repentant sinners who have accepted Christ as Savior. Christ is present, and no one there should be despised because all are part of His body (v. 29). This memorial supper is to be observed **until He comes** (v. 26), looking forward always to the Lamb's Supper (Rv 19:7-9). These distinct truths are communicated in observing the Lord's Supper:

- a memorial to the central truth in Christianity—the atonement of Christ (1 Co 11:24-25),

- the fellowship within the body of Christ (v. 18),

- a diagnostic feast in which the believer examines his own walk with Christ (v. 28),

- a feast of thanksgiving for salvation (v. 24),

- an evangelistic witness to Christ's death (v. 26), and

- an eschatological feast of hope (v. 26).[4]

11:27-34 Paul took the Corinthians back to the most important issue, their defaming the person and sacrifice of Jesus. Their unruly behavior was a great insult to the life and ministry of Christ. Paul wanted them to view the ordinance of the Lord's Supper in sobriety and solemnity. Their misuse of this memorial

feast as **sin against the body and blood of the Lord** (v. 27) was not a small matter, and Paul wanted them to get it right. Paul awakened them to this devastating reality in hopes of expediting their attitude change.

This serious offense prompted Paul to encourage everyone to EXAMINE (Gk. *dokimazetō*, "put to the test, prove by testing") himself honestly before partaking in the Lord's Supper (v. 28), which should be observed seriously and with reverence. The idea is to put yourself on trial, not in the sense of exposing yourself to the judgment of others but to do an intense searching of your own heart and life to find anything that is unacceptable to God. The Lord's Supper is a perfect time to reevaluate oneself and determine whether the heart is pure or standing in offense against God. It is a time to seek forgiveness and restoration with the Almighty and to remember His mercy. The Lord's Supper is also protection for the church because believers ought also to deal with offenses against one another. In this way, the Lord's Supper purifies the church and keeps the body healthy as together the members honor and glorify God.

The Corinthian church, however, was misusing the Lord's Supper. This abuse was so severe that Paul noted that many were SICK (Gk. *astheneis*, "weak, feeble," often used to describe a person's condition after a long and debilitating illness) and ILL (Gk. *arrōstoi*, "sick," in which the alpha privative is added to the verb *hrōnnumi*, " move with speed," and evolving into a word used to describe someone who is healthy—thus here with negation, "one without health") because of their blasphemous behavior and carelessness with the Lord's Supper. He considered this consequence the judgment of God (vv. 29-30). The judgment was not the loss of salvation; rather, the sickness was to bring a sinning believer to repentance and restoration. Many would postulate that God would never take the life of someone just because of his carnal lifestyle, but consider Ananias and Sapphira (Ac 5:1-10), Uzzah (2 Sm 6:6-7), and Achan (Jos 7:16-26). God would not allow them to continue in sin, harming the church's reputation. The alternative to God's judgment was personal spiritual introspection.

God's discipline, while often painful, is a blessing. Instead of allowing His children to fall into gross sin, He will exercise judgment. Believers are encouraged to avoid this discipline by evaluating themselves. People who make selfish, evil choices have arduous work repairing and rebuilding their lives. To make good, wise decisions is much easier—evaluating your life and exercising self-control.

Paul returned to his common theme of believers' caring for one another and putting the needs of others before self-pleasure (1 Co 11:33). He warned the believers not to treat the Lord's Supper like any other meal. They should only participate if their hearts are right and consciences clear (v. 34).

Spiritual Gifts and the Body of Christ (12:1-31)

12:1-3 Paul described the gifts distributed by the Spirit and the ministry opportunities through these gifts. He made a distinction between God's gifts and what came out of pagan religions, which provided little understanding but demanded great commitment.

This congregation had serious problems with factions. They were not unified as they were intended to be, and this controversy over the gifts was evidence of the deeper problem. Paul wanted them to understand the doctrine behind the gifts of the Holy Spirit and how these gifts practically affected church life.

ABOUT MATTERS OF THE SPIRIT (Gk. *pneumatikōn*, "spiritual," v. 1) or "that which pertains to the Spirit" is a phrase in English but one word in Greek—either masculine (as in "spiritual people") or neuter (as in "spiritual things" or gifts). Another word is used in the phrase "different **GIFTS**" (Gk. *charismatōn*, "gift or favor or grace," v. 4). Paul mentioned about 20 different gifts in his epistles, arranged in four passages according to purpose:

- Romans 12:6-8, discussing gifts in a general way
- Ephesians 4:7-13, introducing gifts that work toward unity in the body of Christ
- 1 Peter 4:10-11, emphasizing the service rendered by the gifts
- 1 Corinthians 12:8-10; 28-30, setting forth some of the more extraordinary gifts in importance.

These gifts were undoubtedly supernaturally endowed and not merely natural or human giftedness.

The Holy Spirit gives one or more gifts to every believer (vv. 7,11). There were clear purposes noted for these gifts:

- the common good or **what is beneficial** (v. 7)
- the proper functioning of believers within the body of Christ (vv. 14-27)
- edification and equipping of believers (14:3-12)
- affirmation of the preached word—the gospel (14:24; Ac 1:8; Heb 2:3-4)
- cooperation among believers (1 Co 12:14-26).

You were led to dumb idols expressed the reality that the church in Corinth was being led astray by pagans who were under the influence of evil spirits (v. 2).

They needed a tool for discernment to know what was inspired by the Holy Spirit, and the ultimate test was Jesus— **no one speaking** under direction of **the Spirit of God** would say **Jesus is cursed** (v. 3; see also 1 Jn 4:1-6).

The triunity is found: "Spirit" (1 Co 12:4), "Lord" or Jesus (v. 5), and "God" the Father (v. 6). This wonderful model illustrates for the church how all should function according to responsibility and gifting to accomplish a unified purpose. In the Godhead, there is no competition, division, or jealousy and neither should there be in the church.

12:4-7 When spiritual **gifts** are divisive and distracting, something is wrong. The problem is not with the distributor of the gifts but with the recipients. The people obviously wanted to control what they received from God. They had not fully surrendered to God and instead were struggling within themselves.

Paul further explained that there are differing **ministries** but that all come under the authority of the Lord (v. 5). The emphasis again is on the importance of harmony and cooperation. Competition and pride are a natural part of life with which all must struggle, but here Paul was explaining that the lordship of Jesus Christ should overcome competitive spirits and allow the church body to function with cooperating **ministries**, that build up the entire church.

God can work in different people and in many different ways to accomplish His purposes. Instead of seeking to be the best or placing too much emphasis on one particular gift, Paul encouraged the congregation to recognize the multifaceted ministry of spiritual gifts and embrace them fully (vv. 6-7). The gifting was not randomly distributed but perfectly selected for a particular person in the work of the kingdom and for building up of the body of Christ.

The people in this church did not understand the role of gifts and the importance and place of each gift in the ministry of the church. They were placing too much importance on certain gifts. Paul began by clarifying the gifts and purposes. His list was not meant to be exhaustive but instructive.

12:8 Generally, **a message of wisdom** is understood to be knowing God's Word, understanding His will, and being able to make known God's wisdom to individuals in a particular situation (cp. Ac 6:1-6; 15:13-21). This gift could benefit the church in a variety of ways, such as a pastor who effectively applies God's Word to the problems of a congregation or someone who provides godly counsel for another who needs a clear direction.

The **message of knowledge** indicates a sharp mind with the ability to study and understand difficult principles and truths that many cannot grasp on their own. In this gifting the Holy Spirit reveals the facts of a situation to benefit and buttress other gifts in relating God's truths more accurately.

12:9 The gift of **faith** is an important and unusual ability to trust God, a great benefit in particularly difficult circumstances (13:2). The person with the gift of faith trusts God to do tremendous and supernatural things in the face of great obstacles, knowing how to appeal to God through prayer and motivate people to lay hold on God's promises (12:9; cp. Jms 5:17-18).

Healing is a supernatural work that has always been accomplished by God. In New Testament times, God healed through the apostles, the 70, and some associates of the apostles. Many conservative scholars believe the **gifts of healing** have ceased (12:9). Yet, God does continue to heal. However, these gifts of healing are not distributed in the same way they were in the early church era. Christians may freely seek God for healing but must realize that even in New Testament times, as today, some may receive healing and some may not. God may work through the medical profession or through simply willing the healing to come to pass. God is still good no matter the outcome. Even Paul could not heal indiscriminately (2 Tm 4:20).

12:10 The performing of miracles involved the temporary suspension of the commonly observed laws governing the world. They were a sign to show the glory of God so that people would believe in Jesus (Heb 2:3-4). Jesus and the apostles performed miracles, and these brought many to a saving knowledge of Jesus and belief in Him as God and in the truth of the gospel message. They were primarily used to authenticate the apostolic office (2 Co 12:12) and thus are not as prominent today. God does still perform miracles but usually directly instead of through a human agent.

PROPHECY (Gk. *prophēteia*, linking *pro*, a preposition meaning "before," with *phēmi*, a verb meaning "speak") carries a breadth of meaning from the speaking of the words of God before people to speaking about an event before it occurs. Either way, the gift from God is expected to be used and appreciated.

The gift of **distinguishing between spirits** has also been called discernment and is an important gift in protecting and guiding the church (1 Co 12:10). Because Satan is so skilled at distorting the truth and confusing well-meaning people, believers must be armed with discernment. Clearly, the Word of God is the objective truth from which to judge; however, discernment must be used to determine the spirit of a matter. Distinguishing between what came from the Holy Spirit and the satanic counterfeit coming from the Devil is an important gift that can pre-

vent many harmful situations both personally and for the congregation as a whole.

Different kinds of languages identified a gift considered by some scholars to have ceased. On the day of Pentecost, the disciples spoke in languages they had never studied but that were recognized by the people (Ac 2:4-11). The same phenomenon occurred at Caesarea (Ac 10:46) and at Ephesus (Ac 19:6) since the same descriptive Greek word (Gk. *glōssais*, "tongue, speech, language") is used for all. These gifts were certainly used in New Testament churches and given by God. However, they were being misused in the Corinthian church, as Paul explained in 1 Corinthians 14; he provided very clear guidelines to direct the use of this gift in church meetings.

Luke seemed to recognize a continuity in these events. However, in Corinth, the words they were speaking were apparently not understood by anyone, including the speaker, without divinely inspired interpretation (1 Co 14:2,14). The Greek word *glōssa* seems to refer to a person with the ability to speak in a language that was not native to him, one that he himself did not understand. The interpreter's role was to explain the message from God to others who did not have the ability to understand.

While it would be presumptuous to say that God will never work in this way again, it is also important to note that the initial purpose of the "different kinds of languages" and of the **interpretation of languages** was to authenticate the spoken word from God. Since the revealed Word of God is found in the Old and New Testaments, that verification is no longer needed in the same way. The interpretation of languages was given in accordance with the gift of languages so that this gift did not minister solely to an individual but also to the entire church body (v. 10). The interpretation also helped with the judgment of whether or not the message was true.

12:11 Paul concluded the naming of the gifts by reminding his readers that the Holy **Spirit is active** and involved in all these gifts (cp. v. 6), and He determines who will receive the gift(s). Every believer is given just the right gift to accomplish her God-ordained purpose, and every believer is partnered with the Holy Spirit to use these gifts to build up the body of Christ. No believer should feel unimportant or unnoticed by God. And all must realize that the Holy Spirit does not give gifts in a vacuum. They are all given to unify and build the church. Therefore, division because of gifts is in direct contradiction to God's purpose in bestowing the gifts.

12:12-26 Paul began this lengthy discourse on the difference between diversity and division by explaining that with division comes strife, but conversely, with diversity also comes unity and completion. Paul used the human body as a great metaphor describing the universal and local body of Christ (v. 12).

The human body works with incredible efficiency and drive. A body often compensates for a weakness, such as lack of sight, by overdeveloping other senses. There have been many remarkable cases of the resiliency of the human body working to overcome incredible odds, doing things that would seem impossible.

The body's ability to cooperate and function is so intricate and complex that the number of medical disciplines required to understand and explain this phenomenon are too numerous to name. However, all doctors would agree that the understanding and treatment of any part of the body must be calculated and work in conjunction with the overall function of the entire body. Only when there is a problem, such as a disease, does a part of the body withhold service to another part,

attack a part, or isolate its services from another part. This behavior in the body causes sickness, pain, and ultimately death.

These same principles function in the church body. The members of the body must unify, work together, and efficiently learn to live in the most effective way. No matter the circumstances, ethnic or financial background, weakness or strength, limitation or talent, the gift given by the Spirit has been **placed** according to a purpose.

At conversion the believer is **baptized by one Spirit** and simultaneously united to the body of Christ—the church (v. 13). He is in Christ (Gl 3:26-27). Jesus sent the Spirit as His ascension gift at Pentecost (cp. Ac 2). The Holy Spirit does the baptizing of the believer into the Lord's body. Baptism of the Holy Spirit occurs once at conversion, assuring your position in Christ. The filling of the Spirit is repeated again and again (Ac 2:4; 4:31; Eph 5:18), bringing power; it is experiential. At Pentecost the two experiences—baptism and filling—happened almost simultaneously.

Paul described the dysfunctional body using words such as **I don't need you** (1 Co 12:21) and **I don't belong to the body** (vv. 15-16). These phrases may have been used by people against one another. Some members of the body are so full of pride they do not see others as necessary or helpful to the work of God. Paul forcefully contended with this idea.

12:27-31 The first three offices were specifically ordered and belonged to the pastoral leadership of the church (v. 28). Paul used **apostles** in its particular or restrictive sense to mean the Twelve (v. 28; Lk 6:13). The Spirit inspired and empowered them in unique ways. An "apostle" had to be a witness of the resurrection (cp. 1 Co 12:28; Ac 1:21-24). These men had no successors. However, public proclamation and teaching continue in the church (see commentary on Ac 1:15-26).

Loving Others and Spiritual Maturity (13:1–14:40)

13:1-3 True, complete, Christlike love is the overarching theme of this epistle. The love of which Paul spoke is so profound and life changing that it should diminish many of the problems faced by the church, such as pride, selfishness, and division. The Corinthians were overwhelmed with self-love. Paul certainly knew about self-love. He had formerly hated and persecuted Christians. Paul knew firsthand the transforming power of Christ's love. He strongly desired that the Corinthians know and experience this love.

The Corinthian church could never utilize its spiritual gifts without the genuine love of Jesus Christ. In fact, the Corinthians' lack of love caused even the wonderfully positive gifts of the Spirit to become a source of contention and strife. Their behavior was not the only thing that needed to change. The Corinthians needed a new heart attitude and a new motivation (12:31).

Paul's first phrase would have been particularly interesting to the Corinthians, who highly prized the gift of **languages**. He explained that even this most desired gift, when exercised without love, was like the terrible sound of an instrument being misused (13:1).

Understanding **all mysteries** and obtaining **all knowledge** would be an unbelievably profitable position from which you could minister; but without love, you are worth nothing (v. 2). Even the great **faith** of being able to trust God for impossible things was empty without love (v. 2).

Much easier than genuinely loving the unlovable would be to serve them (v. 3). The alleviation of guilt and the recognition of others are only a few ways that deeds can bolster a person. Even the incredible sacrifice of giving one's life in martyrdom can be totally empty if done for self-recognition rather than for love for Christ and others. Those who were trying to find and establish their identity by using their gifts were stung by this realization.

13:4-7 Obviously, Jesus Christ was the picture of this **love** (Gk. *agapē*). God Himself came to earth to exhibit perfectly all these previously unknown qualities. Jesus did not merely possess the qualities of love; He exercised them naturally and consistently. He did not merely create the attributes of love; He also practiced them. He was not only able to understand love, but He was also able to share love with the deepest intensity, becoming the greatest sacrifice for others. In perfect harmony with God's sacrificial love, the Holy Spirit indwells believers, allowing them also to exhibit supernaturally the amazing love described.

13:8-10 Evangelicals divide into three different camps in regard to the "sign gifts." Charismatic Christians view these gifts as continuing and even normative for the church. More cautious theologians assign less importance to the gifts but maintain that, while some of these gifts are no longer frequently bestowed, God could certainly grant them at any time. Cessationists note that at least one gift (apostleship) has ceased altogether since no living individual could have been with Jesus in His lifetime or a witness to His resurrection (see Ac 1:21-22). These theologians are convinced that the "sign gifts" ceased with the close of the apostolic era and the ensuing availability of Scripture, often citing as evidence of their position 1 Corinthians 13:10 and the decreasing reference to these gifts in the New Testament documents. Regardless of your position on the matter, Paul has made it clear in chapters 12–14 that the significance of gifts such as tongues or "languages" is to be reckoned as far less important that the much weightier matters of theology and practice.

When Paul discussed **the perfect**, he was referring to the perfect state to which God will bring all believers when they are living in heaven and to the idea of completion of their assignments from God (vv. 11-12). **Prophecies** and **knowledge** will end. The passive is used in the sense that these will be acted upon by "the perfect" when it comes (v. 10), which can mean:

- the completion of the canon of Scripture;
- the maturity of the church at the end of the apostolic age;
- the death of believers who are ushered immediately into the presence of the Lord;
- the rapture or snatching away of the church;
- the return of Christ;
- the eternal state of believers;
- the entering of the end times as a unified whole.

13:11-13 Paul used the illustration of growing from **a child** to **a man** to explain that with knowledge and maturity come responsibility to react the right way. As God's people learn, spiritual truth ought to shape their behavior and interaction with others. Once in heaven, God will finally sanctify His children, but here on earth God's children must strive for maturity, working through awkward and difficult periods. However, Christians should come to a point of maturity and experience real love and sacrifice for one another. This verse has a natural application for mothers who are intensely involved in the nurturing of their children (v. 11).

Every woman loves **a mirror**, and Corinth is said to have produced very fine bronze mirrors. Until heaven, one can see

things honestly, as a mirror shows, but not perfectly or **face to face** (v. 12). Not all things on earth will be revealed or totally understandable, but in heaven the reality will be clear. The understanding will also be deepened, and this state can be anticipated with great hope by all Christians.

LOVE (Gk. *agapē*) in this nominal form only has seven possible appearances in secular Greek writings. Its frequent appearance in the New Testament would attest that the word was virtually coined to describe Christian love. *Eros*, appetitive or self-interested love, is common in Greek literature but is not found in the New Testament. *Philos* is often used in the New Testament with a general sense of esteem and affection, which is heightened within a Christian context. In fact, it is sometimes used interchangeably or synonymously with *agapē*. In this chapter Christian love was defined in terms of loving acts—not by words or feelings.

14:1-5 Paul brought this letter to a close with some final directives. The abuse of the gift of languages was a problem to which women were contributing in the church. Paul devoted an entire chapter to this particular problem. He built on the teaching from previous sections. Clearly love was lacking in this often counterfeit gift being exercised virtually without restraint. Paul wanted to take the Spirit's good gift and put it in proper perspective and practice.

Paul began with the challenge to pursue "the greatest" thing, which he had already identified as love. While Paul's language is tough and direct, he did not leave the Corinthians in confusion as to how to solve their problems. He stayed with them, struggling to work toward a positive result.

Paul stressed the importance of the gift of prophecy because this gift, like no other, would edify, encourage, and comfort. The **languages** could not be understood directly by most people and therefore could not be an encouragement to many. In addition, the gift was being misused at Corinth for personal edification alone (v. 5). Paul's use of this line of reasoning was natural since most of the letter deals with building others up.

Paul explained that the gift of "languages" was good and desirable, but he emphasized the gift of prophecy as better for the whole body (v. 5). Since the Holy Spirit perfectly and intentionally distributes the gifts, no person should seek gifts they have not been granted. Instead, one should fully exercise and enjoy the gift selected and bestowed by God. Paul encouraged the entire congregation to desire prophecy because it was a benefit to the whole group. Paul reaffirmed his own intention to pray and sing with full understanding. Far more important than ecstatic utterances were prayers and singing that were understood by all (v. 15).

The issue of languages was a major question in the Corinthian church, and great confusion and disorder accompanied the exercising of this gift. When Paul used the word **language** in this chapter, he likely had in mind two different practices, even though the same word was used to describe both. In the first instance he was describing the use of **other languages** as the term first appeared in Acts 2 (see the discussion of tongues, Ac 12:10). At other times Paul was referring to the Corinthians' imitation of this gift as described in later verses (1 Co 12:23). Some translators distinguish the meaning by designating the unintelligible sounds as "*unknown* tongues," which clarifies the phrase **I wish all of you spoke in other languages** (14:5). Corinthian ecstatic utterance was a poor imitation of the gift of languages given by the Holy Spirit at Pentecost (cp. Ac 2). A reference to this speaking of diverse languages is seen (1 Co 12:21).

The alleged contradiction between verses 22 and 23 is easily resolved. Verse 22 refers to languages "as a sign" to "unbelievers," a reference to the Acts 2 account in which unbelievers did indeed hear the gospel in their own respective languages, resulting in their amazement and the conversion of many. On the other hand, the reference to unbelievers as saying "you are out of your minds" is a warning to the Corinthians of the potential harm from their imitation of the earlier gift by using a frenzied concoction of unintelligible sounds, which could evoke a reaction of disgust from unbelievers.

14:6-12 Using strong examples, Paul appealed to the people to seek order and clarity. Even if Paul, as their teacher, shared incredible truths, they would not benefit if they could not understand the language. Paul had already explained that the Holy Spirit gives gifts to build up the body, not to build up the individual. The gift of languages was useless unless it was **building up** the other believers.

14:13-19 Paul affirmed the gift of languages but stressed the importance of **understanding** (v. 14), which would allow more people to grow. Paul, as the consummate soul winner and spiritual father, always desired growth and maturity among his converts. The person speaking in the language should have control of heart, mind, and body. Likewise, the person listening ought to have enough understanding to affirm and learn from the message.

14:20-25 Be infants in evil and adult in your thinking—naïve, inexperienced, unable to cause or participate in evil, but trained in clear and wise thinking (v. 20). The Corinthians knew well how to cause division, strife, and evil, just as children instinctively know how to manipulate and sin. Paul said that they should mature in their thinking regarding the spiritual gifts and regarding their love for others. They should no longer be experts at evil but at good.

Paul paraphrased the prophet Isaiah, who spoke very simply to the people, proclaiming judgment if they did not turn from their wicked ways and toward God (v. 21; Is 28:11-12). The people would recognize God's judgment when they were conquered by foreigners with a strange tongue. Knowing this history, the New Testament Jews would have recognized that the gift of tongues spoken at Pentecost had given them an opportunity to accept Jesus as Savior. As recorded, many Jews rejected this sign and the gospel became available to Gentiles from every nation.

The languages were also a sign to unbelieving Gentiles, validating the authority of the apostles through signs, wonders, and miracles. If the gift of languages was used improperly and indiscriminately, it would baffle and confuse not only believers but unbelievers as well. Those people would be hindered from accepting the gospel message because they could not understand what was happening in the church. The improper use of the gift would act as an obstacle to the growth of the kingdom rather than a blessing to the body.

14:26-28 Paul began addressing the group as **brothers**, a generic term including men and women. He was coming, still with authority, but as a fellow heir of Christ Jesus. Through his question, he was forcing them to think about their ridiculous behavior. The various elements of the church service were being overused and abused by nearly everyone.

Paul did not forbid ecstatic utterance, but he placed limitations upon its practice (v. 26):

- Everything done must edify the church members (v. 26), ruling out anything for personal promotion.

- No more than **three** people were allowed to speak during a service (v. 27).

- They must **each** speak **in turn**, one at a time (v. 27).

- An **interpreter** must be present (vv. 27-28).

- Women were never to speak in ecstatic language (v. 34).

- All **must be done decently and in order** (v. 40).

14:29-33 Paul also gave instruction for the gift of prophecy. He listed the number of prophets who should be allowed to convey a message. He explained that they were to be evaluated in order to remain faithful to the truth already revealed and to protect the congregation (v. 29). The prophets were not to speak simultaneously but were to share in deference and politeness toward one another (v. 31). This kind of behavior showed love and respect toward others with the gift of prophecy. This order also allowed everyone present to learn from the message shared. The prophets were always to be in control of themselves (v. 32).

Paul knew that a God of order would not be pleased with a church of disorder. Paul also equipped the church with a great tool of discernment. Any group that refused to comply with God's order of worship was not honoring God. A lack of order was evidence of a deeper, more serious problem.

14:34-35 This controversial section grabs the attention of women. In a sense Paul was saying, if you are really trying to build up others, why does each one of you want your own ministry showcased? They were not concerned if things were organized or orderly, only whether or not they got to speak and have their own way. The problems the church faced were not caused by women alone. Certainly, men were contributing to the chaos and disorder experienced by the church. However, clearly the women were out of order, misusing gifts in ways that were harmful to the church and its mission.

Paul had previously affirmed women and acknowledged that, along with men, they would receive spiritual gifts. He encouraged all believers, both male and female, to use their respective gifts in ministry within the body. However, women as well as men were required to follow guidelines in church meetings. Paul stood against disorder and disobedience.

The possible interpretations of verse 34 include these:

- Women were not to speak at all, which would seem to contradict the earlier passages where Paul commended the women who prayed and prophesied under the headship of their respective husbands (11:5; 14:26).

- This verse was addressed only to the Corinthians and to no other church beyond them, which would seem to unravel the entire point of the letter since Paul's instructions have been carefully presented with clear theological foundations and as principles transcending time.

- Women were to refrain from ecstatic utterances only, due to the previous discussion in chapter 14.

These conclusions can be made:

- The context of the passage concerns the use of ecstatic utterance in the assembly.

- The temple prostitutes, who worshiped the goddess Delphi, had a practice of talking in gibberish or an unintelligible language. Some have speculated that Paul was afraid that the women of the church would be identified with this practice by speaking in tongues in the public worship.

- Consistent with the reason women should cover their heads to identify themselves as submissive to their husbands' leadership and not identify themselves with ungodly women, is observing the prohibition against tongues, thereby setting Christian women apart.

- Women who spoke out of turn were critical and disorderly. They did not reflect God's order in the church (v. 40).

God has set guidelines for the roles of men and women in the church and home. These guidelines include the servant leadership of men in the church and home and the willing submission of women. God has designed the church to reflect His ordered character. He has also designed men and women to reflect His image.

Women speaking out of turn and critically evaluating teaching or interpretations would show an obvious lack of submission and a rebellion against God's order. Therefore, Paul instructed the women to hold their tongues and refrain from speaking out in the meetings of the congregation. This command to **be silent** was not reflecting a prejudice against women. BE SILENT (Gk. *sigatōsan*, "say nothing, become silent, keep still") was a word that meant to close the mouth and not talk at all, in contrast to the word translated SILENT (Gk. *hēsuchia*) found in other passages (1 Tm 2:11,12; 1 Pt 3:4). The Old Testament law prohibited women from speaking in the Jewish synagogues, and the New Testament affirmed the leadership of men. Undoubtedly, God gifted women with intellect, leadership ability, and spiritual gifts. The restriction was based not on inherent value or ability but on order. This restriction would also allow women, who previously were given no encouragement in learning, the opportunity to participate in education and to ask questions in the proper setting—

one in which their husbands were encouraged to teach them (v. 35).

By encouraging a woman to ask spiritual questions of her own husband, Paul was allowing a wife's spiritual desires to fuel the growth of her husband, who would be challenged to immerse himself in studying God's Word and prayer in order to answer the questions of his wife.

14:36-40 Paul was also keeping the lines of authority clear. Men should have the major part of teaching and leading in the church to follow and affirm God's plan of male headship. There were many disruptions in the church service, including women trying to speak and promote their own agendas rather than God's.

Paul did encourage the use of spiritual gifts. But, he discouraged an atmosphere marked by disorder and warned about the misuse of gifts. Again, the focus was removed from the individual to God and others. Love for God should overshadow personal rights and preferences. Love for others should control personal behavior and attitudes.

TEACHINGS ABOUT THE RESURRECTION (15:1-58)

15:1-11 Paul brought the Corinthians back to the main thing: Christ and the gospel. Nowhere is there a clearer and more concise rendering of the essence of the gospel:

- **Christ died for our sins** (v. 3).
- **He was buried** (v. 4).
- He arose **on the third day** (v. 4).
- He was seen by many eyewitnesses (vv. 5-7).
- He also appeared to Paul (v. 8).

The resurrection body was unusual. Christ could pass through closed doors (Jn 20:19,25). He could vanish before the eyes of His disciples (Lk 24:31). Yet His body of flesh and bones could be touched and felt (Lk 24:39; Jn 20:17,27). The evidence pointed to a historical event—not merely a spiritual apparition. Those who deny the resurrection cannot explain away the empty tomb and the eyewitness observations of the risen Christ. The resurrection became the Father's signature that He accepted the atonement—the sin-bearing death—of His Son Jesus and that now Jesus reigns as Lord over all (Php 2:9-11), guaranteeing for all believers the final victory over death (1 Co 15:12-13).

Christ's Resurrection Appearances

- Mary Magdalene and the other Mary (Mt 28:9; Jn 20:16-17)
- Peter (1 Co 15:5; Lk 24:34)
- Cleopas and his friend (Lk 24:13-32)
- The apostles without Thomas (Lk 24:36-39; Jn 20:19-24)
- The apostles with Thomas (Jn 20:26-29)
- A group of over 500 people (1 Co 15:6)
- The seven disciples by the sea (Jn 21:1-23)
- James (1 Co 15:7)
- The apostles for the Great Commission and ascension (Mt 28:16-20; Lk 24:50; Ac 1:6-11)
- Paul (1 Co 15:8; Ac 9:3-6)

Clear

Paul's personal encounter with the resurrected Christ was vivid in His mind. He compared that event to a premature birth (v. 8). In the first century, survival by children born prematurely was unlikely. Can Paul be saying that his becoming a Christian and an apostle was a highly unexpected and unlikely event? AB-NORMALLY BORN (Gk. *ektrōmati*, "miscarriage") is not in the sense of an abortion preceding the regular time for birth. Rather, the unexpected appearance of the resurrected Christ to Paul came at an unexpected moment as an untimely termination of a hopeful pregnancy with delivery at an unannounced moment. What comes in this premature birth is incapable of sustaining life on its own volition and requires divine intervention if it is to continue. The emphasis was on Paul's weakness and his dependence upon God's grace.

Paul humbly noted that he was not one of the original Twelve. He also shared the failures of his former life. Had it not been for Christ's miraculous appearance to Him, Paul never would have experienced salvation or apostleship (vv. 9-10). Paul did not doubt his authority but acknowledged the power of God to forgive him and use him to advance the kingdom he had formerly stifled. God extended grace to him and was using him and others to further the gospel message (v. 11).

15:12-19 Some attempted to refute the resurrection of Christ. Paul explained that without the resurrection the gospel is a useless message (v. 13). Without preaching the resurrection, the prophet is a false witness, going against the testimony of God Himself (v. 15). He likened the ability of God to be raised from the dead with God's ability to forgive sin. Paul explained that if the resurrection is impossible, then so is the forgiveness of sin and eternal hope in Jesus Christ (v. 17).

15:20 In Paul's teaching on the future resurrection of believers, he described Jesus' resurrection as **the firstfruits**. Jesus was the first to be raised from the dead to live forever; and, therefore, all who are in Him will also be raised from the dead (v. 20).

The Greek noun *aparchē* comes from the preposition *apo*, meaning "from," and *archē*, meaning "beginning or first." The word is used to describe the first installment of the crop, which would then be a foreshadowing and pledge of what was to come in the harvest. In ancient Greek, *aparchē* was often used to announce the beginning of an event and became the official name for a certificate of birth. Twice Paul used *aparchē* in reference to the believers who were the first converts of a certain province (Rm 16:5; 1 Co 16:15). A special group of believers in the end times are also called **FIRSTFRUITS** (Rv 14:4). The Holy Spirit is received by believers as the "firstfruits" of their salvation (Rm 8:23; Jms 1:18). In discussing the resurrection in the current context, Paul referred to Christ as "the firstfruits of those who have fallen asleep" (1 Co 15:20). Christ was the first to arise from the dead (v. 23), and His resurrection is the basis for the resurrection of all believers.

15:21-28 God has an order: Christ is the first to be resurrected; when He returns again, believers will be caught up to meet Him (v. 23); and the end will come when Christ conquers the antichrist and has ultimate victory in the earth (v. 24). Christ's resurrection guarantees the resurrection of all believers. He will reign, and all enemies will be placed **under His feet** (v. 25); then Christ will totally overcome death symbolizing total victory (v. 26).

Paul explained that for Christ to "put everything under His feet" does not change His eternal position within the

Godhead. God the Father is the One who places everything under the rule of Jesus, and only the Father is not under the feet of Jesus (v. 28). Jesus will deliver the earthly, millennial kingdom to the Father. While Jesus had a position and purpose different than God the Father, He continued to have equal value. He is coeternal and coequal with the Father.

15:29-34 This concept is difficult to interpret and must be understood in light of other clearer passages regarding baptism. Biblical doctrine cannot be built on any one verse as difficult and obscure as this one (v. 29). Nowhere does Scripture encourage a person to be baptized for a dead person. Since baptism saves no one, being baptized in the place of those who are already dead cannot be of value to anyone. However, baptism is closely associated with salvation since it was the first step of obedience in the life of a new Christian.

There are several possible interpretations:

- It can be understood as the testimony of those who died for the faith. Those who lived faithful lives and died were catalysts, through the testimony of their lives, for others who would at a later time accept Christ as Lord and Savior and subsequently experience baptism.

- It could suggest a hypothetical situation: If Jesus cannot be raised from the dead, then Christianity and baptism mean nothing. If there is no hope of resurrection, then what is the point of following Christ in baptism? Baptism is a symbol of the resurrection that will come; a symbol that has no meaning without the reality of a future resurrection.

- The preposition **FOR** (Gk. *huper*, "over or instead of") can also mean "concerning" (see Jn 1:30). The idea is that baptism "concerning"

death and the resurrection is meaningless unless the resurrection is a reality.

Paul understood that listening to and associating with evil company would only corrupt the believers (vv. 33-34). He commanded them to stop living in this foolish way and to be wise about the things of God. He told them to stop sinning and shamed them for allowing others to influence them wrongly when they should be influencing others for God.

15:35-46 Paul began a discussion about the resurrection body. He explained, in line with his teaching on earthly life, that the earthly body would have only a slight likeness to the heavenly body. The glorified body is beyond human understanding and cannot be explained (v. 35), but Paul did provide a helpful analogy (vv. 36-37). God has a plan for the earthly bodies as a gardener has a plan for his seeds and eventual harvest. The resurrected body is related to the old body in some sense, but it is also a new creation (v. 44).

Believers will be given glory and power in their spiritual bodies. Paul also pointed out that the **natural body** viewed as a seed is evidence that a **spiritual**, everlasting **body** will come. For unbelievers, this body will dwell eternally in hell. For believers, this body will reside eternally in heaven. Paul logically explained that **the natural** must precede **the spiritual** just as Adam preceded Jesus, falling perfectly in line with the order of God's plan.

15:47-49 All are born like Adam with a natural bent toward sinning. Like Adam, all need forgiveness of that sin and a supernatural Savior. Only those who receive forgiveness of sin and accept Jesus as Savior and Lord can be reborn as heavenly or spiritual people. The resurrection body was obviously an important concept. Jesus also addressed this subject in His teaching to Mary and Martha (cp. Jn 11).

15:50-58 A mystery is a revealed truth that cannot be discerned by human wisdom (v. 51). Paul addressed the "mystery" that not all believers will face death (v. 51). **The dead** in Christ **will be raised** (v. 52) before the great tribulation, and they will have received glorified bodies. Believers still living will be instantly caught up in the air and changed into their glorified bodies (vv. 51-52; cf. 1 Th 4:14-17). Once Christ has accomplished His work, as predicted in Isaiah 25:8, death will be **swallowed up** (1 Co 15:54) in the **victory** of Jesus Christ. All acknowledge death as the unavoidable ultimate enemy; but Jesus will conquer even death, removing its power and **sting**. God will give His people victory over sin and death because of the sacrifice and work of Jesus Christ.

CONCLUDING PERSONAL REMINDERS (16:1-24)

The Gift for the Church in Jerusalem (16:1-4)

16:1-4 Since Paul was a traveling missionary, he could easily assess the needs of the churches and share news among congregations, which apparently he did regularly. Paul not only admonished the Corinthians to give to other believers who were in need, but he also told them how to give (v. 1). Paul assumed that the church met on Sunday, **on the first day of the week** (cp. Ac 20:7; Jn 20:19,26). Believers had exchanged the Sabbath as a primary day of worship for Sunday to commemorate Christ's resurrection and victory over the grave. He explained setting aside money systematically, according to the family's prosperity, before the money was spent on other things (1 Co 16:2). The money was to be set aside before he arrived as a measure of account-

ability or a test for their maturity. He explained that he would make sure the gift was given to the Jerusalem church, which was suffering because of great persecution (v. 3). Paul had balance: He was zealous for his beliefs and always ready to share excitement, but he also understood the importance of practical living.

Plans for Paul's Travel (16:5-12)

16:5-9 Because Paul had a great love for the church, he let them know the route of his journey (vv. 5-6). He requested extended time with them, assuring them that the chiding in his letter did not hinder his love for them (v. 7).

16:10-12 Paul feared that Timothy might be mistreated (vv. 10-11). He reminded the Corinthians that **Timothy** was sincerely and effectively **doing the Lord's work** and that they should not **look down on him**. Paul also made clear that Timothy would return and give him a report, thus providing accountability to the church for their behavior.

Paul also mentioned **Apollos**, who was known to be a great preacher (v. 12). Paul was letting the people know that he wanted them to experience spiritual nurturing and thereby grow in Christ. Paul was able to accept the fact that God was directing Apollos, and God's timing must be trusted. He assured the people that Apollos would come when he was able. Paul was able to distinguish between his own personal desires and the clear revelation of God's will. Apollos understood God's will for himself to be other than what Paul desired. Apostolic authority did not manifest itself in coercion.

A Final Exhortation from Paul (16:13-24)

16:13-18 These were difficult days for the New Testament church, and Paul's challenging words were needed (v. 13).

Paul cited the family of **Stephanas**, affirming their genuine faith, and asked the people **to submit** to them (v. 15). He affirmed those who were living the Spirit-filled life, holding them up as examples of what he had been teaching in the letter. He also identified those men who came to minister to him in Ephesus, acknowledging that they had been a blessing to him (v. 18).

16:19-20 These verses are significant because Paul left the Corinthians with the impression that many believers were standing with them and supporting them in their efforts to become like Christ and to promote the kingdom of God. This accountability was healthy and encouraging. Paul was reminding the Corinthians that all believers are fighting an important fight. This great motivation provided an appropriate closing for Paul's powerful letter.

16:21-23 Paul reaffirmed his authorship. He also revealed the truth of his heart when he exclaimed, *Maranatha,* "Our Lord, come!" MARANATHA is a transliteration of two Aramaic words. It can be understood in two ways: either *marana tha*, meaning "Our Lord, come!" or *maran atha*, meaning "Our Lord has come!" In the New Testament this exclamation occurs only here (v. 22). Since Paul had expounded on Christ's coming kingdom in chapter 15, he likely meant "Our Lord, come!"—which was an appropriate expression of joy and hope regarding Christ's return. Paul extended God's blessing, and he extended his great love for the Corinthian church in the name of the Lord Jesus Christ (vv. 23-24).

Bibliography

*Calvin, John. *Commentary on the Epistles of Paul the Apostle to the Corinthians.* Grand Rapids, MI: Baker Books, 2003.

*Garland, David, E. I *Corinthians.* Baker Exegetical Commentary on the New Testament. Grand Rapids: Baker Academic, 2003.

*Kistemaker, Simon J. *I Corinthians.* Grand Rapids: Baker Books, 1993.

MacArthur, John. *I Corinthians.* The MacArthur New Testament Commentary. Chicago: Moody Press, 1984.

MacLaren, Alexander. *I & II Corinthians, Galatians, and Philippians.* Expositions of Holy Scripture, vol 14. Grand Rapids: Baker Book House, 1974.

Murray, Andrew. *Humility.* New Kensington, PA.: Whitaker House, 1982.

Patterson, Paige. *The Troubled, Triumphant Church.* Eugene: Wipf and Stock Publishing, 2002.

*Prior, David, *The Message of I Corinthians.* Downers Grove, IL: InterVarsity Press, 1985.

Wiersbe, Warren. *Be Wise.* Wheaton, IL: Victor Books, 1983.

*For advanced study

Notes

1 Adapted from the *Woman's Study Bible*, ed. by Dorothy Kelley Patterson and Rhonda Harrington Kelley (Nashville: Thomas Nelson, 1995), 1908.
2 Letha Scanzoni and Nancy Hardesty, *All We're Meant to Be: Biblical Feminism for Today* (Grand Rapids: W. B. Eerdmans, 1992), 30-31. See also the exhaustive work of Wayne Grudem on this word in *Recovering Biblical Manhood and Womanhood*, ed. by John Piper and Wayne Grudem (Wheaton: Crossway Books, 1991), 424–76.
3 Adapted from the *Woman's Study Bible*, 1940.
4 Paige Patterson, *The Troubled, Triumphant Church*: *An Exposition of First Corinthians* (Nashville: Thomas Nelson Publishers, 1983), 196–203.

2 CORINTHIANS

Introduction

Paul had a long and intense relationship with the Corinthians. They spent much time together, enjoyed warm fellowship in Christ, and had many confrontations. This letter was written to the church in order to prepare them for Paul's coming visit. The beginning is very positive, but the second part of the letter is strongly confrontational and straightforward as Paul defended his own authority and opposed false apostles. Paul was motivated by love to defend his ministry and thus point to Christ. (For more information regarding Corinth, see the introduction to 1 Corinthians.)

Title

Paul wrote at least three letters "To God's church at Corinth" (1:1; 1 Co 1:2). Some scholars posit four or more. The Greek title of the letter known in English as "2 Corinthians" is *pros Korinthiogē B*, "To the Corinthians B," derived from the letter's immediate recipients. In 1 Corinthians, Paul mentioned having written a previous letter (5:9), which is not extant; and in 2 Corinthians he mentioned previously writing another "painful" letter (2:3-4; 7:8,12), which also is not extant. Although 2 Corinthians is actually the fourth written correspondence, its title acknowledges this letter as the second of the two Corinthian letters accepted in the New Testament canon.

Setting

Paul spent a great deal of time mentoring and leading the Corinthians. At times the church was very responsive, while at others they were hostile. They experienced much growth as a result of Paul's efforts, but at times they regressed in their attitudes and behavior. One visit was incredibly painful for Paul as his authority and apostleship were challenged by a defiant man. He addressed this lack of respect for authority in his lost letter and then met with Titus to discuss the results in the church. The good report brought by Titus must have been a great encouragement to Paul. However, he also brought news that a small fraction still opposed the apostle. Not one to ignore problems, Paul followed this letter with a personal visit, which appears to have been successful.

Genre

Second Corinthians is a letter from the Apostle Paul to the church in Corinth. The letter begins with the three-part salutation typical of ancient Greco-Roman written correspondence: name of the writer, identification of the recipients, and words of greeting. Unlike other Pauline letters, these preliminaries are followed by an extended blessing (1:3-11) that introduced the nature of the epistle's contents. Paul addressed the persistent problems in the church with apostolic authority, but he had to make the case for this authority in order to be heard. His sufferings for

Christ's sake proved the authenticity of his apostleship and of his genuine love for the Corinthians. Paul reiterated these themes in closing the letter and concluded with final exhortations, greeting, and benediction.

Author
Paul is the undisputed author of this epistle, which contains many characteristics of his style. He wrote with a familiarity of the people, including many references and much autobiographical information. Paul and Timothy had a close relationship. He mentored Timothy and respected him. Paul involved this younger man in ministry, inviting him to become his helper and sending him on missionary journeys.

Timothy had also spent time with the Corinthian congregation. Paul did not identify Timothy as an apostle but instead as a fellow brother in Christ. Possibly Timothy had returned from a visit with the Corinthians and was with Paul at the writing of the letter.

Date
Paul wrote this letter during his third missionary journey, probably while in Macedonia with another congregation. Several letters were written to Corinth over a period of time. The first and third letters are no longer in existence. The second letter is known to be 1 Corinthians and was written to resolve a number of ethical and doctrinal problems the church was facing. The fourth letter was the book of 2 Corinthians, which was written in the year AD 56, not long after the writing of 1 Corinthians.

Recipients
Paul felt a real affection for the people as he personally shared Christ with many. He planted this church and spent much time with them. While they had baggage from their past, they were also very blessed with spiritual gifts. They were living in a wicked and ostentatious society and had much to learn regarding Christian maturity. Paul was intensely concerned about their preparation for spiritual welfare.

Major Themes
The first and most obvious theme is Paul's strong defense of his apostolic authority. He clearly disliked commending himself to the Corinthians. However, Paul understood that their recognition of his apostolic office was closely tied to their acceptance of the gospel message. Because the message was so important, he provided a clear, thorough, and convincing defense.

A related theme is compliance to godly leadership. Many Corinthians enjoyed having their own way, even though they were accountable to God, who has clearly designed all areas of life with structure and authority. Paul laid the foundation for following godly pastoral leadership in this book. His love and subsequent actions provided a good training manual for pastors facing conflict.

In addition, Paul boldly warned against the deception of false teaching. The Corinthians had obviously been duped and suffered serious consequences. All churches would be wise to protect themselves from false teachers and doctrines.

Finally, looking toward heaven is a concept Paul discussed at great length in this epistle. He contrasted the earthly life with the heavenly life and offered believers an eternal perspective of a glorious future.

Pronunciation Guide

Achaia	*uh KAY yuh*	Judea	*joo DEE uh*
Aretas	*EHR uh tuhs*	Macedonia	*mass uh DOH nih uh*
Damascenes	*DAM uh seens*	Silvanus	*sil VAY nuhs*
Damascus	*duh MASS kuhs*	Troas	*TROH az*

Outline

I. INTRODUCTION (1:1-11)
   A. Words of Greeting (1:1-2)
   B. An Expression of Thanksgiving (1:3-11)
     1. For God's comfort (1:3-7)
     2. For God's deliverance (1:8-11)

II. THE DEFENSE OF THE APOSTLE (1:12–2:11)
   A. His Trustworthiness (1:12-14)
   B. His Explanation for Postponing His Visit (1:15–2:4)
   C. His Call for Forgiveness (2:5-11)

III. THE MINISTRY OF THE APOSTLE (2:12–6:10)
   A. The Trip to Macedonia (2:12-13)
   B. A Testimony of God's Sufficiency (2:14–3:6)
   C. The Glorious New Covenant (3:7-18)
   D. The Heart of the Gospel (4:1-6)
   E. The Treasure of the Gospel (4:7-15)
   F. The Eternal Perspective of the Gospel (4:16–5:21)
   G. A Ministry Commendation (6:1-10)

IV. THE WORK OF THE APOSTLE AMONG THE CORINTHIANS (6:11–7:16)
   A. Paul's Challenge to the Corinthians (6:11–7:1)
   B. Paul's Response to the Corinthians (7:2-16)
     1. Affection for them (7:2-4)
     2. Joy over their repentance (7:5-16)

V. THE OUTGROWTH OF PAUL'S MINISTRY (8:1–9:15)
   A. A Testimony from the Macedonians (8:1-7)
   B. The Example of Christ (8:8-9)
   C. An Appeal for the Collection (8:10-15)
   D. The Response to the Collection (8:16–9:5)
   E. Lessons Learned from Giving (9:6-15)

VI. AN AUTHENTICATION OF PAUL'S MINISTRY (10:1–12:13)
   A. Paul's Authority (10:1-18)
   B. Judging between Genuine and False Apostles (11:1-15)
   C. Paul's Genuine Apostleship (11:16–12:13)

VII. PAUL'S PROPOSED VISIT TO CORINTH (12:14-21)

VIII. PAUL'S BENEDICTION AND CHALLENGE (13:1-13)
   A. The Apostle's Warning (13:1-4)
   B. The Apostle's Admonition (13:5-10)
   C. A Final Exhortation (13:11-13)

Exposition of the Text

INTRODUCTION (1:1-11)

Words of Greeting (1:1-2)

1:1-2 Paul identified himself **and Timothy** as the authors of this letter **to God's church at Corinth**. As **an apostle of Christ Jesus** Paul spoke with the authority of the divine Messiah and Savior who had sent him to proclaim the gospel in His name. Paul humbly recognized that he was an apostle only **by God's will** (v. 1). Later in the epistle, Paul openly defended his apostleship and the church's need to submit to his authority, which in turn was subject to God's authority.

> *Spiritual regeneration cannot be undone by human frailties or reversed by satanic forces, which are at work even among believers.*

Paul had a wonderful ability to open the hearts and minds of people to the majesty of God and His ability to use ordinary people. By identifying the Corinthian believers as "God's church," he reminded them of their high calling and of God's great love. The letter was also addressed to the **saints ... throughout Achaia**. SAINTS (Gk. *hagiois*, "separate from common condition, dedicated, righteous, holy") allowed for the inconsistencies and deficiencies of daily life since the emphasis is upon the regenerating and sanctifying of the Holy Spirit who indwelled those who called themselves Christians. Spiritual regeneration cannot be undone by human frailties or reversed by satanic forces, which are at work even among believers.

Paul extended to all these believers a greeting of **grace** (Gk. *charis*, "free, unmerited favor") **to you and peace from God our Father and the Lord Jesus Christ** (v. 2). PEACE (Gk. *eirēnē*, "tranquility," anglicized in the name "Irene") was a Hebrew greeting emphasizing holiness and prosperity of life, more than expressing good wishes but rather in the sense of offering a benediction or blessing. It suggested freedom from external enmity with others and from internal distractions. Its thoughtful placement by Paul in each of his salutations (Rm 1:7; 1 Co 1:3; Gl 1:3; Eph 1:2; Php 1:2; Col 1:2; 1 Th 1:1; 2 Th 1:2; 1 Tm 1:2; 2 Tm 1:2; Ti 1:4; Phm 3) affirmed its subordination to grace since in fact "grace" produces "peace."

An Expression of Thanksgiving (1:3-11)

For God's comfort (1:3-7)

1:3 Paul was so acquainted with the character of God and His magnificent attributes that he was always able to praise and to bless Him. BLESSED (Gk. *eulogētos*) is a Jewish ascription of praise acknowledging God as the source of all blessings. This word is used eight times in the Greek New Testament, chiefly by Paul and always in reference to God. In this section Paul praised God as **the Father of mercies** (Gk. *oiktirmōn*, "compassion, pity"; cp. Ps 103:13) **and the God of all comfort**. COMFORT (Gk. *paraklēseōs*, "consolation, solace, encouragement"; in other contexts, "exhortation") appears 16 times in the letter (cp. 2 Co 1:3-7; 7:7-13; 8:4,17). Literally a "calling near, entreaty, or summons for help," the word usually denotes an active giving of your personal presence to someone in need. Jesus referred to the Holy Spirit as a *paraklēton* ("counselor, advocate, helper") in John 14:16, and the apostles gave the name BARNABAS, "Son of Encouragement" (*paraklēseōs*), to the man who discipled Paul and John Mark. In the Old Testament, COMFORT (Hb. *nacham*) is an action often ascribed to the Lord, particularly in Messianic prophecy (e.g., Ps 23:4; Is 40:1; 49:13; 51:3,12; 52:9; 61:2; 66:13). In 2 Corinthians the word suggests both the unique "consolation" of Jesus the Messiah (cp. Lk 2:25) and God's personal provision of the kind of comfort an attentive, tender-hearted mother gives her hurting or distressed child (cp. Is 66:13). "All" emphasizes a complete adequacy of God's "comfort for any and every circumstance that might arise (see Php 4:19).

The apostle has a beautiful way of identifying the interconnectedness of the trinity with such ease. Because Jesus was the willing sacrifice for the sin of man, God is able to extend mercy. This mercy is here revealed in God's willingness and ability to comfort His children who are experiencing affliction.

1:4-7 Having faced numerous hardships, Paul was familiar with **affliction**. AFFLICTION (Gk. *thlipsei*, "pressure, oppression, distress, tribulation") and the related verb forms occur 10 times in 2 Corinthians. The word literally suggests "pressing firmly together," particularly referring to the squeezing of grapes as in a winepress. One severe beating could forever change, perhaps even handicap, a person for life. Paul faced such beatings and more. Rather than being cast into self-pity, he was able to delight in the **comfort** God provided. He was also able to look beyond himself and realize that his "affliction" better equipped him to minister to others.

While not enjoyable, suffering is part of the Christian life. Coming into the kingdom of Christ introduces believers to **the sufferings of Christ** (v. 5) as one way of

being identified with Jesus. Nevertheless, Jesus is very near to those who are hurting. A believer is blessed to remember Christ, ever seated in majesty at the right hand of the Father, as He was actually standing at the martyrdom of Stephen (Ac 7:54-56) to offer immediate comfort to this precious saint at his time of greatest need.

Paul spoke of affliction for the cause of Christ. Paul was willing to do anything, to suffer at any cost, in order to win people to the kingdom of God and fulfill his calling. Women can easily relate to this commitment as they are willing to suffer and sacrifice incredibly in order to give life to a child. Paul had this same driving passion for unbelievers and for the church. That his affliction had a purpose gave him **comfort** and **endurance**. ENDURANCE (Gk. *hupomenē*, "remaining under, patient expectation") was used to describe a constant bearing up under whatever the burden might be. In classical Greek the word was used to describe the ability of a plant to live under harsh and unfavorable conditions and even evolved to indicate a willingness on the part of a Greek mortal to die for his gods. Paul was able to focus not merely on the hardship itself but on the joy and comfort God provides.

For God's deliverance (1:8-11)

1:8-11 Scripture addresses many of the life-threatening trials faced by Paul and others. Paul mentioned a situation already familiar to the church, so he did not elaborate on the **affliction that took place in the province of Asia**. He did, however, focus on the devastation he and others felt. You CAN JOIN (Gk. *sunupourgountōn*, "cooperate with") indicated the sense of "helping together." The present active participle suggests an ongoing spirit of working together with another and with God. Although Paul would be considered strong and courageous by any standard, he admitted having reached the end of his **strength** (v. 8). The Corinthians knew of Paul's sufferings, but the apostle wanted them to know also the intensity of these "afflictions"— so intense he could not have survived without divine intervention—so that the Corinthians would accept their own afflictions with greater patience. Paul conveyed an expectation of imminent death but trusted **in God who raises the dead** (v. 9). He acknowledged that God had miraculously saved their lives, and he expressed confidence that God could and would do so **again** (v. 10). Paul linked the Corinthians' prayers to his deliverance and expressed gratitude for their petition on his **behalf**. Paul was COMPLETELY OVERWHELMED (Gk. *huperbolēn*, "excess, exceedingly," lit. "throw beyond" in the sense of beyond the normal power of endurance). Paul considered their **prayers** a precious gift. This account of deliverance attests to the power of prayer and its importance in life (v. 11). Philip Hughes describes prayer as "human impotence at the feet of divine omnipotence." Intercession is simply a part of the divine means at work in executing deliverance, which depends wholly on God.

THE DEFENSE OF THE APOSTLE (1:12–2:11)

His Trustworthiness (1:12-14)

1:12-14 Paul was obviously willing to give his life for Christ, and he lived every day with this goal in mind. His life and **conscience** showed his commitment to the Lord (v. 12). He fulfilled his calling to win others to Jesus. He trusted God to help him fulfill his role, and he lived in such a way that he had no regrets or any sins to hide. He was humble, recognizing that his clear conscience and wisdom were the result of God's work in his life.

Paul began to refute the false apostles who were challenging him. Some believed that Paul's letters were difficult to **understand**, but he underscored his desire and intent for the people to "understand" his teaching **completely** (v. 13). Paul wanted the Corinthians to take pride in the fact that he had ministered to them **with God-given sincerity and purity** (v. 12). SINCERITY (Gk. *eilikrineia*, "clearness, purity of motive") is more literally "checked or judged by the sun."

His Explanation for Postponing His Visit (1:15–2:4)

1:15-24 Paul had previously told the Corinthians that he **planned to come** for a visit and stay for an extended amount of time. He had to change his plans and was unable to visit the church at the time they expected. Some in the church took this opportunity to attack Paul's character and trustworthiness. These adversaries seemed to be promoting the idea that he could not be trusted, that he was acting like people of the world who only sought their own best interest, even at the expense of others.

Paul denied this charge, explaining that he was not fickle, self-centered, or **irresponsible**. Instead, Paul explained that the message of the gospel he and others **preached** is reliable and true (v. 19). If they were honest in bringing God's truth, they certainly could be trusted with his change of plans. Paul appealed to the Holy **Spirit** within believers. This Spirit should unify them in Christ and confirm to the church that Paul was a genuine and trustworthy apostle. AMEN (Hb. word first transliterated into Greek and then anglicized) conveys firmness and reliability, meaning "true, trustworthy" and used here to affirm Paul's statement of confidence in the faithfulness of God. The article used in the Greek text (*to*, "the") adds emphasis to the certainty of God's promises. Jesus Himself used this word at the beginning of His utterances to affirm the authenticity and immutability of His words. The word has served as a keystone for Christian prayer, preserving the continuity of the Judeo-Christian faith (Dt 27:15; 1 Ch 16:36; Ps 106:48). Paul was so convinced that he had made the right decision in delaying his visit that he called on **God** as his **witness** (v. 23). This is an incredibly strong defense conveying the idea that Paul believed he was being obedient to God. How could the Corinthians find fault with obedience?

Paul did not specifically address the reason he chose not to come, but he did explain that the delay was for the good of the church. He acknowledged that he could not force the church to obey God, so he appealed to them in the Spirit to be obedient and exercise the virtues of faith and joy. He desired for them to be strong and happy in the Lord.

2:1-4 Paul revealed the reason for choosing not to make the **visit**. After he had written 1 Corinthians, Paul was made aware that the church was not responding in the right fashion. He felt it was necessary to make a personal visit to straighten out some of the problems. Sadly, this visit was very troubling, and Paul had been personally attacked by a man in the congregation. After this visit Paul felt compelled to send the church a powerful and confrontational letter (v. 4). He did not want to cause them undue grief by returning too quickly. He deeply desired to restore relationships and to encourage Christian behavior and attitudes within the congregation. Even though Paul had been deeply hurt and humiliated, he still loved the people. He was obviously not prideful, bitter, or resentful of the poor treatment he had received but eager to move on in Christian love and unity.

His Call for Forgiveness (2:5-11)

2:5-11 Thankfully, Paul included this section, which is helpful in dealing with conflicts faced by most churches. These situations are always delicate and require forgiveness. Church discipline, while required by the Bible, is difficult for churches to exercise. Paul spent time teaching the church the importance of this kind of discipline and teaching them how to carry it out. Paul realized that such discipline was not meant merely to be retributive but also to be remedial for the penitent wrongdoer.

Sadly, when the apostle's authority was challenged, the church did nothing to support Paul or to punish the offender. The person's action and the church's refusal to deal with the offense were harmful to Paul but even more damaging to the entire congregation since the members were vitally interconnected.

Evidently, upon receiving Paul's follow-up letter, the church carried out a **punishment** that was severe. Paul encouraged them to **forgive and comfort** (Gk. *parakalesai*, see 1:3) the offender, who had expressed repentance (2:7). FORGIVE (Gk. *charisasthai*, "give freely, grant, cancel, remit, pardon") has as its Greek root *charis*, "grace or unmerited favor." The idea is to be gracious in the sense of "giving a gift," which is exactly what transpires in forgiveness. COMFORT (Gk. *parakalesai*, "encourage, exhort, urge on") is a word used in the speeches of leaders and military officers who would urge their followers and soldiers courageously onward. Both words are infinitives in Greek, emphasizing the idea of expressing results rather than merely projecting a vision. Paul graciously extended his own forgiveness, refusing to name or humiliate the offender and encouraging others to restore him (v. 10). Paul encouraged forgiveness among the people because he realized the importance of unity and love. Without unity, forgiveness, and love, the body could not be what God intended. In an environment of unforgiveness, **Satan** would easily intervene and cause great damage to the church (v. 11). Paul and the church were aware that Satan was seeking to destroy them, so the apostle called them to look to the greater purpose of Christ Jesus rather than to become caught up in temporal affairs.

IGNORANT (Gk. *agnooumen*, "not know or understand") comes from the verb *noeō*, "think or understand." The *-men* ending indicates the result of thinking, i.e., the thought itself, perception, or understanding. Thus *noema* can mean "mind, thought, or intention." In the New Testament the term occurs in a positive sense only in Philippians 4:7, where Paul stated that "the peace of God will guard" believers' "hearts and *minds*." Three times in 2 Corinthians Paul connected the work of Satan with the Christian's mind (*noema*):

- believers are "not ignorant of his [Satan's] intentions" to destroy them (2:11);

- Satan blinds the "minds of unbelievers" so they cannot be saved (4:4);

- like Eve who was "deceived" by Satan's "cunning," believers' minds can be "corrupted" (11:3).

In 2 Corinthians the other two uses of *noema* refer to the Israelites' "closed" minds that keep them from believing in Christ (3:14) and to thoughts that keep believers from obeying Christ (10:5).

THE MINISTRY OF THE APOSTLE (2:12–6:10)

The Trip to Macedonia (2:12-13)

2:12-13 Paul was a missionary evangelist, traveling from place to place sharing the message of Jesus Christ. **Troas** was located in the northwest corner of Asia Minor. When Paul came to Troas and shared **the gospel**, the Spirit moved in a powerful way, and many accepted Christ. Although Paul wanted to stay there and continue to see the fruit of his ministry, he was willing to leave because he was so concerned about the well-being of the Corinthians.

Titus had been with the Corinthian church and was scheduled to meet Paul in Troas with a full report. When Paul waited patiently and still did not connect with Titus, he determined to go to **Macedonia** in hopes of meeting him there. Paul experienced great unrest at the possibility of missing Titus. This thought is not brought to conclusion until chapter seven.

A Testimony of God's Sufficiency (2:14–3:6)

2:14-17 Paul interrupted his previous thoughts with an exclamation of thanksgiving for God's sending him so many places to proclaim the gospel. PUTS US ON DISPLAY (Gk. *thriambeuonti*, "triumph, celebrate," v. 14; cp. Col 2:15) would likely bring to mind a triumphal procession in which a general promoted his victory by publicly displaying his captured enemies as he led them to their deaths. Customarily, the victorious general marched into Rome in a long procession. The city magistrates and trumpeters were followed by the spoils taken from the defeated enemies and by white oxen to be offered as sacrifices to the gods. Then came the captives with the king of the conquered country and officials with the defeated army accompanied by musicians who were celebrating the defeat. The general himself then appeared as the one in whose honor the entire pageant was presented. In this imagery, Paul was representing himself as a soldier of the victorious general sharing in the glorious triumph. Paul had fully surrendered to Christ and gave testimony to God's greatness through his life and death.

The metaphors of being **the scent of knowing** Christ (v. 14) and **the fragrance of Christ** (v. 15) are especially appropriate for Paul as he traveled far and wide spreading the love of Jesus. SCENT (Gk. *osmēn*, "smell") is translated as "fragrance" in John 12:3 to describe the luxurious aroma of the perfume with which Mary anointed Jesus' feet. However, it is a generic term used for smells both good and bad. FRAGRANCE (Gk. *euōdia*, "sweet smell, as of incense") is deeply associated with the sacrificial system (Lv 1:9,13,17; Nm 15:7). Both words are paired in Ephesians 5:2 and Philippians 4:18 (*osmēn euōdias*, "fragrant offering") as metaphors comparing the sweet-smelling aroma of a burnt offering to a sacrifice "pleasing to God." Paul was honored that through his sacrifice of obedience, he could spread the aroma of Christ.

Paul recognized that sharing the message of Jesus would confront people with the choice of life or death. Acceptance of Jesus as Lord means eternal life in heaven. Rejection of Jesus means eternal death in hell. Therefore, "the fragrance of Christ" may be appreciated by **those who are being saved** (Gk. *sōzomenois*, "being rescued from peril, saved or preserved from danger," 2 Co 2:15; cp. 1 Co 1:18; Eph 2:8) as **a scent** (Gk. *osmē*) **of life leading to life,** or it can be the stench (Gk. *osmē*; cp. Jn 11:39) **of death leading to death** (2 Co 2:16) to **those who are perishing** (Gk. *apollumenois*, "being

destroyed, killed, or lost"; the word can also describe those whose death sentence is being declared, v. 15; cp. 4:3; 1 Co 1:18-19). Those who share the gospel can be a life-giving perfume to those who accept salvation or a death-giving drug to those who reject it.

Paul felt unworthy of the opportunity to know Christ and act as His ambassador. He was able to fulfill his responsibility only as a result of God's grace. However, he also acknowledged that there are some who use the message of Christ not to honor God but to **make a trade**. FOR PROFIT (Gk. *kapēleuontes*, "making money by selling as retail, peddling, corrupting") is used in the LXX (Greek translation of the Old Testament) for those who mix wine with water in order to cheat the buyers (Is 1:22). In classical Greek Plato used the word to condemn those he considered to be pseudo-philosophers. Here the word refers to those who would peddle or sell God's Word for profit. Paul explained that he and Timothy, by contrast, ministered **with sincerity**. SINCERITY (Gk. *eilikrineias*, "purity, righteousness," from *eilē*, "sunlight" and *krinō*, "examine, judge") literally means proven to be "unsullied" when brought out in the open, under the scrutinizing rays of the sun. Paul supported himself financially so that others would not view him as one peddling the gospel for money. He acknowledged his call from God and his accountability to God.

3:1-3 When Paul first visited Corinth and founded the church, he came only with his apostolic authority and the power of God. He became their spiritual father and needed no **letters of recommendation** (v. 1). After he left, imposters had come into the church with pseudo-letters, trying to peddle the gospel and seeking to undermine Paul's authority. Letters of recommendation were often appeals for aid or even pleas for instruction. Paul was not

Heart to Heart:
Spreading the Fragrance of Jesus

Studies have shown that the sense of smell has a very strong link to emotions, hunger, and memory. Real estate agents suggest lighting a pleasantly scented candle or baking brownies when showing a home to prospective buyers. The right aroma makes a house feel warm and welcoming. When a woman wearing a familiar perfume walks by, your mind may race back to memories of your grandmother or a time in your life when you wore that scent. Yet for others, the scent of a certain candle or cologne can lead to a migraine headache lasting for days. One woman's fragrance can be another woman's bane.

God puts His children "on display" and through them "spreads . . . the scent of knowing" Christ "in every place" (v. 14). For some, the "scent" will stir up a hunger or evoke emotions that draw them to Christ. For others, the "scent" will repel or evoke anger or rejection. The "scent" is the same, but the nose decides how to respond.

Should you choose not to light the candle or spray on the perfume because you don't want to offend anyone? You do want to exercise restraint for the good of the guests in your home or the woman sitting behind you in church, but the aroma of Christ is different. The woman in whom Christ dwells should keep on pleasing God by leaving the "fragrance of Christ" every-where she goes.

disparaging the use of these letters. He himself had sought such a letter from the high priest at Jerusalem to present his credentials to the synagogues in Damascus (Ac 9:2; 22:5). He, in turn, furnished "letters of commendation" (Rm 16:1-2; 1 Co 16:3,10-11; 2 Co 8:16-24). These letters were requests for help or hospitality, an opportunity for the recipient to express his loyalty to the writer of the letter. The believers themselves were the only **letter** (Gk. *epistolē*, "epistle, written message") Paul and Timothy needed to authenticate their ministry in the Corinthian church. Paul described them as:

- being **written** (Gk. *eggegrammenē*, "inscribed, engraved, recorded"; cp. Lk 10:20) **on our hearts** (2 Co 3:2)—

Paul and Timothy cherished the Corinthians and would never forget them;

- being **recognized** (Gk. *ginōskomenē*, "known, perceived,") **and read** (Gk. *anaginōskomenē*, "known accurately, distinguished or recognized"; cp. 3:15; 1 Th 5:27) **by everyone** (2 Co 3:2);

- plainly **Christ's letter** (v. 3)—IT IS PLAIN (Gk. *phaneroumenoi*, "made manifest, known, or apparent; plainly recognized") is one of the 10 words in the Greek text of 2 Corinthians derived from the verb *phainō*, "bring into the light, cause to shine, become evident," v. 3. (See 2:14; 4:10,11; 5:10,11; 7:12; 11:6; 13:7; cp. Eph 5:13);

- the product of their ministry (2 Co 3:3)—Having been **PRODUCED** (Gk. *diakonētheisa*, "served, ministered to") by Paul and Timothy meant that the Corinthians' faith and the existence of a Christian community in that city were evidence of the distinctive ministry of the apostle and his partner;

- **not written with ink but with the Spirit of the living God** (v. 3)—the Holy Spirit within them would testify that they genuinely belonged to God;

- written **not on stone tablets but on tablets that are hearts of flesh** (v. 3)—the Spirit had plainly engraved God's law ("stone tablets," Ex 32:15; 34:1,4) on their hearts (cp. Jer 31:33; Ezk 36:26), sealed within Paul as a papyrus roll to be opened and revealed to all who would listen to his message. Christ composed the letter. The Holy Spirit as the *amanuensis* recorded it. Paul was the publisher or the one who distributed and delivered the letter to its destination.

3:4-6 Paul and Timothy, ever careful of arrogance, reminded the Corinthian believers that any success in ministry is a result of God's work in the human life. As **ministers of a new covenant** (v. 6; cp. v. 3; Jer 31:31), they acknowledged that their **competence** did not come from their own abilities but **from God** (2 Co 3:5). **COMPETENT** (Gk. *hikanoi*, "fit, able, qualified, sufficient, authorized") appears three times in the Greek text in verses 5-6, emphasizing that God alone can adequately equip the saints for His service; cp. 2:16; Mt 3:11; 8:8; Col 1:12. The "new covenant" was provided in the death of Jesus Christ (1 Co 11:25; Heb 8:6-13; 9:15). In contrast, many Jews still followed and relied on the "old covenant" for salvation, but **the letter** (Gk. *gramma*, "written document," a metaphor

for the law; cp. Rm 2:27-28; 7:6) **kills**, i.e., attempting to earn salvation by keeping the law only brings death and eternity in hell. **The Spirit produces life** (Gk. *zōopoiei*, "causes to live, makes alive," lit. to bear and give birth to live offspring; cp. Gl 3:12) and eternity with God (2 Co 3:6).

The Glorious New Covenant (3:7-18)

Paul used this section to make an important and excellent comparison between the old covenant and the new covenant. He explained why the new covenant is superior and glorious.

3:7-11 First, Paul described the old covenant given through Moses to the Israelite people in the book of Exodus (v. 7). After spending time with God on Mount Sinai, Moses was given the Ten Commandments written on tablets of stone (Ex 31:18). These commandments were the law for the people, making them aware of their sin and the law of God, leading to righteousness. By believing in God and obeying His principles, the people could have a relationship with God. This magnificent and glorious revelation showed the provision and love of God and His willingness to form this covenant with the people through Moses.

Scripture records that Moses had to veil his **face** after being in the presence of God because the **glory** frightened the people (vv. 7,13). The glory of God actually shone on Moses, so that the pores of his face radiated with God's glory. The radiation from Moses' skin was so bright that the people were not able **to look directly at Moses' face**; he had to put a veil over his face (v. 7; Ex 34:29-35). The old covenant of the law **was fading away** upon the completion of Christ's sacrifice and the institution of the new covenant just as God's glory must have subsided in order for Moses to be able to remove the veil (Gk. *katargoumenon*, "make ineffective, nullify, abolish, release" in the sense of rendering inoperative). The glory was splendid but transient.

Paul contrasted the glory of **the Spirit** (v. 8) to the fading glory of **the ministry of condemnation**, given through the law and Moses. **The ministry of righteousness** through Christ is shown to be far greater and **more glorious** (v. 11). The reason "the ministry of righteousness" is so far superior is based on the unending **glory** of eternity. The new covenant will never cease to exist. It is an all-powerful, never-changing, continuing glory (vv. 10-11).

Contrasts between the Old and the New

Old Covenant	New Covenant
The law was written on stone tablets (v. 3).	The new covenant is written on hearts of flesh (v. 3).
The letter of the law kills (v. 6).	The Spirit of the Lord gives freedom (v. 17)
The law brings condemnation (v. 9).	The new covenant brings righteousness (v. 9).
The old covenant glory is temporal (v. 10).	The new covenant brings eternal glory (v. 11).
The old covenant was fading away (v. 11).	The new covenant endures forever (v. 11).
The Israelites could not view the glory of God without a veil (v. 13).	Believers can look upon the glory of the Lord (vv. 16,18).
The old covenant was delivered by Moses (v. 13).	The new covenant is from Christ Jesus (vv. 14-18).
The glory of the old covenant was fading (v. 11).	The new covenant is ever reflecting the glory of the Lord (v. 18).
One who remains behind the veil of the old covenant was characterized by a closed mind (v. 14).	One who belongs to the new covenant is characterized by boldness (v. 12).
The old covenant was marked by bondage to a closed mind (vv. 14-15).	The new covenant is marked by freedom (vv. 16-17) and transformation (v. 18).
The Law	**The Gospel**
• Is a promise	• Is a fulfillment
• Is lesser—not inferior	• Is greater because it fulfills the law
• Is weak due to the flesh	• Is powerful via the Spirit
• Is external—overt acts	• Is internal—attitudes
• Makes demands, rules	• Gives principles
• Provides no power to obey	• Gives power to obey
• Allows you to be deceived by sin	• Strengthens you unto sanctification through its admonitions
• Leads to remorse	• Leads to forgiveness

3:12-18 Paul exclaimed that Christians should be bold expressing the **hope** that is within, based on the truth of the never-ending, superior covenant (v. 12).

BOLDNESS (Gk. *parrēsia*, "openness and frankness in speech, freedom to speak without reservation," lit. "speaking all" and thus understood as "speaking openly") conveys a sense of "confidence." Paul proclaimed and taught the gospel "with full boldness" (Ac 28:31), and the "boldness" of the apostles Peter and John drew attention to their having "been with Jesus" (Ac 4:13). Such courage to speak openly about Christ comes from the Spirit and was, therefore, requested in prayer (Ac 4:29-31; Eph 3:12; 6:19; Php 1:20). Moses had **to put a veil over his face** because **the sons of Israel could not look at** the glory of God, which **was fading away** from Moses' face (2 Co 3:13). Since the new covenant's glory will not fade, believers should let the glory shine brightly.

The Israelites' **minds were closed** (Gk. *epōrōthē,* "calloused, blinded, hardened," v. 14; cp. Mk 6:52; 8:17; Jn 12:40; Rm 11:7) to the glory and majesty of God. Some scholars suggest that they wanted Moses to cover his face so that they would not be convicted of their sins and therefore be required to repent. Even **to this day**, the Jews turn their hearts and minds away from Jesus and His covenant (2 Co 3:14). With the rejection of Jesus Christ, only the old covenant of the law remains. All who attempt to fulfill the covenant of the law will surely fail and be sentenced to death. Jesus is the covenant of grace, and those who refuse Him will experience death and separation from God.

Paul expanded the illustration by describing **a veil . . . over their hearts** (2 Co 3:15). Paul acknowledged that the minds as well as the hearts of many are closed to Christ. **Whenever a person turns to the Lord** for forgiveness and mercy, **the veil** over their hearts **is removed** permanently (Gk. *periaireitai,* "take away what surrounds or envelopes," with the idea of removing completely, v. 16; cp. Heb 10:11), and they are able to display **the glory** of God (2 Co 3:18).

The Spirit of Jesus Christ brings **freedom** (Gk. *eleutheria,* "liberty," from the adjective *eleutheros,* "free from obligation, not bound by, exempt from," in contrast to one under the yoke of slavery) from the law (v. 17). No longer must people rely on obedience to the law, but now by grace, the children of God have been set free from sin and shame. This freedom is glorious and unending. It is even more far-reaching than the glory on **Moses' face** (vv. 7-8). The glory that blessed believers should have is stronger, brighter, and more radiant than the glory of God on Moses. He had "a fading glory" (v. 7), but believers have a permanent glory. His glory faded, but the believers' glory will continue until ultimate glorification in heaven (v. 11).

Having such close association with God Himself transforms people into His likeness (v. 18). This transformation (Gk. *metamorphoumetha,* "change") allows people actually to reflect **the glory of the Lord** in His majesty. It suggests changing the inward reality to something new and different. This transformation and enjoyment of His presence is never-ending. It will continue **from glory to glory** (v. 18). This magnificent truth should delight the heart of every believer.

The Heart of the Gospel (4:1-6)

4:1 After conveying the incredible truth of the new covenant, Paul identified this treasure of truth as the work of his **ministry**. He was not waiting for a gift, talent, or opportunity but was expressing the truth that the message of the gospel in itself is enough ministry for every Christian. He seems to be referring to his own faithfulness in ministry and his obedience as an apostle. He suggested that he and others only obtained that ministry by the **mercy** of God. This mercy ought to be, and was for Paul, a constant force—a passion driving him to refuse fatigue or discouragement. He would **not give up**

(Gk. *egkakoumen*, "lose enthusiasm, become tired, become afraid") as a faint-hearted coward. Paul realized that despite opposition and conflict, difficulty and suffering, he must move forward because of the importance of the task committed to him. He could never do his ministry through his own human ability, nor could he depend upon performance, achievement or public affirmations to propel his witness; rather his motivation came from the divine mercy he had received.

4:2 Paul reminded readers of his wholehearted commitment to Christ. He had forsaken his old life as evidenced by the fact that he had given up **shameful ... things**. Rather, he and other leaders were focused on living a life of purity in Christ. They had nothing to hide or to bring shame because they were **walking in** obedience to Christ and had received forgiveness for their past sins. He also explained that they were not deceiving people or **distorting God's message**. While he did not mention the imposters here, he no doubt had them in mind. Paul was contrasting himself with others who were inconsistent in life and witness. He warned against "secret things," which would result in shame when brought into the light.

4:3-4 Again, Paul used his ministry as evidence of his authenticity. The false teachers claimed that some did not accept Paul's message because it was difficult to understand and therefore untrue. Paul refuted this idea saying that no one's heart **is veiled** as a result of the message presented. The heart would only be **veiled** because of hardness and rejection of Jesus. These people who reject the gospel message are turning from Christ and toward sin and death.

Scripture explains that God does not desire that any perish (2 Pt 3:9). He wants all to come to repentance. **The god of this age has blinded the minds of the unbelievers** so they do not accept Jesus (v. 4). "The god of this age" or "the ruler of the world" (Jn 14:30) or "the ruler of the atmospheric domain" (Eph 2:2) is a reference to Satan. Although Satan does hold a certain sway over the world during this present age, his power has been usurped, and it is temporary and in no sense absolute. Satan has tried in vain to set himself up as God, but he is merely a rebellious creature and stands under the judgment of *Yahweh* God. When unbelievers bring themselves under Satan's rule, they come under divine condemnation. One dreadful consequence of these tragic choices is that their minds are blinded, and that spiritual blindness ultimately leads to destruction and death (Jn 8:44). IMAGE (Gk. *eikōn*, "image, form, or statue," anglicized as "icon") in ancient Greek culture could refer to an image such as a portrait, a reflection in a mirror, or a phantom. Two main ideas emerge from the various usages of *eikōn* in the New Testament: representation and manifestation. In the context of 2 Co 4:4, Paul proclaimed that Christ, "the image of God" rejected by unbelievers, is the full manifestation of God.

4:5 Paul and Timothy, because they were committed to sharing the gospel with all men, explained that they were **slaves because of Jesus**, not promoting themselves but only the message of the gospel. In other words, they lived to serve by introducing others to Jesus. Paul was not really a slave to men; he was a slave to God. The point was that he and Timothy owed God a debt, which they paid back by seeking the salvation of all to whom they could bear witness.

4:6 God alone can bring "**Light ... out of darkness.**" He alone can make a sinful heart pure. He alone can offer righteousness to the unrighteous. This verse is easily a description of creation when God brought light into the dark universe (Gn 1). If God is able to do all of these things, certainly He is able to bring light within the dark **hearts** of men and women. God brought His **glory** to the dark world through the life **of Jesus Christ**. Christ displayed the exact "image of God" and opened many hearts to **the light** of an eternal relationship (v. 6). Paul shared this true proclamation with enthusiasm.

The Treasure of the Gospel (4:7-15)

4:7 Paul was a master of language. To describe the gospel and God Himself, he enlisted lofty and righteous expressions of worship. However, being exposed to the clear light of God's glory, you cannot help but see, even more clearly, the inadequacies of the flesh. Paul recognized this dichotomy and felt compelled to address the situation. How odd for the greatest treasure to be contained in weak, fragile, and common containers. Yet, the perfect God of holiness has chosen to make His sanctuary in the lives of unworthy sinners. This indwelling places inestimable value on the **clay jars** and rightly shows that a clay jar in itself, no matter how clean and shiny, can produce no power. Rather, God's illumination of the clay jar can bring **extraordinary power**. Further, the fact that He can and does make one who is as a clay jar powerful and righteous testifies to the fact that no individual has ultimate power, but God in His omnipotence is the power and the One who empowers. There is a paradox between the indescribable value of the gospel treasure and the apparent unworthiness of the ministers who bear the gospel just as between the bearers of the light, who are insignificant in comparison to the Light Himself who has inestimable worth and beauty. Human weakness is never a barrier to the purposes of God. It merely enhances God's glory.

Paul Compared the Corinthian Believers to . . .		
Illustration	**Insight**	**Instruction**
Perfume (2:14-16)	"The fragrance of Christ" leading to life for those who believe and death for those who reject	Speak for Christ as from God and before God, spreading the scent of knowing Him.
Letters (3:1-3)	The validation of Paul's ministry, from those whom he had taught and led to the Lord	Judge your ministry based on what Christ has done in your life through Paul and Timothy.
Clay Jars (4:7-18)	The "clay jars" or temporary vessels, which are indwelt by Jesus Christ so that the inner person is being renewed daily, though the jar may be broken	Don't give up in the face of earthly trials; focus on the eternal rather than what is seen.
The Bride (11:2-3)	The "pure virgin," whose devotion to Christ Paul is zealous about guarding	Don't be deceived and led away from your devotion to Christ.

4:8-9 In order to illustrate further the power of God in the weakness of men, Paul offered four profound examples of human weakness, which increase in severity. Using antithesis in each devastating example, Paul illustrated the inadequacy of human beings in discharging their ministry juxtaposed with the power of God, which provided a way of escape. Knowing the real difficulties Paul faced, clearly his word choices are not just literary technique but rather the result of personal experience. He was testifying to the power of God in the human life.

- "We are **PRESSURED** (Gk. *thlibomenoi*, "hard-pressed, oppressed, afflicted," that which burdens the spirit, v. 8; see 1:6; cp. 7:5) in every way but not **CRUSHED**" (Gk. *stenochōroumenoi*, "compressed into a narrow space, restricted, restrained," referring to the confined space of a narrow room and in this context probably to social pressures);

- "we are **PERPLEXED** (Gk. *aporoumenoi*, "at a loss, uncertain about which way to go or what to do," used in the papyri in reference to one who was at his wit's end because of pursuing creditors who would bring him ruin) but not in **DESPAIR**" (Gk. *exaporoumenoi*, "utterly at a loss, out of options, giving up hope, completely baffled"), perhaps a reference to mental anxieties;

- "we are **PERSECUTED** (Gk. *diōkomenoi*, "pursued, hunted down like an animal, harassed, mistreated") but not **ABANDONED**" (Gk. *egkataleipomenoi*, "deserted, left helpless, utterly forsaken," the same word used in the LXX for God's promise not to forsake His own [Dt 31:6-8; Jos 1:5; 1 Ch 28:20; Ps 36:25]), an allusion to physical adversities;

- "we are **STRUCK DOWN** (Gk. *kataballomenoi*, "thrown to the ground, cast down to a lower position," a word used in reference to throwing an opponent down in wrestling or striking someone with a sword) but not **DESTROYED**"

(Gk. *apollumenoi*, "rendered useless, totally ruined"), a reference to personal attack.

Paul had compared himself to a combatant, hard-pressed, then hemmed in, pursued, and finally cast down—a perfect description of the uninterrupted succession of indignities the apostle had suffered throughout his ministry.

4:10-12 Paul mentioned **the death of Jesus** to emphasize the Savior's suffering in His earthly life and agonizing death (v. 10). Paul was identifying his own hardships with the sufferings of Jesus. Paul was so committed to living out the gospel message that Paul could not imagine a life without suffering. His life, so filled with suffering, pointed to the death of Jesus and the subsequent eternal life offered through Him.

Paul believed that he and others could be so victorious in their sufferings that through the power of God, Jesus would **be revealed** (Gk. *phanerōthē*, "make manifest what was hidden, exposed to view, recognized," vv. 10-11). Therefore, the triumphant hardships of believers would bring life to unbelievers as they witnessed the real power of God. How convicting is this passage. Paul was taking real joy in his suffering in the hope that it would bring others to Christ. Most Christians simply desire to be relieved of pressures and hardships, but Paul was able and willing to endure great pain for the sake of future glory. GIVEN OVER (Gk. *paradidometha*, "delivered or handed over into another's power or custody") in this context has the sense of God's "allowing or permitting" believers to be put to death (v. 11). Suffering and death in themselves were not meritorious. However, through Paul's endurance the gospel had been delivered to the Corinthians.

4:13-14 Just as many readers today may find Paul's perspective on hardship beyond reach, surely some Corinthians thought this perspective too lofty to attain. Paul referred to Psalm 116:10 in which the psalmist experienced great deliverance from God and could not help but proclaim the truth. Paul shared the **spirit of faith** with the psalmist and must have believed others could experience this spirit as well (v. 13). Although the afflictions and dangers to which Paul was exposed should have driven him to despair, he was not discouraged. As the psalmist, he affirmed his confidence in God (cp. Ps 116).

Paul took confidence in the power of the resurrection and the assurance that God would **raise** (Gk. *egerei*, "recall from death to life") believers (2 Co 4:14). This testimony to the power of God and the unity of believers affirmed that all believers would be raised up together, so that the leaders and the converts would share in the great miracle.

4:15 Naturally, **grace, extended** (Gk. *pleonasasa*, "made to increase greatly, have too much, cause to grow," cp. 1 Th 3:12; 2 Th 1:3; 2 Pt 1:8) **through more and more people** who come into relationship with God will cause God to receive even more **glory**. "More people" will praise Him and experience His "grace." This love, glory, and grace will **overflow** (Gk. *perisseusē*, "become abundant, increase, make extremely rich, abound"; cp. 1:5; 3:9; 8:2,7; 9:8,12) in superabundance. Paul's love for God is already overflowing and surely he could see nothing better than that others would overflow with praise toward God.

The Eternal Perspective of the Gospel (4:16–5:21)

4:16-18 Paul revealed a key to the thriving Christian life. A person with a great command of the rich doctrinal truths can be RENEWED (Gk. *anakainoutai*, "cause to grow up, make new," in the sense of changing from a former state of corruption to a new kind of life") daily by the mercy and truth of God, thereby sustaining the outer body, which faces great trials. Paul had already shared the severity of the afflictions he and others faced. Yet, with this practice of daily renewal, he was able to view severe hardship as **light affliction** (v. 17). He refused to "give up" (Gk. *egkakoumen*, "be utterly worn out, exhausted, hopeless," in the sense of losing heart and enthusiasm, v. 16), even though he felt he was **being destroyed** (Gk. *diaphtheiretai*, "corrupted, ruined, consumed; decaying"; cp. Lk 12:33), because the Spirit was renewing his **inner person** (Gk. *esō*, "within, internal; inner man, soul, conscience"; cp. Rm 7:22; Eph 3:16). The frailty of the human life and the afflictions sustained in the cause of the gospel only magnified by means of contrast the all-transcending glory and power of God. Ever holding his life up to the assurance of God's truth and glory, Paul realized that once in **eternal** glory, his hardships would become light as a feather (2 Co 4:17).

Paul must have had a real picture of heaven; so much so that he could almost experience it. Facing such constant hardships, he must have imagined himself in his heavenly home many times. What a sweet expectation Paul had, looking to eternity with such desire. He allowed every hardship to deepen his longing for Jesus and eternal life. Paul's hardships fulfilled an important purpose not only in the lives of others but also in his ability to appreciate the prize awaiting him because of his commitment to Christ.

Paul concluded with more personal expressions of his theology of hope in suffering. Do not focus on the world, which is quickly fading away. Although it may seem real and tangible, focus rather on **what is unseen**, that which is truly genuine (v. 18). Eternity is worth living for. Don't be confused by the fake, fading, **temporary** things of this life; instead be consumed with the real, the "unseen," and the **eternal** (v. 18). AN ABSOLUTELY INCOMPARABLE (Gk. *huperbolēn*, "beyond measure, excessive, extraordinary," v. 17), though translated as a descriptive phrase, is actually a noun, lit. "a throwing beyond." Modified by a prepositional phrase repeating the noun—*eis huperbolēn*, "unto beyond measure"—underscores an already superlative characterization of the "eternal weight of glory." See uses of the verb form, "exceed, surpass, transcend," in 3:10; 9:14; Eph 1:19; 2:7; 3:19. The anglicized word "hyperbole" denotes the use of exaggeration to make a point.

Life is complex and difficult. Should it be lived with great planning and intention? Should it be enjoyed with a relaxed attitude toward the future? Paul seemed to promote the idea that the best attitude for living is dying. This perspective of impending death actually brings incredible freedom, joy, and purpose. He showed Christians how to live on earth, how to die, and how to think about the hereafter. Paul determined to "FOCUS ON (Gk. *skopountōn*, "observe, fix one's gaze upon, direct one's attention to," v. 18) what is SEEN" (Gk. *blepomena*, "seen, discerned, perceived," with physical eyesight or, figuratively, "understood" with "the mind's eye," v. 18) because he knew the age to come was "eternal" while his affections were merely "temporary."

5:1-4 Paul defined the **earthly house**, or the body, as **a tent** (v. 1), which while serving an important purpose, is still just a tent. Though providing some shelter, it does not provide total protection; nor is it permanent. Paul encouraged believers to view their earthly lives and bodies as very temporary.

Today, most do not live in tents. However, during Paul's time, tents were used as more permanent homes. As a tentmaker, Paul was very familiar with the strengths and weaknesses of tents. And, as a businessman, Paul must have frequently compared the temporary, albeit strong, tent with the more permanent building.

Many enjoy camping, when they know they have a nice home to which they can return. Even a tent that is dysfunctional can be tolerated for a period of time as you think about the comfortable home awaiting.

Paul's attitude in regard to the heavenly home and the "earthly" body was that the "earthly house" should be viewed as temporary, imperfect, and destructible. In contrast, the **eternal** home, constructed by God, is permanent (v. 1). Understanding the superiority of a building "from God," how could anyone not GROAN (Gk. *stenazomen*, "sigh, complain, make weary, weigh down," as with grief or weariness; from *stenos*, "narrow, straight"; cp. Rm 8:23) "to put on" this heavenly home even now? Certainly, a Christian who knows that something infinitely better is coming would desire to put off this tired, hurting, uncomfortable house and LONG (Gk. *epipothountes*, "desiring, pursuing with love, yearning for," 2 Co 5:2) to put on the "HOUSE (Gk. *oikētērion*, "abode, dwelling place, habitation") from heaven." What Paul longed for was not that he might be alive when Christ came to avoid dissolution of his body or physical tent, but rather to enter his heavenly abode earlier and experience blessedness and glory. Apparently for the first time in his apostolic career Paul reckoned seriously with the possibility, rapidly becoming a probability, of his own death before the return of Christ.

Paul, in discussing the state of the soul after death, identified the sources of divine comfort for the believer facing imminent death:

- the certainty of a glorified, spiritual body (v. 1),

- the presence of an indwelling Holy Spirit as a pledge for future immortality (vv. 4b,5), and

- knowledge that death is not the end but rather the beginning (v. 7) with immediate translation into the presence of the Lord (v. 8).

Paul seemed to express his desire to be taken up with Jesus in the rapture rather than experience death before the return of Christ. For Christians, a tug of war is present in the earthly life. There is an innate will to live in the heart of every human being. Even for the Christian who is confident of a future life with Christ, this present world is well-known and comfortable; and so there is resistance to leaving. Even when you know a projected change will be better, there are still many unknowns.

Paul described himself as **burdened** (Gk. *baroumenoi*, "weighed down," v. 4; see 1:8; 4:17) with his mortality on the one hand but, on the other hand, **swallowed up** (Gk. *katapothē*, more lit. "drank down, devoured, overwhelmed," 5:4; cp. 2:7; 1 Co 15:54) with confidence coming from the promise of eternal life.

5:5 Christians however, can rest confidently in the hope to come. God has **prepared** the way, and God has given every believer a guarantee of what is to come, **the Spirit**. A promise of the future brings great, immediate joy, but even greater future joy. This guarantee, or **DOWN PAYMENT** (Gk. *arrabōna*, "earnest, pledge"; cp. 1:22; Eph 1:14) has two basic meanings in commercial usage:

- a pledge, which differs from final payment, although still making it obligatory, or

- a partial payment, which serves as a first installment or down payment and gives the payee a legal claim to the goods in question. In redemption, however, there is no reciprocal bargaining nor any contractually binding mutual agreement. Rather God bestows on believers His Spirit as an unsolicited gift, according to His grace. Interestingly, in modern Greek the word carries the meaning of an "engagement ring." The Holy Spirit is a pledge from God (2 Co 3:18; 4:16; cp. Rm 8:11), which prefigures and guarantees His future completion of the work begun (Php 1:6) when the believer enters the heavenly abode.

5:6-8 The familiar state of walking in the earthly body should not cause insecurity. Because of the Holy Spirit, you can enjoy a close relationship to God and possess the hope of future glory. On the other hand, a Christian should not have any fear of death because death expedites her union with Christ in heaven.

Women are particularly fascinated with engagements, weddings, and marriage. You must be thankful that God has provided such an enjoyable and exciting picture of what many in the world view morbidly through fear of death. Since the Lord is in control of the engagement, the Christian can simply take joy in pleasing God. Paul, to avoid misunderstanding, observed that believers do **walk by faith**. The Lord is present not to physical eyes but to the eyes of faith (v. 7). **AT HOME IN** (Gk. *endēmountes*, "living in one's own country, among one's own people") and **AWAY FROM** (Gk. *ekdēmoumen*, "live or go abroad, be away from one's own country or people, be absent from") are both from the root *demos*, "people." The prefix differentiates this pair of words: *en-*, "in," and *ek-*, "from." For the Christian, being "at home *in* the body" means temporarily being "away *from* the Lord," invisible to earthly eyes. The confidence enjoyed by believers is not merely a temporary feeling but a permanent state of mind.

5:9-10 In the same way that all brides desire to please their bridegroom, the primary goal of believers should be to please their groom, Jesus. The profound doctrines Paul introduced in verses 1-8 lead naturally to implications for behavior (v. 9). Paul's constant desire to please Christ was the direct outcome of his awareness that death would usher him into the presence of Christ. **All** will come **before the judgment seat of Christ**. THE JUDGMENT SEAT (Gk. *bēmatos*, "judge's official seat, speaker's platform," v. 10) in secular usage denoted the raised platform, approached by ascending steps, where the judge of a case sat, as on a throne or presiding over a tribunal. Jesus appeared before Pilate (Mt 27:19; Jn 19:13) and Paul before both secular and religious officials at the *bēmatos*. Christians, of course, will not have to worry about losing or earning their salvation, which has been won through Christ and His once-for-all atonement for sin. However, believers will be judged and rewarded for the work and ministry entrusted to them. Therefore, every Christian should be consumed with obedience to Christ and His commands. This appearance in the court of heaven will give opportunity for divine illumination of what has been hidden by darkness and is then exposed. The assessment of works and character is done, not with the determination of destiny but with the assignment of rewards. At this time the believer may suffer loss by forfeiting Christ's praise or by losing a reward that might have been given. Paul used words to convey an earnest request by way of personal testimony. **We make it our aim**

(Gk. *philotimoumetha*, "aspire, strive earnestly, have as our ambition"; cp. Rm 15:20; 1 Th 4:11) expresses the apostle's personal commitment to living a life "pleasing to Him" (2 Co 5:9). You ought to be consumed with the ministry He has entrusted and look to the rewards with hope rather than dread. There is a strong sense of accountability in the text. Life consumed with self is not pleasing to the Lord. A life consumed with passion for Christ is worthwhile and will bring satisfying joy.

5:11 Having just discussed the judgment to come, Paul expressed the proper response. While Christians do not need to fear the judgment of hell for themselves, they should fear it for unbelievers and thus be motivated to share with them. The motivation is **fear of the Lord,** who has shown them mercy, and the pending judgment to be experienced by unbelievers. Likewise, they must realize the sure destruction of the lost and spend their lives seeking to persuade men to come to Christ.

Paul used this argument further to support his authenticity as an apostle. He was **open** to scrutiny, both of people and of the Lord. He encouraged the Corinthians to examine his life for evidence of His sincerity and commitment to Jesus Christ. Obviously, the church was torn between trusting Paul as their spiritual father and accepting the persuasive false apostles who had their own letters of commendation.

5:12 Paul placed himself in opposition to the false apostles, **those who take pride** (Gk. *kauchōmenous*, "glory in, boast"; the word or its derivative is used 21 times in the Greek text of 2 Corinthians) **in the outward appearance rather than in the heart**. Rather than **commending** their talents, Paul and Timothy expressed their attitude of surrender to Christ. They were not comparing their own fleshly abilities with other men, but rather they were exposing genuine hearts for God through obedience in evangelism and ministry. This evidence should mandate the church's defense and support of Paul.

5:13-15 Paul was saying that the love of Christ so dominated his life that he was no longer able to live for himself—an odd statement, but Paul's expression of utter commitment to Christ (v. 13). This love COMPELS (Gk. *sunechei*, "constrain, torment, press hard, embrace, rule, holds fast as a prisoner," a verb that implies pressure that confines and restricts as well as controls) his commitment to present the gospel message and subsequent teaching clearly and effectively to the church for their benefit. Paul was not caught up in fads or moved by whim; he was consumed with his task because of the sacrifice of Christ. Whether Paul's way of describing himself was modest or extravagant, sane or insane, he spoke from a heart of sincere passion for the glory of God and of compassion for the Corinthians.

Paul first expressed incongruous feelings OUT OF OUR MIND (Gk. *exestēmen*, "displaced, confused, amazed, astonished, thrown off balance, insane," v. 13; cp. Mk 3:21), an expression suggesting mental imbalance. Then he used an antithetical expression to affirm their feelings for the Corinthians, "we have a SOUND MIND" (Gk. *sōphronoumen*, "in one's right mind, sensible, serious, exercising self-control"; cp. Mk 5:15), an indication of being in control of one's faculties.

Paul has isolated two motives for Christian service: the understanding that every believer is accountable to Christ (2 Co 5:11) and the awareness of Christ's example of self-sacrificing devotion (v. 14).

Christ is then acknowledged as both Savior and Judge.

Paul concluded this personal defense with sobering thoughtfulness and an appeal to godly surrender. Christ's death had released the captives of sin. He enabled all to die to sin and self. Therefore, those who accept Christ are free to live for Christ rather than to live only for themselves. The person who dies to self and lives for Christ is liberated not only from sin but also from eternal damnation. The person who rejects Christ is living only for self, remains captive to sin, and thus is destined for eternal punishment in hell. Ultimately, an individual ruined by the sin of Adam (1 Co 15:22) is restored by the work of Christ. A believing woman is so united with Christ that His death becomes her death, and His life becomes her life.

5:16 The reality of Christ's death should so change the way a woman views life, the world, and eternity, that she can no longer see people in the same way. The gospel became the lens through which Paul saw every person. No individual is excluded from the scope of redemption—God's offer of salvation is universally available; but all do not appropriate the benefits afforded by this universally offered salvation, giving redemption a particularity in application. Before his conversion Paul viewed Jesus as merely a man. After his conversion, he could see **Christ** as the Savior/Redeemer. Paul realized that through receiving Christ he was totally transformed. He also viewed others not in terms of nationality (Jew or Gentile), as he had before, but in regard to spiritual status—believer or unbeliever. The expression **even if** (Gk. *ei kai*) introduces a condition assumed to be true. Paul and others did have knowledge of Christ in **a purely human way** (Gk. *kata sarka*, "according to the flesh"). However, now his understanding of Christ is beyond the factual knowledge of the historical Jesus. Paul does not belittle the example, teachings, and historical observations of Christ, but he now knows the Lord in a new and higher way by faith and through the Holy Spirit.

5:17 Paul's black-and-white view of life must be appreciated. Seemingly he would have hardly recognized his old self. He looked to the change in his life and the lives of others with awe and excitement. Paul wasn't even able to think in the way he had prior to his conversion. He viewed everything from the perspective of God and of the reconciliation required as well as considering the ministry entrusted to him. CREATION (Gk. *ktisis*, "anything created") in rabbinical usage referred to one who had been converted from idolatry to Judaism. This expression not only indicated the greatness and radical nature of the change effected but also pointed to the divine origin of the change. Such divine change sparked the commencement of a new state of being.

5:18-19 Although the Corinthians were certainly familiar with the gospel message, Paul took joy in explaining it again. The sacrifice of Christ satisfied God's righteous demands. Acceptance of this reality and of the person of Jesus allows men and women to avoid continuing to be estranged from God; they can be **reconciled**. RECONCILED (Gk. *katallazantos*, "change, exchange") was often used as a monetary term for changing or exchanging money. In general, though, it referred to exchanging one thing for another as when an enemy becomes a friend. All 10 appearances of the derivatives of this Greek word in the New Testament appear in Paul's writings, and in each case "reconciliation" means the bringing together of two people or parties who were at odds with each other (v. 18; see Rm 5:11; 11:15; 2 Co

5:18-19), e.g., the reconciliation of a wife with her husband (1 Co 7:11). The compound verb *apokatallassō* also means "reconcile" and occurs in the New Testament only in Paul's letters (Eph 2:16; Col 1:20,22). An individual seeking reconciliation with God does not make reconciliation happen. Rather he experiences or embraces what God has already offered through regeneration and sanctification. God reconciles His creation to Himself (2 Co 5:19) before they can respond to the call to be reconciled (v. 20).

5:20-21 Christ is the agent of reconciliation (v. 21). Because of sin, unbelievers are God's enemies (Rm 5:10), but they can **be reconciled to God** through faith in Christ. Consequently, believers are Christ's **ambassadors** (Gk. *presbeuomen*, verb meaning "being a representative"). An ambassador is a messenger and representative. He does not speak in his own name or act on his own authority. He never communicates his own opinions or demands. Rather he delivers the message with which he has been entrusted. The trustworthiness and importance of the message does not emanate from him. Yet he is more than a perfunctory messenger because he actually represents his sovereign and is invested with the authority to speak and act in the stead of his master or sovereign. If he suffers contempt or injustice during that official assignment, the offence is not to him personally but to the one who commissioned him.

Christ's "ambassadors" take God's "message of reconciliation" (2 Co 5:19) to the world. Upon receiving Christ, "the ministry of reconciliation" (v. 18) requires sharing with others and is the assignment to each believer, who, therefore, acts as an "ambassador," bringing the good news of Jesus to those around them (v. 20). Certain that God was **appealing** to unbelievers through him and Timothy, Paul would

plead on Christ's behalf. He was so excited about the message that he repeated it in a different way: Jesus took on sin so that you might take on righteousness. COUNTING (Gk. *logizomenos*, "reckoning, considering, taking into account") is used in the Greek text 19 times in Romans, e.g., 4:3-24; 6:11. TRESPASSES (Gk. *paraptōmata*, "sins, false steps, offenses, wrongdoing, lapses or deviations from truth") is a broad term portraying the need for reconciliation with God (v. 19). Paul was so excited that he wanted to tell everyone to "be reconciled to God" (v. 20). Paul could not imagine anyone turning away from this marvelous reconciliation.

He made the One who did not know sin to be sin for us sets forth clearly the idea of substitution in the sense that what is done by one in the place of another avails just as if the other had done it himself. The victim was the substitute for the offender. Christ did not become a sinner by experience because He bore our sins anymore than you become God by accepting His righteousness. Rather Christ satisfies and redeems so that His righteousness becomes the judicial ground for your acceptance with God.

𝒜 𝑀inistry 𝒞ommendation (6:1-10)

6:1-2 Paul defended himself as an apostle. Then he asked the Corinthians to accept his leadership and to work with him instead of against him. He was very concerned about their faith and ministry; he did not want his efforts and their love for Christ to be misdirected.

Paul made a strong appeal, citing Isaiah, an Old Testament prophet who spoke on behalf of God (v. 2; see Is 49:8). Paul applied this proclamation to the Corinthians and stressed the importance of his message, which was under the directive of God. God's message of reconciliation was clear. He had provided salvation, and he had provided a ministry for the Corinthian church through Paul. Paul further appealed to them by encouraging them to accept that message thankfully, **working together** (Gk. *sunergountes*, "partnering in labor, cooperating with, helping, exerting power together") with him in fulfilling the ministry and obeying God. He warned them not to suggest that God's grace was poured out without content or result, **in vain** (Gk. *kenon*, "empty, with no purpose, for nothing"; cp. 1 Co 15:10).

6:3 Paul proclaimed that his ministry and apostleship were above reproach. He used the plural **we** in order to affirm his own humility and to include other genuine leaders of God. While the imposters would confuse and disappoint the people, Paul said that his message and **ministry** were in line with the pure gospel and should not cause **stumbling to anyone**. Paul was concerned not merely with protecting himself but with honoring God's message and ministry. This time was crucial in the life of the church. Would they accept Paul and the true gospel, or would they accept the imposters and be led down a path of destruction? Paul did not take this matter lightly. He loved the people, the church, and the ministry so much that he was willing to fight for its survival.

6:4-10 Pushed into a defensive posture, Paul commended himself to the people. He listed his sufferings as his first credentials. He clearly viewed his sufferings as enabling him to partner with Christ and His sufferings and as a clear indication of the genuineness of his apostleship (vv. 4-5). He referred to general sufferings (tribulations, deprivations, and distresses), to suffering administered by others, as **beatings** (Gk. *plēgais*, "wounds or bruises" from blows to the body), imprisonments, and **riots** (Gk. *akatastasiais*, "state of disorder, instability, insurrections, disturbances"), and even to the effects of personal disciplines in his own life (**labors**, sleeplessness, and fasting).

Paul did not stop with describing his sufferings. He continued with a listing of the inner resources to be cultivated and used, including the Holy Spirit (vv. 6-7). Paul considered his Christian character to be evidence of his genuine conversion and ability to lead. This insight should not be considered as arrogance but as real evidence of the Holy Spirit's work of transformation in his own life. Only the power of God could transform Paul the persecutor "by **PURITY** (Gk. *agnotēti*, "upright living"; cp. 11:3) . . . by patience, by kindness, . . . by **SINCERE** (Gk. *anupokritō*, "unfeigned, undisguised," lit. "without hypocrisy") love."

Paul affirmed the fact that his message was truth and came from God. Then he directed words to his attackers, indicating the spiritual warfare in which he had been involved. He defined himself as a righteous soldier who was armed both offensively and defensively. He was ready with **weapons of righteousness on the right hand and the left** (v. 7). He recognized that a good soldier faces good times and bad, experiencing fierce battles and easy victories. He was ready to face whatever challenge was placed before him. In concluding this section, Paul proposed antithetical contrasting pairs of paradoxes between the worldly and divine perspectives through which he had been judged (vv. 8-10). For example, **SLANDER** (Gk. *dusphēmias*, "use of language that defames," in the sense of falsely giving someone a bad reputation) and **GOOD REPORT** (Gk. *euphēmias*, "use of language that praises, that is good or auspicious") both combine a prefix with *pheme*, "fame, report"—*dus-* conveys "difficulty or opposition"; *eu-* means "good"—and both appear only here in the New Testament (v. 8).

Paul expressed his confidence in God's sovereignty. He knew he would come close to death, but God would **always** provide either through escape or eternal security. While there would be times for grieving, there would be more times of **rejoicing** because of Jesus (v. 10). Even though his life was **poor** (Gk. *ptōchoi*, "destitute, needy, lowly," v. 10; cp. 8:9) by earthly standards, he possessed heavenly treasures. He was satisfied with this life and able to see it as a wonderful possession.

THE WORK OF THE APOSTLE AMONG THE CORINTHIANS (6:11–7:16)

Paul's Challenge to the Corinthians (6:11–7:1)

6:11-13 The last verses of this section are heart-wrenching as Paul pleaded with the **Corinthians** to return his genuine love. **LIMITED** (Gk. *stenochōreisthe*, "pressed into a narrow place, restricted, restrained, cramped," v. 12) has various shades of meaning in this letter, including "crushed" (4:8) and "pressures" (6:4). **OPENED WIDE** (Gk. *peplatuntai*, "enlarged, broadened," v. 11) and **BE OPEN** (Gk. *platunthēte*, "open wide, enlarge," v. 13) reinforce the sense of unlimited or unhindered **AFFECTIONS** (Gk. *splagchnois*, "mercy-filled heart," lit. "bowels" as the seat of tenderness and compassion; cp. Jms 5:11; 1 Pt 3:8). He did not want them to hold back or reject his love. He wholeheartedly accepted them and hoped for the same in return. He then appealed to them as family members. As their spiritual father, he had a special connection with them, one that could not easily be replaced.

6:14-16a While this admonition easily and accurately applies to the marriage relationship, seemingly here Paul was addressing the temptations faced by the Corinthians when they followed false apostles and false religions. He reminded the Corinthians of the righteousness available to them by means of their unending relationship with Christ. With this purity and glory, how could they stoop to partnering with the lawless, those who rejected Christ?

Paul reminded them of the seriousness of a **partnership** as being binding and powerful. After making several strong comparisons, Paul made his strongest argument comparing Christ and BELIAL (Gk. *Beliar*, originating in Hb. as "worthless" and used in extrabiblical Jewish writings to represent Satan, the prince of lawlessness and darkness and the highest enemy of God). God and Satan are polar opposites. There is no possibility that Satan can be linked with God, just as there should be no possibility for **a believer** to be linked with **an unbeliever**. Among other applications, this principle would certainly forbid marriage between a believer and an unbeliever. Such a union would be MISMATCHED (Gk. *heterozugountes*, "coming under a different or unequal yoke," from *heteros*, "other, different," and *zugos*, "yoke," which is a metaphor for "burden or slavery"; cp. Gl 5:1).

The alliances Paul had in mind could have been marriage, business associations, or even social relationships (cp. 1 Co 10:14). Perhaps the context suggests that the apostle's concern here would be more their involvement with false apostles, whom he held responsible for the schism that had developed in his own relationship with the Corinthian believers. A believer should not have involvement with false religions; he must be solely committed to Christianity. Separation of the believer from the world and dedication to the Lord would be marked by these characteristics, which Paul sets forth in a series of rhetorical questions:

- PARTNERSHIP (Gk. *metochē*, "sharing or partaking, fellowship," v. 14). Interestingly, this Greek word has been used for the organization of student wives on the campus of Southwestern Baptist Theological Seminary (*Metochai*) because of the concept that was clearly established and affirmed in the creation order and thus a part of ministry marriages (Gn 2:18).

- **FELLOWSHIP** (Gk. *koinōnia*, "joint participation, community, association," 2 Co 6:14);

- **AGREEMENT** (Gk. *sumphōnēsis*, "concord, harmony," suggesting the idea of "agreeing together," as in making a bargain, and providing the English word "symphony," v. 15);

- **HAVE IN COMMON** (Gk. *meris*, "share, part, portion," v. 15; cp. Ac 8:21; Col 1:12);

- "AGREEMENT" (Gk. *sugkatathesis*, "joint deposit or vote, union, consent," 2 Co 6:16), a word used in the papyri to describe a decision made by a group.

6:16b-18 Paul combined truths from a number of Old Testament passages regarding the role of believers as the **sanctuary** or dwelling place **of the living God**. These verses beautifully depict the exclusive covenant relationship God has established with His people. Covenant means love, closeness, and commitment. It involves changed behavior, acceptance, and reconciliation with God. Paul emphasized the incredible willingness of God to establish this relationship and its exclusivity. None could be a part of both God and Satan. The people could no longer stand on the fence. They had to choose between God and

Satan. Their behavior would be evidence of their choices. Paul made this distinction clear, hoping that the Corinthians' behavior and attitudes would quickly change.

7:1 Based on the wonderful truth of the relationship provided through the gospel message, Paul appealed for purity both in **the flesh and spirit**. Paul encouraged the entire person to be pure in every way. The Corinthians were surrounded by idol worship and wicked living; they had so many temptations. Paul wanted the church to cooperate with God in their **sanctification** process.

Paul's Response to the Corinthians (7:2-16)

Affection for them (7:2-4)

7:2-4 Again, Paul asked them to open their "hearts" and accept him. He appealed to the Corinthians with purity of heart, affirming that he had not treated them wrongly. He reaffirmed his love for them and let them know he was not trying to make them feel guilty over their treatment of him. He expressed his love for them regardless of their actions toward him.

Paul loved the Corinthians unconditionally. He wanted the best for them, but he did not expect them to be perfect. His love for them was not affected by their behavior. His love for them was expressed in teaching them about God's love and their appropriate response. He strengthened his relationship with them by showing their mutual connection in Christ Jesus. Since believers are all children of God, they had all determined to die to self and live for Christ. They had a common bond and spirit to which Paul was appealing.

By this time, no doubt many were feeling guilty for their lack of support for Paul. He lavished affection on the church and expressed his hope for their future. He testified that this church made him so

happy that he was able to overcome the afflictions he was facing. Yet Paul continued to appeal to the Corinthians, TAKE US INTO YOUR HEARTS (Gk. *chōrēsate,* "yield in order to leave space, make room, hold, contain, accept," v. 2) for their full affection and confidence.

Joy over their repentance (7:5-16)

7:5-7 Paul picked up here from his earlier discussion in chapter 2 regarding his earnest desire to meet with **Titus** and receive an update on the church and their acceptance of him. He reminded them of his unrest because of his great concern for them and due to the opposition he faced in **Macedonia**. Not only was he intensely worried about the church he desperately loved, but he was also in physical danger and was **afflicted** (Gk. *thlibomenoi,* "press upon, oppress" in the sense of exercising pressure on someone) **in every way** (v. 5; see 1:6; 4:8).

Paul was expressing his great discouragement at the possibility of missing Titus and his joy at God's provision of comfort through the meeting with Titus. Although **humble** (Gk. *tapeinous,* "lowly, poor, brought low with grief, depressed," 7:6), used here in the sense of being downcast or depressed, Paul was encouraged that the people had treated Titus kindly, and he was comforted by the presence of Titus and the news he brought. The people expressed **sorrow** (Gk. *odurmon,* "mourning, loud lamentation," v. 7; cp. Mt 2:18) for their poor treatment of Paul; they longed to see him, and they expressed love for him.

7:8 Paul referenced the earlier scathing letter he had sent the Corinthians. He recognized that his words had stung them, and he sincerely regretted hurting them. However, he was pleased that the letter accomplished the intended outcome. This result made the hurt worthwhile. He was exercising tough love with the Corinthian church. While hard for parents, especially mothers, at times this tough love is necessary and greatly profitable. Although it was hard for Paul, he was willing to challenge them lovingly, a willingness modern parents should emulate.

7:9-10 Paul did not dwell on the "sorrow" his discipline caused but on the happy ending. His letter produced godly REPENTANCE (Gk. *metanoian*, "change of mind, remorse"), also translated "conversion," a word pointing to a change in thinking in contrast to "regret" in the sense of sorrow or grief (Gk. *metamelomai*) over one's action. Judas repented (Gk. *metamelomai*), regretting the way things developed (Mt 27:3; Ac 1:16). However, here "repentance" means a complete reversal (Gk. *metanoian*, lit., "thinking after" or "having a second mind") so that one who recognizes her own sinfulness has a mind to reverse completely her direction in life and seek God. Such genuine repentance generates a renewed interest in spiritual matters (2 Co 7:11). As vividly illustrated here in the lives of the Corinthians, repentance is not reserved for conversion but must continue even unto glorification. The godly sorrow of repentance led the Corinthians to be diligent in their service to Christ, to be determined to clear themselves of charges against them, to reject sinful behavior, to fear God, and to pursue righteousness, zeal, and vindication (vv. 11-12).

Paul also described **godly grief**. The noun GRIEF (Gk. *lupē* "pain, affliction, sorrow") and its related verb *lupeō*, "cause pain, grieve," occur 26 times in the Greek New Testament (15 times in Paul's writings, of which 12 are found in 2 Corinthians). Both forms could refer to pain experienced by the physical body, but they usually conveyed mental and emotional anguish. In the New Testament, the literal meaning of the noun is used only once (Jn 16:21); the verb is always used figuratively.

Four times in Paul's writings *lupē* referred, in a negative sense, to the apostle's deep concern about spiritual matters, such as Israel's unbelief (Rm 9:2), the attitude of other Christians to his ministry (2 Co 2:1,3), and the near death of a fellow worker in the Lord (Php 2:27). Paul also used *lupē* to describe the grief caused by sin in the life of a Christian (2 Co 2:7) and to explain that Christian giving should not be motivated by "regret" (*lupē*) but by a cheerful heart (2 Co 9:7). Here, Paul contrasted the false grief of the world with the "godly grief" that leads to repentance and warned against the notion held by some that any form of repentance would be considered genuine (7:10). Paul acknowledged repentance as the will of God. He was thrilled that he remained related to the Corinthians as their spiritual father. Rejecting Paul meant rejecting his message and accepting a different message. Paul considered the situation very serious and was greatly concerned that the people choose life in Christ rather than the destruction awaiting unbelievers.

7:11-13a The people had proven their loyalty to Paul and the gospel. They had dealt with the situation, apparently in a way that pleased the apostle. He reminded them that his harsh letter was not a prideful attempt to exercise his personal rights or to ostracize the one who did wrong but rather to make the situation right and to bring the proper perspective. Because the outcome was so positive and the people had been obedient, accepting the truths of God and the authority of Paul, he was happily **comforted**.

7:13b This section is an incredibly joyful part of Paul's letter, expressing a full range of emotion. Paul was already filled with joy because of the Corinthians' thorough handling of the aforementioned situation; however, he was additionally comforted by their further ministry efforts toward **Titus**. In effect, not only did the Corinthians correct their wrongdoing, but they went a step further and began doing right.

Paul commended the Corinthians for their faithful service to Titus and let them know that they had sincerely RE-FRESHED (Gk. *anapepautai*, "allow or cause someone to stop working long enough to recover strength, provide rest") him. Titus had been blessed by his time with them. The Corinthians must have been smiling upon hearing Paul's extravagant compliments. They had certainly worked hard to do the right thing, and Paul's words must have brought great pleasure and the motivation to continue in doing good.

7:14-16 As if this were not enough, Paul let them know that he believed they would continue doing the right thing. He had even boasted to Titus about how the people lived up to his expectations. Few ministers would enjoy going to a church with so many problems. It is so much easier to love those who are lovable and who seem to have everything together. Yet, Paul was even more proud of this church because they worked through their problems and behaved so honorably. His confidence in them was increased, and Titus's **affection** (Gk. *splagchna*, "inward parts, heart, love," v. 15; see 6:12) was **even greater**. It was cause for celebration.

Many women feel that they will always be second-class Christians because of a wounded spirit or impure background. The testimony of this church shows clearly that even those who have endured tragedy and failure can be transformed by God. Those who make mistakes can correct behavior. The Lord showed Himself to be the God of victories.

THE OUTGROWTH OF PAUL'S MINISTRY (8:1–9:15)

A Testimony from the Macedonians (8:1-7)

8:1-2 Paul had commended the Corinthians for their excellent behavior and spiritual growth. He then moved to share about the generosity of the Macedonian church in hopes of spurring the Corinthians on to more good works. The Macedonian church was a fairly new work. Unlike Corinth, this area had a very poor economy and suffered much **deep** (Gk. *bathous*, "extreme") **poverty** (Gk. *ptōcheia*, "condition of being destitute"). The church had experienced more persecution than the Corinthians. Perhaps, because they had experienced the pains of poverty and in the midst of their trials and struggles had seen God meeting their needs, their hearts were attentive to the needs of the saints in Jerusalem. Paul explained that their "abundance of joy" in the Lord "overflowed" into an immediate desire to give from "the WEALTH (Gk. *ploutos*, "riches, abundance of possessions, plenty") of their GENEROSITY" (Gk. *haplotētos*, "open-heartedness evident by one's generosity"; cp. 9:11,13; Rm 12:8; in other contexts "sincerity, simplicity," as opposed to being self-seeking, e.g., 2 Co 1:12) to others.

8:3-4 The Macedonians did not have to be prompted and reminded to give; rather they asked **on their own** (Gk. *authairetoi*, "of one's own accord, self-chosen, voluntarily") how they could participate. Paul explained that they gave all they could and more, showing that they considered the opportunity to give a privilege. Knowing their own needs, this attitude of giving is to be admired.

8:5 The Macedonians showed great spiritual maturity, far beyond the expectations of Paul and the other leaders. This congregation had tremendous love for God and others. Their love was shown in the fact that they desired to give out of their love and appreciation for **the Lord** and because of their acceptance and aid to the Jerusalem church, which was primarily Jewish. They also demonstrated appreciation of and kindness toward Paul and the others for bringing the gospel to them. Many early churches struggled with the tensions between Jews and Gentiles, but this church clearly moved forward in unity. Paul explained that the Macedonians gave out of the grace of God and according to His **will**, not to hurt the Corinthians or to cause them to be jealous but to encourage their generosity.

8:6-7 Paul and Timothy had **urged Titus** to complete the collection. This collection for the great need of the Jerusalem church had probably been delayed in efforts to solve the church's greater and more immediate issues. Paul urged them now to remember this need and **excel** (Gk. *perisseuete*, "overflow, be abundant, abound, exceed expectation"; occurring 11 times in the Greek text of this letter— 1:5; 3:9; 4:15; 8:2; 9:8,12) in giving.

The Example of Christ (8:8-9)

8:8 Although bearing full apostolic authority as would all God-breathed words (10:8; 13:10), Paul chose to request and suggest, with no hint of coercion, that the Corinthians complete the collection, which was probably a sensitive issue. He was not commanding them to give but suggesting that their generosity would be a display of the **genuineness** (Gk. *gnēsion*, "sincerity, legitimacy, truth," a word used to describe a child born in wedlock) of their **love** for him and for all believers. Paul even suggested that their response would be a **testing** (Gk. *dokimazōn*, "examining, scrutinizing to prove genuine"), a means of proving their genuine love.

8:9 Giving money is usually hard. It is much easier to be selfish and meet personal needs, whether they are simple desires or pressing necessities. Life for New Testament believers regularly offered enticements and demands. Paul taught the people to deal with these demands by viewing them in light of Christ's sacrifice. **Christ** gave up His immeasurable riches for poverty so that others could join in His riches. Once a person has tasted of wealth, it is very difficult to endure poverty, but Jesus was willing to do just that because of His great love.

Jesus **WAS RICH** (Gk. *plousios*, "wealthy, having abundant resources or possessions") and **BECAME POOR** (Gk. *eptōcheusen*, "became destitute" from the same root as "poverty"), so that by His **POVERTY** (Gk. *ptōcheia*, "condition of being destitute of possessions"; also 8:2) you might **BECOME RICH** (Gk. *ploutēsēte*, "become affluent" from the same root as "wealth" in 8:2).

An Appeal for the Collection (8:10-15)

8:10-12 While Paul's greatest encouragement comes from the example of Christ, he did not fail to mention the commitment the Corinthians had made a year ago in regard to the collection (v. 10). They had not been forced to make this commitment but voluntarily did so. He indicated the importance of the fulfillment of their pledge (v. 11). He explained that as long as they had the desire to give, which he described as eagerness (Gk. *prothumia*, "readiness, willingness, goodwill, inclination, zeal," a word used repeatedly by Paul to describe their enthusiasm, vv. 11-12,19; cp. 9:2; Ac 17:11), they need not give beyond what they were able to give (2 Co 8:12).

8:13-14 Paul already expressed his approval of the extremely generous gift from the Macedonian church. However, he let the Corinthians know that the amount of the gift was not as important as the desire to express love and unity in the body of Christ. Paul was hoping that believers everywhere would have concern and compassion for their fellow brothers and sisters, thus desiring to provide **relief** (Gk. *anesis*, "rest," as from persecution; "loosening or relaxing" of conditions, making an unpleasant situation more tolerable; cp. 2:13; 7:5) and meet their needs. SURPLUS and ABUNDANCE (Gk. *perisseuma*, "more than enough, excess, fullness, what remains, scraps, filled to overflowing") both appear in verse 14 and are the same Greek word translated in different ways but emphasizing the principle of reciprocity in giving. In the course of a lifetime, most people experience both "abundance" and NEED (Gk. *husterēma*, "deficiency, absence, shortcoming, lack of resources, poverty, destitution"; cp. 9:12; 11:9). There exists an EQUALITY (Gk. *isotēs*, "fairness") in the sense of equitable treatment for all. Paul wanted to cultivate awareness and generosity among Christians and eliminate prejudice and strife.

8:15 Paul used this illustration of God's provision for the Israelites during their desert journey (Ex 16:18) to encourage sharing among Christians. The Israelites gathered the manna daily. However, when the amounts were measured, those who gathered more than they needed still had only as much as those who gathered less. There was neither surplus nor insufficiency, but each had his needs met. Paul was not suggesting an artificial equalization of property or possessions, nor was he asking the Corinthians to impoverish themselves and their families in order to meet needs in Jerusalem. He simply appealed to

meeting the needs of others when God's blessings enable them to do so. Paul's challenge to the Corinthians was to be generous in sharing their own abundance with those in poverty. Yet their generous sharing with the poor was not to replace the efforts of the poor to work and support themselves as they could (2 Th 3:10).

The Response to the Collection (8:16–9:5)

8:16-19 Paul was well practiced in expressing gratitude. He was grateful that God had **put** a love for the Corinthians **into the heart of Titus**. Paul later commended the ministry of Titus and expressed thanks for him (v. 23). Paul noted that Titus **went out . . . by his own choice** (Gk. *authairetos*, "voluntarily, of one's own accord," v. 17; see v. 3). Along with Titus, Paul mentioned **the brother who is praised**. The church obviously knew the identity of "the brother," although this person is not named in the text. He was also **appointed** (Gk. *cheirotonētheis*, "elected, chosen by raising hands or stretching out hands," v. 19; cp. Ac 14:23) to help with the distribution of the **gift** to the Jerusalem church. This "brother" may have been elected by vote of the congregation, or he may simply have been selected for the task because of his interest and/or availability.

8:20-23 Paul was wise to protect himself from the attacks of others and their inappropriate rumors because of **this large sum** (Gk. *hadrotēti*, "bountiful, abundant collection," from *hadros*, "stout," v. 20). Rather than give anyone an opportunity for grumbling, Paul explained that he was taking an extra **precaution** to make sure the gift was distributed properly. As if this were not enough, Paul also assigned another person to assist with the gift, thereby ensuring his own integrity. The Corinthians probably did not know this person, so Paul commended him as

diligent and faithful and noted that he was one **we have often tested** (Gk. *edokimasamen*, "examined, approved" in the sense of proving the man's reliability by testing in some way, v. 22; see 8:8)

8:24 Paul and the others were clearly excited about this effort and were ready to bring it to completion. He encouraged them to offer **proof** (Gk. *endeiknumenoi*, "demonstration, visible evidence"; see 8:8) of their **love**, while reminding them of his confidence in them. Paul had been bragging about them because he wanted others to think highly of them even as he did.

9:1-2 Paul continued the encouragement regarding the gift for the Jerusalem church. He had previously told the Corinthians of his pride in them and his belief that they desired to add to the contribution. Paul seemed to include all of the churches he had founded in Achaia in this commendation. He expressed strong belief in their good intentions to add to the monetary gift as they had promised. He used a precise word to express that confidence. ZEAL (Gk. *zēlos*, "fervor, ardor, jealousy, rivalry, extravagance" and its related verb *zeloō*, "to be zealous or jealous," occur 11 times in the Greek New Testament, 8 of these in Paul's writings). In the Septuagint, the word often refers to the Lord's zeal or jealousy. The related noun *zēlōtes*, "one who is zealous," is used twice in reference to Simon, who was one of the Twelve and had been a member of the militaristic Jewish sect called the Zealots (Lk 6:15; Ac 1:13). King David's "zeal" for the Lord's house was epitomized in the life of Jesus (Ps 69:9; Jn 2:17). "Zeal" was also used in the negative sense of "envy or jealousy" (Ac 5:17; 13:45; Rm 10:12; 13:13; 1 Co 3:3; 2 Co 12:20; Gl 5:20; Php 3:6; Jms 3:14,16), but in this letter it is used four times in a positive sense to describe:

- the eagerness of the Corinthian believers to serve Paul (2 Co 7:7,11; 9:2; 11:2);

- their desire to act righteously regarding a brother in sin (7:11);

- their eagerness to contribute to the needs of other believers (9:2); and

- Paul's "jealous" desire to present the Corinthian believers to Christ as "a pure virgin" (11:2) who had remained faithful to the truth of the gospel.

Paul did not want to hurt them by giving the impression that his words of affirmation were empty.

Paul further explained how their **eagerness** to give to the struggling saints in Jerusalem was so profound that their testimony was worthy of sharing with other congregations, namely **to the Macedonians** (v. 2). Corinth was the capital of the province of **Achaia**, the term Paul used as inclusive of all the churches associated with and surrounding Corinth. After hearing the commitment of this group of churches to contribute to the offering, Paul went on to Macedonia and shared the positive attitude of the Corinthians. Paul was thrilled because this knowledge **stirred** the Macedonians themselves to give a significant gift.

9:3-5 Although the Corinthians were not struggling financially, they were certainly struggling with unity and had probably delayed their giving in order to settle their difficult and challenging situation regarding Paul and the false prophets. Not wanting to make them feel badly about the delay, Paul gently let them know that he was sending some Christian **brothers** to expedite the collection.

Paul explained his reason for sending these men. Should other churches, especially the Macedonian church, hear that the Corinthians had not completed their commitment, the Corinthians would be terribly **embarrassed** (Gk. *kataischunthōmen*, "dishonored, put to shame, disgraced, disappointed," v. 4) as would Paul, due to all his **boasting** about their sacrificial giving. The Corinthians were happy to participate in the giving project. Paul did not want the gift to be so delayed that the people no longer felt the desire to give, nor did he want the people to develop bitterness because of the delay in expediting their generous commitment. Paul's plan included these admonitions and warnings:

- **to go on ahead** (Gk. *proelthōsin*, "precede, go before, go forward, come out");

- **arrange in advance** (Gk. *prokatartisōsin*, "prepare or equip beforehand, get ready");

- **the generous gift you promised** (Gk. *proepēggelmenēn*, "announce before or previously"; cp. Rm 1:2);

- **will be ready** (Gk. *hetoimēn*, "prepared to do or to receive"; cp. Ti 3:1; 1 Pt 1:5; 3:15) **as a gift**; and

- **not an extortion** (Gk. *pleonexian*, "greediness, covetousness, avarice") in the sense of something forced.

Lessons Learned from Giving (9:6-15)

9:6 Giving is a blessing, especially when you see the receiver enjoy and benefit from that gift. However, this sincere and well-intentioned desire is often clouded by personal need. How does one give to another when facing great personal need? Even beyond Paul's good-hearted plea are the real concerns of jealousy, selfishness, and greed.

Paul wisely reminded the Corinthians: **Remember**. Even when a woman is ready to do the right thing, she can be blessed by a reminder of the reason for the righteous act in view. And, when she does not want to do the right thing, a reminder will often adjust her attitude so that the heart, behavior, and will all come into line. Paul was emphasizing the great blessings that come from giving. He knew that those who give will be rewarded and used a special word to describe such giving. GENEROUSLY (Gk. *eulogiais*, "praise, flattery, consecration, bounty, blessing, benefit") is used here as an adjective. More literally the compound word is "good speaking" or "good words" and thus "praise, invocation of blessing, benediction," as in the anglicized word "eulogy."

> *The more generous and happy-spirited the giving, the more beautiful and satisfying the rewards.*

9:7 Paul emphasized the **heart** attitude, explaining that giving should not be done out of guilt, mere need, or for any other negative reason. Giving should be an expression of gratitude for God and love for others. With this godly motivation, you can cheerfully give what you have **decided** (Gk. *proērētai*, "bring out, make up your mind" in the sense of bringing forward from what you have stored away). Paul encouraged the people to think about their giving, taking time to determine the gift that would be pleasing to the Lord and then to be obedient to give. **God loves a cheerful** (Gk. *hilaron*, "joyous, glad," anglicized as "hilarious") **giver.** "Cheerful" or joyful giving is the antithesis of begrudging release. The more generous and happy-spirited the giving, the more beautiful and satisfying the rewards. To give according to divine standards is to receive gifts completely beyond the proportion of what has been given (cp. Pr 11:24-25; 19:17). Giving for a believer should be an act of worship, accompanied by preparation of the heart, purpose in the plan, and joy in the attitude.

9:8 Paul described the character of God, whose generosity goes beyond the comprehension of His creation. God delights in giving good things to His children. If He was willing to give His only begotten Son, than surely He can make His **grace overflow** on the Christian giver, so that you have **everything you need** (Gk. *autarkeian*, "sufficiency, contentment" in the sense of a condition in which no help or support is needed; cp. 1 Tm 6:6).

God is aware of the needs of each one, and He is able abundantly to care for those needs. This confidence in God should encourage the believer and provide joy in giving. Paul understood God in majestic and holy terms, yet he also knew God intimately and personally.

9:9 Paul loved to call on Scripture to support his arguments. He used Psalm 112:9 to describe the pleasure of God toward one who is generous. While Christianity is not an escape from difficulty, God desires to protect His obedient children and cause them to prosper—especially those who are obedient in giving to others.

9:10-15 Paul rightly placed the emphasis on God. Those who are obedient in giving will be blessed by God. Although this blessing might be prosperity, the greatest blessing is an outpouring of God's grace, an **indescribable gift** (v. 15). In this case, those who have benefited from this incomparable spiritual gift should above all others desire to give material gifts to relieve the physical needs of others.

Next, Paul explained the exciting results of giving: God blesses the giver. The receiver of the gift has cause to thank and praise God. The giver rejoices in, and has a part in, bringing this glorious thanks to God. Therefore, the act of giving pleases God, helps the receiver, and rewards the giver. The act of giving also strengthens the love and unity among all. God has already expressed His desire for the love

and unity of His children. Here, the gifts please God not only because His children are obedient but also because they are expressing love for one another. God is also pleased because He is receiving praise and glory. His plan is accomplished in the lives of His children, and He delights in extending grace. This cycle can only be strengthened and deepened with repetition. It is therefore an indescribable gift and one which also brought Paul great delight, and he obviously wanted others to enjoy this gift to the fullest. Many believe Paul was also thinking of the gift of Jesus Christ. God, in giving His Son, gave not only His best but also His all. How much more should believers through their **obedience** (Gk. *hupotagē*, "submissiveness, subjection" in the sense of subordinating yourself to God; v. 13; cp. Gl 2:5; 1 Tm 2:11; 3:4) look for God's lofty purposes in their own lives. Paul included an allusion to **prayers** (Gk. *deēsei*, "entreaties, seeking, asking," out of a sense of need, 2 Co 9:14), implying special petitions for supplying wants.

AN AUTHENTICATION OF PAUL'S MINISTRY (10:1–12:13)

In the previous chapters, Paul had been very warm and encouraging. Yet he was bold and straightforward regarding the recent controversy challenging his authority in the church. In this section he took a strong pastoral tone as he exerted clear leadership.

Paul's Authority (10:1-18)

10:1-3 Paul spoke to the Corinthians in a personal way, identifying their connection and imploring them to action based on their experiences together. When using the words GENTLENESS (Gk. *prautētos*, "meekness, humility, courtesy"), denoting an attitude of patient submissiveness in the face of offenses and exhibiting freedom from malice or desire for revenge, and **GRACIOUS-NESS** (Gk. *epieikeias*, "gentleness, fairness, clemency" in the sense of what is fitting, reasonable, and fair, often suggesting lenience and indulgence as in patient steadfastness even when there is injustice and maltreatment), Paul was identifying himself with the characteristics of Jesus (v. 1). He was committed to Christlike behavior despite the circumstances, however unfair, and he wanted the people to remember that Christ, though meek and gentle, was able to exert strong leadership and authority. The end of the first verse is a straightforward attempt to answer his opponents. The false prophets were probably Judaizers, who tried to wed a legalistic system of salvation through obedience to the Old Testament law, to salvation by grace through Christ. They were attempting to thwart the growth of the early church by bringing a different message, slandering Paul, and challenging his apostleship. Apparently these men were accusing Paul of being weak and unable to meet the needs of the congregation in his personal visits, on the one hand, and insulting and rude during his absence, on the other. They were attempting to slander his character and question the consistency of his actions. They also faulted him for sending letters rather than making personal visits.

Paul testified to being **humble among you in person**. HUMBLE (Gk. *tapeinos*, "lowly, poor, subservient, downcast") is in a family of words. The verb *tapeinoō*, "humiliate, humble, or make ashamed," occurs 14 times in the Greek New Testament (four times in Paul's writings). The noun *tapeinosis*, "humiliation or humble condition," occurs four times in the Greek text (Lk 1:48; Ac 8:33; Php 3:21; Jms 1:10); another term, *tapeinophrosune*, meaning "humility," occurs seven times (Ac 20:19; Eph 4:2; Php 2:3; Col 2:18,23; 3:12; 1 Pt 5:5).

The ancient Greeks so emphasized personal strength and self-sufficiency that *tapeinos* and its related words were almost always used in a negative sense. To be "humble" or "lowly" was considered in a negative way. However, Jesus elevated *tapeinos*, which the Greeks considered a vice, to the status of a virtue when He said, "I am gentle and humble in heart" (Mt 11:29). Paul also used *tapeinoō* to describe the divine incarnation (Php 2:8). Jesus warned that those who promote themselves will be judged by God, but He also said that those who "humble" themselves will be rewarded (cp. 2 Co 11:7; Mt 18:4; 23:12; Lk 14:11; 18:14). True humility is the opposite of putting self first. Humility means that a person does not think of self at all but instead thinks of the needs of others and makes their needs a priority (Php 2:3-4). God gives grace to those who practice such humility (Jms 4:6; 1 Pt 5:5).

Paul then assured the Corinthians that he was taking care of them and would be coming in person. He wanted them to expect his visit. He explained his desire for the situation to be resolved so that he did not need to exercise discipline. He had already expressed sadness at having to send them the previous letter, which had strongly condemned their behavior and "grieved" them (2 Co 7:8). He did not want to hurt the people he dearly loved. However, he made it clear that he would be **bold** in addressing those who opposed and slandered him.

These imposters presented themselves with extreme confidence and flamboyance, thereby trying to make Paul seem ordinary and unable. He did not deny the fact that he was an ordinary man, but he testified that his power and authority came from the power of God. This explanation would clearly draw the Corinthians to a comparison.

10:4-6 Paul brought a very serious message. He wanted the people to understand that they were in a spiritual battle between light and darkness. They must choose Christ, which meant accepting Paul's leadership, or follow Satan, who was represented by the false apostles. The apostle was trying to draw the lines with such clarity that there could be no mistake.

Some in the church had been very captivated by these imposters. These STRONGHOLDS (Gk. *ochurōmatōn,* "castles, fortresses, prisons") needed "demolition" (Gk. *kathairesin* and *kathairountes,* "destruction, a pulling down," two similar words in v. 4) through the power of God. He was forcing the people to see that the false prophets presented anti-Christian ARGUMENTS (Gk. *logismous,* "reasonings, decisions, thoughts") and placed importance on themselves and "every HIGH-MINDED THING" (Gk. *hupsōma,* "height," as a barrier, Rm 8:39; "elevated structure," such as a "rampart or bulwark," as in an obstacle lifted up and in the figurative sense leading to pride, i.e., exalting oneself, 2 Co 10:5) rather than Jesus (v. 4). Paul wanted the Corinthians to begin thinking critically, seeing for themselves that these men were enemies of God. He wanted them to understand the truth and obey Christ. He was urging their support and decisiveness in the matter so that upon his coming they would be ready to comply fully, refusing the influence of these false apostles. They would accomplish this victory by "taking every THOUGHT (Gk. *noēma,* "intention, scheme, mind," 10:5; cp. 2:11; 3:14; 4:4; 11:3) CAPTIVE" (Gk. *aichmalōtizontes,* "lead away, capture," v. 5; see 2 Tm 3:6) in the sense of bringing into subjection. The present tense of this active participle points to an ongoing and continual struggle.

10:7-9 Paul implored the entire body of believers to examine this important situation. Although the imposters and some in the church claimed a special relationship with God, Paul reminded the Corinthians that he was a genuine believer. He also made reference to his unique conversion and special call as an apostle. He did not place weight on any human attributes but rather on the **authority** (Gk. *exousias,* "power, right, or privilege") given to him by God (v. 8). Paul explained that this "authority" and power are evidenced in the fact that he founded and built Corinthian church. Paul was **not ashamed** of the work God had done through him, and he reiterated the fact that he was continuing to build the church, not tear it down (v. 8).

10:10-11 Paul spoke strongly against the claim of inconsistency in his life. His language was direct. He did not apologize or make any excuses. He simply affirmed that he had been consistent whether in person or absent; he would continue to be just as consistent in the future.

10:12-14 Paul was very convincing in his argument here, using a bold verb, **dare** (Gk. *tolmōmen,* "be bold, bring myself to, presume, am courageous, not dreading or shunning out of fear," v. 12; cp. 10:2; 11:21). The false apostles came in with great commendation, excessive boasting, and impressive qualities. They seemed to have no problem bragging on themselves and tearing others down, especially Paul.

Paul refused even to enter into this kind of worldly comparison. Surely Paul had strengths and weaknesses like every other human being. Certainly, he was insecure about his inadequacies. However, Paul had moved beyond his need to impress others or build his own self-esteem. He needed only to serve Christ and lift Him up. God's call on Paul's life and evidence of

Heart to Heart:
A Mind at War

Women, in comparison to men, have four times as many neurons connecting the two sides of the brain, making them capable of thinking about and solving more than one problem at a time and using both sides of the brain—the logical and the creative—to do it. This blessing equips women to fill many roles simultaneously as is often the case when they don't have the luxury of thinking about one thing at a time. This unique gift can also be a curse. A woman's thought life can be her worst enemy. Paul spoke to this issue, saying that the battle being waged for the mind is not a fleshly one but a spiritual one. He strongly suggested the use of "weapons" that are "powerful through God for the demolition of strongholds" (10:4). Paul spoke about these powerful weapons in Ephesians 6:17-18 when he described the spiritual armor. They are the word of God and prayer—the only offensive weapons listed in the armor. The world is full of "arguments" and prideful opinions, which serve as barriers to obeying God; but through the power of God's word and prayer, women can take these—and even their own imaginations—"captive to the obedience of Christ" (2 Co 10:5). Know the truth of God's word. Commune with Him in prayer. These two weapons, when employed together against wrong thinking, are powerful forces.

an effective **AREA OF MINISTRY** (Gk. *metron tou kanonos*, "measure, extent or limit of a defined sphere of activity, standard, rule or influence," vv. 13,15–16) was enough to validate his apostleship. The church should have seen that those who relied on human strength were clearly serving self and Satan rather than truth and God. God had **ASSIGNED** (Gk. *emerisen*, "bestowed, divided, separated, apportioned, imparted, allotted," in the sense of divided for distribution, v. 13; cp. Rm 12:3; 1 Co 7:17; Heb 7:2) to Paul precisely what He wanted Paul to do. Paul was not **OVEREXTENDING** (Gk. *huperekteinomen*, "overreaching, extending beyond prescribed boundaries, stretching

beyond measure," 2 Co 10:14) his ministry assignment.

10:15-18 Wisely, Paul helped the people to think beyond their present difficulties. In their hearts, they knew God had worked powerfully among them through Paul's sharing of the gospel message. Their spiritual father wanted them to begin thinking about the further ministry God had for them, a ministry that included other regions. They had already wasted time in the confusion caused by the imposters. With unity in the gospel and obedience, they could have an enlarged ministry. How could they have this **greatly enlarged** (Gk. *megalunthēnai*, "magnified, made conspicuous, highly esteemed, extended," v. 15) ministry? They must seek the direction and approval of the Lord Jesus Christ.

Judging between Genuine and False Apostles (11:1-15)

11:1-4 Paul obviously felt forced to present his credentials yet again. He did not desire to do this. His strategy was magnificent. He told a love story. Surely, the ears of the women were at attention.

Paul thought so highly of his Savior. He recognized the Lord as magnificent and worthy of the bride He desired. Paul felt the Corinthians should be joined **in marriage to one husband**. He wanted this impure bride to receive purity, love, and protection (v. 2). This analogy is strong, opening their eyes to the binding significance of their union. And still, the analogy is tender, assuring them of the strong love of Paul and of Jesus, the Bridegroom.

Paul brought further solemnity to the situation when he compared their confusion to the deception of **Eve** in the garden (v. 3). The fall of man is the most tragic event in all of history, affecting the entire world and sealing the need for redemption. Satan slipped in and by his **cunning** (Gk. *panourgia*, "craftiness, trickery, false wisdom," v. 3; cp. Lk 20:23; 1 Co 3:19; Eph 4:14) the mind of Eve was **corrupted**. **The serpent** shared a different message with Eve. Just like Eve in the garden, the Corinthians were being confused with **a different gospel** and **a different spirit** (v. 4). If their mistake was not remedied, their ministry would be tainted and even lost. They had been so tolerant and accepting of this false message; they **put up with it** (Gk. *anecheesthe*, "endured, bore, accepted, stood tall, held up," v. 4) without a fight. This tragic capitulation must have seemed unbelievable to Paul, who saw the situation so clearly.

11:5-6 You have to respect a man who is not afraid to stand up for what he believes. Paul readily acknowledged his weakness but denied that his human weakness would disqualify his effectiveness in ministry. He was not intimidated by those who enjoyed arrogant pretensions. He was confident in the truth of his message and he knew that God had well-prepared him for the task.

Paul defended his actions. These **"super-apostles"** (Gk. *huperlian apostolōn*, "over-and-above or beyond, exceedingly-beyond-measure apostles"), as they must have identified themselves, were obviously seeking monetary gain (v. 5). Paul compared his generous conduct by identifying the foolishness of doubting his apostleship based on his refusal to accept their funding.

KNOWLEDGE (Gk. *gnōsei*, "understanding," v. 6) refers mainly to the knowledge of God and the things of God. It is a key term for Paul in describing various aspects of salvation (2:14; 4:6; 6:6; 8:7; 10:5; 1 Co 1:5; Php 3:8; Col 2:3). In 1 Corinthians "a message of knowledge" is listed as a spiritual gift, probably a revelatory one (12:8; 13:2,8; 14:6). Though "knowledge" can cause pride (1 Co 8:1), "knowledge" is also essential for Christians to enjoy their liberty in Christ (1 Co 8:7,10,11). *Gnōsis* in its positive sense is never merely intellectual knowledge or information that has no effect on the way a person lives. Instead, it is experiential knowledge that changes a person's worldview and lifestyle. Thus, believers must guard against false knowledge (1 Tm 6:20).

11:7-15 On the contrary, Paul wanted them to see that he was not seeking personal gain. He was only seeking the promotion of the gospel and the saving of souls. So committed was he, that he denied their support. He worked long hours to supply his own needs in order not to **burden** (Gk. *katenarkēsa*, "weigh heavily upon," from *kata*, "down," and *narkaō*, "make numb," v. 9; cp. 12:13-14) **anyone** and again to avoid **burdening** (Gk. *abarē*, "not heavy, lightweight," 11:9) the Corinthians. While many might have considered him in a lower class because of his work, he made it clear that he would rather have people think lowly of him than bring doubt upon the great **gospel** message (v. 7). Paul intended to continue this practice. He would not BE STOPPED (Gk. *phragēsetai*, "fenced in, blocked, shut, closed, silenced," v. 10). The refusal of funds was done out of his love for them, which he readily affirmed (v. 9). However, he would CUT OFF (Gk. *ekkopsō*, "cut out or off," as from a tree or "cutting short" a possibility, v. 12) the imposters from OPPORTUNITY (Gk. *aphormēn*, "occasion, pretext, excuse," as a base of operations from which an attack would be launched, i.e., an incentive or occasion to move forward, or the resources used to undertake a project, v. 12; cp. 5:12; Rm 7:8,11; Gl 5:13; 1 Tm 5:14) to receive the privilege of influence and authority among the Corinthians.

In verse 12 Paul further distinguished himself from the "super-apostles" (v.13). Those with opposing messages cannot both be true. He boldly named them as

- **false apostles** (Gk. *pseudapostoloi*, anglicized as "pseudo-apostles"),

- **deceitful workers**,

- **disguising** (Gk. *metaschēmatizomenoi*, "changing the figure of, transforming") **themselves** (vv. 13-15).

Satan's most destructive force is accomplished when he is **disguised as an angel of light**. This deception enables him to masquerade and present himself as good and holy. Those who serve him can do the same as they outwardly appear to obey God. Paul went even further, intentionally

allying them with **Satan** (vv. 14-15). They were not merely naïve, confused men; they were puppets of the enemy. They used Satan's strategies of **disguise** and deception (vv. 14-15). Of course, these men first appeared as **servants of righteousness**, a tactic they used to gain the confidence of the Corinthians. However, Paul minced no words in explaining that their clear **destiny** is hell (v. 15).

Paul's Genuine Apostleship (11:16–12:13)

11:16-21 In previous verses Paul defended himself based on God's calling. Even though he did not feel that he should be required to defend himself with **human** credentials, he acquiesced to their desires, asking that they accept his defense as a final word on the issue. They were obviously accustomed to the **boasting** of the false apostles (vv. 17-18). It seems they had become so comfortable with the tactics of these imposters that they hardly realized that they were enslaved by them, harmed and controlled by them (v. 20). Paul openly identified their weakness, calling himself A FOOL (Gk. *aphrona*, "mindless, without reason, ignorant, senseless, stupid," v. 16) in a play on words in which he used the plural of the word again in verse 19 and its derivative FOOLISHLY (Gk. *aphrosunē*, "folly, senselessness, thoughtlessness, recklessness," v. 17; cp. 11:1,21; 12:6,11), hoping to fully convince them of their deception. SMART (Gk. *phronimoi*, "intelligent, sensible, thoughtful, wise," 11:19; cp. 1 Co 4:10) conveys the sense of being "mindful or aware" and is used with a tone of sarcasm to emphasize the extent to which the Corinthians had been deceived without being aware of it. Elsewhere, Paul warned believers against being "conceited" (Rm 11:25) or "wise in your own estimation" (Rm

12:16). Five conditional clauses identify what the Corinthians **put up with** (v. 20):

- **if someone enslaves** (Gk. *katadouloi*, "puts into bondage, takes advantage of," from the same root as the noun *doulos*, "servant or slave"; cp. Gl 2:4) **you**;

- **if someone devours** (Gk. *katesthiei*, "consumes by eating up, ruins by stripping of possessions or causing injury, destroys"; cp. Lk 15:30) **you**;

- **if someone captures** (Gk. *lambanei*, "takes or catches by craft or fraud, receives, takes in order to carry away as one's own"; cp. 12:16; 1 Co 10:13) **you**;

- **if someone dominates** (Gk. *epairetai*, "lifts oneself up with pride, raises oneself against or in opposition to"; cp. 10:5) **you**; or

- **if someone hits** (Gk. *derei*, "strikes, beats, skins" as in Jn 18:23; in other contexts used for severe beating, e.g., "flogged" in Ac 5:40, but also to express verbal assaults) **you in the face**.

In these verses, Paul intended to prove that his commitment to Christ was much stronger than that of the "super-apostles." He began on the terms of the opposition. He compared first his equal credentials as a Jew from the chosen race of God.

11:22-33 Paul hated listing his own "human" credentials. He obviously preferred talking about Christ rather than himself. He hated being pushed to this level. Who was the real servant of Christ (v. 23)? His extensive list showed his strong devotion to the Lord. This remarkable passage showed clearly Paul's passion for Christ as being far superior to the imposters' worldly, limited display of righteousness.

Paul claimed to be a diligent worker for the Lord. He exhausted himself with a rigorous schedule governed by his passion for the lost. Surely the Corinthians were aware of his work ethic. His imprisonments were well known as were the accounts of numerous **beatings** that nearly took his life (vv. 23-25). Obviously he did not hold his life dear, as did the false apostles.

Suffering for Christ set Paul apart as an authentic and superior servant in contrast with the false apostles. If he was talking "like a MADMAN" (Gk. *paraphronōn*, "being out of one's mind, without understanding, insane"),

- he was "a BETTER (Gk. *huper*, "more so, beyond") one" than they;

- he had experienced "FAR MORE (Gk. *perissoterōs*, "exceedingly, beyond measure") labors";

- had faced "MANY MORE (Gk. *perissoterōs*) imprisonments"; and

- had suffered "FAR WORSE (Gk. *huperballontōs*, "above measure, exceedingly surpassing") beatings" (v. 23).

Paul moved into a discussion of his traveling lifestyle—not glamorous and exciting, but rather dangerous, tiresome, and filled with tragedy (vv. 25-27). He also encountered many enemies of the gospel. Seemingly at every turn, he faced opposition and **dangers** (Gk. *kindunois*, "perils, risks," v. 26; cp. Rm 8:35). How amazing that Paul did not close up shop and live as a hermit in safety. No, his message was far too important to be delayed by fear, pain, and uncertainty.

Paul failed to be deterred even by physical weariness, **hunger, and thirst . . . cold** (2 Co 11:27). Although the people surely knew of the afflictions he had faced, they probably pushed those images of Paul's suffering far from their minds, away from frequent thought. However, his personal and honest recount must have been a painful reminder to them as they remembered again his suffering, even in the process of bringing the gospel to their own ears. Those with a tender conscience must have been deeply burdened.

With personal humility, Paul did add the emotional strain as he would "BURN (Gk. *puroumai*, "burn," as with fire, "be inflamed, made red hot," v. 29) with indignation," expressing his sincere love and genuine CARE (Gk *merimna*, "concern, anxiety, worry," v. 28) for his spiritual children. Just as children need to hear the expression of their parents' love, Paul understood the Corinthians' need for his expression of love and concern.

Paul seemed to soften, knowing that his words must have been painful for them as they were for him. He based his integrity ("I am not lying," Gk. *pseudomai*, "deliberately speaking falsehood, deceiving," v. 31) on the witness of the heavenly **Father**. He had confidence in God and believed that God had confidence in him.

12:1 Understanding the Corinthians' strong background in pagan religions, no wonder they were intrigued by ecstatic and miraculous experiences. Many of these satanic forces were directed at people with spiritual sensitivities. In the Old and New Testament times, God also used **visions**, dreams, and **revelations** to communicate with His people. While accounts like this seem odd to many today, they were of real interest to Paul's readers. In addition, the false apostles had extravagant stories to tell and challenged Paul to see if he had any of his own.

REVELATIONS (Gk. *apokalupseis*, "disclosures," linking *apo*, "away from," and *kaluptō*, "hide, veil," thus "unveilings"). Similarly, the verb *apokaluptō* has the sense of "exposing that which was hidden, revealing." *Kalumma*, a related noun, is a "veil or covering."

In the New Testament, *apokalupsis* always refers to God's revelation of Himself. In Luke 2:32, this revelation comes in the person of Christ, while in Romans 8:19 it is in His "sons." God often revealed Himself through supernatural means to apostles and prophets such as Paul (Rm 16:25; 2 Co 12:1,7; Gl 1:12; 2:2; Eph 3:3). In the end times, God's judgment will be revealed (Rm 2:5), as will Christ (1 Co 1:7; 2 Th 1:7; 1 Pt 1:7,13; 4:13).

The last occurrence of *apokalupsis* in the New Testament is in Revelation 1:1 as the first word of the Greek text. It eventually became the name of the book and the only reference of *apokalupsis* to written revelation, i.e., Scripture. Revelation 1:1 used *apokalupsis* in its noblest sense, as it introduces the main theme of the book: "The revelation of Jesus Christ." Paul may have been trying to differentiate between "visions" (Ac 9:3-9,12; 16:9-10; 18:9-10; 22:17-21; 23:11; 26:19; 27:23-24; Gl 1:16) as something seen and "revelations" as something that can be seen or merely perceived. Not all "revelations" came through visions.

Paul expressed again that he hated **to boast** of himself. He realized the danger that boasting or thinking too much of self can cause. He knew that while he was empowered by God, he was not above sin. Paul loved fellowship with God too much to risk separating himself from God because of pride. He wanted instead to have pure and high thoughts of God.

12:2-4 To confirm his apostleship fully to the church, Paul continued with the "revelations" and "visions" he received from God; but so as not to draw too much attention to himself, he spoke as if these experiences had happened to another man. Perhaps he had not often, if ever, shared this information concerning an event that occurred **14 years** prior.

In Paul's account, he did not offer any extra information. In fact, he used some restraint in details, and seemingly from his comment he was not fully aware of the details on how God performed this miraculous event. This admission does not detract from the truthfulness of Paul's message; rather it supports his humanity.

Paul **was caught up** (Gk. *hērpagē*, "seized, stolen, snatched out or away," vv. 2,4; cp. Ac 8:39; 23:10; 1 Th 4:17) **into the third heaven** (2 Co 12:2), a reference to **paradise** (v. 4), the greatest heights of heaven. Much attention was given to these unusual experiences. Was the whole person transported to heaven or only the soul, mind, or spirit? No doubt, the audience was rapt with attention. Rather than focusing on the details of the experience, Paul drew attention to the power of God manifested through the revelation. Paul also refused to be distracted by the desire of the people to learn what he had actually heard.

12:5-6 Paul still was not comfortable with the idea of sharing such private information. His difficulty was apparent, and his struggle showed his humanity (v. 5). He was also drawing attention to the difference between himself and his detractors. They clearly loved **to boast** about themselves. He obviously did not and was quick to relate his weaknesses.

Paul admitted that he had had incredible and unique experiences with God. So convinced of his apostolic calling, he certainly realized that God had an unusual purpose for his life, which included great suffering and amazing revelations. He was not so foolish or disillusioned as to reject this **truth** (v. 6). However, as comfortable and happy as he was in his apostolic position, he never lost touch with his ordinary humanity.

12:7-8 God ensured that Paul remained close to the frailty of his humanity with the constant, painful

pressing of the **THORN** (Gk. *skolops*, "sharp, pointed piece of wood, splinter," representing an unspecified injury or ailment; a *hapax* or word used only here in the New Testament, v. 7). Paul seemed to know exactly why the **thorn** remained. He knew the temptation of self-exaltation. While Jesus was able to defend Himself in His time of testing, the loving Father knew the limits of Paul. Although Paul obviously wanted the "thorn" to be removed, he clearly admitted that he understood its presence and agreed with its purpose.

12:9-10 Everyone runs from suffering. Paul wanted to escape as well. He was vulnerable in sharing the sheer **torment** it caused. Surely, all wonder what in the world this "thorn" could have been. Wisely, Paul did not describe the "thorn." Yet, the short sentence, **"My grace is sufficient for you,"** has brought untold strength to generations of Christians. The pain so real in Paul's life has encouraged and sustained many weary believers. How gracious for Paul to share his suffering and the grace of God he experienced with the Corinthians. This selfless service was typical of Paul's life.

Paul was not just being an empathetic pastor. He was also offering the reason and purpose for the pain; Christ's **power is perfected in weakness**. The amazing work of God as seen in creation is a similar element here. God created something out of nothing. In human **weaknesses**, Christ is able to perfect His strength (v. 9). Why would God desire, or even be willing, to partner with such handicapped souls? Great comfort comes from understanding pain as a partnership with God. Suffering is a way to bring God glory. Trials are a way to show Him strong. Heartache is a way to demonstrate His sufficiency. Affliction is a way to experience His nearness. Acceptance is a way to bring Him pleasure. Isn't this life really about Him?

Certainly, Paul lived his life for the Father. This dominating reality gave him complete freedom to boast, even take pleasure, in his "weaknesses" (v. 10). If weakness meant the nearness of Christ, then Paul wanted to be the first to announce his weakness. He loved with such abandon. Paul would suffer anything to experience the nearness and the **power** of Christ (v. 9). The strength that came from Christ was invigorating. Paul was driven by his passion for Christ.

12:11 Paul did what they wanted—he defended his credentials. Even though they knew him well enough to affirm his apostleship, even though they had experienced the miracles of God through his authority, even though they should have been the ones defending his leadership, he accepted the fact that they had not. Paul defended his apostleship, not for his sake, but for the good of the Corinthians. Truth was at stake. The **"super-apostles"** were false, and as a genuine apostle, he had the responsibility to defend the church.

12:12 God used **signs** and **miracles** to authenticate His message and His servants. The book of 1 Corinthians explained how much the people valued the showy gifts. Paul knew the people wanted to be reminded of this fact in regard to his leadership. He reminded them of the truth that the "signs" were given in order to bring God glory, not to bring glory to His creation.

12:13 Paul had spent a great deal of time with this church, almost more than any other church. Other groups might have been jealous of Paul's attention and affection for the Corinthians. This verse is a somewhat sarcastic reminder of the extra attention they received. Even with all this extra attention they received, Paul never accepted any payment or support from them. And yet, this act of sacrifice and service was actually being used against him.

This situation was incredibly ironic, yet sadly many pastors have experienced a similar situation with their respective congregations. Often the flock for which they sacrifice so much turns against them. Paul was certainly sympathetic to those who had been betrayed and rejected. He learned to walk in acceptance and in rejection. He knew how to offer love whether it was returned or denied.

PAUL'S PROPOSED VISIT TO CORINTH (12:14-21)

12:14-18 Amid all the difficulty, Paul still desired to see them, and he needed to be with the Corinthians. He assured them that he was not coming to them for any personal gain nor to **take advantage of** them in any way (v. 17). Surely by this time, they were feeling vulnerable for allowing themselves to be so foolish.

Paul expressed his love. He wanted them, not their money, not their perfection, and not their ability. He wanted them exactly the way they were, imperfections and all. Few people experience love with this all-encompassing acceptance. But Paul offered this selfless love to the Corinthians freely. He had already taught them about this love (1 Co 13); here he acted it out for them.

With thoroughness, Paul addressed yet another concern of his opponents. Since they could not claim that Paul was selfishly seeking money from the church, they attempted to convince many that the collection for the Jerusalem church was a fraud. They wanted people to believe that Paul would take the money for himself. They went so far as to blame the visit of **Titus** and the other **brother** as a **sly** (Gk. *panourgos*, "clever, crafty, treacherous, deceitful," v. 16) cover-up in which the two would take the money and keep it for themselves. In light of the constant suffering Paul endured in behalf of the churches, he must have considered this rumor utterly ridiculous. Yet he asked the Corinthians to consider the integrity of the men he **sent** (v. 18). He also asked them to consider the **spirit** of the men. Paul was certain that those he sent affirmed his message and behaved properly. In fact, he was so confident that he asked the Corinthians to scrutinize their behavior.

12:19 Paul must have been exhausted from such a defense. Although difficult for him, he believed his defense was important and mandated by God. He conveyed the idea that their approval was not nearly as important as the approval **of God**. He had been transparent before God and for the benefit of the people.

Sympathy must be extended to Paul. He openly shared his desire to be loved by the people who had deeply hurt him. He had done immeasurable things for the Corinthians, and he went to great personal and emotional expense to prove himself to them. Although this relationship was important to Paul, their relationship with Christ was more important. Paul's purpose was clear—**building you up** (Gk. *oikodomēs*, "edification"; cp. 5:1; 10:8; 13:10).

12:20-21 While the rebellion against his authority was a problem, Paul realized there were many other problems, which he feared would be ignored. He also feared the difficulty of a hurtful and challenging visit. Paul knew that if the problems were still there upon his arrival, he would be forced to address them; so he must have encouraged the people to deal with these problems on their own. He sounded like an experienced father who invites his child to pick a switch from the tree for the inevitable spanking. The child knows that if he does not pick the right switch, the parent will select one that will deliver a more painful blow.

To avoid any confusion and keep the needed focus, Paul listed the terrible sins he wanted the Corinthians to address. He expressed the **fear** that the church might **again humiliate** him and consequently God might allow more pain. He also expressed the personal grief he felt when his spiritual children sinned and refused to repent. He ached over their depravity and the consequences they would face. He dreaded the confrontation but would not let that deter him from his responsibility. He desired to see them live in purity before the Lord. He was willing to sacrifice his relationship with them if it would strengthen their relationship with the Lord.

PAUL'S BENEDICTION AND CHALLENGE (13:1-13)

The Apostle's Warning (13:1-4)

13:1-2 Paul stressed the importance of this **third** visit by announcing it again. Paul had invested so much in this church, and he would stop at nothing to strengthen and purify it. Their problems were intense and had been addressed on numerous occasions. While the church definitely experienced much growth, it was also filled with problems. Although you can look at the Corinthians judgmentally, many believers can relate to their "two steps forward, one step back" pattern.

Paul wanted them to know that he was serious about their behavior change and he was serious about discipline. He quoted Old Testament passages regarding court practices. The testimony of one witness in court was considered insufficient. **Two or three witnesses** were required for a trial (cp. Dt 17:6; 19:15). If the problems still remained, he would hold court! These issues would not be ignored. Paul let them know that he would not overlook any sin.

CONFIRMED (Gk. *stathēsetai*, "stand") has 47 related words that occur in the Greek New Testament, such as *anistemi* ("raise or stand up") and *anastasis* ("resurrection"). In the narrative portions (Matthew to Acts), *histemi* usually means "stand" in a literal sense, but it can also mean "stand firm or endure." The meaning "stand" gave rise to several figurative meanings including that which is "firm, confirmed, established, appointed, or ordained"; these ideas are the most common ones for *histemi* in the epistles and Revelation.

For Paul, *histemi* most often served as a term for standing by faith (Rm 5:2; 11:20; 14:4; 1 Co 10:12; 15:1; 2 Co 1:24; Eph 6:11,13-14; Col 4:12). In discussing the nature of the law, Paul used *histemi* in teaching that righteousness "upholds" rather than cancels the law, since the law also teaches salvation by faith and not works (Rm 3:31; see Rm 4:1-8). Similarly, Paul referred to those who "establish their own righteousness" as opposed to those who submit to God's righteousness (Rm 10:3)—another contrast between faith and works as the basis of salvation. The word also appears in the LXX, the Greek translation of the Old Testament (Dt 19:15), which Paul quoted to establish a principle for church discipline that he would apply on his next visit.

13:3-4 Paul explained that he was modeling his behavior after the Savior. Jesus is **not weak** but **powerful**. The description of the crucifixion speaks to Christ's determination to set people free from sin. Paul had regularly taught the church the significance of the power of the resurrection. Jesus is alive by power! While the apostles were not perfect like Jesus, they would be strengthened by Jesus. "God's power" would allow them to accomplish their calling, which offered

PROOF (Gk. *dokimēn*, "tried character, a test or trial to prove authenticity," v. 3; cp. 2:9; 8:2; 9:13) of Paul's anointing with that power.

The Apostle's Admonition (13:5-10)

13:5 The question must be addressed: Were these rebellious sinners genuine believers? Paul gave a clear answer. They must honestly **examine** (Gk. *dokimazete*, "test, approve, demonstrate to be genuine"; cp. 8:8,22) their own lives to determine if they are in the faith. In other words, he was looking for evidence. Did the person express love for God, changed behavior, and responsiveness to rebuke? Did he experience the power of the Holy Spirit and the change brought by Jesus? Hopefully, these questions would encourage the believers to repent and seek God in purity because of their great love and gratitude toward Him.

On a less positive note, Paul let them know that some might not be genuine believers. He wanted them to consider what rejection of Christ would mean. He wanted them to become stronger in their convictions and more serious minded regarding their faith and purity. He wanted them to be more grateful for their relationship with Christ.

13:6-9 Paul affirmed his assurance of his relationship with the Lord. He had examined himself. He was not asking them to do anything he had not already done. He expressed the idea that he wanted them **to pass the test** (Gk. *dokimoi*, "approved, genuine, respected, accepted," v. 7; cp. 10:18). He had high hopes for them. He was not a mean and vindictive father but a loving and hopeful father.

Far beyond Paul's desire for vindication was his passion that the Corinthians behave rightly. He held **truth** as the great standard by which all things must be judged (13:8). Paul's life was simplified by the fact that his mind was completely clear and able to focus **only** on the truth. He was not confused by things of lesser worth.

Paul had died to himself. He sought only the pleasure of God. Even if his work with the Corinthians appeared to be a failure and he seemed **weak** and unsuccessful, he could be satisfied if they were **strong** (v. 9). In other words, their success was more important than his reputation.

He prayed for their **maturity** and their independence. A parent spends many years preparing a child to be independent and mature. Paul worked tenaciously for the spiritual maturity of his children, and he let them know he desired the best for them.

13:10 Paul expressed his hope that this maturity would come quickly and that their repentance would be evidenced by their own initiative. He explained that he was writing with **severity** in hopes that as pure hearted, restored believers they could enjoy their visit together. He desired to enjoy them, to grow with them, and to build them up.

A Final Exhortation (13:11-13)

13:11-13 While much of the letter had seemed like great anguish, Paul ended very optimistically. This change in tone must have been a relief to the Corinthians. He encouraged them to take joy in the Lord and experience full restoration. This message must have been needed by those who were convicted. He wanted them to be encouraged and unified. He wanted them to function as a healthy and peaceful church; he believed they could do so. This spiritual health was God's expressed desire and the assurance of His presence.

Paul ended his letter with typical and meaningful closing. Most prominent was his commitment to uplifting the triune God and calling attention to His wonder-

ful attributes and benefits. While it is well-known that the Corinthian church had many weaknesses and struggles, God worked powerfully in their lives and used them significantly. This wonderful truth offers hope for many in a degenerate generation. Paul's third visit with them probably lasted three months. Based on later writings, apparently their relationship was restored, and the church grew in maturity and godliness.

During this visit Paul wrote the book of Romans, which is filled with great spiritual truths, and probably the seminal theological treatise of all time. Martin Luther believed Romans—rich with theological insight, brilliant writing, and masterful logic—was the most important book in the Bible. Since Paul wrote Romans while in Corinth, you can safely assume that the Corinthians heard it first. His most profound doctrinal teachings were probably first given to the church at Corinth while he was writing to the church in Rome.

What a special blessing to the Corinthians and a testament to God's grace. Here the prolific apostle was giving church doctrine and theological truths to perhaps the most unruly group of Christians in the New Testament. In this case God was giving the very best truth to the very worst of the disobedient churches. And yet, this metaphor is fitting for the entire book. Paul spent much of his time defending his apostleship to the once ungodly Corinthians. Some may wonder if this personal defense has any application to the modern Christian. Yet, the testimony of the book itself is that God sent Paul, His faithful servant to a challenging ministry. Thus we can have faith that God often gives His very best to those who understand it the least. He gave His Son for sinners, giving them confidence that even those who are disobedient can repent and experience the riches of God's grace. Believers praise Him because of His grace toward them. Thus, Paul fittingly closes with **the grace of the Lord Jesus Christ, and the love of God, and the fellowship of the Holy Spirit be with all of you**.

Bibliography

Barnett, Paul. *The Message of 2 Corinthians: Power in Weakness.* Downers Grove: Inter-Varsity Press, 1988.

*Calvin, John. *Commentary on the Epistles of Paul the Apostle to the Corinthians.* Grand Rapids: Baker Books, 2003.

Garland, David E. *2 Corinthians.* New American Commentary, vol. 29. Nashville: Broadman and Holman, 1999.

Harris, Murray J. "2 Corinthians." In *The Expositor's Bible Commentary,* vol. 10. Edited by Frank E. Gaebelein. Grand Rapids: Zondervan, 1976.

*Kistemaker, Simon J. *New Testament Commentary: Exposition of the Second Epistle to the Corinthians.* Grand Rapids: Baker Books, 1997.

MacLaren, Alexander. *Expositions of Holy Scripture,* vol. 14. Grand Rapids: Baker Book House, 1974.

Richardson, Alan (ed.). *A Dictionary of Christian Theology.* Philadelphia: The Westminster Press, 1969.

*For advanced study

GALATIANS

Introduction

Title

The book of Galatians derives its title (Gk. *pros Galatas*, "to the Galatians") from the region in Asia Minor (modern Turkey) where the churches addressed were located. Only this epistle from the pen of Paul was specifically addressed to churches in more than one city.

Setting

Paul stated the occasion for writing this passionate letter: He was concerned that the Galatians were deserting the gospel that he had preached to them and turning to another gospel (1:6-7). A group commonly referred to as the "Judaizers" were presenting a gospel based on works of the Law, and Paul decried this "different gospel" as no gospel at all (Gl 1:7).[1] This group was spreading a dangerous teaching that Gentiles must first become Jewish proselytes and submit to all the Mosaic law before they could become Christians (Gl 1:7; 4:17,21; 5:2-12; 6:12-13). Shocked by the Galatians' openness to this dangerous heresy, Paul wrote this letter to defend justification by faith and warn these churches of the dire consequences of abandoning the essential doctrine he had faithfully taught them.

Genre

Galatians follows a typical format for a first-century Greco-Roman epistle, which would include a salutation or greeting, commendation, body, exhortation, and conclusion. However, this Pauline letter is the only one that does not contain a commendation of its readers—an obvious omission reflecting the urgency Paul felt about confronting the defection of the Galatian believers and defending the central doctrine of justification by faith alone.

Author

Galatians is one of the first books written by the Apostle Paul, and his authorship has never been seriously questioned since the book lists Paul (Gk. *Paulos*, "little") as the author (1:1; 5:2). The lengthy autobiographical section (1:1–2:23) lends support to this assumption. The early church fathers uniformly accepted Pauline authorship, which was never seriously questioned until the 1800s.

Date

Chapter 2 describes Paul's visit to the Jerusalem Council outlined in Acts 15 (Gl 2:1; see also the commentary on the Jerusalem Council in Ac 15:1-21), so he must have written Galatians after that event. Since most scholars date the Jerusalem

Council as occurring around AD 49, the most likely date for Galatians is shortly thereafter, sometime in the early 50s.

Recipients

Scholars have debated to whom Paul was referring when he addressed "the churches of Galatia" (1:2). The letter could have been sent to the ethnic Galatians, three Celtic tribes akin to the Gauls, who invaded central Asia Minor in the third century BC (known as the "North Galatian" theory). The other possibility is that the letter was written to the racially mixed inhabitants of the Roman province of Galatia, in which case the name "Galatians" was simply used as a general term to cover them all (known as the "South Galatian" theory). The strongest evidence supports the South Galatian theory and means that the letter was addressed to the churches that Paul founded in the southern area of Galatia (Antioch, Iconium, Lystra, and Derbe; see Ac 13:14–14:23).[2]

Major Theme

The central theme of Galatians is justification by faith. Paul vigorously defended this doctrine first from a theological standpoint in chapters 3–4 and then looked at the practical ramifications in chapters 5–6. Paul was adamant in his defense that keeping the law would not save a person, and he offered Abraham as proof of this fact, declaring that Abraham was saved as a result of his believing faith.

Pronunciation Guide			
Antioch	*AN tih ahk*	Galatians	*guh LAY shuhnz*
Barnabus	*BAHR nuh buhs*	Hagar	*HAY gahr*
Cephas	*SEE fuhs*	Sinai	*SIGH nigh*
Cilicia	*sih LISH ih uh*	Titus	*TIGH tuhs*
Damascus	*duh MASS kuhs*		

Outline

I. PAUL'S INTRODUCTORY GREETING (1:1-5)

II. PAUL'S DEFENSE OF THE GOSPEL (1:6-10)

III. PAUL'S DEFENSE OF HIS APOSTLESHIP (1:11–2:21)
   A. His Conversion and Testimony (1:11-24)
   B. His Message and Witness (2:1-21)

IV. THE DOCTRINE OF JUSTIFICATION THROUGH FAITH ALONE (3:1–4:31)
   A. The Response of the Galatian Christians to the Gospel (3:1-5)
   B. The Example of Abraham (3:6-9)
   C. The Relationship Between the Law and the Promises of God (3:10-26)

D. The Inheritance of Sons and Heirs (3:27–4:7)
E. Paul's Concern for the Galatians (4:8-20)
F. Two Covenants: Sarah Versus Hagar (4:21-31)

V. LIFE IN THE SPIRIT (5:1-26)
   A. The Role of Freedom (5:1-15)
   B. The Spirit Versus the Flesh (5:16-26)

VI. CONCLUDING EXHORTATIONS (6:1-18)
   A. Carrying the Burdens of Others (6:1-5)
   B. Doing Good (6:6-10)
   C. Responding to the Cross of Christ (6:11-18)

Exposition of the Text

On his first missionary journey, Paul traveled through Galatia preaching and establishing churches. Within a very short time, however, a number of prominent Jewish legalists infiltrated the congregation of new believers and began teaching that faith in Christ alone was not enough to make a person right with God. Paul defended the purity of the gospel he had preached to the believers in Galatia.

PAUL'S INTRODUCTORY GREETING (1:1-5)

1:1-2 Paul began his letter by immediately establishing his credentials as **an apostle—not from men or by man, but by Jesus Christ and God the Father who raised Him from the dead**. Paul was in a battle for the very souls of the people in the Galatian churches due to a contaminated gospel that was being proclaimed by a divisive group. To defend his apostleship against the attack of false teachers, Paul emphasized that Christ Himself had appointed him as an apostle before he met the other apostles (see vv. 17-18; Ac 9:3-9). Paul included the phrase "raised Him from the dead" to show that the risen and ascended Christ Himself had selected him; thus Paul was a qualified witness of Christ's resurrection (see Ac 1:22). The phrase **churches of Galatia** refers to the churches Paul founded at Antioch of Pisidia, Iconium, Lystra, and Derbe during his first missionary journey (Ac 13:15–14:23).

1:3-5 Grace to you and peace—even Paul's typical greeting attacked the Judaizers' legalistic system. A salvation by works, as these legalists claimed, was not by **GRACE** (Gk. *charis,* "unmerited favor") and could not result in **PEACE** (Gk. *eirēnē*, "peace" indicating a sense of security due to a relationship with Christ that is unaltered by the circumstances of life). Christ gave Himself for our sins (Gk. *hamartiōn*, "offense, guilt")—no one can avoid sin by human effort or lawkeeping (Rm 3:20). Therefore sins must be forgiven, which Christ accomplished through His atoning death on the cross (Gl 3:13). Christ's death on the cross rescued us from **this present evil age.** AGE (Gk. *aiōnos*, "present order of nature") does not refer in this context to a period of time but to an order or system and, in particular, to the current world system ruled by Satan (Rm 12:2; 1 Jn 2:15-16; 5:19). Paul pointed out that Christ's sacrifice on the cross was **the will of our God and Father**; this act was designed and fulfilled for God's glory (see Mt 26:42; Jn 6:38-40).

PAUL'S DEFENSE OF THE GOSPEL (1:6-10)

1:6-8 Paul was amazed that the Galatians were so quickly TURNING AWAY (Gk. *metatithesthe*, "turn away or desert"). This same word described military desertion, which was punishable by death. Paul's use of this word indicated that the Galatian believers were voluntarily abandoning grace to pursue the legalism taught by the false teachers. God's call to the Galatian believers was His effectual call to salvation. **The grace of Christ** refers to God's free and sovereign act of mercy in granting salvation through the death and resurrection of Christ—totally apart from any human work or merit. The "DIFFERENT (Gk. *heteron*, "another of a different kind," v. 6) gospel" to which the Galatians were turning was the Judaizers' perversion of the true gospel, "ANOTHER (Gk. *allo*, "some other of

the same kind," v. 7) gospel." This group added the requirements, ceremonies, and standards of the old covenant as necessary prerequisites to salvation. Paul warned that to bind salvation to Mosaic law demanded more than justification by faith alone and was thus **a different gospel**. The genuine gospel must remain unchanged—the same forever.

TROUBLING (Gk. *tarassontes*, "unsettling, frightening") could be understood as "disturbing," and suggests "shaking back and forth, agitating, or stirring up" (v. 7). Here it referred to the deep emotional disturbance that the Galatian believers experienced at the hands of the Judaizers. CHANGE (Gk. *metastrepsai*, "alter") can be translated "pervert," i.e., turning something into its opposite (v. 7). By adding the law to the gospel of Christ, the false teachers were effectively destroying grace, turning the message of God's undeserved favor toward sinners into the opposite idea of earned and merited favor.

Paul made a hypothetical point when he stated that **if we or an angel from heaven** preached another gospel; he was calling out the most unlikely example for false teaching—Paul himself and holy angels (v. 8). The Galatians should receive no messenger, regardless of how impeccable his credentials, if his doctrine of salvation differed in the slightest degree from God's truth. The phrase "A CURSE (Gk. *anathema*, "a devoted thing" but usually in a bad sense, transliterated into English as "anathema") be on him" referred to devoting someone to destruction in eternal hell (v. 8; see Rm 9:3; 1 Co 12:3; 16:22). False teachers were often given this fate in the New Testament (Mt 24:24; Jn 8:44; 1 Tm 1:20; Ti 1:16).

1:9-10 As we have said before referred to what Paul taught during an earlier visit to these churches, not to a previous comment in this letter. Paul turned from the hypothetical case, the preaching of a false gospel by him or by heavenly angels, to the real situation faced by the Galatians. The Judaizers were doing just that and were to be devoted to destruction because of their damning heresy. Paul concluded this section with two questions that can be summed up by asking, "Who is Paul trying **to please**?" The answer was clear— only God. He admitted that he had tried to please men, but now Paul was **a slave** (Gk. *doulos*, "servant") **of Christ**. Paul had become a willing slave of Christ, which cost him a great deal of suffering from others (6:17). Such personal sacrifice was the exact opposite of the goal of trying to pleasing men (6:12).

PAUL'S DEFENSE OF HIS APOSTLESHIP (1:11–2:21)

His Conversion and Testimony (1:11-24)

1:11-12 In Paul's statement **I want you to know** (Gk. *gnōrizō*, "make known, reveal"), he used a strong verb, which often introduced an important and emphatic statement. **The gospel** Paul **preached** was **not based on a human point of view** (v. 11), or it would have been like all other human religions, permeated with a works' righteousness that was born of human pride and Satan's deception. In contrast to the Judaizers, who received their religious instruction from rabbinic tradition, Paul stated, "I **did not receive it from a human source and I was not taught it**" (v. 12). Most Jews did not study the actual Scriptures; instead, they used human interpretations of Scripture as their religious authority and guide. Many of their traditions were not taught in Scripture and even contradicted God's word. Paul's gospel **came by a revelation from Jesus Christ**, a reference to the unveiling of Christ before Paul

on the Damascus road where he received the truth of the gospel (v. 12; see Ac 9:1-16).

1:13-17 Paul then began to discuss his life before Christ. **Judaism** refers to the Jewish religious system of works' righteousness, based not primarily on the Old Testament but on rabbinic interpretations and traditions. In fact, Paul later argued that a proper understanding of the Old Testament can lead only to Christ and His gospel of grace through faith (3:6-29). Paul had PERSECUTED (Gk. *eporthoun*, "try to destroy, annihilate") God's church. The tense of this Greek verb emphasizes Paul's persistent and continual effort to hurt and ultimately to exterminate Christians (1:13). Not only did he persecute **God's church**, but he also **advanced in Judaism beyond many contemporaries** of his people (v. 14). ADVANCED (Gk. *proekopton*, "progress, go forward") suggests "chopping ahead," much like one would blaze a trail through a forest. Paul blazed his path in Judaism (see Php 3:5-6); and because he saw Jewish Christians as obstacles to his advancement, he worked to cut them down. The phrase **traditions of my ancestors** refers to the oral teachings about Old Testament law commonly known as "Halakah" (Gl 1:14). This collection of interpretations of the law eventually carried the same or even greater authority than the Law (the *Torah*) itself; its regulations were so hopelessly complex and burdensome that even the most astute rabbinical scholars could not master its contents either by interpretation or conduct.

Paul recognized God's sovereignty in his life because he was separated **from my mother's womb . . . and called . . . by His grace** (v. 15). God gave him the life, light, and faith to believe in Him and gave him a calling or vocation that he **preach** Christ **among the Gentiles** (v. 16). Paul did not look to Ananias or other Christians in Damascus for clarification of or addition to the revelation he received from Christ. Rather than immediately traveling **to Jerusalem** to be instructed by the **apostles**, Paul instead went to Nabatean **Arabia**, a wilderness that stretched east of Damascus down to the Sinai Peninsula. After being prepared for ministry by the Lord, he returned to minister in nearby **Damascus** (v. 17). Paul considered the establishing of his validity as an apostle important. Undoubtedly, he was concerned that the false teachers would try to cast doubt on his apostleship, thereby causing the Galatian believers to call into question the message they heard from him. Paul was determined to convince the Galatians that he, and not the Judaizers, preached the true gospel.

1:18-24 The time from Paul's conversion to his first journey **to Jerusalem** extended approximately **three years** (v. 18). During those years he made a visit to Damascus (Ac 9:26-30) and resided in Arabia, under the instruction of the Lord. Paul went "up to Jerusalem" (Gl 1:18); travelers in Israel always spoke of going up to Jerusalem because of its higher elevation. Paul went to Jerusalem **to get to know Cephas,** otherwise known as Peter, the apostle who was the personal companion of the Lord and the most powerful spokesman in the early years of the Jerusalem church (Ac 1–12). Paul wrote **I'm not lying**, and the directness of this statement indicated that he had been accused by the Jewish legalists of being a shameless or deluded liar (Gl 1:20). After going to Jerusalem, Paul **went to the regions of Syria and Cilicia** (v. 21). He preached in that region, including his hometown of Tarsus, for several years. When word reached Jerusalem of revival in that area, they sent Barnabas to investigate (Ac 11:20-26). Paul stayed as a pastor of the church at Antioch. Then, with Barnabas,

he went from there on his first missionary journey (Ac 13:1-3) and, afterward, returned to Antioch. From there they were sent to the Jerusalem Council (Ac 14:26–15:22).

His Message and Witness (2:1-21)

2:1-5 After 14 years referred to the period from the time of his first visit to Jerusalem to the meeting of the Jerusalem Council, which was called to resolve the issue of how Gentiles were saved (v. 1; see Ac 15:1-22). Linguistically, the word AGAIN (Gk. *palin*, suggesting "repetition or continuation") need not refer to the next chronological visit but can just as easily mean "once again" without respect to how many visits took place in between. Paul did, in fact, visit Jerusalem during that 14-year period to deliver famine relief to the church there (see Ac 11:27-30), but he does not refer to that visit here since it has no bearing upon his apostolic authority.

Barnabas was Paul's first ally who vouched for him before the apostles at Jerusalem and who became Paul's traveling companion (Gl 2:1). **Titus** was a spiritual child of Paul and a coworker (v. 3; Ti 1:4-5); as an uncircumcised Gentile, Titus was fitting proof of the effectiveness of Paul's ministry.

Paul went to Jerusalem **because of a revelation** (Gl 2:2). This revelation from God was the voice of the Holy Spirit. Paul referred to the divine commissioning of his visit in order to refute any suggestion by the Judaizers that they had sent Paul to Jerusalem to have the apostles correct his doctrine. He stated that not even Titus **was compelled to be circumcised** (v. 3). At the core of the Judaizers' system of works was the Mosaic prescription of circumcision. They were teaching that there could be no salvation without circumcision. Paul and the apostles denied that assertion, and it was settled at the Jerusalem Council. The **false brothers** are the Judaizers, who pretended to be true Christians; yet their doctrine, because it claimed allegiance to Christ, was opposed to traditional Judaism, and, by demanding circumcision and obedience to the Mosaic law as the prerequisite for salvation, it was also opposed to Christianity (v. 4). TO SPY ON (Gk. *kataskopēsai*, "lie in wait for") comes from a word that pictures spies or traitors entering by stealth into an enemy's camp (v. 4). The Judaizers were Satan's undercover agents sent into the midst of the church to sabotage the true gospel.

2:6-10 Paul described his meeting with **those recognized as important**, referring to James and Peter and John, using a device known as anacoluthon in which he began a thought and then interrupted himself, causing a break in grammatical sequence (v. 6). He said that those three apostles (whose names are listed in v. 9) did not add anything to the gospel he preached. In this interruption in verse 6, Paul used a Greek word (*prosōpon*, "face, countenance"), which referred to a person's appearance physically in some instances but is more accurately translated in this verse as a person's status, conveying the idea that it did not matter if Peter and John were apostles and James was the Lord's brother. The status of these men did not give them special consideration. However, Paul added that even if a person were to give special credence to Peter and James and John, these men also recognized his apostolic authority and validated his mission to the Gentiles.

Paul called James and Peter and John PILLARS (Gk. *stuloi*, "columns," v. 9). The use of this word could be a carry over from the concept of the patriarchs as found in Judaism. Also, the naming of James first may appear odd, but Paul might have named him first because

James at that time was considered a leader in ecclesiastical matters. This section concluded with the apostles asking Paul to **remember the poor**, which may signify their desire for Paul not to forget the Jerusalem church as he fulfilled his mission **to the Gentiles** (v. 10).

2:11-21 Antioch was the location of the first Gentile church (v. 11). Paul **opposed** Peter because he was guilty of sin by aligning himself with men he knew to be in error and because of the harm and confusion he caused his Gentile brethren. Peter, knowing the decision of the Jerusalem Council, had been in Antioch for some time eating with Gentiles. When Judaizers came, pretending to be sent by James, they lied, giving false claims of support from the apostles. Peter had already given up all Mosaic ceremony (Ac 10:9-22), and James had, at times, held only to some of it (Ac 21:18-26). Peter's withdrawal was gradual and deceptive. To eat with Judaizers and decline invitations **to eat with the Gentiles**, which he had previously done, meant that Peter was affirming the very dietary restrictions he knew God had abolished. Thus he was striking a blow to the gospel of grace. The rest of the Jewish believers at Antioch joined Peter's HYPOCRISY (Gk. *hupokrisei*, "pretense, outward show," anglicized as "hypocrisy"). The word referred to an actor who would wear a mask to depict a mood or certain character. In the spiritual sense, it referred to someone who masked his true character by pretending to be something he was not (v. 13).

Keeping **the works of the law** was not a means of salvation because the root of sinfulness is in the fallenness of a person's heart, not his actions (v. 16). The law served as a mirror to reveal sin, not a cure for it. If the Judaizers' doctrine was correct, then Paul, Peter, Barnabas, and the other Jewish believers had fallen back into the category of sinners because they had been eating and fellowshipping with Gentiles, who, according to the Judaizers, were unclean. **Those things that I** [Paul] **tore down** alluded to the false system of salvation through legalism, abolished by the preaching of salvation by grace alone through faith alone (v. 18). Paul and the Galatian believers had **died to the law** (v. 19). When a person was convicted of a capital crime and executed, the law had no further claim on that person. So with the Christian who has died in Christ and risen to new life in Him, justice has been satisfied and the believer is forever free from any further penalty. Paul proclaimed that he had **been crucified with Christ . . . Christ lives in** him (v. 19). A person who trusts in Christ for salvation spiritually participates with the Lord in His crucifixion and receives victory over sin and death. The believer's old self is dead, having been crucified with Christ (Rm 6:3). The believer's new person has the privilege of the indwelling Holy Spirit empowering him and living through him.

Heart to Heart:
Identifying with Christ

When Paul spoke of ethical Christian conduct and relationships, he often held himself up as a role model, saying "imitate me" (e.g., Gl 4:12; Php 3:17; 2 Th 3:8-10). Role models, godly women with behavior worthy of emulation, are important to the believer who desires to glorify God in her life. Imitating the behavior of another can be difficult, if not impossible, for the woman who struggles with difficult relationships, hormonal mood swings, or circumstances beyond her control.

Paul gives a life strategy that goes well beyond imitation—one that is much more effective. He boldly proclaims, "I have been crucified with Christ; and I no longer live, but Christ lives in me" (Gl 2:19-20).

Paul let go of all he was and all he owned, in order to identify with Christ. He released the fantasy that he was somehow good or worthy in and of himself; he saw himself through God's eyes. He let go of his right to live his life his own way in order that Christ might live in him. When he let go, he was able to take hold of something much better—the life lived in faith in the Son of God.

When a believer identifies with Christ in His crucifixion, the cross event becomes more than a work Christ did for her. It becomes something He accomplishes in her. Although she must continue to deal with the circumstances of day-to-day living in the flesh, she lives a different sort of life. She lives a surrendered life, a victorious life, a righteous life.

THE DOCTRINE OF JUSTIFICATION THROUGH FAITH ALONE (3:1–4:31)

The Response of the Galatian Christians to the Gospel (3:1-5)

3:1-5 This section follows directly after Paul's declaration that Jews and Gentiles are saved by the same means, which is faith in the Lord Jesus. Chapter 3 begins with Paul's appeal to the Galatians' experience as proof of their salvation by faith and not by keeping works of the law. He asked the Galatians a rhetorical question—**Who has hypnotized you, before whose eyes Jesus Christ was vividly portrayed as crucified?** (v. 1). Paul used the present verb **want** (Gk. *thelō*, "exercise the will, be inclined or disposed"), followed by the infinitive **to learn** (Gk. *mathein*, "find out") to introduce the second rhetorical question of this section—**Did you receive the Spirit by the works of the law or by hearing with faith?** (v. 2). Paul was not questioning whether or not the Galatians did receive the Spirit; he was simply questioning how they received the Spirit.

Paul repeated the word **foolish** (Gk. *anoētoi*, "unintelligent," see also 3:1), showing how strong an appeal he was making to the Galatian believers. He was incredulous at how easily they had been duped. **After beginning in the Spirit . . . by the flesh**—the notion that sinful, weak, fallen human nature could improve on the saving work of the Holy Spirit was ludicrous to Paul. Paul used the word SUFFER (Gk. *epathete*, "afflict" with its derivative anglicized as "pathos") to describe the Galatians' personal experience of salvation in Jesus Christ (v. 4). The Greek word has the basic nuance of "experienced" and does not necessarily imply pain or hardship but can connote "passion or emotion."

The Example of Abraham (3:6-9)

3:6-9 Paul moved to an example of Abraham who was justified by faith alone (see Gn 15:6). The phrase **Abraham's sons** refers to the truth that believing Jews and Gentiles are the true spiritual children of Abraham because they follow his example of faith (Gl 3:7). The phrase **Scripture foresaw** is a personification of Scripture and a common Jewish figure of speech (v. 8). Because Scripture is God's word, when it speaks, God speaks.

The good news to Abraham was the news of salvation for **all the nations**. Salvation has always been by faith. So those who are of faith, whether Jew or Gentile, are blessed as Abraham. The Old Testament predicted that Gentiles would receive the blessings of justification by faith, as did Abraham; those blessings are poured out on all because of Christ.

The Relationship Between the Law and the Promises of God (3:10-26)

3:10-14 Those people who try to **rely on the works of the law** to be saved **are under a curse** (v. 10). Paul quoted from Deuteronomy 27:26 to show that failure to keep the law perfectly brings divine judgment and condemnation; one violation of the law deserves the curse of God. The curse cannot simply be abolished, but redemption can be made as Christ becomes the substitutionary recipient of the curse (see Dt 21:23). **No one** can keep all the commands of the law (Jms 2:10). Paul then quoted Habakkuk 2:4 to show that justification is by faith alone. Justification by faith and justification by keeping the law are mutually exclusive, as Paul's Old Testament quote from Leviticus 18:5 proved (Gl 3:12). REDEEMED (Gk. *exēgorasen*, "buy") was often used to speak of purchasing the freedom of a slave or debtor (v. 13). Christ's death, because it was a death of substitution for sin, satisfied God's justice and exhausted His wrath, so that Christ actually purchased believers, delivering them from slavery to sin and from the sentence of eternal death. By bearing God's wrath for the sins of believers, Christ took upon Himself on the cross the curse pronounced on those who violated the law.

3:15-18 Brothers, a term of endearment, revealed Paul's compassionate love for the Galatians, which they may have begun to question in light of his stern rebuke (v. 15). Paul then gave the Galatians an example of human covenants, which once confirmed are considered unchangeable. How much more irrevocable a covenant made by an unchanging God. The concept of SEED (Gk. *spermati*, "semen, progeny, posterity," transliterated into English as "sperm") finds its roots in the Old Testament (vv. 16,19; see also Gn 12:7; 13:15; 17:8; 24:7). The singular form of the Greek word, as its English and Hebrew counterparts, can be used in a collective sense in reference to a group, or in this case, to successive generations. Paul's point was that in some Old Testament passages **seed** referred to the greatest of Abraham's descendants, Jesus Christ; but it could also be a reference to Abraham's descendants. **The promises** were those associated with the Abrahamic covenant (Gl 3:16). Because these promises were made both to Abraham and to his descendants, they did not become void when Abraham died or when the law came. The time frame of **430 years** extended from Israel's sojourn in Egypt to the giving of the law at Sinai (1445 BC). The law actually came 645 years after the initial promise to Abraham, but the promise was repeated to Isaac and later to Jacob. The last known reaffirmation of the Abrahamic covenant was made to Jacob (Gn 46:2-4) just before he went to Egypt—430 years before the Mosaic law was given. Paul used the length of sojourn in Egypt as recorded in Exodus 12:40. The number is rounded off to 400 years elsewhere (Gn 15:13; Ac 7:6).

Law and Grace[3]			
The Function		**The Effect**	
Of Law	**Of Grace**	**Of Law**	**Of Grace**
Depends upon works alone (3:10)	Depends upon exercising faith (3:11-12)	Places all under a curse (3:10)	Justifies by faith (3:3,24)
Confines and imprisons (3:23; 4:2)	Confirms position in Christ (3:24)	Imprisons until faith comes (3:24)	Offers life within (2:20)
Functions as a guardian (3:24)	Certifies freedom (4:30-31)	Points the way to Christ (3:24)	Assures adoption as heirs (4:7)
The law precedes Christ and points to Him. It could not be abrogated but was fulfilled by Christ.			

3:19-22 The law **was added because of transgressions until the Seed to whom the promise was made would come** (v. 19). Paul's persuasive argument that the promise was superior to the law raises an obvious question: What was the purpose of the law? Paul answered that the law revealed the utter sinfulness of every man and woman, its inability in itself to save, and the desperate need for a Savior—the law was never intended to be the way of salvation. The Bible notes that **through**

angels the law **was ordered** (see Heb 2:2), but the precise role the "angels" played is not explained (Gl 3:19). The **mediator** was required when more than one party was involved, but God alone ratified the covenant with Abraham (v. 20).

Paul used the strongest Greek negative **absolutely not** *(mē genoito)* to dismiss with scorn the idea that the law and the promise were at opposite purposes (v. 21). Since God gave them both and does not work against Himself, law and promise work in harmony; the law reveals the sinfulness of men and women and the need for the salvation freely offered in the promise. If the law could have provided righteousness and eternal life, there would be no gracious promise. "But the Scripture had **IMPRISONED** (Gk. *sunekleisen*, "confine, catch") everything under sin's power" suggesting the idea of "enclosing on all sides" (v. 22). Paul portrayed all humankind as hopelessly trapped in sin like a school of fish caught in a net; the express teaching of Scripture is that all people are sinners (Is 53:6; Rm 3:23).

3:23-24 "Before this faith came" is a subordinate clause set off in the Greek text by the conjunction *de* ("but") and thus establishing a time period (v. 23). The *de* is not fully adversative and so continued the subject of the Law in relation to faith by explaining a person's condition before faith; the very explanation, however, included a contrast. The faith referenced in this verse is the faith discussed in verse 22.

The use of *pistin* in these verses (vv. 22,23,25) links together its extreme senses, passing from the one to the other, (1) Faith, the subjective state of the Christian,

(2) *The* faith, the Gospel, the objective teaching, the system of which 'faith' is the leading feature.[4]

The second meaning is most appropriate for "this faith" in verse 23.

The imagery of imprisonment is present in the first verb **CONFINED** (Gk. *ephrouroumetha*, "hold in custody, protect, keep"). The second verb **IMPRISONED** (Gk. *sugkleiomenoi*, "enclose, catch") adds to the emphasis representing the law as a jailer or guardian under whose custody the people were placed (v. 23). The Greek phrase *hupo nomon* ("under the law") is unique to Pauline writing, and the anarthrous (appearing without the article "the") use of law in verse 23 distinguishes it from "the law" referred to in verse 24, which can be understood as "the general principle of the law." The law, when activated by its verb, takes on a positive role by providing a protective custody or serving a supervisory function to those under its custody.

GUARDIAN (Gk. *paidagōgos*, "attendant, custodian, guide") presented some challenges in translation. "Tutor" in the sense of a guide or guardian for young boys is another option, and Thayer traces the use of the word among the Greeks and Romans:

Among the Greeks and Romans the name was applied to trustworthy slaves who were charged with the duty of supervising the life and morals of boys belonging to the better class. The boys were not allowed so much as to step out of the house without them [the *paidagōgos*] before arriving at the age of manhood.... The name carries with it an idea of severity (as of stern censor and enforcer of morals) in 1 Co. iv. 15, where the father is distinguished from the tutor as one whose discipline is usually milder, and in Gal. iii 24sq. where the Mosaic law is likened to a tutor because it arouses the consciousness of sin, and is called *paidagōgos eis christon*, i.e., preparing the soul for Christ, because those who have learned by experience with the law that they are not and cannot be commended to God by their works, welcome the more eagerly the hope of salvation offered them through the death and resurrection of Christ, the Son of God.[5]

The *paidagōgos* was entrusted with a supervisory role that involved protecting, guarding, instructing, correction, and rebuke; he was given care over activities ranging from overseeing good hygiene to overseeing the studies of the child in his charge from his infancy to puberty. Many commentators are quick to point out that the role of the *paidagōgos* was not limited to, or even primarily focused on, formal education. It is an overstatement to consider the *paidagōgos* as a harsh warden or prison guard and an understatement to dismiss him as nothing more than a babysitter. Maybe "custodian" or "supervisory guardian" is the best translation. Jerome said that "The custodian guards another person's son and will depart from him when the lawful time of inheritance arrives."[6]

The purpose for having a custodian or **guardian** until Christ came was delineated with the clause **so that we could be justified by faith** (v. 24). The aorist passive verb "justified" (Gk. *dikaiōthōmen*, "make or render right or just, to be acquit-

ted, to be cleansed") conveyed a forensic sense and brings to mind a picture of a judge who declares Christians as righteous when they accept Christ. Christ's death on the cross accomplished an open and shut case for any person willing to accept Him as Lord and Savior. The law was given to show men and women their need of a Savior.

3:25-26 Verse 25 acts as a transition or bridge between the imagery of life under the guardianship or protective custody of the *paidagōgos* and the life lived under the faith. This faith in the Lord Jesus Christ is the long awaited fulfillment of the promised inheritance. Since **faith** (Gk. *tēs pisteōs*) is preceded by the article in the Greek text, the idea is not some abstract concept but a concrete image that is in contrast to the life under the law. In the words of Chrysostom:

> Now if the law was a custodian and we were confined under its direction, it was not opposed to grace but cooperated with it. But if it continues to bind us after grace has come then it is opposed to grace. . . . Those who maintain their custody at this point are the ones who bring the child into the greatest disrepute. The custodian makes the child ridiculous when he keeps him close at hand even after the time has come for his departure.[7]

Verse 25 signaled a "changing of the guards" and further draws attention to the different gospel that the Judaizers were proclaiming as a false gospel because they were trying to hold onto the vestiges of the life lived under the law, when clearly that time had past.

Notice the shift from the first person plural to the second person in verse 26. Paul simply wanted to address the Galatians directly, and for the first time since

3:1-5, he does so. The conjunction **for** (Gk. *gar*) is used in an explanatory and continuative sense, and it makes an appearance in the following two verses to signal three "sayings." This conjunction indicates the continuity of Paul's thought and gives structure to the verses. Verse 26 explains verse 25 and answers the question of why the people are no longer under a guardian—because they are now sons of God through faith in Jesus Christ.

All is emphatic by being placed at the beginning of the phrase in the Greek text, underscoring that Jews and Gentiles together have been admitted to a new spiritual status as equal partners **in Christ Jesus**, a favorite phrase of Paul, which he used to express the most intimate relationship imaginable while being careful not to destroy the identity of the Christian or of Christ.

The Inheritance of Sons and Heirs (3:27–4:7)

3:27-29 Verses 27 and 28 may have been a part of a confessional statement used during the baptismal rite. While this cannot be proven, the reference to baptism in verse 27 is enigmatic. The verb **have been baptized** (Gk. *ebaptisthēte*) is the only reference to baptism in Galatians and may refer either to actual water baptism or to a metaphor representing what it means to be "in Christ." If one assumes that the Galatian believers would take this reference to be actual water baptism (see also 1 Co 1:13), the difficult question arises: Does Paul attach soteriological significance to baptism? While some may want to argue this position, to understand baptism by metonymy (a figure of speech in which the part represents the whole) is far more consistent with the entirety of Scripture. In this case, the part (i.e., baptism) represents the whole conversion experience. Even though the ordinance of baptism and the act of justification are not one in the same, they were so closely related in the early church that one would not think of baptism without understanding that justification had already taken place.

The verb **PUT ON** (Gk. *enedusasthe*, "dress, wear") may also be understood as "clothed with" and acts as a metaphor for what occurs when a person is no longer under the law and has been accepted in Christ. This word may suggest "becoming so possessed of the mind of Christ in thought, feeling, and action as resembling Him and even reproducing the life He lived." This verb, having a personal object, expresses the idea of taking on the character or standing of its object. The imagery of being "clothed" points to Old Testament precedents (see Ps 132:9; Is 61:10, in which the verb used in the Septuagint, the Greek translation of the Old Testament, is the same verb found in Gl 3:27). Being "clothed" in the sense of taking on the characteristics or standing of an object is a Jewish concept and thus the most plausible explanation for the metaphor used in verse 27.

In verse 28, **there is** (Gk. *eni*), the emphatic form of the verb, is used to introduce each of the couplets. The origin of these three couplets has been a matter of considerable debate. One option is to understand these phrases as a direct attack against the Jewish prayer:

> Blessed art thou who hast not made me a Gentile,
> Blessed art thou who hast not made me an uneducated man,
> Blessed are thou who hast not made me a woman.

Another option is to understand these couplets as a baptismal formula that Paul cited because he was concerned only with the first pairing of Jew and Gentile. However, if one examines the other occurrences of "baptismal formulas" in

1 Corinthians and Colossians, there are differences among the examples. Another option is seeing Galatians 3:28 as directly related to distinguishing how a person "got in" under the old covenant versus the new covenant (Gn 17:9-14). Whatever your interpretation of this verse, the couplets together must be interpreted in light of the reason given for their negation, i.e., **you are all one in Christ**.

What does it mean to be "one in Christ"? Augustine wrote:

> Difference of race or condition or sex is indeed taken away by the unity of faith, but it remains embedded in our moral interactions, and in the journey of this life the apostles themselves teach that it is to be respected. For we observe in the unity of faith that there are no such distinctions. Yet within the orders of this life they persist.[8]

The word "one" does not appear in the Greek text; rather "all" (Gk. *pantes*) is the word of inclusion, and its lexical meanings do not include "equal." The idea is unity in contrast to diversity—the common ground shared in Christ. Unity or oneness does not mean uniformity. Oneness does not mean equal in an unqualified sense; it usually connects different things that have something in common. In this case, what the Jew/Gentile, slave/free, and male/female have in common is a shared spiritual status before the Lord. Within God's household, all are in Christ. What it means to be one in Christ is that all people no matter what their race, gender, or status are equal at the foot of the cross and enter into a relationship with God in the same way, unlike the requirements found in the circumcision covenant.

Verse 29 serves as a concluding statement in which Paul moved from speaking about the relationship between the life lived "under law" and the new life of faith lived "in Christ" (3:23-29) to the status of an heir (4:1-7). The first class conditional construction of this sentence in the Greek text assumes the truth of the statement following the "if." When Paul stated **if you are Christ's**, he was not calling into question whether or not the Galatians were true believers. Perhaps this phrase is better understood as "since you are of Christ."

One becomes a seed of Abraham and an heir to the promise by belonging to Christ and not by keeping the works of the law. Jerome comments that being called Abraham's offspring must be understood as spiritual offspring whereby a person "believes in Christ and assumes the dignity of Abraham's race, to whom the promise was made."[9]

Excursus: The Context of Galatians 3:28

Galatians 3:28 is one of the most debated verses concerning the roles of women. In order to properly understand this verse, a person must consider its context within the book of Galatians. Four observations support the theory that Galatians 3:28 is found in the midst of a discussion on the progression of salvation-history:

- *Paul utilized temporal, salvific-historical references in discussing the specific situation in the Galatian churches (3:8,17,19,22,23,25; 4:2-4).*

- *Paul used terms such as promise, heir/inheritance, blessed/blessing, and covenant, indicating that he considered salvation history important to the discussion at hand.*

- *Paul alluded to the fulfillment of at least three events that were associated with the arrival of the new covenant: (1) the promise God would "pour out my spirit on all the people" (Gl 4:4-6; see Jl 2:28); (2) the promise that Gentiles would be included in the new covenant (Gl 3:26-29; see Gn 12:3); and (3) the promised inheritance, which Paul affirmed for those who are "in Christ" (Gl 3:29; 4:7; see Is 58:13-14; Jr 12:14-15).*

- *Christ's death and resurrection are presented as the "means" by which the promise was accomplished (see Gl 3:14; 4:4-5).[10] Christ is presented as redeeming the people "so that" they could receive the promised blessing and the privileges of sonship.*

Why is it so important to establish Galatians 3–4 in terms of salvation history? Just consider how interpretations of the statement in Galatians 3:28 have been used by scholars to support very different theological positions:

> *Galatians 3:28 is not intended to address the social evils that can exist between opposing sides of each of the three contrasting pairs. Paul's point is not the oppressive relationship that can exist between male and female. His point is that in the promised inheritance there is no distinction between male and female. How male and female relate to each other after salvation is not the issue here.[11]*

In other words, the text and context place this verse in the framework of soteriology or the doctrine of salvation. Paul was discussing the nature of salvation and not the proper social relationships of men and women in or out of the church and home. On the other hand, egalitarian commentators espouse a completely different interpretation:

> *He [Paul] is concerned with practical church life in which men and women like Jews and Gentiles, slaves and free persons are here and now fellow-members. It is not their distinctiveness, but their inequality of religious role, that is abolished "in Christ Jesus."[12]*

The interpretation of this passage cannot be divorced from its context, and so the argument for the salvation history context of chapters 3 and 4 is important in the interpretation and application of the passage. In summary, one verse of Scripture, in the view of its author, cannot represent two different and diametrically opposite viewpoints. The key to its interpretation must be found in the author's intent, and one must be cautious about imposing contemporary situations and agendas about the nature of equality upon selected texts in the Bible. In the modern era the emotion-laden issues such as authority patterns in marriage and role interchangeability in the church do have biblical texts that speak explicitly and pointedly to the matter of authority in each relationship. Galatians 3:28 is not such a text, but this verse within its salvific context does address equality:

- *All in Christ are equally justified (v. 24).*

- *All in Christ are equally free from the bondage of legalism (v. 25).*

- *All in Christ are equally children of God (v. 26).*

- *All in Christ are clothed in Christ (v. 27).*

- *All in Christ are equally possessed by Christ (v. 29).*

- *All in Christ are equally heirs of the promises of Abraham (v. 29).*

The equality and unity found in Christ transcends all racial, ethnic, social, and sexual distinctions.

In verse 28 the recipients "who are all one in Christ Jesus" are described vividly as:

- *Jew or Greek,*

- *slave or free,*

- *male or female.*

Paul's assertion does not obliterate social or role distinctions. Rather the impartial nature of God's love is affirmed in salvation (Ac 10:34-35). Fully equal before God, women and men receive the same grace, must adhere to the same obedience, and experience the same blessing of being recipients of spiritual gifts and blessings. They are equal in worth but have received different assignments in the divine economy fashioned within the God-designed creation order.

4:1-7 This passage is the culmination of Paul's argument concerning who is a genuine son and heir of God (3:21). In verses 1-2, Paul referred again to the concept of guardianship for an **heir** (Gk. *klēronomos*, usually denoted a son who represented his father and assumed his responsibilities and duties). In the ancient world, parents would entrust the care of their children to **guardians and stewards** until a set time or fixed day when their children entered adulthood. So too, Christ **came** into the world at a set, fixed time determined by the Father. "Came" (an aorist verb in Greek) points to **the completion of time**, a specific point in time, when God **sent** His Son. Paul gives two reasons why God sent His Son (v. 5):

- He could **redeem those under the law** (see word study on "redeemed" in Gl 3:13).

- They might **receive adoption as sons**.

ADOPTION (Gk. *huithesian*, a term used only by Paul in the New Testament, Gl 4:5; see Rm 8:15,23; 9:4; Eph 1:5) refers to how God takes both Jews and Gentiles into His spiritual family. The person who is adopted into God's family receives all the rights, privileges, and responsibilities afforded to Christ. This adoption is not based on merit; it is always dependent on God's grace. Here in Galatians, the receiving of sonship through adoption occurs simultaneously as a person is freed from the law.

Paul's Concern for the Galatians (4:8-20)

4:8-11 When you didn't know God refers to the time before a person comes to saving faith in Christ. Paul referred to the worship of idols because of the Greco-Roman pantheon of nonexistent deities the Galatians could have worshiped before their conversion (v. 8). You can know God only because He first knew you, just as you choose Him only because He first chose you (Jn 6:44). On the Jewish religious calendar the Galatians observed the **special days** marking the rituals, ceremonies, and festivals that God had given to Israel; but these were never required for the church. Paul warned the Galatians, as he did the Colossians, against legalistically observing them as if they were required by God or could earn favor with Him (Gl 4:10-11; see Col 2:16). Paul feared that his effort in establishing and building the Galatian churches might prove to be futile if they fell back into legalism.

4:12-20 Paul changed his approach drastically as he moved from purely doctrinal argumentation to personal pleading, and these verses contain stronger words of affection than found in any of Paul's letters. He was not so much preaching or teaching as he was simply pouring out his heart in personal exhortation. He wrote, in effect, "I care about you more than I can say. I love you dearly just as you have loved me. Please listen to what I'm saying, because it is vitally essential." He appealed to them, fondly remembering their loving acceptance of him; he warned them about the ulterior motives of the Judaizers and told them of his desire to be with them again in person.

Paul had been a proud, self-righteous Pharisee, trusting in his own righteousness to save him. But when he came to Christ, he abandoned all efforts to save himself, trusting wholly in God's grace. He urged the Galatians to follow his example and avoid the legalism of the Judaizers. Though the Jews had persecuted him during his first trip to Galatia, the Galatian believers had not harmed Paul but had enthusiastically received him when he preached the gospel to them. So he asked how they could reject him now.

The **physical weakness** (v. 13) Paul mentioned could be malaria, possibly contracted in the coastal lowlands of Pamphylia. That could explain why Paul and Barnabas apparently did not preach at Perga, a city in Pamphylia. The cooler and healthier weather in Galatia and especially at Pisidian Antioch where Paul went when he left Perga would have brought some relief to the fever caused by malaria. Although malaria is a serious, debilitating disease, its attacks are not continuous; Paul could have ministered between bouts. The Galatians had welcomed Paul despite his illness, which in no way had been a barrier to his credibility or acceptance. The term BLESSEDNESS (Gk. *makarismos*, "blessing or happiness," v. 15) can also be understood as satisfaction. Paul pointed out that the Galatians had been happy and content with his gospel preaching, so he wondered why they had turned against him.

The Galatians had become so confused that, despite their previous affection for Paul, some had come to regard him as an **enemy**. The apostle reminded them that he had not harmed them but had merely told them the **truth**, which once had brought them great joy (v. 16). Paul encouraged the Galatians to have the same zeal for the true gospel of grace that they had had when he was with them (v. 18). He called them his **children**, an affectionate phrase (v. 19). In contrast to the evil motives of the Judaizers, Paul sought to help the Galatians to become more like Christ.

Two Covenants: Sarah Versus Hagar (4:21-31)

4:21-31 Paul continued to contrast grace with law and faith with works, using an Old Testament story as an analogy or illustration of what he had been teaching. Specifically, he compared the two sons of Abraham, Ishmael and Isaac (v. 22). Many years after God first promised a son to Abraham, Sarah had not yet conceived. When he was 86 and she 76, Abraham feared that, according to the custom of the day, his chief servant, Eliezer of Damascus, would be his only heir. He cried out to God in despair, and the Lord reaffirmed His original promise, saying, "This one shall not be your heir; but one who will come from your own body, shall be your heir" (Gn 15:1-4). But when after several more years Sarah still had not conceived, she persuaded Abraham to father a child by her female slave Hagar.

The birth of that son, whose name was Ishmael, was **according to the flesh**, not because it was physical but because the scheme for conception, devised by Sarah and carried out by Abraham, was motivated by purely selfish desires and fulfilled by purely human means (Gl 3:23). The birth of Isaac, however, was through the **promise**. His conception was supernatural, not in the sense that he was conceived directly by the Holy Spirit as Jesus was, but the Holy Spirit miraculously enabled Abraham and Sarah to produce a child after she was far past normal childbearing age and had been barren all her life. When Isaac was born, his father was 100 and his mother was 90.

The conception of Ishmael represents the way of the flesh, whereas that of Isaac represents God's way—the way of promise. The first is analogous to the way of religious self-effort and works' righteousness. The one is the way of legalism; the other is the way of grace. Ishmael symbolized those who have had only natural birth and who trusted in their own works. Isaac symbolized those who also have had spiritual birth because they have trusted in the work of Jesus Christ.

Hagar and Sarah[13]	
Hagar	**Sarah**
Mother of Ishmael (Gn 16:15)	Mother of Isaac (Gn 21:2-3)
Slave (Gl 4:22-23)	Free woman (Gl 4:22-23)
Covenant of the flesh (Gl 4:23)	Covenant of promise (Gl 4:23)
Based on the Law given at Mount Sinai (Gl 4:24)	Based on the new covenant provided in Christ (Gl 4:4-7)
Lived under the Law (Gl 4:21-23)	Lived under grace (Gl 3:13-14)
Born according to the flesh (Gl 4:29)	Born by the Spirit (Gl 4:29-30)

LIFE IN THE SPIRIT (5:1–26)

The Role of Freedom (5:1-15)

The final two chapters of Paul's epistle are a portrait of the Spirit-filled life, of the believer's implementation of the life of faith under the control and in the energy of the Holy Spirit. The Spirit-filled life thereby becomes a powerful testimony to the power of justification by faith. Paul began with a warning against false doctrine (vv. 2-6) and false teachers (vv. 7-12).

5:1-6 Paul objected to the notion that **circumcision** had some spiritual benefit or merit with God and thus was a prerequisite or necessary component of salvation. Circumcision had meaning in Israel when it was a physical symbol of a cleansed heart and served as a reminder of God's covenant of salvation promise. The atoning sacrifice of Christ cannot benefit anyone who trusts in law and ceremony for salvation. God's standard is perfect righteousness, and thus a failure to keep only one part of the law falls short of the standard. The word **fallen** (Gk. *exepesate*, "lose, fail, run aground") suggests losing one's grasp on something (v. 4). Some use this verse to discredit the doctrine of eternal security. However, Paul's clear meaning is that any attempt to be justified by the law is to reject salvation by grace and faith alone; those once exposed to the gracious truth of the gospel who then turn their backs on Christ and seek to be justified by the law are separated from Christ and lose all prospects of God's gracious salvation. Their desertion of Christ and the gospel proves that their faith was never genuine. Christians already possess the imputed righteousness of Christ, but they still await the completed and perfected righteousness that is yet to come at glorification. Nothing done or not done in the flesh, even religious ceremony, makes any difference in your relationship to God.

5:7-12 Paul compared the Galatians' life of faith with an athletic race. They had a good beginning—they had received the gospel message by faith and had begun to live their Christian lives by faith as well. **Obeying the truth** referred to the believers' way of living, including both their response to the true gospel in salvation and their consequent response to obey the word of God in sanctification (v. 7). Paul wrote more about salvation and sanctification as being a matter of obedience (Rm 1:5; 6:16-17; 16:26). The legalistic influence of the Judaizers prevented the unsaved from responding in faith to the gospel of grace and true believers from living by faith. The **persuasion** to which Paul refers is the notion of salvation by works (Gl 5:8). God does not promote legalism; any doctrine that claims His gracious work is insufficient to save is false.

The influence of **yeast** in dough, because of its permeating or leavening power, was often used in Scripture as an

axiomatic way of denoting sin (v. 9). Paul had **confidence** that the Lord would be faithful to keep His own from falling into gross heresy; they would persevere and be preserved (v. 10). However, all false teachers would incur strict and devastating eternal condemnation. The Judaizers had falsely claimed that Paul agreed with their teaching; he made the point, however, that if he was preaching circumcision as necessary for salvation, why were the Judaizers persecuting him instead of supporting him?

5:13-15 OPPORTUNITY (Gk. *aph-ormēn*, "occasion, pretext, excuse") was often used to refer to a central base of military operations. In context FLESH (Gk. *sarki*, "pertaining to the body, physical") referred to the sinful inclinations of fallen humanity; the freedom Christians have is not a base from which they can sin freely and without consequence (v. 13). Christian **freedom** is not for selfish fulfillment but for serving others. **The entire law**—the ethics of the former Old Testament law—are the same as those of the New Testament gospel, as indicated in the quote from Leviticus 19:18 (v. 14). When a Christian genuinely loves others, she fulfills all the moral requirements of the former Mosaic law; this law is the ruling principle of Christian freedom. Paul's language—**bite and devour one another**—creates the imagery of wild animals savagely attacking and killing each other (v. 15), a graphic picture of what happens in the spiritual realm when believers do not love and serve each other.

The Spirit Versus the Flesh (5:16-26)

5:16-18 All believers have the presence of the indwelling Holy Spirit as the personal power for living to please God. The verbal tense of **walk** (Gk. *peripateite*, "a course of life or conduct") indicated continuous action or a habitual lifestyle. Walking also implies progress; as a believer submits to the Spirit's control, responding in obedience to the simple commands of Scripture, she grows in her spiritual life. **The flesh** is not simply the physical body (v. 17). It includes the mind, will, and emotions, which are all subject to sin, and refers in general to unredeemed humanity. The flesh opposes the work of the Spirit and leads the believers toward sinful behavior that they would not otherwise be compelled to do.

Believers have a choice—they can be **led by the Spirit**, which results in righteous behavior and spiritual attitudes; or they live by the law, which can only produce unrighteous behavior and attitudes (v. 18).

5:19-21 Works of the flesh—these sins listed characterize all the unredeemed, though not every person manifests all these sins to the same degree. Paul's list encompasses three areas of human life: sex, religion, and human relationships.

The Spirit versus the Flesh "These are opposed to each other" (Gl 5:17)			
Fruit of the Spirit Living fruit is evidenced in the life of the believer who is walking by the Spirit Gl 5:22-23		**Works of the Flesh** Dead works are obvious in the life of the unbeliever living life in the flesh Gl 5:19-21	
Love Joy Peace	The Spirit-filled life expressed toward God	**Religious sins** Idolatry Sorcery	**Social sins** Hatreds Strife
Patience Kindness Goodness	The Spirit-filled life expressed toward others	**Sensual sins** Sexual immorality Moral impurity	Jealousy Outbursts of anger Selfish ambitions
Faith Gentleness Self-Control	The Spirit-filled life expressed within yourself	Promiscuity Drunkenness Carousing	Dissensions Factions Envy

The flesh manifests itself in obvious and certain ways. SEXUAL IMMORALITY (Gk. *porneia*, "unlawful sexual intercourse, fornication", from which the English word "pornography" comes) refers to all illicit sexual activity, including (but not limited to) adultery, premarital sex, homosexuality, bestiality, incest, and prostitution. PROMISCUITY (Gk. *aselgeia*, "licentiousness, sensuality, debauchery") originally referred to any excessive behavior or lack of restraint but eventually became associated with sexual excess and indulgence. SORCERY (Gk.

pharmakeia, "magic," anglicized as "pharmacy") originally referred to medicines in general but eventually only to mood- and mind-altering drugs, as well as the occult, witchcraft, and magic. Many pagan religious practices required the use of these drugs to aid in their attempts to communicate with deities. The key word in Paul's warning is the verb PRACTICE (Gk. *prassontes*, "execute, perform"), describing continual, habitual action (v. 21). Although believers undoubtedly can commit these sins, those people whose basic character is summed up in the uninterrupted and unrepentant practice of these acts cannot belong to God.

5:22-26 Fruit of the Spirit refers to fruit produced **by the Spirit** of God. These nine characteristics or attitudes are so inextricably linked that they are all commanded of believers throughout the New Testament. These traits are manifestations of the presence of the Holy Spirit at work so that a believer, by emulating them, can become more like Christ both in character and activities. They are not to indicate maturity but spiritual life in general. They are the best evidence of the presence of the Holy Spirit living within.

The phrase **crucified the flesh** does not refer to Christ's crucifixion (v. 24). Paul stated that the flesh had been executed, yet the spiritual battle still raged in the believer. Paul was looking back to the cross of Christ, where the putting to death of the flesh and the ending of its power to reign over believers was actually accomplished. Christians must wait until their glorification before they are finally rid of their unredeemed humanness; yet by walking in the Spirit, they can please God in this world.

CONCLUDING EXHORTATIONS (6:1-18)

Carrying the Burdens of Others (6:1-5)

6:1-5 Paul used the word **caught**, which may imply the person was actually seen committing the sin, or that he was caught or snared by the sin itself. Those believers who are walking in the Spirit, filled with the Spirit and evidencing the fruit of the Spirit, are to help **restore** the one who has fallen into sin (v. 1). The word RESTORE (Gk. *katartizete*, "put in order, prepare, make sufficient") is sometimes used metaphorically of settling disputes or arguments, and it has the nuance of mending or repairing,

sometimes used of setting a broken bone or repairing a dislocated limb (v. 1). BURDENS (Gk. *barē*, "weights, fullness") are extra heavy loads, which here represent difficulties or problems that people have trouble handling. CARRY (Gk. *bastazete*, "take up, bear, sustain, remove") denotes bearing or carrying something with endurance (v. 2).

The law of Christ is the law of love, which fulfills the entire law. Believers first must be sure their own lives are right with God before giving spiritual help to others. They should rejoice or boast in the Lord only for what God has done in their respective lives, not for what they supposedly have accomplished compared to other believers. Verse 5 does not contradict verse 2. **Load** (Gk. *phortion,* "cargo or burden") has no connotation of extraordinary difficulty; it refers to life's routine obligations and each believer's ministry calling. God requires faithfulness even in meeting these mundane responsibilities (v. 5).

Doing Good (6:6-10)

6:6-10 Paul used an agricultural example, applied metaphorically to the moral and spiritual realm, to show a biblical truth. The word CORRUPTION (Gk. *phthoran,* "deterioration, depravity, destruction") describes degeneration, as in decaying food; sin always corrupts and, when left unchecked, makes a person progressively worse in character (v. 8). TIME (Gk. *kairō,* "limited period of time, fitting season") is the appointed and suitable opportunity, referring to a distinct, fixed time period rather than occasional moments. Paul's point is that the believer's entire life provides the unique privilege by which she can serve others in Christ's name.

Heart to Heart:
Let Us Not Grow Weary

No one understands like a woman what it means "not to grow weary doing good." In the workplace a woman is often underpaid and overworked. In the church she goes unrecognized, using her spiritual gifts and natural talents behind the scenes. At home mothers discover that socks reproduce under the sofa right after the "last" load of laundry is folded and put away. Children roll their eyes and turn up their noses at offerings of wisdom, nourishment, and care. Husbands notice only the work that goes undone when there is a momentary lapse in routine.

For a woman to sow to the Spirit and not to the flesh is a good thing. If she seeks the favor and recognition of others, she will be disappointed and will surely grow weary. If she seeks the fine things of life and satisfaction through worldly entertainments, she will reap only dissatisfaction and corruption.

But, if a woman sows to the Spirit, she will not grow weary. In time, she will see the fruit of her labors. Her coworkers will call her friend, as they are drawn to the image of Christ in her. Her sisters in Christ will call her mentor, as they mature and are edified through her. For a woman who is married, her children and her husband will call her blessed, as they are nurtured in their faith. Above all, her Lord will call her faithful, as she shares all the good things she has been given.

Responding to the Cross of Christ (6:11-18)

6:11-18 Paul's expression **what large letters** can be interpreted in two ways:

- Paul's poor eyesight forced him to use large letters; or

- instead of the normal cursive style of writing used by professional scribes, Paul used the large, block letters (frequently employed in public notices) to emphasize the letter's content rather than its form.

In any case, Paul's words painted a visible picture in contrast to his concern with the content of the gospel for the Judaizers only concern, which was how something appeared to others. The expression served as a transition to Paul's concluding remarks. The Judaizers were motivated by religious pride and wanted to impress others with their external piety. By adhering more to the Mosaic law than to the gospel of Jesus, they hoped to avoid social and financial ostracism from the other Jews and maintain their protected status as Jews within the Roman Empire.

Bibliography

*Bruce, F. F. *The Epistle to the Galatians: A Commentary on the Greek Text.* The New International Greek Testament Commentary. Grand Rapids: William B. Eerdmans Publishing Company, 1982.

*Ellicott, C. J. *A Critical and Grammatical Commentary on St. Paul's Epistle to the Galatians with a Revised Translation.* London: John W. Parker and Son, 1854.

George, Timothy. *Galatians.* The New American Commentary, vol. 30. Nashville: Broadman and Holman Publishers, 1994.

Hove, Richard. *Equality in Christ? Galatians 3:28 and the Gender Dispute.* Wheaton: Crossway Books, 1999.

*Lightfoot, J. B. *St. Paul's Epistle to the Galatians: A Revised Text with Introduction, Notes and Dissertations,* 6th ed. London: Macmillan and Co., 1865.

*Longenecker, Richard N. *Galatians.* Word Biblical Commentary, vol. 41, ed. Ralph P. Martin. Dallas: Word, 1990.

MacArthur, John. *Galatians: The Wondrous Grace of God.* Nashville: W Publishing Group, 2000.

Strauch, Alexander. *Men and Women Equal Yet Different: A Brief Study of the Biblical Passages on Gender.* Littleton, CO: Lewis and Roth Publishers, 1999.

Notes

[1] For a discussion on who the opponents were in Galatia, see Richard Longenecker, *Galatians*, Word Biblical Commentary, vol. 41, ed. by Ralph P. Martin (Dallas: Word, 1990), lxxxviii-c.

[2] For a good treatment on the pros and cons of the South Galatia vs. North Galatia views, see Longenecker, *Galatians*, lxiii-lxx.

[3] Adapted from *The Woman's Study Bible*, ed. by Dorothy Kelley Patterson and Rhonda Harrington Kelley (Nashville: Thomas Nelson, 1995), 1950.

[4] J. B. Lightfoot, *St. Paul's Epistle to the Galatians: A Revised Text with Introduction, Notes and Dissertations*, 6th ed (London: Macmillan and Co., 1865), 148.

[5] Joseph H. Thayer, *Greek-English Lexicon of the New Testament* (Peabody: Hendrickson Publishers, 2002; originally published by T. & T. Clark, 1896), 472.

[6] Jerome, *Epistle to the Galatians,* in Patrologia Latina, ed. by J. P. Migne (Paris: Migne, 1844–1864), 26:368 A-B [443].

[7] John Chrysostom, *Interpretatio Omnium Epistularum Paulinarum*, ed. by F. Field (Oxford: Clarendon, 1849-1862), 4:64.

[8] Augustine, *Epistle to the Galatians,* in Patrologia Latina, ed. by J. P. Migne (Paris: Migne, 1844–1864), 35: 2125.

[9] Jerome, 26:369D-370A [445–46].

[10] See Richard Hove, *Equality in Christ? Galatians 3:28 and the Gender Dispute* (Wheaton: Crossway, 1999) for an excellent and complete discussion of this passage. In the commentary by Ronald Fung, *The Epistle to the Galatians*, New International Commentary on the New Testament (Grand Rapids: Eerdmans, 1988), he interprets the passage from this perspective as well, seeing verse 13 as introducing the perspective of salvation history.

[11] Alexander Strauch, *Men and Women Equal Yet Different: A Brief Study of the Biblical Passages on Gender* (Littleton, CO: Lewis and Roth Publishers, 1999), 100.

[12] F. F. Bruce, *The Epistle to the Galatians: A Commentary on the Greek Text*, The New International Greek Testament Commentary (Grand Rapids: William B. Eerdmans Publishing Company, 1982), 189.

[13] Adapted from *The Woman's Study Bible*, 1952.

EPHESIANS

Introduction

The church in Ephesus was meaningful to Paul because of the time and effort he spent working with this group of believers, who would prove to be a major influence on the world for Christ. Accompanied by Aquila and Priscilla, he went to the city on his second missionary journey. On his third missionary journey, he spent three years with the people and had incredible spiritual experiences with them. This body of believers understood the persecution he faced and the importance of the gospel message. Many consider this epistle to hold some of the greatest Pauline theology, coupled with practical truths for living, and the brief letter continues to influence the church today.

Title

The Greek title for the epistle is *Pros Ephesious*, "To the Ephesians." The title's accuracy has been contested because the phrase "in Ephesus" (1:1), identifying the letter's recipients, does not appear in the earliest reliable manuscripts. Of the various hypotheses for this omission, the best explanation is that Paul intended for the letter to be taken to Ephesus, the capital of the Roman province of Asia, and from there to be distributed to churches throughout the province. The early church almost universally referred to the letter with the title, "To the Ephesians."

Setting

Ephesus (modern-day Kusadasi) was a very influential city located on the eastern portion of the Aegean Sea in what is now Turkey. It was the capital of proconsular Asia and boasted the world-renowned temple of Diana (or "Artemis" in Greek mythology). Interestingly this city was given over to paganism and temple prostitution. Ephesus was deeply ingrained in selfish ambition and worldly living.

Genre

The book of Ephesians is framed as a letter and, like other letters of the ancient Greco-Roman world and of the Pauline corpus, opens with the typical identification of author and recipients followed by greetings. The distinctively Christian greeting, "Grace to you and peace," appears in each of the Pauline letters included in the New Testament. The Ephesian letter also closes with a conventional commendation of the one who would deliver the letter and a benediction. In terms of content, the letter follows more closely the form of a sermon or homily. Despite various attempts to place Ephesians in a different genre, the book is clearly couched as a letter with greater emphasis on doctrinal and ethical issues than on particular ecclesiastical problems or issues relating to church polity.

Author

Paul, originally named Saul, was a Jew from the tribe of Benjamin. He may have been named after one of the most prominent Benjamites in history, Israel's first king Saul. Paul was well-educated, trained under Gamaliel, and later a member of the Sanhedrin, the elitist and influential council for Judaism. He was one of the fiercest persecutors of Christians until his conversion on the Damascus road (Ac 9:1-18; 26:12-23). After receiving Christ, he spent his life planting churches and serving as a special apostle to the Gentiles.

Date

Paul was imprisoned for preaching the gospel in Rome. Most scholars believe that he wrote this letter and others during his imprisonment between AD 60 and 62.

Recipients

Most commentators agree that this epistle was intended to circulate among churches and was first sent to the Ephesian church in Asia Minor. This church contained both Jewish and Gentile converts who certainly represented a plethora of backgrounds in the church body. They saw God perform spectacular miracles through Paul and helped save his life from angry mobs. Many helped Paul in his evangelistic efforts both in the city and other areas.

Major Themes

Several themes emerge in this letter. First, Paul continually brought readers to an understanding of God the Father as the one who blesses, God the Son as Christ glorified, and God the Holy Spirit as the divine seal on believers. You can learn much about God's character through this letter as Paul lovingly shared God's wonderful attributes.

The mystery of the body of Christ as revealed in the church is another prominent theme. For the new church, this information must have been a crucial puzzle piece, revealing God's marvelous plan of working in and through His people to accomplish His worldwide eternal purposes.

Another significant theme in Ephesians is unity within the Godhead and its implications for the unity within the church. Paul spent time explaining the importance of unity in the family as well as among believers in varied situations. The call to view life from God's perspective is clear.

Pronunciation Guide			
Ephesus	*EF uh suhs*	Tychicus	*TIK ih kuhs*

Outline

I. SALUTATION (1:1-2)

II. SALVATION IN CHRIST (1:3–2:10)
   A. The Favor of the Beloved (1:3-6)
   B. The Glorious Redemption (1:7-14)
   C. Paul's Prayer for Believers (1:15-23)
   D. Those Dead in Trespasses (2:1-10)

III. UNITY IN THE BODY OF CHRIST (2:11–4:16)
   A. Unity to the Body through Christ's Sacrifice (2:11-22)
   B. Ministry to the Gentiles in the Body (3:1-13)
   C. Paul's Prayer (3:14-21)
   D. Unity in the Body through the Spirit (4:1-6)
   E. Unity in the Body through Gifts (4:7-11)
   F. Unifying the Body around Truth (4:12-16)

IV. WALKING LIKE CHRIST (4:17–5:21)
   A. A Warning Not to Walk in Your Former Life (4:17-32)
   B. An Admonition to Walk in Love (5:1-21)

V. RELATIONSHIPS IN CHRIST (5:22–6:9)
   A. Between Husband and Wife (5:22-33)
   B. Between Parent and Child (6:1-4)
   C. Between Employee and Employer (6:5-9)

VI. STRENGTH IN CHRIST (6:10-20)

VII. BENEDICTION (6:21-24)

Exposition of the Text

SALUTATION (1:1-2)

1:1-2 As is typical of New Testament letters, **Paul** began by identifying himself as the author and defined his position as **an apostle of Christ Jesus**. Paul was considered an apostle, together with the original 12 disciples (except Judas, who was replaced by Matthias). Interestingly, Paul explained his apostleship not by his credentials, his rights, his abilities, or any other human qualification. In this first sentence, he humbly conceded that he was an apostle only **by God's will** (v. 1).

Like Paul, all must come to the place where their respective roles, rights, or assignments mean less than their desire to obey God and serve in the capacity He has selected for each. Paul placed the emphasis on God, not on himself or temporal circumstances. He kept an eternal perspective and here acknowledged the sovereignty of God in the beginning words of the letter.

While this letter was first addressed to the influential believers **at Ephesus**, it obviously was also intended to be circulated among other believers (v. 1). As was customary for Paul, he began by offering **grace** and **peace** from Christ, a warm and sincere greeting of Christian love and unity (v. 2).

SALVATION IN CHRIST (1:3–2:10)

The Favor of the Beloved (1:3-6)

1:3 Paul began with great praise by honoring **God** the **Father** and acknowledging Him as the ultimate Giver of blessings for all people. Recognizing that God is the One bestowing blessings affirms the idea that He alone holds all power, might, wisdom, and resources to bless whomever, whenever, and under whatever circumstances He sees fit. This great sentence places the emphasis of blessing not on the one being blessed but first on the One who **has blessed**.

Here, Paul showed that God, not a man or a woman, must be the starting point. This concept is difficult to keep in perspective because of the immediate concerns and pressing struggles, which seem tangible and urgent in this earthly life. However, identifying God first and glorifying Him continually will keep the proper balance.

> *You are not deserving of a blessing but are blessed despite who you are and what you deserve.*

While Paul was often the first to bring the focus back to God, he was not unaware or unsympathetic to human need. All must be encouraged and enthralled by the extent of Paul's claim in verse 3. We, as believers, have been blessed **with every spiritual blessing in the heavens!** Although this verse is difficult to comprehend, the closing words, in Christ, help to determine the meaning. Only because of the redemptive work of Jesus Christ's sacrificial death on the cross can any person have the blessings described in verse 3. Again, a wonderful reminder: People are blessed, not by any human work or merit, but only by the goodness and mercy of God. You are not deserving of a blessing but are blessed despite who you are and what you deserve.

God has the desire to bless people and takes the initiative to do so. In difficult circumstances, you may feel neglected or unimportant to God, but His Word explains clearly that He can and will abundantly bless. "Every spiritual blessing" should be an encouragement that God has already

given all that you need to accomplish His purposes and live successfully. Interestingly Paul did not write about material blessings, which are easy to identify, but rather directed his attention to the more important, and sometimes difficult to identify "spiritual" blessings that God lavishes on His children.

1:4-6 God gives because "He **CHOSE** (Gk. *exelexato*, "picked out, selected") us in Him, before the foundation of the world." The next verse takes the idea even further saying He **PREDESTINED** (Gk. *proorisas*, "determined, decided, or appointed beforehand"; cp. v. 11; Ac 4:28; Rm 8:29-30; 1 Co 2:7) us for adoption "through Jesus Christ" and all this "according to His FAVOR (Gk. *eudokian*, "desire, good intention, pleasure, wish, delight"; cp. Eph 1:9) and will," not according to the works of man. God's abundant blessings heaped upon believers are consistent with His selection of those who place their trust in Him and are obedient to His plan, established in eternity past, to be devoted unto Himself (cp. Rm 8:29). God predetermined that these ones should become a part of His own family through adoption with all the rights, privileges, and inheritance of natural-born children (Rm 8:15-17; Gl 4:4-7).

God's foreknowledge precedes His predestinative act or election. On earth, men and women are totally responsible for their actions, choosing either to reject or to accept Christ's sacrifice on the cross. In heaven, however, a new dimension of God's elective purpose is unveiled. All that transpires in heaven and on earth ultimately conforms to His purpose. Included in that purpose is salvation for the elect. Harmonizing predestination and election is ultimately understood only by God (Rm 11:34). However, you can be certain of these truths understood by all:

Heart to Heart:
Making the Right Choices

Imagine a young woman who was loved and received provision from her family. She was nurtured and cherished and had much as a result of the care of those around her. But, this young girl refused the provision and love of her family and instead sought the love of an evil young man. He abused and mistreated her for years and encouraged her to make poor life choices. She lived in destitution, filth, and poverty, feeling rejected and unloved. The resources and acceptance of her family were still available to her, but she did not want to accept them. She did not want to let go of her life with this man. She was deceived. Sadly she chose to live in misery when she could have enjoyed the treasures and blessing of a family who genuinely loved her rather than being in bondage to one who used her.

Often Christian women make poor choices. God has given you "every spiritual blessing" in heaven, but you live by earthly means as though you have depleted resources, unable to thrive and enjoy the life given in Jesus Christ. You refuse to accept the gifts of the Heavenly Father and instead embrace the troubles of the world. Many are like this young woman, seeking love and acceptance in the wrong places. Because of insecurity, you are deceived. Just as Eve questioned the goodness of God in the garden, many women today question the goodness of God based on their respective circumstances or feelings. Satan is an eager participant, waiting for the right moment to bring doubt, deception, and fear. Rather than trusting God, the loving Blesser, to meet spiritual needs, many turn to the world to meet temporal desires.

- Salvation from start to finish is God's work.

- Salvation is secured and kept by God.

- Election assures God's providential care for believers.

- Election extends throughout the world and history.

Paul was acknowledging the truth of election, God's selecting those who would enter a relationship with Him through Jesus Christ. This idea may seem to be in contrast to other Scripture that indicates the free will of man to choose to accept Christ and the willingness of God to accept and forgive those who come to Him of their own free will. While these two ideas seem to be irreconcilable in the human mind, in the mind and heart of God they are not only compatible but interwoven. With limited understanding, you may not be able to bring clarity to the paradox, but God in His infinite wisdom views the compatibility of election and human choice. Therefore, you must believe the teaching of Scripture and accept this hard-to-understand truth in balance with belief in both the goodness and holiness of God.

The reality of being chosen "before the foundation of the world" and "predestined" to a loving relationship with God should not bring heartache and confusion but joy and gladness. Just as Genesis beautifully describes the purpose and plan of God in creating mankind, so these verses should remind readers that joy and thanksgiving must come from the understanding that they are wanted and intended by God. He has a purpose and plan for His children and a great love for His creation. These beautiful truths should not be overlooked because of limited human ability to reconcile these wonderful teachings.

Even the idea of adoption in verse 5 is significant, realizing the rigors and expense that earthly adoptive parents must face in order to gain a child who was previously unwanted. The next verse speaks lovingly of His desire for His children and means of coming through **the Beloved**, Jesus Christ (v. 6).

The Glorious Redemption (1:7-14)

1:7-8 Paul called believers to realize the incredible REDEMPTION (Gk. *apolutrōsin*, "liberation or release upon payment of a ransom"; cp. v. 14; 4:30; Rm 3:24; 8:23; 1 Co 1:30; Col 1:14) and FORGIVENESS (Gk. *aphesin*, "pardon, remission of penalty, release from imprisonment"; cp. Col 1:14) because of the shedding of the "blood" of Jesus. Although "redemption" and "forgiveness" are not identical, forgiveness of sins is a central component in redemption. Paul identified this incredible sacrifice to remind believers of the riches of His grace. Christ is able to give beyond normal means and to extend grace where all others would be unable or unwilling. Yet, knowing how unworthy and despicable individuals are, He **lavished** (Gk *eperisseusen*, "abundantly furnished") this "grace" on believers in **wisdom and understanding** (Eph 1:8).

Only God could or would conceive of the perfect plan to reconcile to Himself sin-ful men and women in a sinful world. Only a perfect God of holiness could rightly determine how to punish sin, and only a perfect God of love would be willing to sacrifice Himself to pay the sin debt of His chosen people. Christ's substitutionary death on the cross fully satisfied God's first requirements (Rm 3:23-24; Eph 2:13). This willingness to reconcile men and women to Himself through the life, humiliation, and death of Jesus is **the riches** (Gk. *ploutos*, "wealth, abundance of possessions," v. 7; cp. v. 18; 2:7; 3:8,16) **of His grace** "lavished" on mankind through the "understanding" and "wisdom" of God.

1:9-11 Paul further discussed the work of Jesus and explained that through the life, work, and words of Jesus, God **made known to us the mystery of His will** (v. 9). MYSTERY (Gk. *mustērion*, "something hidden or kept secret, hidden purpose") is used six times in Ephesians (1:9; 3:3,4,9; 5:32; 6:19). This "mystery" of reconciliation was not known by previous generations. Abraham and Moses and others believed by faith in a **Messiah**, but they did not know exactly how the plan of God would be revealed or worked out. They believed in God's unknown plan by faith. But thankfully, New Testament Christians can enjoy the understanding of this "mystery" because of God's **good pleasure** (Gk. *eudokian*, see v. 5) in revealing the plan and carrying it to completion, which will finally come in the last days when Jesus reigns supreme and all things are settled once and for all (vv. 9-10).

Another aspect of the blessing believers receive because of Christ Jesus is **His inheritance** (Gk. *eklērōthemen,* "allotted to another as a possession," v. 11). Now, an inheritance is something to get excited about. An inheritance is especially anticipated when the giver is not a poor, weak, or foolish person, but a mighty, wise, and glorious King. You can treasure the

Heart to Heart:
Jesus, the Beloved,
and His Great Love for Women

" *The* church is the only place left where women are treated unequally."

"Women cannot relate to a 'male' God."

"Christianity downplays the importance and ability of women."

"The Bible and its writers are derogatory toward women."

These views, while common in the last few decades, are completely false. Some women hold these ideas and are bound by prejudices because they have a wrong understanding of God or because they have been hurt in the past. However, embracing such claims only brings deception and eventual destruction.

God loves women. He created the woman, and He knows the minds, hearts, and souls of women more intimately than they know themselves. Psalm 139 speaks of the intention with which God created His children.

God so loves women that He revealed Himself in the Bible, a passionate love letter filled with honesty, romance, and affection. The Word of God is written in such a way that women love to read it. It is filled with poetry, love stories, amazing characters, and detailed stories. The Bible speaks of clothing, jewelry, and travels. The Bible identifies beauty and hospitality, which are enjoyed by women. The Bible upholds the important influential role women play in the lives of those around them. Scripture shares many examples of godly women who were praised for their righteousness and contributions to the kingdom.

Jesus held significant and close relationships with women. They were a part of His ministry, and He spent much time training and teaching them. He believed in the intellectual acumen and giftedness of women. He spoke to women tenderly and gave them a place of importance they had not yet known in any society. Jesus raised the status and value of women as no one else in history.

Women should not need to come to the Word of God with fear of suppression or rejection. The Bible reveals God's amazing purpose and design through womanhood. He created women with a special assignment that brings dignity and fulfillment. His Word shares the accountability men have in protecting and caring for women they lead. God cares for the hurting, the lonely, and the lost. God cares for women. Do not be deceived by a world seeking self pleasure, but embrace God's unique call for women and experience life as He intended.

thought that one day you will no longer struggle with heartache, pain, abuse, uncertainty, insecurity, and loss. You can love to dream of days lavished in comfort, perfection, and satisfaction. Yet you realize that this life is temporary and much less significant than eternal heaven.

Believers are **predestined** (Gk. *prooristhentes*, see v. 5), **according to** His **purpose** and plan, to enjoy the good things of heaven, especially communion with God. They have been planned and prepared for heaven. For believers to take up eternal residence in heaven is no surprise. "Before the foundation of the world" (v. 4), before believers were even conceived, their enjoyment of the blessedness of heaven and of the intimacy of a personal relationship with God was predetermined in Christ.

1:12-14 The cooperation of believers with God is His plan—their acceptance of His will and His Son **bring praise to His glory**. They are affirming with a great "cloud of witnesses" (Heb 12:1) that He is wonderful and glorious. Although God does not need them to bring Him glory, they are allowed the privilege of being a small part in praising and honoring Him.

Verse 13 refers to the balance between an individual's free will and God's elective purpose, saying that upon the hearing of **the word of truth**, **the gospel** message, and believing it, you **were sealed with the promised Holy Spirit** (v. 13). To be SEALED (Gk. *esphragisthēte*, "marked with a seal, certified") is to be authenticated, proven to belong to God. Being "sealed" also conveys the sense of being secured from Satan, to whom the seal would identify one as "off limits"; cp. 4:30; 2 Co 1:22. He is the DOWN PAYMENT (Gk. *arrabōn*, "earnest money, first installment, deposit, pledge that full payment will follow"; cp. 2 Co 1:22; 5:5) or assurance of the INHER-

ITANCE (Gk. *klēronomias*, "property received by inheritance, that which has been allotted as a possession for inheritance"; cp. Eph 1:18; 5:5) to come (v. 14) and completion of the transaction.

This long section of Scripture explains the glory and blessing of God the Father, the sacrificial redemptive work of Jesus the Son, and the completing and cooperating work of the Holy Spirit in accomplishing the redemptive plan of God. Like Paul, the understanding of this massive, difficult-to-imagine truth, should make all **praise . . . His glory!**

Paul's Prayer for Believers (1:15-23)

1:15-19 Paul began this section with a magnificent truth showing His motivation and reasoning in praying for other believers. Because of all that God the Father, the Son, and the Holy Spirit have done to redeem mankind and to give value and purpose and because the saints have faith in God and His plan for the church, Paul could not stop giving thanks. Again, he was excited about what God had initiated in their lives and how they were responding. Paul experienced great joy. As a loving and affirming spiritual father, he told the people how he prayed for them. This affirmation must have been a great encouragement to the Ephesians as Paul was praying that they would be wise and discerning, making good choices based on the truth of God.

Paul prayed that believers, with their whole being, might be able to know

- **what is the hope of His calling**—not just for those in "professional ministry," but for all who are called to be His children (v. 18);

- **what are the glorious riches of His inheritance** (Gk. *klēronomias*, v. 18; see v. 14) **among the saints**; and

- **what is the immeasurable** (Gk. *huperballon*, "exceeding, excellent, surpassing," v. 19) **greatness of His power** (Gk. *dunameōs*, "inherent power, strength, ability") **to us who believe, according to the working of His vast** (Gk. *ischuos*, "ability, force, strength, might"; cp. 6:10) **strength** (Gk. *kratous*, "dominion, might, force, power" v. 19; cp. 6:10).

1:20-23 In typical Pauline style, the apostle did not just stop with the idea or the statement but went on to demonstrate the great truth. The "power" of God referenced in verse 19 is associated with God's work in the life of the believer and is illustrated in the next verse by His **power** to raise Christ **from the dead** and the decision to place Him high, lofty, and ruling in heaven, **far above** (Gk. *huperanō*, "above," in place, rank or power, v. 21) **every**

- **ruler** (Gk. *archēs*, "first, leader, rule, principality"; cp. 3:10; 6:12),

- **authority** (Gk. *exousias*, "power of government, of one who commands others"; cp. 2:2; 3:10; 6:12),

- **power** (Gk. *dunameōs*, see v. 19),

- **dominion** (Gk. *kuriotētos*, "lordship, power"), and

- **title** (*onomatos onomazomenou*, "name that is named").

Paul did not lack for drama or majesty (v. 21). He said to his readers: If God can do this for Jesus, remember your inheritance; He can do mighty things for you. Paul lived expecting God to do mighty things based on the truth of the resurrection of Jesus. He probably faced less fear and anxiety than most believers because he understood the magnitude of God's power and His ability to meet needs.

Interestingly, while the first chapter is full of incredibly important and encourag-

ing truths for believers, Paul began and ended with God. The picture is as if while describing the benefits of the creation, he got so wrapped up in who God is as the Creator that he started praising and magnifying God. His perspective was perfect.

Jesus is above **everything** that was, is, or will come. He is the ruler, the **head** (Gk. *kephalēn*, v. 22), and Jesus knows His purpose and position, especially in relation to His beloved church. This is an incredible Scripture identifying Jesus' indissoluble union with His church. Paul does not limit Christ to being "head" of the church; rather here he acknowledged the rule of Christ over the world and everything in it. By the plan of God, He and His fullness are linked to all believers. Until the fulfillment of time, when all of His children are accounted for and **His body** is complete, Jesus is waiting for His complete glorification. No one will ever know why God would choose to give sinful and fickle individuals such a place of importance and association with Jesus Christ, the Mediator and eternally reigning Messiah.

Those Dead in Trespasses (2:1-10)

2:1-3 While chapter 1 begins and ends with the glories of God, chapter 2 begins with the failures of mankind as if Paul was drawing the strict comparison between the perfect God and imperfect man. The next verses explain the desperate state of the sinner before association with Jesus. This information is not shared in order to discourage or degrade but rather to allow the realization of the magnificence and importance of the salvation offered through Jesus Christ.

John Calvin explained that since spiritual death is alienation of the soul from God, then all are born dead and live as if dead until they are made alive in Christ. Spiritual death is a terrible state: cold, dysfunctional, and sad. Because of your trespasses and sin, Paul explained that you are the walking dead.

In verse 2, he began to explain this walking death. First, Paul said it is walking **according to this worldly age**; instead of doing things God's way it is doing things the world's way, the way enemies of God do things. THIS (Gk. *toutou*, "of this one") implies that the "worldly age" is neither the only time or only place in existence. The word is not the definite article "the," which would designate *one* "worldly age" and effectively rule out the possibility of any other. The word is not the indefinite article "a" as though there were many "worldly ages." The word is "this," implying another, "that" one, in which Christ's sovereignty will be manifest.

Satan is the **RULER** (Gk. *archonta*, "commander, leader, chief"; cp. 1 Co 2:6,8) of the **ATMOSPHERIC DOMAIN** (Gk. *exousias*, "power or authority"), "the spirit now **WORKING** (Gk. *energountos*, "operative, putting forth power, producing, bringing about") in the **DISOBEDIENT**" (Gk. *huiois tēs apeitheias*, lit. "sons of disobedience," a Hebrew idiom indicating people who are characterized by "obstinacy or stubborn opposition" to God's will). Therefore, doing things as the world would do them is doing things according to Satan's way.

The **fleshly desires** of people draw them to do evil things, and Satan and his demons work along with the world to draw them away from God. The **flesh** and Satan work as enemies of God's plan and design; therefore, those who have not accepted Christ as Savior are partners with the Devil. This thought is frightening but realistic.

Because they forgot what their lives were like before they accepted Christ, Paul reminded his readers: **You were dead in your trespasses and sins** (v. 1),

living according to their own evil "desires" (v. 2). This idea is basically the heart of humanism, placing yourself above everything else and your own desires above the needs of others or true righteousness. The phrase, **carrying out the inclinations of our flesh and thoughts** (v. 3), is a description of the life lived by one who is not controlled by the Spirit. Note the change in pronouns from the second person ("you" in v. 1), which suggested Gentile background, to the first person ("we" in v. 3), which would be inclusive of Paul himself, a Jew. INCLINATIONS (Gk. *thelēmata*, "that which one wishes to be done, what one chooses or determines to be done, desires") is otherwise used in this letter and in the New Testament to denote God's "will" (v. 3; cp. 1:1,5,9; 5:17; 6:6). All do things they carnally desire without regard for consequences. There are many desires in life, which, if taken to their natural conclusion, would cause incredible heartache and pain. Thus, many unbelievers experience undue suffering. Refusing to live by God's principles removes an umbrella of protection and guidance, which ought to be enjoyed by believers. Life is hard enough without adding your own foolish mistakes; you are wiser to live a life of obedience and blessing.

Paul also explained that without the shelter of a relationship with Jesus, you are **children** living **under wrath** (v. 3). Anyone who has lived under an abusive and angry father can testify that this miserable existence has dangerous and undesirable consequences. While God is not abusive or unreasonable, He is righteous; and He will proclaim the fierce judgment of His wrath. Biblical descriptions of God's wrath and the judgment of hell are not exaggerated or inaccurate but true and far less than the reality they convey. These pictures of eternal damnation should spur you on to godly living and evangelism.

2:4-7 Verse 4 is a reassuring reminder that you are alive in Christ because of **His great love**. The fact that God has been **abundant** (Gk. *plousios*, "wealthy, rich," v. 4) **in mercy** on children of wrath and the fact that He loved them when they **were dead in trespasses**, should challenge any thought that God enjoys punishing the wicked or is overzealous in His judgment (v. 5). "Mercy" suggests the divine withholding of what is deserved— divine judgment (v. 4); on the other hand, "grace" offers what is not deserved (v. 5). His trustworthy Word explains the abundance of His love.

Verse 6 further explains God's love regarding the future resurrection of believers and the ability to be **seated** with Christ **in the heavens**. Not only are believers **raised** from a dead position, but they are also "raised" higher to an exalted position in the heavens in Christ Jesus— inexplicable honor and value. Although they are not yet in heaven, Paul referred to this truth as if it had already happened and encouraged believers to live differently as a result of the reality to come. Capturing this idea and living free from the past moves to living as changed and new creatures according to the blessings of God.

Paul used three verbs beginning with the prefix *sun* (Gk. "with, together"), conveying Christ's personally effective salvation and incorporation of believers into His kingdom:

- MADE US ALIVE WITH (Gk. *sunezōopoiēsen*, a synonym for the verb "raise," also suggesting the idea of "preserving life," v. 5; cp. Col 2:13)

- RAISED US UP WITH (Gk. *sunēgeiren*, "awaken with," usually from death in the sense of experiencing a resurrection, Eph 2:6; cp. Col 2:12; 3:1),

- SEATED US WITH (Gk. *sunekathisen*, "cause to sit down together, place together," Eph 2:6; cp. Lk 22:55).

These privileges coming with a believer's position in Christ will be realized and enjoyed experientially. As if being "seated" with Christ were not enough, Paul further explained that "the IMMEASURABLE (Gk. *huperballon*, "excelling, surpassing, outdoing, transcending"; see Eph 1:19) RICHES (Gk. *ploutos*, "wealth, abundance, fullness") of His grace in His KINDNESS" (Gk. *chrēstotēti*, "goodwill, benevolence, uprightness, generosity, goodness") toward believers will continue to be revealed (2:7). Not to believe that blessings are only in the future, Paul proclaimed that believers have present blessings because of their salvation through faith.

2:8-10 Verses 8-9 reiterate that salvation is a work of God, not of man. For people to imagine they are able to earn their salvation by doing good things is natural. However, Paul made it clear that no person can do enough good things or live a life perfect enough to merit salvation. GRACE (Gk. *chariti*, lit. "by grace") is an overwhelming expression of God's love in action through which He reveals Himself. God's goodness is understood through its contrast with undeserving humanity. The greatest manifestation of "grace" is found in salvation through Christ's atonement on the cross (cp. Ti 3:5). "Faith" is preceded by a preposition (Gk. *dia*, "through") indicating that this "faith" is the channel through which salvation comes and not the positive work or accomplishment of the individual. YOU ARE SAVED (Gk. *sesōsmenoi*, perfect passive participle, and more lit. "you have been saved," in the sense of something initiated in the past but with effects continuing into the present and beyond).

Heart to Heart:
Overcoming the Past

People often find letting go of their past difficult. Whether a person was raised in an unhealthy environment filled with terrible memories and destructive patterns of behavior or willfully chose to commit terrible sin, to become a new creature takes no small effort. Women often feel undeserving of God's love. Some feel that God's love and forgiveness, while offered to others, is not available to them. Many believe God's promises but can't seem to forget the past or change wrong thought patterns.

These verses should be a treasure for anyone with a tainted past. Paul certainly fit into this category, and he placed the emphasis on God's mercy and love. Many people read about and understand the mercy of God but do not accept or receive it. A woman must make this choice to receive God's love before His love can change her completely. You have a free will and must cooperate with God in accomplishing His purposes for your life. Realizing and accepting the magnificent truths in this section changed Paul and brought him healing from his past. These verses also express the future that God has for His children. God does not powerfully save people and then expect them to continue living in defeat. He saves them for a glorious purpose and a changed future. By accepting God's truth, relying on His power, and obediently walking in the future He has prepared, His children can overcome the past and live in victory.

> *You are not saved by good works but for good works.*

Verse 10 closes this thought with the idea that you belong to God. You are His creation, and salvation is a result of His work, which should bring believers great joy to know that they are created by God with a specific plan in mind. You were not haphazardly created on a whim. Rather, "we are his CREATION" (Gk. *poiēma*, "that which has been made, workmanship" by God, anglicized as "poem," v. 10; cp. Rm 1:20)—"CREATED (Gk. *ktisthentes*, "make, form," Eph 2:10; cp. 2:15; 3:9; 4:24) in Christ Jesus for good works, which God PREPARED AHEAD OF TIME" (Gk. *proētoimasen*, "made ready beforehand," from *pro*, "before," and *etoimazō*, "prepare, make ready," 2:10; cp. Rm 9:23) for believers to carry out. Psychologists say that people with plans are happy people. To know that God has planned for believers to do **good works** as a result and as evidence of their salvation is satisfying indeed. Other Scriptures clearly say that there is no way your "good works" can make you worthy of salvation, but rather, "good works" should follow salvation. You are not saved *by* good works but *for* good works.

UNITY IN THE BODY OF CHRIST (2:11–4:16)

Unity to the Body through Christ's Sacrifice (2:11-22)

2:11-13 Based on the understanding that not one person has earned salvation or is deserving of salvation, believers are called to unity. People will always cause divisions for one reason or another. During New Testament times, there was great division between Jews and Gentiles. While accepting Christ made Jews and Gentiles spiritual equals, for some to overcome their earthly differences was hard. These earthly differences were ingrained with generations of prejudice and wrongdoing. These New Testament Christians, both Jews and Gentiles, were the first to make this adjustment as spiritual equals and thus brothers and sisters in Christ.

Before Christ came and offered salvation to all, the Jews were God's chosen people. Paul used dramatic but accurate language to describe life without God. **Gentiles in the flesh** were

- **without the Messiah;**

- **excluded** (Gk. *apēllotriōmenoi*, "alienated, estranged, shut out from fellowship or intimacy," v. 12; cp. 4:8; Col 1:21) **from the citizenship** (Gk. *politeias*, "rights of a citizen, political body of people under common rule as a nation or state, commonwealth, society," anglicized as "polity," Eph 2:12; Ac 22:28) **of Israel;**

- **foreigners** (Gk. *zenoi*, "strangers, aliens, those who are without knowledge of or a share in"; the root of the English word "xenophobia," fear of foreign people or things; Eph 2:12; cp. v. 19) to the covenants of the promise;

- **with no hope** (Gk. *elpida*, "expectation of good," particularly of eternal salvation in the New Testament);

- **without God** (Gk. *atheoi*, the negative particle *a,* "not," combined with *theos*, "God"; the only appearance of this word in the New Testament) **in the world** (v. 12).

Unfortunately, many know the feeling of being totally alone in the world without any hope or reason to live. Through **Christ Jesus**, those **who were far away** (Gk. *makran*, "far, at a great distance," vv. 13,17) and looked down on are now included and **brought near** because of Jesus' sacrifice.

2:14-19 The following section of Scripture is an incredible and inspiring description of one of the mysteries of the kingdom of God—the unity brought through Jesus Christ. In Christ, **our peace**, all who are saved, both Jews and Gentiles,

- are with the Messiah;

- are included as **fellow citizens with the saints** in Christ's kingdom (v. 19);

- "are no longer foreigners and STRANGERS" (Gk. *paroikoi*, "resident alien, one who dwells in a country without citizenship; sojourner," from *para*, "near," and *oikos*, "house, dwelling place," v. 19; cp. Ac 7:6,29; 1 Pt 2:11) but share in "the covenants of promise" (Eph 2:12);

- have hope; and

- as **members of God's household** (Gk *oikeioi*, "belonging to a house or family," v. 19), belong to God now and for eternity.

Christ Jesus, by His once-for-all sacrifice (Heb 10:10-12) "tore down the DIVIDING (Gk. *phragmou*, "hedge, fence, something that separates or prevents two from coming together, barrier," Eph 2:14) WALL (Gk. *mesotoichon*, "partition wall," from *meso*, "middle," and *toichos*, "wall" in a house; used only here in the New Testament) of HOSTILITY" (Gk. *echthran*, "enmity," from the verb meaning "hate, be hostile toward, oppose as an enemy," vv. 14,16; cp. Jms 4:4). Upon the sacrifice of Jesus, He DID AWAY WITH (Gk. *katargēsas*, "put an end to, annulled, abolished, made ineffective, deprived of force or power, rendered inoperative," Eph 2:15) the law of the COMMANDEMENT (Gk. *entolōn*, "orders, decrees, prescribed rules," v. 15; cp. Col 2:14) in REGULATIONS (Gk. *dogmasin*, "doctrines, decrees, ordinances," anglicized as "dogma," v. 15). Christ thereby PUT . . . TO DEATH (Gk. *apokteinas*, "killed, destroyed," v. 16) "the hostility"; the law was now fulfilled, and salvation was available to all, not only to the Jews.

The spiritual equality for Jews and Gentiles, men and women, slaves and free was a revolutionary concept for the world and was accomplished so that **hostility** would end. In unity, Christ could RECONCILE (Gk. *apokatallaxē*, "restore to a former state of harmony," v. 16; cp. Col 1:20-22) His diverse church "to God." The ability of Christ to accomplish this event was a miracle. Because of Jesus Christ, all "have ACCESS (Gk. *prosagōgēn*, "approach, act of bringing or moving to," v. 18; cp. 3:12; Rm 5:2) by one Spirit to the Father."

2:20-22 The body of Christ is **built** first on **Jesus** as **the cornerstone** with everything being **fitted** (Gk. *sunarmologoumenē*, "framed or joined closely together," esp. parts of a building or of a body) and revolving around Him (v. 21). The **apostles and prophets** built on this "cornerstone," adding **the foundation** and

the inspired word of God. Verse 21 is a magnificent description of Christ's **growing** (Gk. *auxei*, "increasing, growing up"; cp. 4:15) body. This church or **building** is being "fitted" with new members, each according to God's design and specifications. BUILDING (Gk. *oikodomē*, "edifice") refers here to a structure but in its other three uses (4:12,16,29) denotes the act or process of "building up" or "edification." There are no mistakes and no accidents. Each new member comes with purpose and importance to the overall "building," and this adding of members is "growing" the building **into a holy sanctuary**. SANCTUARY (Gk. *naon*, "temple") generally referred to the sacred edifice of the temple in Jerusalem—the holy place and the holy of holies. In both Corinthian letters, Paul applied this imagery both to individuals indwelled by the Holy Spirit and to the church (1 Co 3:16-19; 2 Co 6:16). Jesus also referred to His physical body as "this sanctuary" (Jn 2:19-21). In the Lord, believers "are being BUILT TOGETHER (Gk. *sunoikodomeisthe*, "put together, constructed," from *sun*, "with, together," and the verb *oikodomeō*, "build a house," from the root *oikos*, "house, household") for God's DWELLING (Gk. *katoikētērion*, "place where someone lives, habitation, abode," from the root *oikos*, "house, household") in the Spirit" (v. 22).

Ministry to the Gentiles in the Body (3:1-13)

3:1-7 Incredibly fascinating is the fact that God chose **Paul** to be a special apostle to the **Gentiles**. Remember that Paul was the Jew of Jews and a Pharisee. He was trained by the most prominent Jewish teacher. He was a great defender of Judaism and a persecutor of Christians. As such a devout Jew, he would have been

Heart to Heart: God's Dwelling

Many women feel unimportant or useless in the church, but this verse makes clear the truth that every single member is vital to the accomplishment of God's purpose through His church. This spiritual building, which is slowly coming together, has the supernatural component of growth and protection through the Holy Spirit of God. The spiritual building is also assurance of the permanence of the believer's position in Jesus Christ and the crucial part all believers play in His dwelling place. Remarkably God allows individuals a place of purpose and significance. Two thousand years after Christ and with millions coming into His kingdom all over the world, God still provides importance to and service from each one. It is exciting to be a part of such a massive and magnificent construction project. A life purpose bigger than self is worthwhile and rewarding.

Antonio Gaudi was a famous architect from Spain, doing his primary work in Barcelona. He was approached in 1883 to construct a church dedicated to the Holy Family called El Temple Expiatori de la Sagrada Família. He spent many years devoting his entire energies to this massive project and believed the church would require at least 200 years for completion. This unusual man used ordinary people on the street as models for the magnificent sculptures on the building.

While the building is still incomplete, it is one of Spain's treasures and a "must see" for tourists. Although Gaudi was certain he would never see the completion of the project, he was totally committed to the effort, which he knew was beyond the span of his own life. He realized the vital part that he would play, and he realized that the building was greater than he.

Believers have a much more significant role in building the church of God. They are not working toward something tangible but toward something eternal. They, under the leadership of Christ, are building a holy sanctuary, God's dwelling in the Spirit.

repulsed by any who were not from the chosen race, namely, the Gentiles.

For example, Jonah was given the assignment to go to the people of Nineveh, who were very different from him and in his eyes were detestable. Jonah refused to go and was even disgusted that God asked him to make such a humiliating sacrifice. Paul, on the other hand, was so enraptured by God's forgiveness and grace that he did not question his assignment. Paul was willing to love wholeheartedly and serve selflessly those whom he formerly hated.

Paul began this chapter by directing his comments to the Gentiles themselves, those who were probably used to being despised in the church. Paul wanted to assure the Gentiles and to remind the Jewish believers that opening salvation to the

Gentiles had always been part of God's wonderful and mysterious plan of salvation and redemption. To Paul had been given **the administration** (Gk. *oikonomian*, "management of a household, stewardship, oversight of property," v. 2; cp. 1:10; 3:9) **of God's grace** for the Gentiles. Although at this time true "mystery" had only recently been revealed (v. 4), that "the Gentiles" were considered CO-HEIRS (Gk. *sugklēronoma*, "fellow- or joint-heir, participant in inheritance," v. 6; cp. Rm 8:17), part of the BODY (Gk. *sussōma*, "belonging to the same body," from sun, "with," and *sōma*, "body"; used only here in the New Testament) of Christ, and PARTNERS (Gk. *summetocha*, "joint partakers, sharers"; cp. Eph 5:7) of the gospel was no less a reality (3:6).

Paul was a wonderful model of love and acceptance. Women may allow their natural insecurities to overcome their ability to minister to, accept, and value women who are different. However, women must step out of their comfort zones, overcome prejudice, and extend loving fellowship toward to other women in the unity of Jesus Christ. Just as Paul was given the mandate to spread the gospel message to others, women also have the unique privilege of reaching out to women who have often never heard of Jesus Christ all over the world.

3:8-11 Paul was clearly thrilled about his opportunity to share Christ with "the Gentiles" and reminded the people of "the INCALCULABLE (Gk. *anexichniaston*, "incomprehensible, unfathomable, inscrutable," used only here and in Rm 11:33) RICHES (Gk. *ploutos*, "wealth, abundance") of the Messiah" (Eph 3:8). However, he did not stop at the benefits of God to His people; he reminded the church of his more important desire to make known God's "MULTI-FACETED (Gk. *polupoikilos*,

"marked by great variety, manifold," from *polus*, "many," and *poikilos*, "of various sorts or colors") wisdom" (v. 10).

Everything ought to bring glory to God. Paul was explaining that **the church**, by accepting all of God's elect and living in unity, could make known God's **wisdom** to **the rulers** (Gk. *archais*; see 1:21) **and authorities** (Gk. *exousiais*; see 1:21) **in the heavens**, giving them even more reason to praise and bring Him glory (1:11). Paul explained a unique opportunity to focus on eternity by obeying Jesus now and bringing Him the glory due.

3:12-13 "In the Messiah, Jesus our Lord," believers have

- **boldness** (Gk. *parrhēsian*, "freedom to speak without reserve but openly and frankly, fearless confidence"; cp. 6:19),

- **access** (Gk. *prosagōgēn*, "approach, coming near" Him; see 2:18), through God's favor allowing you, and

- **confidence** (Gk. *pepoithēsei*, "reliance, trust") **through faith in Him** (3:12).

Paul closed this section by reminding them that the affliction he faced was for greater **glory** and therefore worthwhile. Certainly, this church knew of the difficulties Paul was facing as he administered the gospel, for some measure of pain over his suffering was inevitable. Paul realized that the Ephesians were burdened by his sorrows, and so he gave them his perspective on the situation and said, **I ask** (Gk *aitoumai*, "beg, call for," v. 13) **you not to be discouraged**. All of his hardships and sufferings were for God's glory. He was able to find joy and comfort in seeking to glorify God, and he wanted other Christians to experience this same satisfaction.

This century has brought a great rise in Christian persecution around the world. More missionaries are going to dangerous parts of the world in order to share the gospel. Many are dying and experiencing persecution because of their faith. While you should be mindful of the sacrifices of these who suffer for the sake of the kingdom and pray fervently for them, Paul explained that their suffering was for a greater cause.

Paul's Prayer (3:14-21)

3:14-15 Rarely do you have the opportunity to know or hear what others think about you or pray on your behalf, but here, Paul tells believers exactly what he prays for them. Christians who agree in prayer get results (Mt 18:19-20). You can speculate that Paul's openness regarding prayer was an encouragement for them also to pray in this manner. Paul described a posture of humility "before the Father," his King: "I BOW (Gk. kamptō, "bend the knee, bow" in honor, to demonstrate reverence; the posture of worship, Eph 3:14; cp. Rm 11:1; 14:11; Php 2:10) my knees." The validation for his prayer comes from the fact that God has allowed all who come to Him to have a new identity with Him. Whether Jew or Gentile, all are **named** after Him, associated with Him, and continually receive the privileges of one who belongs to God's **family** (Gk. patria, "nation, people, group of families, all those who claim the same ancestry or lineage," Eph 3:15; cp. Lk 2:4; Ac 3:25). Because God has incalculable riches and unfathomable grace, the measure He extends to His children cannot be estimated. He is the perfect **Father** of all who come to Him in faith.

3:16-19 Therefore, with this immeasurable greatness in mind, Paul first prayed for the Holy Spirit's power to strengthen **the inner man** or the deepest recesses of the hearts of believers. For **the Messiah** to **dwell** (Gk. katoikēsai, "settle, inhabit, take up residence," from the root oikos, "house," v. 17) in the hearts of God's people provided an incredible strength and connection with the Father and His power. Scripture abounds with depictions of the incomprehensible power of God.

God has no limits on His **power** or His ability to provide. All of His resources are readily available to Him at all times. Since God provides spiritual power to believers, Paul prayed that believers would be strengthened even to their very core by this power. They do not have to wait to receive strength from God but can call upon the resources He has already provided. The essence of Paul's powerful prayer is that believers would use the resources available to them. Verse 17 first appears misplaced, since Paul was praying for believers who already have "the Messiah" dwelling in their hearts. However, this reference need not apply to the act of salvation but to the deepening relationship that is a result of salvation. Paul prayed that the saints would be "rooted and FIRMLY ESTABLISHED (Gk. tethemeliōmenoi, "founded, made stable, established," Eph 3:17; cp. Mt 7:25; Col 1:23; Heb 1:10; 1 Pt 5:10) in love." ROOTED (Gk. errizōmenoi, "having taken root, having been established or thoroughly grounded," Eph 3:17; cp. Col 2:7) is anglicized as "rhizome," a plant having a horizontal, underground stem that sends out roots and shoots from the buds forming at its joints. "Rootstock" and "rootstalk" are synonyms for a "rhizome" used as stock for propagating more plants. When a rhizome is cut by a cultivating tool, it does not die like other roots but instead produces multiple plants. Ginger is an example, as is crabgrass, which is, consequently, hard to get rid of. He was praying that they would deepen their experiences with and become more like the Lord, increasing their love for Him. This foundation of love should be so firm and solid that it cannot be shaken by anything. Is your love connection with God so strong that absolutely nothing can cause you to doubt His love? Is your love connection with God so strong that you are compelled to love others, even those who are unlovable? Is your love connection with God so strong that you love the lost and long for them to experience the love of Jesus Christ?

When the foundation of love is this strong, Paul prays that believers will "BE ABLE (Gk. *exischusēte*, "have full or eminent ability," from the verb *ischuō*, "have power or strength, be robust or strong") to COMPREHEND" (Gk. *katalabesthai*, "mentally take hold of, understand; seize upon, apprehend, obtain," Eph 3:18; cp. Ac 4:13; 10:34; Rm 9:30; Php 3:12-13; Jn 1:5) and KNOW (Gk. *gnōnai*, "understand or know from personal experience," Eph 3:19) the "depth" and love of God. This **love** is so vast it extends in all directions beyond human comprehension (vv. 17-19). Hopefully, believers will be able to experience and recognize God's love in all circumstances and from any perspective.

Most people, especially leaders, allow others to know a limited amount of personal information and reveal only a portion about who they really are. People of great authority and position have little reason to share private details about themselves with those under their leadership. However, God desires for His people to search the depths of His character and greatness and to participate actively in becoming like Him. He wants people to enjoy Him personally, sink in His love, and live in fellowship with **the fullness of God** (v. 19).

3:20-21 Because Paul was divinely inspired to write this prayer, you can rest in confidence that God's desire is for you to know Him with this magnitude of understanding, realizing that He **is able to do above and beyond** (Gk. *huperekperissou*, "surpassingly or exceedingly abundantly, immeasurably, supremely") **all that we ask** (Gk. *aitoumetha*, "beg, call for"; see 3:13) **or think** (Gk. *nooumen*, "understand, think about, ponder, consider, perceive with the mind"; cp. Rm 1:20; 1 Tm 1:7; 2 Tm 2:7; Heb 11:3). This free access to God and this realization of His ability to work on behalf of believers ought to cause all to bring Him glory for generations to come!

Unity in the Body through the Spirit (4:1-6)

4:1 Paul expected that standing with the heavenly Father through Jesus Christ should spiritually, mentally, and emotionally change an individual. This change should be so profound that you no longer walk as those dead in trespasses but as those **worthy** (Gk. *axiōs*, in a "fitting or suitable" manner) **of the calling**. As noted previously, Paul was imprisoned when he wrote this letter. He mentioned this fact in an effort to acknowledge his all-out surrender to Jesus. He had been changed, and he had a new calling on his life. Paul went to great lengths to explain practically the nature of this changed life. In 1 Samuel, Saul was anointed the first king of Israel. He was not totally prepared to be king or sure of how to behave, so Samuel the prophet explained "the rights of kingship" or expected behavior of royalty (1 Sm 10:25). He also wrote it down so that others would know and remember. Essentially Paul did the same in Ephesians 4. Because of the believer's new standing in Jesus Christ, she is to behave differently. Her behavior should change not just when she is at church, not just when she is around other Christians, and not just when she feels like being different. The calling of Christ is a daily calling that lasts through a lifetime and into eternity.

4:2 Paul explained the character qualities Christians are to develop with the help of the Holy Spirit. He began with HUMILITY (Gk *tapeinophrosunēs*, "modesty, having a humble opinion of oneself," appearing five times in the Greek text of Paul's letters and only once elsewhere in the New Testament; see 1 Pt 5:5). The word has the sense of viewing yourself as small and recognizing God as all-powerful and above all others. Interestingly Paul placed **humility** as the foundation for the Christian life and calling. The Greeks and Romans considered humility to be a great weakness, and this kind of attitude was not encouraged or appreciated. Those with meekness were despised and considered worthless. However, the trait was redeemed among believers to represent a distinctively Christlike virtue, which placed the humility of a believer in stark contrast to the high-mindedness of unbelievers who tended to think more highly of themselves than others and than even God Himself.

No person has a natural inclination toward humility. People want to exalt themselves. A woman may want to be the prettiest or most desirable woman in the room. To build yourself up is a normal desire, and today's culture certainly reinforces this idea through excessive self-help seminars and self-esteem psychology. Paul was calling the Ephesians to live in a way and with an attitude that was contrary to their very nature and experience. However, without genuine humility, no one can seek mercy in Christ with sincere repentance, neither can you remain in right standing with God. This incredibly difficult virtue is crucial to the Christian life.

After "humility," Paul identified GENTLENESS (Gk. *prautētos*, "mild-

mannered or meek in disposition, courteous"). "Gentleness" is a fruit of the Spirit (Gl 5:22-23) and can be characterized by self-control. The element of restraint is included in its meaning, suggesting controlled and steadfast strength rather than reactionary waffling weakness. The idea is to be willing to lay aside selfish desires for the desires of others, as in Paul's description of Jesus in Philippians 2:1-18. This attitude manifests itself in a submissive spirit that accepts even offenses and injustice without malice or vindictiveness (cp. 1 Pt 3:1-7). This **gentleness** is even more important in the Christian community as people from varied backgrounds attempt to live as brothers and sisters. It takes great self-control to live according to Christian principles, and gentleness is a virtue rarely modeled.

PATIENCE (Gk. *makrothumias*, "endurance, steadfastness, forbearance, longsuffering, not quickly provoked") is another attribute necessary for walking "worthy of the calling." This attribute, characteristic of God Himself, suggests a patient endurance even when others have inflicted pain or suffering. In fact, in the New Testament often the word describes a reluctance to return evil for evil, a refusal to seek revenge. While easy to praise, **patience** is extremely difficult to live out. No one wants to be patient, and few enjoy it. However, it is a necessary part of the Christian life. It is incredibly difficult to accept the fact that God sets His own timetable, which is often in contrast to the desires and demands of people. Often God may seem to be overdue or late on His promises, but with patience you will see that He is always faithful; or to put it in the vernacular, He always shows up. In the Old Testament, Sarah, as an elderly woman beyond the years of fertility, finally conceived a child. According to a human timetable, God had passed the deadline, but He planned to reveal His miraculous power through Sarah.

To wait patiently when you are experiencing pain, heartache, or loss is difficult. Many will never know why God allows difficulties in their lives. However, with obedient longsuffering comes great faith and the realization that God will sustain His children. This patience is encouraged by Paul and demanded of those who walk in a worthy way.

Paul spoke of "ACCEPTING (Gk. *anechomenoi*, "holding up, sustaining, enduring, forbearing") one another in love." The word suggests a tenacity, i.e., a patience to accept someone until your provocation has passed. Paul often speaks of **love**. The Bible says that God is love (1 Jn 4:8). In order to believe and accept the Christian faith, you must love. The book of Exodus describes the priestly garments worn in the holy of holies. Reportedly pure gold was melted into small thin sheets and then used as thread to sew parts of the garments. The gold threads brought value, beauty, and importance. Love might be thought of as this gold thread in the life of the church. Love for God is an essential element in relationship to Him. Love for others is required by God and is evidence of your love for Him. Love for the church enables self-control and sacrifice. Love for the lost builds God's kingdom and accomplishes God's purposes.

Walking worthily means accepting others and loving them purely. Jesus is the best example of love as He refused His comforts and kingly position in order to accept mankind in love. He must be the model for loving others, and His acceptance of His children is the true motivation for accepting others.

4:3 Finally, Paul challenged believers to "walk worthy of the calling" by "DILIGENTLY (Gk. *spoudazontes*, "hastening, being zealous, eagerly, making every effort, endeavoring, exerting oneself") KEEPING (Gk. *tērein*, "carefully attending, guarding, observing, taking care of, maintaining") the unity of the Spirit with the peace that BINDS us" (Gk. *sundesmō*, "bonds," in the sense of something holding together securely as fetters would bind a prisoner; also Col 3:14; "ligaments" in Col 2:19). God has made **peace** with those who come to Him through His Son. The Spirit then indwells Christians, uniting them with the Godhead and uniting them with one another. There is no way to describe this miraculous reality. Living with one another in the Spirit's love is a wonderful way to show outsiders the love of Christ. Since Christ first loved believers, they must love others. Living in **unity** with other Christians is a privilege. While often described as a grudging necessity, it is better considered as a strong pillar in sustaining the church.

Attending a Christian event at a large packed stadium fills believers with a sense of oneness and the realization that they are not alone. God has a mighty army of believers who are often spread apart. When a vision is given of the strength of many coming together and praising God, the unity is incredibly uplifting.

When Christians face hardship and conflict, they often easily move away from one another to simplify life. However, a church that will work through problems in love and gentleness is a unified church and is strong enough to thwart the schemes of Satan. A unified church can accomplish God's purposes and find satisfaction in the peace of God's Spirit. When believers walk in a way that is "worthy of the calling," they can experience unity.

4:4-6 Paul gave the Ephesians personal directives and guidelines in regard to behavior toward others. With magnificent consistency, he called them to a single-minded state of living based on God, His **calling**, and His filling. God is unified in His character. He does not separate believers into categories, but all who accept Christ are part of the **one body** of Christ (v. 4). The body is held together by the Holy Spirit of God. There is only **one** true **Spirit** (v. 4), and He indwells each believer. The Spirit is also the **one hope** of what is to come, the eternal heaven that all believers will experience as a result of salvation (v. 4). Salvation only comes through faith in the **one Lord,** Jesus Christ (v. 5). He is the only way of salvation, the **one faith** (v. 5). The **one baptism** (v. 5) is commonly known as a public profession of this faith in Christ. This identification is a step of obedience, which Christians are commanded to take upon receiving Christ as Savior and Lord. Paul summarized in a wonderful comprehensive way with his description of the worthy "calling," which is offered by God, completed in Jesus, and sealed in the Holy Spirit (v. 6).

Unity in the Body through Gifts (4:7-11)

4:7-11 While the previous section spoke of the body of Christ, these verses focus on the individual members with a wonderful confirmation that Jesus has given gifts to His children in order to bless them and help them accomplish His calling. Through His **grace**, or His willingness to reconcile mankind, He measures out the gift to each believer (v. 7). He is able to relate to His church simultaneously as a body and as individuals and precious children. For this reason, Christ measured, or intended, the specific **gift** for each child. Having so many children, for Jesus Christ to be involved in assigning specific portions to every one of His children is remarkable.

Verses 8-10 explain the reason Christ is able to give the **gifts**. Paul referred to David's victory hymn celebrating God's

conquest and triumphant ascent in Psalm 68:18. Paul was identifying the work of Christ on earth and His victory as the validation for distributing "gifts." Jesus **descended** from the high heavens to give His life as a sacrifice; then He rose from the grave and was seated at the right hand of the Father. This miraculous feat proves that He alone accomplished the will of the Father and fulfills **all things**.

Unifying the Body around Truth (4:12-16)

4:12 After His resurrection, but before His ascension into heaven, Jesus assigned different roles to different people in order to train Christians for ministry and build His kingdom. This section outlines the plan accomplished through Christ, the means of further achievement through the saints, and the ultimate goal of reaching unity in the faith and maturity in Christ Jesus (v. 13).

This attention to and distribution of gifts by Jesus also testifies to His loving care for His bride, the church, whom He loved as His own body; He did not leave her alone to struggle until His return. Instead, He took great effort to assign gifts as a means of building and protecting the church. He also sent the Holy Spirit to empower, guide, and teach the church. Jesus lovingly and tenderly cared for His bride. This example is excellent preparation for the instruction to husbands, who are directed to nurture and cherish their wives as their own bodies (chap. 5).

The fact that Jesus also provided leadership for His bride is significant. Beyond individual gifts, he fitted the church with leaders: apostles, prophets, evangelists, pastors, and teachers (v. 11). Every person and every organization needs leadership. The church is no different. The church must also first follow the leadership of Jesus Christ. The church must follow those placed in authority over **the body**.

While Scripture is clear that women are chosen, gifted, and used by God, the Bible is also clear that churchwide leadership positions are to be filled by men. This assignment is a reflection of divine order and purpose rather than ability, but the reality is nonetheless difficult to accept for many. Although individuals can be incredibly grateful for the gifting of God, gifting is not a license for lack of boundaries. God's gifting is perfectly in line with His creation order for the home and the complementary order within the church. Women should fully exercise their gifts in the power of the Spirit for the benefit of the church; but like Paul, they must be willing to devote themselves to function according to the mandates of the word and **to build up** (Gk. *oikodomēn*, "edification, promotion of growth," in the sense of development of people and resources, v. 12; see 2:21) the entire body. The church should not be a showcase for personal ability or an arena for debate; rather, the people of God must gather in humility, love, unity, and service.

4:13 Understanding the deep truths of God revealed in the **Son** is the unifying, maturing material of the church. This maturity and **unity** (Gk. *enotēta*, "oneness, agreement"; cp. v. 3) ought to buttress the church and protect it from erroneous theology and uncertain faith so that believers can spend their time **growing** to know and become like Christ. Of course, becoming like Christ—becoming **mature** (Gk. *teleion*, "complete, finished, initiated, perfect," v. 13; cp. Mt 5:48; 19:21; 1 Co 2:6; 13:10; 14:20; Php 3:15; Col 1:28; 4:12; Heb 5:14; Jms 3:2)—is God's goal for every believer. Whether painful or pleasant, this is God's overarching purpose for each life. A Christian's life should be about accomplishing God's own goals, not her own. A woman should not be consumed with seeking her own glory but instead should

seek the glory of God. A life totally surrendered to Christ is the only life worth living.

4:14-16 Recognizing this truth is to live in maturity and in the fullness of Christ. A fantastic result comes from this maturity; it provides solid footing. Paul compared immaturity to being "tossed by the WAVES" (Gk. *kludōnizomenoi*, from *kludōn*, "surging, violently agitating waves" in the sea, v. 14; cp. Lk 8:24; Jms 1:6), to being "blown around by"

- "every **WIND** (Gk. *anemō*, "very strong, violent, tempestuous wind"; cp. Ac 27:4-15; Jms 3:4) of teaching,"

- "human **CUNNING**" (Gk. *kubeia*, lit. "dice-playing," from *kubos*, anglicized as "cube," e.g., a cube-shaped die or understood figuratively as "cunning," because of the intentional practice of dice players to cheat and defraud each other),

- "**CLEVERNESS** (Gk. *panourgia*, "craftiness, trickery, cunning, false wisdom"; cp Lk 20:23; 1 Co 3:19; 2 Co 4:2; 11:3) in the techniques of deceit."

Growing in the knowledge of Christ provides protection from confusion over false doctrine. Knowing the truths of God is arguably one of the best defenses against the enemy, who clearly has many "techniques of deceit." Growth in Christ is accomplished by **speaking the truth in love**, which means sitting under preaching and leadership that is truthful according to Scripture (Eph 4:15). It also means living in an authentic Christian way, which should protect individuals and the church from evil and deception.

Paul affirmed the importance on the part of individual Christians to exercise their specific gifts. He compared them to the intricate parts of a physical **body** working together to accomplish a task (v. 16). Christ is the **HEAD** (Gk. *kephalē*, v. 15). He explained that "the whole body" is "**FITTED** (Gk. *sunarmologoumenon*, "joined or framed closely together"; see 2:21) and **KNIT TOGETHER** (Gk. *sumbibazomenon*, "joined or put together, united," in reference to the body held together by sinews, ligaments, and joints, i.e., a correlation that steps up to the plate and reports to the job as a working organism, 4:16; cp. Col 2:2,19) by every supporting **LIGAMENT**" (Gk. *haphēs*, "joint, bond, connection"; cp. Col 2:19). Each body part must function according to its own respective purpose and assignment in order to build and support the overall goal of the body. This work should be done out of great love and the understanding that Jesus chose and fills and empowers the body **in love** (v. 16).

WALKING LIKE CHRIST (4:17–5:21)

A Warning Not to Walk in Your Former Life (4:17-32)

4:17 Paul continually brought readers back to the larger picture of salvation. Since believers have been adopted into the family of God and are being "fitted" in the body of Christ, they cannot live as they previously lived and as others around them live. Ephesus was a city filled with great immorality and wickedness. The church was a small and isolated group surrounded by evil and sin. Many converts had doubtless participated in perverse behavior and likely had friends and family who were still immersed in a godless lifestyle and whose thinking was characterized by **FUTILITY** (Gk. *mataiotēti*, "purposelessness, depravity; what is without truth, worthless"; cp. Rm 8:20; 2 Pt 2:18). This word sug-

gests complete vanity or emptiness, an aimlessness without any purpose or end in sight. Coming from such backgrounds and being surrounded by bad influences, Paul reminded his readers to keep their minds pure, noting that wrong behavior begins in the mind with wrong thinking.

4:18-19 The non-Christians were living without success, hopelessly seeking after things that would only bring death and destruction. The "**HARDNESS** (Gk. *pōrōsin*, often used in medical sense as "callous, thickened skin cover, insensibility and dullness") of their hearts" against the Lord prevented them from understanding the truth of God, they were "**EXCLUDED** (*apēllotriōmenoi*, "alienated, estranged, shut out," implying that one is and has been an alien from any enjoyment of a godly lifestyle; see 2:12) from the life of God" (4:18). Because they were so **CALLOUS** (Gk. *apēlgēkotes*, "insensible to pain or grief," in the sense of being past the ability to feel) and self-indulgent, having willfully sold out to **PROMISCUITY** (Gk. *aselgeia*, "licentiousness, sensuality, unrestrained lust," v. 19), they only served their fleshly desires and were eaten up by their behavior, like addicts, only wanting more and more of what ultimately would cause their ruin. You have all known people living in similar situations, so deep into sin that they don't even recognize or care about the depths of depravity into which they have sunk. Inevitably a broadened mind that accepts what God rejects is indicative of a shrinking conscience that embraces the world and rejects Christ.

> *Inevitably a broadened mind that accepts what God rejects is indicative of a shrinking conscience that embraces the world and rejects Christ.*

4:20-24 Paul made a strong contrast between those who had rejected Christ and those who had experienced salvation in Christ, or **learned about the Messiah** (v. 20). When a genuine conversion occurs, the person is forever changed. A Christian can make mistakes or lapse into a **former** (Gk. *proteran*, "previous, earlier, prior") **way of life**, but ultimately, a genuine believer is different and cannot consistently live in wickedness because Jesus is renewing her mind, continually causing her to grow in His **likeness**. This act is initiated by Jesus with the cooperation of the believer, who is diligently seeking to pursue **righteousness** and **truth**.

In the concluding verses of this chapter, Paul gave instructions for how the believer should conduct herself with the help of the Holy Spirit. He listed some very specific actions including four references to controlling the tongue in order to build up others rather than tear them down. He also listed five situations in which right thoughts and attitudes toward others have significance.

4:25 Women love to talk. The use of the tongue comes naturally and is enjoyable. While women use words in many positive ways, there are many ways to use the tongue that are destructive and harmful. The first problem Paul addressed is **lying** (Gk. *pseudos*, "conscious, intentional falsehood or lie"; Jn 8:44; Rm 1:25; 1 Jn 2:21,27). Of course, every Christian knows that lying is wrong and unacceptable, but telling the truth is often very difficult and may seemingly have harmful consequences. "Lying" carries its own heavy weight of consequences; but it is sometimes an easier, faster route than telling the difficult truth straightforwardly. Some Christian women are drawn to lying in the sense of deception, exaggeration, and gossip. You can give an impression or implication without actually saying anything untruthful. All should diligently work at keeping a clean mind and pure speech. Mothers especially have an important duty to train children regarding the use of chaste language and pure speech.

While lying is unacceptable, speaking **the truth** is crucial. To have a word that can be trusted is an important character quality that every Christian should master. You must be proven over time and consistently shown to be dependable. Those who speak falsehood can rarely gain trust, but those who speak the truth are sought after.

The Christian faith demands honesty. People must honestly see themselves as sinners and God as holy and righteous. They must be honest with unbelievers in evangelism. They must be truthful with fellow believers. Truth spoken in love is healthy for the church. Paul not only taught believers to speak truthfully, but he also affirmed the importance of their responsibilities to fellow Christians. The members of the body of Christ are connected to one another. Truthfulness in the body is essential to growth and effectiveness. Unity and love thrive in truth.

4:26-27 Paul offered a strong warning to the church regarding "ANGER (Gk. *parorgismō*, "wrath, indignation, exasperation," in the sense of a violent irritation). This word is used only here in the Greek New Testament and seems to suggest the expression of harmful words or inconsiderate actions or even an antagonistic stare—any or all of which can be hidden beneath the surface as an angry mood just smoldering and waiting to erupt. Opening the door to anger gives **the Devil** an opportunity. This church was certainly familiar with the schemes of the Devil and would not want to leave him an open door of opportunity to overtake the church. Paul recognized anger as an easy target. While he implied that some anger is righteous and necessary to spur Christians to action, he also acknowledged how quickly that righteous anger can turn to bitterness and evil. Paul encouraged the Ephesians to keep their anger in check by dealing with it daily. People should not push their anger down and let it fester into ungodliness. Anger must be confessed, dealt with, and acted upon according to Scripture.

4:28 Paul addressed stealing and contrasted it with **honest work**. There are many ways to steal. Whether someone actually takes a possession, maneuvers an undeserved commission, cheats the government, or steals recognition belonging to someone else, all are considered dishonest dealings. A believer should be involved in honorable, ethical **work with his own hands**. It is often discouraging to behave honorably when those around you prosper through dishonest gain, but Paul indicated that stealing is not ever acceptable under any terms.

While the Devil may bless a **thief** (Gk. *ho kleptōn*, "one who steals, commits a theft") for a time, God will not bless the one who steals. Good "honest work" is rewarded through personal satisfaction and trust of others. However, Paul identified the greatest reward as the ability **to share** with those **in need**. Rather than being self-centered, Christians should look to others with need and gladly give. Materialism and poor financial habits prohibit Christians from being able to give to others; however, giving is considered a blessing and a natural part of the Christian life. All should work hard in order to have the resources to give generously to others.

4:29-30 Paul tackled the untamable tongue once again. People often speak poorly of others in order to make themselves feel important. Instead, Paul said that speech ought to be monitored by what is profitable for others to hear and by what is able to bring them **grace**. Paul

wanted Christians to be accustomed to encouragement. He wanted expressions of love and affirmation to be natural and normal rather than rare and uncomfortable. The church should be a place of safety and comfort, not a place of disparagement.

"**ROTTEN** (Gk. *sapros*, "putrefied, decayed, corrupted, unfit, worthless, unwholesome," in the sense of bad and evil in nature and even disgusting, v. 29) talk" and actions bring grief and heartache to the "Holy Spirit." Mothers often weep when their children harm one another rather than love one another. The Spirit has great concern and involvement in the lives of believers and is grieved when they hurt each other. Paul's motivation for pure speech and **the building up** (Gk. *oikodomēn*, "edifying," v. 29; see 2:21) of others is based on the seal of the **Holy Spirit** (4:30). The Spirit indwells all believers upon salvation and the promise of eternity with God. He has **sealed** (Gk. *esphragisthēte*, "marked, confirmed, certified, secured," v. 30; see 1:13) believers **for the day of redemption** (4:30). This precious helper bearing the promise of heaven should be so greatly loved that believers would readily avoid any behavior that would "grieve" (Gk. *lupeite*, "cause sorrow or make sorrowful, bring pain, offend") Him. Here the verb is a present imperative tense prefaced by a particle of negation (Gk. *mē*) and thus with emphasis and warning against continual and habitual action, such as lying and "rotten talk."

4:31 In case Paul's lengthy discussion on speech, behavior, and attitudes was not enough, he proceeded to leave no back doors for escape. **All bitterness** and **all wickedness** must end. He did not allow a time of adjustment or an acceptable regulation of quantity. All evil things must end, and they must cease immediately.

Things That "Must Be Removed" (5:31)		
Attitudes	"Bitterness" (Gk. *pikria*, "bitter root, harshness" the root word from which "provoked" comes—see Heb 3:10), used figuratively to denote a frame of mind in which one is continually inclined to harsh and uncharitable opinions of others and thus fussy with a scowling face and venomous words	
	"Wrath" (Gk. *thumos*, "heated anger, rage") in the sense of explosions and passionate outburst	
	"Anger" (Gk. *orgē*, "temper, wrath," in the sense of a violent and aggressive emotion), more the deep-seated clamor, churning, simmering, subtle emotions	
Actions	"Insult" (Gk. *kraugē*, "outcry, uproar, clamor"), with the idea of ensuing strife and quarreling	
	"Slander" (Gk. *blasphēmia*, "speech that injures or detracts from another's good name, defamation"), which becomes an enduring expression of a deep-seated angry spirit, often coming forth with reviling and accusatory tones	
Root	"All wickedness" (Gk. *kakia*, "malice, unashamed desire to do harm or evil"), the summarizing, generic term inclusive of the root of all the vices mentioned	

4:32 Replacing those things should be kindness, compassion, and forgiveness. Paul was a wise teacher. He not only explained what not to do, but what to do. He was also gracious to provide reasons for the change. He knew that many of the requirements were difficult, and he offered the best motivation for discipline in these areas. God's love and forgiveness for you should be your motivation for loving and **forgiving** others. How could any true believer deny the depth of God's love and forgiveness. Paul knew that no Christian could argue with this reasoning.

Certainly, there were damaged and scarred people in this congregation who had major offenses to forgive. Paul did not ignore this reality but simply reminded all believers that God has forgiven them, and, therefore, they must forgive others. As much as you may want a loophole or exception, there is none included. Instead, the admonition is to **be**:

- **kind** (Gk. *chrēstoi*, "mild and pleasant," the opposite of being bitter, sharp or harsh), a determination to be useful, good, and benevolent toward others;

- **compassionate** (Gk. *eusplagchnoi*, "tenderhearted," lit. "good or strong bowels," which, in Hebrew idiom, referred to the seat of one's emotions and intentions; strong, expressive emotion, expressing courageous pursuit of good as opposed to giving into the bad emotional responses mentioned in v. 31; see 1 Pt 3:8),

- **forgiving one another** (Gk. *charizomenoi*, "giving freely, granting pardon, graciously restoring" relationships,) in contrast to deliberately harming others by "insult" or "slander" from a heart of "wickedness."

An Admonition to Walk in Love (5:1-21)

5:1-5 Most significant in this chapter is the principle that believers are to **be imitators** (Gk. *mimētai,* in the sense of leaving a "mark, image, form, pattern"; see 1 Th 1:6) **of God**. This vision should guide all thought and behavior. Paul admonished believers to imitate God because of all He had done for them (described in detail in the previous chapters) and because they are **dearly loved**

children. Some view God as strict and rigid, but God expresses Himself as both a righteous and loving Father. He does not stop there but also reminds His children that they have a **Messiah**, a Savior, who **loved us and gave Himself for us.** This great love should be your motivation for following Him and obeying His commands (v. 1).

The love that compelled Christ to give His life for sinful man and reconcile God's creation is said to be a "FRAGRANT offering (Gk. *osmēn*, "smell, odor" and *euōdia*, "sweet smell, aroma, as of incense"; see 2 Co 2:14; a phrase used in a figurative sense to describe an acceptable offering and here a pleasing lifestyle) to God," confirming the fact that the loving Father desires to be unified with His people and recognizing sacrifice as an indispensible part of a life lived unto godliness (v. 2). Living a consistent and pure Christian life is not easy and does require some sacrifice, but Jesus is the ultimate role model showing that God's children can also be a "fragrant offering." Paul listed conduct that is inappropriate for a Christian (vv. 3-4):

- **SEXUAL IMMORALITY** (Gk. *porneia*, "illicit sexual intercourse, prostitution, unchasity, fornication");

- any **IMPURITY** (Gk. *akatharsia*, "uncleanness" in one's behavior or thought life, figuratively "immorality");

- **GREED** (Gk. *pleonexia*, "avarice, greedy desire to have more, covetousness" in the sense of something forced);

- "**COARSE** (Gk. *aischrotēs*, "obscenity, ugliness, filthiness" in the sense of obscenities or shameful, filthy speech) and FOOLISH TALKING"

(Gk. *mōrologia*, "silly talk," from *moros*, "foolish, impious, godless," and *legō*, "talking, speaking," a compound word linking foolishness and sin together);

- **CRUDE JOKING** (Gk. *eutrapelia*, "humor, jest, buffoonery," with a bad connotation in this context, implying a turning of wit or humor to evil or even to use what should be lighthearted interchange to deceive, a practice said to be common among Ephesian orators.

Participation in the behaviors listed would be evidence that someone purporting to be a believer had not experienced real conversion. Scripture is clear that a person who has experienced salvation is a changed person, unable willingly and continually to participate in wrong behavior. For example, being **sexually immoral** (Gk. *pornos*, "one who indulges in illicit sexual intercourse," v. 5) would not cause someone to lose his salvation but rather would suggest that the person may not have been saved in the first place. Being an **impure or greedy person** or an **idolater** does not result in losing your **inheritance** (Gk. *klēronomian*, "possession, property," v. 5; see 1:14,18) **in the kingdom of the Messiah and of God** but demonstrates that you were not actually a member of God's family and therefore had no inheritance to lose.

5:6 Paul acknowledged that many are deceived by **empty arguments** or opinions that are not based on truth and lead to destruction. To do research, come to a right conclusion, and receive positive results based on that decision is rewarding. Conversely to believe an "empty argument" that has no good return and only fatal consequences is devastating. Paul alerted his readers to the seriousness of the situation by saying that "God's wrath is coming on the **DISOBEDIENT**" (Gk. *huious tēs* *apeitheias*, "disbelief"; "sons of disobedience," a Semitic expression denominating disobedience as the chief characteristic of a person; see 2:2). Today's culture is filled with "empty arguments." The world says there is nothing wrong with an immoral lifestyle, no consequences or heartaches; yet this is contrary to God's Word.

5:7 Believing empty lies and participating in wicked behavior is likened to a partnership. There is no good way to disobey God. A partnership has ties that bind, and Paul explained that disobedience to God by default is partnership with darkness. Many do not realize that when they disobey God, they are partnering with Satan to produce pain, heartache, and emptiness.

5:8-14 Paul convincingly argued that the **light** of **the Lord** exposes evil and offers truth and life, inspiring people to produce **fruit** resulting in **goodness, righteous**, **and truth** (v. 9). Essentially, Paul said, don't forget what it was like to be in the dark; let this realization compel you to **expose** (Gk *elegchomena*, "convicted, refuted or corrected by bringing to light") the darkness to **the light** and make **everything clear** (v. 13). **Children of light** have a responsibility not to tamper with **darkness** but to offer hope and clarity (v. 8). As Paul had explained before, don't walk as people dead in your trespasses, but walk alive in the sunshine of Christ Jesus.

5:15-18 This section is a wakeup call. Do not be consumed with the world and the demands of everyday life, but realize what this life means in the greater perspective of eternity. Don't waste your life seeking selfish desires rather than eternal profit. Know God's "will" and UNDERSTAND (Gk. *suniete*, "put together in the mind, comprehend, perceive," in the sense of bringing things together in order to determine how they relate to one another, v. 17) His timing. Realize that life on earth is brief and should not be wasted. Paul urged "MAKING THE MOST OF (Gk. *exagorazomenoi*, "buy up for oneself or one's use, redeem," in the sense of capitalizing on opportunities so the time and energy are well spent, v. 16; cp. Col 4:5) the time." Although you are surrounded by **evil**, you can still live godly lives, honoring the Lord. Do not make choices that will lead you to disobedience, but instead fill your lives with godly things and serve the Holy Spirit. Paul specifically contrasted being "FILLED (Gk. *plērousthe*, "filled to overflowing, rendered complete," Eph 5:18) with the Spirit" to being "drunk with wine, which leads to RECKLESS ACTIONS" (Gk. *asōtia*, "abandoned life of a prodigal, lacking moral restraint, debauchery, v. 5:18; cp. Ti 1:6; 1 Pt 4:4). This word suggests the idea of one who refuses to save and squanders his means through an extravagant lifestyle, which degenerates into a profligate and wasteful life.

5:19-21 Paul explained how Christians were to live in the Spirit. You are to build others up with your speech and actions, you are to continually give thanks **to God**, and you are to treat others as more important than yourself. Believers "filled with the Spirit" should be "speaking to one another in":

- **PSALMS** (Gk. *psalmois*, "pious songs," lit. "striking or plucking" chords on a stringed instrument, used especially of sacred songs that were rendered to the accompaniment of instrumental music, v. 19; cp. 1 Co 14:26; Col 3:16),

- **HYMNS** (Gk. *humnois*, "songs of praise," a reference to sacred compositions that were primarily sung as praise anthems, Eph 5:19; cp. Col 3:16), and

- **SPIRITUAL SONGS** (Gk. *ōdais*, "songs of praise, odes," especially used of lyric poetry, Eph 5:19; cp. Col 3:16, Rv 5:9; 14:3; 15:13).

Christians should always seek the betterment of others and be willing to sacrifice personal preferences for the good of the body of Christ. This **submitting to one another** should be the regular behavior of Christians. It should not be resented or avoided but done as unto the Lord (Eph 5:21). SUBMITTING (Gk. *hupotassomenoi*, "lining oneself up under") is in the present tense and middle voice, thus suggesting the idea of continuing in submission and clearly noting that the action is by personal choice. The word definitely expresses the idea of voluntarily giving up your own rights and bowing your own will to another. In the Greek culture, the word was often used in military terminology in the sense of soldiers standing under the authority of a commanding officer. Verse 21 is a transition verse, addressing generally the appropriate submission within the congregation as a whole. Paul then moved in succeeding verses to specific applications for wives and husbands, children and parents, and even slaves and masters.

RELATIONSHIPS IN CHRIST (5:22–6:9)

Between Husband and Wife (5:22-33)

5:22-24 The final verses in chapter 5 are incredibly meaningful and intriguing. In perfect harmony with the teaching in the previous verses, Paul continued instruction on how to be "imitators of God" and live a Christian life consistent with His word.

This first idea of imitating God is of primary importance. In order to imitate God properly, you must have a proper understanding of His character, which is consis-

tently displayed throughout Scripture from Genesis to Revelation. Both men and women were created to display the image of God, and the Old and New Testaments affirm an equal value, coupled with a differentiation in roles among men and women.

The idea of equal value with differing responsibility is easy to understand by looking at the example of God Himself in the triunity. While the Father, Son, and Holy Spirit are equally God, holy and perfect, each also fulfills a different function. Each member of the triunity has the same authority and importance, but each carries out a function in order to accomplish their unified purpose.

Similarly, men and women can have equal value and importance before the Lord and still carry out different functions. Some view this principle as degrading; however, the complementarity between women and men brings a greater importance to the need for each gender one for the other. If the roles of men and women are interchangeable, then there is no need for both. Men and women should stop demanding equality or sameness in roles and start accepting responsibility before God for whatever He assigns.

Scripture notes that Jesus was totally submissive to the will of the Father (Jn 5; Lk 22). Jesus did not have an identity crisis; rather, He perfectly understood His role and the importance of His responsibility.

Submission **as to the Lord** calls a woman to understand her role of modeling submission in the home and church. Gratefully, the act of submission is against the backdrop of love and respect for Jesus. The previous chapters of Ephesians wonderfully explain all that **Christ** has done for His **church**. With Paul's reminder that submission is to be done unto the Lord, he was encouraging women to look beyond this life and instead consider the eternal implications of their behavior in marriage.

This passage addresses all **WIVES** (Gk. *gunaikes*), which is in the vocative case, yet with the definite article (Gk. *ai*, "the"), affirming that the apostle's words are for wives in a general sense and emphasizing the timelessness of the directive to follow. They are told to imitate God by being submissive to their own husbands. When a Christian woman marries, she should understand that while she is her husband's equal in personhood and in her spiritual accountability to God, she is called to submit herself willingly to her husband's leadership. **Wives** must yield to their **husbands** in love. Their love must be first for the Lord and then for their husbands. There is no escape clause in this passage. The verb "submit" is not found in the Greek text in verse 22 but is clearly understood as the appropriate verb from its mention in the preceding verse. The wife's submission is voluntary (see note on v. 21); it is to a specific authority ("to your own husband") and is regulated ("to one another," Gk., *allēlois*, in the sense of some to others, not everyone to everyone else). For example in 1 Peter 5:5, you see both unique ("submit yourselves to your elders") and mutual ("be submissive to one another") just as here in Ephesians in which there is a general admonition ("Submitting to one another") and a unique application ("wives . . . to your own husbands"). Women with more talent, education, wealth, or wit than their husbands are still under God's command to **submit**. Women who choose to marry ungodly, angry, or unkind men are still under this command. Neither Paul nor anyone else, was advocating abuse. This passage speaks to husbands and wives with the divine standard for the wife's willing submission to servant leadership (vv. 24-25,28-29) as the norm for all marriages of all time, according to the Word of God.

If submission is the norm for every Christian woman in marriage, then for Christian women to select godly mates is incredibly important. **The husband is head of the wife.** HEAD (Gk. *kephalē*) speaks for itself—authority over and direction over what is happening. The word is used 11 times in a single section of Paul's first letter to the Corinthians (1 Co 11:3-13). The word does have two meanings, depending on the context: spiritual (1 Co 11:3,4b,5b; Eph 5:23) and physical (1 Co 11:4a,5a,5c,6,7,10,13). Submission to a husband who loves like Jesus is satisfying, safe, and rewarding. Submission to a husband who loves himself above all else is difficult and draining. The principle of submission must be taught to young women before marriage so that they have an accurate picture of God's expectation as well as wisdom in selecting a life partner. Further, submission is the willing act of the wife, not a response to the threat or demand of the husband. Just as Jesus willingly submitted Himself to the desire of the Father, so women choose submission to their own husbands over personal independence.

Paul was very sensitive to the feelings and insecurities of women. This sensitivity is noteworthy since Paul was known for straightforwardly demanding even difficult behavior when mandated by Scripture. It is difficult to obey a command that you do not understand. God does give some commands with no explanation. A lack of explanation, of course, is no excuse for disobedience. However, Paul offered a clear explanation for submission. Marriage is a model for the church. Jesus **Christ is** the loving **head**, or authority, **of the church**. Husbands are to represent this loving headship in their families. Wives represent the response of the church to Jesus Christ by submitting to and respecting the leadership of their respective husbands.

Paul's sensitivity is shown by his reminder that Christ is the *sacrificial* Savior. Although no one relishes the role of being submissive, you should want to submit if submission accomplishes a greater, more important purpose, beyond personal happiness and the orderliness of a marriage relationship. Your life can and should reflect the church's appropriate response to the Savior, Jesus Christ, in regard to eternal salvation and the completion of God's plan of redeeming the world to Himself. This understanding puts submission in a completely different light. That's a plan with which women can get on board!

The practicalities of submission can be complex, but clearly looking to Jesus is the failsafe way to guide behavior. Jesus showed that He was submissive to the will of the Father, and Scripture unveils how the church is to respond to Jesus by using the metaphor of the wife's relationship to her husband in marriage. Just as the church cannot hold back any area from Jesus, so wives must submit to their husbands **in everything** (v. 24).

God has placed checks and balances in Christian marriage. Husbands are accountable to God Himself. He is a loving and protective Father who deeply cares for His daughters. A man who is under the authority of Jesus will be reminded of his own responsibility to care sacrificially for his wife. A healthy family is characterized by a husband and father who considers even his life less important than the needs of his family and a wife who willingly allows her husband to lead, thus supporting the structure created by God.

5:25 The husband is to represent the sacrificial leadership of Jesus Christ for His bride. **Husbands** are reminded that Jesus **gave** up everything He had of value

to serve His bride and provide not only for her physical and emotional needs but also His greatest sacrifice on the cross to meet her spiritual needs. As Christ is the spiritual head of the church, so husbands ought to be the spiritual heads of their homes, modeled after the loving and serving Savior.

5:26-28 Christ gave His life for the spiritual purity and reconciliation of His bride. The Word of God proclaims this message and the ingredients for right and successful living in Jesus Christ. His Word changes men and women, and His principles will keep you pure and **holy**. Christ went to great lengths to minister to, cleanse, and teach His bride the word of God so that in the final days, when she is presented, she will be without "SPOT (Gk. *spilon*, "stain, fault, moral blemish," v. 27; cp. 2 Pt 2:13) or WRINKLE" (Gk. *putis*, "fold"), but full of SPLENDOR (Gk. *endoxon*, "glorious, illustrious, distinguished, esteemed, held in high repute," Eph 5:27) and BLAMELESS (Gk. *amōmos*, "without blot, unblemished, disgrace," v. 27; cp. 2 Pt 2:13). These terms are used to describe physical beauty and symmetry and figuratively to denote spiritual perfection.

Husbands have a clear command to devote themselves to expediting the spiritual growth of their wives. Wives must feel very honored for God to assign their respective husbands with the responsibility to expend themselves in developing the spiritual purity of their brides.

While many husbands feel comfortable with financial or physical provision, few husbands feel adequate to provide for the spiritual needs of their wives and families. This task is a huge and difficult mandate. Wives must be patient and sensitive to their husbands as they pursue this difficult role.

Heart to Heart:
Paul's View of Women

Much has been said about the Apostle Paul's attitude toward women. In fact, some feminist theologians have reacted so strongly against Paul's words that they construed this passage as simply Paul's opinion and responded by substituting their own theology! Feminist theologians suggest that Jesus loved women but that Paul was speaking within the limitations of his own culture. In other words: Jesus spoke for God, but Paul only spoke for himself. They affirm that Christ reacted against the culture, while Paul merely reflected the culture. A brief look at Paul's historical context shows that nothing could be further from the truth.

Paul, of course, was raised in Judaism. Paul had the right lineage, the right family, and was a member of the strictest religious sect of Judaism (cp. Php 3:4-6). Paul's association with these legalistic religious leaders has perhaps been responsible for an unfortunate prejudice toward him because of the directives his letters contain concerning women in the church. The Pharisees were not known for being accommodating or even kind toward women. Those who were in this order could divorce their wives for any minuscule reason, and these rejected women would have no recourse due to the social and political climate of the day. Paul undoubtedly had been immersed in an atmosphere in which the understanding was that women were not as valuable to society as men.

This historical reality actually makes Paul's words of encouragement toward women more profound. While some interpret Paul's words toward women as pejorative, the truth is that Paul was not reflecting his culture; he was reacting against it. His strong stand on divorce (1 Co 7), his encouragement of the women who ministered to him (Lydia, Ac 16:40; Phoebe, Rm 16:1; Priscilla, Rm 16:3), and even the way he encouraged women who were great participants and patrons for world missions (Priscilla, Ac 18), all illustrate that Paul was bringing to his world a new way of thinking about the value of women within the context of Christianity and their usefulness in the spreading of the gospel. Especially in Ephesians 5:25-30 Paul made three revolutionary statements about women.

First, Paul's teaching style illustrates that men and women are equal. He did not give women unreasonable requirements and leave no instruction for the men. Rather he gave them both instruction. There is no air of superiority in his pedagogy, only the simple pastoral teaching for both men and women. Second, Paul commanded the men to **love their wives as their own bodies** v. 28).

LOVE *(Gk.* agapan*) is an action thoroughly explained by Paul in another letter; cp. 1 Co 13). The verb (Gk.* agapate*) indicates continuous and habitual action (Eph 5:25) and, with its derivatives, occurs a number of times in the Greek text (vv. 25-33).* Paul did not declare that Christ loved the church because of its holiness; rather, he clearly said that Christ's love for the church was a means "to make her holy" (v. 26). This attitude was completely foreign to Paul's views as a Pharisee.

Third, this love led to a man's nourishing and cherishing, usually considered feminine-driven activities, his wife. Paul is saying that men should relate to women on their terms. Nourishment and tangible affection are qualities to which women can relate. Why this charge to men? Paul understood that all are equal in Christ. More important, in this context, Paul thought it important enough for the theology of Christ's relationship to the church to be taught so that he commanded the men to do something often contrary to their nature. This cherishing is a temporal, tangible expression of the eternal truth that Christ loves and nourishes His church. The marriage model, God's model, facilitates more than temporal behavior. This model teaches the eternal truth and so brings glory to Christ in a culture that does not know Him.

The modern culture is contrary to the gospel in the same way that Paul's culture was. Paul amazingly reacted strongly against his upbringing for the purpose of glorifying God by showing the way the Lord values and cherishes women. Praise God that the counter-cultural message of hope Jesus offered to women is echoed in the practical and theological instruction that God gave to women through Paul.

Not only did Christ die for and lead His bride, but He has given the bride access to His own inheritance and His own resources. He does not hold back or resent His bride for His sacrifices. In fact, He considers the bride part of Himself and rushes to meet her need and comfort her. The husband and wife are challenged to "become one flesh" (5:31; cp. Gn 2:24). The wife becomes as important to the husband's well being and functioning as his own body. The husband should meet the needs of his wife and care for her as if he were caring for himself.

5:29-30 Again the example of Christ ministering to His church appears. While a husband may feel inadequate and uncertain of how to provide for his wife, Paul left no escape when he compared the husband to Jesus, who "**PROVIDES** (Gk. *ektrephei*, "nourish, rear, bring up to maturity," just as a parent would nourish children to maturity, v. 29; cp. 6:4) and **CARES FOR**" (Gk. *thalpei*, "keep warm, cherish with tender love and care, in the sense of showing affection and tender love"; see 1 Th 2:7) His body, "the church" (Eph 5:29). Perhaps, there is no greater standard to which a man could rise than the sacrifice of Jesus for the **members of His body** (v. 30). Just as no Christian woman should marry without the commitment to loving submission to her husband, no Christian man should marry without the commitment to loving leadership and sacrifice for his wife. A couple is prepared for marriage when they have both surrendered their lives to the will and design of the Word of God.

5:31 This reference is to Genesis 2:24 and to the account of Adam's first meeting with Eve, at which time he expressed her value (cp. Gn 2:23). With great sensitivity and passion, Adam explained to Eve how important and significant she was to him. This section is completed with the verse proclaiming the exclusive covenant relationship of husband and wife and with Adam's commitment for establishing the home as the spiritual leader, while still viewing Eve as equally valuable and necessary for the success of the family clearly understood. The biblical pattern (v. 31):

- **a man will leave** (Gk. *kataleipsei*, "leave behind because called away to another obligation, abandon") **his father and mother**;

- **and be joined** (Gk. *proskollēthēsetai*, "cleave, join oneself closely to, stick or glue to," from the root *kollaō*, "glue together, cement, fasten firmly") **to his wife**, in the sense of being faithfully devoted to another;

- **and the two will become one flesh**.

The first two parts of the divine pattern suggest one's complete separation from all his former ties, and then the climax comes in the establishment of a new relationship. Nowhere does Scripture allow or encourage homosexual unions, promiscuous unions, or polygamous unions. Marriage is defined by God just as salvation is defined by God. A person cannot follow Jesus and Buddha, or Jesus and Muhammad, or Jesus and self. A union with Jesus is an exclusive commitment just as a marriage between one man and one woman is designed to be exclusive.

5:32 Paul expressed awe that God created marriage in order to explain and show others about the **mystery** of the gos-

pel. By entering into Christian marriage and behaving in marriage as **Christ** intended, Christian families are a witness of Jesus' sacrifice and acceptance of His bride. Marriage is a living example of the mystery of the gospel of Jesus Christ. This bottom line emphasizes the importance for wives to submit to their husbands and for husbands to lead their wives. The commands are so much bigger than relationships, rights, or practical functions. You must get these relationships right because there is much more at stake than just the life of an individual. Monogamous marriage, together with its relationships within the union, is one of the analogies employed to describe Christ and His relationship to the church.

Between Parent and Child (6:1-4)

6:1-3 Certainly, life in the pagan culture of Ephesus was vastly different from God's design. Living the Christian life in the face of opposition has always been challenging and requires self-discipline and an understanding of God's call and purpose. The previous chapter described what a Christian marriage should look like, and chapter 6 continues with more details on relationships in the Christian home.

Paul first commanded **children** to **obey** (Gk. *hupakouete*, "listen, follow, hearken to a command," v. 1) their **parents** because it is the **right** thing to do. A child's obedience to her parents is a reflection of her obedience to the Lord. Then Paul continued with the admonition to **honor** (Gk. *tima*, "revere, to count as valuable") in the sense of treating **father and mother** as precious, an attitude of reverence with a double promise—well-being and longevity. The latter part of the promise is appropriate not as a guarantee of length of days but as a reminder that disobedience to parents is an indication of an undisciplined life, which can put a child on the fast track to sinful patterns that in themselves tend to shorten life. Well-being, too, is greatly enhanced when there is the peace that comes from self-discipline and orderliness in life. A child who honors God will honor her parents. Rebellious children reveal their personal rejection of God and His laws. The Lord has set up the family with authority and structure. He intends for parents to pass this structure on to their children and to enforce His principles graciously but steadfastly. In a society where the father held primary importance in the home, God, through Paul, offers this **commandment with a promise** to the children (v. 2).

Children who learn to obey and honor their parents will have the greatest opportunity to learn from their parents, receive protection from their parents, and benefit from learning valuable lessons through the natural instructions that emanate within their relationship with their parents. Children who are rebellious will make needless mistakes, ruin relationships, and bring hardship on their lives. God has designed the family to be a harmonious and happy environment for children and parents to grow in godliness.

When parents and children cooperate together to accomplish God's goals, the home will be safe, happy, and effective. Parents who are obedient to their assigned roles encourage children to take a position of obedience to divinely placed authorities in the family. Children must submit to authority within the family circle and honor God in order for parents to exercise successful stewardship with the children God has given. Parents must train their children to become godly individuals, contributing to the kingdom. In this way, the entire family cooperates to achieve God's important purposes.

6:4 The primary responsibility of leadership in the home rests upon the shoulders of the father, who must balance love and authority. Paul boldly told **fathers** not to provoke continually or cause anger in their children but instead to **bring them up** in such a way that children will desire to obey and honor their parents and to be open to learning from them about **the Lord**. While Paul could have included many commands for parents and fathers, he only noted one: "**BRING THEM UP** (Gk. *ektrephete*, "nourish, bring to maturity"; also 5:29) in the **TRAINING** (Gk. *paideia*, "upbringing, instruction, discipline, entire educational process" intending not only to impart knowledge but also to cultivate virtuous and healthy lives through reproof, discipline, and correction; to provide with tender care) "and **INSTRUCTION** (Gk. *nouthesia*, "admonition, exhortation, warning, training through words of tender encouragement, coupled when necessary with correction" indicating the complete process of discipline to be used in correcting any transgressions of God's laws within the household) of the Lord." This clear command should cause parents to understand that their most important job is raising godly children. Nothing else should take priority over this goal. God does warn parents in a straightforward way not to push their children toward the wrath of God.

Many parents want children to enrich their own lives and gain personal happiness or because it is simply the thing to do; but God says that parents have a responsibility to raise godly offspring. Both the sections on marriage and parenting uphold a higher and more rewarding standard than many people realize. There doubtless have always been many ineffective parents. However, even in a less than ideal situation, children should honor and obey their parents when such obedience does not require disobedience to God. All authority, good and bad, can be used by

God to accomplish His purpose, for God loves and protects His children.

Between Employee and Employer (6:5-9)

6:5-8 In this section Paul was not endorsing slavery but acknowledging it as a way of life. Slavery is not presented in Scripture as a divinely established institution. These verses are often applied to the employer/employee relationship common today. Christianity brought a whole new perspective to early believers, especially to those who were considered of little worth in society. Jesus brought these people a sense of value and freedom. While Scripture does not require someone to stay in an abusive and harmful situation, it does not give people license to abandon structure and authority. Paul did not endorse slavery but regulated it. He addressed slaves with the same courtesies as he did their masters. Masters were admonished to treat their slaves with justice and consideration (v. 9). Slavery in the New Testament era was complex:

- There were slaves from different races and nations, captives from war;

- There were slaves who volitionally chose to indenture themselves for financial and economic reasons;

- There were slaves among laborers, philosophers, farmers, and even physicians.

The designations of "slave" and "free" were primarily legal distinctions.

Many **slaves** (Gk. *douloi*, "servants, bondsmen," v. 5) who accepted Christ had a new spiritual importance and more freedom but found it necessary to remain in their positions. Everyone at some point in life is required to fulfill positions or responsibilities that he finds unappealing and oppressive. Paul described the attitude with which "slaves" should **obey** their **human masters** (v. 5) or **render service** (v. 7):

- with fear and trembling;

- in the sincerity (Gk. *aplotēti*, "not self-seeking but free from hypocrisy, upright, simple, generous," v. 5) of your heart;

- as to Christ;

- not only while being watched;

- not in order to please men (Gk. *anthrōpareskoi*, "courting the favor of men," especially at the expense of principle, v. 5; cp Col 3:22), but as slaves of Christ;

- doing God's will from your heart;

- with a good attitude (Gk. *eunoias*, "kindness, zeal, enthusiasm, goodwill," without waiting to be compelled, Eph 6:7);

- as to the Lord and not to men;

- knowing that whatever good each one does, . . . he will receive this back (Gk. *komisetai*, "be recompensed, cared or provided for," in the sense of a deposit that presupposes an adequate return, v. 8; 2 Co 5:10) from the Lord.

The struggle is acknowledged but readers are reminded that all things, pleasant and unpleasant, must be done with excellence and sincerity as if they were being done for Jesus Himself. Paul encouraged a strong work ethic, which would make the slave valuable in the master's sight, and an attitude that would endear him to those in authority over him, which would also help protect a slave or anyone who might be in a vulnerable situation.

6:9 Paul, never afraid to address a touchy subject, spoke to husbands, fathers, and now masters. He brought these men in authority to the realistic picture that they themselves were under authority. He told them to **treat** others kindly based on the truth that all are equal spiritually. Paul's teaching would have been humbling to the men of his day. However, Jesus offered examples of how others should be treated, and Paul admonished these in authority to behave rightly because they must answer to their heavenly **Master**, with whom **there is no favoritism** (Gk. *prosōpolēmpsia*, "partiality, discriminating or making judgment based on the face or outward appearance of things," v. 9; cp. Rm 2:11; Col 3:25; Jms 2:1; nominal form in Ac 10:34).

STRENGTH IN CHRIST (6:10-20)

6:10-13 This passage on Christian warfare is a great encouragement since it offers a clear and honest picture of the Christian life. While many would like to believe that accepting Jesus means comfort, wealth, and blessing, the Bible offers quite a different perspective. The book of Ephesians is fraught with examples of God's beneficence and the idea that God desires to bless His children; however, this book also addresses the reality that a Christian has many enemies in the world. Enemies can be Satan, unbelievers, your own flesh, and others. All of these things war against the Christian and the church, strategically seeking to hinder the growth of God's Kingdom and the success of the body. Christians live their lives in victory for Christ Jesus, or they live their lives for self and Satan. There is no unengaged life. Many want to live superficially keeping all options open, but an in-between state is impossible.

Paul was an expert tactician and warrior for Christ. He offered motivation for the battle and trained his followers on how to have success in battle. Interestingly Paul did not encourage believers to wait on the Lord for strength; neither did he discourage action until one felt strong. Quite the opposite, Paul said **be strengthened**. David chose to find strength in the Lord (1 Sm 30:6). He did not wait for someone to come along and counsel Him. He did not wait for a book to be published or for a revival service to attend. David knew God intimately. He knew God's strength and love, and David trained his mind, heart, and body to be strengthened in the Lord. He knew the discipline of a mighty warrior, and so must you.

Since Paul wrote this letter when he was under arrest, he may well have had a guard standing over him. He probably wrote these verses while looking at the armor of a soldier as the Holy Spirit inspired his application of truths about the Christian life.

Paul called the believers to get ready for battle and "put on" the "ARMOR (Gk. *panoplian*, "full or complete armor," from *pas*, "collectively, each individual piece," and *hoplon*, "weapons, instruments of warfare," v. 11) of God" so that he is ready to stand against the tactics of the Devil. This full armor included a shield, sword, lance, helmet, and breastplate and usually made a rather splendid and striking display. Satan will not wait for the Christian to get his act together and dress for battle; he will start his attack when you are most vulnerable.

Paul emphasized that people are not the enemy. For Christians, the **battle** (v. 12) is:

- **against the rulers** (Gk. *archas*; see 1:21; 3:10),

- **against the authorities** (Gk. *exousias*; see 1:21; 3:10),

- against the WORLD POWERS (Gk. *kosmokratoras*, "lord of the world, prince of the age," used only here in the New Testament) of this darkness, and

- against the spiritual forces of evil in the heavens.

A wise Christian will arm himself by putting on the "armor" that God has already provided. Only then can the believer "stand against the TACTICS (Gk. methodeias, "cunning arts, deceit, schemes, craftiness," 6:11) of the Devil" (v. 11) and "be able to RESIST (Gk. antistēnai, "take a stand against, oppose, withstand," v. 13; cp. Jms 4:7; 1 Pt 5:9) in the evil day" (Eph 6:13).

6:14-20 A believer wearing the "full armor of God" is ready to stand firm, having

- "truth like A BELT AROUND YOUR WAIST" (Gk. perizōsamenoi, "wrap around, fasten garments with a belt around;" osphun, "hips, loins," as leather apron to protect the lower abdomen or the sword-belt and special belt designating an officer, v. 14; cp. "ready for service" in Lk 12:35);

- "righteousness like armor on your CHEST" (Gk. thōraka, "thorax, from the neck to where the ribs end, breastplate" what was worn to protect the body between the shoulders and the loins, usually a piece of metal but for those who were wealthier a chain mail that covered all the chest and hips, Eph 6:14; cp 1 Th 5:8);

- "feet SANDALED (Gk. hupodēsamenoi, "bind under, bind or fasten on, tie beneath, put on shoes, wear," Eph 6:15) with READINESS (Gk. etoimasia, "state or condition of being prepared and ready," perhaps figuratively emphasizing firmness and a solid foundation) for the gospel of peace";

- taken up "the SHIELD of faith" (Gk. thureon, probably a door-shaped "shield," since "door" is the root word, usually with an iron frame and sometimes a metal boss in the center, v. 16) with which to "extinguish the flaming ARROWS (Gk. belē, "missile, dart, javelin," v. 16) of the evil one";

- taken "the HELMET (Gk. perikephalaian, from peri, "around," and kephalē, "head," therefore lit. a piece of armor surrounding the head, through which nothing short of an axe or hammer could pierce, v. 17; cp. 1 Th 5:8) of salvation";

- grasped "the SWORD (Gk. machairan, "short, straight sword or saber" used in combat, Eph 6:17; cp. Heb 4:12) of the Spirit, which is God's WORD" (Gk. hrēma, "word or utterance" from a living voice, "verbalized speech, message, or declaration," Eph 6:17; cp. 5:26; Ac 11:6; Rm 10:8,17-18; Heb 6:5; 11:3; 1 Pt 1:25).

Just as any soldier would have to practice with weaponry to be used, so believers must learn to be comfortable with their armor; and this section offers a great training program imbedded with the necessity of prayer. Paul offered details on how to pray:

- pray constantly;

- pray **in the Spirit**;

- **be alert** (Gk. agrupnountes, "attentive, awake, ready, circumspect, watchful," lit. "sleepless or staying awake" in order to guard and keep watch), persevere, and intercede for the saints (Eph 6:18).

Paul closed this section by making himself and his own needs known to the people. He did not consider himself above temptation and knew troubles and suffering well. Paul was certainly on the front lines of battle and needed support from other Christians. He asked for specific prayer regarding the message of the gospel. Few American Christians can envision real spiritual battles or the possibility of actually having to lay down their lives for the cause of Christ. But for many believers around the world, and for Paul, this reality was a daily possibility. No doubt there were some days when Paul wanted to run and hide, escape the danger, abuse, and beatings. Yet, he was committed to standing firm and asked that others would also pray for His **PERSEVERENCE** (Gk. *proskarterēsei*, "devotion or adherence to, patience, undaunted faithfulness in continuing to care or give attention to what would come, being in constant readiness," especially in the sense of waiting for your trial or remaining at your work despite difficulties, v. 18; the only instance of the nominal usage in the New Testament, but cp. various appearances of the verb form: Mk 3:9; Ac 1:14; 2:42,46; 6:4; 8:13; 10:7; Rm 12:12; 13:6; Col 4:2) and **BOLDNESS** (Gk. *parrēsia*, in the sense of speaking openly, Eph 6:19; see 3:12) in proclaiming the gospel even in chains (6:18-19).

BENEDICTION (6:21-24)

6:21-22 Paul had a good balance of sharing honestly about himself and his own needs but not being so overwhelmed in self-struggle that he was unable to recognize the needs of others. Paul was constantly concerned about the needs of those in the churches to whom he ministered. This concern led to his sending **Tychicus** to give a full, thorough, and honest report. Paul commended Tychicus so that he would receive love and respect upon his coming but also encouraged the people to trust and rely on him. Paul was convinced that Tychicus would be an encouragement

to the people, and Paul had an obvious excitement about the coming of this co-laborer to the Ephesian church.

6:23-24 Paul seemed to enjoy sending his final greetings filled with love and blessings, reminding readers of his own love and more importantly of God's love. Paul ended with wise motivation, claiming **grace** for those with **undying** (Gk. *aphtharsia*, "incorruptible, immortal, perpetual, imperishable," v. 24; cp. Rm 2:7; 1 Co 15:42-54; 2 Tm 1:10) **love**. This picture of "undying love" should be the lens through which the apostle's instruction is viewed by the Ephesians. Paul behaved as a wonderful, loving father, caring for his children. Since God is speaking through Paul, you can trust his loving, passionate heart.

Bibliography

*Calvin, John. *Commentaries on the Epistles of Paul to the Galatians and Ephesians.* Grand Rapids: Baker Books, 2003.

Hendriksen, William. *Exposition of Ephesians.* New Testament Commentary. Grand Rapids: Baker Books, 1967.

*Leslie, William Houghton. "The Concept of Woman in the Pauline Corpus in Light of the Social and Religious Environment of the First Century." Ph.D. Dissertation. Northwestern University, 1976.

Lloyd-Jones, D. Martyn. *God's Ultimate Purpose: An Exposition of Ephesians.* Grand Rapids: Baker Books, 1978.

MacArthur, John. *Ephesians.* The MacArthur New Testament Commentary. Chicago: Moody Press, 1986.

MacLaren, Alexander. *Ephesians.* Expositions of Holy Scripture, vol. 13. Grand Rapids: Baker House Books, 1974.

Richardson, Alan. *A Dictionary of Christian Theology.* Philadelphia: The Westminster Press, 1969.

* For advanced study

PHILIPPIANS

Introduction

The book of Philippians, a favorite book of the Bible for many who have read its content, contains memorable verses: "For me, living is Christ and dying is gain" (1:21); "I am able to do all things through Him who strengthens me" (4:13); "And my God will supply all your needs according to His riches in glory in Christ Jesus" (4:19). The encouragement readers receive from Philippians is not surprising, considering its original intent. In this tender letter from the Apostle Paul to the Philippian church, one sees Paul's heart as a mentor in the faith and as a father who deeply cared for his spiritual children. He yearned to see their spiritual growth; thus, he taught them the essence of the Christian life, warning them of those things that might hinder them as they "pursue [the] goal" (3:14).

> *The book of Philippians is a present-day affirmation that what really matters in all of life is the passionate pursuit of Jesus Christ.*

Above all, Paul wanted the Philippian believers to know the surpassing worth of Jesus Christ and to pursue knowing Him (3:7). For Christ gives meaning to life and can transform death into gain (1:21); Christ, the Suffering One, serves as an example and supplies strength in times of suffering (2:5-11); and Christ, the highly exalted Lord and Savior, is the Source of the deepest, truest, and most lasting joy (3:1; 4:4). The book of Philippians is a present-day affirmation that what really matters in all of life is the passionate pursuit of Jesus Christ.

Title

The Greek title of the epistle is simply *pros Philippēsoge*, "to the Philippians." This title reflects that the letter is addressed "To all the saints in Christ Jesus who are in Philippi, including the overseers and deacons" (1:1).

Setting

Paul's letter to the Philippians was born out of an act of giving. In their regular correspondence with Paul, the Philippians heard of his imprisonment in Rome. As was their ministry custom, they promptly sent Paul a gift of support, as well as one of their own members, Epaphroditus, who was a personal embodiment of their love and concern (2:25; 4:18).

Epaphroditus brought their gift, as well as news of the Philippian church, to Paul, who was always anxious to know how they were doing. Likely Epaphroditus updated him on the external opposition and the internal strife facing the Philippians. The resultant letter that Paul felt compelled to write served many purposes:

- Paul *updated* the Philippians on his own circumstances (1:12-18).
- He *challenged* them to stand firm in the faith against all opposition (2:27-30; 4:1).
- Paul *warned* them against those who preach and live contrary to the gospel of Christ (3:1-2,18-19).
- He *reminded* them of the true essence of the gospel (3:3-9).
- He *encouraged* them to press towards the prize (3:12-17).
- He *urged* them to unite for the sake of the gospel (1:27; 2:1-4; 4:2).
- Finally, Paul *thanked* them for their constant support, as well as for their recent gift sent through Epaphroditus (4:10-20), whom they should gladly welcome back into their community (2:25-30).

The most remarkable thing about the setting of this letter is that its message came from a man who was sitting joyfully in prison. Surrounded by the hostile opposition of unbelievers, betrayed by others who were believers (1:15-17), and awaiting a possible death sentence, Paul chose to rejoice—rejoice in the Lord he loved, trusted, and pursued passionately; rejoice in the advancement of the gospel; and rejoice in the Philippians' own joy in Christ.

Genre

Paul's introduction resembles the form of ancient letters written and exchanged between friends in the Graeco-Roman world.[1] Paul began with a greeting (1:1-2), expressed his thanksgiving and affection for the Philippians (1:3-8), then told them how he prayed for them (1:9-11). Although the letter is similar in form to ancient letters, the content is uniquely Christocentric and full of Paul's own articulation of the gospel message.

Author

The authorship of Philippians has rarely been questioned. The book itself claims to have been written by the apostle Paul (1:1); early external attestation verifies Pauline authorship (i.e., Polycarp, AD 135); and the letter has been included in all the lists of canonical writings. Scholars widely agree that the Apostle Paul (Lat. *Paulus*, "little") did indeed pen the letter.

The only portion of the book in which the authorship might be questioned is the Christ Hymn (2:6-11). While some scholars say that Paul cited an existing Christian hymn, others say Paul wrote it himself, a task for which he was clearly capable (e.g., Rm 8:31-39; 11:33-36; etc.).[2]

Date

In contrast to the widely accepted authorship of the book, the dating of Philippians has caused much discussion. The book's date depends upon Paul's location when he wrote it. Speculation on his precise whereabouts at the time has reaped a divergence of opinion.

Clearly from the book itself one notes that Paul was in prison awaiting sentence when he wrote the letter (1:7,13-14,17,20,30; 2:17). The book of Acts records four places where Paul was imprisoned: Philippi (16:23-40), Jerusalem (21:26-36; 22:22-29), Caesarea (23:31–26:32), and Rome (28:16,30-31). Some have also suggested that Paul could have been imprisoned during his two-year, sometimes-tumultuous stay at Ephesus (Ac 19); however, there is no direct evidence of this assertion.

Several facts recorded in Philippians suggest Paul's location. Paul wrote from a place where there was a Roman imperial guard (1:12-13) and where members of Caesar's household were present (4:22). He had apparently been in prison for an extended period of time, for many had heard of the reason for Paul's imprisonment, and there had been time for the gospel to advance (1:12-14). Even more significantly, several journeys had been made in the time lapse during the correspondence between Paul and the Philippians (2:25-30; 4:10-20). At the time of his writing, Paul was facing an upcoming trial and was uncertain of the outcome, whether he would live or die (1:19-26; 2:23). He thought, however, that he would be released and would come to Philippi once again (1:25-26; 2:24). Finally, one should note that, in whatever place he was imprisoned, Paul had a certain measure of freedom, for clearly he was able to write letters (3:1), welcome friends (2:25), and receive gifts (4:18).

Since the time of the early church, the traditional origin for the letter has been Rome. While arguments for other places of origin have some merit (particularly Caesarea),[3] Rome still seems to be the most likely setting for the facts listed above. If indeed Rome is the place of origin for Paul's letter to the Philippians, then the likely date of the book is AD 61–62, toward the end of Paul's Roman imprisonment.

Recipients

Paul wrote this letter to the believers in the city of Philippi. The Philippian church, founded by Paul on his second missionary journey in the early 50s, bears the distinction of being the first Christian congregation in Europe.

Philippi was a cosmopolitan city located on the plain of eastern Macedonia, about 10 miles inland from Neapolis, an important seaport. Founded in 356 BC by Philip of Macedon (the father of Alexander the Great), this Greek city had been made into a Roman military colony in 42 BC. When Paul arrived in Philippi, he saw a "miniature Rome," made up of privileged people who were diverse in nationality and social position.

The details of Paul's first visit to Philippi are recorded in Acts 16:13-40. Paul found no synagogue, meaning that there were not even 10 Jewish male believers. Paul did find a place of prayer not far from the city gate on the Gangites River. Here Paul found a group of God-fearing women. The Philippian church was born.

When Paul left Philippi, he left behind a diverse group of believers in Christ: a Jewish proselyte and wealthy merchant named Lydia, whose home was probably used for their first church (Ac 16:14-16,40); a native Greek slave girl whose spirit of divination Paul cast out (Ac 16:16-21); and a Roman jailer and his household, who had been won to Christ through Paul and Silas's midnight worship in prison (Ac 16:22-34).

The Philippian church was beloved by Paul (Php 1:3-8). They were a praying people (1:19) as well as loyal and liberal givers throughout Paul's ministry. Even when no one else supported him (4:15), they gave out of their own "deep poverty" (2 Co 8:2) to further the gospel message.

Major Themes

Opposition and suffering. Suffering formed the backdrop for Paul's own circumstances, as well as that of the Philippian church. While only four verses in the book speak explicitly about external opposition (1:28; 3:2,18-19), the admonitions throughout to stand firm (1:27; 4:1), to be fearless (1:28; 4:6), and to be obedient followers (2:12; 3:15-17; 4:9) form the context and framework of the entire book.

Joy. The words "joy" and "rejoice" are found more times in this letter than in any other of Paul's letters: "Joy" (Gk. *chara*) is used five times (1:4; 2:2,18,29; 4:1) and "rejoice" (Gk. *chairō*) is used nine times (1:18 [2], 19; 2:17-18, 28; 3:1; 4:4 [2]). Paul discovered the true source of joy in Christ Himself, and Christ enabled Paul to experience joy even in suffering. Paul wanted the Philippians to experience this same joy of faith; thus, he urged them to grow in their knowledge of Christ (3:8) and called them to rejoice in *Him* (3:1; 4:4).

Unity. Paul's emphasized unity within the church as vital for the progress of the gospel in the world (1:27; 2:2-4,14; 4:2). In the face of church disagreement, they were to "agree in the Lord" (4:2). In the face of opposition by the world, they were to stand "firm in one spirit, with one mind" (1:27). The key to their unity was to pursue Christ and His interests, not other things and not their own interests (2:4).

Christ. A list of themes for the book of Philippians would not be complete without mentioning Christ Himself. The Christocentricity of the book is evident by the more than 50 references to Jesus, whom Paul calls "Lord," "Savior," and "Christ." For Paul, "living *is* Christ" (1:21; also Gl 2:19-20).

Pronunciation Guide

Epaphroditus	*ih PAF roh DIGH tuhs*	Neapolis	*nee AP uh lis*
Euodia	*yoo OH dih uh*	Philippi	*FIH lih pigh*
Judaizer	*JOO day ighz uhr*	Philippians	*fih LIP ih uhnz*
Lydia	*LID ih uh*	Proselyte	*PRAHS uh light*
Macedonia	*MASS uh DOH nih uh*	Syntyche	*SIN tih kee*

Outline

I. INTRODUCTORY MATTERS (1:1-11)
  A. Greeting (1:1-2)
  B. Thanksgiving (1:3-8)
  C. Intercession (1:9-11)

II. THE PRESENT AND FUTURE OF PAUL'S IMPRISONMENT (1:12-26)
  A. Paul's Present Joy: Good Outcomes of Imprisonment (1:12-18a)
    1. Unbelievers hear of Christ (1:12-13)
    2. Believers proclaim Christ (1:14-18a)
  B. Paul's Future Joy: Christ's Honor and the Philippians' Joy (1:18b-26)

III. COMMISSION AND FOLLOW-UP (1:27–2:30)
  A. The Philippians' Commission (1:27–2:18)
    1. Be united and humble (1:27–2:4)

2. Be Christlike (2:5-11)
3. Be obedient (2:12-18)
  B. Paul's Follow-Up (2:19-30)
    1. Arrival of Timothy (2:19-24)
    2. Arrival of Epaphroditus (2:25-30)

IV. THE ESSENCE OF THE GOSPEL AND LIFE ITSELF (3:1–4:1)
  A. The Inadequacy of the Flesh (3:1-7)
  B. The Sufficiency of Christ (3:8-14)
  C. The Appeal (3:15–4:1)

V. CONCLUDING MATTERS (4:2-23)
  A. Reiterative Exhortations (4:2-9)
    1. Be united (4:2-3)
    2. Be Christ-focused (4:4-7)
    3. Be obedient (4:8-9)
  B. Appreciation (4:10-20)
  C. Closing Greeting and Benediction (4:21-23)

Exposition of the Text

INTRODUCTORY MATTERS (1:1-11)

Greeting (1:1-2)

1:1 While **Paul** is clearly the author of the letter, he chose to include **Timothy** ("honored of God") in the greeting as well. Timothy had a vested interest in the church as its cofounder (Ac 16–18) and was presently with Paul (Php 2:19). Paul identified them as **slaves** (Gk. *douloi*) **of Christ Jesus** (cf. 2:7), an indication that that they belonged to Jesus, with no rights of their own and an introduction to one of the letter's key themes—humility.

Paul identified the recipients of the letter as **all the saints in Christ Jesus who are in Philippi**. The term "saints" (Gk.

hagiois, "holy or set apart ones") is indicative of the privilege of being recipients of Christ's saving work, as well as of a responsibility to live holy lives, set apart for His use (1 Pt 1:15-16). The inclusion of the **overseers** (Gk. *episkopois*) **and deacons** (Gk. *diakonois*) in the greeting occurs only here in Paul's letters. While it is not certain whether or not these officers were established in the church at the time Philippians was written, at least there were those who performed the functions of overseeing and serving the flock. See notes on 1 Timothy 3:1-13; Titus 1:5-9; and 1 Peter 5:1-4.

1:2 Paul changed the customary Greek greeting, "rejoice" (Gk. *chairein*) to "grace" (Gk. *charis*); then he added "peace" (Gk. *eirēnē*): **Grace to you and peace**. This greeting was probably an adaptation of a Jewish blessing used in synagogue services, but Paul added **from God our Father and the Lord Jesus Christ**, acknowledging Christ's deity.

Thanksgiving (1:3-8)

1:3-6 For Paul, every thought of the Philippian believers was cause for joy, and each prayer turned into one of thanksgiving (v. 3). The basis for his joy in them was their "PARTNERSHIP (Gk. *koinōnia*, "fellowship, sharing") in the gospel" from the very beginning (v. 5), an evidence to him that God had "started a good work" in them (v. 6). The idea of fellowship was closely associated with the early church, highlighting close relationships within the body and interacting participation. This communion also suggested the idea of "gift" or sharing what is held in common.

The "good work" was the work of salvation, a deliberate plan in the mind of God since "before the foundation of the world" (Eph 1:4). Since God had begun a good work in them, He would certainly **carry it on to completion**, for God always finishes what He starts (Php 1:6; 1 Th 5:24; Gl 3:3). The day of completion is **the day of Christ Jesus**, when Christ returns to complete the salvation of the saints and to be worshipped and recognized by all (Php 2:10-11).

1:7-8 Paul saw the good work of God in their lives; thus, he could call them **partners with me in grace** (v. 7). They were partners in that they had supported Paul during his **imprisonment** (v. 7; 4:10-19) and also because they shared in the same trial of suffering for the sake of the gospel (1:27-28). No wonder Paul had such deep, abiding AFFECTION (Gk. *splagchnois*, "inward parts, entrails, heart, love"; v. 8; cp. Lk 15:20; Mk 6:34). The word suggested the strongest expression in Greek for affection.

The word also indicated heart-felt compassion.

Intercession (1:9-11)

Paul continued telling the Philippians how he interceded on their behalf. He prayed that they would grow spiritually (vv. 9-10) so that, in the end, their fruit of righteousness would abound to the glory and praise of God (v. 11).

Paul's eye was on how God would ultimately be glorified through the Philippians. He prayed that their already present love would **keep on growing in knowledge** (i.e., understanding of life situations) **and every kind of discernment** (i.e., perception of what to do in life situations) so that they could **determine what really matters** in life.

Their determination and approval of what really matters in life (cp. 3:8) would result in **pure and blameless** living. The resultant **fruit of righteousness** (cp. 2 Co 9:10; Gl 5:22-23)—ethical actions possible not because of their own effort but because of their union with **Jesus Christ**—would abound **to the glory and praise of God** (cp. Mt 5:16).

THE PRESENT AND FUTURE OF PAUL'S IMPRISONMENT (1:12-26)

Knowing that the Philippians were anxious to be updated on his circumstances, Paul spoke of what was happening at present (1:12-18a), and what he thought might happen in the future (1:18b-26).

Paul's Present Joy: Good Outcomes of Imprisonment (1:12-18a)

Whereas some might have focused on the difficulties of prison, Paul focused on two good outcomes resulting from his imprisonment.

Heart 10 Heart:
Pray for Your Children

In Philippians 1:3-10, one gets a glimpse of the deep love Paul had for the Philippian believers, whom he considered to be his spiritual children. Paul thought of them often, for they were in his heart (1:7). And yet, Paul did not spend time merely thinking of his spiritual children; he spent time praying for them. Intercession was a natural by-product of his Godward focus, which constantly channeled his thinking about the believers into prayers on their behalf.

God has uniquely gifted women to be nurturers and to care for their children. To think about your children is easy; this process is what it means to be a mother! Paul's example, however, causes you to ask yourself: Do I spend as much time praying for my children as I do thinking about them? And do I pray with an eye toward what God's purposes are for them (1:9-11)? And how often do you make your children aware of what you are praying for them (which encourages them to act on what you are praying)? Paul's example is a reminder that caring for your children means offering up fervent, visionary prayers on their behalf.

Unbelievers hear of Christ (1:12-13)

1:12-13 One could easily conclude that imprisonment would hinder the spread of the gospel. **Actually**, Paul concluded that the gospel had spread because of what had happened to him (v. 12).

Paul probably had in mind here the entire chain of events that had led to his imprisonment in Rome, beginning with his arrest in Jerusalem (cp. Ac 21:26–28:31).[4] The gospel had actually forged ahead because of this ordeal of *several years*, for in each circumstance, Paul had the opportunity to testify of the gospel of Jesus Christ. Now in Rome, Paul noted that the **whole imperial guard** and **everyone else** knew why he was in chains (Php 1:13). If, in fact, there were nine thousand praetorian guards in Rome, as some think, this truly was a wonder.[5]

Believers proclaim Christ (1:14-18a)

1:14-18a Paul saw another good outcome of his imprisonment: Most of the Roman believers had a renewed boldness in preaching Christ. These newly emboldened believers fell into two groups.

One group of Roman believers understood that Paul was in prison because he had been **appointed for the defense of the gospel.** Zealous for the gospel and having a **love** for Paul, they sought to aid the rapidly spreading gospel in Rome by their preaching (v. 16).

Another group of Roman believers preached Christ out of entirely different motives—apparently **out of envy and strife** (v. 15) and **rivalry** (v. 17) with Paul. They hoped that their preaching would bother Paul or cause him **trouble in** his **imprisonment** (v. 17).

The reasons for this group's animosity toward Paul are not clear from the text; neither is it clear exactly how they expected their preaching to hurt Paul. RIVALRY, which might also be translated "selfishness" or "self-seeking" (Gk. *eritheias*), suggests that they were preaching to further their own interests or to gain something for themselves. The ambition and self-centeredness expressed in this word further indicated feuding and contention in seeking one's own desires. Perhaps, as the word "envy" (Gk. *phthonon*, "jealousy") seems to suggest, they were jealous of Paul's large following and the attention this outsider was receiving, and they sought to further their own authority by passionately preaching Christ. They were still preaching Christ—not another gospel, so apparently it was not the gospel *content* that was intended to distress Paul.

However, this group misjudged Paul. Although Paul most certainly was hurt by the opposition of fellow believers, he was able to rejoice because Christ was being proclaimed, regardless of the motive (v. 18). Here was a man who looked after the interests and reputation of Christ, not his own. Paul was not oblivious to the hurt; rather Paul's focus on Christ enabled him to choose to rejoice, even in his own difficult circumstances.

Paul's Future Joy: Christ's Honor and the Philippians' Joy (1:18b-26)

1:18-19 Paul turned from his present joy to what he knew would bring him joy in the future: being a vessel for Christ's honor (v. 20). Paul first stated that he would **rejoice** because he knew this would **lead to** his **deliverance** (Gk. *sōtērian*, "salvation" in the sense of preservation from danger or destruction). How could Paul's current situation of suffering lead to his "deliverance"?

More than likely, Paul was not referring here to "deliverance" from his opposition or even death itself. Like Job (cp. Job 13:16), Paul probably meant that he expected his trials to result in his salvation and ultimate vindication before God. Paul therefore relied upon their **prayers and help from the Spirit** in order to remain steadfast to this end (Php 1:19).

1:20 Paul's greatest expectation was that Christ would be honored through him. The word in 1:20 translated EAGER EXPECTATION (Gk. *apokaradokian*; cp. Rom. 8:19) means literally "turning one's head away from something." The idea is straining with outstretched neck to look for that which is expected. What a picture of Paul! By deliberate choice, the apostle had turned away from looking at his opposition and suffering, and he was straining to see the fulfillment of his expectation: "Christ" being "highly honored" (Gk. *megalunthōsetai*, "make great, enlarge, magnify") through the "boldness" of his testimony. The nuance of meaning included praise and extolling. Paul was not worried about being shamed before others; he was concerned about being ashamed before God. Paul would be ashamed to shrink back in fear and timidity, for this cowardice would fail to bring Christ honor.

1:21 The intensity of Paul's desire to honor Christ—whether by his life or his death—becomes understandable with his next statement: **For me, living is Christ and dying is gain**. For Paul, life was all about preaching and pursuing Christ; therefore, death could only be gain, for in death, he gained Christ.

1:22-26 Paul knew his fate was in the Lord's hands, though he considered whether he would choose life or death if the choice were his. If it were left up to him, he would choose death—**far better** because he would **be with Christ** (v. 23). However, he believed he would live because it would mean:

- **fruitful work** for him (v. 22), and

- the Philippians' **advancement and joy in the faith** (v. 25).

If Paul were to survive this ordeal and come back to them, they would have renewed **confidence** (v. 26) and joy in Christ because of their answered prayer. Once again, Paul showed that his joy was found in looking to the interests of others, not his own—the Philippians above himself and Christ above all.

Heart to Heart:
Where Is Your Focus?

Have you ever experienced a life-changing event—an event that changed your perspective on life and altered the way you live, even to this day? Paul experienced such an event when he encountered Jesus Christ on the road to Damascus (Ac 9). The surpassing worth of Jesus caused everything else around Him to pale in comparison. It is not surprising that Paul gave his life for the cause of Christ, for he came to believe that to live is Christ (1:21).

Paul's focus on Christ affected the way he thought and spoke (1:12-26). His longing for Christ to be preached meant that he was able to look past the many difficulties of prison and rejoice in the good outcomes of his suffering. Thus, he did not spend time rehearsing his long list of recent trials (see endnote 4), nor did he lament about how hard life had been lately. Paul was even able to cast fear and timidity aside because of his intense desire to see Christ exalted through his own life and death (1:20).

Where is your focus? Is it on the person of Jesus Christ or on the trials around you? Pray that God might show you the surpassing worth of Christ so that your thoughts and focus might stay on Him.

COMMISSION AND FOLLOW-UP (1:27–2:30)

Paul then turned his attention to the Philippians' spiritual walk. He urged them to live **worthy of the gospel**, standing united for the sake of Christ (1:27-30). He reminded them that church unity can only happen as each believer seeks to live in humility and obedience according to his Christlike nature (2:1-18). Finally in this section, Paul told the Philippians of his plans and reasons for sending Timothy and Epaphroditus, both of whom would follow up on their progress in the faith (2:19-30).

The Philippians' Commission (1:27–2:18)

Be united and humble (1:27–2:4)

1:27 Living in a Roman military colony, the Philippians would have understood well Paul's instruction to "LIVE (Gk. *politeuesthe*, "conduct oneself as a citizen") worthy of the gospel." They were to conduct themselves as citizens of Christ's rule (cp. 3:20), for Christ, not Caesar, is Lord (2:11). Living worthy of Christ means "STANDING FIRM" (Gk. *stēkete*, "standing like a soldier who will not budge"; cp. 4:1), "WORKING SIDE BY SIDE (Gk.

sunathlountes, "contending together like a team") for the faith of the gospel," united in every way. The idea is remaining steadfast while simultaneously working together as a team in spreading the gospel.

1:28 While the identity of the Philippians' **opponents** is not clear, they were apparently pagan because they were headed for **destruction**. The steadfastness of the believers would simultaneously be a sign of their salvation and a sign of their opponents' destruction.

1:29-30 Their command to stand firm is based on the fact that God has GIVEN (Gk. *echaristhē*, "giving graciously," v. 29) them not only the opportunity to believe but also the opportunity to suffer. The term includes the idea of granting freely, bestowing in kindness, and even ultimately canceling, forgiving, pardoning. This **struggle** (v. 30), experienced by both Paul and the Philippian believers, was proof of God's grace in their lives, as they shared in the sufferings of Christ (cp. 3:10).

2:1-2 The chapter break here is awkward since Paul continued his thought on how they were to live as Christians. Adding to the list of that which **has been given** to them by God (1:29), in chapter 2 Paul sought to motivate the Philippians to unity and humility by reminding them of what they had received—**encouragement** from Christ, **consolation** of God's love (cp. 2 Co 1:3-4), and **fellowship with the Spirit**. This trinitarian activity in their lives had equipped them with **affection and mercy** for their relationships with others.

2:3-4 Assuming that this is their spiritual makeup as Christians, they would have had all the resources necessary to be united in every way (2:2, note the repeated emphasis on "same" and "one"). This soul-unity starts at the individual level,

with each person living out his relationships with others in **humility** (v. 3). Humility is a mind-set that acknowledges each person as equally valuable, for each is made in the image of God.[5]

Rather than relating to others in SELFISHNESS ("rivalry," cp. 1:17) and CONCEIT (Gk. *kenodoxian*, "seeking praise though not deserving it"), the Philippians were to put others first (v. 3). Again the idea is vanity that promotes excessive ambition. Paul had already set an example for them in this (1:21-26), and he reminded them of the supreme example of humility—Christ Himself.

Be Christlike (2:5-11)

2:5 In this section, Paul directed his readers' gaze to Christ Himself, the supreme model of humility and obedience, and admonished them to **make** their **attitude that of Christ Jesus**. Paul was calling them not only to imitate what they knew of Christ's attitudes and actions, but even more, to live in accordance with the transformation Christ had already made in their minds and attitudes.

2:6-11 The following section, which is known as the Christ Hymn, could be considered the centerpiece of the New Testament, for it tells the story of Jesus Christ—His preexistence, His incarnation, His death, and His exaltation.[7] This hymn has been central to the church's Christology (the study of the person and work of Christ); thus, whether or not one realizes it, each believer's understanding of who Christ is has been impacted to this day.

The first section of the hymn speaks of Christ's humiliation (vv. 6-8). In this section, the attitude and behavior of the humble Christ stands in stark contrast to Paul's self-seeking opponents in 1:15-17 and the behavior Paul decries in 2:3-4. Although existing [*always* existing, cp. Jn 1:1-3] in the **form** of God—thus, being equal with

God—Christ refused to act selfishly by taking **advantage** of the rights of His Lordship (v. 6).

Instead He emptied Himself (Gk. *ekenōsen*, "make empty or of no effect," v. 7) voluntarily—not of His *deity*, for He was still in the form of God and equal with God, but perhaps of the *display* of His deity. This self-giving God poured Himself out by assuming a new form, that **of a slave** (Gk. *doulou*, cp. 1:1), **taking on the likeness of men.** He was like men, but was not the same as other men, for He was still God. Even so, one should not think He was a man only **in His external form** (Gk. *schēmati*, "appearance"), but to those who saw Him, He looked like other men. This is the incarnation: the One who was fully God becoming fully man, henceforth existing as two natures (deity and humanity) in one person (Jesus Christ).

This, however, was not the extent of Christ's humility. He humbled Himself further by becoming **obedient to the point of death**—and not just any death, but the death reserved for criminals and slaves, **death on a cross** (v. 8). In His act of humility—of putting others above Himself—Christ showed that to be God is to be loving, self-giving, and self-sacrificial.

The subject changes in the second part of this hymn, Christ's exaltation (vv. 9-11). Having traced the work of God the Son, now the hymn traces the work of God the Father. Because of the Son's humble obedience, God has **highly exalted** (Gk. *huperupsōsen*, "exalt to the highest degree") **Him.** The **name that is above every name** (v. 9) seems to refer to **the name of Jesus** (v. 10), but most likely this goes further to mean that God the Father grants Jesus the title of **Lord** (Gk. *kurios*, equivalent to the Hb. title, *Adonai*; v. 11).

One day, the lordship of Jesus will be confessed by **every tongue** (v. 11) on a day when **every knee** will **bow** (v. 10), including those **in heaven** (angels and demons), those **on earth** (those living at the time of Christ's return), and those **under the earth** (the dead to be raised). The early church confession "Jesus Is Lord" still leads today to the salvation of His confessors (cp. Rm 10:9-10); unfortunately, those who wait until that final day to make such a confession will only do so to their condemnation. Paul displayed this portrait of Jesus the Servant-King before the Philippians, so that they could see what it meant truly to be humble and selfless.

Be obedient (2:12-18)

2:12-18 With the phrase **So then** Paul came back to an emphasis on living in a manner appropriate for Christians' contending **for the faith of the gospel** (1:27). Paul spoke of hearing about the Philippians while he was **absent** in 1:27 and exhorted them to **work out** their **salvation with fear and trembling**, especially in his **absence** (2:12). Paul held them accountable to live the faith they professed, whether or not he could see them in person (v. 12; 1:27).

Verse 12 has caused anxiety for many readers who think Paul was calling for attaining salvation by works. One should look at this verse in the context of Paul's other writings, however. If, in every other place, Paul emphasized that salvation is by grace through faith alone (3:9; Rm 3:28; Gl 2:16,21; 3:3,24; Eph 2:8-9; 2 Tm 1:9, etc.), then this verse must not be considered the exception where Paul was contradicting himself or an indication that he had reverted back to his former days of keeping the law. As Paul would say, "May it never be!"

One should also look at the context surrounding the verse. The parallel between 1:27 and 2:12 has been noted above, where 2:12 is part of Paul's one line of thought to live as the Christians that they are. The most important context, however, is found in tandem with the next verse (2:13). The connection between the verses is made with the preposition **for**, indicating that 2:13 is the grounds for 2:12.

In 2:13, **God** is the Worker! Apart from God's action there is no **will** or inclination to act according to God's **good purpose**. At the point of regeneration, however, everything becomes new (Gl 2:20). God's continuing work is to cause believers **to will and to act for His good purpose**. This work He started, and this work He will complete (Php1:6).

If your pastor said, "Work out your relationship to your husband," would you take it to mean you were not already married? In this context, then, the working out of your salvation (2:12) is the working out of the salvation you already have! One should note that the Philippians are *already* **saints in Christ Jesus** (1:1) and **children of God** (2:15). This verse (2:12) is merely confirmation that they must live out the salvation they have been given. Obedience is not intended to gain God's favor; it is the result of salvation and the living out of who one is in Christ.

> *Obedience is not intended to gain God's favor; it is the result of salvation and the living out of who one is in Christ.*

Paul instructed them to live out their salvation by being united, which required humility and putting others first (1:27—2:11). Paul then cautioned them about **grumbling and arguing** (2:14), both of which feed disunity. GRUM-BLING (Gk. *goggusmōn*, "murmuring, muttering") indicates dissatisfaction stemming from self-centeredness, and the word here for ARGUING (Gk. *dialogismōn*, "opinion, reasoning, doubt, dispute") indicated inward questioning

and criticism, resulting in dispute (cp. the Israelites, Nm 11:1). Both of these hinder spiritual maturity, and both prevent the witness of the church in a world that is **crooked and perverted** (Php 2:15). Paul desired for them to stand firm; their spiritual maturity was that for which he had tirelessly labored in ministry (v. 16).

Then, once again, Paul's amazing choice to rejoice: Even if his life had been **poured out as a drink offering**, he would **rejoice** (vv. 17-18). In the Jewish sacrificial system, the drink offering accompanied the main sacrifice (Nm 28:1-7). Amazingly, Paul was picturing the Philippians' **service** of **faith** as the main **sacrifice** (Php 2:17), while the giving of his life in death (cp. 2 Tm 4:6) was the drink offering to accompany it. Paul's joy was neither a feeling of happiness nor dependent on circumstances. Joy stems from a choice one makes when she is satisfied in the Lord (cp. Php 3:1; 4:4).

Paul's Follow-up (2:19-30)

Paul's next section would usually occur at the end of a letter but perhaps is strategically placed here because both Timothy and Epaphroditus were prime examples of what he had been teaching the Philippians. For this reason, both men were perfect candidates to go to Philippi and follow up on the Philippians' spiritual growth.

Arrival of Timothy (2:19-24)

2:19-24 Although Paul expected to see the Philippians soon, he was not able to come yet. He therefore planned to send Timothy first to follow up on their spiritual state (vv. 23-24). Timothy was the best possible candidate to send because he and Paul were **like-minded** (Gk. *isopsuchon*, "equal in soul, like-souled,") in their genuine **care** for the Philippians (v. 20). According to this text, to care for

Heart to Heart:
Do Everything Without Grumbling

The children of Israel were grumblers. God had delivered them from bondage in Egypt and had fed them faithfully with manna as they wandered in the wilderness. Rather than living gratefully with God's deliverance and provision, the Israelites complained about the manna, longing for the food they had in Egypt (Nm 11).

Have you ever been around someone who grumbles about everything? If you have, you know that being around a grumbler is not the most pleasant way to spend your time! God may bless the grumbler a thousand times over, but the grumbler rarely notices due to her negative outlook on life. The grumbler is hardly ever content: What she has is never good enough, and what she does not have is always better. Women often struggle with the sin of grumbling. Sometimes it stems from a pessimistic spirit and sometimes from unmet expectations, but always from dissatisfaction and, ultimately, self-centeredness.

Be a woman who does everything without grumbling. Faithfully practice the act of gratitude, choosing to be satisfied in God and His blessings.

others is what it means to seek the **interests** of **Jesus Christ** (v. 21).

One can imagine that Paul made a sacrifice to send Timothy. Serving with Paul in the ministry **like a son with a father**, Timothy was likely a great encouragement to Paul while he was in prison. Perhaps this is why Paul wanted to wait to find out about his own outcome before he sent Timothy (v. 23). Timothy was the best Paul had, and by example he would show the Philippians what it meant to care for the interests of others (cp. 2:3-4).

Arrival of Epaphroditus (2:25-30)

2:25-30 The arrival of Epaphroditus was without delay; however, he was delivering this very letter. Apparently Ephaphroditus had been the Philippians' **messenger and minister** to Paul when they heard Paul was in prison. They sent Epaphroditus with a gift (4:18) and seemingly intended for him to stay with Paul for a time. Unfortunately, Epaphroditus

became deathly sick, either on the way there or when he arrived. Paul said that **he was so sick that he nearly died** (2:27). Word reached the Philippians of his illness, and they were understandably worried. In that day, death was the assumed outcome for certain sicknesses. Word of their concern traveled back to Epaphroditus, who at some point before or after had been healed by the **mercy** of God. Paul, in seeing Epaphroditus' deep distress over the Philippians' now unnecessary concern, thought it best to send him back home.

Paul commended Epaphroditus for being willing to **RISK HIS LIFE** (Gk. *paraboleusamenos*, "bring into danger, gamble with one's life," v. 30) to minister to Paul. Epaphroditus, too, was an example of looking first to the interests of others. For this, Paul said he deserved **honor** and a joyful **welcome** (v. 29), even though he had not been able to stay longer with Paul.

The phrase **to make up what was lacking in your ministry to me** (v. 30) was probably not a rebuke. The Philippians' only lack was their absence from Paul; Epaphroditus was the completion of this lack.

THE ESSENCE OF THE GOSPEL AND LIFE ITSELF (3:1–4:1)

In 1:21, Paul said that, for him, living was Christ and dying was gain. This section (3:1–4:1) makes clear why Paul viewed Christ as the essence of life itself. Only Christ was sufficient for one to have a right standing with God (3:8-14); all human achievements were woefully inadequate (vv. 1-7). Therefore, believers should not be focused on earthly things (vv. 17-21), but they should make it their goal to pursue knowing Christ (3:10).

The Inadequacy of the Flesh (3:1-7)

Paul hoped that the arrival of Epaphroditus would cause the Philippians joy (2:28), but the only *Person* in whom Paul urged his readers to rejoice is the Lord Jesus Himself (3:1). What follows in chapter 3 provides plenty of reasons for one to **rejoice in the Lord** (v. 1; cp. 4:4).

Not everyone rejoices in the Lord. Some rejoice in their own achievements and, even worse, teach others to do the same. Concerned that the Philippians not fall prey to this "Christ plus" gospel of the Judaizers (cp. Gl 2:1-14), Paul wrote words of warning, using irony to make his point (Php 3:2). These Judaizers may have sounded confident in their standing before God; however, they were in fact **"dogs"** (a label of uncleanness the Jews reserved for the Gentiles); **evil workers** (not keepers of the law, as they claimed); and mutilators of **the flesh** (for their act of circumcision had lost its value).

God's people are no longer constituted by circumcision of the flesh, but circumci-

sion of the heart through faith (Rm 2:29; Gl 5:1-6; 6:15). Those who belong to Him no longer **SERVE** (Gk. *latreuontes*, "worship or serve") God by keeping the law, but they serve "by the Spirit" (Php 3:3; cp. Jn 4:23-24). True believers do not "put confidence in the **FLESH**" (Gk. *sarki*, "fleshly, physical," here referring to external things, advantages, achievements) for their salvation; instead, their confidence and "boast" is "in Christ Jesus" (Php 3:3; cp. Jr 9:23-26).

Paul did not speak about this from lack of experience. At one time, he also **had confidence in the flesh** (Php 3:4). In fact, if anyone had reason to boast, he did.

Paul's Impeccable Credentials
Philippians 3:4-6

Credentials by birth:
- One adopted into the covenant by circumcision
- A man among God's chosen people Israel
- A member of the loyal tribe of Benjamin
- A pure-blooded Hebrew by birth
- One adopted into the covenant by circumcision

Credentials by achievement:
- Being a Pharisee, one most "faithful" to Scripture
- Intensely zealous for the law; persecutor of the church
- Having a blameless record in the eyes of others

If anyone could have achieved a right standing with God based on his credentials, Paul would have qualified. However, when Paul encountered Christ on the Damascus road (Ac 9:1-9), those things which he had previously seen as **gain** appeared worthless in light of the surpassing worth of Christ. In fact, they were not only worthless, but they were **loss** (Gk. *zēmian*, "damage, detriment"); for clinging to his achievements had prevented him from placing full confidence in Christ alone (Php 3:7).

Heart to Heart:
The Ground for Boasting (3:3)

In Philippians 3:3, Paul distinguished a believer from an unbeliever. An unbeliever places her confidence in the flesh (i.e., in external things and achievements) in order to "achieve" a right standing with God, while a believer, having achieved a right standing with God through Christ, places her faith and confidence in Christ alone (3:9). So often a woman confesses with her mouth that she trusts solely in Christ for her salvation, and yet she lives as if her achievements will gain God's favor and approval. Paul gave a reminder that righteousness does not come from living according to a set of rules or from having an impressive set of credentials; righteousness comes by being found in Christ (3:8-9). Being a good woman, wife, and mother will no more save you than Paul's impeccable credentials were able to save him. Instead, Christ must be your ground for boasting.

> *The wise must not boast in his wisdom; the mighty must not boast in his might; the rich must not boast in his riches. But the one who boasts should boast in this, that he understands and knows Me. (Jr 9:23-24a).*

In what or in whom is your boast?

The Sufficiency of Christ (3:8-14)

3:8-9 At his conversion, Paul's life changed radically. Having formerly pursued Christians to kill them (v. 6), now he pursued their Lord, **to know Him** (v. 10). What caused such transformation? Paul caught a glimpse of the infinite greatness and worth of Christ and the **surpassing value of knowing** Him (v. 8). Everything else paled in comparison.

Paul's language intensified in verse 8. Not only did he count his supposed *gain* as loss (v. 7), but he counted **everything** as loss in comparison to knowing Christ (v. 8). Like Isaiah, who said all of one's righteous deeds are like filthy rags (Is 64:6), Paul saw that everything upon which he formerly depended for God's favor was mere **FILTH** (Gk. *skubala*, lit. "human excrement" or "trash

thrown to the dogs," v. 8). Like the man who found a treasure in a field and sold all he had to buy the field (Mt 13:44), so Paul **suffered the loss of all things** (upon which he depended for salvation) in order to **gain Christ and be found in Him**.

To be found in Christ means that one is declared righteous before God (Php 3:9). Here in this one verse is the gospel message. Can a person work out his own salvation (as some seem to think Paul himself said in 2:12)? By no means! You must be found in Christ.

Paul spoke of two different types of **righteousness**: One he referred to as **my own**, and one was **from God**. The former looks to one's own ability to keep the law and conform to its standards in hopes of becoming righteous. This self-conferred righteousness counts for nothing. The righteousness that is from God, on the other hand, is not based on one's ability to keep the law but is based on one's **faith in Christ**. In this case, God declares as righteous the one who is "found in" Christ, who was the only righteous human being (1 Pt 3:18; 1 Jn 2:1-2).

3:10-11 Paul once sought to gain right standing with God based upon his own achievements. His encounter with Christ the righteous One, however, showed him that *only Christ* was sufficient to achieve salvation on his behalf. Now, being "found in Him," Paul's goal was **to know Him** personally and experientially. To know Christ means both experiencing **the power of His resurrection and the fellowship of His sufferings** (v. 10). This process is sanctification. At new birth, the believer experiences resurrection power as he is raised to walk in new life (Rm 6:4). This power of Christ enables the believer to walk where Christ walked, even through His sufferings (cp. Php 1:29-30).

Paul's desire to know Christ was so intense that he yearned to drink deeply even of Christ's sufferings. Although he did not know exactly how it might happen, he knew that such identification with Christ in His sufferings would eventually lead to his **resurrection from among the dead** (3:11).

3:12-14 Lest anyone get the wrong impression that he had already reached his goal of knowing Christ, Paul stressed that he continued to pursue **the prize promised by God's heavenly call in Christ Jesus** (v. 14). While "God's heavenly call" could be the eventual call to heaven each believer receives, more likely here the reference is to the effectual call given in Christ Jesus before salvation (Rm 8:29-39).

Paul used here the imagery of a race (Php 3:13-14). He was the runner who, in his straining towards the goal, knew better than to look back and risk losing the race.

Instead, he focused only on the goal and the prize and pursued it relentlessly (Gk. *diōkō*, same verb as in 3:6a). Although the prize is not clearly stated, one can assume from the context of this passage and the book that Paul looked forward most of all to being with Christ (1:21,23), knowing Him completely (3:10), and being transformed into His image at the resurrection (3:20-21).

The Appeal (3:15–4:1)

3:15-17 Paul was certain of Christ's sufficiency; therefore, he appealed to the Philippian believers to THINK (Gk. *phronōmen*, "ponder, set your mind on"; cp. 2:2,5; 4:2) as he thought on this and to imitate his actions, as well as the actions of others who lived accordingly (3:15-17). In other words, the Philippian believers should, with their minds, value the surpassing worth of Christ and, with their actions, pursue knowing Christ.

3:18-19 Finally, in this section, Paul gave an example of a group they were *not* to imitate (vv. 18-19). The exact identity of this group is not certain. They clearly were not believers, for they were **enemies of the cross of Christ** (v. 18) headed for **destruction** (v. 19). That their **god is their stomach** could be interpreted to mean that

- they focused on strict dietary laws;
- they were gluttonous; or
- they lived according to sensuous appetites.

No matter the interpretation, clearly their deified appetites dictated their lives; thus, being egocentric, they had not made Christ their Lord. Paul also said that **their glory is in their shame**, which means they apparently delighted in something that ought to have brought them shame (cp. Is 5:20).

3:20–4:1 These qualities should not characterize believers (vv. 20-21). The former group is focused on **earthly things** (3:19); they are present-oriented and seeking temporal satisfaction. Believers, however, have a heavenly **citizenship** (v. 20); thus, they are to be future-oriented, with eyes toward Christ, **eagerly** awaiting Him and the day of His return, when by His power, He **will transform** frail, sinful bodies into bodies like His (v. 21; cp. 1 Jn 3:2).

So then, Paul said, knowing of their powerful Lord who is able **to subject everything to Himself** (Php 3:21), they must **stand firm in the Lord** (4:1; cp. 1:27; 2:16), against all false teaching (3:18-19) and in unity (1:27; 4:2-3). Then, with an unprecedented string of vocative terms, Paul reminded them of their bond of love (**dearly loved brothers . . . dear friends**). They were his **joy** (1:4; 2:2), as well as the future reward of his labor (**crown**).

CONCLUDING MATTERS (4:2-23)

Paul's tender language (4:1) cushioned and grounded his final exhortations (4:2-9), which hearkened back to what he had said throughout the letter. Paul then thanked them for their gift (4:10-20) and closed with greetings and a blessing (4:21-23).

Reiterative Exhortations (4:2-9)

Be united (4:2-3)

4:2-3 For brevity, verse 2 is striking for several reasons. First, it is unusual for Paul to mention specific names in his exhortation; second, the names belong to women; third, the Greek here is verbatim to 2:2—but now with specificity, indicating that this is the crux of the unity problem in Philippi.

Apparently two women in the Philippian church—Euodia ("pleasant, fragrant") and Syntyche ("lucky, fortunate")

—were in disagreement on an issue about which no details are given here. Their disagreement was significant enough that word of it had reached Paul and serious enough that he felt the need to address it. The matter apparently threatened church unity (2:2-4; 3:15)—and did so because these women were of some influence.

Who were these ladies of influence? Not much is known about them, except that they **contended for the gospel** with Paul (v. 3). Paul's use of the Greek verb *sunēthlēsan* (a military word meaning "to fight alongside"; cp. 1:27) implies that in the midst of difficult and even dangerous opposition, these women had stood firmly and bravely for the cause of the gospel. Their vigorous and ongoing partnership with Paul was not surprising, considering the involvement of Philippian women in the church since its beginning (cp. Ac 16).

One should not exaggerate the leadership of these women beyond what the text actually says. For example, one cannot argue from this text that women held offices in the church. What *may* be said, however, is that Paul viewed women as equal partners in the ministry and as vital to the spread of the gospel. Their influence could therefore be a help—or a hindrance—to the gospel.

For this very reason, Paul URGED (Gk. *parakalō*, "beseech or beg, call alongside") these women contenders "to agree in the Lord," (Gk. *sunergōn*, "work together," or literally, "to have a common mind," v. 2; cp. 2:2). Considering this phrase's use in the context of doctrinal matters (i.e., to have a common mind with Paul in pursuing Christ and putting no confidence in the flesh; 3:15), these women could have been in a doctrinal dispute. However, the text does not define the matter of dispute—perhaps because the damage came from contention in the church regardless of what caused the quarrel.

Although Paul had already given them instruction on how to be of one mind (2:2-4), he felt it necessary to call upon an unnamed **partner** (4:3) to serve as a mediator for the women. The identities of this partner and of **Clement** (4:3) have long been discussed and are still unknown. The most important thing to note is the premium Paul placed on church unity. This matter was not to be taken lightly. When necessary, division should be discussed openly within the church, and all resources (e.g., mediation) should be used to secure unity for the sake of the church and the gospel.

Euodia and Syntyche *Philippians 4:2-3*		
Their Background	**Their Problem**	**Paul's Solution**
• Two leaders in the church at Philippi	• Disagreed with one another	• Asked them to agree in the Lord (v. 2)
• Spread the gospel with Paul	• Admonished by Paul for their behavior	• Asked other believers to help them reconcile (v. 3)
• Recognized by Paul and other believers		

Be Christ-focused (4:4-7)

4:4-7 Paul then gave three commands (not suggestions), each of which relates to the person of Christ.

Christ is the *object* of the first command: **Rejoice in the *Lord* always** (v. 4, author's emphasis; cp. 3:1). Paul was not merely commanding a mood or an emotion, which would be impossible. Paul was commanding them to glory in the person of Jesus Christ (cp. 3:3)—to express openly their deep satisfaction, which was not dependent upon outward circumstances, in Him.

Christ is the *motivation* for the second command in verse 5: **Let your graciousness be known to everyone** (even your oppressors). GRACIOUSNESS (Gk. *epieikes*, "yielding, gentle, kind") has to do with forbearing the faults of others, being selfless, and not demanding one's rights (cp. 1 Pt 2:23). The warning that the **Lord is near** holds them accountable and promises their vindication (cp. Jms 5:8-9).

Christ's nearness (Php 4:5) may also serve as the grounds for Paul's last command in this section (v. 6): **Don't worry about anything**, even in the face of persecution. Instead, **in everything** about which you are worrying, pray, and do so **with thanksgiving** (cp. 1 Th 5:17-18). Paul could not conceive of bringing specific **requests** to God without thanksgiving (Php 1:3-4), for God's gracious actions are evident in each situation and should be acknowledged.

Trusting God with one's petitions brings God's PEACE (Gk. *eirēnē*, "peace," equivalent to Hb. *shalom*, "wholeness, well-being"). The word GUARD (Gk. *phrourēsei*, "guard, hold in custody, protect, keep") actually pictures soldiers guarding a city gate from *within* the gate. So in entrusting one's petitions to God, God's peace will stand guard within the gates of your mind and heart to prevent the invasion of fear. Such peace, in the midst of trial, is so shocking that it "surpasses every thought" (4:7).

The sphere of peace is **in Christ Jesus**. As one finds joy (satisfaction) in Christ (v. 4), she is able to experience peace, despite the circumstances (v. 7).

Heart to Heart:
Make a Choice to Rejoice

Philippians 4:4 is often interpreted to say that one must be happy in every circumstance. This interpretation of Scripture is not only discouraging when we are not able to "muster up" feelings of happiness, but it may also cause you to think that God holds you to an unrealistic standard of feeling happy when enduring trials.

No doubt, Paul was a man who was joyful in spirit. He was able to rejoice in the Philippians' growing faith (1:4) and in the furtherance of the gospel (1:18), despite the fact that he himself was sitting in prison, facing a possible death sentence. For Paul to say he rejoiced in what God was doing through his trial is not to say, however, that Paul was happy about sitting in a prison cell! Rather, despite an unhappy circumstance, he was choosing to focus on the good and to rejoice in God.

The call is not to be happy about every circumstance—this would deny the authenticity and reality of other emotions that are entirely appropriate for a given situation (Ec 3:4). The call is to rejoice in the Lord Himself during every circumstance. Make a choice to rejoice! Choose to focus on and delight in God Himself.

Be obedient (4:8-9)

4:8-9 Paul was not yet finished with his thought on peace: **and the God of peace will be with you** (v. 9b). The Philippian believers not only had need for the peace of God, but also for the presence of the God of peace. In these verses, the strong "God of peace" (cp. Rm 16:20; Heb 13:20) promises His presence to those who "think" (Gk. *logizesthe*, "consider, with plans to act; calculate, ponder") on certain things (Php 4:8) and then do them (v. 9).

Appreciation (4:10-20)

Finally, Paul came to one of his main reasons for writing this letter. He wanted to express his appreciation to the Philippians for their gift.

4:10-11 Paul let them know that he rejoiced in their **renewed care** for him (v.

10), but—lest they get the wrong impression—his rejoicing was not because his need was met (v. 11). Why? He had "learned" the secret of how "to be CONTENT" (Gk. *autarkēs*, "self-sufficient"), no matter the need or the circumstance. For Greek Stoics in Paul's day, contentment was a fundamental virtue. It was an indication of self-sufficiency—the ability to face any situation by your own resources.

4:12-13 Paul made a wonderful contrast by using this word. Yes, he was content in every circumstance, but not because of his self-sufficiency. Rather, he was content because he was dependent on *Christ* and *His* resources. Paul began like the Stoics ("I have the power to do all things") but then qualified his words by saying it is *Christ* **who strengthens** him (v. 13). One

Heart to Heart:
The Solution for Worry

The book of Philippians says it plainly: Do not worry about anything (4:6). To many women for whom worry has become a way of life, this command not to worry about anything seems ludicrous, not to mention impossible. How do you stop worrying about all that concerns you? Paul says the solution is to pray about everything; then peace will take the place of worry in your hearts and minds (4:7).

If, however, your prayer is merely a pouring out of your concerns before God, you will experience no less worry and no more peace. A mere rehearsal of concerns may be void of any attitude or expression of trust in God, which is necessary for the relief of the burden that you carry. You must not only speak to God about your worries; you must leave your burdens with Him, trusting Him to perfect whatever concerns you (Ps 138:8). Praying "with thanksgiving" (4:6) is the key to convincing your heart to let go and trust God with your concerns, for when you pray "with thanksgiving," you inevitably begin to focus on who God is, what He has done and, consequently, what He is able to do in your current situation.

The solution to your worry problem is prayer—prayer that not only says, "Here is my concern," but that adds, "I cannot handle this, but I know You can, and I trust You will."

should note that **all things** here refers to living in want or in plenty (v. 12); it does not warrant believing Christ enables every Christian to be a superhero!

4:14-20 The Philippians were a uniquely generous people (cp. 2 Co 8:1-5), and they had a one-of-a-kind relationship with Paul (Php 4:15-16). Furthermore, their gift (apparently food) sent through Epaphroditus was exactly what Paul needed (v. 18). Even still, Paul's cause for rejoicing was not the meeting of his need (v. 11). Instead, he rejoiced because their giving resulted in heavenly dividends for *them* (v. 17), as well as God's provision for their needs now (v. 19).

All of this background provides the context for the famous verse 19, **and** [or "now in return"] **my God will supply all your needs.** Because God had seen their act of sacrificial giving and had been pleased by it (v. 18; cp. Gn 8:20-21; Lv 1:9,13), Paul was confident that God would respond and provide for their (material) needs. A repetition of Greek words in this verse affirms the reciprocal nature of this promise: The Philippians had sent gifts for Paul's need (Gk. *chreian*, Php 4:16), and he was "fully supplied" (Gk. *peplērōmai*, "make full, fill up," v. 18). Therefore God "will supply" (Gk. *plērōsei*) their "needs" (Gk. *chreian*) according to "His" abundant "riches," as always "in Christ Jesus" (v. 19). The mere mention of God's graciousness caused Paul to break out in doxology (v. 20).

Closing Greeting and Benediction (4:21-23)

In order to affirm their "worldwide" bond of fellowship and unity in Christ, Paul closed his letter by sending greetings from the saints who were around him: his companions (**Those brothers**, v. 21) and the other believers in Rome (**All the saints**, v. 22).

The greetings from those in **Caesar's household** (v. 22) are noteworthy. At the very least, this phrase suggests that there were disciples in Nero's civil service (e.g., soldiers, government officials). At the most, it means that the gospel had penetrated Nero's own palace. Either way, to know that Christ was proclaimed as Lord in a sphere where only Nero declared himself to be "lord" would be extremely encouraging to the Philippians. Paul began and ended his letter with the same blessing of **grace**, which can only come through **the Lord Jesus Christ** (v. 23).

A Recipe for Spiritual Character from the Book of Philippians

Step 1: Identify ingredients in your character that hinder your relationship with Christ. The book of Philippians is a good starting point for self-examination. Do you . . .

- Shrink back in timidity and fear when faced with opposition (1:29)?
- Live in rivalry with others because of envy or conceit (2:3)?
- Focus more on yourself and your own interests than those of others and their needs (2:4-5)?
- Grumble out of discontentment (2:14)?
- Argue and thus cause dissension around you (2:14; 4:2)?
- Take pride and place confidence in your own achievements (3:3-7)?
- Focus more on present concerns than future hopes (3:18-21)?
- Worry about everything and pray about nothing (4:6-7)?
- Entertain wrong thoughts and engage in harmful thinking processes (4:8)?

Step 2: Realize that *you* are not able to eliminate these ingredients from your character; only the *Holy Spirit* can transform you. Confess any known sin and ask God to complete the good work He has started in you (1:6).

Step 3: Make the decision to pursue the person of Christ passionately (3:8). The value you place on lesser (and sometimes sinful) things will diminish in the light of Christ's surpassing worth (3:8)

Step 4: You are a new creature. Begin to live, therefore, in a manner worthy of the gospel of Christ (1:27). Mirror the strengths of the Philippian women:

- Pray fervently and faithfully (1:19; Ac 16:13).
- Rejoice in Christ and so become a source of joy for others (Php 4:1; 2 Co 8:2).
- Love deeply and show that love to others (Php 1:9).
- Act graciously and hospitably towards other people (Ac 16:15).
- Support, share, and give sacrificially where there is need (2 Co 8:1-5; Php 4:10-20).
- Partner in the ministry and contend for the gospel (Php 1:5,7; 4:3).

Bibliography

Bruce, F. F. *Philippians.* New International Biblical Commentary 11. Peabody, MA: Hendrickson, 1989.

*Fee, Gordon D. *Paul's Letter to the Philippians.* New International Commentary on the New Testament. Grand Rapids, MI: Eerdmans, 1995.

_____. *Philippians.* IVP New Testament Commentary Series. Downers Grove, IL: IVP, 1999.

*Hawthorne, Gerald. *Philippians.* Word Biblical Commentary, vol. 43. Waco, TX: Word, 1983.

*Martin, Ralph P. *Philippians.* New Century Bible Commentary. Grand Rapids: Eerdmans, 1980.

Melick, Richard R., Jr. *Philippians, Colossians, Philemon.* New American Commentary, vol. 32. Nashville: Broadman, 1991.

Motyer, J.A. *The Message of Philippians: Jesus Our Joy.* Downers Grove: IVP, 1984.

*O'Brien, Peter. *The Epistle to the Philippians: A Commentary on the Greek Text.* New International Greek Testament Commentary. Grand Rapids: Eerdmans, 1991.

*Silva, Moisés. *Philippians.* Baker Exegetical Commentary on the New Testament. Grand Rapids: Baker, 1992.

Thielman, Frank. *Philippians.* NIV Application Commentary. Grand Rapids: Zondervan, 1995.

*For advanced study

Notes

[1] Many have noted this similarity in form. For detailed study on ancient letter writing, see John L. White, *Light from Ancient Letters* (Philadelphia: Fortress, 1986).

[2] Literature is extensive concerning the authorship of the Christ Hymn. For an overview of the possibilities, see Ralph P. Martin, *Carmen Christi, Philippians 2:5-11 in Recent Interpretation and in the Setting of Early Christian Worship* (Grand Rapids: Eerdmans, 1983), 42-62. Whether or not Paul wrote this hymn does not change the fact that he *chose* to use these words to illustrate the humility of Christ. The text, then, does indeed reflect Pauline thought and doctrine.

[3] On first glance, Caesarea is an attractive possibility. Paul was imprisoned there for two years (long enough to correspond with the Philippians) amongst Herod's imperial guard and members of Caesar's household who resided in the city. Acts 24:23 indicates that he had some freedom and that his friends could minister to him. Gerald Hawthorne, *Philippians*, Word Biblical Commentary, vol. 43 (Waco, Texas: Word, 1983), xxxvi-xliv. However, if Paul was imprisoned in Caesarea at the time he wrote Philippians, likely he would not have spoken of facing possible death (1:22-26), for he could have always appealed to Caesar in Rome.

[4] Since Paul's initial arrest in the Jerusalem Temple (Ac 21:26f), he had been beaten, scourged, imprisoned; he had his life threatened by ambush; he had been transferred to Caesarea and imprisoned there for two years awaiting a verdict; he had appealed to Caesar; he had experienced shipwreck on the way to Rome; and he was now in prison in yet another city, having waited almost two years for a possible death sentence. All of these experiences gave Paul the opportunity to testify of the gospel of Jesus Christ.

[5] Ralph P. Martin, *Philippians*, New Century Bible Commentary (Grand Rapids: Eerdmans, 1980), 2.

[6] Paul's appeal to humility as a virtue stands in stark contrast to the Greco-Roman mindset in which humility was considered to be a weakness, held only by those of base birth and right. Gordan D. Fee, *Philippians*, IVP New Testament Commentary Series (Downers Grove: IVP, 1999), 88.

[7] As the centerpiece of the book, the Christ Hymn receives extensive treatment in almost every work on the book of Philippians. Entire books have been written on the passage (e.g., Martin, *Carmen Christi*, endnote 2 above). Theologians and scholars go to great lengths to discuss various aspects of the hymn, including its authorship, original setting, meaning, literary form, and poetic structure. Although such detail may not be given here, the reader should be aware of the wealth of insight this one passage may bring to her own understanding of Christ and worship in the early church, and she should be encouraged to pursue self-study on this passage.

COLOSSIANS

Introduction

Title

Colossians was so named because its primary recipients were in the church at Colossae, a small town in western Asia Minor (modern Turkey).

Setting

Colossae, at the base of Mount Cadmus (elevation 8,435 feet), was about 120 miles east of Ephesus in the Lycus River Valley. Historical records are few regarding this fairly insignificant Roman city that is mentioned by only a few writers. Colossae was overshadowed by the larger, more affluent city of Laodicea, only 11 miles to its northwest. Colossae did benefit from a textile industry, however, and from its strategic location on a major trade route, which stretched from the Aegean coast to the center of Asia Minor and on to Syria and further east. There is also evidence supporting a significant Jewish population in the area surrounding Colossae, and probably in the city as well.

THE PROVINCE OF ASIA

Genre

The book of Colossians is an epistle or letter. Letters of ancient times had a particular literary form. Most ancient epistles, including Paul's letter to the Colossians, are in the following form:

- *Salutation*—References are made to the sender and to the recipient of the letter, together with a greeting.

- *Thanksgiving and/or Prayer*—All of Paul's letters, except Galatians, where its absence is significant, include this element.

- *Body*—This section is typically the longest part of Paul's letters.

- *Exhortation*—These specific instructions are directed to the congregation, depending upon their respective situations and needs.

- *Conclusion*—Words calling for peace, greetings to friends, and/or closing blessings are included.[1]

Author

In scholarly circles, questioning the authorship of almost every letter of Paul has been considered fashionable, yet the authorship of Colossians is seldom debated.[2] According to Colossians 1:1, the Apostle Paul and Timothy, Paul's close companion, wrote the letter. In verse 23, however, Paul writes in the first person and then in an autobiographical manner. Paul more probably is the author of Colossians, while Timothy served as Paul's *amanuensis*, an ancient-world secretary or stenographer. Apparently Timothy's task was to record with a stylus on wax tablets Paul's dictated words and then to transcribe the text on a papyrus sheet or roll. Historians suggest that in order to be sure of the correct recording of the dictation, there would most likely have followed a repeated "out-loud" rereading of the document. For Paul to close the letter to the Colossians by saying, "This greeting is in my own hand—Paul" makes perfect sense if an amanuensis were recording the letter. He was affixing his signature to the document for proof of his authorship.

Date

Colossians, along with Ephesians, Philippians, and Philemon, is a part of the group of New Testament books often called the Prison Epistles. These books were most likely written between AD 60 and 63 during Paul's imprisonment at Rome, which is recorded in Acts 28:30-31. Tychicus (Col 4:7) was with Paul in Rome and probably served as the courier for the Colossian letter as well as for the letters to the Ephesians and to Philemon. Since Onesimus, about whom the book of Philemon is written, was a member of the church at Colossae, Tychicus could have first delivered the Ephesian letter, followed by Colossians, and then handed over Philemon to a key member of the church to be read by the congregation at a later time. In fact, the letter to Philemon could have been a "case study" that developed directly out of the household code of Colossians (Col 3:22–4:1).[3]

Recipients

The recipients of the book were the people of the church at Colossae. Evidence suggests that Paul had not visited Colossae at this point in time (2:1), even though he was certainly acquainted with individuals from the church (Phm 19). Epaphras (Col 1:7), and possibly Timothy (Col 1:1), most likely evangelized the city and founded the church during Paul's three-year stay in Ephesus in the midst of his third missionary journey, around AD 52–56 (Ac 19:1,10,26). Although a Jewish community existed around Colossae, the church was probably composed mainly of Gentile believers (Col 1: 27). Apparently, while in Rome, Paul was visited by Epaphras (Phm 23), who informed him of the spiritual state of the Colossian church, especially alerting the apostle to the dangers in the congregation of the influence of heretical teachings, which might lead many to a relapse.

Major Themes

The significant themes of Colossians are twofold and dependent on each other:

- Paul's letter is specifically focused upon combating some dangerous false teachings about Jesus Christ circulating in the church.

- Paul desired to instruct the Colossians in how to live the Christian life based upon a true understanding of the life and person of Christ.

Paul warned of false teachings in Colossians 2:8, where he wrote, "Be careful that no one takes you captive through philosophy and empty deceit." Many writers have speculated as to the nature of the "philosophy" that threatened the faith of the Colossians. Some identify the Colossian heresy as the radical teachings of a specific, identifiable group, such as the Gnostics (see discussion in endnote 2); others suggest that it was syncretistic (i.e., a blending together of Jewish, Christian, and pagan religious elements); still others propose that this heresy arose from the temptations of the pagan culture surrounding Colossae.[4]

The exact nature of the false teaching may never be known with certainty. Yet, by examining how Paul responded to the Colossian heresy, one can deduce at least two important characteristics of the heresy. Its adherents taught these tenets:

- Salvation is not attained through faith in Jesus Christ alone, but by exclusive mystical knowledge and good works.

- Material things are essentially evil, including the world and everything within it, even the human body.

These two beliefs led to the following characteristics found in the Colossian church:

- the strict observance of certain Jewish religious rituals (2:16),

- the practice of specific dietary laws (2:16,21),

- a tendency toward asceticism (i.e., a life characterized by severe self-denial; 2:20-21),

- the dependence upon and promotion of human philosophies and special knowledge (2:8),

- the worship of angels (2:18), and

- attacks upon the centrality, supremacy, and sufficiency of Jesus Christ (1:15-19; 2:9-10).

The truth about the person and work of Christ triumphs over deceptive heresy and teaches Christians to live in fullness and freedom through Him.

After combating the Colossian heresy with the truth of Jesus' divinity and supremacy over all things, Paul also focused on living the Christian life in light of such truth. Paul used two words to describe the Christian life in Colossians: *freedom* and *fullness.* Paul stressed to the church at Colossae that followers of Jesus are free from all laws and regulations of the world because Jesus erased the certificate of debt and its obligations, which were against them and opposed to them, and He removed that debt by nailing it to the cross (2:14). In addition, in the freedom found through Christ, the Christian is provided with fullness of life, because she is God's chosen one,

Pronunciation Guide

Aegean	*uh JEE uhn*	Epaphras	*EP uh frass*
Amanuensis	*uh man yoo EN siss*	Ephesus	*EF uh suhs*
Archippus	*ahr KIP uhs, AHR kip uhs*	Laodicea	*lay AHD ih SEE uh*
Aristarchus	*ehr iss TAHR kuhs*	Nympha	*NIM fuh*
Colossae	*koh LAHS sih*	Onesimus	*oh NESS ih muhs*
Colossians	*kuh LAHSH uhnz*	Philemon	*figh LEE muhn*
Demas	*DEE muhs*	Tychicus	*TIK ih kuhs*

holy and loved (3:12). Paul's message to the Colossians can be summarized in the following way: The truth about the person

Outline

I. INTRODUCTION (1:1-14)
   A. Paul's Salutation to the Colossians (1:1-2)
   B. Paul's Thanksgiving for the Colossians (1:3-8)
   C. Paul's Prayer for the Colossians (1:9-14)

II. CHRIST'S WORK AND PAUL'S MISSION (1:1–2:3)
   A. Christ's Divine Personhood (1:15-18)
   B. Christ's Redemptive Work (1:19-23)
   C. Paul's Ministry to the Whole Church (1:24-29)
   D. Paul's Concern for the Colossians and Their Faith (2:1-3)

III. REFUTATION OF THE FALSE PHILOSOPHY AND RECOGNITION OF THE TRUE FAITH (2:4–3:4)
   A. A Warning against the False Philosophy (2:4-8)

and work of Christ triumphs over deceptive heresy and teaches Christians to live in fullness and freedom through Him.

   B. An Elaboration of Christ's All-Sufficiency (2:9-15)
   C. Warnings against Spiritual Dangers (2:16-19)
   D. Consequences of Death with Christ (2:20-23)
   E. Consequences of Resurrection with Christ (3:1-4)

IV. PRACTICAL APPLICATION TO THE CHRISTIAN LIFE (3:5–4:6)
   A. "Putting Off" Vices (3:5-11)
   B. "Putting On" Virtues (3:12-17)
   C. Examining Household Relationships (3:18–4:1)
   D. Praying and Witnessing (4:2-6)

V. PERSONAL NOTES FROM PAUL (4:7-18)
   A. The Bearers of the Letter (4:7-9)
   B. Greetings from Paul's Companions (4:10-14)
   C. Concluding Messages and Final Blessing (4:15-18)[5]

Exposition of the Text

INTRODUCTION (1:1-14)

Paul's letters often begin with a salutation, an expression of thanksgiving, and a prayer, and Colossians is no different. Although Paul's main purpose for writing to the Colossians was to combat the false teachers in their midst, he began by encouraging them in their faith and sharing his desires for their spiritual growth.

Paul's Salutation to the Colossians (1:1-2)

1:1 Paul began his letter to the Colossians with a typical salutation, one that

reveals the writer and recipients, along with an opening blessing upon the recipients. Both **Paul** and **Timothy** are mentioned in the salutation of this letter, but almost certainly Paul was the primary author of Colossians, using the young Timothy as his *amanuensis* (i.e., secretary or stenographer). Paul identified himself with the other apostles who had also seen the risen Lord, **an apostle of Christ Jesus**. He was an apostle, not by his own choice, but **by God's will**.

1:2 The letter was written to **the saints ... in Colossae**. SAINTS (Gk. *hagiois*, "set apart") is a word often used in the New Testament to describe God's people. A believer is one who has been justified by faith in Christ and hence is by all means set apart by and for God and thus holy. However, this holiness is not by any act of one's self but solely on the basis of the imputed righteousness and holiness of Christ. Consequently, the believer is indeed a "saint" (sanctified and holy) by virtue of that relationship to Christ and Him alone. The Colossian "saints" were **faithful brothers in Christ**, indicating their steadfast commitment to the gospel, as well as their relationship as a spiritual family predicated upon their relationship to Christ. Paul's use of the term "brothers" in reference to the Colossians does not mean that women were not included, for 3:18, with its instruction to "wives," indicates Paul was addressing the women of the church as well as the men. Thus, the term "brothers" is being used generically in this salutation, much as "sons" is used generically in Galatians 4:6-7. Paul sent his blessing to the congregation—**Grace to you and peace**—the standard way of greeting other believers in the first century. Both are acknowledged to be **from God our Father**.[6]

Paul's Thanksgiving for the Colossians (1:3-8)

1:3 As Paul began Colossians, he waited to address his main concern—the dangerous heresy being taught among them. Instead, he offered encouragement by affirming his gratitude for them and for the truths of the gospel, in which the Colossians believed. He also assuredly noted that he prayed for them with much thanksgiving.

1:4 Paul explained that he prayed for them with thanksgiving because of three essential qualities of Christian character evident in their lives: **faith**, **love**, and

hope. These virtues also appear together in Romans 5:2-5; 1 Corinthians 13:13; Galatians 5:5-6; 1 Thessalonians 1:3; 5:8; and Hebrews 10:22-24. Their faith was **in Christ Jesus** and, as a result, they expressed love **for all the saints**. Faith in Christ is incomplete without a love for other believers. Jesus instructed His disciples, saying, "By this all people will know that you are My disciples, if you have love for one another" (Jn 13:35).

1:5 The faith and love present in the lives of the Colossians was dependent upon **hope**. The Greek word *elpis*, translated "hope," has evolved in its meaning. A modern use of hope suggests wishing for something that might not happen, such as "I hope it doesn't rain today" or "I hope my son did his homework." Hope as described in the Bible carries a different meaning. For Paul, hope is an eager and confident expectation for fulfillment of the promises of God. The believer's hope is even more secure because it is **reserved ... in heaven**, safe from any earthly force that could compromise its integrity. Paul then reminded the Colossians that the hope of which he spoke is found in the **message of truth**, which is **the gospel** (1:5-6). He was already making the case that the gospel is complete truth, while the heresy with which the Colossians were being confronted, and which he would address later, was falsehood.

1:6 The word **gospel** means "good news" or "good message." The Colossians had heard this message already, as it was proclaimed to them first by Epaphras (v. 7). Paul assured the Colossians that the gospel message was not just another pagan religion like the many others in their region. Instead, **it** [i.e., the gospel] **is bearing fruit and growing all over the world**. He assured them that the "fruit-bearing" in their lives is mirrored in the experiences of people all over the world who also responded to the gospel in faith. This message has not weakened or changed over time, but it is faithfully the same in every place or time. Though cultures and peoples may change, the message of Jesus Christ and the transformation He brings to human lives is constant.

> *The understanding of salvation as an unearned and free gift of God is a hallmark of true biblical faith.*

Paul also reminded the Colossians that by responding to the gospel **the day** they **heard it**, they also **recognized God's grace in the truth**. God's grace is unmerited favor and undeserved kindness, extended to believers through His divine power. As the Colossians faced a false teaching that promoted rules and regulations as a means to please God, they found that remembering the unearned grace of God was of utmost importance in preserving the truth among themselves. The understanding of salvation as an unearned and free gift of God is a hallmark of true biblical faith.

1:7-8 Anytime the gospel seed takes root and subsequently bears fruit in a person's life, you can be assured someone was there to plant that seed in the first place. Every disciple of Jesus is entrusted with spreading His message. For the Colossians, **Epaphras** taught them the truth and continued to minister on their behalf. You should not be offended by Paul's use of the word **slave** in reference to Epaphras. This word appears in other translations as "servant" or "bondservant," but these translations do not capture the force of the word. Servants are hired, but slaves are bought. Every believer has been purchased by the precious blood of Christ, and, as a result, all believers are His willing and indebted slaves. Apparently, Epaphras visited Paul while he was in prison and informed Paul of the **love** of the Colossians for him. The love of the Colossians was a result of the enabling power of the Holy Spirit in their lives (Gl 5:22).

Paul's Prayer for the Colossians (1:9-14)

1:9 Following his expression of thanksgiving for the Colossians, Paul relates his prayer for them. First, he set forth reasons for his prayers: He was recalling the good report he received from Epaphras concerning the faith of the Colossians. In fact, since the day he heard about them, he had not ceased to offer prayers on their behalf. Paul was eagerly praying for a group of Christians who were doing well. Instead of waiting for a crisis to arise and then pray, Paul was already interceding on behalf of the Colossians. In addition, the requests in his prayer focus upon spiritual instead of material blessings, since spiritual blessings are far more important in light of eternity. Paul's prayer was then a practical reminder for all believers: You must pray for others even when life seems relatively easy for them, and you must pray for spiritual blessings, not just material ones.

Paul clearly expressed his desire for the Colossians to have spiritual intelligence **that you may be filled with the knowledge of His will in all wisdom and spiritual understanding**. The term "be filled" carries the idea of being "fully or completely equipped." Notice, though, that they are not to be fully equipped with the knowledge of God's supernatural mysteries or His mind-boggling miracles. Instead, Paul desires simply that they be filled with the knowledge of God's "will." Just as being filled with the Holy Spirit (Eph 5:18) means being controlled by Him, being filled with knowledge of God's will means being controlled by His will. This knowledge, though, will not happen accidentally but comes through "all wisdom and spiritual understanding." "'Wisdom' refers to the comprehension of truth, while 'understanding' refers to the application of truth. Being controlled by God's will means believers comprehend the principles of Scripture and then put them into practice."[7]

Paul's Steps to a God-Pleasing Life (Colossians 1:10-12)

- Bearing fruit in every good work
- Growing in the knowledge of God
- Enduring with patience
- Giving thanks to the Father with joy

1:10 Spiritual intelligence is for the purpose of practical obedience **so that you may walk worthy of the Lord, fully pleasing to Him**. You may have heard someone described with these words: "She is so heavenly minded, she is of no earthly good." Paul is determined that believers should not get so caught up in absorbing the "deeper truths" of God that they forget about His primary desire that His children live a faithful and Christlike life. Being "fully pleasing" to God means to please Him in every part of your life.

How is this accomplished? Paul answered this question in verses 10-12. First, a God-pleasing life means **bearing fruit in every good work**. Although salvation is a free gift, good works are the natural result of salvation and part of God's plan for each believer in Christ (Eph 2:8-10). Second, God is pleased with your life when you are **growing in the knowledge of God.** You must seek to know more of His character, His will, and His ways if you are ever to conform to what is pleasing to Him. Your primary way of knowing God is through the living Word, Jesus Christ, who is perfectly revealed in the written Word, the Bible. You also grow in your knowledge of God through personal practices like prayer, meditation, and solitude, as well as community practices such as service, worship, and ministry.

1:11 Third, your life is pleasing to God when marked by **endurance and patience**. Endurance might be best understood as continuing to trust and obey God even in the face of difficult trials. Patience, on the other hand, might be put to test as one continues to trust and obey God even in the face of difficult people. Isn't it amazing how often you can endure faithfully through troubling circumstances, only to lose your temper in impatience with friends and loved ones? The need to endure both trials and people goes hand-in-hand as God transforms you into the likeness of Jesus. However, you can only please God through endurance and patience as you are **strengthened with all power, according to His glorious might**. God gives the believer the ability to please Him and you must continually ask Him to do just that. As Jesus said, "You can do nothing without Me" (Jn 15:5).

> *Obviously you do not earn an inheritance; you receive it.*

1:12 Fourth, believers please God when they are **with joy giving thanks to the Father**. A heart full of joy and gratitude should be a distinguishing mark of a believer, for God has done marvelous things for His children. Paul described that gratitude in several ways. God **has enabled you to share in the saints' inheritance in the light**. Undeservedly, every believer has been "enabled" or "qualified," through the work of Christ in the crucifixion and resurrection, to inherit all spiritual blessings with Him. If the term *saint* with its connotation of set apartness means "holy one," then, *through Christ*, you who are unholy have been transformed into "holy ones," worthy of "the inheritance in the light." Obviously you do not earn an inheritance; you receive it.

Heart to Heart:
Your Inheritance in Jesus

Women often struggle with feelings of inadequacy or inferiority. These feelings can have negative effects on their efforts to live the Christian life, preventing them from experiencing the fullness of God's blessings in Christ. Colossians 1:12, though, has good news for women: You have been qualified by God to share in the inheritance of the saints. While before you were unworthy of God's inheritance, Jesus has made you worthy through His death and resurrection. So, what does this inheritance mean for you? First, a glorious reward awaits you in eternity when you are finally in the presence of the Savior. Second, you can live victoriously in this truth right now. You can go to the grocery store, pump gas in your car, and walk to the park knowing that you are heir to a glorious inheritance!

1:13 God has also **rescued us from the domain of darkness**. This phrase communicates an image of the Lord swooping down like a giant bird and plucking His children out of the clutches of Satan, who has chained you within the walls of his evil kingdom. And just as God delivered you from the powers of darkness, He has also **transferred us into the kingdom of the Son He loves**. In this way, God has carried His children up and over the menacing walls of Satan's realm and dropped you gently within Jesus' palace in the kingdom of light. This concept of deliverance and transference is paralleled in the experience of the children of Israel in the Old Testament story of the Exodus. God delivered them from bondage in Egypt (Ex 3–14) and brought them into the promised land of their inheritance (Jos 1–4).

1:14 God's work of salvation is accomplished because, in Jesus Christ, **we have redemption, the forgiveness of sins**. The word *redeem* conveys the idea of buying someone back and then setting him free. The forgiveness of sins has been completed as Jesus offered Himself as payment for sin-debt, and He was raised from the dead as a sign that His payment was acceptable to God. As the Old Testament Exodus was accomplished through shedding the blood of the Passover lamb, in the New Testament redemption was accomplished through shedding the blood of the Lamb of God. Paul even described Jesus elsewhere as "our Passover" (1 Co 5:7).

CHRIST'S WORK AND PAUL'S MISSION (1:15–2:3)

After Paul greeted and encouraged the Colossian church, he took some time to lay out the truths about Jesus Christ and about his own gospel ministry. In a sense, he showed them what is true before he showed them what is false. The person and work of Christ and the missionary endeavors of Paul went hand in hand as the apostle led into the refutation of the false teachers.

Christ's Divine Personhood (1:15-18)

1:15 Paul's prayer for the Colossians became lengthy praise to Jesus Christ. Because of the poetic qualities in verses

15-20, many scholars believe these words are the quotation of a hymn of the early church. While the language and style of the verses are certainly marks of poetic excellence, there is no way to know for certain that they comprise a hymn. Nevertheless, these verses make up one of the most beautiful and eloquent Christological passages of praise regarding Christ in the New Testament.

Verses 15-20 also serve as a challenge to the false teachers in the Colossian church. Apparently, while they did not encourage doing away with worship of Jesus, they did propose to the church that Jesus was not uniquely God, but merely one of many intermediaries between God and man (see discussion of the "Colossian heresy" in *Major Themes*). "The false teachers in Colossae, like the false teachers of our own day, would not *deny* the importance of Jesus Christ. They would simply *dethrone* Him, giving Him prominence, but not preeminence."[8]

Jesus is **the image** of God. The Greek word *eikon*, translated "image," also refers to likenesses placed upon coins, portraits, and statues. It communicates the concept of an equivalence to the original. When a coin was made, a piece of softened metal was stamped by an engraved tool, and the hardened metal coin would contain the exact representation of the engraving from the original stamp. The God-man Jesus Christ is the exact "stamp" of the Father's nature. The writer of Hebrews affirms this concept in a similar way, saying, "He is the radiance of His glory, the exact expression of His nature" (Heb 1:3). In His essence, God is **invisible** to human beings, but Jesus Christ has perfectly revealed Himself to you. Logically, since no mere creature can perfectly reveal God, then Jesus must be God Himself.

Not only does Jesus perfectly reveal God to you, but He also ranks above everything in the universe as **the firstborn over all creation**. "Firstborn" is a term referring to Jesus' rank in creation, not creation in time (see discussion of 1:18). Jehovah's Witnesses have used this verse incorrectly when they teach that Jesus is not God, but only the first created being. But, parallel to verse 18, "firstborn" here refers to Jesus' rank or position of authority, as both the inheritor of the universe and the ruler over it. Isaac is an Old Testament example of someone who was not the firstborn son in time but one who was blessed with the authoritative position and privileges of the firstborn.

1:16 Jesus possesses the most privileged position in creation because He is the Creator of all things. Paul's description of **heaven**, **earth**, **visible**, and **invisible** communicates to the Colossians: "You name it—Jesus created it!" Within the angelic realm He even created the spirit beings whom the false teachers were calling on the Colossians to worship (Col 2:18). Verse 16 essentially teaches that Jesus created everything that exists for His own good pleasure.

1:17 Saying that Jesus **is before all things** means that He is eternally existent, which is an attribute that belongs only to God. At the same time, Jesus sustains the universe, for **by Him all things hold together**. Jesus is like the great "cosmic super-glue" that fastens everything in the universe in its proper place.[9] If for one second Jesus were to relinquish His power over the universe, all would turn from order to chaos. This truth also applies to the Christian life. A marriage without Christ is chaos. Parenting without Christ is chaos. A workplace without Christ is chaos. Essentially, life without Christ is chaos.

1:18 Just as Jesus is sovereign over creation, He is also sovereign over the church. Paul calls Him the **head of the**

body, which is **the church**. The Greek word *kephalē*, translated "head" in this context, without doubt means that Jesus is the "authority" over the church.[10] It is *under* Christ that the church functions in humble obedience.

Jesus' position of supremacy in the church is specifically founded upon His nature as **the firstborn from the dead**. As in verse 15, "firstborn" has nothing to do with time. Others before Jesus rose from

the dead but not in the way Jesus did (see Jn 11:38-44 for one example). Jesus is first in rank. Through His triumph over death, Jesus has led the way for those who, by faith in Him, will likewise be resurrected on the Day of Judgment, never to die again. Because of the resurrection of Christ, a believer can be confident in her own resurrection (1 Co 15:20-23). All this was done that Jesus would **have first place in everything**.

Heart to Heart: Giving Jesus "First Place in Everything"

The last phrase in verse 18 is mainly theological in nature, but it has profound application in the life of a believer. If Jesus has "first place in everything" within the created order, what place does He have in your life? Whether single or married, with children or without, women shoulder many responsibilities in everyday life. Though most are good responsibilities, none should take the place of Christ. You will often have to give yourself a "priority check," making sure that neither your marriage, your home, your church, nor anything else is stealing first place from Jesus. Because everything in your life is dependent upon your relationship with Christ, you must learn to nurture your walk with the Lord and give Him the "first place" position He demands and deserves.

Christ's Redemptive Work (1:19-23)

1:19-20 Jesus is supreme over all things because all of God's **fullness** dwells in Him. The word translated "FULLNESS" (Greek *pleroma*) for the false teachers may have been a technical term that meant "the sum total of all the divine power and attributes." If so, Paul was beating them at their own game, using their term to exalt the true God. Or, *pleroma* could be referring to the many places in the Old Testament where the glory of God inhabited the place He chose to dwell. Ezekiel

exclaimed, "I looked, and the glory of the Lord filled His temple" (Ezk 44:4). Paul elaborated on this concept later in Colossians 2:9, saying, **in Him the entire fullness of God's nature dwells bodily**. It is as though someone could take all of the vastness that makes up God's person and essence and use a gargantuan funnel to pour Him into the person of Jesus Christ.

God was pleased **to reconcile everything to Himself** through Jesus. Humanly speaking, reconciliation refers to someone intervening between two warring parties to establish peace and friendly relations. In this case, man through his rebellion has become the enemy of God, and Christ

through the blood of His cross has reconciled man to Himself and in so doing brought ultimate peace. Without the forgiveness of sin, which offends God's holiness, there would be no peace between God and His creation. And "without the shedding of blood there is no forgiveness" of sin (Heb 9:22). Therefore, Jesus accomplished reconciliation through the shedding of His blood, bringing to those who are willing to be reconciled to Him peace and fellowship with God.

Further, there is a profound theological point in verses 19-20: Paul said all of God's nature dwelt bodily in Jesus Christ, and he declared that Jesus Christ was crucified for the purpose of our reconciliation with God. In another context, Paul put it this way: "He made the One who did not know sin to be sin for us, so that we might become the righteousness of God in Him" (2 Co 5:21). In light of this truth, one must truly "stand amazed in the presence of Jesus the Nazarene."

1:21-22 Yet, this deep theology is also personally relevant for every believer. Prior to Jesus' work of reconciliation, all unbelievers were considered enemies of God. Paul described the status of the unredeemed as God's enemies in two ways: They were **alienated** from Him, i.e., they were outsiders, estranged, and separated forever (Eph 2:11-12). This alienation made them *positional* enemies of God. Figuratively speaking, not only were they locked out of the kingdom of God, but they were standing beyond the gates, hurling angry insults and blasphemies at the King. In this position, they were not only God's enemies, but they were also *mental* enemies of God. Paul describes this condition as being **hostile in mind**. Even as this enemy stood lonely and excluded from the kingdom, in her mind she wanted nothing to do with the King and she thought only evil of Him. Paul indicated that her positional and mental

enmity with God was a direct result of her **evil actions**. Purposeful rebellion against the holiness of God caused a seemingly irreconcilable rift between God and His creation.

Thankfully, that is not the end of the story! Paul continued by saying, **But now He has reconciled you**. Jesus is the peacemaker, who **by His physical body through His death**, was able to venture beyond the kingdom's walls and bring His creation into the presence of God, making peace between God and mankind, once and for all time. Jesus has done all this so that every woman and man may one day stand **holy, faultless, and blameless before Him**. The word "holy" emphasizes the believer's position as set apart from the world; "faultless" emphasizes her purity before God, like an Old Testament sacrifice without any deformity or blemish; and "blameless" emphasizes her status as "free from accusation," because her slate of sins has been wiped clean.

1:23 The word **if** in verse 23 must not be misunderstood. Paul was not casting doubt on the believer's future status before God, as if her eternal salvation is dependent upon her performance here on earth. Instead, Paul was saying, "If you are truly saved, and built upon the solid foundation, Jesus Christ, then you will continue in the faith and nothing will move you. You have heard the gospel and trusted Jesus Christ, and He has saved you." In other words, you are not saved by your steadfastness in the faith. But, you are steadfast in the faith because you are saved.

Paul's Ministry to the Whole Church (1:24-29)

1:24 After establishing the truth about the person and work of Jesus, Paul moved on to establish the truth about his personal ministry—and all ministry for that matter—in the church of Jesus. Paul certainly knew about suffering for the sake of the gospel; and through those experiences he could honestly tell the Colossians, **I rejoice in my sufferings for you**. Suffering in general is not a reason for joy. But, suffering on behalf of Christ and fellow believers is a privilege and honor. When Paul said that he was **completing in** [his] **flesh what is lacking in Christ's afflictions** for the **church**, he was not implying that Christ's atoning sacrifice was incomplete or deficient. Instead, he was acknowledging that because Jesus is not around to be the victim of persecution, the world is persecuting His followers. Paul knew that Jesus took the blows meant for him; he was willing to take the blows meant for Jesus. Elsewhere, Paul considered sufferings as the means by which believers have true "fellowship" with Christ (Php 3:10).

1:25-27 Paul can rejoice in his afflictions because he is a **minister** of the church by God's appointment. He calls the **message** God has given him a **mystery**. When the word *mystery* is used today, one typically thinks of eerie novels and suspenseful detective movies. But, in Paul's day, the word *mystery* was used to describe a secret hidden in the past but now revealed. For the Christian faith, the "mystery" is the sacred secret **hidden for ages and generations** that has now been **revealed** to God's **saints**: that is, Jesus Christ is the promised Messiah of the Jews, who also brings **Gentiles** into the family of God, and dwells within all believers, whether Jew or Gentile, giving all a future **hope of glory**.

1:28-29 By today's standards, these verses might be Paul's formal "mission statement." He considered his primary responsibility to be to **proclaim** Christ, which includes the Lord's life, death, and resurrection. This proclamation of the gospel takes on two different forms: **warning and teaching**. "Teaching" is the positive side of proclamation that involves instruct-

ing believers in the truths of the Word of God. "Warning" is the negative side of proclamation that involves alerting believers to the lies of the enemy. Both are absolutely necessary in order to **present everyone mature in Christ**. The Greek word *teleios*, translated MATURE, means "complete" or "perfect." Paul's goal, which must be yours, was to bring every disciple of Jesus Christ to full maturity in the truths and practices of the faith. More than any other goal in life, the maturity of the believer is accomplished only through much "labor" (exhausting effort) and "striving" (agonizing effort). Yet, you are not alone in this endeavor, for you do all this with "His strength that works powerfully" in you.

Paul's Concern for the Colossians and Their Faith (2:1-3)

2:1-3 Paul closed this section by reminding the Colossians once again **how great a struggle** he had waged for them. This struggle was not as a result of his many sufferings and current imprisonment, as one would expect; rather, it was the result of an internal battle **for all who have not seen** [him] **in person**. Paul was about to share with the Colossians his direct warnings against the false teachings that have spread in the church—the main reason he wrote this letter in the first place. So, he assured them of his motivations: (1) that **their hearts** would be **encouraged**, (2) which happens as they are **joined together in love,** (3) in order that they may be confident in their **knowledge of God's mystery**. The false teachers in Colossae were telling the people that wisdom and knowledge are hidden away and that only a few worthy people are able to find such higher understanding through mystical experiences and strict regulations. But, Paul countered this idea and said that **all the riches of assured understanding** and the "knowledge of God's mystery" are found solely in **Christ**. He was essentially saying, "Jesus is all you need."

REFUTATION OF THE FALSE PHILOSOPHY AND RECOGNITION OF THE TRUE FAITH (2:4–3:4)

In this section, Paul finally attacked the false teaching directly. He first warned the Colossians about the dangers of the false philosophy and then supported those warnings with more truth about Jesus Christ. Then, because of who Jesus is and what He has done for believers, Paul exhorted the Colossians to be aware of spiritual dangers, remembering their privileged position in Christ because of His death and resurrection.

A Warning Against the False Philosophy (2:4-8)

2:4-5 Paul affirmed he had written **so that no one will deceive** them with **persuasive arguments**. The Greek word *pithanologia*, translated "persuasive arguments," was used in courts of law to describe rhetoric that is false and empty but is actually "high sounding nonsense." The falsehood that lures you away from Christ is not usually blatantly wrong. Instead, such teaching is craftily dressed up like a wolf in sheep's clothing: sweet and innocent on the outside, but deceitful and wicked on the inside. It promises everything but delivers nothing.

Along with the Colossians, you can be protected from dangerous "smooth talking" by remaining in **good order** and strong in your **faith in Christ**. These words are military terms that describe an army completely prepared for the enemy's attack. "Good order" refers to the ranks of the army, with every person in his proper place, while **strength** refers to the formation of the soldiers, with no one "breaking rank" under pressure. Like a proud commander, Paul told the Colossians that although he was **absent in body**, he was **rejoicing** in his **spirit** to see them fully prepared to face the enemy.

2:6-7 In order to prepare for the enemy, Paul strongly encourages these Colossian believers to **walk** in their faith just as they **received Christ Jesus** in the first place. The Greek word *peripateite,* translated "walk," is often used in Paul's letters as a metaphor for "live." Essentially, he was saying, "You began your Christian life with Christ, now continue it with Christ. You began your Christian life with faith, now continue it with faith." Four vivid images express Paul's desire for the faith of the Colossians:

- To be **rooted** in Christ suggests a tree planted in good soil and now growing in strength and stability.

- To be **built up in Him** suggests an architectural picture of the Christian building her faith on the firm foundation of Christ.

- To be **established in the faith, just as you were taught** is educational terminology suggesting that the believer must be schooled rightly in the truth.

- To be **overflowing with thankfulness** paints the picture of a mighty river that overflows its banks.

2:8 Even in a state of readiness and faithfulness, though, believers face the real threat of being taken **captive** by false teaching. You can, in effect, be spiritually "kidnapped" by **philosophy and empty deceit**. This warning is not a complete indictment of *all* philosophy, only against those ideologies that are full of "empty deceit," as opposed to having the fullness of Jesus Christ (1:19; 2:9). Such things clearly are not based upon Christ, but upon **human tradition** and **the elemental forces of the world**. By "elemental forces of the world," Paul is probably referring to spirit beings—the "angels" whom the false teachers encouraged the Colossians to worship (2:18). Neither human ideas nor spirit beings are any comparison to the truth and power of Jesus. Any teaching or practice not **based on Christ** should be rejected. Philosophy, a transliterated Greek word meaning "the love of wisdom," describes a legitimate human pursuit. Biblical writers often make use of philosophical concepts (see Jn 1:1). However, philosophy remains a human endeavor for explaining the nature of reality. As with all other human efforts, it must, therefore, be subject to Christ and to the revealed Word of God. Left to itself, philosophy becomes speculative, and unwary individuals can become enslaved to unproven and often unprovable theories. For example, women would do well to examine the tenets of modern feminism in light of Scripture. The only way for a Christian to avoid being kidnapped by false teaching is by knowing the Word of God and understanding the doctrines of the faith.

Feminism versus Biblical Womanhood		
Feministic Ideology	**Biblical Principle**	**Biblical Reference**
Equality of personhood necessitates equal access to roles/position.	Jesus affirmed equality of the man and woman and modeled God's plan for different roles.	1 Pt 3:7; Gn 2:15-18
God did not ordain specific roles at creation. Role differences are a result of the fall.	The fall distorted God's plan, but the differences between men and women can be traced to Creation.	Gn 1:26-27; 3:7-8; 1 Co 11:7-10; Eph 5:23-27; Php 2:5-8
The Bible contradicts itself with regards to its teaching on the role of women (e.g., Jesus vs. Paul). The Bible presents differing opinions on what the role of women ought to be.	All Scripture is God-breathed and is unified and without internal contradiction in its message. Jesus came to fulfill the law.	Mt 5:17-18; 2 Tm 3:16; 4:1-5
Woman's experience is the source and norm—the lens through which women must interpret Scripture.	God's will as revealed in Scripture is the final authority for faith and practice. Personal opinions and preferences are not above the teachings of Scripture.	Dt 10:12-13; Ac 5:29
Women have the right to revisit and revise history/language to incorporate a woman-centered point of view.	God's truth does not change. His words/plan transcend culture. Men and women have the responsibility to submit to His revealed will.	Pr 3:5; Is 3:4-5,12; 4:10; Mt 16:24
God can rightly be referred to as "she." Some argue that goddess imagery can be incorporated into the Christian faith.	God supersedes masculinity and femininity. Though He has submissive/nurturing aspects to His character, interaction with Him must be on the basis of His self-designated identity/names.	Eph 5:21-28; Php 2:5-8

An Elaboration of Christ's All-Sufficiency (2:9-15)

2:9-10 Attacks of false teaching usually focus on two major issues: (1) the person of Jesus Christ and (2) the Christian's identity in Him. False teachers may deny that Jesus Christ is God, or they may undermine His personhood as being fully human. They often propose "something more" as necessary for the completion of salvation. Quasi-Christian[11] cults have an easily identifiable "mathematical" formula: They *subtract* from the person of Jesus Christ and *add* to the method of salvation.

> *Quasi-Christian cults have an easily identifiable "mathematical" formula: They subtract from the person of Jesus Christ and add to the method of salvation.*

Paul confronted both attacks in verses 9-10 by assuring the Colossians that Jesus is completely God and believers are complete in Him, with no need to add anything more. In Jesus, all of the **fullness of God's nature dwells bodily,** and, in turn, believers have **been filled** by Christ. Both concepts of fullness (Gk. *pleroma*)—the fullness of Christ as God and the fullness of the believer—possess the idea of permanence. Jesus is permanently the embodied fullness of God, and Jesus permanently fulfills believers. When you are born again into the family of God, you are born complete in Christ. But, you still have need for spiritual growth. Such growth, however, is not by *addition* (like the false teachers), but by *nutrition*. Feeding on the Word of God in community with fellow believers, you grow in Christ from the inside out.

> *Such growth, however, is not by addition (like the false teachers), but by nutrition. Feeding on the Word of God in community with fellow believers, you grow in Christ from the inside out.*

2:11-13 Paul used two well-known religious rituals to symbolize the spiritual transformation in the life of a Christian: **circumcision** and **baptism**. The circumcision that Paul was discussing is **not done with hands**, as the Old Testament covenant of circumcision instituted by Abraham in Genesis 17. Instead, he was talking about the spiritual surgery by which the **body of flesh**, or the sinful nature, is cut off by Christ through His lordship, which is the **circumcision of the Messiah**. For Paul, baptism is not the replacement of Old Testament circumcision but rather the outward symbol of New Testament circumcision or the New Birth. The New Testament symbol of baptism is another way of illustrating the Christian's death to sin, **having been buried with Him**, and triumphing over both sin and death, **through faith in the working of God** (see Eph 2:4-6). Both of these concepts—circumcision and baptism—remind believers that, when they were **dead in trespasses** and spiritual **uncircumcision**, Jesus made them **alive** with Him, forgiving **all our trespasses**.

2:14-15 These verses are a vivid picture of Jesus' accomplishment in forgiving your sins. The Greek word *cheirographon* (more literally "handwriting"), translated "certificate of debt," comes from Jewish business practices of the era. It was a handwritten note that recorded the various financial debts of the people. Upon payment of the debt, the note would be read aloud, declared to be fulfilled, and then destroyed. The "certificate of debt" for you and me is the violation of God's laws and rebellion against His rule. The **obligations** necessary to fulfill this debt are death and eternal punishment. For this reason, the "certificate of debt" was **against us and opposed to us**, meaning it is always before our faces as an eternal reminder of our sins. Yet, through His death and resurrection, Jesus has **erased** the certificate of debt. In addition, He has **taken it out of the way by nailing it to the cross**. In this way, Jesus has conquered sin and death. Yet, He has also **disarmed** the powers of darkness, which Paul identifies as **rulers and authorities**. Though Satan and his minions labor and scheme to bring shame upon humanity by exposing your sin, Jesus has **disgraced them publicly** and **triumphed over them** through the cross.

Heart to Heart: Forgetting the Past

Many women today are haunted by the sins of the past. Despite knowing about the forgiveness of God and affirming its truth, a woman often finds it difficult to enact that forgiveness in her heart and to forgive herself. Although you are a Christian, your certificate of debt seems to remain against you and opposed to you. There is no magic formula through which you can gain freedom from such self-condemnation, but you can begin to do so by claiming the truth of Colossians 2:14—i.e., Jesus has removed your sins and nailed them to the cross. The Bible says, God has "vanquished our iniquities" and cast all our sins "into the depths of the sea" (Mc 7:19). You can have freedom from the "ghosts" of your past and victory in your Christian life now.

Warnings Against Spiritual Dangers (2:16-19)

2:16-17 Because of what Christ has done for them, Paul instructed the Colossians not to let anyone **judge** them. This reference is specifically to people who "pass unfavorable judgment on" or "find fault with" the faith of other believers. Apparently, there were some people in the Colossian church who were criticizing others because they did not observe certain religious practices, such as dietary laws (**food and drink**) and special days (**festival, new moon, sabbath day**). The keeping of such rules was very much a part of the Old Testament law; and many people, especially Jewish Christians, had difficulty understanding that their salvation was not tied to the observances of such rules. The false teachers at Colossae preyed upon this misunderstanding, attempting to force these laws upon the church. But, Paul reminded them that these regulations were merely **a shadow of what was to come**: the arrival of **Messiah**. As a result, because believers have the Messiah and are complete in Him, there is no need for strict laws or the observance of special days.

2:18-19 Paul warned that there are significant dangers in listening to the teaching of those who insist on **ascetic practices and the worship of angels**: They can be **disqualif[ied]** from the prize. This Greek term *katabrabeueto* ("cheating") carries the idea of being deprived of spiritual reward. Paul used the imperative to emphasize the importance of defending yourself from fraud. The false teachers in Colossae claimed to have **access to a visionary realm**, which made them **inflated** or puffed up with pride. This ongoing danger for Christians manifests itself in getting so caught up in seeking emotional and spiritual experiences that you miss out on true fulfillment in Christ. Neither rules nor experiences can replace the completion you find in Christ alone. Anyone who is drawn away by such rules or experiences **doesn't hold onto the head**; i.e., she has not remained attached to the True Vine and will shrivel up and die without the necessary nourishment and **growth from God** (Jn 15:5-6).

Consequences of Death with Christ (2:20-23)

2:20-23 In addition to rules, special days, and mystical experiences, Paul debunked the idea that depriving the body makes one individual more spiritual than others. He affirmed that, because believers **died with Christ to . . . this world**, they do not need to **submit to regulations** that false teachers desire to foist upon them. The rules of deprivation—**don't handle, don't taste, don't touch**—are probably related to fasting and dietary laws. Paul reminded the Colossians these were merely **human commands and doctrines**. Such human doctrines may appear to be wise and super-spiritual, but, in reality, **they are not of any value**. Christians often try many different methods of self-help and quick-fix to battle **fleshly indulgence**, or the sin nature, but they don't work.

Heart to Heart: Avoiding the Bondage of Legalism

*In your attempts to be the "perfect" woman, whether as a wife, mother, church member, or employee, often you impose upon yourself a personal list of "regulations" and "human commands" (Col 2:20,22). Failing to achieve these super-human standards can become a source of much anxiety and grief. Although it is not easy, you as believers need to free yourselves from these bonds of legalism for, as Colossians 2:23 says, **they are not of any value**. If God's grace has given you eternal life, then why do you attempt to live that life by your rules? Having been saved by grace, you must live by grace. Instead of looking to your own fabricated standards of "perfection," which no one on earth could attain, you must look to Christ. He has fulfilled all of God's law on your behalf so that you do not have to meet the standards of the law, and He lives eternally to empower you day by day with His grace and mercy.*

Consequences of Resurrection with Christ (3:1-4)

3:1-4 Christians have died with Christ and are therefore free from the rules and regulations of the world. But, Christians have also **been raised** with Christ, which provides even more benefits. First, the lives of believers are **hidden with the Messiah in God**. Being HIDDEN (Gk. *kekruptai*) with the Messiah carries the ideas of both safety and security. The perfect tense gives the idea of a continuing completed state resulting from a past action. Christians can take comfort that, even as the world condemns and Satan accuses, they are safe from any attack and secure from any trial because they are "hidden . . . in God." For this reason, Christians should **set** their **minds on things above**, i.e., focus on the eternal things of life, not the temporal things that will soon pass away (1 Jn 2:17). Even **what is on the earth** should be seen against the background of eternity. Second, when **the Messiah . . . is revealed**, Christians who are hidden with Him will also be **revealed with Him in glory**. The believer's identification with Christ means a glorious future as well as a break with sin in the past and security in the present. Paul says in Romans 8:30 that believers have already been glorified. This glory, though, is simply awaiting the return of the Messiah to be fully revealed.

PRACTICAL APPLICATION TO THE CHRISTIAN LIFE (3:5–4:6)

After Paul exposed the false teachings and reminded the Colossians of the truth, he discussed practical application of truth to the Christian life. This section could be called the "So what?" part of the letter. Paul instructed the Colossians that the life of a believer involves doing away with vices and cultivating virtues, especially within the believer's household and in her personal prayer and witness.

"Putting Off" Vices (3:5-11)

3:5-7 Based upon the believer's death and resurrection with Christ (2:20-23; 3:1-4), Paul exhorted believers to **put to death** in their lives **whatever** is **worldly**. This exhortation is not a reference to the careful management of sins in your lives, but it demands the complete extermination of sins from your lives. The first set of worldly things of which Paul spoke are all related to the satisfaction of internal desires. SEXUAL IMMORALITY is from the Greek word *porneia*, referring to any kind of sexual activity outside the bonds of marriage. **Impurity** reminds believers that any illicit sexual encounters are inherently wicked and mock the purity of soul Christ has given you through forgiveness of sins. Beyond the physical acts of sexual immorality, the Christian is not even supposed to give a place to **lust** or **evil desires**, both of which occur primarily in the heart and mind. **Greed** seems like an odd sin to list after those describing sexual immorality. Yet, anything that undermines the proper place of God in your life is **idolatry**, whether it is lust for physical or material satisfaction. Those Christians who continue in these sins are mocking the realities of both their past and their future:

- **They once walked in these things**, in the past, but they have been redeemed from these sins by Christ.

- They await the future **wrath of God** that will come on the Day of Judgment. Both truths should have a here-and-now impact on the way you as believers live your lives.

3:8-10 The metaphor in verse 8 becomes one of changing clothes. The call to **put away** in verse 8, followed by the charge to **put off** and **put on** in verses 9 and 10, communicates a powerful idea: The metaphor suggests that believers discard old, repulsive habits like worn-out clothes in order to adorn themselves with a well-dressed and appropriate lifestyle. Notice that this group of sins is specifically focused on the nature of personal interactions among Christians. ANGER (Gk. *orgen*), also translated indignation, is the slow-burning fuse of emotion that remains smoldering right below the surface, while WRATH (Gk. *thumon*), also translated passion or rage, is the explosive burst of emotion that rises and falls quickly, but with much intensity. MALICE and SLANDER typically

Heart to Heart: Sexual Immorality

One can easily imagine that the passages in the Bible regarding sexual immorality are more applicable to men than women. Surely most women do not struggle with lust or evil desires. But the truth is that women and men have struggles with sexual immorality. A woman's struggles just don't appear in quite the same way as those of their brothers in Christ. For women, more often than not, the sin of sexual immorality begins not only in their thoughts but also involves their emotions. When entertained long enough, even nonsexual romantic thoughts and feelings toward a man who is not your husband can be very damaging to your marriage. For this reason, your emotional need for affection and attention from your spouse should never be transferred to anyone else. Women who desire to avoid any kind of sexual sin must vigorously guard their minds and hearts, catching the "foxes" of sexual immorality that can destroy the "vineyard" of their marriages (Sg 2:15).

go hand in hand, for "malice" (Gk. *kakia*), also translated "badness, wickedness, or trouble," is the "vicious and deliberate intention of doing harm to others," while "slander" (Gk. *blasphemian*) refers to the damaging words spoken to defame a person's character, carrying the suggestion of irreverence. FILTHY LANGUAGE (Gk. *aischrologia*) is a compound Greek word, which combines *aischpos*, meaning "ugly, shameful, or base," with *logos*, meaning "word." The reference is to any crude, obscene, or abusive speech.

All of these things, along with [lying] **to one another**, are a part of **the old man with his practices** and must, therefore, be "put off." The image of "the old man" versus **the new man** is common in Paul's writings and has nothing to do with gender or age. One could translate these phrases "the old self" and "the new self" because Paul was simply referring to the complete transformation of one's identity in Christ. Through faith in Jesus, you have a new self *spiritually*, but you must, in a sense, activate this new self *practically* in

everyday life. This is a constant process because you are continually **being renewed in knowledge according to the image of** [your] **Creator**.

3:11 In this process of sanctification in Christ, there are no longer any distinctions among believers, whether by ethnicity, culture, gender, or social status. Such distinctions do not disappear, but they no longer matter. Because **Christ is all** (central and supreme in everything) **and in all** (indwelling every believer through the Holy Spirit), all believers stand as equals before God. However, this equality is one of *personhood*, not one of *function*. Whether in the home or in the church, according to Scripture, while each person is equal in personhood, each is different in function (see discussion of Col 3:18-23).

"Putting On" Virtues (3:12-17)

3:12-14 After removing the stained clothes of sin from the old self, the Christian must also **put on** the pure and clean clothes of the Spirit that suit the new self. You are able to do this because you are **God's chosen ones**, who are set apart for

Him (**holy**) and cherished by Him (**loved**). Israel was described by these terms in the Old Testament (Dt 4:37; 7:7-8), but now these same words are applied to the body of Christ (1 Pt 2:9-10).

A Christian Woman's Wardrobe *(Colossians 3:8-14)*	
"Put Off" **3:8-10**	**"Put On"** **3:12-14**
• Anger	• Compassion
• Wrath	• Kindness
• Malice	• Humility
• Slander	• Gentleness
• Filthy language	• Patience
• Lying	• Acceptance
	• Forgiveness
	• Love

Heartfelt compassion is the first virtue to make up your new clothing, which is genuine sympathy for those suffering or in need. **Kindness** follows genuine compassion, for it is the helpful and gracious character that works to meet the needs seen in the lives of others. **Humility** is the right view of self in light of the right view of God. Believers are not to think too highly of themselves, nor are they to think too little of themselves. Self-abasing or self-deprecating attitudes are not humility, but a poor attempt to mimic the real thing. The Savior models the best example of **gentleness** or meekness for you. While on earth, He was fully God, with all of His mighty powers and prerogatives, and yet He submitted completely to the Father's will, allowing Himself to be under the Father's control. A woman who is submitted totally to the will of God will have no need for brashness, cruelty, or bullying because she trusts the Lord to meet all of her needs. Gentleness is matched with **patience**, which is the ability to endure injury or injustice without retaliation. Both are rooted in a childlike trust in the Lord.

All of these virtues lead to **accepting one another**, which is the idea of putting up with the offenses and injuries of others. Yet, even more than the acceptance of others' faults, you must also be **forgiving [of] one another**, which is the act of releasing others from the "debt" that their sin against you creates. You must forgive **just as the Lord has forgiven**, completely and without condition. The concept of accepting one another must be balanced, though, with the content of Colossians 2. Paul clearly reveals that false teaching, which is dangerous to the church and offensive to God, should not be endured for any reason. However, if the leaders of such a group turn away from their false teaching to the truth of the gospel, then you as believers should respond to them in forgiveness and love.

The most significant item of virtuous clothing is saved for last: **Above all, put on love**. Paul described love as the **perfect bond of unity**, for love not only binds all of the virtues together to complete the garment of Christian character, but also binds all members of the church together in perfect unity. The kind of love that comes from God is what distinguishes all the other virtues from meaningless moralism (1 Co 13:1-3). This sacrificial love, perfectly revealed in the death and resurrection of Christ, transforms the Christian virtues from a list of "dos and don'ts" to an instinctive lifestyle.

3:15 In order to attain **unity** in the body of Christ, **the peace of the Messiah** must **control [your] hearts**. This peace is not like the world gives, temporary and unstable. Jesus gives peace that is free and eternal, completely independent from the circumstances of life. Christians who allow the peace of Jesus to rule in their hearts will not succumb to the fears and worries

> *And a congregation of believers united in the peace of Christ will avoid most conflict and turmoil because they are allowing themselves to be controlled by Christ, not by the whims, worries, and wishes of the day.*

so common in day-to-day life. And a congregation of believers united in the peace of Christ will avoid most conflict and turmoil because they are allowing themselves to be controlled by Christ, not by the whims, worries, and wishes of the day.

3:16-17 As believers put on biblical virtues and live out the Christian life, you must allow **the message about the Messiah** to **dwell richly among [you]**. When Paul wrote to the Colossian church, the Colossians probably had none of the four Gospels or any other writings of the New Testament. Yet, they had an abundance of teachings about Jesus from the oral tradition of the disciples, brought to them first by Epaphras. Likely their **psalms, hymns, and spiritual songs** also served as teaching tools about Jesus. However, "the message about the Messiah" is contained in the Bible. Therefore, for that message to **dwell richly** in your lives, which means to let it "feel at home," you must study its contents, memorize and meditate on its words, and put its teachings into practice.

Heart to Heart: Community of Faith

*Notice, however, that, for the believer, such study does not take place primarily alone, but in the context of the community of faith. You are to be **teaching and admonishing one another**, which implies doing such things together. Notice also that the **singing** of Christian songs is based upon the message of the Messiah. Without adequate teaching and admonishing, the corporate worship of the church most certainly will be severely lacking. Surely, if Christians seriously implemented the aspects of this passage—the bond of love, the peace of Christ, the message of the gospel, and the teaching of the church—they could resolve and avoid most of the so-called "worship wars" that are raging in churches all over the country today. Certainly, musical preferences fade in comparison to your high calling to Christ-like living in the body of Christ.*

Verse 17 is the "cover-all" statement that both concludes the section on Christian virtues and introduces the following section on specific household relationships. **Whatever you do**, in speech or action, you are to do **everything in the**

name of the Lord Jesus. Many things that are not pleasing to God have been done in Jesus' name. The so-called "Christian" Crusades in the Holy Land, beginning around AD 1095, are a humbling example of something done in Jesus' name that was loathsome and offensive in the eyes of God. Everything from adulterous relationships to religious genocide has been done in the name of Jesus. So, how do you know if what you are doing is rightly "in the name of the Lord Jesus"? The "name" of the Lord corresponds to the character of the Lord. The character of God was perfectly revealed to you in the person of Jesus Christ. Therefore, everything that you do should be matched up against the character of Jesus. "What Would Jesus Do?" isn't simply a cliché after all.

Heart to Heart: Doing All Things in the Name of Jesus

This passage can be a particular challenge for many women because they do countless things in life that they do not enjoy. Whether household chores or any thankless tasks, sometimes really to "do everything in the name of Jesus, giving thanks to God the Father through Him" seems impossible. You may ask, "Are you sure that everything done should be worthy of Jesus' name?" The answer is yes. Many have said that worship is not merely singing and praying; it is a lifestyle. That is what this verse is all about. When you sweep the kitchen floor, you should do even this mundane task in Jesus' name with a heart of gratitude to God. In so doing, you join the seventeenth-century monk Brother Lawrence as he rightly prayed,

> *Lord of all pots and pans and things. . . . Make me a saint by getting meals and washing up the plates!. . . The time of business does not with me differ from the time of prayer, and in the noise and clatter of my kitchen . . . I possess God in as great tranquilly as if I were upon my knees at the blessed sacrament.*[12]

Working out at the gym, bathing your children, walking the dogs, driving to work—anything you do on a regular basis should honor the Lord (1 Co 10:31). In the words of Joni Eareckson Tada, "In God's eyes, all of life's activities are sacred." Accept the challenge of Colossians 3:17 and try turning the unpleasant parts of your day into acts of worship offered unto God in Jesus' name.

Examining Household Relationships (3:18–4:1)

3:18-21 If you are to do everything in the name of the Lord Jesus, then how are you as Christians supposed to act in your own homes? In Paul's day, three sets of relationships existed in the home:

- Husband and wife

- Parent and child

- Slave and master

Heart to Heart:
Submission Is Not Oppression

Submission is meant to be a good and beautiful thing in a Christian marriage (even if it is not always easy to do!). It is important, however, for women to understand the distinction between submission to a servant leader and coercion from an oppressive tyrant. Biblical submission is a voluntary choice. Submission is the willing and loving acceptance of a husband's authority and leadership in marriage. Yet, it is not the passive acceptance of physical, mental, or verbal abuse. Such behavior is oppressive, dangerous, and contemptible to God. If you or someone you know is suffering from abuse, seek help from a trusted and godly confidant, whether a pastor, counselor, or close friend. God's desire is for wives to have healthy and happy marriages. With intervention, repentance, and the grace of God, that can become a reality.

First, **wives** are called to **be submissive** to their **husbands**. Submission is not a demeaning posture for a wife to take, for Jesus is the perfect model of biblical submission. Though equal with the Father, He willingly submits to the authority of the One with whom He is equal (see 1 Co 11:3; 15:28; Php 2:5-11). The Bible clearly teaches that a wife is equal to her husband (Gn 1:27; 1 Pt 3:7). Yet in her equality, she is to place herself voluntarily under her husband's authority. Paul says that this submission is **fitting in the Lord**. All institutions have clear lines of authority; submission as a part of God's design for the home is no different.

The husband, though, is not given the right to treat his wife as a "subject." Instead, he is to honor his wife with sacrificial **love**. This love is selfless, meeting the needs of others regardless of the personal cost. The parallel passage in Ephesians 5:25-26 further illuminates this concept: "Husbands, love your wives, just as also Christ loved the church and gave Himself for her." Clearly this kind of love has no room for bitterness (Gk. *pikraines-*

the), which is also translated "harshness." Husbands are never to use their authority in the home as an excuse to be harsh, domineering, or cruel.

The obedience of children to parents **in everything** is **pleasing in the Lord**. Jesus told His disciples that, if they loved Him, they should obey His commandments (Jn 14:15). In the same way, children must show their love for their parents by obeying them. The authority of parents, specifically **fathers**, over their children, again is not a license for harshness. Paul encouraged fathers not to **exasperate** their children, so that **they [the children] won't become discouraged**. The word translated EXASPERATE (Gk. *erethizete*) reflects a form of bitterness caused by harassment or provocation, and the word translated DISCOURAGED (Gk. *athumōsin*) refers to losing heart or becoming discouraged, having a broken spirit. As parents train up their children, they should seek to harness, not break, the spirits of their children.

3:22–4:1 This section addressing slaves and masters is quite long, compared to the section on the family, likely because of the situation in Colossae, in which the runaway slave Onesimus was returning to his master Philemon with a letter from Paul. Slavery was common in the Roman provinces of Paul's day, even in Christian homes. The church at Colossae would have consisted of both slave owners and slaves. Though the spread of Christianity would eventually dismantle the Roman slave system, Paul gave instructions here for how to function as Christians within this deeply entrenched economic and social structure. For the purpose of application, the present-day relationship of employee to employer is the closest comparison to this concept of slave to master.

Slaves are admonished to **obey** their earthly **masters** in all things. Not only does this mean working while the master is watching closely but also working **wholeheartedly** all the time, so as to please the **Lord**. Similarly, as Christians function in their jobs, they are not to work so as to **please men**, but God. The praise of men will quickly pass away, but the praise of God is a reward stored up for you in eternity (v. 24). The enthusiastic fulfillment of your job is based upon the truth that you work **for the Lord and not for men**. Though people look at the outside, God looks at the heart (1 Sm 16:7).

Masters are likewise encouraged to treat their slaves in ways that are right and fair. Employers are not to take advantage of their employees or treat them with disrespect, for they, **too, have a Master in heaven**. Both employers and employees will give an account to God for their behavior on earth.

Praying and Witnessing (4:2-6)

4:2 Moving away from the household, Paul commanded the Colossians to **devote** themselves to **prayer**. The Greek word *proskartereite*, translated "devote," calls for perseverance, i.e., being busily engaged in or giving constant attention to something. A life busily engaged in prayer is not optional for believers who desire to grow in their faith. There is no other way to stay in close relationship with Christ other than constant communion with Him through prayer. You are also to **stay alert ... with thanksgiving**. Jesus also used the command to "stay awake" when He told His disciples to "Stay awake and pray so that you won't enter into temptation" (Mk 14:38). For the same reason you are to stay alert because "the Devil is prowling around like a roaring lion, looking for anyone he can devour" (1 Pt 5:8). For a meaningful prayer life, your alertness is to be coupled with your gratitude.

4:3-6 Even while the Colossians are praying, though, they must be mindful of the witness of Christians in the world: **Pray also for us that God may open a door to us for the message**. The prayers of God's people opened up doors for Paul before, as chronicled in the Acts of the Apostles. The message, which is the **mystery of the Messiah**, is not always easy to proclaim. So, Paul encouraged the Colossians and all believers to pray that he would **reveal it** as he was **required to speak**, emphasizing the need for clarity as Christians share their faith. Clarity is accomplished through diligent preparation: You must both study the Scriptures and pray that God gives you the right words.

Not only are you to pray for others as they witness in the world, but you are to be witnesses yourselves. This witness is achieved first by **walk[ing] in wisdom toward outsiders**. Walking is a metaphor for living, so Paul was instructing the Colossians to live lives characterized by wisdom, especially among those who were not believers in Jesus. Effective witnessing also occurs as you are **making the most of the time**. The more literal translation of this phrase would be, "buying back the time." The idea is that you are to snatch up any opportunity for Christ that comes along. Your speech is the third important aspect of the Christian witness, **so that you may know how you should answer each person**. Paul described appropriate speech as **seasoned with salt**, which produces a wonderful picture of evangelism. In Paul's day, salt was used to keep food from spoiling and to give flavor to food. As believers interact with unbelievers, their speech should be free from corruption and appealing to them. To summarize this paragraph, the Christian witness is characterized by fervent prayer and clear, gracious speech.

PERSONAL NOTES FROM PAUL (4:7-18)

The letter to the Colossians closes with some personal notes from Paul. He addressed the men who would be bringing the letter to the Colossian church and then sent greetings from the men who were his companions in prison. Paul concluded the letter with some final instructions and a blessing.

The Bearers of the Letter (4:7-9)

4:7-9 In these concluding verses of Colossians, Paul revealed more than just a list of names. He revealed the community of people who rallied around him to accomplish his mission in Christ. Like Paul, you need a community of other believers to support you in your life and ministry.

Tychicus, a trusted colleague of Paul, originally came from Asia Minor (see Ac 20:4). He probably served as the carrier of the letter to the Colossians, along with the letter to the Ephesians. Tychicus was being sent specifically to inform the Colossians about all of Paul's **news** and **so that he may encourage [their] hearts**. **Onesimus**, who was Philemon's fugitive

slave, was returning to Colossae. Apparently, he somehow encountered Paul and became a Christian under his ministry, then served him faithfully while Paul was in prison. The letter to Philemon would explain these circumstances to Onesimus' master and plead for his forgiveness of Onesimus and acceptance of him back into the household.

Greetings from Paul's Companions (4:10-14)

4:10-11 Along with those who would bear the letter, Paul also sent greetings from companions who were with him. **Aristarchus** was with Paul during the Ephesian riot (Ac 19:29) and during his shipwreck (Ac 27:2). Seemingly Aristarchus was always there when Paul needed him. **Mark**, Barnabas' cousin, abandoned Paul on his first missionary journey, but was restored to the ministry with the help of Barnabas. Paul apparently received him back in forgiveness, and at the end of his life Paul called Mark "useful" in ministry (2 Tm 4:11). The Colossians were instructed to **welcome him**. **Jesus**, also called **Justus**, was another **co-worker** of Paul who was a **comfort** to him. Evidently, these three men were the only Jewish believers (**of the circumcision**) who were with Paul in prison.

4:12-14 Of the Gentiles who stayed with Paul during his imprisonment, **Epaphras** was the prayer warrior. He is described as **always contending for you in his prayers**. The word translated "contending" can also carry the meaning of "wrestling" or "battling," which gives a vivid picture of the intensity with which Epaphras interceded for the Colossians. Convinced of their need to **stand mature and fully assured in everything God wills**, he never ceased to pray for them fervently and with purpose. **Luke** the physician was a constant companion of

Paul's and one dearly **loved** by him. Though **Demas** was at Paul's side as he wrote Colossians, he would later defect from the ministry because of his love for the world (2 Tm 4:10).

Concluding Messages and Final Blessing (4:15-18)

4:15-18 Colossians closes with Paul's personal greetings and instructions. Apparently, a letter was sent to the **church of the Laodiceans** that would be valuable to the Colossians as well, but we have no copy of this letter today.

The case of **Nympha and the church in her house** is a reminder that for 200 years the early church met in homes, not "church buildings."

Nympha
Colossian 4:15

- Perhaps a wealthy woman
- Evidently from Laodicea
- A new believer
- The hostess for a fellowship of believers in her home

Archippus is mentioned only here and in Philippians 2, where Paul called him a "fellow soldier," suggesting he labored in a ministry similar to that of Paul. He may have served as the pastor of the church that met in Philemon's home. We have no way of knowing what **ministry** Paul was encouraging him to **accomplish**, but we can be sure that the apostle's exhortation was meaningful to Archippus.

Paul's statement that he wrote the **greeting** in his own **hand** was his way of affixing his signature to the letter. If Timothy served as his secretary, Paul's personal autograph would assure the

Colossians as to the legitimacy of the letter. Paul had dealt with the issue of mistaken identity in his letter writing to the church at Thessalonica (2 Th 2:2). He asked them to **remember [his] imprisonment**, possibly for the purpose of prayer, and offered a blessing for the **grace** of God to be with them.

Bibliography

Anders, Max. *Galatians, Ephesians, Philippians, and Colossians*. Holman New Testament Commentary. Nashville: Broadman and Holman, 1999.

*Bruce, F. F. *The Epistles to the Colossians, to Philemon, and to the Ephesians*. New International Commentary on the New Testament. Grand Rapids: Eerdmans, 1984.

*Dunn, James D. G. *The Epistles to the Colossians and to Philemon*. New International Greek Testament Commentary. Grand Rapids: Eerdmans, 1996.

Elwell, Walter A. *Evangelical Commentary on the Bible*. Grand Rapids: Baker, 1988.

*Harris, Murray J. *Colossians and Philemon*. Exegetical Guide to the Greek New Testament. Grand Rapids: Eerdmans, 1991.

Lucas, R. C. *The Message of Colossians: Fullness and Freedom*. Downers Grove: IVP, 1980.

*Martin, Ralph P. *Colossians and Philemon*. New Century Bible Commentary. Grand Rapids: Eerdmans, 1981.

*O'Brien, Peter T. *Colossians, Philemon*. Word Biblical Commentary, vol. 44. Waco: Word, 1982.

Wiersbe, Warren W. *Be Complete*. Colorado Springs: Chariot Victor Publishing, 1981.

*Advanced Study

Notes

[1] For a helpful discussion regarding the difference between an "epistle" and a "letter," see Robert H. Stein, *A Basic Guide to Interpreting the Bible* (Grand Rapids: Baker, 1994), 169–70.

[2] Some modern critics, however, have challenged Pauline authorship based on the idea that the letter refutes a form of Gnosticism that was only present in the second century AD. (Gnosticism, simply defined, was an early Greek religious movement whose followers believed that they had gained a special kind of spiritual knowledge [the Greek word *gnōsis*, the root of "Gnosticism," means "knowledge"] that was unavailable to most people. Gnostics also tended to emphasize the spiritual realm over the material, with claims often made that the material realm is evil and must be escaped. The greatest influence of Gnosticism occurred in the second century.) A careful study of the so-called "Colossian heresy" (the word *heresy* refers to any teaching rejected by the Christian community as contrary to Scripture), however, does not reveal an established form of Gnosticism from the second century but an emerging mixture of Jewish, Greek, and mystical pagan thought with early Gnostic overtones. Furthermore, the strong internal claims of the book's authorship and the universal witness of the early church affirm the traditional recognition of Paul's authorship of Colossians.

[3] A. Boyd Luter was the source of most of the related material in preliminary research for an unpublished manuscript on the Prison Epistles.

[4] See Max Anders, *Galatians, Ephesians, Philippians, and Colossians*, Holman New Testament Commentary (Nashville: Broadman and Holman, 1999), 288–90, for a concise and helpful discussion of the Colossian heresy and its possibly identity.

[5] The outline is adapted from that of Harris, *Colossians and Philemon,* 5–6.

[6] The HCSB includes a textual note explaining that other ancient manuscripts of Colossians add the phrase "and the Lord Jesus Christ" following the blessing "Grace to you and peace from God our Father." There are not as many manuscripts with this addition, however, so most scholars conclude that the added phrase, "and the Lord Jesus Christ," should be left out (the KJV and the NKJV, though, are two common translations that leave the phrase in the text). The meaning of the verse remains unaffected whether the phrase is in or out of the text. Furthermore, because of the doctrine of the Trinity, anything received as a blessing from "God our Father" is also from "the Lord Jesus Christ" and the Holy Spirit.

[7] Anders, *Galatians, Ephesians, Philippians, and Colossians*, 281.

[8] Warren W. Wiersbe, *Be Complete* (Colorado Springs, CO: Chariot Victor Publishing, 1981), 45.

[9] This illustration for the way Christ holds all things together is used by Ron McGowin.

[10] See Wayne Grudem, "The Meaning of *Kephalē* ("Head"): A Response to Recent Studies," in *Recovering Biblical Manhood and Womanhood: A Response to Evangelical Feminism*, ed. by John Piper and Wayne Grudem (Wheaton, IL: Crossway Books, 1991), 425–68. Egalitarians suggest an infrequent meaning ("source") for *kephalē* in order to minimize headship in the home since the same metaphor (and even the same word) is used in Ephesians 5 concerning how wives are to relate to their husbands. The argument defining *kephalē* as "source" in this passage cannot pass the exegetical test (see 1 Co 11:3) any more than the etymological one. Doubtless Christ is the source of the church in the sense that He established the church (Mt 16:18), but His sovereignty and headship are the clear emphases of this verse.

[11] *Quasi* is Latin, meaning "resembling." A quasi-Christian cult is a group that resembles Christianity but lacks credibility in one area or another.

[12] Brother Lawrence, *The Practice of the Presence of God: With Spiritual Maxims* (Old Tappan, NJ: Fleming H. Revell Company Publishers, 1958), 11–12.

1 THESSALONIANS

Introduction

First Thessalonians is Paul's initial letter to the young church comprised of new believers who had come to faith in Jesus Christ during his brief visit to Thessalonica. Paul had completed his first missionary journey when in a dream he heard a man urging, "Come over to Macedonia and help us" (Ac 16:9). In response Paul, Silas, and Timothy crossed the Aegean Sea for the Roman province of Macedonia to begin the first evangelistic effort in Europe. They arrived at Philippi, and after they established a church, caused a riot, and were imprisoned, Paul and Silas continued down the Egnatian Way to Thessalonica. The *Via Egnatia* was an important Roman highway that served as the primary east-west land route across northern Greece and by way of the Adriatic connected with the Appian Way, the main route to Rome.

Located on the Egnatian Way, Thessalonica, the self-governing capital of Macedonia and seat of Roman power, was situated at the intersection of river trade routes. Named after the half sister of Alexander the Great in 315 BC, Thessalonica, with 200,000 people, was also located on the eastern coast of Macedonia and boasted a deep harbor and protection from dangerous winds. The climate was ideal for crops, rain was abundant, forests provided timber for construction, and the rivers provided fish. Consequently, Thessalonica was not only the largest but also a very strategic city from which to advance the gospel throughout the Roman Empire.

The city's religious climate was diverse and included Judaism, the imperial cult, Greek gods Cabirus and Dionysus, and Egyptian gods. The resident Jews had established a synagogue there. Religious affiliation was not private but had far-reaching civic and social implications. All of the benefits Thessalonica offered to her inhabitants were the very points that attracted Paul to this city.

Title

In the Greek New Testament the title is *pros Thessalonikeis A*, "to the Thessalonians, A." More loosely, the title might be rendered "the first letter to the Thessalonians." Just as "A" indicates that "B" will follow, so "first" implies that a "second" will follow. This letter is, in fact, the first of two letters sent by Paul "to the church of the Thessalonians" (1:1). Although various theories have been advanced to argue that 1 Thessalonians actually followed the other letter chronologically, none of these is thoroughly convincing. The traditional order in the canon reflects that the epistle called 1 Thessalonians has an accurate title.

Setting

Since their arrival in Thessalonica, Paul, Silas, and Timothy were the cause of civil turmoil. Two specific reactions to the apostles caused the unrest: Jews abandoned the synagogue because of their new faith in Jesus, and the apostles' message of another king defied imperial decrees. Some stirred up a riot and attacked the house of Jason, expecting to find the apostles there. When they did not, they proceeded to drag Jason and "some other brothers" before the authorities and accused them of treason (Ac 17:1-9). After spending at least three weeks and perhaps up to six months in Thessalonica, the persecution forced Paul, Silas, and Timothy to flee. Unfortunately that left the new believers in Thessalonica to face the persecution without their trusted mentors.

When Paul, Silas, and Timothy were working in Athens, Paul sent Timothy back to check on his beloved spiritual sons and daughters, "to strengthen and encourage" and "find out about" their faith (1 Th 3:2,5). Paul moved on to Corinth, seemingly discouraged (1 Co 2:3), and Timothy met him there with good news about the Thessalonians. Paul was encouraged and his ministry was affirmed, resulting in a fresh commitment to the work.

Genre

This tenderhearted pastoral epistle follows the basic structure of other letters written during the Greco-Roman period—introduction, body, and conclusion—but in a distinctively Christian manner. The letter opens with the typical identification of the authors and recipients and Paul's unique greeting, "Grace and peace to you" (1:1), but the introductory section consists of a prayer of thanksgiving (1:2-5), and the concluding section (5:23-24) contains a benediction before the closing greetings (5:25-28).

In his letters Paul made use of the various rhetorical strategies taught and employed in his day without being bound by their strictly ordered patterns of argument. Instead, he adapted his approach according to the context of the audiences to whom he wrote. The rhetorical genre of Thessalonians can be best described, however, as "demonstrative" or "epideictic" (lit., "fit for display or appropriate for public discourse"), concentrating primarily on praise and blame, or instruction aimed at the audience's shortcomings. The main argument (1:6–3:13) is actually a lengthy expansion of the letter's thanksgiving section and includes three clear statements of the apostle's thankfulness for the Thessalonian church (1:2-5; 2:13; 3:9-13). The last of these three also functions as a transition to the section in which Paul exhorts, corrects, and encourages the believers. In closing the letter, the apostle specifically charged that his letter, written to be fit for a public audience, "be read to all the brothers" (5:27).

Author

The Apostle Paul was the principal author. However, Timothy and Silvanus (Silas) contributed. Paul used plural pronouns throughout most of the letter referring to the three authors. When Paul left Thessalonica and Berea because of persecution, he went to Athens and from there sent word to Silas and Timothy for them to come to the city quickly. Paul sent them immediately from Athens to the church in Thessalonica (3:1-3).

Paul discovered Timothy, already "a disciple" of whom the believers "spoke highly" (Ac 16:1-2), when he visited Lystra and Derbe a second time. Paul chose him to be one of his companions, and Timothy accompanied the apostle on his second and third missionary journeys until Paul appointed him to stay at the church in Ephesus (1 Tm 1:3).

Silas, who was probably a Roman citizen (Ac 16:37), also accompanied Paul on his second missionary journey. Silas is described in Acts as one of the "leading men among the brothers" at the church in Jerusalem (Ac 15:22) and as a prophet (Ac 15:32). When Paul and Barnabas parted company, Paul turned to Silas (Ac 15:40). Peter also commends Silas (Silvanus) as "a faithful brother" through whom he wrote his first letter (1 Pt 5:12).

Date

The Emperor Claudius responded to a question posed by proconsul Gallio (Ac 18:12). The answer is found on an inscription at Delphi, which dates the service of the proconsul beginning in early summer AD 51. Paul had exercised ministry in Corinth prior to Gallio's arrival and most likely penned his letter in AD 50. First Thessalonians was written shortly after Timothy joined Paul at Corinth (3:6) and not long after Paul had left Thessalonica (2:17). He responded to Timothy's report with this letter within the eighteen months (Ac 18:11) that he remained in Corinth.

Recipients

The letter was written to the church at Thessalonica, to the brothers and sisters who had come to faith in Jesus Christ as a result of Paul's brief ministry there.

Major Themes

The contents of Paul's letter indicate that Timothy brought both good news as well as concerns. He wrote to encourage the church to press on in the midst of persecution, to communicate his thankful heart and joy over their obedience, to defend his integrity and clarify his motives, and to correct their doctrines on work and sexuality. Further, Paul responded to specific questions that may have arrived via a letter carried by Timothy, concerning fraternal Christian love (4:9), earning one's living (4:11), the destiny of the deceased (4:13), and the day of the Lord's return (5:1-2). Paul lovingly communicated his concern for the spiritual well-being of this young church through encouragement and instruction. To Paul, loving this congregation meant correcting their wrong thinking and affirming what they were doing well. He recognized that their lifestyle mistakes were linked to their misunderstanding of doctrinal issues. He did not simply tell them to live differently but corrected the thinking that led to those choices. The connection between orthodoxy ("right thinking") and orthopraxy ("right practice") was vital in Paul's thinking. How this letter made its way back to Thessalonica is unknown.

Pronunciation Guide			
Achaia	*uh KAY yuh*	Silvanus	*sil VAY nuhs*
Macedonia	*MASS uh DOH nih uh*	Thessalonians	*THESS uh LOH nih uhns*
Philippi	*FIH lih pigh*		*(th as in thin)*

Outline[1]

I. DELIVERING A PERSONAL TESTIMONY (1:1–3:13)
  A. Thanksgiving for the Thessalonian Believers (1:1-10)
  B. Paul's Ministry in Thessalonica (2:1-16)
  C. Timothy's Ministry (2:17–3:13)

II. MAKING A PASSIONATE APPEAL FOR LIVING TO PLEASE GOD (4:1-8)

III. RESPONDING TO QUESTIONS (4:9–5:11)
  A. On Brotherly Love (4:9-10)

B. On Earning One's Living
(4:11-12)

C. On Those Who Die before the
Day of the Lord (4:13-18)

D. On the Day of the Lord (5:1-11)

IV. IV. OFFERING A CHALLENGE TO
CHRISTIAN DUTY (5:12-22)

A. Leadership in the Community
(5:12-13)

B. Fellowship in the Community
(5:14-15)

C. Submission to Christ (5:16-22)

V. CONCLUDING PRAYER, GREETINGS,
AND BLESSING (5:23-28)

Exposition of the Text

DELIVERING A PERSONAL TESTIMONY (1:1–3:13)

Thanksgiving for the Thessalonian Believers (1:1-10)

1:1 Paul, Silvanus (Silas), **and Timothy** penned this letter to the entire **church** of Thessalonica. This distinctive greeting **in God the Father and the Lord Jesus Christ** identified the unique relationship between the Father and Son, which gives the church its identity. The social and theological dimensions of the church are inseparably joined in its vertical relationship with God through Jesus.

The salutation ends with **Grace to you and peace**. In the word **GRACE** (Gk. charis, "act of favor, acceptance, free gift") the saving work of Christ and the continuous action of His enabling believers to do His will are communicated. "Peace" (Gk. eirēnē, "tranquility, unity"), the common Jewish greeting, described the ultimate benefit of a saving relationship between God and His people. In Christ, peace results from grace. This simple greeting is a blessing that encapsulated the benefits Paul desired for the Thessalonians.

1:2 Paul informed the Thessalonians that he and his associates regularly thanked God for them, praying diligently and consistently for all the Thessalonian believers. Specifically, they thanked God for the Thessalonians' conversion and for the benefits they received directly from God's hand, as well as for those that came as a result of His work (vv. 5-10).

1:3 The memory of the Thessalonians' Christian virtues—faith, hope, and love—prompted Paul to prayers of thanksgiving. He remembered their **work of faith, labor of love, and endurance of hope**. These classic Christian virtues are evidence of Christian character. Paul mentioned the fruit of these virtues as well—WORK (Gk. ergou, "deed, action, that with which one is occupied"), LABOR (Gk. kopou, "intense work, vexation, travail"), and ENDURANCE (Gk. hupomonēs, from hupo, "under," and menō, "remain, abide," thus "abiding under or bearing up under," suffering with patience and steadfastness, persevering until the point of exhaustion)—all of which could be witnessed. The believers were known by their work. Furthermore, their love (Gk. agapēs) was evidenced in hard, exhausting labor, which was self-sacrificing for the sake of others. They were also able to remain steadfast in the face of suffering because of their hope in the coming of the Lord Jesus Christ.

1:4-5 Paul offered thanks to God in prayer for their Christian character because it was evidence that God had chosen them. God elected them not based on their virtue, but because He loved them. Paul called them **brothers loved by God** (v. 4). God's divine love transformed this diverse group of people into brothers and sisters. Familial love dominated. Paul referred to the believers as "brothers loved by God," not to exclude women but to highlight the nature of the relationship shared by believers who have been born into the family of God (Jn 1:12-13; 3:5). BROTHERS (Gk. *adelphoi*, "associates, members of the Christian community") in its most basic understanding referred to near kinsmen or those "from the same womb." Paul repeatedly called Christians "brothers"—an identity used in the early church. Believers may have been alienated from society, but they formed a new spiritual identity as children of one Father.

Election (Gk. *eklogēn*, "selection, choosing") is a reminder that salvation from start to finish is the work of God. Election is the assurance of God's providence, but it cannot be understood apart from God's foreknowledge (cp. Rm 8:29; 1 Pt 1:2). Clearly it is inextricably linked to the gospel of Christ, the proclamation of the message of salvation, and the work of the Holy Spirit.

The proclamation of the gospel was confirmed by miracles brought about by the Holy Spirit. The message was recognized as divine because of the **power** (Gk. *dunamei*, "able, mighty") of the Spirit— the preaching of the gospel and the work of the Holy Spirit went hand in hand. The Spirit is the one who convinced them of the truth of the message.

Paul then turned to the character of the messengers of the gospel. The Thessalonians themselves should have been able to testify to the integrity of the character of the missionaries and the message they preached. The character of the messengers was a significant part of the message they preached. They lived with integrity, not for their own benefit but for the sake of the hearers.

1:6 Paul shifted emphasis from the apostles' proclamation to the believers' reception of the message. They became **imitators** of God and the messengers. They followed their model of suffering. Believers expected suffering. New believers were taught to do so as well. The **severe** suffering referred to opposition from their contemporaries. Yet, they had **joy** in suffering because they shared in the sufferings of Christ. Joy was the evidence of the Holy Spirit, which adversity could not destroy. IMITATORS (Gk. *mimētai*, "mark, image, form, pattern") was Paul's word used consistently to encourage believers to follow his example or imitate his way of life (see 2:14; 1 Co 4:16; 11:1; Eph 5:1; 2 Th 3:7,9; Heb 6:12). The English word "mime" designates an actor who presents a character or concept only with movements and facial expressions that mimic, imitate, or copy those of his subject. The image of the traditional white-painted face, white-gloved mime illustrates the point Paul makes (1 Th 1:5-6). A mime performs without words, and a convincing performance focuses the audience's attention on the story or message being presented. Paul emphasized the integrity of the gospel by clarifying that the good news had come to the Thessalonians not only in words but also in the Holy Spirit's power to transform lives. Paul could praise the Thessalonians for becoming "imitators" of the apostles and of the Lord because in doing so they recognized that the Holy Spirit changes the way a person acts. Authentic Christians do not present the gospel with words *alone* but also by *imitating* Christ in their lives; Christian living means acting like Jesus.

1:7-10 Because they imitated the **example** Gk. *tupon*, "pattern, model," (v. 7) of God and the missionaries, the Thessalonian church became a model for other churches. The phrase, **to all the believers in Macedonia and Achaia,** specifically referred to the churches in Philippi, Berea, Athens, Corinth, and maybe Cenchrea. Paul, Silvanus, and Timothy spoke about the Thessalonians' faith, love, and steadfastness in relating to all these churches. They were exceptional in the way they handled persecution, and now others could imitate them.

Therefore, the Thessalonians' faith was known everywhere—it **rang out** (v. 8). The Greek verb *exēchētai*, meaning "sound forth, resound," is a *hapax*, used only here in the New Testament. In the perfect tense, this verb conveys an action completed in the past but with a continuing result. "The Lord's message" and the confirming evidence of the Thessalonians' faith have not only been clearly sounded forth but continue to reverberate throughout their scope of influence. They continued Paul's evangelistic effort and looked outward. Paul did not need to preach in certain places because of the evangelism this church had done.

Those **in Macedonia and Achaia** reported to Paul what a good entrance the team had in Thessalonica. They were well received and gained hearers and disciples. For the Thessalonians to convert from idolatry meant abandoning a cult and turning from its immoral practices. The word **turned** (Gk. *epestrepsate*) implies a change in attitude and action, which is necessary for true repentance.

The Thessalonians had hope in the promise that the Son would return. Their hope was manifested in their moral life and steadfastness in face of persecution. God's Son was the object of their expectation. Jesus was described in four ways (v. 10):

- God's Son comes **from heaven**. Only here in 1 Thessalonians is Jesus called God's **Son**. His sovereignty is affirmed because He comes from the place where God is.

- He is the one **whom** God **raised from dead**—the core of Paul's message.

- His name is **Jesus**.

- He **rescues us from the coming wrath**—judgment against those who violate God's law. The Thessalonian believers were assured of their liberation and of the judgment that would come upon those who afflicted them.

In Paul's thinking, hope in Christ and His power to transform empowered the believer to live an upright moral life.

Paul's Ministry in Thessalonica (2:1-16)

2:1-12 Paul reminded the believers of what they already knew of the apostles' conduct. He explained the apostles' move from Philippi to Thessalonica and defended their motive and source of strength for their ministry. God had **emboldened** them **to speak** the truth in the midst of **great opposition** (v. 2). OPPOSITION (Gk. *agōni*, "contest, struggle," anglicized as "agony") may refer to outward conflict or inner turmoil or anxiety. The word was used of athletes competing in the Olympic games to describe their strenuous training or the intense effort required to defeat an opponent in a contest. The term was also used metaphorically of a person's struggle against temptation. Here, Paul speaks of tangible persecution intended to obstruct the progress of the gospel. Further, they referred to their message as **the gospel of God** (v. 2), indicating that God is the source of the good news. Their preaching in the midst of opposition demonstrated their pure motives. Paul's defense suggested that he and his companions had been accused of impure

Heart to Heart:
Caring Deeply

Paul cared deeply about the spiritual well-being of the believers in Thessalonica. He wanted them to know God and live for Him. Paul's passion enabled him to endure persecution, difficult travel, and sickness. You would be wise to emulate Paul and accept your responsibility to affect the spiritual growth of other believers, to grieve when they are mistreated, to correct when they are misinformed, and to redirect when they are misapplying truth. Paul's concern grew out of his view that believers really are one body with many parts that affect the whole (Rm 12:12-27).

motives and a desire for status, fame, or financial gain. Traveling philosophers of the day typically came into cities to gain notoriety and wealth. The apostolic band had left the city quickly, and Paul had not returned, which may have caused criticism from within or from outside the church. Paul may have been distinguishing his ministry from the philosophers' character and methods. He offered three differences:

- Their **exhortation didn't come from error** (Gk. *planēs*, "delusion, deception") **or impurity** (Gk. *akatharsias*, "uncleanness, dirt, refuse" often used figuratively in the New Testament to denote sexual impurity but also associated with impure motives and greed) **or an intent to deceive** (Gk. *dolō*, "treachery, cunning" with the idea of deliberately intending to catch with bait, tricking or deluding," v. 3).

- They **never used flattering speech** (v. 5).

- They **didn't seek glory from people** (v. 6). Instead they spoke to please God.

Paul stated that God Himself had tested and "**approved**" (v. 4) the apostles for their ministry. Once "approved" **by God**, they were **entrusted with the gospel** (v. 4) and sought to serve him. God examined their hearts and could testify to their pure ministry. Paul used the present tense verb **examines**, indicating that, even as Paul penned this letter, God continued to test the hearts of His messengers. Paul offered specifics about their upright behavior: They were **gentle** instead of **a burden** (v. 7); they nurtured the new converts rather than wielding their apostolic authority. Paul used a NURSING MOTHER (Gk. *trophos*, "nurse"), as a vivid simile to convey his tender affection for the believers. Paul fed the baby believers with the gospel, teaching them spiritual survival just as a mother nurtures her children. The Greek verb *thalpē* ("cherish or hold dear, keep warm, comfort") appears only one other time in the New Testament (Eph 5:29) and demonstrates more than a loving attitude but caring activity as well (v. 7).

The apostles' deep affection is evident (v. 8). The phrase CARED SO MUCH (Gk. *homeiromenoi*, "longing or yearning for, desiring greatly") is used only here in the New Testament and appeared rarely elsewhere. One ancient scroll, dated to the fourth century AD contains an example from the inscription on a sepulcher where the word describes the grieving parents as "greatly desiring their son." Their ministry was personal, not simply a message of salvation, but a loving sharing of themselves. They demonstrated their pure motives and love by **working day and night** in tent-making as they preached in order not to be dependent on the Thessalonians (v. 9).

Calling on the converts and God as **witnesses** (v. 10), Paul again defended the apostles' behavior as devout, righteous, and blameless. He also reminded them that after their conversion, the apostles encouraged, comforted, and implored them (v. 12) like a loving **father with his own children.** Just as Paul compared his tender affection for the church with the image of **a nursing mother** (v. 7), here he employed the image of a godly father's encouragement and exhortation of his own children to illustrate his own commitment to teach and encourage those new to the faith. The apostles taught the new believers the basics of Christian ethics so they might live a life **worthy of God** (v. 12). The apostles' fatherly concern drove them to insist that the Thessalonians respond with a certain course of action.

Heart to Heart:
Living the Exemplary Life

*P*aul's setting himself up as an example for the Thessalonians to follow can sound like inappropriate self-righteousness for one who should follow Christ in humility. Much can be learned from Paul. Believers are called to be examples for one another and before a watching world. They might live more carefully and intentionally, pursuing holiness more rigorously, if they were mindful of being examples for other believers (v. 12).

2:13-16 Paul thanked God for the Thessalonians' reception of the gospel, because they had the spiritual insight to recognize it as the word of God with the power to transform believers. As a result of accepting the message, they imitated the steadfast faith and courage of Judean believers who suffered at the hands of Jews.

Paul leveled six accusations at some of the Jews:

• They had **killed** Christ.

• They had killed the prophets.

• They had **persecuted** (Gk. *ekdiōxantōn*, "drove out, banished") believers (Ac 17:5-9).

• They displeased God.

• They showed hostility to anyone who was not Jewish (v. 15).

• They had hindered the apostles from preaching (v. 16).

Paul was personally familiar with this persecution because he had previously participated in it. The hostility engendered hindered the message from making its way to **Gentiles** and thus prevented them from being **saved.** This thwarting of the divine plan was the summary and conclusion of their history of sin as they continued to add to it before judgment was poured out. These Jews who opposed the divine plan did not escape God's judgment.

Paul's strong language against the Jews must be read in light of the totality of his teaching. In Romans he demonstrated his love for his people and desire for their salvation. He also used strong language in Romans against the Gentiles' conduct. This rebuke was in response to the persecution he and his flock received at the hands of the Jews and did not indicate anti-Semitic sentiments; rather, he was confirming that God will judge all, Jews and Gentiles alike.

Timothy's Ministry (2:17–3:13)

2:17-18 Paul apparently felt torn between his call to his itinerant mission and his pastoral concerns for the churches. He longed to return and put plans in place to do so in order to see them **face-to-face**, but Satan himself kept them from returning. Paul conveyed the emotional impact of being **FORCED** (Gk. *aporphanisthentes*) to leave the new believers in Thessalonica (v. 17). The word describes one who is "bereaved," having been "made an orphan by separation," intensifying the images of parental love Paul has already used to express his feelings for the Thessalonians. The noun translated "orphans" appears elsewhere in the New Testament (i.e., Jn 14:18; Jms 1:27), but this verb form appears only in this instance.

2:19-20 The writers provide the reason for their great desire to see the believers—they are the basis of the apostles' hope that on the judgment day there would be evidence that Paul had fulfilled his calling. He will rejoice in the presence of Christ that his missionary work was lasting. At the return of Christ, the Thessalonians will also be the apostle's **crown of boasting** (v. 19). This attitude is not self-aggrandizement or pride, but the reward and satisfaction of knowing God has accomplished His work through one who is His servant.

Heart to Heart: The End in Sight

*P*aul seemed to long to hear his Father say, "Well done, good and faithful slave" (Mt 25:21,23; Lk 19:17). His desire was to please God. His ministry would be validated when the Thessalonians stood before God. Furthermore, God's power to transform hearts and His faithfulness to use the "worst" of sinners (1 Tm 1:15) would be reason for rejoicing. Living with the end in sight can influence your choices, relationships, and commitments. Like Paul, you can find motivation for a holy, service-minded, other-centered life by contemplating the day when you will see the Lord face-to-face.

3:1-5 When the three apostles could not bear the painful separation and lack of knowledge about the Thessalonians' welfare, they **sent Timothy** to check on them. Paul explained his conclusion that "it was better TO BE LEFT ALONE (Gk. *kataleiphthēnai*, "leave behind, abandon, neglect") in Athens" (v. 1). The prefix *kata*, "down," suggested "rejection, defeat, helplessness." The root *leipō* contains the idea of being forsaken, language which indicates that the apostles were in agony over their concern for these new converts. The strong language also affirms why they sent Timothy back to Thessalonica, leaving the other two apostles to travel alone.

Although Timothy was apparently under Paul's authority, Paul recognized him as his **brother and God's co-worker** (v. 2). Timothy was young, and this assignment may have been his first solo ministry. There were obviously some questions that he could or at least did not answer with regard to sexual ethics. Timothy was **to strengthen** their faith in the face of persecution and **encourage** them through Christian teaching. Paul expressed his hope that "no one will be SHAKEN (Gk. *sainesthai*, "disturb") by these persecutions" (v. 3). In the New Testament, this word is only used here. The word metaphorically suggests being "unsettled, disturbed, agitated, or drawn aside." Paul reminded the church that not only was **persecution** predicted for the apostles and the new church, but persecution was an expected, normal part of the Christian life. Reiterating his concern, Paul sent Timothy to make sure the Thessalonians were standing firm in their **faith** so that the apostles had not labored without results (v. 5).

3:6-8 Timothy returned with **good news** of their **faith and love** and their **good memories** of the apostles who longed to see them as well (v. 6). The distressed apostles were encouraged by the good news of the believers' unwavering faith, the fruit of the hope mentioned at the letter's beginning.

3:9-10 Rhetorically, the apostles asked how they could **thank God** properly for all this **joy**, motivated by their gratitude over the Thessalonians' faith, hope, and love. The latter part of Paul's question revealed that the apostles continued in constant prayer to see the Thessalonians **face-to-face** and complete their Christian instruction. Paul set a brilliant example of heartfelt concern for the faith and spiritual

growth of the young church. Likewise, you can demonstrate love for Christ's church by caring deeply for the spiritual state of those within your realm of influence.

3:11-13 Paul followed this commitment *with* a prayer for the Thessalonians. He asked God to **DIRECT** (Gk. *kateuthunai*, "lead, make straight") their way, i.e., to make their path to the Thessalonians free of obstacles. They longed to see the Thessalonians but recognized that God was sovereign over even these details of their ministry so that the apostles' concentrated efforts would not necessarily result in a visit.

Paul described God as **Father** (v. 11), thereby communicating the familial relationship of God's people while also highlighting one of God's relational traits—He is Father to all believers. Paul also linked God the Father and Jesus by treating them as a compound subject with a singular verb, affirming his confidence in the deity of Christ.

Paul prayed that they would increase in **love for one another and for everyone** (v. 12), using the apostles' love as an example. Paul's leadership was evidenced by his willingness to set himself up as an example to be followed. If he could love by God's power, not based on what is deserved, the Thessalonian believers could continue to grow in this area as well.

Paul's attention turned to the future as he prayed that they might be holy at the return of Christ (v. 13). **Holiness** (Gk. *hagiōsunē*) is not emphasizing holy actions but rather an atmosphere saturated with attitudes and actions that are Christlike. Paul prayed for the highest standards, set apartness unto the Lord, until Jesus returned **with all His saints** (Gk. *hagiōn*, "holy ones"), most likely a reference to deceased believers.

Heart to Heart:
Challenged to Pray

Paul's commitment to pray for the Thessalonians is a challenge to us to participate in the sanctification of others. You can love other believers by praying for their holiness as you watch and wait for the Lord to return. Indeed, your holiness and that of other believers should be a continual concern. If it is, you will be moved to pray, teach, and encourage one another toward holiness so that God may be glorified and His people fit for kingdom service.

MAKING A PASSIONATE APPEAL FOR LIVING TO PLEASE GOD (4:1-8)

As was Paul's practice, after laying a theological foundation in the first half of his letter, in the second half he turned to instruction for Christian living.

4:1-2 The word **finally** serves as a transition marking Paul's movement to exhortation. By calling the Thessalonians **brothers** (Gk. *adelphoi*), Paul reinforced the familial relationship he had shared with them. Paul then exhorted the church to **walk and please God**, calling them to continue in their moral living in such a way that befits a follower of Christ. He was instructing them not just on **how** "to walk" but more broadly, how one must live in order to "please God." He affirmed that they were actually living according to their faith but challenged them to **do so even more**. Paul reminded them of the authoritative **commands** he **gave** them earlier, stating that these originated from the **Lord Jesus**, not from Paul himself (v. 2).

4:3-5 Paul began the section on practical instruction with an exhortation to sexual purity, perhaps indicating a predominance of this type of sinful behavior in contemporary Greek society. The Christian call to sexual morality was radical in a culture in which marriage was not enough to prohibit men from pursuing sexual satisfaction wherever they could find it. Perhaps some were finding adherence to the strict ethic the apostles taught difficult. On the other hand, perhaps Paul was warning the Thessalonians to avoid temptation and reminding them of a proper Christian perspective on sexual behavior.

One aspect of **God's will** for the Thessalonians was **sanctification** (Gk. *hagiasmos*, "consecration, holiness") or the daily process of becoming more Christlike (v. 3). Paul suggested three reasons for holy living:

- to fulfill "God's will" (v. 3),
- to honor your spouse (v. 4), and
- to avoid defrauding a brother (v. 6).

Paul was primarily concerned that their sanctification would advance as a result of aligning their will with God's by fully abstaining from **sexual immorality** (Gk. *porneias*, "fornication"), which referred to a broad category of illicit and unnatural sexual indulgence (premarital sex, extramarital sex, homosexuality, lesbianism, sodomy, incest, and bestiality). He was calling them to demonstrate their commitment to sanctification through sexual purity, which would thereby gain them an honorable influence in society.

The one being sanctified will not be overcome with uncontrolled sexual desires as non-Christians are. Paul made the connection between ignorance or rejection of God and giving in to sexual immorality. The implication is that those who have identified with Christ should demonstrate their new identity through having control over their bodies, setting them apart from the ungodly who act on their sexual desires without constraint.

Paul suggested three guidelines for safeguarding sexual intimacy in marriage:

- The mandate to "abstain from sexual immorality" (v. 3),

- The encouragement to **possess his own vessel** (Gk. *skeuos*, "thing, body") **in sanctification and honor** (Gk. *timē*). In rabbinic writings the Hebrew equivalent of VESSEL, *keli*, refers to a "wife," and "to use a vessel" appears to be a Talmudic euphemism for sexual intimacy in marriage. A similar passage (1 Pt 3:7) describes wives as having a "weaker nature" (Gk. *asthenesterō*, "weak, powerless, sick, ill"; *skeuei*, "vessel, thing, body") and calls for husbands to show them "honor" (Gk. *timēn*, "worth, value"), using the same descriptive word as in 1 Thessalonians.

- The warning to avoid defrauding a brother (v. 6).

The implication in this section of the letter is that knowing God should result in self-control and a desire to do God's will with regard to sexuality. **Lustful desires** (Gk. *pathei epithumias*, lit. "hot-after passion") is a strong expression of unrestrained desires. Strength of will in controlling desires within the realm of sexuality is the fruit of knowing God. Paul presupposed that knowledge informs

belief, which, in turn, determines behavior.

4:6-8 Paul's habit of referring to previous teaching demonstrated how thorough he was. Here he referred to his previous teaching against defrauding another through sexual immorality (vv. 3,6). Not only was promiscuity a transgression against those involved in the immoral acts, but it was also an offense against the Christian community and against God. As an AVENGER (Gk. *ekdikos*, "punisher," one who exacts a penalty or satisfies justice by punishing the wrongdoer), God will bring about justice by way of chastisement (v. 6). Offenders would face not only the social consequences of their behavior but also the judgment of God. Sexuality was not simply a personal issue but a community concern.

Paul returned to the concept of **sanctification** with a positive injunction—the Thessalonians were to reject sexual immorality because of the divine call to do so. God's electing and calling the Thessalonians included transformation in their daily lives, particularly with regard to sexual morality and the rejection of moral impurity or uncleanness. **Impurity** or uncleanness must be replaced with holiness.

Paul concluded this section of his letter with **therefore** (v. 8). Based on what has just been established concerning sexual purity, to reject this teaching was to reject God, not man. Because the instruction came from God and was so tied to God's character, disobedience meant rejecting God, not just ignoring Paul and the teaching of men. God gives the Holy Spirit, who brings about sanctification and victory over sexual immorality. The Thessalonians had evidently been given Christian instruction on sexual purity, but some members of the church must have rejected it or continued their sexual practices. Paul used emphatic language to call them to a higher standard than that of their pagan culture. Believers have that same task today in a sex-saturated society; they must embrace the teaching of purity and call the body of Christ to holiness.

RESPONDING TO QUESTIONS (4:9–5:11)

On Brotherly Love (4:9-10)

4:9-10 Paul began with the topic **about brotherly love** and then seemed to address specific issues of concern to the Thessalonians. Perhaps Paul was taking this opportunity to answer questions they had sent him *via* Timothy. Throughout the letter Paul repeatedly praised the Thessalonians for their "brotherly love" (Gk. *philadelphias*) for one another, the mark of one who had faith. Questions arose about the nature of brotherly love, perhaps because this type of love was nor-

mally reserved for familial relationships. The relationships within the fellowship would have been noticeably different since believers were unique in coming from different families, social classes, and religious backgrounds, yet gathering in fellowship and loving one another just as within a family. Because of their new faith, many of the Thessalonians would have been rejected by their birth families. To assure them that they were doing the right thing in the face of rejection, Paul reminded them that God **taught** them **to love one another**.

Paul acknowledged that they were already loving even those believers outside of their Thessalonian fellowship, specifically those in other churches in **Macedonia**—in Philippi and Beroea. Paul did not want them to be satisfied with the love they had already shown but to realize that there were always more opportunities to love.

Heart to Heart: Love for the Body

This exhortation is for believers today as well. Indeed, the effectiveness of the church depends largely on the self-sacrificial love of its women to welcome, feed, hug, listen, encourage, teach, pray for, and set an example for the church family. These are ways you can love, and it is a weighty task. In other passages of the Bible believers demonstrate their love for God by their love for one another. And your love for one another is also your testimony before a watching world.

On Earning One's Living (4:11-12)

4:11-12 Paul encouraged the Thessalonians to strive for **A QUIET LIFE** (Gk. *hēsuchazein*, "quiet, trustful, leading a quiet life"), one of tranquility but not inactivity. He was specific, encouraging them **to mind your own business**. He may have been referring to meddling in the business of church leaders or in rela-

tionships with neighbors. Manual work was relegated to slaves and artisans. Paul was commanding even free men to labor and earn their living, a shocking idea in their culture.

Therefore, Paul provided two reasons for laboring for their bread.

- He asked them to set an example for those outside the church, to **walk**

properly or in a fitting manner, in order to gain respect from outsiders (v. 12).

- He called them to avoid dependence on anyone. Christians were not to be a financial burden, since presuming on the generosity of the brethren was not acting in brotherly love.

To work hard, mind your own business, and concentrate on what God has given you to do will provide for any woman a worthy testimony.

On Those Who Die before the Day of the Lord (4:13-18)

4:13-17 Paul then turned to the topic of the return of the Lord and the resurrection of the dead in Christ. **Those who are asleep** (Gk. *koimōmenōn*, "fall asleep, die") are believers who have died. The euphemistic phrase for death focuses on the status of the body at death, suggesting a temporary state of rest, from which they would awaken. The believer goes immediately into the presence of the Lord at death (2 Co 5:8). Jesus, even in the agony of His own crucifixion, had affirmed this promise to the thief on the cross (Lk 23:39-43). Here Paul affirmed that truth in saying that Jesus would **bring** those **asleep** in Him **with Him** when He returns (1 Th 4:14). He then added the catching up of believers who remain to meet Him in the air (v. 17). Perhaps members of the church had died since Paul had been with them, and the grief of those remaining left them with questions about Christ's return. Paul wanted them to understand rightly, so that they would not **grieve** like those **who have no hope** (v. 13). The promise of Christ's coming was their hope in the midst of sadness over losing loved ones.

Christ's death and resurrection is the reason for the hope. The fact of His resurrection gave the Thessalonians hope for the resurrection of their dead. Paul stated

that when Jesus returned He would bring believers who had already died with Him. His resurrection gave Him power over death. The believers were assured that those who died in Christ were not separated from Him.

Paul assured the recipients that those **still alive at** His coming would **have no advantage over** those who had already died (v. 15). The Thessalonians were comforted by the statement that the dead in Christ would not be excluded from the celebration that will occur at **the Lord's coming** (Gk. *parousia*, "presence, advent, arrival").

Paul taught that Jesus Himself would return in majesty, **with the trumpet** pronouncing a divine command to rise. The SHOUT (Gk. *keleusmati*, "word of command, signal, summons," in the sense of a military order) and "trumpet" were evidence of triumph. The dead in Christ will have the prominence of rising first. Paul offered more reassurance as he informed the believers that they would all, dead and alive, be "caught up together . . . TO MEET (Gk. *apantēsin*) the Lord" (v. 17). This idiom was used to welcome an important person upon his arrival. The leading citizens from a Hellenistic city like Thessalonica would go out to meet a visiting dignitary when he arrived and accompany him to the city. The official visit of such a person was called a COMING (Gk. *parousia*, as in v. 15; see also Mt 25:6 and Ac 28:15). Paul did not seem to be primarily concerned with teaching an order of events as much as providing consolation. **So we will always be with the Lord** is a phrase summarizing Paul's teaching on Christ's return and providing the ultimate satisfaction and reassurance (1 Th 4:17).

4:18 Truth should be a source of comfort and hope! The particular truth of Christ's death and resurrection is the impetus for the hope of believers. Their

Eschatological Glossary[2]

Allegorical Interpretation	A method that looks beyond the literal sense of a historical statement for symbolic meanings of people, places, things, or events.
Apocalypse (Gk. *apokalupsis,* "unveiling")	The anglicized title for the New Testament book of Revelation.
Bēma (Gk. "raised platform")	The judgment seat of God before which every Christian must appear to give an account and to receive rewards (Rm 14:10-12; 2 Co 5:10).
Eschatology (Gk. *eschaton,* "end, last")	The branch of theology focusing on study of "last things, end times, or events to be fulfilled in the future."
Harpazō (Gk. "to catch up, snatch away, seize")	This word is used to describe the way believers will meet the Lord upon His return (1 Th 4:17).
Kingdom	In the New Testament, this word appears in various contexts: • Christ's earthly kingdom, • the Father's heavenly kingdom, or • the sovereign reign of Christ in a believer's heart.
Israel	Most often a reference to the literal national group called "Israel."
Millennium (Lat. "1000 years")	A reference to the 1,000-year reign of Christ during which Satan is imprisoned (Rv 20:1-7).
Rapture (Lat. *rapiemur,* "carried off"; Gk. *harpagēsometha*)	The removal of believers from the world when Christ returns (1 Th 4:17; see *Harpazō* above).
Tribulation	A seven-year period of intense suffering on earth, unlike any other in history (Dn 12:1; Zph 1:15; Mt 24:21-22,29; Mk 13:19,24; Lk 21:25-26; Rv 7:14).

ultimate hope is in the promise of meeting Christ and abiding with Him forever.

On the Day of the Lord (5:1-11)

5:1-5 Perhaps the Thessalonians' experience of persecution made urgent their need to be reassured that **the Day of the Lord** would indeed come. Paul was apparently satisfied with the way the church comprehended that the timing of Christ's return could not be predicted.

Paul used the imagery of A THIEF (Gk. *kleptēs,* "one who comes unexpectedly") IN THE NIGHT (Gk. *en nukti,* "under cover of darkness") to teach the unexpected nature of Christ's return (v.

2). However unexpected, believers should be ready. In contrast, unbelievers would assume all was safe, and then the Day of the Lord would come unexpectedly, suddenly, and inevitably, as the process of giving birth cannot be stopped when the time comes. Life would end, and unbelievers would have no chance of escape. Similarly, Paul set the Thessalonians in stark contrast to unbelievers. Believers will not be caught off guard because they live in the light and not in spiritual DARKNESS (Gk. *skotei,* v. 4). The Thessalonians "are all sons of LIGHT" (Gk. *phōtos,* "light"), even characterized by shining illumination (v. 5), which made their spiritual transformation evident. Here Paul shifted from **you** to **we** as he moved into communal exhortation.

5:6-8 Because believers are of the light and not darkness certain behavior should follow. **Sleep** here is not a reference to death as in 4:13 but describes spiritual apathy characteristic of unbelievers. Believers, however, must be marked by watchfulness and circumspection in light of the Lord's imminent return. The Thessalonians **must stay awake and be sober** (v. 6), watching with a self-controlled, alert mind. They remain alert by not partaking in activities that characterize those in darkness, which would keep them unprepared for the Day of the Lord. The believer's readiness likened him to a soldier who, to prepare himself for battle, must put on faith, hope, and love. As pieces of defensive armor, the breastplate and **helmet** (Gk. *perikephalaian*—from *peri*, "around," and *kephalē*, "head,"—lit. "around the head") would defend the believer against the surprise arrival of the Day of the Lord (v. 8). As in 1:3, **hope** follows **faith** and **love** as the culmination and desired result of the former two. Their hope was the result of their certain conviction concerning their future salvation.

5:9-10 God appointed believers, "sons of light" (v. 5), to be saved, not to incur His **wrath** like those "in darkness" (v. 4). Eschatologically this text seems to affirm that believers are excluded from the tribulation (i.e., the "Day of the Lord" or the "wrath" to come), a position identified as pretribulational premillennialism. Accordingly, believers are taken out of the world before the outpouring of God's wrath, which means the "rapture" of the church is a separate event from the return of Christ, although both are part of the last days or eschaton.[3] God graciously elected the Thessalonians, whom He foreknew would respond to His offer of salvation, to fulfill His purposes. Salvation came through Christ's death and not by the

good works of the Thessalonians. Those in Christ would live with Him, and death would not end the believer's relationship with Christ.

5:11 Paul ended this teaching on the Day of the Lord by reminding the Thessalonians to strengthen **one another** by their words and **build** one another up in faith. While Paul obviously felt some responsibility to strengthen the Thessalonian believers, he was instructing not just the leaders but also all the members of the church to take up this call. This injunction is to mutual edification, which he recognized they were **doing** and called them to continue.

OFFERING A CHALLENGE TO CHRISTIAN DUTY (5:12-22)

Leadership in the Community (5:12-13)

5:12-13 In this last section of the letter, Paul addressed issues of importance to the Thessalonians. Once the apostolic band departed, leadership within the church was crucial. He began by asking them to recognize the worth of those in leadership **who labor among ... lead ... and admonish** members of the body. These leaders, though not given a title, were known by their tasks, working until they were weary, leading with the Lord's authority spiritually to benefit the church, and correcting wrongdoing.

Paul told the believers **to esteem** their leaders **very highly ... because of their work**, not because of their position, status, or personality, and to demonstrate it by love. All believers were called to **be at peace** with one another, to live in harmony, without discord (v. 13). Some could have more authority than others, and all were to admonish one another, but harmony could still be achieved. Especially in light of the persecution they faced, harmony and peace among the members was vital for survival.

Fellowship in the Community (5:14-15)

5:14-15 Paul exhorted the entire church, not just the leaders, in the way they should relate to one another:

- **warn the lazy** (Gk. *ataktous*, "disorderly, unruly, insubordinate, undisciplined"), a word often designating a soldier who is "out of the ranks, out of order, or truant," i.e., one who neglects his duties;

- **comfort the discouraged** (Gk. *oligopsuchous*, "feebleminded, fainthearted," from *oligos*, "small," combined with *psuchē*, "soul"), the only instance of this word in the New Testament, so they would not give up;

- support and take an interest in **the weak**, and **be patient** or tolerant **with everyone** (v. 14);

- **pursue what is good for one another and for all** (v. 15).

In the face of persecution, this weighty injunction flew in the face of the natural human tendency to repay evil for evil. The Thessalonians were instructed always to do good to everyone regardless of what harm they had experienced, setting them apart from the world. Paul's teaching hearkened back to the Lord's Prayer to forgive those who trespass against us (Mt 6:12; Lk 11:4) as well as Jesus' words on the cross, "Father, forgive them" (Lk 23:34).

Submission to Christ (5:16-22)

5:16-18 The Thessalonians should practice prayer and giving thanks **always** (v. 16), **constantly** (Gk. *adialeiptōs,* "without intermission, incessantly," v. 17), and **in everything** (v. 18). The inward joy and peace was rooted in the gospel, and its hope could occur even in the midst of suffering. There is no implication that every trial or tragedy is good. Rather, believers were to look beyond circumstances to see the purpose and providence of God who brings the believer through the difficulty or suffering so that she is edified in some way and God is glorified. Their prayer, expressing their dependence on God, should be done constantly. This fellowship with God would lead to rejoicing. Paul was calling them to be conscious continually of their dependence, not necessarily to utter words continually to God but to be in a spirit of prayer. Their thanks, because they knew God was sovereign over all, could be given in every situation. Christians should be characterized by gratitude, and this reality comes only if they know that God is in control and that He is good.

God has revealed His will for the believer **in Christ Jesus** (v. 18) with this threefold approach toward life, based on an understanding of the gospel and the sovereign hand of God over life circumstances. These should therefore characterize the disposition of a woman of God. How great the influence women would have if rejoicing, prayer, and giving thanks permeate and distinguish their lives.

5:19-20 Paul then gave five exhortations concerning prophecy within the community. He first instructed the believers not "to STIFLE (Gk. *sbennute*, "quench or extinguish," as a fire) the Spirit" (v. 19). The metaphor of stifling suggests that the Spirit has ignited a fire within the fellowship of believers. If the fire remains burning, the testimony issuing forth will be God-glorifying and productive. In this imperative phrase the use of the Greek word *mē* requires the stopping of an action already in progress. Paul was exhorting the believers, "Stop continually suppressing or stifling the Holy Spirit" (v. 19). Paul seemed to be telling them not to hinder prophetic activity by despising or rejecting it but rather to value the role of the prophet in their gatherings. PROPHECIES (Gk. *prophēteias*,

"prophetic activity, setting forth revealed truth, divine truth set fort by special gift," v. 20) suggests the public
proclamation of the word of God. Together with the admonition for attentive
hearing of "prophecies" is the counter-
balance of a warning to TEST (Gk. *dokimazete*, "examine, prove," v. 21),
suggesting the testing was in view of approval. What God has said, once understood properly, is to be acted upon (see
Jms 1:22-25).

While they were to value the prophet,
they were not to welcome everything they
heard but **test all things** (v. 21) to ensure
they were from God. The hearers must be
discerning before embracing prophecy in
order to protect the church from false
teaching. Once something is tested and
determined to be good, the believer
should hold onto it. On the other hand, the
Thessalonians are told to **stay away from
every form** (Gk. *eidous*, "form, kind, external appearance") **of evil** (Gk. *ponērou*,
"bad," what is actively opposed to the
good), or to reject any teaching that does
not come from God (v. 22).

CONCLUDING PRAYER, GREET-INGS, AND BLESSING (5:23-28)

5:23-25 Paul concluded his letter in his
usual style. He prayed for the recipients of
his letter that they would be sanctified
thoroughly. Specifically, he prayed that
their whole person would be **blameless**
and have integrity in all aspects of their
being, until the Lord returned.

5:26-28 The letter changed from first
person plural to first person singular.
Throughout the letter Paul used plural
pronouns referring to him, Silvanus
(Silas), and Timothy. At the end he personalized the message by using **I** (v. 27).
He requested that all be greeted with
affection from him. The **holy kiss** (v. 26)
was the common, affectionate greeting of
believers as they gathered for worship.

Paul charged the Thessalonians to read
this letter aloud so that all, even those
who had been immoral, lazy, or weak,
could hear the letter's contents. A public
reading would contribute to their sense of
community as they shared in Paul's commendation and exhortations. They would
be left with a common commitment to
sanctification, accountability, and joy.
Paul concluded his letter as he began,
with **grace,** which comes from **our Lord
Jesus Christ** (v. 28).

Bibliography

Green, Gene L. *The Letters to the Thessalonians: The Pillar New Testament Commentary.* Grand Rapids: Eerdmans, 2002.

Lineberry, John. *Vital Word Studies in I Thessalonians.* Grand Rapids: Zondervan, 1960.

MacArthur, John. *1 & 2 Thessalonians.* The
MacArthur New Testament Commentary
Series. Chicago: Moody Publishers, 2002.

Martin, D. Michael. *1, 2 Thessalonians.* The
New American Commentary, vol. 33. Nashville: Broadman and Holman, 1995.

Morris, Leon. *The First and Second Epistles to
the Thessalonians.* The New International-
Commentary on the New Testament, ed. F. F.
Bruce. Grand Rapids: Eerdmans, 1991.

Notes

[1] The structure of this outline follows that found in Gene L. Green, *The Letters to the Thessalonians,*
The Pillar New Testament Commentary (Grand Rapids: Eerdmans, 2002).
[2] Adapted from the *Woman's Study Bible*, ed. by Dorothy Kelley Patterson and Rhonda Harrington
Kelley (Nashville: Thomas Nelson, 1995), 1997.
[3] See notes in the *Believer's Study Bible*, ed. by W. A. Criswell and Paige Patterson (Nashville:
Thomas Nelson Publishers, 1991), 1709.

2 THESSALONIANS

Introduction

Paul wrote his second letter to the Thessalonians shortly after his first letter, and most likely from Corinth where he stayed for 18 months during his second missionary journey (Ac 18:11). How information concerning the church at Thessalonica reached Paul is not known, but some assumptions can be made about its well-being.

Title

In the Greek New Testament the title for this letter is *pros Thessalonikeis B*, "to the Thessalonians, B," denoting "the second letter to the Thessalonians," the second of two letters sent by Paul "to the church of the Thessalonians" (1:1). The first letter bears the same title but is designated the first by the *alpha*, or "A." Various theories have been proposed arguing that this letter was actually the first chronologically, but none of these is convincing enough to discard the traditional order reflected in the canon.

Setting

Since their arrival in Thessalonica, Paul, Silvanus (Silas), and Timothy were the cause of civil unrest (Ac 17:1-9). After spending at least three weeks and perhaps up to six months in Thessalonica, persecution forced Paul, Silvanus (Silas), and Timothy to flee. From Athens, Paul sent Timothy back to check on his beloved spiritual sons and daughters (1 Th 3:1-6). Timothy met Paul in Corinth with his report.

Genre

Typical of correspondence in the Greco-Roman period, the letter opened by identifying the authors and recipients. Paul's distinctively Christian greeting (1:2) preceded the introduction of thanksgiving and prayer (1:3-12). In the body of the letter, Paul approached the Thessalonians in a manner different from his first letter. The rhetorical genre of 2 Thessalonians can be best described as "deliberative" because the apostle aimed to persuade the Thessalonians to choose a course of action, particularly in regard to eschatological expectations (chap. 2) and various ethical concerns (3:6-14). The tone of Paul's reproof is more authoritative in this letter than in the first, but he deftly mixed stern exhortation with loving encouragement, reiterating in the closing greeting an emphasis on peace that was much-needed by the persecuted church (3:15-18).

Author

The Apostle Paul was the principal author (3:17). In addition, Timothy and Silvanus (Silas) contributed to the letter, evidenced by Paul's use of plural pronouns throughout most of the letter (see "Author" in the introduction to 1 Thessalonians).

Date

Paul wrote this second letter from Corinth shortly after the first, probably AD 50–51. The biblical record in Acts 18 can be correlated with extrabiblical evidence to date the epistle (see *Date* in 1 Thessalonians).

Recipients

The letter was written to the fellowship of believers at Thessalonica.

Major Themes

The Thessalonian church had apparently taken some of Paul's first letter to heart. He did not consider providing a defense of himself or his work necessary; neither does he discuss sexual morality, church leadership, or brotherly love. However, he did address their persecution and the perseverance that would be necessary. He assured them with the promise of his prayer and the destiny of both the persecutors and the Christians. Paul next dealt with eschatology, specifically the advent of the Day of the Lord. The Thessalonians were, by some means, deceived into believing that the day had already come. This further confused them and threatened their stability. Paul responded by reminding them of the tradition they had received and of the destruction of the "man of lawlessness" (see 2:3). They were instructed to stand firm in the tradition passed on to them. Paul repeated his theme of work and the necessity that each follows his example by earning his own food. He then gives direction on how to handle those members of the church who do not obey this teaching.

Pronunciation Guide	
Silvanus	*sil VAY nuhs*

Outline

I. GREETING (1:1-2)

II. AN EXPRESSION OF THANKSGIVING AND PRAYER (1:3-12)

III. THE BODY OF THE LETTER (2:1–3:15)
   A. The Coming of Jesus Christ (2:1-12)
   B. A Word of Encouragement (2:13-17)
   C. Final Instructions (3:1-15)
      1. Prayer (3:1-5)
      2. Godly discipline (3:6-15)

IV. CONCLUSION (3:16-18)

Exposition of the Text

GREETING (1:1-2)

1:1 The greeting used by **Paul, Silvanus** (Silas), **and Timothy** is similar to that in 1 Thessalonians, reminding the church that they are connected in a familial manner with the apostles and other believers by their relationship with God, which is the foundation for the Christian concept of unity. The authors name themselves, then their recipients.

1:2 Paul pointed to the deity of Christ in linking the Father and Son as both the foundation of the church and the givers of **grace** (Gk. *charis*) and **peace** (Gk. *eirēnē*). Grace and peace summarize the saving benefits to believers and have special significance in view of the situation of the Thessalonian church.

AN EXPRESSION OF THANKSGIVING AND PRAYER (1:3-12)

1:3 Paul noted his duty or obligation to offer thanksgiving to God for the growing **faith** and **love** the Thessalonians were demonstrating. God is worthy to receive thanks because His work among them prompted the production of these virtues. While Paul mentioned their faith and love, he did not speak of hope as elsewhere (1 Th 1:3); rather he implied its presence by praising their perseverance in the midst of persecutions and trials. Paul had exhorted them to love one another more and more (1 Th 4:9-10) and prayed that their love might increase (1 Th 3:12). God responded to his prayers. Love among the Thessalonian believers was mutual and inclusive; no member was excluded from giving or receiving love.

1:4 Paul told other congregations of the young believers' good progress in faith and love. The word **BOAST** (Gk. *egkauchasthai*) appears nowhere else in the New Testament in this compound form. The root *kauchasthai*, "glory in or boast," appears frequently in Paul's letters (cp. Gl 6:14). This boasting would have been a source of encouragement as they encountered adversity. Paul honored them in the presence of their peers, thus giving them an awareness of their participation in the wider movement of evangelization. The boasting also made them an example for other churches to emulate, thereby strengthening both this church and the other congregations.

The content of the boasting was the **endurance and faith in all the persecutions and afflictions you endure.** Their endurance was an example to others and was deeply rooted in the hope of the coming of Christ. Paul had been concerned about their continuing in faith and sent Timothy to check up on them to make sure they had not abandoned their faith. Timothy returned with a good report of their steadfastness.

The persecutions were suffered at the hands of their contemporaries, motivated by Satan. **All** indicates that the persecutions were many and likely varied. The believers were not only emotionally distressed but also facing great hostility, yet their endurance was rooted in God who was the object of their faith and hope.

Paul presented an aspect of the theology of suffering, which plays a central role in God's divine plan and is not to be interpreted as a sign of divine neglect. Indeed, suffering is often a means for God's working His divine plan.

1:5-10 Enduring suffering results in a robust character, lessons learned, opportunities to witness, and evidence of being **COUNTED WORTHY** (Gk. *kataxiōthēnai*, "to account or judge worthy," v. 5; cp. Lk 20:35; Ac 5:41); they would be shaped by God into what He would have them become. God's righteousness is demonstrated in His wrath toward evildoers. His coming will include judgment of the unjust, a recompense for those who have afflicted the Thessalonians. He will also reward the righteous with relief or **rest** (Gk. *anesin*, "relaxation, relief") from affliction at the coming of the Lord.

The apostle, through his own life experience and his knowledge of the present age, knew that trial and tribulation would be ongoing. However, **at the revelation** (Gk. *apokalupsei*, "disclosure, unveiling") **of the Lord Jesus**, when He is revealed "in that day," believers will receive a rest. This phenomenon is not the cessation of activity but rather the replacement of the negative elements of life with that which is positive and edifying (2 Th 1:7). A CLEAR EVIDENCE (Gk. *endeigma*, "plain indication, sure token, or recognizable sign") of God's righteous judgment (v. 5) is the believers' endurance. The word appears only here in the New Testament, but it is related to a verb used more frequently, *endeiknumi*, meaning "to show, demonstrate, point out, or make manifest."

Paul described this revelation as **from heaven** (v. 7), with the **angels**, and **with flaming fire** (v. 8; cp. Is 66:15-16). When He comes from heaven, where He is enjoying the glory of the Father, He will come with all authority to judge. His angels point to His glory. He will administer justice with majesty that is compared with a "flaming fire" (v. 8). God's VENGEANCE (Gk. *ekdikēsin*, "retribution, punishment," cp. Rm 12:19; Dt 32:35) will be against those who have rejected Him and His message. It is not vindictive retaliation but the proper administration of judgment toward those who have not believed. The subjects of this wrath rejected His person and disobeyed His call. The **PENALTY** (Gk. *dikēn*, "just punishment") will be "everlasting **DESTRUCTION**" (Gk. *olethron*, "ruin, death," 2 Th 1:9; see also 1 Th 5:3; 1 Tm 6:9), the opposite of eternal life. This eternal ruin or "destruction" is not annihilation but a cutting off or moving "away from the Lord's presence" (2 Th 1:9) forever. This serious consequence of rejecting God in this life will be meted out with God's **glorious strength** (Gk. *ischuos*, "power, might, ability, force," v. 9; cp. Mk 12:30,33; Eph 1:19, 6:10; 1 Pt 4:11). Believers are reassured of God's justice upon their persecutors. When Jesus returns, He will be glorified in bringing justice.

Believers will take part in this glorification of the Lord, a comforting thought to the Thessalonians who will be numbered among the saints admiring Him **in that day,** a reference to the Day of the Lord. This Old Testament imagery is used to describe all the events in the end times (1 Th 5:1-2; cp. Jl 1:15 and Am 8:3,9), including the glorification of the saints, the ensuing tribulation (Rv 4–19), and the glorious millennium (Rv 21–22).

1:11-12 With the teaching of salvation in mind, Paul continually prayed that **God will consider you worthy** (Gk. *axiōsē*, "deem or make suitable"; cp. Lk 7:7; 1 Tm 5:17; Hb 3:3) **of His calling** (2 Th 1:11). The Thessalonians were unworthy when God called them, but Paul prayed that they might desire to be worthy servants now that they have been called. Even the desire to be worthy is something to be accomplished **by His power** (v. 11). Human power is not sufficient. Paul prayed that they would desire works resulting from their faith **so that the**

name of our Lord Jesus will be glorified by you (v. 12).

Often a person's name summarized his character. Paul was hoping that the virtue of the believers would be evident so that glory would be given to the Giver of the virtue. Then the Lord's character would be more accurately discerned. In addition, the Thessalonians would be glorified on account of him **according to the grace of our God and the Lord Jesus Christ** (v. 12). Any glorification of believers is the result of God's grace and His unmerited kindness to them.

Heart to Heart: Partnering the Persecuted

Most Christians in the United States do not experience the ongoing persecution about which Paul writes in this letter. Yet, in times when western culture affords relative ease for worshiping God, you have a responsibility to encourage, support, and pray for those who are suffering at the hands of evildoers for the sake of the gospel. Brothers and sisters in far away lands desperately need a word of hope, prayer, and encouragement to endure. You can have a vital partnership with them through such intercession.

Theological Terms

Soteriology	Study of the doctrine of salvation effected by Jesus Christ; from Gk. *sotērian*, "salvation" (2 Th 2:13).
Salvation	Deliverance from the guilt and condemnation of sin (Eph 2:8).
Grace	Acceptance and loving mercy is neither deserved nor earned but given freely by God (Eph 2:8).
Faith	Demonstration of total trust in and commitment to the Lord (2 Th 2:13; Php 3:9).
Justification	The first aspect of salvation in which a person's relationship with God is made right through the saving work of Jesus Christ (Rm 3:21-26).
Sanctification	The Holy Spirit indwells, sets apart, and works in the believer to bring about increasing Christlikeness and holiness (2 Th 2:13).
Glorification	The culmination of salvation in which the believer is transformed into Christ's likeness (Rm 8:30; Php 3:21).

THE BODY OF THE LETTER (2:1–3:15)

The Coming of Jesus Christ (2:1-12)

2:1 Although Paul dealt with **the coming** (Gk. *parousia*) of the Lord in his first letter to the Thessalonians, he felt the need to return to this subject. Someone was identifying the present persecution among the Thessalonians as a part of the tribulation and claiming there would be no rapture for which they could hope. *Parousia* may refer to the coming or arrival of either person or event, but most often in the New Testament it refers to the future coming of the Lord Jesus. His return to earth will be preceded by the revelation of "the lawless one," the antichrist (vv. 8-9). Jesus' coming "in the air" (1 Th 4:17) will be accompanied by the resurrection of the dead in Christ and the gathering of saints still living (1 Co 15:23-25; 1 Th 4:15-16).

Perhaps some of Paul's communication had been misunderstood or ignored. Or perhaps his teaching had been confused with the teaching of another with a different message. These imposters were denying the prophetic outline Paul had given in his first letter. As a result, this matter is the primary topic of concern in his second letter. The instruction in this letter is not comprehensive teaching on the return of Christ but assumes prior knowledge.

2:2 Paul began by asking his brothers to be level-headed regarding "the coming of our Lord Jesus Christ and our being gathered to Him." The level-headedness is in contrast to being "easily **UPSET** (Gk. *saleuthēnai*, "agitated, shaken, causing to totter") in mind." They are to maintain their reason so as not to be shaken off balance by sudden false teaching. Further, they are not to be **TROUBLED** (Gk. *throeisthai*, "alarmed, frightened or weighed down by worry and anxiety"). Jesus also used this expression in an eschatological discourse (see Mt 24:6; Mk 13:7). Paul offered three potential causes for the Thessalonians' emotional and mental reactions: **a spirit** (prophecy), **a message** (oral communication), or **a letter**.

Apparently, the Thessalonians received a letter that purported to be from Paul. He was not sure about the details of the letter and denied any responsibility for it. This letter of unknown authorship taught that **the Day of the Lord has come,** activating an emotional reaction from the Thessalonians.

2:3 Paul warned them not to be deceived. He then sought to empower them to withstand such deception by demonstrating the inaccuracy of the anonymous letter. He expounded on this teaching that the **day will not come unless** certain things are in place. First, the **APOSTASY** (Gk. *apostasia*, "abandonment," lit. "standing away from," as in the abandonment of God's law), conveying both the idea of political rebellion and religious revolt against God's authority—perhaps in opposition to civil order, or rebellion—comes; and then the **MAN OF LAWLESSNESS** (Gk. *anthrōpos tēs anomias*) is also called the **SON OF DESTRUCTION** (Gk. *huios tēs apōleias*, 2:3; cp. Ps 88:23; Jn 17:12) and the **LAWLESS ONE** (Gk. *ho anomos*, in which the Greek letter *a*, the first letter of the Greek alphabet, known as the alpha privative when used as a prefix as here, is attached to *nomos* or "law" to negate it, 2 Th 2:8). These expressions depict one who is doomed to destruction and characterized by his repudiation of God's law. Then the "man of lawlessness is REVEALED" (Gk. *apokaluphthē*, "unveiled, uncovered, disclosed"). This man who personifies evil and sin is to be identified with the first beast (Rv 13), the little horn (Dn 7–8), the abomination (Mt 24:15).

Antichrist (1 Jn 2:18) is apparently a person who appears in history at a pivotal moment, receiving incredible power and influence from Satan. His true character is not revealed until the midpoint of the tribulation (Dn 9:24-27). He is finally destroyed at the return of Christ to the earth (2 Th 2:8). These two happenings must have made sense to the Thessalonians and led to a concrete conclusion that, indeed, the Day of the Lord had not arrived.

2:4-9 Many have tried to identify this "man of lawlessness," but who he is or what he represents is unclear. However, he is "the son of destruction" (Gk. *apōleias*, "utter destruction, waste, ruin," v. 3), and he is an eschatological figure who will appear only at the end of the age—these facts are certain. He will be "revealed" (v. 3), which means he existed before he is made manifest to the world. He is further described as one who **exalts himself above every so-called god or object of worship** (v. 4) so that he claims to be first above all else. He goes so far as to publicize **that he himself is God** (v. 4) while residing in some unknown building. The phrase EXALTS HIMSELF (Gk. *huperairomenos*, "lifts or raises above, puffed up with pride") combines the prefix *huper* ("above, over") and the root *airō* ("raise or lift up, elevate"). The word also connotes "being haughty or insolent." The only other instance of this word in the New Testament is Paul's mention of his "thorn in the flesh," given to him so he would not "exalt" himself (2 Co 12:7).

Paul asked a seemingly emotionally charged question: **Don't you remember that when I was still with you I told you about this?** (v. 5). The Thessalonians were previously given all the instruction necessary to evaluate and reject this false teaching. Paul reminded them that something is holding back or restraining "the man of lawlessness." Although many commentators have speculated as to who or what the restrainer might be, and while clear to Paul and the Thessalonians, the text is not explicit. Probably the restraining is done by the Holy Spirit who is active even now in restraining evil. Although the restraining ends during the tribulation, the Holy Spirit does not depart since He is omnipresent. Rather, one of His ministries would cease temporarily. Although the "restrainer" is not named, this power kept "the man of lawlessness" from being revealed until the divinely appointed and permitted time. The believ-ers should have known that the Day of the Lord had not come since this prerequisite had not been fulfilled.

Once the restrainer is removed, "the man of lawlessness" will no longer be hidden or remain a MYSTERY (Gk. *mustērion*, "secret" that would remain beyond human knowledge until divinely revealed). This "mystery" and its revelation are all within God's providence, which Paul emphasized. In his effort to comfort the believers and correct their misinformation, he did not dwell on the details of these events but on the sovereignty of God to bring about His purposes.

"The Lord Jesus will DESTROY" (Gk. *anelei*, "consume, do away with, kill, overthrow") the man of lawlessness with ease, with "the breath of His mouth" (v. 8; cp. Is 11:4). The **lawless one** will be powerless and brought **to nothing** when Jesus comes in splendor and majesty. Paul recognized the power of "the man of lawlessness" by mentioning his FALSE (Gk. *pseudous*, "a lie, counterfeit," anglicized as "pseudo," and used here as a descriptor for all the works of "the man of lawlessness") MIRACLES (Gk. *dunamei*, "power"), SIGNS (Gk. *sēmeiois*, "that which distinguishes someone or something from others, that by which one is known; sign or portent, thus miracles"; cp. "take note" in 2 Th 3:14, "sign" in 3:17), and WONDERS (v. 9; Gk. *terasin*, "awe-inspiring works"). All three of these words are used in the Gospels to describe the miracles of Jesus (see also Ac 2:22 and 2 Co 12:12), but Paul noted here that these acts are done to deceive people into destruction. Then as now the counterfeit nature of these deeds are best exposed when placed alongside the work of Christ. Nevertheless, Paul made clear that Jesus is abundantly more powerful.

2:10-12 Paul turned from discussing "the man of lawlessness" to emphasizing the fate of those who followed the deceiver. Those deceived will **PERISH** (Gk. *apollumenois*, "being destroyed, rendered useless, killed," in present tense as a participle, suggesting ongoing destruction) because they were not rightly related to the "truth"—to Jesus (v. 10). They deliberately did not receive **the truth** of Jesus, revealing the attitude of their hearts. Therefore, they will not **be saved**—an eternal consequence (v. 10).

God has ultimate power—even turning Satan's evil to work out His divine purposes (cp. Rm 8:28). A person's defiance of God and allegiance to Satan is an instrument God ultimately uses to bring about His punishment. These unbelievers "believe what is **FALSE** (Gk. *pseudei*, v. 11; cp. v. 9; Rm 1:25), so that all will be **CONDEMNED**" (Gk. *krithōsin*, "judged, sentenced" 2 Th 2:12). God demonstrated His justice, and Paul clearly noted the reasoning for condemnation—they rejected truth but **ENJOYED** (Gk. *eudokēsantes*, "approved, consented, thought of as good, took pleasure in") **UNRIGHTEOUSNESS** (Gk. *adikia*, "wrongdoing, wickedness, injustice"). Wrong had become good to them, and they delighted in sin (v. 12).

Heart to Heart: Loving Correction

Paul expressed his love for the Thessalonian believers by correcting their wrong beliefs. He knew that their wrong thinking would result in behavior unfitting for believers, so he made every effort to instruct them more perfectly. This methodology remains an important means of expressing love for one another to this day. You can love and serve one another by continually using gentle instruction to help a sister grasp a concept of God more accurately. This responsibility is not the pastor's alone, but each member of the body is competent to minister in this way. Bible studies, discipleship groups, prayer partners, meeting over coffee, taking long walks for discussion together are some venues where this kind of love in action can take place. Asking poignant questions, listening well, and knowing Scripture in order to give wise input into a person's situation are necessary. Discipleship and correction should be an integral part of life within the body of Christ.

A Word of Encouragement (2:13-17)

2:13-15 After Paul instructed the Thessalonians, he turned back to his thankfulness for them, even going so far as to say, he "**MUST** (Gk. *opheilomen*, "obligated, owing or being bound to") always thank" God for choosing the Thessalonians for salvation. Paul was recognizing their salvation, affirming God's sovereignty in it, and declaring that he prayed for them often. He also called the **brothers loved by the Lord**, closely linking being loved with being chosen **for salvation**. The result is the Holy Spirit makes the believer holy. **Sanctification** (Gk. *hagiasmō*, "holiness, consecration") indicates dedication to God. This progressive cleansing of soul and life is part of the salvation process. A believer is initially sanctified in the sense of being set apart unto the Lord by the power of the Holy Spirit and his own act of faith. Paul also mentioned the human part in salvation: Their **belief in the truth** of the gospel and personal commitment to that truth were necessary for their salvation.

In light of the teaching on "the man of lawlessness" and the future glory, Paul told the believers to **STAND FIRM** (Gk. *stēkete*, "persevere, remain steadfast"). They were not to waver but to **HOLD TO** (Gk. *krateite*, "hold fast, not discard or let go") the teaching they received by Paul when he was with them, or by his "letter," a probable reference to 1 Thessalonians. Both of these sources of truth were considered the word of God and therefore authoritative, requiring humble obedience.

2:16-17 Paul transitioned seamlessly from argument to prayer. He recognized they could not accomplish what his teaching required in their own strength. Thus, he prayed that God might **strengthen** them. This prayer attributed deity and supreme power to Jesus Christ. In addition, Paul used singular verbs, **ENCOURAGE** (Gk. *parakalesai*, "console, comfort, encourage") and **STRENGTHEN** (Gk. *stērixai*, "make stable or firm, establish, support," v. 17; cp. 3:3), stressing for the Thessalonians the unity of the Father and Son. The encouragement for which Paul prayed is eternal, abiding amid present difficulties or whatever would come. **Good hope** is a gift from God, enduring within and affecting without the lives of believers (2 Th 2:16). These gifts are meant to encourage and strengthen their whole beings, to bolster them for Christian service, for **every good work and word** (v. 17).

Final Instructions (3:1-15)

Prayer (3:1-5)

3:1 Paul asked the Thessalonians to pray continually for the apostles, recognizing that they, too, were dependent on God to accomplish any good for the kingdom. He specified the issues for prayer. First he asked them to pray that the gospel message may **SPREAD RAPIDLY** (Gk. *trechē*, "spread rapidly") a word for describing runners in a race or of someone moving in haste. It could also mean "to meet with or provoke danger" that would require great effort to overcome. Because the subject of the clause is not a person but "the Lord's message," and the verb is in the present tense, *trechē* suggests Paul's hope is for the gospel to advance swiftly and powerfully, cp. Ps 147:15; Mt 28:8; Lk 15:20; Gl 2:2, 5:7; Php 2:16; 1 Co 9:24-26; Heb 12:1; Rv 9:9. Apparently the gospel had been effective in this way with the Thessalonians. They responded quickly and revered God's word as they saw its impact. Paul had not experienced that kind of response to his ministry since he left Thessalonica.

3:2 Paul also asked his friends to pray that he would be "**DELIVERED** (Gk. *hrusthōmen*, "rescued, saved, preserved"; cp. 1 Th 1:10) from **WICKED** (Gk. *atopōn*, "out of place, wrong, evil, unrighteous") and **EVIL** (Gk. *ponērōn*, "evil, wicked, bad"; cp. 2 Th 3:3) men." This specific situation seems to be one of which the Thessalonians were aware and from which Paul desired to be free. Some Jews were opposing his preaching and hindering the advance of the gospel. Likely Paul referred to this group, whom he described as those without **faith**, i.e., those who do not believe in Jesus Christ.

3:3 As was Paul's custom, he was quick to turn from relating difficulties to lauding the faithfulness of God. God's character is the important factor in the situation. He **is faithful** to bring about His plan, and this provided comfort even in the midst of difficulties. Next Paul affirmed that because God is FAITHFUL (Gk. *pistos*, "trustworthy, credible, sure, relied upon," cp. 1 Th 5:24), He will "STRENGTHEN (Gk. *stērixei*, "make stable or firm or steadfast," cp. 2:17), and GUARD (Gk. *phulaxei*, "protect, have in custody, watch, keep safe") you from the evil one" (Gk. *ponērou*, "evil, wicked, bad"; also in 2 Th 3:2). Interestingly Paul switched from his prayer requests for the Thessalonians to praying *for* them. Again, his own concerns do not dominate his thoughts, and his pastoral heart is evident. Perhaps Paul was concerned that his current difficulties would discourage the Thessalonians' faith, so he reminded them that God would **strengthen** and protect them. If God strengthened them, they would be unwavering in their faith. If He guarded them **from the evil one**, they would be protected from spiritual injury.

3:4 Paul readily went back and forth between praise for God and affirmation of the Thessalonians. This habit testifies to his understanding that God does the work, and His children cooperate. Paul praised whenever possible and seemed delighted to do so, but he always tempered his praise with **in the Lord** or a mention of the real source of his confidence—the Lord—to accomplish the work of sanctification.

3:5 This affirmation of **Christ's endurance** points to a corresponding perseverance on the part of believers. The love and endurance of Christ would serve as the template for their own attitudes.

Godly Discipline (3:6-15)

3:6 After Paul commended the Thessalonians for their response to his command, he returned to a subject discussed in his first letter—irresponsible members. He addressed the Thessalonians as **brothers** but exercised his authority by commanding them, strengthening his commands by delivering them **in the name of our Lord Jesus Christ**. This authoritative message is intended to incite the Thessalonians to obedience. They are told **to keep away** or withhold fellowship from those who are lazy or irresponsible. Laziness is an issue for the brothers to confront, not ignore. Perhaps the irresponsible ones refused to work because they believed the Day of the Lord was imminent. Even so, the refusal to work contradicted **tradition**, or the instruction they had received from Paul during his visit.

3:7 Paul again reminded them of his previous teaching. They knew they were to **imitate** (Gk. *mimeisthai*, "follow an example, emulate" also in v. 9; see 1 Th 1:6) the apostles. The responsible work ethic of the apostles must be emulated. The apostles had toiled, earned their own living, and preached the gospel. The Thessalonians were to do the same.

3:8-9 Paul **labored and toiled** around the clock so that he could provide for himself and not be a **burden** to the young church (v. 8; cp. 1 Th 2:9). Paul reminded them that he had **the right** to have this kind of care. While preachers could rightfully expect the financial support of a church, Paul chose to forego that expectation for the sake of his example among them.

3:10-11 Paul reminded the Thessalonians again of something they had heard earlier (see 1 Th 5:14). **If anyone isn't willing to work**, let him not eat. Scripture notes the provision for one unable to do gainful work (cp. 1 Co 16:1-3), but such benevolent support is not appropriate for those who can work (Ex 20:9). Some did not work at all, and worse, they interfered in the work of others. This meddling may have included dissuading others from their work in light of Christ's return.

> ## Heart to Heart:
> ## Do as I Do, and as I Say
>
> *One might be put off by Paul's tendency to point to himself as an example (1 Co 4:16, 11:1; Php 3:17; 1 Th 1:6; 2 Th 3:7-9). Paul knew that the success of the gospel was related to his determination to live according to it. Surely Paul did not claim to be perfect, but as a man of integrity he had to show congruence between what he said he believed and how he lived. Paul didn't just expect this of himself, but he calls you to the same (1 Th 2:14; 1 Tm 4:12; Ti 2:7). He specifically expects this behavior of older women (Ti 2:3-6) and calls them to teach younger women through their words and example. The success of the church demands from women a willingness to love one another in this way, to be bold enough to say, "Be imitators of me, as I also am of Christ" (1 Co 11:1).*

Apparently Paul had identified these individuals.

3:12-13 Paul wrote directly to the idle ones, referring to them as **such people** (v. 12). In his effort toward reconciling them to the body, he commanded with authority from Jesus Christ, communicating that obedience is the only appropriate response. He exhorted them not only to work but also to do so **quietly**. A calm and consistent approach to work was in order as the fruit of one who trusts Christ and is not in a panic about His return. Believers would earn and **eat their own bread** (v. 12).

Speaking again to the majority who are working, he implored them to **not grow weary in doing good** (v. 13). Perhaps this "good" included restoring the meddlers to fellowship. He was calling them to patience and not to resignation, urging them to continue to work toward restoration.

3:14-15 Paul predicted that some would ignore the **instruction** of his **letter** and disobey it. The upright were to "TAKE NOTE (Gk. *sēmeiousthe*, "mark, distinguish by marking," v. 14; cp. "signs" in 2:9, "sign" in 3:17) of that person," to notice who he is so that action could be taken against him. The believers were to withdraw fellowship from him, with the hope of eventual restored fellowship for all. The willfully and consistently disobedient ignored Paul's face-to-face preaching, his first letter, and now his second letter. Discipline was the right consequence as they were not in good standing with the church. Paul fully expected that the irresponsible ones could be treated as brothers while also being excluded from fellowship. The desired end of this withdrawal was **so that he may be ashamed** (2 Th 3:14; cp. 1 Co 4:14; Ti 2:8). The lack of fellowship ideally would cause the idler to reflect on his behavior, experience the implications of his actions, and repent.

Paul expected that this punishment could be exercised while still regarding the errant one **as a brother**, not **an enemy**. He was warning the majority against being too harsh and not loving. The rebuke was to be done with love, as from a friend who cares for the well-being of the sinner. Still, this response was a strong one, and Paul did not soften the blow.

CONCLUSION (3:16-18)

3:16 Paul prayed that **the Lord of peace** would grant the Thessalonians **peace**, which is a gift from Jesus Christ. He would provide peace even in the midst of discord in the church. God's presence **with all** was the only means of peace for the Thessalonians. Paul's prayer was for all of them, including those who deserved punishment, for whom he continued to care deeply and to whom he communicated his desire that they know the peace of God as well.

3:17 Paul dictated his letters to a scribe. At some point toward the end of his letters, he took the pen in hand and wrote a few lines to punctuate the fact that the letter originated with him. In his own handwriting he wrote, **this is how I write**, which may have served to distinguish his letter from a letter falsely attributed to him. They could now expect any correspondence from him to bear this sign (Gk. *sēmeion*, "mark, token"; cp. "signs" in 2:9, "take note" in 3:14).

3:18 Paul's ending, as in 1 Thessalonians but with the addition of the word **all**, again emphasized his concern for the entire church. He closed this letter as he did the first letter, with **grace**—God's undeserved favor.

Bibliography

Green, Gene L. *The Letters to the Thessalonians: The Pillar New Testament Commentary.* Grand Rapids: Eerdmans, 2002.

Martin, D. Michael. *1, 2 Thessalonians.* The New American Commentary, vol. 33. Nashville: Broadman and Holman, 1995.

Morris, Leon, *The First and Second Epistles to the Thessalonians.* The New International Commentary on the New Testament. Edited by F. F. Bruce. Grand Rapids: Eerdmans, 1991.

1 TIMOTHY

Introduction

Title

First Timothy (Gk. *pros Timotheon A*) bore the name of its intended recipient—Timothy, Paul's son in the faith.

Setting

The city of Ephesus was a thriving commercial and religious center strategically located on the major east-west trade route near the southern coast of Asia Minor. Paul founded the church during a brief stop on his second missionary journey. He left Priscilla and Aquila, later joined by Apollos, to continue the work (Ac 18:18-21,24-28). Paul later stayed there more than three years, probably AD 54 to 57 (Ac 20:31). Ephesus, the gateway city to a large region of Asia Minor, was critical in the spread of the gospel (Ac 19:10). On the return leg of this third missionary journey, he stopped at the port city of Miletus and sent for the Ephesian elders to join him, warning them to watch out for false teachers who would come to destroy God's work in the Ephesian church (Ac 20:17-38).

Paul's words proved to be an apt description of the situation the church faced several years later when he left Timothy there to set things in order. False teachers, who may have been elders from within the church (Ac 20:29-30), had arisen (1:3-11; 4:1-5; cp. Ac 20:17-28). Their identity as Ephesian elders is supported by their self-designation as "teachers of the law" (1:7), which was an elder's responsibility (5:17; cp. 3:2); by the excommunication of Hymenaeus and Alexander by Paul himself (1:19-20) rather than by the church (2 Th 3:14; 1 Co 5:1-5); and by Paul's emphasis on the elder's qualifications (3:1-7) and discipline (5:19-25).

Genre

First Timothy is one of two letters the Apostle Paul wrote to his disciple and son in the faith. These letters, together with a third written to his disciple Titus, are commonly called the Pastoral Epistles since they gave instruction and encouragement to these two younger men who were serving in pastoral roles.

Author

Traditional scholarship has long regarded the Apostle Paul to be the author of the Pastoral Epistles. Each letter explicitly states that Paul is the author (1:1; 2 Tm 1:1; Ti 1:1). Nevertheless, in the early nineteenth century some scholars began to question whether they were written by Paul himself or by someone using his name after his death. While these scholars have raised some legitimate concerns, evidence is sufficient to support Paul as the author.

First, although the events cited in the Pastorals are not mentioned in the book of Acts, nothing in the New Testament precludes the apostle's release from the Roman imprisonment of AD 60–62 described in Acts 26:16-31. The date of Paul's death is generally considered to be the winter of AD 67–68 under the Emperor Nero; the events of the Pastorals could easily have occurred in the intervening years. (See "Date" for a suggested chronology.)

Second, the heresy Paul described in the Pastorals is not the highly developed system found in second-century Gnosticism. The gnostic elements of the heresy Paul attacked in the Pastorals were already present in the first century. The teachers Paul described seem to be Judaizers who taught a combination of pagan speculations and Jewish legalism (e.g., 1 Tm 1:4,7; Ti 1:4).

Third, a church structure consisting of "overseers" (1 Tm 3:1; also translated "elders," 5:17,19) and "deacons" (3:8) is entirely in keeping with the situation during Paul's lifetime. A more complex structure involving a bishop, several elders, and multiple deacons is characteristic of the second century.

Fourth, the wide range of vocabulary used in the Pastorals—but not elsewhere in the New Testament—calls for focusing on the historical context in which the letter was written. Paul was a highly trained scholar, at home in the Greek language of his day, and he used vocabulary that was specific to the situation he was addressing. Some examples include: the teaching and the lifestyle of the specific heretics he was refuting (e.g., "fruitless discussion" in 1:6 or "love of money" in 6:10); teaching directed towards the present situation in the Ephesian church (e.g., "elaborate hairstyles" in 2:9 or "has brought up children" in 5:10); terminology directly related to church leaders (e.g., "not a bully" in 3:3; Ti 1:7 or "new convert" in 1 Tm 3:6); lists of sins prevalent in these churches (e.g., "kidnappers" in 1:10 or "irreconcilable" in 2 Tm 3:3); words of direction or encouragement exactly suited to Timothy's needs (e.g., "stomach" in 1 Tm 5:23 or "share in suffering" in 2 Tm 1:8); quotations from other sources (e.g. "ransom" in 1 Tm 2:6 or "unapproachable" in 6:16); groups of words related to a specific topic (e.g., "gold, silver, wood" in 2 Tm 2:20); and cognates of words found in epistles of unquestioned Pauline authorship (e.g., "older women" in Ti 2:3 and "elderly man" in Phm 9). Paul also may have dictated these letters to a secretary or *amanuensis* (see Rm 16:22; Eph 6:21) who, under the direction of the Holy Spirit, may have taken some liberty in the precise wording. While the use of an amanuensis does not diminish the concept of plenary inspiration, the reasons previously enumerated make this conclusion unnecessary.

Date

Scholars who hold to Pauline authorship generally believe the Pastorals were written between AD 62 and AD 67. Acts 28:16-31 describes a Roman imprisonment of at least two years duration from AD 60 to 62. Paul was evidently set free sometime after the end of the Acts account, since both 1 Timothy and Titus picture him traveling in the eastern Mediterranean region: to Ephesus (1:3; 3:14); to Crete (Ti 1:5); and to Nicopolis on the western coast of Greece (Ti 3:12). His first letter to Timothy and the letter to Titus were written during this period, probably AD 62 to 65. His second letter to Timothy finds him in a much more dire imprisonment than that described in Acts 28:23,30-31, one he clearly expected to end in his execution (2 Tm 4:6). Church historians place his death in the winter of AD 67–68.

Recipients

Timothy was from Lystra, a city in southern Asia Minor, which Paul visited on his first and second missionary journeys (Ac 14:6,21; 16:1). Timothy's father was a Gentile, but his mother and grandmother, who were Jewish, taught him the Scriptures from an early age (Ac 16:1; 2 Tm 1:5; 3:15). He probably heard the gospel during Paul's first journey; and since the apostle referred to him as "my beloved and faithful child in the Lord" (1 Co 4:17; cp. 1:2; 2 Tm 2:1), he possibly led Timothy to personal faith in Christ. Timothy was highly esteemed by the church leaders in Lystra; and during Paul's visit there on his second missionary journey, he asked Timothy to join him in his travels (Ac 16:3). In order to avoid potential conflicts with Jews, who knew Timothy's father was a Gentile, Paul circumcised him (Ac 16:3).

Timothy later traveled extensively with Paul and was sent on missions to various churches, including Thessalonica, Corinth, and Philippi, as his apostolic representative (1 Co 4:17; Php 2:19-24; 1 Th 3:2,6). At the time Paul wrote the letter identified as 1 Timothy, Timothy's role in the church in Ephesus was as Paul's coworker. His purpose was not to become a long-term overseer, but rather to bring doctrinal clarity and organizational stability in a situation plagued with false teachers, as well as lovingly to train up the believers in righteous living. This letter was not intended as a private missive for Timothy only but was to be read aloud in the Ephesian church, thereby giving Timothy written authorization from Paul to make needed changes in the church.

Major Themes

This occasional epistle addresses concerns specific to Timothy and the church in Ephesus. Several recurrent themes appear.

The true nature and the fruit of sound doctrine. Throughout his epistles, Paul's primary strategy for refuting false doctrine is to state clearly sound doctrine and to demonstrate its power to change lives. The truth of God's provision of salvation through Jesus Christ's finished work on the cross is made clear (1:15; 2:3-6), as is the sinful human condition that necessitated it (1:9-10,13,15). In addition, believers have certain hope of eternal life (1:16; 4:8; 6:12). This provision becomes effectual for all who personally place their faith in Christ (1:16; 4:10; cp. 1:13). Paul considered himself to be the chief example of this life-changing power (1:12-16), noting that the result of God's working in a believer's life will be "love from a pure heart, a good conscience, and a sincere faith" (1:5).

Appropriate conduct in the worship assembly. The context of 1 Timothy 2 is the worship assembly, and Paul cited four areas needing correction in this particular church.

- He wanted to ensure the centrality of public prayer, especially for governmental leaders (2:1-7).

- He expected the men to pray with cleansed consciences, free from interpersonal conflicts (2:8).

- He exhorted the women to have both dress and demeanor that would glorify God (2:9-10).

- He directed the women to receive instruction with receptivity and submissiveness to sound doctrine (2:11-15).

The character and conduct of church leaders. The church leadership consisted of two groups: overseers (sometimes also translated "elders") and deacons. Paul delineated both the character and lifestyle qualifications necessary for those who filled each of these offices (3:1-13). Later he returned to the subject of elders, exhorting the Ephesians and Timothy to honor those elders or pastors who fulfilled their responsibilities and to rebuke publicly those who did not (5:17-20).

The necessity of exposing and refuting false doctrine. The primary difficulty within the Ephesian church was the disruption caused by the false teachers. This particular heresy was characterized by reliance on extrabiblical teaching and empty speculations and was filled with a pervasive legalism (1:4,6-11; 4:1-3). These demonically inspired teachings led to a lifestyle characterized by an impure, seared conscience filled with conceit, envy, argumentativeness, and greed (4:1-3; 6:4-10). These teachers had departed from sound teaching (1:5-6).

Lifestyle guidelines for various groups of believers within the church. Paul stated that both elders and deacons must have lives of godliness and maturity, coupled with a good reputation among nonbelievers (3:1-13; 5:17-20). He described appropriate lifestyles for widows and gave Timothy instructions for providing for their care (5:3-16). He gave an encouraging word to slaves describing how they as believers should relate to their masters (6:1-2). Finally, Paul had a special word for those with material wealth in this bustling commercial city (6:17-19).

Paul's goal was to encourage Timothy to refute the false teachers (1:3-11; 6:3-10) and to defend against further attacks through teaching sound doctrine (4:6,13-16; 6:2b,17-18), encouraging righteous living by both leaders (3:1-13; 5:17-25; 6:11-16) and laypeople (5:1-6; 6:1-2,17-19), and setting proper church procedures in place (2:1-15; 3:1-13).

Pronunciation Guide			
Apollos	*uh PAHL uhs*	Hymenaeus	*high meh NEE uhs*
Aquila	*AK wih luh*	Macedonia	*mass uh DOH nih uh*
Ephesus	*EF uh suhs*		

Outline

I. SALUTATION (1:1-2)

II. DIRECTIVES CONCERNING SOUND DOCTRINE (1:3-20)
   A. Description of the False Doctrine and Its Teachers (1:3-11)
   B. Paul as an Example of Transformation through Sound Doctrine (1:12-17)
   C. Timothy's Responsibility to Teach Sound Doctrine (1:18-20)

III. DIRECTIVES CONCERNING THE WORSHIP ASSEMBLY (2:1-15)
   A. How Prayer Should Be Offered in the Worship Assembly (2:1-7)
   B. How the Men Should Pray in the Worship Assembly (2:8)
   C. How the Women Should Be Attired in the Worship Assembly (2:9-10)
   D. How the Women Should Receive Instruction in the Worship Assembly (2:11-15)

IV. DIRECTIVES CONCERNING CHURCH LEADERS (3:1-16)
   A. The Character and Conduct of Leaders or Overseers (3:1-7)

B. The Character and Conduct of Deacons (3:8-13)

C. The Importance of Paul's Directives to the Church (3:14-16)

V. DIRECTIVES CONCERNING FALSE TEACHERS (4:1-16)

  A. The Holy Spirit's Revelation Concerning False Teachers (4:1-5)

  B. Timothy's Response to False Teachers (4:6-10)

  C. Paul's Encouragement for More Effective Ministry (4:11-16)

VI. DIRECTIVES CONCERNING VARIOUS CHURCH MEMBERS (5:1–6:10)

  A. Guidelines for Admonishing Older and Younger Church Members (5:1-2)

B. Guidelines for Caring for Widows (5:3-16)

C. Guidelines for Support, Discipline, and Selection of Pastors (5:17-25)

D. Guidelines Concerning Slaves (6:1-2a)

E. Guidelines Concerning Exposure of False Teachers in Their Greediness (6:2b-10)

VII. DIRECTIVES CONCERNING THOSE WHO SERVE CHRIST (6:11-21)

  A. Exhortation for Timothy to Pursue a Godly Lifestyle (6:11-16)

  B. Exhortation for the Wealthy to Handle Their Wealth Responsibly (6:17-19)

  C. Exhortation for Timothy to Guard Sound Doctrine (6:20-21)

Exposition of the Text

SALUTATION (1:1-2)

1:1 Paul identified himself as the writer of this letter and **an apostle** called by God, a designation that would hardly be necessary if he intended only his spiritual son Timothy to read the letter. This reference to his apostolic office clarified his intention that the letter be read to the congregation, since it would underscore the authority he was delegating to Timothy to carry out the changes mandated in his letter.

1:2 Paul's reference to Timothy is warm and personal, **my true child in the faith**. (See "Recipients" in Introduction.) Although Paul discipled various younger men, such as Silas and Titus, Timothy seems to have held a unique place in his heart (Php 2:20-22).

First-century letters typically began with the identification of the writer and the recipient, followed by a greeting. Paul blessed Timothy (and those in the church who would hear his letter read aloud) with God's **grace, mercy, and peace**.

DIRECTIVES CONCERNING SOUND DOCTRINE (1:3-20)

Description of the False Doctrine and Its Teachers (1:3-11)

1:3-4 The events mentioned in 1 Timothy occurred after Paul was released from the Roman imprisonment (Ac 26:16-31; cp. introduction). During the period from AD 62 to 67 Paul traveled freely, and at some point he and Timothy came to Ephesus. There he left his beloved disciple as his apostolic representative and sailed for Macedonia in Greece. The letter opened with a clear statement of one aspect of Timothy's mission: He was to stop the false teachers who were causing dissension and strife and turning believers away from **God's plan, which operates by faith**. Sound teaching is central both in establishing a personal relationship with God through Jesus Christ (Eph 2:8-9) and in continuing the daily walk of sanctification with Him (1 Th 4:1-3).

The content of this **other doctrine** seemed to have been a mixture of pagan speculations and Jewish legalism, which Paul described as **myths** (Gk. *muthois*, "tale, story, myth, legend, or fable") **and endless genealogies** (Gk. *genealogiais*), probably similar to the heresy in Crete, which Paul termed "Jewish myths" (Ti 1:14). Although proponents of non-Pauline authorship have said these terms indicate that the book was written in the second century, when Gnosticism was in full flower, these particular Greek terms are not used to describe Gnostic systems. The letter suggests that the heresy had Jewish roots and was bolstered by the fact that these individuals desired to be "teachers of the law" (1 Tm 1:7). In addition, a sizable body of extrabiblical literature, such as the *Book of Jubilees*, providing elaborate descriptions of the lives of biblical characters, existed at the time.

1:5 Timothy confronted the false teachers to bring the church back to a core value: love for one another—love with its source in **a pure heart, a good conscience, and a sincere faith**. A "pure heart" reflects the words of David (Pss 24:4; 51:10) or Jesus (Mt 5:8), describing a person who has been cleansed from sin. CONSCIENCE (Gk. *suneidēseōs*, "self-judgment") refers to an innate, God-given ability to distinguish between right and wrong (Rm 2:14-15). It functions both to encourage a person to make right choices and later to approve or disapprove those choices. Here Paul envisioned those whose consciences had been impregnated with biblical values and who had consequently acted in conformity

with them (see 2 Co 1:12; 1 Tm 1:19; 3:9). Although "faith" is an absolute concept—one either has it or does not—Paul added the term "sincere" to place it in contrast to what was peddled by the false teachers.

1:6-7 Paul charged that the false teachers **deviated** from "a pure heart, a good conscience, and a sincere faith." Elsewhere the false teachers were characterized as being deceived, influenced by demonic teachings, being liars, and having seared consciences (4:1-2). Like Hymenaeus and Alexander, their faith had been shipwrecked (1:20). Here Paul highlighted their love of **fruitless discussion.** FRUITLESS DISCUSSION (Gk. *mataiologian*, "vain or useless talk, idle chatter, empty argument," 6:20; also 2 Tm 2:16). These discussions from the outside seem to have substance but in reality are vain and empty, a reference to the EMPTY SPECULATIONS (Gk. *ekzētēseis*, "senseless babble") mentioned earlier in verse 4. These individuals wanted to be **teachers of the law** (see note on 1 Tm 1:3-4) but **they don't understand what they are saying**.

1:8-11 Paul turned his attention from the false teachers to the law itself. He clarified the fact **that the law is good** when used **legitimately**. Its legitimate use pointed out sin in the lives of those who were **lawless and rebellious** (vv. 9-10). He then listed a number of sinful acts and made his case more personal by focusing on the individuals who practiced these sins rather than simply the sins themselves (e.g., "murderer" rather than "murders"). An interesting parallel exists between several of the terms and the Ten Commandments: **those who kill their fathers and mothers** (fifth commandment); **murderers** (sixth commandment); **the sexually immoral and homosexuals** (seventh commandment); **kidnappers** (eighth commandment; lit., "slave traders"); **liars** and **perjurers** (ninth commandment). Rather than necessarily pointing out specific sins in the false teachers' lives, Paul seemed to be emphasizing the fact that God gave the law to reveal human sinfulness rather than to be a source for their myths and endless genealogies (v. 4) as well as for legalistic practices (4:3).

Paul summarized his list of sinful practices with the phrase **and for whatever else is contrary to the sound teaching**. SOUND (Gk. *hugiainousē*, "healthy") is a medical term, used here metaphorically. In the Pastoral Epistles the apostle focused on the "healthiness" of the teaching found in the "glorious gospel," which he taught, in contrast to the "sick interest" of the false teachers in their "disputes over words" (6:4), teachings that "will spread like gangrene" (2 Tm 2:17).

Paul as an Example of Transformation through Sound Doctrine (1:12-17)

Paul ended the preceding sentence with the thought that God Himself entrusted to him the ministry of taking "the glorious gospel" to the world and launched into a personal testimony expressing his unending gratitude that he—the worst of sinners—was given the gift of salvation and entrusted with this privilege (1 Tm 1:11).

1:12-14 Paul often burst into thanksgiving at the thought of what God had done for him (Rm 6:17; 7:25; 1 Co 15:57; 2 Co 2:14; 8:16; 9:15), and here he also transitioned into a personal testimony. He first thanked Christ, **who has strengthened** him. The verb tense here does not point to a continual strengthening to live the Christian life but rather to Christ's initial empowering, calling, and equipping with spiritual gifts for ministry. God chose Paul because He considered him **faithful** (Gk. *piston*, "trustworthy"), which forms a play on words with "entrusted" (Gk. *episteuthēn*) in verse 11. God demon-

strated His trust in Paul by **appointing** him to the ministry even though he was living a sinful lifestyle at the time God called him: **a blasphemer, a persecutor, and an arrogant man** (v. 13).

The apostle went on to say that he **received mercy** from God, the Great Initiator (v. 13; cp. Eph 1:4), not because he deserved it; rather God chose to use him as an example of a person redeemed by His grace (1 Tm 1:16). At the time he received God's mercy, His **grace** also **overflowed** to him, as did **the faith and love** whose source is Christ Jesus (v. 14).

1:15-16 As Paul built his case for God's great grace, he quoted a formulaic expression found only in the Pastoral Epistles: **This saying is trustworthy** (also used in 3:1; 4:9; 2 Tm 2:11; Ti 3:8). Scholars are divided on whether Paul was quoting traditional material or whether he was the originator of the statement. Certainly Paul forcefully stated a foundational fact of the gospel: **Christ Jesus came into the world to save sinners** (cp. Rm 5:8). Paul was awestruck with the greatness of God's mercy and grace, as he declared that he was **the worst of them**, a debatable statement in the absolute sense, since cruel tyrants who have killed their millions have appeared throughout history. Underlying Paul's statement, however, was the fact that he had a healthy sense of his own sinfulness in the presence of a holy God. God extended His mercy to Paul **that He might demonstrate** in him **the utmost patience as an example to those who would believe in Him for eternal life**, and Paul said, in effect, "If God could save me—the very worst of sinners—then there is hope for every other person on earth."

1:17 Paul concluded his testimony with a doxology in which he identified God with a fourfold description: **the King eternal** (lit., "the King of the ages"); **immortal, invisible** (an Old Testament description that made its way into the church; cp. Rm 1:20; Col 1:15); and **the only God** (a strong monotheistic statement in keeping with Old Testament teaching).

Timothy's Responsibility to Teach Sound Doctrine (1:18-20)

1:18-19a With a term of endearment, **my child**, Paul returned to his initial exhortation: Timothy must command the false teachers to stop spreading their heresy (v. 3). Fulfilling **this instruction** (Gk. *paraggelian*, "charge, command, advice"; also v. 5) was **in keeping with the prophecies previously made** about him. In the New Testament, prophecy involved reporting something that God brought to mind spontaneously for the purpose of edification, comfort, and exhortation (1 Co 14:3). This prophetic insight may have come at various times when Timothy was younger, or it may have been given to him at the time Paul singled out later in the letter (1 Tm 4:14; see 2 Ti 1:6) as some spiritual gift was imparted to Timothy when the elders laid their hands on him (1 Tm 4:14), making God's calling on his life for ministry clear through prophetic insight. In 2 Timothy 1:6, a much warmer personal context, Paul focused on the fact that he was among those laying hands on him (2 Tm 1:6). Clearly Paul was referring back in Timothy's life to a landmark event that he would immediately remember and from which he would draw strength, encouragement, and renewed focus so that he could **strongly engage in battle** against the false teachers. He realized that Timothy would be unable to persevere apart from a total reliance on the power of the Holy Spirit in his life. In addition, he encouraged him to hold onto his **faith and a good conscience** (see 1 Tm 1:4-5).

1:19b-20 As an illustration of what can happen when a person rejects **these** (i.e.,

faith and a good conscience), he cited **Hymenaeus and Alexander**. Hymenaeus was mentioned one other time by Paul (2 Tm 2:17). Two Alexanders are mentioned in connection with Ephesus: one early in Paul's ministry (Ac 19:33-34) and another a coppersmith about whom Paul later warned Timothy (2 Tm 4:14-15). These men, probably well-known elders, had **suffered the shipwreck of their faith**. Paul stated that he had **delivered them to Satan**. The parallel passage in 1 Corinthians 5:5 added the statement "for the destruction of the flesh," considered by some commentators as a reference to physical punishment but not necessarily so. Instead, the expression "delivered . . . to Satan" most likely meant that Paul had placed the men back in the world where Satan held sway. In other words, they had been excommunicated from the church and were no longer under its covering and protection (see 1 Tm 5:19-20).

The apostle's purpose in turning them over to Satan was redemptive: **so that they may be taught not to blaspheme.** The verb "blaspheme" seems to be used in the same sense that it was in 1 Timothy 6:4 where the noun form is translated "slanders" and the context was once more the false teachers. These men had consciously rejected God's grace in favor of quarrelling and disputation, and Paul sought to place them in an environment where they would learn to do this no longer.

DIRECTIVES CONCERNING THE WORSHIP ASSEMBLY (2:1-15)

After urging Timothy to stop the false teachers from spreading their heresy, Paul turned to what was taking place in the worship assembly. The word "then" (Gk. *oun*, lit., "therefore") tied this section to the preceding one (1:3-20) and showed that the problems Paul was about to discuss were a consequence of the situation in chapter 1 (i.e., the presence of the heretics). Their influence had gone far beyond mere intellectual discussions about specialized, extrabiblical knowledge. Their teachings had practical ramifications, and the apostle wanted to bring correction in four specific areas:

- the significance and the content of public prayers,

- the need for men to pray with cleansed consciences,

- appropriate attire for the women, and

- the importance of women being submissive to the teaching of God's word in the assembly.

How Prayer Should Be Offered in the Worship Assembly (2:1-7)

2:1 At the top of Paul's list was the matter of prayer in the worship assembly. The issue here was not a lack of prayer in the assembly (see 1:8); rather he addressed the scope of that prayer. He insisted that prayer should **be made for everyone** (v. 1), including "all those who are in authority" (v. 2), since God wanted "everyone to be saved" (v. 4) and gave His Son Jesus as "a ransom for all" (v. 6). This stood in direct contrast to the focus of the Ephesian heretics. Like cult leaders down through the ages, they taught a gospel whose deepest truths were available only to their disciples.

Paul began by directing the believers to offer PETITIONS (Gk. *deēseis*, "requests, specific expressions of need"; Php 4:6), PRAYERS (Gk. *proseuchas*, the most general term for "prayer"; Php 4:6), INTERCESSIONS (Gk., *enteuxeis*, "petitions," possibly with a focus on prayer for others; Php 4:5), and THANKSGIVINGS (Gk. *eucharistias*, "thankfulness"; Php 4:6). His purpose in using varied terms for prayer was not

particularly to distinguish among different sorts of prayer. Rather he used a common Semitic literary device of grouping synonyms together to emphasize that prayer, whatever sort it may be, is important "for everyone."

2:2 Prayers should be offered, in particular, **for kings and all those who are in authority** so that believers may live **a tranquil and quiet life in all godliness and dignity**. The point was not to be free from all trials and stress, which are inevitable (2 Tm 3:12). The statement needs to be seen against the backdrop of the false teachers' actions. Not only were they bringing dissension within the church; but they also were causing the church and the gospel message to be viewed unfavorably by the world (see 1 Tm 3:7; 5:14; 6:1; Ti 2:5,8; 3:1-3). In contrast, Paul was asking the believers to pray for these governmental authorities so that there would be a favorable social climate in which they could live godly lives and the gospel message could spread rapidly. A similar situation had existed earlier in Thessalonica, and there Paul urged the believers to live "a QUIET (Gk. *hēsuchion*, "peaceful," which in this verse and its nominal form in 1 Tm 2:11 clearly cannot mean "silent," as it does in Lk 14:4 and Ac 11:18; 21:14, but rather suggests a "gentle demeanor") life . . . so that you may walk properly in the presence of outsiders" (1 Th 4:11-12).

2:3-4 The apostle returned to prayer for all people and affirmed that such prayer **is good, and it pleases God our Savior**. The expression "God our Savior" (see 1:1) emphasizes the fact that God is the source of salvation. He **wants** (Gk. *thelei*, "desires") **everyone to be saved**, a statement the Apostle John reinforced when he wrote that Jesus Christ is the atoning sacrifice for our sins, "and not only for ours, but also for those of the whole world" (1 Jn 2:2; see Jn 3:16; Ac 17:30; Heb 2:9).

However, not everyone will be saved, since the element of personal faith in Jesus Christ is necessary (see Jn 3:16; 1 Tm 4:10). God also wants everyone **to come to the knowledge of the truth**, emphasizing the objective reception of the facts of the gospel.

2:5-6 Paul used the word **for** to offer evidence that God desired all to come to salvation in the form of three theological affirmations, possibly taken from a creedal statement of the day.

- He stated that **there is one God**, a foundational belief in both the Old and New Testaments (v. 5; e.g., Dt 6:4; 1 Co 8:4).

- He said that there is **one mediator between God and man, a man, Christ Jesus**. Jesus Christ incarnate is both fully God and perfectly human. In His role as "mediator," or intermediary, He has brought reconciliation between a holy God and sinful human beings through His atoning death on the cross (1 Tm 2:5; 2 Co 5:18-19; 1 Jn 2:2).

- Paul affirmed that Jesus **gave Himself—a ransom for all** (1 Tm 2:6; Mk 10:45; Mt 20:28). RANSOM (Gk. *antilutron*) referred to something given in place of the payment—the death penalty, in this case—that Jesus made when He died on the cross (Rm 5:8) FOR (Gk. *huper*, "on behalf of") all mankind as the substitute. As a result, all who receive Him are released from judgment (Rm 3:25-26), sin (Eph 1:7) and death (Rm 8:2), and they are adopted into God's family (Rm 8:15,23; Gl 4:5; Eph 1:5). The final phrase, **a testimony at the proper time**, referred to the whole of verses 5 and 6. In the history of God's redemptive plan, the time had arrived for God's mercy to be shown to all peo-

ple. Jesus' sacrificial death for all stood as a witness to the church in Ephesus that it is essential to pray for all people.

2:7 Paul concluded this section with a word of personal testimony. He said that **for this**—to bear witness to Christ's work on the cross—he **was appointed a herald, an apostle . . . and a teacher of the Gentiles**. Paul was called to bring the gospel to all, both Jews and Gentiles, a fact that he mentions here to underscore the universal availability of salvation. And, as if to place an exclamation point, he added, **I am telling the truth, I am not lying**.

How the Men Should Pray in the Worship Assembly (2:8)

2:8 Now that he had delineated the proper scope of prayer, Paul moved on to conduct in the worship assembly, especially prayer. He said that **I want the men . . . to pray, lifting up holy hands, without anger or argument**. Two clarifications are in order. First, prayer is not limited to men, since in 1 Corinthians 11:5 women received instruction on praying and prophesying. Second, Paul's main focus was not on the physical posture of prayer, although for believers to pray with uplifted hands was not uncommon. This Jewish custom (1 Kg 8:22; Pss 28:2; 63:4; 141:2; 143:6; Lm 3:41) was also practiced by Christians. Instead, the issue in the Ephesian church concerned the heart attitude of the men as they prayed.

The word "holy" carries here the idea of "devout" or "pleasing to God." "Holy hands" serves as a figure of speech representing a cleansed conscience. Cleansing was definitely needed, since Paul highlighted the sins of "anger" and "argument," the fruit of a divisive, argumentative spirit likely related to the false teachers' influence. This problem seems to have been pervasive, since elsewhere in the Pastoral Epistles Paul warned various groups against contentiousness: overseers/elders (3:3; Ti 1:7); deacons (1 Tm 3:8); Timothy (2 Tm 2:24); believers in general (Ti 3:2).

How the Women Should Be Attired in the Worship Assembly (2:9-10)

2:9 The apostle addressed what were appropriate attire and demeanor for women in the worship assembly. First, he made the more general exhortation that they should **dress themselves in modest clothing**. A play on words occurs with the words translated **DRESS** (Gk. *kosmein*, "adorn, trim, decorate, do credit to") and **MODEST** (Gk. *kosmiō*, "in good taste, respectable, honorable"). The inner attitude accompanying the women's clothing choices should be one of **DECENCY** (Gk. *aidous*, "modesty"), and **GOOD SENSE** (Gk. *sōphrosunēs*, "propriety, discretion, reasonableness, self-control"). The apostle then singled out some items of adornment the Ephesian women were wearing that he deemed especially inappropriate: **elaborate hairstyles, gold, pearls, or expensive apparel**. At least two reasons for these instructions are possible. Some of the women may have been dressing in a more sensual manner reminiscent of their former pagan lifestyles, or more probably some of the wealthier women, who could afford to own the accessories Paul named, were dressing in a way to reflect their superior social status. Although the Ephesian church included those who were wealthy (Eph 6:17-19), the majority would have been from the poorer classes, and such conspicuous dress could have been a hindrance to their sharing in the life of the church (see 1 Co 11:20-21 for a similar situation). The emphasis is not to prohibit tasteful accessories but to enjoin modesty and propriety.

2:10 Whichever reason is correct, Paul's main point is clear: A woman's inner adornment is the primary issue in God's eyes. Thus women should adorn themselves **with good works, as is proper for women who affirm that they worship God**. This exhortation to do "good works" appeared again in his instructions concerning widows as well as believers generally and those who were wealthy in particular (5:10,25; 6:18). Good deeds are ever to be the outflow of a believer's life and are, in fact, a form of "worship" (see Eph 2:10).

How the Women Should Receive Instruction in the Worship Assembly (2:11-15)

2:11 Paul's fourth area of concern was that the women receive instruction in the worship assembly with a submissive spirit. His directions are given to women generally, not to wives only, as some commentators have suggested. The nature of his remarks to men generally (not just husbands) concerning worship without anger (2:8) and to women generally (not just wives) concerning attire (2:9-10) affirms this premise. Also, his focus is on the worshiping community rather than family members as in Ephesians 5:22-33.

The apostle stated that **a woman should learn** (Gk. *manthanetō*, "find out"). The verb connotes learning through instruction (see 2 Tm 3:7,14; Jn 7:15; 1 Co 14:31) and underscored Paul's assumption that women both could and would learn. In light of the false teachers' ability to influence their hearers and lead some into heresy (2 Tm 3:6-7), he wanted to insure that the women were thoroughly grounded in sound doctrine.

Two phrases describe the manner in which they should learn: **in silence with full submission**. Earlier the adjectival form of the noun "silence" (Gk. *hēsuchia*) was translated "quiet" (1 Tm 2:2). Since it

Heart to Heart:
Modesty

Throughout Scripture, God gives instruction to His children about lifestyle and behavior. Both Old and New Testaments address modesty, and it continues to be an important virtue to develop and discuss.

The word **MODESTY** *(Lat., modus, lit. "measure") has come to mean a measure of propriety or humility, characterized by reserve and freedom from excess. In the Bible, modesty impacts inner life as well as outer appearance.* Lack of modesty in the Bible is often connected with immorality or sensuality. Therefore, the Christian woman should be modest in all ways.

Paul discussed modesty in several of his letters to first-century churches. He encouraged proper dress for believers and appropriate attire in the church (1 Co 12:23; 1 Tm 2:9). Modesty in appearance reflects godliness in character. A godly woman should develop the virtue of modesty and govern her life accordingly. While people are greatly influenced by culture, a woman's sense of modesty is to be regulated by her personal relationship with Jesus Christ and His example of purity.

would have been normal for the women to speak during the worship assembly (see 1 Co 11:5; 14:26), clearly the apostle was referring to a heart attitude and demeanor of "quietness" rather than to absolute silence. In the second phrase Paul directed the women to learn "with full submission" (Gk. *hupotagē*, "subjection, subordination"). Since the context is not family relationships, Paul is not likely urging the women to be submissive to their husbands, although this is taught elsewhere (see Eph 5:21-22; Col 3:18). In this context of learning in the worship assembly, the object of their submission is best understood either as the pastor ("overseer" in 1 Tm 3:2; "elders" in 5:17) or, more likely, as sound doctrine. In light of the presence of false teachers, a combination of the two is also possible: they were to submit themselves only to those pastors who taught sound doctrine.

2:12 Verses 11 and 12 are connected together in the Greek text with an untranslated "but." Paul's desire is to contrast the behavior pictured in verse 11 with that described in verse 12. He says, **I do not allow a woman to teach or to have authority over a man**. The present tense of "allow" (Gk. *epitrepō*, lit. "I am not permitting") emphasized his reference to a situation currently happening in the Ephesian church. This apostolic directive was more than his personal preference; rather it was what he expected the church to follow. Paul used his apostolic influence to affirm the divine mandate (cp. v. 8).

And what is not permitted? First, a woman is not to **TEACH** (Gk. *didaskein*, "admonish, direct") a man in the worship assembly. A teacher is one who effectively gives systematic explanation of truth to others with an emphasis on its application to daily living (see Mt 28:19-20). This term and its related noun are the most common New Testament words for teaching and are used almost exclusively for teaching in a public forum. Since the context is the worship assembly, the subject matter the women are forbidden to teach is likely Scripture.

Second, a woman is not to HAVE AUTHORITY over a man in the worship assembly. This term (Gk. *authentein*, "to have/exercise/usurp authority, control") appears only here in the New Testament and is rare in existing Greek literature. The limited linguistic data available indicates that either "to exercise authority" or "to usurp authority" is a possible meaning. Paul commonly used the more usual term for having authority (Gk. *exouziaō* or its noun form, *exousias*, Ti 3:1), and thus he probably chose *authentein* because he had a special nuance of meaning in mind.

The apostle completed discussion of the prohibition by reiterating that a woman is TO BE SILENT (Gk. *hēsuchia*), exactly the same phrase he used in verse 11, and in both verses the best translation is "in quietness." By using the identical phrase at the beginning and end of this prohibition to women, Paul emphasized his positive directive that women are to receive instruction with an inner attitude of quietness and submission to the truth of the gospel.

2:13 Paul offered two reasons why the women were to receive instruction quietly and submissively in the worship assembly rather than teaching or exercising authority over men. His reference is to the accounts of the creation and fall of the human race (vv. 13-14; cp. Gn 2–3). He does this by means of summary citation, a common rabbinic method of referring to the Old Testament. In other words, he used the summary statement in verse 13 to

refer to the entire section of Scripture dealing with the creation of man and woman (Gn 2:4-24), and the summary statement in verse 14 to refer to the account of the fall (Gn 3:1-15).

Paul was well-trained in the rabbinic exegetical methods of his day, and he used arguments by analogy (1 Tm 2:13-14). Verse 13 states that **Adam was created first, then Eve**. Paul implied here that Adam's chronological priority in creation carried some degree of authority, although the Genesis 2 account does not state this. According to the Old Testament concept of primogeniture, the firstborn son succeeded his father as the leader of the family and of family worship (Dt 21:15-17). In addition, he received a double portion of the inheritance (Dt 21:17). By appealing to Adam's chronological priority in creation, the apostle may have been asserting that Adam's status as the eldest carried the leadership suitable for a firstborn son. Paul's directive concerning women would stand whether or not he appealed to creation; but in using this argument, he demonstrated how his instruction harmonized with God's design in creation.

2:14 The apostle used the same line of argumentation when he said that **Adam was not deceived, but the woman was deceived and transgressed** (v. 14). Paul was not saying that women are more easily deceived than men or that they are less intelligent. Both Scripture and history demonstrate how easily both men and women have been deceived, especially with regard to doctrine. For example, numerous warnings against deception by false teachers are given to believers generally (Rm 16:17-18; Eph 5:6; Col 2:8; 2 Th 2:3). Rather, Paul was saying that a reversal of roles occurred in Genesis 3. Through deception the serpent tempted Eve to eat the forbidden fruit. After eating, she offered the fruit to Adam and he succumbed, and thus they both fell into sin (Gn 3:7). Scripture makes clear that God held Adam ultimately responsible for their fall into sin (Rm 5:12). However, the Lord asked Adam and Eve to explain their actions (Gn 3:11-13). He later told Adam that the earth would be cursed because he listened to (i.e., obeyed) his wife's voice. Paul's analogy, then, is that just as a reversal in roles caused such problems in the beginning of history, so such a reversal of roles and the resulting problems should be avoided in the Ephesian church.

2:15 A concluding statement is provided concerning the results of women fulfilling their God-given roles: **She will be saved through childbearing**. Although multiple interpretations have been suggested for this notoriously difficult verse, it is best understood as affirming that women will receive salvation, with a focus on eschatological (future) reward, through faithfulness to their proper role, exemplified here in motherhood.

In the New Testament the verb SAVED (Gk. *sōzō*) may refer to physical deliverance (Mt 14:30; Ac 27:20), to physical healing (Mk 5:34; Ac 4:9-10), to deliverance from demonization (Lk 8:36), and, most commonly, to spiritual salvation. Paul sometimes viewed salvation as a whole, and at other times he focused on its component parts. Justification begins the moment a person receives Christ as personal Savior (Eph 2:8) and is completed in the believer's final glorification (Rm 5:9-10). Between justification and glorification lies the believer's daily walk with Christ, called sanctification. This walk begins at the moment a person commits her life to Christ and continues throughout a lifetime of Spirit-empowered, holy living (Rm 6:19; Php 2:12-13; Col 1:10). The believer will be presented to God in complete purity (Eph 5:26-27; 1 Th 3:13; 5:23). Paul underscored his focus on the future aspects of salvation through his

use of the future tense: A holy and obedient lifestyle will lead to future rewards when salvation is consummated in heaven (1 Tm 2:15; Col 1:22-23; 1 Th 5:8-9).

Paul continued by saying that a woman will be saved "through" (Gk. *dia*) childbearing. This preposition may be understood best as describing a circumstance accompanying salvation. **Childbearing** is one of the good works that will typically be part of a godly woman's life. A literal use of the word CHILDBEARING (Gk. *teknogonias*) seems unlikely here, since not all women bear children. Also, *teknogonias* may refer not only to childbearing but also to child-rearing. The term most probably serves as a figure of speech (a synecdoche, in which a part represents the whole); i.e., "childbearing" represents the typical range of activities in a woman's life. This was an apt illustration in Paul's day, since a limited life span meant that most of a woman's adult years would be focused on marriage and motherhood.

Verse 15 is actually a conditional sentence in which the condition is stated at the end: "if she CONTINUES (Gk. *meinōsin*, "continue, remain," carrying the idea of not leaving the sphere in which she finds herself) in faith, love, and holiness, with good sense." The apostle then listed four qualities that must characterize a woman's lifestyle in order for her to receive future, heavenly rewards. **Faith** refers to personal faith in Christ (Eph 1:15; 2:8) that results in good works (Eph 2:10; 1 Th 1:3). **Love** reaches out to serve others (Eph 5:2; Php 1:15-16). **Holiness** relates to the daily process of sanctification, of becoming conformed to the image of Jesus Christ (Rm 8:29). The final word, GOOD SENSE (Gk. *sōphrosunēs*, "reasonableness, self-control, decency, modesty"), is best translated "discretion." Paul also used the word, which includes the ideas of moderation, good judgment, and self-control, in verse 9. In summary, Paul concluded verses 11-15 by encouraging women to fulfill their proper role in life, a concept he summed up by the term "childbearing," a reference to the general scope of activities in which women are involved. These activities should be accompanied by the qualities of faith, love, and propriety, with discretion. The result of such a lifestyle will be future rewards in heaven (2 Co 5:10).

DIRECTIVES CONCERNING CHURCH LEADERS (3:1-16)

The Character and Conduct of Leaders or Overseers (3:1-7)

Paul turned to the subject of church leaders: overseers and deacons. In both cases he discussed the character and conduct qualifying individuals for these roles. The situation in Ephesus was unlike that in Crete, where Titus was to appoint overseers (Ti 1:5). The church in Ephesus was well-established and already had elders. Paul's concern was rather with the character and lifestyle of the elders, which needed to be significantly different from that of the false teachers.

3:1 He introduced this new topic with the second **trustworthy** saying (see 1:15): **If anyone aspires to be an overseer, he desires a noble work**. The term OVER-SEER (Gk. *episkopēs*, Ac 20:28; Ti 1:7) and the term "elder" (*presbuteros*, Ac 20:17; 1 Tm 5:17, 19; Ti 1:5) are used interchangeably by Paul. Their duties included teaching, preaching, and generally giving oversight to the church (1 Tm 3:1-7; 5:17). This "noble work" (lit. "good work") involved protecting and promoting the truth of the gospel.

3:2-3 The list of qualifications that followed underscored the connection between the office itself and the qualifications. The person serving in this position **must be**

above reproach, a more general term seemingly summarizing the 11 qualities that follow. The word is used only here and in reference to widows (5:7) and to Timothy himself (6:14), although a similar word, "blameless," is used for deacons in verse 10. In both cases, the emphasis is on outward, observable behavior.

The overseer is to be THE HUS-BAND OF ONE WIFE (Gk. *mias gunaikos andra*, lit. "a one-woman man"), an expression that Paul repeated in a similar list in his letter to Titus (Ti 1:6). Various interpretations have been offered. That the elder should be married rather than single is unlikely since Paul highly valued his own celibacy (1 Co 7:7-8,17). Likewise, it probably is not merely a prohibition of polygamy, which was a rare occurrence, and not necessarily a prohibition of second marriages, since Paul used the expression "wife of one husband" to refer to older widows wishing to be supported by the church, yet encouraged the younger ones to remarry (5:9,14). The most likely interpretation is that the elder should be faithful to his wife, what could be paraphrased as a "one-woman sort of man." This interpretation honors the emphasis given to the word "one" in the original language's grammatical structure and affirms the divinely mandated permanence of the marital union. Further, immorality was a serious problem, and the overseers were admonished to be examples of marital faithfulness.

Paul presupposed that the elders in Ephesus were both male and married, as would be expected in the patriarchal culture of the Greco-Roman world. The New Testament does not have an example of a woman elder, apart from the rather ambiguous reference in 2 John 1 to "the elect lady and her children."

The apostle continued with his list of positive qualities that overseers should possess. SELF-CONTROLLED (Gk.

nēphalion) often means "temperate," but since abuse of alcohol was specifically mentioned later, the word probably has its broader meaning of "clear-headed, self-controlled." He must also be SENSIBLE (Gk. *sōphrona*, "self-controlled, thoughtful") and RESPECTABLE (Gk. *kosmion*, "well-ordered, honorable," picturing an individual whose well-ordered life reflects a well-ordered mind.) He is to be HOSPITABLE (Gk. *philozenon*, lit. "a lover of strangers"). In contrast to the false teachers, he must be **an able teacher**, which includes the ability both to teach the truth and to refute error, and **not addicted to wine**. The next three qualities seem to go together, since they depict behavior exactly opposite that of the false teachers, whom Paul elsewhere described as given to quarreling and constant disagreements (6:3-5) and greed (6:5,10). Thus an overseer must "not" be a BULLY (Gk. *plēktēn*, "combative, one who strikes with his fists"), "but gentle, not quarrelsome, not GREEDY" (Gk. *aphilarguron*, lit., "not a lover of silver").

3:4-5 An overseer should also be **one who manages his own household competently**. The term MANAGES (Gk. *proistamenon*, "rule, is concerned about") pictures someone who leads, governs, protects, and cares for those in his household, including his children, who should be UNDER CONTROL (Gk. *hupotagē*, "subjection"; cp. 3:12; Ti 1:6). This phrase is much better translated "having submissive children." The manner in which the overseer is to lead, protect, and care for those in his household is **with all dignity**. The overseer who abuses his wife or children is much more likely to be abusive towards his church members. As if to lend an exclamation point to his argument, Paul asked a rhetorical question: If a person **does not know how to manage his own**

household, how will he take care of God's church? The answer, of course, is that he cannot.

3:6-7 Two qualifications remain. First, an overseer should **not be a new convert**. This is positively stated in 5:22 where the role of elder is clearly reserved for those who are more mature. Too rapid a promotion to leadership might place the new convert in the path of temptation, especially to become CONCEITED (Gk. *tuphōtheis*, "puffed up, deluded, inflated with pride"). Such conceit could eventually cause him to **fall into the condemnation of the Devil**. He might experience the same judgment that the Devil himself experienced when, in his pride, he rose up against God. Second, the overseer **must have a good reputation among outsiders**, meaning the unbelievers in Ephesus. The good reputation of both the church as a whole and the individuals within it formed a constant refrain in Paul's writings (e.g., 2:2; 6:1; Ti 2:5,8,10). Failure to have a good standing would open the possibility that the overseer might **fall into disgrace and the Devil's trap**. Paul's picture is of a personal Devil setting a snare for the elder who keeps running God's stop signs in his life, taking down one by one the bricks of his reputation. The result will be disgrace both to him personally and to the church as a whole.

The Character and Conduct of Deacons (3:8-13)

Paul next listed a number of qualifications for DEACONS (an anglicized form of Gk. *diakonous*, "helpers") more commonly translated "servant" in the New Testament. It can refer to either a man or woman, depending on the context. For example, Phoebe is called a servant (Rm 16:1), as are Timothy (1 Tm 4:6) and Paul himself (Eph 3:7). The term also referred to an official group of people in the church (Php 1:1). In this case the translation "deacon" is best. While generally understood to be a position more focused on service, this fact is not explicitly stated in this passage. Although the word "deacon" is not used in Acts 6:1-6, these men handling the food distribution in the Jerusalem church are commonly understood to be the first appointed deacons.

3:8-9 Paul began listing qualifications for deacons with a more general term, WORTHY OF RESPECT (Gk. *semnous*, also "noble, honorable, dignified"), and then moved into more specific items. Deacons should not be HYPOCRITICAL (Gk. *dilogous*, lit. "double-tongued, insincere"), as were the false teachers (4:2). Like the overseers (2:3), they were warned about **not drinking a lot of wine**, or being **greedy for money**. On a more positive note, the deacons should be **holding the mystery of the faith**, an expression Paul used several times in reference to the gospel. The basic meaning of MYSTERY (Gk. *mustērion*) in Pauline literature is not something secret but rather something that was once hidden and has now been revealed (1 Co 2:7; 4:1; Eph 3:3-9). Paul had already brought up the importance of having **a clear conscience** (see 1 Tm 1:5). Here he again spoke of a life lived in congruence with the truth of the gospel where the conscience imbued with the truth of God's word would have no reason to bring inner condemnation—exactly the opposite of the false teachers' lifestyle.

3:10 Deacons are to **be tested first** and those who **prove blameless** are allowed to **serve as deacons**. TEST (Gk. *dokimazesthōsan*, "examine") means here "testing to see whether something is genuine or true." The purpose of the test is to discover those who are BLAMELESS (Gk. *anegklētoi*, "irreproachable"), a term used of pastors

(Ti 1:6-7) and a synonym to the word translated "above reproach" (1 Tm 3:2). This requirement is similar to the one given Timothy regarding pastors (5:22,24). Time should be provided so that the fruit of their lives, whether sin or good works, may become apparent. In the case of deacons, whether Paul was sanctioning a formal examination process, although possible, cannot be determined. Certainly a process of observing their lifestyle, orthodoxy, perseverance, and faithfulness in various situations, their growth in holiness and intimacy with the Lord, and their development in using their spiritual gifts is evident.

3:11 The individuals Paul discussed in verses 8-10 are generally assumed to be men, since verse 12 speaks of their family situations. Verse 11, however, is directed specifically to women. But who are these women? Some commentators have said that they are the **wives** (Gk. *gunaikas*, "women, wives") of the male deacons, but this conclusion is not necessarily so. Two reasons support the position that they were female deacons. First, the term "likewise" previously introduces a separate group of people, the deacons (v. 8). Second, the qualifications are very similar to those of the male deacons. The women are to be **worthy of respect**, the same word used to refer to the male deacons (v. 9). They are not to be SLANDERERS (Gk. *diabolous*), those who spread false and malicious reports about another person. A male elder or pastor must not be double-tongued, a similar sin (v. 8). He must also be SELF-CONTROLLED (Gk. *nēphalious*, "temperate, clear-headed," the term used earlier to describe overseers and male deacons, vv. 2,8). Finally, the women are to be **faithful in everything**. If these women are deaconesses, their ministry would certainly have been one of service and directed especially to women (Ti 2:3-5).

3:12-13 Paul returned to the subject of the male deacons and said that they are to **be husbands of one wife**. This expression is exactly the same used regarding the overseers (see v. 2). Also like the overseers, they are responsible for **managing their children and their own households competently** (see v. 4).

Qualifications of Church Leaders	
Overseer/ Pastor (1 Tm 3:1-7)	**Deacon (1 Tm 3:8-13)**
• Above reproach	• Worthy of respect
• The husband of one wife	• Not hypocritical
• Self-controlled	• Not drinking a lot of wine
• Sensible	• Not greedy for money
• Respectable	• Hold the mystery of the faith with a clear conscience
• Hospitable	• Blameless
• An able teacher	• Wife is worthy of respect
• Not addicted to wine	• Wife is not slanderers
• Not a bully	• Wife is self-controlled
• Gentle	• Wife is faithful in everything
• Not quarrelsome	• Husband of one wife
• Not greedy	• Manages children and household competently
• Manages household well	• Good standing in society
• Controls children	• Great boldness in the faith
• Not a new convert	
• Good reputation	

The Importance of Paul's Directives to the Church (3:14-16)

3:14-15 Paul paused for a moment to clarify his purpose in writing this letter to Timothy. He anticipated that his circumstances might change, although he was **hoping to come** to Ephesus soon. If he **should be delayed**, however, he was writing so that Timothy—and the church at Ephesus who would hear this letter read—would know how **to act in God's household**. By using the term "household" Paul emphasized the fact that the church was much more than its weekly gathering of believers in the worship assembly. This metaphor uses the "family," in which God is the Father, believers are sisters and brothers, and the apostles are the household managers. The apostle then filled out the metaphor by describing the household of God—the church—in two ways. First, it **is the church of the living God** (see 1 Co 3:16-17; 2 Co 6:16; Eph 2:21), calling to mind the image of God's filling His sanctuary in the Old Testament with His presence (2 Ch 7:1-3). Second, the body of believers is **the pillar and foundation of the truth**: The church is the repository of the truth of the gospel message, a message that must be guarded against the heresies of the false teachers.

3:16 The mention of "the truth" (v. 15) of the gospel led Paul into a hymn of praise regarding **the mystery of godliness** similar to "mystery of the faith" (see v. 9). Both referred to the truth of the gospel message that was once hidden and had now been revealed. His subsequent statements together formed a hymn expressing several basic truths of the gospel.

In the original language the hymn has a tight, clear structure in which each line begins with a passive, past tense verb and is followed by a prepositional phrase, usually beginning with the same word (Gk. *en*, "in, by, among"). Jesus Christ is the implied subject of each verb. Some of the statements are quite obvious in their meanings (lines 1, 4, 5) and others are not quite as clear (lines 2, 3, 6). Although the hymn can be understood as composed either of couplets or of triplets, it works best to see it as two groups of three lines each: the first referring to Christ's ministry on earth and the second referring to the church's ministry in the world. The third and sixth lines form a sort of "refrain" with their focus on the gloriousness of Christ's ministry.

- Jesus Christ **was manifested in the flesh**, a transparent affirmation of His incarnation (Jn 1:14; Rm 1:3). Christ, who is God, also took on humanity at His birth and so became the perfect God-man, able to die as the perfect sacrifice for the sins of humanity.

- Jesus Christ was **justified in the Spirit**. Interpreters differ on whether the reference is to the Holy Spirit or to Christ's divine spirit. Although both are theologically possible, understanding the reference as to the Holy Spirit seems preferable. In this case the text is stating that the Holy Spirit vindicated Christ's claims to be God before men: at His baptism and commissioning to ministry (Mt 3:15-17; Lk 3:21-22); at His transfiguration (Mt 17:5; Lk 9:35; Mk 9:7); shortly before His death (Jn 12:27); at His resurrection (Rm 1:4); and at His ascension (Jn 16:7,10).

- Jesus Christ was **seen by angels**, which may refer to the activity of angels in Jesus' life while on earth or to their worship of Him as the risen Son of God. Elsewhere this verb, followed by a prepositional phrase, is used as a formula to describe Jesus' resurrection appearances to His disciples (Lk 24:23; 1 Co 15:5-8). Likely the focus is on the risen Lord as being seen by the heavenly hosts, either while still on earth or after His ascension in glory (Php 2:9-11).

- Jesus Christ was **preached among the Gentiles**, a clear reference to the activity of the believers, who after Pentecost took seriously Jesus' commission to take the gospel to all nations (Mt 28:18-20; Ac 1:8). GENTILES (Gk. *ethnesin*, "nations, Gentiles") is better translated "nations" here, since a distinction between Jews and Gentiles is nowhere in view.

- Jesus Christ was **believed on in the world**, focusing on the response to the gospel by those who heard it preached among the nations.

- Jesus Christ was **taken up in glory**, a verb used elsewhere in the New Testament to refer to Jesus' ascension to heaven (Lk 9:51; Ac 1:2,11,22). If the second three lines of the hymn refer primarily to the spread of the gospel in the world, then this line is best understood as focusing on the phrase "in glory" (Gk. *en doxē*), which may also be translated "gloriously, or accompanied by glory." The emphasis then is not so much on the event of the resurrection as on the gloriousness of this truth that the disciples preached throughout the nations.

Why did Paul choose to include this hymn here? First, these statements concerning Jesus' identity as the incarnate God-Man are likely to have some reference to the heresy of the false teachers, especially if their false teaching was tainted with the heresy of nearby Colossae, where the false teachers denied Christ's full humanity (e.g., Col 2:9-10). Second, Paul is about to return to an attack on the Ephesian false teachers and their doctrine, and this hymn holds up a clear statement of the truth of the gospel, providing a contrast to their perverted teaching.

DIRECTIVES CONCERNING FALSE TEACHERS (4:1-16)

The Holy Spirit's Revelation Concerning False Teachers (4:1-5)

4:1-2 Paul had spoken earlier about the false teachers whom Timothy was to silence in the Ephesian church (1:3-11,19-20). Here he referred to prophetic revelation given by the Holy **Spirit** that **in the latter times some will depart from the faith**. There was no indication as to whether this revelation was given in a public setting (see Ac 13:2 for an example) or to Paul personally. The "latter times" is a general reference to the period between Christ's incarnation and subsequent coming. The season of apostasy pictured here is not the final time when the antichrist will appear but is rather one of many seasons preceding his appearance. What the Spirit had revealed is that "some will depart from the faith." The word "some" referred to members of God's household (see 3:15) who were being deceived by the false teachers, not to the false teachers themselves, whom Paul referred to as "liars" (v. 2). "The faith," of course, referred to the truth of the gospel message.

The source of the false teaching in Ephesus was explicitly demonic, for the apostle said some believers had been **paying attention to deceitful spirits and the teachings of demons**. Paul considered

Satan and his demonic hoards a serious threat to the church's welfare. In his earlier letter to the Ephesian church, the apostle made it clear that both the church and individual believers were in a battle against demonic forces (Eph 6:11-20). Also he told the believers that demonic spirits were both the true reality and the power behind pagan idols (1 Co 10:20-21). Here he stated that the heretics' doctrine was not simply a bad philosophy; it was demonic in its source (see 2 Co 11:3,13-14). In fact, Paul said that the false teachers had been captured by the Devil to do his will (2 Tm 2:26). This diabolical teaching was being brought to the believers in Ephesus **through the hypocrisy of liars**. Not only were these teachers LIARS (Gk. *pseudologōn*, "ones who speak falsely"), they were also guilty of HYPOCRISY (Gk. *hupokrisei*, "pretense, outward show"). This fact underscored that the ascetic practices mentioned in the next sentence were a sham.

Furthermore, their "consciences are SEARED" (Gk. *kekaustēriasmenōn*, "sear, brand with a red-hot iron"), which may mean that their consciences had been cauterized, and thereby rendered inoperative. This idea would correspond to other passages in the New Testament where people's hearts were said to have been hardened (e.g., Eph 4:18). More likely, the reference is to the practice of branding criminals, runaway slaves, members of certain religious cults, and others, in which case the false teachers had been branded by Satan himself as a mark of his ownership (see 1 Tm 5:15, where some believers are said to have become followers of Satan). This interpretation supports the fact that Paul had previously identified the source of their doctrine as demonic (v. 1), plus the fact that the verb is passive, suggesting that the branding was done to them by another.

4:3-5 The apostle moved on to specify two aspects of their false teaching. First, **they forbid marriage and demand abstinence from foods**. The Colossian heresy had the same sort of restrictions (Col 2:16-23). Paul did not expand on the issue of marriage, although he certainly was in favor of the institution (see 5:14). Rather he refuted the dietary restrictions the teachers were imposing by saying that **God created** food and that true believers should receive it **with gratitude** because **everything** God had created was **good** (a truth stated repeatedly in Gn 1). Further, **nothing should be rejected if it is received with thanksgiving, since it is sanctified by the word of God and by prayer**. His point is not that prayer somehow consecrated food, but rather that believers should acknowledge the food to be the bounty of a loving and wise Creator. Also, Paul did not deal here with the issue of whether a believer's food choices may cause another to stumble in his faith (Rm 14:3; 1 Co 10:29-30); instead, he dealt with the teachers who were requiring certain food choices.

Timothy's Response to False Teachers (4:6-10)

4:6 Paul now turned from refuting the false teachers and their doctrine to exhorting his son in the faith, instructing Timothy to **point these things out**, i.e., the fallacies of the heretics, **to the brothers,** the Ephesian believers. His doing so would demonstrate that he was **a good servant of Christ Jesus**. Paul then elaborated on what being "a good servant" involved. NOURISHED (Gk. *entrephomenos*, "bring up, train") is a term associated with child-rearing and was intended to remind Timothy that he was still in the process of discipleship. The past tense translation needs to be considered in light of the present passive participle, which carries the idea that Timothy, having been nourished, would "keep on being trained" with the "words of the faith" (the gospel message), as well as with "the good teaching that you have followed." The nourishment suggested reading and inwardly digesting. The process had begun and was to continue. The latter phrase may be another reference to the content of the gospel, or it may refer to the proper use of Scripture, a theme on which Paul expounded (2 Tm 3:14-16). In either case, the two phrases together highlighted Timothy's long association with the Scriptures and with the truth of the gospel (2 Tm 1:5; 3:14-17).

4:7-8 Paul urged Timothy to **have nothing to do with irreverent and silly myths**, which stand in direct contrast with the true gospel. These were the "myths" favored by the false teachers (see 1:4), centering on extrabiblical revelation. He characterized them as IRREVERENT (Gk. *bebēlous*, "profane, irreligious, godless"), and SILLY (Gk. *graōdeis*, "old-womanish"), the sort of fairy tale an aging grandmother might tell to a child. Rather than pursuing such false knowledge, Timothy should, with the fervor of an athlete, actively "train" himself in GODLINESS (Gk. *eusebeian*, "piety"). In the Pastoral Epistles, the term "godliness" referred to practical, godly living that is observable by others (see 2:2). The apostle explained this further through a contrast between **training of the body**, a reference to physical exercise that **has a limited benefit** and **godliness**, which has wide-ranging benefits both now and in eternity. Paul was by no means denigrating the value of physical exercise, for he said it had a "limited benefit." His point was to focus on the great value of godliness, which benefited the individual and the church as a whole both in **the present life** and in **the life to come**.

4:9 Paul followed this quotation with the third of the **trustworthy** sayings in the Pastoral Epistles (see 1:15; 3:1). The reference was perhaps especially to the latter part of the preceding quote, since his point was to advocate practical, godly living.

4:10 In fact, Paul said, **we labor and strive for this**, namely the promise of benefit both now and in the life to come (v. 8). Both of these verbs were common in Paul's writings and are used in the present tense to stress their ongoing nature (i.e., "we are continually laboring and striving"). LABOR (*kopiōmen*, "labor, toil, become weary, struggle") referred to hard work, such as that performed by farmers (2 Tm 2:6), by the church elders (5:17), and by Christians generally (Rm 16:6,12). STRIVE (*agōnizometha*, "struggle, strive, fight") is an athletic metaphor that underscored the conflict Timothy could expect to face as he did the work of the ministry. Paul used the term again when he told Timothy to "fight the good fight" (6:12) and, at the end of his life, when he testified, "I have fought the good fight" (2 Tm 4:7). These two verbs also appeared together in Colossians 1:29 as Paul described his labor as a minister of the gospel.

Paul was willing to work hard in the ministry **because** he had placed his **hope** in the right place, namely, **the living God**, the One who was continually available to accomplish all He had promised to do. He further described God as **the Savior of everyone, especially of those who believe** (see 2:5). Two clarifications are relevant. First, the term "Savior" focused on God's ability to provide spiritual salvation, and thus is used just as it is in 1:1 and 2:3, when Paul referred to God our Savior who offered His Son Jesus as a ransom for all (2:5). It does not refer to God as One who preserved or delivered humanity in the sense of the Creator who cares for all humanity providentially. Second, while the salvation God provides is available to "everyone," it is "especially" for "those who believe." Salvation is potentially within reach of all men and women throughout time, but it is actually available only to those who "believe" in Jesus Christ as their personal Savior and Lord (Jn 3:16).

Paul's Encouragement for More Effective Ministry (4:11-16)

4:11 Paul returned to his concern for Timothy through a series of exhortations that concern both the younger man's personal walk with the Lord and his ministry in Ephesus. The term **command** carries considerable authority, and probably referred to refuting the false teachers. **Teach** (Gk. *didaske*; 2:12) in the Pastorals especially referred to teaching Christian doctrine. **These things** seems to focus on the doctrine he had just discussed concerning the importance of godliness and the blessings available both in this life and the one to come. These truths are relevant to everyone and should be communicated.

4:12 The next statement, **no one should despise your youth**, with an imperative verb, is better translated, "Let no one despise your youth." Timothy was in his early thirties by this time, and despite his spiritual qualifications some of the Ephesian elders and church members, as well as some of the heretics, would have been older than he. In a culture where age was valued, some would likely DESPISE (Gk. *kataphroneitō*, "look down on, scorn, treat with contempt;" Mt 6:24; 18:10) him because of his comparative youth. As a way of winning the respect of the believers, Paul urged Timothy to **be an example** (lit., "a pattern") **to the believers**. Paul elsewhere referred to himself as a model that others should follow (1 Co 4:6; Php 3:17; 1 Th 1:6). Here the present tense command clearly affirms that Timothy was to continue being an example in five areas: **in speech**, specifically through avoiding the quarreling and empty babbling of the false teachers; **in love**, especially expressed towards others; **in conduct**, a general term referring to personal lifestyle; **in faith**, likely a reference to his personal faith in Christ; and **in purity** (Gk. *hagneia*, "chastity, purity"), a term with sexual connotations used only here and in reference to Timothy's relationships with the younger women in the congregation (5:2).

4:13 Paul exhorted his spiritual son to be devoted to the ministry of the word in Ephesus until he himself was able to come (see 3:14). The term GIVE YOUR ATTENTION (Gk. *proseche*, "care for, devote oneself to, officiate") was used earlier to describe the false teachers' devotion to their perverted teachings (1:4). The three terms that follow all relate to the Scripture. **Public reading** refers to the custom, carrying over from synagogue worship, of formally reading the Scripture aloud during the worship assembly. EXHORTATION (Gk. *paraklēsei*, "encouragement, comfort, exhortation") focuses more on communicating the word to people at the heart level, encouraging and comforting them, motivating them to make practical application of it in their lives. **Teaching** emphasizes the need for doctrinal clarity and correctness in Timothy's preaching.

4:14 Next the apostle urged Timothy to "not NEGLECT (Gk. *amelei*, "disregard, be unconcerned about") the gift that is in you." The term GIFT (Gk. *charismatos*) specifically refers to a spiritual gift, graciously given by the Holy Spirit, such as those Paul discussed at length in other letters (e.g., 1 Co 12–14; Eph 4:11). In this context of public proclamation of the word, likely the gift Paul had in mind was his Spirit-empowered ability to teach and to exhort. Both here and in 2

Timothy 1:6-7 **the gift** was said to be **in you**; it was his present possession. He received this gift **through prophecy**, accompanied by **the laying on of hands by the council of elders**, a custom occurring in both the Old and New Testaments, and used for blessing (Mt 19:13-15), for healing (Ac 9:12,17), for commissioning someone to a specific ministry (Ac 6:6), and as a visible sign of God's promise to pour out His Spirit (Ac 8:17; 19:6). The word "through" here does not mean that a prophetic word (or several of them) caused him to receive the gift, for that is the ministry of the Holy Spirit alone (1 Co 12:7). Rather it described the situation that most probably occurred when the elders in Lystra laid hands on him and, with prayer and prophetic words, commissioned him for ministry. The Spirit thus used the vehicle of prophetic insight to make clear the manner in which He was equipping the young man for service. This procedure is reminiscent of Paul's own commissioning to a traveling ministry when the Holy Spirit spoke, apparently through the prophets who were present (Ac 13:1-3). In response, the teachers and prophets in the church in Antioch fasted, prayed, and laid hands on Paul and Barnabas as they sent them out into ministry.

4:15-16 Paul summarized all his exhortations (vv. 1-14). He exhorted Timothy to **practice these things** and to **be committed to them**. The first verb carried the idea of consistently cultivating them, and the second verb painted the picture of an athlete who was wholly committed to his training regimen. The purpose for such disciplined living was so that his **progress may be evident to all**, including the believing community, the pagan society, and the false teachers. Further, Timothy was to **be conscientious about** himself, referring to his lifestyle and to his **teaching**, a reference to his exposition of the Word. He was to **persevere in these**

things—in living a godly life and in pursuing the work of the ministry—because the result would be that he **will save both** himself and his **hearers**. The word "save" can best be understood here in the light of the ongoing walk of sanctification (Php 2:12-13). On a daily basis Timothy was to work out the salvation that God was continually working in him. Not only would he experience the fruit of salvation in his own life, but he also would be God's instrument to bring salvation to others.

Heart to Heart: Why Have a Women's Ministry? (1 Tm 4:12-16)

God is working through the lives of women who are called to minister to other women. Women's ministries are developing in many churches in order to strengthen women in the church and reach women outside the church. Though women's ministry seems important, the demands of other programs in the church often force the question: "Why have a women's ministry?" Paul answers that question (1 Tm 4:12-16).

Women's ministry programs help Christian women fulfill the calling of God to be an example in word and deed. The instruction is clear, Christians are to

- *be an example to believers in speech, conduct, love, faith, and purity (v. 12),*

- *give attention to public reading, exhortation, and teaching (v. 13),*

- *use spiritual gifts such as prophecy (v. 14),*

- *practice these things in order to grow in righteousness (v. 15),*

- *be conscientious about personal lifestyle and teaching (v. 16), and*

- *persevere in godliness (v. 16).*

Women's ministry programs that include discipleship, evangelism, and missions will help a Christian woman grow in faith and spread the gospel to others.

DIRECTIVES CONCERNING VARIOUS CHURCH MEMBERS (5:1–6:10)

Paul turned his attention to how Timothy should deal with various members of the Ephesian church. Until he once more turned his attention to the false teachers (6:3-10), his advice to the younger man was focused primarily on relationships rather than on theological issues. This section especially demonstrates two things:

- the value of the often hidden, administrative structure of the church;

- the absolute necessity of daily choices for godly living by individual church members.

Guidelines for Admonishing Older and Younger Church Members (5:1-2)

Earlier Paul referred to the church as "God's household" (3:15), and in these two verses he again pictured the church members as part of God's family. The Ephesian church included those who were both older and younger than Timothy, and it was important that Timothy, as their leader, relate to individuals in those groups appropriately.

5:1-2 First, the apostle dealt with what would have been the most difficult situation: needing to bring correction to a man older than he. He must **not rebuke an older man**. The verb REBUKE (Gk. *epiplēxēs*, "strike at, reprove") is a strong term used metaphorically to picture a harsh verbal rebuke. Instead, he should "EXHORT (Gk. *parakalei*, "encourage, appeal to, exhort," e.g., 1:3; 2:1) him as a father," showing respect for him as a person while yet bringing needed correction.

The next three groups of people were also pictured as members of God's family who at some point may need to receive correction. He should exhort the **younger men**—those around his own age or younger—**as brothers**, and the **older women as mothers**. An example of Paul's own attitude of honoring older women is found where he sent his greetings to Rufus' mother, whom he honored as if she were his own mother (Rm 16:13).

As expected by the family analogy, Timothy was also to treat **the younger women as sisters**. Paul, however, added an important warning here: Timothy was to relate to them "with all PROPRIETY" (Gk. *hagneia*, "chastity, purity"; see 1 Tm 4:12, where it is translated "purity"), emphasizing the need for sexual purity—an exhortation

that had special relevance as he dealt with the young widows (5:11-16).

Guidelines for Caring for Widows (5:3-16)

When numerous government and private safety nets are available for aging widows, the dire situation of widows in the ancient world can be misunderstood. The Old Testament law made special provision for those least able to protect and provide for themselves (Ex 22:22; Dt 24:17,19-21). God Himself was seen as being their champion (Ps 68:5), and through the prophet Isaiah He exhorted Israel to do the same (Is 1:17). The early church also made special provision for widows. The first major point of dissension recorded in the early church concerned the care of widows. The Hellenistic Jews felt their widows were being discriminated against in favor of those of Hebrew ethnicity in the daily distribution of food (Ac 6:1). The early believers did what was necessary to resolve this problem (Ac 6:2-6).

Even with this understanding that the church had a primary role to play in the care of its widows, the following section has long been somewhat puzzling to scholars. Why so much attention to the needs of widows when the primary concern elsewhere in the letter was with developing godly church leadership and combating the threat of false teachers? The answer seems to lie in the clear contrast made between those widows who are older and living godly lives, and those who are younger and living lives of idleness and sexual promiscuity. Clearly Paul wanted the needs of those who were "genuinely widows" to be met (1 Tm 5:3-4,8,16). At the same time the apostle seemed to be using their godly lives to highlight the undesirable lifestyles of the younger ones (vv. 11-15), just as he earlier contrasted Timothy's lifestyle with that of the false teachers (4:6-16; 6:11-16). Above all, Paul did not want their behavior to be a cause of reproach to the Christian community (5:14; cp. 3:2; 5:7; 6:14).

5:3 Paul's opening exhortation was for the church to SUPPORT (Gk. *timia*, "honor, revere, respect") those who were "genuinely widows." Used elsewhere simply to mean "respect" (e.g., 6:1), here, as with those who worthily fulfill their role as elders (5:17), the term includes the idea of providing material and financial support. A genuine widow, worthy of support by the church, was not simply one whose husband had died. As the succeeding verses make clear, she must be without any other means of support, and she must have lived a consistently upright Christian life over the years.

5:4 Paul first addressed the issue of alternate support. If she had **children or grandchildren**, they were responsible for supporting her, giving them the opportunity to **learn to practice their religion** within the context of their own family. In the Pastoral Epistles "religion," which is often translated GODLINESS (the Gk. verb *eusebeō*, "show piety, display godliness," and its related noun *eusebeia*, "piety, godliness"; see 2:2; 4:7; 6:5-6,11) referred to practical, godly living that was observable by others. Through fulfilling this responsibility, they would be able **to repay their parents** for the care they received earlier in their lives. Paul declared that this practice **pleases God** (Ex 20:12; Eph 6:2).

5:5-6 Thus the first qualification for a widow to receive church support was that she be a **real widow** (the same phrase used in v. 3) who had been **left all alone** with no family or other means of practical support. The second qualification was that she be living a life of consistent dependency on God alone as the source for all

her needs. She **has put her hope in God** (see 4:10 and 6:17) and made Him the focus of her attention, expressed through prayer as one who **continues night and day** in prayer, a Jewish word picture that meant to pray continually (cp. 1 Th 5:17). Such a woman stood in direct contrast to one who was SELF-INDULGENT (Gk. *spatalōsa*, "living for pleasure"; Jms 5:5), a term that referred to luxurious self-indulgence and likely to the lifestyle of the young widows (vv. 11-13). One who lives this way **is dead** (a reference to spiritual death; e.g., Rm 7:10,24; Eph. 2:1,5; 4:18) **even while she lives**.

5:7-8 Paul paused in his description of this self-indulgent lifestyle to reinforce the seriousness of the situation. Two interpretations are possible.

- The recipients of the command may be the widows. In this case Paul was exhorting Timothy to **command** the widows to become focused and dependent upon the Lord in order that **they won't be blamed** or, more literally, that "they may be without reproach" (see 3:2), an expression that accurately described the behavior Paul described in verse 5.

- Paul may be telling Timothy to "command" the families of widows to fulfill their responsibilities to care for them. This view is slightly preferable since he had already outlined the relatives' responsibilities (5:3-4) and since he turned to this issue again in the very next sentence.

The apostle extended the responsibility to care for widows as broadly as possible by referring to **anyone** who **does not provide for his own relatives**—members of his extended family—**and especially for his household**—members of his immediate family. One who commits such a sin **has denied the faith**, a strong word of judgment clarified by the next clause—

and is worse than an unbeliever. Throughout the letter Paul expressed his concern that the lifestyle of believers be at least as good as that of the members of pagan society (see 3:1; 1 Co 5:1). Care for widows by their families was a social norm, and the believers' failure to support their own was clearly wrong. Their sin, in fact, was greater than that of their pagan neighbors, because they had the clear teaching of Scripture (see v. 4).

5:9-10 Paul gave several specific qualifications for those who **should be placed** (lit., "enrolled") **on the official support list**. Commentators who deny Pauline authorship of the letter contend that this terminology indicated an official "order of widows," such as existed in the second century. Thus these women fulfilled the qualifications detailed in this passage and performed specific duties within the church in return for material support. However, more likely Paul was simply continuing to fill out the picture he was painting of those who were worthy to be supported by the church, and whose lives stood in such contrast to some of the younger widows and their dissolute lifestyles.

The rest of this sentence listed the specific qualifications the Ephesian church should require. First, the widow should be **at least 60 years old**. The use of a specific age probably reflected a cultural understanding of "old age," especially in an era in which the average life span for women was in the mid-thirties. In addition, it likely denotes an age after which marriage would not be considered a possibility. Second, she **has been the wife of one husband** (Gk. *henos andros gunē*, lit. "a one-man woman"). The grammatical construction here is identical to the wording Paul used regarding elders (see 3:2). Most likely the widow must have been faithful to her husband, a "one-man sort of woman." In a society filled with oppor-

tunities for immorality, this value was clearly important. Also, such an interpretation adequately accounts for the emphasis given the word "one" in the Greek text. In addition, the possibility that she could have been twice widowed is left open. This consideration is important, since he so strongly encouraged the younger widows to remarry (5:14).

Third, a widow supported by the church should be **well known for good works**. The qualifications that follow are to be added to the list given (v. 5), where Paul said that she should have placed her hope in God as her source of supply and should have a lifestyle of consistent prayer. Several specific examples of good deeds follow here. To make the rearing of **children** a qualification reflects the cultural norm of the times (see 2:15) and also stands in contradiction to the doctrine of the false teachers, who forbade marriage and, presumably, child-rearing (see 4:3).

A qualified widow has **shown hospitality**. Paul elsewhere cited hospitality as necessary for pastors or elders (3:2) as well as for Christians generally (Rm 12:13). She has **washed the saints' feet**, a practice that would highlight her humility and willingness to serve others (Jn 13:3-11,14). Further, she has **helped the afflicted**. The apostle was not pinpointing a specific type of affliction, such as persecution, since this is a more general term for those in trouble; he was rather emphasizing the widow's willingness to help those with any need.

5:11-12 Paul turned now to a group of **younger widows** whose lifestyles stood in direct contrast to those of the older women he had just described. He instructed Timothy to **refuse to enroll** them on the list of those whom the church supports and stated why they should be excluded. First, he considered it likely that they will be **drawn away from Christ by desire**. The verb DESIRE

(Gk. *katastrēniasōsin*, "have sensual desires against, wanton toward") has explicitly sexual overtones and referred to their feeling sensual impulses that became greater than their commitment to Christ. Rather than offering these natural sexual desires to the Lord Jesus Christ in full submission to His will, they had allowed them to become channeled in the wrong direction. Rather than allowing these desires to be an instrument that would draw them to greater dependency on Christ, they let them become a tool alienating them from Him.

As a result, Paul said, they will **want to marry**. The problem here was not remarriage by the younger women, since later the apostle would specifically urge them to do so (v. 14). Rather he envisioned a remarriage that involved abandoning their Christian commitment. Paul may have had in mind marriage to an unbeliever, a union which he warned against in a similar context of allowing younger widows to remarry (1 Co 7:39).

In any case, should they choose to remarry in this state of withdrawal from Christ, they would **receive condemnation because they have renounced their original pledge** (lit., "because they have set aside their former faith"). The translation "pledge" is possible, although the term (Gk. *pistin*) is most commonly translated "faith." In this context scholars have suggested that the term may refer to a pledge of faithfulness to the woman's first husband, to a vow of celibacy, to a commitment to Christ as her husband, or to her personal faith in Christ. The first is unlikely since Paul argued elsewhere that marriage is binding only so long as the spouse lives (Rm 7:1-3) and since he specifically allowed remarriage for widows (1 Co 7:39; 1 Tm 5:14). The next two options assume vows made within the context of a well-defined order of widows, and records of such orders and their

vows appear only in later centuries. The fourth option best suits the context: She has turned from her personal faith in Christ. This option best explains Paul's use of the strong expression "receive condemnation," also allowing the term to have its usual meaning of "faith."

5:13 Paul continued with a second reason why the younger women should not be included on the list of widows whom the church supports. Simply put, they display a lack of Christian virtue in their lifestyles. First, they **learn to be idle**, a fact emphasized by its repetition in the next clause. They had developed a habitual pattern of idleness, which led them to go **from house to house**. They were wasting not only their own time but that of others. Such a lifestyle stood in direct contrast to that of Dorcas, who was known and loved among the widows of Joppa for her good deeds (Ac 9:36-42), or Anna, a widow who was both a prophetess and a woman of prayer in the Jerusalem temple (Lk 2:36-38).

In addition, these young women "are also **GOSSIPS** (Gk. *phluaroi*, "foolish talkers,"), and busybodies indicating more than simply spreading slander about others and carrying the idea of speaking in a foolish manner or spreading ideas that are foolish.) Paul elsewhere charged the false teachers with spreading ideas that were foolish (1 Tm 1:6; 6:20; 2 Ti 2:23), and these widows themselves possibly were sharing the heretics' various false doctrines as they went from house to house. The apostle also referred to them as **BUSYBODIES** (Gk. *periergoi*), referring to those who are meddlesome and involved in concerns that are none of their business.

5:14-16 In light of these very real dangers faced by the younger widows and others in the Ephesian church, Paul counseled these **younger women to marry, have children**, and **manage their house-**

holds. This picture reflected the typical range of activities that would be of consummate worth to God in a first-century woman's life (see 2:15; Ti 2:4-5).

By being actively involved in their households, women would "give the ADVERSARY (Gk. *antikeimenō*, "the opponent, the enemy, the devil," a reference to Satan, whether he was working directly or through the instrumentality of a human being) no opportunity to accuse. In the Pastoral Epistles Paul repeatedly emphasized the need for the church to protect itself from unnecessary accusations through the antidote of godly living (3:7; 6:1; Ti 2:5,8). Satan had already brought devastation in the lives of some of the widows who **turned away to follow Satan**. The dangers described (1 Tm 5:13-14) were not theoretical, but actual, and needed to be handled immediately.

Guidelines for Support, Discipline, and Selection of Pastors (5:17-25)

The apostle turned his attention to the pastors or elders. He had already discussed the character and conduct required (3:1-7), and those qualities and behaviors formed the background for the three practical issues he discussed in this passage. First, he spoke of financial support for pastors who minister well. Second, he discussed the difficult task of bringing disciplinary action against a pastor when necessary. Third, he offered an important criterion for the selection of pastors.

5:17 The elders (Gk. *presbuteroi*, "pastors") **who are good leaders** are those who serve in positions of authority in the church. The same word is translated as "older man" in 5:1-2, where the context clearly points to believers in various age categories, whereas here Paul was referring to those set apart as leaders in the church. These are the same individuals whom he

called "overseers" (3:1-7; cp. Ac 20:17,28; see also Ti 1:5-7 where he used the terms interchangeably). The term LEADERS (Gk. *proestōtes*) is used by Paul earlier to refer to the elder's role in his household, and here it has the same meaning of leading, directing, governing, and protecting those committed to his care (1 Tm 3:4-5).

Leaders who serve with excellence are to "BE CONSIDERED WORTHY (Gk. *axiousthōsan*, "deserving esteem") of an ample honorarium," literally "double honor." The word HONORARIUM (Gk. *timēs*, "price, value") comes from the same root as "support" in verse 3. Those who lead the church well are worthy of honor and respect, but the meaning is broader here. The church is to provide them, as the widows, with material and financial support. The church was to care financially for its leaders (e.g., 1 Co 9:7-14; 2 Co 11:8-9; 1 Th 2:7).

> *The church was to care financially for its leaders (e.g., 1 Co 9:7-14; 2 Co 11:8-9; 1 Th 2:7).*

While not all pastors would specialize in **preaching and teaching**, some certainly would. And they are to WORK HARD (Gk. *kopiōntes*) to the point of weariness at these tasks. The apostle had used this word to refer to his own and Timothy's service in the Lord (see 4:10; cp. Col 1:29). "Preaching" is the more general term, referring to the various aspects of a leader's ministry involving speech, such as encouraging, admonishing, and comforting. "Teaching" the truth of God's Word involved explaining clearly the harmony and detail of God's revelation so that people learn. While prophecy involves transmitting new revelation from God, teaching focuses on explaining revelation already given.

5:18 The apostle placed an exclamation point after his directive to financially support those elders who fulfill their ministries with excellence by giving reasons from both the Old Testament and the words of Jesus. Paul gave equal authority to the words of the Old Testament and the words of Jesus and referred to both as **Scripture**. First, **You must not muzzle an ox that is threshing grain** (Dt 25:4), permitting an ox that was separating the chaff from the wheat kernels through trampling the grain to eat some of that grain. Paul elsewhere used this verse to make the point that he, as an apostle, had the right to receive support from the churches he served (1 Co 9:1-14). Second, Jesus' words, **The laborer is worthy of his wages** (Lk 10:7; cp. Mt 10:10; 1 Co 9:14).

5:19 Paul's statements on bringing disciplinary action **against an elder** or pastor are particularly relevant in light of the presence of the false teachers in the Ephesian church, some of whom were likely pastors (Ac 20:30). The apostle sought to safeguard those in authority against false accusations. The support **by two or three witnesses** was the normally accepted standard for bringing accusation against someone in the church (2 Co 13:10), a custom with roots in the Mosaic law (Dt 17:6; 19:15) and affirmed by Jesus (Mt 18:16; Jn 8:17; see Heb 10:28). Paul's emphasis was to protect those pastors who were innocent.

5:20-21 The apostle turned his attention to elders who were genuinely guilty. Timothy was to **publicly rebuke those who sin** (Gk. *hamartanontas*, "those who continue in sin"), a reference to pastors who had established a lifestyle of sinning, not to those who did so occasionally. The present tense of the command to "rebuke" these elders indicated that Timothy was to be in the habit of rebuking such individuals and that, once proper investigation has been made and the charges verified, the situation should be handled "publicly." Although **REBUKE** (Gk. *elegche*, "expose, convict, reprove, correct") has a range of meanings, on three other occasions Paul paired it with the term **EXHORT** (Gk. *parakaleō*; 2 Tm 4:2; Ti 1:9; 2:15). The emphasis here seems to be on an exposure of sin leading to repentance and changed behavior.

The purpose for such a "public" (literally "before everyone") reproof is **so that the rest will also be afraid**, probably a reference to the church in general, more likely primarily to the other pastors. The resultant fear may be a reference to a healthy "fear of God," to a fear of public rebuke themselves, or to both. The account of Ananias and Sapphira provides an example of the godly fear such exposure can bring (Ac 5:11).

Paul underscored the urgency and importance of Timothy following this directive by giving him a solemn charge **before God and Christ Jesus and the elect angels**. Given the context of judgment, the angels were probably those who chose to follow God rather than Lucifer (Jd 6; cp. 2 Pt 2:4). Although angels were elsewhere seen as observers of the church (1 Co 4:9; 11:10), the reference here was unusual and served to emphasize the gravity of the apostle's charge to his son in the faith. The manner in which Timothy was to carry out the discipline of sinning elders was twofold. He was to carry out these procedures without **PREJUDICE** (Gk. *prokrimatos*, "prejudgment, discrimination," coming to a conclusion prematurely without giving weight to all the facts). He was to avoid acting out of **FAVORITISM** (Gk. *prosklisin*, "partiality").

5:22 The apostle's third concern in this section on elders had to do with their selection. The removal of some pastors from office would logically require their replacement by others with good character. He began with two negative exhortations.

- Timothy was cautioned: **Don't be too quick to lay hands on anyone**, a reference to setting apart and commissioning a pastor for service officially, as in Timothy's own commissioning (see 4:14; Ac 13:1-3). Paul urged Timothy not to "be too quick" to do this since the whole truth about the person may not be immediately apparent (5:24-25).

- Timothy must not **share in the sins of others** by too quickly setting apart unqualified pastors for ministry and risking becoming involved in the same sins besetting these individuals (cp. 4:12).

5:23 This exhortation to personal purity led Paul to a quick personal aside to Timothy: Instead of **drinking only water,** he should **use a little wine**. In the ancient world "wine" was widely considered to have medicinal qualities and, in light of Timothy's **stomach** and his **frequent illnesses**, Paul clearly believed it would be necessary for him to include "wine" in his diet for the sake of his health.

5:24-25 Paul returned to the sins of the pastors. On a negative note he stated that **some people's sins are evident** and obvious for all to see. **The sins of others**, however, were hidden and would not be exposed until later, although both were destined for **judgment**. By selecting and commissioning pastors too quickly, Timothy might choose some who would be unfit for the office because of hidden sins. The same was true in the matter of **good works**, which in some **are obvious**, while in others are only seen later. By commissioning elders too quickly, he might pass over some who were well qualified. Thus Timothy should take time to observe carefully the lifestyles of potential elders.

Guidelines Concerning Slaves (6:1-2a)

Paul turned to the slaves. Well over half of the people in the Greco-Roman world were slaves, so his words would have had wide relevance in the Ephesian church. The message of the gospel is that all are liberated from the bondage of sin and are made brothers and sisters in Christ. Nevertheless, the social institution of slavery was a fact of life in the first century, and the apostle wanted to encourage the Christian slaves to relate appropriately to their masters. He spoke to slaves generally (v. 1) and specifically to those with Christian masters (v. 2).

6:1 The expression **under the yoke as slaves** is redundant, since "under the yoke" was a common metaphor for slavery. Paul likely added this expression to emphasize the fact that, despite their spiritual freedom in Christ, their social status was unchanged, and obedience to their masters was not optional. They must consider "their own masters to be worthy of all RESPECT" (Gk. *timēs*, "honor, reverence, respect," the same word used earlier to refer to financial support for those who serve well as elders; see 5:17). Yet the present context requires the basic meaning of "honor" or "respect." Paul seemed to be bringing correction to a situation in which some slaves were so focused on their newfound freedom in Christ that they were failing to give proper respect to their masters.

The purpose for their properly honoring their masters was to prevent **God's name and His teaching** from being **blasphemed** (Is 52:5; see Rm 2:24, where Paul also spoke of believers who dishonor God through their lifestyles). Similar warnings were given to church members elsewhere: to the younger widows (1 Tm 5:14); to the younger wives (Ti 2:5); and to slaves (Ti 2:9-10).

6:2a Turning his attention to those slaves with **believing masters**, Paul said that they **should not be disrespectful** towards them **because they are brothers** (Gk. *adelphoi*), commonly used as a general term referring to both male and female believers (e.g., Rm 12:1; 1 Co 14:26; Eph 6:23). BE DISRESPECT-FUL (Gk. *kataphroneitōsan*, "look down on, scorn, despise, treat with contempt") is the same Greek word in 4:12 (see also Mt 6:24; 18:10). The slaves' conduct should be exactly the opposite. They **should serve them better**—not better than nonbelievers, but in the sense of "even more so"—because **those who benefit from their service are believers, and dearly loved**. Paul directed the slaves in the Ephesian church to relate properly to their masters, both unbelievers and believers.

Guidelines Concerning Exposure of False Teachers in Their Greediness (6:2b-10)

The apostle turned once again to his primary concern in the Ephesian church, the false teachers, who were most likely pastors in the church, and Timothy's role as his apostolic representative. He mentioned several teachings that had led to their ungodly lifestyle and then focused on the love of money.

6:2b-5 For the final time in this letter Paul exhorted Timothy to **teach and encourage these things**, a reference to what he had just written (5:1–6:2a; see 3:14; 4:6,11; 5:7,21). He then returned to the false teachers and their doctrine by using a conditional sentence in which he stated the nature of the heretical teaching (6:3) and gave the consequences of their turning away from healthy teaching (vv. 4-5). The true doctrine Timothy was to teach stood in direct contrast to the **other doctrine** the heretics were teaching (Gk. *heterodidaskalei*, "teaching a different

doctrine"; 1:3). He further clarified the heretical nature of their doctrine.

- Those teaching it did **not agree with the sound teaching of our Lord Jesus Christ**, language almost identical to his description of the gospel of Christ as "sound teaching," a medical metaphor for "healthy" teaching (see 1:10). Their teaching was not centered on the person of the "Lord Jesus Christ."

- Those teaching it disagreed **with the teaching that promotes godliness**. The outflow of accurate doctrine will be GODLINESS (Gk. *eusebeian*, "piety"; 2:2; 4:7-8; 6:5-6,11), a reference to godly, Spirit-empowered living.

The second half of the conditional clause gives the conclusion to be drawn about those who teach such things.

- Such a person was CONCEITED (Gk. *tetuphōtai*, "to be puffed up, to be inflated with pride"; 3:6).

- Although this person, in his pride, believed he had great knowledge, he actually understood **nothing**.

- This individual had "A SICK INTEREST (Gk. *noson*, "having a sick or unhealthy craving for something," continuing Paul's medical metaphor of "healthy teaching" in v. 3) in disputes and arguments over words." Paul referred earlier to the false teachers' love of disputation, saying they had "turned aside to fruitless discussion" (1:6).

The results flowing from these unhealthy attitudes affected the entire Christian community and included **envy, quarreling, SLANDERS** (Gk. *blasphēmiai*, "defamation," among these interpersonal sins a likely reference to defilement of others rather than of

God, as was the case with Paul's self-description in 1:13), **evil suspicions** (resulting from "slanders"), **and constant disagreement** (not surprising among false teachers).

Paul came to the climax of his argument against the heretics.

- Their **minds are depraved**. The "mind" especially referred to a person's rational ability to process information and make decisions, which among the false teachers had been corrupted (see 4:2, where their consciences are described as "seared").

- These individuals had consciously departed from the faith, "paying attention to deceitful spirits and the teachings of demons" (4:1) and had been **deprived of the truth** of the gospel.

- They **imagine that godliness is a way to material gain**, the root motivation for the false teachers' ministry. In his second letter to Timothy, Paul described these men as having a form of godliness or making an outer show of religious practices such as asceticism and technical religious discussion. They had, however, denied the life-changing power of the gospel (2 Tm 3:5). Their root motivation was now laid bare: They wanted money, shedding light on Paul's qualifications for deacons and pastors (3:3,8; cp. 1 Th 2:5). Paul had made it clear that pastors who served well were to be paid by the church (5:17), so the issue was paying the pastors. However, these teachers were not only teaching a false gospel, but they were also seeking to get rich from it.

6:6-8 By contrast, true **godliness**—the sort based on the gospel and the empowering of the Holy Spirit—when paired **with contentment**, is a means to **great gain**. Although "contentment," in the sense of "self-sufficiency," was a concept favored by the Stoic philosophers of his day, the apostle's meaning was different. He believed that true contentment involved "Christ-sufficiency," which enabled him to live beyond material abundance or lack of it (see Php 4:11, where a cognate term was used).

Paul described the great value of true godliness accompanied by contentment, giving two reasons for this value (see 5:18).

- You bring **nothing into the world and take nothing out** when you die (cp. Jb 1:21); thus greed is pointless.

- Individuals on earth need simply **food and clothing** in order to **be content** (the cognate verb of the noun used in 1 Tm 6:6), a reflection of Jesus' teaching (Mt 6:25-34; Lk 12:22-32).

6:9 The apostle initially broadened his warning to include all **those who want to be rich** and then focused on the false teachers (v. 10b). He began by painting a graphic picture of the downward path to destruction that awaited those seeking riches. First came TEMPTATION (Gk. *peirasmon*, "testing"), a word used here to describe an enticement to sin (cp. Lk 4:13), leading the prey into the TRAP (Gk. *pagida*, "snare"). Paul likely meant a snare specifically set by Satan (1 Tm 3:7; 2 Tm 2:26). In that trap they were exposed to "many foolish and harmful desires." The fruit of acting on these desires is deadly, plunging "people into RUIN (Gk. *olethron*, "destruction, death," a strong term picturing an unexpected and often sudden outcome; 1 Co 5:5; 1 Th 5:3; 2 Th 1:9) and DESTRUCTION" (Gk. *apōleian*, "waste, ruin"; cp. Php 1:28, adding emphasis to his description of the headlong rush into total devastation that awaited those whose goal was seeking after riches).

6:10 In support of his argument, the apostle offered a common and spiritually accurate proverb: **The love of money is a root of all kinds of evil**. Avarice was not the only root cause of evil, but it did seem to be a central one in the Ephesian church, and so Paul highlighted it. The false teachers, whom he said were **CRAV-ING** (Gk. *oregomenoi*, "strive for, desire") riches, reaching out greedily for all they could get, illustrated this premise. The results had been tragic for them personally, as well as their hearers.

- They had **wandered away from the faith**—the true gospel, and they had embraced false doctrines.

- They had "pierced themselves" through, as with a sword or stake, "with many **PAINS**" (Gk. *odunais*, "woe, sorrow, distress," describing continual, intense, deeply felt pain). The term was elsewhere used to describe the anguish Paul felt over the Jewish nation that had turned against Jesus (Rm 9:2), and the related verb described the pain felt by the rich man as he begged Lazarus for help (Lk 16:19-31).

Through their lust for money the false teachers had fallen into Satan's cunning snare and were already experiencing tremendous anguish.

Heart to Heart:
Godliness with Contentment Is Great Gain (1 Tm 6:6-11)

Contentment is the ultimate acceptance of yourself, your surroundings, your past, and your future. Many women are full of discontent. They seek happiness from others, accumulate material possessions to find joy, move to a new home, or marry another husband in a search for contentment. The Christian woman should learn to be content in Christ.

Though contentment seems illusive, you can be content as you trust in God, relying on Him to provide what you need. You must be confident in yourself. You must be grateful for your family and your friends. Paul challenges you to seek godliness with contentment with whatever you have (1 Tm 6:6-11). If you truly desire to follow God, He will teach you to be content. Godliness with contentment is great gain.

DIRECTIVES CONCERNING THOSE WHO SERVE CHRIST (6:11-21)

Exhortation for Timothy to Pursue a Godly Lifestyle (6:11-16)

In the final section Paul gave a personal exhortation to his beloved son in the faith.

He appealed to Timothy to avoid the error of the false teachers and to fulfill his calling to ministry fearlessly with one last exhortation to the wealthy to use their riches for the benefit of the gospel. He closed with a final warning for Timothy not to be led away by false knowledge.

6:11 Fixing his attention directly on Timothy, Paul addressed him as a **man of God**, a designation used again when in reference to Timothy as a minister of the word of God (2 Tm 3:17). He was calling out the best in his spiritual son, encouraging him to be all God had called Him to be in Christ. "Man of God" was used in the Old Testament (68 times in the Septuagint) to refer to Moses, David, and various prophets (e.g., Dt 33:1; Neh 12:24; 1 Kg 17:18). Like them, Timothy was to stand strong in God's power as he contended against the Ephesian heretics.

The apostle's exhortation was fourfold. First, he warned Timothy to **run from these things**: the false doctrine; the divisiveness; and the greedy, ungodly lifestyles of the false teachers (6:3-10). Second, he urged him actively and continually to **pursue** a life of holiness, which he summed up with three pairs of critical qualities. Only one who had been made righteous through appropriating God's gift of salvation in Christ was able to walk in **righteousness** and **godliness**. Such a life is lived by faith through the power of the Holy Spirit (Rm 8:1-4; 2 Co 5:17,21). **Faith** and **love** often appear together (1 Tm 1:5,14; 2:15; 4:12; 2 Tm 1:13; 2:22; 3:10; Ti 2:2). "Faith" is used in the same sense as in 1:5, where the focus was on personal trust in Jesus Christ. One of the ministries of the Holy Spirit is to pour out lavishly in believers' hearts the Father's love (Rm 5:5), which is then poured out both in worship to God and in ministry to others (Mt 22:37-39). ENDURANCE (Gk. *hupomonēn*, "steadfastness, perseverance"; Ti 2:2) flows from faith and hope (Rm 8:25) in the crucible of suffering (2 Tm 2:10) and results in godly character change (Rm 5:3-4). Timothy had to possess this key Christian virtue, especially as he faced the constant onslaught of the heretics and the devastation wrought by their

teaching. Coupled with this was **gentleness**, a necessary quality in all his relationships, but especially with the false teachers (see 2 Tm 2:25, where a cognate noun is used).

6:12 Paul's third exhortation was to **fight the good fight for the faith**. The verb is in the present tense, emphasizing the need for Timothy to persist. Although the English translation has military overtones, the imagery is actually that of an athlete in competition for the prize. Paul later used this expression to describe both his personal walk with the Lord and his ministry and added the phrase, "I have finished the race" (2 Tm 4:7). "The faith" is first of all a reference to the gospel, but the context here suggests the likely inclusion of Timothy's personal faithfulness in the ministry.

The apostle's fourth exhortation was for Timothy to "TAKE HOLD OF (Gk. *epilabou*, "seize, grab tightly") eternal life," as an athlete would seize the prize of victory. Believers have "eternal life" the moment they receive Jesus Christ as their personal Savior and Lord (Rm 6:23). The opportunity was theirs to experience it abundantly throughout their sojourn on earth (Jn 10:10), although its fullest expression will be in His presence in heaven. Paul affirmed God's initiative in calling women and men to salvation (1 Co 1:9; 7:17-24; 2 Th 2:14) when he stated that Timothy was **called** to **eternal life**. He then referred to the public expression of the young man's response to God's call when he said that he had **made a good confession before many witnesses**, perhaps referring to his baptism, to his setting apart for ministry, or to some other public occasion. Because the immediate context especially focused on Timothy's salvation, likely his baptism is in view. In that setting he would have made a public declaration of his earlier decision to invite

Christ into his life "before many witnesses" (cp. Jn 1:12-13).

6:13-15a Paul followed these exhortations with a solemn charge:

- He made it **in the presence of God, who gives life** (Gk. *zōogonountos*, "make or keep alive") **to all**, probably reflecting words used at the time of Timothy's baptism and a reference both to God's gift of eternal life and to His ongoing role as the One who preserved it.

- He made it **before Christ Jesus, who gave a good confession before Pontius Pilate**. Paul certainly intended to encourage Timothy to persevere no matter how great the difficulties. The exact nature of Christ's "good confession" is less clear, since "before" is more literally translated "in the time of." If "before" or "in the presence of," it could refer to something Jesus actually said to Pilate during His trial. If "in the time of," it may be a more general reference to the witness Jesus bore as He persevered both through His life and especially at His death.

Paul formally charged Timothy **to keep the commandment without spot or blame**. The verb "charge" carries the sense of "command" or "direct" (see 4:11; 5:7). The exact nature of "the commandment" is unclear. The reference may be to something specific, such as Timothy's baptismal vows or commitments he made when he was set apart for ministry; or more probably it may refer to something more general, such as Timothy's commitment to Jesus Christ as Savior and his ensuing commitment to live a godly life and to fulfill his calling to ministry (e.g., 4:16). This command must be kept WITHOUT SPOT (Gk. *aspilon*, better translated "unblemished"; 2 Pt 3:14; Jms 1:27). Further, it must be kept without BLAME (Gk. *anepilēmpton*; 3:2; 5:7), a word elsewhere translated "above reproach." Further, it must be kept **until the appearing of our Lord Jesus Christ**, a reference to Christ's return (2 Tm 4:1,8; Ti 2:13), **which God will bring about in His own time**. The Sovereign Lord, in control of all things, will orchestrate Christ's return to earth at exactly the right time.

6:15b-16 As he reflected on God's sovereignty and omnipotence, Paul broke out into a hymn of praise bearing similarities to his doxology in 1:17. **He is the blessed and only Sovereign**, a phrase that emphasized God's sovereignty and the fact that He is the only God (see 1:17; 2:5). Although originally used to refer to pagan kings (e.g., Dn 2:37), **King of kings** had become a term for *Yahweh* by the time of the Maccabees (2 Macc 13:4), and **Lord of lords** is an Old Testament term that emphasized *Yahweh's* sovereignty over all other pagan gods (e.g., Dt 10:17). The two expressions had been joined in reference to *Yahweh* by the intertestamental period (1 En 9:4) and were used of Christ in the book of Revelation (Rv 17:14; 19:16). In this context the two phrases probably reflect a conscious opposition to the contemporaneous cult of emperor worship.

God alone **has immortality** (see 1 Tm 1:17, where Paul used a different word), and He dwells **in unapproachable light** (see Ps 104:1-2). No one **has seen or can see** Him emphasized His dwelling place in unapproachable light, evoking the familiar Old Testament theme of God's awesome holiness in contrast to humanity's sinfulness (Ex 33:20). Appropriately, Paul closed with **Amen**, an ending to hymns and blessings from Jewish synagogue worship, which had already become part of Christian worship (1 Co 14:16; see also Rm 16:27; Gl 1:5).

Exhortation for the Wealthy to Handle Their Wealth Responsibly (6:17-19)

6:17 Paul's instructions to the wealthy included six brief exhortations followed by the results of obedience. First, "those who are rich in the present age" must not BE ARROGANT (Gk. *hupsēlophronein*, a compound word meaning "thinking about yourself in a proud, haughty way"). Such an attitude of superiority over those who are poor would be a direct repudiation of the fact that God Himself is the source of riches. Second, they must not **set their hope on the uncertainty of wealth** (a common biblical theme; e.g., Ps 52:7; Pr 23:4-5); rather, their confidence must be placed **on God**, the One **who richly provides us with all things to enjoy**. This truth is the antidote to a false asceticism that denies the goodness of God's creation as well as to a false trust in your own resources. God willingly supplied His children's needs (Mt 6:11; Php 4:19; 4:1-5).

6:18 The last three exhortations follow logically from an understanding that God is the source of **all things**. The more general statement, that the wealthy are **to do good**, was clarified, i.e., they should **be rich in good works**. The third exhortation made plain that they are **to be generous, willing to share**. The wealthy, in other words, have a responsibility before the Lord to share with the poor (Rm 12:8; 13:2; 2 Co 9:6-15).

6:19 The apostle concluded this section with compelling motivation for their generosity. In so doing, they were **storing up for themselves a good foundation for the age to come**. He was not speaking of good works as a means to attaining salvation, which comes by grace through faith alone (Eph 2:8-9; 1 Tm 1:12-17). Instead, he used two metaphors—that of "storing up" spiritual riches and of laying "a good foundation" through those riches—to

emphasize the importance of amassing what Jesus called "an inexhaustible treasure in heaven" (Lk 12:33b). The purpose for banking heavenly riches was given in the final clause: **so that they may take hold of life that is real**, a statement that reflects Paul's earlier appeal to Timothy to "take hold of eternal life" (1 Tm 6:12).

Exhortation for Timothy to Guard Sound Doctrine (6:20-21)

6:20-21a As he closed his letter Paul summarized. First, "Timothy" must "guard what has been ENTRUSTED" (Gk. *parathēkēn*, 1:18; 4:11; 2 Tm 1:14; 2:2) to him, referring to something of value that has been given to a person for safekeeping or for passing on to others. He was referring to the gospel in all its fullness, including both its doctrinal structure and its practical outworking in a lifestyle of godliness.

Second, he must avoid "IRREVERENT (Gk. *bebēlous*, "unholy, profane, godless"; 1 Tm 1:9), EMPTY SPEECH (Gk. *kenophōnias*, suggesting fruitless discussion, 1:6) that was devoid of value; 2 Tm 2:16), and contradictions from the 'knowledge' that falsely bears that name." The verb tense of "avoiding" makes clear that continually, day after day, he must avoid the teaching of the heretics. Further, what its adherents falsely called "knowledge" is filled with internal **contradictions**. The false teachers and their followers were those who once believed the gospel but had embraced this false doctrine and so had departed from it.

6:21b The apostle closed his letter to Timothy with a final benediction, **Grace be with all of you**, Paul's common closing blessing, here in the short form (see Col 4:18; 2 Tm 4:22) and sometimes in a lengthened form (e.g., 1 Co 16:23; Ti 3:15). "Grace" may be understood here as God's undeserved blessing, His infinite resources freely available to be experienced by every believer. The word "you" is plural since Paul intended this letter be read to the entire church.

Bibliography

Hendriksen, William. *Exposition of the Pastoral Epistles*. New Testament Commentary. Grand Rapids: Baker Book House, 1957.

*Knight, George. *The Pastoral Epistles: A Commentary on the Greek Text*. The New International Greek Testament Commentary. Grand Rapids: Eerdmans Publishing Co., 1992.

*Köstenberger, Andreas J. and Thomas R. Schreiner, eds. *Women in the Church: An Analysis and Application of 1 Timothy 2:9-15*. 2nd ed. Grand Rapids: Baker Academic, 2005.

Lea, Thomas D. and Hayne P. Griffin, Jr. *1, 2 Timothy, Titus*. The New American Commentary. Nashville: Broadman Press, 1992.

*For advanced study.

2 TIMOTHY

Introduction

Title

Paul's second letter to Timothy is designated as such by its title in the Greek text: *pros Timotheon B*, "To Timothy, B." As the second letter in the Greek alphabet, "B" signifies the "second" of two things in a sequence.

Setting

Paul wrote this letter from a Roman prison where he awaited a second judicial hearing (4:16-18). Timothy received the letter in Ephesus where he served a church founded by Paul but infiltrated by false teachers. The problems addressed in the letter suggest that Paul had in view the same group of heretics as those described in 1 Timothy (2 Tm 2:14-19,23-26; 3:6-9; 4:3-4). Hymenaeus is specifically mentioned in both letters (1 Tm 1:20; 2 Tm 2:17). These opponents of Paul's apostolic authority can be described generally as a group of itinerant Jewish Christians promoting strict ascetic practices and teaching that the resurrection had "already taken place" (2:18), a false doctrine not mentioned in the previous letter. (See introductions to 1 Timothy and Ephesians for additional information about Ephesus and the false teachers addressed in the first letter.)

Genre

Second Timothy has the features of a personal letter typical of the ancient Greco-Roman world and typical of Paul with its uniquely Christian greeting and its personal closing. The letter opens with identification of the writer and recipient and, following the greeting, with an expression of thanksgiving. In closing, Paul sends personal greetings to various fellow believers and ends with a brief benediction.

As one of the "Pastoral Epistles," 2 Timothy is distinguished from other New Testament letters clearly addressed to churches rather than to individuals. However, letters, like most written documents in the ancient world, were regarded as recorded speech, a substitute for the personal presence of the writer. Although 2 Timothy is personally addressed to a particular pastor, its contents provide guidance for both the pastor and the members of the church, and evidence of the letter's circulation in the early church before the middle of the second century does exist.

Author

The salutation of 2 Timothy clearly identifies the Apostle Paul as the writer of the letter. For 18 centuries Pauline authorship was virtually unquestioned. The letter is included in the oldest canon; and the intimate, personal nature of its message renders problematic any hypotheses that it was written by anyone other than

Paul himself. (See "Author" in the introduction to 1 Timothy for additional support of Paul's authorship of the letters to Timothy.)

Date

The testimony of several early Christian leaders, including Clement, bishop of Rome, corroborates the claim that Paul was martyred in AD 67 or 68 in Rome under the emperor Nero. The second letter to Timothy was written around AD 66 or 67, since, as Paul wrote this letter, he clearly expected to be condemned but believed that Timothy had time to reach him in Rome before winter (4:6).

Recipients

Paul had known Timothy for approximately 20 years (c. AD 46–67) years when he wrote to his "dearly loved child" in the faith (1:2). Born of a Jewish Christian mother and a Gentile father, Timothy was uniquely suited to minister with Paul in the mixed urban culture of Hellenistic Judaism and paganism. Timothy had traveled with Paul, had been sent by Paul on several missions to various churches, and had assisted the apostle in writing or personally delivering several of his letters (2 Co 1:1; Php 1:1; Col 1:1; 1 Th 1:1; 2 Th 1:1; Phm 1). Paul had participated in Timothy's ordination (1 Tm 4:14; 2 Tm 1:6) and reminded the younger pastor of the spiritual calling and gifts entrusted to him (1 Tm 1:18; 4:14). One can reasonably infer from this second letter that Timothy had a shy or timid personality and may have needed both the personal encouragement brought by the letter and its usefulness as a source for appealing to Paul's influence when his own authority was being challenged (1:6-8,13-14; 2:1-7; 3:14-15; 4:1-2,5).

Timothy certainly would not have been the only reader of the letter, however, especially since the epistle is included in the canon of Scripture. The letter itself implies that Paul's intended audience included the Christian community. Paul argued for his apostolic authority (e.g., 1:11) and affirmed Timothy's pastoral authority (e.g., 3:10; 4:1-5). Furthermore, the letter provided the rationale for Timothy's sudden departure to Troas and Rome to see Paul for the last time (4:9,13,21). (See "Recipients" in the introduction to 1 Timothy for additional details of Timothy's background and partnership with Paul in ministry.)

Major Themes

Writing to encourage Timothy in his role as a pastor, Paul emphasized at least four major themes.

Faith and Faithfulness instead of Fearfulness and Being Ashamed. Paul commended Timothy for his faith (1:4) and exhorted him to continue in that faith that he had "learned and firmly believed, knowing those from whom" he had learned (1:5; 3:14-15). Having been instructed by the Scriptures "for salvation through faith in Christ Jesus" (3:15), Timothy is charged with committing what he had learned to faithful disciples who could repeat the process (2:2). Ministers of the gospel such as Paul and Timothy must be confident, not "faithless," in their knowledge of Christ whom they "have believed" (1:12) because "He remains faithful" (2:13), having "called" them (1:9) and "entrusted" the Holy Spirit to them (1:14).

Paul reassured Timothy that he did not have to fear being "ashamed" because God has given "power, love, and sound judgment," not "fearfulness" (1:7). Timothy's continued diligence (2:15), pursuit of purity and righteousness (2:21-22), and reliance "on the power of God" (1:8) and Scripture (3:17) set him apart as a "special instrument" who would be "useful," "prepared" (2:21), and "equipped" (3:17) to "do the work of an evangelist" (4:5), "a worker who doesn't need to be ashamed" (2:15). Paul also commended the example of Onesiphorus who had not been "ashamed" of Paul as a prisoner (1:16).

Endurance of Suffering and Persecution. Throughout the letter Paul referred both to his current experience of suffering and to his expectation of "difficult times" and persecution to come (3:1,12). He explained the reason why he suffered (1:12; 2:9) but also the reasons and rewards for enduring (2:10,12; 3:10-11), and he invited Timothy to "share in suffering for the gospel" (1:8) and "as a good soldier of Christ Jesus" (2:3).

Perils of Spiritual Leadership. Timothy was urged to remain faithful and to endure so that he could "proclaim the message" (2:2) of Christ according to Paul's example (1:13-15). Therefore, Paul repeatedly turned Timothy's attention to the glory of the gospel (1:9-10; 2:8-13; 4:1,17). Much of the letter, however, is devoted to the tasks of confronting false teachers and protecting believers from their deception (2:14-19,23-26; 3:6-9; 4:3-4; 4:14-15) and of avoiding and fleeing anything that would undermine Timothy's witness (2:15-16,22-25; 3:1-5,10; 3:14–4:2; 4:5).

Hope of Eternal Life. Despite Paul's impending death, the suffering he described as inevitable for "all those who want to live a godly life in Christ Jesus" (3:12), and the dark picture he painted of "the last days" (3:1-5), an unshakable confidence and hope in Christ's past, present, and future glory and sovereignty remained vibrant in the letter. In the salutation Paul described himself as "an apostle of Christ Jesus by God's will, *for the promise of life in Christ Jesus,*" leaving no doubt about his eternal perspective (1:1). He offered these reminders to Timothy:

- Their "holy calling . . . was given . . . in Christ Jesus before time began" (1:9);

- "with salvation comes "eternal glory" (2:10); and

- Christ "has abolished death and has brought life and immortality to light through the gospel" (1:10).

Paul firmly believed that the Lord would bring him "into His heavenly kingdom" (4:18) and that he would "live" and "reign" with Christ (2:11-12). He also trusted that Christ is the one who will "judge the living and the dead" (4:1). "Until that day" (1:11) Paul would look forward to obtaining "mercy from the Lord on that day" (1:18) and to receiving, "on that day," a "crown of righteousness" from "the Lord, the righteous judge" (4:8).

Pronunciation Guide

Aquila	*uh KWIL uh*	Miletus	*migh LEE tuhs*
Carpus	*KAHR puhs*	Onesiphorus	*ahn ih SIF oh ruhs*
Crescens	*KRESS uhnz*	Philetus	*fih LEE tuhs*
Dalmatia	*dal MAY shih uh*	Phygelus	*fih JEL uhs*
Demas	*DEE muhs*	Prisca	*PRISS kuh*
Erastus	*ih RASS tuhs*	Pudens	*PYOO denz*
Eubulus	*yoo BYOO luhs*	Troas	*TROH az*
Hermogenes	*huhr MAHJ ih neez*	Trophimus	*TRAHF ih muhs*
Hymenaeus	*high meh NEE uhs*	Tychicus	*TIK ih kuhs*

Outline

I. SALUTATION (1:1-2)

II. AN ADMONITION TO TIMOTHY TO
MINISTER FAITHFULLY IN GOD'S
POWER (1:3-18)
   A. Paul's Prayers for Timothy
   (1:3-5)
   B. An Exhortation to Keep Ablaze
   His Spiritual Gift (1:6-7)
   C. An Appeal to Join Paul in
   Suffering for the Gospel
   (1:8-12)
   D. An Exhortation to Guard the
   Gospel Message (1:13-14)
   E. An Example of One Who Has
   Served Faithfully (1:15-18)

III. AN ENCOURAGEMENT TO TIMOTHY
TO ENDURE THE HARDSHIPS THAT
ACCOMPANY MINISTRY (2:1-13)
   A. An Appeal to Commit the
   Gospel to Faithful Persons
   (2:1-2)
   B. An Exhortation to Share in
   Suffering for the Gospel (2:3-7)
   C. Paul's Loyalty to Jesus Christ,
   the Author of Salvation
   (2:8-10)
   D. Christ's Enduring Faithfulness
   to Believers (2:11-13)

IV. A WARNING TO TIMOTHY TO
RESIST AND CORRECT THE FALSE
TEACHERS (2:14-26)
   A. A Warning to Avoid the False
   Teachers' Controversies
   (2:14-19)

   B. An Analogy of Household
   Vessels (2:20-21)
   C. Living Righteously and
   Avoiding the False Teachers'
   Disputes (2:22-26)

V. A PLEA TO TIMOTHY TO STAND
FIRM IN THE FACE OF INEVITABLE
APOSTASY (3:1-17)
   A. Paul's Assurance That a Time
   of Apostasy Is Coming (3:1-9)
   B. Paul's Appeal to Timothy to
   Stand Firm in the Face of
   Persecution (3:10-17)

VI. A SOLEMN CHARGE TO TIMOTHY
TO FULFILL HIS MINISTRY IN ALL
CIRCUMSTANCES (4:1-8)
   A. A Solemn Charge to Proclaim
   the Gospel Consistently (4:1-5)
   B. The Victorious Completion of
   Paul's Ministry (4:6-8)

VII. FINAL INSTRUCTIONS TO TIMOTHY
(4:9-18)
   A. Instruction to Come to Paul in
   Rome (4:9-15)
   B. Paul's Testimony of God's
   Faithfulness During His First
   Trial (4:16-18)

VIII. PAUL'S GREETINGS AND BLESSINGS
(4:19-22)
   A. His Greetings to the Believers
   (4:19-21)
   B. His Final Blessing to Timothy
   (4:22)

Exposition of the Text

SALUTATION (1:1-2)

1:1 Paul identified himself as **an apostle of Christ Jesus** and could, therefore, speak with authority (see 1 Tm 1:1). However, Paul's apostleship was not self-designated—he delivered a message from Christ Jesus **by God's will**. He knew he was not experiencing persecution because he had somehow stepped out of God's will; rather, he was directly in the center of God's will and thus could rejoice in **the promise of life in Christ Jesus** despite his circumstances. This life—elsewhere called "eternal life" (1 Tm 6:11)—begins at the moment of salvation (Jn 3:16,36; Rm 6:23) and may be experienced in abundance in the present age (Jn 10:10). It is also the down payment on the promised fullness of life in heaven with Him (Eph 1:14; see 1 Tm 6:12).

1:2 Paul affectionately referred to **Timothy** as his **dearly loved child** (cp. 1 Co 4:17), and blessed him in three ways: with **grace** (Gk. *charis*, God's "unmerited favor"), **mercy** (Gk. *eleos*, "tender lovingkindness"), **peace** (Gk. *eirēnē*, "security, tranquility"), an experiential peace that flows from an assurance of peace with God (Php 4:6-7). These blessings flow **from God the Father and Christ Jesus our Lord**.

AN ADMONITION TO TIMOTHY TO MINISTER FAITHFULLY IN GOD'S POWER (1:3-18)

Paul's goal was to encourage his beloved son in the faith to continue his ministry without fear or shame. Paul reminded the younger man of his heritage and of how God had gifted him for the task. The power of the Holy Spirit was available to enable Timothy to share in the suffering that would inevitably accompany the gospel ministry. As an encouragement, Paul presented himself as an example of one who had faithfully carried out his calling to ministry. Returning to the gospel message itself, Paul emphasized the need to hold tightly to the true and accurate gospel Timothy had received from him. Furthermore, Timothy must not be like others who had turned away from the truth and from Paul himself. Like Onesiphorus, Timothy must remain faithful to Paul and to the gospel.

Paul's Prayers for Timothy (1:3-5)

1:3 The apostle often began his letters with a word of thanksgiving (Php 1:3-8), a blessing (Eph 1:3-14), or a prayer (Php 1:9-11) for the recipient. While this was a common practice of the secular world of his day, Paul's prayers were always filled with God's grace and were deftly tailored to the situation of the individual or church. Here, as he opened his letter to Timothy, his thoughts immediately turned to the thanksgiving that was an integral part of his continual prayers for his spiritual son.

As he offered his thanks, Paul entered into the presence of **God** with assurance that he was serving Him **with a clear conscience as my forefathers did**. CONSCIENCE (Gk. *suneidēsei*) is an inborn, God-given capacity to distinguish between right and wrong (Rm 2:14-15). It urges an individual to do what is perceived to be right and afterwards approves or disapproves of the action (see 1 Tm 1:5). Trained as a Pharisee, Paul was also ethnically Jewish and had been reared in the rich tradition of Jewish beliefs and under the influence of the Old Testament Scriptures (Php 3:5-6).

His conscience had been shaped by many years of study of the Scriptures and by the ministry of the Holy Spirit in his heart, bringing him into conformity with the character of Christ (Rm 8:29). Here he declared that he had consistently acted in conformity with its standards (e.g., 2 Co 1:12; 1 Tm 1:5,19; 3:9). The reference to his "forefathers" is surprising and probably emphasized the interconnectedness of the Old Testament and the gospel message (cp. 3:14-17). Paul **constantly** remembered Timothy in his **prayers night and day**. Regular times of prayer "night and day" were an ingrained part of his life as an observant Pharisee, and he continued these as a Christian.

1:4-5 In his lonely prison cell, Paul's prayers for Timothy were not only unceasing, they were also filled with deep longing **to see** him again, **so that** he may **be filled with joy** (v. 4). As he prayed, he remembered the last time he saw his spiritual son, probably as they parted when Paul left him in Ephesus as his apostolic representative (1 Tm 1:3). Clearly the parting was emotional, for Paul remembered Timothy's **tears** and doubtless his own as well (cp. Ac 20:36-38 with the Ephesian elders).

The apostle clearly recalled Timothy's **sincere faith** (2 Tm 1:5; see 1 Tm 1:5), probably referring primarily to Timothy's personal faith in Christ rather than to the gospel as a body of teaching. In contrast to the faith of the false teachers, Timothy's faith was SINCERE (Gk. *anupokritou*, "unfeigned, undisguised, genuine," lit. "not hypocritical") and was the primary cause for Paul's thankfulness as he remembered his son, for he knew that this "faith" would keep him faithful to the Lord Jesus despite the hardships.

Timothy's "faith" was nurtured in a faith-filled home environment. Paul reminded Timothy that this faith "first

lived in your GRANDMOTHER (Gk. *mammē*, akin to how a small child addresses his mother or grandmother: "mammy") Lois, then in your MOTHER (Gk. *mētri*) EUNICE" (Gk. *Eunikē*, "good victory," from *eu*, "good" and *nikē*, "victory"), and Paul was CONVINCED (Gk. *pepeismai*, "persuaded, sure, confident"; cp. v. 12) in Timothy also. Although his father was a Gentile, his mother was Jewish (Ac 16:1). "From childhood" he had been taught the Old Testament Scriptures (2 Tm 3:15), which shaped his thought patterns and lifestyle.

An Exhortation to Keep Ablaze His Spiritual Gift (1:6-7)

1:6 Therefore refers back to the basis of Paul's appeal: his spiritual son's life-giving faith in Christ. Because Timothy's faith was real, Paul reminded him **to keep ablaze the gift of God that is in you through the laying on of my hands**. KEEP ABLAZE (Gk. *anazōpurein*, "rekindle, fan into flame"), rather than referring to a fire that has gone out, pictures a fire that has been burning for some time and now needs to be stirred up in order to burn more brightly. Timothy was to rekindle the spiritual "gift" he had been given. Specifically, a GIFT (Gk. *charisma*, "favor, gift of grace") is a way of administering God's grace to others (1 Pt 4:10). The Holy Spirit determines who receives the various gifts (1 Co 12:7-9), but Paul encouraged believers to seek the greater gifts (1 Co 12:31). Here Paul referred to a spiritual gift (or group of gifts), which the Holy Spirit had imparted to Timothy when Paul and other elders laid hands on him, publicly acknowledging his gifting and calling for ministry (1 Tm 4:14). Although the "gift" is unnamed, a composite of gifts, which included teaching, pastoring, and administration, as well as revelatory gifting, was probably involved.

1:7 Timothy was able to stir up his gifting because the Holy Spirit indwelled him. Although the noun **spirit** is sometimes understood as an attitude, much more likely the reference is to the Spirit of God in this verse (see footnote "a" in HCSB). This view is preferable for four reasons.

- Verses 6 and 7 are closely linked grammatically, and the word **for** indicates that verse 7 is an explanation of verse 6, where Paul speaks of a gift given by the Holy Spirit.

- In the closely related passage, 1 Timothy 4:14, the Holy Spirit is named as the One who gives such gifts.

- Paul elsewhere referred to the Holy Spirit as simply the **Spirit** (e.g., Rm 5:5; 1 Co 12:7; 2 Co 1:22; 5:5; 1 Th 4:8).

- Verse 7 follows Paul's "not . . . but" pattern of showing a contrast in which the focus is on the clause beginning with **but** (Rm 8:15; 1 Co 2:12). In this case the apostle was saying, "**God has not given us** a Spirit who imparts **fearfulness**; instead, He has given you the Holy Spirit who imparts **power, love, and sound judgment**"

(Gk. *sōphronismou*, "self-control, moderation, holding to one's duty, sound mind"; cp. Ac 1:8; Rm 15:13; Gl 5:22-23).

In this letter the number of exhortations to endure in the face of suffering makes clear that Timothy was facing tremendous pressure in the ministry. While seemingly very doubtful that Paul was attributing "fearfulness" (*deilias*, "cowardice, timidity") to Timothy, he did want to emphasize the positive quality of endurance. Paul wanted his son in the faith to stand firm, and in order to do that Timothy must rely on the "power" the Holy Spirit imparted to him (Ac 1:8; Rm 15:13,19; 1 Co 2:4). Furthermore, as he faced his lying and hypocritical opponents (1 Tm 4:2), he must draw on the resources of God's **love** that the Holy Spirit had lavishly poured out in his heart (Rm 5:5). Finally, he must embrace the Spirit's supply of **sound judgment** (Gk. *sōphronismou*, "moderation, self-discipline, self-control, sound judgment"). Scholars differ on the exact nuance of this complex word, but closely related terms in the Pastorals indicate that the ideas of both self-control and sensible judgment are present (1 Tm 2:9; 3:2; Ti 1:8; 2:2,5,12).

Lois	Eunice
Lois and Eunice 2 Timothy 1:3-7	
Lois	**Eunice**
• grandmother of Timothy	• mother of Timothy
• mother of Eunice	• wife of a Greek Gentile
• strong faith in God	• strong faith in God
• taught Timothy the Bible	• taught Timothy the Bible
• lived a godly lifestyle	• lived a godly lifestyle
• served God through the church	• served God through the church

An Appeal to Join Paul in Suffering for the Gospel (1:8-12)

1:8 The apostle knew that Timothy's sincere faith (v. 5), as well as Spirit-endued power, love, and practical wisdom, were exactly what the young minister would need to stand unashamed and resolute in the face of persecution. **So,** since he had these resources, Timothy should not **be ashamed** (Gk. *epaischunthēs,* "be disgraced, dishonored"; also vv. 12,14) **of the testimony about our Lord, or of me His prisoner**. Paul had declared to the church in Rome that he was unashamed of the gospel (Rm 1:16), and he expected no less from his spiritual son. From the world's viewpoint, there was much in the gospel message that would bring shame, for it was seen as foolishness (1 Co 1:23), and Paul himself was a man who, rather than exalting himself as did the false teachers, appeared to be a fool and the refuse of the earth (1 Co 4:10-13). Nevertheless, his head was held high as he invited Timothy to **share in suffering for the gospel**. SHARE IN SUFFERING (Gk. *sugkakopathēson,* the prefix *sun,* "with," and the compound of *kakos,* "bad, wrong, troublesome," and *pathos,* "feeling, emotion") is used in a similar context in 2:9, and in both places it seems to emphasize personally sharing with Paul in affliction or hardship. Such endurance is possible through **relying on the power of God**. This life-changing "power" of God is the Holy Spirit of whom he has just spoken in the preceding sentence (v. 7).

1:9 Paul supported his reference to the "power" of God by breaking out into a more formalized statement of belief or creed describing how great God really is. God **has saved us and called us with a holy calling**. He is the One who has initiated and consummated salvation (a common thread in the Pastoral Epistles; e.g.,

1 Tm 1:1; 2:3-4; 4:10; Ti 1:3; 2:10; 3:4-5). In addition, He has "called" individuals to be part of His kingdom family (1 Co 1:9; Rm 8:28-30) with a "calling" that marks them as set apart for His purposes, destined to walk before Him in holiness (1 Co 1:2). He has provided salvation **not according to our works** (Gk. *erga,* "act, deed, product"), for no human merit is involved (Eph 2:8-9). Instead, salvation and calling are **according to His own purpose and grace** (Ti 3:5). **Before time began**, God purposed to provide salvation as a free and gracious gift that **was given to us in Christ Jesus**. It is available to all women and men and becomes effectual for those who believe in Jesus Christ as their personal Savior and Lord (Jn 3:16; 1 Tm 4:10).

1:10 Although God purposed from eternity to provide salvation, **this has now been made evident** (Gk. *phanerōtheisan,* "manifest, make visible or known what has been hidden or unknown") **through the appearing of our Savior Christ Jesus** in the present age (Ti 3:4-7). Paul elsewhere uses the term APPEARING (Gk. *epiphaneias,* "manifestation, making conspicuous," anglicized as "epiphany") to refer to Christ's return (4:1,8; Ti 2:13), but in this verse the past tense of the verb "made evident" clarifies its reference to His first coming. Paul highlighted two purposes of Christ's ministry.

- He **has abolished** (Gk. *katargēsantos,* "wipe out, set aside, break"; cp. 1 Co 15:24,26; Eph 2:15; 2 Th 2:8) **death**. The penalty for sin is death (Rm 5:8), but Jesus, through His substitutionary atonement on the cross has paid that penalty. Thus death has no power over believers, since they stand before God without condemnation (Rm 8:1).

- Christ **has brought life and immortality** (Gk. *aphtharsian,* "incorruption, eternality") **to light through the**

gospel. The gospel alone displays the eternal life that Jesus has made available to each believer.

1:11-12 Paul returned to personal testimony in stating that **for this gospel I was appointed a herald, apostle, and teacher**, almost exactly the same wording as in 1 Timothy 2:7; his purpose was to give a brief summary of key aspects of his ministry (v. 11). HERALD (Gk. *kērux*, "one commissioned to deliver an official message from someone in authority," e.g., a public summons,) in the New Testament denotes a "preacher," one who openly proclaims the gospel, also called by derivation the "kerygma." Paul suffered **these things** specifically because of his gospel ministry. Although imprisoned, however, Paul declared that he was **not ashamed** (Gk. *epaischunomai*; see v. 8; cp. Lk 9:26) for two important reasons (2 Tm 1:12).

- First, **because I know** (Gk. *oida*, "know for certain") **whom I have believed** (Gk. *pepisteuka*, "entrust, regard as true, place confidence in"; cp. 1 Tm 1:11,16; 3:16)—the apostle had come into a personal life-changing relationship with Jesus Christ (2 Tm 1:12). After many years of walking with Him, Paul could say with a deep, settled assurance that he knew Christ intimately and that this relationship was infinitely satisfying to him.

- Second, Paul is **persuaded that He is able to guard** (Gk. *phulaxai*, "keep safe; watch over; protect from loss, theft, or destruction") **what has been entrusted** (Gk. *parathēkēn*, "deposited, consigned to faithful keeping") **to me until that day**.

"Believed" and "persuaded," perfect tense verbs in Greek, both emphasize past decisions with lasting results, which were

as real to Paul then as they had been on the road to Damascus. He was convinced that this personal God whom he served had all the power necessary "to guard" the gospel message that had been "entrusted" to his care (see 1 Tm 6:20, where the wording, focused on Timothy, is nearly identical). In addition, Paul affirmed that Christ Himself is able to protect and keep the message safe "until that day," a reference to the Lord's return.

An Exhortation to Guard the Gospel Message (1:13-14)

1:13 Paul exhorted his son in the faith to "HOLD ON TO (Gk. *eche*, "hold fast, lay hold of, possess, adhere or cling to") the PATTERN (Gk. *hupotupōsin*, "outline, sketch, brief summary of the essentials, example"; cp. 1 Tm 1:16) of SOUND (Gk. *hugiainontōn*, "well, in good health," figuratively "without error, dependable"; cp. 2 Tm 4:3; 1 Tm 1:10; 6:3) teaching," a reference to the gospel message that Timothy had heard from Paul. In making this statement, Paul once more identified loyalty to the gospel with loyalty to himself (cp. 2 Tm 1:8). In addition, while commitment to the gospel matters, so does the manner in which Timothy would live out that covenant. His life and ministry were to be characterized by **the faith and love that are in Christ Jesus** and were the Lord's supernatural gifts to him (1 Tm 1:2,5,14).

1:14 With his personal testimony as the backdrop, Paul exhorted Timothy to **guard** (Gk. *phulaxon*; see v. 12) the gospel message described as **that good thing entrusted** (Gk. *parathēkēn*; see v. 12) **to you** (see 1 Tm 6:20). Paul knew that such a responsibility required more than human ability; so he emphasized that Timothy would guard the treasure of the gospel **through the Holy Spirit** indwelling both Paul and Timothy. For the third time in this opening series of exhortations, the apostle referred to the necessity of reliance on the "Holy Spirit" for accomplishing the work of the ministry. Furthermore, he added that the Spirit **lives in** (Gk. *enoikountos*; "indwell"; cp. 2 Tm 1:5; Rm 8:11; 2 Co 6:16; Col 3:16) them and, by extension, in all other believers (Rm 8:9-11).

An Example of One Who Has Served Faithfully (1:15-18)

1:15 In this section Paul turned from directly exhorting Timothy to reminding him of something he already knew, his loyalty to Paul. First, the apostle gave a negative example: **All those in Asia have turned away from me**. This could mean that a number from the province of Asia came to Rome to meet with Paul but turned back, leaving only Onesiphorus to seek him out. It could also mean that the number of desertions in Asia was so great that even those whom Paul knew well, **including Phygelus** (Gk. "a little fugitive") **and Hermogenes** (Gk. "born of Hermes," a Greek deity), had turned away.

1:16-17 In either case, Paul's reason for bringing up this issue was to focus on one man's faithfulness. He began with a spontaneous prayer that God would **grant mercy** (Gk. *eleos*, "compassion, pity") **to the household of Onesiphorus**. God's "mercy" is His goodness extended to those who are in distress or deep need. Possibly this Christian brother had died, since Paul speaks of Onesiphorus' service in the past tense and since Paul referred to his benefactor's household again in the closing greetings (4:19). However, since Paul asked for God's mercy to be his at the time of Christ's return (1:18), more likely Onesiphorus simply was not with his "household" when Paul was writing. While Onesiphorus was in Rome, "he often REFRESHED" (Gk. *anepsuxen*, figuratively "was a breath of fresh air,"

from *ana*, "in the midst," and *psuchō*, "breathe, cool off, cool by blowing") Paul. This refreshing would certainly have been through meeting his physical needs in the prison, but it would also have included the spiritual and emotional comfort and encouragement he brought as a brother in Christ. More importantly to Paul's overall argument in this section of the letter, Onesiphorus **was not ashamed** (Gk. *epaischunthē*; see vv. 8,12) of Paul's imprisonment. In fact, by actively seeking out Paul he had assumed great personal risk—his friendly association with a prisoner in Rome could have led to his own arrest.

1:18 In response to his faithful ministry, Paul prayed that **he obtain mercy from the Lord on that day**. Paul knew that he would never be able to repay this man's kindness, so he asked God to do so. "That day" is a reference to Christ's return, which will be followed by a time when rewards will be given to believers for faithfulness. Paul added, **and you know how much he ministered at Ephesus**. Thus Paul used this man's example of faithful service, both to himself and to Christ and His gospel, as an object lesson to motivate his beloved son, Timothy, also to serve faithfully and unashamedly.

AN ENCOURAGEMENT TO TIMOTHY TO ENDURE THE HARDSHIPS THAT ACCOMPANY MINISTRY (2:1-13)

In many ways this section of the letter is simply an extension of the themes found in chapter 1. There, however, Paul's focus was more on loyalty to Jesus Christ, to His gospel, and to himself personally. In these verses the apostle focused specifically on the need for Timothy to endure the hardships that are part and parcel of the ministry and to teach God's Word diligently and correctly.

Heart to Heart:
Paul's Be-attitudes to Timothy

As a loving father in the ministry, Paul gave thoughtful advice to young Timothy. He reminded Timothy of his legacy of faith from his grandmother Lois and his mother Eunice. Then, in this final letter, Paul gave Timothy direct instruction. His advice was to affect Timothy's attitudes and actions.

• *Be thankful for God's blessings (1:3-7).*

• *Be bold with the gospel (1:8-12).*

• *Be loyal to the faith (1:13-18).*

• *Be strong in grace (2:1-13).*

• *Be a diligent worker (2:14-26).*

• *Be wary of false teachers (3:1-9).*

• *Be true to God's Word (3:10-17).*

• *Be determined to fulfill your ministry (4:1-8).*

• *Be filled with God's grace (4:19-22).*

The loving counsel of Paul to Timothy is timely advice to Christians today.

An Appeal to Commit the Gospel to Faithful Persons (2:1-2)

2:1 Paul focused his attention directly on Timothy and emphatically addressed him as **You ... my child** (Gk. *teknon*, "son"), highlighting Paul's tender affection for him. **Therefore** refers back to the exhortations of 2 Timothy 1:13-14, where he urged Timothy to hold fast to the gospel message. His exhortation here is to **be strong** (Gk. *endunamou*, "continue being strengthened") **in the grace that is in Christ Jesus**. God Himself is the source of this power (1:8,14). As he allowed the Lord to strengthen him, Timothy must consistently draw on the undeserved yet all-sufficient resources of that "grace," for which the source is "Christ Jesus."

2:2 God's strengthening forms the prerequisite for Paul's next appeal for Timothy to **commit to faithful men** that "pattern of sound teaching" (1:13), i.e. the gospel message, that Timothy had **heard** from Paul **in the presence of many witnesses**. This teaching was not the secret instruction of the false teachers, whose deeper truths were reserved for their initiates; rather, the truth taught by Paul was broadcast freely and was widely attested by many.

The nominal form of the verb **COMMIT** (Gk. *parathou*, "set before, deposit, entrust, commit to another's charge"; cp. 1 Tm 1:18) has been used twice previously in reference to the gospel as "that good thing entrusted to you" (2 Tm 1:12,14; cp. Rm 3:2; 6:17; 1 Co 9:17; Gl 2:7; 1 Th 2:4; 1 Tm 1:11; 6:20; Ti 1:3). Having received the sacred trust of guarding and preaching God's Word, Timothy must entrust it "to FAITHFUL (Gk. *pistois*, "reliable, dependable, trustworthy; believing") MEN" (Gk. *anthrōpois*, "people, human beings," the generic word for "man," unlike *andros*, "male," in 1 Tm 2:12). The next clause delineates a prime characteristic of such people: They "WILL BE ABLE (Gk. *hikanoi*, "fit, sufficient in ability, adequate, worthy") to teach others also." One of Paul's purposes in this letter was to urge Timothy to leave Ephesus, even though his task there had not yet been completed, and to come to him in Rome (2 Tm 4:9). To do so, the younger man would need to appoint leaders who could teach accurately and pastor the flock. Most likely these were the elders described in his previous letter (1 Tm 3:1-7; 5:17-18).

An Exhortation to Share in Suffering for the Gospel (2:3-7)

2:3-4 Paul turned to the second reason why it was critical that Timothy be strengthened in God's grace: He must **share in suffering** (Gk. *sugkakopathēson*, "suffer hardship together," see v. 8) along with Paul for the sake of the gospel. To make his case, Paul used three illustrations, with the second two building on the idea of the first, a military metaphor. Timothy must do this **as a good soldier of Christ Jesus**. Paul often used military imagery in his letters (2 Co 10:3-5; Eph 6:10-17; Phm 2), and the underlying assumption here seems to be that suffering is automatically part of a soldier's life as he does battle. "To PLEASE (Gk. *aresē*, "strive to please" with the sense of making adjustments to accommodate another's goals or outlook) the RECRUITER" (Gk. *stratologēsanti*,

"army commander who enlists soldiers or gathers an army"), a soldier must stay focused and avoid becoming "entangled" in the affairs of civilian life. The root of **ENTANGLED** (Gk. *empleketai*, "involved, woven into, enmeshed") is *plekō*, "weave together, twist, plait, braid," anglicized as the root of "complex." In the Gospels it describes the construction of Jesus' crown of thorns (Mt 27:29; Mk 15:17; Jn 19:2). Peter also warned believers against becoming "entangled" in "the world's impurity" because, like trying to remove a ribbon intricately woven into braided hair, extricating oneself from such compromising lifestyles can prove nearly impossible (2 Pt 2:20). A soldier's single-minded attitude toward fulfilling his duties will please the one who enlisted him. Paul was not speaking against marriage or secular employment, since he himself worked as a tentmaker and also expected that church leaders would most often be married (1 Co 9:5-6; 1 Tm 3:2). Rather, he was simply highlighting the need for single-minded perseverance in the face of suffering. For those who endure, the reward is the pleasure of God Himself.

2:5 Paul's second metaphor is athletic, a common one in his writings (e.g., 4:7; 1 Co 9:24-27). An athlete must also suffer as he endures the rigors of training and of competition, and he cannot be honored as victor in a contest "unless he COMPETES (Gk. *athlēsē*, "wrestles, contends for a prize, engages in a contest") ACCORDING TO THE RULES" (Gk. *nomimōs*, "lawfully"). Just as an athlete's reward is to be CROWNED (Gk. *stephanoutai*, "adorned or honored with the victor's wreath," from the noun *stephanos*, the "crown" awarded to the winner in an athletic contest; cp. Heb 2:7,9), so Timothy's reward would be a future "crown of righteousness" when he would finally stand in his Savior's presence (see 2 Tm 4:8; cp. 1 Co 3:15; 2 Co 5:10).

2:6 The third metaphor is agricultural. Again, Paul drew attention to a profession— **the hardworking farmer** (Gk. *geōrgon*, "tiller of soil, husbandman, vinedresser")—involving not only hard labor and suffering but also a reward. Paul used the term HARDWORKING (Gk. *kopiōnta*, "work or labor to the point of weariness or exhaustion") in his previous letter to Timothy to describe "elders who are good leaders" deserving double honor (1 Tm 5:17). The farmer who has invested his personal labor in cultivating the crop **ought to be** (Gk. *dei*, "it is necessary") **the first** to reap the benefits of his labor.

2:7 Paul instructed Timothy to **consider** (Gk. *noei*, "reflect on, think over, ponder, heed") the meaning of these three word pictures, since he had not taken time to draw out the meanings explicitly. Timothy did not need to rely on his own intellectual effort for this, **for the Lord will give** (Gk. *dōsei*, "supply, furnish") **you understanding** (Gk. *sunesin*, "knowledge, insight," lit. "a flowing or running together"; cp. Lk 2:47; Eph 3:4; Col 1:9; 2:2) **in everything**. God alone would be the source of that true spiritual insight he would need.

Paul's Loyalty to Jesus Christ, the Author of Salvation (2:8-10)

Paul changed the focus slightly and placed the spotlight squarely on Jesus Christ Himself and the gospel message. Timothy's loyalty must always be to Jesus Christ personally but would be demonstrated first by his loyalty to Paul, who was suffering as a prisoner because of his own commitment to Christ, and second by faithfulness to carry out the ministry committed to his care.

2:8 The apostle highlighted two aspects of the gospel here. First, **Jesus Christ** is **risen from the dead**. The empty tomb is a central truth of the gospel message, announcing the effectiveness of Christ's substitutionary sacrifice for the sins of all. The resurrection also ensures the believer's future resurrection and participation in future rewards (see 2:5-6). Second, Jesus is **descended from David**, the true Messiah who has fulfilled Old Testament prophecy. Paul regarded these as core truths of the gospel he preached.

2:9 For that gospel Paul suffered **to the point of being bound** (Gk. *desmōn*, "bonds," from the verb *deō*, "bind, tie, fasten with chains") **like a criminal** (Gk. *kakourgos*, "evildoer"). Paul was not under the sort of house arrest described in Acts 28. Rather, this imprisonment was dark and harsh, and it involved being bound in chains like a particularly dangerous criminal—a clear indignity for someone who was both innocent of wrong-doing and a Roman citizen. But while he, the best-known teacher of the Gospel, is in chains, he victoriously declares that **God's message is not bound** (Gk. *dedetai*, "imprisoned," with the sense of being unhindered or unrestricted from movement; also from the verb *deō*, "bind, tie, fasten with chains"). Although the prevailing government could chain the messenger, the message itself would progress unfettered (cp. Php 1:12-18).

2:10 Paul mentioned his imprisonment here for two reasons. First, it served as a contrast to the gospel that spread freely throughout the earth. Second, he wanted to emphasize that he endured **all things for the elect**, God's chosen people. Paul referred here to those previously saved, those presently saved, and those who will be saved in the future (Rm 8:33; Col 3:12; Ti 1:1). **Endure** (Gk. *hupomenō*, "stand one's ground, hold out, endure"; cp. Rm 12:12; 1 Co 13:7) is central here because it continues the idea of perseverance that reaches from 2 Timothy 1:3 to 2:13 (see 1 Tm 6:11). The implication, of course, was that Timothy should be willing to do the same.

The purpose for Paul's enduring suffering was **so that they also may obtain salvation** centered in the person of **Christ Jesus** accompanied by **eternal glory**. Paul's sufferings certainly did not procure salvation for those who had not yet responded to the gospel message. Salvation is ever and always a free gift (Eph 2:8-9). Rather, Paul saw himself as God's messenger whose sufferings were somehow necessary for spreading the gospel. He especially focused on the "eternal glory" that he and all other believers would experience at the consummation of their salvation in heaven.

Christ's Enduring Faithfulness to Believers (2:11-13)

As Paul approached the end of his appeal to Timothy to endure the hardships that accompany the ministry, he wrapped up his exhortation with the last of the "trustworthy sayings" in the Pastoral Epistles (see 1 Tm 1:15; 3:1; 4:10; Ti 3:8.) The word "for" at the beginning is explanatory, and specifically refers back to 2 Timothy 2:1-10, although endurance in the face of suffering has been the topic since the beginning of the letter (v. 11). "This saying" was probably an early hymn or creedal statement. The clearly poetic structure consists of four lines, each beginning with a protasis (the "if" clause) describing believers' actions. Each protasis is followed by the apodosis (giving the results of the "if" clause) in terms of Christ's actions. A coda (an additional statement) follows the fourth line. The general flow of thought seems to be from conversion (line 1), to a believer's enduring hardships in light of future rewards (line 2), to a warning about the consequences of denying Christ (line 3),

to a word of reassurance that Christ's faithfulness is always greater than a believer's disloyalty to Him (line 4).

2:11 The first line mirrors Romans 6:1-11, especially verse 8, in which Paul spoke of the believer's identification with Christ in His death and resurrection (cp. Gl 2:20). **This saying is trustworthy** (Gk. *pistos ho logos*, "faithful or reliable the word," i.e., "what has been said"): Those who **have died with Him** are assured that Christ's death has paid the penalty for sin and that His resurrection means they will therefore **live with Him**, i.e., experience new life as an eternal reality—both present and future—to be enjoyed one day in His presence. The apostle thus invited Timothy to reflect on his conversion experience and to consider how it should affect his walk with the Lord.

2:12 Paul again invited Timothy to **endure** (Gk. *hupomenomen*, see v. 10) in suffering for the gospel and highlighted the promise of victory and reward. Believers who remain faithful to Christ during trials **will also reign with Him**. The third line directly contrasts the victory of line two: **If we deny Him, He will also deny us**. DENY (Gk. *arnēsometha*, "deny, repudiate, disown") seems to be used in an absolute sense in this verse to refer to complete apostasy (cp. Mt 10:33; 1 Tm 1:16). In the context of this letter, this statement seems to be a warning to Ephesian leaders such as Hymenaeus and Philetus (2 Tm 2:17) and possibly to those from Asia Minor, who earlier deserted the apostle (1:15). The second half of the sentence refers to the time of Christ's future judgment and His consequent denial of those who had apostatized.

2:13 The fourth line is not intended as a word of judgment but rather as one of encouragement to those believers who, in their weakness, have failed to "endure" (line 2). It is not a reference to those who have professed belief but who have later turned to complete apostasy (line 3). Believers are sometimes **faithless** (Gk. *apistoumen*, "unfaithful, betraying a trust, disbelieving"; cp. Mk 16:16; Lk 24:11; Ac 28:24), as was Peter when he told the servant girl that he did not know Jesus (Mt 26:69-75; Mk 14:66-72; Lk 22:54-62; Jn 18:15-17,25-27). Nevertheless, there is a place of repentance and forgiveness for them, as there was for Peter (Jn 21:15-19). The reason for Christ's faithfulness to believers rests in His unchanging nature. He must be true to His character and fulfill His promises to believers (e.g., Php 1:6).

A WARNING TO TIMOTHY TO RESIST AND CORRECT THE FALSE TEACHERS (2:14-26)

Having exhorted Timothy to remain true to his calling to the ministry despite hardship and suffering, Paul turned his attention to the false teachers in Ephesus. Clearly, they had continued their deviant and disruptive ways, as Onesiphorus had probably informed him. Paul appealed to his son Timothy to resist and correct them and to avoid being sucked into their disputes. Instead, Timothy must teach the truth of God's word and continually pursue a lifestyle of godliness.

A Warning to Avoid the False Teachers' Controversies (2:14-19)

2:14 Timothy was to **remind** the Christians at Ephesus **of these things**, most likely a reference to the "trustworthy saying" of verses 11 to 13. With the daily threat of the false teachers' poisonous doctrines, the believers needed to recall the importance of persevering in the truth of the gospel. **Charging** (Gk. *diamarturomenos*, "earnestly testifying, solemnly affirming by testimony"; cp. 4:1; 1 Tm 5:21) **them before** (Gk. *enōpion*, "in the sight or presence of") **God**, Timothy was

to make clear that believers will be held accountable for their obedience to his prohibiting their fighting **about words.** FIGHT ABOUT WORDS (Gk. *logomachein*, "contend about words") translates a compound word—*logos*, "word, what someone has said, doctrine," and *machomai*, "argue, quarrel, wrangle, dispute," also denoting the action of people engaged in hand-to-hand combat. In verse 24, Paul insisted that one who serves Christ must not be "quarrelsome" (Gk. *machesthai*), i.e., not characterized as contentious, causing disagreements to escalate to the level of verbal combat. This characteristic was primarily found among the Ephesian heretics, who had "a sick interest in disputes and arguments over words" (see 1 Tm 2:8; 6:4-5). Paul made clear that such fighting "is IN NO WAY PROFITABLE (Gk. *ouden chrēsimion*, "not useful, useless") and leads to the RUIN (Gk. *katastrophē*, "overthrow, destruction," usually of cities, e.g., of Sodom and Gomorrah in 2 Pt 2:6; anglicized as "catastrophe) of the hearers."

2:15 Turning his attention to Timothy personally, the apostle urged him to **be diligent** (Gk. *spoudason*, "hasten, endeavor, be zealous and eager, sparing no effort"; cp. 4:9,21; Eph 4:3; Ti 3:12) **to present** himself **approved to God**. APPROVED (Gk. *dokimon*, "acceptable, pleasing") also described money changers who refused to circulate coins that had been reduced in weight, i.e., shaved down to steal the precious metal for personal gain. The word is thus associated with integrity and faithfulness. Timothy should aspire to stand before God as one who had lived and proclaimed the gospel message in its entirety and as unadulterated, undistorted truth. Unlike the false teachers, Timothy should be **a worker who doesn't need to be ashamed** before God because of faulty craftsmanship.

Instead, he is to be one who is **correctly teaching the word of truth**. COR-RECTLY TEACHING (Gk. *orthoto-mounta*, "rightly handling") literally means "cutting straight." The word combines *ortho*, "straight, not crooked, correct," and *tomoteros*, "sharper" with the sense of making a single, clean slice or stroke as opposed to the repeated action of chopping. The term occurs only here in the New Testament but appears in the Septuagint: Pr 3:6, "will guide you on the right paths; and 11:5, "clears his path." The emphasis is not so much on accurate biblical interpretation as it is on "teaching" the gospel, "the word of truth," in contrast to participating in arguments over words as the false teachers were doing.

2:16-18 Returning his focus to the heretics, Paul appealed to Timothy to **avoid** (Gk. *periistaso*, "shun, turn around to avoid, turn your back on"; cp. Ti 3:9) the **irreverent** (Gk. *bebēlous*, "profane, ungodly"; cp. 1 Tm 4:7), **empty speech** of the heretics (1 Tm 6:20). Purposeless talk that fails to honor God **will produce** (Gk. *prokopsousin*, "advance, make progress, proceed or lead to") **an even greater measure of godlessness** (Gk. *asebeias*, "impiety, ungodliness, irreverence," 2 Tm 2:16; cp. Ti 2:12). Furthermore, **their word will spread like gangrene** (anglicized from Gk. *gaggraina*, "cancer," from *grainō*, "gnaw"), producing spiritual death, rather than life, in their hearers (2 Tm 2:17).

Hymenaeus (Gk. "regarding marriage," from *Humen*, "god of weddings"; see 1 Tm 1:20) **and Philetus** (Gk. "beloved" from *phileō*) were prime examples of those who **have deviated** (Gk. *ēstochēsan*, "gone astray, missed the mark, fail, aimed badly") **from the truth** (cp. 1 Tm 1:6; 6:21) and **are overturning the faith of some** (v. 17). OVERTURN-ING (Gk. *anatrepousin*, "overthrow-

ing, destroying, upsetting, subverting"; cp. Ti 1:11) vividly describes Jesus' literal "overturning" of the money changers' tables in the temple (Jn 2:15). The heretics' teachings were putting "the faith of some" in disarray and confusion, i.e., a doctrinal mess. These men taught **that the resurrection has already taken place** (v. 18). This particular heresy was not new in the life of the early church (cp. 1 Co 15:12; 2 Th 2:2) and probably came from a Hellenistic misconception that "resurrection" was a purely spiritual concept and that there would be no bodily resurrection of believers. Paul argued elsewhere that such teaching was dangerous and would lead to denial both of Christ's literally rising from the dead (see 1 Co 15:13-14) and of believers' triumph over death and the grave. Paul considered these to be cardinal truths of the gospel, so he urged Timothy to fight against this false teaching (1 Co 15:20-28).

2:19 Nevertheless, Paul continued, despite the false teachers' efforts to draw some away from the truth, **God's solid foundation stands firm**. The foundation is the true gospel itself now intertwined with the lives of those who are living obediently in accordance with its precepts and sharing this good news with others. The foundation has **this inscription: The Lord knows those who are His**—a direct quotation from Numbers 16:5. True conversion involves God placing His INSCRIPTION (Gk. *sphragida*, "seal, signet, mark," as a mark of confirmation or authentication, proof by another's testimony that you are who you claim to be, or security from Satan; cp. Jn 6:27; 2 Co 1:22; Eph 1:13; 4:30) or seal of ownership on the believer whose name He knows. This seal guarantees God's commitment to produce both correct doctrinal belief and a godly lifestyle in each Christian.

An Analogy of Household Vessels (2:20-21)

2:20 Paul followed up with a different analogy involving household vessels. In a wealthier household, **gold and silver bowls** would be reserved **for special** occasions and **wood and earthenware** ones would be used **for ordinary** meals, cooking preparation, and garbage disposal.

2:21 Paul used this analogy to illustrate the need for believers to purify themselves from the contamination of false teaching and "unrighteousness" (v. 19) in order to **be a special instrument** (Gk. *skeuos*, "vessel, implement," the same word translated as "vessel" in v. 20), figuratively one of the gold or silver ones. PURIFIES (Gk. *ekkatharē*, "cleanse, clean out") combines the prefix *ek*, "out of, from," with the verb *kathairō*, "cleanse," in the sense of removing filth or impurity or pruning (Jn 15:2). The English word "catharsis" denotes purging or thoroughly cleansing. The prefix *ek* in this word suggests that believers must not merely identify what is incompatible with Christlikeness or even "loosen" the hold of such vestiges of the sinful nature. Instead, they must completely do away with anything that hinders or detracts from holy living; cp. 1 Co 5:7. Purified vessels are fit to be "SET APART" (Gk. *hēgiasmenon*, "consecrated, dedicated, sanctified") in holiness and to be "useful to the Master, PREPARED (Gk. *hētoimasmenon*, "made ready," in English idiom "fit for a king") for every good work." MASTER (Gk. *despotē*, "ruler with absolute power, lord") did not have the negative connotation acquired by the English word "despot." In the New Testament the word appears in two contexts: (a) as the "master" of a household with servants or slaves committed to obeying him (1 Tm 6:1-2; Ti 2:9; 1 Pt 2:18; 2 Pt

2:1); (b) as the "Master" addressed in prayer (Lk 2:29; Ac 4:24; Jd 4; Rv 6:10). All believers have the privilege of repenting, of allowing God to cleanse them from the filth of false teaching and of being used as instruments of honor in the Master's hands.

Living Righteously and Avoiding the False Teachers' Disputes (2:22-26)

Paul applied the analogy of honorable vessels to Timothy, God's chosen leader of the Ephesian church. Timothy's commitment to a life of inner holiness and practical righteous living must be uncompromising. Paul also introduced the importance of rescuing others from the entrapment of the false teachers. In all his interactions with the heretics, Timothy was to act out of settled peace in his heart.

2:22 The apostle began with negative and positive exhortations. First, Timothy was to **flee from youthful passions** (Gk. *epithumias*, "craving, desire, longing, lust," particularly for something forbidden). "Youthful passions" include sexual sins as well as becoming involved in foolish discussions leading only to arguments (v. 23), pride, love of money, showy display of knowledge, and addictive behaviors. When Timothy ran away from these, he should continually run in pursuit of **righteousness, faith, love, and peace—** key characteristics of God's servant filled and empowered by the Holy Spirit (see 1 Tm 6:11). FLEE (Gk. *pheuge*, "escape from danger by running to safety, shun, run away from"; cp. 1 Co 6:18; 10:14; 1 Tm 6:11) is a present tense verb, making clear that he must continue fleeing every single time temptation rears its ugly head. PURSUE (*diōke*; "run swiftly in order to catch, follow, or reach the goal line; chase after; eagerly strive for or seek after") implies intense effort being directed toward a specific aim. In some contexts this word is translated "persecute," but here the word identifies the actions and qualities that should mark the Christian who is deliberately following His Master (cp. Rm 9:30-31; 12:14; 14:19; 1 Co 14:1; Php 3:12,14; 1 Th 5:15; 1 Tm 6:11; Heb 12:14; 1 Pt 3:11). Timothy was not alone but would run "along with those who call on the Lord from a PURE (Gk. *katharas*, "clean, free from corrupt desires, blameless"; cp. 2 Tm 1:3; 1 Tm 3:9) heart," i.e., free from the domination of sin (1 Tm 1:5).

2:23 Pursuing "peace" would be especially needed when dealing with the quarrelsome false teachers (v. 22), but Timothy must also "REJECT (Gk. *paraitou*, "shun, avoid, express disapproval of"; cp. 1 Tm 4:7; Ti 3:10) foolish and IGNORANT (Gk. *apaideutous*, "uneducated, not discipled") DISPUTES (Gk. *zēteseis*, "questioning, debate, controversy"; cp. 1 Tm 1:4; 6:4; Ti 3:9) knowing that they breed QUARRELS" (Gk. *machas*, "fights, conflicts, disputes"; cp. Ti 3:9; Jms 4:1). No matter how cunningly the hook is baited, Timothy must not become engaged in peripheral questions, which always end up as divisive personal conflicts (see 1 Tm 6:3-6,20-21).

2:24-25a To avoid quarrels, however, would not mean that Timothy should fail to engage the false teachers. Without letting discussion deteriorate into hostile argument, Timothy must:

- **be gentle** (Gk. *ēpion*, "approachable, gracious, mild, kind") to everyone,"

- be **able to teach**,

- be **patient** (Gk. *anexikakon*, "calm endurance of annoyance or provocation, showing restraint though incited to react"),

- instruct **his opponents with gentleness** (Gk. *prautēti*, "humility, meekness, being considerate"; cp. 1 Co 4:21; 2 Co 10:1; Gl 5:23; 6:1; Ti 3:2).

Paul has just stressed the importance of a life filled with "righteousness, faith, love, and peace," and now he adds this new list. Many of these are part of what he elsewhere calls "the fruit of the Spirit," character qualities that the Holy Spirit both imparts and develops in the life of the yielded, cooperative believer (Gl 5:22-23).

2:25b-26 A life filled with Spirit-empowered grace was critical to God's purposes in Ephesus. Timothy's godly attitude toward those who opposed him might be a catalyst for their **repentance** (Gk. *metanoian*, "change of mind"), seen here as a gift from God that would enable them to understand **the truth** of the Gospel (cp. Rm 2:4). They might also **come to their senses** (Gk. *ananēpsōsin*, "sober up, calm down") and have a clear head (cp. 2 Tm 4:5) about their situation, their lifestyle, and what they have believed. God would enable those who repent to "escape the Devil's TRAP" (Gk. *pagidos*, "snare, noose," typically used to entangle and catch birds and having the sense of taking by surprise), for they have "been CAPTURED (Gk. *ezōgrēmenoi*, "taken or caught alive, hunted down or eagerly pursued") by him to do his will." The diabolical, deceptive nature of the false teaching is once again highlighted here; the doctrines are not simply false, they are evil and destructive (see 1 Tm 4:1-2).

A PLEA TO TIMOTHY TO STAND FIRM IN THE FACE OF INEVITABLE APOSTASY (3:1-17)

The preceding section shows that Paul's purpose in refuting the heretics was to proclaim the truth of the gospel and refute error. He also desired redemption for those who were prisoners of Satan. He was not blind to the danger these false teachers presented to the Ephesian church, however; so in this section he gave a final indictment of them, their doctrine, and their lifestyles. He did this against an eschatological backdrop, i.e., a belief that they were living in the last days when evil will increase.

Paul and the other New Testament writers believed that with Christ's incarnation a chain of events was set in motion, to be completed with the Parousia—Christ's return. When Christ came to earth at His incarnation, a corner was turned in divine history. He ministered in the world, died to pay the penalty for the sins of all, rose from the dead, ascended to heaven, and established the church with the coming of the Holy Spirit on Pentecost. New Testament Christians enjoyed the benefits of salvation and a personal relationship with Christ, yet they were aware of a future aspect of their salvation as well, when they would be with Him in heaven and would worship Him forever. As Peter declared at Pentecost, the church now exists in the last days (Ac 2:16-21).

Paul's Assurance That a Time of Apostasy Is Coming (3:1-9)

3:1 But know this, Paul stated, **difficult times will come in the last days**. His goal here was to place the false teachers and their pernicious doctrine in a wider theological perspective. Specifically, a consistent part of the apostles' teaching was that in the times prior to Christ's return there would be an increase of evil (e.g., 1 Co 7:26; 1 Jn 2:18; 2 Pt 3:3). Paul set out to demonstrate that the false teachers were living proof that they are in the last days, and he went through a lengthy list of their sinful characteristics.

3:2-5 Like those listed in Romans 1:29-31 and 1 Timothy 1:9-10, these sins reflected pagan society generally and the false teachers specifically. In "the last days" (v. 1) believers can expect that **people will be**:

- **lovers of self**, an apt place to begin since a focus on self, and consequent disregard for others, opens the door for a multitude of vices (2 Tm 3:2);

- **lovers of money** (2 Tm 3:2; cp. 1 Tm 6:10);

- **boastful** (Gk. *alazones*, "empty pretender, braggart" 2 Tm 3:2; cp. Rm 1:30);

- **proud** (Gk. *huperēphanoi*, "arrogant, haughty," from *huper*, "over, beyond," and *phainō*, "cause to shine, bring into the light," 2 Tm 3:2; cp. Rm 1:30), figuratively suggesting one who seeks the spotlight for himself or sets himself up as better than others;

- **blasphemers** (Gk. *blasphēmoi*, "revilers, slanderers"), speaking evil of God (v. 2);

- **disobedient** (Gk. *apeitheis*, "cannot be persuaded, not compliant, insubordinate, willfully obstinate") **to parents**, which suggests a breaking up of prevailing social values (v. 2; cp. Lk 1:17; Rm 1:30; Ti 1:16; 3:3);

- **ungrateful** (Gk. *acharistoi*, "without grace, ungracious, unthankful," 2 Tm 3:2; cp. Lk 6:35);

- **unholy** (Gk. *anosioi*, "impious, wicked," 2 Tm 3:2; cp. 1 Tm 1:9), lacking respect for anything sacred;

- **unloving** (Gk. *astorgoi*, "unsociable"), lacking the natural affection one has for family members (2 Tm 3:3; cp. Rm 1:31);

- **irreconcilable** (Gk. *aspondoi*, "impossible to please, cannot be persuaded to enter a covenant or treaty in order to set aside hostilities") in relationships (2 Tm 3:3);

- **slanderers** (Gk. *diaboloi*, "accusers, defamers," those who "maliciously attack another's good name, humiliate or malign others"; cp. 2 Tm 2:26; 1 Tm 3:11; Ti 2:3)—like Satan himself, they speak falsehoods for the purpose of damaging others (2 Tm 3:3);

- **without self-control** (Gk. *akrateis*, "dissolute," v. 3);

- **brutal** (Gk. *anēmeroi*, "not tame, cruel, vicious, heartless, fierce," v. 3);

- **without love for what is good** (Gk. *aphilagathoi*, "opposed to goodness or good people," v. 3);

- **traitors** (Gk. *prodotai*, "betrayers") who maliciously deliver others over to destruction (v. 4; cp. Lk 6:16; Ac 7:52);

- **reckless** (Gk. *propeteis*, "impulsive, heedless, rash, impetuous"), acting without thinking, caring nothing for the interests of others, disregarding both possible and known consequences (2 Tm 3:4);

- **conceited** (Gk. *tetuphōmenoi*, "haughty, puffed up or blind with pride," lit. "wrapped in mist or smoke"), having only their own interests in view (v. 4);

- **lovers of pleasure rather than lovers of God** (v. 4);

- **holding to the form of religion but denying** (Gk. *ērnēmenoi*, "reject, refuse, give up"; cp. 2 Tm 3:12–13) **its power**—focusing on ascetic practices and engaging in endless discussions of religious myths, genealogies (1 Tm 1:4; 4:7), and obscure aspects of the Jewish law (1 Tm 1:7)—their disputes and arguments over words may sound religious to some, but they

were only empty speech (1 Tm 6:4-5,20). The outward "form of religion" might have been present, but these teachers were "denying its power" to transform lives through the work of the Holy Spirit. Paul's warning to Timothy and to others in the church is clear: **Avoid these people!** (2 Tm 3:5).

3:6-7 The apostle continued his denunciation of these teachers by citing the specific example of their deceiving some of the women in the Ephesian church. **Among** the hypocrites of the last days would be those who **worm their way into households** (v. 6). WORM (Gk. *endunontes*, "creep in, enter") suggests entry through deceptive means. Not unlike wolves in sheep's clothing (Mt 7:15), these religious charlatans come in "undercover, cloaked," hiding their real agenda. They made a point of proselytizing women. While the term "households" (Gk. *oikias*) could indicate wealthier women, the translation "homes" would be equally accurate and would not presuppose a certain socioeconomic class. Their activities, in fact, clarify a number of facets of the historical situation in the Ephesian church. CAPTURE (Gk. *aichmalōtizontes*, "lead away captive, make prisoner") is a term for capturing a prize of war. The word combines *aichme*, "spear," and *halosis*, "catch or take," as in a hunt (cp. 2 Pt 2:12). The picture is thus of being captured by the enemy and led away at "spear-point," 2 Tm 3:6; cp. Lk 21:24; Rm 7:23; 2 Co 10:5. Paul described the women targeted by these charlatans as IDLE WOMEN (Gk. *gunaikaria*, a diminutive form of "women"), with a negative connotation suggesting contempt (2 Tm 3:6).

- They were "BURDENED DOWN (Gk. *sesōreumena*, "heap up, overwhelmed by a heap of something") with sins" (v. 6) from their past, providing an opportunity for the false teachers to gain a foothold by offering false forgiveness or by convincing them that the sins are of no consequence in God's eyes.

• They were "led along by a variety of PASSIONS" (Gk. *epithumiais*, v. 6; see 2:22), probably sexual sins since the women have been brought under the influence of the false teachers inside their homes. Also, Paul earlier spoke of some young widows who "are self-indulgent" (1 Tm 5:6) and of others who "are drawn away from [their commitment to] Christ by desire" (1 Tm 5:11).

• They were "always LEARNING (Gk. *manthanonta*, "receiving instruction, gaining knowledge"; cp. 2 Tm 3:14; 1 Tm 2:11; 5:4,13; Ti 3:14) and never able to come to a KNOWLEDGE (Gk. *epignōsin*, "precise, full, correct knowledge") of the truth" (2 Tm 3:7).

Since the heretics clearly had a way with words, an endless cycle of teaching in the intricacies of myths, genealogies, and obscure points of the Jewish law, followed by payment for their teaching (1 Tm 6:3-10), is not hard to imagine. Because their spiritual hunger was being directed to the pursuit of countless dead-end religious questions, these ladies were "never able" to find Christ, the truth who sets men and women free (Jn 8:32; 14:6).

3:8-9 Paul concluded his discussion of the false teachers with an analogy. According to Jewish tradition, **Jannes and Jambres** were the names of Pharaoh's chief magicians who **resisted Moses** (Ex 7:11-12,22; 8:7). The apostle compared the deceptive practices of Pha-

raoh's magicians with those of the false teachers and said that **these** (the false teachers) **also**

• **resist** (Gk. *anthistantai*, "oppose, withstand," set themselves against; cp. 4:15) **the truth**,

• **are corrupt** (Gk. *katephtharmenoi*, "depraved") **in mind**, and

• **worthless** (Gk. *adokimoi*, "not approved, not standing the test, unfit, reprobate," in contrast to 2 Tm 2:15; cp. Rm 1:28; 1 Co 9:27; 2 Co 13:5-7; Ti 1:16; Heb 6:8) **in regard to the faith**.

The good news is that these heretics **will not make further progress** (Gk. *prokopsousin*, "go forward, advance," see 2:16). Just as the Egyptian magicians were shown to be ineffective charlatans, so the false teachers will be exposed both in their sinful practices and in their lack of understanding of the true gospel.

Paul's Appeal to Timothy to Stand Firm in the Face of Persecution (3:10-17)

Paul personally addressed his beloved son in the faith, Timothy. In this section he brought together the primary concerns of the first two sections of the letter. First, he returned to the topic of loyalty in the face of persecution (1:6–2:13). Second, he referred to the ongoing threat posed by the false teachers (2:14–3:9).

3:10-13 The apostle deftly switched topics from the false teachers to Timothy himself by opening this new paragraph with an emphatic expression, **but you** (2:1; 3:14; 4:5). Paul pointed out how Timothy had **followed** him in every sense of the word, in contrast to the godless lifestyle of the false teachers. By the first century FOLLOWED (Gk. *parēkolouthēsas*, "follow with the mind, understand, make one's own"; cp. 1 Tm 4:6) could be used as a technical term to describe the relationship between a disciple and his master. In their years of travel and ministry together, Timothy became Paul's closest disciple, described to the Philippians as "like-minded" (Php 2:20-22).

Paul called attention to the specific aspects of his life and ministry that Timothy would need to emulate in the months and years ahead (v. 10):

- his **teaching** or doctrine, the gospel message in all its aspects;
- his **conduct** or way of life;
- his **purpose**, which, from the moment of conversion, was fixed on fulfilling Christ's commission to take the gospel message throughout the earth, particularly to the Gentiles (Ac 26:19-20);
- his personal **faith** in Christ;
- his Spirit-given **patience**;
- his **love**, which enabled him to respond rightly both in personal relationships and in regard to circumstances;
- his **endurance,** enabling him to stand firm in even the most difficult times of persecution;
- **the persecutions and sufferings that came** to him **in Antioch, Iconium, and Lystra** (see Ac 13:13–14:23). Paul's two summary statements say it all: **What persecutions I endured! Yet the Lord rescued me from them all** (2 Tm 3:11).

Next Paul turned his focus from his own experience of persecution to a more general principle: **In fact, all those who want to live a godly life in Christ Jesus will be persecuted** (v. 12). In other words, persecution in some form is simply a normal part of life for all believers who choose to live godly lives (Jn 16:33).

In direct contrast to such believers are those like the false teachers. Paul called them **evil people and imposters** (Gk. *goētes*, "sorcerers, swindlers, deceivers") and said that they would progressively **become worse** (2 Tm 3:13). Their lives would become a downward spiral in which they were both **deceiving** others **and being deceived** as the god of this world led them to ultimate destruction.

3:14-15 Now Paul again turned his attention directly to Timothy with the emphatic expression, **but as for you** (cp. v. 10). Paul exhorted his son to **continue in** the gospel he had **learned** through instruction and which, as a result, he **firmly believed** (v. 14). Timothy could safely hold to what he had learned for two reasons:

- First, he knew **those from whom** he **learned**. Certainly he had learned the "Scriptures" (a reference to the Old Testament) from Paul himself, but **from childhood** (Gk. *brephous*, "infancy," a word consistently used in the New Testament to refer to unborn and newborn babies; cp. Lk 1;41,44; 2:12,16; 18:15; Ac 7:19; 1 Pt 2:2), he had **known the sacred Scriptures** as well (2 Tm 3:15). Although his father was a Gentile, his mother Eunice and his grandmother Lois were Jewish (1:5), and they educated him in the Jewish Scriptures from a very young age.
- Second, he had actually "known the sacred Scriptures." He had learned through experience that these "Scriptures" are true and trustworthy—they **are able to instruct** him **for salvation through faith in Christ Jesus**. Thus Paul called on Timothy's loyalty not only to what he had learned in the past but especially to Scripture itself, in which Jesus Christ is revealed as

"the source and perfecter" of salvation (Heb 12:2).

3:16-17 The apostle reflected on the true character of the Scriptures and their value to him in ministry. First, **all Scripture is inspired by God** (Gk. *theopneustos*, "God-breathed," the only instance of this word in the New Testament), emphasizing God's initiation and control of the process of communicating His thoughts to human beings (v. 16). The Holy Spirit orchestrated this process, so the original writings are without error (2 Pt 1:21). God's written word is authoritative simply because it is *God's* word. It is also infallible—it cannot be broken (Jn 10:35).

"All Scripture" is also **profitable** (2 Tm 3:16):

- **for teaching** (Gk. *didaskalian*, "instructing" in regard to doctrine) God's truth to others, one of Timothy's primary ministry responsibilities (4:3; 1 Tm 4:6,13,16; Ti 1:9; 2:1,7, 10);

- **for rebuking** (Gk. *elegmon*, "proof, conviction"), i.e., enabling him to expose the errors of both the lifestyles and the teaching of the heretics (4:2; 1 Tm 5:20);

- **for correcting** (Gk. *epanorthōsin*, "restoring to an upright position, making straight again") those who are in error and setting them on a path of restoration (2 Tm 2:25; Jn 17:17);

- **for training** (Gk. *paideian*, "discipline, course of instruction" aimed at cultivation of both knowledge and character; cp. Eph 6:4; see Heb 12:5-11) **in righteousness**, providing wisdom in how to grow in an intimate relationship with the Lord and in how to minister in the full power of the Holy Spirit.

Paul climaxed this discussion of the importance of Scripture in the life of Timothy (and, of course, all other believers)

with a purpose clause: **so that the man of God may be complete, equipped** (Gk. *exēptismenos*, "completely or perfectly furnished, accomplished") **for every good work** (see 2 Tm 2:21). COMPLETE (Gk. *artios*, "fitted, perfect") means to be capable and proficient—Timothy would be able to meet all possible demands within the will of God. Paul added this final clause to remind Timothy that he had all the God-given equipment necessary to carry out his responsibilities in Ephesus and in the years ahead.

A SOLEMN CHARGE TO TIMOTHY TO FULFILL HIS MINISTRY IN ALL CIRCUMSTANCES (4:1-8)

As Paul approached the end of his letter, he drew all his concerns together into one final charge to his spiritual son, Timothy. The solemn charge itself (v. 1) is followed by nine imperatives that delineate its various facets (vv. 2,4). These are followed by the reason the timing of this charge is so critical: Paul was well aware that his death was imminent, and he was in the process of turning over his ministry to Timothy (vv. 6-8).

A Solemn Charge to Proclaim the Gospel Consistently (4:1-5)

4:1 In all of Paul's writings, a charge more solemn than this one is hard to imagine (cp. 2:14; 1 Tm 5:21; 6:13). The backdrop is eschatological—he appealed to Timothy as a person whose life was lived out in the very real presence of the living **God and Christ Jesus**. This same Jesus will **judge** (Gk. *krinein*, "separate, decide, pronounce judgment, rule, govern") all humankind (1 Co 4:5; 2 Co 5:10), both **the living and the dead** (Ac 10:42). He will come again to earth at **His appearing** (Gk. *epiphaneian*, "being made manifest or con-

Heart to Heart:
Gullible Women of the World or Godly Women of the Word (2 Tm 3:6-17)

Are you a gullible woman of the world or a godly woman of the Word? Many Christian women today have been led astray by the culture, following its practices and lifestyles. Paul gave a very convicting description of gullible women of the world in 2 Timothy 3:6-9. Gullible women are "burdened down with sins," "led along by a variety of passions," "always learning and never able to come to a knowledge of the truth." The Bible is clear: Christians are to resist these false teachings and "flee" from immorality (2:22-23).

In contrast, Paul challenged believers to be godly women of the Word. Godly women follow true doctrine, live Christlike lives, seek God's purposes, grow in faith, develop patience, extend love, and persevere in persecution. Christians are to live godly lives, remaining set apart from the world.

Throughout the Pauline epistles, the apostle contrasted the gullible life and the godly life. In Colossians 3, Paul instructed believers to "put to death" worldliness (Col 3:5) and "put away" sin (Col 3:8-9). Instead they are to "put on" godliness (Col 3:12-14). In Galatians 5, Paul contrasted "the works of the flesh" (Gl 5:19-21) and "the fruit of the Spirit" (Gl 5:22-23). Christians are not to carry out "the desire of the flesh"; instead, they are to "walk by the Spirit" (Gl 5:16). Daily believers are to crucify "the flesh with its passions and desires" (Gl 5:24), living by the Spirit and following Christ's example. Be a godly woman of the Word, not a gullible woman of the world!

spicuous," anglicized as "epiphany," a revelatory manifestation of God; cp. 2 Tm 1:10; 4:8; 2 Th 2:8; 1 Tm 6:14; Ti 2:13), and He will then rule in His future **kingdom** (2 Tm 4:18). Against this backdrop Paul said, **I solemnly charge you**. His use of the first person "I" reflected both his apostolic authority and the directness of his appeal to Timothy.

4:2 This sentence is rounded out with five of the nine imperatives comprising the charge:

- First, Timothy must **proclaim** (Gk. *kēruxon*, "herald with authority, publicly declare, preach") **the message**. He was to preach the word of God in all its fullness, not philosophize or argue about it.

- Second, he must **persist** (Gk. *epistēthi*, "stand ready, appear, attack, present," with the root meaning "stand firm, be steadfast, uphold or sustain authority, establish or make firm") in his proclamation of the word **whether convenient** (Gk. *eukairōs*, "opportunely," from *eu*, "good," and *kairos*, "the right time," thus when the opportunity is ripe) **or not** (Gk. *akairōs*, "unseasonably," when it's not a good time; cp. verb form, "lacked opportunity," Php 4:10) either to him or to his hearers.

- Third, he must **rebuke** (Gk. *elegxon*, "convict, refute, call to account, correct, admonish, reprove"; cp. 2 Tm 3:16) those who are in error.

- Fourth, he must **correct** (Gk. *epitimēson*, "chide, censure, assign due penalty") those who are in error in doctrine or attitudes and overall lifestyles.

- Fifth, he must **encourage** (Gk. *parakaleson*, "exhort") them to live in obedience to God's word.

Timothy must carry out these last three activities **with great patience and teaching**, not only because life transformation typically takes time in the human heart, but also because—as the following sentence makes clear—there will be resistance to change.

4:3-4 Paul paused to explain why proclaiming God's word will be such a difficult task. A **time will come when** people will not put up with **sound doctrine**, a synonym for God's word, especially in the Pastoral Epistles (e.g., 1:13; 1 Tm 1:10; 6:3), emphasizing the health and life-giving nature of the gospel. Rather than embracing the truth, such people will

- heed **their own desires**;

- **accumulate** (Gk. *episōreusousin*, "heap up, gather in a pile"; cp. related word in 3:6) **teachers for themselves** who appeal to their being enamored with new ideas;

- **have an itch to hear** (Gk. *knēthomenoi tēn akoēn*, "scratch or tickle the ears") **something new**;

- **turn away from** (Gk. *apostrepsousin*, "turn back, turn around to face another direction"; cp. 1:15; Ti 1:14) **hearing the truth**;

- **turn aside to myths** (Gk. *muthous*, "fables, fictions, falsely construed

stories," as the antithesis of truth; cp. 1 Tm 1:4; 4:7; Ti 1:14; 2 Pt 1:16).

Pictured here is a lineup of false teachers, each with a slightly different emphasis that will prove new and interesting to the hearers. There can be no true satisfaction, however, because only God's word, received in humility and with a willingness to obey, can prove truly satisfying to the soul. "Turn aside" (Gk. *ektrapēsontai*, "turn, twist out of joint, shun, avoid association with"; cp. 1 Tm 1:6; 6:20) was used earlier of young widows who turned aside to follow Satan (1 Tm 5:15). The use of the passive voice here (lit. "they *will be turned* aside to myths") suggests people were allowing themselves to come under diabolical influence.

4:5 Paul returned to the final four commands of his charge to Timothy:

- Sixth, in contrast to those who turn aside to lifeless myths, Timothy must **keep a clear head** (Gk. *nēphe*, "be self-controlled, well-balanced, self-possessed"; cp. 1 Th 5:6,8; 1 Pt 1:13; 4:7; 5:8) **about everything**.

- Seventh, he must **endure hardship**, a recurring theme in both Paul's letters to him (cp. 1:8; 2:9).

- Eighth, he must **do the work of an evangelist**. The spiritual gift of evangelism is characterized by an unusual ability to proclaim the message of salvation effectively (Eph 4:11). Paul seemed to be encouraging Timothy not to overlook this aspect of his ministry despite so many other responsibilities at hand.

- Paul's ninth command in many ways summarized them all: **fulfill** (Gk. *plērophorēson*, "accomplish, carry through to the end") **your ministry**. Timothy was to carry out the ministry to which God has called him conscientiously and wholeheartedly.

The Victorious Completion of Paul's Ministry (4:6-8)

4:6 Having called Timothy to step into the fullness of his God-given ministry, Paul revealed why he had so passionately encouraged him to do this. Clearly Paul believed he would not live much longer, and Timothy was invested with the assignment to continue where he left off. Paul described his approaching death as **already being poured out as a drink offering.** Paul understood his ministry to be an offering to the Lord (Rm 15:16; Php 2:17), and his **departure** (i.e., his death) would be the final act of this sacrificial offering.

4:7 Switching to an athletic metaphor, Paul recounted his spiritual legacy. His point, of course, was not to boast about what he had accomplished over the years. Instead, as Timothy's role model, he wanted to provide him encouragement. He made three parallel statements using perfect tense verbs, which gave a sense of finality to his words.

- First, **I have fought the good fight** (cp. 1:8,12; 2:9-10; 3:11). Paul's point was that the fight itself—the gospel ministry—was inherently good and worth the investment of a person's life.

- Second, **I have finished the race** (cp. Ac 20:24). Paul emphasized the fact that he had completed the mission God assigned to him. The larger race—that of bringing the gospel "to the ends of the earth" (Ac 1:8)—still remained, and he was passing the baton to Timothy, asking him to continue the race despite persecution.

- Third, **I have kept the faith**. Paul had accurately preserved the content of the gospel and had faithfully fulfilled his God-given commission (cp. 2 Tm 3:10).

4:8 Looking ahead now to his **future** life in heaven with the Lord, Paul reflected on what **is reserved** (Gk. *apokeitai*, "laid away, placed in safekeeping") for him there: **the crown of righteousness**. This reference may be to a crown given to him because he had pursued a life of practical righteousness through the power of the indwelling Holy Spirit. It may also refer to a crown that would be given to him because Christ, **the righteous Judge,** had imputed His righteousness to him. This "crown" will be awarded to him **on that day** in heaven, but it is not for him alone. Turning his attention once again to Timothy, he encompassed him in the wonderful truth that the reward awaits **all those who have loved His appearing**. As the Apostle John later wrote, the greatest incentive for righteous living is an anticipation of Christ's return (1 Jn 2:2-3).

FINAL INSTRUCTIONS TO TIMOTHY (4:9-18)

In many ways the apostle's final instructions to Timothy read like a checklist of things he wanted him to accomplish, followed by a report on how things were going with him in Rome. What was unexpected was his request that Timothy join him in Rome as soon as possible. In the first letter to Timothy, as well as in this letter, Paul's primary focus had been on other issues, such as building up the Ephesian church and protecting it from the destructive advances of the false teachers. Also, he had made a strong appeal in both letters for Timothy's loyalty to Christ and the gospel, as well as to himself personally, in the face of persecution. Nevertheless, this appeal to come to him in Rome was actually the second reason for the letter.

Charge to Ministry 2 Timothy 4:2-8	
The Task	**Examples and Exhortations**
Proclaim the message (v. 2).	Mt 24:14; Mk 16:15; Lk 24:47; Ac 10:42; Rm 10:14-15; 1 Co 1:23; 2 Co 4:5
Persist in the truth (v. 2).	Ac 26:22; Rm 14:4; 1 Co 15:1-2; 16:13; Gl 5:1; Eph 5:11-14; Php 1:27; 4:1; 1 Th 3:8; 2 Th 2:15; 1 Pt 5:12; Jd 24
Rebuke, correct, and encourage believers with patience and instruction (v. 2).	Mt 18:15; Lk 17:3; Ac 14:22; Rm 12:1; 15:30; 16:17; 1 Co 1:10; 2 Co 5:20; 8:6; Eph 4:1; 5:11; 1 Th 2:11; 4;1,18; 5:11,14; 2 Th 3;12; 1 Tm 5:1,20; 6:2; Ti 1:9,13; 2:6; 2:15; Heb 3:13; 1 Pt 5:12; Jd 3
Teach sound doctrine (v. 3).	Jn 7:16-17; Rm 6:17; 16:17; 1 Tm 1:3; Ti 1:9
Keep a clear head (v. 5).	2 Th 5:6,8; 1 Pt 1:13; 4:7; 5:8
Endure hardship (v. 5).	2 Tm 3:11; Rm 12:12; 1 Co 4:12; Heb 11:25; 12:3; Jms 5:10; 1 Pt 2:19
Do the work of an evangelist (v. 5).	Ac 5:42; 8:4,12,25,35,40; 13:32; 14:7,15; 15:35; 16:10; Rm 1:15; 10:15; 15:20; 1 Co 1:17; 9:16-18; 15:1-2; 2 Co 10:16; 11:7
Fulfill your ministry (v. 5).	Ac 6:4; 20:24; Col 4:12,17; 2 Tm 4:17

Instruction to Come to Paul in Rome (4:9-15)

4:9-11a The apostle's request was quite clear: **Make every effort** (Gk. *spoudason*, "hasten, hurry"; cp. 4:21; Ti 3:12) **to come to me soon** (Gk. *tacheōs*, "quickly, at once, without delay," 2 Tm 4:9). The urgency of the request was reflected in his vocabulary, as well as in his request that Timothy come "before winter" (4:21). The rest of the sentence explained the reason for this request: All of his fellow workers except Luke had left him. **Demas has deserted** Paul, **because he loved this present world, and has gone to Thessalonica** (v. 10). Little else is known of Demas except that he was a co-worker with Paul during his previous Roman imprisonment (Col 4:14; Phm 24). DESERTED (Gk. *egkatelipen*, "forsaken, abandoned, left behind," usually in a helpless state, 2 Tm 4:9; cp. Mt 27:46; Ac 2:27,31; 2 Co 4:9; Heb 13:5) is a strong word, and Paul also used it

in verse 16 to describe how his friends abandoned him at his "first defense." Demas's departure was clearly very painful to Paul, perhaps especially so because this "co-worker" had chosen to embrace the world and its values rather than to remain with the apostle. Two other men had also left, but Paul had likely sent them out on assignments. **Crescens**, of whom nothing else is known, **has gone to Galatia** in central Asia Minor (v. 10). **Titus**, whom Paul earlier sent to the church in Crete (1 Tm 1:5), had by this point been in Rome with Paul and was then in **Dalmatia** up the Adriatic coast. **Only Luke** remained with him (2 Tm 4:11a).

4:11b-12 Mark had earlier traveled with Paul and Barnabas but had left when things became too difficult (Ac 13:13). Whether or not to bring him on a subsequent journey became a matter of contention between Paul and Barnabas, who had earlier discipled Paul, had taken Mark under his fatherly care and had played a key role in Mark's restoration to the ministry (Ac 15:36-41). Paul further noted that he had sent **Tychicus to Ephesus** (2 Tm 4:12; Eph 6:21; Col 4:7; Ti 3:12). He seems to have been the bearer of this letter and was probably the one sent to take over Timothy's responsibilities in the Ephesian church.

4:13 Paul next asked Timothy to bring two important things with him when he came to Rome. First, he asked for **the cloak** that he **left in Troas with Carpus**. He had left a heavy woolen cloak there, perhaps when he was arrested. It would be invaluable to him in his cold, dark prison cell. Second, he asked for "the SCROLLS (Gk. *biblia*, "small books or written documents," the diminutive form of *biblos*, "book"), ESPECIALLY (Gk. *malista*, "above all, chiefly, particularly") the PARCHMENTS" (Gk. *membranas*, from Lat. "membranes"). The nature of these documents is not known, although they may have included sections of the Old Testament.

4:14-15 Next came a warning about **Alexander the coppersmith**, a man who **did great harm** to Paul (v. 14) and **strongly opposed** his **words** (v. 15). In the strongest possible words, Paul warned Timothy to **watch out** (Gk. *phulassou*, "guard, protect") **for him yourself**. Scholars have suggested that this man was the one who had facilitated Paul's arrest, especially since the word translated "did" (Gk. *enedeixato*) commonly means "to show or point out" and in secular texts can have the legal meaning of "inform against." Whatever the case, Paul had placed him in the Lord's hands for judgment (v. 14).

Paul's Testimony of God's Faithfulness During His First Trial (4:16-18)

4:16 The apostle updated Timothy on what had been happening to him since being imprisoned in Rome. He spoke of his "first defense," apparently referring to a preliminary hearing, called a *prima actio* within the Roman legal system, which would have been followed later by a formal trial. During his earlier imprisonment under Felix, there had been a two-year delay (Ac 24:1, 7), so it was not unreasonable for Paul to assume that there would be enough time for Timothy to reach him now. This "first defense" had clearly been a painful time for him—**no one came to my assistance** (Gk. *paregeneto*, "was present, supported, came," also with the sense of publicly standing by him), **but everyone deserted** (Gk. *egkatelipon*, see 2 Tm 4:9) **me**. Despite this, Paul's heart was filled with mercy and forgiveness as he prayed, **May it not be counted against them,** following the example of Jesus (cp. Lk 23:34).

4:17 Although his coworkers did not stand with him at his trial, Paul declared that **the Lord stood with me** (cp. 2 Tm 2:1; 1 Tm 1:12). The presence of the Lord Jesus was completely real and tangible to Paul in that Roman courtroom. The Lord had **strengthened** him (2 Tm 2:1; 1 Tm 1:12) to proclaim the gospel clearly for the Gentiles' sake. Filled with the power and confidence that Jesus alone could give, Paul made the most of the opportunity. Paul had also been **rescued from the lion's mouth**, a metaphor that could refer to Satan or to Nero but more likely refers to death. Some of the same terminology—of being deserted and of being delivered from death—occurs in Psalm 22 (see vv. 1,11,13,21).

4:18 Reflecting on God's mighty deliverance in that courtroom, Paul declared that **the Lord** who so powerfully delivered him then would continue to **rescue** him **from every evil work** and **bring** him **safely** (Gk. *sōsei*, "save, keep safe, rescue from danger or harm"; cp. 1:9) **into His heavenly kingdom.** Paul did not believe that he would always be delivered from death, for he certainly expected to be with the Lord Jesus someday in heaven. What he did believe was that he was held in his Father's loving hands and that the power of evil could not usurp the Lord's sovereignty. To this powerful, loving, sovereign Lord, Paul declared, **be the glory forever and ever! Amen**.

PAUL'S GREETINGS AND BLESSINGS (4:19-22)

His Greetings to the Believers (4:19-21)

4:19 Paul concluded this letter, as he typically did, with personal words and greetings. He extended his greetings to **Prisca** (elsewhere Priscilla) and **Aquila,** close friends whom he met in Corinth on his second missionary journey (Ac 18:2). They had traveled with him (Ac 18:18) and had served in the church in Ephesus (Ac 18:26). He also greeted **the household of Onesiphorus**, who had so bravely stayed with him during his current imprisonment (2 Tm 1:16-18).

4:20-21 Paul's notes about two other mutual friends not only provided information for Timothy but also emphasized the importance of his coming quickly to Paul's side. **Erastus has remained at Corinth,** and at some point prior to this imprisonment Paul had left **Trophimus** (Ac 20:4; 21:29) at **Miletus** due to his ill-

ness. Since only Luke was still with him (2 Tm 4:11), he again urged Timothy to join him **before winter**, when high seas and unpredictable winds would make sailing impossible. Finally, Paul sent greetings to Timothy from some local believers: **Eubulus, Pudens, Linus, Claudia, and all the brothers.**

Claudia
2 Timothy 4:21

These facts are known about Claudia. She was . . .
- a member of the Roman church
- a respected and influential woman
- a Gentile by background
- a convert of the gospel
- a leader in the church
- a personal friend of Timothy
- an encourager to Paul and other believers

His Final Blessing to Timothy (4:22)

4:22 Paul concluded his letter with a final expanded blessing to Timothy: **The Lord be with your spirit** (cp. Gl 6:18; Php 4:23; Phm 25). Second, he offered a benediction to the Ephesian church, for the word "you" is plural: **Grace be with you!**

Bibliography

Hendriksen, William. *Exposition of the Pastoral Epistles*. New Testament Commentary. Grand Rapids: Baker Book House, 1957.

*Knight, George. *The Pastoral Epistles: A Commentary on the Greek Text*. The New International Greek Testament Commentary. Grand Rapids: Eerdmans Publishing Co., 1992.

Lea, Thomas D., and Hayne P. Griffin, Jr. *1, 2 Timothy, Titus*. The New American Commentary, vol. 34. Nashville: Broadman Press, 1992.

*For advanced study

TITUS

Introduction

Title

This epistle, like 1 and 2 Timothy, is called a Pastoral Epistle. It bears the name of its recipient—Titus, the young protégé of Paul. Although Titus was not identified as a pastor, this letter, as those written to Timothy, dealt with practical and timely issues that would have been foremost in the minds of congregants and church leaders—both from an individual perspective and in the life of the congregation. These books have been known as Pastoral Epistles. Titus was mentioned 13 times in the New Testament (2 Co 2:13; 7:6,13,14; 8:6,16,23; 12:18 [twice]; Gl 2:1,3; 2 Tm 4:10; Ti 1:4). Titius Justus mentioned in Acts 18:7 was a different man.

A Greek by ethnic heritage, Titus was converted under the ministry of Paul (1:4). He chose to remain uncircumcised, perhaps as a testimony to the power of the gospel for Gentiles as well as Jews (Gl 2:3). His close association with the apostle is noted:

- Paul commended Titus as his partner (Gk. *koinōnos*) and fellow worker (Gk. *sunergos*) in ministry (2 Co 8:23).

- Paul took him to the Jerusalem Conference (Gl 2:1-5), perhaps to make the point that Gentiles, even without submitting to circumcision, were just as much heirs to salvation as Jews.

- Paul used Titus as his personal messenger to the troubled church at Corinth (an assignment in which the young man seemingly met with both challenges and successes, 2 Co 8:16-24).

- Titus was then sent to Crete where doctrinal aberrations and moral decadence had invaded the churches (Ti 1:5). At some point Paul also sent Titus to Dalmatia (2 Tm 4:10).

In conclusion, for this brief epistle to bear the name of its emissary is indeed appropriate. Titus had distinguished himself, not only with the Apostle Paul but also among the churches, as a man who, though young in years, was mature in the faith and full of wisdom and discernment. He did not waiver in his convictions and held fast to the great doctrines of the faith, and he demonstrated a gracious statesmanship that endeared him to the congregations to whom he was sent, enabling him to work through their difficulties and to bring them back to the center in their kingdom responsibilities.

Setting

During the time these Pastoral Epistles were penned, the Apostle Paul seemed to be on the move—at least out of prison (1 Tm 1:3; 3:14; Ti 1:5). Paul's reference to

an earlier visit to Crete would seem to suggest that he established a church, leaving Titus to organize the congregation and disciple the new believers. Crete is one of the larger islands in the Mediterranean, extending approximately 156 miles in length and up to 30 miles in width. Ancient cities included Knossus, Paistos, Haga Triada, and Fair Havens (Ac 27:8), and all were overshadowed with a mountain range whose top peak, Mount Ida, the traditional birthplace of the Greek god Zeus, reached 8,193 feet.

According to Greek legend, the son of Zeus became king of Crete, and the reign of this powerful and acclaimed King Minos has indeed been documented in history. One can find extensive archaeological excavations with fascinating evidence of this earlier civilization in the ancient Minoan Palace. Perhaps the most unique aspect of the legends surrounding this period of Cretan history has centered upon the ancient legend of the Minotaur, a monster who was half bull and half man and was shut up in Labyrinth. An extensive "bull lore" was associated with the island of Crete. The entire legend is shrouded in immorality and lends understanding to the problems Paul and Titus found in the churches on the island. The Cretans were overwhelmingly stereotyped by ancient writers as immoral and rude and as part of a barbarous culture.

Genre

The reader should not be surprised that Paul chose a very personal medium for sending such an intimate message to a colaborer who was facing the challenging task of correction and encouragement within a difficult congregation. The epistle or letter without doubt came directly from Paul's heart with the intent to accomplish his goals despite his own absence. Note the earlier discussion on this genre in the introductory section of Colossians. The use of this style in personal communication was quite appropriate. Critics err in trying to separate the apostle from a letter bearing his own imprimatur in the salutation (1:1).

Author

When Paul identified himself as the sender of the epistle (1:1-4), believers who honor Scripture as accurate and without error end all discussion on authorship. The church fathers of the ancient world did not question Pauline authorship; nor do evangelical scholars in modernity suggest that the clear statement of the text is inaccurate. However, theologians enamored with the higher critical method of questioning anything and everything about Scripture have not left this question untouched.

Most attacks on Pauline authorship have come on the basis of suggesting a vocabulary difference between words used in the Pastoral Epistles in comparison to Paul's longer letters. Most writers in antiquity or modernity could not survive a vocabulary test based upon common words used in different works whatever the length. Some authors, in fact, work toward a variation in words for interest as well as precision. In addition, one would assume that Paul would use a different approach, and even different words, in speaking to his co-laborers than he would use in writing directly to a congregation. Certainly in the case of the former, appealing to a body of truth already presented as the standard without the need of redeveloping that material at every appropriate point would be sufficient. Perhaps a worthy presupposition for determining authorship would be to accept without question whatever is explicitly stated in the text. From that point, one can enjoy the scholarly pursuit of how the other pieces fit together. The apostle's autograph at the beginning of the epistle and the consistency of his theological teachings, including the language used to express these truths, provide ample internal evidence to support his authorship.

Date

There has been some legitimate discussion about the dating of the epistle of Titus. The question is whether Paul endured one or two imprisonments in Rome. There seems to be good consensus that Paul was not in prison between AD 62 and 64, which allowed for his travel to Nicopolis, evidently by his own choice and thus as a free man, to spend the winter (3:12). The date of AD 63 has been supported for these reasons:

- the optimistic closing words of the capable historian Luke in the Acts/Luke material (Lk 24:52-53);

- the tradition regarding additional, though unrecorded, missionary journeys by Paul;

- other minor historical data that seemed to necessitate Paul's release from prison shortly after the close of the events recorded in Acts.

The writing of 1 Timothy and Titus has been projected as falling between Paul's first Roman imprisonment (as early as AD 61–63) or as late as sometime before his penning of 2 Timothy (as early as AD 64–67), if Paul's death did occur, according to a strong tradition, during the reign of Nero (which ended AD 68).

Recipients

Paul addressed this letter to his Greek convert Titus. Even though an uncircumcised Gentile, Titus accompanied Paul to the Jerusalem Conference and was a strong helper to Paul in pleading the case of salvation by grace alone, without the requirement of circumcision or any other personal work (Gl 2:1-5). Titus might be considered the test case of salvation, which for the Jews required circumcision, by grace alone without the keeping of the law.

Titus also excelled in his handling of the problems among the Corinthians when he did troubleshooting for the apostle in that troubled congregation (2 Co 8:16-23). This letter gave Titus the authority and the encouragement to address issues of doctrine, church polity, and even the spiritual formation of the church in Crete. The apostle used this epistle to instruct Titus on what he should teach and how those teachings would apply to the believers in Crete. Titus received not only a letter but also the apostolic authority carried therewith. Titus certainly played an important part in extending early Christianity beyond the confines of Judaism to Gentiles and unto the ends of the world.

Major Themes

Sound doctrine is at the heart of this brief epistle (2:1-14; 3:4-7). Church polity is clearly a component in that doctrinal foundation. Not only was doctrine addressed, but also the spiritual fervor to incorporate that doctrine as a standard for Christlike living was clearly mandated.

Servant or Christlike living was delineated as the natural and essential outgrowth of understanding sound doctrine. Despite the pagan environment, the Cretans were held to the highest ethical standards, as was expected of every believer. They had no option other than placing themselves under the authority and lordship of Jesus Christ in their everyday lives. Obedience was to be neither optional nor selective. Personal responsibilities were clearly delineated for older men and women as well as for those who were younger. High standards were demanded from those in authority as well as those under their direction (2:1-10). Serious warnings were issued concerning false teachings and the teachers who propagated such (1:10-16; 3:9-11).

Pronunciation Guide

Artemas	*AHR tih mus*	Zenas	*ZEE nuhs*
Tychicus	*TIK ih kuhs*	Apollos	*uh PAWL uhs*
Nicopolis	*nih KAHP oh liss*		

Outline

I. INTRODUCTION (1:1-4)
  A. Author of the Letter (1:1)
  B. Motivation for Writing the Letter (1:2-3)
  C. Recipient to Whom the Letter Is Addressed (1:4a)
  D. Salutation and Greeting (1:4b)

II. THE APPOINTMENT OF PASTORS (1:5-9)
  A. Consistent Patterns in Character (1:5-8)
    1. In the family (1:5-6)
    2. In personal habits and life (1:7)
    3. In faith and practice (1:8)
  B. Passionate Purpose in Ministry (1:9)

III. THE CHALLENGE OF COMBATING HERESY (1:10-16)
  A. Overcoming the General Worldview (1:10-11)
  B. Engaging the Specific Field Assignment (1:12-16)

IV. THE INSTRUCTIONS FOR BELIEVERS (2:1-10)
  A. A General Word (2:1)

B. A Specific Word (2:2-10)
    1. To older ("spiritually mature") men (2:2)
    2. To older ("spiritually mature") women (2:3)
    3. To younger ("new in the faith") women (2:4-5)
    4. To younger ("new in the faith") men (2:6-8)
    5. To slaves (2:9-10)

V. A PERSUASIVE REASON FOR OBEDIENCE (2:11—3:11)
  A. The Gift of Grace in Salvation (2:11-15)
  B. The Outworking of Faith in Life (3:1-11)
    1. The recognition of authorities (3:1)
    2. A respect for others (3:2)
    3. A call to obedience (3:3-8)
    4. A warning against disobedience (3:9-11)

VI. CONCLUSION (3:12-15)
  A. Final Instructions (3:12-14)
  B. A Personal Closing (3:15)

Exposition of the Text[1]

INTRODUCTION (1:1-4)

Author of the Letter (1:1)

1:1 Paul, in his salutation, shared his own personal testimony as well as encapsulating his driving passions and previewing the themes of this brief epistle penned to Titus concerning building the church in Crete. He clearly stated two relationships upon which his life and ministry were based:

- Paul was a **slave** (Gk. *doulos*). Perhaps it is significant that this word was frequently used to describe one born into slavery, and anyone who comes into this relationship with Christ is born again, becoming a bondslave through spiritual birth. Every follower of Christ must become a slave to the Lord, dying to self and committing himself entirely to Him (Rm 6:1-23; Gl 2:20; Eph 6:6).

- Paul also described a unique relationship reserved for only a few selected for a particular service to Christ. He was an **apostle** (Gk. *apostolos*, "messenger" or "one sent," transliterated into English as "apostle") of Jesus Christ. The New Testament clearly delineated the requirements for the esteemed position of apostleship:

  - Apostles were chosen, called, and sent forth by Christ (Mk 3:13-15).

  - They were eyewitnesses to the resurrected Christ (Jn 20:20-29).

  - They were marked by the indwelling of the Holy Spirit (Jn 20:22-23).

  - Seemingly their appointment was for life and reached beyond the influence of the local congregation (Mt 28:18-20; Ac 1:8).

As an apostle, Paul related to the broader kingdom, described here as **God's elect**, who were believers. This designation underscored that election took place according to God's foreknowledge (1 Pt 1:2). The faith of God's elect was of particular interest since Crete had been plagued with doctrinal instability, which was one reason Paul sent Titus to offer wisdom and encouragement to the Cretan congregations. He coupled with faith the knowledge of truth that leads to godliness. There would be no defense of the faith or maturing of the faith without KNOWLEDGE (Gk. *epignōsin*, "know well, perceive, understand, learn"), a word that is amplified with the prefix preposition (Gk. *epi*, "upon"), which would suggest thorough or full knowledge.

Motivation for Writing the Letter (1:2-3)

1:2-3 There are some important words in verses 2 and 3. **Hope** (Gk. *elpidi*) is not to be understood as something without certainty, as the word is popularly used in modernity. Believers must know that their "hope" is a sure thing, based upon a settled expectation and grounded in the very person of God Himself. A believing woman's unique trust in God as being entirely trustworthy enables her to wait patiently for the consummation of her salvation even in the midst of a hostile and destructive world. TIME (Gk. *chronōn*, "period of time") in verse 2 has the sense of a sequence of time, a concept readily understood by anyone. In other words,

Heart to Heart:
Digging Deep into God's Word

Overwhelmingly women purchase more Bibles and more Bible study materials than men do. By all rights, just the amount of materials in the marketplace should make women the best equipped Bible students of the modern era. However, one has only to peruse those materials to see that there is a great gulf fixed between most of what is being produced by women for women and even the most basic devotional commentary. Inspirational thoughts, practical application, and systematic topical studies are all important, but women need more. Women can study the Bible in depth; they can learn to do genuine exposition or verse-by-verse interpretation of God's Word, using the best hermeneutical principles; and this commentary is a step in making available to women resources produced especially for them. Here is a clarion call to women to demand the best in biblical scholarship—even resources prepared by women who have been formally trained in biblical studies—and to spend the time necessary to dig deeply into God's Word and pull out its rich truths and full knowledge.

God's plan for salvation was in place "before time began," a reference to the sequence of events in time. TIME (Gk. *kairois*, "appointed or proper time, season") in verse 3 suggests a particular occasion rather than an extended time. Here the reference is to a time chosen by God to reveal Himself in Christ. Human beings move through a chronology of time, but God often makes His particular intervention in an event in time, such as the proclamation of His message.

Recipient to Whom the Letter Is Addressed (1:4a) and Salutation and Greeting (1:4b)

1:4 Grace and peace presented an enigma. People have continually been looking and working for peace. The question comes again and again: Will there ever be peace in the Middle East? in Ireland? in Africa? in Korea? But how much more believers ought to realize that before peace must come grace. Genuine peace cannot be achieved by war or diplomacy but only by spreading abroad the grace of the Lord Jesus. Both grace and peace come from God alone, but peace will only come after God has done His work of grace in the heart.

THE APPOINTMENT OF PASTORS (1:5-9)

1:5-9 Paul gave to Titus a reminder of his assignment in Crete. Not only was he "to SET RIGHT" (Gk. *epidiorthōsē*, "correct"), but in the process he was to do "what was left undone." The former word was used in medical writings in reference to setting broken limbs and could project the idea that the task was necessary and would require enduring some painful adjustment as well as heeding an urgent demand for getting it right. The spiritual body is as important as the physical body in its care and healing.

Paul also advised Titus **to appoint elders in every town**. The apostle did not intend for Titus to remain on Crete. He followed this assignment with very specific qualifications dictated by the divine requirements as well as the serious spiritual responsibilities that would belong to them. There was no random choice on the part of Titus or the congregation, but Titus had been designated as God's agent for making these important assignments for service in the congregations on Crete.

Interestingly, Paul used two words—ELDERS (Gk. *presbuterous*) in verse 5 and OVERSEER (Gk. *episkopon*, "overseer, guardian, bishop") in verse 7. These words are used interchangeably in Scripture in reference to pastors (see also Gk. *poimenas*, "shepherd," a word used elsewhere in the New Testament in tandem with the former words, Eph 4:11). Four major passages discuss the qualifications and responsibilities of the pastor or elder or overseer (Ti 1:5-7; Ac 20:28-35; 1 Tm 3:1-7; 1 Pt 5:1-4). Most of the early churches seemed to have a plurality of pastors, each of whom probably had an area of oversight of some particular ministry in the church much as is common in large congregations in the modern era. The elders appointed were local, living among the congregants they served, and they had requirements to meet. The word translated "elders" certainly has a connotation related to age, which would make perfect sense in that older men tend to have more wisdom and experience and thus be better prepared to meet such a challenge. However, many scholars accept this designation as a distinction or technical term for a church leader.

The word translated OVERSEER (Gk. *episkopon*, compound word with the preposition *epi*, meaning "over,"

and the noun *skopos*, "one who watches or looks out") is not a reference to another person but carries the nuance of the way a pastor would function in overseeing and guarding or watching over his flock or congregation. The same word was used to describe the Lord as the "Overseer of your souls" in 1 Peter 2:25.

Likewise, the word used in other texts and translated pastor adds to the understanding of this divinely assigned leader of the congregation with an emphasis on his loving care and faithful guidance of those whom God placed in his ministry flock. Not only is this section addressing the requirements for pastoral leadership in the congregation important to men who have been called out to undertake the responsibility for leading the flock of God, but also these verses have lessons for the laity concerning what they should expect from the pastor or any spiritual leader who would relate to the congregation.

THE CHALLENGE OF COMBATING HERESY (1:10-16)

1:10-16 Throughout history those who embrace the gospel, and especially those who present the gospel, have been plagued with persecution and suffering and senseless attacks. The blood-sprinkled trail of martyrs has included godly men and women of faith. Paul here reminded his readers that there have always been opponents to the gospel. These talkers often had much to say about God's glory, but they had no fruit or converts who had come to Christ by their testimonies. The phrase **especially those from Judaism** was a reference to some of the legalistic Jews, who believed themselves to be the only real interpreters of Scripture.

Pattern for Pastors		
Requirements	**Insight**	**Reference**
Blameless	(Gk. *anegklētos*, "irreproachable")—The word meaning "accuse" is prefixed with an alpha privative (*alpha*, first letter in the Greek alphabet), which negates the word. Thus, the word means nonchargeable. The pastor should stand above accusation, maintaining the highest moral character, having an untarnished reputation.	v. 6
The husband of one wife	The emphasis is not that the pastor must be married, for Paul himself is at least single at this time (whether by choice or as a widower). Rather, the emphasis is that the pastor is a one-woman man, having taken very seriously God's plan for marriage (Gn 2:24; Mt 19:5). His marriage must also be exemplary.	v. 6
Having faithful children	(Gk. *tekna echōn pista*, "having believing children")—Seemingly these children are still under their father's authority in the home. The idea here is not just a physical behavior requirement but a spiritual heart condition. Above all, a pastor ought to give his energies and passion to winning his own children to faith in Christ. And his exemplary life should call forth the respect of his children.	v. 6
Not accused of wildness or rebellion	(Gk. *asōtias*, "reckless living, dissipation")—This word for "wildness" was also used in Luke 15:13 to describe the lifestyle of the prodigal son. It was sometimes translated "incurable" in the sense that one was destroying his life so completely that it could not be rebuilt. Rebellion (Gk. *anupotakta*, "undisciplined, disobedient") suggests refusal to submit to authority. Parents cannot control or dictate a child's response to God, but they are responsible for guiding the child's public behavior. It stands to reason that a child who refuses the authority of his parents or teachers would not be likely to honor God or submit to His mandates. No pastor would want his child's outrageous behavior to bring hurt to the church and destroy his credibility as God's servant.	v. 6
God's manager	(Gk. *oikonomon*, "steward, administrator, treasurer")	v. 7
Not arrogant	(Gk. *authadē*, "self-willed, stubborn")—This compound word links the personal pronoun and the verb meaning "enjoy oneself." A pastor should be more concerned with pleasing God than himself.	v. 7
Not quick tempered	(Gk. *orgilon*, "inclined to anger")—Righteous indignation is perfectly acceptable, but there is never a place for eruptive anger or bitter wrath, and most pastors will have many challenges that test their self-control.	v. 7

Pattern for Pastors		
Requirements	**Insight**	**Reference**
Not addicted to wine	The fermented fruit of the vine of Paul's day cannot be compared to the intoxicating alcoholic beverage of the modern-day liquor industry, which wrecks homes and takes lives. Pastors must bring even their habits into subjection to an exemplary standard.	v. 7
Not a bully	(Gk. *plēktēs*, "combative person")—No believer should allow an annoyance to provoke him to violence toward another. Scripture is clear that a believer is to endure suffering with a patient spirit.	v. 7
Not greedy for money	(Gk. *aischrokerdē*, "fond of dishonest gain")—Materialism grips this age, including those who serve the Lord. Doing the best for your family, providing their necessities, and working to give some extras are the happy privileges of every husband and father. However, one must guard against being pulled into a materialistic mindset where things are more important than people and God.	v. 7
Hospitable	(Gk. *philoxenos*, "loving or delighting in a stranger or foreigner")—Rarely used in the New Testament, the word could be appropriate here because of the necessity for travelers to depend on local homes for accommodations, or perhaps the emphasis is on the open door such loving care would provide to share the gospel.	v. 8
Loving what is good	(Gk. *philagathon*, linking the popular word *phileō*, "love," with the word for good)—The admonition is entreating pastors to seek and to embrace with passion the good as a springboard for all they do.	v. 8
Sensible	(Gk. *sōphrona*, "thoughtful, moderate, self-controlled, decent, modest")—The spiritual dimension adds to good intellectual choices a sanctifying presence that permeates all of life with wise and discerning choices of how one thinks, what decisions he makes, what words he utters, and what deeds he does. No trait is more important for a pastor.	v. 8
Righteous	(Gk. *dikaion*, "just")—The pastor must not only be in right standing with God, but he must also be just and fair in dealing with members of his family and congregation, whether in business or community or the affairs of the church.	v. 8
Holy	(Gk. *hosion,* "devout, pious")—This word is not the usual New Testament word for **holy**. The nuance in its meaning suggests going beyond the usual reverence for God with the idea of being accountable to God without any regulation or monitoring. How could a pastor represent God to the people if he himself is not set apart unto the Lord in a unique and all-encompassing way? His task is to model holiness and draw others to walk in the way of the Lord.	v. 8

Pattern for Pastors		
Requirements	**Insight**	**Reference**
Self-controlled	(Gk. *egkratē*, "disciplined")—Certainly a pastor must be master of himself in the sense that he commits his life and decisions to be controlled by the Holy Spirit. He moves from self-control to God-control in his own life and seeks to move all in his congregation to that model.	v. 8
Holding to the faithful message as taught	His task culminates in the mandate to cling to or hold firmly (Gk. *antechomenon*, the verb meaning "have" is prefixed with the preposition "against" so that the idea is literally "to have against," suggesting that your hold is not easy but is buffeted with difficulties that are working against you). What a picture for the pastor who must hold fast and firm the teachings of Scripture in the midst of his own pressures and challenges so that he will have a "faithful message." Clearly this message is one that embodies faith and comes directly from God. It is not only free from error but imparts health and encourages growth. The apostle continued to expound on the nature of that message, using the phrase "sound teaching" (Gk. *didaskalia tē hugiainousē*). The "teaching" or instruction entails both content (OT and NT—the whole counsel of God) and action (lifestyle), and it is further described as "sound" or, more literally, "healthy." This medical term often describes someone in perfect health. No better tool could come to the pastor in his task of discounting false doctrine than to have "healthy teaching" to use in confronting error and distortions that would attack the gospel.	v. 9

Paul was strong in his words concerning the false teachers (v. 11). He recognized that one can be lulled by the call to tolerance so much that he might tolerate doctrinal error, which would be devastating to him and to others. The Greek word *epistomizeon* (*epi* or "upon" is linked with *stoma* or "mouth" so that the idea is "upon" or "over the mouth," i.e., "muzzle") is clear; in other words, Paul himself took the initiative to call for stopping the mouths or silencing those who taught contrary to Scripture.

1:12–16 The quote in verse 12 is from the Cretan poet Epimenides, who inhabited the island in the sixth century BC. Historically the residents of Crete had been known for their immorality. Interestingly Paul was well acquainted with ancient nonbiblical literature. Perhaps here he was using that knowledge to gain a hearing from nonbelievers in Crete. Or he may simply have been using the words of a pagan poet to awaken the people to their profligate lives and thus the need for the life-changing gospel of Jesus Christ.

Doctrinal purity is not optional. To insist on the truthfulness of Scripture is not exercising intolerance or bigotry. Just as a child should be snatched from the dangerous path of an oncoming car, even if against the child's will, the strongest rebuke of those who would deceive was deemed necessary by Paul. The rebuke is to be done **sharply** (Gk. *apotomōs*, linking *apo* or "off" with *tomos* or "cutting" as with a knife). Paul expected such a severe rebuke to produce sound doctrine and have the healthy result of building up faith (v. 13).

Paul described the false teaching as the **Jewish myths and the commandments of men who reject the truth** (v. 14). He did not elaborate on these. However, Jewish rabbis were known for the elevation of their own traditions to a position of importance alongside the law of God. Their legalistic interpretations often added to or even contradicted the divine law recorded in Scripture. They assumed that they could make themselves acceptable to God by their own traditions and rituals, such as their extensive and complicated dietary regulations (vv. 15-16).

The purity to which Paul alluded was not acquired (see Rm 3:10); rather, it was bestowed by God Himself through His atonement (Ti 3:5). Only in this way is the believer distinguished from the unbeliever. The **pure** (Gk., *kathara*, "clean, ritually pure, guiltless") were pure by means of their faith alone (2:15). Of course, Paul was not suggesting that the "pure" could not or would not sin; rather, his point was

that no sinner could make himself pure however religious he might be.

The false teachers were observant of religious traditions. They even professed (Gk. *homologousin*, "confess, promise, declare") **to know God.** Paul had the strongest condemnation for their duplicity (v. 16). C. S. Lewis once observed, "Of all bad men, religious bad men are the worst."[2]

THE INSTRUCTIONS FOR BELIEVERS (2:1-10)

A General Word (2:1)
2:1 Paul moved from the necessity of Christlike holy living for pastors to a call for personal holiness in the lives of believers in the congregation, realizing that living in an unholy day would call for leadership among those in the congregation—both men and women—to provide an example and the necessary encouragement to call all believers to Christlike living.

Self-Control Is the Key

The Group	The Dominant Character Trait	The Faithful Outworking
Older Men	Worthy of respect	Sound in faith, love, and endurance
Older Women	Reverent in behavior, not slanderers, not addicted to much wine	Teaching what is good, encouraging the young women
Younger Women	Sensible about everything, pure lives	Good homemakers, submissive to their husbands
Younger Men	Sensible about everything	Examples of good works and sound speech
Titus—the pastor	Integrity, dignity	Setting an example of good works
Slaves	Well pleasing, not talking back, not stealing	Submission to their masters in everything

A Specific Word (2:2-10)
2:2 Paul began with the men (Gk. *presbutas*), and without question this word denoted older or aged men; and those addressed here were not pastors but rather the natural leaders of the congrega-

tion. No age was specified, but the idea expressed seems to identify men who were mature and settled in their own homes and in their respective spiritual walks. The six requirements for holy living included being **self-controlled,**

worthy of respect, sensible, and sound in faith, love, and endurance. The first group contained ethical considerations and came alongside what had already been noted for pastors. The second group of three was devoted to ministry of life or what the men were to exhibit in their own respective spiritual lives. Character must always be fleshed out in the way one chooses to live and work. Paul expected the scrutiny and judgment of the pagan world on the lives of believers. Teachers give instruction in both doctrine (what to believe) and ethics (how to live), and they model how believing and living are intertwined in holding to certain timeless principles and living out the application of those principles in timely ways. Genuine godliness lived out in word and deed cannot be achieved without a genuine faith built upon the foundation of truth as recorded in God's Word.

> *Spiritually mature women are to teach women who are new to the faith!*

2:3 The section devoted to women began with an adverb (Gk. *hōsautōs*, "in the same way, likewise") connecting these verses with the beginning of the chapter and words of instructions to men. The list of these qualities is very similar to the qualities assigned to wives of deacons (1 Tm 3:11), which is natural since all women in leadership in the local church would be expected to meet high standards in character and lifestyle. The OLDER WOMEN (Gk. *presbutidas*, "old or elderly women") are addressed as the teachers in this woman-to-woman teaching within the church. To suggest that these women or "female elders" are required to be "worthy of the priesthood" has no basis in the text.[3] While the word selected is clear in its meaning, even though it is a *hapax legomenon* (a word used only once in the

Greek New Testament), the passage as a whole made a clear contrast between the teaching women and the pupils identified as young women (Gk. *neas*, "new, fresh, young"), who were not necessarily merely young in years but who were new and fresh to the faith. The context then allows the teachers to be identified as those who are immersed in faith, usually older in years but most of all well versed in God's Word and saturated with His wisdom, or "spiritually mature women" who then would teach women new or fresh to the faith, usually younger women who have not yet been equipped with the knowledge of God's Word and with the discerning wisdom that comes from time in studying Scripture. Spiritually mature women are to teach women who are new to the faith!

Paul then moved to describe the character of these spiritually mature women who would be teaching the younger women. Woman-to-woman teaching goes back to early Christianity where it was tried and proven. Mentoring relationships among women have been God-ordained and profoundly effective. A woman must be "REVERENT (Gk. *hieroprepeis*, "like people engaged in sacred duties, that which is suitable to holiness, temple-like"; *katastēmati*, "demeanor, deportment") in behavior." Certainly this demeanor would be inclusive of dress, suggesting a godly modesty. Most of all the word suggests outward action as emanating from inner character. A woman's everyday activities are as if she were engaged in sacred duties, carrying into daily life the demeanor appropriate for the temple. In fact, the root for the word translated "reverent" is the Greek word for "temple." Jerome, one of the ancient church fathers, summarized the passage in this way: "Their walk and motion, their countenance, speech,

Spiritual Mothering			
The Mentor and Novice	**The Curriculum**	**The Rewards**	**The Biblical Example**
Older Women (Gk. *presbutidas*) could be understood as spiritually mature women. Age definitely gives the edge in spiritual maturity (Ti 2:3).	Lifestyle Example (Ti 2:3) • **reverent behavior**— godly conduct, dress, and conversation Warnings (v. 3) • **not slanderers** (fault-finding, gossip, false accusation) • **not addicted to much wine**	To prevent slandering of God's message (Ti 2:5) To guard the sanctity of the home (2:4-5) To give young women the opportunity for spiritual ministry (2:12-15)	Naomi and Ruth • Naomi won Ruth to faith in *Yahweh* (Ru 1:16-17). • She gave Ruth wise counsel to win the heart of Boaz (Ru 2:20,22; 3:3-6). • She helped nurture Ruth's son Obed (Ru 4:15-16).
To teach the **young women** (Gk. *neas*) is not only a reference to youth but connotes freshness or what is new. New converts and those who have not been discipled are in view (v. 4).	Admonitions (vv. 4, 5) • **to love their husbands** (v. 4, Gk. *philandrous*, connoting "esteem" or "respect") • **to love their children** (v. 4, Gk. *philoteknous*) • to be **sensible** (v. 5, Gk. *sōphron*) • to be chaste or sexually **pure** (v. 5, Gk. *hagnas*) • **homemakers** (v. 5, Gk. *oikourgous*) • **good** (v. 5. Gk. *agathas*) • **submissive to their husbands** (v. 5, Gk. *hupotassō*; also used in Eph 5:21; Col 3:18; 1 Pt 3:1)		Deborah and Barak • Deborah guided him into battle (Jdg 4:6,14). • She accepted Barak's call for help (Jdg 4:9-10). • She celebrated the victory in song (Jdg 5:1-31). Elizabeth and Mary • Elizabeth encouraged Mary (Lk 1:41-45). • She offered Mary hospitality and refuge (Lk 1:56). Priscilla and Apollos • Priscilla, with her husband Aquila, received spiritual preparation from the Apostle Paul (Ac 18:1-4). • They patiently shared their understanding of Scripture (Ac 18:24-28). • Priscilla kept her home open to believers (Rm 16:3-5).

silence, may present a certain dignity of holy propriety."

The apostle continued with some warnings for women who want to be used in this teaching role. They must not be SLANDERERS (Gk. *diabolous*, "devils"). This word is a compound form with *dia*, a preposition meaning "through or by means of," and *ballō*, a verb meaning "throw." In the passive tense, *diaballō* means "bringing charges." Of course, the Devil is the great accuser and uses every opportunity to bring charges against believers or to cast through their lives and characters. Spiritually mature women who are going to be leaders and teachers must not *cast through* or *gossip*. Their words are to be encouraging and uplifting and instructive.

Heart to Heart: What Is the Fruit of Your Mouth?

Women are often accused of wagging their tongues in an ungodly manner. Certainly in the church at Corinth women were evidently caught up in the ecstatic utterances in public worship so much so that the apostle says clearly, "The women should be silent [Gk. sigatosan, "stop talking" or "close your mouth"] in the churches, for they are not permitted to speak" (1 Co 14:34). This warning is a reminder that all coming from the lips of a godly woman must be wholesome and Christ-honoring. Even prayer meetings can be turned away from a holy purpose when intimate and embarrassing details about a sister's tragedy are shared under the guise of requesting prayer but in reality become a conduit for passing along tragically sinful behavior.

The phrase **not addicted** (Gk. *dedoulomenas,* "enslave, subject, bring into bondage") **to much wine** is not surprising in a letter concerning the Cretans, who were known for their drunkenness. Even in contemporary society there are ample warnings in public places directed to women concerning the drinking of alcoholic beverages. Again women who want to be teachers and mentors of other women are to be held to the highest standards.

Perhaps you are wondering why Paul would use the phrase TEACH WHAT IS GOOD (Gk. *kalodidaskalous*, a *hapax legomenon* or word used only one time in the NT and not found outside the NT) rather than encouraging the mentoring women to warn the women they were teaching to avoid bad and evil. Perhaps Paul coined this word to describe a unique method of teaching, which would combine both example (character) and behavior (lifestyle). Actually the apostle showed a prophetic edge as he offered a timely word for subsequent generations. How can you warn against evil effectively when the pattern for what is good and godly has been lost? The spiritually mature women were to instruct and teach what is good in character and life as well as to motivate those women who were fresh in the faith to live godly lives, incorporating what is good and Christlike into their own lives. The emphasis was not on formal instruction but upon the private counsel and encouragement given by word and example. Character was intertwined with duty in the ancient world. Habits and lifestyle were at the heart of character. Thus, for a woman to manage her relationships to husband and children and others demanded certain appropriate traits of character.

2:4-5 The apostle hastened to provide the curriculum for this good teaching. Perhaps you are surprised that the things taught are not on what is considered to be a higher spiritual plane, such as methods in Bible study or skills in evangelism or even information on how to develop strategies for helping the needy. None of these things are unimportant, and all surely come in due course. However, Paul began according to the priorities already set forth from creation. He did not leave this important instruction to chance or assume its duties would be done by natural impulse. The phrase **so that they may encourage the young women to love their husbands and children** certainly catches the sense of the Greek text, but for better understanding one should note that two primary words are used, *philandrous* (Gk. for "husband-loving") and *philo-teknous* (Gk. for "children-loving"), which reminds the reader that these are really two different assignments.[4] You do indeed love husband and children, but your loving deeds and faithful service are offered to each in different ways. Because the woman was created to be a helper to the man before children ever arrived on the scene and because they as husband and wife begin their journey, and usually end it, without their children, it is quite fitting that the first lesson to be taught is for wives to love their husbands. But children are worthy of appropriate lessons in loving as well.

There are different words used in the Greek language for love, and the scope of this discussion does not allow the development of these. Certainly the Holy Spirit inspired certain words for a reason. One possibility is that *agapaō*, uniquely used in the New Testament and having the nuance of self-sacrifice and unconditional love, may have been much more natural for a wife and mother who in her own God-given nature and assignment from creation has a unique bent to self-sacrifice for her family. On the other hand, a wife/ mother may find it more difficult to live for her family over the years than to offer her life in a moment of crisis. Perhaps *phileō* called for a measure of respect and honor, which certainly was inclusive in genuine love. In this case, a woman might find her daily challenge to be in honoring her husband and children and respecting them with her words and actions. Beginning this section with an admonition on how a woman was to relate to her family is then in tandem with instructions given elsewhere by the apostle, as well as by Peter, to wives (Eph 5:21-24,33; Col 3:18; 1 Pt 3:1-6).

Another surprise in the apostle's list is **HOMEMAKERS** (Gk. *oikourous*, "working at home"). This *hapax lego-menon*, a word used only here in the New Testament, is a simple compound word linking "home" and "work."[5] Jewish women were certainly busy in their households according to biblical or extrabiblical sources. They would grind the flour, bake the bread, cook the meals, spin and weave the cloth, sew and launder the family's clothing, keep the house, and care for the children as well as extending hospitality to neighbors and even strangers passing through. To suggest that this term implied "having a home office" would be anachronistic at the least and inconsistent with the context's emphasis on husbands and children.[6] The emphasis seemed to be on a woman's efficient management of her household. Although many scholars do link **good** as a descriptor of the **homemakers**, this commentator prefers to consider it separately as a character trait. In any case, this homemaker is certainly understood to be not only hard-working but also passionately committed to her husband and children. What she did for them was not mere duty but joyful service offered ultimately unto the Lord. Single women would do well not to dismiss this passage as only directed to married women, for there are numerous epithets addressing character traits that should belong to all women. And one must not underestimate the importance of understanding God's plan for the home and relationships therein as a prelude to His revelation of Himself.

Note the consistency of this passage in relationship to other household codes and words directed to wives in Scripture. The household is the basic unit of society and is interconnected with the church and even with the state. The proper ordering of the household, i.e., how husbands and wives as well as parents and children relate to one another, is essential to maintain order in the church and support lawfulness in the community. Even though believers are not of the world, they must live in the world. The phrase "submissive (Gk. *hupotassomenas*, a present middle participle, "submissive to, under the authority of") to their [own] husbands" is completely in harmony with other passages. The word calling for submission is not demeaning; in fact, you cannot submit in the sense the word is used in the New Testament without choosing to do so. Submission is a personal choice, and the obedience it calls forth goes beyond human authority because the mandate comes from the heart of God Himself.

This section addressed to women ended in an unusual way as the apostle made his final appeal a reason for all that has gone before, **so that God's message will not be slandered**. The surprise is in the choice of the Greek word *blasphēmetai*, which probably for some seems a bit

strong. The word is transliterated into English as "blasphemy," a sin not to be taken lightly. The word does mean "to slander" or more precisely "to speak lightly of sacred and holy things" or "to speak against God so that you cast through or make null and void God's word and His truths." Not only must you avoid speaking or doing evil, but you must say and do good in order to avoid dishonoring God and to pursue honoring the Lord and His name (vv. 3,5). Only by obedience to the divine mandate does one magnify the Lord and draw others to Him. Disobedience brings the gospel itself into disrepute and incites reproach against God's Word.

2:6-8 Paul's admonition to the young men, as with the young women, is made with earnest entreaty, **URGING THEM** (Gk. *parakalei*, "call alongside") to be **SENSIBLE** (Gk. *sōphroneō*, "of sound mind, serious"), a word that involves caution and self-control, precluding personal gratification and self-interest. Derivatives from the same word are used elsewhere in this passage (vv. 2,5).

Here Paul found a natural opportunity to call for Timothy to serve as an example for other young men in what he did as well as what he taught. Not only doctrinal purity but also chaste language was included in the apostle's admonition. Nothing is any more important to spiritual leadership than consistency in your character and life. What you teach must be exemplified in how you live. The message in verse 8 is described as an apology, a carefully prepared and persuasively presented testimony of the gospel. Paul surely knew criticisms would come, but his concern was that these young men would be so well equipped that their opponents would not find in their lives weakness or reproach to use against the gospel (v. 8).

2:9-10 Slaves were an essential part of the Roman society, especially its economy. Paul did not express approval of slavery in his comments on how Christian slaves were to relate to their masters. He recognized the situation as it existed without offering judgment on whether it was right or wrong. Without apology, the apostle injected Christian principles into the pagan system so that even slaves could be a witness for Christ. The important issue was how slaves and masters were to treat one another.

Paul referred to himself as a bondslave to Christ. The only exception for a slave's obedience to his master would be a moral or spiritual matter in which the slave would be accountable first and foremost to God (Ac 5:29). The root of the tragic injustices found in slavery issued from the hearts of men. Sinful hearts taint any system just as Christ brings liberty in any situation.

Paul presented character qualities for the slave who wanted to emulate a Christlike demeanor:

- **submissive to their masters in everything** (Ti 2:9a; see also v. 5 and comments on "submissive");

- **well-pleasing** (Gk. *euarestous,* "acceptable") with a sincere desire to please (v. 9b);

- **not talking back** (Gk. *antilegontas,* "speak against") or refraining from argument and contradiction (v. 9c);

- **not stealing** (Gk. *nosphizomenous,* "keep back for myself, embezzle") or pilfering or misappropriating for yourself what belongs to another (v. 10a);

- **demonstrating utter faithfulness,** a cherished virtue of commitment (v. 10b).

All of these qualities associated with a Christian slave are just as appropriate in the right relationship between a Christian employee and his employer. Excellence in the marketplace is a powerful tool for witness.

Neither the words of Paul nor any reference in Scripture endorsed slavery. Scripture spoke to slavery and assumed its continuance without endorsing or supporting its existence. Paul cannot be accused of accommodation or support of slavery based upon the Spirit-inspired words he penned concerning how both slaves and masters were to act within the existing system. Rather the apostle addressed the matter of correct behavior for those who found themselves in slavery. A slave could not change his condition, but he could accept his position with a peace based upon trust in the providence of God to carry him through. There is reward in voluntarily choosing to submit yourself even to what cannot be changed. Voluntary submission is very different from coerced subjection because it looks with hope toward the future and Christ's return and subsequently to the believer's reunion with Christ in the air at His return or in heaven if death comes before Christ's return. Who better than a slave can demonstrate the sufficiency of Christ to provide sustaining grace even in the darkest hour and deepest disappointment!

Paul understood that he himself could not abolish slavery, but he knew that turning hearts to Christ would eventually remove a system with such potential for evil. However, for balance, you must note that even though slaves were owned as property, modern conclusions must be considered in light of a different social context. Some "free" people were even worse off than those slaves who were considered as members of the family and whose needs were provided accordingly and whose lives in some cases were not necessarily lived in suffering and humiliation. Some enjoyed considerable freedom and even held positions of authority. The apostle concentrated his energies on helping slaves—and masters—to live and act in Christlike ways. Even in modernity there are slaves in some places in the world. A slave is responsible for bearing a witness to the living Christ by the way in which he lives (**adorn the teaching of God our Savior in everything**, v. 10c). Instructions to slaves included the same admonition to seek a Christlike standard for character and work, including consistent faithfulness under pressure and loyal commitment even in the midst of injustice. Nothing brings as much credit to Christianity and its doctrines as the quality of character a believer's faith produces in her life.

A PERSUASIVE REASON FOR OBEDIENCE (2:11–3:11)

The Gift of Grace in Salvation (2:11-15)

2:11-12 Here the application seems threefold:

- **Sensible** living expressed a serious reflection that demanded personal restraint and self-control, or better God-control, over your thoughts as well as your actions.

- **Righteous** conduct spoke of absolute integrity and justice with others.

- **Godly way** described an overall attitude of piety that characterizes what you think, say, or do.

2:13-15 Verses 11-14 cast a vision of expectant living, moving through the journey of life renouncing evil and molding your life after that of Christ, but always looking beyond this world to what is to come, **the blessed hope** (Gk. *tēn makarian elpida*). "Blessed" is a word suggesting happiness and good fortune (certainly by-products of the hope

described), and "hope" definitely had a focus on the future. Believers wait for the return of Jesus Christ. He came as a baby in the manger in His incarnation, and He was born to die because redemption and the cross were before Him. However, when He returns, He will come in strength and victory, and that return is the next great event in redemptive history and one to which all who put their trust in Him for salvation can look with expectancy. Redemption, which began with the birth of the Christ Child in a humble manger and moved forward with His great suffering and death on the cruel cross, will culminate with His glorious return.

The Outworking of Faith in Life (3:1-11)

3:1-3 Again the call for submission (Gk. *hupotassesthai*) appeared, coupled with a call for obedience (Gk. *peitharchein*, "listen to"). If obedience to those in authority would impress earthly rulers, how much more would the Heavenly Father be encouraged and glorified when believers are submissive and obedient to Him and His mandates. Obedience is a necessary attribute for anyone who identifies herself with Christ, and that obedience is shallow and unimpressive unless it is complete and unconditional.

3:4-7 Paul undoubtedly believed that God is the author of salvation. God initiates the process by making provision for your salvation and by drawing you to Himself. He extends His mercy, and once you accept that mercy, He completes the work of redemption. You are not saved by your own works of righteousness; rather, Christ provides His work of righteousness. Thus Paul spoke clearly, **not by works of righteousness that we had done, but according to His mercy**. . . . **Salvation**, which comes through God's merciful grace—not works that come from our own imperfect and feeble efforts, **makes the doing of good works possible**. Good works are not possible without a right relationship to God, and a right relationship to God will produce good works as its fruit.

Some have seen **the washing of regeneration** as a reference to baptism, but several considerations make this conclusion impossible:

- Nothing in this passage suggests that any individual can do something equal to Christ's redemptive work.

- On the other hand, these verses do clearly define what God does to make salvation possible. It is clearly God's work from start to finish.

- The apostle even underscored that salvation is not secured by one's "works of righteousness."

What then is meant by "the washing of regeneration"? David spoke of a unique kind of cleansing in Psalm 51: "Wash away my guilt, and cleanse me from my sin" (Ps 51:2). The sweet psalmist of Israel certainly did not have reference to baptism, but his language indicated that he sought and expected to receive a cleansing from his sin. Baptismal waters, as important as they are for obedience and witness, cannot wash away sin. Rather, Jesus shed His blood on the cross, and that blood does indeed cleanse from sin.

3:8-11 "Reject a DIVISIVE (Gk. *hairetikon*, "factious, causing division" from a root meaning "choose" or "decide") person." In English the word has been transliterated as "heretical" and first came to denote self-willed opinions and eventually adapted the connotation of opinions of personal preference that produce divisions. One who decides to go her own way and in the process causes divisions may not hold false doctrine, but she does bring confusion within the assembly of believers.

CONCLUSION (3:12-15)

Final Instructions (3:12-14)

3:12-14 Paul seemed to indicate a changing of personnel in Crete when he called for Titus to join him in Nicopolis, suggesting that he would send Artemis or Tychicus (see Ac 20:4; Eph 6:21; Col 4:7) to continue the work on Crete. Note the mention of the eloquent and brilliant Apollos (v. 13), who had received instruction from Priscilla and Aquilla in Ephesus (Ac 18:24-26). The gospel was proclaimed as the way of salvation, and just as clear was the conclusion that the outcome of salvation would be a change in behavior. The men mentioned in these verses did not seem to be pastors but more probably were committed laymen who were serving in important kingdom positions of leadership.

A Personal Closing (3:15)

3:15 Paul in his final instructions made clear that the pastor or even a team of pastors could not meet all the urgent needs of a congregation—whatever the size. He thus challenged **our people** (v. 14), all believers, to arise and do good works. His final words were a poignant reminder to the congregation that all must be done in love and harmony, which would then draw **grace** or the unmerited favor of God Himself to all **in the faith**.

Bibliography

I & II Timothy, Titus. Shepherd's Notes. Nashville: Broadman & Holman Publishers, 1997.

*Barrett, C.K. *The Pastoral Epistles.* New Clarendon Bible. Oxford: The Clarendon Press, 1963.

Dana, H. E. *The Later Pauline Epistles and Hebrews.* The New Testament Message, vol. 3. Fort Worth: Pioneer Publishing, 1925.

*Ellicott, Charles. *Philippians, Colossians, Philemon, 1 Timothy, 2 Timothy, Titus.* Ellicott's Commentaries, Critical and Grammatical, on the Epistles of Saint Paul with Revised Translations. Minneapolis: The James Family Publishing Co., 1978.

Fairburn, Patrick. *I and II Timothy, Titus.* Classic Commentary Library. Grand Rapids: Zondervan Publishing House, 1956.

Gorday, Peter, ed. *Colossians, 1-2 Thessalonians, 1-2 Timothy, Titus, Philemon.* Ancient Christian Commentary on Scripture, vol. 9. Downers Grove: Intervarsity Press, 2000.

*Hanson, A. T. *The Pastoral Epistles.* The New Century Bible Commentary. Grand Rapids: Wm. B. Eerdmans Publishing Co., 1982.

*Knight, George. *The Pastoral Epistles: A Commentary on the Greek Text.* The New International Greek Testament Commentary. Grand Rapids: Eerdmans Publishing Co., 1992.

Lea, Thomas D., and Hayne P. Griffin. *1,2 Timothy, Titus.* The New American Commentary, vol. 34. Nashville: Broadman Press, 1992.

*Liefeld, Walter L. *1 & 2 Timothy.* The NIV Application Commentary. Grand Rapids: Zondervan Publishing House, 1999.

*Oden, Thomas. *First and Second Timothy and Titus.* Interpretation. Louisville: John Knox Press, 1989.

Patterson, Paige. *Living in Hope of Eternal Life: An Exposition of Titus.* Grand Rapids: Zondervan Publishing House, 1968.

Vine, W. E. *The Epistles to Timothy and Titus.* Grand Rapids: Zondervan Publishing House, 1965.

Young, Frances. *The Theology of the Pastoral Letters.* Cambridge: Cambridge University Press, 1994.

*Advanced Study

Notes

[1] I am most indebted in my understanding of this brief epistle to Paige Patterson's *Living in Hope of Eternal Life: An Exposition of Titus* (Grand Rapids: Zondervan Publishing House, 1968), which is no longer in print.

[2] C. S. Lewis, *Reflections on the Psalms* (London: Collins, 1961), 32.

[3] See Catherine and Richard Clark Kroeger, *I Suffer Not a Woman* (Grand Rapids: Baker Book House, 1992), 91. The Kroegers espouse an egalitarian perspective.

[4] The Holman Christian Standard Bible translators elected to link these two phrases, "to love their husbands and children."

[5] The HCSB translators understood "good" as an adjective modifying "homemakers."

[6] Walter L. Liefeld, *1 & 2 Timothy,* The NIV Application Commentary (Grand Rapids: Zondervan Publishing House, 1999), 328. Written from an egalitarian perspective.

PHILEMON

Introduction

Even though Philemon is the shortest of Paul's letters (only 25 verses—335 words in the Greek text), no other epistle gives its readers a better glance at Paul's skill in handling practical problems within the family of God. A valuable lesson can be learned by studying Paul's use of tact and courtesy as he calls for Christian maturity in handling a difficult situation.

Title

In its shortest form, the Greek title of this epistle is *pros Philēmona*, "to Philemon." The title simply reflects the designated recipient of this letter from Paul.

Setting

Paul wrote Philemon to encourage him to accept Onesimus, not as a slave but "as a dearly loved brother" (v. 16). Although Paul did not state explicitly that Onesimus had run away from Philemon, this fact can be inferred through the letter's content. Along the way Onesimus met Paul and came to faith in Christ (v. 10). He could have faced severe punishment for his crime, yet Paul urged Philemon to exercise mercy and grace. Paul even offered to pay any debt Onesimus owed to Philemon, setting forth one of the most beautiful illustrations of the gospel message. Paul offered to pay a debt that Onesimus could not pay in order for this slave to be reconciled with his master. Christ likewise paid sin's debt so that women and men could be reconciled with God.

Genre

The book of Philemon, together with Ephesians, Philippians, and Colossians, is grouped among Paul's Prison Epistles. This letter is an example of private correspondence describing a real problem between two friends.

Author

Paul is identified as its author (v. 1). Its place in the canon and its authenticity have never been seriously questioned. This short letter's similarity in style and structure to Paul's other writings and the unanimous affirmation of the early church give credibility to Pauline authorship. When such internal (the style and structure of the letter) and external (the testimony of the early church) support is examined, the testimony of this letter concerning its authorship cannot be doubted.

Date

The date and provenance (location from which it was written) of Philemon are tied to its classification as a prison epistle. The traditional view is that this letter was written during Paul's first incarceration in Rome AD 60–63 (Ac 28:30-31). However, another plausible option is that Paul wrote Philemon while he was in prison in Ephesus in the mid 50s. Perhaps the proximity of Colossae to Ephesus (almost 100 miles) and Paul's proposed visit (v. 22) make the Ephesian imprisonment in the mid 50s a more likely option for the dating and provenance of this letter. Additionally, the return trip of Onesimus to Colossae from Ephesus instead of Rome supports the latter option.

Recipients

This semiprivate letter was addressed to Philemon, a believer who opened his home as a place of worship in Colossae. Paul sent the letter with Tychicus and Onesimus, Philemon's runaway slave (Col 4:7-9). Paul also addressed the letter to Apphia and Archippus, who cannot be positively identified; however, it is reasonable to believe that Apphia was Philemon's wife and Archippus their son because Paul addressed the church that met in Philemon's house directly after he greeted Apphia and Archippus.

Major Themes

The major theme of this letter is Christian fellowship. How a person treats both believers and unbelievers reflects upon the Holy Spirit who lives within and will affect her relationships. Paul's entreaty and gentle encouragement to Philemon to treat Onesimus as a brother displayed a vital truth of Christianity: All believers, regardless of race, gender, social status, or economic background, are to be treated with love and respect. This small epistle echoes Christ's words "By this all people will know that you are My disciples, if you have love for one another" (Jn 13:35).

Pronunciation Guide

Apphia	*AF ih uh*	Epaphras	*EP uh frass*
Archippus	*ahr KIP uhs*	Onesimus	*oh NESS ih muhs*
Aristarchus	*ehr iss TAHR kuhs*	Philemon	*figh LEE muhn*
Demas	*DEE muhs*		

Outline

I. INTRODUCTORY GREETING (vv. 1-3)

II. PAUL'S EXPRESSION OF CONFIDENCE IN PHILEMON (vv. 4-7)

III. PAUL'S INTERCESSION FOR ONESIMUS (vv. 8-22)

A. Paul's Account of the Conversion of Onesimus (vv. 8-11)

B. Paul's Assessment of Onesimus (vv. 12-16)

C. Paul's Solution to the Problem (vv. 17-22)

IV. CONCLUDING GREETINGS (vv. 23-25)

Exposition of the text

INTRODUCTORY GREETING (VV. 1-3)

1 Paul began his greeting with a strategic decision to identify himself as **a prisoner of Christ Jesus** instead of an apostle of Christ (see Rm 1:1; 1 Co 1:1; 2 Co 1:1; Gl 1:1; Eph 1:1; Col 1:1, 1 Tm 1:1; 2 Tm 1:1) or as a slave of Christ (see Rm 1:1; Php 1:1). Only here did Paul use "prisoner" (Gk. *desmios*) to identify himself in an epistolary greeting. He used this word or one of its derivatives four times in this short letter (vv. 1,9,10,13). Clearly Paul wanted to stress his present circumstances to Philemon. The phrase "of Christ Jesus" denoted the authority with which Paul wrote. He included greetings from **Timothy,** who was converted during Paul's first missionary journey and who served alongside him as a trusted companion for many years. The phrase "to Philemon" identified the letter's addressee as a "dear friend and co-worker." The term CO-WORKER (Gk. *sunergō*, "helper, fellow worker") is frequently used by Paul to describe those actively engaged in the ministry of the gospel. Philemon was a resident of Colossae who had been saved under Paul's ministry (v. 19) and who then opened his home to local believers.

2 The fact that **Apphia our sister** was greeted immediately after Philemon lends credence to the belief that she was Philemon's wife and hostess for the church that met in their home. The term SISTER (Gk. *adelphē*, "sister or fellow-believer") is best taken in the Christian sense and not as a literal flesh-and-blood sister. She is not mentioned elsewhere in the Bible, but according to tradition, she, alongside Onesimus, Philemon, and Archippus, was stoned to death during the persecution of Nero.[1]

Apphia	
Paul said . . .	She is "our sister," a relationship anchored in Christ rather than a sibling.
Paul implied . . .	She is Philemon's wife and hostess for the house church.
Tradition recorded . . .	She, along with others mentioned in this letter, became a martyr for the faith.

Archippus our fellow soldier was a member of Philemon's household and probably his son. The designation FELLOW SOLDIER (Gk. *sustratiōtē*, "comrade in arms") brings to mind a person who shares similar objectives and goals with another, someone who is engaged in the same conflicts and battles. Archippus may have been the pastor of the church that met in Philemon's house; he was certainly prominent in the church in Colossae (see Col 4:17). **To the church that meets in your house**—before the third century, house churches were the most common place a group of believers met. Many women and men in the early church exercised the gift of hospitality to build up the body of Christ and spread the gospel. The simple act of opening your home to believers or unbelievers had and can still have a huge impact on the kingdom of Christ.

Examples of House Churches in the New Testament	
Mary at Jerusalem (Ac 12:12)	Gaius at Rome (Rm 16:23)
Lydia at Philippi (Ac 16:15,40)	Aquila and Priscilla at Ephesus (1 Co 16:19)
Jason at Thessalonica (Ac 17:5-6)	Nympha at Laodicea (Col 4:15)
Aquila and Priscilla at Rome (Rm 16:3-5)	Philemon at Colossae (Phm 2)

3 Paul used a conventional phrase, **Grace to you and peace**, to close the greeting portion of his letters (see Rm 1:7; Col 1:2).

PAUL'S EXPRESSION OF CONFIDENCE IN PHILEMON (VV. 4-7)

4-5 Before Paul launched into the main reason for his letter, he took a moment to assure Philemon of his continual **prayers** for him. He commended Philemon's **love and faith toward the Lord Jesus and for all the saints** (v. 5; see Col 1:4). Epaphras is most likely the source of Paul's information concerning Philemon's excellent witness (see Col 1:7-8; 4:12; Plm 23).

6 As Paul prayed, he called for Philemon's **participation** to be **effective**. PARTICIPATION (Gk. *koinōnia*, "close relationship") indicates both fellowship and generosity—genuine partnership. Philemon's faith became effective as he participated in the Christian life through knowing and recognizing the good things which were his in Christ. EFFECTIVE (Gk. *energēs*, "powerful, efficient") carried the sense of active and productive and has been anglicized as "energetic." A Christian woman's faith is infused with life and productivity as the great blessings residing in her are used for the glory of Christ. Do not miss that Paul points out this **faith** is to be effective **for the glory of Christ**.

7 Paul had experienced **great joy** because of Philemon's love for his fellow Christians. He used the word REFRESH (Gk. *anapepautai*, "cause to rest") in regard to Philemon, and this key concept appears later in the letter as well (v. 20). The term implied a time for rest or relaxation that prepared a person to begin his labor anew. The outpouring of Philemon's great **love** upon his fellow believers **refreshed** them so that they were energized to devote themselves to the work of the kingdom. What a coveted commendation that every woman would "refresh" the hearts of fellow believers through her great love for them so that they would want to devote themselves afresh to the work of God's kingdom. Such a woman is like a cool stream in the midst of a dry desert—she has a great ministry simply because she loves her brothers and sisters as Christ would love them!

PAUL'S INTERCESSION FOR ONESIMUS (VV. 8-22)

Paul's Account of the Conversion of Onesimus (vv. 8-11)

8-9 For this reason—Paul appealed to Philemon's love, which he had just praised (v. 7). Although Paul had certain rights that would give him great boldness to command Philemon to obey his request, he chose instead to appeal to Philemon's love for his fellow believers. Paul used a masterful rhetorical device (see also v. 19); he told Philemon exactly *why* he should grant his request and then told him why he would dare to deal with him so boldly—because he trusted Philemon to make the right decision. Any mother can appreciate Paul's logic and cunning in this verse. He called himself **an elderly** (Gk. *presbutēs*, "older man, aged person") **man** and **a prisoner of Christ Jesus**, undoubtedly casting himself in a more sympathetic light through gentle self-depreciation. How could Philemon possibly say no to his request?

10-11 Paul appealed to Philemon on behalf of **Onesimus** whom he considered his son in the Lord because Paul more than likely played an instrumental role in bringing the slave to salvation. The metaphor of fatherhood expressed the endearment of Onesimus to Paul, identifying him as a son instead of a slave. Paul was teaching Philemon to renew his thinking—his slave was not only a son but also a brother in Christ. Onesimus's name was common among slaves and meant "useful or profitable." Paul made a play on words because he said that Onesimus was once USELESS (Gk. *achrēston*, "worthless") but had become USEFUL (Gk. *euchrēston*, "serviceable") both to Philemon and Paul—he can now live up to his name. In the latter description, the prefix *eu*, meaning "good," is added to *chrēston*, meaning "profitable," to emphasize the worth and goodness. In the former word, the alpha privative negates the concept of worth. The respective prefix then intensifies the meaning of the words. By ministering to Paul, Onesimus was doing so on Philemon's behalf, and he became "useful" again.

Paul's Assessment of Onesimus (vv. 12-16)

12-13 Paul referred to Onesimus as **part of himself**. Another translation could be that Paul considered Onesimus "his very heart" (see also vv. 7,20), and Philemon had not only refreshed Paul's heart by showing love (v. 7), but Paul requested that Philemon "refresh my HEART (Gk. *splagchna*) in Christ" (v. 20) again by showing grace and mercy towards Onesimus, who had become his heart, A PART OF MYSELF (Gk. *splagchna*, "inward parts, heart," v. 12). This same Greek word is used three times (vv. 7,12,20) and represents the seat of emotions and innermost being. This play on words is very clever in the Greek text and is an example of Paul's eloquence in making a request. Paul made the generous assumption that Philemon wanted to help him; and since Philemon could not minister to Paul during his **imprisonment**, Onesimus could minister to him in Philemon's place.

14 Paul gave up his own rights and preference to give Philemon an opportunity for service. By empowering Philemon to demonstrate his maturity and love for his brothers in Christ, Paul asked Philemon to empower Onesimus with the same opportunity. To help someone make the right choice is not to enslave him but to free him.

15-16 Paul speculated that maybe God used Onesimus's disobedience to bring him to the place where he would accept God's free offer of salvation. God turned a bad situation and worked it for the good. PERMANENTLY (Gk. *aiōnion*, "a significant period of time, illimitable duration") could also mean "eternally"—now Onesimus was not only his slave but also his brother in Christ for the rest of eternity. Paul did not request that Onesimus be emancipated (see 1 Co 7:22; Col 3:22–4:1; Gl 3:28); he urged Philemon instead to change his thinking about Onesimus. Certainly slavery was a terrible evil; Paul's method for handling the situation demonstrated true wisdom.

Heart to Heart:
Doing the "Right" Thing

God empowers you in the same way Paul empowered Philemon. God takes pleasure in obedience. Yet, even though He has the power and authority to enforce obedience, He allows you to choose between right and wrong. He also allows you to choose between exercising your rights and choosing to do the right thing, just as Paul allowed Philemon to choose. You can act within the parameters of your lawful or social rights, yet not profit from that choice (1 Co 6:11-13). You may feel that you have the right to be angry, yet God would ask you to forgive. You might feel that you have the right to indulge your own desires—but God would ask you to be a servant. A woman who insists upon exercising her rights will be unlikely to do the right thing in the end.

Paul knew that until hearts and minds were transformed, social evils such as slavery would not be abolished. Imagine what would have happened if every slave owner treated his slave as a dearly loved brother! Paul knew that salvation does not change a person's circumstances on earth, but in heaven, Onesimus was equally an heir and son of the King of kings.

Paul's Solution to the Problem (vv. 17-22)

17 Paul stated that if Philemon considered him **as a partner** (Gk. *koinōnon*, "companion, sharer"), then he would **accept** Onesimus as if he were accepting Paul. The sentence structure in the Greek is a first class conditional statement, which means that the proposed condition is understood as being true. So, Paul stated that *if* Philemon considered Paul a partner (which he did), then Philemon would grant his request. Paul was already convinced that Philemon would do what he asked.

18-19 These verses are a beautiful picture of the ministry of reconciliation. There is no way to know for sure the exact nature of Onesimus's crime and what he owed Philemon; however, Paul offered to take Onesimus's debt upon himself, which is exactly what Christ did for every woman and man. This illustration is a superb example of precisely what the Bible means when it speaks of substitutionary atonement whereby the righteousness of Christ Jesus is credited to those who accept His gift of salvation. A little bit of tongue in cheek was involved in Paul's comment in verse 19; Paul subtly compared the spiritual debt that Philemon could owe Paul to the material or monetary debt that Onesimus owed Philemon.

20-22 Paul created a deliberate play on words with the use of **REFRESH** (Gk. *anapausan*; see v. 7) and **HEART** (Gk *splagchna*; see vv. 12-13). He simply asked Philemon to do for him what Paul had already commended him for doing for other believers. Paul had complete confidence that Philemon would respond to his call for a loving response.

CONCLUDING GREETINGS (VV. 23-25)

23-25 Paul concluded by sending greetings to Philemon from

- **Epaphras** (Gk. "lovely"), **my fellow-prisoner** (Gk. *sunaichmalōtos*) is identified elsewhere as "our much loved fellow slave" (Col 1:12) and a "slave of Jesus Christ" (Col 4:12). This preacher from Colossae was instrumental in opening Colossae, Hierapolis, and Laodicea to the gospel. He was imprisoned with Paul when he came to Rome seeking Paul's help to fight against incipient Gnosticism.

- John **Mark** (see Ac 12:12,25; 15:37, 39; Col 4:10; 2 Tm 4:11; 1 Pt 5:13), a Jew, was the cousin of Barnabas (Col 4:10).

- **Aristarchus** was a traveling companion of Paul from Macedonia (Ac 19:29). According to tradition, Nero put Aristarchus to death in Rome.

- **Demas,** a companion and coworker of Paul, later deserted him because Demas "loved this present world" (2 Tm 4:10).

- **Luke**, author of the third Gospel and the book of Acts and a close friend and traveling companion of Paul's, was also with Paul shortly before his martyrdom (2 Tm 4:11).

Bibliography

Melick, Richard R. *Philippians, Colossians, and Philemon.* The New American Commentary, vol. 32. Nashville: Broadman Press, 1991.

*O'Brien, Peter T. *Colossians, Philemon.* The Word Biblical Commentary, vol. 44. Waco: Word Books, 1982.

* For advanced study.

Notes

1 Paul Gardner, ed., *The Complete Who's Who in the Bible* (London: Marshall Pickering, 1995), 56.

HEBREWS

Introduction

Hebrews is a book that possesses many deep truths that challenge believers to diligent study and complete reliance on God's Spirit for insight and understanding. Its beautiful imagery conveys the supremacy of Jesus, connecting the truths of the Old and New Testament in a profound manner. In fact, Hebrews has been referred to as the *Reader's Digest* version of Deuteronomy, Numbers, and Leviticus due to the author's dependence on these particular books.

The book of Hebrews was originally addressed to Jewish men and women who recognized and believed that Jesus is the Messiah. Such a declaration of faith, however, meant that they endured persecution, suffering, and the temptation to return to Judaism and reject the claims and teachings of Jesus. Hebrews was written to encourage them to run the race of faith with endurance, recognizing the fullness of Jesus' sacrifice on their behalf. Likewise, this epistle addresses those today who struggle in the Christian walk and need to be reminded of the importance of persevering to the end. The writer motivates his readers throughout this stirring letter, offering encouragement to all who meditate on His word.

Title

The oldest manuscript of Hebrews identifies the letter simply as "To the Hebrews" (Gk. *pros Hebraious*). Unlike most epistles in the New Testament, this letter lacks the typical salutation identifying the author and recipients. Originally the letter had no title and may have circulated briefly without one until it was given a place among collections of other apostolic letters. The title likely reflects an assumption that the letter was written to a predominantly Jewish-Christian audience because of its heavy emphasis on Old Testament themes.

In Acts 6:1 "Hebraic Jews" or "Hebrews" designated a group's ethnicity or culture rather than where they lived or were born. The label identified people who, living primarily in Palestine, maintained various aspects of Hebrew culture, including use of the Hebrew language in worship, in distinction from thoroughly "Hellenistic Jews." Nevertheless, the content of the letter depends heavily on the Greek translation of the Old Testament, so its title may be misleading. Likely, writer and recipients were steeped in the Scriptures and traditions of Hellenistic Judaism before responding to the gospel.

Setting

The author repeatedly stated the need for his readers to hold fast to the confession that they had made that Jesus is the Messiah and Savior of the world. The temptation was to succumb to the pressures of the surrounding community, which urged them to abandon their faith and return to the traditions of Judaism. Judaizers argued that the prophets, angels, and Moses were greater than Jesus, and they attempted to use the Old Testament to bolster their argument. The author of Hebrews, however, demonstrates the superiority of Jesus on all accounts, using Old Testament texts to prove his point. The original audience is described as disheartened and weak (5:11; 6:12; 12:3) due to their sagging faith. They needed a renewed sense of commitment to their new life in Jesus and the reminder that He is the Messiah, the High Priest, the One through whom intimacy with God is possible.

Genre

Hebrews was written in the form of a sermon prepared in response to a crisis of faith. Although the book of Hebrews is correctly regarded as a letter, it lacks many of the features common to other ancient Greco-Roman letters. The author does not identify himself or his recipients, and there are no introductory words of thanksgiving or blessing. The book does, however, close with the personal remarks and greetings customary to the genre of epistle. In fact, in the conclusion, the writer identified the letter as a "word of exhortation" (13:22). This phrase was an idiomatic expression referring to the sermon or homily typically delivered in the synagogue or church setting of Hellenistic Jews who embraced the Christian faith. The rhetorical structure and literary style of the letter's contents support classifying the letter as such a sermon, which would have been read aloud to the assembled body of believers.

Author

Throughout the centuries, scholars have proposed that Paul, Luke, Apollos, Barnabas, or Silvanus penned this letter. It is the only anonymous epistle in the New Testament. The tradition of Pauline authorship remains the majority position, although not positively proven. What is understood from the letter's content is that the author was presumably within the Pauline circle and expected to travel with Timothy (13:23). The author was undoubtedly familiar with the traditions and theological aspects of Judaism, referring repeatedly to the Old Testament. His writing style also indicates that he was skilled in Koinē Greek. However, Clement of Alexandria (c. AD 150–215) believed that Paul wrote the letter originally in Aramaic and that Luke translated it into Greek. Tertullian (c. AD 160–215) believed that Paul's missionary partner Barnabas wrote it. This position could account for the suggested resemblances to Pauline thought in the book of Hebrews. Of course, Barnabas's authorship of the letter cannot be proven more than any other. Martin Luther believed that Hebrews was written by Apollos. Some modern evangelical scholars offer substantial evidence that Luke penned Hebrews. Most, however, decisively conclude, along with the early church leader Origen (AD 185–253), that "who wrote the Epistle, God only knows the truth."

Date

Because allusions to the book of Hebrews seem evident in 1 Clement, an early church manuscript, the date must be before AD 95. Others base the date on the fall of Jerusalem in AD 70, believing that the letter was either written just prior to or just following this time. The letter's internal evidence suggests that the temple had not yet been destroyed as the author seems to regard this system as still existing (9:6-9; 10:1-3). The author's exhortations indicate that persecution was on the rise, which could point either to Nero's reign in AD 64–68 or to Domitian's reign AD 81–82. Given these elements, most commentators place the date of the letter around AD 65–68.

Recipients

The book of Hebrews originally addressed a persecuted group of Jewish believers, many of whom are believed to have been second-generation believers. Scholars are divided on the group's location—some maintain they lived in Rome while others believe they lived in Jerusalem or Antioch of Syria. To recognize that these believers were Jewish helps the reader understand the context of the author's discussion throughout the letter. These believers were obviously familiar with the Old Testament texts the author used (12:16), even though he did elaborate on their meaning (12:17). Furthermore, to note throughout the book the centrality of Moses, a Jewish figure highly venerated in Judaism, is interesting. He served as the supreme example of an individual's access to God; yet the author of Hebrews demonstrated Jesus' superiority. The letter also reflects the author's concern that this group was being pulled away from what they knew to be true and was returning to the tradition they once followed, which conflicted with God's word (13:7-9). Chapter 2 implied that these believers had grown complacent in their walk with Jesus and were dangerously close to returning to their old patterns of life.

The author is concerned that the recipients understand Jesus' complete fulfillment of the Mosaic covenant, a topic that continues to resound especially with modern-day Jewish believers. Having come out of Judaism, within which they were born and raised, these new believers often faced tremendous hostility from their own people who had not yet embraced Jesus as their Messiah (10:32-34). Additionally, many of these new believers struggled in discerning how to marry their Jewish practices and ceremonies with Christian teachings. Many, therefore, were in danger of adopting a ritualistic, legalistic form of Christianity. They needed the reminder that while still Jewish, they were newly identified in Christ and therefore were not bound to the traditions of Judaism. The new covenant, given in grace through Jesus, supercedes the Mosaic covenant and provides individual access and intimacy with God through His Son.

Major Themes

The theme of Hebrews can be summed up with a simple phrase, "Jesus is better." The author used the characteristic phrase "better than" to refer to Jesus 13 times during the course of this letter. Jesus is the great high priest—superior to the angels, to Moses, and to the prophets and priests of the Old Testament. The new covenant, made possible by Jesus, had now superceded all that was present during the Mosaic covenant. This theme ties together the entire letter. Jesus is superior to and preeminent over everything. Living by faith in Jesus is superior to living according to legalism. Believers are encouraged to mature in their faith, daily persevering in their walk with Jesus. Jesus, as the ultimate high priest, has fulfilled the demands of the law and has once and for all provided a way of salvation for all who believe in Him—this is the beautiful message of Hebrews.

Pronunciation Guide

Barak	*BAY rak*	Levitical	*lih VIT ih kuhl*
Enoch	*EE nuhk*	Melchizedek	*mel KIZ uh dek*
Gideon	*GID ih uhn*	Rahab	*RAY hab*
heifer	*HEH fuhr*	testator	*TES tay tuhr*
Jephthah	*JEF thuh (th as in thin)*		

Outline

I. THE SUPERIORITY OF THE PERSON
OF JESUS (1:1–4:16)
A. God's Revelation through Jesus
(1:1-4)
B. Jesus' Superiority over the
Angels (1:5-14)
C. Warning against Neglecting
Salvation (2:1-4)
D. The Glory of Jesus (2:5-18)
E. Jesus' Superiority over Moses
(3:1–4:13)
F. Jesus, the High Priest (4:14-16)

II. THE SUPERIORITY OF THE
PRIESTHOOD OF JESUS (5:1–10:39)
A. Jesus' Perfect Priesthood
(5:1-10)
B. The Problem of Believers'
Immaturity (5:11–6:20)

C. Jesus' Superiority over Aaron
and His Likeness to
Melchizedek (7:1-28)
D. The Superiority of Christ's
New Covenant (8:1–10:39)
1. The nature of the new
covenant (8:1-13)
2. The sacrifice of the new
covenant (9:1-28)
3. The sufficiency of the new
covenant sacrifice (10:1-39)

III. THE SUPERIORITY OF THE POWER
OF CHRIST (11:1–12:29)
A. The Great Hall of Faith
(11:1-40)
B. A Call to Endurance (12:1-29)

IV. CONCLUDING REMARKS (13:1-25)

Exposition of the Text

THE SUPERIORITY OF THE PERSON OF JESUS (1:1–4:16)

God's Revelation through Jesus (1:1-4)

1:1 The epistle begins with a profound Christological passage that beautifully describes the preeminence of Jesus. Verses 1-4 are packed with theological significance, describing the God who reveals, creates, saves, and reigns forever. The author of Hebrews began by introducing his readers to the God who speaks. He stressed in these verses that God is not silent, but rather He reveals Himself to mankind and desires to be known by the men and women He created. His revelation is rooted in His love. God, therefore, is aware of human circumstances, speaking as the *Living God*. The writer, however, contrasted the various ways God has spoken to mankind. God formerly spoke **by the prophets at different times and in different ways** (v. 1). God raised up Moses, Elijah, Nathan, Jeremiah, and others for the purpose of communicating His message to the people. God spoke to them in various ways—through a burning bush (Ex 3:1-10), a quiet voice (1 Kg 19:11-13), and visions (e.g., Gn 15:1; 46:2; Nm 12:6). The Old Testament recorded their authoritative words, "Thus says the Lord . . . " While their ministries were important and vital, the author demonstrated that each was only temporary. Prophetic revelation reached its climax with the birth of Jesus. Verses 1 and 2 establish the contrast between the ministry of the prophets and the ministry of Jesus. The prophets were used by God in former times, while Jesus is now the One through whom the Father "has spoken in these last days" (Heb 1:2). The old paved the way for the new, a truth repeated throughout the epistle.

1:2 The author described the greatness of Jesus, setting the tone and establishing the theme for the entire epistle. Jesus is the One through whom God **has spoken** (v. 2). Jesus is the Superior One, and as John's gospel explains, He is "the way, the truth, and the life" (Jn 14:6), and He is "the word" (Jn 1:1,14). In the opening verses of Hebrews, the writer described Jesus as the eternal Son, the incarnate Son and the exalted Son. Jesus is first described as the **heir of all things**, a title of dignity that demonstrates His supreme position in the universe. Furthermore, through Him **the universe** was created. This truth is important in Christian doctrine. God is the Creator of the world, and through the Son He spoke all of creation into being (Jn 1:3; 1 Co 8:6; Col 1:16).

1:3-4 The Son is described as the **radiance** of God's **glory**, the revelation of God's majesty (v. 3). The whole ministry of Jesus, therefore, was evidence of God's glory. Jesus is also **the exact expression of His nature,** a critical Christological truth speaking directly to the nature of Jesus and His relationship with God the Father. Not only does the Son reflect God's glory, but He also shares God's nature. The EXACT EXPRESSION OF HIS NATURE (Gk. *charaktēr*, "reproduction, representation," anglicized as "character") refers to an engraved character or impression made on a seal or coin—"the very stamp." In other words, the Son's nature is the same as God the Father's. There is no difference (Jn 10:30). Moreover, it is this One who "sustains all things by His POWERFUL WORD (Gk. *hrēmati tēs dunameōs autou*, lit., "by the word of His power"). The noun *hrēma* is not used in the Gospel of John to identify Jesus as "the word" (Gk. *ho logos*). *Hrēma* denotes specifically the spoken word, what is said with one's voice (see also 6:5; 11:3; 12:19). Not only was the world created

through Him, but it is also sustained by Him simply by "His powerful word." What an incredible thought to ponder!

The author continued by explaining that this One made **purification for sins** (v. 3). The entire epistle deals with the reality that the Son came to confront the problem of man's sin; and by His priestly work in offering the ultimate sin offering, the penalty of death was forever removed from those who place their faith in Him. PURIFICATION (Gk. *katharismon*, "ceremonial cleansing") points to the defiling aspect of sin. The same word is used to describe the cleansing of lepers. This truth is underscored by the last phrase in verse 3. **He sat down at the right hand of the Majesty on high.** Sitting at God's right hand affirmed that Jesus' saving work had been completed forever and He now occupies the highest seat of honor. Jesus' supremacy is underscored in His enthronement at the right hand of God, leading naturally to the statement that He is superior to the angels (v. 4) and setting up the argument that the new revelation of Jesus is better than the old revelation mediated by the angels (2:1-4). Interestingly, in these opening statements (1:1-4), Jesus is presented as prophet (God spoke through Him to man), priest (the One who purges our sin), and king (He sat down at the right hand of God to reign forever).

Jesus' Superiority over the Angels (1:5-14)

1:5 Having introduced the Son's superiority to the angels, the writer turned to the Old Testament and cited seven passages to support his point. The writer did not always record these quotations in the same way as found in the Old Testament text. For instance, he applied references to kings to Jesus. He understood that Jesus the Messiah, the King of kings and Lord of lords, is heir to the throne of David. The first passage he quoted demonstrated

God's enthronement of the Son (Ps 2:7). The second quotation comes from 2 Samuel 7:14 (cp. 1 Ch 17:13) and pointed to a father-son relationship that is best exemplified in the relationship of Jesus to God the Father. Angels cannot, as the writer clarified, claim such a unique relationship. In the context of the verse the prophet Nathan promised David that his line would produce an heir who would build a house for God and through whom a throne would be established forever. The prophets and people throughout the time of the Old Testament longed for the establishment of such a kingdom through the Messiah. The writer of Hebrews, therefore, declared that this ancient promise found its fulfillment in the coming of Jesus the Messiah who is the Son of God and from the lineage of David.

1:6 This verse stresses that Jesus is the one and only Son of God and does not imply that He is a created being. He is the **firstborn** Son of God. He is superior to the angels. The writer added that **all God's angels must worship Him**, a quotation from the *Septuagint* or LXX (the Greek translation of the Hebrew Old Testament) rendering of Deuteronomy 32:43. "All" stressed that every angel must worship Him, for, as the writer demonstrated, Jesus is worthy of their worship because He is the Son of God.

1:7-9 The writer pressed his point further by quoting two additional Old Testament passages. First, he quoted Psalm 104:4 to demonstrate again that whereas **the angels** are servants to God, the Son is the ruler of the universe. In verses 8 and 9, the writer quoted Psalm 45:6-7, emphasizing the Sonship of Jesus over the service of the angels. Jesus rules with **a scepter of justice** (Heb 1:8), a distinct characteristic of God, and He despises **lawlessness** (v. 9), pointing to Jesus' earthly obedience to the holiness of God. Furthermore, God **has anointed** His Son

with the oil of joy (v. 9). The Old Testament recounted the special ceremony in which Israel's leaders were anointed with oil as a symbol of the presence of God upon them as the chosen leaders of God's people (i.e., Ex 29:5-7; 1 Sm 9:26–10:1). In the same way, Jesus was anointed with the Holy Spirit at the time of His baptism (Lk 3:21-22).

1:10-12 The sixth quotation in Hebrews 1 comes from Psalm 102:25-27. The comparison is between the eternal Son and the temporal universe. First, the author drew attention to the fact that the Son created the universe and, therefore, preceded it. Furthermore, even when creation is destroyed during the end times, the Son will remain unchanged. The reference is to the transformation of **the heavens and earth** following the time of the millennium (Is 34:4; 2 Pt 3:10-13) when the old creation will be exchanged for the new. The immutability and eternality of the Son is underscored as distinct characteristics of God's nature. He controls the destiny of creation and is not controlled by what He created. His eternal throne and dominion will remain unshaken even during the time when creation is utterly and completely transformed.

1:13-14 The seventh and final quotation in the first chapter comes from Psalm 110:1. Here, the writer showed the superiority of the Son over **the angels** by emphasizing His place of authority at the **right hand** of God. Angels are never spoken of in Scripture as sitting at the right hand of God, but rather they are always standing or moving because their role is one of service to God. This verse also speaks of the Son's final victory over His **enemies**. The victory is His alone. Verse 14 summarizes all that the author has said in the preceding verses. The Son reigns while the angels are ruled. Additionally, however, verse 14 indicates the unique role of angels in the drama of redemption, even though they remain inferior to the Son. The Son's superiority does not negate the important role that angels play in a believer's life. Angels, as this verse demonstrates, minister to God's children while on earth. By serving the Son, they are called **to serve** the saints. Knowing that God has provided His servants to minister to His children should instill encouragement in the heart of the believer. These Jewish believers, in particular, were encouraged not to give up despite the persecution they were enduring because God's final victory is promised, and His provision of angels to minister to His followers offers hope.

Warning against Neglecting Salvation (2:1-4)

2:1 This warning is the first of five given in the book of Hebrews. The purpose of these warnings is to encourage believers to heed the word of God and to obey its commandments faithfully. This warning concerns neglecting salvation (v. 3). The author was not writing concerning "rejecting" salvation, but "neglecting" salvation. This distinction is important as it identified again the audience to whom this warning was directed—not to unbelievers but rather to those who had already embraced Jesus as Messiah and Savior. Believers need to be reminded to pay close attention to the great salvation received from the Lord. Specifically, the Jewish believers to whom this letter was originally written were confronted with the temptation to renounce their faith and return to traditional Judaism. The truth conveyed in chapter 1 has important implications, so the writer used the word **therefore** to point back to the supremacy of Jesus. Since Jesus reigns supreme over all things, including the angels, the readers of Hebrews would be wise to pay careful attention to what they had learned regarding the gospel message. Inability to

focus on one's salvation leads to neglecting the things of God and inevitably to the temptation to sin. It was this danger that concerned the writer and stirred him to write these words of warning. PAY EVEN MORE ATTENTION (Gk. *prosechein*, "care for, devote yourself to, heed, be attentive, attach oneself to, or cleave to") is a strong admonition. The writer stressed the importance of cleaving to the gospel message and not straying from its teaching.

2:2-4 The writer compared **the message** given by **angels** to the message given by the Son. In essence he concluded that if the message given by the angels was LEGALLY BINDING (Gk. *bebaios*, "valid, firm, permanent, steadfast, dependable, guaranteed"; cp. 3:6,14; 6:19; 9:17), how much more respect and honor should be given to the message delivered by the Son. While the Old Testament does not directly state that the angels were present at the giving of the Mosaic law, other New Testament passages imply it (Ac 7:53; Gl 3:19); therefore, seemingly the writer had this idea in mind when penning these verses. He continued by adding that a great **punishment** is in store for those who lose sight of the victory and deliverance promised in the Son's victory over His enemies. He is not concluding that you can lose salvation by neglecting the teaching of the gospel, for this would stand in contradiction to other Scripture. Rather, **salvation** (Heb 2:3) refers here to the glorification of the saints with Jesus upon His triumphant return, just as it did in 1:14. The penalty ultimately entails a loss of opportunity or rewards and glory, which is a terrible punishment for the believer. This salvation experience was proclaimed by Jesus (Lk 12:31-32; 22:29-30) and confirmed, as the writer attests, by the teaching of the apostles as well as through the **various miracles** (Gk. *dunamesin*, "powerful deeds,"

Heb 2:4) of the Spirit displayed by them. Furthermore, God confirmed the message by distributing **gifts from the Holy Spirit** (Heb 2:4) for the purpose of serving God (1 Co 12:4). These gifts, as he noted, were not born from man's capabilities but rather by God's sovereign will.

The Glory of Jesus (2:5-18)

2:5-11 Angels were not given the responsibility for creating the world, and neither were they given the role of authority (Heb 1:5-14). Thus, people, not angels, will be awarded dominion over the world to come. Such a thought caused the writer to recall the words of the psalmist who declared the insignificance of man compared to the rest of creation in Psalm 8. Who are we, as men and women of God, to be remembered by God and committed to His intimate care? Furthermore, who are we to be included in His plan for the world?

Having expressed man's lowly state, the author stated three things about man's nature:

- He is **lower than the angels** (v. 7).

- He is **crowned** with **glory and honor** (v. 7).

- He has been set over the works of God's hands (v. 8).

Man was created "little less than God" (Ps 8:5), not "than angels." Man was also endowed with the image of God and therefore is bestowed "with glory and honor" because of the reflection of God in his nature. Finally, Genesis 1:26-28 teaches that man was given the responsibility to have dominion over the earth, having rule over God's works. Sin, however, makes this mission more difficult, and as things are now, one does not see the subjection of all things to man (v. 8). However, the ultimate fulfillment of this passage is found in Jesus. He is the one who was **made lower than the angels** (at the incarnation) and **crowned with glory and honor because of the suffering of death** (v. 9). **By God's grace,** Jesus tasted **death for everyone** so that we might be shown the grace of God. Jesus fully satisfied God's design for mankind as described in Psalm 8.

By Jesus' humanity He is able to bring men and women **to glory** (v. 10). He is, as Paul declared, the "second Adam" (Rm 5). Jesus, the source of **all things,** is **the source** of salvation. SOURCE (Gk. *archēgon*, "author, leader, ruler, prince, originator, founder, or pioneer"; cp. Heb 12:2) in other Greek writings denoted (1) one who established, named, and guarded a city; (2) the founder of a school of philosophy; or (3) the head of a family. The word also connoted a military captain who forged the way in front of his men. Jesus could lead man into salvation because He was made **perfect through sufferings** (2:10) experienced throughout His life and consummated on the cross. There is no indication that prior to His death Jesus was not perfect in the sense that He was tainted with sin. Rather, His perfection—the completion of His purpose in redeeming mankind to God through the suffering He endured on the cross—is in view here. Likewise, one should not neglect the purpose and calling He has given to cling to the message of salvation.

2:12-13 Verses 12-13 stress the bond between the Son of God and believers resulting from Jesus' work on the cross. By His death, Jesus makes you holy, and thus you are identified with Him before the Father. The writer quotes three passages from the Old Testament to support the statement about Christ's oneness with His brethren (v. 11). The first, Psalm 22, is a messianic psalm describing Jesus' crucifixion and establishing the basis for unity with Him found only in His death upon the cross for your sin. The second and third quotations are from Isaiah 8:17-18 (from the LXX). Jesus trusted in His Father, and His brethren must do the same. In the original context of the Isaiah passage, Isaiah saw himself linked with his children in service to God. Likewise, the writer of Hebrews draws the comparison of Jesus' link to His people.

2:14-18 The fellowship between Jesus and His brethren is further emphasized as the writer demonstrated His continued involvement in the life of the believer (vv. 14-18). In order to deliver man from the bondage of sin, Jesus had to become like man by becoming **flesh and blood** (v. 14). The Greek word used to describe Jesus' act of sharing man's nature, *meteschen* ("share, participate, belong, enjoy") literally conveys the idea of "becoming partners." It also emphasizes that Jesus Himself, not another, became flesh on our account. Jesus became partners with men and women for the purpose of saving them from the penalty of sin. In doing so, therefore, Jesus, **through His death**, destroyed **the power of death** that held man in captivity. He became sin for you and me so that through Him we might receive the righteousness of God (2 Co 5:21). As a result, **the Devil** is destroyed. DESTROY (Gk. *katargēsē*, "render inoperative or powerless, make ineffective, nullify, abolish, release, put an end to, do away with, deprive of power") is similarly used in 1 Co 15:24,26; Eph 2:15; 2 Th 2:8; 2 Tm 1:10. Clearly, death is still a reality, but it does not hold power over those who believe in Jesus. We can face death with the same confidence and assurance that Jesus displayed on the cross. As Paul stated, death has lost its sting (1 Co 15:55).

Furthermore, Jesus ministered to mankind, **Abraham's offspring** (Heb 2:16), **and did not reach out to help angels**. Through Abraham and his seed all of mankind would be blessed. Paul identified this seed as being Jesus (Gl 3:16), the One who brings redemption. Those who believe in Him, therefore, are Abraham's seed and heirs according to His promise. Jesus' death, burial, and resurrection made the way of salvation possible to all who believe.

The writer introduced a picture of Jesus as a **high priest**, which emerges numerous times throughout the pages of Hebrews and is one with which the original readers were quite familiar (Heb 2:17; cp. notes on chapter 5). Jesus' identity with mankind as a "high priest" underscored His being made like them so that He could **make propitiation for the sins of the people**. His role as priest enabled Him to display mercy as He acted on our behalf in service to God. He ministered before God to MAKE PROPITIATION (Gk. *hilaskesthai*, "make atonement for, satisfy") for man's sin through a once-and-for-all sacrifice. Not only did He atone for man's sin, but **He Himself** (emphatic in the Greek) also **was tested and has suffered** and is, therefore, **able to help those who are tested** (v. 18). TO HELP (Gk. *boēthēsai*, "bring help, aid, succour") appears in the *Septuagint* (LXX) in the nominal form to translate the Hebrew word *'ezer*, "help" or "helper" (see Gn 2:18, 20; cp. Ex 18:4; Dt 33:7,26,29; Ps 20:2; 33:20; 70:5; 89:19; 115:9-11; 121:1-2; 124:8; 146:5). The writer of Hebrews had much more to say on this topic in the chapters that followed, but for now He stressed that Jesus stands ready to help believers when they are tempted to sin or when they suffer. He has defeated their enemy and released them from the captivity of sin. While angels are able to minister to you through service, Jesus is superior in that He is able to deliver you from sin and is able to identify with you in your suffering. Jesus is our Savior, the One who knows our weaknesses and when and how we are tempted. He is our substitute, our sympathizer, and the one who reigns supreme. Praise to God for His provision of grace through Jesus!

Heart to Heart: Resist Temptation

Every Christian is tempted by someone or something at some time in life. Jesus Himself was tempted, but because of His deity He did not sin. Luke 4 recorded Jesus' encounter with the Devil. He was tempted in three different ways:

- *to turn stone to bread, thereby demonstrating His power (Lk 4:3);*

- *to worship the Devil, thereby gaining dominion over the kingdoms (Lk 4:6-7); and*

- *to throw Himself from the temple pinnacle, thus allowing God to protect Him (Lk 4:9).*

The responses of Jesus give us wisdom on how to resist temptation today:

- *obey God always (Lk 4:4; Dt 8:3);*

- *worship God alone (Lk 4:8; Dt 6:13); and*

- *trust God unconditionally (Lk 4:12; Dt 6: 16).*

The example of Jesus and the power of the Holy Spirit enable Christians to overcome temptation. Temptation is an "enticement to sin" arising from human desires and passions (see Jms 1:14 and 1 Jn 2:16). God does not tempt His children, but He does allow the Devil to test you in order to strengthen your faith. The Lord promises to protect you from temptation beyond what you are able to bear—He provides "a way of escape" (1 Co 10:13) and strength to endure (2 Pt 2:9). Christians must resist temptation and repel evil influence. Then you will receive "the crown of life," which the Lord "has promised to those who love Him" (Jms 1:12).

Jesus' Superiority over Moses (3:1–4:13)

Having shown the reader Jesus' superiority over the prophets and angels and having introduced His priesthood, the author of Hebrews turned his attention to demonstrating how Jesus is better than Moses, the one through whom the Mosaic covenant was given. In order to appreciate the argument the author is making, one must recall the place of prominence that Moses is given in Judaism. Otherwise, the author's purpose in declaring Jesus better than Moses is not fully understood. The Old Testament recorded the special relationship Moses enjoyed with God the Father. The account of the burning bush, for instance, highlighted Moses' interaction with the Father. He was the one chosen to lead God's people from Egyptian slavery into the promised land. Moreover, he brought the Ten Commandments down from Mount Sinai to the people and wrote the Pentateuch, which outlines the Levitical laws dictating Jewish ceremony. Exodus 34 recorded Moses' face-to-face interaction with God to the extent that his face shone before the people, radiating the very glory of God. He was undoubtedly a special man of God. The Jewish people recognized His prominence in the Old Testament. Yet, the writer of Hebrews pointed to Moses here in chapter 3 and declared that there is One even better. Jesus is shown to be better in His person and in His work.

3:1 The writer exhorted his readers to **consider Jesus**, who is greater in His person because He is the "merciful and faithful high priest" (2:17), CONSIDER (Gk. *katanoēsate*, "notice, look, contemplate") implies "fixing one's mind or eyes upon." The writer used the imperative to emphasize the duty of being a Christian and, in this case, looking to the Mediator of salvation. Jesus is **the apostle and high priest of our confession.** CONFESSION (Gk. *homologias*, "acknowledgment, profession") is a combination of the root *homo*, meaning "same" and *logos*, "spoken word," or *lego*, meaning "to say or speak" (and various synonyms dependent on context). The verb literally means "to say the same thing as another," but it can express the idea of "confession," admitting that one is guilty as accused, or "profession," openly declaring one's allegiance to a person or cause. In various forms the word appears also in 4:14; 10:23; 11:13; and 13:15, where it means "to praise, celebrate, or give thanks." Since the writer addressed "holy brothers and companions" in the plural, this passage seems to imply that Jesus is the one of whom Christians

"speak together," the One whom the church openly worships. The reader is encouraged to look continuously to Jesus alone. Only here in the New Testament Jesus is referenced as "apostle" (Gk. *apostolon*). The idea, however, that Jesus was sent or "appointed" (3:2) by God the Father to accomplish His purpose is a theme found throughout the Gospels. You must consider Him in all you do. While Moses was a good man, he was not perfect. He prepared the way for the coming of Messiah, the sinless Jesus who is fully able to represent men before God.

3:2-6 Jesus is also greater in His work. Although **Moses** is described as a **faithful** (Gk. *piston*) member of **God's household** (Gk. *oikō*, vv. 2,5), he was unable to enter the promised land on account of his disobedience to God's instructions (Nm 20:6-12). Yet, the writer of Hebrews did not focus on such instances, but rather concluded that despite his shortcomings as a man, he was still considered **faithful as a servant** of God (Heb 3:5). SERVANT (Gk. *therapōn*, "one who ministers willingly") is related to the verb *therapeuō*, "heal, serve," and the noun *therapeia*, "service, care," from which the English words "therapy" and "therapeutic" are derived. The word lends dignity to Moses' careful attendance to the assignments God gave him. Just as Moses was faithful to God, however, even more so was Jesus **faithful** to the author of His redemptive mission. In fact, **Jesus is considered worthy of more glory than Moses** (v. 3) because of His work as the builder of God's household. Moses was no more than part of the house, but Jesus built the house and rules over it. The writer was not criticizing Moses but rather was demonstrating that as a faithful servant he was just that—a servant. Jesus is better in the sense that He is more than a servant—He is actually God's Son, faithful to His Father's commission to build and rule over the household of faith. The author concluded this section by reminding the reader that membership to this house is limited to those who have trusted in Jesus and cling to the confidence that they are children of God.

3:7-19 The author issued a second warning to his readers. The first warning concerned neglecting one's salvation (2:1-4). This second warning, echoing Psalm 95:7-11, illustrated through the rebellion of the Israelites in the wilderness the danger of doubting and disbelieving the word due to hardness of heart. The Old Testament recorded how the Israelites grumbled against the Lord and doubted the promise of God even though He had walked closely by them during their wanderings in the wilderness (Ex 17:1-7; Nm 13–14). Psalm 95:8 specified "at *Meribah*" (Hb. "strife, contention") as the place and described the incident "on that day at *Massah*" (Hb. "temptation"). As a result of their unbelief, the Israelites missed their inheritance and died outside the borders of Canaan. The next generation took possession of the promised land and entered into the rest God had prepared.

The author warned believers against making the same mistake of hardening their hearts to the Lord and acting instead according to their own will. The people of Israel had exhibited an erring heart that did not trust God, resulting in a hard heart that **provoked** God (v. 10). Verses 8 and 15 speak of a day of testing or trial when Israel "provoked" God. PROVOKED (Gk. *parapikrasmō*, "exasperate, revolt, rebel, incite one's indignation") also appears in 3:16. Its concrete meaning suggests "producing a bitter taste in the stomach" (see Rv 10:9-10). The verb root *pikrainō* has the sense of "embitter, exasperate, make indignant, deal bitterly with, grieve." The noun *pikrias* denotes a "bitter root" and appears in Hebrews 12:15. The sin of Israel is stated in verse 12, having **an evil, unbelieving heart that departs from the living God**. DEPARTS (Gk. *apostēnai*, "leave someone, desert, mislead, defect, cause to rebel, fall away or withdraw from, cause to be faithless," coming into English as "apostasy") is understood from the context of these verses by some commentators as meaning "not abandoning one's faith completely" and therefore being condemned by God, but rather pointing to a departure from the living God by refusing to live according to His will. Therefore, discipline by God is inevitable. However, others maintain that the very nature of "apostasy" relates only to unbelievers who have turned completely away from God. What is meant by **rest** (v. 11) is discussed more thoroughly in chapter 4. In summary, the quotation from Psalm 95 accomplished the following three things:

- It served as a sober reminder of the unfaithfulness of God's people.

- It stressed the importance of faithfully listening to the voice of God.

- It described the tragic cost that accompanies unbelief and faithlessness.

Verses 12-19 elaborate on the quotation. In verse 12, the writer addressed **brothers** (Gk. *adelphoi*), again emphasizing the audience to whom he was writing—believers in Jesus the Messiah. Every believer must be careful to guard against an "unbelieving heart." The writer stressed the sternness of this warning by urging his reader to **watch out** (Gk. *blepete*, "see, beware"). One preventative against a tendency to stray from God's word is specified in verse 13. Believers are exhorted to **encourage each other daily** so that their hearts would not grow

hardened by sin. ENCOURAGE (Gk. *parakaleite*, a form of the word used by Jesus to identify the Holy Spirit, Jn 14:16). The root meaning is "coming alongside another to help." Additionally, the writer used the word **today** in reference to the time in which the believer has an opportunity to respond and act according to God's will. Believers must be careful *today* to guard themselves against a heart that grows complacent and unmoved by the word of God.

In verse 14, the writer described believers as **companions of the Messiah**. COMPANIONS (Gk. *metochoi*, "sharing in, participating with the sense of being partners or partakers") is used in 1:9 and 3:1 to describe the companions of the King (see also 6:4 and 12:8). Elsewhere in the New Testament, the word appears to refer to fishermen on separate boats as "partners" (Lk 5:7). For decades, the wives of students at Southwestern Baptist Theological Seminary have used the name "Metochai" to describe their organization in the sense that they are partners with their husbands in ministry. The writer was stressing the privilege of serving among the many sons of God, whom He has designated to rule with Him. Yet, he warned again that this privilege of serving alongside Jesus is contingent on the faithfulness of the believer. The idea is expressed elsewhere: "The victor and the one who keeps My works to the end: I will give him authority over the nations" (Rv 2:26). Therefore, believers must hold firmly until the end and not harden their hearts as did the Israelites **in the rebellion** (Gk. *parapikrasmō*, Heb 3:15). In verses 16-19, the writer posed a number of questions that all drive at the point of this passage.

4:1 The writer continued to consider the blessing the Israelites missed due to their lack of trust and confidence in God.

Believers have **the promise** of **entering His rest** as well, but they must be careful lest they **miss it**. As long as a promise **remains**, there is still an opportunity to enter God's rest. The writer's concept of REST (Gk. *katapausin*) cannot be separated from its Old Testament roots. In the books of Deuteronomy and Joshua, "rest" implies the entrance of the people of Israel into Canaan (Dt 3:20; 12:10; Josh 1:13,15; 21:43-44; 22:4). In Psalm 95:11, however, the concept of rest refers also to the future rest promised to the people of God.

4:2-6 The writer referred to **the good news** (Gk. *euēggelismenoi*) that believers had received, just as the good news was received by the Israelites. The good news concerned the future rest for God's people. As verse 2 clarified, the Israelites heard **the message** (Gk. *ho logos*, lit., "the word") concerning rest, but it was of no value to them because of their lack of **faith**. Therefore, believers today must exercise faith in order to profit from God's promise of rest. The writer's concern was with his readers' perseverance in faith and trust in the promise of God. This theme is seen throughout the pages of Hebrews as the writer continuously exhorted his readers not to give up in running the race of faith (cp. Heb 12:1-2). In verses 4-5, the writer linked God's Sabbath **rest** with the rest that the Israelites missed in the desert. When God completed the acts of creation, Scripture records that He **rested** from His work (Gn 2:2-3). The nation of Israel, however, did not complete the work God set before them and, therefore, missed the rest that was promised to them. God's grace is seen in that His rest is still offered to those who believe in Him and trust in His word.

4:7-11 Quoting again from Psalm 95:7-8, the writer further described the grace of God in mentioning that God's rest is promised to those who **do not**

harden their hearts to His voice. Even though Joshua did conquer the land promised to the Israelites, the writer of Hebrews indicated that God's perfect rest still had not been fully realized, and thus, He spoke the promise again **through David** (v. 7). There remains, then, **a Sabbath rest** (v. 9) for the people of God. This rest can be reached by persevering to the end and completing the tasks God has laid before the believer, namely, living according to His will. You need to model your lives after Jesus and hold firmly to the end, confident that God will provide you with the promised rest that is yours in the future. Based on this point, the writer seized the opportunity to issue the reminder for the believer to **make every effort to enter that rest** (v. 11) by doing His will to the very end, unlike the Israelites who fell into a **pattern of disobedience**. Notice as well that throughout this chapter the writer included himself in these exhortations—**let us** (4:1,11). He recognized his own need, as a believer in Jesus, to be reminded of these warnings lest he, too, grow hardened in his heart toward the truth of God.

4:12-13 Having completed the exposition from Psalm 95, the writer concluded this section with a reminder of the uniqueness of the word of God, for upon this word the promises of God are revealed. Verse 12 is often quoted as a statement summarizing the awesome nature of God's word. The writer used a number of key descriptions of God's word: **living and effective and sharper than any two-edged sword**, **penetrating**. Its penetrating power reaches the innermost part of man's being so that it judges even **the ideas and thoughts of the heart**. In doing so, the word of God divides **soul, spirit, joints, and marrow**. All unbelief, insincerity, lack of faith, all things can be detected by God through His word. The sense is, then, that the truth of God penetrates the heart of man to such an extent that one's motives and intents are brought to light. By piercing the soul and spirit and the joints and marrow, the word of God is seen as penetrating the whole person so that it is able to divide that which seems indivisible. Nothing, not even your innermost thoughts and feelings, is shielded from the power of the word of God. His word affects every part of your being. For this reason each believer must be diligent to heed God's word and to trust completely in its truthfulness. You must be aware of your propensity to develop a heart of unbelief that fails to acknowledge that God's word is eternally true. As a means of ensuring that his readers understand the importance of grasping this truth, the writer continued in verse 13 by stating that **no creature is hidden from God** but rather **all things** are laid bare before Him.

Jesus, the High Priest (4:14–16)

4:14-16 Yet, believers are encouraged because they have a high priest who intercedes on their behalf; therefore, they can approach Him boldly because of their confidence in Him and what He has done for them. The writer had previously explained some of the ways in which Jesus' superiority is demonstrated in His priesthood—His being made in the nature of man, tempted in every way, able to help you in our weakness (2:17-18). In verses 14-16, however, Jesus' priesthood is considered in greater detail. Jesus, as **a great high priest** (v. 14), is able **to sympathize with our weaknesses**, because He has been **tested in every way** just as we are tested, yet He was **without sin** (v. 15). What a word of encouragement and hope to the believer! The Savior knows the trials of your hearts and understands the struggles you endure, and, at the same time, He sets the example for you of how to live in a way that pleases the Father.

Unlike the priests of the Old Testament, Jesus is set apart as one who can identify with you on an intimate level. He is **the Son of God**, as verse 14 states, a reiteration of the humanity and divinity of Jesus. With such a high priest, who is compassionate and understanding, believers should **approach the throne of grace with boldness** or confidence (v. 16). Notice that the word "grace" is used to describe God's throne. This grace is extended because of Jesus' ultimate act of love and submission to the Father on your behalf when He offered Himself as the sacrifice for sin. The grace and mercy of God is available to the believer at her time of need; and thus, the invitation is issued for every believer, regardless of gender, age, or race, based solely on the love and grace of God.

"Let Us" Exhortations

God's followers are called to godly living through these exhortations (Heb 4).

- **Let us** fear the Lord (v. 1).
- **Let us** rest in God's grace (v. 11).
- **Let us** hold fast to our confession of faith (v. 14).
- **Let us** approach God's throne boldly (v. 16).

THE SUPERIORITY OF THE PRIESTHOOD OF JESUS (5:1–10:39)

Jesus' Perfect Priesthood (5:1-10)

Before launching into the writer's discussion on the priesthood of Jesus, one should review the requirements, duties, and purpose of the high priest as established in the Old Testament. The word for **HIGH PRIEST** (Gk. *archiereus*) is a combination of *arche*, meaning "first or leader" and *hiereus*, meaning "priest, one consecrated to God." In the Old Testament, the word for "priest" (Hb.

kohen) first appears in Genesis 14:18 in which Melchizedek is identified as "a priest to God Most High." The original readers would have been thoroughly acquainted with this as it remained an important aspect in Judaism. The priest was central to the order of worship because he was the one designated to bring the offerings to the Lord on behalf of the people. Their sins could not be forgiven without his intercession. Additionally, the priesthood was restricted to those from the tribe of Levi. Leviticus, Numbers, and Deuteronomy describe the many tasks of the priests, as well as the specific instructions they were to follow to ensure that they remained holy unto the Lord. For instance, as the author further illustrated in chapter 9, only the high priest was able to enter the holy of holies, the special place where God's presence resided. Furthermore, he was only able to enter this place once a year on the Day of Atonement (Lv 16:1-25). At this time, he would enter the holy of holies and sprinkle blood on the mercy seat following the sacrifice of a young bull as a sin offering on behalf of him and his family. The priest then would take two goats, one offered as a sin offering for the people and the other presented alive as a scapegoat. The blood from the goat used in the sin offering was sprinkled on the mercy seat to make atonement for the people. The high priest then confessed the sins of the people over the head of the second goat, which was led away and released into the wilderness. This practice was repeated each year on the Day of Atonement when the people returned to the temple in order for the high priest to intercede for them so that their sins might be forgiven. The writer of Hebrews used these images throughout the epistle to demonstrate that Jesus, the Son of God, serves as the ultimate high priest since he has once-and-for-all removed all of the sins of believers today and forevermore.

5:1-7 With this picture in mind, chapter 5 continues the writer's description of the superiority of Jesus as the "great high priest" (4:14). In verses 1-3, the author reminded the reader that a high priest is selected from among men and is able, therefore, to serve as their representative in offering "GIFTS (Gk. *dōra*) and SACRIFICES (Gk. *thusias*) for sins" (v. 1). Additionally, he is also described as a compassionate man who deals "gently" with "those who are IGNORANT (Gk. *agnoousin*, "lack understanding or knowledge, do not know, err or sin in ignorance or by mistake") and are going astray." GENTLY (Gk. *metriopathein*) is a compound of *metrios*, "measured, moderate," and *pathos*, "passion, feeling." The word conveys the picture of one who chooses not to be upset by another's errors or sins. In Greek philosophy, its antonym is the adjective *apathēs*, "indifferent, or dispassionate," which describes the Stoic ideal. To show compassion instead of anger represented a "happy medium" between the extremes of an absence of feeling and overly soft-hearted leniency or between harsh treatment and indulgence. This instance is the only use of the word in the New Testament. "Those who are GOING ASTRAY" (Gk. *planōmenois*, v. 2) also appears in 3:10 in the quotation from Psalm 95 and in 11:38 where it denotes physical "wandering." Part of this compassion is born from the recognition that he, too, is **subject to weakness** and is prone to fail, although such compassion was warranted only for unintentional sin (cp. 9:7; Lv 4:2,22,27; 5:2-4). This reason lay behind the high priest's need to offer sacrifice first for him and his family before making **a sin offering** on behalf of the people (Heb 5:3). The compassion of Jesus, however, is far greater since He, though "subject to weakness," did not fail in perfectly following God's commands (4:15). One thing is absolutely certain, as verse 4 states. The office of high priest is one ordained **by God** and not an **honor** that you can take upon yourself. Just as a high priest is chosen by God, so Jesus was chosen by God to serve as the intercessor on behalf of all mankind. The author quoted from Psalms 2 and 110 to demonstrate that Jesus is the One chosen by God to serve as **priest forever in the order of Melchizedek** (v. 6); the meaning of this designation is more fully discussed in chapter 7. The writer brought together these two quotes in declaring God's appointment of His Son to the office of high priest. The description of Jesus' ministry in verse 7 is striking. The author has asserted that He fully participated in the human condition, being tested as we are tested. It is **with loud cries and tears** that He offered prayers to God on our behalf (Lk 22:39-44; 23:34-46; Jn 17). These were accepted by God because of Jesus' submission to Him. He was ultimately saved from death, rising from the dead, offering decisive proof of God's acceptance of His sacrifice for mankind.

5:8-10 These verses are mysterious in their meaning but nonetheless important to try to understand. Jesus had to experience the true meaning of obedience through suffering and did so in such a way that He WAS PERFECTED (Gk. *teleiōtheis*, "made complete," describing the accomplishment of a goal or purpose, v. 9; cp. 2:10; 7:19,28; 9:9; 10:1,14,40; 12:23). As the Son of God, He was infinitely perfect in His divinity. At the time of the incarnation when He took on the form of humanity, however, He acquired the experience of the human condition, and through His suffering became perfect in His humanity. Jesus, the boy, was perfect—man and God. But because he had entered time, He was subject to the human process of becoming complete—becoming a man. In one sense, He was perfect at each stage, but He was becoming or being made perfect for the purpose God had for Him. The writer then affirmed that **He became the source** (Gk. *aitios*, "cause, author," v. 9) **of eternal salvation**. Jesus is the example of one who placed His trust fully in God. His obedience to God, described in verse 8, demands that believers respond in obedience to Him. Such obedience flows from one's faith in Jesus. Truly, Jesus is better than the Old Testament priests, specifically Aaron, who is mentioned in this chapter. Furthermore, verse 10 describes Jesus as being **declared by God a high priest**. What was the reason, given the superiority of Jesus as the great high priest, for these Jewish believers to be tempted to return to the legalistic system of Judaism? The answer is found in the final verses of this chapter. They lacked maturity in their spiritual walk. So, the writer paused from his discussion on the priesthood of Jesus and "the order of Melchizedek" to encourage these readers to grow diligently in the Lord.

The Problem of Believers' Immaturity (5:11–6:20)

5:11-14 These verses serve as the writer's third warning to believers and concerns the immaturity and sluggishness that often marks the spiritual walk. He sensed the danger of their becoming SLOW TO UNDERSTAND (Gk. *nōthroi*, "lazy, sluggish or dull of hearing," also in 6:12; and *akoais*, "hearing," especially in the sense of listening to oral instruction), which prevented them from fully digesting the truth of God. Given the importance of the points he made in chapter 5 regarding the priesthood of Jesus, the writer paused to address their immaturity. As he says in

verse 11, he has **a great deal to say** regarding the priesthood of Jesus (7:1–10:18) that would be **difficult to explain** given their slowness **to understand**. He rebuked them for being so immature that they were not able to teach others—they still required **milk** instead of **solid food** (5:12). What he seemed to have in mind was their instability in confidently holding fast to their faith in Jesus as the Messiah and their temptation to return to trappings of Judaism. Therefore, they needed to be trained again in **the basic principles** of God. Though sanctified, these believers had seemingly made little progress in continuing to grow in their knowledge and service and thus are described in terms fitting for babies and not growing, maturing children. What a tragedy that these believers, who should be fully grown, are instead babies in their sense of understanding the wondrous truths of God. INFANT (Gk. *nēpios*, "minor, immature, innocent") can be translated literally as "one who is incapable of speech." These spiritual "babblers" did not possess divine wisdom because they had not meditated on God's truth. These believers were incapable of telling others about **the message about righteousness** (v. 13).

Mature (Gk. *teleiōn*, "perfect, complete, initiated, or adult") believers, on the other hand, were described as those who are skilled in sharing with others and **have been trained to distinguish between good and evil.** The concept of training comes from two phrases in the Greek text: (1) *dia tēn hexis*, "through practice"; and (2) *gegumnasmena*, "exercise," as an athlete training for competition. Use of the verb *gumnazō* demonstrates the intentionality of those who desire to grow in their spiritual walk. The marks of spiritual immaturity from these verses are:

- slowness to understand the word of God,

- inability to share with others,

- inexperience with the deep things of God, and

- lack of discernment.

Discipleship is marked by a deepening understanding of and dependence on the word of God and demands that believers grow consistently in their walk with God. This matter of maturity is addressed in chapter 6.

Jesus the High Priest

Jesus Christ had unique qualifications to serve as High Priest. He was . . .

- appointed by God (5:1,4-6),
- confirmed by Scripture (5:4-6),
- interceding with God the Father (5:7),
- sinless even when tempted (4:15),
- the source of eternal salvation (5:9), and
- perfected in His suffering (5:8).

6:1-6 The writer began chapter 6 by issuing the challenge to press on toward spiritual **maturity** by leaving the safety of understanding only the elementary ABCs of Christianity and plunging into the deeper waters of spiritual maturity. God enables believers to press forward in their growth as His children and provides them with all that they need for life and godliness (2 Pt 1:3). The author listed those areas he considered **elementary** (Gk. *tēs archēs,* "the beginning, the rudiments," v. 1) to their spiritual walk including— **repentance from dead works, faith in God, teaching about ritual washings** (Gk. *baptismōn didachēs,* "teaching about baptisms"; the plural form indicates that the phrase probably refers to the various cleansing rites practiced in Judaism, but the instruction may also focus on distinguishing among baptismal practices), **lay-**

ing on of hands, the resurrection of the dead, and eternal judgment (Heb 6:1-2). If they were to progress as believers maturing in their faith, they would avoid the danger of **laying again the foundation of repentance from dead works** (v. 1). As some understand verses 4-6, if these were to fall away (6:6), then a foundation would have been laid for a new repentance, but this falling away is impossible, so they must press on toward maturity. The writer explained that returning to dead works, in the form of ordinances and legalism, would only result in taking a backward step instead of a forward step in maturity. Such a step backward would eventually require one to be taught again that salvation comes by faith and not by works. The author acknowledged that believers are able to take a step forward in maturity only with God's permission (v. 3).

There are four primary ways in which this difficult passage (vv. 4-6) has been interpreted:

- Some believe these verses teach that a believer who refuses to grow, and has thus **fallen away,** will lose his salvation. This view is rejected as it stands in contradiction to other Scriptures that plainly articulate the believer's eternal security in Jesus (Jn 5:24; 10:27-29; Rm 8:28-39). Salvation is a work of God and not of man.

- The second view states that perhaps the ones to whom the writer was referring were not true believers. They have, in essence, tasted salvation but have not partaken of salvation. However, some see this interpretation as a problem since the writer clearly articulated in verses 4 and 5 that these have experienced at one time the blessings of salvation. They **became companions with the Holy Spirit** (Heb 6:4) and experienced the goodness of God's word. These traits, they argue, are true only of believers. God's presence is a reality in their lives.

- Third, others argue that the writer is describing a hypothetical situation. In other words, *if* believers could lose their salvation, then it would be impossible for them to be restored to the community of faith later. Some commentators argue, however, that the original language does not allow for such a conditional situation. The Greek makes clear that **it is impossible** (v. 4) for these to be restored to repentance. Additionally, it hardly seems like a stern warning for believers if such renewal is an impossibility, discussed only as a hypothetical situation.

- Fourth, these verses refer to a believer's progression, from true faith to a life that is marked by an inability to be of service to God and to inherit millennial glory. The reason such believers cannot be rendered effective in the kingdom of God is due to the fact that, as verse 6 clarifies, **they are recrucifying** Jesus and publicly disgracing Him. In essence, for Jewish converts to revert back to reliance on Judaism for their salvation would be to endorse those who crucified Jesus. Also, it would be indicative of the hardening effect on their hearts, moving them away from their commitment to Jesus as their Messiah. At this point, it is helpful to recall the author's discussion in chapter 3 concerning the Israelites' failure to obtain the privilege of entering the promised land. They were not utterly rejected by the Lord, but they were ineffective in their service to Him due to their lack of trust and faith. The writer is noting that these Jewish believers

were in danger of doing the same and would, therefore, not be used by God in their service to Him.

While many different views are presented in theological discussions on this passage, most can be distilled down to whether or not the writer is addressing the case of believers or unbelievers, with both groups agreeing that he is directing his comments to believers. Those who hold that the writer is addressing believers argue that these verses describe the fate of the one who refuses to move forward in maturity, thus the impossibility of restoring them in repentance. They understand the inheritance mentioned in these verses as a reference to the blessings or rewards that a believer will receive in the millennial kingdom. However, those who argue that the writer is addressing the case of unbelievers maintain that the warning is addressed to believers to be careful of those who profess to believe in Jesus and yet have ultimately rejected Jesus and, therefore, will not possess the inheritance of heaven.

6:7-8 The author used an example from nature to illustrate his point. When the rain-soaked ground **produces vegetation**, it is blessed by God by proving **useful to those** for whom **it is cultivated** (v. 7). **If it produces thorns**, however, **it is worthless** (v. 8). Again, some suggest that this reference is to an unproductive Christian life, which may ultimately fall under God's punishment. While the text also uses the picture of fire in describing the punishment of such ones, they argue that this cannot be absolutely linked with the "fire of hell," supposing then that these are cursed and damned to eternal separation from God. Indeed, fire is often used as a picture of hell, but fire is also used in other senses as well. For instance, burning a field to destroy the undesirable growth it had produced was something familiar to these ancient people. Their desire was not to burn the field to the point that it would be completely destroyed, but rather that the undesirable produce would be destroyed. However, those who believe this text refers to unbelievers maintain that ultimate destruction and judgment is the proper understanding.

6:9-12 These verses instill hope in the reader following the author's stern warning. Having warned them severely of the danger of not maturing in their faith and returning to dead works, he encouraged them that he does not expect this to be the case for them. He trusted that they will heed his warnings and persevere to the end, acquiring the blessings that are theirs in reigning with Jesus. His tender words reminded them that God saw their good works and would reward them accordingly (v. 10). Having encouraged them, though, the writer sensed the need to add one final word of warning again and said, in essence, "Just make sure you do not **become lazy** and forget what I have told you!" He exhorted his readers to guard themselves from this danger by recalling and imitating those who had inherited the promises of God through their faith and perseverance (v. 12). Later, the writer listed such great men and women of faith who were to serve as encouragement to believers (chap. 11).

6:13-15 At this point, the author of Hebrews provided an example of one great man of faith—**Abraham**, who, like Moses, was a great figure in Judaism. As the text explains, he received a blessing and **promise** from God who **swore** to Abraham that He would **bless** and **multiply** his seed. The writer, of course, was referring to the Abrahamic covenant recorded in Genesis 22:17. In spite of Abraham's failings as a man, God still kept His promise, and Abraham received his son, Isaac. Abraham waited **patiently** (Gk. *makrothumēsas*, "enduring patiently,

longsuffering") for this promise of God—an attitude that was the exact opposite of the laziness and slothfulness condemned in verse 12. The writer seemed to be encouraging his readers to continue in the walk of faith, not giving up, maturing in Jesus; and they, too, could be assured that they would receive the promises of God.

6:16-20 In addition, the blessings promised to Abraham are also guaranteed for all believers. The Messianic hope that was evident in the words of the Abrahamic covenant (Gn 15) also applies to those who have placed their hope in Jesus, the promised seed of Abraham. This promise is guaranteed for two reasons. First, God has sworn **an oath** to Abraham (Heb 6:17). Second, God cannot lie (v. 18). This promise forms the basis for your security in the hope that you have in Him. Verse 19 describes an ANCHOR (Gk. *agkuran*, as the anchor of a ship, a symbol of hope in both ancient and modern times) that holds the soul secure and enables the believer to stand firm and sure on her hope in Christ. Such security also comes in knowing that Jesus has gone before and has led the way as **a forerunner**, a topic that the writer revisited in chapter 12. The writer returned to his thought on the priesthood of Jesus and recalled that Jesus stepped **behind the curtain** (v. 19) of the holy of holies and intercedes **on our behalf** (v. 20). Once again, because of this act of grace you are able to stand firm in your faith in Jesus, knowing that He will be faithful to His promises. Your salvation is secure in Him.

Jesus' Superiority over Aaron and His Likeness to Melchizedek (7:1-28)

7:1 Melchizedek takes center stage at the beginning of chapter 7, for the writer turned his attention to demonstrating how Jesus is superior to this great Old Testament figure. Verses 1-10 provide background information on Melchizedek as the writer of Hebrews reminded his readers of the account recorded in Genesis 14 in which this figure emerged on the Old Testament scene. He is described as both a **priest** and a **king**, and these are titles also given to the Son of God. The first mention of Melchizedek described his encounter with **Abraham** when he blessed Abraham and Abraham responded by offering him a tithe. This encounter reinforced the recognized superiority of Melchizedek by Abraham's receiving the blessing and paying him a tithe. In verse 4, he even emphasized, "Abraham *the patriarch* gave a tenth." Abraham is typically venerated for his greatness, especially by Jewish people; however, in this passage, the writer is holding Melchizedek in higher regard. The writer seems to take great pains to ensure that his readers see this distinction clearly.

7:2-4 As verse 2 explains, Melchizedek's name means both **king of righteousness** and **king of peace**. MELCHIZEDEK is actually a compound of two Hebrew words: *melek*, "king," and *tsedeq*, "righteousness," and thus means, "My king (is) Righteousness," or "king of righteousness." The Hebrew place-name SALEM, like the word *shalom*, means "Peace." Salem was generally believed to be Jerusalem. Interestingly, both righteousness and peace are Messianic attributes. Furthermore, verse 3 described him as a man without a known genealogy; despite the importance Genesis placed on human origins, the times of his birth and death or the names of his family are not provided. He is, in essence, the Old Testament "man of mystery." To add to the mysterious nature of this man, the writer ended verse 3 with two curious statements. First, Melchizedek resembled the Son of God. Some have taken the fact that he did not have a genealogy as making him like Jesus, who is the eternal Son of God. To be sure,

Jesus had a genealogy, recorded in both Matthew 1 and Luke 3, but His lineage is traced not to Aaron or Levi but to Judah. While His humanity can be traced back to Judah, as the Son of God He has **neither beginning of days nor end of life.** Second, Melchizedek **remains a priest forever**, which some argue resembles the Son of God, since there is no account of his death. In this way, Melchizedek is a picture of Jesus, who overcame death in His resurrection. The conclusion, then, is that Melchizedek's priestly ministry is eternal. It is argued that the author meant that Melchizedek belonged to a priestly order in which there was no end, since no record is available of his death or of any successive priests.

7:5-10 Especially curious is Melchizedek's recognition as a priest, even though he was not a descendent from the tribe of Levi (vv. 5-6). The writer emphasized again the singularity of Abraham's recognition of his priesthood both by accepting the blessing and by offering him a tithe. As verse 7 declares, **Without a doubt, the inferior is blessed by the superior.** The greatness of Melchizedek in light of both the patriarch Abraham and the priestly order of Aaron is the point of the entire passage. The argument that the writer presented in these opening verses laid the groundwork for the thesis of this passage—there is a promised priest who is like Melchizedek but even greater.

7:11-24 The writer emphasized the many ways in which Jesus is like Melchizedek but is not like the Levitical priests. As he proved, **the Levitical priesthood** was imperfect because **another** priesthood was established **in the order of Melchizedek** (v. 11). The Levitical priesthood was inadequate and thus had to be replaced by something even better. The writer used Psalm 110:4 later in this passage to demonstrate that God promised a different priesthood than the

Levitical priesthood. God was announcing a CHANGE (Gk. *metathesis*, "alteration, removal, transfer, change in something established") in the law (v. 12). Psalm 110:4 prophesied of the coming of Jesus as our high priest and declared that He is a **priest forever in the order of Melchizedek** (vv. 15-17). He is from a tribe other than Levi, the tribe of Judah. A further proof of Jesus' fulfillment of Psalm 110:4 is that He will be a priest forever (Heb 7:15,21), like Melchizedek's priesthood (v. 17). Jesus' priesthood is not WEAK (Gk. *asthenes*, "infirm, powerless, sick, feeble," an antonym for "strength") and UNPROFITABLE (Gk. *anōpheles*, "useless, harmful" an antonym for "profitable"; cp. Ti 3:9) because He offers man "a better hope" for eternally drawing near to God (Heb 7:18-19). The law or the old priesthood was not evil in the sense of being carnal or fleshly. Rather, the description pertained to people who died, while the new priesthood pertains to One who lives forever. The new priest, Jesus, has replaced the old order of priests and provides "a better hope" **through which we draw near to God** (v. 19). His priesthood is perfect, while the old was imperfect. Jesus is **the guarantee of a better covenant** (v. 22). He guarantees to us that God, based on His oath, will fulfill His promises in the new covenant, a covenant of grace.

7:25 The permanence of Jesus' priesthood enables Him continually **to save those who come to God through Him**, and He saves to the uttermost. Because He is the eternal high priest, He saves completely and forever. What wonderful assurance for the believer and a reminder of God's faithfulness in fulfilling His promises. Verse 25 further instills hope in the heart of the believer by testifying that Jesus not only saves completely, but He also lives eternally to INTERCEDE

(Gk. *entugchanein*, "make intercession, plead, appeal, petition, entreat someone to do something"; in the New Testament, used only here and in Ac 25:24; Rm 8:27,34; 11:2) on behalf of those who place their faith in Him. Intercession, as the writer will demonstrate later in this epistle, is a key component to the duty of a priest, since he stands as a mediator between God and man. Jesus, the perfect Son of God, is the only person who completely fulfills the law and is able, therefore, to stand as a mediator on behalf of the believer. He is the innocent, undefiled Lamb of God. These remarkable statements undoubtedly made an impression on the epistle's original readers as they considered the permanence of the priesthood of Jesus, their Messiah, and the richness of the writer's points in this passage concerning the atonement for sin.

7:26-28 The writer called for a high priest such as Jesus who is HOLY (Gk. *hosios*, "morally faultless or unblemished, holy, pious, devout"; cp. Rv 15:4; 16:5), INNOCENT (Gk. *akokos*, "harmless; devoid of evil, guile, or guilt"), UNDEFILED (Gk. *amiantos*, "unsoiled, stainless, untainted"; cp. 13:4; Jms 1:27; 1 Pt 1:4) by sin, "separated from sinners," and "exalted above the heavens," because only such a priest can eternally save those who are lost. While the Old Testament priests were "holy" in their service to God, they were still sinners just like the people for whom they ministered daily. Furthermore, verse 27 indicated that Jesus **doesn't need to offer sacrifices every day** as required of the priests of old. Neither does He offer a sacrifice first for Himself and then for the people, because He is without sin. His sacrifice was offered **once for all** (Heb 7:28) upon the cross and forever met God's requirement for a blood sacrifice for sin. Truly, in all these ways, He is a better high priest, superior to the Levitical priests and in the order of Melchizedek.

The Superiority of Christ's New Covenant (8:1–10:39)

The nature of the new covenant (8:1-13)

8:1-6 In capturing the reader's attention, the writer began chapter 8 by emphasizing **the main point** (Gk. *kephalaion*, from *kephalē*, "head," hence "the leading or overall idea") of what he has just shown in chapter 7 by, in essence, saying, "Listen up; this information is important." Jesus is our **high priest** who is seated in heaven **at the right hand** of God. Knowing that Jesus is our high priest, the writer explained the duties of our high priest. He is "a MINISTER (Gk. *leitourgos*, "servant") of the sanctuary" and of "the *true tabernacle*" which *God* built "and not man" (v. 2). He phrased verse 2 in this way because he demonstrated the superiority of the tabernacle of heaven compared to the tabernacle of earth (vv. 2-5). The idea is not that the tabernacle built by man is *not good*; rather, it is inadequate as a permanent dwelling place for Almighty God. It simply serves as a pattern for the heavenly one, which is eternal. As with many of the practices and elements of Old Testament worship, the earthly tabernacle, too, points to something better that is coming, ultimately found in the person and work of Jesus the Messiah (v. 5). Why would anyone be satisfied with **a copy** as opposed to the real thing? The writer is urging this Jewish audience to recognize the perfection of the new tabernacle compared to the old.

The heavenly tabernacle is also better because it is crafted by God and not by man. Since the role of priest involved both **gifts and sacrifices**, the writer concluded that our high priest, Jesus, also has **something to offer** (v. 3)—His sacrifice for our sins. In order to serve in this way, Jesus could not administer the old offerings in the earthly tabernacle, but rather He administers the new offerings in the heavenly sanctuary (v. 4). Jesus now occupies the new tabernacle and serves as **the mediator of a better covenant** (v. 6). MEDIATOR (Gk. *mesitēs*, "one who intervenes to restore peace or friendship, one who ratifies a covenant"; cp. 9:15; 12:24; Gl 3:19-20) appears in the Septuagint in Job 9:33. Job observed that there is no man who can serve as a mediator between mankind and God, but without a mediator to remove the gap separating sinful mankind from the holy God, man's condition is hopeless. A mediator is someone who stands between two parties and brings them together. As Job recognized, the only mediator who could eternally bring man and God together would have to represent both. While Moses, the prophets, and the priests all served as mediators between the people of Israel and God, they were only reflections of the true mediator who would perfectly join man and God together. Paul announced that "There is one God and one mediator between God and man, a man, Christ Jesus" (1 Tm 2:5). The writer of Hebrews echoed this declaration of praise that One has come who is "the mediator of a better covenant," which is founded **on better promises**. The better covenant to which he referred is more fully explained in verses 7-13.

8:7-13 The Mosaic covenant was not wrong, but it was limited. The prophet Jeremiah, whom the writer of Hebrews quoted in verses 8-12, recognized its limitations because of the people's sin. Jeremiah's own words revealed the superiority of the new covenant compared to the Mosaic covenant. The **new covenant**, just as the Mosaic, will be made **with the house of Israel**. Israel's place in

God's redemptive plan for the nations is key. God has never made a covenant with the Gentiles but rather makes His covenant with the Jewish people. Gentiles are grafted in, as Paul explained (Rm 11:23-24), to the unique relationship God has with Israel, and, thus, all believers are recipients of the blessings and promises of the new covenant. Second, the Mosaic covenant was based on the law (Heb 8:9). The blessings of the old covenant were dependent on the people's obedience to the law of God. The new covenant, however, is based on grace. Third, the new covenant will emphasize the internal versus the external (v. 10). The Mosaic covenant was written on tablets of stone, whereas the new covenant is written on the hearts and minds of those who follow God. While Deuteronomy 6:6 commanded the people to write the law of God **on their hearts**, they could not accomplish this task completely without the work of the Spirit. The Spirit, however, was not given until following the time of Jesus. Fourth, as verse 12 tells us, man's sins will be completely forgiven, never to be remembered by God again. These are all the "better promises" to which the writer alluded in verse 6.

Old Testament prophecy, including the one just quoted from Jeremiah 31, demonstrated the superiority of the new covenant over the Mosaic covenant. Verse 13 drew the conclusion, therefore, that this old covenant was aging and would soon disappear. The author's words suggest that he remembered the words of Jesus in Matthew 24:1-2 that the temple would soon be destroyed and, therefore, all of the sacrifices and ceremonies still being conducted according to the Mosaic covenant would soon vanish. In all likelihood, this prophecy was soon fulfilled following the writing of Hebrews (see "Date" in the introduction). In a spiritual sense, however, the Mosaic covenant was void when

the veil in the temple was torn in two (Mt 27:50-51; Lk 23:44-46) following the sacrifice of Jesus on the cross. Jesus' once-and-for-all sacrifice was offered up unto God and was accepted by Him as the perfect and final payment for man's sin. Truly, the new covenant is superior to the old because of Jesus' role as our high priest.

The sacrifice of the new covenant (9:1-28)

9:1 Chapter 9 provides a beautiful description of the **regulations** and practices of worship under the Mosaic covenant compared with Jesus' fulfillment in the new covenant. The writer painstakingly illustrated the parallels between the two to emphasize once more the superiority of the new covenant because of Jesus. Chapter 9 picks up where chapter 8 left off by describing in verses 1-10 the ministry of the Mosaic covenant as seen in the **earthly** tabernacle. He clearly demonstrated that the Mosaic covenant, or old covenant, was not worthless or pointless, but rather it was divinely instituted for the purpose of preparing the people for the greater covenant. Although temporary, it nonetheless was of importance in the redemptive plan of God.

9:2 Verses 2-10 provide a brief description of the earthly tabernacle, described in detail in Exodus 25–40. Made of raw materials, including animal's skins, the original structure by its very nature reflected the essence of impermanence. It was never intended to serve as an eternal place of worship. The tabernacle, however, paints a beautiful picture of the coming Messiah, and this aspect of its beauty demands the reader's attention. The tabernacle was constructed in such a way that there were outer and inner parts. **The lampstand, the table and the presentation loaves** were placed in the sanctuary. The lampstand was near the table where twelve loaves were placed as a representation of the twelve tribes of Israel. This outer part of the tabernacle **is called the holy place** in verse 2, for it was erected as an act of worship to God to represent man's need for holiness.

9:3-5 However, the inner part of the tabernacle was described as **the holy of holies** (v. 3). In fact, it was separated from the outer part by a **curtain**. It held the **altar of incense and the ark of the covenant**. The ark of the covenant contained **a gold jar** holding pieces of **manna, Aaron's rod**, and the stone **tablets** on which **the covenant** of God was written. It represents the true basis for relations between God and man. On the lid of the ark of the covenant was **the mercy seat** on which stood **the cherubim of glory**. The mercy seat was found between the wings of these two cherubim (Ex 25:22). Verse 5 mentioned "the cherubim of glory" briefly because, as the writer indicated, these descriptions were not discussed **in detail**. He wished, rather, to focus on services performed in this special place.

9:6-10 In verses 6-10, the writer showed the limited access to God, which was permitted under the Mosaic covenant. The descriptions in Exodus, as well as here in verse 6, explained that only **the priests** could **enter the first room**, the outer part of the tabernacle. In this holy place they conducted their assigned ministries. Only **the high priest** was able to enter the holy of holies and **only once a year** on the Day of Atonement. The most significant symbolism seen in the earthly tabernacle is the arrangement of the furniture and other objects. The division between the inner and outer parts, separated by a veil at the door of the holy place and by one at the holy of holies, demonstrated the separation between God and the sinner. Additionally, the symbol of **blood** is strongly emphasized in the

description of the duty of the high priest in entering the holy of holies with blood, which he offered to God for his and the people's sins that were **committed in ignorance** (Gk. *agnoēmatēn*, v. 7). Such an arrangement and sacrifice, as the writer explained, demonstrated that this was temporary and limited. The people could only reach God through the priests and high priest, serving as mediators between them and God. The old covenant sacrificial system could not meet man's deepest need by perfecting **the worshiper's conscience** (v. 9). Ceremonies and rituals could not permanently touch the worshiper's inner defilement, which prevented fellowship with God. These ceremonies were external in nature. Therefore, these external rituals and ceremonies, with which the original readers would have been very familiar, were only meant to apply **until the time of restoration**. The readers must remember that these ceremonies were only temporary under the old covenant and would be replaced in the new covenant through the person of Jesus.

9:11-15 Having shown the limited nature of the old covenant, the author sets forth the superiority of the new covenant by describing Jesus' role as **the mediator of a new covenant** (v. 15). In verses 11-15, the Messiah's arrival is announced as He is described as the **high priest** who has appeared and entered the **more perfect** sanctuary, the heavenly **tabernacle** (v. 11). Jesus ministers for believers in heaven at God's right hand, as the writer has stressed throughout this epistle. His tabernacle is not made of earthly things but is formed and fashioned by God in heaven. It is a tabernacle prophesied in Zechariah 6:12-13 when the "Branch," Jesus, would come to build the house of God.

But, what does Jesus do as the high priest? First, **He entered the holy of** holies with **His own blood**, not that **of goats and calves** (v. 12). This high priest served as our sacrifice. Second, Jesus made His sacrifice *once and for all* (9:28; 10:10). It is not something He must repeat every year, as did the former high priests who repeated this sacrifice on the Day of Atonement. Third, He **obtained eternal redemption** (9:12) on our behalf. He has cleansed all of our past, present, and future sins by His one, complete sacrifice. He is the perfect Lamb of God, slain for the sins of mankind, offered as a pleasing sacrifice to Almighty God. This perfect sacrifice is able to **cleanse our consciences** completely (v. 14). Chapter 8 explained how the ministry of the new covenant is internal as opposed to external. Jesus cleansed man from the inside. Second Corinthians 5:17 explained that Jesus makes the believer "a new creation" at the point of salvation. The old is gone and is replaced by a redeemed creature. Our salvation is based on this final act of Calvary, a sacrifice that makes us perfect and complete in Him. The original readers, in particular, needed the reassurance that their faith in Jesus' sacrifice frees them from the added works of the law (v. 15). A believer can have confidence in the promised **eternal inheritance** (v. 15), because of all she has in Jesus.

9:16-23 The promise of an eternal inheritance caused the writer of Hebrews to consider the figure of **a will** (Gk. *diathēkē*, the same word rendered "covenant" in previous verses). In the legal sense, Jesus wrote all believers' names in His will for eternal life. Such a will, however, can become effective only upon the death of the one making the will, **the testator** (vv. 16–17). Jesus died and declared, "It is finished" (Jn 19:30). In dying, He paid the price for believers to inherit eternal life at the cost of His blood. The old covenant was also sealed in blood, but with animal's blood (v. 18).

The writer described the inauguration of the old covenant through the ceremony of sprinkling the sacrificial blood based on Exodus 24:3-8. The law was **sprinkled** with blood as were **the people**, the tabernacle and the furniture inside the tabernacle (vv. 19-21). In this way, blood was used in the establishment of the old covenant as well as throughout its time of ministry. God's principle, clearly articulated in Leviticus 17:11, is that blood is required before sin can be forgiven (v. 22).

The Passover celebration also demonstrates the centrality of blood. The people were commanded to use blood on the doorposts of their homes in order to avoid the judgment of God upon Egypt. There is power and life in the blood. God has ordained **the shedding of blood** (v. 22) for removal of sin; and with the new covenant, blood must be shed (v. 23). In summary, the writer proved the superiority of the new covenant by demonstrating that just as the old covenant was established with blood, so was the new covenant. Furthermore, the new covenant was established **with better sacrifices** (v. 23), a sacrifice that purifies man's conscience. Lastly, the new covenant is established in a better place, in the heavenly realm.

9:24-26 The fulfillment of the new covenant is seen in the high priest, Jesus, who has entered once and for all the eternal sanctuary and ministered on our behalf (v. 24). There He represents us before God. Jesus does not stand in the *earthly* holy of holies, but rather stands **in the presence of God** in heaven (v. 24). He has ushered believers into the very presence of God. Roman Catholic teaching that began with Gregory the Great (AD 540–604) does not embrace the fact that Jesus' sacrifice for sin was **offered once** (v. 28) and cannot be repeated. The perpetual offering of Jesus' body and blood as a sacrifice for sin is contrary to the biblical teaching found here in Hebrews. The "Lord's Supper" symbolizes the sacrifice Jesus made and celebrates the unity believers have with God because of Jesus' blood and broken body, but it does not reenact it (vv. 25-26).

9:27-28 People (Gk. *anthrōpois*), as sinful creatures, are destined **to die once** and then to face **judgment** (v. 27). Furthermore, you cannot atone for your own sins and escape the judgment of God. The allusion in verse 28 is most likely to the Day of Atonement, at which time the high priest emerged from the holy of holies after having offered the people's sacrifice for sin. The people experienced temporary relief that, for the time being, they had satisfied God's requirement for "the removal of sin" (9:26). But, an even greater anticipation awaits believers who will behold the great high priest, the One who has forever removed sin from us and satisfied God's wrath because He has brought us eternal salvation through His precious blood. As Scripture promises, He **will appear a second time** (v. 28), and this time for the purpose of gathering those who have believed in Him for salvation in order that they might obtain the inheritance of eternal life with Him that He has promised them.

The sufficiency of the new covenant sacrifice (10:1-39)

A cursory reading of chapter 10 may leave the impression that the writer is merely repeating what has already been said about Jesus' sacrifice, which ushered in the new covenant. However, while chapter 9 focuses on the necessity of Jesus' sacrifice, chapter 10 emphasizes how this sacrifice perfects those who worship Him. These two chapters could be considered as the primary blocks of the epistle, since they reflect the heart of the writer. Jesus is superior to all, and His superiority allows access into God's presence.

10:1-10 The writer began in verse one by explaining once more that the law (old covenant) was only a **SHADOW** (Gk. *skian*, "shadow, an image cast by an object intercepting the light; sketch or outline"; cp. 8:5; Col 2:17) of what was to come through Jesus' sacrifice (new covenant). It could not **PERFECT** (Gk. *teleiōsin*, "make perfect, accomplish, fulfill, or complete") those who offered sacrifices year after year. The annual and daily ceremonies present during the old covenant testified to its temporal nature. Besides, as verse 2 highlights, if perfection had been possible under the old covenant, then the sacrifices would have ceased. Indeed, the people of Israel continued to offer sacrifices **year after year** (v. 1) because of their **consciousness of sins** (v. 2). The yearly rituals associated with the Day of Atonement served as a sober **reminder of sins** (v. 3) present in the people's lives, and continues to do so for Jewish people who have not yet recognized Jesus as their Messiah. The finality of Jesus' sacrifice on the cross perfects His people and eliminates the need for the continuation of these old ceremonial practices. As one evangelical scholar observes, "Worshippers in the Old Testament age were provided with a means of grace, but that means was never able to achieve a complete removal of sins, which could be voluntarily accomplished only by a perfect human, in contrast to an animal sacrifice."[1] This principle can also be understood with the contemporary illustration of a credit card. Consider the case of a person who has charged this limit on a credit card only to be faced with the impossibility of paying for all of the charges. He is simply able to pay the minimum monthly payment. The creditors do not trouble him so long as he makes these monthly payments at the designated time, yet the person knows that the entire debt cannot be paid. The animal sacrifices are like those monthly payments in that they provided for a provisional atonement, but there was still a debt that remained unpaid. The debt could only be paid in full by the Messiah and His perfect sacrifice.

Given the inadequacy, therefore, of animal sacrifices, the writer reflected on the words of the psalmist in Psalm 40:6-8. This Messianic passage declared the ultimate ineffectiveness of sin offerings and the anticipation of One who would fulfill God's will by satisfying the payment for sin forever. Jesus' incarnation in verse 5 refers to the BODY (Gk. *sōma*) that was PREPARED (Gk. *katērtisō*, "made, created, put in order, restore, make sufficient, fit or shaped for"; cp. 11:3; 13:21) for Him. He came to achieve the will of God by perfecting those who worship under the new covenant. Jesus' consciousness of the purpose of His mission in the incarnation is made clear in John's Gospel (Jn 5:30; 6:38; 7:16; 10:17; 12:49-50). He was sent by God for the purpose of redeeming mankind, and He completed His mission perfectly and completely (Jn 6:40).

10:11-13 God does not, as the writer articulated, desire any SACRIFICES (Gk. *thusias*, "act of offering") or OFFERINGS (Gk. *prosphoras*, "sacrifice, gift") but rather delights in the obedience of His Son (vv. 8-9). By Jesus' obedience believers are allowed the blessing of sanctification. The words used in verses 10 and 14 demonstrate that our *sanctification* is an accomplished, completed action (v. 10) because Jesus **has perfected** (Gk. *teteleiōken*, "made perfect or complete") us **forever** (v. 14). In the Greek text, both "perfected" and **sanctified** are written in the perfect tense, indicating an action completed in the past and with ongoing effects. This truth stands in con-

trast to the Levitical priesthood since their sacrificial duties were never truly completed (v. 11). As the writer of Hebrews stressed again, **But this man**, Jesus, **after offering one sacrifice for sins forever, sat down at the right hand of God** (v. 12). His seat "at the right hand of God" signals the finality of His sacrifice. Such an act also revealed that He was simply WAITING (Gk. *ekdechomenos*, "expecting, awaiting, looking for, receiving," also in 11:10) for "His enemies" to be made "His FOOTSTOOL" (Gk. *hupopodion*, literally "under foot," particularly as a conqueror demonstrated victory by placing his foot on the conquered enemy's neck). Making Christ's enemies "His footstool" thus entails their "subjecting to His power," a demonstration of His victory. This reoccurring point is found in the epistle as the writer has already referred to Jesus' enthronement and victory as King. As King, He will not allow His enemies to triumph but rather will utterly crush them.

10:14-18 At this point, the discussion turned again to the new covenant that God promised to His people. The writer used Jeremiah 31:33-34 to illustrate his point. **The Holy Spirit . . . testifies** that a new covenant was coming, at which time the law of God would be written on the hearts and minds of believers, and their sins would no longer be remembered (vv. 16-17). This passage was also quoted in 8:8-12. There is no further need for sacrifice, and thus, as he concluded verse 18, the one who is forgiven under the new covenant has no other **offering for sin.**

10:19-21 The latter part of the chapter turned from the subject of Jesus' final and complete sacrifice to another warning for those who have been perfected by Him. This section has been argued as the climactic point of the entire epistle as the writer concluded his thoughts on the priesthood of Jesus and turned to pointing out the implications of His sacrifice. The writer's words of encouragement, mixed with stern instruction, create an unusual tone at this point in the book. Yet, compassion for fellow believers has driven the writer to both tasks. Verse 19 referred back to all that has been said previously. In tracing back his steps, we are reminded of the superiority of Jesus the Son of God over the angels, prophets, and priests and of His ministry as the high priest. Due to the sacrifice He made in covering our sin, **we have boldness** (Gk. *parrēsian*, "confidence, assurance"; cp. 3:6; 4:16; 10:35) **to enter** the holy place **through** His **blood** (v. 19). While this is awe-inspiring for all believers, it is especially meaningful for a woman. Because of Jesus' blood, women are able to enter the holy of holies without fear of death. Under the old covenant only men could enter this special place, and furthermore, only men from the tribe of Levi who had been ordained to serve as priests could enter. Now all men and women who believe in Jesus are able to enter this sacred place because of Jesus' blood. His blood purifies men and women of their sin and thus enables us to stand in the very presence of the holy God. As His daughter, robed in His righteousness, sanctified by Him and sealed with His grace, I am able to come *boldly* before Him. Believers have confidence to enter His presence by a **new and living way** (v. 20), by Jesus' body which is **the curtain** that separated man from God. This picture is of the veil in the old sanctuary that separated the holy from the unholy. Only through Jesus mankind can have access to God the Father. The NEW WAY (Gk. *prosphaton*, meaning "freshly slain" or "recently made new") is used only here in the New Testament, drawing attention to the *recent* access that believers have to God compared to the old covenant.

10:22-25 Based on these fundamental truths, the writer exercised his gift of exhortation by encouraging believers to do the following things:

- **Let us draw near** (v. 22): Because of the access we have to God through Jesus, we can enter His presence by faith in Jesus' sacrifice. He has **sprinkled** us, **washed** us and cleansed us from all of our impurities, making us holy as He is holy. The reference here is to believer's baptism when one demonstrates outwardly what has already taken place inwardly. Baptism represents the cleansing of sin in the life of a believer. Every believer should approach God with a sense of personal holiness that is made possible only by Jesus. It is expressed by **a true heart in full assurance of faith**. There should be no wavering in regard to one's standing before God. Instead, we are called to stand confidently before Him not because of what we have done, but because of what Jesus has done on our behalf. We stand before God because of God's Son.

- **Let us hold on to the confession of our hope** (v. 23): There is a need for believers to remain steadfast in the faith. Endurance and perseverance in the Christian walk are central themes of this epistle, and the writer makes this point again in these verses. A believer must hold fast to what is true **without wavering** or looking back to the life left behind based on the faithfulness of God in fulfilling His promises. The writer demonstrated this even further in the next chapter as he recorded the lives of faithful men and women as well as the faithfulness of God.

- **Let us be concerned about one another** (v. 24): The third exhortation focused on a believer's relationship to others. Believers must be attentive to the needs of fellow brothers and sisters in Christ. The writer encouraged attentiveness to loving one another and promoting **good works**. TO PROMOTE (Gk. *paroxusmon*, "provoking, encouraging, sharp disagreement") implies stimulating something to action. It can also mean, "to incite, urge, spur on or sharpen." It suggests that one must work at loving others in such a way that they are stimulated to demonstrate this love in tangible ways. Given the persecutions in particular, there was a need for believers to love and encourage one another as the body of Christ. This loving encouragement remains important today. The writer continued by encouraging believers not to abandon "OUR MEETINGS (Gk. *episunagōgēn*, "gathering together, assembling" as a religious body), as some habitually do" (v. 25). Evidently some were already neglecting Christian fellowship, perhaps because of their temptation to return to old patterns of life. The writer was concerned, as he had been throughout his letter, that believers needed to stand firm in their faith. Encouragement is essential to the progress believers make together, and it should increase as the day approaches when Jesus will reappear. Interestingly, the well-known trio from 1 Corinthians 13:13 is included in these verses: faith (v. 22), hope (v. 23) and love (v. 24), evidence of the Spirit's work in the life of a believer who was exercising godliness.

10:26-39 Following these exhortations, the writer issued a fourth strong warning— against the dangers of apostasy. There are similarities between this section and

Hebrews 6. With the thought of the imminent return of Jesus fresh on his mind, the writer felt compelled to address this topic in light of the day of judgment "drawing near" (Gk. *eggizousan*, "approaching, coming near," v. 25). The situation that could result in serious judgment is that of apostasy. As verse 26 explains, those who have received **the knowledge of the truth** (v. 26) but who continue to sin deliberately and knowingly, can expect a **terrifying** display of **judgment**. TERRIFYING (Gk. *phobera*, "inspiring fear, terrible") was also used in 10:31 and 12:21. The related word *phobos*, "fear, dread, terror," appears in v. 27; 2:15. Again, evangelical scholars are divided on whether this passage refers to believers or unbelievers. There are reasons to believe that either could be the case, but the difficulty arises in interpreting the meaning of key phrases such as **there no longer remains a sacrifice** (v. 26) and **by which he was sanctified** (v. 29), as well as **those who draw back and are destroyed** (v. 39). Nevertheless, a number of conclusions can be made from this difficult passage. For instance, the position of the word **deliberately** (Gk. *hekousiōs*, "willingly, intentionally") as first in the Greek sentence, highlights the seriousness of consciously or willfully sinning (v. 26). By "deliberately" sinning, one rejects the truth of God and therefore insults the sacrifice of Jesus, a serious offense indeed. By renouncing the efficacious sacrifice of Jesus, no other available sacrifice that can save man from God's ultimate judgment remains. This sacrifice is God's provision for sin and is the means by which we receive grace. Under the old covenant, no sacrifices were made for deliberate sins (Ex 21:12-14; Nm 15:27-31). Instead, any who despised or disregarded the law of Moses were executed (Dt 17:1-7). Within this context David pleaded before God in Psalm 51 regarding the sin of adultery, which he had willingly committed. He recognized that he deserved to die on account of this sin and cried out for God's mercy. There was no sacrifice available to cleanse him from this sin, and thus all he could offer God were the sacrifices of a broken heart and a contrite spirit (Ps 51:16-17). God promised to deal severely with these as the writer attested in verses 30-31. The argument proceeded to demonstrate that if the punishment was severe under the old covenant, imagine how much more severe it is under the new covenant. This serious offense is evident when one:

- has "TRAMPLED ON (Gk. *katapatēsas*, "tread upon, treat with disdain," with the implication of insulting or spurning), or rebelled against God (v. 29); the Son of God"

- has **regarded as profane the blood of the covenant**, understood as treating the holy as common or cheap;

- has INSULTED (Gk. *enubrisas*, "outraged," from *hubrizō*, "being insolent, treating shamefully"; cp. Mt 22:6; Lk 18:32) the Spirit of grace, or rejected the Holy Spirit who dispenses grace (Heb 10:29).

Clearly, such a one is promised that she will **fall into the hands of the living God** (v. 31).

As he has done with other warning passages, the writer encouraged his readers in the verses following this stern warning. He called upon them to recall the steadfastness with which they had stood against hard persecutions. Verses 32-34 provide insight into the persecutions that these believers had already faced. They were publicly humiliated and persecuted and had supported others who were treated this way (v. 33). They had also shown compassion for those who were imprisoned and had suffered the loss of property with an attitude of joy, knowing that their greatest riches were yet to be received in heaven (v. 34). Whatever they were now facing, they needed to be reminded of the steadfastness they had faithfully exhibited in the past and be spurred on to continuing in the same manner. Perseverance and **endurance** (v. 36) are central to the writer's theme, and in these closing verses of chapter 10, he encouraged both among believers. ENDURANCE (Gk. *hupomonēs*, "steadfastness," lit., the act of "remaining under") in the New Testament was usually ascribed to the believer who remains undeterred from loyalty to Christ despite great trials and suffering. See also 12:1. The purpose of our endurance is to do the will of God (10:36). The writer concluded by encouraging believers to stand fast, remain true, exercise confidence in God, and press on in faith, because the Lord is returning soon and will give life to those who follow Him. He used Isaiah 26:20 (from the LXX) and Habakkuk 2:3-4 to show that the Lord will reward those who stand firm but will find "no pleasure in" those who DRAW BACK (Gk. *huposteilētai*, the "fear and hesitation" with which one would sneak away or fail to acknowledge one's beliefs; cp. Ac 20:20,27; Gl 2:12) from Him (v. 38). God's favor cannot rest on one who has shrunk back from Him. The call has been issued to enter God's presence boldly, recognizing Jesus' ministry as high priest, and therefore to be faithful in drawing near to God with a heart of faith that trusts in His provision for our sin and of the grace that we need to live faithful lives before Him.

THE SUPERIORITY OF THE POWER OF CHRIST (11:1–13:19)

The Great Hall of Faith (11:1-40)

11:1-3 Faith (Gk. *pistis*, v. 1) is what is needed in order to fulfill with confidence the will of God in exhibiting Christlikeness. The original recipients of this epistle were being tempted to return to the practice of Judaism and to place their faith in the law. Their confidence lay in the visible things of the world instead of the invisible, and thus the writer understood their need to be reminded of the fullness of true faith in God and His promises. Faith serves as the foundation for the Christian life and results in a life that perseveres in trusting in God. Verse 1 provides the description of faith. Biblical faith is confidently believing what God says despite the circumstances or consequences. It is not "wishful thinking" but a confident expectation that God will do all He says He will do. Faith also relates to the manner in which one understands the world as being something created by God, not with visible but invisible things (v. 3). Faith will produce endurance and confidence in God, as evidenced in the lives of those the writer mentions in the verses that follow (vv. 2-3).

11:4-6 Listed first in this "hall of faith" is **Abel,** whose acceptance by God was based on the **better sacrifice** he offered (v. 4). Genesis 4:4 referred to Abel's sacrifice but does not explicitly describe the faith he exhibited. In contrast, however, **Cain** was told that if he offered the same sacrifice as Abel, he, too, would be accepted (Gn 4:7). The inference is that Abel's attitude in offering his sacrifice was found pleasing to God. It is also possible that his offering a blood sacrifice was pleasing to God. He was deemed **a righteous man** who, although **dead**, still testified to faith in God. He still serves as a source of inspiration for men of faith.

So, too, **Enoch** exhibited faith and thus **did not experience death** (v. 5). He was **approved** by God and taken by Him before death (Gn 5:21-24), an unusual man of faith in the Old Testament. Given Enoch's example, the writer stressed the impossibility of pleasing God **without faith** (Heb 11:6). One must have faith in order to draw near to God, because this one must also **believe that He exists**. Since He is not seen visibly, faith must be exercised.

11:7 God rewards "those who seek Him" (v. 6), which is particularly evident in the life of **Noah**. In the midst of wickedness and corruption, Noah obeyed God and **built an ark to deliver his family** from the promise of destruction. As a result of his faith in God and His promises, Noah was declared **an heir** of **righteousness**. Moreover, Noah's faith not only affected him, but his entire household. Interestingly, Noah was the first man described as "righteous" in the Old Testament.

11:8-10 Once again, the writer of Hebrews was captivated by the example of **Abraham** and recounted in greater detail his faith and obedience to God. This great patriarch of the Old Testament moved from his home, followed the call of God, and became a stranger in a new place where it was promised he would receive his **inheritance** (v. 8). The first aspect of his faith noted is his obedience to follow God's call. He left the home that was visible and moved to a place he had never seen, simply because God said, "Go." As a result, his sons were also linked with him as **co-heirs of the same promise** (v. 9). Abraham's faith was more than just leaving the home he knew for a land he did not know. It consisted of his faith that God would build **the city** that has a foundation, unlike the tents Abraham dwelt in, a city that was much farther off than the borders of Canaan. It is this perspective and trust in God that the writer highlighted. Abraham serves as one of the greatest models of Christian faith because of his tenacious commitment to follow God wherever He led and to trust in the promises He made with His people. In fact, the writer was so moved by the example of faith of Abraham that he mentioned him again later in the chapter (vv. 17-19).

11:11-12 Not only was Abraham commended for his example of faith, but **Sarah** his wife was also mentioned in verses 11-12. She is the first woman to be referenced in this "hall of faith." Her faith is set apart from her husband's by the words in verse 11, **even Sarah herself**. Well **past the age** of childbearing, Sarah believed the promise of God that she would bear a child and that from him would come **offspring** that would number **the stars of heaven** (v. 12). Although Genesis 18:12 records Sarah's initial laughter upon hearing the news that she would bear children, still the writer drew attention to the faith that she developed before the birth of her son Isaac. Like her husband, Sarah believed the promises of God and therefore shared in His blessings. She is revered in the Old and New Testaments as a woman who exhibited the qualities of godly womanhood, both in her life of faith and her life of submission to her husband and to the Lord.

11:13-16 The writer seemed to pause in verses 13-16 from his record of those in the "hall of faith" in order to add further comment on those he had already described. By faith these Old Testament saints **saw** the promises made to them only **from a distance** (Gk. *porrōthen*, "afar off"), and yet they pressed on in aspiring for their heavenly inheritance (v. 13). They did not, as the writer observes, receive the promises while they lived, but they still believed that these promises would be fulfilled. The Old Testament

recorded that the patriarchs never obtained a true HOMELAND (Gk. *patrida*, "fatherland, one's native country, permanent abode," v. 14) during their lifetime, but welcomed it "from a distance." God honors such an expression of faith and **is not ashamed to be called their God** (v. 16; cp. 2:11). What an incredible statement to ponder! Despite their weaknesses, God is not ashamed to be identified with these great men and women of faith because of their lives of faith. He has prepared a better homeland for them, one that is built on spiritual things and not material possessions.

11:17-19 Following these general comments, the writer returned to the example of **Abraham** as one of the greatest men of faith. The reference in verses 17-19 is to the account in Genesis 22 when Abraham is commanded to offer Isaac as a sacrifice to the Lord. The writer reminded the reader that **Isaac** was the very one who was promised to Abraham as the **seed** (v. 18) through whom the nations would be blessed, and yet, God tested Abraham's faith in this way. Abraham's faith was so steadfast and true that he believed that somehow God would honor His promise even if Isaac were offered as a sacrifice (v. 19). The writer highlighted the remarkableness of Abraham's faith by reminding the reader that Isaac was Abraham's **unique son** (Gk. *monogenē*, "only begotten, one of a kind," v. 17), which is understood in relation to the promise. While Ishmael was also one of Abraham's sons, he was not related to the promise of God to be the heir of the promise that God would bless nations through him. The maturity of Abraham's faith is seen in verse 19 when the writer pointed out that **he considered God to be able** to do something that did not even seem possible. Clearly, Abraham carefully reasoned that God would somehow do the impossible. Truly, Abraham exhibited faith like no other and is praised by the writer for his obedience to God.

11:20-22 Likewise, Isaac, Jacob, and Joseph also modeled lives of faith before God. Each one believed that God would do what He promised, namely, in giving the people of Israel a homeland. A common denominator among all of these was that they displayed faith until the end of their lives. In the same manner, the readers are encouraged to maintain lives of faith until the end of their time.

11:23-31 Moses, too, was a key figure in Old Testament literature and in Judaism. He, too, exercised faith by choosing **to suffer with** (v. 25) the Israelites in spite of his privileged status in the Egyptian kingdom (vv. 24,26). But, before the writer drew attention to Moses' faith, he mentioned the faith of **his parents** in hiding their baby because they trusted in God's protection. **They didn't fear the king's edict** (v. 23) to kill the sons of the Israelites. God rewarded their faith by empowering Moses to lead His people out of Egypt. Moses' spiritual perspective rather than his worldly point of view motivated him to live a life of faith in God. Refusing **to be called the son of Pharaoh's daughter** (v. 24), Moses instead identified himself with the slaves of Egypt and suffered alongside his people. He did this simply because he recognized the **greater** reward that would come from **the Messiah** versus the worldly pleasures of Egypt. Leaving Egypt behind and, like his parents, not fearing **the king's anger** (v. 27), **he persevered** (Gk. *ekarkerēsen*, "was steadfast or strong," v. 27), following instead the One from whom he received instruction. **He instituted the Passover** (v. 28), the Israelites' **sprinkling** of **blood** on their doorposts to protect the lives of their firstborn from the death angel of God.

The Passover remains a highly celebrated time in Judaism because of the deliverance that came as a result of God's promise to lead his people to the promised land under Moses' leadership. While this monumental event in Israel's history was no doubt familiar to the original readers of this epistle, nonetheless, the writer reminded them of certain details. It was **by faith** that the Israelites **crossed the Red Sea** and, as a result, witnessed the destruction of the Egyptian army (v. 29). Additionally, they watched as **the walls of Jericho fell down** (v. 30). In verse 31, the second woman in this "hall of faith" is also mentioned.

The inclusion of **Rahab** is especially noteworthy since she was a Gentile woman and a **prostitute**. Her faith is applauded because her faith was not without works. She risked her life for the people of Israel and identified herself with the God of Israel. The account in Joshua 2:8-11 recounted Rahab's declaration of faith to **the spies** by disclosing that she believed that the Lord God of Israel had given them the land to conquer. Second, she also revealed that everyone in the region was fearful of the Israelites. Third, she declared her own personal faith in Israel's God. As a result, she **didn't perish** with those in Jericho.

11:32-40 Having only mentioned great men and women of faith from Genesis to Joshua, the writer began to summarize the stories of other known heroes of the faith. The rhetorical question in this verse does not imply that the writer has exhausted all that he could say, but rather that those already mentioned are sufficiently impressive. Yet, it seems essential to include a few more. He lists six more champions of faith by name—four judges (**Gideon, Barak, Samson, Jephthah**), a king (**David**), and a prophet (**Samuel**)— **and the prophets** (v. 32). Verses 33-37 list the many things they, along with other men and women of faith, encountered and endured as they walked by faith in God.

Heart to Heart:
Heroines of Faith

People naturally look to others for examples of living. Christians need to imitate godly lives. Christian women must follow their holy heroines, women of great faith.

The writer of Hebrews recorded in one chapter the names of many champions of faith. Men and women who lived out their faith are mentioned. They loved the Lord, followed His will, and obeyed His commandments. Two women were listed specifically by name.

Sarah was included with her husband Abraham (11:8-12). Although Sarah laughed when she heard that she was to have a much longed for child at her advanced age, her disbelief eventually turned to faith before the birth of her son Isaac (Gn 18:12). While Abraham's strong faith was the seed of a great people, his faithful wife also left a godly legacy. Sarah's attitude changed, her faith grew, and her life became an example of great faith for centuries.

The prostitute Rahab was also listed in Hebrews 11 as a holy heroine. The immoral Gentile woman was used by God to hide the spies and deliver His children. She turned away from her gods and trusted in the one true God. She became a role model because she made wise decisions and remained steadfast in her faith. Rahab's lineage included Boaz, the godly husband of Ruth; David, the great king of Israel; and Jesus Christ, the Savior of the world. God granted her a lasting legacy.

Though Sarah and Rahab initially seemed lacking in their faith, their hearts were transformed by their love for God. They were remembered for their faithfulness, not their unfaithfulness, and they have remained holy heroines.

Some **conquered kingdoms** (David, v. 33) while others **shut the mouths of lions** (Daniel, v. 33), and yet others **were stoned** (Zechariah, v. 37) for their faith in God. Undoubtedly, readers could identify others such as Paul, Stephen, and John the Baptist who had also endured to the very end of their lives in faithful obedience to God. Yet with all of these, the writer attested, **the world was not worthy of them** (v. 38). This commendation of faith is underscored in the closing verses of this chapter as the author summarized his point: These had not yet received what had been **promised** to them through the salvation of the Messiah (v. 39). They longed for Him, believed in Him, and yet did not live to see His appearance. Indeed, it is **better for us** (v. 40) since we enjoy the benefits of being joined with our Messiah. As a result, the perfection and eternal home for which the Old Testament saints longed also await us as believers in Jesus.

A Call to Endurance (12:1-29)

Chapter 12 begins with the writer turning from a historical recital to a pastoral exhortation. Some argue that there should be no chapter division here, since 12:1-3 is really the climactic point in the writer's argument concerning the importance of a life of faith. The beginning of verse 1, intensified by the conjunction THERE-FORE (Gk. *toigaroun*, "consequently, for which reason"), which is found only here and in 1 Thessalonians 4:8, serves as the crescendo in the writer's composition.

12:1-4 The two groups of saints to whom the writer had just referred at the end of chapter 11 are mentioned again in 12:1. He was careful to connect their lives with the exhortation to the fellow heirs of the promise of salvation. In verse 1, believers were called to faithfulness, knowing that they were surrounded by **a large crowd of witnesses** identified in chapter 11. The focus of verse 1 is not, however, that the host of witnesses *watches us*, but rather that they *looked unto Jesus* and therefore were able to run with endurance. The Greek word for WITNESSES, *marturōn*, does not denote that they are mere spectators, but rather the word implies that they testify from their own experience in the Christian walk. The fact that the writer mentioned them in terms of a "cloud of witnesses" demonstrated the vast number of those who surround believers for the purpose of cheering them on toward running strong and hard as we look to Jesus (v. 2).

The first paragraph of chapter 12 identified three actions that are required of the believer in running **with endurance** (Gk. *hupomonēs*; see 10:36). First, we must look back to those described in chapter 11 and recount their lives of faith. This flashback will spur you on to running the race of faith. Their commitment and zeal for the promise of God should inspire believers to do likewise.

Second, as believers we must **lay aside every weight and the sin that so easily**

entangles us (v. 1). The picture is of a runner who must remove some of his clothing in order to run unhindered. In the same way, believers must remove everything that would hinder them from running with endurance. Sin is at the forefront of the writer's mind in this regard. A life of faithfulness is one marked by a lifestyle that reflects devotion to God. Sin handicaps the believer and prevents her from running with perseverance. The author is not thinking of running a short sprint, but rather a long-distance race that requires determined persistence to continue to the finish. He made this point in chapter 11 by describing the lives of faith of ones such as Abraham and Joseph who continued running, believing that God would fulfill His promises. Sin hampers consistent running and ENTANGLES (Gk. *euperistaton*), conveying the idea of taking off a long heavy robe that keeps you from running. Sin ultimately distracts us from running the race consistently. We must therefore make every effort to rid our lives of its presence.

Third, in order to run with endurance, the believer must keep her eyes on Jesus. The Greek word *aphorōntes*, is derived from *apo*, a prefix denoting "separation," and *horaō*, "to see." It carries the meaning of turning one's sight *away from* what originally held the attention *to* something else. The appeal is for concentrated attention that is much more than a mere gaze. It describes an intense looking with the focus squarely on the object at hand (v. 2). The writer identified the object on which we should focus our attention. **Jesus** is the ultimate example of one who ran with endurance, displaying a life of complete faithfulness to God. The writer described Him as **the source** (Gk. *archegon*; see 2:10) **and perfecter of our faith**. Jesus not only pioneered the path of faith; He is also the one in whom faith finds perfection, since He reached the end of the race successfully. Furthermore, Jesus kept His eyes fixed on **the joy** set before Him. He ran perfectly because He never sinned, and therefore, His focus remained consistently on His Father. His earthly life provided the perfect example of trust in God. He accomplished this despite the humiliation and suffering He endured at the cross. His sacrifice cannot be forgotten at this important juncture in the epistle. He has also **sat down at the right hand of God**, a phrase the writer has used several times throughout the epistle to note Jesus' triumphant position and final work upon the cross (v. 2; 1:3; 8:1; 10:12). His endurance under such circumstances should encourage the believer to continue to run and not to **grow weary and lose heart** (v. 3).

The writer acknowledged that discouragement and fatigue are inevitable but can be overcome when considering Jesus' example. He issued the reminder that while the readers struggled against the temptations of sin, they had **not yet resisted to the point of shedding** their **blood** (v. 4). Jesus, however, did endure pain and suffering to the point of shedding His blood in order that we might not be enslaved to sin. It is through Him and His power that we are able to run with endurance. His example of faithfulness should motivate us not to lose heart but to keep running and to run well!

12:5-13 Additionally, believers are reminded that they should not lose heart when they **endure** hardship and face **discipline** for they are being trained by God for His glory (vv. 5-11). DISCIPLINE (Gk. *paideias*, referring to a child's overall "education and training—of mind, morals, and body") has the sense not only of instruction but also of correction, chastisement, and of a father's punishment of his son. Discipline testifies to a believer's position as a member

of the family of God. The writer used Proverbs 3:11-12 to remind the readers that those who are disciplined are the ones the Lord loves. God deals with believers as sons who need discipline, but such training and correction are evidences of His love. The fact that a believer receives discipline should encourage and not discourage, since those who do not receive discipline are considered **illegitimate children and not sons** (v. 8). The writer drew on the analogy of an earthly father who disciplines his children to demonstrate the respect and submission they should have for their heavenly Father. He disciplines them out of love, for their benefit, so that they can reflect Him more and thereby **share His holiness** (v. 10).

Discipline also produces **peace and righteousness** in the life of the believer being trained through God's correction. The thought of disciplined training relates back to the illustration of the race. The believer's response towards discipline should be a renewed resolve to persevere. With this in mind, the writer exhorts the reader to **strengthen your tired hands and weakened knees** (v. 12). Believers must ready themselves for the contest, bracing themselves for what lies ahead. According to this passage, the goal of discipline is maturity and participation in the holiness of God. Whenever a believer endures hardship or suffering, she can be reminded of God's love for her and His desire that she become more like Him. It is a call to strengthen one's resolve to run this long-distance race with endurance, not being tripped up by sin.

12:14-29 Believers are also exhorted to **Pursue peace with everyone** (v. 14). The verb PURSUE (Gk. *diōkete*, "earnestly seek after; run after swiftly, as one in a race runs toward the goal line; eagerly seek to obtain; press on") is used several times in the New Testament to convey the intensity, effort, and focus with which believers should strive to fulfill their holy calling. Occasionally, Scripture specifies what *not* to run after. See Lk 17:23; Rm 9:30-31; 12:13; 14:19; 1 Co 14:1; Php 3:12,14; 1 Th 5:15; 1 Tm 6:11; 2 Tm 2:22; 1 Pt 3:11. In other contexts, the word is translated "persecute"; see, for example, Mt 5:10,11,12, 14. There is a direct parallel with this verse and Romans 12:18. Peace with everyone, however, is limited by doing what is right. This is hardly a call to abandon one's beliefs simply as a means to pursuing peace with another. As much as possible, however, peace should be something for which we strive in our relationships with others. Furthermore, verse 14 exhorts believers to pursue **holiness**, since **without it no one will see the Lord**. Believers are made holy through the effective power of Jesus' death on the cross, but they are also called to a lifestyle of holiness that is pleasing to God. Accompanying this exhortation is the command to make every effort to cultivate **the grace of God** (v. 15).

There is no room for **bitterness** (Gk. *pikrias*) if you recognize the grace of God in your life each and every day. When you forget this precious gift, bitterness brought on by discouragement creeps back into your heart and defiles others just as a plant's root affects the fruit it produces. A spirit of bitterness could also be likened to a disease that infects those around you. The writer encouraged his readers to depend on God's grace and to avoid becoming bitter by looking at faith in three directions:

- *Look back: the example of Esau (Gn 25:27-34).* Esau is a prime example of one who neglected the grace of God. He is described by the writer of Hebrews as an **immoral or irreverent person** (v. 16), not recognizing the grace of God. As a result, he for-

feited his blessing, exchanging it **for one meal**. Once he realized what he had done, it was too late, and he could not receive it back. God's grace never fails, but you can fail in depending on God's grace in your life.

- *Look up: the glory of heaven.* Verses 18-24 contrast the awesome delivery of the law of God to the people of Israel with the majesty of the new covenant. So great and powerful was the giving of the law to Moses that he literally trembled before God (v. 21), and the people were afraid to hear the voice of God (v. 19). Juxtaposed to this event is the new covenant depicted by Mount Zion, God's heavenly city (v. 22; Ps 2; 110:1-2). It represented the grace of God available through Jesus. The patriarchs longed and waited until the time of their deaths for reaching this city (Heb 11:10,14-17). The citizens of this kingdom include **myriads of angels** who gather in celebration, as well as those **whose names have been written** (Gk. *apogegrammenōn*, "register, especially entering in a public record; enroll"; cp. Lk 2:1,3,5) **in heaven** (Heb 11:22; Lk 10:20). **Firstborn** is a title of privilege and relates **to the assembly** (Gk. *ekklēsia*) of those gathered in heaven (v. 23). Whereas the word "firstborn" (Gk. *prōtotokōn*) is understood from the Old Testament as being a couple's firstborn son, the implied meaning here in verse 23 is that all believers stand on an equal plane of privilege before God because they have all inherited the blessing of salvation. God is also present, of course, in Mount Zion and is described as **the judge of all**, the One who can discern the hearts of men. **Jesus**, identified as the **mediator**, is also there. He is the One who shed

His blood that you might enjoy the kingdom of heaven. Because of His blood you have redemption. Unlike Abel's blood that cried out to God from the earth (Gn 4:10), Jesus' blood frees mankind from guilt and opens the door for communion with God. This picture illustrates the glory of heaven that awaits the believer. When discouragement comes and endurance in the race of faith seems impossible, the believer is encouraged to look up and meditate on the glories of heaven.

- *Look ahead: the unshakable kingdom.* Not only should the believer, the runner in the race of faith, look back and look up, but she must also look ahead to the unshakable kingdom of God. After providing the contrast between Mount Sinai and Mount Zion, the writer strongly urged his readers, **See that you do not reject the One who speaks** (v. 25). If men were held accountable for carefully listening to the words of God when He spoke from Mount Sinai, how much more must believers heed the words He speaks from Mount Zion! The writer used this line of argument before, emphasizing the greatness of the new covenant that demands faithful obedience. The responsibility required of those who have received the new covenant outweighs that required of those under the old covenant. Furthermore, God's **voice shook the earth** at the time He gave the law to Moses on Mount Sinai (v. 26). Quoting Haggai 2:6, the writer stressed that one day God will **not only** shake **the earth but also heaven** (2 Pt 3:10,12; Rv 6:12-14). At the end of time everything physical will be destroyed. Only the eternal things will remain and these are described as "unshakable." God has prepared "a new heaven and

a new earth" (Rv 21:1-2), i.e., **a kingdom that cannot be shaken** (Heb 11:28). It is unchangeable and immovable, serving as further motivation for the believer to run with endurance, holding firmly to the grace of God, since believers are promised an unshakable kingdom. Your response to God's grace should be one of reverent service to God. The writer ends chapter 12 with one of the severest descriptions of God: He **is a consuming fire** (v. 29). These words should inspire the believer to stand in awe of Him. The reminder of God's holiness must impact our worship and service to Him.

CONCLUDING REMARKS (13:1-25)

Having provided the great examples of faith in chapter 11 and the encouragement to faith in chapter 12, the writer concluded his letter with the evidences of faith in chapter 13, which should be reflected in a believer's life.

13:1 Brotherly love (Gk. *philadelphia*) is the first evidence mentioned (v.1). Jesus commanded brotherly love among believers: "Love one another just as I have loved you. . . . By this all people will know that you are my disciples if you have love for one another" (Jn 13:34-35). Both Peter and Paul also emphasized the importance of brotherly love in their letters to the church (Rm 12:10; 1 Th 4:9; 1 Pt 1:22; 3:8; 2 Pt 1:7; cp. Gl 5:13; 1 Pt 4:8). The fact that the original readers were enduring persecutions from a hostile culture made this command even more necessary. By loving one another they would not only encourage one another but also serve as a witness to those around them.

13:2 Additionally, the exhortation is given to practice HOSPITALITY (Gk.

philoxenias, a combination of *philos*, "friend," and *xenos*, "stranger, foreigner"; thus, "one who receives another hospitably"). "Hospitality," then is "the practice of welcoming, sheltering, feeding—with no thought of personal gain—those who come to your door."[2] The writer may have recalled the words of Jesus in Matthew 25:35-44 when He spoke of taking in a stranger and feeding and clothing him without realizing that they were ministering to Him. The writer may also have recalled Abraham's hospitality in feeding strangers who approached his tent; unbeknownst to him, they were angels (Gn 18).

13:3 Believers are also called to **remember the prisoners** and their needs (cp. 10:34). These are presumably fellow believers who were imprisoned because of their testimony. Often it is easy to forget or neglect those who have been imprisoned simply because of other distractions, yet the writer urged his readers not to forget these. They, too, needed encouragement to persevere in continuing their walk of faith.

13:4 Next, the writer turned to exhortations that refer more to a believer's private life. He began with marriage and encouraged married believers to keep their marriage bed undefiled, for **marriage** (Gk. *gamos*) **must be respected by all**. In the Greek text, RESPECT (*timios*, an adjective describing something as "precious, expensive, especially dear" and therefore "held in honor") is the first word in the sentence. Peter used this word to describe the blood of Christ (1 Pt 1:19) and His promises (2 Pt 1:4). Established in Eden (Gn 2:24) for the purpose of bringing glory to God by fulfilling His purposes, marriage is to be held in highest regard, therefore, by "all" (Gk. *pasin*, a word referring both to individuals and groups). Marriage can be held in honor in a number of ways, including

the mutual love and respect of a husband and wife. This idea is best displayed in their relationship to the Lord and to one another. IMMORAL PEOPLE (Gk. *pornous*, "fornicators, men who indulge in illicit sex," the same word used to describe Esau as "immoral" in 12:16) and ADULTERERS (Gk. *moichous*, "adulterers," those who have sexual relations with someone other than their spouse) who do not keep THE MARRIAGE BED (Gk. *hē koitē*) UNDEFILED (Gk. *amiantos*, "unsoiled, pure"; cp. 7:26) will be judged by God. Such behavior, according to Ephesians 5:3, is not even to be named among believers.

13:5-6 Additionally, a believer must also be careful not to love money, but rather should remain **satisfied** (Gk. *arkoumenoi*, "to be contented, sufficient, enough") with the good gifts of God which she has received. Materialism will rob the heart of the believer of trusting in the provisions of God. It is important to note that it is not money that is to be avoided, but **the love of money** that is to be carefully guarded against. The sentence begins with the compound Greek word *aphilarguros*, linking the prefix *a* or alpha privative, "not," with *phileō*, "love," and *arguros*, "silver." The word *philarguros* describes in a negative light those who do love money (Lk 16:14; 2 Tm 3:2). The writer quoted the Old Testament again (Dt. 31:6) to add the assurance believers have in the Lord's continual presence. These words instill in believers' hearts the hope that God knows what they need and provides accordingly. One's contentment should be securely fastened on the Lord and not on worldly possessions.

The writer also appealed to Psalm 118:6, a psalm used in the celebration of Passover. The words are suitable because of their affirmation of God's character in helping His children, thereby eliminating the fear of man. These words continue to encourage believers who are faced with circumstances that might tempt them to become fearful of human actions. One recent example is the response of Jewish believers in Israel at the time of the Gulf War in 1991. In the midst of unsettling circumstances, both spiritually and physically, many Jewish believers turned to the words of this psalm for comfort. Despite the persecutions they endured because of their faith and the physical threat of Saddam Hussein's missiles, these faithful believers sang the words of the psalmist, **The Lord is my helper, I will not be afraid** (Heb 13:6). However, in the last sentence they substituted the name of their enemy for the word "man"; instead of singing, **What can man do to me?** they sang, "What can Saddam do to me?" This rhetorical question does not require an answer for it is obvious that with the Lord's help, no man can harm a believer apart from God's permission.

13:7-9 The reader's attention is now drawn to remembering their **leaders** who faithfully taught them the word of God. The implication is that these have already died but have left a legacy of faith behind them. The writer exhorted believers to recall **their lives** and to **imitate their faith** (v. 7), similar to the exhortation in 12:1. Ultimately, Jesus serves as the primary example of faith as has been shown throughout the pages of this epistle. Therefore, it is not surprising that the writer added that He **is the same yesterday, today, and forever** (v. 8). Only this One is changeless throughout time, and only He serves as the high priest who continually intercedes on the believer's behalf. The writer warned believers to avoid those who propagate **strange** (Gk. *xenias*, "foreign"; cp. Ac 17:18) **teachings** that stand in contradiction to these truths (Heb 13:9).

13:10-17 Drawing the letter to a close, the writer returned to the topic of Jesus' priesthood one last time and painted the picture of Jesus' perfect sacrifice made to atone for man's sins. Just as the sin offering was **burned outside the camp** (v. 11), so, too, Jesus' sacrifice was made outside the city of Jerusalem where He sanctified **the people** with **His own blood** (v. 12). The exhortation is then given that believers go **outside the camp, bearing His disgrace**. Rather than return to the trappings of Judaism, the writer encouraged his readers to identify themselves completely with Jesus and His sacrifice. After all, as he explained in verse 14, our home is not on earth but is the **enduring city**. This hope causes the believer to rejoice and thereby to offer **a sacrifice of praise** to God (v. 15). It should also motivate the believer continually to share with others this good gift (v. 16) and to exercise submission to their spiritual leaders (v. 17).

13:18-21 Hebrews ends on a note of praise as the writer offered one of the most beautiful prayers in the New Testament. He prays that God will enable them **to do His will** in order that they will be **pleasing in His sight** (v. 21). The writer used the imagery of a shepherd to depict Jesus who leads the flock of God. He is **the great Shepherd** whom God brought up **from the dead** (v. 20). Under the new covenant, inaugurated by Jesus' shed blood, believers are able to accomplish what is pleasing in God's sight by remaining faithful until the end.

13:22-25 The writer ended by sending the good news that Timothy has been released from prison and that both of them hoped to see this group of believers soon (v. 23). He sent greetings to all that are gathered with them and relayed greetings to them from **Those who are from Italy** (v. 24). It is debatable whether this should be interpreted as those "from" Italy send greeting or those "in" Italy send greeting.

Regardless of the interpretation, however, the purpose and meaning of the epistle is not affected. The writer ended the letter with the Christian greeting, **Grace be with all of you** (v. 25). Only believers can appreciate the wonderful gift of grace that God gives to all those who believe in Him and recognize His superiority as the great prophet, priest, and king. The first chapter of this beautiful epistle declared that God had spoken in various ways in the past, but now He has spoken through His Son, Jesus. May you heed the words He has spoken through His inspired word and by so doing live lives that are faithful to Him.

Bibliography

*Greenlee, J. Harold. *An Exegetical Summary of Hebrews.* Dallas: Summer Institute of Linguistics, 1998.

Guthrie, Donald. *Hebrews.* Tyndale New Testament Commentaries. Grand Rapids: William B. Eerdmans Publishing Company, 1999.

Hobbs, Herschel H. *Hebrews: Challenges to Bold Discipleship.* Nashville: Broadman Press, 1971.

Hughes, Philip Edgcumbe. *A Commentary on the Epistle to the Hebrews.* Grand Rapids: William B. Eerdmans Publishing Company, 1977.

Lane, William. *Call to Commitment: Responding to the Message of Hebrews.* Nashville: Thomas Nelson Publishers, 1985.

*Lane, William L. *Hebrews.* Word Biblical Commentary, vols. 47A and 47B. Dallas: Word Books Publisher, 1991.

MacArthur, John. *Hebrews.* The MacArthur New Testament Commentary Series. Chicago: Moody Press, 1983.

Morris, Leon. *Hebrews.* The Expositor's Bible Commentary, vol. 12. Grand Rapids: Zondervan Publishing House, 1981.

Sacks, Stuart. *Hebrews through a Hebrew's Eyes: Hope in the Midst of a Hopeless World.* Baltimore: Lederer Messianic Publishers, 1995.

Wiersbe, Warren. *Be Confident.* Wheaton: Victor Books, 1982.

*For advanced study

Notes

1 Donald Guthrie, *Hebrews*, Tyndale New Testament Commentaries (Grand Rapids: William B. Eerdmans Publishing Company, 1999), 203.
2 Dorothy Kelley Patterson and Rhonda Harrington Kelley, eds., *The Woman's Study Bible* (Nashville: Thomas Nelson, 1995), 2071.

JAMES

Introduction

The Greek heading "*Iakōbos*" identifies this epistle. *Iakōbos* is the Greek form of the Hebrew *Iakōb* or Jacob and was a common name among the Jews.

Setting

James wrote the letter in order to strengthen and encourage the faith of Jewish Christians who were being persecuted and oppressed. He primarily addressed social and ethical aspects of the gospel instead of purely doctrinal matters because he knew that the believers were struggling with questions of how their faith should impact their daily lives. James encouraged his readers to display love, Christlike attitudes and speech, and perseverance during trials.

Genre

The letter from James is the first of seven denominated as "General" or "Catholic" Epistles (terms first used by the historian Eusebius). Also included in this grouping are 1 and 2 Peter, Jude, and 1, 2, and 3 John. The term "catholic" (Gk. *katholikos*, "general, universal") refers to the fact that these seven epistles were not addressed to any particular church and thus meant to be distributed to a number of churches. A unique feature of this letter is its format as a collection of brief sermons and ethical teachings rather than just a letter. It has been called "the Proverbs of the New Testament."

Author

James, the brother of the Lord (Mt 13:55), is the author of this book; however, he did not mention this familial relationship in the epistle. His authorship has been disputed because four men bearing the name of James are mentioned in the New Testament. James, Jesus' brother, was bitterly opposed to the Lord during Jesus' earthly ministry, but he was converted by a special and private interview with Jesus following His resurrection (1 Co 15:7). He became a man of prayer, emerged as the leader of the Jerusalem Church, and was slain by Jews in AD 62. He claimed as his authority for penning this message his position as "a slave of God and of the Lord Jesus Christ" (1:1).

Date

Since James was martyred in AD 62, this letter must have been written before that date. Some believe James is one of the oldest New Testament books, but specific references to events or dates are not found. However, internal evidence suggests that the letter may have been written before the Jerusalem Council outlined in Acts 15 (Gl 2:1; see also the commentary on the Jerusalem Council in Ac

Four Men Named James	
James, the father of Judas	James was the father of one of the twelve disciples of Jesus, the lesser known Judas, who was a witness to the resurrected Christ and His ascension (see Lk 6:16; Ac 1:13).
James, the son of Alphaeus	James, the son of Alphaeus, was one of the twelve disciples of Jesus, though not as prominent as James, the brother of John. He, too, was a witness to the resurrected Christ and His ascension (see Lk 6:15; Ac 1:13).
James, the brother of John	One of the two sons of Zebedee, to whom Jesus gave the name "sons of thunder," James was one of the Twelve and part of the inner circle of Jesus. He witnessed the transfiguration, offered to call fire down from heaven to consume those who did not receive Jesus, and fell asleep when Jesus asked him to pray in the garden. He was a witness to the resurrected Christ and His ascension. Herod had him put to death with a sword (see Mk 3:17; 14:33-42; Lk 5:10; 9:28,54; Ac 1:13; 12:2).
James, the brother of Jesus	Jesus' brother did not become a follower of Christ during Jesus' three-year ministry but did so after he witnessed the resurrected Christ. In time, James came to play a significant role in the Jerusalem Council, hearing the reports of the missionaries, welcoming Paul, and judging the situation with Gentile believers. He, along with his brother Jude, considered themselves bondservants of Christ (see Jn 7:2-5; Ac 1:14; 12:17; 15:13; 21:18; 1 Co 15:7; Gl 1:19; 2:9,12; Jms 1:1; Jd 1).

15:1-21). Since most scholars date the Jerusalem Council around AD 49, a likely date for James can be determined as predating the council. In addition, if James was written before AD 49, the notion that James wrote his epistle to combat the Pauline view of justification by faith as unfolded in Romans or Galatians would become a moot issue since both letters were probably written after AD 49. However, Paul's preaching of the gospel was well known; and if James wrote his letter after Galatians or Romans, his teaching was not so much combating Paul's teaching as correcting the wrong conclusions of some concerning justification by faith (see commentary on Jms 2:14-26).

Recipients

From its content several things become clear about the people to whom the letter was written. Almost certainly the readers were Jews (Jms 1:1; cp. Gn 49:28; Ex 24:4; Ezk 47:13; Mt 19:28; Ac 26:7; Rv 21:12). James identified himself as a follower of Christ and acknowledged his readers as believers (cp. 1:18; 2:1,7; 5:7). The letter implies that the Jewish believers were mainly poor people who were caught in a situation of considerable social tension. Oppressed by wealthy landlords and hauled into court by rich people who also scorned their Christian faith, the readers were exhorted to be patient and endure these trials to the end. In any case, most agree that the letter was prepared to be circulated among the churches since no single geographical location is identified.

Major Themes

Maligned by Martin Luther as a "strawy epistle," the book of James has often been misunderstood, yet the pivotal theme in James is how faith and works relate to one another. In a pastoral tone and straightforward manner, James instructed Christians in practical ways of living out their faith. Once a person accepts Christ as Lord and Savior, the indwelling Holy Spirit should bring a noticeable difference into her life. However, some people mistakenly believe that one can trust Christ for salvation and yet continue to live like an unbeliever. James was trying to combat this thinking by saying that if Christ does come into your life, then you will act differently. Your lifestyle will reflect and give evidence of the life of the One who lives within you.

Other key themes addressed in James include these:

- trials and temptations,
- the power of speech,
- wisdom, and
- the relationship between the poor and the rich.

> *Your lifestyle will reflect and give evidence of the life of the One who lives within you.*

Pronunciation Guide

| Dispersion | *diss PUHR zhuhn* | Rahab | *RAY hab* |

Outline[1]

I. ADDRESS AND SALUTATION (1:1)

II. TRIALS AND CHRISTIAN MATURITY (1:2-18)
   A. The Purpose of Trials (1:2-4)
   B. Wisdom, Prayer, and Faith (1:5-8)
   C. A Word Regarding Poverty and Wealth (1:9-11)
   D. The Source of Trials and Temptations (1:12-18)

III. TRUE CHRISTIANITY AS SEEN IN ITS WORKS (1:19–2:26)
   A. An Exhortation Regarding Speech and Anger (1:19-21)
   B. Doers of the Word (1:22-27)
   C. Impartiality and the Law of Love (2:1-13)
   D. Faith That Saves (2:14-26)

IV. DISSENSIONS WITHIN THE COMMUNITY (3:1–4:12)
   A. A Warning About the Uncontrolled Tongue (3:1-12)
   B. An Explanation of True Wisdom (3:13-18)
   C. A Condemnation of Evil Passions (4:1-3)
   D. A Summons to Repentance (4:4-10)
   E. A Prohibition of Critical Speech (4:11-12)

V. IMPLICATIONS OF A CHRISTIAN WORLDVIEW (4:13–5:11)
   A. A Condemnation of Arrogance (4:13-17)
   B. A Condemnation of Those Who Misuse Wealth (5:1-6)
   C. An Encouragement to Endure Patiently (5:7-11)

VI. CONCLUDING EXHORTATIONS (5:12-20)
   A. Oaths (5:12)
   B. Prayer and Healing (5:13-18)
   C. A Closing Summons to Action (5:19-20)

Exposition of the Text

ADDRESS AND SALUTATION (1:1)

1:1 The author of the letter introduced himself as **James**, and the simplicity of the identification points to the well-known "James the Just," the half-brother of the Lord (see Mt 13:55; Mk 6:3). James did not claim apostolic authority, although Paul called him an apostle in Galatians 1:19. Rather, James chose to characterize himself simply as **a slave of God and of the Lord Jesus Christ**. By calling himself a "slave" (Gk. *doulos,* "servant, slave, bondservant"), James showed that he considered his position to be one of humble service to his master, the Lord Jesus. He identified the recipients of the letter as **the 12 tribes in the Dispersion**. DISPERSION (Gk. *diaspora,* "scattering") indicates those who are exiles in a foreign country; this word became the technical name for the Jewish community living outside of Palestine. However, in 1 Peter the term "dispersion" is used to refer to Christians on earth who are temporarily exiled from their heavenly home (1 Pt 1:1). Linking "dispersion" with "12 tribes," though, almost certainly indicates that James was addressing Jewish Christians and not all Christians.

TRIALS AND CHRISTIAN MATURITY (1:2-18)

The Purpose of Trials (1:2-4)

1:2-4 James opened the body of his letter by addressing his readers as **brothers**, a term he used 14 times, often to introduce a new section. This affectionate address set a strong pastoral tone for the many exhortations of the letter. Then, James issued a command: **Consider it a great joy**. The command is categorical, suggesting the need for a definitive decision to take up a joyful attitude. Believers should react with joy when faced with **various trials** (Gk. *peirasmois,* "tests, testings") because these outward circumstances—whether suffering, troubles, or conflicts—are the means through which God works in believers to prove a perfect faith or build **endurance** (Gk. *hupomonēn,* in the sense of a staying power that surpasses simply hanging in there through afflictions to include a determination to work through difficulties with purpose and focus) in the believer. The **testing of your faith** was not a means of affliction and destruction but rather a way to refine and purify. Abraham's faith was tested in this way (cp. Gn 22:1-8). The believer is asked to respond to trials with joy, then, because she knows that trials are tools working to produce a deeper, stronger, more certain faith. The goal specified, "that you may be MATURE (Gk. *teleioi,* "perfect, complete," in the sense of the completion of a process, an Old Testament idea that defines perfection as a right relationship with God, unstained by worldly pursuits) and COMPLETE" (Gk. *holoklēroi,* "whole, sound complete, blameless") is something for which the Christian is to strive constantly, with all her power, even though she will not in fact attain that goal until she sees her Savior in heaven. Only then will Christians be **lacking nothing**. Although God does allow testing through "trials" in the lives of believers, He cannot by His own nature and character test with the intent toward evil (v. 13). On the other hand, Satan does tempt to do evil, and believers may fall into evil because of their own fallen natures (Eph 2:1-3). INDECISIVE

(Gk. *dipsuchos*, "double-minded, hesitating," lit. "two souls") describes one who is divided and has one part of her set on God and the other on the world (Mt 6:24).

Wisdom, Prayer, and Faith (1:5-8)

1:5-8 One of the most important virtues a Christian may lack is **WISDOM** (Gk. *sophias*, "knowledge, wisdom"). This term can refer to prudence (Col 4:5), skill (1 Co 1:17), human knowledge or philosophy (1 Co 1:19), divine wisdom (Rm 11:33), and even Christian enlightenment (Col 1:9). The idea is more than a temporary solving of difficulties or problems and includes learning and profiting through the challenging experience (v. 5). It is this last nuance of meaning to which James referred in this context, and Christian enlightenment only comes through the work of God in a believer's life since He is the source and giver of wisdom. In promising his readers that God will give wisdom to those who ask, James reflected Old Testament teaching (Pr 2:6a). He probably had in mind Jesus' promise: "Keep asking, and it will be given to you" (Mt 7:7a). And, like Jesus, James based his confidence in God's response on the character of God because He **gives to all generously and without criticizing**.

Heart to Heart:
Wisdom Is Knowing When to Ask for Help

God delights to answer your prayers; He encourages His children to seek Him. When you are faced with a situation that you do not know how to handle, turn to God. He will give you wisdom. Unfortunately, when they are faced with difficult circumstances, many women turn to friends, family members, co-workers, or even worldly distractions to take their minds off their problems. God wants to be your first oasis; He desires to meet your needs and for you to want Him to do so. Just like a husband or father who delights to care for his wife or children, God, your heavenly Father, eagerly waits for you to seek Him.

When James exhorted his readers to "ask in faith without doubting" (v. 6), many women may think, "That is a lot easier said than done!" Even though God is so faithful to meet your needs, there are times when the circumstances of life are just overwhelming, and it is easy to lose sight of God. Like Peter when he tried to walk on the water, Christians sometimes focus on the storms instead of the Savior. James used a metaphor to illustrate that when a person lacks faith, she, like the surf of the sea, will be "driven and tossed by the wind." God has navigated every storm you will face, and He waits to give you the wisdom to help overcome each one. Trust your Savior and seek Him first. Who else could guide you better?

A Word Regarding Poverty and Wealth (1:9-11)

1:9-11 When approaching verses 9-11, the crucial question lies in the identity of **the one who is rich**—is he a believer or an unbeliever? Unfortunately, the answer cannot be easily surmised. Commentators tend to be evenly divided over this issue, and authors differ on the basis for their respective conclusions, depending on the weight you give to syntactical arguments, lexical appeals, structural considerations, and contextual evidence.

Other passages in James where the "rich" are mentioned clearly seem to indicate that the rich are unbelievers (see 2:1-6; 5:1-6). James presented the rich in these two later passages as "wicked oppressors of the people of God." Nevertheless, "rich" is not analogous to the "wicked" in the Bible; in the Old and New Testament, rich people are seen as fallible but also capable of entering into a genuine relationship with the Lord. The word "rich" (Gk. *plousios*, "wealthy") in itself does not settle the matter of the spiritual status of the person James addresses. Perhaps the balance of evidence points toward this person's being a believer who is warned not to think too highly of his wealth and who is encouraged to identify with the humility Jesus suffered on the path of redemption. In fact, James may be making the case that poverty *and* wealth are the greatest tests for a Christian.

The contrast James set up between the status of the poor in contrast to the rich within the Christian community can be seen as an allusion to the sayings of Jesus, who stated that all who exalt themselves will be humbled and all who humble themselves will be exalted (Mt 23:12; Lk 14:11; 18:14).

On the other hand, some identify the rich person to be an unbeliever, holding that the "rich" in James always refers to someone outside the believing commu-nity. According to this interpretation, James used the term *plousios* specifically to refer to unbelievers and referred to wealthier members of the Christian com-munity by describing them but never call-ing them rich (Jms 2:2 or 4:13). However, the context seems to support the contrast as applicable to believers. James was well aware of the human tendency to trust in possessions. For that reason he empha-sized the dangers inherent in having riches or wealth and used imagery to underscore the transiency of physical things—the allusion to the flowers and grasses of Israel, which began to bloom and grow in February but disappeared before the summer's heat and drought (Is 40:6-8; cp. Ps 102:4,11). The ultimate les-son for the man with an abundance of pos-sessions would be to rejoice even in trial because they teach him that life is short and transitory in nature and any loss of material things ought to drive him closer to the Lord. Whether poor or rich matters not; what is important is how you relate to the Lord who provides for all spiritual riches. Someone has described trials and difficulties as "equalizers," which drive every child of God—rich or poor—to the bosom of the Father (cp. Heb 4:16).

The Source of Trials and Temptations (1:12-18)

1:12-18 James returned to the theme of **trials** (v. 12). The relationship of this verse to the earlier paragraph (vv. 2-4) is obvious from the verbal resemblances between them. The word "trials" occurs in both places, **test** in verse 12 picks up the "testing "of verse 3 and the word **endures** in verse 12 is simply the verbal form of the word translated "steadfastness" in verses 3 and 4. A reward, **the crown of life**, is promised to the Christian who suc-cessfully meets the test. There are those who react against the notion of a reward for faithful Christian living. And, indeed, service to God that is motivated by a calculated desire for reward is the very antithesis of Christian commitment. But the New Testament consistently invites the believer to contemplate the inheritance awaiting her.

James then made several important points regarding trials and temptations:

- **God is not tempted by evil** (v. 13; cp. Dt 32:4; Jb 34:10).

- God does not **tempt anyone** (Jms 1:13).

- The source of temptations is in a person's **own evil desires** (v. 14).

- Giving in to desires leads to **sin** and **death** (v. 15; cp. Rm 6:21-23; 8:6).

DRAWN AWAY (Gk. *exelkomenos*, "drag away, lure away," a hunting term used to describe a trap designed to lure and catch an unsuspecting animal) and ENTICED (Gk. *deleazomenos*, "lure," a term suggesting luring pray from safety to capture and even death) add intensity to the desires that pull toward sin. No one sins without questioning the wisdom of God and choosing to turn away from God's word. Sin is attractive and addictive (v. 14). DESIRE (Gk. *epithumia*, lit. "hot after") or lust, although long associated exclusively with evil and especially sexual promiscuity, is not bad in itself but simply describes a strong, deep-seated desire or longing for anything—good or bad. However, when that desire grows out of control and becomes a governing habit, the bent toward sinning takes charge. Clearly the fault for inappropriate "desires" rests entirely with the individual. God cannot be blamed. The human desire becomes so overwhelming that you overlook or ignore the trap until there is no turning back. FULLY GROWN (Gk. *apotelestheisa*, "finish, complete, perform") acknowledges completion of a goal—in this case, sin has reached its height and engulfed the sinner. So by enduring trials (vv. 2-4), a Christian has the opportunity to become more mature and complete in her walk with God; on the other hand, giving into trials and temptations only leads to sin and death.

TRUE CHRISTIANITY AS SEEN IN ITS WORKS (1:19–2:26)

An Exhortation Regarding Speech and Anger (1:19-21)

1:19-21 James' brief admonition to avoid hasty speech and uncontrolled anger was introduced with his familiar address, **my dearly loved brothers**. The prohibition of unrestrained **anger** is based on the fact that anger **does not accomplish God's righteousness**. James apparently used "righteousness" and the cognate verb "justify" with the general meaning of the righteous status that God confers on believers.

Doers of the Word (1:22-27)

1:22-27 Those who fail to do the word, who are **hearers only**, are guilty of a dangerous and potentially fatal self-delusion. If the gospel, by nature, contains both saving power and summons to obedience, those who neglect obedience have not truly embraced the gospel. Thus James can say that people who only hear the word are **deceiving** themselves. They think that they have a relationship with God because they regularly attend church, go to Bible studies or read the Bible. But if their listening is not accompanied by obedience, their true situation before God is far different. "Obedience," says Calvin, "is the mother of the true knowledge of God."

Orphans and widows were among the most vulnerable in society. They needed protection and provision (cp. Ezk 22:7). **Pure and undefiled religion** was not based on knee-jerk relief but on compassionate care and provision (Jms 1:27).

Impartiality and the Law of Love (2:1-13)

2:1-13 In this section, James signaled a change of subject by addressing **my brothers** and then decried the sin of **favoritism**. FAVORITISM (Gk. *prosōpolēmpsiais*, "partiality, receiving one's face,") comes from two Greek words *prosōpon*, "face," and *lambanein*, "to take or hold." This word is a form of the Hebrew idiom *panim nasa*, "to lift up the face of a person" and so in turn to be partial to that person (cp. Rm 2:11; Col 3:25; Eph 6:9). James used a hypothetical situation to illustrate his point; he described a person who discriminates against a person just because he is **dressed in dirty clothes** instead of **fine clothes** (Jms 2:2-4). This type of conduct should not characterize a believer; however, there are many ways today that believers show the sin of favoritism:

- belonging to cliques;
- classifying people depending on their economic status;
- showing callousness or hardness of heart to those who are in need;
- comparing people; and
- trying to control people because you think you are better or smarter than they are.

Consider the example of Christ who did not view people in terms of what they could do for Him. He saw people through the eyes of their potential and through the eyes of eternity, knowing that what mattered most was whether or not they had a relationship with Him. James reminded his readers of the Lord's **royal** (Gk. *basilikon*) **law** (Gk. *nomom*), the law of love, the command to **love your neighbor as yourself** (v. 9; cp. 1:25; Lv 19:18; Mt

22:39). This designation, based on Leviticus 19:18, may be so named because

- the "law" came from God, the King of kings; or
- this law is the highest authority governing human relationships.

The second reasoning seems more appropriate. This law is superior to all others. When you consider others' needs first and love them, you are obeying the highest authority, and in the process you also combat the sin of favoritism. God affirms and defines obedience (v. 10). There is no option for selective obedience—choosing what part of the law is pleasing to you and worthy of your doing. James declares the whole law to be from God, and disobedience of any part defies God.

Faith That Saves (2:14-26)

Does the Bible contradict itself? Absolutely not! However, one must admit that at first glance James 2:21 may appear to contradict Paul's statement in Romans 4:3. Was Abraham justified because he believed God, as Romans indicates, or did works, as James states, justify him? In order to answer this question, a person must understand the terminology of faith, works, and justification as used by Paul and James. One commentator astutely observed, "James uses Paul's vocabulary, but not his dictionary."[2]

2:14-26 These verses are not in isolation but are woven into a book with a definite message and within a precise contextual background. The heartbeat of James' letter is the concept of true religion. Those addressed are admonished to live so that their "confession" (lifestyle) matches their profession of faith (their words of commitment). The themes of hearing and doing (1:19-26; 3:12-18) and the interaction between partiality and observing the law, in which showing partiality contradicts a person's claim to faith (2:1-13), culminate in 2:14-26 where James insists that faith and works are completely inseparable. To rephrase this concept in a contemporary understanding: James felt that a person's walk must match his or her talk; if it did not, the talk was false.

James 2:14-26 is often viewed as a form of Hellenistic diatribe in which James set up a proposition (faith without works cannot save, v. 14), gave rationale or proof for the proposition (vv. 15-16), confirmed the proposition through use of an imaginary opponent (vv. 17-19), and amplified the truth of the proposition through use of examples (vv. 20-26). The terms **faith** (Gk. *pistin*, "belief, firm persuasion") and **works** (Gk. *erga*, "anything done or to be done, action") are introduced (vv. 14-16). In verse 14 James stated his proposition by asking a question that demanded a negative response. Is faith that produces no works saving faith? No! Perhaps to translate *erga* as "deeds" instead of works will avoid confusion with Paul's use of the same word. James used *erga* to refer to acts of mercy and help for the poor and oppressed. This concept is not some abstract—in James' thought, "works" or deeds are primary in the sense that they are the only way to validate that your faith is real.

Faith is a God-given trust in God—effected within the individual's heart by God. Ultimately faith is vertical, linking you to God. On the other hand, works are outward manifestations of a right relationship with God expressed in horizontal relationships you have with others. Certainly service to God (the essence of your faith) cannot be separated from what you do for others in His name. Especially is this principle true when placed before the backdrop of obedience to Christ, which has always meant putting feet to or acting upon your faith.

Faith must be understood in relation to a person's deeds, and James was concerned with attacking a false understanding of faith. He used faith in two ways in his letter:

- to refer to true faith (1:3,6; 2:1,5; 5:15) and

- to refer to a "claimed" faith that is false.

Clearly this second meaning of faith is addressed in 2:14-26; James used faith in these verses to refer to a sanctimonious emotion or an intellectual acceptance of doctrine. This kind of faith is dead and gives no evidence of genuine salvation. In verse 18 James introduces an imaginary interlocutor, and much has been written about the identity of this opponent. However, in Hellenistic diatribe, the author often introduced an imaginary opponent to prove a point. The point of this interlocutor is to stress the necessary outcome of faith and the ridiculousness of true, saving faith existing as an inward commitment without any outward manifestation. **The demons** have faith (v. 19), but their faith is not the faith that saves anyone.

James then made the statement that sparked the controversy over understanding how Abraham was **justified** (v. 21). Both James and Paul quoted Genesis 15:6; however, James expressed his conclusion saying that Abraham was justified by works. The confusion can be cleared through understanding the meaning of justification as expressed by Paul and James. James stated that Abraham was "justified" or made righteous **by works**. Why is "works" in verse 21 plural when he cited the "deed" or "work" of sacrificing Isaac on the altar? Abraham's offering of Isaac acts as a synecdoche (a figure of speech in which the part represents the whole) to refer to all of Abraham's deeds—his deeds of hospitality when he entertained the three strangers and other instances in which he bore testimony to his faith. So, by implication, James stressed the deeds during Abraham's lifespan as evidence of his complete trust in God. Genuine faith will produce works, and works complete faith. Abraham demonstrated his faith by his work of obedience. James used the word "justified" in the sense of proving—you prove or testify to others of your genuine faith through acts of obedience.

Paul and James expressed themselves using the same vocabulary in different ways. In this case, each addressed a different aspect of justification, and both together give believers a clear and comprehensive understanding. Paul described the justification that comes at the beginning of a believer's walk in faith; James focused on justification as occurring within a believer's life. Paul gave attention to the importance of justification when a believer initially makes her commitment to Christ. James gave his emphasis to the believer's commitment to faith and the acceptance of its demand for obedience.

> *Faith is the key to salvation; works are the path to obedience and Christian living.*

Paul never used "faith" to refer to a mental agreement or intellectual assent without implications on a person's behavior as James did when he referred to the belief of demons. Faith, for Paul, is the response of someone who has accepted Jesus as Lord; James saw two kinds of faith: genuine faith, which is lived out with deeds, and false faith. In the same manner, "works" in Paul's writings are understood as acts someone would perform in order to earn God's initial acceptance or approval; whereas James saw "works" as the byproduct of a changed life, such as the rendering of mercy or kindness. Paul expressed this concept of the products of a changed life most often with the metaphor of "fruit" in a believer's life. Both Paul and James saw the importance of "fruit" or "deeds" in a believer's life—they just stressed the importance of this ingredient in different ways. You might consider Paul as pushing the need for "preconversion work" in the sense of relying on Christ alone for salvation, while James was caught up in the necessity of "postconversion works" or giving evidence to the faith embraced. To attempt to separate faith and works is **foolish** (v. 20). Faith and works are inextricably linked in God's plan. They have never been enemies but are partners. Faith is the key to salvation; works are the path to obedience and Christian living.

DISSENSIONS WITHIN THE COMMUNITY (3:1–4:12)

A Warning About the Uncontrolled Tongue (3:1-12)

3:1-12 Again, James signaled a change of subject by addressing **my brothers** (v. 1) and turned his attention to the destructive nature of the **tongue**. James used three metaphors (**horses** and **bits**, **ships** and **rudder**, and **a small fire** and **a forest**, vv. 3-5) to illustrate the powerful force of the tongue before moving to the heart of his warning against uncontrolled speech (v. 6).

At first glance, verse 6 appears to suggest a simple straightforward meaning; however, while the general meaning is not hard to grasp, the detailed parts of the verse are difficult and complex. Within the first part of this verse, there are five nominative expressions with one indicative verb, and the obscure yet poetical nature of the verse must be taken into account when seeking to understand the meaning of James' words. James used these nominative expressions to explain the destructive nature of the tongue:

- **The tongue is a fire**. This image would have been very familiar to the Jews, for several texts in the Old Testament speak of the lips or the tongue being like a scorching fire (v. 5; see Ps 120:4; Pr 16:27; 26:18-22).

- **The tongue, a world of unrighteousness**. The reading found in the Peshitta states, "the tongue is a fire, the world of unrighteousness is a wood." While the Peshitta may be seen as a paraphrase instead of a translation of James' words, it gives an allegorical understanding of the wicked world; however, what does this phrase mean? "World" (Gk. *kosmos*) always has a negative connotation in James' epistle (Jms 3:6; see 1:27; 2:5; 4:4), referring to the ordered world or the sinful world. Perhaps the "tongue" was considered representative of the world because this tiny member of the body is the means by which you communicate with others. If that is the case, the tongue becomes the primary conduit for temptation from person to person. If this understanding is true, by implication, the tongue can lead to demonstrations of wickedness throughout the world.

- **It pollutes the whole body**. The participle "pollutes" (Gk. *spilousa*, "stain or defile") should be understood in a symbolic sense of "spiritual and moral corruption" (v. 6; see Jd 23). Indeed the tongue can defile the whole body because this tiny organ so necessary in speech can be the primary means of expressing hostility to God and leading others to do the same.

- **And is set on fire by hell**. The final phrase contains a word that occurs only 12 times in the Greek New Testament (v. 6). HELL (Gk. *geennēs*, "the valley of Hinnon, hell, Gehenna") or Gehenna is found 11 times in the Synoptic Gospels (all in the words of Jesus); the only other occurrence is here in James. The word is derived from the valley called "the Valley of the Sons of Hinnom," which was a ravine south of Jerusalem once used for pagan fire sacrifices (see 2 Kg 23:10; Jr 7:31). This valley was also described as being used as a garbage dump where trash was burned and fires were going continually, an idea which can be traced to Rabbi David Kimhi's commentary on Psalm 27:13. This valley eventually became linked to the idea of punishment for the wicked, and by New Testament times it was synonymous with the concept of hell. The unique feature of James' use of *Gehenna* is that he linked the potential evil of the tongue to hell, perhaps because of the irreparable damage done by evil speaking.

The main point cannot be missed—the tongue can be the source of wickedness that affects the entire course of a person's life. Evil speaking cannot be tolerated within a true child of God.

> *Evil speaking cannot be tolerated within a true child of God.*

An Explanation of True Wisdom (3:13-18)

3:13-18 What gives this section and the next its unity is the problem of **envy** (3:14,16; 4:2) and the related ideas of **selfish ambition**, selfish desires and arrogance. This sinful attitude is set in contrast to **the wisdom from above** (v. 17), describing the effects of this attitude as **disorder and every kind of evil** (v. 16). The whole section is reminiscent of, and perhaps modeled after, a popular Hellenistic-Jewish moral tradition that traced social ills back to jealousy and envy. Particularly close to James' teaching are some sections of *The Testaments of the Twelve Patriarchs,* a Jewish pseudepigraphal work, most of which was written around 100 BC. In this book, slander, violence, and murder are all connected to jealousy—and these are topics treated by James. Moreover, the problem of double-mindedness is frequently mentioned in the Testaments, striking another familiar chord for the reader of James. Since James directed his letter to Jewish Christians, likely he used concepts familiar to them to drive home his ethical teachings.

A Condemnation of Evil Passions (4:1-3)

4:1-3 James uses a question to introduce his next topic (v. 10), which arises naturally from the preceding discussion. James suggested a connection between "envy" and "selfish ambition" and "disorder," and he specified more clearly what he meant by "disorder," portraying its production by "envy" and other desires. How tragic that the Christian church has so often been characterized by bitter controversies. Some battles are worth fighting to be sure; but even then they must be fought without sacrificing Christian principles and virtues. James' specific reference to **the wars and the fights** is unclear. However, he seemed to be bothered more by selfish spirits and bitterness in quarreling than by the right and wrong of the various viewpoints.

A Summons to Repentance (4:4-10)

4:4-10 James concluded his series of commands with a summarizing exhortation, **Humble yourselves,** reflecting the promise found in Proverbs 3:34—**God . . . gives grace to the humble**. To humble yourself before the Lord means to recognize your desperate need of God's help and to submit to His will for all your life. This humility is beautifully exemplified in the tax-collector of Jesus' parable, who, deeply conscious of his sin, called out to God for mercy. In response, Jesus pronounced him "justified," and said, "Everyone who exalts himself will be humbled, but the one who humbles himself will be exalted" (Lk 18:14).

This saying was taken up as a popular motto in the early church expressing this fundamentally important principle that the enjoyment of spiritual vitality and victory comes not through independent efforts of your own but through complete dependence on the Lord. To try to exalt yourself by relying on your own abilities or status or money brings only failure and condemnation—God humbles His children. James expressed this principle earlier in his letter when he encouraged the poor Christian to boast in his humiliation.

A Prohibition of Critical Speech (4:11-12)

4:11-12 The connection between this section and its context is not immediately clear. It may be that speaking evil of others is to be seen as a manifestation of pride God resists, which is to be avoided by humility before God (4:10). On the other hand, speaking evil is often linked to jealousy (2 Co 12:20), selfishness, quarrels, and pride; it is also seen as a manifestation of double-mindedness. Finally, the prominence of law and judging in verses 11 and 12 corresponds to the theme of 2:8-13. Just as Leviticus 19:18 was quoted, James might have had in mind Leviticus 19:16, which prohibits slander; the shift from **brother** to **neighbor** in verse 12 makes this interpretation especially plausible. These several possibilities suggest that verses 11-12 should basically be seen as an independent section that picks up a number of James' favorite themes. But the prominence of the tradition that links "speaking evil" to the sins of jealousy, quarreling, and pride—which have been the focus of 3:13–4:10—suggests that these topics belong generally to this larger discussion. Perhaps verses 11-12 should be seen as a brief reprise of the larger discussion of sins of speech, which opened the section (3:1-12).

IMPLICATIONS OF A CHRISTIAN WORLDVIEW (4:13–5:11)

A Condemnation of Arrogance (4:13-17)

4:13-17 This section singles out arrogance or worldliness; however, while the attitude of those who presume to stand in judgment of others may be labeled arrogant, James did not highlight this. The identical introductions to 4:13-17 and 5:1-6 strongly suggest that James saw them as closely linked. Moreover, these sections are associated also by the theme of wealth. To be sure, those described in 4:13-17 are not explicitly said to be rich, but the extensive travel plans mentioned in verse 13 imply that they were well-off and that their intention was to get gain. Those who leave God and His values out of their way of life are criticized (4:13-17; 5:1-6). They are warned about the sin of omission or neglecting to do what is right. Indeed, you sin when you know what is right and choose not to do it (cp. Lk 16:19-31). However, while the rich in 5:1-6 are unreservedly condemned, the businessmen in 4:13-17 are exhorted to

change their boastful attitudes. James criticized, not their wealth, but rather their boastful arrogance, suggesting that the businessmen addressed in this paragraph are probably Christians. However, James' failure to address them as brethren and the lack of overtly Christian presuppositions suggests that he might also have had in mind people outside the church.

A Condemnation of Those Who Misuse Wealth (5:1-6)

5:1-6 This section, as well as 4:13-17, is introduced with the imperative. Both sections address and condemn a pursuit of wealth that disregards God and His purposes in history. The rebuke is so strong that at first glance the words seem to be directed to those outside the church. However, James's use of the second person seems more likely to suggest that he was still addressing those in the church or associated with the body of believers in some way. These straightforward words, however, could fall upon the ears of some in the church who claimed to be believers but who had not been genuinely saved. James condemned any employer who treated his employees unjustly (cp. Is 3:14-15; 10:2) just as he promised judgment on all who oppressed the poor. The rich people pictured are clearly wealthy landowners, a class accused of economic exploitation and oppression from early times. In James' surroundings, one may think particularly of Palestinian Jewish landlords, who owned large estates and were often concerned only about how much profit could be gained from their lands. James proceeded to announce the condemnation of these rich landholders and justified their condemnation on the grounds of their selfish hoarding of wealth (Jms 5:2-3), their defrauding of their workers, their self-indulgent lifestyle, and their oppression of the righteous.

James preached this message of denunciation to the church, knowing that non-Christians would also hear and be convicted. James also reminded the faithful that they, hearing of the miserable end of the rich, might not envy their fortune. Also knowing that God would be the avenger of the wrongs they suffered, with a calm and resigned mind they might bear them.

An Encouragement to Endure Patiently (5:7-11)

5:7-11 Psalm 37 is a marvelous song of encouragement directed to the righteous. They are described as afflicted and needy (Ps 37:14) and as suffering persecution at the hand of the wicked (Ps 37:12-15, 32-33). They are tempted to be envious of the prosperity and well-being of the wicked (Ps 37:1,7) and, somewhat paradoxically, also to be impatient for the wicked to receive judgment. In this situation, the psalmist encouraged the righteous to be silent before the Lord (Ps 37:7); to refrain from anger (Ps 37:8), for God will certainly vindicate the righteous people, mainly poor, who were suffering from similar circumstances. James' advice was the same as what the psalmist offered: **be patient until the Lord's coming** (Jms 5:7), when the wicked will be judged and the righteous delivered.

CONCLUDING EXHORTATIONS (5:12-20)

Oaths (5:12)

5:12 Although this verse stands essentially on its own, the introductory statement **Now, above all** (Gk. *pro pantōn de*) does appear to suggest some connection with the previous context. Certainly James cannot mean that taking oaths is a worse sin than others he mentioned in the epistle. The swearing that James prohibits is not dirty language as such but the

invoking of God's name, or substitutes for His name, to guarantee the truth of what you say. In the Old Testament, God is frequently presented as guaranteeing the fulfillment of His promises with an oath. The law does not prohibit oaths but demands that a person be true to any oath he has sworn. Concern about the devaluation of oaths because of their indiscriminate use and the tendency to try to avoid fulfilling them by swearing by less sacred things led to warnings against using them too often. Jesus apparently went even further, when He commanded His disciples not to swear at all (Mt 5:34).

Prayer and Healing (5:13-18)

5:13-18 As James began the concluding section of his epistle, he took a decidedly pastoral tone and addressed the subject of pastoral and community prayer. The tricky part of these verses occurs when the issue of healing is discussed: Does James intend his readers to understand the healing that occurs after a person receives prayer and/or anointing with oil to be a physical or spiritual healing? Or, was James intentionally ambiguous so as to allow both understandings?

Verses 13-16 open with a series of rapid-fire questions followed by third person imperatives, which are commonly used in diatribe. The third question asked in verse 14 states, **Is anyone among you sick? He should call for the elders of the church** . . . and these elders are to pray over the sick person and anoint him with oil.

James used the word **SICK** (Gk. *asthenei*), which can mean weakness of any kind, i.e., moral weakness (v. 14; see Rm 4:19; 1 Co 8:7, 11-12). Physical weakness is by far the most common connotation for this word in the New Testament and the best rendering for the word in James 5:14 (see also Mt 10:8; 25:36; Lk 9:2; Jn 4:46; 5:3; Ac

9:37; Php 2:26). This person who is physically sick is to call on the elders[3] or the leaders of his local body of believers to have them pray over him and anoint him with oil. Anointing a person with oil was a Jewish custom, which was portrayed by Herod when he sat in a tub of warm oil to cure his ailments or as in Isa- iah 6:1 where oil is offered as a remedy to soften sores and wounds. The word OIL (Gk. *elaiō*, "olive oil") was used for cooking food, fuel for lamps, various kinds of anointings, and as a treatment for wounds or a means for healing. Two main reasons for anointing a person can be found in the Bible:

Historical Excursus: James 5:14 and Extreme Unction

Understanding how this verse has been used in the history of Christian interpretation in ecclesiastical practices is important. Verse 14 has often been reviewed as an important text concerning the power of prayer in healing and how the forgiveness of sins plays into that equation. The Roman Catholic Church bases its doctrine of "Extreme Unction," the practice of anointing a sick person—likely near death—as an instrument or vehicle of grace, on this verse. It was named as one of the seven sacraments of the Roman Catholic Church in the twelfth century and officially defined at the Council of Trent. The doctrine that developed has no connection to the true meaning of James 5:14. In James it was understood to be used for the remission of sins and spiritual comfort of the dying. The Roman Catholic Church used it in a sacramental and nontherapeutic manner and administered it to help prepare a person for death, not to help restore him to health (whether that be spiritual or physical health). There is no indication in verse 14 that James encouraged believers to anoint sick people strictly to prepare them for death.

- for medicinal or practical purposes or

- for symbolic reasons.

Mark 6:13 is the closest parallel in the New Testament of the anointing with oil of a sick person for the purposes of being physically healed.

Verse 15 includes two words that prove to be difficult because of their seemingly ambiguous nature in the context and the various connotations that can be attached to them. The first word is *sōzei* or SAVE, with a broad range of meanings including saving one from physical death, saving a person from a dangerous situation, freeing someone from disease, keeping something or someone in good condition, and saving someone from eternal death. This last definition of saving someone from eternal death is most commonly used in James (see 1:21; 2:14; 4:12; 5:20), but that does not mean that it cannot mean to free a person from disease in 5:15 since it is used frequently in the Synoptic Gospels and other New Testament books to refer to physical healing (see Mt 9:21-22; Mk 3:4; 5:23; Lk 18:42; Jn 1:12; Ac 4:9; 14:9). The comparison of James' letter to the Gospels, and especially to the words of Jesus, offers support that James would not restrict his understanding of "save" to include only saving from eternal death. The second term is RAISE UP (Gk. *egerei*). Is James' reference to God's raising a person as from the sickbed in the present, or is the reference to an act of God in the eschaton, such as the resurrection of believers? The dual meaning may be confusing, but there is no indication within the context that James is talking about the resurrection of the body during the endtimes, a plausible possibility but not a probable interpretation. The most natural reading would be to interpret the account as a sick man who has been "raised up" from his sickbed.

The end of verse 15 and verse 16 include the mention of sins in regard to the sick person; this fact has led some people to infer that James must be talking about spiritual healing. However, this leap should not be made too quickly. Sin can be a factor in illness; yet sickness is not the same thing as sin. Nor did James suggest that sickness is derived from sin. But sickness is *analogous* to sin in its social effects. Therefore, the healing of the sick person and the healing of the community must take into account the spiritual dimensions of this threat. For this reason, James encouraged believers to confess their sins to one another. Confession is offered as a help to the believer and a way to gain spiritual wholeness. The encouragement of corporate confession and prayer also showed that prayer for the sick did not have to be done by the elders alone, for it is a corporate responsibility. Sickness was seen as an opportunity to minister to the physical needs of other members of the body instead of as a reason to exclude someone from the body.

What relevance does this text have for believers today? Since James seems to be talking about physical healing, should this practice continue in the church? Is anointing a person with oil a timely manifestation of a timeless principle that should be at work in the church? Certainly not everybody is healed—Paul was not healed of his thorn in the flesh, and every person will eventually die unless the Lord returns. However, should "anointing a person with oil" still take place? There is no reason why it should not, but the spiritual undertones of this practice should not be ignored. While James did speak of physical healing, believers also experience spiritual healing as they minister one to another. As believers confess their sins to one another, they experience spiritual unity and healing; as spiritual healing takes place, the prayers of these believers will be the most effective in appealing to God to heal a person who is physically sick.

A Closing Summons to Action (5:19-20)

5:19-20 James closed his letter not with the greetings and benediction typical of epistolary endings, but with a summons to action. In this regard, his letter is typical of other more formal New Testament letters, which read almost like sermons (see 1 John especially). For a last time, James addressed his **brothers**. He had spoken to them in his letter about many problems: sinful speech, disobedience, lack of concern about others, worldliness, quarreling, arrogance. Now he encouraged every believer to take the initiative in bringing those who have wandered **from the truth** in any of these ways back into fellowship with God and the community.

Bibliography

*Adamson, James. *The Epistle of James*. The New International Commentary on the New Testament. Grand Rapids: Wm. B. Eerdmans Publishing Company, 1976.

*Johnson, Luke Timothy. *The Letter of James*. The Anchor Bible, vol. 37a. New York: Doubleday, 1995.

Laws, Sophie. *A Commentary on the Epistle of James*. Peabody, MA: Hendrickson Publishers, 1980.

*Martin, Ralph P. *James*. Word Biblical Commentary, vol. 48. Nashville: Thomas Nelson Publishers, 1988.

Moo, Douglas. *James*. The Tyndale New Testament Commentaries, vol. 16. Grand Rapids: Wm. B. Eerdmans, 1985.

Richardson, Kurt. *James*. The New American Commentary, vol. 36. Nashville: Broadman and Holman Publishers, 2002.

Zodhiates, Spiros. *The Labor of Love: An Exposition of James 2:14–4:12*. Grand Rapids: Wm. B. Eerdmans Publishing Company, 1960.

_____. *The Patience of Hope: An Exposition of James 4:13–5:20*. Grand Rapids: Wm. B. Eerdmans Publishing Company, 1960.

_____. *The Work of Faith: An Exposition of James 1:1–2:13*. Grand Rapids: Wm. B. Eerdmans Publishing Company, 1960.

*For advanced study

Notes

[1] Adapted from Douglas Moo, *James,* The Tyndale New Testament Commentaries, vol. 16 (Grand Rapids: Wm. B. Eerdmans Publishing Company, 1985), 56.

[2] Sharyn Dowd, "Faith That Works: James 2:14-26," Review and Expositor 97 (2000): 202.

[3] The Roman Catholic Church at the Council of Trent voted that this word meant a "priest ordained by a bishop"; however, there is no textual warrant for restricting the meaning of *presbuterous* in this way. Rather this word is better understood as a reference to the leaders of a local church.

1 PETER

Introduction

Contemporary evangelical scholarship classifies 1 Peter as one of the "general epistles," along with James, 2 Peter, Jude, and 1, 2, 3 John. In five short chapters, the author covered a variety of topics with a tone that conveyed deep compassion and concern for those to whom he was writing. First Peter was written to believers who were experiencing persecution because of their faith in Jesus Christ. These were men and women who lived in a place in which they were considered "aliens" or "strangers," pilgrims of a pagan culture with practices foreign to them. Peter exhorted these believers to stand strong in their faith by giving glory to God through their Christlike behavior toward those who persecuted them. His warm tone and practical advice make this beloved epistle one that continues to encourage believers to remain steadfast in giving a testimony of their faith.

First Peter is especially helpful to women in that it teaches what biblical submission truly means and how it works. Considering how this biblical quality of womanhood is often misunderstood, for women to grasp its rich meaning and profound implications is particularly important. Peter's letter not only provides clear instructions but also encourages women not to abandon the call of God on their lives as wives, mothers, and daughters of the Lord God.

Title

The Greek heading "*Petrou A*," identifying the text as the first epistle "of Peter," appears on the oldest manuscripts of this letter. On later manuscripts the title is variously amended to include the letter's designation as a "catholic" epistle, to specify "Peter" as "the holy apostle," or to highlight the letter's recipients as Gentiles.

Setting

At least 15 times in this epistle, Peter referred to suffering. Persecution was common to these first-century Christians. Following the death of Jesus during the tremendous growth that marked the early church, believers were often the target of persecution by both Jewish and Roman authorities. This persecution only intensified during the first and second centuries. Peter wrote to provide counsel to believers on how to live in difficult times in such a way that others would be drawn to their witness for Christ. His purpose was to teach them how to live victoriously even in the midst of trials. In doing so, he addressed several important doctrines in this letter, including salvation, the atonement, and baptism.

Genre

First Peter opens with the three-part formula of a typical early Christian letter—the self-identification of the writer, designation of recipients, and the greeting, which features the words "grace and peace" common in other New Testament epistles. The letter also closes with typical greetings addressed to specific people along with the writer's final admonitions. In terms of content and style, the letter is not characterized by a personal tone, and it does not seem to address specific situations or questions particular to certain localized churches. Instead, 1 Peter is a circular or "encyclical" letter addressed predominantly to churches in five Roman provinces in Asia Minor (1:2). First Peter, written from "Babylon" (5:13), is also a *diaspora* letter akin to the Jewish letters written from Jerusalem to the Jewish people dispersed among Assyria, Egypt, and Babylon (see Jr 29:4-23 for an example of this genre). Like other *diaspora* letters addressed specifically to God's chosen people in exile, 1 Peter offered exhortation, encouragement, and hope to Christians, "chosen" by God (1:1), suffering intense persecution as "temporary residents of the Dispersion" (1:1; 2:11).

Author

The author of this small but significant letter was undeniably Peter—he identified himself in the opening verse, "Peter, an apostle of Jesus Christ." He further identified himself at the close of the letter by referring to himself as "a witness to the sufferings of the Messiah" (5:1). Indeed, Peter is known as one of the foremost leaders among the early disciples. His original name in Hebrew was "Simeon," although the New Testament referred to him 49 times as "Simon." Jesus gave him the Aramaic name "Cephas" or "Petros" (Gk., lit. "rock or stone"; Jn 1:42; Mt 16:18).

Peter was the son of Jonah (Mt 16:17) and the older brother of Andrew, who introduced Peter to Jesus (Jn 1:40-42). Peter was raised on the shores of the Sea of Galilee where he acquired the skills of a fisherman. Additionally, Peter was married; his wife apparently traveled with him on many of his missionary journeys (1 Co 9:5). Along with Paul, Peter had a heart for carrying the message of the gospel to "the ends of the earth" (Ac 1:8). The book of Acts links him with Jewish evangelism, as well as mission endeavors among the Samaritans and the Gentiles. As one of the 12 disciples, Peter was also one of three individuals considered closest to Jesus. Christian tradition holds he was martyred in Rome between AD 64 and 67, crucified upside down.

Date

According to most biblical scholarship, 1 Peter was written shortly before Nero began his brutal persecutions in Rome in AD 64. The letter's origin is still debatable as commentators argue whether Peter composed this letter in Babylon on the Euphrates or in Rome. First Peter 5:13 alluded to Peter's location as he sent greetings from the church in Babylon. However, some commentators understand this as a secretive reference to Rome, since the city symbolized the corruption and godlessness that marked Babylon in the Old Testament. Some evidence also indicates that Peter resided in Rome prior to his death. Other commentators prefer the literal reading of the text and argue that indeed Peter wrote from Babylon on the Euphrates. There is historical evidence that a large Jewish population was present in Babylon at that time.

Recipients

First Peter 1:1 clearly addressed the recipients of this letter as "the temporary residents of the Dispersion." This common designation primarily applied to Jews throughout the Roman Empire. Peter mentioned the various regions in his letter, with the intention that his epistle would circulate to these different areas. He wrote to a people who were under tremendous persecution, people who faced the daily challenges of living in a pagan society that was becoming increasingly more hostile to the gospel message.

Major Themes

- The grace (Gk. *charis*, "favor," especially when unmerited) of God (1:2,10,13; 3:7; 4:10; 5:5,10,12) has been expressed in a popular acrostic: God's Riches At Christ's Expense. Nothing is better interwoven with the sufferings of believers than a reminder of the Savior's unique sacrifice.

- Encouragement during suffering (4:12). Peter reminds his readers that they will suffer, and he reminds them of what God provides.

Only when you depend on the immeasurable, matchless grace of God can you glorify Him in times of suffering. The sufferings experienced on earth are overshadowed by the agonies of Christ Himself.

Pronunciation Guide.			
Bithynia	*bih THIN ih uh*	Pontus	*PAHN tuhs*
Cappadocia	*kap uh DOH shih uh*	Silvanus	*sil VAY nuhs*
Galatia	*guh LAY shuh*		

Outline

I. GOD'S GRACE IS THE POWER OF GOD UNTO SALVATION (1:1–2:12)
   - A. Greeting (1:1-2)
   - B. The Blessing of Salvation (1:3-12)
   - C. The Responsibility of Salvation (1:13–2:3)
      1. Holy living (1:13-21)
      2. Love (1:22-25)
      3. Spiritual growth (2:1-3)
   - D. The Chosen Stone and His People (2:4-12)

II. GOD'S GRACE IS THE POWER OF GOD UNTO SUBMISSION (2:13–3:7)
   - A. Submission to Government (2:13-17)
   - B. Submission in the Workplace (2:18-25)
   - C. Submission in the Home (3:1-7)

III. GOD'S GRACE IS THE POWER OF GOD UNTO SUFFERING AND SERVICE (3:8–5:14)
   - A. Principles of Godly Living (3:8-12)
   - B. Suffering for Righteousness' Sake (3:13-22)
   - C. Suffering as Christ Suffered (4:1-6)
   - D. Serving for God's Glory (4:7-11)
   - E. Suffering for God's Glory (4:12-19)
   - F. The Responsibility of Elders (5:1-4)
   - G. Submission to Elders (5:5-7)
   - H. A Final Warning (5:8-11)
   - I. Farewell (5:12-14)

Exposition of the Text

GOD'S GRACE IS THE POWER OF GOD UNTO SALVATION (1:1–2:12)

Greeting (1:1-2)

1:1-2 Peter began the epistle by defining his audience *geographically*. Those described as **temporary residents of the Dispersion** (Gk. *diasporas*) were primarily Jewish believers who were scattered throughout the region due to persecution. Notice the language Peter used to describe them. The term TEMPORARY RESIDENTS (Gk. *parepidēmois*, "foreigners, resident aliens, sojourners") indicates that they were not residing at home. See also 2:11; Heb 11:13. Interestingly, these believers settled in areas mentioned in Acts 2. Peter specified these provinces in verse 1: **Pontus, Galatia, Cappadocia, Asia, and Bithynia** (see the map of the Seven Churches in Revelation, which includes these provinces).

Peter moved from recognizing the believers' geographic location to their *spiritual* position (v. 2). The doctrine of election is reflected in this verse, as Peter recounted God's purposeful act of choosing believers to be called His children. The word FOREKNOWLEDGE (Gk. *prognōsin*, lit., "knowing beforehand, predetermination") highlights an important attribute of God, for it contrasts finite human knowledge with His perfect knowledge of His creation and His desire and ability to rescue all from the penalty of death. The only other nominal usage of this word in the New Testament is in Peter's sermon at Pentecost in Acts 2:23. In Ephesians 1:4, Paul likewise declared that God "chose us

in Him [Christ] before the foundation of the world." The **chosen** (Gk. *eklektois*, "selected, picked out, excellent, elect" 1 Pt 1:1; cp. 2:4,6,9) sojourners are sanctified—**set apart** (Gk. *hagiosmō*, "consecrated, purified, separated out for God's purposes," v. 2; cp. 2 Th 2:13)—**by the Spirit**, because of His Son's death upon the cross.

Furthermore, Peter emphasized that God has chosen us and set us apart **for obedience and for the sprinkling with the blood of Jesus Christ** (v. 2). The call for holiness is at the heart of Peter's greeting. OBEDIENCE (Gk. *hupakōn*) denotes "submission, allegiance." lit., "hearing under," i.e., "hearkening" in the sense of listening and complying with instructions. In the New Testament the word is usually used in close connection with the "gospel" (as in Rm 10:16) or the "faith" (as in Ac 6:7) in the sense of a person's willing reception of Christ as Lord. "Sprinkling with the blood of Jesus Christ" is a reference to the sacrificial atonement of Jesus the Messiah. Exodus 24 recorded the account of Moses' sprinkling the people with blood to demonstrate the covenant between God and man. Hebrews used this same imagery in speaking of Jesus' death (Heb 9:18-22; 12:24). Likewise, believers in Jesus at the point of salvation are ushered into the new covenant with God because of the blood Jesus shed on their behalf. Though the word "Trinity" is not used explicitly here, the concept of the triunity is conveyed strongly by the language Peter used in referring to the Father, Son, and Spirit.

The Blessing of Salvation (1:3-12)

1:3 Peter's focus at the beginning of this letter was on God and all He has done for us, contrasted with the self-pity that often characterizes those troubled by difficult circumstances. As His children you are part of God's creation, but Peter traced this relationship to God not through creation but through Calvary. Believers are in Jesus and He is in God. Peter first praised God for who He is and then for what He has done.

The doctrine of the new birth is explained more fully in verse 3. Peter demonstrated that the **new birth** (Gk. *anagennēsas*, "born again or anew," found only here and in v. 23; cp. similar usage of "born again" in Jn 3:3,7) comes as a result of God's **mercy**. The new birth provides **a living hope**. It is active and vibrant. In the New Testament, "living" also describes water (Jn 4:10), bread (Jn 6:51), sacrifice (Rm 12:1), and God's Word (Heb 4:12). Furthermore, the new birth is accomplished **through the resurrection of Jesus Christ from the dead**. Peter testified that the new birth promises an inheritance to those who have placed their faith in Jesus. Salvation comes through Jesus and provides the assurance that His children will never be separated from His love (cp. Rm 8:26-39).

1:4-5 Peter used specific words to describe the believers' inheritance (v. 4):

- IMPERISHABLE (Gk. *aphtharton*, "incorruptible, immortal") is derived from the verb *phtheirō*, "destroy or corrupt." Jews regarded the temple as "destroyed" when it was defiled or damaged in the slightest way. The adjective *aphtharton* thus describes an inheritance that is in no way subject to decay or corruption, one that cannot perish. In Romans 1:23 and 1 Timothy 1:17, the word described

God as "immortal" in contrast to "mortal man" and animals. See also 1 Peter 1:23 and 3:4.

- UNCORRUPTED (Gk. *amianton*, "undefiled, pure") described the believer's inheritance as "unsoiled, stainless, untainted" (cp. Heb 7:26; 13:4; Jms 1:27).

- UNFADING (Gk. *amaranton*, "dried up or withered, wasted away") appears once, in James 1:11, comparing grass and flowers that have been dried up and destroyed by the sun's heat with the temporality of a rich man consumed by his pursuits. Another form of the adjective also appears in 1 Peter 5:4.

Unlike the things around you (and Peter's original audience), what believers inherit as God's children is not subject to decay and cannot be destroyed or marred; it is permanent and unfading in its purity and beauty, unlike anything in the temporal world. These pilgrims must have been encouraged that an everlasting home was being reserved for them! The word **kept** (Gk. *tetērēmenēn*, "guarded, carefully attended to, took care of, stored away") reinforced the picture of how secure the inheritance is **in heaven**. In God's domain, nothing can damage or diminish what He continually protects and preserves for His own.

Likewise, believers themselves **are being protected by God's power**—the doctrine of eternal security. The verb BEING PROTECTED (Gk. *phrouroumenous*, "being watched over or guarded, protected, held in custody" from a root verb *phroreuō*, "garrison.") is a military term for the protection soldiers would provide against enemy invasion. "God's power" (Gk. *dunamei*, "inherent strength, military might") accessed **through faith** (Gk. *pisteōs*, "continuing trust, maintaining allegiance, fidelity") is impregnable protection for those who enjoy new life and hope as citizens of heaven. Peter began the body of this letter by praising God (1:1) because he was so keenly aware of the eternal, unfading nature of salvation that is not dependent on what an individual accomplishes or fails to accomplish (cp. Gl 4:7; Eph 2:8-9). God's grace expressed and your response to Him in faith initiate your birth into His family. The consummation of a believer's relationship with Christ is set for the future when He returns and believers inhabit the place He has kept for them.

1:6-7 Peter affirmed that believers **rejoice** because of **this** future hope, even in the midst of **trials** (v. 6). REJOICE (Gk. *agalliasthe*, "be overjoyed, be exceedingly glad, exult") also appears in 1:8 and 4:13, echoing the way Jesus' followers were commanded to respond to persecution (Mt 5:12; see also Lk 1:47; 10:21; Jn 5:35; 8:56; Ac 2:26; 16:34; Rv 19:7). Believers can rejoice in the Lord despite the most adverse circumstances, for they are motivated by the promise that their joy ultimately will bring glory to God (1 Pt 1:7).

Peter outlined four important aspects of the "trials" (Gk. *peirasmois*, "tests, ordeals," v. 6) believers face:

- Trials are **various,** practically unlimited in variety (v. 6).

- Trials are temporal, occurring **now for a short time,** only during this earthly life (v. 6; cp. 2 Co 4:17-18).

- Trials are necessary. The phrase YOU HAVE TO BE (Gk. *deon*, "it is necessary, there is need of") DISTRESSED (Gk. *lupēthentes*, "grieved, made sorrowful, offended") conveys this idea of necessity. The verb *deō* typically means "to bind or put under obligation." The sense is that trials are bound to afflict believers.

- Trials are ordained. God allows trials for the purpose of refining believers to resemble Jesus more perfectly. Difficult trials purify and solidify faith.

The process of purifying gold requires extreme heat. An ancient goldsmith knew when all impurities had been burned away because he could see his own reflection in the molten gold. In like manner, God looks for His reflection in His children. Faith is much **more valuable than gold** and will be rewarded by God. Peter explained what results from the testing of one's faith—**praise, glory, and honor** (v. 7). These are all Christlike qualities. The beautiful reality is that because we as believers serve a God of grace, in giving He receives. In honoring, He is honored. In glorifying, He is glorified. In praising, He is praised.

1:8-9 The result of daily placing one's trust fully in the Lord is joy **inexpressible** (v. 8). You should have **joy** in the midst of trials, but your daily fellowship with Jesus gives cause for even greater joy.

In verses 1-9, Peter emphasized the greatness of God's grace and further elaborated on the gift of salvation in verses 10-12. Salvation was the subject of many messianic prophecies recorded in the Old Testament. The grace of the new covenant was prophesied in such passages as Isaiah 9:6-7; 51:11; Joel 2:28-32; Jeremiah 31:31-34; and Zechariah 3:1-10.

1:10-12 Longing to understand all that they recorded about **salvation** (Gk. *sōtrēias*, v. 10), the prophets **inquired** and **carefully** searched for answers. The phrase "searched and carefully investigated" translates a pair of verbs similar in form and meaning. SEARCHED (Gk. *exezētēsan*, "searched out, charge with") often applies to seeking God (e.g., Heb 11:6) and suggests diligent and thorough investigation. CAREFULLY INVESTIGATED (Gk.

Heart to Heart:
Suffering for a Season (1 Pt 1:6)

No one likes to suffer! However, suffering is a part of life. All people will suffer various trials, but the Bible assures Christians that suffering is only for a season.

The book of 1 Peter discusses the reality of suffering. In chapters 1 to 5, biblical counsel is given to Christians who face suffering. Here is a summary of the basic teachings of Peter. Suffering . . .

- *is inevitable (1:6);*
- *is short-lived (1:6);*
- *is varied (1:6);*
- *may result in praise, glory, and honor (1:7);*
- *was experienced by Christ (1:11; 4:1);*
- *is redemptive (1:18-19);*
- *is commendable before God (2:20-21);*
- *brings blessing (3:14; 4:14);*
- *may be the will of God (3:17);*
- *is sometimes unjust (3:18);*
- *should not be a surprise (4:12);*
- *should be cause for rejoicing (4:13);*
- *is sharing in His suffering (4:13);*
- *is an opportunity to glorify the name of Christ (4:16);*
- *reflects an act of commitment (4:19);*
- *may be instigated by the Devil (5:8);*
- *is experienced by all believers (5:9);*
- *is temporary (1:6; 5:10).*

Though suffering is painful, for the Christian it is only for a season. God will sustain and strengthen His suffering children. He promises eternal life without suffering and rewards for patient endurance. You can claim His promises as you face your trials.

exēraunēsan, "inquired with great care") usually referred to searching out a place (such as a tent or a city) in order to find someone or something. This word appears only here in the New Testament, but the related word INQUIRED (Gk. *eraunōntes,* "searched, examined, investigated" v. 11) appears in other contexts (Jn 5:39; 7:52; Rm 8:27; 1 Co 2:10; Rv 2:23).

Verse 11 conveys Peter's view on the inspiration of Scripture. Peter clarified that the Holy Spirit operated in the minds and hearts of the prophets in such a way that they wrote the truths of God clearly and accurately (cp. Heb 1:1). Furthermore, he emphasized that **angels desire** (Gk. *epithumousin,* "long for, eagerly desire") **to look into** salvation, but they cannot because it is reserved for mankind (v. 12). TO LOOK INTO (Gk. *parakupsai,* "stoop or bow one's head in order to look") is the same expression used for the posture of Peter and John (Jn 20:5) and of Mary Magdalene (Jn 20:11) as they stooped down to see inside Jesus' tomb. In James 1:25, the word suggests how "intently" the believer "looks into" God's word in order to act on it. While the Scriptures reveal the angels' keen and active interest in the matter of salvation and although angels rejoice at a believer's conversion (Lk 15:10), they can only watch and delight in God's redemptive activity as His plan unfolds.

How could this gospel (v. 12) not instill a profound sense of joy in the believer? Joy should be the response to God for His gift of salvation, but Peter also delineated a believer's outward response that should accompany his inner elation.

The Responsibility of Salvation (1:13–2:3)

Salvation carries certain responsibilities, which Peter illustrated throughout the remainder of the epistle. He began with believers' responsibilities to God, then their responsibilities to others, and finally to the church body. Considering all that God has done for us, "Therefore" (v. 13), we are to live differently than before. Holiness is an absolute requirement in the believer's life.

Holy living (1:13-21)

1:13-16 Peter addressed the importance of disciplining both the mind and heart in order to **be holy** like Christ (v. 15). First, he encouraged sharpened spiritual thinking. GET YOUR MINDS READY FOR ACTION (Gk. *anazōsamenoi tas osphuas,* "gird up the loins" with *tēs dianoias humōn* "of your minds, thoughts, understanding") metaphorically applies the ancient custom of tucking in long robes around the waist for comfort and ease of movement. The idea is similar in meaning to "roll up your sleeves." Of primary importance in holy living is getting out of the way the thoughts or thinking patterns that would hinder progress in spiritual growth. Believers are instructed throughout the Scripture that a disciplined mind results from abiding in God's word, meditating on it, and then being faithful to obey it (Ps 119:9-11; 19:7-11; Jms 1:22-25). Believers also discipline their minds by binding up loosely flowing thoughts (2 Co 10:3-6).

However, Peter knew how easily you can lose your spiritual alertness through mental intoxication with the things of the world. BEING SELF-DISCIPLINED (Gk. *nēphontes,* "being sober, temperate; watching, being circumspect," from the root verb *nēphō,* "to be free from every form of mental and spiritual drunkenness, free from excess, passion, rashness; to be well balanced"), also used in 4:7 and 5:8, implies overall self-control—sobriety in conduct, speech, and judgment.

Being holy also requires a disciplined heart. Peter instructed believers to "SET their HOPE" (Gk. *elpisate*), much stronger than "wish for or dream about." It conveys a sense of confident expectation) COMPLETELY (Gk. *teleiōs*, "perfectly, to the end") on the grace" that Jesus will bring when He is revealed. Likewise, "OBEDIENT (Gk. *hupakoēs*, v. 14; see 1:2) children" are not "conformed to the desires" of their "former ignorance." CONFORMED (Gk. *suschēmatizomenoi*, combining the prefix *sun*, "with," and the verb *schēmatizō*, "conform to an outward pattern") is the source of the English word "schema" denoting a "a pattern imposed on reality or experience, a way of organizing or shaping the perception of reality." The word appears only here and in Romans 12:2. DESIRES (Gk. *epithumiais*, "cravings, longings") here and elsewhere in the letter (2:11; 4:2,3) has the negative sense of sinful desires or "lusts." Those who have been born anew into God's family, having willingly submitted to His authority, must no longer operate according to the sinful thought patterns, false hopes, and destructive desires that characterized their former life of IGNORANCE (Gk. *agnoia*, "lack of knowledge," particularly of God; "moral blindness"). Instead, Paul commanded believers to "be transformed by the renewing of your mind" (Rm 12:2), and Peter underscored the believer's obligation to BE (Gk. *genēthēte*, "become, be made") holy in all CONDUCT (Gk. *anastrophē*, "manner of life, behavior," v. 15), a weighty concern for Peter (see also 1:18; 2:12; 3:1,2,16; 2 Pt 2:7; 3:11).

1:17-21 Those who believe in Christ may **address** God **as Father**, but Scripture also testifies that He is **the One who judges** (v. 17). God's word teaches that all of mankind will stand before Him, yet

believers will not be condemned (Rm 8:1). Peter again addressed how believers should **conduct** themselves during their time on earth (cp. v. 15). A sense of reverential awe for God should remain in the Christian life. What makes the difference is an accurate view of the "EMPTY (Gk. *mataias*, "without purpose, devoid of truth") way of life" from which "you were REDEEMED" (Gk. *elutrōthēte*, "released, delivered, or liberated by payment of a ransom," v. 18) and an appreciation for the inestimable value of the price paid for that redemption, "the PRECIOUS (Gk. *timiō*, "of great price, very costly, especially dear"; cp. 1:7) blood of Christ" (v. 19). Peter identified Jesus with the innocent Passover lamb, which had to be **without defect or blemish** (Ex 12:5; Heb 9:14). On account of Christ, believers can fully rely on God in the present and also have complete confidence in God regarding their future. Before creation, God determined to redeem mankind by His Son's blood (v. 20). Not only did God pay the ransom, but He also **raised** Jesus **from the dead and gave Him glory** (v. 21).

Love (1:22-25)

1:22-25 Love is the response that we should have to God's salvation. One of the first marks of a believer's genuine growth in holiness is love for God that overflows as love for others. Believers are in a position to demonstrate "SINCERE (Gk. *anupokriton*, "unfeigned, undisguised," lit., "without hypocrisy"; see 2:1) love of the brothers" because they are obedient to the truth, having purified themselves (see 1:2,14). Peter pictured the believer as one who had **purified** himself in the metaphorical sense of the ceremonial cleansing required before celebration of the Passover (Jn 11:55). To obey the truth, that is, to submit one's life to Christ's lordship, goes hand in hand with forsaking the sin that is forgiven and cleansed by the blood of the sinless Lamb of God. Having BEEN BORN AGAIN (Gk. *anagegennēmenoi*, 1 Pt 1:23; see 1:3) uniquely enables the Christian to comply with the command in verse 22—"love one another earnestly from a pure heart." The LOVE (Gk. *agapēsate*) commanded here is the unconditional and self-sacrificing love of Christ that pervades the New Testament. EARNESTLY (Gk. *ektenōs*, "intently, fervently," from *ekteinō*, "stretch out, stretch forth") suggests that Christians must love each other actively, reaching outward to embrace other believers as family members. You cannot love "earnestly" without putting forth effort and becoming involved in the lives of others. To love **from a pure heart** parallels the qualification of being "purified." Genuine love overflows from a heart cleansed of impure motives and sinful desires, a heart ruled by Christ.

Peter drew an important parallel in verses 23-25. Believers and their inheritance are **imperishable** (v. 23), as he also indicated at the beginning of the chapter (1:4). Peter quoted Isaiah 40:6-8 to remind his readers that God's word, the vehicle by which believers come to know Him, is likewise "imperishable." Significantly when Isaiah first gave this message to the Jewish people at the time of their exile in Babylon, they were a scattered and oppressed people. Interestingly, the same is true at Peter's time as well.

Spiritual growth (2:1-3)

2:1-3 In the process of growing in Christ we are called to "take off" and "put on" certain things. Peter painted a picture of taking off clothes, indicating that believers are to cast off these things entirely (v. 1; cp. Eph 4:22). Peter outlined two things that sanctification involves. First, believers should reject the

harmful (1 Pt 2:1). Peter specified several characteristics that are harmful to the believer:

- **WICKEDNESS** (Gk. *kakian*, "unashamed wickedness, malice, evil") characterizes one who lives in opposition to God and seeks to hurt others.

- **ALL DECEIT** (Gk. *dolon*, "guile," from *deloō*, "catch with bait or decoy") implies deliberate dishonesty. Jacob is one example of an Old Testament figure whose intentional dishonesty cost him a great deal (Gn 27).

- **HYPOCRISY** (Gk. *hupokriseis*, "insincerity, pretense, outward show, dissembling"; from *hupo*, "under," and *krinō*, "give an answer, think, have an opinion, pass judgment"; cp. 1 Pt 1:22) is the profession of beliefs or opinions one does not hold, i.e., being two-faced. In secular usage, "hypocrite" did not have a negative connotation but literally referred to a stage actor, who in ancient Greek theater originally answered questions posed by the chorus, a group of men who functioned as a unit to narrate or comment on the story through music and movement. The "hypocrite" not only played a role but also wore a mask. "Hypocrisy" naturally acquired the sense of pretending to be something you are not by assuming the false appearance of being religious. Jesus clearly disdained hypocrisy (Mt 15:1-9).

- **ENVY** (Gk. *phthonous*, "jealousy") denotes an embittered awareness of another's advantage combined with the desire to possess the same. In Greek mythology, Phthonos was the personification of envy, described in one epic poem as "self-tormenting" and "stung with his own poison." Having a "crafty heart," he devised "a crooked plan" in which he donned "the false image of counterfeit Ares" and smeared his armor with poison dyed red to imitate blood. Also certain Greek poets likened *phthonos* to greed and associated such envy with the destructive power of the "evil eye," an idiom for greed and a quality never ascribed to a good person.

- **ALL SLANDER** (Gk. *katalalias*, "evil speaking, defamation") refers to any speech that harms another. James 3 described the dangerous weapon of the tongue that is full of poison.

All of these are aimed at hurting other people as opposed to loving them. The one who is characteristically deceitful, cunning, crafty, and malicious cannot be called a child of God.

Second, just as there are things that believers are to take off, Peter reminded his readers that there are also healthy habits and characteristics that should distinguish believers from the world and identify them as Christians (2:2). Peter used the metaphor of **newborn infants** to convey the dependence we should have on the Lord. **DESIRE** (Gk. *epipothēsate*, "fervently long for, pursue with love, yearn for") could also be translated "crave." Throughout Scripture, believers are commanded to develop an insatiable appetite for God's word (Jb 23:11-12; Ps 42:1-2). Indeed, a believer's growth in Christ is contingent on her appetite for the word of God.

The Chosen Stone and His People (2:4-12)

2:4-5 Beginning a new section, Peter used Old Testament imagery to communicate a New Testament reality: Jesus brought salvation both to the Jew and Gentile who are now known as "God's people" (v. 10). Peter referred to Jesus as a stone in three different ways, describing Him as a living stone (Gk. *lithon*, "stone, rock," v. 4), "cornerstone" (vv. 6,7), the **rejected** stone (vv. 4,7), and "a stone that causes men to stumble" (v. 8).

Interestingly Peter is the one to whom Jesus referred as the rock upon which He would build His church (Mt 16:18). A careful reading of this text combined with Matthew 16:18-20 invalidates any attempt to maintain that Jesus named Peter as the chief rock or foundation for His body. Clearly, Jesus reserved this role for Himself—Peter himself described Christ here as "the cornerstone" (v. 7), the foundational stone for the entire structure (cp. 1 Co 3:11). More likely Jesus was using a play on words with Peter's name (Gk. *Petros*, "stone"). Furthermore, Peter also makes the point that the church is built with living stones, those who confess Jesus as Christ (1 Pt 2:5; see Mt 16:15-18). Believers are identified with *the* "living stone" (1 Pt 2:4) who fashions them into His image, building them into **a spiritual house** (v. 5). Peter affirmed that all believers are priests in that they rely on no other mediator than Jesus in order to approach God (v. 5; cp. Heb 4:16).

The Jewish people prided themselves on the beauty of the temple in Jerusalem, one of the great structures in Palestine. Yet, Peter pointed out that the worship of God is accomplished in an even greater and more beautiful manner through Jesus. The special abiding presence of God, once limited to the Jerusalem structure, is now reserved for those who have understood and embraced the new covenant. All who believe in Jesus are considered a part of God's spiritual house. One can speculate that this must have come as a great comfort to the pilgrims who worshiped

God far from Jerusalem and that it took on even greater meaning when the temple was destroyed by the Romans in AD 70.

2:6-10 Peter used a number of Old Testament passages to elaborate on the beautiful reality of Jesus serving as the "chief cornerstone." For instance, he quoted Isaiah 28:16 where Jesus is **a chosen and valuable cornerstone**. CORNERSTONE (Gk. *akrogōniaion*) denotes the corner foundation stone of a building (v. 6). In verse 7, however, "cornerstone" (Gk. *kephalēn gōnias*, lit., "head of [the] corner") means the "chief" or "first" corner. The cornerstone is used symbolically in Scripture as a picture of stability. Jesus is the foundation for the believer's faith. However, to those who do not recognize Jesus as Christ but instead reject Him, He is described as the "stumbling stone." The quotation from Isaiah 8:14, "A stone that causes men to stumble and a rock that trips them up," contains two metaphors illustrating the results of disobedience. The first, literally a "stone of stumbling" (Gk. *lithos proskommatos*, "stone that cuts or strikes against" by accident), refers to a "stumbling block" or an "obstacle." Paul also applied Isaiah 8:14, urging believers to avoid actions that would cause fellow Christians to stumble or be offended (Rm 9:32-33; 14:13,20; 1 Co 8:9). The ROCK THAT TRIPS THEM UP (Gk. *petra skandalou*, "trap, snare," an obstacle deliberately placed in the way to cause stumbling; "offense"), however, is the cause of a fall. Jesus used this word when He rebuked Peter for objecting to His telling the disciples of His imminent death in Jerusalem (Mt. 16:23) and when He acknowledged the inevitability of impediments to belief and of people who cause the downfall of others (Mt 18:6-7; Lk17:1). He did not excuse these, and neither did Peter. See also Rm 9:33; 11:19; 14:13; 16:17; 1 Co 1:23; Gl 5:11.

Quoting Psalm 118:22, Peter stated that unbelievers stumble because of their disobedient failure to recognize Jesus as Lord. These were not appointed to disobedience, but rather to the judgment of God in response to their unbelief (1 Pt 2:7).

God's people (v. 10), the "spiritual house" (v. 5), are described as **a chosen race, a royal priesthood**, **a holy nation**, **a people for His possession** (Gk. *perioiēsin*, "one's own property"; something "obtained, purchased, reserved, preserved for oneself"; special possession that is "laid by or kept safe"; v. 9). In contrast to those who reject Christ, believers are considered a part of God's family, adopted heirs of the King, and a nation set apart for Him, not constricted by geographical boundaries. Peter was not teaching that the church replaced the nation of Israel, once described as God's "holy nation" (Ex 19:6), God's chosen people (Dt 7:6). Peter added that God's own special people are so called for the purpose of proclaiming His **praises** to the nations (1 Pt 2:9). In light of the **mercy** received in being saved **out of darkness**, believers are called to live holy lives that are pleasing to Him and to serve as a light to the world of the truth of the gospel (v. 10). Peter's argument prompts, as a whispered response to, "But how does one accomplish this?"

2:11-12 Peter's answer to this question was both general and specific. The grace of God is displayed through a believer's submission. As in chapter 1, Peter began by explaining what to reject and then addressed what to accept and do. He begged his audience to "abstain from FLESHLY (Gk. *sarkikōn*, "carnal," controlled by the human nature in opposition to the Spirit) DESIRES" (Gk. *epithumiōn*, "cravings, longings, lusts, desires for what is forbidden," v. 11; see 1:14; 4:2-3; 2 Pt 1:4; 2:10,18; 3:3), and encouraged them to live in such a way that their conduct stood as a witness (v. 12; see Mt 5:16). He stressed that a real spiritual battle continued to rage around them, seeking to attack believers at their weakest point. The seriousness of this battle is illustrated by the words Peter chose in verse 11, **desires that war** (Gk. *strateuontai*, "fight, serve in active military duty, lead an army unit into battle"; cp. Jms 4:1) **against you**. Verse 12 expresses a central element of Peter's epistle and turns from the negative to the positive—the grace of God should always be evident in a believer's life. How humbling to realize that a believer's conduct has the potential for causing others to **glorify God** as they observe Christlike behavior.

GOD'S GRACE IS THE POWER OF GOD UNTO SUBMISSION (2:13–3:7)

Peter also specifically defined the manner in which believers are called to submission by outlining how differently believers should behave in relation to government, slaves, and spouses. Under the guidance of the Holy Spirit, he addressed these three areas in which believers are to exercise submission.

Submission (Gk. hupotassō, *"lining up under authority")*

What it does not mean	What it does mean
• Subjecting oneself to abusive tyranny; • Forced obedience; • Inequality in essence and worth; • Selective submission, an attitude of "I'll submit when I want to submit."	• Willingly choosing to obey; • Placing oneself under another's authority; • Equality in essence and personhood but difference in role and assignment; • Obedience in all situations and circumstances according to God's word—not choosing when you will and will not obey; • An attitude of the will, void of stubbornness; • Voluntary commitment of service to others.

Submission to Government (2:13-17)

2:13-15 Because a believer's outward conduct is a witness to others of God's grace, Peter issued the command that we are to submit ourselves to the civil authorities (v. 13). Christians are expected to obey the law (see Mt 22:15-22; Rm 13:1-7). Paul likewise exhorted Titus to remind believers to obey rulers and authorities in a Christlike manner (Ti 3:1-2). As both Peter and Paul explained, the government has been instituted for the purpose of punishing the wicked and protecting the good (1 Pt 2:14). The motivation, however, for submitting to government authorities should not be simply for the sake of avoiding punishment, but rather **because of the Lord** (v. 13). God has ordained ruling authorities to whom believers are to submit themselves (v. 15). There is no hint that human government is superior to God. God's law always stands above human law. Yet, God's expectation is that His children will submit themselves to human government in order that their excellent behavior might draw others to Him (v. 15).

Peter explained that by DOING GOOD (Gk. *agathopoiountas*, "doing right, doing what is good, excellent, honorable, upright," vv. 14-15,20; 3:6,17; cp. 3 Jn 1:11), believers would "silence" the ignorant and foolish talk of those who falsely accused them. Bear in mind that while widespread, intense persecution may not have yet faced these pilgrims, they did encounter verbal and even physical abuse due to the lies charged against them. Peter issued the reminder again that the weapons with which believers are to fight are contrary to the sword that the government must wield (cp. 2 Co 10:3). He argued that the enemy will be defeated by your good works, which will literally shut the mouths of those who oppose you. SILENCE (Gk. *phimoun*, "muzzle, harness") is used elsewhere in Scripture to speak of harnessing an ox (1 Co 9:9 and 1 Tm 5:18). In the Gospels the verb expresses the authority with which Jesus "silenced" the Sadducees when they questioned Him on the resurrection of the dead (Mt 22:34), the demon confronting Him through a man in the synagogue (Mk 1:25; Lk 4:35), and the wind and seas threatening the disciples' boat (Mk 4:39). Also, in Jesus' parable of the wedding banquet, the man without wedding clothes "was speechless" or "silenced" when the offended king confronted him (Mt. 22:12). Peter's point is very clear as he teaches that, likewise, a believer's good works will also put to "silence" the lies and false accusations lodged against him by the world. Peter encouraged his readers to recognize the supernatural response they should have, which will lead to supernatural results.

2:16 Christians are **free** yet under God's authority. They have been made free by Jesus (Jn 8:32,36) and are free from sin and condemnation (Rm 8:1-2). Freedom is often misunderstood as the right to do whatever you want—living without boundaries. Real freedom is not found in being under one's own authority, which Paul equated with slavery to sin (Rm 6:16), but in being under Christ's authority, "enslaved to righteousness" (Rm 6:18; cp. Gl 5:1). Believers are free from sin; nevertheless, they are children of God.

Submission is inherent in the language used in these verses.

2:17 Peter reminded that your submission should be exemplified in such a way that believers **honor everyone**, including those government authorities over you. Believers are also called to **love** the Christian brethren and, ultimately, to **fear God**. As in 1:17, fearing the Lord does not mean living in terror of God in the sense of paralyzing fear, but rather being in awe of Him and dedicating yourself to obeying Him. Finally, believers are called to **honor the Emperor** (Gk. *basilei*, "king, prince"; cp. 2:13). Peter summarized the point that you are to submit yourselves to the ruling authorities. When you submit yourselves to the government, love your Christian brothers and sisters, honor all men, and fear God, then you are effective witnesses for Christ to the world. Other Scriptures support this conclusion. For example, Jesus commanded His followers to love one another just as He had loved them because it would mark them as His disciples (Jn 13:35).

Submission in the Workplace (2:18-25)

2:18-20 The institution of slavery was prominent in the first century. Although this letter is not a treatise on slavery, Peter further specified the extent of submission to others and, ultimately, to God. Submission is not dependent on a master's treatment of his slave or on an employer's treatment of an employee. Many masters are kind and fair, yet Peter acknowledged that some are harsh or CRUEL (Gk. *skoliois*, "curved, crooked," from which is derived the medical term "scoliosis," a curved or bent spine, v. 18). Taking into account what Peter articulated in 2:1 regarding putting off all deceit, envy and evil speaking, your example to the world will be far greater when patience is displayed in the midst of hardship. The power of God's grace is evident when submission is present. In light of salvation, consider the privilege of living as His daughters in this manner. God is honored when His children endure hardship from a crooked master, and yet He does not delight in your suffering but rather in how you reflect His Son.

2:21-25 The sacrifice of Jesus is the most powerful **example** of submission. EXAMPLE (Gk. *hupogrammon*, from *hupo*, "by," and *grammos*, "write," the only occurrence of this compound word in the New Testament) referred literally to a writing or drawing, such as the letters of the alphabet, which a student would be instructed to trace or copy. In Christian literature, the word quickly acquired the metaphorical sense of a moral example. Jesus' example provides the pattern for how His children should live. Believers are called upon to trace their lives over His. He **suffered** tremendous physical and verbal abuse yet responded with silence. These verses speak of the doctrine of the atonement, namely, that Christ died in your place to remove the horrible separation between man and God. Peter illustrated Jesus' example of submission by using Isaiah 53, a key Messianic passage (see chart).

Tracing Isaiah 53 in 1 Peter 2	
ISAIAH 53	**1 PETER 2**
"He Himself bore our sicknesses, and He carried our pains" (v. 4).	"He Himself bore our sins" (v. 24).
" . . . although He had done no violence and had not spoken deceitfully" (v. 9).	"He did not commit sin, and no deceit was found in His mouth" (v. 22).
"He was oppressed and afflicted, yet He did not open His mouth" (v. 7).	"When reviled, He did not revile in return; when suffering, He did not threaten" (v. 23).
"We are healed by His wounds" (v. 5).	"By His wounding you have been healed" (v. 24).
"We all went astray like sheep; we all have turned to our own way" (v. 6).	"For you were like sheep going astray" (v. 25).

Believers are commissioned to live according to Jesus' example of suffering under hardship yet without committing sin, speaking no deceit, refusing to revile others even when reviled or threatened, and entrusting yourself wholly to God. In this high calling, you are to "consider Him who endured such hostility" (Heb 12:3) on your account, thereby being renewed and not losing heart. God considered your sins as belonging to Christ and punished Him with the anger He had against you.

"Our SINS" (Gk. *hamartias*, "missing the mark, doing wrong, going astray, offense, violation of divine law") appears at the beginning of the sentence, emphasizing the purpose of the crucifixion (v. 24). BORE (Gk. *anēnegken*, "brought or carried to a higher place, lifted up and took upon oneself") has the sense of carrying a sacrifice to the altar, as in 2:5; cp. Dt 21:22; Is 53:12; Jms 2:21; Heb 9:28. Peter was stressing that Christ died for the sins of you and me. Our need for a Savior is evident. **He Himself** is also emphatic in Greek, stressing that Jesus alone **bore our sins** (cp. Heb 1:3). Jesus redeemed us by taking the curse we deserve and allowing Himself to be hung **on the tree** (cp. Dt 21:22).

Some understand verse 24 as a proclamation of physical healing promised
to a believer, but Peter's point, as well
as Isaiah's, was that you and I HAVE
BEEN HEALED (Gk. *iathēte*, "cured,
restored, made whole," with the verb
tense here indicating a completed
action) from sin, our salvation having
been accomplished in Jesus' suffering
on the cross. His death provided the healing for man's spiritual sickness and promises salvation to all who trust in Him as
their Savior. Peter added that Jesus not
only sets the example and provides salvation, but He also offers the guidance and
protection needed as **the shepherd and
guardian of your souls** (v. 25). Jesus
spoke of Himself as the "Great Shepherd"
who knows His sheep and willingly "lays
down His life" on their behalf (Jn
10:11-18). Furthermore, Jesus commissioned Peter to feed and shepherd His
sheep (Jn 21:16-17). This imagery instills
hope in the heart of the believer in trusting
that Jesus promises to guide and protect
you as you entrust yourself to His loving
care.

Submission in the Home (3:1-7)

Peter described the model of living as a
submissive citizen and employee in chapter 2 and then extended this principle by
describing submission in the home.

3:1-2 Often, this passage is taught only
in the immediate context of **wives** submitting to **husbands**, and therefore conclusions that are not consistent with the text
are drawn. Peter linked this passage to the
preceding chapters with the phrase **in the
same way** (Gk. *homoiōs*, "likewise, in the
same manner," v. 1).

In chapter 1, Peter described for believers the wonderful gift of grace and those
behaviors and attitudes that should be evident in the Christian life. Chapter 2 continued by specifying the growth that
should mark believers—craving the word

of God, living holy lives, and drawing
attention to the grace of God by their
treatment of other believers, citizens, and
employees. Peter's concluding illustration
in chapter 2 served as a reminder of the
submissive spirit believers are to reflect in
imitating Jesus' submission to God the
Father. All of this is important to recall
when interpreting chapter 3. A wife is to
be submissive not because of any merit on
her husband's part but as an act of obedience to the Lord. Submission is an act of
worship motivated by love for the Lord
and a desire to follow Christ's example; it
is neither a wife's escape route for avoiding unpleasant circumstances nor a tool
for manipulating her husband. Rather,
biblical submission is part of a wife's
response to God in light of His marvelous
love (see chart on "Submission" in chapter 2). Furthermore, a wife's submission
to her husband demonstrates the importance and uniqueness of the marriage relationship in which God has chosen to
display His power and glory in the midst
of a corrupt society.

SUBMIT (Gk. *hupotassomenai*, "subordinate, be subject to, yield to") was a
military term for "arranging [troops]
under" a commander's leadership, but
it was also used for voluntarily giving
in, carrying a burden, placing in a certain order, assigning a place. Elsewhere
in Scripture the word describes Jesus'
obedience to His parents (Lk 2:51), citizens to governing authorities (Rm 13:1;
Ti 3:1), believers to church officials
(1 Pt 5:5), and ultimately respect given
to God (Jms 4:7; Heb 12:9). Here, the
verb is in the middle voice, implying an
action that results from a woman's own
choice. The perfect illustration of this
concept is found in the example of Jesus
who subjected Himself to the Father (1 Co
15:28). While being essentially equal to
their husbands, wives are called upon,

nonetheless, to submit themselves voluntarily to their husbands.

Submission involves both a woman's *outward* actions and *inward* disposition. Peter first addressed the former. Most commentators agree that women were well represented in the churches in the geographic region to which Peter originally sent this letter, and some of their husbands were not believers (cp. 1 Co 7:1-10). Peter anticipated that these women were likely questioning the relevance of submission to their husbands because of their marital situation. His response is powerful. The purity of a godly woman's life exercised in submission can soften her husband's heart without her speaking a word. While verbal communication has an important place in the marriage relationship, words are not always needed as much as the example of one's behavior. The word *logos* is used twice in verse 1. Both the presence of the definite article and the context of THE [Christian] MESSAGE (Gk. *tō logō,* "spoken message, doctrine, or teaching," lit. "the word") suggest that this use of "*the* word" refers to the gospel message. The second usage (Gk *logou*), preceded by the preposition WITHOUT (Gk. *aneu,* "apart from one's will") and void of the article, indicates general communication—"without word, without saying anything." Peter's comments center on the powerful witness of a woman's behavior and response to her husband and the enormous impact these have on him and others who observe her.

Submission does not mean inferiority. When Peter spoke of submission to government and employers he never implied inferiority. Neither did he do that here. Rather, he demonstrated the importance of living according to God's pattern established in Genesis. He provided both husbands and wives with principles needed to combat the effects that sin made on God's original design of male and female. A woman's submissive spirit serves as one of the greatest evangelistic tools in her home and community.

The submissive attitude described in verse 1 is complemented with PURE (Gk. *agnēn,* "chaste, modest"; cp. Ti 2:5), "reverent" behavior in verse 2. REVERENT (Gk. *phobō,* "fearful") in this context does not mean being afraid but rather indicates a "respectful" attitude toward husbands and a humble recognition of Christ's lordship (1 Pt 2:18; 3:15). The "fear of the Lord" should be the mainspring of a woman's life (Pr 31:30). Husbands observe this attitude and the conduct it inspires. Just as good works can lead a watching world to give God credit for what He has done to transform believers' lives (1 Pt 2:12; 3:2), so a wife's behavior and attitude in the eyes of her husband can witness powerfully either for or against the gospel.

3:3-4 Peter turned to the inward appearance that also characterizes a godly woman. Some completely misinterpret this passage by maintaining that women are not to wear certain things or even care for their appearance. This idea is not what Peter is saying. Such a reading of the text would also mandate that a woman should not wear clothing. Besides, Scripture speaks of godly women as dressing in **fine clothes** (v. 3), as did Queen Esther in the court of ancient Persia and as the Shulammite in Song of Songs, and certainly they were considered godly women. Peter does not simply leave his readers with a prohibition but rather continues in verse 4 with this teaching point. He is not laying down a legalistic code of what can and cannot be worn; rather he is saying, your outward appearance is not primarily what matters to God but rather what is inward, your character (1 Sm 16:7). Peter noted three aspects of internal beauty:

Submission[1]			
Definition	**Method**	**Example**	**Rewards**
• An attitude of the will	"As to the Lord" (Eph 5:22)	**Jesus:** • He had no other purpose (Heb 10:7) • To submit was joy (Ps 40:7-8) • He did not consider His will (Jn 5:30)	A vibrant witness (1 Pt 3:1)
• More than obedience	"To your own husbands" (Eph 5:22; 1 Pt 3:1)		A means of glorifying God (1 Pt 3:5-6)
• Resting, leaning, trusting, abandoning yourself to the Lord	An act of the will (1 Pt 3:1-2)		A means for teaching spiritual truths (Eph 5:25-32)
• Void of stubbornness	Extends to "everything" (Eph 5:24)		A way to train children (Ti 2:3-5)
• Confidence that His will is best	Patterned after the relationship between Christ and the church (Eph 5:25-32)	**Esther:** "I will go . . . if I perish, I perish" (Est 4:16)	The object of human love and divine protection (Eph 5:25; 1 Pt 3:7)
	A response to love (Eph 5:24-25)	**Sarah** (1 Pt 3:5-6)	A way to increase worth (1 Pt 3:4)
	Extends to everyone:		A means for liberating creativity (1 Pt 3:7)
	• The church to Christ (Eph 5:24)	**Rebekah** (Gn 24:58)	
	• All believers to God (Heb 12:9; Jms 4:7)	**Abigail** (1 Sm 2:5)	
	• All believers to spiritual leaders (Heb 13:17)	**Michal** (2 Sm 6:23; 21:8)	
	• All believers to governing authorities (Rm 13:1,5; Ti 3:1; 1 Pt 2:13)		
	• All believers to one another (Eph 5:21)	**Mary:** "May it be done to me" (Lk 1:38)	
	• Wives to husbands (Eph 5:22,24; Col 3:18; Ti 2:5; 1 Pt 3:1,5)		
	• Children to parents (Eph 6:1-3)		
	• Slaves to masters (Ti 2:9; 1 Pt 2:18)		

- It is **hidden**—internal, not external (v. 4).

- It is **imperishable** (Gk. *aphthartō*, "incorruptible," v. 4). The same word is used in 1:4 to describe the believer's inheritance and salvation. Internal beauty will not fade away, unlike the fleeting beauty of your outward appearance.

- It is precious to God. VERY VALUABLE (Gk. *poluteles*, "very costly, precious, of surpassing worth," from *polus*, "much," and *telos*, "end, goal,") also describes the "pure and *expensive* fragrant oil of nard" poured on Jesus' head by the woman in Bethany (Mk. 14:3). Peter used two words to describe godly beauty: gentleness and quietness.

Being GENTLE (Gk. *praeōs*, "meek, humble") is a mark of strength rather than weakness. The word was frequently used in ancient literature to refer to a wild beast that had been tamed, suggesting that the characteristic is acquired rather than natural. Jesus described His own disposition as "gentle" (Mt 11:29), and He included this quality in the Beatitudes (Mt 5:5). "Gentleness" is also commended as a fruit of the Spirit (Gl 5:23). Equally important, being QUIET (Gk. *hēsuchiou*) does not mean being totally silent, neither does it suggest being devoid of personality. Instead, the idea is "self-control" and "trust," closely connected with meekness, as in this verse. Both of these characteristics of a godly woman are described as "very valuable" or "precious" in the eyes of God, as well as an "imperishable quality" in contrast to gold, jewels, and other ornaments that will eventually fade away. The quiet and gentle woman, however, will be admired by those who observe her behavior, and she is approved by God for her faithfulness in living according to His pattern. This demeanor is in keeping with Peter's earlier focus on aspects of faith that are considered "precious" and "incorruptible" to God—your salvation and His Son's blood.

3:5-6 Peter identified women who have exhibited such godly beauty **in the past**. He referred to them as **the holy women** who served as wives, **submitting** (Gk. *hupotassomenai*; see v. 1) **to their own husbands**. These women "BEAUTIFIED (Gk. *ekosmoun*, "adorned, prepared, arranged, put in order," from which comes the anglicized "cosmetic") themselves" with the qualities described earlier. The imperfect tense of this verb indicates a continuous action on their part. Some believe Peter had in mind the four matriarchs of Jewish tradition: Sarah, Rebekah, Rachel and Leah. However, Peter specifically mentioned only Sarah, his primary example of a woman who lived in submission to her husband. A central figure in Jewish life today, Sarah is still honored for her role as matriarch of Israel. She often found herself in precarious and difficult situations, yet she demonstrated the godly qualities described in this chapter. She even called Abraham **lord,** also translated "master," as an expression of her submission to his leadership in their home (v. 6). As Peter clearly indicated, Sarah's reverence for her husband did not reflect subjection to a cultural view of women as inferior or a cultural mandate for wives to be subservient to their husbands without dignity. Sarah was not coerced into calling Abraham "lord" but rather willingly chose to place herself under his leadership and care, thereby exhibiting the very quality of submission Peter was encouraging in the lives of his readers. He underscored throughout his letter the equal standing that women and men share spiritually. Peter also consistently demonstrated that submission is an inward spirit of obedience to the Lord exhibited outwardly by a woman's gentle spirit. Sarah's submission, therefore, was commended.

Peter also explained that wives who exhibit these godly qualities and are not unsettled by trying circumstances are "daughters of Sarah," **her children** (v. 6). A wife characterized by "a gentle and quiet spirit" is a woman of strength under control, able to avoid panic in the most difficult situations and relying on the Holy Spirit rather than on herself (vv. 4,6).

3:7 Peter turned his attention to the **husbands**. Verse 7, like verse 1, addressed to "wives," employs the expression **in the same way** (Gk. *homoiōs*, "likewise") to connect this exhortation to the previous chapters; it does not suggest that husbands submit to their wives, which would be a contradiction of Scripture; but rather, husbands, too, are to follow God's established pattern for them, i.e., to lead the family unit with the attitude of Christ. Peter exhorted husbands to love their wives by offering two specific gifts of love: respect and **understanding** (Gk. *gnōsin*, "intimate, experiential knowledge, wisdom"). Husbands must strive to understand their wives, seeking to know them as intimately as possible—emotionally, intellectually, spiritually, and physically. They must understand the purpose and will of God that their marriages be "one-flesh" relationships with their respective spouses (Gn 2:24; Mt 19:5-8). Husbands are also expected to bestow **honor** on their wives. HONOR (Gk. *timēn*, "value") describes the attitude of reverence appropriate to a great treasure that is to be nurtured and protected. The word fits precisely what God ordained from the beginning in the establishment of male headship (Gn 1–2). The husband is to love his wife by protecting her emotionally, intellectually, spiritually, and physically. Paul also exhorted husbands to love their wives "as also Christ loved the church" (Eph 5:25).

The description of a woman as having a WEAKER (Gk. *asthenesterō*, "weak, lacking strength, not made to be strong") NATURE (Gk. *skeuei*, "vessel," an idiom referring to the body) invites discussion about what Peter was truly saying about women (v. 7). Most commentators agree that "weaker nature" (or "vessel") is a reference to biological differences between men and women, with women being weaker *physically.* While a woman is fully equal to a man in her essence and personhood, not inferior simply because she is a woman, she is physically weaker simply due to her biological nature. In no way is she weaker intellectually, but rather generally her body does not possess the same physical strength as does a man. Peter was not demeaning women, but he was exhorting the husband to recognize that women are created differently, and, therefore, a wife is to be treated as a special gift from God. Wives are to be honored as **co-heirs** of grace (v. 7)—husbands and wives have the same spiritual standing, having been chosen by Jesus Christ as His children. The husband is called to love his wife, to care for her, and to respect her as his confidant, lover, and gift of grace from God. His motivation for adhering to these commands is found at the end of the verse: **so that your prayers will not be hindered**. Clearly, God takes the role of husband and wife seriously. These verses highlight the coequality and unity of a husband and wife. A wife is to demonstrate her submissiveness before the Lord in relationship to her husband, and a husband is to demonstrate his submissiveness to the Lord in his gentle and understanding treatment of his wife.

While some object that Peter wrote little to the men while expending more ink in words to the women, quantity does not always indicate the weight of the words. Peter may have used fewer words to address the men, but he delivered to husbands a substantial charge packed with emphatic speech. This powerful message, just as that delivered to the women, demands the reader's attention. The home, as Peter demonstrated, serves as a central sphere of influence in radically impacting the world with the gospel, in keeping with God's plan that the family reflects the Lord's relationship with His people. A husband and wife's relationship, therefore, has the potential to issue the clarion call to all people to deny themselves, submit their hearts to the Lord Jesus, and to live in obedience to His plan for their lives and homes.

GOD'S GRACE IS THE POWER OF GOD UNTO SUFFERING AND SERVICE (3:8–5:14)

Principles of Godly Living (3:8-12)

3:8 Peter returned to his general theme (2:11-12) and addressed **all of you**, giving specific guidelines for living in a hostile culture. Verses 8 and 9 outline the importance of general attitudes that should mark the believer:

- *Unity.* **Be likeminded** regarding spiritual attitudes and actions. Jesus prayed that His disciples would be united together (Jn 17:11), and Paul spoke of the importance of unity referring to believers as "one body in Christ" (Rm 12:5-8; 1 Co 12:27-30). For Paul, the unity of the church was important partly because of its reflection of the unity of the Godhead (1 Co 12:6; Eph 4:5). Unity is expressed in the fellowship of believers one with another, as well as in a shared burden for the mission of the Church (Php 2:2), common beliefs and purpose (Eph 4:5), and suffering for His sake (2 Co 1:6; 1 Pt 5:9).

- *Sympathy.* Be **sympathetic**, i.e., suffer with others, exercising compassion. Jesus serves as the primary example of this Christian virtue, being able "to sympathize with our weaknesses" (Heb 4:15) because of the suffering He endured.

- *Brotherly Love.* **Love believers**, not just suffering with one another because it is the right thing to do but genuinely loving one another.

- *Compassion.* Be COMPASSIONATE (Gk. *eusplagchnoi,* "tender-hearted," from *eu,* "good" and *splagchnois,* "inward parts, bowels," an idiom for deep, abiding "affection'" cp. Eph 4:32; Php 1:7-8).

- *Humility.* Be **humble** (Gk. *tapeinophrones,* "humbleminded").

3:9 The necessity for returning good for evil is the crux of verse 9. Believers, rather than **paying back evil for evil**, should give **a blessing** in return for insult. BLESSING (Gk. *eulogountes,* "praise," from *eu,* "good," and *logos,* "word, speech"), literally means "speak a good word or speak well of," just as the anglicized word "eulogy" denotes a speech or tribute that gives praise or commendation. Responding to "evil" and "insult" with "blessing" is to follow Jesus' teaching (Mt 5:11-12,44) and example (1 Pt 2:23). As with other promises God makes in His word, and specifically in this epistle, His assurance here is that **blessing** will likewise follow obedience when one adheres to these commands.

3:10-12 Psalm 34:12-16 was the basis for a further outline of the blessings believers will experience based on their obedience. Such blessings include, "loving life," "seeing good days," and "having the eyes of the Lord" on her. This does not promise prosperity, good health and fame. Rather, these blessings relate to the contentment found in rejoicing in the Lord regardless of your circumstances. Contentment in the Lord leads to such blessings. You should also be encouraged that God knows your struggles, God hears your prayers, and God sets His face against those who do evil. If you trust that God knows of your trial, hears your cries for help, and promises to oppose those who persecute you, then you have all that you need to motivate you to return good for evil. The wicked are in the Lord's hands, not yours. You are only responsible for your response to the wicked. Believers are also challenged to seek peace and to pursue it when opposition comes. Peace should always be the believer's goal in any situation.

Suffering for Righteousness' Sake (3:13-22)

3:13-14 Persecution occurred, however, even though believers pursued peace and sought to do good. Peter encouraged his readers that the right response to unde-served suffering will result in blessing. While their enemies may cause great physical harm to them, ultimately these enemies cannot injure a believer's spiri-tual position in Christ. Jesus has secured this position on behalf of believers (1:5). Peter asked the rhetorical question, "What can man do to you if you belong to God?" Indeed, he has reiterated numerous times already that believers are to fear God, not man, and not with trembling for what will be done to them, but because of what God has already done for them (Is 43:1-3; Mt 5:10; Rm 8:31-39). Believers should not fear man, but rather direct their energies and focus on doing good and living righ-teously in order to serve as living exam-ples of Jesus. It is possible that Peter recalled Jesus' words from the Sermon on the Mount, "Blessed are those who are persecuted for righteousness" (1 Pt 3:14; see Mt 5:10).

3:15 The inward reverence that we are to have for Christ as Lord will be demon-strated in an outward readiness **to give a defense . . . for the hope that is in you**. TO GIVE A DEFENSE (Gk. *apologian*, "verbal defense, formal justification"),

like the legal term "apologia" or "apol-ogy," is to make your case, to provide a "reasoned argument." "Apologetics" is a branch of theology that focuses upon defending the faith and proving the truths of Scripture. To give a "defense" or "apology" in this sense does not involve "apologizing," i.e., making excuses or expressing shame for being a Christian. When **anyone** recognizes your changed life and **asks you for a reason**, as a believer you should enthusiastically provide the reason for such hope—Jesus **the Messiah**. Early in this epistle, Peter reminded his readers of the "living hope" that comes because of Christ and His res-urrection (1:3,21). What do you say when people ask about your happiness, your friendly smile, your sense of peace? Do you merely thank them and continue on, or do you take the opportunity, as Peter urged, to tell them the source and motiva-tion for the difference they see in you? Peter assumed that a believer's life would be markedly different from the world.

3:16 Peter carefully described the man-ner in which believers are to tell others the reason for their hope—with **gentleness** (meekness) **and respect**. These are the same qualities that are required of women in chapter 3, and promising the same result to serve as a witness of Christ's working within the believer's heart. What Christ had accomplished in Peter, who had denied Jesus three times out of fear of man, was exhibited in his zeal for pro-claiming the gospel regardless of personal cost. He feared God more than he feared man. He had stood before crowds and unashamedly preached the gospel (Ac 4–5). Peter stressed that if suffering does indeed come, it is the will of God. There is security in the assurance that God cares for believers and protects them even when permitting their suffering.

3:17 There are many examples in the Old and New Testament of ones who exhibited such a response to suffering (Joseph, Daniel, Esther, Mary), yet Peter chose the example of Jesus as the perfect illustration of the innocent and sinless man who suffered and died in submission to God the Father for the purpose of your redemption.

3:18 This verse has been described by some as one of the shortest but richest summaries of the cross of Jesus in the New Testament. Peter's explanation of the motivation and cost of Jesus' death highlighted once again the doctrine of the atonement. Peter revealed five important aspects of Jesus' example:

- He died and suffered for sins.

- He died once for all.

- He died in the place of sinners—the righteous for the unrighteous.

- He suffered and died in order to bring you to God.

- His suffering and death was followed by resurrection.

3:19-20 In contrast, Peter's exposition on Jesus' activities after His death and prior to His resurrection constitutes one of the most difficult passages to interpret in the New Testament. A number of questions are raised in these verses. Who were **the spirits in prison**? Did Jesus visit hell? When did He visit these spirits? What did He preach? Theologians offer at least four explanations:

- Jesus descended into *Sheol* (Hb. "the realm of the dead," equivalent to the Gk. *Hades*) to preach the gospel either to fallen angels or primitives.

- He descended into *Sheol* to proclaim judgment on the primitives.

- He descended into *Sheol* to proclaim judgment on the fallen angels.

- There was no descent. The reference is to Christ's preaching by means of

the Spirit through Noah to those in the time of Noah.

SPIRITS (Gk. *pneumasin*) can refer either to human (Ec 12:7; Mt 27:50; Heb 12:23) or angelic spirits (Heb 1:14). Commentators who argue for the last aforementioned explanation cite that the word "spirits" is linked to the descriptive clause "who in the past were disobedient" (Gk. *apeithēsasin*, "refused to believe or be persuaded, refused to comply or obey"; cp. 1 Pt 2:8; 3:1; 4:17), which is tied to "in the days of Noah while an ark was being prepared" (1 Pt 3:20). Their point is that Scripture gives no evidence that angelic spirits were disobedient at the time of Noah, but rather such was indeed the case in human spirits. Furthermore, the text reads that **God patiently waited** for these to repent, and Scripture never gives any indication that God waits for angelic spirits to repent. Scripture is replete with examples of human spirits for whom God has exercised great patience (see 2 Pt 2:4; Jd 6). So, these human spirits from the time of Noah seemingly await the final judgment of God.

The problem remains, however, as to when Jesus preached to these spirits. As some commentators point out, the plausibility is that Jesus preached to these spirits, not at the intermediate time between His death and resurrection, but rather through the lips of Noah during the days he was building the ark. The Spirit of Christ preached through Noah the message of repentance. Interestingly, this view is supported in 2 Peter 2:5 where Noah is referred to as a "preacher of righteousness." Furthermore, Peter's example of Noah is in keeping with the points made in chapter 3 about standing strong in the faith while enduring persecution. Genesis 6 recounts that Noah and his family lived in a culture that was hostile to their witness. Noah, however, did not fear man but obeyed God and trusted that God would deliver him and his family. Other commentators argue that Jesus Himself preached to these spirits following His death and prior to His resurrection.

Those who argue for the third interpretation maintain that Jesus preached to the evil spirits in *Sheol* following His death for the purpose of declaring His victory over Satan. These spirits could be the ones referred to as the "sons of God" who disobeyed by having sexual relations with women (Gn 6:1-4). Such an interpretation of Genesis 6 is debatable as well, however.

3:21-22 The interpretation of the verses that follow depends, of course, on how one interprets verse 19 and the first part of verse 20. What is clearly understood is that the judgment of the flood destroyed most but that some were saved. Peter indicated that "eight" souls, traditionally understood to be Noah and his family, "were saved through water" (v. 20). Peter explicitly compared the water that saved Noah and his family with **baptism** (Gk. *baptisma*, "immersion, submersion," v. 21). While Peter may appear to be saying that baptism saves a person in the sense that salvation itself depends on baptism, a careful examination of the text affirms that this is not what he is saying. Rather, the water is an antitype for baptism. In other words, just as Noah and his family were saved and brought safely through the water, so, too, believers are saved through the gift of salvation demonstrated by baptism. Baptism is an outward testimony of a believer's decision to follow Christ. It represents a complete break with the former way of life and commitment to follow Christ. Just as the flood destroyed a sinful world, so, too, baptism serves as a picture of the destruction of the believer's sinful life and his new birth in Christ.

The text explains that baptism is **the pledge** (Gk. *eperōtēma*, "appeal, demand, intense desire") **of a good conscience toward God**, and **not the removal of the filth of the flesh** (v. 21). It is not equivalent to salvation but an important expression of the believer's faith in God (Rm 6:3-5; Gl 3:27). Peter reminded believers that they should have the courage to take a public stand for Jesus through baptism as a testimony of God's grace. For Peter's original audience, public baptism often meant death. Reformers, such as the Anabaptists of the sixteenth century, also faced death because of their commitment to believer's baptism as an act of obedience to Christ. Yet, Peter exhorted believers to obey the Lord in the act of baptism regardless of the consequences.

Jesus triumphed over death and reigns as the resurrected Lord. He faced persecution, suffered death, and rose victoriously. Likewise, believers should be encouraged to follow His example in the way they respond to suffering. The authority and power of the resurrected Lord should comfort those who trust in Him. All things are in His hands, and He alone will judge those who judge His own.

Suffering as Christ Suffered (4:1-6)

4:1 Believers are urged to live with a Christlike attitude, even in the midst of suffering. Peter provided the example of Jesus in chapters 2 and 3 and in chapter 4 encouraged his readers to live for God's will and not their own. **Therefore** refers back to 3:18 when Peter spoke of Jesus' example in suffering and His victory over death. He encouraged believers to have the same Christlike attitude and mindset in suffering (Php 2:5), trusting that just as Jesus' suffering led to glory and victory, so a believer's suffering is a pathway to reward, especially that of living in His Presence. Believers must remain obedient to God's call regardless of the cost, running with endurance and resolve. The language Peter employs in verse 1 is reminiscent of Paul's depiction of a warrior preparing himself for spiritual battle (Rm 13:12; Eph 6:10-18, 1 Th 5:8). **ARM YOURSELVES** (Gk. *hoplisasthe*, "furnish with weapons, equip, provide"; metaphorically, "take on the same mind") is a military expression and appears as a verb only here in the New Testament. Like soldiers preparing themselves for battle, so believers must be diligent in preparing themselves for suffering.

4:2-5 Believers are not to live as they did prior to life in Christ because they are free from the bondage of sin. Furthermore, believers should not be driven by their own **desires** (see 2:11), but by **God's will**, which should remain at the center of their hearts. Peter bluntly exhorted believers to break from their former lives, counting as wasted the time spent on living according to the world's desires. "Pagans" (Gk. *ethnōn*, or "Gentiles") conveyed the idea that Gentile Christians have been grafted into Israel on account of Jesus the Messiah. Believers now belong to Him and, therefore, should live accordingly. This changed identity and behavior will attract the attention of the world. A Christlike heart and mind capture the interest of those who walk in darkness but can also provoke hostility in unbelievers as an offense to their own lifestyle. As verse 4 warns, **they slander you** (Gk. *blasphēmountes*, "blaspheme, revile, malign, speak reproachfully, give an evil report" v. 4; cp. 2 Pt 2:2,10,12), but they will one day face **the One** who will **judge** them for their acts against God's children. No man escapes giving **an account** to God (v. 5).

4:6 Those who died due to persecution did not die in vain, as God will judge those who persecuted them (v. 6). This promise is tied to verse 5. For this reason

the gospel was preached to them before they died. They would be assured that while they may not be saved from physical death, they would know of their spiritual salvation and rest in knowing that God would handle the punishment due their oppressors. Unfortunately, some interpret this passage in such a way that all men who have died are given a "second chance" for salvation. This interpretation must be rejected as it does not reflect the message of salvation found in the context of these immediate verses nor in other Scriptures.

Serving for God's Glory (4:7-11)

4:7-11 In light of all of this, Peter referred to the return of Christ. The shortness of time, in light of eternity, should motivate believers to live for and serve Jesus. Rather than becoming fearful and discouraged by the promise of suffering, they should arm themselves with the spiritual weapons God has provided, recall His promises, and commit themselves to exhibiting the qualities of Christlikeness. As a result, believers will:

- **BE CLEAR-HEADED** (Gk. *sōphronēsate*, "of sound mind, self-controlled, thinking soberly of oneself, curbing one's desires, temperate," v. 8);

- be "**DISCIPLINED** (Gk. *nēpsate*, "sober, alert," with the sense of being unruffled or undeterred by emotions or competing desires) for prayer";

- "keep your love for one another at **FULL STRENGTH**" (Gk. *ektenē*, "stretched out, fervent," and *echontes*, "hold fast, adhere, cling," v. 8);

- **BE HOSPITABLE** (Gk. *philozenoi*, "generous with your friendship toward guests," specifically toward other believers, v. 9).

Believers should also be attentive to using the spiritual **gift** (Gk. *charisma*) given by God for the edification of the body and as a further means of bringing glory to Him (v. 11; 1 Co 12). This spiritual gift originates with God's grace. First Corinthians 12 and Ephesians 4:11-16 list some of the spiritual gifts given to believers by God, and throughout Scripture many of these are clearly evident in women who faithfully served the Lord (e.g., Deborah, Esther, Lydia, and Mary). Peter divided the gifts into two categories: speaking and serving. He affirmed that both depend on God's grace and should be exercised in such a manner that you are keenly aware of whom you serve or for whom you speak. ORACLES OF GOD (Gk. *logia theou*, "brief utterances or laws of God") refers to God's written word, which Peter has already described as the incorruptible and everlasting truth of God (1:25). Hence, the reference is not to any spoken word based on what someone feels is special revelation from God. God's strength and His word manifested in a believer exercising her gift will result in praise and glory for God. Peter offered a closing word of praise in this section with the doxology, **To Him belong the glory and power forever and ever. Amen** (v. 11).

Suffering for God's Glory (4:12-19)

4:12-16 Peter anticipated the **sufferings** that believers would face shortly; and so, in this portion of his letter, he encouraged endurance in suffering with Christlike faith, knowing that you will be identified with Him (v. 13). He returned to the subject of trials addressed earlier in his epistle, prompting his readers to recall that trials are to be expected. The world stands in opposition to the truth of God, as he has discussed; and he summarized again the nature of these trials believers will

encounter. They are intense, they are inevitable, and they will test a believer. These trials are part of the refining fire that God uses to mold and shape His children into more of His likeness (1:7). Trials should also cause believers to **rejoic**e, not in a sadistic way, but in the **joy** of knowing that they are identifying with Christ's death in a very real sense and with the hope of seeing Him face-to-face (v. 13). Peter referred again to Jesus' teaching in Matthew 5:11 to encourage believers to consider themselves **blessed** when persecuted **for the name of Christ** (1 Pt 4:14). Peter stressed that regardless of how severe the persecution might become, believers are never to be involved in lawlessness by retaliating in a way that could be deemed criminal. A Christian should never do anything that would justify being punished as a **murderer** or **thief**. Furthermore, disobedience would contradict Peter's point in chapter 2 regarding a believer's submission to government. A Christian who does suffer **should not be ashamed** even when publicly punished (v. 16; cp. Rm 1:16). The use of the word CHRISTIAN (Gk. *Christianos*, "little Christ," v. 16) is startling, since it is not used often by New Testament writers (only in Ac 11:26; 26:28). Its usage, however, fits beautifully with Peter's comments since it is a term originally ascribed to believers by those outside of the community of faith who observed their reflection of Christ (Ac 11:26).

4:17-19 Verse 17 may appear harsh at first glance, but Peter simply argues that God's **judgment** begins with His people as part of the refining process in disciplining His children (cp. Heb 12:7). At the same time, Peter rhetorically asks, "Just imagine if God's judgment is on us as His beloved, chosen people, what will God's judgment be like for those who reject Him?" This "judgment" is meant to lead to brokenness on behalf of believers for

Heart to Heart: Hospitality or Entertainment

Hospitality with grumbling is not hospitality at all! The Bible clearly says that Christians are to extend hospitality to others without complaining (1 Pt 4:10). In fact, if you grumble about your efforts, you are working. If you rejoice in your efforts, you are serving. God's way is service, i.e., hospitality without complaining.

There is a distinctive difference between biblical hospitality and worldly entertaining. Biblical hospitality is opening your home and heart to others in Jesus' name. It is much more than elaborate menus, elegant table settings, or lavish entertaining. It is sharing what you have and who you are with whomever God sends your way. Christians are to extend love and grace to friends and strangers while enjoying their fellowship.

Peter included hospitality in his passage on the ministry of spiritual gifts. Biblical hospitality truly ministers to all givers as well as receivers. The Bible promotes hospitality that:

• *provides a safe place (Pr 31:21);*

• *does not seek reward or compensation in return (Mt 6:1-4);*

• *puts people before things (Mt 10:42);*

• *shares all possessions (Ac 2:44);*

• *offers freedom and forgiveness (Rm 8:2);*

• *seeks to serve others (1 Pt 4:8-9); and*

• *does not complain (1 Pt 4:10).*

Practice biblical hospitality—serve others without complaining.

those who refuse to accept the gospel and, therefore, are promised a much more severe and eternal punishment. Peter summarized the thrust of this passage— **entrust** (Gk. *paratithesthōsan*, "deposit, commit or commend to another's charge," v. 19; cp. Lk 23:46; Ac 14:23; 20:32; 1 Tm 1:18; 2 Tm 2:2) yourself to your **faithful Creator**, for **those who suffer according to God's will** do share in His sufferings. The reference to God as Creator implies His sovereignty in knowing

and creating all things for a purpose. He is the One who has created you perfectly for His pleasure; and, therefore, He intimately knows you and the suffering that you must endure. You must trust in God and Him alone and demonstrate this trust to others by doing good.

The Responsibility of Elders (5:1-4)

Chapter 5 focuses on service as Peter first addressed the pastors or leaders in these congregations. Since this body of believers was suffering together, Peter first addressed the leadership of the congregations and then turned his attention to the community as a whole.

5:1-4 He began by addressing THE ELDERS (Gk. *presbuterous*, with a meaning suggesting maturity and the respect and esteem that entails referring to a pastoral title or identifying leaders of the congregation, v. 1). Peter called himself **a fellow elder**, and furthermore, an apostle, speaking with the authority of one who had physically walked with Jesus, witnessed His death, resurrection and ascension, and been given the mandate to take His commandments and instruct others in His truth. While reminding them of his authority as an elder and apostle, he also intentionally identified himself with them in his suffering. Peter described the role of pastors or elders with two other key words: **shepherd** and **overseeing** (v. 1; cp. Jesus' words to Peter, Jn 21:16). SHEPHERD (Gk. *poimanate*, "tend a flock of sheep") depicts the role of a spiritual leader who must faithfully care for "God's flock" by serving them, feeding them the Word of God, guiding, leading by example, and protecting them from spiritual corruption, 1 Pt 5:2. This word describing the ministries of the leader of a congregation, even more than the others, has inspired the term of respect and affection in churches with congregational government, i.e., "pastor." The imagery Peter used of a shepherd and flock was something to which the people of Israel, in particular, could relate. They understood the responsibility required to protect and provide for their flocks. However, Peter continued with the reminder that this flock does not ultimately belong to the shepherd, but to God (v. 2). The shepherd's job is to lead and care for the sheep, willingly, lovingly, and humbly. He is to strive for his heavenly reward by faithfully fulfilling his tasks as a shepherd, rather than being preoccupied with financial gain (v. 3). Pastors are called to lead their sheep and not to drive them like cattle. They are to lead by example, and in doing so will receive a great reward (vv. 2-3). Peter does not promise the fading pleasures of worldly rewards but rather affirms that Jesus, **the chief Shepherd**, will reward them with **the unfading crown of glory** (v. 4). UNFADING (Gk. *amarantinon*) more literally is "composed of amaranth," a flower symbolizing immortality. "Amaranth" reflects the merging of two Greek words—*anthos*, "flower," and *amarantos*, the prefix *a-*, "not," combined with *mainō* "wither, decay," to form *amarantos*, an "unfading flower." Pliny, a first-century Roman naturalist, wrote of the amaranth as an imaginary, never-fading flower. Clement of Alexandria, a second-century Christian leader, described the amaranth as a flower only heaven could produce and contrasted the "fair crown of amaranth . . . laid up for those who have lived well" with the fading glory "of those who have not believed on the Lord."[2] Flowers in the amaranth family serve well in dried flower arrangements— they do have small, densely clustered blooms that do not fade or wither when picked.[3]

The third term describing the pastor's role, **overseeing** (Gk. *episkopountes*, "look at, take care, care for"), emphasizes the administrative responsibilities of this leader in the congregation (v. 2). Although each descriptive term emphasizes a different aspect of the pastor's responsibilities, all are synonymous in referring to the same office.

Submission to Elders (5:5-7)

5:5-7 Peter turned his attention from the shepherd to the sheep and called them to be submissive to the Lord as well as to their shepherds. He admonished the **younger men** to be submissive to **the elders** (v. 5). These younger members of the body are encouraged to willingly submit themselves to those who had been given the responsibility of leadership. Quoting Proverbs 3:34 from the LXX, Peter also exhorted young and old alike to exercise **humility** toward one another. CLOTHE (Gk. *egkombōsasthe*, "fasten or gird oneself," v. 5)) is formed from the root word used to describe the apron a humble slave would wear in serving others. The imagery is powerful, and one has to wonder if Peter might have recalled how Jesus had demonstrated humility by tenderly washing His disciples' feet on the night before His death (Jn 13:1-17). HUMILITY (*tapeinophrosunēn*, "modestly," from *tapeinos*, "lowly, of low degree, low to the ground," and *phrēn*, "heart, mind, intellect, thinking") denotes a "lowliness of mind" as opposed to thinking too highly of oneself, "a deep sense of one's smallness" in comparison with others rather than an attitude of superiority, "a sense of modesty" instead of braggadocio, and "a humble opinion of yourself" rather than one of proud self-promotion; v. 5; cp. Ac 20:19; Eph 4:2; Php 2:3; Col 3:12. God honors humility. In humbling yourself, you will be lifted up by **the mighty hand of God** (1 Pt 5:6). What a comfort to those who were being persecuted.

Echoing Jesus' Sermon on the Mount (Mt 6:25-32) and specifically quoting Psalm 52:22, Peter instructed believers to cast their cares upon God (1 Pt 5:7). CASTING (Gk. *epiripsantes*, "throwing or placing upon") requires the deliberate release of control and the intentional placement of worries and concerns "upon God." The only other occurrence of this word in the New Testament provides a vivid illustration—the disciples' "*throwing* their robes on the donkey" Jesus was about to ride into Jerusalem (Lk 19:35). God is not indifferent to your sufferings. He desires that you cast not some, but **all** of **your care** (Gk. *merimnan*, "anxiety, worry") **upon Him**. The anxieties that trouble your hearts and minds, the fears tied to your past, present and future circumstances, are all to be cast at His feet as you entrust yourselves to His tender care. Unlike the pagan gods that are esteemed as ones so lofty that they do not trouble themselves with human affairs, Christians serve Almighty God who is highly exalted yet also notices the affairs of His creation and **cares** about them as a Father.

A Final Warning (5:8-11)

5:8 Two commands grab the reader's attention: **Be sober!** and **Be on the alert!** Peter issued the same command in 1:13, speaking of the need to prepare your minds "for action." In this verse, he adds a further reason for the necessity of doing so: You have an **adversary** (Gk. *antidikos*, "enemy, opponent," particularly in a lawsuit; cp. Mt 5:25; Lk 12:58; 18:3), **the Devil**. Believers must both *recognize* and *resist* the enemy, because he is dangerous. Peter described the dangers of this personal enemy:

- he **is prowling around like a roaring lion**, vicious and ready to attack;

- he is **looking for anyone he can devour** (Gk. *katapiein*, "swallow, destroy, overwhelm," 1 Pt 5:8; cp. 1 Th 5:6).

Believers must remain alert and on guard at all times. When they sense Satan's subtle presence, believers are commanded to RESIST (Gk. *antistēte*, "oppose, set oneself against," 1 Pt 5:9; cp. Gl 2:11; Eph 6:13; Jms 4:7) him by taking a FIRM (Gk. *stereoi*, "steadfast, immovable, strong, hard, solid"; cp. 2 Tm 2:19) stand against him. Taking a stand against Satan does not imply rebuking Satan. The instruction Peter gives is to "resist him" by standing firmly in your faith. Believers know God is in control, cares for them, hears their prayers, and will cause Satan to flee; and, therefore, they entrust themselves to His protection.

5:9 Peter also reminded his readers that they were not the only ones suffering under Satan's attacks, but rather these are also experienced by the body of Christ throughout the world. This principle holds true today and is increasingly apparent with reports of modern-day martyrs for the Christian faith.

5:10-11 In the midst of discussing the suffering that God's children must endure, Peter focused once more on the **grace** of God. He reminded his readers that God will use such trials to perfect and **strengthen** them, the picture of the refining fire once again (v. 10). Just the thought of God's grace and His immense care captivated Peter, and he broke forth with praise focusing on the **eternal** power of God alone (v. 11).

Farewell (5:12-14)

5:12 Peter addressed the important role **Silvanus** (or Silas, as he is identified in the book of Acts) had played in the epistle's composition. Most commentators understand that he served as Peter's secretary or messenger. Silvanus is mentioned numerous times in Acts and is specifically identified as a messenger who carried the words from the apostles and elders in Jerusalem to the believers in Antioch (Ac 15:22). There is no evidence that he actually penned the words of this epistle. Peter makes clear throughout the letter, by both the words and imagery he uses, that the letter is his. Nevertheless, Peter mentioned his **faithful brother**, Silvanus, as a tribute to his help in delivering this letter. More importantly, Peter ensured that his readers understood the letter's purpose of **encouraging** believers to endure persecution by standing fast, knowing that the **grace of God** is **true** and perfect.

5:13-14 Peter closed the letter with greetings and a benediction. The greeting comes from the church **in Babylon**, taken by most commentators to mean either the literal city of Babylon on the Euphrates or a "code word" for Rome (v. 13). Since Babylon in the Old Testament represented those who opposed God, some argue that Peter's reference here is to Rome, regarded as the enemy of God. Peter also sent greetings from **Mark**, certainly a reference to John Mark, one of Peter's "students," whom he lovingly addressed as **my son**. This reference to Mark as his son indicated the fatherly love Peter expressed for his young student (v. 13).

The final verse exhorted believers, **Greet one another with a kiss of love**, referring to the common ancient greeting that marked warm fellowship. Pauline letters include similar greetings (Rm 16:16; 1 Co 16:20; 1 Th 5:26). Peter encouraged believers throughout this letter to love one another as an expression of love in Christ, so it is altogether fitting that he close with this final exhortation. He also concluded by wishing **Peace to all**, saying in essence, "Remember God's grace. Don't give up. Rest in Him in such a way that your spirit is stilled even when life is tough." Nevertheless, the peace of God only applies to those who have met and accepted the Prince of Peace, the giver of grace, the hope for salvation. Peter called for believers to continue to hope in the Lord regardless of the difficulties faced and to remain mindful that, in the end, they will be witnesses to others of God's marvelous grace in their lives. As he so beautifully prayed at the beginning of this letter, **May grace and peace be multiplied to you** (1:2).

Bibliography

Brown, John. *Expository Discourses on the First Epistle of the Apostle Peter.* Geneva Series of Commentaries, vols. 2–3 Carlisle, PA: Banner of Truth Trust, 1975.

Grudem, Wayne. *The First Epistle of Peter: An Introduction and Commentary.* Tyndale New Testament Commentaries. Leicester, England: InterVarsity Press and Grand Rapids: Eerdmans, 1988.

Patterson, Dorothy. "Roles in Marriage: A Study in Submission: 1 Peter 3:1-7." *Theological Educator* 13:2 (Spring 1983): 70–79.

Patterson, Paige. *A Pilgrim Priesthood: An Exposition of the Epistle of First Peter.* Nashville: Thomas Nelson Publishers, 1982.

Grudem, Wayne. "Wives Like Sarah, and the Husbands Who Honor Them: 1 Peter 3:1-7," in *Recovering Biblical Manhood and Womanhood,* eds. John Piper and Wayne Grudem. Wheaton: Crossway Books, 1991, 193–210.

Schreiner, Thomas R. *1, 2 Peter, Jude.* The New American Commentary, vol. 37. Nashville: Broadman and Holman Publishers, 2003.

*Selwyn, E. G. *The First Epistle of Peter.* New York: Macmillan Co., 1964.

Slaughter, James R. "Submission of Wives (1 Pet. 3:1a) in the Context of 1 Peter," *Bibliotheca Sacra* 153:611 (Jan.–Mar. 1996): 63–74.

_____. "Sarah as a Model for Christian Wives (1 Pt 3:5-6)." *Bibliotheca Sacra* 153:611 (Jul.–Sep.1996): 357–65.

Vaughan, Curtis, and Thomas Lea. *I and II Peter, Jude.* Bible Study Commentary. Grand Rapids: Zondervan Publishing, 1988.

Wiersbe, Warren. *Be Hopeful.* Wheaton: Scripture Press Publications, Victor Books, 1982.

*For advanced study

Notes

[1] Adapted from *The Woman's Study Bible.* ed. by Dorothy Kelley Patterson and Rhonda Harrington Kelley (Nashville: Thomas Nelson, 1995), 2068.

[2] *The Instructor*, 2.8.16-17.

[3] Flowers in the amaranth family include: Love-Lies-Bleeding or Tassel Flower, Prince's-Feather, Joseph's-Coat, and the deep red cockscomb.

2 PETER

Introduction

Unlike Peter's first letter, his second epistle has been described by modern evangelical scholars as "obscure," "oft-ignored," and "perplexing." Yet, these also contend that its content is essential for believers throughout the ages as is all of the eternal word of God. Classified as one of the "general epistles," along with James, 1 Peter, Jude, and the Epistles of John, 2 Peter can be characterized both as an exhortation and a farewell speech all packed within three short chapters. The fervency and urgency of Peter's words suggest the probability of his impending death (1:14). Peter, therefore, seized the opportunity both to encourage fellow believers and to warn them of the attacks that would be made against their faith. As with Peter's first letter, his warm tone is evident as he writes to "dear friends" whom he loves (3:1,8,14,17).

Second Peter carries a very important message for contemporary times, just as it did in the life of the early church. Believers, living in a time when the fundamentals of the Christian faith are questioned, ridiculed, and dismissed as "primitive" and ostensibly "irrelevant" to changing times, diverse peoples, and divergent spiritual beliefs, continue to engage in a spiritual battle waged against the truthfulness of God's word. Peter demonstrated the sheer importance of recognizing and making preparations for these attacks by living in worthy manner and continuing to grow in the knowledge of Jesus Christ. Discipleship remained at the center of Peter's heart and overflowed onto the pages of 2 Peter. He was concerned for believers to be reminded that the Christian faith is the bulwark against error. Combating the proliferation of erroneous teaching both within and outside the church, 2 Peter continues to encourage women and men to grow continually in the grace and knowledge of Christ, looking expectantly for His return.

Title

In the earliest manuscripts, 2 Peter is entitled simply "*Petrou B*" (Gk. "of Peter"), meaning the second letter of Peter. The writer introduced himself in the first verse as "Simeon Peter" the "apostle of Jesus Christ."

Setting

Trouble developed in these congregations as they battled against false teachers. Peter, a champion of theological orthodoxy, warned of the seriousness of false teachers and exhorted his readers not to neglect growing in their faith. A believer's faith must continue to grow in knowledge, and the church must remain alert to erroneous teaching. Peter further defined the knowledge that believers are to attain as being based solely on the word of God, "the prophetic word strongly confirmed" (1:19). Such knowledge originates with God and not with man. The Christian life is more than just a conversion experience—it involves growing in Christ by walking with Him, studying His Word, and depending on Him for all things. Peter's second epistle acknowledges the dangers posed by false teachers and provides an urgent reminder of how a believer guards herself from falling prey to destructive heresies.

Genre

The introductory section of 2 Peter contains the essential elements of a letter written in the ancient Greco-Roman world. The letter opens by naming the writer, designating the recipients, and greeting the audience. The content resembles that of the "testament" or "farewell speech," a genre of Jewish literature popular during the intertestamental period. The genre's major characteristics include the dying person's ethical instructions and prophetic message along with an eschatological emphasis. As Peter anticipated his imminent "departure" (1:11-15), he reminded believers to live godly lives as evidence of their own future "entry into the eternal kingdom" of Jesus Christ. Also in view of his "soon" laying aside his "tent," Peter admonished the believers (1:3-10; 3:11,14,18), predicted the emergence of false teachers (2:1-3a; 2:10b–3:1-5,16-17), and defended his ethical teachings against them (1:16-21). The letter also emphasized the judgment in store for the false teachers (2:4-10a) and the certainty of the Day of the Lord (3:6-10,12-16). However, unlike "testaments" in Jewish literature, 2 Peter was written as an epistle—neither a work of fiction nor an elaboration on Peter's life. Second Peter is a letter conveying the testament, or "last words," of a shepherd deeply concerned for the continued purity and protection of his sheep, his "dear friends" in Christ (3:1,8,14,17).

Author

Interestingly, some commentators note that this book has suffered more than any other New Testament book at the hand of critics. This challenge is due, in part, to the question of the epistle's authorship. Differences between 1 and 2 Peter in style, vocabulary, and content cause some to maintain that Peter simply could not have been the author of the second epistle. Many of these critics identify the letter as a "pseudonymous" writing, composed in Peter's name for authoritative purposes yet written by someone else at a time following Peter's death. However, the external and internal evidence available counters such claims.

Possible traces of 2 Peter can be found in 1 Clement and other documents dated as early as AD 95. However, 2 Peter was not cited by name until Origen quoted 2 Peter as Scripture in the third century. In the fourth century, the letter was considered a "genuine" part of the divine word and was included by Jerome in the Latin Vulgate translation of the Bible (AD 346–420). More importantly, the letter itself identified Peter as the author of the book (1:1). Additionally, the author attested to witnessing the transfiguration of Jesus (1:18), a monumental event that Peter watched with his own eyes. The author of this epistle acknowledged this letter as his second, claimed by most evangelical commentators as a reference to 1 Peter as the earlier document. Finally, the author referred to his own death as noted by Jesus (1:14), which was also recorded in John 21:18-19.

Of the several objections to Peter's authorship of 2 Peter, the most significant relate to differences in style and thought. Critics observe that the Greek used in 1 Peter is polished and cultured, while that of 2 Peter is awkward and somewhat disjointed. However, any difference in the language can and has been overemphasized to the point of concluding that the same person could not have authored both letters. For a variety of reasons, however, an author does not always use the same words or ideas in all of his writings, which may have been the case with Peter. It is also conceivable that he may have used a different *amanuensis* or secretary in writing this second epistle. Many believe the letter may represent Peter's last will and testament since it follows the same pattern used by Moses and others for writing final directions, warnings, and encouragement to those under their authority. Certainly such circumstances can account for the differences in the language used in the second epistle as compared to the first, but one can argue that the similarities in style are just as notable. Second Peter also includes the unique vocabulary of Peter's sermons recorded in the book of Acts.

Second, those who argue against Petrine authorship maintain that the difference in thought between 1 and 2 Peter is evidence that someone other than Peter penned the second epistle. First Peter addressed the suffering church, while 2 Peter addressed the issue of false teachers who denied Jesus' return. That the material in the two letters is different to some degree is not a sufficient argument for denying that Peter wrote both letters. The letters were written for two different situations and times, so the author used various lines of thought for each. Though differences in content, vocabulary, and writing style do exist between 1 and 2 Peter, the external and internal evidence affirm Petrine authorship.

Any discussion of 2 Peter must also address the book of Jude, as the similarities between the two are noteworthy. Scholars in the early church believed that Jude relied somewhat on 2 Peter, while many who argue against Petrine authorship of 2 Peter place the writing of Jude first. The dating of Jude, however, is equally problematic and has no bearing on whether Peter borrowed from Jude's thought or vice versa. This observation does not affect the authorship or authenticity of 2 Peter; neither does it threaten the inspiration of Scripture. Clearly, both letters address a topic that appears to have been paramount in the minds of those writing during Peter's last days, as the threat of persecution mounted. Both Jude and 2 Peter issued to believers the warning not to neglect their faith and to use discernment in evaluating the clever but distorted teachings disseminated by false teachers.

Date

The content of 2 Peter gives every indication that the letter was written just prior to Peter's death between AD 64 and 67. Since 1 Peter was probably written around AD 64, conceivably 2 Peter followed a short time later (3:1), most likely from Rome where, according to Christian tradition, he was crucified.

Recipients

Second Peter 3:1 indicates that this letter is the second that Peter had written to his designated audience, so he was probably addressing the churches in Asia Minor identified in his first letter—Galatia, Cappadocia, Asia, and Bithynia (1 Pt 1:1). Clearly, the text also conveys that Peter wrote to "those who have obtained a faith of equal privilege with ours" (2 Pt 1:1), believers to whom he had previously written (3:1).

Major Themes

Second Peter centers on growing in the knowledge of Jesus Christ in order to identify and discern false teachings. Peter used the word "knowledge" numerous times throughout the epistle and chose this word for both his greeting and farewell. His purpose was to stir within his readers a passion for growing in the grace and knowledge of Jesus as they looked forward to His return.

<table>
<tr><td colspan="4" align="center">*Pronunciation Guide.*</td></tr>
<tr><td>Balaam</td><td>*BAY luhm*</td><td>Gomorrah</td><td>*guh MAHR uh*</td></tr>
<tr><td>Bosor</td><td>*BOH sawr*</td><td>Sodom</td><td>*SAHD uhm*</td></tr>
</table>

Outline

I. A REMINDER OF GOD'S PROVISION FOR GROWTH (1:1-21)
  A. Greeting (1:1-2)
  B. The Need for Faithful Growth in Christ (1:3-11)
  C. The Reliability of Scripture (1:12-21)

II. A REMINDER OF DESTRUCTIVE TEACHERS (2:1-22)
  A. The Power of Deception (2:1-3)

B. The Doom of False Teachers (2:4-11)
C. The Deception of False Teachers (2:12-22)

III. A REMINDER OF GOD'S PROMISES (3:1-18)
  A. The Assurance of Jesus' Return (3:1-13)
  B. Farewell (3:14-18)

Exposition of the Text

A REMINDER OF GOD'S PROVISION FOR GROWTH (1:1-21)

Greeting (1:1-2)

1:1-2 The author of 2 Peter identified himself as **Simeon Peter, a slave and an apostle of Jesus Christ** (v. 1). SLAVE (Gk. *doulos*, "bond-servant," from the root verb *deō*, "bind, tie, fasten; be bound to one's spouse") stressed Peter's humility before Christ; cp. 1 Pt 2:16. As a "slave," Peter not only was willingly devoted to his Master without regard for his own interests, but also he was a man under orders, bound to obey the One who had purchased him with His own blood (1 Pt 1:18-19). Throughout the New Testament *doulos* refers to actual slaves or servants (e.g., Mt 8:9; 10:24-25), but the word frequently carries spiritual implications with the sense that everyone serves *either* Christ *or* a counterfeit, i.e., someone or something claiming authority that belongs to

Christ alone. Being an authentic believer, therefore, is synonymous with being a "slave" of Christ (e.g., Ac 4:29; 16:17; 2 Co 4:5; Gl 1:10; Col 4:12; 2 Tm 2:24; Rv 19:5). This word also characterizes Moses' role as God's "servant" (Rv 15:3), indicates the scope of the outpouring of God's Spirit at Pentecost (Ac 2:18; Jl 2:28-32), and expresses the humility of Jesus' incarnation (Php 2:7). Mary, the mother of Jesus, called herself "the Lord's slave" to indicate her complete submission to God's plan (Lk 1:38; cp. v. 48), and Simeon, who recognized the infant Jesus as God's "salvation," called the Lord "Master" and himself God's "slave" (Lk 2:29). The majority of the New Testament writers affirmed their submission to the lordship of Christ by introducing themselves as His *doulos* (Rm 1:1; Php 1:1; Ti 1:1; Jms 1:1; Jd 1; Rv 1:1). **APOSTLE** (Gk. *apostolos*, "messenger, delegate, one who has been sent," as in delivering a message from a higher authority) stressed Peter's authority. The New Testament designates the 12 disciples[1] and Paul as "apostles," men specifically chosen by God and empowered by the Spirit to proclaim Christ's salvation as eyewitnesses of His Passion and disciples whom Jesus had personally instructed and commissioned.

Peter also identified his audience as those who, like himself, had received righteousness through Jesus by faith, stressing that the faith of the apostles is no different than that which belongs to any believer. OBTAINED (Gk. *lachousin*, "chosen or obtained by lot, received by divine allotment," 2 Pt 1:1; cp. Lk 1:9; Jn 19:24; Ac 1:17) implies that the gift of salvation originates with God and not with man. Peter stressed the coequality of God and Jesus Christ, perhaps in response to the emergence of heretical teachings that questioned Jesus' divinity. Peter clearly recognized **Jesus Christ** as both **God and Savior**. Peter used the term SAVIOR (Gk. *sōteros*, "deliverer, preserver") five times in this letter (2 Pt 1:1,11; 2:20; 3:2,18). Here "God" is paired with "Savior," but the other four combine "Lord (Gk. *kuriou*) and Savior." All three terms indicate the divinity of "Jesus Christ." For Jews like Peter who recognized and embraced Jesus as their Messiah (Hb., equivalent to Gk. *Christos*), to call Jesus "Savior" implicitly acknowledged His deity, since the Scriptures ascribed salvation to God alone.

Peter greeted his readers with a blessing of **grace and peace** (cp. 1 Pt 1:2). However, here he specified that grace and peace come **through the knowledge of God and of Jesus our Lord.** KNOWLEDGE (Gk. *epignōsei*, "certain, decisive, true knowledge") refers to the believer's "coming to know" Christ in conversion (cp. 2 Pt 1:2-3,8; 2:20). True

"peace" and abundant "grace" are only attainable through a personal knowledge of Jesus. "Knowledge" served as a key term for the author and is a theme traced throughout Scripture. Knowledge of God must remain at the heart of a believer's spiritual journey (Pr 9:10; Hs 6:6). It is described not merely in intellectual terms but includes experiential knowledge of God. In the New Testament, in particular, this knowledge of God comes through a relationship with Jesus (Jn 8:19; Col 2:2-3).

The Need for Faithful Growth in Christ (1:3-11)

1:3 Goodness (Gk. *aretē*, "moral excellence, virtue"; cp. v. 5) comes as a result of **the knowledge** of God. Peter explained that the Lord's **divine power** provides the believer with **everything required** for spiritual vitality and growth. This assurance is both encouraging and challenging at the same time. Believers are equipped with everything needed to grow in a vibrant, solid walk with the Lord, which is available only through "the knowledge" **of Him**. Peter added that "the knowledge" of God is only available because of God's call to be one of His children, which should motivate the believer to live a holy life, committed to the Lord and His word. He has **called us**, lavished believers with His love, and enabled them to know Him intimately. He may not provide all that they desire, but Peter clearly states that God does give all that is needed **for life and godliness.**

1:4 Peter continued the thought he began in verse 3. Through "His own glory and goodness" (v. 3), God "has GIVEN" (Gk. *dedōrētai*, "presented as a gift, bestowed, granted," used only here and v. 3; Mk 15:45) His "very great and **PRECIOUS** (Gk. *timia*, "highly honored, costly, highly valued, very dear"; cp. 1 Pt 1:19) promises"

(2 Pt 1:4). Some of these Peter already described in his first epistle, such as the **precious** promise of a believer's "inheritance" (1:4) and the return of Jesus (1:7). He also promised His protection (1:5) and His care (5:7). These **promises** enable the believer to **share in** (Gk. *genēsthe . . . konōnoi*, "become, be made . . . partners, partakers") **the divine nature** of God as His new creation (2 Co 5:17) and have been given for the purpose of allowing the believer to live a holy life, **escaping** the sin of **the world**. This promise does not mean that the believer will be "deified" in the sense of becoming God; neither does it mean that the believer will be free from all sin. Instead, Peter maintained that believers will share in the nature of God by becoming like Him, as His children, at the point of conversion. With the guidance of the Holy Spirit, believers mature in their knowledge and reflection of Christ and thereby escape **the corruption** of the world. This process will reach its ultimate consummation in the future when Jesus returns.

Heart to Heart:
The Precious Promises of God
(2 Pt 1:4)

How true it is! God has granted you His precious and magnificent promises. The Bible reveals many of those promises, as many as 30,000 are recorded in Scripture. A promise is the pledge to another to fulfill a specified act. Scripture records promises by God to His children (Jn 14:13), by God to Jesus (Jn 13:3-5), by one person to another (Neh 5:12), and by a believer to God (Ec 5:4-10). Christians can claim God's promises of forgiveness, eternal life, answered prayer, guidance, comfort, provision, and protection!

While the promises of God are available to all believers, there are some conditions. God's children must humble themselves, pray, seek God's will, and turn from evil (2 Ch 7:14). The fulfillment of God's promises is directly related to the obedient responses of God's children. If you obey Him, you will experience God's precious promises.

1:5-7 Some evangelical scholars call these verses the "ladder of faith" or "the symphony of faith." In this beautiful passage, Peter described the qualities that should be evident and ever increasing in the believer's life as she grows in the knowledge of God. **For this very reason** refers back to "the divine nature" that believers share with Christ. Because believers belong to Christ, they should reflect Him by exhibiting the virtues described in the verses that follow. Peter was not espousing a works-based righteousness as though salvation were based on a believer's ability to do these things. Rather, he grounded his exhortations in the grace and love of God. Because of God's grace, believers should be motivated to live in a way that pleases and honors Him. The new birth does not exclude human activity altogether, for Peter instructed believers to **make every effort** to add these qualities to **your faith**. This challenge requires a zealous pursuit of holiness rooted in the active grace of God. The Bible clearly teaches that God expects His children to exercise diligence in growing in their spiritual walk (Col 2:6-7; 3:12-17; 1 Th 4:1-2). Godly character is born from an active, personal walk with the Lord, not from passivity.

The list of virtues is not exhaustive, but Peter identified eight key virtues beginning with faith and ending with love. The point of the passage is not the order in which these are done, but rather that they are evident in the believer's life and that there be a diligent cultivation of these over time. "Faith" is the foundation of all qualities characterizing the Christian life and serves as Peter's springboard for a discussion on these qualities. Faith sets apart believers from other people. **Goodness** (Gk. *aretēn*, "moral excellence or virtue"; cp. Php 4:8) is to be added to faith (2 Pt 1:5).

Knowledge (Gk. *gnōsin*) is to accompany self-control. It is not merely an intellectual pursuit but rather relates to spiritual discernment that comes through the work of the Holy Spirit and that is rooted in the word of God. This discernment distinguishes, in part, believers from false teachers. While false teachers promote the knowledge they have attained through their own abilities and talents, Peter encouraged knowledge of God that comes by the truth of God founded in Scripture.

Those who pursue such knowledge should also be SELF-CONTROLLED (Gk. *egkrateian*, "mastery of one's desires and passions, power to restrain oneself"), which is identified as a fruit of the Spirit (Gl 5:23) and as a qualification of an overseer (Ti 1:7-8). The word here implies that believers are to control their appetites for fleshly lusts by surrendering to the control of the Spirit in their lives.

ENDURANCE (Gk. *hupomonē*, "perseverance," from *hupo*, "under," and *menō*, "stay, abide, remain"), which concerns a believer's "steadfastness" to "endure" without giving up regardless of the adversities encountered along the way, is the ability to continue patiently in the faith while simultaneously resisting the pressures of the world that can distract the believer from her ultimate goal of reflecting Christ. Such "endurance" can only spring from a heart that is surrendered to Christ, expressed in personal faith, and set on knowing Jesus in a deeper way.

To such endurance is added the quality of **godliness** (Gk. *eusebeian*, "piety, reverence for God"), which is displayed in faithfulness and holiness. **Brotherly affection** (Gk. *philadelphina*) and **love** (Gk. *agapēn*), which complete Peter's list, highlight a believer's relationship with others. Whereas the first six qualities primarily concern one's relationship with God, these final two qualities represent the overflow of that relationship to one's treatment of others. Warm fellowship and genuine love should characterize the relationships among believers (1 Co 13:13). Love flows from God who is described by John as the author of love (1 Jn 4:8). Those who desire to follow Christ, participating in the divine nature, must increase in their love for God and consequently in their love for others. Jesus Christ is the perfect example of love characterized by self-sacrifice (Jn 3:16). All of these qualities should be evident in a maturing believer.

1:8-11 In verses 8-11 Peter provides a "formula" for distinguishing the outcomes of living in pursuit of **these qualities** versus neglecting such discipline. Christian growth will produce fruitfulness while inactivity in pursuing such things will render the believer ineffective (cp. Jms 2:17-22). **The person who lacks** the qualities described in verses 5-7 **is blind and shortsighted** (2 Pt 1:9).

SHORT-SIGHTED (Gk. *muōpazōn*, "seeing dimly, near-sighted"), used only here in the Greek New Testament, is the source of the anglicized word "myopia," the description of a condition in which one is able to see clearly only things that are close by. The metaphor figuratively illustrates the spiritual condition of those who do not apply all that Christ's "divine power has given" to move beyond "faith" to "increasing" Christlikeness (vv. 3,5,8). They are "blind" to the nature they have as God's children purchased with His blood, and they are unable to grasp the fullness of the richness of life in Christ. They cannot "see" far off, their perspective is skewed, and the scope of their understanding is limited. They have consequently **forgotten the cleansing from his past sins** (v. 9).

For this reason Peter encouraged his readers to remain determined and steadfast to walk with the Lord and to please Him by living a holy life. This theme is reminiscent of Peter's exhortation in 1 Peter 1:13-22. A believer is to grow in grace, practicing the virtues listed in the preceding verses, thereby confirming her **calling and election** of God (2 Pt 1:10). While calling and election are God's work in salvation, the emphasis here is on the responsibility of the believer to live faithfully according to her calling as a child of God. The call of God and godly living go hand in hand, contradicting the tenets of false teachers who claim that God's grace provides license for living however one desires. The Christian life does not end at the point of conversion, which is only the beginning. Believers live in service and submission to the Lord, as Peter so eloquently reminded his readers in his first epistle.

Peter maintained that two things would result from living in conformity to God's calling. First, the believer **will never stumble** (Gk. *ptaisēte*, "trip up, go wrong, fall into misery," v. 10). Peter did not suggest, as some argue, that a believer could lose her salvation, as though salvation were dependent on spiritual growth. Scripture affirms that salvation is by faith alone, not by one's works (Eph 2:8-9). Rather, Peter was saying that mature believers who pursue godliness by growing in their knowledge of God and reflecting Him through their actions will never trip up, unlike those who are "blind and shortsighted" in their spiritual walk. Maturing believers will not fall prey to false teachings that could otherwise lure them away from the truth of God's word. Second, the one who lives in conformity to God's calling will also be rewarded with **entry into the eternal kingdom**.

The phrase RICHLY (Gk. *plousiōs*, "abundantly") SUPPLIED (Gk. *epichorēgēthēsetai*, "furnished, granted, given") is related to terminology in Greek drama. The root verb for "supplied" (Gk. *choregeō*) literally means "furnish a chorus at one's own expense." The *choregos* was a wealthy citizen chosen and appointed by the state to finance and organize the training of the *chorus*, the people performing as a group in a theatrical production. Like the *choregos*, Jesus Christ has provided believers with an "all-expense-paid" entrance into His "kingdom," having paid dearly with His own life for their "cleansing" from sin (v. 11).

The ultimate reward for the believer is the welcome that she will receive from the Lord. That believers will receive a rich welcome by the Savior supplies hope to those struggling to persevere in their walk with the Lord. Peter encouraged his readers to view the Christian walk not simply as an intellectual endeavor based primarily on personal works but rather as an active response to the Lord for the grace He has provided in salvation. In the end, believers can look forward to being richly welcomed by Jesus into His eternal kingdom.

Heart to Heart:
Persevering in Faith (2 Pt 1:5-11)

Peter wrote to Christians in Asia Minor urging them to continue in the faith. He warned of false doctrines and heretical teachers who were distorting the truth of the gospel. He challenged them to live the Christian life diligently and receive the rewards of heaven. Peter's wise counsel should be followed by Christians today—persevere in the faith.

There are many virtues to be added to faith, not for salvation but for righteous living. Goodness, knowledge and self-control are godly virtues, but the key to faithfulness is perseverance. Peter explained and repeated the need for endurance in the faith when he said increase in these things (v. 9), be diligent, keep practicing. Perseverance in the faith enables the believer to receive all that God has promised. If you continue in the faith, then you will enter the everlasting kingdom of the Lord Jesus Christ.

Are you persevering in the faith? Are you abounding in godly virtues? Are you walking in His ways without stumbling? If so, you can be assured of the abundant promises of God. You will enter the everlasting kingdom of the Lord Jesus Christ.

The Reliability of Scripture (1:12-21)

1:12-15 Peter digressed for a couple of verses from his theological treatise to address his readers on a more personal note. He expressed concern that his audience be constantly reminded of what he taught them (v. 12). Peter desired believers to remain unwavering in their faith, so he exhorted them not to forget all that they had learned. Believers can easily grow lethargic in their spiritual walk and fail to recall all that they have learned and know in relation to what God has done for them and what He expects from them. The danger still exists that believers can slip into doctrinal error or serious sin, should the Lord's teaching be neglected.

Perhaps Peter remembered the words of Jesus in Luke 22:32: "When you have turned back, strengthen your brothers." Peter strengthened his fellow believers by encouraging them **to recall** all that he had written. Knowing the time of his death was imminent, Peter wrote with a sense of urgency (2 Pt 1:14). Peter also shared his desire to leave a record of the things he had taught so that they could be recalled at a later time (v. 15). God has preserved these through His written word. What a blessing to possess the infallible, eternal word of God and to be encouraged and challenged as you recall what it teaches. Your responsibility is to remember the truths you have learned (Col 2:6-7).

1:16-18 Peter stressed the importance of apostolic authority in the matter of discerning truth from error. True faith is founded not upon clever stories but rather on historical facts, which **eyewitnesses**, such as the apostles, saw with their own eyes. False teaching, however, relied on clever stories and fabrications of the truth of God's word. Peter distinguished between the two in the effort both to defend the apostolic witness as well as to instruct his readers regarding the dangers of straying from what God has revealed in His written word and through His Son, Jesus.

Peter was an "eyewitness" of the Lord Jesus Christ and **His majesty** (v. 17). He heard the **voice** of God on the Mount of Transfiguration, where he, along with John and James, stood and beheld the majesty of Jesus (v. 17; Mt 17:1-5). Jesus' sonship was confirmed **on the holy mountain** (2 Pt 1:18–19) as the Lord God spoke saying, **This is My beloved Son. I take delight in Him!** (v. 17; Mt 17:5). Jesus is the Messiah, the promised Son of God, and the transfiguration was only a preview of His coming glory as the King of kings (2 Pt 1:19). But, how does this eyewitness account relate to verse 16? Peter was pointing out that what he had taught regarding Jesus' **coming** (Gk. *parousian*, "advent, arrival, presence," v. 16; cp. 1 Th 2:19; 3:13; Jms 5:7-8; 1 Jn 2:28) was based not on a clever tale, but rather on what he knew to be true based on what he saw with his eyes and heard with his ears. Jesus promised that He would return in **power** (2 Pt 1:16). Peter was foreshadowing his disagreement with the false teachers who denied Jesus' future return. He spoke to this issue more specifically in chapter 3. The apostles taught that Jesus would return in power, and this day would mark the time when a decision on who will enter Jesus' eternal kingdom would be made.

1:19 The prophetic word testified to Jesus' return. Even as he passionately recalled the miraculous event on the Mount of Transfiguration, Peter turned his attention to the surer testimony of Scripture. Peter emphasized that just as the transfiguration has "confirmed" what was taught in the Old Testament, all of Scripture is vitally important to the believer as **a lamp** illuminating the darkness. The metaphor of light is used elsewhere to speak of Scripture given to guide, protect, and illuminate a believer's understanding of God and His revelation (e.g., Ps 119:105). Believers are exhorted **to pay attention** to God's word **until the day dawns and the morning star arises in your hearts**. Peter was referring to the Day of the Lord in which judgment would be issued on all mankind whether it be salvation or punishment. Again, this day had been confirmed both by Peter's witness of the transfiguration as well as "the prophetic word" of Scripture. THE MORNING STAR (Gk. *phōsphoros*, "bringing light, light-bringer") is a metaphorical reference to Jesus used only here in the Greek New Testament. With different wording in Revelation 22:16, Jesus calls Himself "the Bright Morning Star" (Gk. *ho astēr*, "the star"; *ho lampros*, "the shining, splendid, magnificent"; *ho prōinos*, "of the morning"). At that promised day, believers will see all things clearer when they come face-to-face with the eternal Light of the World. Until then, Peter exhorted, believers to heed "the prophetic word" of Scripture.

1:20-21 Peter strengthened his argument by emphasizing that **no prophecy** originates with man but rather with God. He says several important things here about the inspiration and interpretation of **Scripture**:

- Scripture should not be interpreted according to an individual's private **interpretation** (v. 20).

- Scripture is willed by God, not by man (v. 21).

- God is the Divine author of Scripture. The human authors who penned the words of Scripture were "MOVED (Gk. *pheromenoi,* "borne or carried along") by the Holy Spirit." In Acts 27:15,17 the word is used to describe a sailing vessel being "driven along" by the wind. The human authors were certainly involved in the process—but only as **men** who **spoke from God** (v. 21).

A REMINDER OF DESTRUCTIVE TEACHERS (2:1-22)

The Power of Deception (2:1-3)

2:1-3 Peter concluded that there had always been **FALSE PROPHETS** (Gk. *pseudophrophētai,* combining *pseudēs,* "lying, deliberately deceitful, fake, untrue" and *prophētes,* "prophets," thus someone proclaiming falsehoods while speaking under the pretext of being a divinely appointed spokesperson for God) and always would be "FALSE TEACHERS (Gk. *pseudodidaskaloi,* combining *pseudēs,* "lying, deliberately deceitful, fake, untrue" and *didaskaloi,* "teachers," thus someone teaching falsehoods under the pretext of correctly explaining the truths of Scripture) among" God's people (v. 1). Peter compared the false prophets of the Old Testament to false teachers emerging in the early church and identified several common characteristics. False prophets and teachers will:

- **SECRETLY BRING IN** (Gk. *pareisaxousin,* lit., "lead in by the side, introduce") false doctrines, with the sense of introducing doctrinal error "through the back door" (v. 1);

- introduce false teachings that are **DESTRUCTIVE** (Gk. *apōleias,* marked by bringing to "ruin, waste" or causing to "perish," v. 1);

- inject **HERESIES** (Gk. *haireseis,* "choices, factions, sects; false teachings," v. 1), i.e., will introduce doctrines that deviate from the truth and thereby foster the formation of dissenting groups, each following its own doctrine;

- gain a large following of people who imitate their **UNRESTRAINED WAYS** (Gk. *aselgeiais,* "sensuality, licentiousness, shameless conduct," v. 2; cp. vv. 7,18; 1 Pt 4:3);

- incite blasphemy of **THE WAY OF TRUTH**—God's word and His name will be reproached, maligned, and reviled "because of them" (2 Pt 2:2);

- be motivated by **GREED** (Gk. *pleonexia,* "unsated desire for more, avarice, covetousness," v. 3; cp. v. 14);

- **EXPLOIT YOU** (Gk. *emporeusontai,* "use for gain or as a source of profit"; related to *emporiou,* which is anglicized as "emporium, marketplace" in Jn 2:16);

- use "**DECEPTIVE** (Gk. *plastois,* "molded, fabricated, shaped," lit. used of forming clay; source of the English word "plastic") words" in order to "exploit you" (2 Pt 2:3).

Peter was most appalled, perhaps, by the fact that they denied the sovereign Lord who purchased their salvation. Even in light of the grace demonstrated to them by Almighty God, they consciously chose to follow their own ways and teach what was contrary to Scripture. They led others astray to the point that the word of God was blasphemed.

Peter made clear the nature of punishment awaiting such false teachers—utter **destruction**. The question is raised then as to how destruction can be promised for those who have been redeemed by the Lord. Evangelical commentators offer a variety of answers:

- They were saved at one time, but lost their salvation. This position must be rejected because it contradicts Scripture (Rm 8:28-39; Php 1:6).

- In verse 1, the word **bought** (Gk. *agorasanta*, "buy or sell, do business in a marketplace") must mean something other than "redeem" or "save." This explanation is plausible but stretches the meaning of the original word used in this passage.

- The false prophets *said* they were "bought" by Jesus, but perhaps they were only misleading others with such a statement. Again, this interpretation is plausible but not stated in the text itself.

- They were "bought" in the sense that Jesus did pay the price for their salvation, but they did not accept this gift of grace and thus were not truly saved (1 Tm 2:6; Heb 2:9). This answer to the question seems to be preferred and is an argument for the position of "unlimited atonement." Such a view argues that Jesus died for all mankind, but that salvation is dependent on one individual's acceptance of this gift of grace. "Limited atonement" maintains that Jesus died only for those who were predetermined to accept the gift of salvation.

Peter warned that the destruction belonging to false teachers **does not sleep**. God will judge them severely for their shameful ways. They are shameful in part because of the devastation they reap among God's people by the influence they have on those within the church.

The Doom of False Teachers (2:4-11)

2:4-6 Peter addressed the judgment of God by speaking of the fallen **angels**, the **flood**, and **the cities of Sodom and Gomorrah**. He sets up an equation: If God did not spare A, B or C, then . . . He certainly would not **spare** the false prophets. Yet, while making this conclusion, he seemed to focus more on God's mercy than on His wrath (vv. 4-9). As in his first letter, Peter again referred to the flood. He described **Noah** as **a preacher of righteousness** who heralded the justice of God, though surrounded by ungodliness (vv. 4-5). God destroyed many people and flooded the earth, but He saved Noah and his family. God not only judges the wicked, but He also saves the righteous. Likewise, God will destroy false teachers, regardless of their number, but He will save those who follow Him.

2:7-11 Peter cited the example of **Lot** who was saved from the destruction of Sodom and Gomorrah (v. 7). Just as Noah and his family were protected from death, so, too, God delivered Lot from the fires that burned against these two rebellious cities. To readers familiar with the biblical account of Lot's less than exemplary life (Gn 19), Peter's describing him as **righteous** may seem surprising (2 Pt 2:7-8). Peter explained, nevertheless, that Lot was "DISTRESSED (Gk. *kataponoumenon*, "oppressed, afflicted, subdued, exhausted, troubled") by the UNRESTRAINED (Gk. *aselgeia*, "sensual, licentious" v. 7; see v. 2) behavior of the IMMORAL" (Gk. *athesmōn*, "lawless, unprincipled" describing those who set aside the law in their pursuit of self-gratification) among whom he lived (vv. 7-8). Ultimately, God rescues the righteous and punishes the wicked (v. 9). Notice, too, that God does not keep His people from trials; He gives them victory in the midst of trials. As Peter instructed in his first letter, God uses such trials to refine the believer and to impact the ungodly. The wicked are in God's hands for His proclamation of judgment.

Peter also addressed the reasons why future judgment would be fitting for false teachers (v. 10):

- They **follow the polluting desires of the flesh** over His desires. Believing that future judgment and the *parousia* are obsolete, they abandoned the believer's responsibility to live holy lives before the Lord. Instead, they embraced a lifestyle of "freedom" to live as they wish.

- They "despise AUTHORITY" (Gk. *kuriotētos*, "lordship, power, dominion"; cp. Jd 8), namely, the authority of Christ. They refused to submit themselves to anyone, being confident of their own authority to decide for themselves what is truth and what is not.

- They are **BOLD** (Gk. *tolmētai*, "daring, audacious, reckless" with the sense of being unrestrained by fear or respect for authority) and **ARROGANT** (Gk. *authadeis*, "self-pleasing, self-willed" in the sense of being determined to do what they want, 2 Pt 2:10).

- They carelessly "blaspheme" angels (Gk. *doxas*, "glories, glorious ones," v. 10). To magnify the false teachers' foolish audacity, Peter pointed out that although the angels are of superior ability "and power," even they do not dare to "bring a SLANDEROUS (Gk. *blasphēmon*, "blasphemous, reviling") CHARGE (Gk.

krisin, "judgment, condemnation") against" the human heretics (v. 11).

The Deception of False Teachers (2:12-22)

2:12-16 Peter compared false teachers to **irrational** (Gk. *aloga*, "without or contrary to reasoning") **animals** following their natural passions rather than the truth. Their doom will be the same as an animal's—they will **be caught** (Gk. *halōsin*, "taken, captured") **and destroyed** (v. 12). Though they try to deceive others concerning their spiritual well-standing and special knowledge, they are so caught in their own web of self-destruction that they parade their sin **in the daytime** (v. 13). They claim to be more spiritually astute than the apostles yet do not even bother to hide their orgies. Hence, they are **BLOTS** (Gk. *spiloi*, "spots, stains, faults") and **BLEMISHES** (Gk. *mōmoi*, "defects, disgraces, insults") among God's people (v. 13). What a stark contrast to Jesus' cleansing of the church from every "spot or wrinkle," making her "blameless" (Gk. *amomos*, in which the Greek alpha ["a"] is a prefix of negation or alpha privative, thus "without blemishes," Eph 5:27). So extensive is their sin and rebellion that they look for ways to sin, deceive others to do the same, and have **hearts trained in greed** (2 Pt 2:14). Their habitual sin indicated the self-serving motivation of their hearts. There seems to be little doubt now about whether or not they are redeemed children of God (v. 14; cp. 1 Jn 3:9).

The false teachers resemble **Balaam**, the Old Testament prophet who rebelled against God in order to follow his own way. He, too, reveled in leading people away from God's truth. Likewise, the false prophets were wandering off the right path, foolishly believing they could sin without being punished. Balaam's greed led him to believe he could thwart

God's will, but ironically his **speechless donkey** had more spiritual perception and insight than the prophet and **restrained** Balaam's **madness** (2 Pt 2:15-16; Nm 22:27-35).

2:17-19 False teachers are able to bring destruction into the church because of the vulnerability of those whom they seek to destroy. Knowing the weakness of sinful human nature, **they** use the sensuality of the flesh to **seduce** (Gk. *deleazousin*, "allure, catch with bait, entice") others (v. 18). Peter described them as **springs without water** and **mists driven by a whirlwind** (v. 17). They exchange the "living water" (Jn 4:10-14) for **empty** beliefs and **promise** liberty that they themselves do not even possess (2 Pt 2:19). Their coming judgment promises utter **darkness** (v. 17). False teachers prey on those **who have barely escaped from those who live in error**. Both new believers who are relatively unstable in their walk with the Lord and people who are being introduced to the gospel are vulnerable (v. 18).

2:20-22 Verses 20 and 21 are much more complex and debated among scholars. Is this teaching that someone can lose her salvation? Is this a reference to the false teachers or to those whom they led astray or to both? The passage seems similar to Hebrews 6. In the context of the whole of Scripture, certainly these verses are not teaching that believers can lose their salvation. Rather, here seemingly the reference is to people who had intellectual knowledge of Christ yet failed to place their faith in Him, following the ways of the world instead. Peter noted that **it would have been better for them not to have known about the way of righteousness than** to have known the truth and deliberately rebelled against it. Peter used two shocking images to convey this point. He compared false teachers to the animals that Jewish people considered to

be the most unclean—dogs and pigs. While false teachers tried to present themselves as "spiritual leaders," like dogs returning to **vomit** and washed pigs wallowing **in the mud,** they were steeped in spiritual filth and could not hide it.

A REMINDER OF GOD'S PROMISES (3:1-18)

The Assurance of Jesus' Return (3:1-13)

3:1-4 Peter's urgency is evident as he reminded his **dear friends** to **remember** God's word delivered by **prophets** and **apostles** so that the truth could protect them from false teachers (vv. 1-2). One of the issues raised by false teachers concerned the return of the Lord. They questioned the promise that Jesus made regarding His imminent return. Peter urged believers to wait and watch for the return of Jesus.

3:5-7 Furthermore, false teachers **willfully ignore** (Gk. *lanthanei*, "forget, overlook") the fact that the earth is the Lord's and that He controls its processes (v. 5). The false teachers believed that the universe must follow a natural course, meaning that Jesus' return would be impossible. Peter referred back to the creation account in Genesis 1 to remind them that God is Creator and has all dominion and authority over creation. He alone is the supreme Creator of heaven and earth, and He alone determines how and when His creation could be destroyed and restored. While God used flood waters to destroy the earth in the time of Noah, He will use **fire** for the future destruction of the world. God will judge ungodliness, and He will destroy the present heavens and earth through fire (v. 7; cp. Is 66:15-16; Ezk 38:22; Am 7:4; Zph 1:18; Mal 4:1-2; 2 Th 1:8).

3:8-9 Peter addressed an unsettling question: In light of the wickedness and evil present around us, why should the Lord wait to come? First, God counts time differently than you do (v. 8; cp. Ps 90:4). What may seem like a long time to you is very short in the Lord's eyes. Second, God has waited to bring destruction on the world because of His desire for **all to come to repentance** (Gk. *metanoian*, "change of mind or purpose, remorse" 2 Pt 3:9; cp. Mt 4:17; Rv 3:3). The seeming **delay** in Christ's return is not due to His indifference but rather reveals His patience and mercy. Peter was not teaching universalism—that God will save all mankind. He was simply stating that God desires that all will be saved, while knowing that many will reject Him (cp. 1 Tm 2:4).

3:10-18 When **the Day of the Lord** does **come**, it will be a surprise, **like a thief** (Gk. *kleptēs*, "one who takes away by stealth, who steals," v. 10; cp. Mt 24:43; Lk 12:39; 1 Th 5:2,4; Rv 3:3; 16:15). The Lord will appear and destroy the world. The end-time events described as "the Day of the Lord" will be marked by devastation and catastrophe. What will be annihilated is sin. The present order will be completely renewed as the new creation becomes the dwelling place of righteousness for the children of God. Peter asked a key question: In light of certain, future destruction, what kind of people should believers be? Believers should be motivated towards **holy conduct**, living godly, Christ-centered lives set apart from the world and from false teachers (2 Pt 3:11; contrast 2:7). All is to be done with an attitude of waiting and trusting in the Lord's return. Believers are to continue steadfast in righteousness until the Lord returns.

Peter urged believers to **be found in peace** (v. 14) and to live spotless and blameless lives. MAKE EVERY EFFORT (Gk. *spoudasate*, "endeavor, be diligent, exert oneself, hasten") stresses both the importance and urgency of the manner in which believers await the Lord's return (v. 14). Rather than being frantic or fearful, believers should be actively and eagerly "keeping the house in order," ready at any moment for the Lord's arrival. Unlike those who "are blots and blemishes" openly indulging in sin (2:13), believers should endeavor to be "WITHOUT SPOT (Gk. *aspiloi*, "unsullied, irreproachable, blameless," 3:14; cp. 1 Tm 6:14; Jms 1:27) or BLEMISH" (Gk. *amōmētoi*, "faultless, blameless," 2 Pt 3:14). The Lord's longsuffering in delaying His return gives the world time to repent, but the Day of the Lord will soon usher in judgment.

Peter concurred with **Paul** who also **has written** concerning **these things** in **his letters** (cp. Rm 2:4; 6:1). Peter acknowledged that some things contained in Paul's letters "are hard to understand" and thus are misused by ignorant men who TWIST (Gk. *streblousin*, "pervert, distort," in this context having the figurative sense of torturing the language to make it confess falsehood, 2 Pt 3:16) Paul's words to fit their own motivations. They do this, Peter indicated, not just with Paul's letters but with all of Scripture. Peter did not specify which Pauline passages are difficult to understand but rather placed the emphasis on the perversion and distortion, which characterized those who manipulated God's Word.

Peter encouraged believers to **guard** themselves from being led astray (v. 17). The believers had been FOREWARNED (Gk. *proginōskontes*, "know beforehand, choose in advance" from *pro*, "before," and *ginoskō*, "learn, come to know, understand," the root for the English word "prognosis"). Just as a medical prognosis helps a patient know beforehand the expected outcomes of her illness, God's word helps believers know beforehand the dangerous consequences of following false teachers. Believers must remain alert, actively on the lookout for deceptive ploys to lead them "to fall" from their "own STABILITY" (Gk. *stērigmou*, "firm position, firm footing, steadfastness"), i.e., from their secure position in the truth of God's word. FALL (Gk. *ekpesēte*, "fall from, down, or away") implies harm caused by the movement away from firm footing (v. 17). In Acts 27 this verb is used four times in the description of a shipwreck—the vessel "runs aground," and the ropes to its skiff are cut to let it "drop away" (Ac 27:17,26,29,32). **The possibility of being led away by the error of the immoral (Gk. *athesmōn*, "lawless," see 2:7) is a major threat.** LED AWAY (Gk. *sunapachthentes*, "lead away with or together," from *sun*, "with," and *apagō*, "lead away") is typically used in the context of leading or taking someone away to trial or prison (cp. Mk 14:44,53; Ac 12;19; 1 Co 12:2).

Peter concluded his letter by urging his readers not to neglect their personal relationship with Jesus but to continue to **grow in the grace and knowledge** of Jesus (2 Pt 3:18). GROW (Gk. *auxanete*, "increase") in the present imperative tense here suggests a continual growing process that is absolutely necessary. Peter knew from first-hand experience the joys that accompany the one who walks with the Savior. This old fisherman from Galilee, a servant and apostle of Jesus, closed with an humble expression of praise for the One to whom all **glory** is due (v. 18).

Bibliography

*Blum, Edwin A. "2 Peter" in *The Expositor's Bible Commentary: Hebrews–Revelation*, vol. 12. Grand Rapids: Zondervan Publishing House, 1981.

*Green, Michael. *II Peter and Jude.* Tyndale New Testament Commentary, vol. 18. Leicester, England: InterVarsity, 1999.

Hiebert, Edward. "The Necessary Growth in the Christian Life: An Exposition of 2 Peter 1:5-11." *Bibliotheca Sacra,* 141:561 (Jan.–Mar. 1984): 43–53.

Schreiner, Thomas R. *1, 2 Peter, Jude.* The New American Commentary, vol. 37. Nashville: Broadman and Holman Publishers, 2003.

Vaughan, Curtis, and Thomas Lea. *I and II Peter, Jude.* Bible Study Commentary. Grand Rapids: Zondervan Publishing House, 1988.

Walvoord, John F., and Roy B. Zuck. *The Bible Knowledge Commentary: New Testament.* Colorado Springs: Chariot Victor Publishing, 1983.

* For advanced study

Notes

[1] Matthias was chosen to replace Judas Iscariot.

1 JOHN

Introduction

First John was written to teach the fellowship of believers how to protect themselves against the heretical doctrines of false teachers, who were claiming that the historical Jesus was not the Christ. Likely they were those holding to some form of the heresy that became known as Gnosticism, a set of beliefs that began its development even prior to the expansion of Christianity.

Cerinthus of Ephesus, a contemporary of Polycarp—one of John's students—taught that the Christ came in spirit form upon Jesus some time during the beginning of His ministry, possibly at the time of His baptism. Since the false teaching addressed seems closest to the heresy taught by Cerinthus, the point of reference seems to be the incipient Gnosticism, which did not develop fully until the second century, spreading through Asia Minor. People, having been introduced to this view by false teachers, left the church and then returned to disrupt its fellowship (2:19). They were dualists who viewed spiritual things as good and all physical things as evil. Christ was deity, but Jesus was only human. They refused to recognize Christ Jesus as the God-man He claimed to be. The Gnostic problem with the body of Christ led them to an ethical challenge in two ways, both of them antithetical to genuine truth:

- *asceticism*, which rigorously denies the body as an attempt to overcome its evil nature; and

- *antinomianism*, which also views the body as inherently evil and so without hope that its activities are unimportant and can thus be pursued without restraint.

First John is a response to these opponents. This epistle provides the reader with a way to distinguish between true and false teachers and to strengthen these believers in their faith (1:4). The author provided a series of tests—obedience to God, love for one another, and pure doctrine—to confirm to the believers their salvation. He also provided a clear distinction between the lives and actions of believers who held to truth and the heretics who embraced false teaching. The author referred to the actions and teachings of the opposition as the work of "antichrists." John admonished the struggling believers to hold to the truth, which had been taught them by the apostles, and to manifest that truth through a lifestyle reflecting obedience to Christ and love for others (2:1,26).

Title

First John bears the name of its author, John the beloved apostle.

Setting

The audience to whom John wrote was encountering false teachings from former members of the church. Early Christian tradition and the consensus of evangelical scholars is that John wrote this epistle while he was ministering in Ephesus. John was writing in response to these false teachers. He also wrote to bring assurance to the true fellowship of believers and to teach them the distinctions that exist between a believer and a heretic.

Genre

The structure of 1 John does not fit the typical format of a letter for this time period. However, the author used terms of endearment and salutations that affirmed his connection to his readers. Also the contents of the letter suggest its intention to be instruction from the heart of a pastor to his people, identifying 1 John as an epistle with a pastoral quality similar to Paul's Pastoral Epistles (1, 2 Timothy and Titus).

Author

The name of the author is not mentioned in the epistle; however, there is external and internal evidence to support John, the son of Zebedee and brother of James (Mk 1:19-20) and the beloved disciple, as the author.

- *External evidence:* Only the Apostle John was ever suggested by the early church to be the author of 1 John. Polycarp, a disciple of John, attributed the epistle to him. Others citing 1 John as the work of the beloved disciple included Irenaeus, Papias, Tertullian, and Clement of Alexandria (AD 130–200). These men are respected and trusted church fathers.

- *Internal evidence:* The opening of the epistle proves the author was an eyewitness to the life, ministry, death, and resurrection of Christ. Much of the internal evidence is based on the similarities in theology, writing style, and grammar between the Gospel of John and the epistle of 1 John. One example of such similarities is the word *paraclete* (Gk. *paraklētos*, "one called or sent to assist another, an advocate, one who pleads the case of another") used especially to identify the one whose influence and work were to compensate and continue the work of Christ Himself after His departure. All five appearances of this word in the New Testament are found in John's writings.

Date

The epistle provides little evidence as to the time of writing. Much of the supposition as to its date is based on the similarities between the epistle and the Gospel of John, while allowing adequate time for the opposing belief system to develop within the churches. The dates lie between the early sixties and the last decade of the first century. For those who oppose Johannine authorship, the date has been estimated as late as the beginning of the second century, but conservative scholars are consistent in assigning a date between AD 80 and 95 during John's ministry in Ephesus.

Recipients

The internal evidence is obscure as to the destination of the epistle. Scholars have suggested Asia Minor due to the connection of the Gnostic teachings to that area as well as to its geographic connection to the book of Revelation.

Although the geographic region is difficult to discern, one can infer more about the readers based on John's topics and how he referred to the readers. John referred to the ones to whom he wrote as "my little children" (2:1) and "dear friends" (2:7), showing an affectionate relationship with his readers. Apparently those to whom he wrote were being infiltrated by a group of heretical teachers. More likely, the readers were members of a particular congregation. Doubtless the letter also circulated among multiple congregations throughout Asia Minor.

Major Themes

Love. One of John's favorite themes is God's love. Love was always important to "the disciple whom Jesus loved" (Jn 21:7). In 1 John, he emphasized that God's love should permeate the believer so that the evidence of salvation prompted the believer to be obedient to the commands of God and to give attention to how she treats members of the fellowship. However this love would be hypocritical unless grounded in God's truth. You cannot separate right belief in your heart from righteous conduct in your lifestyle.

> *You cannot separate right belief in your heart from righteous conduct in your lifestyle.*

Jesus is the Christ. Due to the heretical teachings, John found it necessary to address the issue of Christ's humanity. He stressed that the historical Jesus is indeed the Messiah; to believe otherwise resulted in heresy and damnation. He also called attention to the connection between God the Father and God the Son. Every genuine believer must acknowledge Jesus as both fully God and fully man.

Light versus darkness. To show the inaccuracies of the teaching of his opponents in comparison to the truth of God, John used extreme metaphors. He used polar opposites such as: light and darkness (1:5-7), Christ and the antichrist (2:18-25), life and death (3:11-15). John clearly defined genuine faith as providing eternal life and affirmed assurance of salvation. He was careful to note its by-products, i.e., mercy in forgiveness, power in prayer, and victory over the evil one.

Pronunciation Guide

Cerinthus	*suh REN thus* (th as in thin)	Gnosticism	*NAHS tuh SIH zuhm*

Outline

I. THE PROLOGUE: WHAT IS TRUE (1:1-4)

II. TRUE FELLOWSHIP IS IN CHRIST (1:5–3:10)

    A. Living in Obedience to God (1:5–2:11)

      1. Walking in the light (1:5–2:2)

      2. Following God's commands (2:3-11)

    B. Experiencing the Love of God and the Hatred of the World (2:12–3:10)

      1. The Christian's response to the world (2:12-17)

      2. A warning against antichrists (2:18-27)

      3. The love of God the Father (2:28–3:3)

      4. An admonition to avoid lawlessness and abide in God (3:4-10)

III. GOD IS LOVE (3:11–5:17)
  A. The Necessity of God's Love
     (3:11-24)
     1. Life and death (3:11-18)
     2. Assurance of salvation
        (3:19-24)
  B. Testing the Spirits (4:1-6)
  C. Loving the Fellowship (4:7-21)

  D. Being Victorious through Faith
     (5:1-5)
  E. Accepting the Witness of the
     Spirit (5:6-13)
  F. Receiving the Bounty of Prayer
     (5:14-17)

IV. CONCLUSION: WHAT THE BELIEVER
    KNOWS (5:18-21)

Exposition of the Text

THE PROLOGUE: WHAT IS TRUE (1:1-4)

1:1-4 Because 1 John lacks a salutation, the recipients of the epistle must have known the author so well that the name was unnecessary. Also, John's reference to his readers as his **children** (2:1,12,14,18,28; 3:7,18; 4:4; 5:21) is evidence of a loving relationship between the beloved apostle and those to whom he wrote.

John went right to the heart of the controversy: The historical man Jesus is also the Christ. John wrote a clear progression of the gospel: It **was from the beginning** (v. 1); it **was revealed** (v. 2); it was proclaimed by the apostles (v. 3) and shared with others to complete their joy (v. 4).

"What was from the beginning" are the first words. Questions have arisen among scholars about what John meant by the word "beginning." Since the Gospel of John opens with a similar phrase, "In the beginning was the Word" (Jn 1:1), some scholars believe the author was discussing Jesus' pre-incarnate existence. However, based on context and the issue at hand, more probably John was referring to the life and message of the historical Jesus. Jesus was not just the messenger; He was also the message. What He shared verbally during His time on earth, He acted out in life.

The main verb of the prologue, **PROCLAIM** (Gk. *apangellomen*, "report, announce, tell, proclaim"), occurs in the third verse. All that was stated prior to the appearance of this verb was witnessed by and attested to by the apostles. John could speak with authority about Jesus because he was a witness to the life and ministry of Jesus during His early ministry. John saw and could testify to the truth of Christ as the embodiment of the gospel. He witnessed the works of Jesus and could share with confidence that He is the truth. Not only had John seen Jesus, but he also touched Christ. He knew the Word became flesh because he had touched the flesh. John had a full sensory experience with his Redeemer.

John provided his reasons for writing (vv. 3-4): fellowship and joy. The word **FELLOWSHIP** (Gk. *koinōnia*, "close relationship, participation") suggests that a group, corporately or with each possessing an equal part, has joint ownership of something. In this instance, all believers are equal heirs of heaven. The fellowship that believers have with one another requires their own respective individual fellowship with God. This fellowship is eternal; it is perfected in the presence of God.

John wrote this epistle showing his feeling of responsibility for his flock as their pastor. He wrote **so that our joy may be**

complete (1:4). As a pastor, he could not be completely full of joy until those to whom he has a responsibility were aware and participating in the fellowship.

TRUE FELLOWSHIP IS IN CHRIST (1:5–3:10)

Living in Obedience to God (1:5–2:11)

Walking in the light (1:5–2:2)

1:5-7 In this section John laid out the qualifications for members of the fellowship and the characteristics of unbelievers. John used a series of **if we say** clauses in these verses to show the cause and effect of the life of a true believer in contrast to an unbeliever. He often began with describing the life of the sinner and followed with a description of the life of the believer.

John began by defining God as **light**. The Hellenistic culture of the first century used light as a symbol of goodness and as an indication of safety. Therefore, John's use of "light" as a metaphor would not be difficult for his readers or others living in the first century to follow.

"Light" is a metaphor for salvation or life in Scripture. Light provides one with the ability to see. John emphasized that God is the ultimate good, and He is the complete source of "light" for Christians. In Him there is **no darkness**, just the radiation of His goodness. Therefore, the antithesis would be darkness, which is one of the most graphic metaphors for evil.

The first **if we say** clause shows that the life of an unbeliever personifies lying (v. 6). In opposition, the next clause reveals the life of a Christian as resulting in two things (v. 7):

- fellowship with other believers, and

- cleansing from sin through Jesus' blood. CLEANSES (Gk. *katharizei*, v. 7) is in the perfect tense, which indicates that the cleansing is a completed action with continuing results. As the Christian is sinning, Christ is cleansing him.

Salvation is immediate upon request; sanctification is progressive. Being sanctified is a result of being in the light God provides.

1:8 These false teachers imported an elitism into Christianity. To be a Christian gave one a position higher than others; therefore, the Christian was considered perfect. Since the Christian was viewed as perfect, all she did was flawless, meaning that even in doing things that would be sinful for others to do, she would not be sinning. In response, John wrote his third clause, **If we say, "We have no sin," we are deceiving ourselves, and the truth is not in us.** God is faithful to forgive because those who are His creation are without faith and in need of forgiveness.

1:9-10 Confession of sin is the first step to forgiveness from God. The word CONFESSION is a combination of two Greek words, *homos*, meaning "same," and *legō*, meaning "to say." "Confession" then is "saying the same" or "agreeing." Believers are called to say the same thing about sin that God says—to see sin as God sees it. When a believer confesses personal sin and professes faith in Christ, then God will faithfully and justly **forgive** sin and cleanse unrighteousness. Confession is essential to the believer's relationship with God and to fellowship with other people.

2:1-2 For the first time in the letter, John addressed his audience directly and intimately as his LITTLE CHILDREN (Gk. *teknia*, the diminutive form of the Greek noun used in the New Testament only by John in this letter, 2:12,28; 3:7,18; 4:4; 5:21. and in his Gospel, Jn 13:33). Jesus tenderly addressed His disciples as *teknia*). The

Heart to Heart: God's Faithfulness

You can be encouraged with the faithfulness of God. God is fully reliable. John attributed any capacity for righteousness within the Christian to God's faithfulness and trustworthiness. Paul wrote, "If we are faithless, He remains faithful, for He cannot deny Himself" (2 Tm 2:13). Christ cannot deny His own existence. Every believer can trust Him to forgive and to pass judgment. God's forgiveness of believers coexists with God's judgment of unbelievers; otherwise He would not be a just God.

phrase introduced John's parental concern in admonishing Christians to avoid sinful behavior.

John reminded his readers that when sin occurs, believers **have an advocate** in Jesus (v. 1). ADVOCATE (Gk. *paraklēton*, more literally "one called alongside") is found five times in the Greek New Testament, all in John's writings. Here the term refers to the intercessory ministry of Christ as He stands before God the Father on behalf of His children. The word especially denotes one who is summoned to another's aid or one who pleads another's cause in a court of law, or before a judge, somewhat like a defense attorney. Jesus thwarts the evil one's accusations of sin against God's children by being "the righteous One" and "the propitiation for our sins" (v. 1). Jesus effectively pleads the sinner's case before the Father because as the sinless Lamb of God He has fulfilled the death penalty incurred by the sinner's crimes. The word is used only four other times, each time in reference to the Holy Spirit as "Counselor" (in Jn 14:16,26; 15:26; 16:7).

Following God's commands (2:3-11)

2:3-4 The word KNOW (Gk. *ginōskomen*, "perceive, understand") is in the perfect tense, again affirming that an action from the past has a continual effect through history (v. 3). This Greek word is used 25 times in the epistle with the idea of having experiential knowledge or understanding, knowing on the basis of life experience or personal observation. John did not use the common word for "know" (Gk. *gnōsis*), which usually signifies general knowledge or understanding of right and wrong. Gnostics used this word to indicate "intellectual, advanced, or secret knowledge." John may have chosen not to use *gnōsis* possibly because of the heresy, which his opponents embraced, so that the distinction between their position and the true Christianity about which He wrote was clear. However, this possibility cannot be proven. To know God in the biblical sense is to have a personal relationship with Him through forgiveness of sin, not, as the false teachers claimed, merely to achieve release from ignorance.

At this great distance from the New Testament documents, how much the tenets of Gnosticism appearing in a later era had already begun to take hold in the first-century ministry of John is not clear, but from the text apparently some of the same ideas later integral to Gnosticism were even then being presented to the

Christians in Asia Minor. The teachings of this incipient gnostic heresy were already causing confusion among believers. Thus, John here offered a series of tests to provide the believer with assurance of salvation, beginning with the test of obedience.

Obeying God's commandments is the natural and inevitable fruit of salvation—of knowing Christ. If believers are not obedient to His command, they may well question whether they have saving knowledge of Him. John used the strongest possible language about the person who claims to know Him but does not obey: That person **is a liar**. On the other hand, the believer's obedience to Him gives her assurance that she has **come to know Him**.

2:5-6 The use of the objective genitive in the phrase **the love of God** renders the statement to be understood as "your love for God" (v. 5). In John 15:1-8 believers are reminded that God allows them to be extensions of His work on earth when they remain connected to Him: "I am the vine; you are the branches. The one who remains in Me and I in him produces much fruit, because you can do nothing without Me" (Jn 15:5). Christ is the light of the world, but He asserts that His followers are also the light of the world (Mt 5:14-16). If He is light and no darkness is found in Him, then when believers abide in Him, they too have no darkness. The one John was referencing with the pronoun "Him" is unclear. The ambiguity could be to show the permanent oneness of God the Father and God the Son.

2:7-8 John referred to his instruction as a familiar old commandment; then he restated it as a new commandment—both **old** (v. 7) and **new** (v. 8). Within this paradox, which some seem to consider confusing, lies the second test—a test of active love.

2:9-11 The law of love, which has existed since before creation, is one that John's readers understood. In this sense, the law of love is an old commandment, not one invented by John but one that had been "known from the beginning" (Jn 3:11; 4:21; see Lv 19:18). However, the law of love takes on a new approach through the life of Christ (Jn 13:34) because of the dimension of love introduced by Christ's death on the cross. He is the fulfillment of the law of love: "I give you a new commandment: love one another. Just as I have loved you, you must also love one another. By this all people will know that you are My disciples, if you have love for one another" (Jn 13:34-35). Believers are commanded to love people in their fellowship. This command ran contrary to that of those espousing the heresy whose focus was just intellectual. Their lack of love actually diminished their knowledge. Their condition is analogous to physical blindness. The result is that they do not know where they are going. Acting properly toward Christian brothers and sisters in obedience to God demonstrates your love for Him.

Experiencing the Love of God and the Hatred of the World (2:12–3:10)

The Christian's response to the world (2:12-17)

2:12-14 These verses may seem to function as a separate unit not clearly connected to the surrounding text, but John merely shifted to a more direct form of address to convey his personal concern for the believers. The style of this section, particularly with the repeated phrases **I am writing to you** (vv. 12,13) and **I have written to you** (v. 14), also reinforced a sense of John's apostolic authority. These phrases had already appeared in the letter in the same or similar form (1:3,4,5; 2:1,7,8), and they were repeated in the remainder (2:21,26; 3:13). Furthermore,

John consistently addressed his readers as "little children" (Gk. *teknia*) throughout the letter (see commentary on v. 1). Overall, these verses emphasize the differences between believers and pseudo-Christians:

- the **sins** of God's children **have been forgiven** (v. 12);

- believers **have come to know the One who is from the beginning** (vv. 13,14), the **Father** (v. 14);

- believers **are strong** (v. 14) and **have had victory over the evil one** (vv. 13,14);

- **God's word remains in** those who belong to Him (v. 14).

Some have suggested that the three categories of believers—**children**, **fathers** and **young men**—are physical members of John's fellowship. However, John referred to all his readers as "children." The three groups could refer to stages of spiritual development within the fellowship of believers to whom he was writing. The "children" were those who had recently received salvation. "Young men" were beginning and growing in their relationship with the Lord. They were looking for guidance and wisdom as would a young person. The "fathers" were seasoned Christians, those who had an intimate relationship with the Father, resulting in greater spiritual maturity. These believers had been through the valleys and the mountaintop experiences and were now enjoying having fellowship with "the One who is from the beginning."

John's greatest focus in these verses was the "young men" who were engaged in daily spiritual battles. Apparently, they were achieving their intended victory because John commended them for overcoming Satan. His commendation was prefaced with the protection and truth of their victory, "because you are strong, God's word remains in you" (v. 14).

Because of God and His power, they had overcome "the evil one."

2:15-17 In John 3:16, John referred to God's overwhelming love for His creation and His desire to secure their redemption, while here John was referring to the tragedy of what sin has done to society in turning God's own creation against Him (1 Jn 2:15-17). **The world** (Gk. *kosmon*) has an attitude of self-serving that is characteristic of a godless society. John's reference is not to a physical entity but to His creation, which as a whole is in rebellion against God. Worldliness resides in one's attachment to material things and within philosophies and religious ideologies that contain accusations that stray from Scripture.

In each verse John showed the gradual progression of what results from loving the world and from loving the Father. Loving the world is depicted with an explicit description of the nature of worldliness:

- **the lust of the flesh**, sensuality or lack of restraint in desire for food, drink, or sexual gratification;

- **the lust of the eyes**, envious or greedy, engulfed in materialism;

- **the pride** of life, controlled by arrogance or motivated by thinking more highly of yourself, demanding power and position.

Each of the three snares of the world is a corruption of one of God's good gifts. God gave the body or flesh; eyes are a gift from Him; possessions and opportunities for leadership come from Him as well. All these can make service to Christ more effective. However, here the warning speaks to a lack of restraint or a misuse of the appetites, to a tarnished and distorted understanding of aesthetic beauty, and to the danger of unbridled or inordinate ambition. When tainted by sin, what is good and wholesome can be distorted and twisted so as to put you in opposition to God. Actually, Satan used these exact areas to make his appeal to Eve in the garden (Gn 3:6) and even to Jesus in the wilderness (Mt 4:1-11). The things of the world entice you to embrace gains that are temporal and passing. Love for the Father, on the other hand, results in rewards that are eternal and everlasting.

During this time Christianity was rejected and Christians were persecuted. However, as persecution began to subside, John was warning against the temptation to become relaxed in belief and practice. He was also warning against the lax attitude about sin taught by the false teachers.

A warning against antichrists (2:18-27)

2:18 John began this section referring to **the last hour**, the only time "the last hour" is seen in Scripture, and questions have been raised as to what John may have meant by that statement. Most scholars agree that the term is in reference to the time following Christ's ascension and before His return.

The word **ANTICHRIST** (Gk. *antichristos,* "adversary of the Messiah," from the prefix *anti*, meaning "against, opposite to, instead of," and *Christos* or "anointed one, Messiah") is found only in John's letters (vv. 18,22; 4:3; 2 Jn 1:7). Perhaps John coined the word himself. The perception of **antichrist** by John's audience was inspired by people such as Gaius (Roman emperor AD 37-41), who set up an image of himself in Jerusalem's temple as a reminder to his Jewish faction that they were to honor him as a god. Hence, John referred to such individuals as the **many antichrists** who would precede the antichrist expected at the end time.

2:19 The views of these false teachers were heretical in that they left the fellowship and abandoned their faith. The issue was not merely joining another fellowship but intentionally leaving the Christian faith.

2:20 John described the differences between believers and antichrists. He started with a reminder to the believers that they **have an anointing** (Gk. *chrisma*, "unction, appointment," lit. "anything applied by smearing, ointment"). Some believe the reference is to Scripture, but the Bible has never been referenced as an "anointing." Most likely the anointing is the work of the Holy Spirit in helping the believer understand the truth of Scripture.

2:21-27 John was trying to confirm to the readers that the knowledge they possessed through the Holy Spirit was the true knowledge. Information alone cannot result in knowledge of God, since to know Him requires supernatural assistance. The information claimed as knowledge by the false teachers had to be counterfeit because they said that Jesus was not the Messiah. The third test provided by John was a test of doctrine. You cannot claim to know God the Father without embracing God the Son. Complete truth requires belief that Jesus is the Christ.

The true believer holds to the revealed truth of God. John elaborated on this point. The work of anointing was all that was necessary for the believer to grow and remain in the truth. John did not mean to suggest avoiding the instruction of godly people; otherwise, he would have been contradicting himself by writing the epistle. The Holy Spirit's instruction can come through people indwelt by the Holy Spirit. The believer can gain the truth through instruction due to the moving of the Holy Spirit both in the teacher and the student. Moreover, the discernment of the Spirit should give the believer the necessary perception to differentiate between true and false teachings. Merely claiming that something is Christian does not make it so.

The love of God the Father (2:28–3:3)

2:28–3:3 John began a new section in the epistle with **so now** and an encouragement to **remain** diligent in seeking God. He desired this discipline for his readers so that they would **not be ashamed** when facing God with an accounting of their lives. The word BOLDNESS (Gk. *parrēsian*) suggests the idea of "freedom, assurance, courage." The verb BE ASHAMED (Gk. *aischunthōmen*, "disgraced") is defined as being separated from God due to guilt or humiliation (v. 28). John again referred to the fellowship of believers as **little children** (v. 28); he challenged believers to be bold and unashamed.

> *Being accepted by God is different than being acceptable to God.*

All believers are accepted into the body of Christ; yet there are those believers who do not seek to be holy. Being an active part of the fellowship is evidence that the believer is committed to God's purpose for the church. If you claim to be a member of the family of Christ, you must live in a Christlike way. Actions speak louder than words. Being accepted by God is different than being acceptable to God.

John continued with the familial tone in his reference to the fatherhood of God. He referred to the **love** of the Father as being **great** (3:1). The lavishness of the Father's love provides for believers to be adopted as His children. The original meaning for the adjective translated HOW GREAT (Gk. *potapēn*, "what sort, what kind, how great, how glorious") expresses degrees, especially the superlative. The Father's love for His children is so inexplicable that it must come from a source outside of human limits; it is divine love—beyond human ability or comprehension. Due to the fact that God's love is beyond worldly understanding, the world rejected His Son because they did not fathom God's unlimited love. The

world also rejects believers, which is symbolic that they have passed from death to life, from fear of hell to security in heaven.

In the final two verses of this section, John affirmed that although believers are the **children** of the Father, the process of sanctification has yet to be completed. In order to be holy, your focus must be on Jesus. The sanctification process that has begun will come to completion upon seeing Christ. All the joys and privileges the believer receives in part now will be experienced fully in looking upon the face of Christ. Her obedience will be perfect, her life complete; she will be fully alive and standing in the light of His presence.

An admonition to avoid lawlessness and abide in God (3:4-10)

3:4-7 John began in these verses to set up signs that mark an authentic Christian faith:

- Righteousness, which is the moral or ethical test—how you handle your own conscience and make your own choices (3:4-10a);

- Love, which is the social or personal test—how you relate to others (3:10b-18);

- Doctrinal orthodoxy, which is the doctrinal test—how you determine truth and thus how you relate to God (4:1-6).

These false teachers failed the very test that John used to affirm their actual spiritual condition as being against God and His truth.

John defined sin as breaking **the law** (Gk. *anomia*). The lawlessness to which he referred was not the breaking of civil laws, but a person's willful intent to go against God, being rebellious toward Him and aligning herself with the forces of evil. John focused on the response of the human nature, despite its redemption, with the natural bent to sin.

The lawless person commits sin; whereas the believer, through the work of Christ, will not willfully and continually sin. The key to understanding what seems to be a conundrum—**everyone who remains in Him does not sin** (v. 6a) in contrast to "if we say, 'We have not sinned,'" we make Him a liar" (1:10)—lies in the understanding of tenses in the Greek language in which these verses were originally penned. There is no teaching that a believer will never commit an act of sin (3:6a), for the Greek verb is in the present tense carrying with it the idea of continuing action. No believer reaches perfection and freedom from sin in this earthly life. However, genuine conversion does free an individual from the continued hold of sin on her life so that the sense of the verse is "everyone who remains or lives in Christ does not keep on habitually and continually sinning."

John was also clear on how the believer manages this difficult challenge. Her position in Christ and the indwelling Holy Spirit enables the believer to overcome habitual sinning (5:18). In addition, the believer has "His seed" (Gk. *sperma*, "offspring, progeny, posterity," v. 9) and figuratively the principle of spiritual life. Whether the word of God itself (see Jms 1:18; 1 Pt 1:23-25) or the principles emanating from the word or a reference to the indwelling Holy Spirit (Jn 3:5-8)—all these serve to equip and strengthen the believer, on one hand, to do battle with the evil one and, on the other, to emulate Christ in her lifestyle. Still, you cannot escape the most natural interpretation of the text: that the believer has been implanted with new life—a new nature—through the new birth so that God is firmly and permanently in her life, making habitual and continuing sin impossible.

Jesus is perfect. As a result, all who come to a saving knowledge of Him obtain a perfect nature. When acting through that nature, a believer is incapable of habitual sin. However, to sin is inevitable due to the sin nature with which every human being is born. Sanctification is a work in process.

For believers, sin should not be veiled as righteousness. Only righteous deeds provide the peace of righteousness. Unfortunately, the heretics not only permitted sin, but they purported to be sinless.

3:8-10 John identified the root of evil as **the Devil.** Sin and evil began with Satan. God is perfectly good. Consequently, He cannot contain within Himself any evil. John also reminded his readers that Jesus came for the purpose of defeating Satan. Satan is the enemy who has already lost the battle. The ultimate victory belongs to Jesus Christ.

GOD IS LOVE (3:11–5:17)

The Necessity of God's Love (3:11-24)

John continued to show extremities between the truth of God and the evil of Satan by using physical examples of both. He reminded his readers that loving one another has been a command for believers from the beginning of their salvation. He then showed the polar opposite through the actions of Cain, who murdered his brother Abel.

Life and death (3:11-18)

3:11-14 Cain bore evidence of being a child of the Devil. Cain hated Abel because Abel was more righteous than he. For the same reason the world hates believers. John again used **world** (Gk. *kosmos*) to describe an evil society systematically working against God (v. 13). The conditional clause **if the world hates you** suggests that the world's hatred of believers is not only a present existing reality but also a condition that will continue to exist in the future.

3:15-18 Proof of eternal life is given through the believer's love for his brothers in Christ. John contrasted love for fellow believers with its opposite—ultimate hatred, even murder of one's brother. The book of Acts records how Paul persecuted and killed Christians before he came to salvation (Ac 22:4). A murderer using his own merit—even a religious man like Saul of Tarsus—cannot get into heaven, but a person cleansed by the blood of Jesus of all sin, including murder, will be welcomed into heaven.

In contrast to Cain's evil action, John defined practical love through the actions of Jesus. He connected love with the sacrificial act of Jesus. Because of His actions believers can experience and act out the indwelling love John defined. The verb **SHUTS OFF** (Gk. *kleisē*, "shut, bar, close, lock") is used here metaphorically to illustrate the obstacles that hinder active love (v. 17). If the focus is on spirituality to the degree that love for others is ignored, then the thought is hypocritical. Conversely, God's truth is necessary lest the action be hypocritical (v. 18).

Assurance of salvation (3:19-24)

3:19-24 The heretical teachings must have caused even genuine believers in the fellowship to question their salvation. For that reason, John provided evidence of the readers' **confidence** (Gk. *parrēsian*, v. 21; cp. 2:28; 4:17; 5:14) **before God**:

- An active love—**that is how we will know** (vv. 18-19)—is a practical and working love.

- The omniscience and omnipresence of God—despite our hearts, God knows the truth. Time is fashioned by divine design and operates under divine direction; therefore, God is in

the past, present, and future all at the same time. He knows all you have done and will do in the future; nothing is hidden from Him. He knows the believer and confirms her salvation. Salvation is controlled by God, not the person: "I [Paul] planted, Apollos watered, but God gave the growth" (1 Co 3:6).

- Answered prayer, through which the believer can find assurance—if you ask anything in God's will, you are asking in obedience; therefore, selfish desires are not a factor.

- Obedience to God's commands, a theme expressed several times in the epistle, especially as the result of abiding in Christ.

- The personal indwelling of the Holy Spirit.

Testing the Spirits (4:1-6)

4:1-3 John returned to the topic of the **false prophets** (Gk. *pseudoprophētai*, v. 1) and **spirit of the antichrist** (v. 3). The fellowship needed to be reminded of the power of demonic forces and what such forces can do to a church. In Deuteronomy, Moses provided tests to distinguish genuine prophets from false prophets:

- If what the prophet said does happen, he is a true prophet (Dt 18:22).

- If what the prophet said does happen but he leads the people to false gods, he is a false prophet (Dt 13:1-5).

John's audience also needed to be reminded how to distinguish evil spirits from the Holy Spirit. For this discernment, John returned to the doctrine of the historical Jesus as the Christ.

4:4-6 John created a distinction between believers and those working for the spirit of the antichrist (v. 4). Even though the influence of these evil forces could be daunting, John reminded them that they were indwelled by the Holy Spirit. Satan can only attack with God's permission. Satan was created by God, and the creation cannot be greater than the Creator. John also reminded the readers that those who belong to the world listen to others who speak on the world's terms. False prophets and teachers speak on the world's terms. John emphasized the power of being a child of God (v. 6). If the person is open to hearing from a child of God, he is not from the spirit of deception.

Loving the Fellowship (4:7-21)

4:7-8 For the last time John addressed brotherly **love**. The believer's new birth and authentic knowledge of God are shown in her relationships with others. Since **love is from God**, the one born of God will manifest love. The converse is also true: **One who does not love does not know God** since **God is love**.

4:9-16 The greatly loved verse in the Gospel of John is restated (v. 9; see Jn 3:16). The structure of the sentence focuses on the distinctiveness of Jesus. John mentioned life through and in Jesus six times (1 Jn 4:9-16). The verb **sent** is in the perfect tense, showing the work of Jesus for the believer's salvation as having staying power. All the love shown by believers is an extension of the work of Christ. Any love shown by those who are unredeemed is also due to the work of God. All have been created in the image of God. The image was defiled but not destroyed; therefore, what exists of love within the creature is a reflection of the Creator. The believer not only should have God's love but also should display that **love**. God made the ultimate sacrifice to display His love, and His children are commanded to do likewise.

In the early church, prophecy was evidence of the work of the Holy Spirit. Yet John stressed that this manifestation of the Holy Spirit resided only in the Christian who maintains an intimate relationship with God (v. 13).

In opposition to the teaching of his opponents, when John spoke of needing Jesus, the Son of God, he was referring to the historical Jesus as the Christ, not a separate spirit. John presented three characteristics of the believer (vv. 13-16):

- the indwelling of the Holy Spirit,
- the confessing of **Jesus** as **the Son of God**, and
- living in God's love.

Faith must have substance, for it is the source of true knowledge. God's love for and dwelling in the believer is defined (vv. 17-21). His love is the reason no one in the fellowship should fear **the day of judgment**. God provides believers with love since its beginning resides in Him. God will always reciprocate with His love, leaving the believer no reason for **fear**; she can love God without the worry of betrayal or denial (v. 18). Since God's love is unfailing, believers should also display this love toward one another. Love for God that does not manifest itself in love for humanity is not genuine love. Empty love suggests disobedience to His commands and is therefore meaningless.

Being Victorious through Faith (5:1-5)

5:1-2 John began the final section of this letter (chap. 5) by repeating that obedience to God is evidence of His love. "By this we know that we love the children of God when we love God and keep His commands" is a more literal translation of verse 2. You are expected to love your family; in the family of God, you should love your brothers and sisters in Christ if you love God the Father.

5:3-5 God's **commands are not a burden**. God will provide what you need to

Love			
WHO	• The Father loves His children (3:1). • Believers (God's children) love the Father (2:15; 4:20). • Believers love one another, their brothers (1:7; 2:10; 3:14,23; 4:21).		
WHAT	• God loved us and sent His Son to be the propitiation for our sins (4:10). • God is love (4:16). • Laying down one's life for our brothers (3:16). • Compassion demonstrated by sharing one's possessions with brothers in need (3:17). • Keeping God's commands (5:2-3).		
WHEN	Present tense—here and now (4:7-16).		
WHERE	In this world (4:17).		
HOW	• In deed and truth (3:18). • Doing what is right (3:10). • Without fear (4:18).		
WHY	• Christ laid down His life for us (3:16; 4:10). • Love is from God (4:7,10). • God first loved us (3:1; 4:19). • Christ's command (3:23; 4:21; 5:2).		

overcome the world and will create in you a new desire to be obedient to Him. Jesus offers you His yoke (Mt 11:30), proving that to be in God's will and to be obedient are not burdensome.

Some believers may get discouraged with the human propensity to sin and feel that they have not overcome the world, but John reminded his readers that through union with Jesus the world is defeated (vv. 4-5). People do not have in themselves the capacity to become Christians. To do so requires the saving power of Jesus. Through Christ you receive a new nature and the power to live like Him.

Accepting the Witness of the Spirit (5:6-13)

5:6 John recorded in sequential order Jesus' baptism and His crucifixion. Cerinthus taught that Christ came upon the man Jesus at baptism but left Him before the crucifixion. In his view, Christ could have revealed truths and knowledge to the man Jesus. John countered this heresy by reminding his readers that the Spirit attested to the baptism and to the crucifixion of Jesus the Christ.

5:7-8 These verses are not in some of the earliest texts and were often found as side notes before they were officially added to the text in the 1520s. Despite the question, their addition, or lack thereof, does not change the context or authority of John's writings. They only confirm that the Holy **Spirit** is the testimony upon which believers should depend. John bore witness to the baptism, crucifixion, and resurrection of Jesus, but he stated that the Holy Spirit should be the believer's proof and affirmation of the baptism (**water**) and crucifixion (**blood**). Thus, the same Holy Spirit who witnessed the passion also clarifies the truth of it for all who believe. The Holy Spirit is God's witness of Jesus. He should be accepted because He is "God's testimony."

5:9-13 God the Father also testified to the ministry of Jesus. When the Holy Spirit came down upon Jesus at His baptism, God the Father spoke, "This is My beloved Son. I take delight in Him!" (Mt 3:17). God also caused the earthquake and

Heart to Heart: Confidence in Prayer (1 Jn 5:14)

Christians can have confidence in God! Prayer is the means of communication between God and His children. Through prayer God's children can speak to Him and be confident that He hears: If you pray, <u>then</u> He will listen. God hears you when you pray, and He answers according to His will.

*In His model prayer, Jesus told the disciples to ask according to the will of God (Mt 6:10). When a believer talks to the Father, each request for help and every desire for guidance should be asked in the name of Jesus. All of the conditions related to prayer are bound up in the phrase, **according to His will**. If you pray in His name and ask according to His will, then He will hear and answer. You can have confidence in prayer!*

split the curtain in the temple at the time of the death of Jesus (Mt 27:51).

Receiving the Bounty of Prayer (5:14-17)

5:14-17 John closed the epistle with reminders of how the readers could be assured of their salvation, both through the stated evidence and the tests provided in the epistle. They could and should have **confidence** in the authenticity of their relationship with God. John also reminded them that prayer comes with a requirement—it must be done in harmony with God's will (v. 14). The purpose of prayer is not to obtain selfish desires but to make believers more holy and better prepared for intimacy with God. As the believer yields herself to God through prayer, obedience, and learning Scripture, God accomplishes His will through the believer.

Questions have arisen among scholars as to what sin resulted in **death**. Some see a reference to physical death, while others hold that this allusion is to the spiritual death that would come to those false teachers who had heard a clear presentation of the gospel but openly rejected it.

Considering the context and noting the heretical teachings that were being introduced to the fellowship would suggest that the **sin that brings death** (Gk. *thanaton*) was probably apostasy (v. 16). The heretics were committing this sin.

Believers should have "confidence" (Gk. *parrhēsia*) in their prayers. However, God's answering of prayer is not indiscriminate. The effectiveness of praying for believers is acknowledged if prayers are offered **according to His will** (v. 14) and from the hearts of those who "do what is pleasing in His sight" (3:22), in contrast to the prayers of unbelievers, who lack confidence in their relationship with God (5:14-17). John did encourage the believers to pray for those who have committed **a sin that does not bring death** (vv. 16-17).

CONCLUSION: WHAT THE BELIEVER KNOWS (5:18-21)

5:18-20 Know (Gk. *oidamen*) does not mean a knowledge to be gained by natural means but refers to a present certainty and assurance, which manifests a confidence based on the character God showed in salvation and held by all in the body of believers.

John began a synopsis of what he had written.

- Christians no longer habitually and continually sin (v. 18; cp. 3:6).

- The child of God is confident because she has a position assured and the marks of a believer. Just as Satan has no dominion over God, he is also ultimately powerless against those under God's protection (v. 19; see Eph 6:10-18), who have the arsenal of heaven available.

- Jesus is the **true** God and the **One** through whom all believers are related to God.

5:21 John was not just referring to false gods (Gk. *eidōlōn*, "idols, images"). His opponents were teaching about the Christian God but in a false manner. Taking part in pagan rituals would not be an intended choice for Christians; however, the present world is presided over by Satan and is thereby permeated with the opportunity to idolize everything that takes away from the glorification of God.

Heart to Heart:
Lessons from 1 John

There are many lessons to be found in 1 John. First, you are reminded of the necessity of believing in Jesus as the Christ. Today's society is no exception to the skepticism about Jesus. Many believe there are alternate paths to heaven. Yet, Jesus made Himself clear, "I am the way, the truth, and the life. No one comes to the Father except through Me" (Jn 14:6). He did not say he was some of the way, part of the truth, and most of the life; He said He was all. He is the only way to God, and to deny Jesus' deity is to deny God's as well. You cannot believe in one person of the triunity without accepting all three persons. To deny any one of the three is to deny God. Anyone claiming to be a believer must claim all the truth of God.

John did not try to lessen the need to love sinners, but his focus was to love those within the church. Those with whom we get along are easy to love, but what of those who betray you? What about those people who are hard to love? What about those people who are members of the fellowship, yet they do something so heinous that you find yourself questioning their salvation? John wrote that lack of love for your brother in Christ is living in darkness (2:9-11).

Believers in themselves are incapable of love. The love shown by the unredeemed is residual from being born in God's image. All love expended is rooted in God. When you face the seemingly insurmountable obstacle to love someone you do not want to love, you must reach further into the source of love found only in the Lord. You love through Christ because His love is perfect.

Lessons from 1 John (continued)

In order to love in perfection, abiding in God is necessary. John heavily reinforced this in 1 John. Abiding in God requires obedience to Him. God loves you so much that He calls you His child (3:1). Children are not supposed to obey their parents merely to avoid punishment. Children are supposed to obey out of love and respect for their parents. You are to obey God, grow in God, and love God, because He is your Father. To obey for the sake of pleasing Him is to do so in joy, not requirement. God does not want you to obey because "He said so." He wants you to obey because He loves you! The more you understand the love of God, the more you desire and love Him.

As you grow in your relationship with God, you will desire more of the eternal and less of the temporal. Craving temporal things is ridiculous for two reasons. First, they can stifle your relationship with God. If your desire for material possessions, wealth, power, or anything else becomes an obsession, then it has become more important to you than God. Second, you cannot take your possessions with you.

Everything you work for on this earth will eventually be destroyed. Yet, heavenly rewards are eternal. Jesus commands,

> *Don't collect for yourselves treasures on earth, where moth and rust destroy and where thieves break in and steal. But collect for yourselves treasures in heaven, where neither moth nor rust destroys, and where thieves don't break in and steal. For where your treasure is, there your heart will be also (Mt 6:19-21).*

Where does your heart lie?

Bibliography

Akin, Daniel. *1,2,3 John*. The New American Commentary, vol. 38. Nashville: Broadman and Holman, 2001.

Anders, Max, and David Walls. *I & II Peter, I, II, & III John, Jude*. Holman New Testament Commentary. Nashville: Holman Reference, 1999.

*Brown, Raymond E. *The Epistles of John*. The Anchor Bible, vol. 30. Garden City: Doubleday and Company, Inc., 1982.

Bruce, F. F. *The Epistles of John*. Grand Rapids: William B. Eerdmans Publishing Company, 1970.

*Dodd, C. H. *The Johannine Epistles*. The Moffatt New Testament Commentary. New York: Harper and Brothers, 1946.

*Marshall, Howard I. *The Epistles of John*. The New International Commentary on the New Testament. Grand Rapids: William B. Eerdmans Publishing Company, 1978.

Stott, John R. W. *The Letters of John*. Tyndale New Testament Commentaries, vol. 19. Grand Rapids: William B. Eerdmans Publishing Company, 1995.

Tozer, A. W. *Knowledge of the Holy*. New York: HarperSanFrancisco, 1964.

Vines, Jerry. *Exploring 1, 2, 3 John*. Neptune, NJ: Loizeaux Brothers, 1989.

*For advanced study

2 JOHN

Second John is the second shortest book in the New Testament. The letter was possibly written to the same community as 1 John. The author wrote on issues similar to those he addressed to the community of 1 John—heretical teachings about Jesus not being the Christ, loving the fellowship, and abiding in God.

Title

In the Greek New Testament, the title is simply "*Iōannou B*," designating it as John's second letter.

Setting

The church had apparently been encountering the same heretical teachings as those addressed in 1 John. John, ministering to churches throughout Asia Minor, probably wrote from Ephesus to encourage the believers to continue to grow in their love for one another, to remain in the truth, and to avoid welcoming the heretics into their homes.

Genre

Second John is a personal letter. Like other first-century letters of the Greco-Roman world, it opened with identification of the writer and recipients, followed by a distinctively Christian greeting. The form of the letter's conclusion and its brevity (only 245 Greek words) are also typical of private letters of the first century. Rhetorically, 2 John is a good example of hortatory discourse since the writer seemed to aim at modifying the recipients' conduct or moving them to action.

Author

Unlike 1 John, the author does identify himself, referring to himself as "The Elder" (Gk. *presbuteros*, "older one," suggesting one in a position of authority and influence, v. 1). This designation supports the fact that John would have written these letters in his senior years when he seemingly held a position of influence in the church. External and internal evidence points primarily to the Apostle John, the son of Zebedee and brother of James (Mk 1:19-20), as the author. Obviously the author knew the recipients personally (v. 1). All the works attributed to John (the Gospel of John; 1, 2, 3 John; Revelation) have similarities in style and content. Other scholars claim there was an "Elder John" but without evidence to prove his existence.

Date

Due to the striking similarities between 1 and 2 John, the dates of the two writings are supposed to be close together. Scholars typically ascribe a late first-century date to the epistles, AD 80 to 95, probably around AD 90.

Recipients

The letter was written "to the elect lady and her children" (v. 1). Some believe these recipients included an actual woman in history; however, the content seems more directed to a group of people beyond a family circle. The church was typically personified in a feminine manner in the New Testament (cp. Rv 21:9 in which the church is personified as a "bride"). Therefore, the letter is more likely addressed to a church, quite possibly the same church to whom 1 John was written, either to a corporate body or to the individuals in the church.

Major Themes

The themes of 2 John are the same as those of 1 John—"love" and "truth"—but addressed in greater brevity. John proclaimed clearly the "truth" of the gospel and of Jesus Christ, whom he clearly noted is both perfect deity and full humanity (v. 7; see 1 Jn 4:3), as well as continually calling for "love" from believers (2 Jn 1; see 1 Jn 5:3). He refuted heretical theology, especially concerning the incarnation, as departing from "truth" and urged his readers to use God-given discernment with the itinerant teachers who had come upon the scene (2 Jn 10-11).

A Comparison of 1, 2, 3 John

	1 John	2 John	3 John
Author	John, the son of Zebedee	same	same
Date of Writing	AD 80 to 95	same	same
Place of Writing	Ephesus	same	same
Recipients	Churches in Asia Minor	same	same
Length of Epistle	5 chapters or 105 verses	1 chapter or 13 verses	1 chapter or 14 verses
Purpose	• Strengthen the faith of believers • Focus on apostolic teaching • Spread the gospel	• Warn about false teachings • Prepare for John's coming visit	• Encourage Gaius to hold the truth • Rebuke Diotrephes for his disobedience • Commend Demetrius for his godly conduct

Outline

I. ADDRESS AND SALUTATION (VV. 1-3)

II. FOLLOWING GOD'S COMMANDS (VV. 4-6)

III. THE TRUTH VS. THE DECEIVERS (VV. 7-11)

IV. CONCLUSION (VV. 12-13)

Exposition of the Text

ADDRESS AND SALUTATION (VV.1-3)

1 The elder (Gk. *ho presbuteros*, "the presbyter or older man") in this context is a title of authority. His authority was evidence of his spiritual maturity. The letter was written **to the elect lady and her children,** most likely alluding to a local congregation of believers. LADY (Gk. *kuria*) is the feminine form of *kurios,* "lord," a term showing respect for the recipient(s) of the letter. ELECT (Gk. *eklektē,* "chosen, selected, picked out") also suggests the idea of "excellence."

Heart to Heart: The "Elect Lady"

The "elect lady" of 2 John is thought by some scholars to have been an actual woman. Her name could have been "Electa" (a play off of eklektos *meaning "elect") or "Kuria" (a play off of* kurios*). Some even say her name was "Electa Kuria." However, through context and the frequent feminine personification of the church in the New Testament, most have concluded that the "elect lady" was a reference to a church.*

The church has been described in Scripture as the bride of Christ. In Ephesians 5:22-32 Paul compared a biblical marriage to Christ's relationship with the church. The husband is to love his wife as Christ loved the church, as a servant leader. The wife is to love her husband as the church is to love Christ, in an attitude of gracious submission. God intentionally developed marriage in this fashion so that it would be a beautiful active witness of the gospel.

Although formal titles were used, John showed authentic affection for the church. When he said he loved them, John made sure to include that he loved them **in truth** (Gk. *agapō en alētheia*). Here "truth" was a reference to what is ultimately real and genuine—God Himself and more especially to His Son Jesus who identified Himself as the truth (Jn 14:6). He used the Greek verb *agapaō* ("value, esteem, be faithful towards"), suggesting "love" that was unconditional, a word for the "love" uniquely characteristic of Christ and His followers. John affirmed his love as genuine because it was from God. John's inclusion of **all who have come to know the truth** in his expression of love for "the elect lady" is another confirmation that he was writing to a church.

2-3 John emphasized the necessity of truth through repetition. In verse 2, John affirmed that God's truth **remains in** (Gk. *menousan*, "remains, abides, continues to be present, does not depart, lasts or endures") the believer and never leaves. Believers are capable of love because of the truth.

In his blessing, John did not wish anything for the church because of his confidence of God's blessing on them. His order of **grace** (Gk. *charis*, "benefit, favor, gracious provision"), **mercy** (Gk. *eleos*, "compassion, pity," an emotion that is aroused when you see someone experience an affliction that is undeserved), **and peace** (Gk. *eirēnē*, "tranquility, unity") was intentional. Mercy and peace result from grace. Grace is unmerited favor, God's path of mercy, which in turn brings peace due to the rewards of salvation poured out upon the believer. Salvation is given by God the Father and provided through Jesus, and all of this is done because God extended His love to His children through His truth and love.

FOLLOWING GOD'S COMMANDS (VV. 4-6)

4-6 John used the word **command** (Gk. *entolēn*, "commandment, order, charge, precept," v. 5) to provide cohesion to this section. Believers are commanded to walk in truth (v. 4) and to love one another (v. 5). John began by praising the obedience of some of the members of the church. Three things stand out:

- The verb **find** is in the perfect tense, having the sense that John received this command in the past, and these believers were continuing in obedience to truth and in love.

- John said **some**, implying that not all the members of the church were **walking in truth** and love.

- "Walking" is meant to define behavior throughout life, not for just a brief time.

John addressed the entire church when he wrote, **So now I urge you, lady** (v. 5). He was urging the same action as in his first letter—active love in truth for the fellowship of believers. Belief and action are inextricably intertwined. If you believe the "truth," you will walk in it by expressing love to others (vv. 5-6). This walking in truth gives the ultimate veracity to the Christian message.

The commands of verses 4 and 5 mandate the active love of obedience to God's commands (v. 6). Scholars have questioned why John used singular and plural forms of **command** (Gk. *entolēn*, singular "a new command," v. 5; *entolas*, plural, "His commands," and *entolē*, singular, "the command," v. 6) in this section. In the singular the word seems to be directed toward a particular command, such as "walk in love"; whereas the plural usage represented the larger understanding of obeying all God's commands, in the sense of a general exhortation. Perhaps coupling the singular with the plural emphasizes the importance of the command for love within the series of admonitions to believers.

THE TRUTH VERSUS THE DECEIVERS (VV. 7-11)

7 In the Greek text this verse begins with the word *hoti* or "because," signaling a transitional link between the sections before and after. John began by warning the fellowship about **deceivers** (Gk. *planos*, "leading astray, deceitful") who may try to propagate false doctrine about Christ. These "deceivers" seem to embrace the same false knowledge about Jesus as did the individuals referenced in 1 John. They believed that Christ was a spirit who came upon the man Jesus at the start of His ministry but left Him before the crucifixion.

To distinguish the true teachers from the false ones, John provided the church with a test of confession. True believers would confess the historical Jesus as the Christ. **The coming of Jesus Christ in the flesh** is a present active participle, meaning that

Jesus Christ came in the flesh and continues to remain in the flesh—He never stopped being human. John labeled one advocating the heretical view as **the deceiver and the antichrist**. The word DECEIVER (Gk. *planos*, "wandering or roving"), figuratively meaning wandering from the truth, designates one who "leads into error, an imposter or deceiver." John also identified those who denied Jesus' humanity as ANTICHRIST (Gk. *antichristos*) or actively opposed to Christ. The choice of words underscores Scripture's uncompromising distinction between truth and error. John was clear in identifying those false teachers who pedaled heretical doctrine as having an inadequate understanding of Jesus.

8-9 John issued a warning, **watch yourselves** (Gk. *blepete*), in the sense of stressing vigilance both in the negative sense ("don't lose what we have worked for") and the positive ("you may receive a full reward"). This present active imperative form underscored that John wanted those in the fellowship to be continually on alert and to avoid becoming complacent. Complacency could result in some loss, not of salvation but of heavenly reward (v. 8). However, if a person had completely turned away from God's teachings, he never was a believer (v. 9).

Promoters of the heresy that John refuted viewed themselves as superior to others because they believed they had a special knowledge of God that made them Christians. However, their knowledge was outside of Scripture or "beyond it" (Gk. *proagōn*, "lead out, go before" in the sense of "running ahead"), which meant they were actually separated from the truth. John used a bit of sarcasm. They claimed advanced teaching, but actually they had moved beyond the boundaries of biblical truth. They had tried to separate

God the Father from God the Son, resulting in heresy. Christianity requires the connection; otherwise Jesus' death would be senseless and without meaning or purpose.

10-11 John did not mean that believers could not have false teachers in their homes for the purpose of loving confrontation concerning God's truth. John warned that believers were not to welcome these deceivers into their homes for the purpose of furthering the heresy. The **welcome** (Gk. *chairein*, a verb lit. meaning "to greet" in the sense of extending "joy" or "health"—a cordial and warm greeting) to which John referred would have resulted in the believer's alignment with the deceiver—at least in public perception. You can be gracious without embracing those who are trying to seduce others into accepting false doctrine by their twisting and maligning the word of God. The believer would be showing hospitality as well as providing opportunity for the false teachers if he welcomed these deceivers in the fashion to which John referred. Doctrinal heresy is a grave matter with serious and even eternal consequences. Heretical teaching can result in eternal damnation in hell for those who reject Christ.

CONCLUSION (VV. 12-13)

12-13 The conclusions of 2 and 3 John are quite similar. Both are worded in a proper manner but express the authentic love coming from the author. John assumed that the church would welcome him. He also felt that upon visiting the church their **joy may be complete**. If "the elect lady" is a church, the **elect sister** (Gk. *adelphēs*, "sister, fellow-believer") was possibly a reference to another church under John's care.

Heart to Heart:
Life Lessons from 2 John

John emphasized love for one another within the fellowship of believers. To love is not usually natural. Loving requires supernatural assistance. To hold a grudge or to hate someone who has caused you suffering is the typical human response. Yet, when your sins caused Christ to suffer, He forgave you. In fact, His reason for living on earth was to provide you a way to eternal life through the path of His suffering.

Second John also teaches that everything entitled "Christian" does not live up to its designation. There are many people, philosophies, religions, and materials that claim to be from God. However, upon closer examination, those things are actually "deceivers" (v. 7).

In a society of instant gratification, you can easily become passive and accept as truth many things claiming to be "Christian." However, just as John wrote, "Watch yourselves so that you don't lose what we have worked for, but you may receive a full reward" (v. 8). Be diligent and steadfast in obedience to Scripture and in prayer. Otherwise, intimacy with God is replaced with complacency and false philosophies.

Bibliography

*Akin, Daniel. *1, 2, 3 John*. The New American Commentary, vol. 38. Nashville: Broadman and Holman Publishers, 2001.

Anders, Max, and David Walls. *I & II Peter, I, II, & III John, Jude.* Holman New Testament Commentary. Nashville: Holman Reference, 1999.

*Brown, Raymond E. *The Epistles of John*. The Anchor Bible, vol. 30. Garden City: Doubleday and Company, Inc., 1982.

*Bruce, F. F. *The Epistles of John*. Grand Rapids: William B. Eerdmans Publishing Company, 1970.

*Dodd, C. H. *The Johannine Epistles*. The Moffatt New Testament Commentary. New York: Harper and Brothers, 1946.

*Marshall, Howard I. *The Epistles of John.* The New International Commentary on the New Testament. Grand Rapids: William B. Eerdmans Publishing Company, 1978.

Stott, John R. W. *The Letters of John*. Tyndale New Testament Commentaries, vol. 19. Grand Rapids: William B. Eerdmans Publishing Company, 1995.

Tozer, A. W. *Knowledge of the Holy*. New York: HarperSanFrancisco, 1964.

Vines, Jerry. *Exploring 1, 2, 3 John*. Neptune, NJ: Loizeaux Brothers, 1989.

*For advanced study

3 JOHN

Introduction

Third John is the shortest book in the New Testament with striking similarities to 2 John in structure, thus inviting the designation of "twin epistles," although they are not identical in purpose or content. They could be described as "fraternal" because of the many similarities.

Title

In the *Greek* New Testament, the title is simply *"Iōannou C,"* designating it as John's third letter.

Setting

Because the tradition that John lived in Ephesus and worked from his residence there in ministries among the churches in Asia Minor is strong and widespread, to assume he wrote this letter from Ephesus is a good conclusion.

Genres

Third John is a personal letter that follows the basic pattern of other ancient letters, beginning with an introduction that identified the writer and recipient and closing with typical personal greetings. John wrote this epistle primarily to address the actions of Diotrephes and give an alternate response to his behavior. Diotrephes had been rebellious toward John and those sent by John.

Author

Like 2 John, the author identified himself as "The Elder" (Gk. *presbuteros*, v. 1). "The Elder" in 2 John is thought to be the Apostle John; however, external evidence is lacking. Certainly his advanced age and position of influence among the churches would qualify the apostle for this endearing term of respect. The similarities in content, style, and vocabulary found in the structure of 2 and 3 John constitute the strongest evidence for John as the author, but the association of the apostle with this epistle is a strong tradition virtually unchallenged.

Date

The only speculation about the date is that 3 John was written around the same time as 2 John, AD 80–95.

Recipients

One of the differences from 2 John is that this letter of encouragement was explicitly written to a person, John's "dear friend Gaius" (v. 1). Gaius was a common name during this time, mentioned three other times in Scripture (Rm 16:23;

Ac 19:29; 20:4); yet, it is highly unlikely that any one of these men was John's friend. Two other men are mentioned: Diotrephes, who was causing trouble and thus received a rebuke, and Demetrius, who received a commendation from John and was probably the bearer of the letter.

Major Themes

Several themes are found in this brief epistle:

- Personal messages to Gaius (appreciation, vv. 1-3), Diotrephes (rebuke, vv. 9-10), and Demetrius (commendation, v. 12).

- General admonition: to extend Christian hospitality to those who minister in the name of Christ (vv. 5-8) and to encourage the sharing of a Christian testimony (v. 12).

Pronunciation Guide			
Demetrius	*dih MEE trih uhs*	Gaius	*GAY yuhs*
Diotrephes	*digh AHT rih feez*		

Outline

I. SALUTATION (VV. 1-4)

II. EXHORTATION TO GAIUS (VV. 5-8)

III. DIOTREPHES AND DEMETRIUS (VV. 9-12)

    A. Condemnation of Diotrephes (vv. 9-10)

    B. Commendation of Demetrius (vv. 11-12)

IV. CONCLUSION (VV. 13-14)

Exposition Of The Text

SALUTATION (VV. 1-4)

1-4 John referred to himself as **the Elder** (Gk. *presbuteros*), which provided a sense of authority for the letter (see section on author in introduction). Although the introduction is formal, the affection of the author is felt by the readers through his tender words to Gaius, his **dear friend** (Gk. *agapētō*, "one who is loved, beloved"). Although no other information is available on Gaius in Scripture, clearly he occupied a position of responsibility, and probably leadership, in the church.

John wrote that he was praying for Gaius' **GOOD HEALTH** (Gk. *hugiainein*, "in good health, healthy," a common greeting and expression of good intent for the recipient to have well-being). The phrase "just as your SOUL (Gk. *psuchē*) prospers" suggested that John was concerned for the spiritual health of Gaius as well as his physical health (v. 2).

The remainder of this section praised Gaius for his hospitality towards those sent by John. John first praised his obedience to God's commands (v. 3). Evidence of Gaius' obedience and active love in the truth came in the form of reports to John from other Christians (v. 4). Gaius might have been one of John's converts since the apostles often referred to their converts as their children, and John wrote of the **joy** he felt to learn that his **children are walking in the truth** (v. 4).

EXHORTATION TO GAIUS (VV. 5-8)

5 John praised Gaius for his hospitality to the traveling teachers whom he had sent to minister the word. The teachers may have been asked to report to John upon their return, or they may have spoken of their experience as a testimony at a church meeting. Either way, their descriptions of Gaius were such that John felt the need to commend Gaius' and his work.

6-8 John also wrote about the need to treat the traveling teachers with proper hospitality and respect so as to honor the Lord's name because they were traveling as His ambassadors. Christians should assume responsibility to support those who give themselves totally to the work of the kingdom. Customarily **to send them on their journey** would mean providing basic necessities—food and money for whatever was needed to help them travel comfortably—as appropriate for those who were dedicated to the service of God. To be supported by fellow believers put them in contrast to the itinerant philosophers and the beggar priests of pagan deities. False teachers and philosophers of the time were requesting compensation and favors in exchange for their instruction, while Christian teachers were only accepting the kindnesses offered to them.

DIOTREPHES AND DEMETRIUS (VV. 9-12)

9-12 John addressed the behavior of Diotrephes. He had sent a letter to the church (**I wrote**), which seems to be a reference to an earlier letter that is no longer extant. Although the contents of the letter are unknown, one could surmise from the context of this section that the lost letter

might have been commending a teacher sent by John or giving instruction to the church (v. 9). When **Diotrephes** learned the content of the letter, he refused to comply with the requests of John. Not only did Diotrephes in pride and arrogance refuse the teachers, but he also spoke out against John and spurned his authority. He also prevented other members of the church from welcoming the teachers (v. 10).

John described Diotrephes as one who LOVES TO HAVE FIRST PLACE (Gk. *philoprōteuōn*, "wish to be first, like to be leader"), suggesting that Diotrephes "aspired to preeminence" (v. 9). In this combination of two Greek words, *philos* denotes the love between friends, appearing in plural form in v. 14 as "friends," and *prōtos* means "first." The word expresses the ambitious desire to be above everyone else, and the present tense adds the idea of continual and habitual action. Diotrephes loved the power of authority more than obedience to God. The rebellion of Diotrephes occurred at these points:

- He demonstrated pride and arrogance in seeking the **first place**.

- He spread **malicious** untruths about John, "the elder."

- He refused to extend hospitality to brothers in Christ from other churches and chastised those who did extend hospitality.

John planned to use his authority to address the matter with Diotrephes. Discipline within the church is demanded in Scripture (Mt 18:15-20; 1 Co 5:1-13) and necessary to keep the church holy. Due to the fact that John wrote about Diotrephes, Gaius may have been unaware of the man's actions. He may have been a member of another church, or his home may have been simply a stopping place for missionaries.

When John wrote for Gaius to **imitate good**, he entreated Gaius to continue his hospitality and walk in the truth. John also provided a physical example of **what is good** (Gk. *agathon*, v. 11). **Demetrius** was probably John's carrier for the letter to Gaius, and John shared a commendation of the one who had helped him.

Demetrius had a threefold witness to his life and behavior:

- testimony from everyone,
- the truth itself (which was the self-evidence of his behavior), and
- John—we also testify for him (v. 12).

Three Men in 3 John		
Gaius (vv. 1-8)	**Diotrephes (vv. 9-12)**	**Demetrius (vv. 9-12)**
• Committed to the truth • Demonstrated his faith • Loved others unconditionally • Extended hospitality to friends and strangers • Was an example to all Christians	• Prominent member of the church • Refused to assist workers in the kingdom • Spurned the authority of John • Caused division in the church	• Good reputation among believers • Accepted God's truth • Walked in faith • Had a testimony of faithfulness

CONCLUSION (VV. 13-14)

13-14 This conclusion is similar to 2 John in that the apostle did not want **to write** everything in his heart to Gaius. Instead he wrote, **I hope to see you soon, and we will talk face to face** (v. 14; 2 Jn 12). The phrase translated FACE TO FACE (Gk. *stoma pros stoma,* lit. "mouth to mouth") is an idiom conveying the sense of speaking to one another in person rather than in writing. Use of this idiom acknowledges the limitations of written communication and reinforces the writer's desire to talk with Gaius personally. If they had any authority, **the friends** (Gk. *philoi*, v. 14) to whom John referred would serve as support for his response against Diotrephes.

Heart ❧ Heart:
Humble Obedience to God

Living for your personal glory cannot result in glorification of God. Diotrephes was choosing personal status and power over a life of humble obedience to God.

Women have been given the responsibility of being helpers (Gn 2:18). Your responsibility is to live out this role with gracious submission. Yet, the world tells you that you are to be superwomen. You should be able to have the wealth, power, status, and perfect family life, all while wearing stilettos and modeling perfectly styled tresses. In reality, trying to achieve what the world decides you need only results in frustration and chaos. The world is constantly changing, so the fads projected also change. God is unchanging. He designed the paradigm for biblical womanhood to complement perfectly biblical manhood, so that ultimately the Creator God is glorified. He created both the man and the woman, so He knows what is best for both.

Bibliography

Akin, Daniel. *1,2,3 John*. The New American Commentary, vol. 38. Nashville: Broadman and Holman Publishers, 2001.

Anders, Max, and David Walls. *I & II Peter, I, II, & III John, Jude*. Holman New Testament Commentary. Nashville: Holman Reference, 1999.

*Brown, Raymond E. *The Epistles of John*. The Anchor Bible, vol. 30. Garden City: Doubleday and Company, Inc., 1982.

*Bruce, F. F. *The Epistles of John*. Grand Rapids: William B. Eerdmans Publishing Company, 1970.

*Dodd, C. H. *The Johannine Epistles*. The Moffatt New Testament Commentary. New York: Harper and Brothers, 1946.

*Marshall, Howard I. *The Epistles of John*. The New International Commentary on the New Testament. Grand Rapids: William B. Eerdmans Publishing Company, 1978.

Stott, John R. W. *The Letters of John*. Tyndale New Testament Commentaries, vol. 19. Grand Rapids: William B. Eerdmans Publishing Company, 1995.

Tozer, A. W. *Knowledge of the Holy*. New York: HarperSanFrancisco, 1964.

Vines, Jerry. *Exploring 1, 2, 3 John*. Neptune, NJ: Loizeaux Brothers, 1989.

*For advanced study

JUDE

Introduction

Title

Like other public epistles written by first-century Christians, the title "Jude" reflects its authorship. In the Greek New Testament the title is simply the name *Ioudas*, "Jude," based on the self-identification of the writer in the salutation: "Jude (Gk. *Ioudas*), a slave of Jesus Christ, and a brother of James" (v. 1).

Setting

Jude did not specify the church or churches to whom he was writing, but his main concern was the dangerous influence of false teachers who had apparently infiltrated a particular congregation. The letter itself provides no clear evidence for certain identification of these false teachers, but Jude's characterization of their beliefs and practices reflects heretical ideas that emerged during the first century as the gospel spread throughout Asia Minor.

Jude targeted at least two particularly deceptive heresies, antinomianism and spiritual elitism. "Antinomianism" (Gk. *anti*, "against" and *nomos*, "law") is a mis-interpretation of Christian freedom as meaning to be set free from the moral imperatives of Old Testament law. Having cast off the obligation to pursue righteousness as prescribed in Scripture, those who subscribed to the heresy also cast off moral restraint in the name of freedom. Jude refers to the distinctly unchristian manifestations of this thinking in verse 4 ("turning the grace of our God into promiscuity") and his description of the "sexual immorality" that mirrored the perverted lifestyles of Sodom and Gomorrah (v. 7). Jude also countered the false teachers' claims to spiritual authority on the basis of ecstatic visions and private spiritual experience. He denounced such imposters as "not having the Spirit" at all (v. 19).

The content and style of the letter also reflect the outlook of a believer whose worldview was thoroughly Jewish. Jude's use of Old Testament typology and allusions to first-century Jewish literature indicate that his outlook was typical of Jewish Christians who believed they were living in the last days and interpreted Scripture from this apocalyptic point of view.

Genre

Jude is a personal letter, which opens with the elements typical of most ancient letters—sender, recipients, and greeting (vv. 1-2)—and closes with a doxology typical of early Christian epistles (vv. 24-25). The body of the letter reflects Jude's familiarity with Greek rhetorical patterns, but some scholars also argue that Jude basically penned a sermon in the form of a letter because he could not visit his audience in person. Although it is typically grouped among the "catholic" or "general" epistles, the epistle was written to a particular church or group of churches Jude had identified as needing its message. In either case, Jude addressed straightforwardly the heresies being peddled by rebellious opponents of the grace of God. His purpose was to persuade his readers to "contend for the faith" (v. 3).

Author

The introductory words "Jude, the slave of Jesus Christ, and brother of James" are clear indication that Jude, who was also a brother of Jesus, wrote this letter. Jude identified himself as the "brother" of James and the "slave" of Jesus, denoting a marked change in the way Jude related to his brother Jesus. By the time of the writing of this epistle, Jude had begun a salvific relationship with Jesus that differed from his fraternal relationship to Christ before the cross (Mt 13:55; Mk 6:3). The humility exhibited in this title sets the stage for the rest of Jude's letter.

Date

This letter was probably written between AD 65 and 80. The exact year of its origin is difficult to establish since nothing in the context of the epistle lends itself to establishing a timeline. However, since Jude, the brother of Jesus and James, is the author, the date would have to be sometime before his death in the latter part of the first century.

Recipients

Jude does not specifically identify his recipients. He described them as those "who are the called, loved by God the Father and kept by Jesus Christ" (v. 1) and "dear friends" (v. 3), which would seem to indicate that he knew the people to whom he was writing. A careful observation of the letter, however, does divulge some details about the recipients. Jude referred to much Old Testament history. He also referred to some first-century Jewish literature (vv. 9,14). These facts indicate that the recipients were well acquainted with Jewish history. Hence, Jude was probably writing to Jewish believers in the region of Asia Minor.

Major Theme

At the heart of the epistle of Jude is the importance of sound doctrine evidenced in pure living. Jude does not detail the nature of the heresy because the lives of those "certain men" condemn their teaching. Jude called for an accurate understanding of authority and submission. For women today, this lesson is timely. Jude reminded his readers of the destinies of people who did not heed the authority of the Lord or humbly walk in His ways. The Day of the Lord will be terrible for those who have not obeyed (vv. 14-16) but glorious for those who do persevere in this age (vv. 17-25).

Pronunciation Guide			
Balaam	*BAY luhm*	Korah	*KOH ruh*
Enoch	*EE nuhk*	Sodom	*SAHD uhm*
Gomorrah	*guh MAHR uh*		

Outline

I. INTRODUCTORY GREETING (VV. 1-2)

II. A PURPOSE FOR WRITING THE LETTER (VV. 3-4)

III. A REMINDER FOR THE RECIPIENTS (VV. 5-11)

IV. A DESCRIPTION OF THE INTRUDERS (VV. 12-16)

V. AN EXHORTATION FOR BELIEVERS (VV. 17-23)

VI. CONCLUDING DOXOLOGY (VV. 24-25)

Exposition of the Text

INTRODUCTORY GREETING (VV. 1-2)

1-2 The Gospels sometimes describe the relationship of Jesus' brothers to Him during His earthly ministry as less than admirable (Mk 6:3-4). However, at some point Jude realized that Jesus as God deserved to be served and worshiped. For contemporary women, the same kind of change in relationship must occur. A realization of Jesus' divine nature and His offering salvation must transcend into daily living as worthy of absolute and complete obedience.

Heart to Heart: Greetings in Relationships

Jude expressed his heart and his relationship to the Lord as His "slave" (v. 1), but he also expressed his heart for his fellow brothers and sisters. In your relationships with other women, do you have a desire, as did Jude, for God's blessing to be on the lives of your dear friends? Do you communicate that to them? In conversations with other women, are mercy, peace, and love the center of your conversation with them?

As you relate to your dear friends by speaking psalms, hymns, and spiritual songs, may you continue to grow in your ability to bless them (Eph 5:19-21). May your prayers for your friends be intercessions of mercy, peace, and love on their behalf. May you follow Jude's example by addressing serious concerns with your dear friends with boldness and honesty and with blessing as well.

A PURPOSE FOR WRITING THE LETTER (VV. 3-4)

3-4 While Jude set out to write to Jewish believers concerning their **common salvation** (v. 3), he changed the tone and spirit of his letter and instead zealously challenged the recipients of his letter **to contend for the faith that was delivered to the saints once for all** (v. 3). His fervent encouragement for this action by the Jewish believers was precipitated by the presence of false teachers in the church. These ungodly men had crept in, denying the lordship of Christ. Their teaching had to be confronted and corrected for the good of the church.

CONTEND (Gk. *epagōnizesthai*, "fight") includes the idea of contending strenuously in defense, even in athletic or military action. The word denotes intense struggle and effort. The common salvation entrusted to the saints was precious and worth protecting. Jude challenged the recipients of his letter with strong exhortations to protect their faith.

> *Women today do well to consider not only the words but also the lives of their teachers.*

Jude described the methodology of these "certain men" (v. 4) who had crept into the believers' midst as coming in BY STEALTH (Gk. *pareisedusan*, "sneak in, enter privately," v. 4), a term with vivid illustrative significance. These rebellious men did not blatantly proclaim their heresy, but they deceitfully infiltrated the fellowship of the church. At first false doctrine may not be clearly obvious. However, the nature of the heresy becomes more evident as you compare the false teaching to the truth of the gospel. Jude's description of "stealthy" practices is followed by his description of the false teachers who **are ungodly, turning the grace of our God into promiscuity and denying our only Master and Lord, Jesus Christ** (v. 4). Jude pushed his readers to consider the connection between doctrine and practice. He illustrated his condemnation of the false teachers using their own behaviors and practices. Women today do well to consider not only the words but also the lives of their teachers.

DEAR FRIENDS (Gk. *agapētoi*, "beloved, worthy of love") is a warm term denoting God's love and care for His people. By using this term repeatedly, Jude reminded his readers of their relationship with Christ as Savior. In the context of the full letter, Jude linked this relationship to the last judgment. For those persevering through the difficulties of this life, the view of eternal reward and punishment was paramount. In this way, Jude admonished them to be faithful by reminding them they were dearly loved by God.

CERTAIN MEN (Gk. *tines anthrōpoi*) assumed the identity of these deceivers was apparent since the phrase is one of generality. Jude continued by describing their behavior to give specific indicators as to who they were. He described them as DREAMERS (Gk. *enupniazomenoi*, "receive some supernatural impression or information in a dream or cherish vain opinions," v. 8). Jude was not condemning all those who dream or have ambition, but he was condemning those who base their entire lives on these vain visions. Their dreams were selfish and autonomous and without respect to any authority, including God's. Jude also called these men GRUMBLERS (Gk. *goggustai*, "speak privately in a low voice, mutter, utter secret and sullen discontent," v. 16). They were arrogant, selfish, and flatterers. In this sense Jude rejected his opponents on theological and moral grounds. The **certain men**, in contrast to Jude's **dear friends**, were neither sound in doctrine nor sound in practice. Therefore, their lives and message had to be opposed for the sake of the gospel and their "common salvation" (v. 3).

A REMINDER FOR THE RECIPIENTS (VV. 5-11)

5-11 Jude included seven examples of **people** and **angels** who exhibited various responses to the mercy of God. These historical accounts served to remind the Jewish believers of both good and bad choices made in the salvific history of Israel.

The exodus of the Israelites from Egypt and their rescue from Egyptian slavery were pivotal in the history of Israel (v. 5; see Ex 1–6). Every Jew knew and understood the magnanimity of this event of deliverance. Jude reminded them of God's faithfulness and warned them of the consequences of infidelity. The people of Israel rebelled against the Lord with grumbling and disbelief in the desert; therefore, they were not allowed into the promised land (Nm 14).

Jude made reference to the precosmic rebellion of Satan and his coterie of angels who rebelled against God (see Lk 10:18; Is 14:1-15; Ezk 28:1-19). In this rebellion, Satan, together with his followers, was cast out of heaven. Jude declared that most of these would be held in chains of darkness until the day of final judgment. Apparently, however, some, as Satan himself, remain at large in the world, constituting the group that the Bible references as demons.

The example of **Sodom and Gomorrah** served as an especially poignant reminder for Jude's contemporary readers since the **sexual immorality** rampant in those cities was similar to the sexual immorality of the intruders Jude described. Jude reminded the believers that **eternal fire** awaited all those who indulged in this sort of rebellion (v. 7).

In contrast to these kinds of subversive activities, Jude reminded them of the archangel **Michael**. According to Jewish history Michael refused to rebuke **the Devil** when arguing with him over **Moses' body**. Even when God's will was difficult to understand, Michael humbly stayed within his allotted position as a servant of God. He could have rebuked the Devil but chose to trust God to do that.

The example of the archangel Michael stands in contradistinction to that of those who disobeyed God (v. 8).

Finally, Jude compared the false teachers with those who had **traveled in the way of Cain**, embraced **the error of Balaam**, and **perished in Korah's rebellion** (v. 11). This threefold oracle of woe was a common Jewish literary device used in the Old Testament: "The use of a woe implies prophetic consciousness on the part of the speaker or writer, as one authorized to announce divine judgment."[1]

Cain was the first man to commit murder—the malicious homicide of his own brother (Gn 4:8). When God rebuked Cain for his insufficient offering of "some of the land's produce" (Gn 4:3), he chose to rebel by killing his brother rather than correcting his own wrongs. The "error of Balaam" (Jd 11) lay in Balaam's defiant unwillingness to bless Israel for the sake of his own greed (Nm 22–24; Dt 23:4-5). When Balaam refused to bless Israel, his donkey would not obey him in his persistent insolence. Korah rebelled against the leadership of Moses and Aaron (Nm 16). God clearly communicated His mandates through these two men, yet Korah did not respect the authority of God's servants. As a result, the earth consumed Korah and his allies. The false teachers with whom Jude was admonishing the Jewish believers to contend were similar to Cain, Balaam, and Korah in their defiance, greed, and insubordinate attitude toward authority. Their actions were not without consequences, as Jude tersely reminded his readers.

A DESCRIPTION OF THE INTRUDERS (VV. 12-16)

12-16 Jude likened the false teachers to **dangerous reefs at your love feasts** (v. 12). Common among the practices of the early church was the sharing of a large

Heart to Heart:
Understanding Authority

For the Christian woman today, Jude's lesson concerning authority and its place in her life is of special importance. Many see relationships of authority as having no significance. Feminist ideology has taught women and men that they are completely autonomous with the right to define themselves, their world, and their God.[2]

However, Scripture teaches that understanding authority is essential to understanding how you properly relate to God and others. Jude confronted "certain men" who had crept into the fellowship of believers by giving examples of others who had despised authority. He urged his readers to consider negative and positive examples of those in relationships of authority. For the Christian woman, the example of Michael is appropriate as he willingly submitted to God to take care of the Devil in His own way (vv. 8-9). Christian women also do well to obey God through submission to authority while trusting Him to take care of the outcome.

meal, which ended with the Lord's Supper. Reefs are large underwater rocks that cause trouble for ships because they are difficult to see. So these false teachers were difficult to identify at their fellowships. Although they mixed and mingled among the congregation in the love feasts, everything was not as it seemed. As the reefs cause unexpected damage and shipwreck, these false teachers in a similar way caused damage to the faith.

Waterless clouds and **trees in late autumn** (v. 12) refer to the lack of depth and true help found in those who had stealthily crept into their midst with false teachings. Both of these analogies articulate the idea of help and life, while in fact being dead and of no use. The false teachers were the same in the fellowship of the church. Although it might have seemed that their teaching could offer help, no source of assistance or life was found therein.

Jude then compared these teachers to **wild waves of the sea** and **wandering stars** (v. 13). In the analogy of the waves Jude referred to their licentious lifestyles. The surging waves of the sea produce sticky foam. The immoral lifestyle of these men produced shameful deeds. They were like "wandering stars" that provided no navigational assistance. The false teachers could not provide genuine assurance. Jude, in this way, likened them to be no help whatsoever.

Jude was reminding his audience that even though the false prophets were able to fool some, they could not fool God, who knows the nature of their teaching and misdeeds and is able **to execute** judgment **on all** (vv. 14-15). Like those who grumbled in the desert, these men were complainers who indulged their flesh in whatever way best suited their passions. God cannot be mocked, however, and Jude concluded his description of the false teachers with this reminder.

Heart to Heart:
Is Everything as It Seems?

Among Christians, new teachers and Bible study products abound. How does the discerning Christian woman decide what to study or implement in her women's ministry programs? Jude exhorted his readers to consider the source. He admonished his readers to observe their favorite teachers and leaders. How did they live their lives? What fruit was produced in their ministries? What were their relationships like? Was there any evidence of God or godliness in their lives? Jude's word pictures describe deficits in these areas in the lives of the intruders.

The same principles exist today for the Christian woman who is deciding what to study and with whom to study: Consider the source. There should be fruit of righteousness in the lives of leaders in your local church. What beliefs does a Bible study author hold? Jude warned his readers to guard against certain character traits. The same holds true today.

AN EXHORTATION FOR BELIEVERS (VV. 17-23)

17-23 Jude continued his reminder to the Jewish believers by contrasting the behavior and lifestyle of those who truly belong to God as compared to the false teachers. He exhorted them to remember the words of the apostles, suggesting that eyewitnesses of the resurrected and ascended Lord Jesus had taught the recipients of Jude's letter. The apostles warned them that **scoffers** (v. 18) would come, and indeed they had—hence, the occasion of this epistle.

Jude contrasted the impure lives of the false teachers with the proper behavior of those who truly know the Lord. He urged believers to **keep yourselves in the love of God** (v. 20). This ongoing effort is motivated by their **expecting the mercy of our Lord Jesus Christ for eternal life** (v. 21). Those who doubt will appear, and

Jude admonished believers to show mercy (v. 22).

For those more seriously in trouble with regard to their faith, Jude instructed that the Jewish believers **save others by snatching them from the fire** (v. 23). This phrase does not mean that they were already in the fire, but rather that they were in danger of fire. Therefore, they must be admonished strongly and carefully so as to restore their faith.

The final group Jude mentioned was in even more danger due to the false teaching. These people were to be shown **mercy in fear** (v. 23). This mercy was not without recognition of the consequences of sin. The believers were to respond lovingly to those with garments **defiled by the flesh**, while also deeply despising their sin (v. 23). The destruction brought about by actions rooted in the false teaching was to be intensely abhorred out of the fear and respect for the perfect and righteous God.

CONCLUDING DOXOLOGY (vv. 24-25)

24-25 Jude concluded his letter just as graciously as he began. He reminded the believers of the power and ability of God to keep them pure and holy for eternity. He ascribed **glory, majesty, power, and authority** (v. 25) ultimately to God because He is the one **who is able to protect you from stumbling** and to present you **blameless and with great joy** (v. 24). Appropriately, Jude exhorted the believers that whatever difficulties they experienced in this life would be fully worth their persevering to the end. Jude closed his letter with a reminder to his audience of the nature and character of God who alone is powerful and able to hold them in His hand, no matter what they might face. God existed before time and will reign in excellence forever. In praise and adulation Jude concluded his letter to those who are "the called, loved by God the Father and kept by Jesus Christ" (v. 1). In the exhortation to "contend for the faith," Jude reminded believers that their struggle was not in vain and that the day would come when they would see Him face to face so that He who is matchless in "glory, majesty, power and authority" would reward their efforts (v. 25).

Bibliography

Anders, Max., ed. *I & II Peter, I, II, III John, Jude.* Holman New Testament Commentary, vol. 11. Nashville: Holman Reference, 1999.

*Bauckham, Richard J. *Jude, 2 Peter.* Word Biblical Commentary, vol. 50. Waco: Word Books, 1983.

Carson, D. A., Douglas Moo, and Leon Morris. *An Introduction to the New Testament.* Grand Rapids: Zondervan, 1992.

Schreiner, Thomas. *1, 2 Peter, Jude.* New American Commentary, vol 37. Nashville: Broadman and Holman, 2003.

* For advanced study

Notes

[1] Richard J. Bauckham, *Jude, 2 Peter*, Word Biblical Commentary, vol. 50 (Waco: Word Books, 1983), 78.
[2] See Mary Kassian, *The Feminist Mistake* (Wheaton: Crossway Books, 2005) for discussion of feminist ideology and its impact on women.

REVELATION

Introduction

Title

Though simply titled "Revelation" in most Bibles, the full title is "The revelation of Jesus Christ" (v. 1). In the Greek text, the title is literally "A Revelation of John" (Gk. *Apokalupsis Iōannou*, "revelation recorded by John"). "Revelation" (Gk. *apokalupsis*, "unveiling or revealing") suggests a great secret or mystery, which the reader has the privilege to observe as it is uncovered; but this mystery is not ordinary, for it is "of Jesus Christ" or "belonging to Jesus Christ." Such divine mysteries are not discovered by human ability but must be revealed by God alone. So, this book is "an unveiling message belonging to Jesus Christ." Even though the man John is said to be the author of the book, verse 1 specifies that God gave Jesus Christ the revelation to give to believers, God's slaves. A special blessing is stated, which is available for those who read, hear, and obey the words of Revelation (1:3). If verses 1 and 2 make up the title and subtitle of the book, then the blessing of verse 3 could be an author's note: "Blessed is the one who reads and blessed are those who hear the words of this prophecy and keep what is written in it, because the time is near!" Blessed are those who read and hear the words of this prophecy. Nevertheless, the primary concern of Revelation is not merely looking at events in the future but living life in personal obedience in the present.

Setting

A description of Revelation's setting depends on one's conclusions about the book's authorship and date. Here, John the apostle is identified as the human author, and that he wrote the book sometime after the fall of Jerusalem in AD 70 is assumed. John's testimony reveals three key facts about his personal situation:

- He "was on the island called Patmos" as an exile (1:9; see commentary).

- He was there "because of God's word and the testimony about Jesus" (1:9).

- He "was in the Spirit on the Lord's day" when the initial vision arrested his attention (1:10).

These facts, along with the apocalyptic message found in the book, underscore that John did not independently decide to compose the book of Revelation based merely on his immediate historical situation but that the Holy Spirit disclosed to him "the revelation of Jesus Christ that God gave Him" to challenge and comfort believers from the first century unto generations to come and to the end portrayed in its pages (1:1).

The circumstances of John's original readers differed greatly from the modern era. Although many people assume that a mid-90s date for Revelation meant the existence of widespread persecution in the empire, current historical evidence does not necessarily support this conclusion. Random persecution is documented, but it may not have been as widespread as many have assumed. Within the book itself, persecution had been experienced by Smyrna and Pergamum (2:13), with more on the way for Smyrna (2:10) and Philadelphia (3:10); internal division due to false teaching within the churches was also a threat in Pergamum (2:14-15) and Thyatira (2:20); yet, complacency represented the greatest threat at Ephesus (2:4-5), Sardis (3:1-2), and Laodicea (3:15-19). The internal struggles of these churches were similar to those of modern congregations: apathy, complacency, division due to false teaching, and gratuitous harshness, or lack of love— issues rarely experienced by churches suffering intense persecution.

In order to gain victory over the forces of evil (embodied by the dragon of chap. 12, two beasts of chap. 13, and the great prostitute of chap. 17), Christians must become the "victor" (2:7,11,17,26; 3:5,12,21; 21:7) through the "blood of the Lamb" and "the word of their testimony" (12:11).

John's visions urged the churches to take up their spiritual weapons and report for active duty within a hostile environment. The first-century Christians encountered opposition from Jews who sought to distinguish themselves from Christians and from the pressure to conform to Roman life, particularly on social and economic levels. For example, Christian workers who belonged to trade guilds faced unemployment and social ostracism for refusing to participate in the idolatrous practices devoted to the guilds' patron deities. The message of the book of Revelation insists that believers must not compromise with pagan society, even though such a posture would necessarily and inevitably incite persecution against them.

Genre

Many different kinds of literature appear in the Bible. However, the book of Revelation is not easy to categorize. It has characteristics of the following genres:

- an apocalypse, in which a being from another world delivers to a human recipient a written document containing a supernatural message with its basis in the present world as well as an emphasis on the age to come (1:1);

- a prophecy, making claims about the future while demanding present-day obedience to the word of God (1:3); and

- an epistle, formatted as a letter addressed to a specific audience (1:4) with a formal greeting (1:1-8) and conclusion (22:6-21), and seven messages written to seven historical churches in between.

In summary, Revelation is an apocalyptic prophecy written in the form of a letter.

Author

The writer of Revelation identified himself simply as "John," a "slave" (1:1) and the "brother and partner" (1:9) in the faith of the believing readers. Obviously he was a man of authority in the churches, well acquainted with the conditions in which the people lived. Traditionally, the author of Revelation has been identified as the son of Zebedee and brother of James, the Apostle John, who also wrote the Fourth Gospel and the three letters of John in the New Testament.

Yet, because the writing style, vocabulary, and thought patterns of Revelation are quite different from the Gospel of John and of 1, 2, and 3 John, some interpreters have followed the reasoning of Dionysius, a church leader in North Africa in the third century, who suggested that Revelation was written by a different "John," known in that day as "the Elder," who was also an authoritative leader in the Ephesian church. The great church historian Eusebius also corroborated this view, claiming "John the Elder" as the author of Revelation. Support for this position also comes from the fact that the John of Revelation does not claim to be an apostle but refers to the "12 apostles" (21:14) as if he is not one of them. However, these facts must also be considered:

- Revelation has many themes and theological ideas in common with John's Gospel and letters (i.e., Jesus as the "Lamb" and the "Word of God").

- If there were another John besides the apostle in Ephesus, surely the author would have to distinguish himself in such a way as to prevent confusion.

- Other early church fathers writing about Revelation almost unanimously attribute the book to John the apostle, including Irenaeus of Lyons (d. AD 190), who was a student of Polycarp, the pastor of the church at Smyrna and a student of the Apostle John. Irenaeus testified that Polycarp had spoken of John as writing Revelation during the reign of Emperor Domitian.

The traditional view is further supported by the fact that:

- The writer of Revelation was suffering in circumstances historically associated with John the apostle.

- Apostolic authority would appear important to justify the author's bold transformation of so many Old Testament images.

- The stylistic differences between Revelation and other writings of John may be explained by his use of an *amanuensis* (i.e., a secretary or stenographer).

There is no compelling reason to go against the longstanding tradition that John the apostle is the writer of Revelation.

Date

Although there has never been unanimity regarding the question of when Revelation was written, two major views exist among evangelicals: (1) the mid-90s of the first century AD, during the reign of the Roman Emperor Domitian, and (2) the late 60s, just before the fall of Jerusalem to Roman armies in AD 70. Three considerations are pertinent:

- John's vision of a "new Jerusalem" (21:2) suggests that the old Jerusalem had already been destroyed.

- There is no evidence that "Babylon" (17:5) was used as a name for the city of Rome prior to AD 70.

- Time for the circulation of a certain rumor (formally called *Nero Redivivus*, or "Nero brought back to life"), which was said to be behind the imagery of the terrible "beast" (17:8) throughout the book, called for a later date.

A date in the mid-90s seems the most plausible.

Recipients

The immediate recipients of the book were seven churches of Asia Minor, located in the cities of Ephesus, Smyrna, Pergamum, Thyatira, Sardis, Philadelphia, and Laodicea, not the only churches in Asia Minor at the time but singled out by the Lord for respectively receiving the book's messages. Apparently the seven churches were conveniently located on an ancient postal route of the Asian mainland. In western Asia Minor, the imperial cult was entrenched, and Christianity was well established.

Some have speculated that these churches were chosen in order to illustrate a downward course in church history, culminating in Laodicean lukewarmness. More likely the choice of seven churches is a purposeful literary device pointing toward the universal application of the directives to the individual churches. In truth, the problems they faced seem ever present and have emerged in congregations throughout various cultures and ages. Revelation was written first to the seven churches and then distributed throughout the region for the edification of all the churches.

Special Issues for Interpretation

People have approached the interpretation of Revelation in four major ways.

- According to the "preterist" view, the events recorded in Revelation were fulfilled in the days of the first century under the emperors Nero or Domitian, with little or no future fulfillment to be expected apart from the return of Christ. This position eventually removed any message for future generations.

- The "historicist" (or postmillennial) view proposes that Revelation depicts the broad sweep of church history, from the time of the apostles to the consummation of the age. Christ returns at the conclusion of the millennial age. Espoused by most of the Reformers (except the Anabaptists), this view is weakened by inevitable subjectivity in its interpretation of the symbolism.

- The "idealist" (or amillennial) view proposes that Revelation is not to be considered an ordered presentation of actual events but a symbolic depiction of the ongoing battle between God and Satan, good and evil. There is no literal millennial reign of Christ on earth.

- The "futurist" (or premillennial) view interprets the events beginning with chapter 4 to be a marvelous prophecy of what is to come in the future age. Christ ushers in the millennium. The early church fathers were united, with a few exceptions, in interpreting Revelation as in some sense actual history. Anabaptists also held this view.

Revelation is to be interpreted as an apocalyptic prophecy primarily referring to the end times, yet speaking to the problems and needs of first-century churches, while communicating principles equally binding and applicable to hearers at any point in history until the end of the age. Aiming both to interpret and apply the contents of Revelation, three questions must be answered:

- What did the text mean specifically to the ancient readers?

- What is the "timeless principle" being conveyed by the text?

- How does this "timeless principle" apply to you today?

Although time lines continue to be popular in the study of Revelation, its chronology cannot be established with absolute certainty. Revelation opens and closes with promises of blessing to those who *obey* its teachings (1:3; 22:7), not to those who dwell on deciphering the future fulfillment of its prophecies. Revelation was given so that you may know "what must quickly take place" (1:1). Yet, as you watch eagerly for the Savior's return, you are wiser to focus on obedience to the book's teachings than to speculate needlessly about the minute details of the ultimate fulfillment of its prophecies.

The Use of the Old Testament and Symbols

Revelation can be intimidating because of its use of the Old Testament and symbolic elements, such as numbers, which are often unfamiliar to modern readers. While such unique elements may complicate your understanding of the book, some can be clarified prior to its study in order to make comprehension easier.

No direct quotations of the Old Testament appear in Revelation, but estimates for the number of allusions to the Hebrew Bible range between 275 and 600. The message of Revelation was written to an audience likely familiar with the Old Testament. Studying the book in this light should lead you to a greater appreciation of the Hebrew Scripture.

Major Old Testament Allusions in the Book of Revelation	
Revelation	**Old Testament**
1:7	Dn 7:13-14; Zch 12:10
4:1-11	Ezk 1
6:1-8	Zch 1:8-10
6:12-17	Jl 2:30-31
9:1-12	Jl 1:1-12
10:1-7	Dn 10:2-9
10:8-11	Ezk 3:1-4
11:1-4	Ezk 40:2-5; Zch 4:11-14
12:1-6	Gn 3:15
13:1-17	Dn 7:7-8,23-25
14:17-19	Jl 3:13
17:7-14	Dn 7:23-27
18:1-24	Jr 51
20:4-10	Ezk 38–39
21:1–22:5	Is 65–66; Ezk 40–48; Gn 2:8-14

Revelation is completely saturated in symbolism. From the image of the glorified "Son of Man" (chap. 1) to the "river of living water" (chap. 22), God uses astonishing and often mind-boggling images over and over to convey His message. Mysterious pictures are painted of terrifying horned beasts, a virtuous sky-woman crowned with stars, mighty angels with trumpets of judgment, and, maybe more familiarly, the gold-paved streets of the new Jerusalem.

You must not conclude that the symbolism is so prevalent as to require a completely figurative approach to the book. All symbolism is intended to communicate something. You must consider each symbol on its own terms within the text. You must also not interpret the symbolism of Revelation so literally as to lose touch with the original intent of John's writing. From the opening line of the book, clearly God desires "to show" His revelation to His people, but even the word "signified" (Gk. *esēmanen*, "make known, report, indicate clearly") contains the idea of "showing *by signs or symbols*" (1:1). Interpretation requires a balance between using the simplest, most consistent explanation possible while respecting the symbols within their proper framework in the book. All symbols within Revelation are to encourage and exhort readers toward obedience.

Numbers are the obvious and puzzling symbols in the book of Revelation. The three major numbers from which the majority of other numbers are derived are four, seven, and twelve. Based on other uses throughout Scripture, the following ideas can be associated with each of these numbers:

- *Four*: The earth with four seasons, directions, winds, and quadrants (Rv 7:1; 20:8); even the fourfold designation of "tribe, language, people, and nation" (5:9; see variations in 7:9; 10:11; 13:7).

- *Seven*: Earth (the number four) crowned with heaven (the number three as representing the triunity), leading to perfection and completeness. The number seven appears often: seven churches (1:4,11); seven spirits (1:4; 3:1; 4:5; 5:6); sevenfold doxologies (1:3; 14:13; 16:15; 19:9; 20:6; 22:7,14); seven seals (5:1,5; 6:1); seven trumpets (8:2,6); seven bowls (15:7; 16:1; 17:1); and seven blessings (1:3; 14:13; 16:15; 19:9; 20:6; 22:7,14).

- *Twelve*: God's perfect manifestation of Himself in His created order. There were 12 tribes of Israel (7:5-8; 21:12) and 12 apostles (21:14), as well as 12 foundations (21:14) and 12 gates (21:12,21) in the new Jerusalem.

The interpretation of these three numbers finds almost complete agreement among scholars. Yet, once these numbers are divided (i.e., "two witnesses" in 11:3), multiplied (i.e., "144,000" in 7:4), or subtracted from (i.e., "666," in 13:18), there seems to be less agreement among interpreters. To interpret Revelation's symbols, including its numbers, will call for understanding historical background in both the Old Testament and first-century society as well as careful examination of immediate contexts in the book.

Major Themes

The most central theme of Revelation is inherently a practical one: the division between the followers of the Lamb and the followers of the beast (Revelation's "antichrist"). The earth dwellers are the unbelievers whose rebellion against God and His Messiah makes them completely "earthbound." The heaven dwellers are the believers whose obedience to God and the Lamb makes them eternally "heavenbound." The earth dwellers, because of their many crimes, will end up in a place of eternal suffering, while the heaven dwellers will end up united with God in a place of eternal bliss. The dominating imagery of the book, which we will consider in more detail in the commentary, also supports this division. There are two harvests, two women, two cities, two banquets, and two resurrections, all of which pertain to these divisions.

For those who are followers of the Lamb, the message of Revelation also emphasizes practical obedience. The church is warned not to compromise with the sinfulness of the world, for only the person who is victorious over temptation will be rewarded in the new Jerusalem. In the end, the person who fails to remain loyal to Christ exposes himself as a fraud, one whose name was not written in the Lamb's book of life. The church is also confronted with the truth that disciples of Jesus should not only expect suffering and persecu-

Followers				
Of the Lamb		**Of the Beast**		
Heaven dwellers	5:9-11; 7:9; 12:12; 19:1,6,14; 20:4,6	Earth dwellers	3:10; 6:9-11; 8:13; 11:10; 13:8; 17:2,6,8; 18:24–19:2
Harvest of wheat	14:14-16	Harvest of grapes	14:17-20
"Bride" of Christ	19:7; 21:9	"Notorious prostitute"	17:1
New Jerusalem	21:1,10	Babylon the Great	17:5; 18:1
Marriage Feast of the Lamb	19:9	Great supper of God	19:17
First resurrection (unto life)	20:6	Second resurrection (unto death)	20:12

tion but also should be willing to endure whatever cost is involved. In Revelation, true Christ followers imitate their Savior by triumphing over evil through suffering and death. Clearly, the church must consider no price too high to pay for loyalty to the Son of God.

Beyond the practical themes of Revelation, there are themes pertaining to Christian doctrine, such as the doctrine of God, which focuses primarily on His sovereign rule over the world. The titles used for God illustrate this point (chap. 1):

- "The One who is, who was, and who is coming" (1:4,8) affirms that God is always in control—past, present, and future. His omnipresent sovereignty guarantees the future fulfillment of His promises to His people.

- "The Alpha and the Omega" (1:8) points to divine sufficiency. God is not only in charge of the past and future but also everything in between.

- "The Almighty" (1:8) signifies the omnipotence of God, which ensures His ultimate triumph over the forces of evil.

- The exalted One "seated on the throne" (4:2-3) emphasizes His holiness and incomprehensible wisdom.

Encountering the God of Revelation, readers are left with the assurance that the all-wise and all-powerful Creator of the universe is able to bring the world to its ultimate and most glorious consummation.

The Christological language is the most exalted in the New Testament. "The revelation of Jesus Christ" (1:1) is the title of the book, and the first vision of John is a Christophany, a heavenly and bodily appearance of Christ (1:12-16). The book of Revelation consistently identifies Jesus Christ, not just as fully divine, as in many New Testament books, but as equal to God in nature and status. John communicated this doctrine by using similar phrases to describe Christ and the Father. Jesus is characterized as:

- "the faithful witness" (1:5);
- the glorified "Son of Man" (1:12-16);
- "the Lion from the tribe of Judah, the Root of David" (5:5);
- "a slaughtered lamb" (5:6);
- the universal ruler (12:5);
- the bridegroom (19:7-9);

- the victorious warrior (19:11); and
- "the Word of God" (19:13).

Finally, Revelation also deals at great length with eschatology, the doctrine of last things with the absolute certainty that God will triumph over evil in the end. Satan and his minions will be defeated and punished, along with all people of the earth who rebel against the rule of God. Those who follow the Lord Jesus and remain faithful to Him until the end will be rewarded with eternal life in the city of God. The judgment of God serves to reveal His righteous character and to vindicate His righteous people. On these key themes all interpreters agree. Yet, the detailed events of the end times, along with their timing, are issues of dispute even among evangelical Bible scholars.

Pronunciation Guide

Abaddon	*uh BAD uhn*	Millennium	*muh LEN ih uhm*
Alpha	*AL fuh*	Nicolaitans	*nik oh LAY uh tuhns*
Apollyon	*uh PAHL yuhn*	Omega	*oh MAY guh*
Armageddon	*ahr muh GED uhn*	Pergamum	*PUHR guh muhm*
Babylon	*BAB ih lahn*	Philadelphia	*fil uh DEL fih uh*
Ephesus	*EF uh suhs*	Sardis	*SAHR diss*
Euphrates	*yoo FRAY teez*	Smyrna	*SMUHR nuh*
Laodicea	*lay ahd ih SEE uh*	Thyatira	*thigh uh TIGH ruh*

Outline

I. THE PROLOGUE (1:1-20)
  A. The Title (1:1-3)
  B. Greetings and Praise to Jesus (1:4-8)
  C. John's Vision and Commission to Write (1:9-20)

II. THE MESSAGES TO SEVEN CHURCHES OF ASIA (2:1–3:22)
  A. The Message to Ephesus (2:1-7)
  B. The Message to Smyrna (2:8-11)
  C. The Message to Pergamum (2:12-17)
  D. The Message to Thyatira (2:18-29)
  E. The Message to Sardis (3:1-6)
  F. The Message to Philadelphia (3:7-13)
  G. The Message to Laodicea (3:14-22)

III. ADORATION IN THE THRONE ROOM OF HEAVEN (4:1–5:14)
  A. The Throne and Its Surroundings (4:1-11)
  B. The Lamb and the Seven-sealed Scroll (5:1-14)

IV. THE SEVEN SEALS (6:1–8:6)
  A. The Opening of the First Four Seals (6:1-8)
  B. The Opening of the Fifth Seal (6:9-11)
  C. The Opening of the Sixth Seal (6:12-17)
  D. The First Interlude Vision (7:1-8)
  E. The Second Interlude Vision (7:9-17)

F. The Opening of the Seventh
Seal (8:1-6)

V. THE SEVEN TRUMPETS (8:7–11:19)
A. The First Four Trumpets
(8:7-13)
B. The Fifth Trumpet or First Woe
(9:1-12)
C. The Sixth Trumpet or Second
Woe (9:13-21)
D. The First Interlude Vision
(10:1-11)
E. The Second Interlude Vision
(11:1-14)
F. The Seventh Trumpet or Third
Woe (11:15-19)

VI. TWO GREAT SIGNS AND THEIR
INTERPRETATION (12:1-17)
A. Two Signs in Heaven: The
Woman and the Dragon
(12:1-6)
B. The Dragon Thrown Out of
Heaven (12:7-17)

VII. THE TWO BEASTS AND THEIR
DECEPTION (12:18–13:18)
A. The Beast from the Sea
(12:18–13:10)
B. The Beast from the Earth
(13:11-18)

VIII. THE FIRSTFRUITS AND THE
HARVEST (14:1-20)
A. The Redeemed of the Earth
(14:1-5)
B. The Messages of Three Angels
(14:6-13)
C. The Harvest of the Earth: Part
One (14:14-16)
D. The Harvest of the Earth: Part
Two (14:17-20)

IX. THE SEVEN LAST PLAGUES
(15:1–16:21)
A. The Third Great Sign in Heaven
(15:1-8)

B. The First Three Bowls of Wrath
(16:1-7)
C. The Fourth Bowl (16:8-9)
D. The Fifth Bowl (16:10-11)
E. The Sixth Bowl (16:12-16)
F. The Seventh Bowl (16:17-21)

X. BABYLON AND HER DESTINY
(17:1–19:5)
A. The Vision of the Woman and
the Scarlet Beast (17:1-6)
B. The Angel's Interpretation of
the Vision (17:7-18)
C. The Announcement of
Babylon's Fall (18:1-8)
D. The World Mourns Babylon's
Fall (18:9-20)
E. The Finality of Babylon's
Destruction (18:21-24)
F. The Rejoicing of Heaven
(19:1-5)

XI. THE FINAL VICTORY (19:6–20:15)
A. The Marriage of the Lamb
Announced (19:6-10)
B. The Victorious Messiah
Appears (19:11-16)
C. Antichrist and Allies Destroyed
(19:17-21)
D. The Binding of Satan (20:1-3)
E. Christ's Millennial Reign
(20:4-6)
F. Satan's Final Destruction
(20:7-10)
G. The Final Judgment (20:11-15)

XII. THE NEW HEAVEN AND NEW
EARTH (21:1–22:5)
A. The New Creation (21:1-8)
B. The New Jerusalem (21:9-27)
C. Eden's Restoration (22:1-5)

XIII. EPILOGUE (22:6-21)
A. John and the Angel (22:6-11)
B. Conclusion (22:12-21)

Exposition of the Text

THE PROLOGUE (1:1-20)

Chapter 1 is the introduction to Revelation, providing several keys vital to understanding the rest of the book. The first three verses, its "title page," include the name of the book, "The Revelation of Jesus Christ," the identity of its author John, and an "author's note" providing insight into God's intent for the apocalypse and its importance for the Christian life. Then follows a formal greeting from the author (1:4-5a), an extended doxology (i.e., words of praise) to Jesus Christ (1:5b-8) and the "theme verse" of the book (1:7)—a vivid collage of Daniel 7:13 and Zechariah 12:10—as well as a reminder of Who will bring all the prophecies to pass. Then, in verses 9-20, the setting in which John received the revelation is described, as well as Jesus' commission to record it.

The Title (1:1-3)

1:1-3 REVELATION (Gk. *apokalupsis*, "unveiling, uncovering, laying bare, disclosure," anglicized as "apocalypse") indicates the book is categorized as "apocalyptic literature," comparable to the Old Testament book of Daniel. "Revelation" specifically refers to God's unveiling of His plan for the world to John. The word has come to be used more broadly, however, to include an entire genre of ancient literature characterized by the prediction of future events, accounts of visionary experiences or journeys, and vivid symbolism. Ancient apocalyptic literature was generally written during times of intense internal and external threat to a religious community. These writings flourished in the Jewish community between 100 BC and AD 150, especially following the destruction of the temple and Jerusalem in AD 70.

The revelation of Jesus Christ could mean it is the revelation *about* Jesus Christ, *from* Jesus Christ, or *belonging to* Jesus Christ—all true, but the idea of possession fits best in this context, especially in light of the succeeding words **that God gave Him to show** (Gk. *deixai*, "expose to view, give evidence or proof"; also 4:1; 17:1; 21:9-10; 22:1,6,8) **His slaves what must quickly take place** (v. 1). The word SLAVES (Gk. *doulois*, "servants, bond-servants," commonly used in the New Testament for followers of Jesus) vividly illustrates the status of Christians: They have been purchased at a high price—the life of God's Son—and belong solely to Jesus as a result. The phrase "must quickly take place," coupled with the statement at the end of verse 3 that **the time is near**, has been difficult for many to understand for almost 2,000 years after the book was written. MUST (Gk. *dei*, "of necessity or necessarily will"; cp. 4:1; 22:6) confirms the events being disclosed. Their fulfillment is not only a fixed certainty but a necessity demanded by the character and sovereignty of God. QUICKLY (Gk. *tachei*, "shortly, soon, speedily, hastily"; cp. Lk 18:8; Ac 12:7; 22:18; 25:4; Rm 16:20) conveys a sense of urgency and swift action or movement. Yet, while Christ's return is near at hand when the events within the body of the book begin to take place, the prophecies will be fulfilled "quickly" (vv. 1,3). With God, a thousand years is like one day (1 Pt 3:8).

The revelation was **sent** and **signified** by way of **His angel** (Gk. *aggelou*, "messenger"). Often portrayed as God's heavenly couriers throughout the Bible, in the book of Revelation angels play a particularly important role. The angel brought the revelation **to His slave John**, who identified himself through this designation with those for whom he was writing.

Figuratively speaking, John was raising his right hand and swearing to "tell the truth, the whole truth, and nothing but the truth." He in no way embellished his story but merely **testified** (Gk. *emarturēsen*, "bore witness, affirmed having seen or experienced," v. 2) **to God's word and to the testimony** (Gk. *marturian*, "witness, the content of what one testifies") **about Jesus Christ, in all he saw**. Believers affirm the entire Bible as "the word of God," and the book of Revelation claims the title for itself.

In John's time, because literacy was unusual among the common people, "readers" were appointed to be responsible for reading the Scriptures aloud in their assemblies. However, **blessed is the one who reads** (Gk. *anaginōskōn*, "recognizes, acknowledges, knows accurately, distinguishes between") should not be misunderstood to mean that one is "blessed" simply for reading or studying Revelation. Both to **hear** and to **keep** (Gk. *tērountes*, "guard, attend, or observe carefully"; also 2:26; 3:3,8,10; 12:17; 14:12; 16:15; 22:7,9) **what is written in it** is necessary. To "hear" the message of the book is not merely listening to it passively but absorbing it eagerly into the mind and considering its significance in obedience. Revelation is not intended as merely a book of mysterious prophecies and futuristic predictions. Its contents are for the purpose of teaching the followers of Jesus, guiding them toward living every day in light of the fact that "the time is near." The blessing for those who "read," "hear," and "keep" the things written in Revelation is also for every generation of Jesus' followers. Thus appears the first of

seven "blessing" statements, or beatitudes, in the book (see also 14:13; 16:15; 19:9; 20:6; 22:7,14).

John referred to the book of Revelation as a **prophecy** (Gk. *prophēteias*, "message from God" in the sense of both "foretelling" [future prediction] of God's plans and "forth-telling" [present direction] of God's will; also 19:10; 22:7,10,18,19). Some parts of the book await future fulfillment, but every teaching demands obedience in the present. Many focus on the future fulfillments of prophecy, speculating wildly as to the specific "who, what, where, when, and how" of the return of Christ and consummation of the age, missing the treasure trove of precious teachings on here-and-now application to the Christian life within the book.

Greetings and Praise to Jesus (1:4-8)

1:4-5a As with the other letters in the New Testament, the salutation names the author, **John**; specifies an audience, **the seven churches**; and includes the characteristic greeting **grace and peace** (v. 4). The source of the "grace and peace" is **the One who is, who was, and who is coming**, referring to God the Father as God in the past, present, and future—striking evidence for the doctrine of the triunity of God, one God existing eternally in three persons of the Father, the Son, and the Spirit (see also 1:8 and 4:8). Although the syntax of the Greek text is awkward, John seemed to be expanding God's Old Testament name: "I AM WHO I AM" (Ex 3:14). "The One who IS" (Gk. *ōn*, "being," the present participle of "be, exist, be present") affirms God's self-existence. **The seven spirits before His throne** is a rather strange phrase and may refer to the angels of the seven churches (2:1,8,12,18; 3:1,7,14) or other angels (e.g., 8:2). Keeping in mind that the number seven often symbolizes completion or perfection in the Bible, the "seven spirits" probably represent the fullness of the Holy Spirit (cp. Is 11:2).

Following the Father and the Holy Spirit, the Son is presented. **Jesus Christ** is first described as **the faithful witness** (Gk. *martus*, "one who testifies, provides a testimony, or attests to the veracity of a claim," from which is derived the English word *martyr*). "Witnesses" are those who remain faithful in their allegiance to Christ even in the face of suffering and death. Jesus modeled that kind of faithfulness in His obedience unto death (Php 2:8), while also leading the way for the Christian victory through the resurrection. Jesus, **the firstborn from the dead,** was not the first person to be raised from the dead (v. 5; see 2 Kg 4:32-35; Jn 11), but He was the first person to be raised from the dead with a resurrected body, never to die again.

RULER (Gk. *archēn*, "commander, leader, chief," the only use of the word in Revelation) appears in Stephen's recounting of Moses' role in the history of God's people. In Egypt, when Moses "tried to reconcile" two Israelites, "the one who was mistreating his neighbor" resisted Moses' intervention with the question, "Who appointed you a ruler and a judge over us?" Stephen pointed out that the same Moses was the "one God sent as a ruler and a redeemer" (Ac 7:26-27,35; Ex 2:14). Stephen later characterized his audience as "stiff-necked people with uncircumcised hearts and ears ... always resisting the Holy Spirit" and as the "betrayers and murderers" of Christ, "the Righteous One," having "received the law under the direction of angels and yet have not kept it" (Ac 7:51-53). The first verses of Revelation identify Jesus Christ as "the ruler of the KINGS (Gk. *basileōn*, "leaders of the people, commanders, lords, princes")

of the earth." Unlike those who aggressively resisted God's kingdom by putting His Son to death, "the kings of the earth" are described as hiding from His wrath (6:15) and facing defeat when they gather with the beast "to wage war against" Christ. Revelation makes clear that God who is "King of the Nations" (15:3) has made Christ the "King of kings" (17:14; 19:16), the "ruler and judge" over all.

1:5b-6 Glory and dominion (Gk. *kratos*, "great power, might, strength; the force by which one rules or dominates," v. 6; cp. 5:13; 1 Tm 6:16; 1 Pt 4:11; 5:11; Jd 25) belong to Him:

- He **loves** (Gk. *agapōnti*, "loving unconditionally and self-sacrificially," as only God can; appearing more often in John's writings than in any other New Testament books, Rv 1:5; Rm 5:8).

- He **has set us free** (Gk. *lusanti*, "loose or release from that which binds, untie, release, break, destroy, overthrow," Rv 1:5) **from our sins**.

- He has **made us a kingdom** (Gk. *basileian*, "people or territory subject to a king, under a king's dominion, reign or sovereign rule and protection," v. 6; cp. 5:10), **priests to His God and Father** (1:5). This language recalled Israel's rescue from Egypt (Ex 19:6).

God deserves all praise, honor, and power because He has loved us, freed us, and made us His people. These aspects of the people of God—kingdom, priests, and those washed in Christ's blood—will become signifiers of the "heaven dwellers" or the saints of God.

1:7-8 What is often identified as the theme verse of Revelation is a prediction of the return of Christ and emphasizes the contrast between His incarnation and His return (v. 7). It contains strong allusions to two Old Testament messianic verses (cp. Dn 7:13; Zch 12:10). While Jesus' incarnation was marked by lowliness and humility, His return will be with majesty and power. Only a few people noticed His birth and a few hundred witnessed His resurrection (1 Co 15:5-8); but when Jesus returns, **every eye will see Him**. While the return of Christ will be a joyous occasion for His followers, those who deny Him will experience a day of great sorrow (cp. Mt 24:30).

John described the return of Christ as **certain** (Gk. *nai*, "indeed, yes, even so, truly, assuredly," v. 7) and continued with a declaration of God's nature. **Alpha** and **Omega**, the first and last letters of the Greek alphabet, affirm God's eternal nature.

John's Vision and Commission to Write (1:9-20)

1:9 Historical tradition indicates John was exiled by the Roman Emperor Domitian to the isle of Patmos about AD 95 and released after Domitian's death in 96. His exile was a result of **God's word and the testimony about Jesus**, suggesting that John's preaching and teaching somehow offended Roman law.

Patmos, a small **island** (about 10 by 6 miles) 37 miles southwest of Asia Minor in the Aegean Sea, is beautiful with a mild and temperate climate. It was used by Rome as a penal colony for many years. For John, the longtime pastor of the Ephesian church, to live imprisoned on Patmos, knowing that his beloved community was only 40 miles away, must have been very difficult.

In relating to the churches, John considered himself their "partner in the TRIBULATION (Gk. *thlipsei*, "pressure, a pressing together, oppression, distress"), KINGDOM (Gk. *basileia*, "kingship, dominion, royal power,

authority to rule") and PERSEVERANCE (Gk. *hupomonē*, "patient endurance, steadfastness") in Jesus." Interestingly, "tribulation" seems to suggest the common experience of all who are "in Jesus" rather than something Christians should try to avoid or escape.

1:10-11 John received the Revelation **on the Lord's Day,** a common way of referring to the first day of the week in celebration of the resurrection of Jesus. The phrase **in the Spirit** occurs three other times in the book (4:2; 17:3; 21:10), each time meaning, "I had a vision inspired by the Spirit of God," possibly used by John to organize the book around the four major visions.

A loud voice like a trumpet ordered him to **write on a scroll** (Gk. *biblion*, "small book or written document," appearing 24 times in the Greek text of Revelation), the form in which "books" existed in those days. Papyrus plants were used to create sheets of paper, which were then glued into strips about a foot wide and as long as 30 feet. Such scrolls were handwritten with ink and then easily rolled or unrolled for use and transportation.

1:12-16 John **turned to see** (Gk. *blepein*, "perceive with the eyes, discern with the mind's eye") **the voice**, that is, to see who was talking to him, a strange phenomenon to see the voice (v. 12). The first thing he **saw** (Gk. *eidon*, "perceived with the eyes or senses, observed, noticed") upon turning around was **seven gold lampstands** with seven branches holding oil and wick like those in the Mosaic tabernacle (v. 12; Ex 27:20-21), representing **the seven churches** (Rv 1:20). As the lampstands bring light to darkness, so should the churches of Jesus bring light to a dark world (Is 49:6; Mt 5:14-16).

More amazing, though, is that **among the lampstands** stood **One like the Son of Man**, (v. 13). This favorite self-designation was used by Jesus and appears 82 times in the four Gospels. Yet, neither His friends nor enemies referred to Jesus as "Son of Man," nor did the early church use this title for Him. It is absent from the Epistles, except in a citation from Psalms (Heb 2:6). Many accepted the notion that "Son of Man" is simply a synonym for the humanity of Christ (in contrast to His deity, as expressed in the title "Son of God"). The term is used this way in Ezekiel, as God refers to the prophet, His human mouthpiece, as "son of man." Yet, in more recent studies, many have come to appreciate another context for the title based on Daniel 7:13 in which the coming Messiah is referenced so that Jesus was indirectly calling Himself "Messiah" without awakening in the Jewish community the inevitable misunderstanding that using the term "Messiah" would have created.

John had seen Jesus Christ in a glorified state on the Mount of Transfiguration (Mt 17:2) and had seen His resurrected body after He was raised until the ascension (Jn 20; Ac 1:2-11), but the appearance of Jesus in this first vision outstrips them all. The LONG ROBE (Gk. *podērē*, "garment reaching to the ankles or feet," from the root *podos* meaning "foot"; used only here in the New Testament) and "gold sash WRAPPED AROUND (Gk. *periezōsmenon*, "fastened with a belt, girded") His chest" indicate Christ's position as both King and High Priest (Rv 1:13; Ex 39:2-4). His "head and hair," which appear "WHITE (Gk. *leukai*, "brilliant from whiteness, shining or dazzling white") like wool—white as snow," suggest the wisdom and all-knowing nature of Jesus (Rv 1:14). For followers of Christ, it is comforting to know that not only does He know all things, but He also knows what is best for you. Christ's "eyes" looked "like a

fiery flame," suggesting that He sees all things with piercing clarity (v. 14). His feet, "like FINE BRONZE (*chalkolibanō*, a compound of Gk. *chalkos*, "brass," and Hb. *libanos*, "frankincense," a white resin burned as fragrant incense) fired in a furnace," pictures Jesus as a conqueror who subdues all forces of evil, natural and supernatural, by trampling them underfoot. The **voice** of Jesus was deafening and powerful, **like the sound of cascading waters**, and **in his right hand** were **seven stars** (vv. 15-16). The identities of these stars have been the subject of much debate, for they are interpreted as "the angels (Gk. *aggeloi*, "ones who are sent, messengers, envoys," v. 20) of the seven churches." Some say the angels are representatives for each congregation, while others see the angels as human messengers, identified with the pastors of the churches. Either interpretation is possible, but the main point is that Jesus has them in His hand, a sign of care and protection. The TWO-EDGED SWORD (Gk. *hromphaia*, most likely a long, straight broad-sword used in cavalry charges; cp. 2:12,16; 6:8; 19:15,21; Lk 2:34-35) proceeding from Jesus' "mouth" is the strangest part of this picture, but it represents the power of Christ to conquer and judge His enemies (v. 16; cp. 19:15; Is 49:2). John could not gaze fully upon the face of Christ (v. 16). This glory shows Christ's deity in all its fullness.

1:17-20 The only possible and appropriate response when God reveals Himself is worship. Jesus blessed John by laying **His right hand** on him, the same way He touched the sick and needy in His days on earth (v. 17). The firm hand of Jesus upon John surely brought back a flood of memories from the many times John felt the touch of the Lord while He was still among the disciples on earth. Though Jesus was glorified before him and splendid to behold, this same Jesus had walked, talked, and eaten with John during at least three years of ministry.

The touch of comfort from Jesus reminded John that he did not have to be **afraid** (v. 17):

- "I am the **FIRST** (Gk. *prōtos*, "first in time, first in any succession or rank, principal, chief") and the **LAST**" (Gk. *eschatos*, "last in a succession, extreme, the last, end," the root for the word "eschatology" or the doctrine of "last things"): Christ has power over time.

- **I am ... the Living One**: Christ has power over life.

- **I was dead, but look—I am alive forever and ever**: Christ has power over sin.

- **I hold the keys of death and Hades**: Christ has power over death.

These statements reveal the comforting truth that there is nothing over which Jesus does not reign supremely.

John worshiped and received a blessing from Christ (vv. 17-18), then he received a mission from Christ (vv. 19-20): **Write what you have seen, what is, and what will take place after this**. He was responsible for recording the vision revealed to him and everything that would be revealed afterwards. The natural divisions within the book are set forth:

- "what you have seen," i.e., John's own vision of the resurrected and glorified Christ (chap. 1);

- "what is," i.e., a description of the representative churches (chaps. 2–3); and

- "what will take place after this," i.e., an unfolding of future events (chaps. 4–22).

This verse (1:19) then becomes the key for unlocking the structure of the book.

Jesus disclosed to John **the secret of the seven stars**, which represented **the angels of the seven churches** (vv. 16,20), and **the seven** gold **lampstands**, which represented **the seven churches** to whom Revelation was being written (vv. 12,20). Both the communities of believers and their leaders were presented as bearers of light, and both of them are clearly of special concern to the Lord.

THE MESSAGES TO SEVEN CHURCHES OF ASIA (2:1–3:22)

The messages in chapters 2 and 3 have none of the normal characteristics of ancient letters (see *Genre*); rather they are styled as prophetic oracles or messages (cp. Am 1:2–2:16). There is no evidence they were ever sent out independently from the book. The phrase, "Anyone who has an ear should listen to what the Spirit says to the churches" (2:7,11,17,29; 3:6,13,22) is similar to the Old Testament formula of the prophets, "Thus says the Lord."

The arrangement of these messages is fairly uniform. Each is prefaced with a charge to write to the angel of the specific church (2:1,8,12,18; 3:1,7,14). Whether each angel is understood as the "guardian angel" of the church or the human "messenger" of the church (see discussion of 1:16), he serves as a representative of the entire congregation. The message to the church is generally ordered in the following way:

- a *characteristic* of Christ is described;

- a *compliment* of the church is given;

- a *criticism* of the church is made (except for the churches at Smyrna and Philadelphia);

- a *command* to the church is given; and

- a *commitment* from Christ is made to those who are obedient to Christ until death.

The messages address the practical problems of individual churches in light of the imminent return of Jesus Christ. They are the practical and historical "lens" through which the rest of Revelation must be viewed. Remember that the message of Revelation is to be read, heard, and *obeyed* by followers of Jesus (1:3). Further, the content of the messages sets the moral and ethical stage upon which the rest of Revelation is played out. The themes of moral purity, overcoming evil, endurance amidst suffering, and eternal reward are threads woven throughout the book of Revelation.

The Message to Ephesus (2:1-7)

Ephesus (modern Kusadasi), located on a major harbor in western Asia Minor, was one of the most powerful cities in the Roman Empire. Religiously, Ephesus was devoted to the worship of Artemis, the fertility goddess, and to the Emperor of Rome, who was also considered a god. The church apparently was planted by Priscilla and Aquila around AD 52 and later visited by Paul for at least two years while he used the city as a center for evangelizing the region. The New Testament also reveals that the Ephesian church struggled with false teachers (2:2,6; cp. Eph 4:14; 1 Tm 1:18-20; 6:3-10; 2 Tm 2:14-19).

2:1 *Characteristic.* Jesus reminded the church at Ephesus that He is the one protecting the church in the heavenly realm and abiding in their midst. Because Jesus is walking among the churches, He can rightly criticize their actions and motives (v. 1; see 1:20).

2:2-3 *Compliment.* The Ephesian believers were praised for their **works** . . . **labor**, and **endurance** for the cause of

Christ. Apparently they were intent upon ridding the church of evil. Specifically, they ejected those from their congregation who were evildoers and investigated and rejected some falsely claiming to be **apostles**. Jesus commended the Ephesians for hating "the practices of the Nicolaitans," a heretical group that appeared again in the church of Pergamum (v. 6). The Nicolaitans (from Gk. *nikaō*, "conquer," and *laos*, "people"—the "people conquerors" or "overcomers" in the sense of inappropriate authoritarianism) may have referred to a group trying to subject those in the church to certain powerful leaders or to those who had compromised their faith for a life of immorality and idolatry. Along with their zeal for truth and purity, the Ephesians are commended for possessing **endurance** and for having **tolerated many things** for Jesus' sake without growing **weary** (v. 3). They had suffered much hostility from those worshiping other gods but had remained firm in the faith (cp. Ac 19:23-41).

2:4 *Criticism.* In their passion for the truth, however, the Ephesian church had drifted into grave error: **You have abandoned the love you had at first**, which may have been a reference to the love for Christ they had as new converts (Mt 6:33) or to their lack of love for one another, which is supposed to be the hallmark of Christ's church (Jn 13:35).

2:5-6 *Command.* Christ, even after words of commendation, had a stinging reprimand for this loveless church. He urged them:

- "Remember then **HOW FAR** (Gk. *pothen*, "from where, from what condition or place; from what origin or source") you have fallen";

- **REPENT** (Gk. *metanoēsēs*, "change one's mind," esp. for the better, forsaking sin; a key word in Revelation—see also 2:16,21,22; 3:3,19; 9:20-21; 16:9,11), and

• **do the works you did at first**.

If they refused to do so, Christ said, **I will . . . remove your lampstand from its place**. While Christ has vowed that His church will flourish worldwide (Mt 16:18), He gave no promise of permanence to any individual congregation. Jesus was threatening to remove His Holy Spirit from their congregation. The message is clear: A loveless church, no matter how theologically and ethically pure, is no longer a Christ-honoring church.

2:7 *Commitment*. The entreaty for all to **listen to what the Spirit says to the churches** is a reminder that the messages to the churches are for all of Christ's followers. Jesus promised the Ephesians that **the victor**—the one who is faithful to Christ and His teachings unto death—will be given **the right to eat from the tree of life, which is in the paradise of God**.

Jesus referred to the believer as a VICTOR (Gk. *nikōnti*, "one who conquers, prevails, or is victorious over enemies") from *nikē* (Gk. "victory"), the name of a mythological Greek goddess personifying triumph and victory in both military and athletic arenas. Of the 28 times the verb is used in the Greek New Testament, 24 appear in John's writings, including 17 in Revelation. First John describes believers as those who "have had victory over the evil one" (1 Jn 2:13,14), who have "conquered" because Christ, in whom they have placed their faith, is "greater" than "the world" (1 Jn 4:4; 5:4,5). In Revelation, the word most often describes Jesus as conqueror (Rv 3:21; 5:5; 6:2; 17:14; 21:7) and saints as victors (12:11; 15:2); only twice is "the beast" the subject of the verb and then only by divine permission (11:7; 13:7). The book is filled with Jesus' personal promises of rewards to those in and through whom Christ displays His complete triumph over evil (2:7,11,17, 26,28; 3:5,12,21). Revelation thus depicts the fulfillment of Jesus' promise of victory to His disciples (Jn 16:33).

In Revelation, the victorious ones are all those who overcome the world and its sufferings even to the point of death. In fact, Revelation never distinguishes between martyrs and the rest of the church. All endure suffering, and all are victorious.

The Message to Smyrna (2:8-11)

Smyrna (Hb., "myrrh, bitterness," modern Ismir), another harbor city known for its architectural beauty, an imposing array of pagan temples, material wealth, and civic pride, had a large Jewish population that bitterly opposed Christianity. When Domitian issued an edict declaring emperor worship mandatory for all inhabitants of Rome, Christians became easy targets for persecution, especially as Jews in the city denounced them to the authorities. Rome had exempted the Jews from emperor worship, and they did not want this privilege extended to what they considered a heretical and divisive group. The church at Smyrna was likely founded during Paul's third missionary journey (cp. Ac 19).

2:8 *Characteristic*. Jesus reminded the church at Smyrna that He is the eternal God—**the First and the Last**—as well as the God-man, who came to earth, died, and rose from the grave.

2:9 *Compliment*. The church at Smyrna lived in a city known for its wealth, yet its Christian inhabitants were in **poverty** (Gk. *ptōcheian*, "destitution"; cp. 2 Co 8:2,9). In this Roman city, as well as many others, any craftsperson (merchants, potters, metalworkers, sellers of cloth) desiring to conduct business was required to become a member of a guild. However, worship of the emperor and the gods of Rome was required for membership, eliminating faithful Christians as members. Without guild membership, Smyrnan Christians could not work or earn a reasonable living. Their unwillingness to conform may have contributed to their poverty, making them victims of imprisonment, mob violence, and looting.

Jesus assured them that although they were materially poor and experiencing much **tribulation**, they were truly **rich** (Gk. *plousios*, "wealthy, abounding in material resources") in the spiritual sense. Jesus also acknowledged their struggle with the Jews of Smyrna, who zealously opposed the spread of Christianity, even using **slander** (Gk. *blasphēmian*, "blasphemy, speech intended to harm another's good name") to get their way. Christ asserted that, while these Jews believed they were the people of God, they had become the tool of Satan to persecute the true people of God.

2:10 *Command.* The suffering was unavoidable for them, but Christ promised divine comfort and blessing in the midst of these experiences. Some of them would be thrown **into prison** by **the Devil**. Romans used imprisonment for detention pending trial or detention awaiting execution, which meant that some of them faced the real possibility of **death**. Though Satan would be allowed to afflict them, God would limit the time of such **tribulation** to **10 days**, which could have been literal or figurative, but probably alluded to the 10-day testing of Daniel (Dn 1:12-14). The tribulation would be quite severe, yet limited by God in its duration. The purpose of these experiences is TO TEST (Gk. *peirasthēte*, "ascertain by trial"; cp. 2:2; 3:10) them. The verb can be understood to have a double meaning. Satan desires to "tempt" them to apostatize, and God desires to "test" their faith.

2:11 *Commitment.* Jesus once again assured that the one who is victorious **will never be harmed** (Gk. *adikēthē*, "damaged, hurt") **by the second death**. "Second death" is used elsewhere in Revelation (20:6,14; 21:8) and specifically referred to the final eternal death in the "lake of fire" (20:14-15). For those who overcome this world, even if through martyrdom, there would be no "second death" beyond the mere physical death that ends life on earth.

The Message to Pergamum (2:12-17)

In the first century AD, the city of Pergamum (Gk., "height, elevation," modern Bergama) was the leading religious center of Asia Minor. Countless temples, shrines, and altars were dedicated to the many gods of the area. The temple of Asklepius, the Greek god of healing, was the most famous for its cultic worship. It was a center of emperor worship, and Christians were persecuted harshly for their refusal to participate in this expression of civic loyalty and patriotism. They were considered "atheists" for refusing to acknowledge other gods; "haters of the human race" for refusing to show political loyalty to Rome; and "superstitious" for worshiping a "new" God and being intolerant to the gods of Rome.[1] Jesus called Pergamum the place "where Satan's throne is" (v. 13).

2:12 *Characteristic.* The **sharp, two-edged sword** (Gk. *hromphaian*; see 1:16), symbolized to the church at **Pergamum** the justice of Christ (cp. Is 11:4). Jesus transformed Rome's symbol of the might and power for the church at Pergamum, though, telling them that it is Christ, not the Roman government, who is the true and ultimate judge.

2:13 *Compliment.* Jesus commended the church at Pergamum for **holding on to My name** and not denying their **faith** in

Him even though they lived **where Satan's throne is** with all of the pressures to conform and submit to the gods of Rome, an incredible burden to Christ's followers. The church had seen **Antipas** killed for his steadfast loyalty to Christ (according to tradition he was publicly slowly roasted to death in a large kettle); yet they stood firm. Jesus reminded believers that churches facing persecution for their faith are not warring against flesh and blood but against the powers of darkness and the reign of Satan (Eph 6:12).

2:14-15 *Criticism.* Even in their faithfulness, Jesus had **a few things** against the church. They tolerated the presence of heretics in their church, **those who hold to the teaching of Balaam**, a Gentile prophet enlisted by **Balak**, king of Moab (Nm 22–24), to place a curse on the Israelites. Yet, by the power of God, Balaam could only proclaim blessings. The Israelites committed immorality with Moabite women and worshiped Baal, which Moses attributed to "Balaam's advice" (Nm 31:1; cp. 25:1-3). Apparently, the teaching of the Nicolaitans was causing similar sin among its followers in the church at Pergamum. Their tolerance of the sins of eating **meat sacrificed to idols and** committing **sexual immorality**, which went against the commands of the Holy Spirit and the apostles (cp. Ac 15:28-29), were shared by the church in Thyatira (Rv 2:20).

2:16 *Command.* In light of the heresy infecting the church, Jesus commanded them to **repent** of their immorality and antinomianism immediately. If they refused to repent, He warned: "I will come to you quickly and **FIGHT** (Gk. *polemēsō*, "carry on a war," anglicized as "polemic," a word denoting controversial argument and refutation of or opposition to a particular opinion or doctrine) against them with the

SWORD (Gk. *hromphaia*) of My mouth." Jesus promised to execute swift judgment upon the heretics and their followers, as well as on the church for harboring them. Any time false doctrine arises within a local congregation, that church is responsible to root out the heresy, correct those teaching it, and exercise discipline upon those who refuse to repent. If the church shirks this responsibility, Jesus will deal with those inflicting damage.

2:17 *Commitment.* Once again, the reward for the victorious ones is eternal life in fellowship with God, symbolized by **the hidden manna**—divine, spiritual sustenance—and **a white stone** with **a new name**. A WHITE STONE (Gk. *psēphon*, "small pebble or stone that has been worn smooth") served as a type of ancient "ticket" into a feast or community gathering, figuratively here, the feast of the Messiah in the kingdom of God. White and black stones were also used in ancient Greek courts to indicate acquittal or condemnation, respectively, and as a means of voting in elections. NEW (Gk. *kainon*, "unused, novel, unprecedented") signifies God's activity, particularly in terms of the future fulfillment of His redemptive purpose and in contrast to the lament that "there is nothing new under the sun," i.e., in man's time-bound, earthbound existence apart from God's intervention in Christ (Ec 1:9). When Christ's reign is revealed to all, the victors receive "a new name" (Rv 2:17); a "new Jerusalem" comes "down out of heaven from God" (3:12; 21:2) and is "called by a new name" (Is 62:2; cp. Is 1:26; 60:14,18; Jr 33:16; Ezk 48:35); the saints sing "a new song" (Rv 5:9; 14:3); and there is "a new heaven and a new earth" (21:1; cp. Is 66:22; 2 Pt 3:13). Ultimately, "the One seated on the throne" exclaims, "Look! I am making everything new" (Rv 21:5).

The Message to Thyatira (2:18-29)

Thyatira (Gk., "unceasing sacrifice, odor of affliction," modern Akhisar) was a commercial town located on the Lycus River and the smallest and least important of the seven cities. Although the economy and social life of most Roman cities centered around trade guilds, those of Thyatira were especially prominent, notably shoemakers, sellers of dyed cloth (such as Lydia, Ac 16:12-15), and bronzesmiths. Each guild had a patron god or goddess and social events centered on their worship. The pressure for Christians to participate in this idolatrous and immoral lifestyle was great for economic and social reasons. The message to Thyatira is the longest and is placed in the center of the seven, thus drawing attention to its words and imagery.

2:18 *Characteristic*. Jesus reminded the church at Thyatira that He is **the Son of God**, who sees or knows all things— **whose eyes are like a fiery flame**—and has dominion over all things—**whose feet are like fine bronze** (Gk. *chalkolibanō*; see 1:15). The combination of these two images for the Thyatiran church was especially important in light of the false prophetess "Jezebel," who was deceiving a significant portion of the church (2:20). Jesus sees through all of her destructive arguments, and His judgment upon her and her followers is imminent.

2:19 *Compliment*. The works of the Thyatiran Christians are pleasing to Jesus: **love, faithfulness, service, and endurance** (Gk. *hupomonēn*, "patient endurance, steadfastness," esp. active perseverance in the midst of pressure and suffering). Not only were they active in ministry, but unlike the Ephesian church, they did so for the love of God and one another. In addition, the quality of their Christian life was

increasing, for their **last works are greater than at first**. The church at Thyatira was continuing to grow in their good deeds.

2:20-23 *Criticism*. Unfortunately, the weaknesses of the Thyatiran believers far outweighed their strengths. They were tolerating, or permitting, **the woman Jezebel, who calls herself a prophetess**, and who was teaching Christians **to commit sexual immorality and to eat meat sacrificed to idols**. The female oracle *Sambath* had a large and lucrative business telling fortunes, which may have desensitized the Thyatiran believers for the corruption of Jezebel, the evil and immoral female false teacher.

WOMAN (Gk. *gunaika*, "wife," v. 20) occurs 19 times in the Greek text. With the exception of two minor uses in Rv 9:8 and 14:4, each time the word occurs, a significant character in Revelation's drama is being addressed. Here the word is used in reference to the false prophetess named "Jezebel," probably metaphorically describing her character (2:20; cp. 1 Kg 21:5-29). In chapter 12 derivatives of the word are used eight times as the "great sign" in heaven portrays "a woman clothed with the sun" (12:1) who gives birth to "a Son" (12:5), a symbol of Christ. The word appears six times in the description of the mysterious "notorious prostitute" identified as "Babylon the Great" (17:15,18; 18:2). The final two uses are for the bride of the Lamb making herself ready for her bridegroom (19:7) and then for the bride of Christ in the eternal state (21:9). Each of these women described is essential to the meaning and purpose of the book of Revelation.

In the Old Testament "Jezebel" was the infamous Phoenician wife of Israel's king Ahab. As queen, Jezebel led the northern kingdom into idolatry and sorcery (1 Kg

16:31-34; 21:25-26; 2 Kg 9:22) and persecuted the prophets of God, including Elijah (1 Kg 19:1-2). Here Jezebel was using the facade of what she claimed to be oracles and pronouncements from God to spread falsehood and lies. She also possessed a close affinity to Babylon the Great (Rv 18:23), for both women seduced their followers into sexual immorality and idolatry, and both encouraged believers, the **slaves** of Christ, to compromise with the world.

Three groups received judgment from Jesus. First, Jesus affirmed to the Thyatirans that He **gave** Jezebel **time to repent, but she does not want to repent of her sexual immorality** (v. 21). Those who had been deceived by her, though, would be given a little more time. Yet, **unless they repent of her practices**, Jesus would **throw** them **into great tribulation** (v. 22). GREAT TRIBULATION (Gk. *thlipsin*; see 1:9) refers to a general time of intense affliction, the nature of which is not known. Its use foreshadows the affliction to come upon the whole earth (3:10; 7:14). The **children** of Jezebel are spiritual "children" who had committed themselves to her teaching. This group would be killed **with the plague** (Gk. *thanatō*, physical "death"), another foreshadowing of widespread death by plague to come (2:23; 6:8). The purpose was that **all the churches** would **know** that Jesus is **the One who examines minds and hearts** and gives to **each** person **according to** his **works**. Our Lord is jealous of the purity of His bride, the church, and is willing to do whatever it takes to purify her.

2:24-25 *Command.* The believers in Thyatira who did not follow Jezebel are described as not having **known the deep things of Satan**. Although puzzling, this phrase is likely a sarcastic reference to Jezebel's claim to know "the deep things of God." Like "Satan's synagogue" in Smyrna (2:9), Jezebel thought she knew

the ways of God but was really teaching the ways of Satan. Those who were not followers of Jezebel received no **other burden** from the Lord except to **hold on to what** they **have**, keeping a firm grip on the core of accepted Christian doctrine in contrast to the heretical teaching they were to oppose, **until** Christ comes. Maintaining the truth and opposing falsehood must continue in the church until Jesus returns.

2:26-29 *Commitment.* Jesus promised that the victorious **one who keeps My works to the end** will be given **authority** (Gk. *exousian*, "power of rule or government"; used over 20 times in Revelation) **over the nations** (v. 26). The saints' "authority" is described with a paraphrase of Psalm 2:8-9, where the Messiah is prophesied to **shepherd** (Gk. *poimanei*, "feed, tend, or keep a flock of sheep; rule or govern") the nations **with an iron scepter** (Gk. *hrabdō*, "staff or rod") and **shatter** (Gk. *suntribetai*, "break in pieces, crush"; cp. Rm 16:20) **them like pottery** (Rv 2:27). Both images depict the authoritative rule and devastating judgment of Christ upon the nations of the world. How the saints will share this authority with Christ is not fully understood, but elsewhere in the New Testament the saints' reign and judgment with Christ over the earth are described (1 Tm 2:12; 1 Co 6:2-3). **The morning star** is likely an allusion to the messianic prophecy in which the star and scepter are symbols of the coming Messiah (Nm 24:17).

The Message to Sardis (3:1-6)

Sardis (modern Sart), founded around 1200 BC and one of the most glorious and ancient cities in Asia Minor, was built on the slope of Mount Tmolus and thus was almost impregnable to intruders unless its precipitous walls were left unguarded (v. 3). In AD 17 an earthquake destroyed Sardis and Philadelphia, but both were later rebuilt with the help of Emperor Augustus. Sardis, the extremely prosperous seat of government for the Lydians, was home to an enormous, yet unfinished, temple to Artemis, the patron goddess of the city, and a sacred hot springs associated with the god of the underworld. The people of Sardis, who were especially interested in death and immortality, sought after the divine in the fertility cycles of nature and the worship of Artemis, the goddess of fertility.

3:1a *Characteristic.* Jesus described Himself in the address to **the church in Sardis** as **the One who has the seven spirits of God** (likely a reference to the Holy Spirit, cp. Is 11:2; Zch 4:2,10) **and the seven stars** (the angels of the seven churches, Rv 1:20), indicating His authority over these angels and the churches they represent.

3:1b *Criticism.* Jesus had no words of praise for the church in Sardis. While His message did not name specific enemies, whether internal or external, no other message has as much urgency as this one. The church had many **works** and **a reputation for being alive**, but it was spiritually **dead**. They were supposed to be representatives of the living God, but without the vitality of the Holy Spirit they were more like walking corpses. The good "works" and common rituals of Christianity can lull you to sleep if you are not careful to preserve the life of the Spirit within your own heart.

3:2-3 *Command.* Because their works had not been found **complete** before God the Father, Jesus urged them to do five things:

- BE ALERT (Gk. *grēgorōn*, "watch, be cautious and actively attentive, take heed") is an admonition frequently describing the correct approach for a believer anticipating Christ's return or standing firm

against false teachings (cp. 16:15; Mt 24:42-43; 25:13; 26:38-41; Mk 14:34-38; Lk 12:37; Ac 20:31; 1 Co 16:13; Col 4:2; 1 Th 5:6; 1 Pt 5:8). The idea here was that the Sardians had not met the standards of God. Like Belshazzar in the book of Daniel, this church had been "weighed in the balance and found deficient" (Dn 5:27). In response, they must regain an attitude of watchfulness or readiness (Mk 13:34-37) and give sustenance to the small minority in the church who remained faithful to Christ.

- **Strengthen what remains**.

- Jesus also commanded, **Remember therefore what you have received and heard**, which means to recall what had been passed onto them from the apostles.

- **Keep** (Gk. *tērei*, "carefully attend to, guard, take care of"; cp. 1:3) **it**, putting these truths to practice in everyday life.

- **Repent** (Gk. *metanoeson*, "change one's mind," v. 3; see 2:5) of their spiritual collapse.

The consequence for not being **alert** is that He **will come like a thief** and they would not be ready for Him. This imagery of imminency is clear here as elsewhere (16:15; Mt 24:43; 1 Th 5:2-4).

3:4-6 *Commitment.* The **few people in Sardis who have not defiled** (Gk. *emolunan*, "contaminated, stained, made unclean, polluted"; cp. 14:4; 1 Co 8:7) **their clothes** are promised the privilege of walking with Jesus **in white** (Gk. *leukois*; see Rv 1:14). They are already pure because they have not been polluted with sin as the others, yet they will be further rewarded with the virtuous white clothes of those reigning victoriously with Christ **because they are worthy** (Gk. *axioi*, "having value, weight, or merit"; see 7:9; 19:8,14). In addition, **the victor, dressed in white clothes**, is further promised two things: a permanent place in **the book of life** and the acknowledgement of **his name before** the **Father** (Mt 10:32).

There are two possible ways of understanding the promise, **I will never erase** (Gk. *exaleipsō*, "wipe off or away, obliterate, blot out, cancel"; cp. 7:17 21:4; Ac 3:19; Col 2:14) **his name from "**the book of life." First, the book of life contains the names of everyone who ever lived because Jesus died to redeem all. Yet, those who do not choose to put their faith in Christ before death will be blotted out and sent to eternal destruction. Second, the book of life contains the names of everyone who claims allegiance to Christ, but only those who remain faithful to the end will stay in it. Any suggested removal from the Lamb's book of life is rejected since the Greek text has the emphatic double negative in the sense of "I will no not blot out," making this verse a promise that every true believer cannot under any circumstance be removed from this book. However you understand the promises, true Christ followers are victorious and will receive the eternal rewards promised by Jesus.

The Message to Philadelphia (3:7-13)

Philadelphia (Gk. "brotherly love," combining *philos*, "love," and *adelphos*, "brother, sibling," modern Alasehir) was an agriculturally prosperous city on the main trade route to the east coast of Asia Minor where Mysia, Lydia, and Phrygia came together. Although the earthquake of AD 17 affected Sardis as well, Philadelphia was nearer the epicenter and suffered more long-term effects. Thus, the people made long-term and short-term plans with earthquakes in mind.

3:7 *Characteristic*. The Philadelphian church heard from Jesus, **the Holy One**, a frequent Old Testament title for God (see Ps 16:10; Is 1:4; 37:23; Hab 3:3), and **the True One**, probably a reference to His being the true Messiah, in contrast to the "lying" Jewish community in the city (Rv 3:9). Jesus is also **the One who has the key of David**. God ordered that Eliakim replace Shebna as the steward of Hezekiah's household. Eliakim was to be given "the key of the House of David . . . what he opens, no one can close; what he closes, no one can open" (Is 22:22). The key emphasized the power and authority of Eliakim in the king's household, but for Jesus it means much more. The Philadelphian Christians, having been persecuted by the Jewish community, were assured that Jesus alone has absolute control over entrance into the kingdom of heaven.

3:8-10 *Compliment*. The church at Philadelphia had **limited strength**, yet they had **kept** the **word** of Christ and **not denied** Him. They were a small church, with little influence or status in the community. Keeping the word of Christ and not denying His name go hand in hand: The church had guarded the gospel and obeyed it in the midst of severe persecution. For these reasons, Jesus gave the cryptic promise, **I have placed before you an open door that no one is able to close**. The "open door" is theorized to be the way of salvation or a greater missionary opportunity. A better fit for the context would be to understand it as a word of encouragement to believers who have experienced overwhelming persecution—a promise of comforting support more than a plea for greater service. The promise of entrance to the messianic kingdom is an appropriate reward for faithful service.

A part of the Philadelphian church's reward for their faithfulness was their *vindication* by Christ before **the synagogue** of Satan, who claim to be Jews and are not (note the parallel to 2:9). Jesus promised to **make** these enemies **come and bow down at your feet**, and demonstrate beyond doubt that Jesus has **loved** them. To **BOW DOWN** (Gk. *proskunēsousin*, "worship") in Oriental custom was to kneel and bow to the floor, touching your forehead to the ground, as an expression of reverence. The root word is *kuōn*, "dog," expressing the kind of loyalty demonstrated by a dog licking its master's hand. The word generally portrays kneeling or prostrating oneself to demonstrate homage or respect to one of superior rank and therefore often denotes worship. The Old Testament taught that the Gentile nations would be forced to bow down to the Jews in the kingdom of God (Is 60:14), but here the promise was given a new meaning. Israel will have a different attitude toward the church and turn to pay homage even to Gentile believers.

The second part of the church's reward is their *protection* **from the hour of testing that is going to come over the whole world** (Gk *oikoumenēs*, "the inhabited earth," from the root *oikos*, "dwelling, house"; also Rv 12:9; 16:14). This cataclysmic upheaval is beyond persecution (as in 1:9; 2:9-10,22) and a reference to God's judgment on the world (compare the uses of "hour" in 3:3; 9:15; 11:13; 14:7,15; 17:12; 18:10,17,19). The purpose of the hour of testing is explicit in verse 10: **to test those who live on the earth**. The identity of "those who LIVE ON (Gk. *katoikountas*, "inhabit, dwell, settle," from the root *oikos*, "dwelling, house," v.10) the earth," or the "earth dwellers," is key to understanding the events described in the book of Revelation. A study of the phrase reveals that the earth dwellers are unbelievers (17:8), who are held responsible for the deaths of believing martyrs (6:10)

and upon whom the "hour of testing" is focused (3:10). They make themselves the enemies of God by worshiping the beast and persecuting believers.

The hour of testing, then, is the period of time preceding the return of Christ in which God will pour out His wrath upon the earth dwellers or the unbelieving world. Jesus would **keep** (Gk. *tērēsō*, "protect or remove from") the Philadelphian believers—identified here with all faithful believers—from that experience (v. 10). The church, meaning all believers, will be taken out of the world before this tribulation (cp. chaps. 6–19).

3:11 *Command.* In light of the return of Christ, which is coming upon them **quickly**, the Philadelphians are commanded, **Hold on to what you have**, that is, the "open door that no one is able to close" (3:8). They were assured a place in the kingdom of God, vindication (3:10), and protection by God (v. 11). Though Christ had declared them victorious in their Christian walk, they had to continue to persevere, so as not to lose their **crown**, meaning their heavenly reward (see 1 Co 9:24-27).

3:12-13 *Commitment.* For **the victor**, Jesus promised two symbolic rewards. First, the victor will be made **a pillar** (Gk. *stulon*, "column, support"; cp. 10:1; Gl 2:9; 1 Tm 3:15) **in the sanctuary of My God and he will never go out again**. The idea is one of permanence and stability, a comforting promise to people living in a region frequently stricken by earthquakes. There will be no literal sanctuary in heaven (Rv 21:22), but the pillar was a structure that stood firm in its service in God's temple. No one would be able to remove the victorious one from God's presence. Second, with the "pillar" imagery still in mind, the victor will have written upon him **the name of My God, and the name of the city of My God—the**

new Jerusalem (3:12), and Jesus' **new name** (see 19:12). The essence of this threefold promise is overwhelming, including a permanent place in God's family through bearing His name, citizenship in God's kingdom through the name of God's city, and the privilege of sharing the authority and title of God's Son through His new name.

The Message to Laodicea (3:14-22)

Laodicea was an important city for both trade and communications in the eastern region of Asia Minor. It was famous as an administrative and judicial center, a banking center for the region, and for its school of medicine. Laodicea also lay in a region prone to earthquakes and had no water supply. Laodicea had to pipe in water six miles from Denizli through an aqueduct, leaving the city vulnerable to harsh weather and attack. Likely the Laodicean church, along with the churches of Hierapolis (about six miles north) and Colossae (about 10 miles east), was planted by Epaphras, who was probably a native of Colossae, serving as Paul's representative there (Col 1:7) during the apostle's three-year ministry at Ephesus (Ac 19). Tradition suggests the possibility of Archippus as pastor at Laodicea. Both he and Philemon were leaders among the churches in this area.

3:14 *Characteristic.* To the Laodicean Christians, Jesus called Himself

- **The Amen** (Hb. transliterated directly into Gk., "so it is, truly, surely"; also 1:6-7; 5:14; 7:12; 19:4; 22:20). God is literally called "the God of amen" or "the God of truth" (Is 65:16). Jesus was probably referring to Himself in this way as an emphasis upon the certainty of the true and divine origin of His words.

- **The faithful and true Witness** (Gk. *martus*, "one who can give a firsthand account; one who furnishes evidence, testifies, publicly affirms, or attests to the authenticity of a transaction, statement, or event") stands in stark contrast to the Laodiceans who were not faithful to Christ and whose witness was meaningless.

- **The Originator** (Gk. *archē*, "beginning, that which causes to be, first or leader"; also Rv 21:6; 22:13) **of God's creation**.

3:15-17 *Criticism.* Jesus had no words of commendation for the Laodiceans. Christ's accusation that they **are neither cold nor hot** (Gk. *zestos*, "boiling hot, fervent, zealous"), but **lukewarm** (Gk. *chliaros*, "tepid, mildly warm, indifferent," used only here in the New Testament), has been often misunderstood (v. 15). Because the Laodiceans did not have a water supply, they had to pipe in their water from a hot springs four miles away. By the time the water reached the city, it was lukewarm in contrast to water in the nearby cities of Colossae, whose waters were famously cold, pure, and refreshing to drink, and Hierapolis, whose hot springs were well known for their healing and therapeutic effect on the body. Either hot or cold water is useful for something, but lukewarm water is not. You can relate to the unpleasant experience of expecting a cool drink of water or a hot cup of coffee, only to find it lukewarm. Christ was saying that their deeds were worthless to Him, and for that reason He was going **to vomit** them out of His **mouth**. Jesus has no use for a church that is not serving its proper purpose (v. 16).

Jesus' further criticism of the Laodicean congregation was just as scathing. Apparently, like the city, the Laodicean church's immense wealth had led to self-sufficiency, complacency, and pride. They may have thought, **I have become wealthy** (Gk. *peploutēka*, "rich, affluent, having an abundance of possessions or resources," v. 17; cp. Lk 12:21; 1 Co 4:8), **and need nothing**, but Jesus exposed the truth: they were

- **wretched** (Gk. *talaipōros*, "afflicted, miserable, distressed, enduring trouble," from *talanton*, "scale, balance, or that which is weighed," and *peira*, "trial, attempt, experience," suggesting the miserable experience of not measuring up; used only here and Rm 7:24),

- **pitiful** (Gk. *eleeinos*, "pitiable, needing mercy," used only here and 1 Co 15:19),

- **poor** (Gk. *ptōchos*, "reduced to begging; destitute of wealth, position, honor, or influence"; cp. Rv 13:16),

- **blind** (Gk. *tuphlos*, "blinded by pride or conceit"), **and**

- **naked** (Gk. *gumnos*, "totally without clothing or dressed in rags, without an outer garment").

All these were elements of shame and degradation in the ancient world (3:17).

3:18-20 *Command.* In order to remedy these sins, Jesus advised three things:

- for their poverty: **Buy from Me gold refined in the fire**;

- for their nakedness: Buy **white clothes to cover themselves**;

- for their blindness: Buy **ointment** (Gk. *kollourion*, "salve," used for tender eyelids) **to spread** (Gk. *egchrisai*, "rub, anoint") **on your eyes so that you may see**.

The essence of Christ's advice here is threefold—they needed spiritual riches, not earthly wealth; clothing of righteousness, not earthly attire; and spiritual discernment, not earthly vision.

The church was urged to **be committed** to these matters and to **repent**. Christ

explained, "As many as I LOVE (Gk. *philō*, "am fond of, treat affectionately, approve of"; cp. Jn 5:20; 16:27; 21:15-17), I REBUKE (Gk. *elegchō*, in word—"correct, chide, admonish, reprove, convict, call to account;" in action—"chasten, punish") and DISCIPLINE" (Gk. *paideuō*, "train, instruct, cause to learn; chastise or correct" as part of a process of molding the student's character; e.g., a father punishing his son, Rv 3:19; cp. Pr 3:11-12; 13:24; Heb 12:5-6). Christ used another illustration. Jesus is standing **at the door** of the church, a group of believers, announcing His presence and eagerness to join them in sweet fellowship (v. 20). Although suggested to be an evangelistic appeal, the context here does not permit this interpretation. The person who **hears** Christ's **voice** has a personal responsibility to open the door, for Christ does not share an intimate meal with someone who does not want Him. The dining imagery is one rich in meaning for the Near Eastern cultures, for whom sharing a meal meant sharing a life.

3:21-22 *Commitment.* The victorious one is promised **the right to sit** with Jesus on His **throne**, just as He **won the victory** through His death and resurrection and **sat down** with His **Father on His throne**. This commitment goes beyond promised thrones upon which the apostles will judge the twelve tribes of Israel (Mt 19:28). The victorious saints will sit with Christ on His throne, sharing in His authority and reigning for all eternity. The throne imagery also seems to anticipate the coming scene of God's throne room, where John saw "One . . . seated on the throne" (Rv 4:2). HAVE DINNER (Gk. *deipnēsō*, "eat supper, dine"; also Lk 22:20; 1 Co 11:25) and the noun *deipnon* (Gk. "supper, dinner, or feast," especially a formal evening meal) in John's writings and 1 Corinthians refer either to Jesus's last Passover meal, celebrated as "the Lord's Supper" in commemoration of the new covenant established in His body and blood (Jn 12:2; 13:2,4; 21:20; 1 Co 11:20-21), to "the marriage feast of the Lamb" (Rv 19:9), or to "the great supper of God" (19:17), a supper of judgment.

ADORATION IN THE THRONE ROOM OF HEAVEN (4:1–5:14)

Chapters 4 and 5 are united around John's vision of the heavenly throne room. Two aspects are highlighted: The God of creation (chap. 4, in which the Father is central) and the God of redemption (chap. 5, in which the Son is the focus). Worship dominates the atmosphere of the vision, with a glorious progression from the living creatures (4:8), to the elders (4:10-11), to both groups together (5:8-9), to the countless angels (5:11-12), to "every creature" (5:13). What a choir is assembled as all join in worship! Jesus Christ is introduced as the "slaughtered lamb" (5:6), and the victory of Christ through His death and resurrection is the event upon which everything else is based and without which there would be no Revelation. Christ's followers receive eternal rewards, and His enemies receive eternal punishment.

The Throne and Its Surroundings (4:1-11)

Important parallels to this vision of the throne and the throne room of heaven can be found in Ezekiel 1:4-28; Isaiah 6:1-4; and Daniel 7:9-10.

4:1 After this, referring to an unspecified length of time but probably a brief break after John's reception of the messages to the seven churches, John **looked, and there in heaven was an open door**. In Revelation, the concept of an "open" heaven is used as a message of hope for

believers (11:19; 12:10; 15:5; 19:11). Yet, in this case, **the first voice ... like a trumpet** (i.e., the voice of Jesus, 1:10-13) invited John to **come up**. The purpose of John's transport into heaven was that he might be shown **what must take place after this**. God, who sovereignly controls history, would reveal to John His intended progression of events for the conclusion of redemption history. This revelation points beyond a picture of the glorified Christ as He walks among the churches and delivers His message to each in the throne room of the Father in heaven (chaps. 4–5).

4:2-3 As in 1:10, John's being **in the Spirit** refers to a Holy Spirit-sent visionary experience, yet in this vision he is taken up into **heaven**. Some view this transportation of John into heaven as a picture of the pre-tribulation "rapture" of the church. Actually the two exodus events are not the same since John's body remained on Patmos during this extraordinary experience, while the bodies of believers disappear into heaven. John has the purpose of receiving additional revelation, but the believers raptured simply move into the final installment of salvation with their glorified bodies. The rapture of the church is not likely the reference here, but the context does not give any evidence of the church on earth until the inauguration of the millennial kingdom. Therefore, the body of Christ is raptured at some point before the events of the coming Great Tribulation with its terrible judgments (chaps. 6–19, which include God's rationale for His judgment on a rebellious people; cp. 3:10).

The Greek language uses the same word (*ouranos*) to refer to both "sky" and "heaven." Three "heavens" are mentioned in the New Testament. The first heaven is the atmosphere or "sky" where the weather of earth is generated and birds fly (Mt 16:3). When John saw

Heart to Heart:
What the Spirit Says to the Churches

As stated above, the messages to the seven churches set the moral and ethical stage for the rest of the book of Revelation. They affirm that faithfulness, holiness, and perseverance are the vital components of following Jesus. Yet, they also remind you that the Christian life is not lived out alone, but in community with other followers of Jesus. Although this community is never perfect, the messages to the seven churches give you instruction from Christ as to how you are to address certain pressing issues:

- *The message to the Ephesian church affirms that doctrinal purity is no replacement for the teaching of Christ that you are to love one another as He has loved you. Love for others is predicated upon first loving Christ. Nothing is more important than loving Jesus first and above all others.*

- *The message to the church at Smyrna reveals that when you experience hard times for the cause of Christ, you must persevere, knowing that God causes all things to work together for good (Rm 8:28) and that one day He will vindicate His people.*

- *The message to the church at Pergamum reminds you that in light of the intense pressure from the culture to conform to its ways, as well as from the false teachers deceiving fellow Christians all over the world, you must be careful not to water down the truth of Christian theology or compromise the integrity of the Christian life.*

- *The message to the Thyatiran church teaches that, as the church continues to struggle with heretical cult movements, believers must persevere, knowing that behind the everyday battles they face is the spiritual realm, constantly at war for the souls of men and women.*

- *The message to the church at Sardis affirms that you must not get caught up in maintaining your outward "reputation" (Rv 3:1) but instead focus on your internal obedience to the supremacy of Jesus over all parts of life.*

- *The message to the Philadelphian church teaches that, while you may fall prey to the notion that bigger and flashier churches are more "successful," clearly Jesus considers faithfulness to Him the true measure of success.*

- *The message to the Laodicean church is a reminder that, while the Western church may think that affluence and "success" are signs of divine blessing, God is more interested in your hearts than your numbers.*

As women aiming to serve the Lord faithfully in your local churches, you are responsible to listen intently and personally to what the Spirit says to the churches.

an "open door" in "heaven" (Rv 4:1), he saw an opening in the "sky." The second heaven is also commonly referenced as the "sky," but it contains the planets and other heavenly bodies, such as the sun, moon, and stars (Heb 11:12). When speaking of appearances, instead of science, distinguishing between these two heavens is difficult. The third heaven is the place where God and His celestial beings dwell. "A throne" John saw in "heaven" (Rv 4:2) was in the third heaven, the dwelling place of God. Jews of the first century closely connected God with heaven and often substituted "heaven" for "God" (e.g., "kingdom of heaven" in Mt 5:3; 21:25). Although heaven is often conceived and referenced as "up" and hell as "down," the location of these eternal places in terms of space and time cannot be known with certainty. One is always wise not to speculate beyond the teachings of Scripture.

The first thing John saw in heaven was **a throne** and **One ... seated on the throne**. John was unable to describe God on His throne any more specifically than that He **looked like jasper** (an opaque jewel found in many different colors, especially associated with the glory of God, 21:11) **and carnelian stone** (fiery red in color and very popular in the ancient world). In addition, **a rainbow that looked like an emerald surrounded the throne**. Like sunlight passing through a crystal chandelier, the emerald-like rainbow refers to a halo of multicolored light surrounding the throne of God.

4:4 The throne is also surrounded by **24 thrones, and on the thrones ... 24 elders**. These thrones make up the third layer of concentric circles around the throne, with the rainbow of light first (4:3), then the four living creatures (4:6b), and finally the 24 thrones. These elders are **dressed in white clothes, with gold crowns on their heads**, perhaps indicating that the elders are human beings, in which case they are without doubt representative of the redeemed. Some have suggested that the 12 sons of Jacob, or the patriarchs, are a reference to the 12 tribes of Israel in the Old Testament, coupled with the 12 apostles in the New Testament. However, other appearances of the elders tend to militate against this conclusion (5:8; 7:13-14; 11:18; 14:3; 19:4). There is no certainty of the identity of the 24 elders, but clearly they are part of the heavenly court with some special authority that distinguishes them from others in the court.

4:5-6a The **flashes of lightning, rumblings, and thunder** coming from the throne recalls the appearance of God to the Israelites at Mount Sinai (Ex 19:16-19). The awesomeness of God's nature and the fierceness of God's judgment are emphasized in these things. THUNDER (Gk. *brontai*) appears repeatedly in Revelation (6:1; 8:5; 10:3-4; 11:19; 14:2; 16:18; 19:6). Elsewhere, the apostles James and John are called "Sons of Thunder" (Mk 3:17), and "thunder" describes how God's voice sounded when He declared His name from heaven: in affirmation of Jesus' predicting His crucifixion (Jn 12:28). In front of the throne burned **seven fiery torches**, which John interpreted as **the seven spirits of God**. These are not the same as the "lampstands" of 1:12. The symbolic number "seven" represents the Holy Spirit (Is 11:2; Zch 4:1-10), by whom God will administer judgment upon His creation.

Before the throne was also **something like a sea of glass, similar to crystal**, an allusion to the "expanse" separating the waters in Genesis 1:7 (also Pss 104:3; 148:4). Just as the expanse separated the waters from the waters, so God's holiness and transcendence separate Him from His creation—but not in space and time. In fact, the holy and transcendent God is not bound by time and space like an earthly being but is omnipresent for all, closer and more intimately available than in human relationships.

4:6b-8a Four living creatures were in the middle circle that surrounded the throne, and they were **covered with eyes in front and in back**. Although God alone is all-knowing, in some measure His supernatural knowledge has been granted to these creatures, as nothing in creation escapes their vigilant and ever-watchful gaze. Each creature had a different likeness: one like a **lion**, one **like a calf**, one with **a face like a man**, and one **like a flying eagle**. Possibly these beings purposefully represented the noblest, strongest, wisest, and swiftest among God's living beings, similar in appearance to those seen by Ezekiel (Ezk 1:5-6,10-11). Having **six wings and eyes around and inside** seems also to combine the descriptions of the cherubim (Ezk 1; 10) and of the seraphim (Is 6), representing the highest order of celestial beings who lead in worship and judgment (Rv 6:1,3,5,7).

4:8b-11 The four living beings (Gk. *zōa*, "living ones") never ceased to proclaim God's greatness in heaven. In their chant they celebrated:

- God's holiness—**Holy, holy, holy**,

- God's power—**Lord God, the Almighty**, and

- God's eternality—**who was, who is, and who is coming** (v.8).

This first hymn of worship in Revelation, one of many purposely highlighting the sovereignty of God and His worthiness to be worshiped by all created beings, gives **glory, honor, and thanks to the One seated on the throne** (v. 9).

Following the chorus of the creatures' voices, **the 24 elders** (Gk. *presbuteroi*, "forefathers," a term of rank or office) respond in four ways (v. 10):

- they **fall down before** the throne;

- they **worship** God;

- they "CAST (Gk. *balousin*, "throw or let go of something without concern about where it falls, give over to one's care without concern about the result") their crowns" before Him; and

- they offer their own praises.

In the secular realm of John's day, lesser rulers signified their submission to the Roman emperor by bowing before him and laying their crowns at his feet. Clearly only the Lord is worthy of the bowing of the elders before the throne of God. Eventually, even the powerful kings of earth will be forced to bow the knee before **the One who lives forever and ever** (v. 10; Php 2:10-11).

While the four living creatures proclaimed truths *about* God, the 24 elders address their hymn of adoration *to* God, who alone is worthy to be worshiped. TO RECEIVE (Gk. *labein*, "take what is one's own, claim, receive what is offered") should not suggest that your worship gives something to God that He does not already possess. Instead, you are to give Him your recognition of those attributes (i.e., glory, honor, and power) that He already holds (v. 11). The Lord's worthiness for worship is grounded in His role as the Creator of all things (v. 11). The One who created all things also knows the wisest and most just way to bring all things to an end. Truly, God is and will be "the beginning and the end" of His creation.

Heart to Heart:
On Earth as It Is in Heaven

This glimpse into the heavenly realm provides a whole new perspective on Jesus' teaching that you should pray "Your will be done on earth as it is in heaven" (Mt 6:10). The question begs to be asked: How is God's will done "in heaven"? The worship of the angels, the 24 elders, and the four living creatures in Revelation 4 reveal that God's will is done perfectly through worship of Him in heaven. "Worship" (Gk. proskuneō, *lit. "prostrating oneself before") in modern terms suggests falling flat on your face. To have God's will done in your life, "as it is in heaven," you must assume this spiritual posture of prostration before God on a daily basis. You may say that you desire God's will, but you are not actively submitting to whatever He desires. Learning from the heavenly worshipers, you must lay your life down in daily submission before God, ready and willing to do whatever He may ask of you.*

The Lamb and the Seven-Sealed Scroll (5:1-14)

5:1 As elsewhere in Scripture, **the right hand** of God symbolizes power and authority. Scrolls (Gk. *biblion*, "small book") were common in John's day. Strips of thin paper made from a papyrus plant were lined up end to end and glued together, forming a long piece, which was then rolled up for storage (see Ezk 2:9-10). The **scroll** John saw not only included lamentation and woe but also God's perfect plan (symbolized by the number **seven**) for redeeming His creation, which will culminate in the end times. The contents of the scroll could only be revealed, however, when all **seven seals** affixed to the outside of the scroll were removed. "Seals" (Gk. *sphragidas*, "signet, mark, that which affirms") usually consisted of the writer's personalized sign—often embedded in a ring, which would be dipped in hot wax and then affixed to the document to prohibit unauthorized reading. The scroll contained those judgments that will fall upon the

earth within a relatively brief timeframe, which some have suggested is a "history of the future," leading to the establishment of Christ's kingdom on earth. The contents of this very comprehensive (noted by its words extending to the back side of the scroll) account of the outpouring of God's wrath are obviously enacted, not merely read.

5:2-5 The One on the throne desired another person to open the scroll, because Jesus, the Lamb, would usher in the last days. John **saw a mighty angel** call out for one **who is worthy to open the scroll and break its seals** (v. 2). This same mighty angel, whose identity is unknown, appears at two other critical points (10:1-2; 18:21). Only One in His very being is worthy to reveal God's redemptive plan and the events of the end times. That is why **no one** in the entire universe could be **found worthy to open the scroll or even to look in it** (5:3). John began to weep, mourning the thought that the events comprising God's redemptive plan would be thwarted (v. 4).

One of the 24 elders of Revelation 4:4 calms John's fears and presents the solution. The **Lion from the tribe of Judah** and **the Root of David** are titles with messianic origins in the Old Testament (Gn 49:9-10). The rabbis often suggested that the kings of Israel would all come from Judah, including their Messiah (v. 10; see Is 11:1-10). Jesus was the ancestor of Jesse—and, therefore, of David—and a descendant from the tribe of Judah.

5:6-7 John expected to see the Lion appear to open the scroll. Instead, he encountered **one like a slaughtered** (Gk. *esphagmenon*, "slain, violently put to death," used only in John's writings—see 5:12; 6:4,9; 13:3,8; 18:24; 1 Jn 3:12) **lamb standing between the throne and the four living creatures and among the elders**. The "victorious" nature of Jesus (Rv 5:5) is rooted in the fact that He was slain for the sins of the world. Interestingly, even in His glorified state in heaven, the Lamb is pictured as one slaughtered. The scars He bears, though, are not a source of shame but of victory. The first emphasis of this vision is on Jesus' role as sacrificial lamb. Yet, the lamb also has **seven horns**, which in other Jewish writings outside the Bible is seen as symbolic of the Messiah-Warrior who would lead the people of God to victory, the characteristic likely pictured here.

The **seven eyes** of the Lamb are identified **as the seven spirits of God sent into all the earth**. The sevenfold Holy Spirit has been mentioned before, but this time His description as "sent" emphasizes His role in the gospel's proliferation throughout the world. As the Lamb takes **the scroll out of the right hand** of God, a transfer of authority takes place, and Jesus will now execute God's plan for redeeming the saints and judging the world. The lamb is significant, beginning in the Old Testament when the death angel moved through Egypt killing the firstborn son in every household except those marked by the blood of an unblemished lamb on the doorpost (Ex 12:13). The Feast (Festival, HCSB) of Passover has been celebrated among the Jews in all the succeeding centuries as a memorial to God's deliverance. John the Baptist picked up this imagery in identifying Jesus as the Lamb of God (Jn 1:29), and the word (Gk. *arnion*) appears almost 30 times in the book of Revelation.

5:8-10 After the Lamb takes **the scroll** from the hand of God, He receives the universal adoration that God received in 4:8-11, a phenomenal testimony to the full deity of Jesus Christ. As **the four living creatures and the 24 elders** fall at the feet of **the Lamb**, each one holds **a harp and gold bowls filled with incense**. The harp of John's day was a 10- or 12-stringed lyre, which was used in temple worship as an accompaniment to hymns. The golden bowls, placed on the table of the bread of the Presence (Ex 25:29; 37:16), are another reference to the temple. These bowls contained incense, described as **the prayers of the saints** (v. 8; see also 6:9-11 and 8:3-4), affirming that the worship and petitions by God's saints on earth make up a key part of the worship taking place in the heavenly throne room.

In addition, the celestial beings sang **a new song** to the Lamb, praising the worthiness of the Lamb (5:9b), the salvation provided by the Lamb (5:9c), and the rewards given to the followers of the Lamb (5:10). Central to this hymn is that the Lamb's worthiness is directly tied to His sacrificial death, a glorious irony through which the Lamb's death gave victory for Him and all humanity. The fourfold reference to **tribe and language and people and nation** occurs seven more times in the book with different word orders (5:9; 7:9; 10:11; 11:9; 13:7; 14:6; 17:15).

The phrase "tribe and language and people and nation" is not meant as a standard list of categories for humanity, whether political, ethnic, cultural, etc. Instead, until chapter 7, the phrase emphasizes in a dramatic way the universal character of the body of Christ. Unlike the exclusive nature of Judaism, which in John's day prided itself on having been specially chosen out of the nations, the church is genuinely universal and worldwide in its scope. Truly, to "make disciples of all nations" (Mt 28:19), calling out people from all parts of the earth to be part of His Son's pure and holy bride is in the heart of God (Rv 19:7-8).

Only the Lamb could gather His people from the innumerable nations of the world and mold them as individual **priests** into a united **kingdom**. As priests, believers will serve God in worship and witness. As royalty, **they will reign** with God in His kingdom (see the millennial reign, Rv 20:4; and the eternal age, 22:5).

5:11-12 Next, John saw **and heard** the worship of **many angels around the throne** added to that **of the living creatures** and the 24 **elders**. "The number" of the angels "was COUNTLESS THOUSANDS (Gk. *muriades muriadōn*, "ten thousand times ten thousand; innumerable multitiude," anglicized as "myriads"), plus THOUSANDS UPON THOUSANDS" (Gk. *xiliades xiliadōn*, "a thousand times a thousand"), essentially pointing to an infinite number of angelic worshipers seen elsewhere in Scripture (Dt 33:2; Jb 25:3; Pss 68:17; 89:7; Dn 7:10). Their hymn contains seven things ascribed to the Lamb: **power and riches and wisdom and strength and honor and glory and blessing**. With the exception of "riches," these same things are ascribed to God on His throne (Rv 7:12). Once again, qualities normally ascribed to God are

given to the Lamb, stressing the unity and equality of God the Father and God the Son.

5:13-14 The worship reaches its crescendo in this powerful and electrifying scene where all created beings without exception worship God and His Son. **The One seated on the throne** (chap. 4) and **the Lamb** (chap. 5) come together for all creation to worship them in a final surge of praise. Having begun the world together (Jn 1:1-3), Father and Son will end history together (Rv 6:16-17), inhabit the new Jerusalem together (21:22-23), and receive the worship of their creation together forever (22:3).

THE SEVEN SEALS (6:1–8:6)

As the seals are opened, apparently each of the first four seals represents the judgment of God on the tribulation earth. The seven-year period of retribution upon a world that has rejected Christ and His lordship is a time of personal and cosmic retribution. This period is marked by the wrath and judgment of God on the one hand and the awakening of Israel's longing for the Messiah coupled with the preparation for Christ's return on the other. The great tribulation focuses primarily upon three series of seven judgments each:

- the seals (6:1-17),
- the trumpets (8:1–9:21), and
- the bowls (16:1-17).

These judgments are seemingly best interpreted as operating partially concurrently. This telescopic approach interprets the seventh seal as introducing and containing the seven trumpets and then the seventh trumpet as introducing and containing the seven bowls. The mention of the great tribulation (Rv 7:14) or "the great day of Their wrath" (6:17) would lend natural support that the events begin-

---

Heart to Heart:
Finding Comfort in the Midst of Turmoil

As you live busy and hectic lives in the midst of what has become an increasingly traumatic and disastrous world, to find and hold onto any kind of hope for the future is often difficult. Yet, the book of Revelation, originally written to believers living in uncertain times, presents the truth that history, however painful and difficult, is headed in the direction God intends (Jn 16:33). God intentionally revealed to John a scene of powerful worship prior to the revelation of the end times. With John all believers must be reminded of God's supreme worthiness and unrivaled majesty before they see the trouble and distress awaiting them as the end draws near. In His wisdom, justice, and mercy, God is propelling world history toward a glorious and climactic ending in which He will vindicate the followers of the Lamb and set all things right again.

---

ning in Revelation 6 belong to the seven-year or "42 months" of tribulation (11:2; 13:5). That the events described in this section will occur in the future within the tribulation seems most convincing:

- the vision (chaps. 4–5) is described as "after this," i.e., after the revelation to the seven churches;

- the opening of the sealed scroll does not readily find fulfillment in one clear sequence of historical events;

- the lack of mention of the church or its rapture would suggest that the rapture precedes these events and the tribulation.

The Opening of the First Four Seals (6:1-8)

The first four seals are grouped together in both their imagery and content. The four horsemen imagery depicts white, red, black, and pale green (Gk. *chlōros*, the same word used for vegetation, Rv 8:7; 9:4) horses (Zch 1:7-11; 6:1-8; the colors

differ in Zch 1:8). Yet, the horsemen of Zechariah go out, finding the earth "calm and quiet" (Zch 1:11), in stark contrast to the horsemen of Revelation (Rv 6:2,4,5, 8). The first four seals flow together, as each horseman brings escalating suffering on the earth: from the lust for conquest to widespread war to famine to pestilence and death. Some attribute these horsemen to demons, but demonic forces are not necessary in order for humanity to self-destruct. The first four seals, then, are not necessarily demons or unique judgments of God upon the earth but merely the complete "turning over" of men and women to their sinful ways. God allows the consequences of human sinfulness to come full circle in the imagery of the four horsemen of the Apocalypse.

6:1-2 The opening of the seal by **the Lamb** and the command of the living creature is the pattern for the following three seals as well. John looked for the one receiving the order, and he saw **a white horse. The horseman** was described:

- he **had a bow,**

- **a crown** (Gk. *stephanos*, "wreath, reward," or the victor's crown) **was given to him,** and

- **he went out as a victor to conquer**.

Despite the presence of the white horse, this rider cannot be Jesus, for His appearance differs greatly from the first horseman (Rv 19:11-16) since He returns as a conqueror at the end, not the beginning of the tribulation. Instead, the white horse and bow would have reminded the original readers of the much-feared Parthians of Asia, whose trademarks were white horses and skill with the bow and whose successful attacks against Rome in the 60s and 70s terrified the land. However, perhaps this conqueror was the future world ruler, referred to elsewhere in Scripture as antichrist (1 Jn 2:18) or "the coming prince" (Dn 9:26). The sovereignty of God over this first horseman, though, is emphasized by the phrase "was given to him," which is used elsewhere in the book to highlight the authority of God over the destructive events of the end times (e.g., 6:11; 7:2; 8:2-3; 9:1,3,5: 11:2-3; 12:14; repeatedly in chap. 13). Although God allows His creation free reign in their depravity, He is never without ultimate authority and oversight.

6:3-4 The opening of **the second seal** revealed a second horse that was **fiery red**. The rider of this horse is given two things: **a large sword** (a sign of political power as expected from a world ruler) and the power **to take peace from the earth** (civil peace; see Mk 13:7). Clearly the result of the lust for conquest (the first seal) is war when people are enticed to brutally **slaughter one another**. Interestingly, the color of the horse is the same as that of the "great fiery red dragon" (Rv 12:3) whose hatred and murder of God's people is mirrored in this horse of war. When the earth dwellers or unbelievers turn on one another in violent bloodshed, they are revealing their true spiritual parent, the Devil, and they are carrying out their "father's desires" (Jn 8:44).

6:5-6 The famine that this horseman on **a black horse** brought naturally followed the red war that preceded it. The **balance scale** in the hand of the horseman is typical of those pictured in ancient texts: a balance beam with a scale at each end. In ancient times, food was distributed by rationed amounts in times of scarcity. The **voice** heard by John **among the four living creatures** was most likely God Himself still clearly in control. **Wheat** and **barley** were the staple foods of the Roman Empire, with a **quart** being enough food for one person for one day. The **denarius** (a Roman coin) was the average day's wage for a laborer. So, with the inflation of prices during the famine (which according to ancient records may have been 10 to 12 times the normal rate), a man could barely afford to feed himself for a day, let alone his entire family. The order not to **harm the olive oil and the wine** is puzzling, but probably referred to the famine as limited, with some products still available.

6:7-8 The horse of **the fourth seal** was **pale green**, or greenish gray, the color of dead human flesh. Its rider is named "Death," and his companion "Hades" (or the grave) was FOLLOWING (Gk. *ēkolouthei*, "accompanying as an attendant," v. 8) on foot behind him. John was depicting the grave as a lowly squire scampering on foot behind the horse of Death, gathering up the corpses left by his rampage. The authority given to this horseman encompassed the horrors of the other three, and then some, for he would KILL (Gk. *apokteinai*, "destroy, allow to perish, extinguish, deprive of life"; appears 15 times in Rv, always by God's permission) "by the sword, by famine, by plague, and by the wild animals of the earth." The stalking of Death and Hades would occur **over a fourth of the earth**, that is, where a quarter of the world's population live, indicating staggering loss of life; but even more widespread death is still to come (cp. 9:18).

The Opening of the Fifth Seal (6:9-11)

6:9 After the four horsemen on earth had been unsealed, the scene shifted to a vision in heaven. At the opening of **the fifth seal**, John saw **the souls of those slaughtered** (Gk. *esphagmenōn*, "slain, put to violent death"; see 5:6) **because of God's word and the testimony they had**. The reason given for their deaths ties these souls to other instances of martyrdom in the book (12:17; 14:12; 20:4). Strangely, they are seen **under the altar** (Gk. *thusiastēriou*, derived from *thusia*, "sacrifice, victim"), for the altars mentioned elsewhere in the book are altars where incense is placed *on* the altar not *under* it (8:3,5; 9:13; 11:1; 14:18; 16:7). This unique altar recalled the Old Testament sacrificial system, in which the blood of the sacrificial animal was poured at the base of the altar of burnt offering. The "soul" and the "blood" are both symbols of life in the Bible, so the presence of the martyrs' souls at the base of the altar pictured them as slain sacrifices for the cause of Christ.

6:10 Together, the martyrs **cried out with a loud voice: "O Lord, holy and true, how long until You judge and avenge** (Gk. *ekdikeis*, "vindicate, do justice"; cp. 19:2) **our blood from those who live on the earth?"** Their plea for vengeance does not violate Jesus' teachings of mercy and forgiveness, for this is a righteous call for divine justice mirrored elsewhere in Scripture (Ps 6:3; 74:10; 79:5: 80:4). Just as Jesus "committed Himself to the One who judges justly"

(1 Pt 2:23), so do the martyred saints. The question is not *will* God avenge the martyrs' blood upon the earth dwellers (Rv 6:10) but *how soon* until He does so. The completion of God's justice, though sometimes delayed, is never lacking (2 Pt 3:8-9).

6:11 The Lord responded to the martyrs' prayers in two ways: **A white robe was given to each of them**, and **they were told to rest a little while longer**. The **ROBE** (Gk. *stolē*), referring to a loose outer garment extending to the feet, was worn by men who were persons of rank, such as kings and priests. A white robe symbolized the spotless purity of the martyrs and the end-time joy awaiting them (cp. 7:9,13,14; 22:14; Mk 12:38; 16:5; Lk 15:22; 20:46). Before the vengeance of God could be poured out in fullness upon "those who live on the earth," more of God's **slaves** and the martyrs' **brothers** must be killed. **BROTHERS** (Gk. *adelphoi*) is used here in a generic sense to refer to all Christians who share in the fate of the martyrs. The promise of God's judgment for the martyrs will finally be fulfilled (Rv 19:2), and their total vindication is shown (20:4-6,11-14). Through this vision, God reveals that, in the midst of the suffering meted out by the seals, a faithful and persevering witness will be required of all believers. For their faith, some will suffer persecution and death, but in the end God will vindicate His people and avenge their blood.

The Opening of the Sixth Seal (6:12-17)

6:12-14 The breaking of **the sixth seal** revealed phenomena more violent and disturbing than anything John had seen thus far.

- The earth was affected with **a violent earthquake** (Gk. *seismos*, "shaking, trembling, agitation, commotion," the first of five references in Revelation to earthquakes of great magnitude and devastation—8:5; 11:13,19; 16:18).

- **The sun** was affected, turning **black, like sackcloth made of goat hair** (6:12; see Jl 2:31). Sackcloth, some made of coarse black goat wool, was a symbol for death, disaster, or mourning in ancient Israel.

- Other heavenly bodies are affected as the **moon** becomes **like blood** and **the stars of heaven fell to the earth** like **unripe figs when shaken** (Gk. *sei-omenē*, "agitated, caused to tremble," the root of *seismos*, "earthquake") **by a high wind** (Gk. *anemou*, "violent or tempestuous wind," Rv 6:13).

- **The sky** itself appeared to separate (Gk. *apechōristhē*, "sever, split in two, part"), rolling back **like a scroll** (v. 14). The picture here is of a long scroll stretched across the heavens, which when cut in the middle, suddenly spins back in either direction. The movement of **every mountain and island** from its place was the result of the earthquake (v. 12).

With these catastrophes, everything that could be considered stable and secure, whether in the heavens, earth, or sea, was violently shaken. Though the severity of these things makes you think that the Day of the Lord is at hand, Jesus taught that such happenings are "the beginning of birth pains" (Mk 13:8), for the end is still to come. The events, which John purposefully presented in exaggerated and general language, emphasized that nature will go horribly awry between the incarnation of Christ and His return. Just as the conquest, war, famine, death, and martyrdom of the first five seals have run rampant since the ascension of Christ, you can expect the natural disasters of the sixth seal to occur intermittently as well.

6:15-17 John saw all peoples **of the earth** quake in terror at the onset of these disasters, with people fending for themselves against the wrath of God. This initial act of self-preservation turns into utter desperation as they begged **the mountains** and **the rocks** to **fall on** them, a purposeful exaggeration for effect. The earth dwellers would rather be buried in an avalanche of rock than face **the One seated on the throne** and **the wrath of the Lamb**. The **great day of Their wrath** refers to the approaching "great tribulation" period in which the earth dwellers will be tested (3:10). Although their rhetorical question, **"Who is able to stand?"** is intended to be answered in the negative, yet God's servants may stand even in the midst of these natural disasters (7:1-8 and 7:9-17). The sad irony of the earth dwellers' desire to die is that even in death they would not escape the judgment of God (20:11-14).

The reference to the coming "WRATH (Gk. *orgēs*, "violent anger, indignation") of the Lamb" can appear to be contradictory to divine love. Yet, the revelation of God's wrath is absolutely necessary for the revelation of God's love. In His desire to redeem humankind for Himself, God sacrificed His Son, allowing Him to be humiliated, brutally beaten, and crucified. As the earth dwellers had consistently rejected His love, they had also spurned the precious sacrifice of God's Son. God's wrath is not that of one quick-tempered and raging but of a scorned lover whose offer of restored relationship to Himself, through Jesus Christ, had been repeatedly rejected. In light of the earth dwellers' rejection, the wickedness of their sins remained upon them, and the wrath of God is continuously kindled against them.

Although the wrath of God against sin has already been revealed in Jesus (Jn 3:36; Rm 1:18), the great day of God's wrath (called "the day of the Lord" in the Old Testament; see Is 13:9; Zph 1:14-15) is still to come. Therefore, in "the day of the Lord," after God has handed over the judgment of the world to His Son, the Lamb must take up the same wrath held by the Father and mete out the punishment earned by those who rejected Him.

The First Interlude Vision (7:1-8)

A parenthesis or interlude between the sixth and seventh seals (chap. 7) is mirrored later between the sixth and seventh trumpets (chaps. 10–11). This first interlude seemingly serves one main purpose: to disclose a more detailed revelation to John, which would abruptly interrupt "the beginning of birth pains" and usher in the Day of the Lord (or "great tribulation"), which commences with the seventh seal and the trumpet judgments that follow. The interlude's significance is also marked by two periods of silence, one on the earth (7:1) and another in heaven (8:1), which are before-and-after brackets for its contents.

The interlude is made up of two parts: the sealing of the "144,000" (a number representing the fullest completeness and an absolute and unchanging fixedness) and the appearance of a "vast multitude" in heaven, whose identities remain one of the most debated issues in the interpretation of Revelation. Out of several possibilities, the one seeming to fit best both the biblical witness and the overall progress of the book is to identify the "144,000" as the full number of God's people (Israel) to come safely through the tribulation and the "vast multitude" as Gentile and Jewish believers who died or were martyred during the tribulation. God remains faithful to His covenant with Israel, His beloved people and the recipients of His promises. The care with which John listed each tribe (vv. 5-8) affirms this fact.

7:1 After the sixth seal, John **saw four angels standing at the four corners** or in the four quadrants **of the earth** (cp. Mk 13:27; Mt 24:31) to restrain **the four winds** from blowing on the earth, sea, or trees. The cessation of the winds could be intended literally as a kind of eerie stillness following the escalation of natural disasters thus far. Or, they could be identified with the four horsemen (chap. 6) and represent a temporary cessation of the seals' destruction (see Zch 6:1-5, where the four spirits—literally "winds"—are connected to the four horses) prior to the beginning of the "great tribulation" (Rv 7:14).[2] The stillness on the earth must have produced an "eye of the hurricane" effect paralleling the silence in heaven, which will mark the beginning of the "hour of testing" (8:1).

7:2-3 After this, John **saw another angel** come **from the east, who had the seal of the living God**. He ordered continued restraint so that he could **seal the slaves** of **God on their foreheads** (Gk. metōpōn, "space between the eyes," used only in Rv; cp. 9:4; 13:16; 14:1,9; 17:5; 20:4; 22:4). Whether this seal was visible or invisible, a mark, picture, or name, it set the people apart as belonging to God and covered them with His protection. The "seal" of God was meant to contrast with the "mark" of the beast received by the earth dwellers (13:16).

7:4-8 John did not see the sealed slaves of God but instead heard **the number of those who were sealed: 144,000 ... from every tribe of the sons of Israel** (v. 4). The 144,000 are then listed in what resembles a military census (cp. Nm 1:3,17-46), with **12,000** present from "every tribe." There are some peculiarities about the listing of tribal names. However, the tribe of Judah is listed first, though in all other biblical accounts Reuben is first; Joseph is listed with only one of his sons, though Joseph is normally left out, and both his sons are usually listed; and the tribe of Dan is missing altogether (some attribute this to their history of idolatry; see Jdg 18:14-15,18-21, 30-31; 1 Kg 12:25-30). The irregularities suggest that these tribes had been chosen and so listed for a reason. The further identification of the 144,000 as "of the sons of Israel," which is always used of the Jewish people in both the Old and New Testaments, indicates that they are Jews—a remnant of Israel who will follow Jesus as the Messiah in the last days.

The appearance of these "sons of Israel" at the very beginning of the "hour of testing" is indicative of the fact that God is not through with Israel. God will draw the faithful remnant of His chosen people back to Himself (Rm 11:25-27). With the 144,000 under God's protection, they will serve as His spiritual army on the earth during the Day of the Lord, calling the earth dwellers to repentance in light of coming judgment. When they appear again, they are relocated to heavenly "Zion," probably as martyrs (Rv 14:1-5). These chosen witnesses are protected from the wrath of God, manifested in the trumpets and bowl judgments but not from the persecution of the earth dwellers.

Numbers have a particularly symbolic function in Revelation, and whether the number 144,000 should be taken as literal or symbolic is debated. If taken literally, as the hour of testing is about to begin, God will assemble a believing remnant from the scattered tribes of Israel to fulfill this exact number. If taken figuratively, however, then 12 times a thousand, from each of the 12 tribes serves to emphasize the completeness of the group—not one is missing. Either way, out of the nation of Israel the 144,000 comprise a compara-

tively small yet complete remnant who will faithfully serve the Lamb in the last days.

The Second Interlude Vision (7:9-17)

7:9-12 After *hearing* of the 144,000, John now *saw* a different group in a different location. The group John saw **was a vast multitude** (Gk. *ochlos*, "crowd of people gathered in one place, throng," v. 9; cp. 17:15; 19:1,6) from **every nation, tribe, people, and language**. They were too numerous to count. Rejoicing was evident in their being **robed in white** and **holding palm branches**, as **they cried out** praises to **God** and **to the Lamb** for their salvation (5:12).

7:13-17 John did not know the identity of this group. John was informed by the elder that, **These are the ones coming out of the great tribulation**, who had also **washed their robes and made them white in the blood of the Lamb** (v. 14).

GREAT TRIBULATION (Gk. *thlipseōs tēs megalēs*) is often misunderstood because of its broader use in the New Testament. Though there are 43 appearances of *thlipsis*, often translated "tribulation" but also "affliction," "suffering," or "distress," only five to seven refer specifically to end-times events. The remaining uses have to do with suffering in the Christian life (e.g., Ac 14:22).

By focusing on the handful of times *thlipsis* is used in reference to end times, some assume wrongly that there is *no* "tribulation" now but "tribulation" or "great tribulation" at the end of the age. However, a more balanced way of understanding the way *thlipsis* is used in the New Testament is that there is significant "tribulation" during the course of the age (see Rv 1:9 and 2:9-10) but unparalleled "great tribulation" at the end of the age (7:14). Followers of Jesus cannot escape the tribulation promised (Jn 16:33), but they can look forward with eager expectation to their protection from the "great tribulation" (Rv 7:14) or the "hour of testing" (3:10) at the end of the age.

The reference to blood initially suggests that this is an innumerable group of martyrs, but the blood of the Lamb, not of the people, is in view here. All followers of Jesus are made clean by His blood, this scene depicts all believers from the earth (7:9) in heaven serving God in a priestly manner **day and night in His sanctuary** (v. 15). "The One seated on the throne WILL SHELTER" (Gk. *skēnōsei*, "fix one's tabernacle over, abide or live in one's tabernacle or tent"; cp. 12:12; 13:6; 21:3; Jn 1:14), provide for, and protect them (Rv 7:15) "because the Lamb" who purchased them also "will shepherd them" and "GUIDE (Gk. *hodēgēsei*, "lead the way"; cp. Jn 16:13) them to SPRINGS (Gk. *pēgas*, "fountain, well fed by a spring"; cp. Jn 4:6,14) of living waters (Rv 7:17). After the reign of war, famine, death, and destruction over the earth, this vast multitude will finally find eternal peace and comfort from their Savior, who is also their Shepherd (note that some of the wording here echoes Ps 23). The description of this vast multitude in heaven also links this group to both John's doxology (1:6) and the song of the 24 elders (5:9-10). All three passages seem to address the same group of people, who are revealed as the "heaven dwellers" in contrast to the "earth dwellers" (12:12). Although interpretations vary considerably on this issue, seemingly chapter 7 is a twofold picture:

- the assembling of a faithful remnant out of the nation of Israel, and

- those believers (Jews and Gentiles) who died or were martyred during the tribulation.

If the time of great tribulation is specifically intended to test the earth dwellers or unbelievers, then the church (exempt from the wrath of God; see 1 Th 1:10; 5:9) will be removed from the earth before that time begins (referred to as the "rapture" of the church). The "vast multitude," i.e., the church of Christ, does not have to stand on the earth during the Day of the Lord because the Lord has removed them to stand before Him in heaven. According to Old Testament prophecies, however, the 144,000, as a faithful remnant of Israel, will undergo the period of great tribulation with the promise of their vindication when it is over (see Jr 30:4-22; Dn 9:24). The faithful remnant of Israel will "stand" victoriously before the Lord on the earth.

The Opening of the Seventh Seal (8:1-6)

8:1 With the end of the first interlude in the book (chap. 7), John's vision returned to the lifting of the seals. One would expect more catastrophic events with the opening of **the seventh seal**. Yet, there is **silence** (Gk. *sigē*, "a hush") **in heaven for about half an hour**, mirroring the stillness on the earth prior to the sealing of God's people (7:1). The myriads of angels, the 24 elders, and the four living creatures, who had previously been united in ceaseless praise to God, fell silent with the opening of the seventh seal, depicting the awe and anticipation of those in heaven before the grim reality of God's fierce judgments was unleashed upon the earth.

8:2-4 John saw **seven angels** given **seven trumpets** (Gk. *salpigges*, "bugles"; cp. 1:10; 4:1; 8:2,6,13; 9:14; 1 Co 14:8; 1 Th 4:16; Heb 12:19)—evidently not the Old Testament ram's horns (Hb. *shophar*) but the long metal tube, with a mouthpiece and a flared end, of the New Testament. Trumpets announced the arrival of events in the end times (Mt 24:31; 1 Co 15:52; 1 Th 4:16). The sounding of these "seven trumpets" would bring forth a judgment of plagues to fall upon the earth and its inhabitants.

Then **another angel, with a gold incense burner**, was seen standing **at the altar** and was given much **incense** (Gk. *thumiamatōn*, "aromatic substance for burning," Rv 8:3-4; cp. 18:13; Lk 1:10-11) **to offer with the prayers of all the saints . . . in front of the throne**. This incense is similar to the golden bowls the elders held (Rv 5:8). In the Old Testament, incense stood both for protection of the people (Lv 16:13; Nm 16:47-48) and for the people's prayers as they ascended before God (Ps 141:2). Here, **the smoke of the incense** was seen bearing up **the prayers of the saints . . . in the presence of God** (Rv 8:4). God had already accepted the prayers of His people, which were in **the angel's hand**, and He was answering their cries.

8:5-6 In Ezekiel 10:2-7 coals of fire, symbolizing fiery judgment from the throne, are scattered over the city. Here, the imagery is more meaningful, for the fiery judgment about to fall upon the earth was God's direct response to the cries of His people and reflected His desire to vindicate them for their sufferings at the hands of the earth dwellers. As the fire from the altar struck the earth, it caused **thunders, rumblings, lightnings, and an earthquake** (v. 5)—only a preview of what was to come, for John saw that **the seven angels who had the seven trumpets prepared to blow** (Gk. *salpisōsin*, "sound a trumpet"; cp. vv. 7,8,10,12,13; 9:1,13; 10:7; 11:15; Mt 6:2; 1 Co 15:52) **them**.

Heart to Heart: The Significance of Prayer

The appearance of the saints' prayers in heaven before the throne is surprising for many readers. Often while you pay lip service to the importance of prayer in the Christian life, your personal prayer life remains less than meaningful. Possibly this "prayer depression" comes because you do not understand how precious and important your prayers are to God. The prayers of the saints are of such significance that a special angel has been given the role of offering them before the Lord (Rv 8:4-5). In addition, in some mysterious way your prayers have an effect on the outworking of God's plan. In response to the saints' prayers, judgment begins with "thunders, rumblings, lightnings, and an earthquake" (8:5b). From this passage, two things are clear: Your prayers are a delightful gift to God, the Father, as well as a powerful tool in bringing about God's will on earth. To paraphrase James 5:16, the fervent prayer of a godly woman is very powerful!

Apparently the important issue in the sequence of seven seals, including the sealing of the 144,000 and the appearance of the vast multitude in heaven, is not necessarily things like "Who?" "Where?" and "When?" but "*What*?"—i.e., *what* are we supposed to do in light of these revelations? The Christians portrayed present a challenging model for Christian living (chaps. 6–7). Although the martyrs are persecuted and killed for their faith, they trust in God alone to vindicate them (chap. 6). Human nature resists affliction and retaliates when attacked. Seemingly from this passage the Lord desires you to become the kind of woman who is undaunted by the suffering endured in this life, choosing instead to see yourself as victorious through the blood of the Lamb. Contrary to popular ideas about so-called "health and wealth" promises in the gospel, believers will go through trials throughout life. Yet, joy and peace await them when they stand before the throne of God to serve Him day and night. The main issue is not discovering the exact timing of Revelation's events but preparing yourself to become a woman who is watching and ready when they do happen.

THE SEVEN TRUMPETS (8:7–11:19)

The seven trumpets introduced with the opening of the seventh seal (Rv 8:1) are interpreted by some as overlapping and portraying the same events as the seals in different ways, but a more natural explanation is to view them as successive, sounded following the seven seals in an ordered progression. The trumpet judgments, like the seals, are arranged in a 4 + 2 + 1 order, with the first four trumpets grouped together, followed by the next two trumpets, then an extensive interlude before the last trumpet is sounded.

The seals and trumpets differ, however, in both their source and content. The seals were the "beginning of birth pains" (Mk 13:7), events caused primarily by human sinfulness that spanned the period of time from the ascension of Jesus to the beginning of the great tribulation, the "Day of the Lord." After all seven seals were lifted, the scroll was open for viewing.

Thus, the trumpets were the first part of the scroll's contents (Rv 5:1) and the beginning of God's outpouring of wrath upon the earth dwellers. For this reason, the church has been removed from the earth (7:9-17; see 1 Th 5:9), keeping them from the wrath of God.

The First Four Trumpets (8:7-13)

The destruction meted out by the first four trumpets closely mirrors the plagues visited upon Egypt (Ex 7–11). In this case, though, they are visited upon the whole world. As the trumpets are considered, John was not concerned with recording the means by which these disasters take place. He wrote only what he saw and heard. You should not concern yourself with speculation as to how these disasters might take place (such as nuclear war or "global warming") but focus on the truth that they come from the hand of God.

8:7 When **the first angel blew** his trumpet, **hail and fire, mixed with blood, were hurled to the earth** (see Ex 9:13-35, in which God sent hail mixed with lightning and thunder, destroying all of their vegetation and creating the worst storm in Egyptian history). With the first trumpet, however, "fire" and "blood" were added to the hail, (see Jl 2:30). The result of the fiery hail mixed with blood was that **a third of the earth was burned up, a third of the trees were burned up**, and all the green grass was burned up. Terrible forest fires leave charred black remains, yet even the worst forest fires of world history have been localized. The breadth of this natural disaster is unimaginable.

8:8-9 When **the second angel** sounded **his trumpet**, John saw **something like a great mountain ablaze with fire** being **hurled into the sea**. With the impact of the object, **a third of the ships** were destroyed. And, when **a third of the sea became blood**, a third of the sea **crea-**

tures perished (see Ex 7:14-21, in which God turned the Nile and all of the Egyptians' water into blood). Some have suggested a reference to volcanic eruptions, but what kind of volcano begins in the sky and is cast into the sea?

8:10-11 This **star** had a name, **Wormwood**, which is also the name of a shrub, which in the Old Testament became a symbol for bitter sorrow, judgment, and death (see Pr 5:4; Jr 9:15; 23:15; Lm 3:15,19). With the impact of Wormwood upon the earth's fresh water sources, **a third of the waters became wormwood**, or bitter, with many people dying as a result. Wormwood itself was not poisonous, but in this case its affected waters represented the bitterness of judgment and death.

8:12 The puzzling phrase, **a third of the day was without light, and the night as well**, likely indicated a complete darkening of all heavenly bodies (the sun, moon, and stars) for eight hours of every twenty-four-hour day. The effects of this "heavenly plague" would be disastrous for life on earth.

No specific timeline is given here for the ordering of the first four trumpets. Yet, because of the interconnected nature of the earth's environmental systems, you can infer that when the first four angels sound their trumpets, one plague will quickly follow another.

8:13 After the first four trumpets were sounded, John saw a bird of prey (Gk. *aetou*, "eagle or vulture") **flying in mid-heaven**. While the first four trumpets were catastrophic, their attacks were limited to nature. The next judgments, however, would attack the earth dwellers directly. Interestingly, the Greek version of the eagle's threefold cry, WOE! WOE! WOE! (*ouai ouai ouai*, "alas, alas, alas") was probably pronounced "wee," which is close in sound to the natural shriek of an eagle. Contemporary English would render the cry,

"Horror! Horror! Horror!" which is surely an ominous introduction to the coming fifth and sixth trumpets.

The Fifth Trumpet or First Woe (9:1-12)

The fifth and sixth trumpets, or the first and second woes, contain two demonic plagues, which directly attack the earth dwellers. The empire of Satan is pictured in an all-out invasion of earth, appearing first in a plague of torturing locust demons and then in an army of killing warrior demons. Once again, the book of Joel appears to serve as a loose background for these plagues (Jl 1:4-6).

9:1-2 At the sounding of the fifth trumpet, John **saw a star**, representing an angel, that **had fallen from heaven to earth**. Although the term "fallen" could suggest a demon, this angel is given **the key to the shaft** (Gk. *phreatos*, "well, pit") **of the abyss**, which houses a horde of demonic fiends (9:3,7-11). God would not likely entrust a key to the demonic prison to another demon. Instead, this angel later chains and locks up the Devil inside the abyss (20:1).

The "theological geography" of Revelation's universe is three-tiered: heaven, earth, and the ABYSS (Gk. *abussou*, "bottomless, unbounded, immeasurable depth," from the negative alpha privative prefix, *a*, "no, not, without," and *buthos*, "depth, the deep"; cp. Lk 8:31; Rm 10:7). Angels come *down* to earth from heaven and demons come *up* to earth from the abyss. "Abyss" generally refers to an underground pit considered to be a present holding place and the eventual destination for the Devil and his demons (Rv 9:1-2,11; 11:7; 17:8; 20:1,3). The imagery of the abyss is as the prison for evil spirits (Jd 6), where angels are described as "kept with eternal chains in darkness for the judgment of the great day." Wherever the abyss is actually located and whatever its appearance, the final dwelling place of wicked humans and the demons is not the abyss but the "lake of fire" (Rv 20:14).

9:3-6 Emerging from the depths of the smoke-filled shaft are hordes of **locusts**. People of the ancient Near East feared locust plagues because of the widespread devastation wreaked on the land. In the five months spanning spring and late summer, millions of locusts could emerge from the desert, devouring all vegetation and bringing economic ruin on the region.

In contrast to the plagues of locusts common to the ancient world, the locusts John saw were ordered **not to harm the grass of the earth, or any green plant, or any tree, but only people who do not have God's seal on their foreheads**. Those with "God's seal" would presumably include the 144,000 and any converts (see 7:2-8). To bring "harm" upon the earth dwellers, the locusts were given power like that of earthly **scorpions** with stingers to **torment** the earth dwellers for a limited period of time, **five months**, but the plague's severity would be such that the **people** would **seek death** in vain. The stings would not kill the earth dwellers, for **death will flee from them**. Their torture would continue until the demonic army came forth to slaughter them at the sixth trumpet. Rather than devouring vegetation, these demonic locusts brought the earth dwellers pain, terrorizing and demoralizing them without mercy. TORMENT (Gk. *basanisthēsontai*, "torture, inflicting severe pain or distress," 9:5; see also 14:11; 18:7,10,15) refers to the testing of metals by a touchstone. The purity of gold or silver would be determined, for example, by the color of the streak left when rubbed against the black stone. See also 11:10; 12:2; 14:10; 20:10; Mk 5:7; Lk 8:28.

9:7-10 The imagery John used to describe the locusts' appearance is lurid and repulsive. The repeated word **like** speaks of comparison, not bare literalism.

- **On their heads were something like gold crowns** (v. 7), as crowns of usurpers claiming authority and power they do not possess. God ultimately loans them the temporary power to accomplish their fiendish task.

- **Their faces were like men's faces; they had hair like women's hair** (vv. 7-8). The locusts' human faces depicted intelligence, suggesting that they are not inanimate objects but rather spiritual beings.

- **They had chests like iron breastplates** (v. 9), a description emphasizing their preparedness for battle and their terrifying invincibility. No one will be able to defeat this fierce military.

9:11-12 The leader, or **king**, of the destructive locusts is called **the angel of the abyss**, whose name is given as **Abaddon** (Heb.) or **Apollyon** (Gk.). Both words are literally translated "destroyer." Just as Death and Hades were personified in the fourth seal, here destruction took on similar form. Even as the earth dwellers persisted in their worship of demons (Rv 9:20), the very objects of their worship turn on them in violent contempt and cruelty, eager to destroy them—a sad irony.

The Sixth Trumpet or Second Woe (9:13-21)

9:13-14 The blowing of the sixth **trumpet** is followed by **a voice**, probably from the angel who offered the prayers at the altar of incense coming **from the four horns of the gold altar that is before God** (cp. 8:3). He ordered **the sixth angel** to **release the four angels bound at the great river Euphrates**, who like generals, led into battle a fearsome army. This army is a literal combat force.

The **EUPHRATES**, sometimes simply called "the great river," figures prominently throughout the Bible (9:14) beginning as one of the rivers flowing out of the garden of Eden (Gn 2:14) and later coming to be associated with the dreaded enemies of Israel such as Assyria, Babylon, and Persia, who attacked Israel by crossing over the great river. In the first century, the Euphrates served as the eastern border of the Roman Empire, and it was again connected with feared enemies, primarily the Parthians (see Rv 6:2). This judgment from the four angels of the Euphrates prepared the way for the sixth bowl (16:12) in which the river dried up completely, allowing safe passage for the "kings from the east" to assemble their vast armies for the "the battle of the great day of God" (16:14).

9:15-16 The four angels, by inference with God's permission, were released with a singular purpose: **to kill a third of the human race** (v. 15). This number sounds outlandish and impossible until this army's size is noted: **200 million**. Can you imagine the deaths of a third of the human population? With a world population of about six billion today, two billion people would be dead, with some 30 people killed by each of the mounted troops—more than the accumulated deaths of all twentieth-century wars. The horror of this disaster was compounded by the fact that God had prepared them beforehand for this very **hour, day, month, and year**. The timing of this massacre was not only within the predetermined plan of God but also precisely timed to the very hour. The Devil, a murderer from the beginning (Jn 8:44), would surely feel great satisfaction from this terrible conquest, but his eternal doom was fast approaching.

John's statements **I heard their number** (Rv 9:16), "I saw . . . in my vision"

(v. 17) may express his urgency to remind his readers that he heard and saw what he was recording. John could well have been stating insistently what he saw and heard because the vision was so astounding that his readers might not believe him.

9:17-19 What did this destructive cavalry look like? The **breastplates** of the **horsemen** were multicolored—**fiery red, hyacinth blue, and sulfur yellow**—and their horses have heads like lions. The three colors probably correspond to what was spewed from the horses' **mouths—fire, smoke, and sulfur** (Gk. *theiou*, "brimstone," vv. 17-18; cp. Lk 17:29)—all of which were said to be the cause of death for **a third of the human race**. Surely the horror one would feel upon encountering one of these evil warriors cannot be exaggerated.

9:20-21 The chief sin **of the people** is described as their worship of **demons and idols**. How astounding that this outpouring of destruction and bloodthirsty hatred for mankind would not prompt the earth dwellers to seek God's mercy. Once again they turned to their idolatry and demon worship! Even with a third of the earth's population dead, they do not cease from their

- **murders** (Gk. *phonōn*, "slaughter"; cp. Mt 15:19; Rm 1:29; Heb 11:37),

- **sorceries** (Gk. *pharmakōn*, "magic arts" associated with idolatry, "preparation, use, or administration of drugs or poison, i.e., a magic potion or remedy"; cp. Rv 18:23; Gl 5:20),

- **sexual immorality** (Gk. *porneias*, "illicit sexual intercourse"), or

- **thefts** (Gk. *klemmatōn*, "stolen goods, act of stealing").

This lengthy reference to the earth dwellers' unwillingness to repent reveals that even in these horrific plagues, God's purpose was for them to repent and be saved.

Heart to Heart:
How Could God Let This Happen?

As we come face to face with the horrors of the fifth and sixth trumpets, an important, yet difficult question inevitably arises: How could a good God allow the powers of darkness to commit such atrocities against a world He is supposed to love (Jn 3:16)? This question is not new to the Bible or human experience. Upon witnessing the spiritual decay of Israel and then the nation's approaching invasion by the Babylonian Empire, the prophet Habakkuk asked: "Why do You tolerate wrongdoing?" (Hab 1:3a). The Lord's answer is twofold:

* *God has the right to use whatever tools He desires, even the wicked, to bring about His will (Hab 1:6-11).*

* *Although in God's purposes the wicked may be allowed to triumph for a time, their judgment is assuredly coming (Hab 2:2-20).*

In considering the terrors of the demonic forces that will one day ravage the earth dwellers, these truths, however difficult to understand, are true. In some way, demons can be used by a good and just God to bring about His higher purpose. And, while the demons are given power for a season, the time is short until they take their place in the lake of fire forever.

The First Interlude Vision
(10:1-11)

Like chapter 7, the interlude between the sixth and seventh trumpets is divided into two major visions: John and "the little scroll" and the two witnesses who prophesy. The interlude magnifies the role of God's people during the events described, encouraging them in light of the terrible nature of the trumpets. Both visions present a running theme of prophecy—not in the sense of foretelling (future predictions), but of forth-telling (present commands), wherein God's people speak His truth to their respective generations. This interlude also introduces the symbolic time span of the great tribulation, "42 months" (11:2) plus "1,260 days" (11:3), along with the "beast" (11:7).

10:1-4 With the angel's booming cry, **like a roaring lion**, John heard **the seven thunders** speak (v. 3; cp. Ps 29:3). John attempted to record what "the seven thunders" said in obedience to his commission to write (Rv 1:19), but he was prevented from doing so by **a voice from heaven** (10:4). Instead, he was to **seal up** (Gk. *sphragison*, "set a seal upon for safekeeping, to keep hidden or secret, to authenticate," v. 4; cp. 7:3-5,8; 10:4; 20:3; 22:10; Jn 3:33; 6:27) what they said, emphasizing the prerogative of God to decide what will be revealed to His people and what will remain hidden (see Dt 29:29).

10:5-7 The angel assumed a familiar posture of oath-taking—he **raised his right hand to heaven**, swearing by the eternal God (v. 6):

- **There will no longer be an interval of time** (v. 6). In Daniel 12:6-7, the important question was, "How long until the end?" but the response to Daniel was that only God knows. Yet, the angel proclaimed that there would be no more delay before the end.

- **God's hidden plan** (Gk. *mustērion*, "secret, mystery," probably referring to all of redemption history, especially Old Testament verses about the return of Christ and the establishment of His kingdom on earth) **will be completed** (Gk. *etelesthē*, "brought to a close, executed or fulfilled according to a plan, promise, or command; finished") when the seventh angel's trumpet sounds. Without saying the Day of the Lord was not in progress with the beginning of the trumpets, the delay of its swiftness to completion was noted. The aorist passive phrase "will be completed" is probably an instance in which a future event coming as the consequence of a condition is being looked upon as though it had already happened. The emphasis would be on the certainty of its completion.

- **God announced** (Gk. *euēggelisen*, "proclaimed good news, delivered glad tidings"; cp. 14:6) the plan **to His servants the prophets** (10:7; see Am 3:7). Both the Old and New Testament prophets announced and awaited the consummation of God's "hidden plan," to which they were privy to only a small portion.

10:8-11 The events of this section closely parallel the commissioning of the prophet Ezekiel (Ezk 3:1-3), while also containing allusions back to Jesus taking the scroll (Rv 5:1-8). Debate has arisen over the identity of **the little scroll** (Gk. *biblaridion*, "small book, or written document") lying open in **the angel's hand** (vv. 9-10; 10:2,9,10). It is either the same scroll as in 5:8 (now appearing "little" in the hand of the immense angel) or a different scroll still intended to parallel the Lamb's scroll in significant ways. Possibly, in John's scroll a portion of the end times prophecy originally contained in the first scroll is to be seen.

John participated in a living parable designed by God to illustrate both the sweet and bitter nature of the prophecy for His people (10:9-11; cp. Ezk 1:1-3). The angel instructed John to **eat it** (Rv 10:9). Consuming God's word, a common theme in the Old Testament (Ps 19:10; Pr 24:13-14; Jr 15:16), means to take Scripture's message to heart and put it to work in your life. The angel also warned John that it would be **bitter** in his **stomach** (Gk. *koilia*, "the whole belly," figuratively "the innermost part of man," from *koilos*, "hollow," Rv 10:9-10) but **sweet as honey** in his **mouth**.

The point here is twofold.

- For John and all heralds of God's word, the message of God is pleasing to consume, yet often bitter in its delivery. Tension arose between the heavy burden of being God's mouthpiece and the probable rejection by those who refused to receive God's message.

- While the end times hold much sweetness and promise for those who are followers of Jesus, much sorrow and bitterness will also come, especially for those followers of Christ still on the earth (such as the 144,000). As witnesses to God, this truth is a difficult burden to bear.

Only after John consumed and digested the scroll did his further orders arrive. The word translated **about** (Gk. *epi*, "against, concerning") should probably be rendered "against" in keeping with John's prophecies concerning the nations throughout the remainder of the book. While the appearance of this fourfold list (Rv 1–9) referred positively to the worldwide distribution of God's people, its appearance from now on refers negatively to the nations in rebellion against God and His people (see 13:7; 17:15). Yet, these same rebellious nations remain the aim of God's redemptive purposes (14:6).

The Second Interlude Vision (11:1-14)

11:1-2 The second part of the interlude vision is considered by many to be the most difficult vision to interpret. There seem to be as many different interpretations of this chapter as there are interpreters.

After John's consumption of "the little scroll" and his command to prophesy, he was included in yet another living parable. He **was given a measuring reed like a rod**, which would have been a long, lightweight, hollow cane often used to measure the length of things. John was told to **measure God's sanctuary**, along with **the altar** and the worshipers, instructions paralleling Ezekiel's vision (Ezk 40:3,5) in which the measuring of the temple represents God's possession and protection of His people. In John's case, the meaning is similar: God will preserve those who worship Him during the great tribulation.

Throughout Revelation, SANCTU- ARY (Gk. *naon*, "temple") is used to describe only the heavenly temple of God, specifically referring to the sanctuary, i.e., the holy place and the holy of holies, in the temple at Jerusalem, but the earthly temple had actually been destroyed by the Romans in AD 70. Some interpreters conclude from the presence of the temple in this vision that there will be a rebuilding of the temple in Jerusalem prior to the great tribulation.

Scripture speaks of five different temples:

- Solomon's temple, which was destroyed by Nebuchadnezzar in 587 BC;

- the temple of Zeruabbabel, which Antiochus Epiphanes pillaged and desecrated in 168 BC;

- Herod's temple, which was destroyed by Titus in AD 70;

- the temple described here (Rv 11), which will be built during the great tribulation; and

- the millennial temple described in Ezekiel 40–47.

Yet, those who were in **the courtyard outside the sanctuary**, probably referring to God's people who were not yet in His presence (like the 144,000), would suffer violence and persecution from **the nations**. God limited the time that the nations had to **trample** (Gk. *patēsousin*, "tread on, crush under foot, desecrate, insult, treat with contempt"; cp. 14:20; 19:15; Lk 10:19; 21:24) **the holy city**, however, to **42 months** (Rv 11:2). God would deliver the faithful still on the earth into the hands of sinners for a limited amount of time (see Mk 9:31). Though they would be conquered physically (Rv 13:7), they were "sealed" by God and could not be conquered spiritually. The fate of those in the "courtyard outside of the sanctuary" was further described in the vision of God's "two witnesses," which followed.

This time period of "42 months" is one of three ways Daniel expressed his prophecy:

- three and a half years (11:2; Dn 7:25; 9:27; 12:7,11-12)

- "1,260 days" (Rv 11:3; 12:6) and

- "times, time, and half a time" (12:4).

Due to its connection to Daniel's prophesied seven-year period, along with its events, such as the reign of antichrist and the persecution of believers, one can conclude that the "42 months" refers to a limited time in which God allows Satan through antichrist to triumph while God's people, particularly the faithful remnant of Israel, are to be persecuted and killed.

Although these time measurements appear cryptic to modern readers, people in John's day would have recognized instantly the connection of his words to Daniel's prophecy (cp. Dn 9:24). There is no reason to doubt that these time references are precisely literal in their fulfillment. The great tribulation period will be terribly intense but ultimately limited by God.

11:3-6 Directly connected to John's prophetic "measuring" of the temple is the episode involving God's **two witnesses**, who will personally embody and generally represent the fate of God's people left on the earth—the 144,000 and all those who repent—throughout the great tribulation period. The fact that these men die and are resurrected would suggest viewing these two figures as historical men who will appear and function as prophets of God during the end times.

Just as the Lord gives these "witnesses" to the nations to be trampled (11:2), He also gives them **power** to **prophesy** in His name (v. 3). Their prophetic ministry is for a limited time, **1,260 days**, like the "42 months" above, and is accompanied by sorrow and mourning for the sins of the people. The description of the witnesses—as **the two olive trees and the two lampstands that stand before the Lord of the earth** (v. 4)—connects them with a similar vision (Zch 4:2-6), in which the gold lampstand represents the Spirit of God and the olive trees represent two men of God—namely, Joshua the high priest and Zerubbabel the governor (Zch 4:14).

Apparently a similar meaning is intended here but with different men and in a different time. The emphasis, however, is clear: The Holy Spirit will be upon the two witnesses as they prophesy upon the earth.

The earthly ministries of Moses and Elijah serve as the background for the signs the two witnesses could perform **if anyone wants to harm them**:

- **fire comes from their mouths and consumes their enemies** (Rv 11:5);

- **power** (Gk. *exousian*, "authority") **to close the sky so that it does not rain**;

- **power over the waters to turn them into blood**; and

- power **to strike the earth with any plague whenever they want** (v. 6).

In this way, the witnesses will proclaim the word of God and manifest the judgment of God to the earth dwellers.

11:7-10 Following their three-and-a-half-year ministry, the two witnesses will **finish their testimony**, and God will allow the forces of evil to **conquer** (Gk. *nikēsei*, "be victorious," v. 7; see 2:7) **them** for a time (recalling the vision of the "courtyard outside the sanctuary," 11:2). The perpetrator of the witnesses' murder is **the beast that comes up out of the abyss**, a character identified with the antichrist figure later in the book (13:1; 17:8), who is joined by the earth dwellers in hating God's people and who **celebrate** and **gloat over** the witnesses' deaths **for three and a half days** following their murder (11:10). Their contempt is so great that they even refuse to bury the two dead **bodies**, a sign of great scorn and disrespect in the ancient world.

The "witnesses" are said to remain **in the public square of the great city, which is called, prophetically, Sodom and Egypt, where also their Lord was crucified**, indicating that John had Jerusalem in mind. What an incredible tragedy that the city of Jerusalem—once the center of worship for the one true God—would by this point in history be so wicked and unrepentant as to be identified with the godless regions of Sodom and Egypt (see Hs 8:13; 9:3; Jl 3:19). Clearly the task of the two witnesses and all other witnesses for Christ during this time is to maintain their faithfulness to the Lord Jesus even in the face of persecution and death.

11:11-12 The earth dwellers' rejoicing is short-lived, for **after the three and a half days**, God resurrects the two witnesses, powerfully displaying their triumph over death and the evil one. When faced with the power of God, all who saw the two witnesses were filled with **great fear**. The exaltation of the two witnesses teaches that while the faithful will be persecuted and killed, those who persevere to the end will be vindicated by God in due time (6:11; 19:2). God's elect will not be defeated by death. Even against overwhelming odds, God's people will ultimately be victorious.

11:13-14 Following the ascension of the witnesses, another **violent earthquake** strikes the earth. This time **a tenth of the city** (of Jerusalem) **fell, and 7,000 people were killed**. Yet, as is always the case in the judgments of God, the outpouring of wrath was accompanied by a desire for repentance. While the previous instances of God's judgment were met with unrepentant hearts in the earth dwellers, apparently in this case, many were actually converted to Christ. This interpretation is debated by some, for it only says, **the survivors** (Gk. *loipoi*, "the rest, those remaining") . . . **gave glory to the God of heaven** (v. 13). Even in the midst of tremendous suffering and worldwide upheaval, some will indeed respond to God's judgment and turn to Christ. The gospel remains "God's power

for salvation to everyone who believes" (Rm 1:16).

The Seventh Trumpet or Third Woe (11:15-19)

11:15 With the sounding of the seventh **trumpet**, the reader is surely expecting another terrible judgment to befall the earth. Instead, attention is directed back to **heaven**, where John heard **loud voices** exuberantly announcing the reign of God in the world. Though Satan claimed kingship over the world for a time, even being called the "prince of this world" (Jn 12:31; 14:30; 16:11), God would publicly denounce his reign and remove him from power. With the end of God's judgment approaching, these heavenly voices are focusing attention on what is to come: the eternal and blessed reign **of our Lord and of His Messiah**.

11:16-18 Because of this great and powerful announcement, **the 24 elders** present a statement of praise to God with expressions of thanks for His person and work as well as anticipatory remarks about what was to come. These references to future events included the judgment of **the dead**, the rewarding of God's **servants**, and the complete destruction of **those who destroy the earth**, probably a reference to the earth dwellers (v. 18).

11:19 At the end of the 24 elders' worship, John witnessed **God's sanctuary** open **in heaven**. The depiction of God's dwelling place began as a throne room (chap. 4), but the addition of an incense altar unveils God's heavenly temple (8:3; 9:13). The appearance of **the ark of His covenant**, one of the most important religious symbols for the Israelite religion, is a climactic moment in this vision of heaven. The "ark" was the central sign of God's presence among them and so sacred that it was closed off by a veil to prevent human contact. Yet, when the Babylonians invaded and destroyed Jerusalem in 586 BC, it was lost to the Israelites and never recovered. Thus, John was seeing the heavenly counterpart to the ancient ark, which had been missing for centuries (Heb 8:5; 9:23-24).

TWO GREAT SIGNS AND THEIR INTERPRETATION (12:1-17)

In the Roman culture of John's day, emperors commonly used the Greek myths to explain and affirm belief in their own divinity. Emperor Domitian, who was reigning when John received Revelation, exploited his identification with the Greek sun god Apollo for this very purpose, giving him and others like him a convenient excuse for persecuting Christians.

John witnessed a story of cosmic proportions—a great spectacle displayed in the sky, telling the dramatic story of God's plan to redeem His people and triumph over the forces of evil through His Son. The first part of the drama displays what had happened in salvation history up to the time of John's writing (12:1-6), while the second part discloses events yet to come in the drama's outworking (12:7-18).

Two Signs in Heaven: The Woman and the Dragon (12:1-6)

12:1-6 The great cosmic story begins with **a great sign** (Gk. *sēmeion*, "portent, unusual or miraculous occurrence serving as an omen, warning or forecast," v. 1; also 12:3; 13:13,14; 15:1; 16:14; 19:20). The sky becomes the stage for God's dramatic story of salvation history. **A woman** appeared, **pregnant** and crying out in **labor** (Gk. *ōdinousa*, "feeling the pains of childbirth, being in travail") **and agony** (Gk. *basanizomenē*, "torment, distress"; see 9:5) as the time of her delivery drew near (12:2).

To Roman Catholics, this glorious woman is the Virgin Mary, "Queen of Heaven." However, the symbolism of the vision suggests a deeper meaning. The threefold description of her splendor arises out of Joseph's dream of "the sun, the moon, and 11 stars" bowing down to him (Gn 37:1-9). In ancient Jewish literature, 12 stars often represented the 12 tribes of Israel. The Old Testament also contains imagery of Israel as the bride of *Yahweh*. This woman then represents the people of God, particularly the nation Israel, anticipating the coming Messiah. The woman's beauty stands in stark contrast to the next signs of the **great fiery red dragon** (Rv 12:3) as well as the "notorious prostitute" (17:1).

The "**WOMAN** (Gk. *gunē*, 12:1) clothed with the sun" is the first of three major female characters that play a significant part in the drama of Revelation. The woman of chapter 12 represents Israel, the nation through whom would come Messiah. Yet, what becomes of her and the nation she represents, following her escape from the "dragon" under the protection by God (12:6,14)? The other two female characters are: "Babylon the Great, the Mother of Prostitutes" (17:5) and the "wife" of the Lamb (19:7). The Old Testament imagery of the "wife of *Yahweh*" (chap. 12) seems to merge with the New Testament concept of the "bride of Christ" (chap. 19) so that by the triumphant "marriage of the Lamb," the two women have essentially become one (19:7). This understanding is further supported by the imagery in the new Jerusalem combining Israel and the church, which is also described as the "wife of the Lamb" (21:9).

Another sign appeared in heaven—"a great fiery red dragon" (Gk. *drakōn*, "great serpent") with **seven heads and 10 horns, and on his heads were seven dia-**

dems. The "seven heads" suggest cunning, while the "seven diadems" represent blasphemous claims of supremacy. From Daniel's vision of a 10-horned beast, the 10 horns seem to indicate immense power (Dn 7:7,20), which was illustrated as the "dragon" **swept away** (Gk. *surei*, "draw or drag away" as before a judge or to punishment or prison; cp. Jn 21:8; Ac 8:3; 14:19; 17:6) **a third of the stars in heaven**, throwing **them to the earth** (Rv 12:4). Some have suggested that "a third of the stars" is a reference to the angels who followed Satan in his rebellion against God and were thus cast to the earth. Who is this fearsome dragon?— "the Devil and Satan, the one who deceives the whole world" (v. 9). The **dragon** (Gk. *drakōn*, a synonym for the word translated "serpent"; cp. Gn 3:1) represents Satan (Rv 12:9). The multiple heads, horns, and diadems were allusions to his power, wealth, and prestige (v. 3; cp. Dn 8:10; 2 Co 4:4). He was intent on destroying the child (Rv 12:4). The great **dragon** situated himself **in front of the woman**, so that when she gave birth, **he might devour her child** (v. 4), a **Son**, the promised Messiah of Israel (v. 5). This dramatic account alludes to the prophecy found in Genesis 3:15. Both Herod's slaughter of Bethlehem's babies and the crucifixion are examples of the Devil's attempts to annihilate the Messiah.

If the woman is the protagonist of the heavenly drama and the dragon is the antagonist, then the woman's "Son" is the hero. He is **a male** (Gk. *arsen*, a word specifically denoting the male gender; cp. v. 13; Mt 19:4; Mk 10:6; Lk 2:23; Rm 1:27; Gl 3:28) **who is going to shepherd all nations with an iron scepter**, a reference to the messianic king of Israel (Ps 2). The "nations" are not the people of God, and the Son's use of the "iron scepter" to shepherd them is a reference to His judgment (Rv 2:27). Before the dragon could

devour him, the Son **was caught up** (Gk. *hērpasthē*, "snatched up or away") **to God and to His throne** (v. 5). John fast-forwarded from the birth to the ascension of Jesus with a focus on His destiny to rule the nations. This heavenly drama does not gloss over the crucifixion and resurrection of Jesus, which truths have already been recognized (chap. 5) with Christ as the slain yet risen Lamb. The vision that John was seeing emphasized protection by God, the same theme played out in detail in chapters 10 and 11.

Under God's nurturing care, the woman would be **fed** (Gk. *trephōsin*, "nourished, supported, nurtured," Rv 12:6) **there for 1,260 days** (11:2-3). During the limited time of great suffering at the end of the age, God would spiritually protect the remnant of faithful Israel still on the earth, also pictured in the sealing of the 144,000 (7:1-8). Many will still be persecuted, conquered, and killed, but they will overcome Satan through "the blood of the Lamb and by the word of their testimony" (12:11). The 1,260 days synchronizes with the timeframe during which the two witnesses were prophesying.

The Dragon Thrown Out of Heaven (12:7-17)

12:7-9 The dragon would not triumph in this battle (v. 8) but experience humiliating defeat, as he is unmasked and revealed as **the ancient serpent** (Gk. *ophis*, "snake") . . . **the Devil and Satan**. Many have asked when this "war in heaven" occurred. Didn't Jesus ultimately defeat Satan on the cross? Why did the Devil have a "place" in heaven in the first place? The Devil appeared in the garden of Eden as the already fallen serpent (Gn 3:1-15), which assumes that sometime in the unrecorded past he had sinned and been cast down to earth. This fall of Satan's angels from heaven is clearly chronicled by Peter (2 Pt 2:4) and Jude

(Jd 6) as well as Jesus, who reported that he saw Satan "fall from heaven like a lightning flash" when the apostles returned from casting out demons (Lk 10:18), and very probably by Isaiah (Is 14) and Ezekiel (Ezk 28) in the dirges on the kings of Tyre and Babylon, which appear to focus on more than just the monarchs of those two countries.

This reference seems to point to a future time shortly before the return of Christ, when the Devil is finally excluded from *any* access to the presence of God (Rv 12:7). Up to this point, he had been allowed limited admission to heaven's throne room, where he went to appear before God and accuse God's people (12:10; Jb 1:6-12). Yet, after this final battle between the angels of light and the angels of darkness, Satan and his demons will be cast out forever and take their "last stand" on the earth before being cast into the lake of fire (Rv 20:10).

12:10-12 The drama halts momentarily as **a loud voice in heaven** proclaims the threefold significance of Satan's expulsion:

- It reveals **the salvation ... power** and **kingdom of our God**.

- It reveals **the authority of His Messiah**.

- It means that **the accuser** (Gk. *katēgōr*, "one who blames, attacks, incriminates, brings charges against another," from *kata*, "toward," and *agora*, "assembly or public place of assembly" for public debate or trial, v. 10) **of our brothers has been thrown out**.

Just as the prayers of the saints have been ascending before the throne of God, the accusations of the Devil have been going up in a similar way. For this reason Jesus' intercession for believers in heaven is important (Rm 8:34; Heb 7:25).

Even though Christians have been accused and tormented by the Devil on a regular basis, they have also been overcoming him day by day. How is this victory accomplished?

- **The blood of the Lamb** cleanses them from the stain and guilt of sin, enabling them to stand before God spotless and undefiled (Rv 12:11). Because Christians are justified and forgiven in God's sight through faith, the Devil's accusations against them fail.

- They possess **the word of their testimony**, which also leads to a willingness to give up their lives for the cause of Christ (v. 11). Whether that means daily dying to self or literally dying a martyr's death, Christians overcome the Devil through their allegiance to Christ in the midst of suffering and persecution. In response to the Devil's downfall, the **heavens** and those **who dwell in them** are called to rejoice.

12:13-17 The scene of the drama now shifts from heaven to earth. After being cast out of heaven in the end times, **the dragon** now pursues **the woman who gave birth to the male**, hoping that, even if he cannot beat Michael and his angels, he can wipe out the people of God before his time is up (v. 13). Yet, God comes to the aid of the woman, giving her **two wings of a great eagle**, so that she may flee **to her place in the wilderness** (see 12:6) and be protected from **the serpent** (the serpent and the dragon are now John's interchangeable terms for the Devil) for **a time, times, and half a time** (v. 14; see discussion of "1,260 days" and "42 months" in chap. 11). The wings of an eagle are also pictured in the exodus of Israel from the Egyptian nation (Ex 19:4), in both cases serving as symbolic instruments of God's swift and powerful protection.

The story took a bizarre turn when John saw **the serpent spewed water like a river from his mouth**, desiring to **sweep her away** in the torrential flood (Rv 12:15). The attack comes from the mouth of the serpent, but the aid comes from the mouth of the earth, an unusual personification for Scripture, but **the earth opened its mouth and swallowed up** (Gk. *katepien*, "drank down, devoured, destroyed, overwhelmed"; cp. Heb 11:29) the floodwaters that **the dragon had spewed** (Rv 12:16).

Furious with his inability to destroy **the woman**, the dragon gave up and decided to go after the individual followers of Jesus instead, i.e., **the rest of her offspring** (Gk. *spermatos*, "seed, progeny, children, descendants" cp. Jn 7:42; 8:33,37; 1 Jn 3:9). If the woman is faithful Israel, then **her offspring** must also include the people converted to Christ throughout the time of tribulation (Rv 12:17). The Devil's rampage is described as waging **war**, indicating an all-out assault on the Christ followers remaining in the last days, most likely resulting in innumerable new martyrs (v. 17). The description of these believers as the woman's "offspring" refers again to Genesis 3:15, where hostility is prophesied between the "seed of the woman" and the "seed of the serpent." All the offspring of the woman—whether Jew or Gentile— **are those who keep the commandments of God and have the testimony about Jesus**. Faithful believers now and in the end times:

- have been personally transformed by the power of God through the atoning death of Jesus Christ (v. 11a);

- are faithful to their testimony regarding the eternal life found in Christ (vv. 11b); and

- do not falter in their personal allegiance to Jesus even in the face of intense opposition (v. 11).

THE TWO BEASTS AND THEIR DECEPTION (12:18–13:18)

Chapter 13 focuses on the "fury" of the dragon (12:12) and how he goes about waging "war" against the "offspring" of the woman (12:17). A "satanic trinity" emerges—the dragon, the antichrist, and the false prophet—in direct opposition to the holy triunity—the Father, the Son, and the Holy Spirit. The Devil's work is surely at its most deceitful when he is mimicking the person and works of God. Further, from an earthly perspective, the first beast (or antichrist) is political evil incarnated, while the second beast (or false prophet) is religious evil incarnated. These earthly evils have been around throughout world history, but in the last days political and religious abomination will come alive in two human beings—the antichrist and the false prophet. While John's descriptions accurately describe the beasts he saw, the language is purposely exaggerated and symbolic. Yet, even as the two beasts dominate and terrify the earth, clearly the Lord is still sovereign over their every move. They are "given" power (i.e., allowed by the Lord) for a time, but their destruction is imminent (vv. 5,7,15).

The Beast from the Sea (12:18–13:10)

12:18–13:4 Verse 18 serves as the transition between chapters 12 and 13. As the Devil waged war against the Christians still on the earth, he took a stand **on the sand of the sea**. Then, as if by the dragon's own evil creative design, **a beast** was raised from the ocean's depths. What John saw is probably better understood in the vernacular as a "monster."

Heart to Heart:
Waging Spiritual Warfare

Christian women easily can become "earth-bound" in their thinking, virtually unable to see beyond the material world into the heavenly realm, especially when the days seem like endless cycles of meals, errands, and other duties. Everyday activities, frequently thought of as boring or humdrum, do not seem to have any eternal significance. Yet, Revelation 12 offers a rare behind-the-scenes glimpse into the age-long struggle between the "serpent of old" and the God of the universe. The battle between good and evil for the souls of women and men is raging. Godly women participate in this timeless struggle in two ways.

- *You must remember that every action makes a difference. Obeying the commands of God must be foremost in your priorities (v. 17).*

- *You must hold fast to what you have. Your testimony regarding the abundant life found in Jesus Christ is your most valuable possession, to be cherished and nurtured, as well as shared (v. 17). You know and anticipate the triumph of God and His children in the end, but in the mean time, you must pursue the victorious Christian life with holy vigor and focused intensity.*

On the beast's heads, **blasphemous names** are written, an image probably alluding to the titles of divinity given to the Roman emperors of John's day. The water monster's description connects him to the four beasts seen by Daniel (v. 2; Dn 7:4-7). Each of the four beasts in Daniel's vision represented a separate evil empire, so this beast of the end times is a composite of all the evil empires throughout human history. As a political and military leader representing a major political power, this monster's purpose is to rival the kingdom of God in every way. For this reason, **the dragon gave** the beast **his power, his throne, and great authority** (v. 2).

13:5-8 Along with his assault of God, the antichrist blasphemed **His dwelling** (Gk. *skēnēn*, "tent, tabernacle"; also 15:5; 21:3)—**those who dwell** (Gk. *skēnountas*, "have or fix one's tabernacle, abide in a

tabernacle," 13:8; cp. 7:15; 12:12; 21:3; Jn 1:14) **in heaven** (cp. Rv 12:11), the believers before God's throne. These heaven dwellers were also seen rejoicing at the expulsion of Satan from heaven (12:12). Although the beast could not reach the heaven dwellers in God's presence, he could do great physical harm to those Christ followers still on the earth, i.e., the 144,000 and their converts. Although the beast **was permitted to wage war against the saints and to conquer them** (13:7), the martyrs of the earth could say with Paul, "For me, living is Christ and dying is gain" (Php 1:21). The people of God may be conquered in this life, but they will triumph over the Devil and his beast in the end. Even in the face of the antichrist's horrible cruelty and murderous intentions, the earth dwellers **will worship him**, revealing their true nature as those whose names were **not**

written from the foundation of the world in the book of life.

13:9-10 These verses form a parenthetical explanation by John designed to highlight the response expected from the church in light of these revelations. The phrase, **If anyone has an ear, he should listen**, was a "hallmark" of Jesus' teaching, and John's use of it would have drawn the church's attention back to their Lord. Verse 10 mirrors a prophecy proclaiming the inevitable coming of God's judgment (Jr 15:2). The parallel prophecy here probably focuses on a similar concept: Despite the horrific nature of the antichrist and his persecution of the saints, his coming is inevitable and should be anticipated. The people of God still on the earth will surely suffer during the reign of the beast. **Endurance** and **faith** are necessary in the lives of the saints.

The Beast from the Earth (13:11-18)

13:11-12 Following the rise of "the beast," John witnessed the ascent of **another beast**, the second helper and one who is to implement the agenda of the first beast in the dragon's cause (v. 11). The connection between these beasts of the water and earth is not found elsewhere in Scripture. This beast is characterized by deceit and purposely masks himself in the likeness of the Lord Jesus, but he speaks only the words of his true master, the Devil (see Mt 7:15). The second beast mimics the activity of the Holy Spirit, for he **exercises all the authority** of the antichrist; and as the world leader of what is an apostate religion, he **compels** the earth dwellers to **worship** him (Rv 13:12). Just as the Spirit of God glorifies the Son of God, so the earth monster glorifies the antichrist (Jn 16:14). John later referred to the second beast as the "false prophet" (Rv 16:13; 19:20; 20:10), a title empha-

sizing his role in propagating the worship of the first beast.

13:13-15 The works performed by the false prophet can be understood in a general way, yet their precise fulfillment cannot be known until they are revealed. His **great signs** mirror those of Elijah, Jesus, and even the two witnesses of chapter 11, and he uses them to seduce the allegiance of people to the antichrist.

The **GREAT** (Gk. *megala*, "strong, of great importance") **SIGNS** (Gk. *sēmeia*, "portent, unusual or miraculous occurrence serving as an omen, warning or forecast," vv. 13-14; also 12:1,3; 15:1; 16:14; 19:20) of the false prophet are a major focus of his work (cp. 2 Th 2:9). Through them, he mimics Jesus, the messianic prophet whose "signs" became the basis for His messianic claim in John's Gospel. But, unlike Christ and His miracles, the false prophet performs his works "**BEFORE** (Gk. *enōpion*, "in the presence or full view of") people" (Rv 13:13). The signs of Christ glorified the Father, but the signs of the false prophet glorify himself and the antichrist. The performance of such "great signs" by the false prophet reveals the satanic trinity's pretentious claim that the beast is the Christ. Whether the great signs of the second beast will be real or simply illusionary, Scripture clearly states how to deal with them (Dt 13:1-3a).

Through the display of his miraculous powers, the second beast **deceives** (Gk. *plana*, "leads away from the right way, causes to go astray") the earth dwellers and convinces them **to make an image of the beast** (v. 14). The readers in John's day would be very familiar with the construction of statues and images for worship by the Roman emperors. The false prophet will continue this idolatrous and profane practice, spreading its influence throughout the world.

In the pagan religious practices of Rome the people believed that the spirits of the gods actually came and resided inside the statues and sacred places dedicated to their worship. Many magicians and sorcerers capitalized on these beliefs, fabricating "miracles" that would give them both the praise of men and favor of the gods. The false prophet is essentially able to make the image "live" or at least give the impression of breathing and speaking much as a computerized robot or ventriloquist might do. The image is convincing to the people, inducing them to worship and instigating the murdering of those who refuse to pay it homage (v. 15). John does not indicate sleight of hand in his description.

13:16-18 The false prophet is not satisfied to require only the occasional acts of worship from the people, however. Every person on the earth, from the greatest and richest to the smallest and poorest, must give allegiance to the antichrist by receiving the beast's **mark** (Gk. *charagma*, "stamp, imprint, brand; idolatrous graven image," vv. 16-17; also 14:9,11; 16:2; 19:20; 20:4; Ac 17:29) on his person—the much debated "mark of the beast." The mark must be received on the person's **right hand** or **forehead**, a satanic parody of God's "marking" of His people in the sealing of the 144,000 (7:2-4). With the natural world and global economy in a state of distress throughout the great tribulation, the threat of being unable to **buy or sell unless he has the mark** would be persuasive indeed. Here, the possibility of a horrible scenario arises: When faced with your own death, you might find remaining faithful to Christ relatively easy, but what if your faithfulness to Him meant the deprivation of and possible death of your family? The emphasis on **everyone** being compelled to receive the beast's mark reveals one of the main themes (if not *the* main theme) of Revela-

tion: There is no neutral ground in the war between God and Satan. Not to belong to the Lord Jesus i**s to belong to the beast. All must choose whom they will serve.**

The mark of the beast is further described as **the beast's name or the number of his name ... 666** (13:18). The meaning of the number "666" compels consideration of at least three possibilities.

- In John's day giving proper names a distinguishing number by adding up the numerical value of their letters, a Hebrew system of numerology called *gematria*, was common. Some suggest that the murderous emperor Nero (AD 54–68), who forms the historical background for Revelation's antichrist figure, may be the "man" indicated by the number 666. The name "Nero Caesar," after being transliterated into Hebrew adds up to the value 666. However, the antichrist is not Nero.

- Some have suggested a more simplified explanation—that in Hebrew the numerical value of the Greek word for "beast" (*therion*) is 666.

- Seven is the symbolic number of completion and perfection and was often considered a heavenly number. Thus, the threefold rendering of the number six, falling just short of seven, is a symbolic reference to the absolute depravity of the beast. The satanic trinity sets itself up as a rival to the persons and work of the godhead, but it will always fail.

John's prescription that "the one who has **UNDERSTANDING** (Gk. *noun*, "mental or intellectual ability, reason as a capacity for recognizing spiritual truth or distinguishing good from evil"; cp. 17:9) must **CALCULATE** (Gk. *psēphisatō*, "count with pebbles, compute, reckon"; cp. *psēphon* in 2:17) the number of the beast" indicates that the early readers of Revelation probably understood exactly what John meant by 666. For contemporary interpreters, however, to admit your ignorance of the full understanding of the beast's name and number and accept the mystery is wiser. Whether or not the various theories have any merit, the truth remains: The number of the beast represents his imperfect and wicked nature. Therefore, anyone who receives his "mark" is also identifying himself with the beast's perverse character (13:16-17).

The sovereignty of God remains even in the face of the troubling and puzzling truths. Notice the frequency of the phrases "he was given" and "he was permitted" throughout chapter 13. Who exactly *gives* and *permits* the evil things in this period of time? Even the dragon, the antichrist, and the false prophet are dependent upon the permission and authority from God to accomplish their purposes. Although the Lord will ultimately destroy the Devil, for the sake of higher purposes beyond human comprehension, He allows Satan a small window of time during the great tribulation to have his way upon on the earth.

THE FIRSTFRUITS AND THE HARVEST (14:1-20)

Chapter 13 describes the war of the dragon against God and His saints. Chapter 14 describes the assured victory of God's purposes despite the dragon's rage in the last of a cycle of visions, which began in chapter 12. Seven "signs" mirroring the seven seals and trumpets can be observed:

- the conflict of the woman and the dragon (12:1-17);

- the persecution wrought by the beast from the sea (13:1-10);

- the persecution wrought by the beast from the earth (13:11-18);

- the appearance of the Lamb and the 144,000 on Mount Zion (14:1-5);

- the proclamation of the gospel by the first angel and the announcement of judgment by the second and third angels (14:6-13);

- the message of the Son of Man's harvest of the earth's believers (14:14-16); and

- the pronouncement of the wrath of God on the earth's unbelievers (14:17-20).

Each vision contained in these chapters contributes to the same overall theme of an urgent call: Whom will you follow—the beast or the Lamb? Following this theme, the first section of chapter 14 focuses on the fate of the redeemed 144,000 (14:1-5); the second section announces the last opportunity to repent before God's wrath is made complete (14:6-13); the third section is a picture of God's harvest of believers (14:14-16); and the fourth section is a picture of God's harvest of unbelievers (14:17-20).

The Redeemed of the Earth (14:1-5)

The scenes of chapter 14 are puzzling for many interpreters because the location and timing of their contents are inherently vague, probably because the subject matter is very broad—redemption and reward along with warning and final judgment. Yet, these pictures do indeed portray literal future events.

14:1 John's statement, **Then I looked**, changes the focus of the scene from the earth to heaven. We again encounter the **Lamb** and the **144,000** (7:1-8), but this time they are together standing **on Mount**

Zion, symbolizing in Jewish prophecy the place where the Messiah would gather His people. Here, Zion probably represents the heavenly Jerusalem (21:10), possibly indicating that the 144,000 have been martyred by this time. The point is that the Lamb stands in solidarity with the representatives of faithful Israel whether they are in heaven or still on the earth. Several contrasts stand out between the antichrist and his followers and the Lamb and the 144,000:

- The earth dwellers had the beast's mark on their foreheads (13:16-17), while the 144,000 **had His name and His Father's name written on their foreheads** (14:1).

- The dragon "stood on the sand of the sea" awaiting the rise of Antichrist (12:18), while the Lamb **stood** on Mount Zion in the presence of His victorious people (14:1).

- "The mark" of the beast was a brand of ownership and subservience, while "the name" of the Lamb was one of honor and blessing.

14:2-3 As John observed the 144,000 and the Lamb on Mount Zion, he heard offered unto God the incredible and joyous sound of singing **from heaven** (v. 2) with **a new song** that was so unique only they were able to **learn** it (v. 3). Its content most likely reflected another "new song" (5:9). The 144,000 are those **who had been redeemed** (Gk. *ēgorasmenoi*, "purchased," the vocabulary of buying and selling or doing business in the marketplace, 14:3-4; cp. 3:18; 5:9; 13:17; 18:11) **from the earth**; and while they are distinct from the church, both the church and they will share in the same blessings in the world to come (14:3).

14:4-5 The description of the 144,000 emphasizes their **blameless** (Gk. *amōmoi*,

"faultless; without blot, blemish, or disgrace," v. 5) character before God:

- **They have kept their virginity**; i.e., they were pure in their hearts.

- They **follow the Lamb wherever He goes**; i.e., they were faithful in their actions.

- **They were redeemed from the human race as the firstfruits for God and the Lamb**; i.e., they were sanctified in their character.

- **No lie** (Gk. *pseudos*, "conscious or deliberate falsehood," v. 5; cp. 21:27; 22:15; Jn 8:44; 1 Jn 2:21,27) **was found in their mouths**; i.e., they were virtuous in their speech.

FIRSTFRUITS (Gk. *aparchē*) is an Old Testament sacrificial image. The first and best parts of a farmer's crop were offered to the Lord as a sign of gratitude and as humble admission that the crop belonged to God. In the New Testament, "firstfruits" means "first among many." In His resurrection, Jesus is "the firstfruits of those who have fallen asleep" (1 Co 15:20); i.e., His resurrection guarantees the future resurrection of all believers. In Romans 11:16, the conversion of the Gentiles is perceived as the "firstfuits," the blessed beginning, of a great harvest still to come. In a similar way, John saw the 144,000 as a sacrificial offering to God in the last days, a guarantee of the great final harvest of all believers from the earth (Rv 14:14-16).

John's statement that the 144,000 are **the ones not defiled** (Gk. *emolunthēsan*, "soiled, stained, polluted," v. 4; cp. 3:4; 1 Co 8:7) **with women** is considered by many to be puzzling. Some have concluded from this statement that the 144,000 are all men who are literally celibate. Yet, it seems that since sexual immorality is used elsewhere in Revelation as representative of both spiritual and physical adultery, together with the appearance of "the mother of prostitutes" (chap. 17) as the embodiment of opposition to God, that the reference to the 144,000 as "not defiled with women" is primarily spiritual in its implication. The 144,000, then, refers to all Jewish believers who are morally and ethically pure and united to the Lord Jesus with **undefiled and uncompromised love.**

The Messages of Three Angels (14:6-13)

Next in the vision, John was confronted with the messages of three different angels. They progressively announce a final opportunity for the earth dwellers to repent, the looming judgment of Babylon the Great, and the eternal torment of those who follow the beast.

14:6-7 The content of this gospel message is similar to the way the apparent mass conversion in 11:13 was described: In light of His imminent judgment, **Fear** (Gk. *phobēthēte*, "have reverence or awe for, be afraid of") **God and give Him glory … Worship** (Gk. *proskunēsate*, "bow down, submit oneself to," 14:7; see 3:9) **the Maker of heaven and earth.** Just as the "violent earthquake" gave some earth dwellers the opportunity to "fear God" and "give Him glory" (chap. 11), this angel was offering the same to the entire world. The choice for all people is clear: Worship the Lamb and receive salvation, or worship the beast and receive judgment.

14:8 The **second angel** introduced **Babylon the Great**, an end-times empire of evil personified as a "notorious prostitute" (chap. 17). In Revelation, allusions to Babylon are cryptic references to historical Rome, the capital of the Roman world and also the center for propagating many abominable acts, including the persecution of Christians. The angel spoke of Babylon as **fallen**. Even though the city's destruction apparently will not be complete until chapter 19, this word choice emphasizes the absolute certainty of her judgment. In contrast to the purity of the 144,000, Babylon the Great **made all nations drink the wine of her sexual immorality** (used primarily in a spiritual sense), **which brings wrath**.

In the ancient world, WINE (14:8,10) was often used as a symbol of joyous merrymaking and of sinful decadence. In Scripture "wine" also can also refer to God's wrath as if it were being poured down the throats of the wicked. Here it refers to the adulterous practices of Babylon the Great, which inflames all the nations with passion for her immorality, like alcoholics being drawn irresistibly to the bottle. Yet, because both Babylon and the nations share in the debauchery, they will also share in the "wine of God's wrath," which is "mixed full strength" (v. 10). In John's day to dilute wine with water at least by half was common. To drink wine at its full strength, without water, was foolishness, leading inevitably to drunkenness. Here God has mixed His wine undiluted, thereby, in a sense, getting them "drunk" on His wrath. Unlike the effects of earthly wine, however, which wear off over time, the effects of God's wine of fury will never go away.

14:9-11 Babylon the Great is in league with the antichrist (chap. 17). She is to the beast what the bride of Christ is to the Lamb (19:7-8). Naturally then the declaration of judgment moves from the evil empire of Babylon to the people who are a part of it: **Anyone** who **worships the beast and his image and receives a mark on his forehead or on his hand**. Because they have spurned the love of God and His Son, those who follow after the Devil must receive the full extent of

God's wrath, which is depicted as wine at full strength, holding nothing back.

The idea of unbelievers being tormented (Gk. *basanisthēsetai*, "inflicted with pain, tortured," 14:10; see 9:5) with fire and sulfur before the holy angels and the Lamb is a disturbing image. That the Lamb and His angels will observe the suffering of unbelievers for all eternity is unlikely. More likely this reference is to their witnessing the proclamation of judgment and the beginning of the unbelievers' sentence in hell. In familiar biblical language, hell is described as a place of suffering that goes on forever and ever, with no rest (Gk. *anapausin*, "intermission," i.e., when activity, movement, and work stop for awhile, 14:11; cp. verb in v. 13) for its inhabitants. Those who swear allegiance to the antichrist instead of the Lamb have chosen their fate. God will not force His love on those who are determined to spurn it.

14:12-13 As in chapter 13, a message to the saints appeared within this vision. In light of the coming judgment of God, the saints must have endurance, implying that only those who keep (Gk. *tērountes*, "observe, guard"; see 1:3) the commandments of God and the faith in Jesus will be able to persevere (v. 12). A voice from heaven adds reassurance: Those who die in the Lord from now on are considered blessed. Far from being deemed a tragedy, martyrdom is considered a victory over Satan throughout the book of Revelation. The saints on the earth during the great tribulation must be prepared to join in "the fellowship of [Christ's] sufferings" (Php 3:10). Amazingly, the Spirit voices a response to this exhortation (Rv 22:17 is the only other place in the book where the Spirit speaks). In contrast to the eternal torment of unbelievers, those who persevere in their faith unto death will find rest (Gk. *anapaēsontai*, "cause or permit one to stop activity, movement or work for

awhile; refresh, recover strength," 14:13; cp. noun in v. 11) from their labors (Gk. *kopōn*, "troubles, intense work or toil," v. 13; cp. 2:2). And, the rewards of their works will await them in eternity. While the decision to defy the beast and worship the Lamb will not be easily made, the reward will be worth any sacrifice.

The Harvest of the Earth: Part One (14:14-16)

14:14-16 In the third vision of chapter 14, a continuation of the themes of redemption and judgment, the Greek text actually reads: "the one who was sitting on the cloud was like *a* son of man" instead of "*the* Son of Man" (v. 14), and there is considerable debate over whether or not this figure is Christ or simply another angel. The obvious allusion is to Daniel 7:13, where the "one like a son of man" is seen "coming with the clouds of heaven." In Revelation "Son of Man" refers to Christ (see 1:13).

The Son of Man has three characteristics (14:14):

• He was seated on a white cloud, a kind of ethereal throne indicating the glory and victory of Christ (cp. 4:4; 19:11,14).

• He had a gold crown on His head, indicating Christ's royal authority.

• He had a sharp sickle (Gk. *drepanon*, "pruning hook or curved knife" such as a reaper or vinedresser would use, from *drepō*, "pluck"; used only in Rv 14 and Mk 4:29) in His hand, conveying the finality and power of the last judgment.

While Jesus was on the earth, He did only those things that the Father told Him (Jn 5:19), and the harvest of the earth is no different. He receives the acknowledgement that the time ... has come from an angel of God's sanctuary and

Heart to Heart:
The Beatitudes of Revelation

" *B*lessed are the dead who die in the Lord from now on," is one of seven blessing statements in Revelation (14:13). These "beatitudes" of the Revelation, like the beatitudes in the Sermon on the Mount (Mt 5:2-12), are promises of God that frame the entire book with exhortations for our obedience (1:3; 22:14) and interrupt the narrative of Revelation (14:13; 16:15; 19:9; 20:6; 22:7) in order to direct the reader's attention to the rewards of those who are faithful to the Lord Jesus. Although the messages to the seven churches end in chapter 3, these blessings statements continue to urge believers to faithfulness and holy living. Below is a list of Revelation's seven beatitudes:

- "Blessed is the one who reads and blessed are those who hear the words of this prophecy and keep what is written in it, because the time is near" (1:3).

- "Blessed are the dead who die in the Lord from now on" (14:13).

- "Blessed is the one who is alert and remains clothed" (16:15).

- "Blessed are those invited to the marriage feast of the Lamb!" (19:9).

- "Blessed and holy is the one who shares in the first resurrection" (20:6).

- "Blessed is the one who keeps the prophetic words of this book" (22:7).

- "Blessed are those who wash their robes," i.e., are redeemed by the Lamb and rewarded for their obedience (22:14).

then begins His work (Rv 14:15). If the 144,000 were the "firstfruits" for God (14:4), then this gathering is the final great harvest of the redeemed, for at this time **the earth is ripe** (Gk. *exēranthē*, "dried up, withered, wasted away," v. 15; cp. 16:12; Mt 13:6; 21:19-20; Mk 3:1; 4:6; 5:29; 9:18; 11:20-21; Lk 8:6; Jn 15:6; Jms 1:11; 1 Pt 1:24). The Son of Man obeyed the will of His Father and **swung His sickle over the earth**, and it **was harvested** (Gk. *etheristhē*, "reaped; cut off or destroyed," Rv 14:16). Notice that this **harvest** (Gk. *therison*, "act of reaping, an ingathering," v. 15) is akin to the "gathering fruit for eternal life" described by Jesus (Jn 4:35-38).

The Harvest of the Earth: Part Two (14:17-20)

14:17-20 Another angel emerged from **the sanctuary in heaven** and, like the Son of Man, also carried **a sharp sickle** (v. 17) and received his orders from **yet another angel**, who was **from the altar** and **had authority over fire** (v. 18). The duties of the second angel associate him with the altar of incense, where the prayers of God's saints are heard before the throne (6:9; 8:3). This judgment is most certainly a response to those cries for justice. Instead of grain, this harvest is of **the clusters of grapes from earth's vineyard** (v. 18; cp. the grape harvest as a metaphor for God's judgment in Is 5:5;

63:2-3; Lm 1:15; and Jl 3:13). The **rip-ened** (Gk. *ēkmasan*, "flourish, reach maturity," from *akmē*, "climax, point, extremity, present," anglicized as "acme") state of the earth's **grapes** probably indicates that the full measure of sin and evil has been reached.

A WINEPRESS (Gk. *lēnon*, "tub, trough, or vat in which grapes were trodden," Rv 14:19) was a circular or square pit carved out of rock, lined with rocks, and then sealed with plaster. The exposed pit would be filled with grapes and then trampled by foot by several individuals. The grape juice then drained through a channel to collect in a vat below the pit, where it would be allowed to ferment. To imagine the blood of human beings being collected in this way is truly gruesome. The genuine severity of the judgment awaiting unrepentant humanity is beyond human comprehension.

The press is then **trampled** (Gk. *epatēthē*, "tread upon, crushed with the feet"; see 11:2) **outside the city** (14:20), probably a reference to the city of Jerusalem (11:8). To the Jews of John's day, being executed outside the city gate meant being cut off from the covenant people of God (Heb 13:12). Who does the trampling is most likely Christ's agent of divine wrath (cp. Rv 19:15). This picture of final judgment is truly horrifying. The distance covered by the **blood, about 180 miles**, is the length of Palestine from its northern to southern borders, depicting the greatest slaughter in history with the entire Holy Land covered in the blood of the wicked.

THE SEVEN LAST PLAGUES (15:1–16:21)

After the completion of the seven trumpets (11:15-19), a large interlude spanning chapters 12–14 reveals from a "bird's eye view" the great conflict between Satan and God's people (chaps. 12–13) and the promised final judgment of both the righteous and the wicked (chap. 14). Chapters 15 and 16 return to the sevenfold judgments by which God will carry out the final destruction of evil. Chapter 15 is an introduction to the seven bowl judgments, focusing on the preparation of the seven angels and the joy of the victorious martyrs. Chapter 16 details the "seven bowls of God's wrath" (16:1) as they are poured out upon the earth. The first four bowls affect the entire planet, but the last three bowls are concentrated upon the kingdom of the beast.

The Third Great Sign in Heaven (15:1-8)

15:1 This third **sign** (Gk. *sēmeion*; see 12:1,3) appears **in heaven**, but unlike the first two it is called **great and awe-inspiring** (Gk. *thaumaston*, "wonderful, marvelous, amazing, beyond human comprehension"). Why is this one so marvelous in John's sight? The sign is **seven angels with the seven last** (Gk. *eschatas*; see 1:17) **plagues**, and with them, **God's wrath will be completed** (Gk. *etelesthē*, "finished"; see 10:7). These bowls are not just last in the series of sevenfold judgments, but they are also the last judgments of history.

15:2-4 Beyond this sign, John **also saw** a vision of victorious saints standing on **a sea of glass mixed with fire** in front of the throne of God itself (cp. 4:6). They had **harps from God**, instruments of rejoicing and worship to be played as they sang praises to their Lord. This vision of their blessed state proves that when the beast conquers the saints by killing them (11:7; 13:7), he is actually conquered by the saints who are victorious over the temptations to compromise, over the burdens of this world, and over the powers of evil (12:11) and the Lamb (17:14).

The saints were singing **the song of God's servant Moses, and the song of the Lamb**. The "song of Moses" (Ex 15:1-19) differs greatly from the "song of the Lamb" (vv. 3-4). The two titles used for God here—**Lord God, the Almighty** and **King of the Nations**—are the two aspects most magnified in the book (cp. Ps 22:28; 47:8; 96:10; 97:1). The saints further worship the Lord by affirming that everyone will **fear and glorify** Him for three reasons:

• God's unique holiness;

• God's reign over **all the nations**; and,

• God's revelation of His **righteous acts**.

Although all the nations will certainly come and worship before the only true God, all people will not come to faith in Christ. Even in Revelation clearly most of the nations will refuse to repent (Rv 9:20-21; 16:9,11) and will face the final judgment (20:13-14). Yet, in the end, whether by force or by choice, "every knee" will bow and "every tongue . . . confess that Jesus Christ is Lord, to the glory of God the Father" (Php 2:10-11).

15:5-6 After seeing the victorious saints, John looked to see that the **heavenly sanctuary—tabernacle of the testimony—was opened** (v. 5), linking the heavenly temple with the tabernacle or tent of Israel's wilderness wanderings. The "testimony" refers to the stone tablets, which signified the Ten Commandments and the covenant of God with Israel stored in the ark (Ex 25:16; Dt 10:1-2). In the Old Testament, the holy of holies or the ark itself were often referred to as "the Testimony" (Ex 16:34; 27:21; Lv 16:13; Nm 1:50). **The seven angels** who emerge from the tabernacle with **seven plagues** were clothed in the **linen** garments of priests (Rv 15:6; cp. 1:13) and were the

instruments chosen by God to administer the final punishment to the nations.

15:7-8 Continuing the priestly imagery, **the seven angels** were given **seven gold bowls**, which are probably alluding to the golden saucers found on the table of showbread in the tabernacle, used for drink offerings to God (Ex 25:29; 27:3). These bowls are also connected to the "golden bowls" filled with incense and the prayers of the saints (Rv 5:8). This time, however, they are **filled with the wrath of God** (15:7), a response to the prayers of the saints (5:8; 8:3-5) and a sacred offering to the Lord.

After the angels received the bowls of wrath, **the sanctuary was filled with smoke from God's glory and from His power**. Throughout the Old Testament, smoke symbolizes the awe-inspiring presence of God, which makes understandable that **no one could enter the sanctuary**. "Moses was unable to enter the tent of meeting because the cloud rested on it, and the glory of the Lord filled the tabernacle" (Ex 40:34-35). The images of smoke, glory, and power are so closely tied to Old Testament worship that the outpouring of judgment must be viewed as a mysterious act of worship (chap. 16).

The First Three Bowls of Wrath (16:1-7)

16:1-2 The **loud voice from the sanctuary** (v. 1) probably belonged to God, and at His command, the first angel **poured out** (Gk. *ekcheete*, "distribute widely") **his bowl on the earth** (v. 2). This first of four plagues is focused upon the earth in a general sense. All people with the "mark of the beast" break out in SEVERELY PAINFUL SORES (Gk. *elkos*, "an abscessed or ulcerous sore, infected wound," v. 2; cp. Lk 16:21). With such affliction a person cannot walk, sit, or recline without acute pain, echoing the sixth Egyptian plague of boils on both people and animals (Ex 9:9-11).

16:3 The second bowl was **poured** directly **into the sea**, turning it **to blood like a dead man's**. The sea was the life-blood of the Roman Empire, so this total contamination of the waters would have spelled the complete ruin of their civilization. The sheer number of the rotting, stinking corpses of all the creatures of the sea is beyond imagination.

16:4-7 The third bowl was **poured out** on all of the fresh water sources—**the rivers and the springs of water**—and they also **became blood** (v. 4). Drinkable water is more necessary to sustain life on earth than anything but breathable air. This plague shortens the time for survival of the human race.

Almost as if anticipating the horror at this judgment, **the angel of the waters** responded with a defense of God's justice (v. 5). Just as the earth dwellers **poured out the blood of the saints and the prophets**, God has rightfully given them **blood to drink** (v. 6). This judgment was the beginning of what was promised to the martyrs (6:9-11). The full expression of their punishment, though, will not come until the judgment of Babylon the Great (19:2). In the midst of this judgment, God is still **righteous** and **the Holy One** (16:5). The threefold title "the one who is, who was, and who is coming" (1:4,8; 4:8) has been altered in the angel's praise, no longer including "who is coming," probably because the future had, in a sense, arrived, as the divine judgment was reaching its completion. He is no longer coming, for He is already here. **Someone from the altar**, probably the angel who presented the prayers of the saints (8:3-5), affirms this short doxology (16:7).

The Fourth Bowl (16:8-9)

16:8-9 The fourth angel's bowl is **poured out . . . on the sun**. Whereas in the fourth trumpet the power of the sun was taken away, in this judgment the sun's **power** is intensified, enabling it **to burn** (Gk. *kaumatisai*, "scorch"; cp. Mt 13:6; Mk 4:6) **people with fire** (Rv 16:8). Whether this is a scattered occurrence of deadly solar flares or one horrible blast of heat, the result is the same. The hearts of the earth dwellers are so hardened against the Lord that instead of turning for help to God, who holds **the power over these plagues**, they curse His **name** and refuse to **give Him glory** (v. 9). This response ties the earth dwellers' unrepentant hearts to a rejection of the "eternal gospel" preached by the angel (14:6-7; 16:11,21).

The Fifth Bowl (16:10-11)

16:10-11 The judgment of **the fifth** bowl is the first of three directly related to the beast and his kingdom. The angel **poured out** the plague **on the throne of the beast** and the effect is that **his kingdom was plunged into darkness** (v. 10), alluding first to the Egyptian plague of darkness described as so thick that it "can be felt" (Ex 10:21) and yet also resembling references to the place of final judgment, the "outer darkness" where there will be "weeping and gnashing of teeth" (Mt 8:12; 22:13; 25:30; Lk 13:28; 2 Pt 2:17). That the earth dwellers **gnawed** (Gk. *emasōnto*, "chewed," from *massō*, "handle, squeeze," v. 10) **their tongues from pain** suggests that they were receiving a small preview of an eternity in "outer darkness." How long the darkness remained is not known, but the earth dwellers again refused to **repent of their actions** (v. 11).

The Sixth Bowl (16:12-16)

16:12 The contents of **the sixth** bowl are **poured out . . . on the great river Euphrates** and it causes **its water** to be **dried up** (Gk. *exēranthē*, "wither, stop";

see 14:15). This event mirrors the drying of the Red Sea for the safe crossing of the Israelites but for the purpose of invasion, not protection. God intended this judgment to make **way for the kings from the east** who are joining all the nations of the earth for the "battle of the great day of God, the Almighty" (16:14; 19:19).

16:13-14 In reaction to the judgments poured out upon them and their followers, the satanic trinity finally responded. John saw **three unclean spirits like frogs** come out of the mouths of the dragon, beast, and false prophet (v. 13). The action of these unclean spirits gives insight into what they represent: **They are spirits of demons performing signs, who travel to the kings of the whole world to assemble them for the battle of the great day of God, the Almighty**. Seemingly, then, the false trinity was sending out its messengers to proclaim its deceptive message through the three unclean spirits. Satan's main purpose is to incite all nations of the world to join him and his beast in the battle against God and His Christ (see 19:17-21).

16:15 As the forces of evil joined forces to wage war against the Lord Jesus and His people, the people of God still on the earth were in grave danger. Jesus Himself interrupted the flow of the narrative to issue a direct warning: **Look, I am coming like a thief. Blessed is the one who is alert** (Gk. *grēgorōn*, "take heed, watch"; see 3:2-3) **and remains clothed** in a state of constant readiness for Christ's return. The one who goes **naked**, revealing **his shame**, is in what might be called a "backslidden" state. As if the Lord realizes the possibility of distraction by the looming battle, He intervenes to redirect the focus of believers, who must "turn our eyes upon Jesus."

16:16 The kings of the earth gathered "at the place called in Hebrew ARMA-GEDON" ("mountain or hill of Megiddo," from Hb. *har*, "mountain, hill" and Megiddo, "place of crowds"). The ancient city of Megiddo, located in northern Palestine, in the Valley of Jezreel, does not have a mountain. Megiddo is important to Revelation's imagery, probably because it was the site of many famous battles (Jdg 4–5; 5:19; 6:33–7:13; 1 Sm 31; 2 Kg 9:27; 23:29-30). "The plain of Megiddo" is also the place where the "residents of Jerusalem" will mourn over the One "whom they pierced" (Zch 12:10-11). Although knowledge of any specific details is lacking, one can conclude that those who stand against God will mourn as they face the swift judgment of God and His Messiah.

The Seventh Bowl (16:17-21)

16:17 God confirmed the promise that with the completion of the seven plagues, the wrath of God would be spent (Rv 15:1). Although the punishment of Babylon the Great is yet to come (chaps. 17–18), one can understand this more specific judgment as occurring sometime within the sequence of bowls. God repeats the same phrase at the creation of the "new heaven and new earth" (21:6).

16:18-19 With this announcement, there is a "heaven-quake" and an earthquake. The quaking of heaven, including **lightnings, rumblings, and thunders**, later followed by **hail**, is an intensified parallel of the same phenomena mentioned earlier (4:5; 8:5; 11:19). The quaking of the sky was accompanied by **a severe earthquake** of unprecedented magnitude. Foreshadowing Babylon's judgment, **the great city**, identified as Babylon (17:18; 18:10), was **split into three parts** by the earthquake. Likewise, **the cities of the nations** were destroyed. God **remembered** the many abominations of **Babylon the Great**—she had made the nations drunk with "the wine of her sexual immorality" (14:8). God forced her to drink of **the wine of His fierce anger** (v. 19). The details of Babylon's many sins, as well as her punishment, is coming (chaps. 17–18).

16:20-21 The catastrophic effects of the heaven-quake and earthquake continued. The surface of the earth was completely overturned, mirroring the sixth seal (6:14), and from the sky fell **enormous hailstones**, weighing **about 100 pounds** each. Someone has calculated that such a stone would have to be about 17.6 inches in diameter, and the largest hailstones in recorded history weighed only 2.25 pounds, falling on Bangladesh April 14, 1986, and killing 92 people.[3] Faced with destruction of this enormity, the people still did not repent but **blasphemed God** for His judgment. This third and final time the earth dwellers' impenitence is noted.

In these final bowl judgments, God's earthly judgment was proclaimed complete (16:17). All that remained were the details regarding the destruction of the evil empire, Babylon the Great, along with the beast and his armies (chaps. 17–19). Next comes a small glimpse into the millennial reign of Christ upon the earth (20:1-10) and the final judgment (20:11-15), preparing the way for the eternal union of Christ and His people in the new Jerusalem (chaps. 21–22).

BABYLON AND HER DESTINY (17:1–19:5)

Chapters 17 and 18 serve as the "up-close" look at the final punishment of Babylon personified as a "notorious prostitute" (16:19; 17:1). In similar fashion, the role of God's people is magnified (chaps. 7–11), but in this case the enemies of God are the objects of scrutiny. In many ways, the mysterious figure Babylon the Great is the most difficult one for modern readers of Revelation to grasp.

Babylon the Great is the capital of the end-times civilization, which rises up in flagrant opposition to God and His Messiah. While Babylon is understood first as a city in opposition to the city of God (21:2), she also serves as the representative for the entire civilization.

The Vision of the Woman and the Scarlet Beast (17:1-6)

17:1-2 After the display of God's final judgment through the seven bowls, John is approached by **one of the seven angels who had the seven bowls**. This indicates a very close connection between the bowl judgments (chap. 16) and what John was about to see. The judgment of 17:1–19:5 is best understood as an extension of the bowl judgments, specifically as an elaboration of the last two bowls, which led to the destruction of Babylon the Great.

The angel informed John that he was going to show him **the judgment of the notorious prostitute who sits on many waters**. Later in the chapter, the "many waters" are interpreted globally as all the peoples of the world over whom the prostitute reigned (17:15).

Once again **sexual immorality** is used as a metaphor for spiritual abomination. The Old Testament prophets sometimes used the image of a prostitute to describe powerful cities, such as Tyre (Is 23:15-17), whose corrupt combination of politics and religion reveled in widespread injustice and oppression of the masses. This woman seduces the nations with promises of luxury and power, but their drunken stupor of greed will lead to nothing but destruction (18:3,7,9,11-16,19,23).

The description of this harlot continues throughout the chapter. She sits on "seven mountains" (17:9); she has committed "sexual immorality" with the **kings of the earth** (v. 2); she is "THE MOTHER OF PROSTITUTES" (v. 5); she is involved in persecution of "the saints" and "witnesses to Jesus" (v. 6). Finally, she is given the name "Babylon the Great" (18:2), doubtless a reminder of the idolatry beginning with Nimrod (cp. Gn 10:9-10). The ancient mother and child cult arising from the Babylonians' mystery religions was continued by the Romans and Greeks and even embraced by some within nominal Christianity. This "notorious prostitute" (v. 1), "the woman dressed in purple and scarlet" (v. 4), "BABYLON THE GREAT" (v. 5), personifies wickedness, spiritual corruption, and erroneous doctrine.

17:3-6 In order for John to see the judgment of this woman, the angel **carried** him away **in the Spirit** (cp. 1:10; 4:2), referring to a visionary experience inspired by the Spirit of God. His relocation **to a desert** (Gk. *erēmon*, "solitary, lonely, uninhabited, or desolate place; wilderness," 17:3) sets up "the notorious prostitute" he saw there in opposition to the sun-clothed woman (12:1,6) who was protected by God. The woman of chapter 17 was pampered by **a scarlet beast** (17:3). Although the description of the beast from the sea (13:1) did not include his color, these beasts are one and the same. As when this sea monster first appeared, he represents unrestrained political power personified in the end-times antichrist. The union of these two figures shows that the evil empire moves forward in the seduction of the nations with the aid of the antichrist's military and political might.

The description of the woman emphasizes both her luxuriant living and moral corruption (17:4). In the first century, the price of dyed cloth was so expensive that only the very wealthy could afford it. The woman's clothing of **purple and scarlet** distinguished her as particularly prosperous. She was also glittering with **gold, precious stones, and pearls**, which most likely adorned her entire person, from the arrangement of her hair to the hem of her

robes. What should have been a gloriously beautiful sight, however, is unveiled by what follows. In her hand was **a gold cup** that was **filled with everything vile and with the impurities of her prostitution** (v. 4). The immoral acts and perverse trysts of the prostitute must have produced a loathsome wine that was collected and poured into this gilded goblet. Yet, instead of feeling shame, the prostitute held it out for all to see, as if offering a gleeful toast to her abominations. The woman's brazen attitude toward her sin brings to mind the evil queen Jezebel from the Old Testament. Her numerous personal similarities to Babylon the Great suggest that a close affinity between the two women is intended.

Historians have supposed that the aristocratic prostitutes of ancient Rome would place their names on the headbands they wore. In a similar way, "the notorious prostitute" wore **a cryptic name** on **her forehead** (v. 5). The first title, **BABYLON THE GREAT**, reveals her connection with a rebellious and godless civilization. The arrogant king Nebuchadnezzar described his kingdom as "Babylon the Great" right before God executed judgment upon him (Dn 4:30). In the first century, "Babylon" was also frequently used to identify Rome (see 1 Pt 5:13) because, like Babylon, Rome conquered the Jews, destroyed their temple, and flaunted the worship of false gods.

The woman is further called **THE MOTHER OF PROSTITUTES AND OF THE VILE THINGS** (Gk. *bdelugmatōn*, "foul, detestable, abhorrent things," usually referring to idols, Rv 17:4-5; cp. 21:27; Mt 24:15; Mk 13:14; Lk 16:15) **OF THE EARTH** (Rv 17:5). For her to be termed the "mother" of prostitutes and vile things means that she not only is characterized by these traits but has also reproduced them in others. John's original readers would have immediately assumed that this woman's title alluded in some way to the Roman Empire, but her identity clearly transcends their historical setting. The prostitute's identification as the very *source* of all "vile things" shows that she is the embodiment of every evil empire throughout history. In her, the corruption and immorality of human civilization is magnified to a horrifying degree.

"The notorious prostitute" was more than just the source of all impure things, however. She was also a jubilant persecutor of God's people: **the woman was drunk on the blood of the saints**, who were **the witnesses to Jesus**. While the Christians of John's day were not suffering the kind of intense persecution that came earlier and would come later, the martyrdom of the saints has surely become a resounding theme for the faithful church throughout history. In Babylon the Great, this persecution of Christ-followers will reach a horrific highpoint. Upon experiencing all of this, no wonder John **was utterly astounded** (Gk. *ethaumasa*, "wonder, marvel at," vv. 6-8; see 13:3). He was told that he would see Babylon's judgment, but he had only seen her power, luxury, and triumph over the saints. Understandably, he did not know what to think of this amazing vision and needed the help of the angel in order to understand (17:7).

The Angel's Interpretation of the Vision (17:7-18)

17:7 The angel assured John that he need not be **astounded**, for the **secret meaning** of both **the woman** and **the beast** would be explained to him. In the explanation that followed, the angel actually spent more time explaining "the beast" (vv. 8-14) than the prostitute (vv. 15-18).

17:8 Twice in verse 8 the angel noted the bizarre history of the beast with two cryptic titles:

- **the beast that ... was, and is not, and is about to come up from the abyss and go to destruction** (Gk. *apōleian*, "ruin, perishing, utter destruction," vv. 8,11; cp. Mt 7:13; Jn 17:12; Rm 9:22; Php 1:28; 3:19; 2 Th 2:3; 2 Pt 2:3; 3:7);

- **the beast that was, and is not, and will be present again**.

These titles obviously served to mock the threefold title of God in Revelation: "the One who is, who was, and who is coming" (1:4). These titles also refer to the antichrist figure who had one head that "appeared to be fatally wounded, but his fatal wound was healed" (chap. 13). The reference to arising "from the abyss" identified antichrist's power with the same evil that brought forth the demonic hordes (9:2-3).

The angel repeated the prophecy that in light of the beast's false resurrection the earth dwellers would **be astounded** and follow him (13:3). Unlike John's restrained wonder at "the notorious prostitute," the earth dwellers' astonishment implies worship (13:3,8). Those who were deceived by the antichrist revealed their true nature as those **whose names were not written in the book of life from the foundation of the world**. The book of life is an eternal roster of the citizenship of heaven, which has been prepared since before the creation of the world. From the beginning God's plan has been to redeem a people for His pleasure, and all of their names are included in the Lamb's book of life. All those who are not among the redeemed, therefore, are a part of Babylon's debauchery and worship the antichrist.

17:9-11 These verses are among the most difficult to interpret in all of Revelation, and the angel called for discernment: **Here is the mind with wisdom** (v. 9). A similar note appeared before the riddle of the beast's number 666 (13:18).

First, the angel explained that **the seven heads** of the monster were **seven mountains on which the woman** was sitting (17:9). The first-century city of Rome was known as "the city on seven hills." John's immediate audience would have understood this identification quickly. The woman was enthroned upon a kingdom with the same power and prestige of ancient Rome.

Second, the seven heads of the beast were also **seven kings** (v. 10). The identification of these "kings" has been puzzling interpreters for centuries and numerous theories abound. The angel invited investigation into this matter by noting that **five have fallen, one is, the other has not yet come, and when he comes, he must remain for a little while**. Then, the antichrist was identified as **the eighth**, yet still **of the seven** and destined for **destruction** (Gk. *apōleian*, v. 11; see v. 8). Many have suggested that these "kings" represent Roman emperors up to John's day or include antichrist as the end-times figure following in their footsteps. Others have said that the "kings" represent major world empires throughout history, anticipating a future empire to follow the fall of Rome. While both of these theories have some merit, the matter cannot be settled with certainty.

Clearly, however, the beast is considered "the eighth" in whatever list is chosen. This choice is confusing since "the beast" was described as having seven heads, not eight. The answer to this puzzle is that the antichrist figure will actually be "of the seven," in the sense that he will be a kind of reappearance of one of the earlier "kings." In the same way John the Baptist was seen as a type of Elijah, preaching in the same power and spirit as the earlier prophet (Mal 4:5; Mt 11:14; 17:12). Historical evidence exists from

John's day that following the death of the wicked emperor Nero (AD 54–68), the first to persecute Christians, a myth began to circulate in Rome that he would come back to life and return to the throne as *Nero redivivus*, meaning "Nero brought back to life." This "urban legend" served as the historical background for the return of the eighth king.

17:12-14 The antichrist figure will receive support from the **10 horns**, which are **10 kings who have not yet received a kingdom** (v. 12). The ten-horned beast of Daniel 7:7-24 has already been recorded, but the specific identification of either set of kings is equally baffling. Regardless, clearly they will be given **authority** with the beast for a limited time: **one hour**. They unite with the beast in **one purpose** (Gk. *gnōmēn*, "mind, intention, faculty of reason"; cp. v. 17) and hand over their **power and authority** so as to accomplish this purpose: to **make war against the Lamb** (v. 13).

It appears that this scene is an expansion of the earlier reference to the satanic trinity gathering the "kings of the east" and "kings of the whole world" for battle (16:12-14). The number "10" probably symbolizes completion, thereby representing all of the future military allies of the antichrist. The limitation of their alliance to "one hour" is probably to be identified with the period of great tribulation (cp. 3:10) and the final battle of Armageddon.

Once again, however, the sovereignty of God is evident. These allied kings will wage war against the Lamb, but their efforts are in vain. The **Lord of lords and King of kings** cannot be defeated by mere men, and in the end, **the Lamb will conquer** (Gk. *nikēsai*, "have victory over, overcome"; see 2:7) **them** all (17:14). The corpses of the kings will serve as supper for the birds (19:21), and the beast and false prophet will be cast into "the lake of fire" (19:20). Those who fight with the Lamb, in contrast to those who fight with the beast, are

- **called** (Gk. *klētoi*, "invited" as to a banquet, divinely "appointed, selected") and

- **elect** (Gk. *eklektoi*, "picked out, chosen out of many") **and**

- **faithful** (Gk. *pistoi*, "trustworthy, believing or trusting," 17:14).

Here, the vindication of the saints is evident by their participation in the final war. Though how they will serve is unclear, God allows them the honor of contributing in some way to the great victory over those who had martyred them.

17:15-18 So far, the angel has described "the beast" rather than "the notorious prostitute." Finally he turned his attention to the identity and destiny of Babylon the Great. **The waters** that she was sitting on **are peoples, multitudes, nations, and languages** (v. 15). These are the earth dwellers, all the peoples of the world who are deceived by the beast and ally themselves with his kingdom. The harlot's posture sitting on the waters indicates her domination over and control of the world's inhabitants.

Even with this power, however, Babylon the Great proved to be vulnerable. While they use and placate her for a time, **the 10 horns** and **the beast** grow to **hate the prostitute**. Out of this hatred, they will **make her desolate** (Gk. *ērēmōmenēn*, "lay waste, ruin, despoil, strip of treasures,") **and naked, devour her flesh, and burn her up with fire** (v. 16; cp. Mt 12:25; Lk 11:7). In this way, the antichrist and his allies will turn inward to make war against their own people, and "every man's sword will be against his brother" (Ezk 38:21). Being made "desolate" refers to Babylon's de-population as the kings murder her inhabitants, while her being stripped "naked" refers to her unconcealed shame.

In this betrayal, the self-loathing nature of evil is evident once again. The four horsemen (chap. 6) represented the sins of humanity coming "full circle" in self-destruction. The demonic armies (chap. 9) revealed the powers of darkness attacking their own followers in bloodthirsty rage. And here again, the hatred of the evil powers for their followers is exposed. Satan and his demons have no affection for human beings who, even in an unredeemed state, still bear the image of God and are dearly loved by Him. Perhaps, by turning on the people who make up "the great city," the demonic realm imagines that they are getting back at God in some way.

Nevertheless, the beast and the kings of the earth are merely acting in accordance with **God's words**. Although they thought that they were serving their own ends, God had actually **put it into their hearts to carry out His plan** (Gk. *gnōmēn*, "intention," Rv 17:17; see v. 13). In the end "God's words" **are accomplished** (Gk. *telesthēsontai*, "accomplished, fulfilled, executed according to command," v. 17; cp. 10:7; 11:7; 15:1,8; 20:3,5,7; Jn 19:28,30) and cannot be frustrated.

After proceeding through so much symbolism in chapter 17 thus far, the last part of the angel's interpretation seems obvious (Rv 17:18). The angel explained that **the woman . . . is the great city that has an empire over the kings of the earth**. John and his readers would have immediately associated this statement with Rome and the Roman Empire. Ultimately, though, this prophecy concerns the final evil civilization of the world: a Rome-like empire established and ruled by the antichrist.

The Announcement of Babylon's Fall (18:1-8)

18:1-3 John now sees **another angel with great authority** descending **from**

heaven. The glorious **splendor** (Gk. *doxēs*, "glory, brightness") of this angel probably reflected his being in God's presence (v. 1). The image of the angel's holy radiance illuminating the darkness of antichrist's kingdom (16:10) was poignant as judgment was about to fall on Babylon the Great.

The pronouncement of the angel recalls the "second angel" (14:8), for he announced, **It has fallen, Babylon the Great has fallen!** (v. 2; see Is 21:9 for a similar declaration regarding ancient Babylon). The connection between these two prophecies reveals that the final destruction of Babylon the Great is grounded in the eternal decrees of God. Also, the judgment of end-times Babylon will include the judgment of her "idols," namely antichrist and his image.

In her desolation Babylon the Great became **a dwelling** place (Gk. *katoikētērion*, "abode, habitation, home"; cp. Eph 2:22) **for demons** and **a haunt** (Gk. *phulakē*, "prison," as a place that is under "guard or watch, a place of banishment," Rv 18:2; cp. 2:10; 20:7) **for every unclean spirit, . . . every unclean bird, and . . . every unclean and despicable beast** (18:2). The unclean birds and beasts that John's readers would have imagined include vultures, bats, ravens, and owls, along with hyenas, wild dogs, and pigs (see Lv 11). The image of these creatures roaming freely about the ruined city is symbolic and poetic in nature, effectively communicating the total destruction and desolation of Babylon the Great when God's wrath is poured out upon her (cp. Jr 50).

The angel reiterated the reason for Babylon's punishment: **all the nations have drunk the wine of her sexual immorality**. The **kings of the earth** and **the merchants of the earth** are two groups specifically mentioned as benefiting from Babylon's idolatry, wealth, and indulgent **luxury**. This gross materialism

is the primary reason for Babylon's condemnation (chap. 18).

Rome is definitely the primary historical background for the materialism described here. The Roman government of John's day skillfully exploited its subjects in order both to dominate the people and to build national wealth. The heavy tax burden and quickly amassed debts of common people prevented them from ever rising above their poverty. As the Roman Empire expanded through the conquering of other nations, the additional sources of trade and commerce made the ruling and merchant classes very rich. Even the Roman religious cults propagated the social and economic corruption by choosing their priests from among the wealthy and powerful. These economic sins are despicable to God and have been punished by Him as Tyre was in the past (Ezk 27–28).

18:4-5 John **heard another voice from heaven** (vv. 4-20). Although unclear, the direct command addressed to Christians suggests that the voice belonged to God Himself. He said, **Come out of her, My people, so that you will not share in** (Gk. *sugkoinōnēsēte*, "become partaker together with," from *sun*, "with," and *koinōneō*, "have communion or fellowship with, become partners"; cp. Eph 5:11) **her sins, or receive any of her plagues** (Rv 18:4). This address to Christians, although surprising here, mirrors several Old Testament warnings where the Israelites are ordered to "flee" ancient Babylon (Is 48:20; 52:11; Jr 51:6,45). Here the fleeing is intended primarily in a spiritual sense, for God's method of missions in every age has been to set apart a people and call them out from the world, even though they still resided in the world. As followers of Jesus, believers are to be in the world but not of the world (1 Jn 2:17). At the end of the age, those few believers residing in the kingdom of the beast will likely flee in a literal sense from the coming destruction of Babylon the Great.

The **sins** of Babylon the Great are like one huge garbage heap that has been **piled up** to the point of touching **heaven** (Rv 18:5; Jr 51:9). God has delayed the hour of her judgment, but the time has come (vv. 6-8). **God has remembered her crimes** and will bring retribution swiftly to the great city (v. 5; cp. 16:19). Elsewhere in Scripture, when God "remembers" sins, judgment is coming (see Ps 109:14; Jr 14:10; Hs 8:13; 9:9).

18:6-8 The voice who spoke to the people of God now speaks to the unnamed carriers of God's judgment—presumably heavenly beings. The famous biblical law, "eye for an eye and a tooth for a tooth" (Ex 21:24; Lv 24:20; Dt 19:21), is the basis for Babylon's destruction. She will receive exactly as "her crimes" deserve (Rv 18:5). The commands to **pay her back** (Gk. *apodote*, "reward, deliver, render or pay what is due, requite, recompense," v. 6), to **double it**, and to mix **a double portion for her** simply mean to pay her back in full measure (cp. 14:10). The messengers of judgment are to hold nothing back. According to the teachings of Jesus, believers are not allowed to seek vengeance for themselves (Mt 5:38-42). The justice of God, however, will be meted out in His time and His ways (Dt 32:35).

Babylon the Great deserved to be given **torment and grief**, for **she glorified herself and lived luxuriously** (Gk. *estrēniasen*, "with unrestrained excess, extravagantly, immorally, sensually," vv. 7,9; cp. *strēnous*, "luxury," 18:3). To have GLORIFIED (Gk. *edoxasen*, "praised, honored, magnified, clothed oneself with splendor," v. 7) oneself is to have claimed what rightfully belongs only to God. This Greek verb appears 23 times in the Gospel of John, and each time

the one "glorified" is either God the Father or God the Son. Jesus refused to "glorify" Himself (Jn 8:54). Three related statements summarize her arrogant posture in the world (Rv 18:7; cp. Is 47:7-9):

- **I sit as queen**, ruling over the entire world as the finest civilization of all time.

- **I am not a widow**, for my many lovers are the kings of the earth.

- **I will never see grief** (Gk. *penthos*, "mourning," Rv 18:7; cp. 21:4), for I am in complete control of my own destiny.

The empire of Babylon the Great will surely seem invincible until there is a sudden, unexpected collapse. Like the neo-Babylonian Empire, which was conquered by the Persians in one fateful day (Dn 5:30), the empire of antichrist will receive her punishment without warning. The citizens will suffer with **death, and grief, and famine**, while the city's glorious architecture **will be burned up with fire**. Truly, the swiftness and finality of her judgment are due to the **mighty** character of **the Lord God who judges her**.

The World Mourns Babylon's Fall (18:9-20)

This section has been called the "funeral dirge" for Babylon the Great. Three groups who profited greatly from the wealth and power of Babylon lament over the fate of the great city. Their purely selfish mourning is for the lavish lifestyle they have lost. They do not mourn their sins. In addition, they will "stand far off" so that they do not have to participate in her suffering (18:10,15,17b), deserting her in her time of agony. The three parts of the funeral dirge are based upon the lament over Tyre (Ezk 27), a powerful city of trade and commerce in Ezekiel's day. Both the Old Testament city and end-times empire portray the final end of those who traffic in evil and corruption.

18:9-10 The first mourners over Babylon the Great are **the kings of the earth who** joined her in **sexual immorality** and luxurious living (v. 9). Undoubtedly, these are not the "10 kings" who fought with the beast to bring about Babylon's destruction. Although the kings shared both her bed and her wares, they are unwilling to take the risk of coming to her aid. Instead, they **will weep and mourn** while **they stand far off** (v. 10). Their cries recall the shrieking eagle (8:13) proclaiming the disasters of the fifth, sixth, and seventh trumpets.

18:11-17a The second group of mourners are **the merchants** (typically citizens and ship-owners of the exporting city that used the trade routes of the sea to bring their goods to Rome, v. 11), who got very wealthy from trade with the great city. Historians identify Rome as the first nation to develop an international market with China, Arabia, India, and Africa. The wealth of Babylon the Great will at least rival the greatness of ancient Rome.

The merchants mourn specifically because **no one buys their merchandise** (Gk. *gomon*, "ship's freight, cargo carried by ship" vv. 11-12) **any longer**. The inventory of their goods has 29 items and mirrors the list of Tyre's goods (Ezk 27), seven categories of wares familiar to modern readers:

- precious stones and metals—**gold, silver, precious stones, and pearls**;

- luxurious fabrics—**linen, purple, silk, and scarlet**;

- expensive wood and building materials—**fragrant wood products, ... ivory, ... wood, brass, iron, and marble** (Rv 18:12);

- spices and perfumes—**cinnamon, spice, incense, myrrh, and frankincense**;

- food items—**wine, olive oil, fine wheat flour, and grain**;

- animals—**cattle and sheep, horses and carriages**; and

- human slaves—**human bodies and souls** (v. 13).

Appropriately shocking is the listing of HUMAN (Gk. *anthrōpōn*, "of man," a generic reference) BODIES (Gk. *sōmatōn*, "physical bodies," used of Jesus' "body," Jn 2:21; 19:31,38,40; 20:12) and SOULS (Gk. *psuchas*, "breath of life," thus "souls" in distinction from "bodies") alongside "cattle and sheep; horses and carriages" in the inventory of Babylon's merchant wealth. The Roman Empire of John's day is estimated to have had a slave labor force of 10 million, nearly 20 percent of their total population. Slaves were obtained primarily by conquering other nations but also through the payment of debts, kidnapping, punishment of criminals, children sold by their parents for money, and even by the gathering of unwanted children left to die by exposure to the elements. The elite of Roman society often based their social status on the number of slaves they owned. The connection of "bodies" with "souls" (v. 13) serves as a reminder that the slave traders were not just dealing with dispensable bodies but with infinitely valuable human souls. Clearly, the wealth of Babylon the Great is particularly despicable in God's sight because she has attained it while standing on the flogged and broken backs of enslaved human beings, all of whom were fashioned in God's image. Today, any culture aspiring to prosper through similar means is wor-

thy of the same punishment meted out
for Babylon the Great.

All of these items were among the most
costly and coveted in the Roman Empire
and, apart from the food items, possessed
only by the wealthy elite. The materialism
of any society is not far different from that
of Rome. This list of costly merchandise
reveals the reason for God's wrath—
self-centered and self-glorifying materialism.

Like the kings of the earth, the merchants made rich from the luxurious
indulgences of Babylon the Great also
stand far off in fear of her torment (v.
15). Their proclamation of woe (v. 16)
recalls the prostitute's splendid description (chap. 17). Yet, in the grief of personal loss, the merchants declare that **in a
single hour** her **fabulous wealth was
destroyed** (18:17). The financial disaster
pictured here, along with the personal loss
felt by the merchants, would be comparable to the crashing of all of the world's
stock markets in a single day.

18:17b-19 The third group in mourning
for Babylon the Great is everyone who
plays a part in her profitable sea trade (v.
17): **every shipmaster** (or sea captain),
seafarer (or commercial passenger), **the
sailors, and all who do business by sea**
(probably fisherman). Once again, this
group's lament is a result of their material
losses. The gesture of throwing **dust on
their heads** refers to a common sign of
mourning and sorrow in the ancient world
(1 Sm 4:12; 2 Sm 13:19; 15:32; Jb 2:12).
The seamen's declarations of **woe** are a
result of their realization that the large
profits of their trade are a complete loss
with the fall of Babylon **in a single hour**
(v. 19).

18:20 While those who participated in
the prostitute's economic sins despair
over her destruction, those who were
faithful to God **rejoice** at His triumph.
Rejoicing is in order for all—**heaven** and

saints, apostles, and prophets—because
God's judgment on Babylon the Great is
the vindication of His people. The final
annihilation of Babylon the Great fulfills
God's promise of justice to the martyrs
(6:9-11). Since the bowl judgments and
the fall of Babylon the Great appear to
coincide, when Babylon is punished, the
earth dwellers are punished. All believers
will be among these jubilant celebrants
savoring the triumph of God over the
vainglorious empire of the antichrist.

The Finality of Babylon's Destruction (18:21-24)

18:21 The casting of the **millstone** into
the sea is another enacted parable (cp.
10:8,10; 11:1-2) mirroring a similar deed
(Jr 51:63-64). The millstone's plunge into
the water and speedy descent to the murky
sea floor illustrates the way **the great city
will be thrown down violently** (Gk.
hormēmati, in a "rush" or by "impulse,"
used only here in the NT) **and never be
found again** (Rv 18:21).

18:22-23a These next verses detail the
particulars of Babylon's civilization,
which will be lost forever:

- The *music* of her jovial debauchery
will be lost forever, with **the sound of
harpists, musicians, flutists, and
trumpeters** vanishing completely.

- All aspects of Babylon's *commerce*
will be lost, leaving **no craftsman of
any trade** to turn another profit for
her treasury.

- The distinguishing marks of *domestic
life* will become extinct as well. **The
sound of a mill** refers to the practice
of ancient homes to grind their own
grain by hand during the day (v. 22).
The light of a lamp served to illuminate the homes of the people at night.

- The absence of the **groom and bride**
indicates the complete departure of

joy and gladness from the streets of Babylon (v. 23a; see Jr 25:10).

18:23b-24 Like the "rap sheet" of a condemned criminal, Babylon the Great must receive just punishment for the following convictions:

- *corrupt commercial exploits* achieved by partnering with the rich and powerful while oppressing the poor;

- *religious idolatry* that was propagated by seducing all the nations into rebellion against the Lord;

- *persecution of God's people*, including His prophets and saints; and

- *wanton slaughter of innocents* throughout the world.

The fact that **the blood** of **all those slaughtered on the earth** was found in the prostitute points to the way this civilization's sins transcend time (v. 24). Although the appearance of Babylon the Great is yet to come, she embodies all of the godless and corrupt empires that have stood against the Lord since the beginning of human history. Any world culture that reflects the narcissistic materialism seen in Babylon the Great, along with the same willingness to oppress other peoples to maintain prosperity, must realize that God's judgment is neither slack nor far away (chap. 18; cp. Gl 6:7).

The Rejoicing of Heaven (19:1-5)

There is a striking comparison between the three laments given for Babylon the Great (18:9-19) and the three songs of worship from heaven (19:1-5). Heaven, along with the saints, apostles, and prophets, had been told to rejoice over Babylon's judgment (18:20), but the celebration is finally recorded here in three "hallelujah" choruses praising the justice of God.

19:1-3 The joy of this **vast multitude** is complete through the fulfillment of God's promised vindication, when as a heavenly choir they sing praises to their Lord. The beginning word of their praise, HAL-LELUJAH, is actually an un-translated Hebrew word meaning "Praise the Lord." *Hallelu* is the commanding form of the word "praise," while *yah* is a short form for *Yahweh*, the name of God often rendered as "Lord" in English translations. This phrase became a common expression of worship in Israel, appearing throughout the Psalms (e.g., 103-106; 146-150), but it appears in the New Testament only in Revelation 19:1,3,4,6.

The **judgments** of God **are** considered **true** (Gk. *alēthinai*, "genuine, real") **and righteous** because He has demonstrated them by punishing **the notorious prostitute** (v. 2). Babylon's guilt in the **sexual immorality** (probably a metaphorical reference to spiritual adultery with idols) of the whole earth and **the blood of His servants** demanded the execution of God's wrath upon her. God promised the martyrs that He would avenge their blood (6:9-11), and now this promise is fulfilled. By punishing Babylon the Great, the Lord has also punished her citizens, who are guilty of "the blood of His servants." For His faithfulness to do so, **salvation, glory, and power belong** to God alone.

The second **Hallelujah** is followed by the acknowledgement that Babylon the Great has been judged with no possibility for a reprieve or reversal (v. 3). The righteous punishment God metes out must also endure forever (15:7).

19:4-5 This **praise** is a call to the saints still on earth to join the worship of the Lord. Although waiting for the final triumph of God's people, believers in every generation praise Him in the confident expectation of what is sure to come.

THE FINAL VICTORY
(19:6–20:15)

Chapters 17 and 18 have focused on the evil empire, Babylon the Great and her judgment by God in the end times. Although "the notorious prostitute" aligned with the antichrist for a time, he turned on her with great ferocity and was used by God to bring her to ruin. Now that Babylon the Great has been punished for her many sins and heaven has rejoiced at the display of God's justice (19:1-5), the rest of God's victory over evil will be revealed in all its fullness.

The announcement of the marriage supper of the Lamb (19:6-10) is followed by the return of Christ as the warrior Messiah (19:11-16), then by the final destruction of the antichrist and his allies (19:17-21) and the imprisonment of Satan (20:1-3), and finally the glorious thousand-year reign of Christ upon the earth is proclaimed (20:4-6), indicating the definitive end to Satan's reign (20:7-10) and the judgment of all people (20:11-15). Unlike some visions in Revelation with uncertain timing, these visions (chaps. 19–20) will most likely be fulfilled in the chronological order suggested by the text. They portray Jesus in three glorious ways: the faithful *Bridegroom*, the conquering *King*, and the righteous *Judge*. One central truth emerges: God is in sovereign control of His world, and His righteousness will reign supreme for all eternity.

The Marriage of the Lamb Announced (19:6-10)

19:6-8 "The notorious prostitute" will never be seen in the book of Revelation again. Her judgment is complete. The arrival of **the marriage** (Gk. *gamos*, "wedding, wedding banquet or festival, matrimony," vv. 7,9; the anglicized root in words relating to marriage, including "mono*gamy*," the marriage of one man to

one woman) **of the Lamb** is a cause for all people to **be glad, rejoice, and give Him glory** (v. 7). BE GLAD (Gk. *chairōmen*, "rejoice, be joyful"; as a greeting, "Welcome or Hail!") and REJOICE (Gk. *agalliōmen*, "exult, rejoice greatly or exceedingly," from *agan*, "much," and *allomai*, "leap, gush or spring up") convey the jubilant attitude of joyous celebration that would accompany a king's long-awaited wedding, particularly when the event followed triumphant military victory. *Chairō* appears frequently in the New Testament, but in John's writings, the word usually appears in a context emphasizing that Christ is divine, eternal, and personal (Jn 3:29; 4:36; 8:56; 11:15; 14:28; 16:22; 20:20). In all but one of the 11 times it is used in the New Testament, *agallialō* refers to uncontainable joy expressed by Jesus or by believers on His account (Mt 5:12; Lk 1:47; 10:21; Jn 8:56; Ac 2:26; 16:34; 1 Pt 1;6,8; 4:13). An intended contrast is between "the notorious prostitute" and the **wife** of the Lamb. Israel as the bride of *Yahweh* is a rich theme in the Old Testament (Is 54:5; 61:10; Jr 31:32; Ezk 16:7-14; Hs 2:16-20). The same theme is seen in the New Testament, with the church as Christ's bride (2 Co 11:2; Eph 5:25-27).

In Jewish marriages of the ancient world:

- There was an extended betrothal period after an agreement for marriage had been made. Although the consummation was delayed, during this time the bride and groom called each other "husband" and "wife" and remained faithful in their commitment to each another (see Mt 1:18-19).

- The glorious wedding ceremony begins when the groom, with the permission of his father, proceeds to the bride's house and escorts her back to his home. An elaborate feast of celebration followed for several days (see Mt 22:1-10; 25:1-13).

Here the bride and Bridegroom will be united for all of eternity (Rv 19:7-9).

Interestingly the bride is depicted as having **prepared herself**, and she has been **permitted to wear fine linen, bright** (Gk. *lampron*, "brilliant, splendid, magnificent"; also 15:6; 18:14; 22:1,16) **and pure**, which are **the righteous acts of the saints** (19:8). This twofold description emphasizes both the responsibility of believers and the sovereignty of God. As congregations and individual Christians live in faithful obedience to Jesus Christ, they prepare themselves for His return with clothing of "righteous acts." Yet, God Himself bestows righteousness upon believers, giving them the very ability to "wear" such righteous deeds (cp. Php 2:12b-13).

19:9-10 In this beatitude, the sovereignty of God in the Lamb's marriage is clear, for only those who are **invited** (Gk. *keklēmenoi*, "called, invited by name") will be present at **the marriage feast**. These chosen ones are **blessed** indeed. The angel (see 17:1-3) assured John of the authenticity of what he was seeing, for **these words of God are true** (Gk. *alēthinoi*, "genuine, veracious," 19:9).

Apparently at this point John became overwhelmed. The "hallelujahs" of God's people had created such an atmosphere of worship that he **fell** on his knees **to worship**. The angel would not accept such adoration, however, and corrected John's impulsive mistake. Instead, he must **worship God**, for **the testimony about Jesus is the spirit of prophecy** (v. 10), that is, the essence of the proclamation of God's word is the message of Jesus Christ. Anyone who claims to have a word from God

must be measured against the message of Jesus.

The Victorious Messiah Appears (19:11-16)

19:11-16 The first time that heaven was opened to John, the rest of Revelation was revealed to him (4:1). Seeing **heaven opened** this time, John saw "heaven standing open," the gates swiftly thrown wide in anticipation of the **rider** emerging **on a white horse** (19:11). Watch this scene as a motion picture: A valiant white horse gallops swiftly through the open gates, and many banners held by the rider billow sharply in the wind. One of them is emblazoned with the phrase **Faithful and True** (v. 11), and the other says **Word of God** (v. 13). Another banner has **a name** in a language that apparently **no one knows except Himself** (v. 12). As He rides forth, the eyes of the rider blaze **like a fiery flame, and on His head** sit **many** gleaming **crowns** (v. 12). The dark trim of the rider's **robe** is actually **stained** (Gk. *bebammenon*, "dipped"; cp. Jn 13:26) **with blood** (Rv 19:13). When **a sharp sword** (Gk. *hromphaia*, v. 15; see 1:16) appears from **His mouth**, the voice again clarified that He will **strike** (Gk. *patei*, "smite, cut down, kill," esp. with a sword; cp. 11:6; Mt 26:31,51; Lk 22:49; Ac 7:24; 12:23) **the nations** with it and **will shepherd them with an iron scepter** (cp. Rv 2:27; 12:5). Suddenly, a vast army, also riding **on white horses**, thunders forth from the gates, following this incredible rider. But, unlike Him, their robes are of **pure white linen**, without spot or blemish (19:14). As we look closer at the "robe" of the rider, His identity is clear, for written **on His robe** and **His thigh** is another **name written: King of Kings and Lord of Lords** (v. 16). Excitement builds: The glorious Savior rides forth to earth as He triumphs over evil in victorious conquest (19:6b).

Antichrist and Allies Destroyed (19:17-21)

19:17-18 The scene now shifts away from the conquering Messiah to the armies of the antichrist who have assembled to oppose Him. From the start clearly there is not a "fair fight." Even before the battle begins, **an angel** appears in the midst of the blazing **sun** to proclaim the downfall of the antichrist and his allies. The picture is truly gruesome, for with **a loud voice** he invites **the birds** circling the sky to **eat the flesh** of the slain armies at what he calls **the great supper of God** (v. 17). There is a stark contrast here between the joyous "marriage feast of the Lamb" (19:9) and the tragic "great supper of God." Two great messianic feasts will take place at the end of history: the feast with the Lamb for the saints and the feast *on* the sinners for the birds. No one will be exempted from the carnage of this last battle, for the list of the dead includes **everyone, both free and slave, small and great** (see Ezk 39:17-20).

19:19-21 This vision has returned to Armagedon (16:16), where **the beast, the kings of the earth, and their armies gathered** for battle. The satanic trinity has been preparing for this battle since the sixth bowl (16:12-16), but they prove to be no match for **the rider** on the white **horse** and **His army** (19:19). Not even one blow is delivered before the fight comes to an end. In the "battle of Armagedon," as soon as the sword comes out of the Lord's mouth (19:21), the battle is over. **The beast** and **the false prophet**, whose sins are recounted (see 13:12-15), are captured (probably by Jesus Himself) and immediately **thrown alive into the lake of fire that burns with sulfur** (19:20). For the first time in Scripture the place of eternal punishment for the wicked is described with this imagery, which will appear several more times (20:10,14,15; 21:8). With their powerful

leader defeated forever, the armies assembled to fight against the Lamb have no defense. They are all are **killed with the sword** of Christ's **mouth** and, as prophesied (19:17-18), the **birds** gorge themselves on **their flesh** (v. 21).

The Binding of Satan (20:1-3)

20:1-3 The last time the dragon appeared, he was gathering the armies of the earth to battle the Lamb in Armagedon. Now, the reality of his powerlessness and ultimate condemnation is exposed. The **angel** with **the key to the abyss** (9:1-2) now does God's bidding again. But, this time, the angel does not release but imprisons, using **a great chain** (Gk. *halusin*, "bond" used to restrict movement of the body, esp. the hands or feet, 20:1). Seizing the **ancient serpent**—who has been opposing God since the garden of Eden—the angel **bound him** with the iron chain and **threw him into the abyss**, the prison for evil spirits (9:1; Jd 6). The **seal** of God upon the abyss will ensure the imprisonment of Satan **for 1,000 years** (Rv 20:2), after which the Devil will be released **for a short time** (v. 3).

The different understandings of the millennium typically hinge on different interpretations of Revelation 20:1-10. These various interpretations can be divided into three major views.

- The *premillennial* ("before the millennium") view follows what appears to be the straightforward movement of the text, affirming that Jesus will return to earth after the defeat of the antichrist (19:11-15) and set up His kingdom for a period of 1,000 years.

- The *amillennial* ("no millennium") view sees the 1,000 years figuratively and as descriptive of the period of time currently experienced by the church before the return of Christ. The "binding" of Satan (20:2-3) during that time period refers not to his literal imprisonment but to a limitation in his powers.

- The *postmillennial* (meaning "after the millennium") view asserts that Christ will return after the world has become progressively "Christianized" by the spread of the gospel. When that process is complete, there will be a "millennium" of peace on the earth.

Using a more literal approach to understanding both the events prophesied in Revelation and the timing of their fulfillment leads to the *premillennial* view as the most plausible in light of biblical evidence. Although the specific time period of "1,000 years" is not attached to the Messiah's reign elsewhere in the Bible, its conditions of peace, prosperity, and justice are described in numerous places (see, among others, Ps 110:3; Is 2:1-4; 11:1–16; 19:23-25; 35:1–10; 65:17-25; Jr 23:5; Ezk 40–48; Dn 2:44-45; 7:23-27; Am 9:11-15; Mc 4:1-4; Zch 14:3-12; Mt 19:28; Lk 1:31-33; Rm 11:26-27). The purpose of the millennium, then, in the *premillennial* view is threefold:

- to fulfill the prophecies of the Old and New Testaments proclaiming such an age;

- to demonstrate the blessings of God and His Messiah when He reigns on the earth; and

- to reveal the need for the eternal judgment of the wicked since even with Satan bound and a genuine utopia established, some people will still rebel against a good and merciful God when the Devil is released.

With this interpretation in mind, the details of the millennium will now be considered.

Christ's Millennial Reign (20:4-6)

20:4-6 The disembodied **souls** were of those martyrs **who had been beheaded because of their testimony about Jesus and because of God's word** (v. 4). In Rome, beheading was a favored method of execution for Christians of the upper class, with burning, crucifixion, and exposure to wild animals being reserved for foreigners and lower classes. Here, beheading probably serves as a summary term for all martyrdom. Those who were martyred in the great tribulation had refused to worship **the beast or his image** and were without his **mark** (v. 4). After the binding of Satan, God will bring the faithful dead to life and allow them to reign with His Son in **the first resurrection** (Gk. *anastasis*, "raising up or rising from the dead," v. 5).

Some have suggested that the ruling saints portrayed here only include the martyrs of the great tribulation (based on the description of their faithfulness to death, v. 4), who are singled out for special privilege. Yet, the authority to reign with Christ was promised to *all* the "victors" in the messages to the churches (2:26-27; 3:21). Other Scripture passages affirm that all the saints of God will reign with Christ (Dn 7:22; Mt 19:28; 1 Co 6:2). The martyrs here are representatives of all who have remained faithful to Jesus throughout the ages.

Because they refused to serve Christ in their earthly life, **the rest of the dead** must await judgment while the saints of God throughout history participate **in the first resurrection** (Rv 20:6). **The second death** (eternal death) awaits unbelievers, but the Christ-followers **will be priests of God and the Messiah** throughout the **1,000 years**. This picture of the saints serving as priests and reigning as kings fulfills the desire of God to have a "kingdom of priests" (Ex 19:6). The people of God will perform this function on earth during the millennium and will continue their service in the new Jerusalem.

Satan's Final Destruction (20:7-10)

20:7-10 As prophesied, **Satan will be released** (Gk. *luthēnai*, "loose from bondage, unbind, break free or break loose," vv. 3,7; see 1:5; cp. 5:2; 9:14-15) **from his prison** following the **1,000 years.** Although difficult to understand, the wording—"he *must* be released"—shows that the release is part of God's overall plan (20:3). When the Devil is released, he will **deceive** (Gk. *planēsai*, "lead astray, lead into error or sin," vv. 8,10; also 2:20; 12:9; 13:14; 18:23; 19:20) **the nations**. With Christ reigning with the saints on the earth, who is there in His kingdom to be deceived by Satan? Apparently the Devil's final deception will center on two groups of people: (1) those who survive the tribulation (19:17-21), and (2) any children born during the millennial reign of Christ (1,000 years provides for the possibility of 30 to 40 generations of people) who never submitted their individual souls to Christ.

Apparently the Devil will find many unbelievers willing to rebel against God, and he gathers them together from **the four corners of the earth** for another **battle**. The number of people in this final insurgence is staggering, **like the sand of the sea** (v. 8). **Gog** (the king of the northern lands) **and Magog** (the people of Gog) come to wage war against God's people (cp. Ezk 38–39). In Ezekiel, as in Revelation, the rebels are destroyed (Ezk 39), and the people of God reign victorious in the glorified temple (Ezk 40–48). John probably had this prophecy in mind as he observed the confederation of sinners led by the Devil rise up against the Messiah King.

The beloved city where **the saints** are encamped (v. 9) is Jerusalem, often called the city God loves in the Old Testament

(Pss 78:68; 87:2; 122:6; Jr 11:15; Zph 3:17); and it has probably been established as the capital of Christ's kingdom during the millennium. The wicked have come again expecting to battle the Lord Almighty, but nothing materialized (cp. Rv 19:17-21). Instead, John saw **fire** come **down from heaven** and consume the entire confederation of the wicked (20:9). Not one person is left alive. After the armies have been destroyed by fire, God turns His attention to his primary adversary, **the Devil**. At this point, finally, the father of lies and ruler of darkness (Jn 8:44; Eph 6:12) takes his place with the rest of the satanic trinity in **the lake of fire and sulfur** (Rv 20:10). Together, these wicked allies **will be tormented day and night forever**.

The Final Judgment (20:11-15)

The next event that naturally flows from the punishment of Satan in eternal fire is the judging of his followers. In Revelation, one is either with the Lamb or with the Devil. There is no neutral or middle ground position. A rejection of the Savior is an acceptance of Satan. By not declaring absolute allegiance to the Lamb, one declares allegiance to the Devil. With this in mind the judgment of the unbelieving dead takes place.

20:11 The **white** color of the **throne** recalls the purity and holiness of God emphasized throughout the book. The "judge of all the earth" (Gn 18:25) will dispense justice based upon His holy character. The fleeing of **earth and heaven** from God's **presence** emphasizes the awesome grandeur and fearsomeness of His character. Also, this literal dissolution of the universe must be preparation for the "new heaven and new earth" (21:1), which will shortly appear (cp. Is 51:6).

20:12-15 Those who stood before God in this judgment were **the dead, the great**

and the small, whose bodies were surrendered by **the sea**, and by **Death and Hades** (Gk., "the place of the dead"; Hb. *Sheol*). "The rest of the dead" remained in their graves throughout the millennial reign of Christ (20:5). The unredeemed dead are not immune to the "second death" (20:6), the lake of fire (v. 15).

At the "great white throne," God's justice will be meted out to unbelievers (in contrast to the *bēma*, the judgment seat of Christ, before which only believers appear, 1 Co 3:8-15) based upon two criteria:

- **books**, or records, of the **works** performed in earthly life, both good and evil; and

- **the book of lif**e, which contains the names of all the redeemed (Rv 20:12).

All were judged according to their works (v. 13). The rejection of Jesus excludes the recording of a person's name in the book of life; thus the only basis of judgment left is their earthly works (Is 64:6), and true righteousness before God is available only through Christ. Based upon both the absence of their names from the book of life and their wicked acts in the books of their deeds, the dead are found worthy of punishment in **the lake of fire** (Rv 20:15).

The LAKE OF FIRE (19:20; 20:10,14,15) is an image unique to the book of Revelation. While the background of the fiery lake is uncertain, the best corresponding New Testament concept comes from *Gehenna* (Gk., usually translated "hell" or "hellfire"; Mt 5:22,29,30; 10:28; 18:9; 23:15,33; Mk 9:43,45,47; Lk 12:5; Jms 3:6). The name was originally derived from the Valley of Hinnom on the southern slope of Jerusalem, which became notorious during the evil reigns of Ahab and Manasseh when they burned their own children there as offerings to the god Molech (2 Ch 28:3; 33:6). The site of this wickedness was condemned and became a symbol for future punishment (Is 66:24; Jr 7:30-33). In Jesus' day, this place became the city dump where garbage kept the fires constantly burning. *Gehenna*, then, was a rich metaphor for the place of eternal fiery punishment for the wicked (see Dn 7:9-11).

Is the lake of fire a literal place of fiery torment for the wicked? The teachings of Jesus in the Gospels assume the reality of such a place. Clearly John believed in the unending fiery anguish of the wicked. Many interpreters, though, interpret descriptions of hell as metaphors for something so terrible that it defies the possibility of literal description. With or without a literal burning, the "lake of fire" gives the most agonizing description of hell in the Bible (2 Th 1:9).

With irrevocable separation and eternal torment of all who once stood in opposition to God—Babylon the Great, the antichrist and false prophet, Satan, all unbelievers, and "Death and Hades"—the heavenly state of eternal bliss between Christ and His people can now begin.

THE NEW HEAVEN AND NEW EARTH (21:1–22:5)

The fulfillment of God's promise to "create a new heaven and a new earth" for His people (Is 65:17; 66:22) now begins to unfold as John recorded his vision of the new Jerusalem coming down out of heaven from God. The presence of elements such as the "tree of life" (Rv 22:2) and the "river of living water" (22:1) recalls the original garden of Eden (Gn 2:8-14) and invites the reader to see this vision as a restoration of the state of humanity in Eden. When the perfect created order is restored, believers will inhabit the magnificent new Jerusalem, and God will come to dwell there forever (Rv 21:3; 22:22-23). The lines of demarcation between the sinful world and the exalted throne room of God are destroyed (chaps. 21–22), for God's dwelling is now with His people (21:3).

The New Creation (21:1-8)

21:1-2 After the vanishing of earth and heaven before "the great white throne" of God (20:11), John must have wondered what would happen next (21:1; Is 65:19-25). Whether **a new heaven and a new earth** (Rv 21:1) means a transformation of the old elements of the universe or a completely new creation of God remains unclear. What John saw, however, transcends anything that presently exists in the universe (such as living without a sun or moon, 21:23).

John's observation that **the sea existed no longer** stems from the ancient Jewish belief that the sea represented all the things in opposition to the rule of God (v. 1). Leviathan, for example, was an Old Testament sea monster representing the forces of evil (Ps 74:13-14; Jb 41:1; Is 27:1). Isaiah also compared the wicked to the ocean (Is 57:20), and the first beast of Revelation arose from the sea (Rv 13:1). The vanishing of the sea from "the new heaven and new earth" symbolized the disappearance of disorder, chaos, and wickedness.

John **also saw the Holy City, new Jerusalem**, descending **out of heaven from God**, conveying the truth that the final home of the redeemed is the new earth for all eternity. Her description as **a bride adorned** (Gk. *kekosmēmenēn*, "arrange, put in order, ornament, embellish with honor," 21:2; cp. Mt 25:7; Lk 11:25; 21:5; 1 Tm 2:9; 1 Pt 3:5) **for her husband** connects her to the heaven-dwelling saints who participated in the marriage supper of the Lamb (19:7-8). This imagery also contrasts the holy city or bride, "new Jerusalem," with the wicked city or prostitute, "Babylon the Great" (17:1).

21:3-4 For the last time John **heard a loud voice from the throne**, and it proclaimed the significance of the heavenly city for believers. The promise of God personally "dwelling" with His people was very important in the Old Testament (see Ex 29:45; Lv 26:11-12; Jr 31:33; Ezk 37:27; Zch 2:11; 8:8). The fulfillment of this promise developed throughout Scripture:

- Both the tabernacle of Moses in the wilderness and the temple in Jerusalem "housed" the presence of God through the symbol of a cloud and pillar of fire.

- The glory of God became incarnate and literally "tabernacled" (Gk. *skenoō*) with believers through the person of Jesus Christ (Jn 1:14).

- After His ascension, Jesus sent the Holy Spirit to dwell within His individual followers so that Paul could say: A Christian's body is "a sanctuary of the Holy Spirit" (1 Co 6:19).

- The final development of the promise will be fulfilled in the new Jerusalem, when God will dwell eternally and visibly among His people: **God's dwelling** (Gk. *skēnēn*, "tent, tabernacle"; see Rv 13:6) **is with men, and He will live** (Gk. *skēnōsei*, "abide, dwell"; see 7:15) **with them** (21:3).

The dwelling of God with His people has many benefits:

- God **will wipe away** (Gk. *exaleipsi*, "wipe off, erase, anoint or wash completely"; in other contexts, "erase, cancel, obliterate"; cp. 3:5; 7:17; Ac 3:19; Col 2:14) **every tear from their eyes** (Rv 21:4). These tears of suffering and sacrifice have been shed by those who have left everything to fol-

Revelation's Tale of Two Cities and Two Women

Babylon the Great	Bride of Christ
• A woman (chap. 17) and • a city (chaps. 16,18); • "dressed in purple and scarlet" (17:4)	• A woman (chap. 19) and • a city (chap. 21); • clothed in "fine linen, white and clean" (19:8)
Pseudo-queen and consort of the beast (17:3-4; 18:7)	Bride of the Lamb who is King of kings (19:7,9,16)
Dwelling place for demons (18:2)	Dwelling place for God (21:3,11,22-23)
"A woman sitting on a scarlet beast, that was covered with blasphemous names" (17:3)	An army sitting on "white horses," clothed in "fine linen" following Him whose names include "the Word of God," and "King of kings and Lord of lords" (19:13-14,16)
"The notorious prostitute" who kills the saints (17:1,5-6)	"A vast multitude praises God for avenging the saints' blood on 'the notorious prostitute'" (19:1-2)
Closely related to the earth dwellers (17:8)	Closely related to the "vast multitude" who are the heaven dwellers (7:9-15; 12:12; 13:6; 19:1,6)
• "The great city" (16:19; 17:18; 18:10); • "Babylon the Great" (16:19; 17:5; 18:2)	• "The holy city" (21:2,10); • "new Jerusalem" (21:2,10)
The earth dwellers' names are not written in "the book of life" (17:8; cp. 13:8).	No one enters whose name is not written in the "book of life" (21:27).
"She glorified herself" (18:7).	She is "arrayed with God's glory" (21:11).
"In a single hour such fabulous wealth was destroyed" (18:17).	"Her radiance was like a very precious stone" (21:11).
"The voice of groom and bride will never be heard . . . again" (18:23).	"The marriage feast of the Lamb" (19:9), for which the bride has made herself ready (19:7,9; 21:2); "The bride, the wife of the Lamb . . . coming down out of heaven from God" (21:9-10).

low Christ and endured the many heartaches and sorrows of this world.

• All sources of sadness will be removed: **Death** as well as **grief, crying, and pain** (Rv 21:4). God will replace the effects of sin and suffering once plaguing the faithful with joy and bliss. All bear heavy burdens and have sources of sorrow, which cause groaning within (Rm 8:23). You can look with eager hope toward the fulfillment of this precious promise.

All will occur **because the previous things have passed away** (Gk. *apēlthan*, "gone away, departed, left," Rv 21:4). The trials of the old world have no place among the pleasures of the new world. This new Jerusalem where God eternally dwells with His people is the place anticipated with great longing by all faithful saints of both Old and New Testaments (cp. Heb 11:13,16).

21:5-8 This announcement **"Look! I am making everything new"** (Gk. *kaina*, "unprecedented," v. 5; see 2:17) affirms the process and the settled certainty that God will establish the eternal realm portrayed. A voice had declared after the seven bowls of wrath that, "It is done!" (16:17), but now God makes the same declaration, **"It is done!"** in referring to the new Jerusalem (v. 6).

The last part of this section contrasts the destinies of the believer and unbeliever. The character of God as both the source—**Alpha and Beginning**—and goal—**Omega** and **End**—of creation assures the truth of these pronouncements (v. 6). The believer, who is **thirsty** for the things of God, will be able to drink **from the spring of living water** (v. 6; cp. 7:17) **as a gift** (Gk. *dōrean*, "freely, without charge or cost," from *doron*, "gift," v. 6; cp. Mt 10:8). This person is described as **the victor** (see chaps. 2–3) who will be considered a **son** of **God**. For the faithful, the images of quenched thirst and family relationship are sweet promises, but unbelievers, characterized by their many sins, will not share in them; they will receive a **share** in **the lake that burns with fire and sulfur** (Rv 21:8).

Of the numerous lists of sins in the New Testament (e.g., Rm 1:29-31; Eph 5:3-5; Col 3:5-8), only here are COWARDS, (Gk. *deilois*, "timid, fearful") included (Rv 21:8). Why is the sin of cowardice at the top of this list? The answer lies in the realization that this condemnation of "cowards" (v. 8) is meant to contrast with the "victor" (v. 7). While the rest of the sins describe the unbelieving world outside the church, cowardice is a trait of those who, though inside the church, were not genuine believers, giving in to the pressures of the world. The victorious ones, on the other hand, overcame the world and with genuine faith remained faithful until the end. At the final judgment, the cowardly will take their place in the "lake of fire" because they were never truly part of the redeemed (1 Jn 2:19).

The New Jerusalem (21:9-27)

21:9-11 This invitation (v. 9) parallels the one John received in 17:1 to see the judgment of the "notorious prostitute." This time, instead of going into the "desert" (17:3), John was carried **in the Spirit** to the top of a huge **mountain**. The view from such a height must have been breathtaking as John watched **the holy city, Jerusalem, coming down out of heaven from God** (21:10). The city, like a bride, was **arrayed with God's glory**, and **her radiance** (Gk. *phōstēr*, "that which gives light or illuminates, brightness, brilliance" in the sense of the radiation of concentrated light; cp. Php 2:15) **was like a very precious stone**. John provided a detailed description of the city, including its walls and gates (Rv 21:12-14), its measurements (vv. 15-17), its building materials and adornments (vv. 18-21), and the conditions within the city (vv. 22-27).

21:12-14 *Walls and gates.* All the ancient cities of John's day had walls surrounding them for the purpose of protection in times of war. These walls had a number of reinforced gates, each guarded by armed men. The **wall** of the new Jerusalem (v. 12) was not for protection, however, for "nothing profane will ever enter it" (v. 27). The placement of the **12 gates**, with three on each side (v. 13), makes clear that the shape of the city is **a square** (v. 16). Each of the 12 gates bears **the names of the 12 tribes of the sons of Israel** and is manned by **12 angels** (v. 12). Further, the **12 foundations** beneath the massive walls of the city have on them **the 12 names of the Lamb's 12 apostles** (v. 14; see Eph 2:19-20). The prominence of the 12 tribes of Israel and the 12 apostles in the city emphasizes the unity of ancient Israel and the New Testament church as the people of God.

21:15-17 *Measurements.* The angel serving as John's guide to the city measured it for him (cp. Ezk 40-41), appropriately, using **a gold measuring rod** since the city itself is made of pure gold (Rv 21:18). The city is not just **a square** but a cube, with **its length, width, and height** being **equal**. Each side of the city is **12,000 stadia** long, which equals about 1,400 miles, the distance from Dallas to Los Angeles. The thickness of the walls at **144 cubits** equals about 200 feet. The dimensions of this city defy both imagination and the natural laws of physics, for its walls stretch 1,400 miles into the sky, with only 200 feet of support at the base! The emphasis in these measurements, with multiples of 10 and 12, is on the perfect proportions of the new Jerusalem.

21:18-21 *Building materials and adornments.* Constructed of exceptional materials, the city was shining like a **jasper** stone (v. 11), possibly a bright green color. From the vision of God's throne room (4:3), it is closely associated with God's glory. **The city** itself is made of a **pure gold** that is **like clear glass**.

John listed the 12 jewels that **adorned** the **foundations of the city wall**. The arrangement of these multicolored precious stones on the foundations of the city walls would give the impression that the city rests on a shimmering rainbow. The corresponding modern versions of these jewels, along with their possible colors, are as follows:[4]

- **jasper**—perhaps a green quartz;
- **sapphire**—dark blue like the modern sapphire;
- **chalcedony**—gray or green stone;
- **emerald**—bright, cloudy green, like modern natural emerald;
- **sardonyx**—possibly a banded stone like agate or onyx;
- **carnelian**—deep red semiprecious stone;
- **chrysolite**—yellow semiprecious stone;
- **beryl**—blue-green stone, like modern aquamarine;
- **topaz**—dark yellow or orange, like modern topaz;
- **chrysoprase**—yellow-green semiprecious stone;
- **jacinth**—violet-blue semiprecious stone;
- **amethyst**—light purple, perhaps like modern amethyst (21:19-20).

The "pearly gates" fit within the dimensions of the wall already described; they would have to be **12 pearls** of colossal size—at least 200 feet in diameter (v. 21). Pearls were considered the most luxurious of all jewels in the ancient world (see Mt 13:45-46). The last part of the city John described was **the broad street**, paved with **pure gold**, once again **like transparent glass** (Rv 21:21). The priests of Israel's ancient temple used to walk on gold floors (1 Kg 6:30), but now every citizen of heaven will have that same privilege and more.

21:22 *Conditions within the city.* There is no need for a sanctuary or temple or formal location to meet with God, **because the Lord God the Almighty and the Lamb are its sanctuary**. In the temple of ancient Israel, the presence of God in the holy of holies made the temple sacred. But, in the new Jerusalem, the presence of God makes the entire city a holy of holies.

21:23-24 The second aspect of life in the holy city is a natural result of God's presence there: the radiant **glory** of the "Lord God the Almighty and the Lamb" far outshines any created light source. With the luminous glory of God filling the new Jerusalem, the **sun** and the **moon** are unnecessary.

The **glory** that **the kings of the earth** bring to the city refers to the earthly "glory" possessed by the nations, which is now given back to the One who alone deserves it (v. 24). The presence of such "kings" in the holy city is interesting since we saw the "kings of the earth" aligned with the beast earlier in the book (17:2,18). Apparently, God's mercy and grace so triumph over evil that He redeems some even from the rebellious "kings of the earth" (cp. Is 60:1-3).

21:25-27 The third characteristic of life in the new Jerusalem is complete protection and absolute purity, concepts expressed in the notion that **each day the gates will never close**. Unlike the typical ancient city, there is no need for inhabitants of the new Jerusalem to fear unwelcome nightly visitors. Also, the gates of the holy city do not need to protect the citizens from anything **profane** (Gk. *koinon*, "common, ordinary," but in Jewish usage, "unclean, unhallowed") and from anyone **who does what is vile** (Gk. *bdelugma*, "something detestable, abhorrent or foul," esp. associated with idolatry; cp. 17:4-5; Mt 24:15; Mk 13:14; Lk 16:15) **or false** (Rv 21:27). People characterized in this way are not **in the Lamb's book of life** and so will not be present in the new Jerusalem (v. 27). Because of the safety and purity of the city, **the nations** can freely come and go, bringing their worship offerings—**glory and honor**—to the Lamb at any time (v. 26).

Eden's Restoration (22:1-5)

In the previous sections, John has described the city of new Jerusalem beginning from the outside (the wall, gates, and foundations) and moving to the inside (the "sanctuary" and its worshipers). John's continued description will reveal the treasures kept at the city's center. What Adam and Eve forfeited through their disobedience, namely, dwelling in a garden of delight in perfect fellowship with God, the Lord will return to His creation. Here, though, Eden has not only

been restored but also elevated and expanded for the enjoyment of God's people throughout eternity.

22:1-2a An angel "showed" John the "holy city, new Jerusalem" (21:9-10), and the same angel **showed** John the rest of the glorious vision. First, John saw **the river of living water, sparkling** (Gk. *lampron*, "shining, brilliant; transparent, clear"; see 19:8) **like crystal** (22:1), recalling the river that "went out from Eden" (Gn 2:10). Yet, the "river of living water" in new Jerusalem was **flowing . . . down the middle of the broad street of the city** (Rv 22:1-2), fulfilling prophecy (Zch 14:8). The source of the river is God Himself, for it flows **from the throne of God and of the Lamb**. These life-giving waters also recall the images of Jesus as the "living water" (Jn 4:10-14) and the Holy Spirit as "streams of living water" flowing from deep within the believer (Jn 7:38).

22:2b-3a The garden of Eden also had within it the "tree of life" (Gn 3:22), which was the source of eternal life. After the fall, Adam and Eve were driven from the garden so that they would not eat of the tree and find immortality in the midst of their sin. In the new Jerusalem, however, **the tree of life** is restored to humanity. The tree is said to be **on both sides of the river**, either one gigantic plant or "tree" collectively in the sense of an "orchard," with individual trees lining both sides of the river. What is certain, however, is that the presence of the tree of life indicates the removal of **any curse** from God's people. All are permitted to eat freely from the tree, having the choice of **12 kinds of fruit,** which it produces **every month**. Fruit production is normally dependent on the proper season, but in the new Jerusalem there will be no such seasons. The "right to eat from the tree of life" was promised by Jesus to the victorious saints in the message to Ephesus (Rv 2:7).

The use of **the leaves of the tree** for the **healing** of **the nations** has its background in a vision of Ezekiel in which the restored Jerusalem had fruit-producing trees whose "leaves" would be used "for medicine" (Ezk 47:12). The "healing" imagery is also probably connected to the overall symbol that the tree of life represents the lifting of humanity's former curse. The combined images of the river of living water and fruit-producing trees have Ezekiel 47 as their background.

22:3b-5 The garden of Eden had a river and the tree of life, but it did not have **the throne of God and of the Lamb**. Now, instead of ruling from a lofty throne room like the one in chapter 4, the Father and Son will reign in the midst of **the city**:

- With the lifting of sin's curse, the **servants** of God can faithfully **serve Him** in the city (v. 3). Although what kinds of activities such service will require is unclear, certainly life in eternity will never be boring. The picture here is a city bustling with activity as the people of God carry out their appointed duties in the new Jerusalem. Work will no longer be laborious (Gn 3:17) but a joyous expression of worship to the Lord.

- With God ruling in the city, its inhabitants will actually **see His face** (Rv 22:4) in contrast to the days when no one could see God's face and live (Ex 33:20). In eternity somehow the saints will be enabled to behold the glory of God without fear. This intimate knowledge of God cannot be imagined, but it surely surpasses even the most wonderful spiritual experience that this earthly life holds.

- The **name** of God will be on the **foreheads** of His servants. As Aaron the

priest wore on the front of his turban and forehead a gold plate inscribed with the words "Holy to the Lord" (Ex 28:36-38), the saints of the new Jerusalem will all be set apart as a kingdom of priests "holy to the Lord" (Rv 22:4; Ex 19:6). Also, Jesus had promised the victorious saints of Philadelphia that they would bear the name of God (Rv 3:12).

The description of the holy city concluded with what appears to be the most important point about the new Jerusalem—the presence of God among the people. The absence of night and the needlessness of sun and lamp are all **because the Lord God will give them light** (Gk. *phōtisei*, "shine, illumine," 22:5; cp. 18:1; 21:23; Jn 1:9). The proclamation announced by voices in heaven (Rv 11:15) is fully accomplished as God and His faithful servants **reign** (Gk. *basileusousin*, "exercise power, govern, rule," 22:5; cp. 5:10; 20:4,6) in the new Jerusalem **forever and ever**.

EPILOGUE (22:6-21)

The splendid visions that John had seen slowly faded away, and he was back in prison on the island of Patmos. John still recorded the messages given to him by several voices. In the Greek text, because these messages do not follow any discernible pattern, determining exactly who is speaking can be difficult. They begin with John's interactions with the angel (22:6-11), followed by words from Jesus Himself (22:12-16), and then, possibly, some concluding remarks from John (22:17-21). This apocalyptic book of prophecy revealed to John was written as a letter to the churches of Asia Minor. John's expression of the saints' confident expectation of Christ's return is the closing theme of the entire book.

Heart to Heart:
It Is Well with Your Soul

At times in the Christian life, faith can become like a weighty burden and hope like an elusive dream. While everyone else seems to enjoy all the pleasures this earthly life can offer, you must forge ahead as "pilgrims" on this earth, aspiring to "a better land—a heavenly one" (Heb 11:16). The Lord surely knows how difficult the life of faith can be for His followers, and seemingly He provided the vision of the "new Jerusalem" (Rv 21–22) for that very reason. Because His children sometimes lose sight of His promises, God gave John a magnificent glimpse into eternity and allowed him to share its wonders with you. When you arrive at the gates of the new Jerusalem, there will finally be an end to both faith and hope. Seeing God face to face will remove any need for either, and all that will remain is love. In light of this truth, you can press on through whatever difficulties life sends your way and declare with hymn writer Horatio Spafford that "It is well with my soul."

John and the Angel (22:6-11)

22:6-7 The angel who guided John through the vision of new Jerusalem assured him that the **words are faithful and true**. They are reliable because the same **Lord** who inspired **the spirits of the prophets** of old (1 Pt 1:20-21) now speaks through **His angel**, reminding one of the "title page" of Revelation (Rv 1:1), for the angel affirmed that God revealed all this to John in order **to show His servants what must quickly take place** (22:6). The events "must" take place because they are settled in the predetermined plan of God. You can trust that what God has said He will certainly bring to pass.

The speaker changes unexpectedly from the angel to Christ Himself (v. 7). His voice affirmed what the angel had said— He is **coming quickly**, the first of three times that Jesus announced His own return in the epilogue (vv. 7,12,20). Repeating the theme of obedience from the very beginning of the book (1:3), Jesus also affirmed that **the one who keeps the prophetic words** of Revelation will be **blessed**. Although certainly a vision of the end times, the "revelation of Jesus Christ" (1:1) remains the word of God to which His people must submit their lives even now.

22:8-9 As if to verify Revelation's human authorship, **John** stated that he was **the one who heard and saw these things**. In great wonder at the incredible revelation he had seen, John once again **fell down to worship at the feet of the angel**. He may have been so overwhelmed by the surpassing greatness of the vision that he thought the angel before him was Jesus Himself. The angel rebuked this mistake, though, and affirmed his humble role as a fellow created being (cp. 19:10). John must **worship God** alone. Though the angel was an appointed messenger of God, he was **a fellow slave** (Gk. *sundoulos*, "one who serves the same master with another, ministers to the same king, acknowledges the same Lord, is subject to the same authority"; cp. 6:11; 19:10; Mt 18:28-33; 24:49; Col 1:7; 4:7) with John, the prophets, and all **who keep the words** of Revelation (Rv 22:9). Both the angels of heaven and redeemed humanity exist to serve their Creator.

22:10-11 God intends the truths revealed in Scripture to be shared with all who will hear them. So, the angel's next admonition, **"Don't seal the prophetic words of this book,"** can be puzzling. Why would John even want to conceal such great revelations from the world? Consider the parallel instructions to the prophet Daniel at the close of his visions (Dn 12:4). The angel seemingly intended to contrast Daniel's revelation with John's revelation, for one was to be "sealed" while the other was to be "unsealed." In Daniel's day the time was not right to reveal the plan of God for the redemption of the world, but by John's day the right time was at hand. Indeed, he says, **the time** (Gk. *kairos*, "a decisive, appointed time; the right or due time or season"; cp. Jn 7:6,8) **is near** (Rv 22:10).

A fourfold announcement is made regarding the certainty that a person's character will be revealed in their deeds (v. 11). On the one hand, **the unrighteous** will live in **unrighteousness** and **the filthy** will remain **filthy**. On the other hand, **the righteous** will live **in righteousness** and **the holy** will remain **holy**. These character traits will be judged by God in the last days.

Conclusion (22:12-21)

22:12-16 At this point, the angel had completed his task, and John would never hear from him again. Instead, the book of Revelation drew to a close with the voice of the Lord Jesus. In light of Christ's imminent return, the Lord emphasized the **reward** (Gk. *misthos*, "wages, payment for work completed"; cp. 11:18; Jn 4:36; 2 Jn 1:8) and punishment earned by **each person according to what he has done** (Rv 22:12) and expands on this theme of

reward and punishment (vv. 14-15). First, **those who wash their robes** in Christ's blood are **blessed**, because they may eat from **the tree of life** and **enter** the new Jerusalem **by the gates** (v. 14). The symbolism of "washed robes" was first introduced where the rescued church is identified by their purification in the "blood of the Lamb" (7:14). All those who are cleansed in the blood of Christ will have both eternal life ("tree of life") and unhindered access to God's presence ("enter the city by the gates"). Yet, those who are not cleansed by the Lamb will have no part of such blessings. Left **outside** the city of God are those characterized by lives of impurity, idolatry, and selfishness (22:15). These sins are not so heinous that they are beyond God's forgiveness, but such sins *characterize* unredeemed human beings who are thus excluded from heaven. The symbolic term **dogs** is used throughout Scripture to refer to various kinds of impure and unclean persons (see Dt 23:17-18; Php 3:2).

Christ's dispensation of justice upon humanity is grounded in the fact that He is the One who is equal in nature and status with God. The three divine titles here applied to Jesus—**the Alpha and the Omega, the First and the Last, the Beginning and the End**—have also been used throughout the book for God the Father (Rv 22:13; see 1:8,17; 2:8; 21:6). Thus, as the God of all times and all places, God who is the source of all and the goal of all, Jesus also has the power and right to judge all.

Jesus confirmed the authenticity of the message John has recorded by corroborating John's confession that an **angel** was **sent** by Christ **to attest these things . . . for the churches** (22:16). "Church" (Gk. *ekklēsias*) was last mentioned at the end of the messages to the seven churches (3:22). Now the truth is affirmed that the entire content of Revelation, not just the individual messages, is for the edification of the churches. All Christians in every generation are meant to benefit from the message of Revelation.

In affirmation of His authority, Jesus concluded with two more titles previously mentioned in the book. As **the Root and the Offspring of David**, Christ fulfills all of Scripture's messianic prophecies, revealing Himself as the goal to which all of the Old Testament was headed. As **the Bright Morning Star**, Christ is the literal "guiding light" for all believers as they forge ahead toward the end of the age (22:16). Morning stars appear in the sky only when night is almost over. Likewise, believers wait and watch with eager expectation for the glorious appearance of their Savior because this age is almost at an end.

22:17 In the final verses of this epilogue, John wrote his own urgent comments. First, he offered a kind of "invitation" to respond to the book's message. This verbal "altar call" of the book contains the aged preacher's pleading with the unredeemed reader to **Come!** (v. 17). **Whoever desires** may freely drink of **the living water**, meaning eternal life, offered by **the Spirit** of God and **the bride** of Christ. Clearly, the blessings of the redeemed will not be fully enjoyed until the consummation of all things, but the heavenly blessings of eternal life are meant to begin immediately. The gospel of Jesus Christ is offered **as a gift** (Gk. *dōrean*, "freely, without payment"; see 21:6) to anyone who will receive it.

22:18-19 John included a stern message of warning as the one who recorded **the prophetic words of this book**, extraordinary evidence that John was aware what he had written was "God-breathed" (2 Tm 3:16) and authoritative as Scripture. These warnings were not just for the future copyists or scribes who might accidentally add or delete words from the book.

Instead, John's harsh warnings are specifically for **everyone who hears** the book. The one who **adds to** or **takes away from** the prophetic words are those who hear the message of Revelation and then distort its truths. Such people will bring upon themselves the judgment of God, both by receiving **the plagues** of the book and not receiving eternal life in **the holy city** of God.

This warning against deliberate tampering with the word of God also echoes Eve's temptation by the serpent in the garden of Eden, which resulted in the original curse of humankind. The Devil enticed Eve to doubt the word of God with the question, "Did God *really* say . . . ?" In response, Eve *added to* God's command by saying that they cannot "even touch" the fruit of the tree, while the serpent *took away* from God's command by suggesting, "You will not die" (Gn 3:1-7). Anyone who tampers with the words of Revelation in a similar way truly reveals the corruption of his character. This stern warning is for any so-called "prophecy experts" who presume dogmatically to proclaim the contents and timing of Revelation's events with authoritative certainty. In interpreting the book, nothing is to be added or taken away from what God actually revealed.

22:20-21 The ultimate reason for these warnings is that John is not the author of the book. **He who testifies about these things** is Jesus Himself. All of Revelation is true and urgent for the churches because of the imminency of Christ's return.

"Yes, I am coming quickly" are the last spoken words of Jesus recorded in Scripture (v. 20). The Lord put an end to any doubts about His imminent return. Christ's gentle but firm affirmation of His return is the steady echo of hope ringing true throughout all churches, in all places, at all times. When life is difficult and sorrows come—Jesus is coming soon. When joy overflows and blessings abound—Jesus is coming soon. When death is certain and life is at an end—Jesus is coming soon. In all situations, no matter what the circumstances, you can proclaim with John, **"Amen! Come, Lord Jesus!"** The conclusion of Revelation is that of an ancient epistle, as John wished **the grace of the Lord Jesus** upon **all the saints** (v. 21).

Heart to Heart: Proclaim the Message of Revelation

Most of you probably would not consider the message of Revelation to be particularly "evangelistic" since it does not necessarily include the "plan of salvation" or any further instructions for baptism and discipleship. If you consider the overall themes of the book, however, you will see that, while the content *may not be obviously evangelistic, the* goal *of the book most certainly* is. *The stark contrast between the worshipers of the Lamb and the worshipers of the beast makes it impossible for you to remain neutral in your alliances. Both the Lamb and the beast demand that you take a side. In the end, this choice becomes the greatest decision you will ever make, determining your eternal destiny: either in the new Jerusalem or the lake of fire. John's closing remarks bring this decision once again to the forefront, for with the Holy Spirit and the bride of Christ, he pleads, "Come to the Lamb!" Those who have already sworn their allegiance to Christ must echo John's invitation to everyone the Lord brings their way. The glorious return of Christ will also bring His righteous judgment of the world. In the time that you have left before that great day, you must faithfully declare God's message to the world: "Worship the Lamb!"*

Bibliography

Criswell, W. A. *Expository Sermons on Revelation*, vols. 1–5. Grand Rapids: Zondervan, 1962–1966.

Johnson, Alan F. *Revelation*. The Expositor's Bible Commentary, vol. 12. Grand Rapids: Zondervan, 1981.

Pate, C. Marvin, ed. *Four Views on the Book of Revelation*. Grand Rapids: Zondervan, 1998.

Scott, Walter. *Exposition of the Revelation of Jesus*. Westwood: Revell, 1968.

*Thomas, Robert. *Revelation 1–7: An Exegetical Commentary*. Chicago: Moody Press, 1992.

*_____. *Revelation 8–22: An Exegetical Commentary*. Chicago: Moody Press, 1995.

Walvoord, John. *The Revelation of Jesus Christ*. Chicago: Moody Press, 1968.

* For advanced study

Notes

[1] Kendell H. Easley, *Revelation*, Holman New Testament Commentary (Nashville: Broadman and Holman, 1998), 138–139.

[2] Grant R. Osborne, *Revelation*, BECNT (Grand Rapids, Baker, 2002), 305.

[3] Ibid., 600.

[4] Easley, *Revelation*, 400.

INDEX OF FEATURES

Key:

Chart	plain text
Map	**boldface**
Heart to Heart	*italics*
<u>Excursus</u>	<u>underline</u>

Abide in Him 240
Acts, Old Testament Quotes in 282
Adulteress, The Forgiven 220
Anna 144
Aphrodite 414
Apphia 743
Asia, The Province of 595
Authority, Understanding 892
Baptism and Salvation 265
Beatitudes for Women 32
Beatitudes of Revelation, The 956
Bernice 345
Blood of Martyrs Is the Seed of the Church, The 280
Boasting, The Ground for 587
Body, Love for the 635
Canaanite Woman, The: A Desperate Mother Encounters Jesus 56
Candace 288
Caring Deeply 629
Chloe 417
Choices, Making the Right 537
Christ, Becoming Like 385
Christ, Heresies and the Doctrine of 200
Christ, Identifying with 516
Christ's Resurrection Appearances 458
Christian Liberty, Helpful Hints for Exercising Your 440
Christian Woman's Wardrobe, A 614
Church Government 314
Church Leaders, Qualifications of 670
Churches, What the Spirit Says to the 922
Claudia 719
Comfort in the Midst of Turmoil, Finding 928
Comparison of 1, 2, 3 John, A 876
Confession of Faith, The Early 392
Contrasts between the Old and the New (Covenants) 474
Corinthian Church, Divisions in the 418
Critical Spirit, A 401
Damaris 324
Daughter of Jairus, The 99
Daughters of Philip, The 338
Deacons 275
Demons 97

Disabled Woman, The 171
Discipleship, The Cost of 108
Divorce, Reasons God Rejects 62
Do as I Do, and as I Say 651
Doing the "Right" Thing 746
Dorcas 292
Drusilla 343
Dwelling, God's 547
"Elect Lady," The 877
Election, Understanding 389
Elizabeth 142
End in Sight, The 631
Eschatological Glossary 637
Essenes (Jewish Sects in the New Testament) 27
Euodia and Syntyche 590
Faith, Community of 615
Faith, The Obstacle Course of 435
Faith, Persevering in 849
Faithfulness, God's 862
Feminism versus Biblical Womanhood. 608
Focus?, Where Is Your 581
Forgetting the Past 610
Forgiveness and Light 219
Friends, Forever 42
Galatia 510
Galatians 3:28, The Context of 522
Galilee in the Time of Jesus 3
Gender-Inclusive Language 40
Gentleness in the Gender Lens 36
Goddess Worship 331
Godliness with Contentment Is Great Gain 686
God's Word, Digging Deep into 726
Good News! 370
Greco-Roman Goddesses 333
Grumbling, Do Everything Without 585
Gullible Women of the World or Godly Women of the Word 714
Hagar and Sarah 526
Head Coverings for Women 447
Healing and Revelation 107
Heaven, On Earth as It Is in 925
Herodians (Jewish Sects in the New Testament) 26
Herodias 55
Heroines of Faith 783
Home, Your Ministry in Your. 47
Hospitality or Entertainment 835
House Churches in the New Testament, Examples of 744
Household Baptisms in Acts 296
How Could God Let This Happen? 940
Humble Obedience to God 885
Inclusive Language 89
Influence 41
Inheritance in Jesus, Your 602
Is Everything as It Seems? 893
Isaiah 53 in 1 Peter 2, Tracing 823
Issues Addressed in 1 Corinthians. 415

It Is Well with Your Soul 983
James 5:14 and Extreme Unction 805
James, Four Men Named 792
Jesus, Doing All Things in the Name of 616
Jesus, The Family Tree of 151
Jesus "First Place in Everything", Giving 604
Jesus the High Priest 766
Jesus, Spreading the Fragrance of 472
Jesus, the Beloved, and His Great Love for Women 539
Jesus?, What Is Your Reaction to 21
Jesus' Disciples 48
Jewish Feasts and Festivals 121
Jewish Sects in the New Testament 24
Joanna and Susanna: Women Who Supported Jesus 160
1 John, Lessons from 872
2 John, Life Lessons from 880
3 John, Three Men in 884
Journeys of Mary 19
Junia 410
Keeping the Main Thing the Main Thing 105
Kingdom of Heaven, The 54
Lamb and of the Beast, Followers of the 901
Law and Grace 518
Legalism, Avoiding the Bondage of 611
"Let Us" Exhortations 763
Liberation Theology 235
Living the Exemplary Life 630
Lois and Eunice 697
Lord's Prayer, Teachings from the 43
Lost and Found 173
Love 870
Love for You, God's 386
Loving Care, The Truth of God's 387
Loving Your Neighbor 116
Loving Correction 648
Luke, Themes in 135
Luke's Central Section, The Teachings of 165
Lydia 319
Mark, Controversial Encounters Found in 93
Mark, Parallel Events in 106
Marriage Dilemma, The 434
Mary and Martha, The Discipleship of 230
Mary and Martha of Bethany 229
Mary, Mother of Jesus 72, 140
Mary's Song 142
Mary Magdalene 161
Mary Magdalene 247
Mind at War, A 498
Ministry, Charge to 717
Modesty 664
Money in the Bible 183
Mouth?, What Is the Fruit of Your 734
New Beginning, A 34
Nympha 620
Old Testament Allusions in the Book of Revelation, Major 899

Overcoming the Past 544
Palestine, Expansion of the Early Church in 287
Palestine in the Time of Jesus 7
Pastors, Pattern for.. 730
Paul Compared the Corinthian Believers to 477
Paul, The First Missionary Journey of 308
Paul, The Second Missionary Journey of 323
Paul, The Third Missionary Journey of 332
Paul, The Timeline of 316
Paul's Be-attitudes to Timothy 701
Paul's Conversion and Early Ministry 291
Paul's Impeccable Credentials 586
Paul's Life after Acts 352
Paul's Steps to a God-Pleasing Life 601
Paul's View of Women 564
Paul's Voyage to Rome 350
Persecuted, Partnering the 645
Pharisees (Jewish Sects in the New Testament) 24
Philippians, A Recipe for Spiritual Character from the Book of .. 593
Phoebe 407
Pilate's Wife 72
Pray, Challenged to 633
Pray for Your Children 579
Prayer, Confidence in 871
Prayer, Intercessory 406
Prayer of Jesus, The 242
Prayer, The Significance of 935
Priscilla, Aquila, and Apollos 328
Promises of God, The Precious 846
Prophecies Fulfilled at the Cross 306
Queens of the New Testament, The 101
Rejoice, Make a Choice to 591
Relationships, Greetings in 889
Religious Leaders in the New Testament 182
Revelation, Proclaim the Message of 986
Revelation's Tale of Two Cities and Two Women 978
Rhoda 301
Sadducees (Jewish Sects in the New Testament) 25
Salvation in Christ Alone 270
Samaritan Woman, The 212
Samaritan Woman, The 213
Sapphira 273
Scripture in Matthew (OT Prophecy), Jesus' Ministry as Fulfillment of .. 29
Sea of Galilee, Ministry of Jesus Around the 31
Self-Control Is the Key 731
Servant Girl 71
Sexual Immorality 613
She Did What She Could 120
Simon's Mother-in-Law 90
Sin and Temptation, Victory over 381
Sinner at Simon's House 159
Slave Girl, A Fortune-Telling 319
Sorrow, The Blessing of 157
Spirit versus the Flesh, The 528
Spiritual Mothering 733

Spiritual Warfare, Waging 949
Submission 821,826
Submission Is Not Oppression 617
Suffering for a Season 815
Synagogue (Capernaum), First Century 30
Temptation, Resist 758
Theological Terms 645
Things That "Must Be Removed" 558
Virgins, Foolish and Sensible 67
Weary, Let Us Not Grow 530
Wedding at Cana, The 207
Who He Is 56
Widow of Nain 158
Widow, Persistent 178
Wisdom Is Knowing When to Ask for Help 795
Wisdom, The Two Types of 421
Wives of Herod the Great, King of Judea 20
Woman with an Issue of Blood, The 98
Women and the Great Commission 74
Women and the Parables of Jesus 68
Women as Witnesses 211
Women Associated with Jesus' Birth, The 145
Women at the Cross 187
Women Healed by Jesus 46
Women in the Life of Jesus 9
Women Mentioned by Paul in Romans 409
Women Ministering to Jesus 117
Women of Worship and Work 167
Women with Jesus in His Last Days 69
Women's Ministry?, Why Have a 676
Worry, The Solution for 592
Zealots (Jewish Sects in the New Testament) 26
Zebedee's Wife 63

PALESTINE IN THE TIME OF JESUS

- • City
- ○ City (uncertain location)
- ◉ Decapolis city
- ○ Decapolis city (uncertain location)
- ★ Administrative capital
- ▲ Mountain peak
- — Major roads
- — Other roads
- First procuratorship
- Territory of Antipas
- Territory of Philip
- Syrian territory

Coponius was named the first prefect and established the administrative capital at Caesarea Marítima

ABILENE

35 E

36 E

Sidon

ITUREA

Damascus

Abana R.

Mt. Hermon ▲

Caesarea-Philippi (Panias)

Pharpar R.

PHOENICIA (TYRE)

Tyre

Litani R.

Cadasa (Kedesh)

Gischala (Gush Halav)

L. Huleh

GAULANITIS

Raphana

King's Highway

BATANEA

TR

Ptolemais (Acco)

Capernaum

Bethsaida

GALILEE

Sea of Galilee

Gergesa (Kursi)

Hippos

Gamala

Jotapata

Mt. Carmel ▲

Sepphoris

Geba

Nazareth

Tiberias

Abila

Adraa (Edrei)

AUR

Xaloth (Chesulloth)

Mt. Tabor ▲

Gadara

Bostra

Dora

Legio (Megiddo)

Esdraelon Valley

Kishon R.

Scythopolis (Beth-shan)

Dion

DECAPOLIS

Ca

MEDITERRANEAN SEA

Caesarea Marítima (Strato's Tower) ★

Ginae (Jenin)

Pella

Aenon

Salim

SAMARIA

Gerasa (Jerash)

Jordan R.

Jabbok R.

Apollonia

Yarkon R.

Antipatris (Aphek)

Sebaste (Samaria)

Mt. Ebal ▲

Neapolis (Shechem)

Mt. Gerizim ▲

Coreae

Amathus

Joppa

Lydda

Ephraim (Ophrah)

Alexandrium

Gedor (Gadara)

PEREA

32 N

Jamnia

Emmaus (Nicopolis)

JUDEA

Archelais

Philadelphia (Amman)

Azotus (Ashdod)

Jerusalem

Jericho

Cypros

Esbus (Heshbon)

Bethany

Ascalon (Ashkelon)

Hyrcania

Mesad Hasidim (Qumran)

Mt. Nebo ▲

Medeba

Betogabris (Beth-guvrin)

Hebron

En-gedi

DEAD SEA

Machaerus

Callirrhoe (Zereth-shahar)

Eastern Desert

Gaza

IDUMEA

Masada

Arnon R.

Raphia

N. Besor

Malatha

Arad

King's Highway

Beersheba

NABATEA

Arabah

31 N

Zered R.

Khirbet Tannur

35 E

0   10   20   30   40

0   10   20   30   40   50 Kilometers

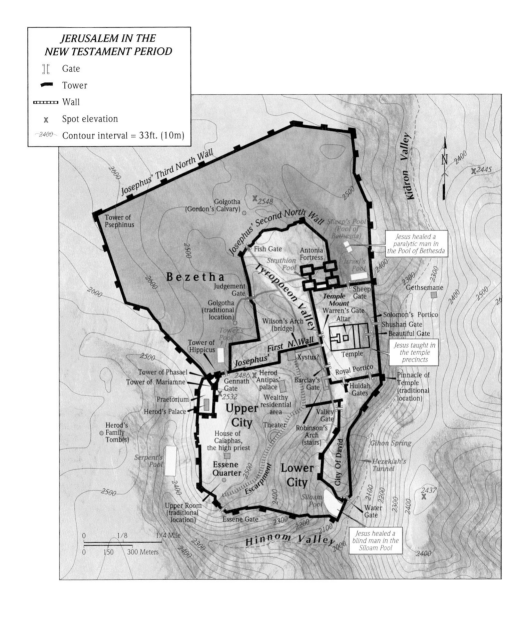

Josephus' Third North Wall

Kidron Valley

N

x 2445

2600

2500

Tower of
Psephinus

Golgotha
(Gordon's Calvary)   x 2548

Josephus' Second North Wall

Sheep's Pool
(Pool of
Bethesda)

Jesus healed a
paralytic man in
the Pool of Bethesda

Fish Gate

Antonia
Fortress

Struthion
Pool

Israel's
Pool

2400

2300   2300

Bezetha

Tyropoeon Valley

Gethsemane

2500

2500

Judgement
Gate

Temple
Mount

Sheep
Gate

2600

2600

Golgotha
(traditional
location)

Warren's Gate

Altar

Solomon's Portico

Shushan Gate

Beautiful Gate

Wilson's Arch
(bridge)

Tower of
Hippicus

Tower's
Pool

2500

First N. Wall

Josephus'

Xystus?

Temple

Jesus taught in
the temple
precincts

Tower of Phasael

Tower of Mariamne

2486 x Herod
Antipas'
palace

Gennath
Gate

x 2532

Barclay's
Gate

Royal Portico

Huldah
Gates

Pinnacle of
Temple
(traditional
location)

Praetorium

Herod's Palace

Upper
City

Wealthy
residential
area

Herod's
Family
Tomb(s)

House of
Caiaphas,
the high priest

Theater

Valley
Gate

Robinson's
Arch
(stairs)

City Of David

Gihon Spring

Hezekiah's
Tunnel

2100   2200   2300   2400

2437
x

Serpent's
Pool

Essene
Quarter

Escarpment

Lower
City

Siloam
Pool

2500

2500

2400

Upper Room
(traditional
location)

Essene Gate

2300

2200   2100

2000

Water
Gate

Jesus healed a
blind man in the
Siloam Pool

Hinnom Valley

2400

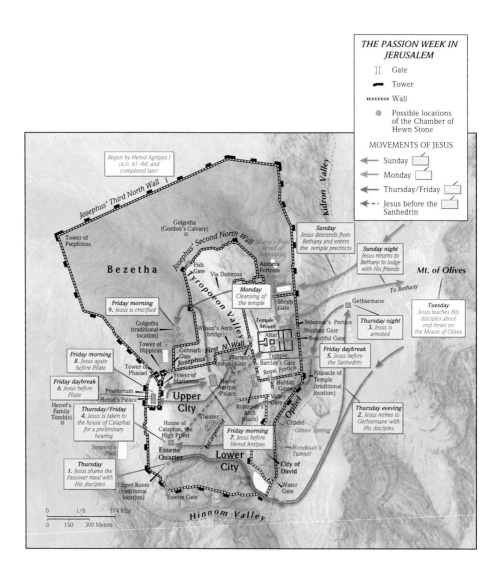

THE PASSION WEEK IN
JERUSALEM

][Gate

— Tower

┅┅ Wall

◉ Possible locations
of the Chamber of
Hewn Stone

MOVEMENTS OF JESUS

← Sunday

← Monday

← Thursday/Friday

←- - Jesus before the
Sanhedrin

Begun by Herod Agrippa I
(A.D. 41–44) and
completed later

Josephus' Third North Wall

Tower of
Psephinus

Golgotha
(Gordon's Calvary)

Josephus' Second North Wall

Sheep's Pool
(Pool of
Bethsaida)

Bezetha

Fish
Gate

Via Dolorosa

Antonia
Fortress

Israel's
Pool

Kidron Valley

Sunday
Jesus descends from
Bethany and enters
the temple precincts

Sunday night
Jesus returns to
Bethany to lodge
with His friends

Mt. of Olives

To Bethany

Tyropoeon Valley

Monday
Cleansing of
the temple

Gethsemane

Tuesday
Jesus teaches His
disciples about
end times on
the Mount of Olives

Friday morning
9. Jesus is crucified

Golgotha
(traditional
location)

Tower's
Pool

Wilson's Arch
(bridge)

Temple
Mount

Altar

Solomon's Portico
Shushan Gate
Beautiful Gate

Thursday night
3. Jesus is
arrested

Tower of
Hippicus

Gennath
Gate
Josephus'
Xystus

First N. Wall

Temple

Friday morning
8. Jesus again
before Pilate

Tower of
Phasael

Warren's
Gate

Barclay's Gate
Royal Portico

Friday daybreak
5. Jesus before
the Sanhedrin

Friday daybreak
6. Jesus before
Pilate

Tower of
Mariamne

Herod
Antipas'
Palace

Huldah
Gates

Valley
Gate

Pinnacle of
Temple
(traditional
location)

Praetorium

Herod's Palace

Upper
City

Robinson's
Arch
(stairs)

Ophel

Thursday eveing
2. Jesus retires to
Gethsemane with
His disciples

Herod's
Family
Tomb(s)

Thursday/Friday
4. Jesus is taken to
the house of Caiaphas
for a preliminary
hearing

House of
Caiaphas,
the High Priest

Theater

Escarpment

Citadel

Gihon Spring

Hezekiah's
Tunnel

Serpent's
Pool

Friday morning
7. Jesus before
Herod Antipas

Essene
Quarter

Lower
City

City of
David

Water
Gate

Thursday
1. Jesus shares the
Passover meal with
His disciples

Upper Room
(traditional
location)

Essene Gate

Siloam
Pool

Hinnom Valley

0   1/8   1/4 Mile

0   150   300 Meters

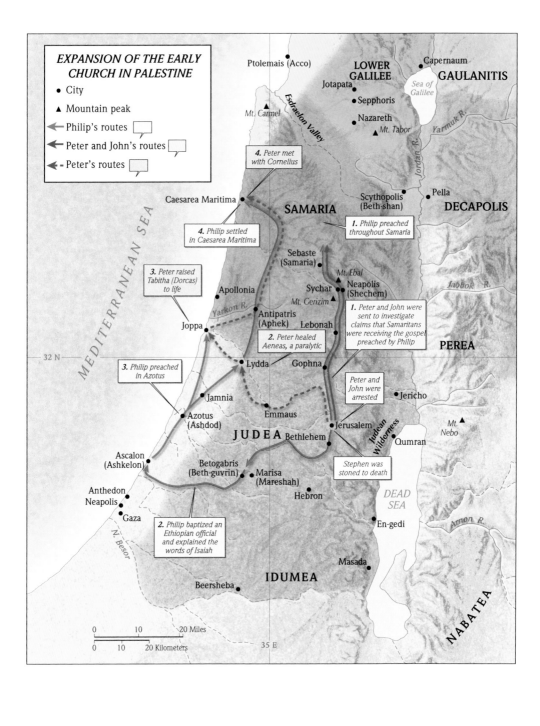

EXPANSION OF THE EARLY
CHURCH IN PALESTINE
● City
▲ Mountain peak
← Philip's routes
← Peter and John's routes
← - Peter's routes

Ptolemais (Acco)
LOWER GALILEE
Capernaum
GAULANITIS
Jotapata
Sea of Galilee
Sepphoris
Mt. Carmel
Esdraelon Valley
Nazareth
Mt. Tabor
Yarmuk R.
Jordan R.

4. Peter met with Cornelius

Caesarea Maritima
SAMARIA
Scythopolis (Beth-shan)
Pella
DECAPOLIS

4. Philip settled in Caesarea Maritima

1. Philip preached throughout Samaria

Sebaste (Samaria)
Mt. Ebal
Neapolis (Shechem)
Jabbok R.

3. Peter raised Tabitha (Dorcas) to life

Apollonia
Sychar
Mt. Gerizim

MEDITERRANEAN SEA

Yarkon R.
Antipatris (Aphek)
Lebonah

1. Peter and John were sent to investigate claims that Samaritans were receiving the gospel preached by Philip

PEREA

Joppa

2. Peter healed Aeneas, a paralytic

32 N

3. Philip preached in Azotus

Lydda
Gophna

Peter and John were arrested

Jericho
Mt. Nebo

Jamnia
Emmaus

Azotus (Ashdod)

JUDEA
Bethlehem
Jerusalem
Qumran
Judean Wilderness

Ascalon (Ashkelon)
Betogabris (Beth-guvrin)
Marisa (Mareshah)

Stephen was stoned to death

DEAD SEA

Anthedon
Neapolis
Hebron

En-gedi

Gaza

2. Philip baptized an Ethiopian official and explained the words of Isaiah

Amon R.

Masada

IDUMEA

Beersheba

NABATEA

N. Besor

0   10   20 Miles
0   10   20 Kilometers
35 E

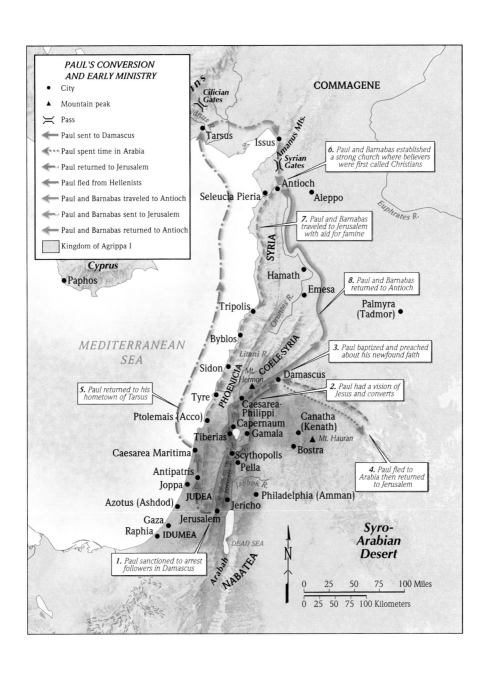

PAUL'S CONVERSION
AND EARLY MINISTRY

- • City
- ▲ Mountain peak
- ⋈ Pass
- ← Paul sent to Damascus
- ←··· Paul spent time in Arabia
- ← Paul returned to Jerusalem
- ← Paul fled from Hellenists
- ← Paul and Barnabas traveled to Antioch
- ← Paul and Barnabas sent to Jerusalem
- ← Paul and Barnabas returned to Antioch
- ▦ Kingdom of Agrippa I

COMMAGENE

Cilician
Gates

Tarsus

Issus

Syrian
Gates

Amanus Mts.

Antioch

6. Paul and Barnabas established
a strong church where believers
were first called Christians

Seleucia Pieria

Aleppo

Euphrates R.

7. Paul and Barnabas
traveled to Jerusalem
with aid for famine

SYRIA

Cyprus

Paphos

Hamath

Emesa

8. Paul and Barnabas
returned to Antioch

Palmyra
(Tadmor)

Tripolis

Orontes R.

Byblos

MEDITERRANEAN
SEA

Litani R.

COELE-SYRIA

3. Paul baptized and preached
about his newfound faith

Sidon

PHOENICIA

Mt.
Hermon

Damascus

2. Paul had a vision of
Jesus and converts

5. Paul returned to his
hometown of Tarsus

Tyre

Caesarea-
Philippi

Canatha
(Kenath)

Ptolemais (Acco)

Capernaum

Tiberias

Gamala

▲ Mt. Hauran

Caesarea Maritima

Scythopolis

Bostra

Antipatris

Pella

4. Paul fled to
Arabia then returned
to Jerusalem

Joppa

Jabbok R.

Azotus (Ashdod)

JUDEA

Philadelphia (Amman)

Gaza

Jericho

Raphia

Jerusalem

IDUMEA

DEAD SEA

Syro-
Arabian
Desert

1. Paul sanctioned to arrest
followers in Damascus

Arabah

NABATEA

N

0   25   50   75   100 Miles

0 25 50 75 100 Kilometers

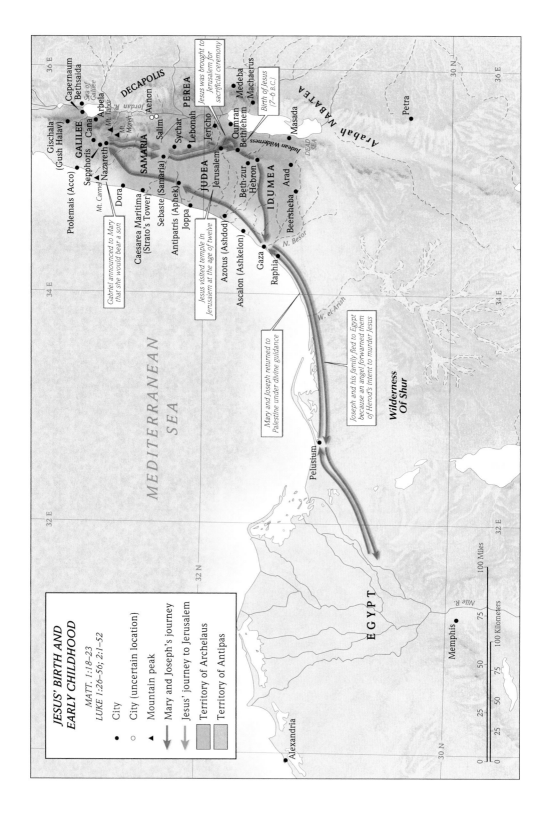

JESUS' BIRTH AND
EARLY CHILDHOOD

MATT. 1:18–23
LUKE 1:26–56; 2:1–52

• City
○ City (uncertain location)
▲ Mountain peak
→ Mary and Joseph's journey
→ Jesus' journey to Jerusalem
Territory of Archelaus
Territory of Antipas

MEDITERRANEAN
SEA

EGYPT

Memphis

Alexandria

Nile R.

Wilderness
Of Shur

W. el-Arish

Pelusium

NABATEA

Arabah

Petra

DECAPOLIS

PEREA

SAMARIA

GALILEE

JUDEA

IDUMEA

Capernaum
Bethsaida
Sea of
Galilee
Abela
Arbela
Cana
Mt. Tabor
Mt. Moreh
Aenon
Salim
Gischala
(Gush Halav)
Sepphoris
Nazareth
Mt. Carmel
Dora
Ptolemais (Acco)
Caesarea Maritima
(Strato's Tower)
Sebaste (Samaria)
Antipatris (Aphek)
Joppa
Azotus (Ashdod)
Ascalon (Ashkelon)
Gaza
Raphia
Sychar
Lebonah
Jericho
Jerusalem
Qumran
Bethlehem
Beth-zur
Hebron
Arad
Beersheba
N. Besor
Jordan R.
Judean Wilderness
DEAD
SEA
Masada
Machaerus
Medeba
Birth of Jesus
(7–6 B.C.)

Gabriel announced to Mary
that she would bear a son

Jesus visited temple in
Jerusalem at the age of twelve

Jesus was brought to
Jerusalem for
sacrificial ceremony

Mary and Joseph returned to
Palestine under divine guidance

Joseph and his family fled to Egypt
because an angel forewarned them
of Herod's intent to murder Jesus

0   25   50   75   100 Miles
0 25 50 75 100 Kilometers

36 E
34 E
32 E
30 N
32 N

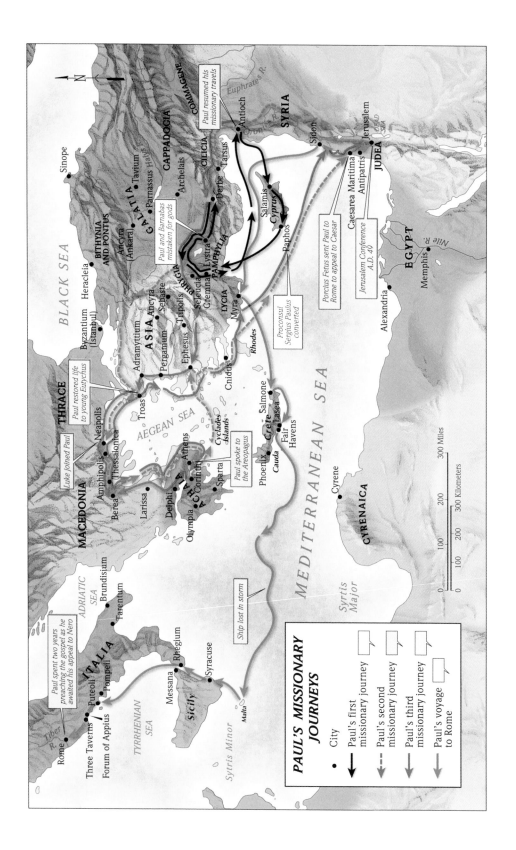

PAUL'S MISSIONARY JOURNEYS

- Paul's first missionary journey
- Paul's second missionary journey
- Paul's third missionary journey
- Paul's voyage to Rome
- City

Paul spent two years preaching the gospel as he awaited his appeal to Nero

Ship lost in storm

Luke joined Paul

Paul restored life to young Eutychus

Paul spoke to the Areopagus

Proconsul Sergius Paulus converted

Paul and Barnabas mistaken for gods

Paul resumed his missionary travels

Porcius Fettus sent Paul to Rome to appeal to Caesar

Jerusalem Conference A.D. 49

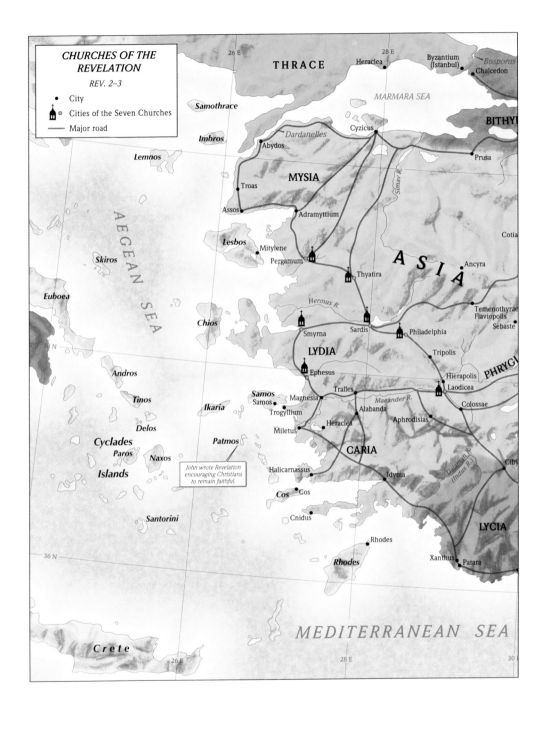

CHURCHES OF THE REVELATION
REV. 2–3

- • City
- Cities of the Seven Churches
- —— Major road

THRACE

Heraclea

Byzantium
(Istanbul)
Chalcedon

Bosporus

MARMARA SEA

BITHYI

Samothrace

Dardanelles

Cyzicus

Prusa

Imbros

Abydos

Lemnos

MYSIA

Simav R.

Troas

Adramyttium

ASIA

Cotia

Assos

Lesbos

Mitylene

Pergamum

Ancyra

Skiros

Thyatira

Temenothyrae
Flaviopolis

Euboea

AEGEAN SEA

Hermus R.

Sebaste

Chios

Smyrna

Sardis

Philadelphia

LYDIA

Tripolis

PHRYGI

Andros

Ephesus

Hierapolis

Tinos

Tralles

Magnesia

Maeander R.

Laodicea

Colossae

Ikaria

Samos
Samos

Alabanda

Aphrodisias

Delos

Trogyllium

Heraclea

Cyclades

Miletus

Patmos

CARIA

*Dalaman R.
(Indus R.)*

Ciby

Paros

Naxos

Islands

John wrote Revelation
encouraging Christians
to remain faithful.

Halicarnassus

Idyma

LYCIA

Cos
Cos

Santorini

Cnidus

Rhodes

36 N

Xanthus
Patara

Crete

Rhodes

MEDITERRANEAN SEA

26 E

28 E

30